Literature Criticism from 1400 to 1800

Guide to Gale Literary Criticism Series

For criticism on	Consult these Gale series
Authors now living or who died after December 31, 1999	*CONTEMPORARY LITERARY CRITICISM (CLC)*
Authors who died between 1900 and 1999	*TWENTIETH-CENTURY LITERARY CRITICISM (TCLC)*
Authors who died between 1800 and 1899	*NINETEENTH-CENTURY LITERATURE CRITICISM (NCLC)*
Authors who died between 1400 and 1799	*LITERATURE CRITICISM FROM 1400 TO 1800 (LC)* *SHAKESPEAREAN CRITICISM (SC)*
Authors who died before 1400	*CLASSICAL AND MEDIEVAL LITERATURE CRITICISM (CMLC)*
Authors of books for children and young adults	*CHILDREN'S LITERATURE REVIEW (CLR)*
Dramatists	*DRAMA CRITICISM (DC)*
Poets	*POETRY CRITICISM (PC)*
Short story writers	*SHORT STORY CRITICISM (SSC)*
Literary topics and movements	*HARLEM RENAISSANCE: A GALE CRITICAL COMPANION (HR)* *THE BEAT GENERATION: A GALE CRITICAL COMPANION (BG)*
Asian American writers of the last two hundred years	*ASIAN AMERICAN LITERATURE (AAL)*
Black writers of the past two hundred years	*BLACK LITERATURE CRITICISM (BLC)* *BLACK LITERATURE CRITICISM SUPPLEMENT (BLCS)*
Hispanic writers of the late nineteenth and twentieth centuries	*HISPANIC LITERATURE CRITICISM (HLC)* *HISPANIC LITERATURE CRITICISM SUPPLEMENT (HLCS)*
Native North American writers and orators of the eighteenth, nineteenth, and twentieth centuries	*NATIVE NORTH AMERICAN LITERATURE (NNAL)*
Major authors from the Renaissance to the present	*WORLD LITERATURE CRITICISM, 1500 TO THE PRESENT (WLC)* *WORLD LITERATURE CRITICISM SUPPLEMENT (WLCS)*

Volume 90

Literature Criticism from 1400 to 1800

Critical Discussion of the Works of Fifteenth-, Sixteenth-, Seventeenth-, and Eighteenth-Century Novelists, Poets, Playwrights, Philosophers, and Other Creative Writers

Michael L. LaBlanc
Project Editor

Detroit • New York • San Diego • San Francisco • Cleveland • New Haven, Conn. • Waterville, Maine • London • Munich

THOMSON
GALE

Literature Criticism from 1400 to 1800, Vol. 90

Project Editor
Michael L. LaBlanc

Editorial
Jessica Bomarito, Jenny Cromie, Kathy D. Darrow, Elisabeth Gellert, Jelena O. Krstović Michelle Lee, Thomas J. Schoenberg, Lawrence J. Trudeau, Lemma Shomali, Russel Whitaker

Research
Nicodemus Ford, Sarah Genik, Tamara C. Nott, Tracie A. Richardson

Permissions
Shalice Shah-Caldwell

Imaging and Multimedia
Dean Dauphinais, Robert Duncan, Leitha Etheridge-Sims, Mary K. Grimes, Lezlie Light,

Dan Newell, David G. Oblender, Christine O'Bryan, Kelly A. Quin, Luke Rademacher

Composition and Electronic Capture
Kathy Sauer

Manufacturing
Stacy L. Melson

LIBRARY OF CONGRESS CATALOG CARD NUMBER 94-29718

ISBN 0-7876-6971-7
ISSN 0740-2880

Printed in the United States of America
10 9 8 7 6 5 4 3 2 1

Contents

Preface vii

Acknowledgments xi

Literary Criticism Series Advisory Board xiii

Preface

Literature Criticism from 1400 to 1800 (*LC*) presents critical discussion of world literature from the fifteenth through the eighteenth centuries. The literature of this period is especially vital: the years 1400 to 1800 saw the rise of modern European drama, the birth of the novel and personal essay forms, the emergence of newspapers and periodicals, and major achievements in poetry and philosophy. *LC* provides valuable insight into the art, life, thought, and cultural transformations that took place during these centuries.

Scope of the Series

LC provides an introduction to the great poets, dramatists, novelists, essayists, and philosophers of the fifteenth through eighteenth centuries, and to the most significant interpretations of these authors' works. Because criticism of this literature spans nearly six hundred years, an overwhelming amount of scholarship confronts the student. *LC* organizes this material concisely and logically. Every attempt is made to reprint the most noteworthy, relevant, and educationally valuable essays available.

A separate Gale reference series, *Shakespearean Criticism,* is devoted exclusively to Shakespearean studies. Although properly belonging to the period covered in *LC*, William Shakespeare has inspired such a tremendous and ever-growing body of secondary material that a separate series was deemed essential.

Each entry in *LC* presents a representative selection of critical response to an author, a literary topic, or to a single important work of literature. Early commentary is offered to indicate initial responses, later selections document changes in literary reputations, and retrospective analyses provide the reader with modern views. The size of each author entry is a relative reflection of the scope of the criticism available in English. Every attempt has been made to identify and include the seminal essays on each author's work and to include recent commentary providing modern perspectives.

Volumes 1 through 12 of the series feature author entries arranged alphabetically by author. Volumes 13-47 of the series feature a thematic arrangement. Each volume includes an entry devoted to the general study of a specific literary or philosophical movement, writings surrounding important political and historical events, the philosophy and art associated with eras of cultural transformation, or the literature of specific social or ethnic groups. Each of these volumes also includes several author entries devoted to major representatives of the featured period, genre, or national literature. With volume 48, the series returns to a standard author approach, with some entries devoted to a single important work of world literature and others devoted to literary topics.

Organization of the Book

An *LC* entry consists of the following elements:

- The **Author Heading** cites the name under which the author most commonly wrote, followed by birth and death dates. Also located here are any name variations under which an author wrote, including transliterated forms for authors whose native languages use nonroman alphabets. If the author wrote consistently under a pseudonym, the pseudonym will be listed in the author heading and the author's actual name given in parenthesis on the first line of the biographical and critical information. Uncertain birth or death dates are indicated by question marks. Topic entries are preceded by a **Thematic Heading,** which simply states the subject of the entry. Single-work entries are preceded by the title of the work and its date of publication.

- The **Introduction** contains background information that introduces the reader to the author, work, or topic that is the subject of the entry.

- A **Portrait of the Author** is included when available.

- The list of **Principal Works** is ordered chronologically by date of first publication and lists the most important works by the author. The genre and publication date of each work is given. In the case of foreign authors whose works have been translated into English, the title and date (if available) of the first English-language edition is given in brackets following the original title. Unless otherwise indicated, dramas are dated by first performance, not first publication. Lists of **Representative Works** by different authors appear with topic entries.

- Reprinted **Criticism** is arranged chronologically in each entry to provide a useful perspective on changes in critical evaluation over time. The critic's name and the date of composition or publication of the critical work are given at the beginning of each piece of criticism. Unsigned criticism is preceded by the title of the source in which it appeared. All titles by the author featured in the text are printed in boldface type. Footnotes are reprinted at the end of each essay or excerpt. In the case of excerpted criticism, only those footnotes that pertain to the excerpted texts are included. Criticism in topic entries is arranged chronologically under a variety of subheadings to facilitate the study of different aspects of the topic.

- Critical essays are prefaced by brief **Annotations** explicating each piece.

- A complete **Bibliographical Citation** of the original essay or book precedes each piece of criticism. Source citations in the Literary Criticism Series follow University of Chicago Press style, as outlined in *The Chicago Manual of Style,* 14th ed. (Chicago: The University of Chicago Press, 1993).

- An annotated bibliography of **Further Reading** appears at the end of each entry and suggests resources for additional study. In some cases, significant essays for which the editors could not obtain reprint rights are included here. Boxed material following the further reading list provides references to other biographical and critical sources on the author in series published by Gale.

Indexes

A **Cumulative Author Index** lists all of the authors that appear in a wide variety of reference sources published by the Gale Group, including *LC*. A complete list of these sources is found facing the first page of the Author Index. The index also includes birth and death dates and cross references between pseudonyms and actual names.

A **Cumulative Nationality Index** lists all authors featured in *LC* by nationality, followed by the number of the *LC* volume in which their entry appears.

A **Cumulative Topic Index** lists the literary themes and topics treated in the series as well as in *Nineteenth-Century Literature Criticism, Twentieth-Century Literary Criticism,* and the *Contemporary Literature Criticism* Yearbook, which was discontinued in 1998.

An alphabetical **Title Index** accompanies each volume of *LC*. Listings of titles by authors covered in the given volume are followed by the author's name and the corresponding page numbers on which the titles are discussed. English translations of foreign titles and variations of titles are cross-referenced to the title under which a work was originally published. Titles of novels, dramas, nonfiction books, and poetry, short story, or essay collections are printed in italics, while individual poems, short stories, and essays are printed in roman type within quotation marks.

In response to numerous suggestions from librarians, Gale also produces an annual paperbound edition of the LC cumulative title index. This annual cumulation, which alphabetically lists all titles reviewed in the series, is available to all customers. Additional copies of this index are available upon request. Librarians and patrons will welcome this separate index; it saves shelf space, is easy to use, and is recyclable upon receipt of the next edition.

Citing *Literature Criticism from 1400 to 1800*

When citing criticism reprinted in the Literary Criticism Series, students should provide complete bibliographic information so that the cited essay can be located in the original print or electronic source. Students who quote directly from reprinted criticism may use any accepted bibliographic format, such as University of Chicago Press style or Modern Language Association (MLA) style. Both the MLA and the University of Chicago formats are acceptable and recognized as being the current standards for citations. It is important, however, to choose one format for all citations; do not mix the two formats within a list of citations.

The examples below follow recommendations for preparing a bibliography set forth in *The Chicago Manual of Style,* 14th ed. (Chicago: The University of Chicago Press, 1993); the first example pertains to material drawn from periodicals, the second to material reprinted from books:

Morrison, Jago. "Narration and Unease in Ian McEwan's Later Fiction." *Critique* 42, no. 3 (spring 2001): 253-68. Reprinted in *Literary Criticism from 1400-1800.* Vol. 76, edited by Michael L. LaBlanc, 212-20. Detroit: Gale, 2003.

Brossard, Nicole. "Poetic Politics." In *The Politics of Poetic Form: Poetry and Public Policy,* edited by Charles Bernstein, 73-82. New York: Roof Books, 1990. Reprinted in *Literary Criticism from 1400-1800.* Vol. 82, edited by Michael L. LaBlanc, 3-8. Detroit: Gale, 2003.

The examples below follow recommendations for preparing a works cited list set forth in the *MLA Handbook for Writers of Research Papers,* 5th ed. (New York: The Modern Language Association of America, 1999); the first example pertains to material drawn from periodicals, the second to material reprinted from books:

Morrison, Jago. "Narration and Unease in Ian McEwan's Later Fiction." *Critique* 42. 3 (spring 2001): 253-68. Reprinted in *Literary Criticism from 1400-1800.* Ed. Michael L. LaBlanc. Vol. 76. Detroit: Gale, 2003. 212-20.

Brossard, Nicole. "Poetic Politics." *The Politics of Poetic Form: Poetry and Public Policy.* Ed. Charles Bernstein. New York: Roof Books, 1990. 73-82. Reprinted in *Contemporary Literary Criticism.* Ed. Michael L. LaBlanc. Vol. 82. Detroit: Gale, 2003. 3-8.

Suggestions are Welcome

Readers who wish to suggest new features, topics, or authors to appear in future volumes, or who have other suggestions or comments are cordially invited to call, write, or fax the Project Editor:

Project Editor, Literary Criticism Series
The Gale Group
27500 Drake Road
Farmington Hills, MI 48331-3535
1-800-347-4253 (GALE)
Fax: 248-699-8054

Acknowledgments

The editors wish to thank the copyright holders of the excerpted criticism included in this volume and the permissions managers of many book and magazine publishing companies for assisting us in securing reproduction rights. We are also grateful to the staffs of the Detroit Public Library, the Library of Congress, the University of Detroit Mercy Library, Wayne State University Purdy/Kresge Library Complex, and the University of Michigan Libraries for making their resources available to us. Following is a list of the copyright holders who have granted us permission to reproduce material in this volume of *LC*. Every effort has been made to trace copyright, but if omissions have been made, please let us know.

COPYRIGHTED MATERIAL IN *LC*, VOLUME 90, WAS REPRODUCED FROM THE FOLLOWING PERIODICALS:

American Political Science Review, v. 95, September, 2001 for "Mary Wollstonecraft's Nurturing Liberalism: Between an Ethic of Justice and Care," by Daniel Engster. Copyright © 2001, by American Political Science Association. Reproduced by permission of Cambridge University Press and the author.—*Cahiers Elisabethains,* v. 57, April, 2000 for "Penitence in 1590's Weeping Texts," by Ceri Sullivan. All rights reserved. Reproduced by permission of the publisher and the author.—*Comitatus,* v. 4, 1973. Reproduced by permission.—*Communication Studies,* v. 47, Winter, 1996 for "A Web of Reasons: Mary Wollstonecraft's 'A Vindication of the Rights of Woman' and the Re-weaving of Form," by Cindy L. Griffin. Reproduced by permission of the publisher and the author.—*Comparative Literature Studies,* v. 12, March, 1975. Copyright © 1975 by The Pennsylvania State University. Reproduced by permission of The Pennsylvania State University Press.—*European Romantic Review,* v. 11, Summer, 2000. Reproduced by permission.—*Dalhousie Review,* v. 60, Autumn, 1980 for "Mary Wollstonecraft's Mask of Reason in 'A Vindication of the Rights of Woman,' by Anca Vlasopolos. Reproduced by permission of the publisher and author.—*Feminist Review,* Autumn, 1992 for "Mary Wollstonecraft and the Problematic Slavery," by Moira Ferguson. Reproduced by permission of the author.—*Feminist Studies,* v. 20, Fall, 1994. Reproduced by permission of Feminist Studies, Inc., Department of Women's Studies, University of Maryland, College Park, MD 20724.—*Hypatia,* v. 8, Fall, 1993; v. 14, Summer, 1999. © by Catriona Mackenzie and Ruth Abbey. Both reproduced by permission.—*Journal of Ecclesiastical History,* v. 48, October, 1997. © 1997 Cambridge University Press. Reprinted with permission of Cambridge University Press and the author.—*Journal of the History of Ideas,* v. 39, April-June, 1978; v. 57, July, 1996. © The Johns Hopkins University Press. Both reproduced by permission.—*Modern Language Review,* v. 89, April, 1994. © Modern Humanities Research Association 1994. Reproduced by permission of the publisher.—*Recusant History,* v. 19, October, 1988 for "William Alabaster: Rhetor, Meditator, Devotional Poet II," by Robert V. Caro, S.J. Reproduced by permission of the publisher and the author.—*Studies in Burke and His Time,* v. 18, Autumn, 1977 for "Radical Politics in Mary Wollstonecraft's 'A Vindication of the Rights of Woman,'" by Elissa S. Guralnick. Reproduced by permission of the author.—*Studies in English Literature,* v. 32, Summer, 1992. © The Johns Hopkins University Press. Reproduced by permission.—*Studies in Romanticism,* v. 32, Summer, 1993; v. 39, Winter, 2000. Copyright 1993, 2000 by the Trustees of Boston University. Both reproduced by permission.—*Texas Studies in Literature and Language,* v. 34, Winter, 1992 for "Rebellious Reading: The Doubleness of Wollstonecraft's Subversion of 'Paradise Lost,'" by Steven Blakemore. © 1992 by the University of Texas Press. Reproduced by permission of the publisher and author.—*Textual Practice,* v. 9, Summer, 1995 for "The Dream of Common Language: Hannah More and Mary Wollstonecraft," by Harriet Guest. © 1995 Routledge. Reproduced by permission of the publisher and the author.—*Tulsa Studies in Women's Literature,* v. 17, Fall, 1998 for "The Anorexic body of Liberal Feminism: Mary Wollstonecraft's 'A Vindication of the Rights of Woman,'" by Ewa Badowska. © 1998, The University of Tulsa. Reproduced by permission of the publisher and the author.—*University of Hartford Studies in Literature,* Vol. 15-16, 1983-84. Reproduced by permission.—*The Yale Journal of Criticism,* v. 5, Fall, 1991. © The Johns Hopkins University Press. Reproduced by permission.

COPYRIGHTED MATERIAL IN *LC*, VOLUME 90, WAS REPRODUCED FROM THE FOLLOWING BOOKS:

Bergvall, Ake. From *Cultural Exchange between European Nations during the Renaissance.* Edited by Gunnar Sorelius and Michael Srigley. Uppsala University, 1994. © Ake Bergvall. Reproduced by permission.—Binns, J. W. From *Seneca.* Edited by C. D. N. Costa. Routledge & Kegan Paul, 1974. © Routledge & Kegan Paul Ltd. 1974. Reproduced by permission.—Buzogany, Deszo. From *Melanchthon in Europe: His World and Influence beyond Wittenberg.* Edited by Karin Maag. Baker Books, 1999. Copyright © 1999 by Karin Maag. All rights reserved. Reproduced by permission of Baker

Literary Criticism Series Advisory Board

William Alabaster
1568-1640

English poet, playwright, and essayist.

INTRODUCTION

Alabaster is best remembered for his sequence of devotional sonnets, which anticipate the works of the metaphysical poets such as John Donne and George Herbert. Written during the late Elizabethan age, these sonnets often employ the stylistic elements of paradox and extended metaphor which characterize the poems of these later writers. A Cambridge scholar and cleric who converted from the Anglican church to Catholicism and back twice, Alabaster also wrote Latin verse, drama, and theological works. Since the rediscovery of his works, critical interest in Alabaster has been primarily historical, though some have examined his style as well.

BIOGRAPHICAL INFORMATION

Born in 1568 to a Protestant family in Hadleigh, Suffolk, Alabaster grew up studying classical languages. In 1584, partly through the influence of his uncle, he was elected a Queen's Scholar to Trinity College, Cambridge. While there he made a promising start to his literary career, beginning *Elisaeis* (composed c. 1588), an unfinished verse epic in Latin on the career of Elizabeth I. Alabaster presented a copy of the first volume of the poem to the queen, and Edmund Spenser highly extolled the work in his *Colin Clout's come Home Again*: "Who lives that can match that heroic song / Which he hath of that mighty Princess made? / . . . / No braver Poem can be under Sun." Alabaster received a B.A. from Cambridge in 1588 and an M.A. in 1591; five years later he became chaplain to the Earl of Essex. His theological career, newly begun, took a drastically different route in 1597, when Alabaster converted to Roman Catholicism. He sent a letter to the Earl of Essex containing "Seven Motives" for his conversion, but the government intercepted this correspondence. Alabaster was arrested and taken to London, where for the most part he was treated gently. A number of Anglican authorities urged him to recant, but he refused. Alabaster escaped from his unguarded confinement, making his way to the English College in Rome. He probably finished the majority of his devotional sonnets before he escaped to the continent. While attempting to return to

England in 1599, he was captured at La Rochelle, France, and taken to the Tower of London, where he began to cooperate with the authorities, giving them information about Catholic plots. Soon after his release in 1603, Alabaster was again arrested for engaging in pro-Catholic teachings and writings, and he was held for two years. He then moved to Belgium, where he wrote his first essay in mystical theology, but he soon became disillusioned with the Catholic institutions of the Inquisition and the Jesuits. After being imprisoned by the Inquisition, released, then imprisoned by the Dutch government, Alabaster declared his intention to return to the Protestant church and was handed over to English authorities. While being confined at the house of the Dean of St. Paul's, however, he repented and re-declared his Catholic faith. Little is known about the next few years of Alabaster's life, but three years later he had once again converted to the Church of England and found himself in favor with King James. In 1618 Alabaster married Katherine Fludd and settled into a life of study and writing about mystical theology, as well as continuing to write epigrams and elegies, until his death in London on April 28, 1640.

MAJOR WORKS

Alabaster is best known for the neo-Latin works he completed while still at Cambridge. The first of these, *Elisaeis,* is an epic about Elizabeth I originally intended to be twelve books in length. The extant volume shows a preoccupation with stylistic experimentation as well as the use of extended rhetorical speeches. However, Alabaster published only the first book—concerning Elizabeth's early difficulties during the reign of Mary I—before he became a Catholic and lost motivation to pursue the anti-Catholic project. Also while at Cambridge, Alabaster wrote *Roxana,* an adaptation of an Italian tragedy written by Luigi Groto concerning the ghost of a murdered king seeking revenge upon his nephew. The play, featuring allegorized figures such as Death and Jealousy, includes many rhetorical speeches and epigrams, recalling *Elisaeis.* After his conversion to Catholicism in 1597, Alabaster began work on a sequence of devotional sonnets in English that later editors have titled *Divine Meditations.* These sonnets, save one, were not published in Alabaster's lifetime, but were circulated in manuscript form. The wit and subtle argument of these poems, as well as their frequent use of extended conceits, have earned Alabaster his modern reputation as an important precursor to the metaphysical poetry of the seventeenth century.

CRITICAL RECEPTION

Alabaster's reputation among his contemporaries rests solely on his Latin verse—Samuel Johnson considered the Latin verse of *Roxana* among the best created in England. Alabaster's devotional sonnets were not known until Bertram Dobell published several in 1903. It was at this point that Alabaster was first recognized as a proto-metaphysical poet, and only after G. M. Story and Helen Gardner's 1959 edition of *Divine Meditations* did he begin to receive much critical attention. Since then, critical interest has been divided between Alabaster's early Latin works and his English poetry. The interest in the neo-Latin texts is largely scholarly and uses these works as examples of period academic literature. Alabaster's devotional poetry has attracted a more diverse attention—critics such as George Klawitter have analyzed the style and language of the sonnets, while Ceri Sullivan and others have discussed their thematic content. While Alabaster is noted as a talented Latin poet and an important predecessor to the later Metaphysical movement in poetry, his career also illustrates the religious and political divisions of his time.

PRINCIPAL WORKS

*Elisaeis (poetry) c. 1588
Roxana (play) c. 1592
Apparatus in Revelationem Jesu Christi (prose) 1607
De Bestia Apocalyptica (prose) 1621
Ecce sponsus venit (prose) 1633
Spiraculum tubarum sive fons spiritualium expositionum ex aequivocis Pentaglotti significationibus (prose) 1633
The Sonnets of William Alabaster [edited by G. M. Story and Helen Gardner] (poetry) 1959
Unpublished Works by William Alabaster (1568-1640) [edited by Dana F. Sutton] (poetry) 1997

*Only the first book of this projected twelve-volume work survives. Alabaster reported that a second book was completed, but it was apparently destroyed.

CRITICISM

Bertram Dobell (essay date 26 December 1903)

SOURCE: Dobell, Bertram. "The Sonnets of William Alabaster." *The Athenaeum,* no. 3974 (26 December 1903): 856-58.

[*In the following essay, Dobell announces his recovery of Alabaster's sonnet series and discusses the nature of the works.*]

Considering what an amount of study and research has been devoted to the literary history of England during the sixteenth and seventeenth centuries, it might be thought that no fresh discoveries of any importance were likely to be made in so well-explored a field. Nevertheless I have been so fortunate myself in the recovery of unknown or only imperfectly known treasure-trove of those periods, that I am convinced that this is by no means the case. Much, I am sure, remains to be discovered, and only requires to be searched for with half the diligence which has been devoted to the search, in Egypt and elsewhere, for the remains of classical antiquity. Who would have imagined that within a brief period it would be possible to discover the unknown works of three considerable poets, whose names, whatever the verdict ultimately passed upon them may be, cannot henceforth be omitted in any general survey of English literature? Of one of these poets—Thomas Traherne—I need not speak here. Of the other two it must be allowed that they are not so absolutely unknown to readers of the present day as Traherne was, since their names at least are to be found in the *Dictionary of National Biography* and other standard works of reference.

Of these poets the one I now propose to speak of—leaving the other to a later occasion—is William Alabaster, one of the many "inheritors of unfulfilled renown" who, after enjoying a great reputation among their contemporaries, survive only in later ages in the pages of bibliographies or biographical dictionaries.

Any one who glances through Wood's *Athenæ Oxonienses* will be surprised at the number of persons on whom the author bestows high eulogiums, but who are now entirely, or almost entirely, forgotten. One of these is Alabaster, whom Wood calls "the rarest poet and Grecian that any one age or nation produced." Fuller also praised him in a similar manner, but the verses which Spenser devoted to him in *Colin Clout's come Home Again* have, up to the present time, constituted his best claim to remembrance:—

> And there is Alabaster throughly taught
> In all this skill, though knowen yet to few;
> Yet were he known to Cynthia as he ought,
> His 'Eliseïs' would be read anew.
> Who lives that can match that heroic song
> Which he hath of that mighty Princess made?
> O, dreaded Dread, do not thyself that wrong
> To let thy fame lie so in hidden shade:
> But call it forth, O call him forth to thee
> To end thy glory which he hath begun;
> That when he finisht hath as it should be
> No braver Poem can be under Sun.
> Nor Po nor Tyber's swans so much renown'd,
> Nor all the brood of Greece so highly prais'd,
> Can match that Muse when it with bays is crown'd,
> And to the pitch of her perfection rais'd.

Eliseïs, of which only the first book—perhaps all that was written—survives in MS., is in Latin, as is the tragedy of *Roxana,* the only other considerable poetic work of Alabaster's which has hitherto been known to exist. It is hard to imagine that Wood, Fuller, and other of Alabaster's contemporaries would have bestowed so much praise upon him unless they had been acquainted with further evidences of his poetic genius. It seems probable that he wrote a good deal of English verse, which, according to the custom of the time, was handed about in MS., and on which his reputation with his contemporaries was partly founded. At all events, it is reasonable to suppose that they knew of the existence of the series of sonnets which, by a fortunate accident, has lately fallen into my hands.

Mr. A. H. Bullen, in the *Dictionary of National Biography,* gives an excellent account of Alabaster's career. A fuller, though not better account of him is given in Dr. Drake's *Noontide Leisure,* vol. i. pp. 242-58. Referring the more curious reader to these sources of information, I will here summarize as briefly as possible the chief events of Alabaster's life. He was born in 1565, and died in 1640, thus living through the whole, or nearly the whole, of the great period of English literature. In

1596 Alabaster, as chaplain to the Earl of Essex, accompanied the expedition against Cadiz. While in Spain he fell in with a Jesuit priest, by whose arguments he was converted to Roman Catholicism. Returning to England, he published a pamphlet apologizing for his change of religion. For this he was promptly committed to the Tower, where he must have remained several months. I think it is pretty certain that most, if not all, of the sonnets which I now possess were written during his imprisonment. On his release it seems that Alabaster went abroad, for in 1607 he published at Antwerp a strange treatise on cabalistical divinity. This seems to have given offence to his co-religionists, for it was placed in 1610 on the 'Index Librorum Prohibitorum.' Being induced by some Jesuits to go to Rome, he was there thrown into the prison of the Inquisition. Making his escape with much difficulty, he returned to England, and became reconciled to Protestantism. Receiving promotion in the Church, he spent the remainder of his days in the study of philology and mystical divinity.

Dr. Drake concludes his account of Alabaster by saying that his memoir

> "will show that he filled during his lifetime a large space in the public eye, and that he was deservedly esteemed, as well for the depth and variety of his erudition as for the elegance of his classical acquirements. It is the record, however, of an individual who unhappily trusted not his fame to his native language, and who has therefore only been preserved from oblivion by the casual notice of his contemporaries and the occasional retrospect of the learned critic."

In writing thus Dr. Drake was speaking according to the knowledge which was then available. Apart from his writings on mystical divinity, the only English works of Alabaster's which were then known to exist were two sonnets which Malone had discovered in the Bodleian Library, and which were printed in the *Variorum Shakespeare,* 1821. Of these sonnets Malone had said "that their piety was more obvious than their poetry." Perhaps that judgment was not altogether unjust as regards the two sonnets which Malone had before him. When, however, John Payne Collier, in the second volume of his *History of Dramatic Poetry* (ed. 1830), endorsed Malone's opinion, I cannot help thinking that he spoke without proper reflection, or after an insufficient examination of the better means which he possessed of coming to a true judgment. Collier at that time owned a manuscript which contained seventeen sonnets by Alabaster. Of these he printed two, and from them alone (though the second is so deformed by misprints or misreadings that it is scarcely intelligible) I think he might have arrived at a different conclusion.

Collier, as I have stated, possessed seventeen of Alabaster's sonnets. But a manuscript which I have recently purchased contains no fewer than forty-three. A poet cannot write so many sonnets as this without giving us a sufficient idea of his quality and capabilities; and I hope to convince the reader that Alabaster was a true poet, and that his sonnets, as a whole, are worthy of a place beside the best of the sonnet-sequences of the Elizabethan period, with the single exception of Shakespeare's.

The whole of Alabaster's sonnets are of a devotional or religious cast. Four or five of them, it is true, are concerned with his personal feelings, or relate to his sufferings for conscience' sake; but these are so closely connected with his main subject that they do not in reality form an exception. There is, I believe, only one other sequence of sonnets of the time of which the themes are wholly religious, so that Alabaster can claim to have been one of the first to discover the capabilities of the sonnet for the expression of religious emotions. If only on this account, my discovery has a certain importance, because it adds another chapter to the history of the sonnet as used by the Elizabethan poets.

To reach perfection in the sonnet form is so difficult a task that no English writer has yet succeeded in producing a sequence in which there are no weak or unequal links. If in a series of forty or fifty the author produces one of first-rate excellence, and (say) a dozen of fine accomplishment, while the remainder reach a fair level of achievement, I think we must allow that he has done very well. The sonneteers who have accomplished so much as this are by no means numerous. Judging him by this standard, I think we may claim that Alabaster is the equal of all but two or three of our English sonneteers.

All authors are usually at their best when expressing the emotions which have moved them most profoundly, or which bear the most intimate relation to their own inner life. It is clear that Alabaster's conversion to Roman Catholicism was an event which stirred his deepest feelings, and awakened his intellect to its greatest efforts. In the following sonnet he gives eloquent expression to the feelings which were aroused within him by the persecutions which he underwent in consequence of his change of faith:—

> My friends whose kindness doth their judgments bind,
> know you (say they) the dangers where you run,
> which zeal hides from you, but compassion
> tells us? You feel the blow, the smart we find.
> I know it well: and as I call to mind
> this is the bill; dearness, affection,
> friends, fortunes, pleasures, fame, hope, life undone,
> want, prison, torment, death, shame, what behind?
> Is then my sense transmettled to steel
> that neither this nor that nor all can feel,
> nor can it bend my mind that thrice doth break?
> Not so, nor so, for I am not insensate,
> but feel a double grief that for Christ's sake
> I have no more to spend, and have not spent that.

The allusion to "prison" in the above sonnet seems to prove that it was written either during the author's imprisonment in the Tower, or not long afterwards.

The following is one of the sonnets which Collier printed, but (as I have already said) very incorrectly. I print it here because I think it is almost a duty to clear it from the errors which deform it in Collier's version, and render it almost unintelligible:—

> Away fear with thy projects! No false fire
> which thou dost make can ought my courage quail,
> or make me backward run, or strike my sail;
> what if the world do frown at my retire?
> what if denial dash my wish'd desire,
> and purblind pity do my state bewail,
> and wonder cross itself and free speech rail,
> and greatness take it not, and death show nigher?
> Tell them, my soul, the fears that make me quake,
> the smothering brimstone and the burning lake,
> life feeding death, death ever life devouring,
> torments not moved, unheard, and yet still roaring,
> God lost, hell found, ever never begun,
> now bid me into flame from smoke to run.

Collier said of the last six lines that he could not pretend to solve the mystery of them; but it seems to me that there is no mystery in them as given above, except possibly in the thirteenth line. The copyist has here probably mistaken the sense. I think Alabaster's line ran something like this:—

> God lost, hell found, pain ever new begun.

The three following sonnets are fair specimens of Alabaster's devotional verse:—

"A Preface to the Incarnation."

> I sing of Christ: O endless argument!
> profaner thoughts and cares begone, begone,
> lest thunder push down your presumption.
> I sing of Christ: let many words be lent
> to enrobe my thoughts with all their ornament,
> and tongues of men and angels join in one
> to shew the riches of invention
> before the eyes of all the firmament.
> The Temple where I sing is Heaven: the quire
> are my soul's powers: the book's a living story:
> each take his time, but with a bow retire
> that modesty may after reach his glory:
> and let the humble base beneath begin
> to shew when he descended for our sin.

Exaltatio Humanæ Naturæ.

> Humanity the field of miseries,
> nature's abortive table of mischance,
> stage of complaint, the fair that doth enhance
> the price of error and of vanities
> whither who seek it: whither doth it rise,[1]
> or do I see or am I in a trance?

I see it far above the clouds advance,
and under it to tread the starry skies.
My dazzling thoughts do hold this sight for pain,
Vouchsafe me, Christ, to look. See! now again
above the angels it bath distance won,
and left the winged cherubims behind,
and is within God's secret curtain gone,
and still it soareth! Gaze no more, my mind.

The sun begins upon my heart to shine:
now let a cloud of thoughts in order train
as dewy spangles wont, and entertain
in many drops his Passion divine,
that on them as a rainbow may recline
the white of innocence, the black of pain,
the blue of stripes, the yellow of disdain,
and purple, which his blood doth well design:
and let those thousand thoughts pour on mine eyes
a thousand tears as glasses to behold him,
and thousand tears thousand sweet words devise
upon my lips as pictures to unfold him:
so shall reflect three rainbows from one sun,
thoughts, tears, and words; all end in action.

I have, I think, now quoted enough to show that Alabaster was at least a fine poetic craftsman, but not enough perhaps to show that he could on occasion rise to the height of a great argument. That he could do so, however, is proved beyond doubt by the following sonnet:—

Incarnatio Est Maximum Dei Donum.

Like as the fountain of all light created
doth pour out streams of brightness undefin'd
through all the conduits of transparent kind,
that heaven and air are both illuminated,
and yet his light is not thereby abated,
so God's eternal bounty ever shin'd
the beams of being, moving, life, sense, mind,
and to all things himself communicated
but for the violent diffusive pleasure
of goodness that left not till God had spent
himself by giving us himself his treasure
in making man a God omnipotent.
How might this goodness draw ourselves above
which drew down God with such attractive love!

Surely this is a poem which should, like the one splendid sonnet of Blanco White, suffice to secure its author's fame while the English language endures. Coleridge, writing to White, said that he considered his single poetical essay as "the finest and most grandly conceived sonnet in our language." That was written immediately after he had become acquainted with it; and it is possible that he might not have cared, on further reflection, to make quite so high a claim for it. For myself I must confess that my feelings on first becoming acquainted with Alabaster's sonnet resembled those of Coleridge on first reading Blanco White's. I think that Coleridge, on mature reflection, would have altered his verdict so far as to term **'Death and Night'** not *the* finest, but "one of the finest and most grandly con-

ceived sonnets in our language," and that is the claim which I cannot help thinking that I am justified in making for Alabaster's sonnet. The sublimity of its thought is matched by the splendour of its expression; it is a rounded and perfect work of art, yet such a work as no art could produce, unless under the influence of that exaltation of mind which we term inspiration. It bears every mark of having been produced in one of those happy periods when the glow of thought overcomes the inertness of words, and easily and victoriously moulds them to its purpose.

There is one word in the sonnet to which objection may possibly be made—I mean "violent," which occurs in the ninth line. It is a good word, a fine word, in itself, but it is certainly not the word which a modern poet would have chosen to use in its place. But it should be remembered that "violent" did not in Alabaster's time bear so exclusively the sense which now attaches to it. We may take it to mean here simply immense, extensive, or infinite.[2]

Notes

1. I suspect an error of the copyist's in this line. I think we should read "to all who seek it," for the first "whither" yields only a strained sense, if any; and Alabaster would naturally have avoided the repetition of the word in the same line.

2. Shakespeare, in 'Troilus and Cressida,' uses the word in much the same sense as Alabaster:—

   Why tell you me of moderation?
   The grief is fine, full, perfect, that I taste,
   And violenteth in a sense as strong
   As that which causeth it.

G. M. Story (essay date 1959)

SOURCE: Story, G. M. "William Alabaster and the Devotional Tradition." In *The Sonnets of William Alabaster,* edited by G. M. Story and Helen Gardner, pp. xxiii-xxxvi. Oxford: Oxford University Press, 1959.

[*In the following excerpt from the introduction to the definitive publication of Alabaster's sonnets, Story overviews the sequence within the tradition of devotional poetry and highlights its distinctive elements.*]

Not the least interesting paradox of Alabaster's eminently paradoxical verse is that its special quality comes from the fusion of an old and widespread devotional tradition with the new poetic temper of the last decade of the sixteenth century. His *Divine Meditations* are an early document for the study of the new school of poets (the 'metaphysical' Donne and his followers) which arose in the closing years of the Elizabethan era, and at the same time they lay bare that continuing tradition which is such a pronounced feature of the devotional literature of medieval and Renaissance England.

The continuity of devotional literature in England down to the seventeenth century is easy to over-emphasize. But in spite of the revolutionary temper of the sixteenth century, the persistence of the devotional tradition throughout the period is striking. It is to be found not so much in a continuing poetic tradition as in the religious spirit itself, and in the literature of prose devotion.[1] It is perhaps most apparent in the continuing vitality of certain devotional classics of the Middle Ages. A good many medieval texts might cease to be used, except perhaps in Catholic circles, after the Reformation; but others, such as *The Imitation of Christ,* than which few works could be more outwardly 'monastic', enjoyed undiminished favour in the sixteenth century, and indeed reached an even wider public through dissemination by the printing press. Even more interesting here is the history of the pseudo-Augustinian *Liber Meditationum,* a devotional manual much used from the thirteenth century onwards, with its popularity increasing, if anything, in the sixteenth century until it became a favourite book not only with Catholics but, 'edited' in English dress, for Protestants as well. Its continuing influence on sacred poetry is attested when we find Alabaster, like an anonymous poet three centuries earlier, drawing upon it for his devotional needs.[2]

Not all the medieval devotional works which continued in use in post-Reformation England did so with quite so much of their original form and spirit unimpaired as the two books just mentioned. Here as elsewhere the reformers used traditional material as an instrument of change. The *Primer* for instance was adapted and modified with this purpose in mind by the authorities. Yet the surprising thing is not so much that its traditional character has changed as that so much of its old form remains. The Protestant temper of the sixteenth century was wary of certain kinds of Catholic devotion. Yet in a collection of prayers like the celebrated *Fifteen Oes,* the warm humanity of the contemplations of the Passion which on *a priori* grounds would seem inimical to the Protestant spirit of the time, remains a prominent feature of the book as late as 1578, demonstrating, as Miss White points out, 'the extraordinary substratum of continuity through all the changes of the period'.[3]

But it is of course the Scriptures which are the most important bond between the devotional life of the Middle Ages and the Renaissance, especially the Psalter, amenable as it was to use by individual Christians for specific needs and occasions.[4]

The mere fact that religious writers of both the Middle Ages and Renaissance alike read and were influenced by largely the same sources is only part of the case for the continuity of English devotional literature. More significant is the extent to which they responded in the same way to the traditional body of Christian literature, the way in which they used it. When, in **'Sonnet 3,'** Alabaster writes of Christ crossing Cedron like David fleeing from Absolom, a complex tissue of allegory and 'moralization' is involved. For David fleeing from his son across the brook Kidron was interpreted in the Middle Ages and Renaissance alike as prefiguring Christ in His Passion. Further, Psalm 3, sung by David when he fled, was moralized as the struggle of the individual soul. The sonnet contains a scriptural allusion, a meditation on an incident in the life of Christ, and a reflection on the poet's own predicament, all three 'meanings' simultaneously explicit within the framework of the tradition of scriptural allegory. And when we find Richard Rolle in the fourteenth century extracting the same meaning from the Psalm,[5] the persistence of an ancient mode of thought in the sixteenth century becomes very clear. What Rolle and Alabaster share is of course the allegorical mind. It was this which produced the interpretations of the Scriptures embodied in texts such as the *Sentences* of Peter Lombard and the twelfth-century *Glossa Ordinaria,* themselves deriving in part from Christian tradition reaching back through the Church Fathers to the New Testament.[6]

The allegorical way of seeing things produced a vast body of Christian symbolism upon which the sacred poet drew just as the secular poet drew upon classical legend. When Alabaster writes in **'Sonnet 39'** of the Virgin's womb as a 'golden cabin', he is alluding to the traditional gloss on the 'tabernacle' of Psalm 19. And it is to traditional Christian symbolism that we must go for an explanation of such conceits as Christ the giant-like runner (**'2'**), the second Adam (**'20'**), the grape-cluster (**'32'**), and St. John as the eagle (**'77'**).

In passages such as these Alabaster is not parading recondite learning. He was a very learned scholar, but the tradition in which such symbolism was embedded was not the preserve of the learned. Christ as the grapecluster, for instance, is a conceit explained by a relatively inaccessible commentator like Rabanus Maurus, and in the Glossed Bible at Numbers xiii. 23. But it was equally accessible to learned and unlearned alike in the stained glass of church windows, or in the illustrated pages of popular devotional manuals. The allegorical mode of thought was a living tradition, and as such it must be seen by the modern reader, not as the quaint lore of a distant past. Its importance for the appreciation as well as the understanding of the sacred poetry which made use of it should not be underrated.

This is also true of more obvious influences on the devotional poetry of the past. The ordinary literate men and women of the seventeenth century would not have needed an elaborate scholarly apparatus to recognize the liturgical influence on Herbert's 'The Sacrifice'. We might even be surprised to learn the extent to which a contemporary of Donne's would have noticed the way he wove into the fabric of the first of the *La Corona* sonnets, phrases from the Advent Offices in the Roman Breviary.[7] It is not mere antiquarian interest which draws attention to these features of sacred verse as much as a desire to uncover a vital aspect of devotional poetry, the all-pervasive influence of the great body of literature, Scriptures, patristic and scholastic writings, liturgy, hymns, and art in which is embodied the Christian experience and apart from which the Christian poet cannot write of his own religious predicament.

The traditionalism of Alabaster's *Divine Meditations,* as well as their interest to the student of the origins of the metaphysical poetry of devotion, can be illustrated in another way as well, for they belong to that ancient Christian exercise, the meditation. The purpose of the exercise is to help the Christian to realize Divine Truth. It seeks to arouse the affections, through which alone the end of the exercise may be achieved, by the use of what St. Ignatius Loyola called the 'three powers of the soul', the memory, the understanding, and the will.[8] The most obvious way in which to move the affections, to arouse devotional fervour, is by appealing to the imagination, and because of its imaginative possibilities verse is one of the most common vehicles of meditation. Alabaster's method is thoroughly traditional. He uses the material of Scripture, variously embellished, or intellectual inquiry, or penitential reflection, to arouse devotion. His method is illustrated by the sonnet **'My soul a world is by contraction'** (**'15'**), in which he elaborates a conceit drawn from the traditional account of the heavenly universe.

> My soul a world is by contraction,
> The heavens therein is my internal sense,
> Moved by my will as an intelligence,
> My heart the element, my love the sun.
> And as the sun about the earth doth run,
> And with his beams doth draw thin vapours thence,
> Which after in the air do condense,
> And pour down rain upon the earth anon,
> So moves my love about the heavenly sphere,
> And draweth thence with an attractive fire
> The purest argument wit can desire,
> Whereby devotion after may arise.
> And these conceits, digest by thoughts' retire,
> Are turned into april showers of tears.

This is the immemorial method of Christian meditation; yet it is so with a difference. For one thing the sonnet form in which the meditation is cast belongs to the sixteenth century, and for another the temper of the verse is new. It is a metaphysical poem.

A reader's opinion of Alabaster's success in a number of sonnets will depend largely on whether he reads them as poems or as devotional exercises. It will be suggested later on that one of Alabaster's purposes in writing his meditations may have been to achieve what he called 'newness of life': he seems to have written them, at least in part, as exercises to arouse religious fervour, as well as to express the religious exaltation he felt on embracing the Roman faith. It may be that the mere presentation of a religious subject for contemplation is sufficient to effect the desired response not only from the poet himself, but also perhaps from the reader. It must be confessed that a good many of the *Divine Meditations* can only be regarded as successful if the criterion adopted be a religious one. Some of them are not so much poetry as the raw material of poetry. The first sequence, *The Portrait of Christ's Death,* for instance, contains many such sonnets. Alabaster presents various incidents or moments in Christ's life and reflects upon the moral consequences for himself. The presentation is often flat, the incidents have not fired his imagination with a passionate apprehension of their significance, in short, they have not been transmuted into poetry. Sonnets such as **''Tis not enough over the brook to stride'** (**'5'**), **'Alas, our shepherd now is struck again'** (**'8'**), or **'His death begins within a farm'** (**'11'**) might just as well have been written in prose. As it is they are neither good verse nor good prose. 'The piety', as Malone remarked of the two sonnets he knew, 'is more obvious than the poetry.'[9]

The failure of other sonnets is often less a matter of lack of poetic feeling than of breakdown in the conclusion. **'Sonnet 10,'** for example, begins well:

> Though all forsake thee, lord, yet I will die,
> For I have chained so my will to thine
> That I have no will left my will to untwine,
> But will abide with thee most willingly.
> Though all forsake thee, lord, yet cannot I,
> For love hath wrought in me thy form divine
> That thou art more my heart than heart is mine:
> How can I then from myself, thyself, fly?

These lines have real vigour, with the powerful cumulative effect of the piling up of vowels and the strong emphasis on personal pronouns. The repetition of the opening phrase of the first line in the fifth is effective, and the paradox of lines 7 and 8 closes the octave strikingly. Alabaster's power of condensed phrasing, often found in his best verse and one of its great distinctions, is very noticeable in the passage (the ellipsis of 'so' after 'hath' in line 6 is characteristic). Unfortunately the sonnet is spoiled by the weak sestet:

> Thus thought St. Peter and thus thinking fell,
> And by his fall did warn us not to swell,
> Yet still in love I say I would not fall,
> And say in hope I trust I never shall,
> But cannot say in faith, what might I do
> To learn to say it, by hearing Christ say so!

Weak conclusions are one of the greatest flaws in Alabaster's sonnets; too often they fall off from the modest level of most of his poems. It may be that the couplet ending which he uses in many of the poems contributes to this tendency in his work, witness the lamentable effect it has on **'Sonnets 59'** and **'73'**. The couplet ending demands great skill if it is to avoid such lameness, and even Shakespeare does not always escape its pitfall. To be fair we must take into account the conditions under which the poems were written and also the way they have come down to us. They appear to have been composed either in prison or when he was hiding from the authorities as a fugitive, and while he was still under the stress, as well as the exaltation, of a profound religious experience. To this, perhaps, are to be attributed some of the occasional passages in which there is a breakdown in sense. In addition, Alabaster probably lacked the opportunity of polishing his work; certainly he never had the poems printed and text established, and textual corruption, the inevitable accompaniment of manuscript transmission, has marred some of them. Nevertheless, the chief cause of the poor quality of many of the *Divine Meditations* is Alabaster's limited poetic talent. He is undoubtedly a poet; but he is a minor poet.

Alabaster was not the only poet who, about this time, was using the sonnet for devotional purposes. In the mid-fifteen-nineties, the indefatigable Henry Lok was turning out more than a 'century' of divine sonnets, and Barnabe Barnes had just turned from his Parthenophe to write spiritual sonnets. Similarly, Henry Constable, having written his sequence to Diana, wrote religious sonnets, like Alabaster, after he became a Catholic, though probably somewhat later. But when poets like Barnes and Constable left Parnassus for Calvary, they wrote, not indeed worse sonnets, but sonnets which are indistinguishable in style from the conventional 'Elizabethan' manner of their secular poems. Alabaster uses the same poetic form, but he does something rather different with it. He is a different *kind* of poet. Malone recognized this when, after his unflattering remark about the 'piety' as opposed to the 'poetry' of the two *Divine Meditations* he had before him, he went on, 'yet Donne, and those in that age who admired Donne, doubtless thought them excellent'. Alabaster is a metaphysical poet, and his sonnets have special interest because, written as they appear to have been in 1597/8, they are among the earliest metaphysical poems of devotion that we have.

It is unnecessary here to describe the rise of the metaphysical school of poets. One of the most perceptive recent studies[10] has explored these poets through their common use of the sixteenth-century methods of devotion alluded to earlier. Perhaps it is this common dependence on recognized exercises in meditation that explains the qualities shared by Alabaster and Southwell, the only other claimant for the honour of anticipating the great devotional poets of the seventeenth century. At the same time, some more general explanation would

probably be needed to make clear the relation to the new movement of poets such as Chapman, 'mannerists', yet not 'metaphysicals'. It was, indeed, Chapman who wrote: 'that Poesy should be as pervial as Oratory, and plainness her special ornament, were the plain way to barbarism', a manifesto to which all the metaphysical writers could, in varying degrees, subscribe.[11] It accounts for the quality of close thought, the conciseness, the tough texture of their writing, as opposed to the loose and decorative effects of 'Elizabethan' verse and, for that matter, 'Ciceronian' prose.

These are the qualities which the sonnet form itself encourages: concentration, the dialectical quality. It is especially useful for religious poetry, in which diffuseness and vague emotion are distressingly frequent. The form is eminently suited to 'intellectual' poetry. And this is especially true of the particular sonnet form which Alabaster often uses, the dramatic Petrarchan sonnet introduced by Wyatt and used frequently by Sidney and Donne. In his best work, Alabaster exhibits these qualities. In addition, one frequently finds another distinctive quality: the firm discipline of controlled rhetoric. The strength and economy with which he achieves his effect in the octave of the sonnet **'Though all forsake thee, lord, yet I will die'** (**'10'**), is also found in another sonnet, number **'7'**, where it is not marred by a weak sestet:

What should there be in Christ to give offence?
His corded hands, why they for thee were bound,
His mangled brows, why they for thee were crowned,
His pierced breast, thy life did flow from thence.
What though some arrows glance with violence
From him to thee, shall this thy friendship wound?
What though some stones upon thee do rebound,
Shall such small fillips break thy patience?
Those shafts which raze thy skin, ran through his
    heart;
Those stones which touch thy hands, first broke his
    head;
But those small drops of pain he doth impart
To show what he did bear, what thou hast fled.
And yet we grieve to suffer for his sake:
'Tis night, or else how could we so mistake.

This is Alabaster in one of his most moving poems, and at the same time, based as it is on the old Complaint of Christ motif, one of his most traditional. While the liturgical overtones in the sonnet give it an impersonal flavour, it is also an intensely personal poem. It has, indeed, an almost Herbertian quality which appears even more strikingly in the fine sonnet, **'Jesu, thy love within me is so main'** (**'19'**). In many of the poems one notices the familiar and argumentative tone of the sonnets. In **'Sonnet 7'** the poet speaks of the 'friendship' between Man and his Redeemer; in **'Sonnet 10'** he tells of a divine love which makes him one with Christ; and in **'Sonnet 77'** he, like St. John, 'on thy breast will lean', nay, 'through thy breast unto thy heart will run'. The vigorous questioning note of the opening line of

'Sonnet 7', so like Donne in his *Divine Poems,* recurs in other poems:

> When all forsake, whose courage dare abide?
>
> (9)

> Lo here I am, lord, whither wilt thou send me?
>
> (41)

and **'Sonnet 65',**

> Why put he on the web of human nature,
> That with his wardrobe did the world invest?

Earlier in this essay we saw that Alabaster frequently draws upon a very old and living Christian tradition for his imagery; and in quoting the sonnet **'My soul a world is by contraction'** (**'15'**), the more specifically metaphysical nature of its imagery was mentioned. Conceits in which the poet makes use of the system of the universe recur in other sonnets, for example, in **'O wretched man, the knot of contraries'** (**'73'**), and **'The first beginning of creation'** (**'63'**). But Alabaster's imagery is not confined to the product of learned inquiry or to traditional symbolism; he has a place for images drawn from the daily life of the world around him. For instance, Christ as the owner of a farm, and Man the tenant who withholds the rent (**'11'**), the poet's will as a parliamentary session, his love, the steward of affection (**'41'**), the poet as a ship, his faith the sail which will never be struck to an enemy (**'46'**), the Incarnation likened to the grafting of one tree to another (**'66'**), and the tears through which he looks on Christ as optics (**'71'**). But whatever the source or nature of the imagery, most of the sonnets have one thing in common, the use of paradox.

Paradox is, indeed, implicit in the very subject of Alabaster's poetry: Christianity, and the great mysteries in which the Christian religion is expressed. To mention one example, the Incarnation has inspired a whole sequence in which the poet strives to apprehend the mystery of God, Who is Infinite, assuming the finite form of Man. And throughout the *Divine Meditations* recurs the penitential theme, the sinfulness of Man who is yet redeemed by the mercy of God. Alabaster's mind works through paradox, and with it he achieves some of his most striking effects. In particular, this quality of paradox in his verse still further strengthens his power of condensed phrasing. Sometimes it appears only in a few lines of a sonnet, and as might be expected this quality of condensed paradox is especially frequent in the sequence on the Incarnation. The opening lines, for instance, of **'Sonnet 54', 'Incarnationem Ratione Probare Impossibile'**:

> Two, yet but one, which either other is,
> One, yet in two, which neither other be,

> God and man in one personality,
> Humanity assumed unto bliss,
> Man unassumed, God being man, not this.

A Christian commonplace, but tersely written. Sometimes Alabaster uses paradox to give a fine epigrammatic turn to his final couplet, for instance in sonnets **'19', '50', '68',** and **'71'.** More rarely it is sustained throughout a sonnet, as in number **'43',** one of the best he wrote:

> Thrice happy souls and spirits unbodied,
> Who in the school of heaven do always see
> The three-leaved bible of one Trinity,
> In whose unfolded page are to be read
> The incomprehended secrets of the Godhead,
> Who only read by love that mystery,
> And what you read is love's infinity,
> Who learn by love, and love is what is learned.
> O happy school whose master is the book,
> Which book is only text, which text unwrit
> Doth read itself, and they that on it look
> Do read by being read, nor do they flit
> From word to word: for all is but one letter,
> Which still is learnt, but never learnt the better.

This quality of paradox in the *Divine Meditations* means that Alabaster's is sometimes difficult poetry. It is not always good; it is usually interesting. The meaning often has to be teased out of the lines, full as they are of close thought, double meaning, and grammatical ellipsis. Readers who like their poetry 'pervial' and 'plain' may protest that the 'poetic' pleasure derived from reading passages such as these is not commensurate with the effort required to understand them. Alabaster does not always write in this way, and some of his paradoxical turns are no more complex than the Christian commonplaces about which he is writing. Nor is it implied that he cannot write, on occasion, simply and movingly. But in other passages, and these in much of his best work, the complexity comes from his dialectical teasing of his subject. This is something he shares with the great metaphysical poets, of whom he is a forerunner, though he never reaches their higher levels. But while the student of sixteenth-century poetry will need no inducement to read these three-score or more sonnets (a considerable addition to the body of devotional verse written on the threshold of England's great age of religious poetry), the lover of minor poetry will also find them of some interest. They are the work of an arresting figure, the vicissitudes of whose career suggest something of the complexity of his era, and whose personality is stamped upon verse which, for all its unevenness has its own distinctive quality.

Notes

1. See Helen C. White, 'Some Continuing Traditions in English Devotional Literature', *P.M.L.A.* (1942), lxvii. 966-80, and *Tudor Books of Private Devotion* (Wisconsin, 1951).

2. Compare sonnet '35' with the first poem (and note) in Carleton Brown's *Religious Lyrics of the XIVth Century* (1924).

3. *Tudor Books of Private Devotion,* p. 229. The *Primer* as an instrument of religious change (the phrase is Miss White's) is described in chapter vi, and the *Fifteen Oes* in chapter xiii.

4. One of the earliest guides to this use of the Psalms is the well-known letter of Athanasius to Marullinus, 'On the Interpretation of the Psalms' (found conveniently with the treatise *On the Incarnation,* tr. A Religious of C.S.M.V., 2nd edn. 1953). It is worth noting as an example of the common approach to the Psalms in both periods that the editors of the 1567 Sternhold and Hopkins version printed with it this 'Table of Athanasius'.

5. *English Writings,* ed. H. E. Allen (1931), p. 125, note.

6. For an account of biblical exegesis in the Middle Ages, and the tradition upon which it drew, see Beryl Smalley, *The Study of the Bible in the Middle Ages* (2nd edn. 1952).

7. The dependence of 'The Sacrifice' on the liturgical offices of Holy Week, the *Improperia* or Reproaches of Good Friday, was independently worked out by Miss R. Freeman, *The English Emblem Books* (1948), p. 162, and by Miss R. Tuve, *A Reading of George Herbert* (1952). Donne's use of the Breviary is noted by Miss Helen Gardner in her edition of *The Divine Poems* (1952), pp. 57-58.

8. *The Spiritual Exercises,* tr. W. H. Longridge (4th edn. 1950), p. 52, and note C. The Jesuit, John Gerard, gave Alabaster the Exercises in 1598 (see above, p. xvi). The significance of this will not be lost on readers of L. L. Martz, *The Poetry of Meditation* (Yale, 1954) which explores the connexions between the rise of 'metaphysical' poetry and the methods of sixteenth-century meditation.

9. (Third Variorum) *Shakespeare* (1821), ii. 263.

10. L. L. Martz, *The Poetry of Meditation* (Yale, 1954).

11. 'Epistle Dedicatory' to *Ovid's Banquet of Sense* (1595). Perhaps this should not be pressed too far. It is usual to distinguish between the deliberate, 'hermetic' obscurity of Chapman, and the kind of difficulty found in metaphysical verse which arises from the nature of the poetic experience.

Abbreviation

P.M.L.A. *Publications of the Modern Language Association of America.*

J. W. Binns (essay date 1974)

SOURCE: Binns, J. W. "Seneca and Neo-Latin Tragedy in England." In *Seneca,* edited by C. D. N. Costa, pp. 205-34. London: Routledge & Kegan Paul Limited, 1974.

[*In the following excerpt from his essay on three neo-Latin tragedies from the Elizabethan age, Binns determines the influence of Seneca upon Alabaster's* Roxana.]

A large number of Renaissance plays which were written in Latin survive today from all the countries of Europe.[1] In England, the plays which are extant from the sixteenth and early seventeenth centuries form an interesting by-way of the Elizabethan drama.[2] A number of tragedies in particular remain, which, cast in Senecan mould, constitute an aspect of Seneca's influence which has been little discussed. The extent of Seneca's influence on the popular drama of the Elizabethan age continues to be debated.[3]

On the Latin drama of the age, the drama written by educated men, who were often members of the Universities of Oxford or Cambridge, the extent of Seneca's influence is less open to doubt. Seneca, as the only surviving ancient writer of Latin tragedy, would be familiar to any cultivated man of the times with an interest in literature, especially in view of the pre-eminent position which tragedy then occupied among the literary *genres.* The plays of Seneca were almost certainly on the syllabus at Westminster School,[4] which was attended by two important writers of Academic drama, William Gager and William Alabaster. William Gager, in the prologue to an expanded version of Seneca's *Hippolytus* which was performed at Christ Church, Oxford, in February 1591/2, could assume that at any rate all the men in the audience, even if not the women, would be familiar with the play.[5]

Modern scholars tend to consider that Seneca's plays were not written for performance on the stage. Renaissance critics, however, generally believed that Seneca's plays had been performed;[6] and several performances are indeed recorded at Oxford and Cambridge during the sixteenth century. G. C. Moore Smith records the performance at Trinity College, Cambridge, of a *Troades* in 1551/2 and 1560/1, of an *Oedipus* in 1559/60, and of a *Medea* in 1560/1 (the 1551/2 performance being certainly of Seneca's play, and the other performances mentioned almost certainly of his plays); of a *Hecuba,* again at Trinity College, in 1559/60 (probably Seneca's *Troades*); and of a *Medea,* perhaps Seneca's *Medea,* at Queens' College, Cambridge, in 1563.[7] G. C. Moore Smith came to the conclusion that 'the original Latin tragedies of Seneca continued to be given on College stages at least down to 1583',[8] and writing of Cambridge Academic plays performed before 1585, he states: 'Judging from the titles of acted plays, Plautus, Terence, and Seneca were the Latin authors most drawn upon'.[9] At Oxford, F. S. Boas lists a performance at Christ Church of *Octavia* (probably the pseudo-Senecan play) in 1588, as well as the performance which I have already mentioned of *Hippolytus* with additional scenes written by Gager in February 1591/2 at Christ Church.[10] Gager himself writing in defence of Academic drama refers to the acting of Seneca as a commonplace event:[11]

> We contrarywise doe it [i.e. come upon the stage] to recreate owre selves, owre House, and the better parte of the *Vniversitye*, with some learned *Poeme* or other; to practyse owre owne style eyther in prose or verse; to be well acquaynted with *Seneca* or *Plautus*; honestly to embowlden owre yuthe; to trye their voyces, and confirme their memoryes; to frame their speeche; to conforme them to convenient action; to trye what mettell is in evrye one, and of what disposition thay are of; wherby never any one amongst vs, that I knowe, was made the worse, many have byn much the better.

Academic acting, then, served the twin ends of amusement and education. It also helped to diffuse a knowledge of and interest in Seneca's tragedies throughout the universities. In all probability, anyone who sat down in the sixteenth century to compose a tragedy written in Latin was thoroughly familiar with Senecan tragedy. Latin tragedies on Senecan lines both are a reflection of the contemporary fascination with Seneca, and help to propagate this interest.

I propose to discuss in this chapter three Latin tragedies to which little attention has been paid, and then to try to see whether it is possible to draw any conclusions which may help us to modify our view of Seneca's influence on the Elizabethan drama.

The first play I shall discuss is ***Roxana,*** a Latin tragedy by William Alabaster, the minor English poet and writer of works of mystical theology.[12] This play was first published in a pirated edition in 1632, and was followed in the same year by an authorized edition described on the title page as: *A plagiarii unguibus vindicata, aucta, et agnita ab Authore* (claimed from the claws of the plagiarist, expanded, and acknowledged as his own by the author). Alabaster states, in a dedicatory letter to Sir Ralph Freeman,[13] also a dramatist, that the play had, however, been written and acted about forty years previously (at Trinity College, Cambridge, in *c.* 1592), when Elizabethan drama was entering the period of its greatest florescence. As in most of Seneca's tragedies, the action of ***Roxana*** commences when events are approaching a crisis: much that is important for the narrative had already happened before the play begins, and in the authorized version of the play to which I shall refer in my discussion, a brief summary outlines these events for the reader. In performance these would have been explained by an early speech of the ghost of Moleon, who recounts his past history on his return from the underworld.

When Oxiartes, king of Bactria, lay dying, he entrusted to his brother Moleon the tutelage of his kingdom and his son, Oromasdes, until the latter should be of an age to rule. When Moleon found excuses for not handing over the kingdom, Oromasdes fled to India and married Atossa, the daughter of an Indian king. Returning with a military force, he deposed and executed Moleon. Moleon had a daughter, Roxana, whom, lest she fall into the victor's hands, he had sent away to a secret hideout in the depths of the forest, accompanied by faithful attendants and all necessary supplies. Oromasdes, separated from his companions whilst out hunting, chanced upon Roxana's hideaway, made her his mistress, and had a son and a daughter by her.

Oromasdes has known Roxana for ten years when the action of the play begins with the return from the underworld to Bactria, his old kingdom, of the ghost of Moleon. Moleon had been promised his revenge by the ruler of the underworld. The figure of Death approaches and offers his aid. To him Moleon outlines his tale, maintaining that he had always intended to deliver up the kingdom to Oromasdes when the latter was ready for it, but Oromasdes had acted too precipitately. The seduction of his daughter was a further wrong to be avenged. Roxana too must pay for loving her father's murderer and for bearing children by him. Moleon decides to set his vengeance in motion by use of the figure of Suspicion, who enters, and is briefed by Moleon. A chorus concludes the act, telling of strange omens: the howling of an owl, a wolf entering the court, two snakes entering Atossa's bedroom. Suspicion begins now to poison the minds of the characters.

Act II opens with Oromasdes beset by ill-defined feelings of unease. He wonders whether his wife Atossa has found out about the existence of his mistress Roxana. He sends his counsellor, Bessus, to make sure that all is well with Roxana. Bessus is afraid lest the king believe that he has betrayed his secret. He begins to fall in love with Atossa and to her he recounts his love. Bessus informs Atossa of the existence of Roxana and her two children, and says that the king is thinking of divorcing Atossa. Atossa is outraged at the news, pledges her love to Bessus, and plots vengeance against her husband. In Act III Oromasdes debates with a senator, Arsaces, the advisability of divorcing his wife on the grounds that she has produced him no heir. Meanwhile Bessus has brought Roxana and her children from her forest retreat to the court, under the pretence that she is to be made queen. Atossa, pretending to be Oromasdes's mother, greets Roxana fulsomely. In the next scene, Arsaces soliloquizes on the vices of the court.

At the beginning of Act IV a messenger enters, overwhelmed with the atrociousness of the news with which he is burdened. He proceeds to relate this piece by piece to the chorus. The messenger describes a secret chamber to the north of the palace, shaded by trees of yew and cypress. The chamber is haunted, and used for black-magic rites. When Roxana, who thought she was about to go through a marriage ceremony with Oromasdes, entered the chamber, Atossa had chained her hands together, taunted her, and then had her flogged. The ghost of Moleon now appears and interrupts the messenger's narration with exclamations of delight. Atossa had placed a sword in Roxana's hands and then forced her to kill her own children. In the next scene, Oromasdes, ignorant of what has just occurred, begins to suspect Bessus's loyalty; he hears him speaking of his love for Atossa and kills him, thinking that the secret of Roxana is now quite safe.

In the first scene of Act V Atossa is boasting that she has outdone Medea in monstrous crime. She is preparing a banquet at which she will serve up the bodies of Roxana and her children. She has prepared a poisoned garland for Oromasdes, which will drip into his goblet of wine and cause him to die. Oromasdes is meanwhile plotting to murder Atossa in exactly the same way. The ghost of Moleon arrives to watch the consummation of his vengeance. When they have eaten, Oromasdes reveals to Atossa the head of Bessus. In return, she reveals to Oromasdes that he has eaten from the bodies of Roxana and her two children. Both now begin to die from the poison they had prepared for each other. Atossa looks forward to the glory she will enjoy in the lower world for her deeds. Oromasdes dies, and Atossa dies immediately afterwards.

The prefatory material to the authorized printed version of the play tells us a good deal about its composition. In the dedicatory letter to Ralph Freeman, Alabaster calls the play a *morticinum . . . abortum* (a dead, unfinished piece), written in two weeks, and intended, not for immortality, but for one performance only. He had hoped that his play could rest undisturbed, but a plagiarist brought the play to light, and printed it from a corrupt manuscript; the plagiarist was responsible for increasing the number of blemishes caused by the hasty composition of the play. Alabaster had been faced with the choice of allowing this faulty version to be perpetuated, or else of supplicating again his youthful Muses, although he was now nearly seventy. He had therefore chosen to issue under his own name a more correct version of the play.

In fact, the pirated version is a good deal closer to the authorized version than one would think from Alabaster's protestations. The pirated version is indeed rather more handsomely printed than the authorized version. The choruses in particular are set out more elegantly. Moreover, the authorized version contains a long list of *errata* at the end of the play, and the first scene of Act II is headed 'Actus Secundus, Scena Quarta'. There are numerous differences of word order, of accidence, and of punctuation between the two versions, together with many small differences of phraseology, but otherwise it is the same play, virtually line for line. The title page of the authorized version advertises the work as *aucta* (expanded), but the expansions are few and far between. The plot summary of events immediately antecedent to the opening of the play does not appear in the pirated version. On the other hand, the authorized version lacks the scene-by-scene summaries which the pirated version possesses. Otherwise the chief additions to the authorized version are nine lines at the end of the first speech of Death in Act I, scene 2; five lines in the middle of his second speech in the same scene; six lines of stichomythia between Death and Suspicion in Act I, scene 4; a short interchange of seven lines between the chorus and Atossa in Act V, scene 1; and four and a half lines added to Oromasdes's last speech in the final scene of the play. It may be that Alabaster wrote these lines especially for his edition of the play, and that this is what he means when he says that he had to supplicate the Muses of his youth once again. The surviving manuscripts of the play,[14] strangely enough, stand in close relation to the pirated version of the play, not to the authorized version. Alabaster's indignation is undoubtedly overstated in the dedicatory letter which prefaces the play.

He states furthermore that the authorized edition of the play is *crebra linearum interpelatione caperata* (wrinkled with interpellation of many lines), although the additions amount to less than thirtyfive lines. Alabaster considered that the style of the play was extravagant throughout. He refers to its *dictionis . . . lolium* (the weeds of its diction). In addition he made a plea for the play to be declaimed in a ranting manner (sig. A5r.):

> cum spuma soni, ut solent poetae tragoedias suas, quia in grandius quodammodo excoluntur, quae cum ampulla oris leguntur.

> (with a foaming sound, in the manner in which poets are accustomed to recite their tragedies, because works which are read in a bombastic voice become even more perfect.)

This suggests that Alabaster prized **Roxana** for its grandiose, inflated style, the Latin equivalent, perhaps, of the ranting bombast of Elizabethan popular tragedy.

It may well be that, as I shall suggest below (p. 229), Renaissance Latin tragedies, and the tragedies of Seneca himself, were valued more for their style than for their dramatic qualities. Commendatory verses by Hugh Holland,[15] who also contributed a dedicatory poem to Shakespeare's *First Folio*, commend the fluency of the inflated style of **Roxana** (sig. A5v.):

> Quis Graium tonat ore tam rotundo,
> Cuius tam cita Musa tamque pressa?

(Which of the Greeks thunders in voice so orotund?
Whose Muse is so swift and so concise?)

In another dedicatory poem, Thomas Farnaby,[16] the brilliant Elizabethan scholar, renowned for his editions of Seneca and other classical authors, praised the exalted style of the play:

> Roxana scenae emancipata pulpitis
> Olim, ubi, cothurno nixa, contempsit solum,
> Calcavit astra, condidit coelo caput.
>
> (Roxana is freed from the boards of the stage, where once, supported by her tragic buskin, she contemned the ground, trampled the stars, and hid her head in the heavens.)

(sig. A6v)

Modern taste may tend to disparage as inferior imitations the Latin writings of the sixteenth and seventeenth centuries; yet for *Roxana* to merit the praises of such a one as Farnaby was in its day no mean achievement. Moreover, in his *Index Poeticus* (London, 1634), a glossary of poetical commonplaces, giving references to treatments of various themes in ancient and modern Latin authors, Farnaby lists Alabaster as one of the seven modern Anglo-Latin authors on whom he has drawn for illustrative material. Although he refers on occasion to Alabaster's poems, most of his allusions to Alabaster are to *Roxana.* He refers the reader to the chorus at the end of Act III for a description of the power of love; to Act III, scene 4 for the arts of the courtier; to Act II, scene 2 for the mutability of Fortune; to Act II, scene 3 for the Furies; to Act IV, scene 1 for omens; to Act II, scene 4 and Act III, scene 2 for dreams; and to Act II, scene 4 for vengeance. Thomas Fuller too, in his *Worthies of England,*[17] describes Alabaster as 'a most rare poet as any our age or nation hath produced; witness his tragedy of *Roxana* admirably acted in [Trinity] college, and so pathetically, that a gentlewoman present thereat (Reader, I had it from an author whose credit it is sin with me to suspect), at the hearing of the last words thereof, *Sequar, sequar,* so hideously pronounced, fell distracted, and never after fully recovered her senses.'

Dr Johnson too remarked that 'Milton was the first Englishman who, after the revival of letters, wrote Latin verses with classick elegance. . . . If we produced anything worthy of notice before the elegies of Milton, it was perhaps Alabaster's *Roxana.*'[18]

Thus Alabaster himself and those who commend the play seem to stress its stylistic virtues, and we should bear this in mind in any discussion of the play. Although Alabaster complains that a plagiarist has made free with his play, *Roxana* is an adaptation, with some omissions and additions, of an Italian play, Luigi Groto's *La Dalida* (Venice, 1572); Alabaster however reduces by about half the great length (some 4,000 lines) of Groto's play. Alabaster's reliance on Groto for the details of his plot again suggests that his interest in literary composition lay not so much in the invention of his material but in his manner of treating it.

None the less, Alabaster's play, by virtue alone of being written in Latin, can succeed in coming much closer to the Senecan style and mood. The Senecan qualities are not transposed by being rendered into another language, as tends to happen in the Elizabethan translations of Seneca, where the language of the translation takes on a life of its own. *Roxana* is certainly bloodthirsty and horrific; the atmosphere is extravagant and exotic. The setting is the kingdom of Bactria in the Balkans; Oromasdes's wife, Atossa, is an Indian princess; and the names of the other characters too are Oriental: Arsaces, the senator; Sisimithres and Ariaspe, Roxana's children; Damiana, attendant upon Atossa. The whole of the first act is devoted to Moleon's account of his wrongs and his desire for vengeance. He, and the stylized figures of Death and Suspicion, are the only characters to appear in the act. Human characters do not appear until Act II, unless one counts the chorus at the end of Act I. The play is economically constructed with few characters. There is no sub-plot. Bessus and Atossa are balanced by Oromasdes and Roxana, and this symmetry is emphasized by the way in which Oromasdes and Atossa choose to kill each other with poisoned flowers, after having first killed each other's lovers.

That episode provides the horrific climax of the play. Earlier, however, a lengthy and explicit description of the sadistic torture of Roxana by Atossa had been given (sig. D6v.):

>   creber et roseam cutem
> Plagis aravit, lividi vibicibus
> Sulci tumescunt, corpus et totum fuit
> Pro vulnere uno; . . .
> . . .   saepe ceu tubulis latex
> Ruptis, aqualis exilit, fusus cruor,
> In ora Atossae purpurae guttas pluit
> Tingens pudore debito invitas genas.
> At illa spumas sanguinis laeta accipit,
> Ut sicca tellus lucidos imbres bibit
> Torrente Cancro.

([the assistant] ploughed frequent blows across her rosy skin; the livid furrows swell with weals, her whole body was as one wound. . . . Her blood, spilt like water when it spurts from burst pipes, showers bright drops on Atossa's face, staining her cheeks with the colour which they ought to have had, but were unwilling to assume. Atossa however happily receives these drops of blood, just as the parched earth drinks up the shining rain at the height of the summer.)

The play dwells lovingly on moments of unnatural horror, on the compelled slaughter by Roxana of her own children, on Oromasdes's feelings when he knows he has eaten his own wife and children. Atossa sees herself consciously acting like a character in a Senecan tragedy. When she hears that her husband has a mistress, she suffers more than Medea (sig. C4v.):

> non sic ruit
> Medea, laesi stimulo amoris saucia,
> Quando astra, et omnes ad suos gemitus Deos
> Deduxit: hoc maior mihi incumbit dolor,
> Furorque maior.

(Medea, wounded by the goad of her injured love, did not rush thus when she drew down to her groaning the stars and all the gods. I am possessed by a greater grief and a greater madness.)

Atossa decorates the chamber where Roxana is tortured with pictures of, amongst others, Medea dividing the limbs of her brother, Hippolytus dragged along by his father's chariot, and Thyestes eating his own children. She boasts that she has excelled the crimes of Medea (sig. E2v.):

> Haec dicta Medeae date; haud superbiat
> Cristasque tollat propter antiquum scelus:
> Atossa maius hoc dedit, maius dabit.

(Bear these words to Medea: let her not be proud, let her not preen herself on her ancient crime. Atossa has committed a greater one, and will commit a greater.)

Nor has Atossa relied on supernatural help, as Medea did, but on her own resources (sig. Ezv.):

> Hoc quicquid est ab uno, in uno pectore
> Natum et petitum est, nemo laudem hanc dividet.

(Whatever I have done has been conceived and attempted by and in one heart. No one will share the praise with me.)

After Atossa has killed Roxana and her children, and has made from their bodies a dish to be served to Oromasdes, she prepares to kill him too by means of a poisoned garland and replies to the remonstrating chorus (sig. E3r.):

> Nihil Thyestem, Tantalum nihil supra
> Conabor?

(Shall I not attempt more than Thyestes or Tantalus did?)

Oromasdes sees Atossa as worse than Medea (sig. E5v.):

> O Furia Scyllae quoque
> Pudenda vel Medeae, et orci faecibus.

(O Fury of whom Scylla, or Medea, and the dregs of hell would be ashamed.)

The chorus too compares her crime with that of Atreus in *Thyestes* (sig. E1v.-E2r.):

> Ad tua quondam fata Thyestes
> Flexit refugam lampada Phoebus,
> Et caeruleo proluit haustu
> Nondum emeritos fine iugales:
> Non minor haec est causa latendi,
> Et digna tuo Phoebe exilio.

(Phoebus once guided a lamp which shunned to look upon your fates, Thyestes; and he bathed in the sky-blue draught the team that had not served their course. There is here no less cause for hiding away, no less cause for your absence, O Phoebus.)

The messenger also says that Atossa has equalled the crime of Atreus (sig. D4r.). The number of such allusions suggests that the play is to be seen within the Senecan tradition. And this suggestion is indeed borne out by the play, with its vengeful ghost, its moralizing chorus, its long speeches on stock themes, its horrific incidents, its stichomythia and *sententiae*.

· · · · ·

Renaissance Latin tragedy is, then, another channel through which the influence of Seneca distils itself. Written in Latin, free from the inevitable distortions which the constraints of another language imposed upon Senecan tragedy in the vernacular, these tragedies constitute a neglected but important aspect of Seneca's influence in the sixteenth century. When performed at a university they would come to the notice of an influential section of educated men. These tragedies would both meet and help to shape the assumptions of such an audience about tragedy, assumptions which they would then carry away with them from the university to regions far beyond.

Notes

1. A list of original Neo-Latin plays printed before 1650 is given by Leicester Bradner in 'The Latin drama of the Renaissance (1340-1640), *Studies in the Renaissance,* IV (1957), pp. 31-70.

2. The best accounts of this drama are Frederick Samuel Boas, *University Drama in the Tudor Age* (Oxford, 1914), and George Charles Moore Smith, *College Plays Performed in the University of Cambridge* (Cambridge, 1923). Plot summaries of most of the important plays were given by George B. Churchill and Wolfgang Keller, 'Die lateinischen Universitäts-Dramen Englands in der Zeit der Königin Elisabeth', *Shakespeare Jahrbuch,* XXXIV (1898), pp. 221-323. There is a brief account of Seneca's connections with University drama in Henry Buckley Charlton, *The Senecan Tradition in Renaissance Tragedy* (Manchester, 1946), pp. clxxi-clxxii. Ghost scenes in Elizabethan drama, including those in Alabaster's *Roxana* and the *Perfidus Hetruscus* are discussed by Gisela Dahinten, *Die Geisterszene in der Tragödie vor Shakespeare* (Palaestra, 225) (Göttingen, 1958).

3. For a recent article arguing against the influence of Seneca, see G. K. Hunter, 'Seneca and the Elizabethans: a case study in "Influence"', *Shakespeare Survey,* xx (1967), pp. 17-26.

4. See Thomas Whitfield Baldwin, *William Shakspere's Small Latine and Lesse Greeke* (Urbana, 1944), ii, p. 560. From the evidence he concludes: 'It looks as if Westminster was the grammar school center of propagation for Seneca in the sixteenth century.'

5. 'Tragoediae summam eloqui, non est opus; Quem Seneca, vestrum lateat?' (Prologue, lines 29-30). Gager's addition to *Hippolytus* are edited in my 'William Gager's additions to Seneca's *Hippolytus*', *Studies in the Renaissance,* xvii (1970), pp. 153-91.

6. See e.g. George Puttenham, 'The Arte of Englishe Poesie', *Elizabethan Critical Essays,* ed. George Gregory Smith (London, 1950), II, p. 27; Martino Antonio Delrio, 'Prolegomena De Tragoedia', esp. chapters vi-viii in *L. Annaei Senecae Tragoediae,* ed. Joannes Casper Schröderus (Delft, 1728), sigs f3v.-g3v.; Daniel Heinsius, *De Tragoediarum Auctoribus Dissertatio,* also in Schröderus's edition, esp. sig. b4v.

7. G. C. Moore Smith, *College Plays . . . ,* pp. 53-7, 106, and 'Plays performed in Cambridge Colleges before 1585', *Fasciculus Ioanni Willis Clark dicatus* (Cambridge, 1909), pp. 269-70.

8. *College Plays,* p.5.

9. 'Plays performed in Cambridge Colleges before 1585', p. 272.

10. Boas, op. cit., p. 389.

11. See Karl Young, 'William Gager's Defence of the Academic Stage', *Transactions of the Wisconsin Academy of Sciences, Arts and Letters,* xviii (1916), pp. 593-638. The extract quoted is on p. 614.

12. See *DNB* [*Dictionary of National Biography*] s.v., 'Alabaster'; the introduction to *The Sonnets of William Alabaster,* ed. George Morley Story and Helen Gardner. Oxford English Monographs (London, 1959); and Louise Imogen Guiney, 'William Alabaster 1567/8-1640', *Recusant Poets* (New York, 1939), i, pp. 335-46.

13. See *DNB,* s.v., 'Freeman, Ralph'.

14. Cambridge University MS. Ff, 11.9; Lambeth Palace MS. 838; Emmanuel College, Cambridge MS., III.1.17; Trinity College, Cambridge MS. R. 17.10. There is a further MS. which I have not seen in Yale University Library. Alfred Harbage, *Annals of English Drama 975-1700,* rev. by Samuel Schoenbaum (London, 1964), p. 307 records also a MS. of an English translation which I have not seen: Folger Shakespeare Library MS. V b. 222.

15. See *DNB* s.v. 'Holland, Hugh'.

16. See *DNB* s.v. 'Farnaby, Thomas'.

17. (London, 1840), iii, 185.

18. 'Milton', *Lives of the English Poets* (London, 1959), I, p. 65.

Lance K. Donaldson-Evans (essay date March 1975)

SOURCE: Donaldson-Evans, Lance K. "Two Baroque Devotional Poets: La Ceppéde and Alabaster." *Comparative Literature Studies* 12, no. 1 (March 1975): 21-31.

[*In the following essay, Donaldson-Evans compares Alabaster's sonnets to those of the French poet La Ceppéde in order to suggest similarities in devotional poetry across Europe.*]

The rediscovery and ensuing re-evaluation of the devotional poetry of the baroque period has been one of the literary phenomena of the twentieth century. It is as though literary critics and readers alike have felt an intellectual and emotional kinship with the political, religious, and social upheavals which shook Europe after the Renaissance. In spite of L. P. Hartley's observation that "the past is a foreign country: they do things differently there,"[1] one is tempted to speculate that the twentieth-century reader has seen in the late sixteenth and early seventeenth centuries a prefiguration of the turmoil of his own era and that he has found solace in the attempts of the devotional poets to come to grips with a world apparently gone awry. Whatever the explanation may be, devotional poetry has been the object of much critical attention in our time so that many poets whose work had been all but forgotten, have now found their rightful place in the official canon of European literature.

In England, the Metaphysical poets have received close scrutiny with the happy result that the works of Donne, Crashaw, Herbert and many others have been resurrected. Interest in the literary baroque, inspired in part by the rediscovery of the English Metaphysicals, has led to the realisation that similar poetic tendencies exist in other European literatures, and so in France, Jean de Sponde, Jean de La Ceppède, and Jean-Baptiste Chassignet have all come into prominence after three centuries of neglect. They are now seen as the most gifted of a large group of poets, whose work bears striking resemblances to that of the English devotional poets. Similar poetic constellations have been rediscovered in Germany, Holland, Italy, and Spain and each national literature now enjoys its own corpus of critical material devoted to its baroque religious poetry. What is surprising, however, is that very few attempts have been made to cross the national literary boundaries and compare devotional poetry from country to country. Of course, parallels have been suggested. Alan Boase, for example, the "inventor" (in the Renaissance sense) of Sponde, has referred to this poet (somewhat unfairly) as "une sorte de Donne manqué."[2] However, the only major attempts to go further in this domain have been made by Odette de Mourgues and Frank J. Warnke.[3] Unfortunately, the excellent works of both these critics are regrettably brief (given the scope of the subject) and their preliminary explorations have been pursued only too rarely by other scholars. It is high time to remedy this situation and to begin to investigate more fully the similarities between devotional poets of the late sixteenth and early seventeenth centuries throughout Europe.

With this aim in view, I would like to set side by side, for purposes of comparison and contrast, the work of two fairly recently "rehabilitated" poets, one French, the other English: Jean de La Ceppède and William Alabaster. La Ceppède, born in Marseilles around 1548 is, by some twenty years, the senior of Alabaster (born 1567-8)[4] and led a considerably more tranquil life than the English poet, in spite of the fact that he was a contemporary of the bloody French Wars of Religion. Alabaster's career was marked by his conversion from Protestantism to Catholicism and by subsequent reconversions which, predictably, involved him in a great deal of secular and religious strife, led to imprisonment, and cloak-and-dagger journeys in England and on the Continent, all of which did not prevent him from living until 1640. La Ceppède, a magistrate who spent most of his life in the Aix-Marseilles region, was born a Catholic and remained one. His only problem in the context of the religious wars (at least as far as we know) was a brush with the radical *Ligue* (he was always a devoted royalist) in 1589, which forced him to flee Aix for a number of years before resuming his magisterial functions in 1594. He died in 1623.

Alabaster's religious verse was written around 1597[5] but not published in his lifetime. La Ceppède saw the publication of all his works, beginning in 1594 with the *Imitation des Pseaumes de la Penitence de David,* a paraphrase in French of the penitential psalms[6] together with twelve devotional sonnets which were to provide a nucleus for his later *Théorèmes.* A second edition of the *Imitation,* dated 1612, was attached to his magnum opus, the *Théorèmes sur le sacré mystère de notre Redemption* (1613), a series of 300 sonnets with extensive notes and prose commentary by the author retracing the last hours of Christ's life. A continuation of the

Théorèmes,[7] dealing with the events between the entombment of Christ and Pentecost, appeared in 1622.

Although the devotional poetry of La Ceppède is considerably more extensive (520 sonnets plus his paraphrases of the psalms and several other religious poems) than that of Alabaster (77 sonnets and two other sonnets of doubtful origin), both bear the clear imprint of what Louis Martz[8] has called the meditative tradition. The works of both poets show unmistakable traces of the techniques of formal meditation which Martz has so skilfully analyzed. The influence of the *Spiritual Exercises* and the numerous other treatises of meditation spawned by the *devotia moderna* is omnipresent, so that the individual poems are often at once formal meditations by the poets themselves and rhetorical exercises in the art of persuasion, whose purpose is to encourage the reader to emulate the meditation performed by the poet or his persona. This is not to say that each individual poem displays the tripartite structure of the traditional Ignatian meditation: composition of place, reflection, and resolve (corresponding to the actions of the imagination aided by the senses, of the intellect as it analyzes what has been presented to the mind's eye by the imagination, and of the will which enflames the heart to take whatever resolves have been suggested by the intellect). The partly epic structure of the *Théorèmes,* which is a vehicle for the narrative of the events of the last hours of Christ's life, usually precludes this possibility, so that while certain poems do represent a complete meditation, most often the exercise of the three powers of the soul is spread over several poems. In La Ceppède's case, then, we must take Jean Rousset's lead[9] and speak of meditative clusters rather than individual meditations. Alabaster's sonnets are much more traditional in that they are, for the most part, self-contained units dealing with various aspects of the life of Christ and the Christian experience, brought together by their common theme but rarely connected in narrative or even in *canzoniere*-like fashion, as are La Ceppède's poems. The major exception to this tendency is found in the eleven sonnets which begin Story and Gardner's edition of Alabaster's **Divine Meditations** and which the editors have subtitled **"The Portrait of Christ's Death."** Although Alabaster does devote a number of sonnets to the Incarnation (unlike La Ceppède), it is significant that both poets begin their works with portraits of Christ's death and begin at precisely the same point in the Gospel narrative, immediately after the Last Supper.

While each poet chooses to meditate on a different aspect of Christ's drama, both present him at the outset of his Passion within the framework of a military metaphor. La Ceppède immediately gives his Christ epic stature as he introduces him in the first sonnet with an evocation of the *Aeneid*: "Je chante les amours, les armes, la victoire / Du Ciel. . . ."[10] ("I sing of the loves, the arms and the victory of Heaven. . . .”). In the following sonnet, La Ceppède describes his protagonist as “Cet Alcide non feint de l’horloge eternele / Oit l’heure qui fatale au combat l’appeloit. . . .”[11] (“This true Alcide hears the hour struck by the clock of eternity, which, as his destiny decreed, was summoning him to the fray.”) Alabaster’s opening lines do not evoke the heroes of antiquity and yet the picture of Christ-the-warrior is no less skillfully painted in the introductory lines of his first two sonnets:

> The night, the starless night of passion,
> From heaven began, on heaven beneath to fall
> When Christ did sound the onset martial.
> A sacred hymn, upon his foes to run. . . .
>
> **(“Sonnet I,”** 1-4)

> What meaneth this, that Christ an hymn did sing,
> An hymn triumphant for an happy fight,
> As if his enemies were put to flight
> When yet he was not come within the ring?
> So giantlike did this victorious king
> Exult to run the race he had in sight. . . .
>
> **(“Sonnet II,”** 1-6)

Each poet then goes on to describe Christ’s crossing of the Brook of Cedron and each attaches symbolic significance to this event. Both have recourse to biblical typology, Alabaster implicitly, La Ceppède explicitly, as they draw the parallel between this New Testament crossing of the brook and David’s crossing of the same water in the Old Testament:[12]

> Over the brook of Cedron Christ is gone,
> To entertain the combat with his death
> Where David fled beforetime void of breath,
> To scape the treacheries of Absolom. . . .
>
> **(“Sonnet III,”** 1-4)

> Comme David predit, il passe le Cedron:
> Mais non pas comme luy pour gauchir l’escadron
> De ses haineux, mais bien pour aider leur poursuite
> . . .
>
> (I, I, iv)

> (As David predicted, he crosses Cedron
> Not, like David, to flee the host of his enemies
> But to assist their pursuit of him. . . .)

Both poets then interpret the crossing of the brook allegorically and, in sonnets **“three”** and **“four,”** Alabaster uses it as a symbolic expression of his own spiritual dilemma and as the basis for a moving colloquy. For him, the brook becomes the symbol of the world, which washes away our resolution and threatens to drown us. We should follow Christ’s example and go beyond it, but this is not possible without divine aid:

> Leave we, O leave we then this miry flood,
> Friends, pleasures, and unfaithful good.
> Now we are up, now down, but cannot stand,
> We sink, we reel, Jesu stretch forth thy hand.
>
> **(“Sonnet III,”** 11-14)

For La Ceppède, the brook is also invested with a symbolic meaning, but at this juncture in his narrative, the whole focus of his attention is on Christ and it is only later that the personal element of the colloquy will make its appearance:

> Et ce torrent qu’il passe est le commencement
> Des flots injurieux, dont l’obscure entresuite
> Le fait crier à Dieu par son vieux truchement.
>
> (I, I, iv, 12-14)

> (And this torrent he crosses is the beginning
> Of the waves of humiliation, whose dark mysterious sequel
> Makes him cry out to God through the mouth of his Old Testament prophet.)

For La Ceppède, each step of Christ’s last journey is a fulfilment of the Old Testament, so that every detail of the Gospel is polysemic. Thus, in his notes, he refers us to Psalm 69, verse 1 (“Save me O Lord, for the waters threaten my life”) to illustrate how Christ’s life sheds new light on the Scriptures (hence his use of the adjective “obscure”) and how his every action is charged with religious meaning. It is only at the end of sonnet **“five”** that the meditative aspect of the epic appears:

> O voyage, ô village, ô jardin, ô montaigne
> Si devot maintenant le Sauveur j’accompaigne
> Permetés qu’à ce coup je gouste vostre fruit.
>
> (I, I, v, 12-14)

> (O journey, o village, o garden, o mountain,
> If I now devoutly accompany the Saviour
> Allow me to taste of your fruit at this moment.)

and it is only in the last tercet of sonnet **“eight”** that we find a fully developed colloquy:

> Mon Roy puisque pour moy vous courez au trespas
> Faites que vostre grace à ce coup m’encourage,
> Et me donne pouvoir de talonner vos pas.
>
> (I, I, viii)

> (My King, since for me you now run to your death,
> Let your grace now encourage me
> And give me the power to follow in your footsteps.)

Because of their tendency to be isolated units rather than links in a poetic chain, Alabaster’s sonnets have more concision, are more tightly structured and perhaps, because of the nature of the English sonnet, make more use of word play and conceits than La Ceppède's works. This is particularly true when Alabaster uses a rhyme scheme which terminates the sonnet with a rhyming couplet (this is never found in a regular French sonnet, where the rhyme scheme of the sestet is either CCDEED or CCDEDE). A case in point is sonnet **"twenty-two,"** in which Alabaster, in dealing with Christ's descent into Hell, plays on contrasting verbs of motion (to ascend and to descend) in order to show how Christ's going down to Hell enables the sinner to go up to Heaven, provided that he, like Christ, first accomplishes a descent into his own soul and a death unto himself. This sonnet is also an interesting example of an individual poetic meditation, with the variation that the colloquy is contained in the first tercet, while the closing tercet contains an intellectual and rhetorical exercise on the Christian paradox that the only way *up* to Heaven is to go *down* to Hell and death:

> Sink down, my soul, into the lowest cell,
> Into the anguish of thy sins descend,
> There think how Christ for thee his blood did spend,
> And afterward went down as low as hell.
> Rise up, my soul, as high as God doth dwell,
> Unto the hope of heaven, and there expend
> How Christ did from the gates of hell ascend,
> In height of glory which no thought can tell.
> Descend in patience with him to die,
> Ascend in confidence with him to reign,
> And upwards, downwards by humility.
> Since man fell upwards, down by Satan's train,
> Look for no fairer way unto thy crown,
> Than that that Christ went up by going down.
>
> **("Sonnet XXII")**

Because of the structure of his work, La Ceppède does not deal with Christ's descent into Hell and subsequent resurrection until the second part of his *Théorèmes*. When he does treat this subject, there are some interesting parallels with Alabaster's sonnet. Christ's descent to Hell is individualized and applied to the poet's own soul. However, whereas in Alabaster's sonnet the poet's soul imitates Christ by descending to and then rising from the hell of sin, in La Ceppède's poem the soul itself is the centre of the metaphor and *itself* becomes Hell waiting patiently for the visit of Christ to release it from the bondage of sin and death. La Ceppède's poem is a prayer to Christ rather than an apostrophe to the soul. By concentrating on the descent of Christ into Hell, it avoids the artificial and somewhat laboured juxtaposition of up/down we find in the English poem and, in place of a paradoxical and strained conceit, it closes with a paraphrase of scripture:

> Fay mon Sauveur descente en l'Enfer de mon ame:
> Mon ame est un Enfer tout noir d'aveuglement
> Que l'acéré trenchant de cent remors entame,
> Que sept traistres Demons traictent journellement.
> D'un seul point mon Enfer, le nom d'Enfer dement
> (Dissemblable à l'Enfer de l'eternelle flame)

> C'est qu'on n'espere plus en l'eternel tourment:
> Et dans le mien j'espere, et ta grace reclame.
> Descends donc par ta grace, ô Christ dans mon Enfer:
> Fay moy de ces demons desormais triompher,
> Pour te suivre là haut, fay qu'icy je patisse.
> Fay que j'aille tousjours mes crimes souspirant,
> Et fay qu'en mon esprit je craigne ta Justice.
> "Car le salut consiste à craindre en esperant".
>
> (II, I, xiv)

> (Descend, o my Lord into the Hell of my soul:
> My soul is a hell black with the blindness of sin.
> Pierced by the hundreds of sharp blades of remorse,
> Which seven treacherous demons torture every day.
> In one thing alone does my Hell belie the name of Hell
> (In this it differs from the Hell of eternal flames)
> In the eternal suffering of the other Hell there is no more hope
> Whereas in my Hell I do hope and call for your grace.
> So descend by thy grace, O Christ into my Hell:
> Give me henceforth the power to triumph over these demons
> So that I may follow thee on high let me suffer here below.
> Let me be constantly a-sighing for my crimes
> And let me fear thy justice in my spirit.
> "For salvation consists in fearing in hope".)

Perhaps the most striking examples of the two poets' common inspiration and similarity of approach are encountered when each concentrates his poetic skill on what Alabaster calls "The Ensigns of Christ's Crucifying." When both poets treat this part of Christ's drama, the crown of thorns placed in mockery on his head becomes the symbol for man's revolt against God and of man's transformation of the Garden of Paradise into the thorny wilderness of Fallen Creation. The contrast between the bounteousness of Eden and the barrenness of the world after the Fall serves as the starting point for both poets. Alabaster:

> The earth, which in delicious Paradise
> Did bud forth man like cedars stately tall,
> From barren womb accursed by the Fall
> Doth thrust forth man as thorns in armed wise,
> Darting the points of sin against the skies.
>
> **("Sonnet XXVI," 1-5)**

La Ceppède:

> O Pere dont jadis les mains industrieuses
> Cette vigne ont planté, voy comme au lieu du fruict
> Qu'elle deut rapporter, ingrate elle produit
> Pour couronner ton fils des ronces épineuses.
> Ces Epines estoient les peines crimineuses
> Des revoltes de l'homme au Paradis seduit:
> Et ce Christ qui sa coulpe, et ses peines détruict
> Ces épines arrose, et les rend fructueuses.
>
> (I, II, lxiv)

(O Father whose industrious hands did once
This vine plant, see how instead of the fruit
It was to bear, thankless it produced
To crown thy son, thorny brambles.
    These thorns were the criminal penalties
Of man's revolts when he was led astray in Paradise
And this Christ who destroys man's guilt and penal-
   ties
Waters these thorns [with his blood] and makes them
   bear fruit.)

Here, it is Alabaster who is the more expansive, for in the tercets of his sonnet he develops the theme of Christ-as-gardener who makes the thorns fruitful, a subject La Ceppède deals with in the second part of the octet quoted above:

For with the purple tincture of his blood,
Which out the furrows of his brows did rain,
He hath transformed us thorns from baser wood,
To raise our nature and odious strain,
That we, who with our thorny sins did wound him,
Hereafter should with roseal virtues crown him.

                      ("Sonnet XXVI," 9-14)

Once again, Alabaster's conclusion is in the form of a play on a paradox, in this case that while our thorns (that is, both the crown and our sins) wound Christ, he, by virtue of the redemptive power of his blood, can transform the crown of thorns into a laurel of rosy virtues.

La Ceppède, on the other hand, ever interested in biblical typology, seeks another example of the association of thorns with redemption, so that Christ's crown of thorns not only evokes the Garden of Eden and Man's Fall, but also Moses, the deliverer of the Jews and a prefiguration of Christ the Redeemer:

Pour delivrer Juda le Pere descendant
D'épines entouré dans un halier ardant
Fit l'effort merveilleux de sa forte puissance.
    Et le Fils descendant du sejour paternel,
Bruslant dans cet halier d'un amour eternel,
Fait l'épineux effort de nostre délivrance.

                      (I, II, lxiv)

(To deliver Judah the Father came down
And surrounded by thorns appeared in a burning bush
As a miraculous demonstration of his mighty power.
    And the Son descending from his Father's home
Burning in this bush of thorns with eternal love
Takes on the thorny task of our deliverance.)

It is interesting that neither poet can resist the pun on the word "thorny" ("épineux"), so that Alabaster talks of thorny sins while La Ceppède uses "épineux effort." However, this is not mere verbal pyrotechnics on their part, but reflects the prevalent Renaissance belief that such word-play was not simply gratuitous, but a revelation of hidden truth.

The contemplation of the reed held by Christ during his trial evokes similar emotions in both poets. Each one alludes to the tradition that the reed had the power to stun or to entrance snakes. For Alabaster, the reed is also an instrument which shepherds use to delight their flocks with music. Christ, with reed in hand, becomes, in a somewhat contrived riddle, both the joy of his flock and the foe of serpents, which are natural enemies of sheep and symbolic of Man's sin:

Conceive a Lamb that should a kingdom weigh,
And judge what sceptre such a prince might bear;
Now turn your thoughts and see Christ sitting here,
Who in his hand a waving reed doth sway.
Conceive how diverse natures should obey
Under one prince, and both be awed with fear,
Serpents and sheep, if they united were,
And judge what sceptre should the kingdom stay.
If nature's penman hath defined right,
A serpent is amazed with a reed,
And shepherds with the same their flocks delight;
Now turn your thoughts and see both these agreed:
Christ's sheep do draw heaven's comfort from his
  breath,
But serpents from the same receive their death.

                      ("Sonnet XXVII")

La Ceppède evokes the miraculous property of the reed, but characteristically sees in it the fulfilment of Biblical prophecy that Christ shall crush the serpent of Eden:

Nature n'a rien fait qu'on doive mépriser.
Sa moindre petite oeuvre est encor' fructueuse
Elle a mis au Roseau la vertu merveilleuse
De pouvoir des Serpens les testes écrazer.
    Mocqueurs, ce vieux Serpent qui vous a fait ozer
Moquer de ce grand Roy la dextre glorieuse,
Par ce vile Roseau, vous faict prophetizer
Qu'il en écrazera sa teste sourcilleuse.

                      (I, II, lxvi)

    (Nature has created nothing which is to be de-
  spised.
Its tiniest work is ever fruitful.
She has given the reed the miraculous power
Of being able to crush the heads of serpents.
    O mockers, the serpent of old who has given you
  the audacity
To mock the glorious right hand of this great king
By this lowly reed, makes you prophesy
That he will crush Satan's proud and supercilious
  head.)

However, La Ceppède sees yet another symbol here and finds in the Old Testament that the Gentiles are referred to by Ezekiel (chapter 29, verse 6) as a reed, so that it now symbolises not only Christ's victory over Satan but also the universality of the redemption this victory brings:

Mais, ô Christ, ce Roseau que tu prens en ta main,
N'est-il pas bien encor le Symbole germain
De ce vile Gentil que ton Royaume embrasse?

(But O Christ, this reed which you take in your
hand
Is it not also the symbol
Of the lowly Gentile your kingdom includes?)

And this figure takes on yet another connotation, as in
an interesting prefiguration of Pascal, La Ceppède pictures the frailness of man as a reed blown about in the
wind:

> Suis-je pas ce Roseau, qui te couste si cher,
> Qu'or l'un, or' l'autre vent de ce monde terrasse,
> Si tant soit peu ta main se lasche à me lascher?

> (Am I not this reed which costs thee so dear
> Which is blown over by every wind of this world
> If thy hand should ever so lightly loosen its grasp on
> me.)

La Ceppède's constant search for hidden meaning in
the events and props of Christ's Passion and his perpetual seeking for secret "figures" in the Old Testament,
add a density and an epic stature to his *Théorèmes*
which are absent from Alabaster's poems. The latter is
too fond of conceits and of playing verbally with the
great paradoxes of Christianity. He is a much more successful poet when he manages to keep his proclivity for
such linguistic gymnastics in check.

The few examples of Alabaster's and La Ceppède's
verse we have had space to examine here are interesting
in many respects. It is perhaps not unexpected to find
certain similarities in poetry dealing with a common
subject, and yet the similarities between the inspiration,
imagery, and treatment of the common material obviously go much deeper than just fortuitous likeness. Although there are, understandably, many differences
which give to each poet his individuality and originality, it is obvious that both are drawing from the same
font of devotional inspiration and are looking at their
subject in much the same way. While the meditative
tradition is not the only factor to be considered, its imprint is unmistakable, as is the influence of the post-
Renaissance devotional revival. It is apparent that we
are dealing with a literary phenomenon that has repercussions throughout Europe, a phenomenon that needs
to be studied from the broadest possible perspective.
The relationships and differences between individual
poets and groups of poets need to be explored in a
much more thorough fashion that has been possible in
this short introduction to the similarities between two
poets. It is only in this way that we will be able to do
justice to the unparalleled revival of devotional poetry
which occurred in the Europe of the Baroque era and
only when we have more precisely charted the scope of
this revival will we be able to determine the full significance of this literary phenomenon.

Notes

1. L. P. Hartley, *The Go-Between.*

2. Jean de Sponde, *Poésies,* ed. F. Ruchon and A.
   Boase (Geneva, 1949), p. 140.

3. Odette de Mourgues, *Metaphysical, Baroque and
   Précieux Poetry* (Oxford, 1953). Frank J. Warnke,
   European Metaphysical Poetry (New Haven and
   London, 1972). We should also mention the un-
   published dissertation of Albert J. Divver,
   "Seventeenth-Century English and French Devo-
   tional Poetry" (Michigan, 1972).

4. Biographical details and the texts quoted from
   Alabaster's work are taken from *The Sonnets of
   William Alabaster,* ed. G. M. Story and Helen
   Gardner (Oxford, 1959).

5. See Story and Gardner, op. cit. p. xxxi.

6. See Michel Jeanneret, *Poésie et tradition biblique
   au XVIè siècle* (Paris, 1969).

7. Jean de La Ceppède, *Théorèmes sur le sacré
   mystère de notre rédemption* (Geneva: Droz,
   1966).

8. Louis L. Martz, *The Poetry of Meditation* (New
   Haven and London, 1954).

9. See the "Introduction" to the Droz edition of the
   Théorèmes, op. cit.

10. *Théorèmes,* Part I, Book I, sonnet i, 1-2.

11. *Théorèmes,* Part I, Book I, sonnet ii, 3-4.

12. Kings 1.15.14-23.

George Klawitter (essay date 1983-4)

SOURCE: Klawitter, George. "Craft and Purpose in
Alabaster's Incarnation Sonnets." *University of Hartford Studies in Literature* 15-16, no. 3-1 (1983-4): 60-
66.

*[In the following essay, Klawitter provides a focused
analysis of the fifteen of Alabaster's sonnets on the Incarnation of Christ.]*

In *An Apology for Poetry,* Sidney divides verse into
three kinds, none of which precisely describes the kind
of religious verse which began to appear in the decades
after his death. His first category, "they that did imitate
the inconceivable excellencies of God," refers to poets
praising the Divinity, like "David in his Psalms," but
the category cannot accommodate a religious poem like
Herbert's "The Priesthood."[1] Nor can Sidney's second
group, the philosophical poems, account for a genre of
verse that blends theology with lyricism. A poem purely
theological might be cataloged with group two, a group
which Sidney hints might not be poetry at all ("let gram-
marians dispute" the laurels of Lucretius and Lucan),

but it cannot rest comfortably there next to the rhetoric of *De Rerum Natura* if it sings with the elegance of Herbert's lines. Sidney's third category, which seems to embrace everything left over ("Heroic, Lyric, Tragic, Comic, Satiric, Iambic, Elegiac, Pastoral"), cannot accommodate didactic religious verse unless we imagine a separate grouping for it among his "certain others, some of these being termed according to the matter they deal with." It seems obvious that philosophically religious verse, which purports to explain divine mysteries, straddles two of Sidney's categories, the philosophical and the imitative. Only then can we appreciate the genre of lines that explicate the holy unknowable, lines like these from William Alabaster's sonnet **"Incarnationem Ratione Probare Impossibile"**:

> Two, yet but one, which either other is,
> One, yet in two, which neither other be,
> God and man in one personality,
> Humanity assumed unto bliss.
>
> (1-4)[2]

The clinical analysis of the God/man mystery is carried in lines that echo the scholasticism of medieval theological prose. The genre of philosophically religious verse was not widely practiced, but it had its adherents.

William Alabaster was not a prolific poet, nor was he an extremely popular one. A recusant who later recanted, he was better known for his controversial tracts and sermons than for the poems he wrote, most of them in 1597-98 when he underwent a first conversion to Rome. The almost fourscore poems attributed to him serve a dual purpose: many of them are personal, therapeutic verses in which he works through his conversion and prison terms; more of them explicate the divine mysteries of Crucifixion, Resurrection, and Incarnation.

Of Alabaster's sonnet sequences assembled by Story and Gardner, only two occur in two major manuscripts (four on the New Jerusalem, and fifteen on the Incarnation), and of these two sequences, that on the Incarnation is the longest sequence in the entire body of poems. It will serve best, therefore, as a focal point to assess Alabaster's minor art, neglected in his own day and barely appreciated in our own, because it affords us ample opportunities to observe his craftsmanship and purpose.[3]

The fifteen sonnets which form the sequence on the Incarnation are an attempt to struggle with the concept of hypostatic union and render it by metaphor. The poet, intent on finding the perfect comparison, spins no fewer than sixteen conceits, each sonnet having one except sonnets **"54"** and **"67,"** which have none, and **"66,"** which has five. The overall design of the sequence justifies these deviations from the norm, however, letting the poems fall into an order that is far from haphazard. The group begins with an invocation (**"53"**) which is followed by a sonnet sans conceit (**"54"**) and then by twelve sonnets with conceits. The sequence ends with a conceitless sonnet (**"67"**) which serves as a match to **"54."** Thus, only two poems are without metaphor, and they serve as a frame for the dozen poems which do attempt to explain the Incarnation through metaphor.

The invocation (**"53"**) sets a joyful tone for the entire sequence by using song to carry the poet's intention:

> I sing of Christ, O endless argument,
> Profaner thoughts and ears begone, begone,
> Lest thunder push down your presumption.
> I sing of Christ, let many worlds be lent
> To enrobe my thoughts with all their ornament,
> And tongues of men and angels join in one,
> To spread the carpets of invention
> Before the eyes of all the firmament.
> The temple where I sing is heaven, the choir
> Are my soul's powers, the book's a living story,
> Each takes his tune, but with a low retire,
> That modesty may after reach his glory.
> And let the humble bass beneath begin
> To show how he descended for our sin.

Alabaster is among scores of English poets who "sing" their way through verse, his lines evocative of both "I sing of a maiden" centuries before him and "Sing Heav'nly Muse" a Puritan regime after him. The lines also vibrate with the same upbeat quality of Whitman's "I sing the body electric." Alabaster repeats the verb "sing" twice, once in identical phrase, next as he begins the sestet and explains his method for the sequence. Singing in heaven, he tells us, will allow his soul's choir to draw on all possibilities of voice range to explicate his theme, but although each poem may be sung by a different voice (soprano, alto, countertenor, tenor), underneath will pulse the bass voice, a kind of "basso continuo" that forms the foundation upon which each voice will build an edifice of metaphor. The bass itself, holding the fundamental, will not embroider theme but will serve to hold the weave of melodies together: "And let the humble bass beneath begin." The method can be illustrated by a well-known baroque piece, Johann Pachelbel's Canon in D, in which measures of continuo preface the ornamentation by upper register strings and never rest, even outlasting the ornamental filigree. In **"Sonnet 54"** the continuo established for the sequence is a philosophical basis on which Alabaster will build all sixteen of the subsequent metaphors for hypostatic union. He thus attempts to render poetically what the "basso continuo" underscores in forthright theological language. Essentially a paradox ("Two, yet but one, which either other is"), the Incarnation, we are told, is a given: we cannot understand it, but we, who cannot "fathom God's omnipotence," accept its reality. Admitting its "possibility / Of being," however, does not prevent the poet from attempting to illuminate it by the sonnets following and their individual metaphors.

"Sonnet 55" begins the queue of metaphorical sonnets by comparing the Incarnation to an "unbounded sea," unfathomable and limitless. The poet ticks off four qualities of God which bear meditation on this mystery and defines each. In lines 6 and 7 they are named "bounty," "power," "wisdom," "justice"; in lines 9 through 12 each receives a short definition. In the couplet the poet encourages himself to select one quality to investigate, calling the action a choice of death "Where diving never hath an end of sinking." The reader, naturally, wonders which of the qualities the poet will choose to investigate in the sequence, but a careful reading indicates that the poet does not choose one to investigate, although he chooses one to ignore. Sonnets **"56"** and **"59"** employ the word "bounty," **"Sonnet 60"** "wisdom," and **"Sonnet 62"** "power." Only "justice" does not occur in the metaphor sonnets. Moreover, the word "good" in **"Sonnet 61"** suggests we label that poem a "bounty" sonnet since "goodness" is tantamount to "bounty" and in fact does occur in tandem with "bounty" in **"Sonnet 59,"** line 11. **"Sonnet 57"** emphasizes God's power, and sonnets **"58"** and **"63"** his wisdom, and although in none of these do any of the four signature words appear, the character of each poem indicates its signature. **"Sonnet 58,"** for example, employs a conceit of God's taking inventory of the world's "parcels of created glory" which "In the world's storehouse did lie undigest / To man." The inventory "is Christ, within whose sacred breast / Entabled is the sum of nature's digest, / Where all may learn a brief introductory." Christ as a "brief" whereby men may be "introduced" to God is a being that we "learn" (line 8) by becoming wise in God's wisdom. **"Sonnet 63"** likewise employs the word "learnt" in emphasizing man's participation in God's wisdom. Both sonnets, therefore, may be considered "wisdom" sonnets. The configuration of qualities fits into a careful pattern of eight consecutive sonnets stressing each quality in turn, with only power omitted where we might expect it: bounty (**"56"**), power (**"57"**), wisdom (**"58"**), bounty (**"59"**), wisdom (**"60"**), bounty (**"61"**), power (**"62"**), wisdom (**"63"**). The omission of a "power" sonnet in the second set indicates the poet's hierarchy of values: God's bounty and wisdom are more significant than power in his solution to man's Fall. It should be noted that the sonnets occur in the sequence in exactly the same order in which the qualities were originally named in **"Sonnet 55"**: bounty, power, wisdom. The omission of "justice" from the sonnets of metaphor has a significance which becomes apparent when the reader reaches the end of the sequence.

Before appreciating the overall pattern of the sequence, however, a reader cannot help being struck by the forcefulness of many of the metaphors Alabaster uses in the internal sonnets. Number **"56,"** a "bounty" sonnet, figures Christ as a fountain of light which, unabated by all the other "streams of brightness" with which God created all things, draws "our souls above." In **"Sonnet 57"** the humanity which Christ embraces is a "field" of miseries, a "table" of ill luck, a "stage" of wailing, and a vanity "fair," but despite its shortcomings, this humanity is wafted heavenward, "within God's secret curtain gone," beyond the cherubim, by a power which dazzles the poet's mind. In **"Sonnet 59,"** Christ is a lamp, in **"Sonnet 60"** a remedy to ease pain, in **"Sonnet 61"** a drawing of divinity. As conceits these metaphors are tame, but that of **"Sonnet 62"** is striking:

> God and man, though in this amphitheatre
> Are many works with beauty varnished,
> Yet all for thee, by thee were polished,
> And first intended by the world's creator;
> Like as a picture of fair grace and stature
> That with a margent is embroidered,
> Wherein are thousand smaller fancies spread,
> Thou art the picture, and the border nature.
> Not that the world is ornament to thee,
> But thou to it that daignst therewith to be;
> Yet as a step it doth thy greatness show
> And workman's power, whose art so high could rise
> In thee, and in thy border fall so low,
> No border unto thee, but to our eyes.

The amphitheater of the world becomes a picture of the God/man, the border being nature, but the poet is careful in the sestet to explain that the frame does not ornament Christ, since the "workman" God the Creator used his "power" of high art to paint Christ. He used, in turn, his low art to design us, who remain a decoration in our own view only, not in his.

The final sonnet of single metaphor, number **"63,"** a "wisdom" sonnet, presents Alabaster's most richly developed conceit, Christ as a single "pale" knitting two rings together, the ring of nature and the ring of Godhead. At the juncture are met:

> Finite and infinite, more and one,
> Alpha and Omega in that fair tablet,
> Wherein is drawn the angels' alphabet,
> Jesus.
>
> (11-14)

As beginning and end, God meets man in Christ, who forms all the wisdom angels need ever know and man need ever "learn." The sonnet offers an extended metaphor, probably inspired by Renaissance double rings, which is also the only conceit Alabaster uses in his recapitulation sonnet, number **"66."** It is not his only brave conceit, however, since the sequence grows more boldly metaphorical as it nears finality. The last three sonnets of the metaphor set are all phrased as question sonnets. Number **"64"** addresses Christ as the "handle of the world's great ball" and asks why "God should become so low and man so tall?" Alabaster does not try to answer the question, nor does he answer the question of **"Sonnet 65,"** Why did Christ dress the world with his robe? As the sequence accelerates, Alabaster seems more intent on jarring our thinking processes than in offering solutions to the basic paradox of two natures in one being.

Thus it is with **"Sonnet 66,"** in which the poet employs no fewer than five metaphors for Christ, hoping vainly to hit upon the finest "glass of resemblance." He seeks a metaphor that will carry the illumination of God in man, a metaphor that will like a mirror unite seer and seen within one object. Is Christ like the union of body and soul? Is he like a tree graft? Is he the diamond fastening two rings? Is he musician united in man? Is he iron fused in fire? No metaphors ultimately capture the mystery, and the poet acknowledges humbly: "No, no, for these resemblances are dead. / How are they then conjoined? As God would" (13-14). The cry for a response is answered at the end of the sonnet with as simple a sentiment of resignation as Herbert used to accept his "collar." It is interesting that this sonnet is the only one so far in the sequence to lack a distinct *volta* or rhetorical "turn" at the sestet. It moves in anguished waves of questions. There is no "but" opening line nine to signal a sestet of answer as there is in half a dozen of the previous sonnets. Having given up on the "how" of the hypostatic paradox, still droning beneath in the bass, the poet must satisfy himself with the "why."

The "why" answer comes quite subtly in the final sonnet, number **"67."** Without metaphor, because the poet has given up on metaphor, the last poem takes us back to the four qualities of the signature tune, as persistent throughout the sequence as the musical progression of major chords I_3^6-IV-V^7-I.

> That power that tied God and man in one,
> (Nature admiring how that was, might be)
> That goodness, which impossibility
> Could gather to bestow his union,
> That wisdom, which knit up affection
> Of finite creature with infinity,
> That mercy, which redeemed misery
> With price of our endless salvation,
> That justice, which might with all laws dispence,
> Yet for us to itself bore our offence:
> Such goodness, justice, mercy, wisdom, power,
> Beyond example, reason or compare,
> Makes me forget myself that they be ours,
> And look about to see for whom they are.

We notice that woven into the musical bass line along with power, goodness, wisdom, and justice, there appears a new quality: mercy. For the first time in the sequence, the poet suggests that his quadrivium is insufficient to explain the *why* of God as Christ. The mystery lies not simply in God's being powerful, good, and

wise, nor in that he saved mankind. It is the combination of these qualities with mercy that prompted his gift. Alabaster places "mercy" in the hierarchy at the end of the octave and reserves justice for mention in the sestet, where it is tempered again by juxtaposition with "mercy" in line 11. The "why" of God's hypostatic gift cannot be explained by justice alone.

Thus, there are no "justice" signature sonnets, for it is not God's justice but his mercy that dispenses bounty, power, and wisdom to humankind. In acknowledging this gift, the poet gains a compelling insight. He shakes off his egocentric intellectualizing and turns to all people in need of God's grace:

> Such goodness, justice, mercy, wisdom, power,
> Beyond example, reason or compare,
> Makes me forget myself that they be ours,
> And look about to see for whom they are.
>
> (11-14)

By the end of the sequence, then, Alabaster returns to what was originally his calling, the ministry. He speaks not only to himself but to all who struggle to comprehend the mystery of his topic, the Incarnation.

Notes

1. Sir Philip Sidney, *An Apology for Poetry* in *Criticism: The Major Texts,* ed. Walter J. Bate (New York: Harcourt, Brace, Jovanovich, 1970), p. 86.

2. William Alabaster, *The Sonnets,* ed. G. M. Story and Helen Gardner (Oxford: Oxford University Press, 1959), p. 30.

3. See, however, William L. Stull, "'Why Are Not *Sonnets* Made of Thee?': A New Context for the 'Holy Sonnets' of Donne, Herbert, and Milton," *Modern Philology,* 80 (1982), 129-35.

Robert B. Caro (essay date October 1988)

SOURCE: Caro, Robert B. "William Alabaster: Rhetor, Meditator, Devotional Poet—II: Alabaster's Meditative Sonnets." *Recusant History* 19, no. 2 (October 1988): 155-70.

[*In the following essay, Caro examines the style of Alabaster's meditative sonnets and demonstrates how they anticipate subsequent developments in the rhetorical and meditative traditions.*]

As we approach Alabaster's sonnets[1] our expectation is enhanced not by the promise of poetic greatness but by the prospect of exploring pure instances of the kind of poetry born in the convergence of rhetoric and meditation. We will focus first on a sequence of sonnets remarkable for their rhetorical techniques; then we will consider a group of sonnets each of which has meditation as its subject. In all the poems, however, it will be apparent that Alabaster as poet is simultaneously rhetor and meditator.

In the corpus of Alabaster's sonnets there is a sequence of fifteen poems on the Incarnation (nos. '53'-'67') which reflect a convergence of rhetoric and meditation similar to that which we have seen in Wright's discourse on love. Just as Wright offered his discourse as an example of amplification, so too Alabaster conceives his sonnet sequence as a project in rhetorical invention. Both are concerned to stir up affections in their own hearts, and so they engage in dialogue with their inner selves or in colloquies with God. Their stance, in other words, becomes meditative, even while they are engaged in what they otherwise consider rhetorical exercises.

'Sonnet 53', 'A Preface to the Incarnation', sets the theme for Alabaster's sequence and also provides clues to his conception of the rhetorical techniques he will use in the poems which follow:

> I sing of Christ, O endless argument,
>
> * * *
>
> I sing of Christ, let many worlds be lent
> To enrobe my thoughts with all their ornament,
> And tongues of men and angels join in one,
> To spread the carpets of invention
> Before the eyes of all the firmament.
> The temple where I sing is heaven, the choir
> Are my soul's powers . . .
>
> ('53')

Christ, considered as God's incarnate Son, will provide the 'endless argument' for the sequence of poems. The discovery of arguments was, of course, the goal of logical invention, but when one trained in divinity addressed himself to a central mystery of the Christian faith, he would already have at hand a supply of theological commonplaces, or topics, in terms of which he could treat his subject. Clearly this was Alabaster's situation. The Latin titles he gave to nine of the fifteen sonnets in his sequence hover around such obvious commonplaces as 'Incarnatio est Maximum Dei Donum' ('56'), 'Convenientia Incarnationis' ('60'), and 'Incarnatio Divini Amoris Argumentum' ('61'). Only one, 'Veni Mittere Ignem' ('59') is directly scriptural (Lk 12:49). These commonplaces are the arguments he will develop, or, alternatively, the points for his meditations.

The traditional difference between logical and rhetorical invention, as we have seen, was measured by the rhetorician's concern to amplify his arguments, elaborating them as to involve not only reason but also the senses

and passions. It is just such a conception of his poetic project that informs Alabaster's concern 'to spread the carpets of invention', i.e., to amplify his arguments. The process he describes is not merely a matter of language (rhetorical style), for it is his very thoughts which he hopes 'to enrobe . . . with all their ornament'. He seeks the aid of 'many worlds', by which we may understand imagination and metaphor, invoked in the interest of making abstract theological arguments vivid and memorable. In amplifying his arguments he also welcomes the aid of other 'tongues', perhaps indicating thereby a willingness (quite proper to rhetorical invention) to borrow his images and ideas from other sources.

Besides Alabaster's conscious and explicit interest in amplification, we will find further similarities between his work and Wright's. Given the prevailing Renaissance aesthetic, the very fact of his writing poetry (albeit under the metaphor of singing songs) implies a rhetorical intention—somehow to move his prospective readers, whoever they might be, to an affective response as well as a notional assent to the mystery of the Incarnation.

The heavenly audience appropriate to his basic meditative stance and suggested by 'the eyes of all the firmament' was obviously not the exclusive audience for these meditations—made-poems. But the readers of such poems, in which rhetorical intention and meditative stance come together, would find themselves in the third-person position of listening in on the conversation of another. 'Sonnet 55', for example, addresses 'my thoughts'. 'Sonnet 62' speaks to Christ as 'God and man', addressing him throughout in the second person. 'Sonnet 57' is part personal exhortation ('gaze no more my mind!') and part divine colloquy ('Vouchsafe me, Christ').

It would be convenient to suggest that Alabaster's sequence of fifteen sonnets on the Incarnation constituted a single meditation; but in spite of a definitive beginning in the prefatory poem, the collection does not grow into an organic whole with a discernible middle and end. The sequence is best thought of, then, as a series of generically related meditations, or parts of meditations, involving 'my soul's powers'—presumably the conventional powers of memory/imagination, understanding, and will. Now one, now another, now all three powers seem to come into play as Alabaster amplifies the arguments which provide the thematic subjects of the individual poems.

It will not be necessary to explicate all fifteen sonnets; it will suffice to consider several representative poems as illustrations of Alabaster's rhetorical technique as he 'spreads the carpets of invention'. His most characteristic method of amplification involves frequent similitudes—sometimes single images, sometimes extended metaphors—as he grapples with his mystery of the Incarnation, and then moves away from attempts at understanding to an affective response. **'Sonnet 56'** is a successful example employing an extended comparison. The title sums up the theological argument which is amplified in the poem:

'Incarnatio est Maximum Dei Donum'

> Like as the fountain of all light created,
> Doth pour out streams of brightness undefined,
> Through all the conduits of transparent kind,
> That heaven and air are both illuminated,
> And yet his light is not thereby abated:
> So God's eternal bounty ever shined
> The beams of being, moving, life, sense, mind,
> And to all things himself communicated.
> But see the violent diffusive pleasure
> Of goodness, that left not till God has spent
> Himself by giving us himself, his treasure,
> In making man a God omnipotent.
> How might this goodness draw our souls above,
> Which drew God down with such attractive love!

('56')

A close reading of this sonnet is necessary to appreciate the fact that the extended simile which fills the octave does not tell the full story of God's bounty; indeed, His greatest gift is revealed precisely in the way that His goodness is not like the sun's.

In terms of the simile, the sun continues to pour out streams of brightness, illuminating heaven and earth, 'and yet his light is not thereby abated'. The present tense of the verbs expressing the sun's activity is significant, insofar as it contrasts with and calls attention to the past tense of God's comparable activity: 'So God's eternal bounty ever shined'. God gave his gifts of being and life, and, in the past, 'communicated' Himself without expending Himself.

But God's present time has changed that economy, as the sestet explains. God could not be content (unlike the sun) to give Himself and still possess Himself. He had to spend Himself completely 'by giving us himself, his treasure'. This divine self-emptying and the consequent lifting up of man (cf. Ph 2:7-9) is God's greatest gift, the ultimate expression of His goodness. It is the mystery and paradox of the Incarnation, effectively summed up as a motive for love in the chiasmus of the final couplet:

> How might this goodness draw our souls above,
> Which drew God down with such attractive love!

The simile which we have just seen in **'Sonnet 56'** is effectively developed to involve a telling contrast, as well as a comparison. **'Sonnet 57',** which continues to meditate on the exaltation of human nature, also em-

ploys a comparison and a contrast, but with a difference: the introductory similitudes are cumulative in their effect rather than extended throughout the poem, and the contrasted elements are opposed as contraries. The basic strategy is quite simple: a series of metaphors which demean man is juxtaposed against a dramatic vision of the heights to which transformed humanity rises:

'Exaltatio Humanae Naturae'

> Humanity, the field of miseries,
> Nature's abortive tale of mischance,
> Stage of complaints, the fair that doth enhance
> The price of error and of vanities,
> Whither? who seeth it? whither doth it rise?
> Or do I see, or am I in a trance?
> I see it far above the clouds advance,
> And under it to tread the starry skies.
> My dazzling thoughts do hold this sight for pain,
> Vouchsafe me, Christ, to look: see, now again
> Above the angels it hath distance won,
> And left the winged cherubims behind,
> And is within God's secret curtain gone,
> And still it soareth: gaze no more my mind!

('57')

The opening quatrain, linked grammatically by apposition to the rhetorical questions of line 5, denigrates humanity in four comparisons which, although unconnected, produce as their cumulative effect a heightened sense of the perverseness of man. Over against this view is set the poet's vision of the exaltation of human nature—a phenomenon not so much described in itself as dramatized in its effects.

Thus the ethereal progression of humanity above the clouds and stars, above the angels and cherubim, and finally into the secret presence of God, never loses its immediacy in the speaker's own experience. He cannot say whether he is in a trance or not. The sight dazzles; his eyes pain; he beseeches Christ to let him look again. And finally, although the vision continues to soar, he must recall himself to earth: 'gaze no more my mind!'

The opposition of contraries, which undergirds the dramatic vision of **'Sonnet 57',** was a conventional topic of invention used in both logic and rhetoric. So to in **'Sonnet 60',** the next poem we wish to consider, the theological argument converges with a rhetorical topic familiar to the Renaissance:

'Convenientia Incarnationis'

> To free our nature from captivity,
> Was requisite our sins' remission,
> Which doth suppose the debt's solution.
> Through impotence man could not satisfy,
> And through omnipotence God was too high.
> The exigent was great, but O compassion,
> O wisdom, God conjoined hath in one
> Both God and man to make a remedy;

That by the one he might deserve of right,
And by the other make it infinite,
That as a man he might descend to pain
And as a God raise up himself again:
For if he were not God he had no powers,
And if he were not man they were not ours.

('60')

Convenientia was a frequent commonplace in theological argumentation. In Wright's meditative discourse, for example, it was the topic he developed in his eleventh motive for love (pp. 219-23). It was also included in his general list of the places of invention, where he observed in passing that it is a denial of *convenientia* to assert that the Incarnation abases God's majesty (p. 186). To be *conveniens* did not mean convenient in the modern sense, but appropriate or fitting. Thus, the exercise Alabaster sets for himself in the present meditation is to discover reasons why it was fitting that God should have become man.

He portrays the human condition before the Incarnation in terms of the theology of redemption commonly associated with St Anselm. In this view, man was held captive by Satan but was unable to pay the infinite ransom demanded for his freedom. To meet this exigency God devised a 'remedy' that would effect the redemption without sacrificing His own prerogatives. It was, in other words, a 'convenient' remedy, if a paradoxical one—and this for the reasons developed in the sestet: it joined finite and infinite, descent and ascent, man and God.

Within its theological framework, Alabaster's meditation is tightly reasoned and, as a poem, succinctly expressed. Although its conception is without benefit of imagery (except for the latent metaphor of captivity), its amplification by paradox carries a power of its own which suggests wonder at God's compassion and wisdom, and thereby proposes to the will a motive for gratitude.

Another poem in which the amplification depends largely on intellectual considerations is **'Sonnet 54'**, **'Incarnationem Ratione Probare Impossible'**. The problem is explained in the octave:

Two, yet one, which either other is,
One, yet two, which neither other be,
God and man in one personality,

* * *

I see it so; but how I do not see.
Nor could I reach the possibility
Of being, if it were not so in practice.

Alabaster develops the basic argument proposed in his title by using the familiar axiom of logic that an inference cannot be drawn validly from the possibility of a

thing to its actuality, but only the other way around (*ab esse ad posse valet illatio*). In other words, apart from the revealed fact of the Incarnation, man could never know even its possibility:

For who can fathom God's omnipotence,
Or sound the creature's large obedience?

The logical conclusion comes in the humbling admission of the final lines:

We must confess that God can do
What we confess we cannot reach unto.

('54')

Alabaster's movement toward acceptance of his own limitations in the face of the mystery he meditates is fairly typical of these poems, but the almost exclusively intellectual development is not.

Intellect and imagination play together in producing the similes and metaphors which are the striking feature of the remaining poems we will examine as examples of rhetorical amplification. **'Sonnet 55'**, a poem written from a clearly meditative stance, employs an extended metaphor to develop the theological topic announced in its title:

'Incarnationis Profundum Mysterium'

The unbounded sea of the Incarnation!
Whither, my thoughts, O whither do ye tend,
To touch the limits of untermed end?
For though I quarter to each region,
Yet find I nought to rest my thoughts upon;
For if to bounty or to power I bend,
Or wisdom or to justice I extend,
I cannot sound the depth of any one:
Power, by which God is finite man become,
Bounty, that did baseness so dear esteem,
Wisdom that hath upspun man's fatal doom,
And justice that by man would man redeem.
Then choose thy death, my thought, or else leave thinking
Where diving never hath an end of sinking.

('55')

It is easy to see how the central conceit of the poem—comparing the depth of a mystery of faith to the unbounded sea—emerges from the topic proposed in the title. The metaphorical sense of *profundus* (as referring to the sea) was already present in the dictionary meaning, yet Alabaster makes the cliché work anew, giving it an original twist in his final line. In **'Sonnet 54'**, hints of the same basic image had coloured his diction when he spoke of man's inability to 'fathom' God's omnipotence or to 'sound' Christ's obedience, but the potential of the metaphor was not exploited until the present poem.

The conceit is announced in the opening line and explicitly recurs at the end of the octave and again in the concluding line of the poem. The metaphor of the unbounded sea clearly provides the framework for amplifying the profundity of the Incarnation. In the present context, though, we may also think of it as providing the imaginative ambience of a meditation, and so the opening line comes to be seen for what it is—a composition by similitude.

The meditative stance is made apparent in the following lines as the speaker addresses a part of his soul:

> Whither, my thoughts, O whither do ye tend,
> To touch the limits of untermed end?

In his imagination he is lost on a boundless ocean and cannot 'sound the depth'. The imaginative experience is, of course, an analogue for his real subject, and the specific attributes of the Incarnation which elude his thoughts are spelled out in lines 9-12. The concluding couplet highlights the fact that the poem has been in interior dialogue with 'my thought' and, resuming the central metaphor, cautions against the dangers of speculation in the mysterious sea 'where diving never hath an end of sinking'.

If Alabaster at times succeeds in giving life to an old image, at other times his conceits are quite original, even metaphysical, in their comparisons based on functions and relations. **'Sonnet 66'** proposes five such comparisons as it searches for an apt simile to reveal 'how God and man, two natures, meet in one':

> By what glass of resemblance may we see
> How God and man, two natures, meet in one?
> Or is it like unto the union
> Whereby the soul and body do agree?
> Or like as when the graft of foreign tree
> Grows in some other by incision?
> Or like as when about one diamond
> Two rings are fasten'd which one jewel be?
> Or as when one same party is both man
> And is together a musician?
> Or like as iron is unbodied
> With interfused fire into one mould?
> No, no, for these resemblances are dead.
> How are they then conjoined? As God would.
>
> ('66')

In his conclusion the poet pretends to leave behind imagination and intellection as he moves to simple acceptance of what God has revealed. Still, his rejection, in the penultimate line, of all five images as stillborn should not be taken literally, as though predication about the divine attributes were not always by analogy. It should be seen rather as rhetorical exaggeration serving to amplify in the context of the present poem the ultimate incomprehensibility of the mystery which many striking similitudes scarcely begin to explain. Elsewhere the same comparisons might be used without any hint of rejection. Thus **'Sonnet 63'** elaborates the image of two rings joined in one diamond as an extended metaphor suggesting the union of created nature and Godhead in Christ. The conceit also helps the understanding to appreciate the Incarnation as

> The knot of both and either, where are met
> Finite and infinite, more and One,
> Alpha and Omega . . .
>
> ('63')

'Sonnet 64' also employs a carefully developed, original conceit. The speaker addresses 'Jesu' in the opening line as 'the handle of the world's great ball' and again in line 5 as 'the handle consubstantial / of God'. The octave develops the image as a metaphor of what happens in the Incarnation: God takes hold of man, and man takes hold of God. The sestet continues the meditation on the marvels of this mystery, but finally rejects attempts to grasp it intellectually, preferring instead a resolution suggested by the central image:

> And let us hold Christ sure for fear we fall,
> Yea, let Christ hold us sure or else we shall.
>
> ('64')

One final example of amplification in the Incarnation poems involves another extended metaphor. **'Sonnet 61'** portrays God as a romantic lover wooing the human race:

'Incarnatio Divini Amoris Argumentum'

> God was in love with man, and sued then
> To get return of love by all those ways
> Which lovers use to compass in their praise.
> His image he did draw with nature's pen,
> To show his beauty and his worth to men;
> His tokens were all good, that our life says;
> His agents were the prophets that did raise
> Man's heart to love where he had loved been.
> But man did love the gift, and not the giver,
> Yet see how God did in his love persever:
> He gave himself, that as a gift he might
> Be loved by taking, putting on our feature
> So to be seen in more familiar sight.
> How must we love him that so loves his creature!
>
> ('61')

The amplification of the argument follows the same strategy we saw above in **'Sonnet 56'**. In that poem the comparison of God's bounty to the shining of the sun, although valid up to a point, was inadequate to express the totality of God's gift of Himself. So here, where His image, tokens, and agents elicit a response of love for what is given but not precisely for the giver, God is not satisfied until He has given Himself, 'putting on our feature'. Thus the Incarnation becomes an argument proving God's love of man and is at the same time a motive for man's love of God—as the poem finally insists: 'How must we love him that so loves his creature!'

This concluding exhortation is a further echo of **'Sonnet 56'** ('How might this goodness draw our souls above') and no doubt epitomizes the effective thrust of the entire Incarnation sequence.[2] As in Wright's discourse, so here in Alabaster's sonnets, arguments amplified become motives for love as rhetoric and meditation converge.

The next poems we will consider are all meditations about meditation. Our explications will look beyond rhetorical technique to the devotional theory and practice about which the poet writes. Very much in the Ignatian tradition, and with no less concern than Wright's for the geography of the mind, Alabaster betrays a conscious familiarity with the so-called powers, or faculties, of the soul. There are at least two sonnets (Nos. **'41'** and **'15'**) in which writes specifically about them, acknowledging their tri-partite division and suggesting their relevance to his devotional exercises. In **'Sonnet 41'** he addresses the Lord, his opening and closing lines echoing the words of Samuel (1 S 3) in the classic Old Testament response to the call of God:

> Lo here I am, lord, whither wilt thou send me?
> To which part of my soul, which region?
> Whether the palace of my whole dominion,
> My mind? which does not rightly apprehend thee,
> And needs more light of knowledge to amend me;
> Or to the parliamental session,
> My will? that doth design all action,
> And doth not as it ought attend thee,
> But suffers sin and pleasures, which offend thee,
> Within thy kingdom to continue faction;
> Or to my heart's great lordship shall I bend me?
> Where love, the steward of affection,
> On vain and barren pleasures doth dispend me?
> Lord I am here, O give me thy commission.
>
> ('41')

The opening line is not only paraphrased in the conclusion, but is itself a repetition of the concluding line of the previous poem.[3] Discernment of an apostolic vocation, suggested by the scriptural allusion, is thereby established as the thematic context for both poems. **'Sonnet 40'** is weaker and less personal but, considered in tandem with **'Sonnet 41',** reveals a kind of progression from the situation of the angels, to that of Christian 'saints' on earth, to that of the speaker himself. The earlier poem compares the attitude of dedicated Christians to the readiness of angels who attend at God's throne waiting to be sent on special missions, some to build up the Church, some to defend it. So too human disciples 'expect thy motion', that is, listen for indications of God's will as they seek to discern the work he wants them to do

> Whether in faith or in devotion
> Or exercise of hope . . .
>
> ('40')

The attitude of ready expectation is the same for angels and those on earth who seek to do God's will. Still, the projects of faith, hope and devotion envisioned for the latter, while not excluding energetic apostolic enterprises, pale by comparison with the specific missions imagined for God's 'winged spirits':

> To help the Church to get the upper hand,
> Or else to break the heads of heresy,
> And scatter them in their apostasy,
> Or against the Turkish swads to make a stand.
>
> ('40')

The implied contrast between such imagined exploits and the primary requirements of cultivating the theological virtues points up the realism (as over against romantic illusions) demanded of the saints on earth, especially of those who have only recently experienced conversion and now hope to make progress in a life of apostolic, or missionary, service. This was, of course, Alabaster's own situation, and one around which the Ignatian Spiritual Exercises would have focussed his attention in the key meditation on the Kingdom of Christ.

It is in this meditation, which is made only after an exercitant has renewed the experience of conversion in the first week of the Exercises, that the demands of an apostolic vocation are spelled out for the first time. Christ is portrayed as a great leader, the eternal King, inviting His followers to share with Him in the work of Redemption: '. . . whoever wishes to join me in this enterprise must be willing to labor with me, that by following me in suffering, he may follow me in glory'.[4] This basic call appeals to the generosity of the exercitant but remains undifferentiated in terms of the specific projects he might eventually accomplish for the spread of the Kingdom. Nonetheless, the third point of the meditation makes clear what must be the starting point of every apostolic vocation, since those who respond to the call of the eternal King 'will not only offer themselves entirely for the work, but will act against their sensuality and carnal and worldly love . . .'.[5] As summarized by a recent commentator, the exercitant's primary response is thus 'to work with Christ in overcoming the disorder that is in the universe and that is in himself'.[6]

This latter phrase—'overcoming the disorder . . . that is in himself'—perfectly epitomizes the apostolic dimension of the question Alabaster meditates in **'Sonnet 41'** and elaborates metaphorically in terms of the kingdom within his soul:

> Lo here I am, lord, whither wilt thou send me?
> To which part of my soul, which region?

The remainder of the sonnet develops the question by dividing the soul into its several parts and suggesting the disorders to which each is subject: the mind, 'which doth not rightly apprehend thee'; the will, which 'doth not as it ought attend thee'; and the heart,

> Where love . . .
> On vain and barren pleasures doth dispend me.

In Alabaster's kingdom metaphor the three powers correspond respectively to a palace, a parliament, and a country estate. This microcosmic view of the soul is a variation of a Renaissance commonplace, but, more importantly, its resonance with the Kingdom theme in the Spiritual Exercises serves to confirm the impression that the discernment which provides the thematic context for the poem is really discernment about the apostolic value of personal asceticism. The rhetorical questions on which the poem turns, effectively heightening the speaker's dramatic stance, do not so much require an answer as suggest one. Against the background of the previous poem, **'Sonnet 41'** leaves no doubt that the immediate and obvious field of the poet's apostolic labors is his own soul ('thy kingdom'). The means for taming the powers of his soul is meditation.

Alabaster's concern, like Wright's in his lengthy meditative discourse, is to find accord between mind and will on the one hand, and his affections on the other, as he prayerfully strives for a heartfelt union of all his powers in the love of God. That a particular devotional discipline answerable to this psychology provided the method of Alabaster's meditation is made explicit in **'Sonnet 15'**:

> My soul a world is by contraction,
> The heavens therein is my internal sense,
> Moved by my will as an intelligence,
> My heart the element, my love the sun.
> And as the sun about the earth doth run,
> And with his beams doth draw thin vapours thence,
> Which after in the air do condense,
> And pour down rain upon the earth anon,
> So moves my love about the heavenly sphere,
> And draweth thence with an attractive fire
> The purest arguments wit can desire,
> Whereby devotion after may arise.
> And these conceits, digest by thoughts' retire,
> Are turned into april showers of tears.

                                                                    ('15')

Again we find Alabaster viewing his soul as a microcosm. He makes his soul a contracted 'world' in the composition by similitude which opens the meditation (lines 1-4)[7] and then proceeds to draw out the conceit in terms of the Ptolemaic cosmology: 'as the sun . . . So moves my love . . .' It is the 'heavenly sphere' of mind (or 'internal sense') which constitutes the geocentre of his soul's universe. Just as the sun draws vapours from the earth, which then condense and return as rain, so love draws from his mind arguments conducive to devotion:

> And these conceits, digest by thoughts' retire,
> And turned into april showers of tears.

The poet reveals his familiarity with a method of meditation employing and harmonizing the powers of the soul, even though his terminology does not correspond in every respect to the traditional division of memory, understanding, and will. What is more significant is that he does depict the operations of both rational and sensitive powers as interacting to produce tears of devotion—which we may take as representing in the present instance the affective response toward which every meditation tends, even those involving prolonged intellectualizing.

Because tears recur frequently in Alabaster's sonnets, it is important to recognize that for him, no less than for the devotional tradition of the Counter-Reformation generally, there are times when actual tears are the appropriate and desired response to God's grace in prayer. St Ignatius teaches his followers, as part of their immediate preparation for meditation, always to ask for a grace that will be in accord with the subject matter of their prayer,[8] and there are two subjects—sin and Christ's Passion—where he repeatedly recommends asking for sorrow and tears.

For example, in the second prelude of the meditation on personal sins the exercitant is instructed 'to ask for a growing and intense sorrow and tears'.[9] In contemplating scenes from the Passion the fourth point is always 'to consider what Christ our Lord suffers in his human nature, or . . . what he desires to suffer. Then I will begin with great effort to strive to grieve, be sad, and weep'.[10] And finally, we read in St Ignatius' Rules for the Discernment of Spirits that 'it is likewise consolation when one sheds tears that move to the love of God, whether it be because of sorrow for sins, or because of the sufferings of Christ our Lord, or for any other reason that is immediately directed to the praise and service of God'.[11]

Such tears of consolation play a part in the two final poems (nos. **'68'** and **'70'**) we will consider. Both are titled **'A Morning Meditation'**. In **'Sonnet 70'**, as in the 'april showers' of **'Sonnet 15'**, tears flow from thoughts. Once more the sun is the agent, but it exerts its force amid quite a different constellation of images from those of the Ptolemaic universe in the earlier poem:

'A Morning Meditation'

> The sun begins upon my heart to shine,
> Now let a cloud of thoughts in order train
> As dewy spangles wont, and entertain
> In many drops his passion divine,
> That on them, as a rainbow, may recline
> The white of innocence, the black of pain,

The blue of stripes, the yellow of disdain,
And purple which his blood doth well resign;
And let these thousand thoughts pour on mine eyes
A thousand tears as glasses to behold him,
And thousand tears, thousand sweet words devise
Upon my lips as pictures to unfold him:
So shall reflect three rainbows from one sun,
Thoughts, tears, and words, yet acting all in one.

('70')

The sun which begins to shine in the opening line is at once literal and metaphorical—literal in that it fixes the time of day and anticipates the images of morning which will recur in the rest of the poem; metaphorical in that the real scene is set not in the outside world of nature but 'upon my heart', where the interior gaze of graced understanding and love provides the analogue for the light and warmth of the sun. In this metaphorical sunshine, thoughts of the Passion extend themselves one after another as 'dewy spangles wont', reflecting a virtual rainbow of colours. The ensuing phantasmagoria makes clear that this meditation of the Passion is not just an intellectual exercise but also a highly imaginative one.

This intellectual-imaginative recreation of Christ's Passion yields an affective response in tears and also in 'sweet words'. Like the speaker's thoughts, his tears and words are portrayed metaphorically in visual terms—'glasses to behold him' and 'pictures to unfold him'. These means of seeing, which also involve feeling, depend on the same light and warmth of understanding and love which have guided his prayer from the outset. The poem clearly dramatizes the method of meditation according to the diverse powers of the soul, yet its final couplet bespeaks their integration in a unified and total response:

So shall reflect three rainbows from one sun,
Thoughts, tears, and words, yet acting all in one.

Turning now to **'Sonnet 68'**, we again find Alabaster using metaphors of light and perception (and their opposites) to portray certain dynamics of meditation:

'A Morning Meditation'

Mine eyes are open, yet perceive I nought,
The day is born, and yet continues night,
Thus do mine eyes want day, the day wants light:
No marvel, for of Christ I have not thought.
Then how can clearness to my soul be brought,
To see and to be seen, that hath his sight
From Christ, and what it sees is his fair spright,
That sense and object both by him are wrought?
Then let my shame a blazing morning spread,
And from mine eyes let crystal dew be shed,
Dew of repentance to wash out this blot,
And shame to blush that Christ was so forgot,
that Christ arising may wipe from my face,
My tears with mercy and my shame with grace.

('68')

The central conceit of this sonnet builds to a comparison between a morning meditation and the sunrise. The first four lines juxtapose the experience of darkness before dawn and darkness within the poet's soul. The ensuing quatrain attempts to develop the notion of Christ as the light of the soul, and at the same time poses a problem: since Christ gives the soul the power of seeing, and what is thus seen interiorly in His Spirit, how can there be any clarity of vision in one who has failed to turn his thoughts to Christ in prayer? The situation implies the speaker's sadness at Christ's apparent absence from his soul. However, the desolation of the octave yields to consolation as awareness of his forgetfulness turns to shame and tears of repentance.

Shame and tears, of course, are signs of conversion—of a change of heart—which is signalled in the sestet by shifts in the imagery away from the lingering night of the poem's opening lines. The poet's blush of shame becomes a 'blazing morning' and his tears are 'crystal dew'. In this experience of a new dawn, the sun which has arisen is Christ, who, gaining the ascendancy once more in his soul, wipes away 'my tears with mercy and my shame with grace'.

Alabaster's poems about the experience of meditation are of a piece with his descriptions of his experience at the time of his conversion to Catholicism when, as we have seen in his autobiography, 'I retired into solitude, and gave myself up to prayers, tears, mourning, and fasting'. Again, he tells us, 'I spent much time in secret and familiar colloquies between God and my soul . . . through diligent mental prayer and meditation uniting my will with the divine [will]'.

On the basis of the poems, we are able to elaborate these generalizations as follows: Alabaster felt himself called to a mode of ascetical discipline that was at once interior and apostolic; work for the 'kingdom' must begin in his own soul in a struggle to achieve mastery over 'vain and barren pleasures' by means of greater knowledge and a more attentive will (**'Sonnet 41'**). Meditation employing the powers of the soul was an apt discipline for this purpose, under the influence of love transforming arguments to affection—even to tears of devotion (**'Sonnet 15'**). Such arguments were seen as both intellectual and imaginative and thus able to encompass the whole man in a response of understanding and affection. Metaphorically, the light which flooded the poet's soul in the consolation of prayer both illuminated his mind and warmed his heart (**'Sonnet 70'**). This experience of light and warmth was, finally, the awareness of Christ present through His grace (**'Sonnet 68'**).

Stylistically, our concerns in the poems analyzed have revolved around Alabaster's explicit use of rhetorical amplification in his sequence of sonnets on the Incarnation and his conscious understanding of the dynamics of meditation as revealed in four further poems. As was true of Wright, so with Alabaster, techniques of amplification—developing a topic through appeals to reason (logical arguments, figures of thought) and to imagination (images and metaphors) in order to engage the passions—converge with practices consciously cultivated in the ascetical discipline of meditation. This convergence implies a 'privatizing' of the ordinarily public world of rhetoric. Thus the poetry (or any public utterance) born of such a convergence is deeply interior, the immediate audience being the speaker's thoughts, some part of his soul, or God. In a word, the rhetoric of meditation is not oratorical but dramatic.

This theory of what happens when rhetoric and meditation converge is demonstrated in the sonnets we have seen. On the view that the dramatic element is the essential note in metaphysical poetry, the theory helps us to understand the close affinity between the devotional tradition and seventeenth-century metaphysical style. William Alabaster, simultaneously rhetor, meditator, and devotional poet, was a harbinger and early exponent of that style.

At their best, Alabaster's poems engage the diverse powers of the speaker's soul in a unifying moment of experience. It does not seem too much to say that such an achievement, while unquestionably a function of the converging disciplines of rhetoric and meditation, is finally inspired—spirit-filled and liberating. In this sense, Alabaster's most successful poems become for him an experience of transcendence.

Alabaster wrote relatively few sonnets. Moreover, he wrote them during a brief span of years and in troubled circumstances which presumably did not allow much leisure for revision. Still, it was for him a time of intense religious devotion, of opening his soul to God and expanding the previous limits of his awareness. It is experiences such as these which are dramatized and realized in the best poems, as the speaker—imaging forth the poet—lets fall his public face, with its pretensions and self-consciousness, and creates himself anew.

Notes

1. The edition used is that of G. M. Story and Helen Gardner (1959), whose numbering is here followed and cited in parenthesis following quotations.

2. The argument corresponds to that developed in the Ignatian Contemplation to Attain the Love of God; see note 34 to part 1 of this article

    3. Like as thy winged spirits always stand,
    Before thy presence with defixed eye,
    The becks attending of thy majesty
    Whether you give them charge of Christian land,

    To help the Church to get the upper hand,
    Or else to break the heads of heresy,
    And scatter them in their apostasy,
    Or gainst the Turkish swads* to make a stand;
    So do thy saints expect thy motion,
    In what religious work thou wilt bestow them,
    Whether in faith or in devotion,
    Or exercise of hope, for thou dost know them:
    In faith, in hope, and love they will attend thee,
    Lo here I am, lord, whither wilt thou send me?

                         (40)

    *Swad: a sixteenth-century term of abuse meaning, *e.g.,* 'lout' (*O.E.D*).

4. *S.E.* [95].

5. *S.E.* [97].

6. John J. English, S.J., *Spiritual Freedom* (Guelph, 1973), p. 109.

7. *Cf.* the opening lines of Donne's 'Goodfriday, 1613': 'Let mans Soule be a Spheare, and then, in this, / The intelligence that moves, devotion . . .' in *The Complete Poetry of John Donne*, ed. John T. Shawcross (Garden City, 1967), p. 366.

8. *S.E.* [48].

9. *S.E.* [55].

10. *S.E.* [195].

11. *S.E.* [316].

Abbreviation

S.E. Luis J. Puhl, S. J., trans., *The Spiritual Exercises of St Ignatius* (Westminster, Md., 1962). Citations in square brackets refer to the standard paragraph numbers used in this edition.

Elizabeth M. Richmond-Garza (essay date 1997)

SOURCE: Richmond-Garza, Elizabeth M. "'She Never Recovered Her Senses': *Roxana* and Dramatic Representations of Women at Oxbridge in the Elizabethan Age." In *Sex and Gender in Medieval and Renaissance Texts: The Latin Tradition*, edited by Barbara K. Gold, Paul Allen Miller, and Charles Platter, pp. 223-46. Albany: State University of New York Press, 1997.

[*In the following essay, Richmond-Garza highlights the thematic treatment of the woman and the Oriental in Elizabethan academic plays such as Alabaster's* Roxana.]

Neoclassical theories of tragedy privilege the plays of the seventeenth and eighteenth centuries, with their careful observations of neo-Aristotelian decorum in language, characterization, and staging. Certainly the praise accorded to John Dryden's experiments in the forms of classical tragedy has been quite substantial, and yet the earlier plays on the same theme often suffer from a scholarly love of restraint and measured heroic elegance. Even, as in the case of the Neo-Latin academic tragedy of *Roxana,* when Dryden merely revised the work of an earlier playwright, it is his later neoclassically purified version that will be remembered. If in 1642 the London Puritan City Council was able finally to achieve its goals of closing the doors of the dangerously entropic and vital Elizabethan, Jacobean, and Carolean stages, although only briefly, its conservative legacy perhaps extends even further. Critical doors are still closed on many plays of that period. Those plays that have suffered most are those that remain unrescued by the critical reception that saves a prominent name, that violate or offend, and that, either publicly or privately, affront both the substantive and the formal conventions that later periods will value. If T. S. Eliot can be offended by even *Hamlet*'s indecorous construction and hybridized content,[1] a much greater potential to affront is offered by the less canonized texts of the period. In their obscurity, both linguistic and archival, lies more than a boldness in style. These plays offer a false appearance of recondite disengagement with the polyphonic and often dissonant counterpoint of the public London stages, both those that we enjoy calling theaters and those that we place in the realm of official politics.

Any reading of a dramatic text in this period, or perhaps in any period, will involve a reading of its performance, that is to say of the complex cultural, political, and ideological material out of which the play's text is constructed and with which the audience who attends its presentation is permeated. With drama we cannot limit the text to the words on the page but must, instead, assess the whole variety of semiotically overdetermined acoustic and visual appeals that the text makes when it is performed to an individual audience in a particular performance space. The elision of such performative considerations as audience expectations and visual iconography permits a privileging of the word as transhistorically and hermeneutically available to the modern reader without the need for a careful meditation on the performative implications of the play, which are connected to the historical. The connection between Elizabethan theater and the political debates of the period has often been noted, both by traditional and new historicist critics. And yet their conclusions have varied widely about the nature of this ideological and iconographic homology, depending very often on the care taken to reconstruct not only a reading of the text but also a subtly nuanced performative context and audience reception of that text.

For decades, modern university students have been trained in the history of the London stage, even as they have ignored other performances of the period. Informed by varying modern ideological agendas, whether following the optimistic universalism of critics like Alfred Harbage, the savage elitism of Ann Jennalie Cook, Martin Butler's proletarian refutations, or Andrew Gurr's careful reconstruction of a diversified and complex nexus of reception, modern scholars have been much concerned over the nature of the Elizabethan audience and of its immediate responses to the plays it witnessed.[2] This preoccupation has often superseded scholarly inquiry into the texts and performances themselves. *Roxana* offers a case in point of this appropriative strategy. Even such basic texts as the *Riverside Shakespeare,* while not adopting a particularly aggressive stance on the nature of this audience in social, political, economic, or gender terms, do place great emphasis upon the construction of the space of performance, if not in ideological at least in architectural terms. Along with the famous sketches and engravings of particular Elizabethan theaters like the Swan, a striking image of the role and positioning of the audience in period theaters is offered.[3] The small woodcut, which is taken from an edition of the largely ignored first *Roxana* play by William Alabaster, is enlarged from its two square inches to show a socially diverse audience, placed both in front of and in galleries to the side of the stage, viewing a performance taking place in the outer stage, which is divided from the inner by a transverse.[4] The popularity of this image for teaching theater history constitutes this play's only reception. Through its reinscription of the fantasy of Elizabethan social integration, the image ironically has been used to obscure the subversive content of the play that it covers. The return to the performative details, as well as the text itself, of the play promises a rescue from such ideologically informed modern conjecture. The original image is, moreover, always cropped in modern editions. Even those critics who concern themselves particularly with the university drama at most indicate that the image is but one of eight woodcuts from the frontispiece of the author's imprint of William Alabaster's *Roxana.*[5]

It is with these censored images that I wish to reintroduce not only a metonymic representative of a marginalized body of Neo-Latin dramatic texts but also another doubled and thus doubly excluded body, that of the woman and of the Oriental. The seven other images that constitute the full frontispiece include female and Oriental nudes in various suggestive and yet graceful postures. Clothed, but only partially, in the flowing garments of European fantasies of the luxurious East, these women have been excluded from the critical reception, such as it is, of the play. Already on the margins of the ideal image of the Elizabethan stage even in the original print, they have failed to infiltrate modern constructions of the Renaissance English stage. With our excluding focus on London theaters and politics, we have not been concerned with the academic experiments occurring only a few miles to the east and west of the capital, where the drama's academic status permitted experiments that would have startled not only later neo-classical formalists but also the contemporary government in London.

In addition to and precisely because of such opportunistic pedagogical manipulations of the image from this text, the play now elicits critical and theoretical scrutiny as a neglected site of ideological experimentation, one that at least Renaissance audiences found compellingly unbearable. Its modern critics however, are more contemptuous. F. S. Boas, for example, launches a threefold attack on *Roxana,* even as he seeks in his seminal study of the academic drama to rescue it from oblivion. The play, he claims, is not only unoriginal; it is indecorous, and it traumatized its original audience. Alabaster's play is derived and condensed from an Italian tragic original, Luigi Grotto's *La Dalida* published in Venice in 1567. Alabaster's play has been praised only for its elegant Latin verses, and not for its philosophical or dramatic content, by Thomas Fuller and Samuel Johnson, who were unaware of Alabaster's plagiarized source. Boas is only able to summon an interest in the play's language and a damningly invidious comparison to Shakespeare's *Titus Andronicus* that argues for *Roxana*'s ascendancy in brutality.[6]

William Alabaster entered Trinity College, Cambridge, from Westminster School in 1583 and went on to complete his M.A. at Oxford University in 1592. He was successively chaplain on the Cadiz expedition to the Earl of Essex (Queen Elizabeth's favorite and later her betrayer) and, after a brief period of conversion to Roman Catholicism, prebendary of St. Paul's, and rector of Tharfield. Indeed, one of his poetic productions, a "heroick song" of praise for Elizabeth entitled the *Eliseïs,* was even well received by his eminent contemporary, Edmund Spenser, in *Colin Clouts come Home Againe.*[7] Little more is known of Alabaster, and, indeed, even this much biographical information is uncommon for the authors of texts such as the university drama whose identities are often preserved in name alone. Although biographical criticism must be approached with care, the details of Alabaster's life are emblems, if not proofs, of the direct connection between the two great universities of Oxford and Cambridge and the expanding world of the early English empire under Queen Elizabeth. It is perhaps not surprising then that Alabaster, in an age preoccupied with empire and with the expansion of England's and Europe's frontiers, should appropriate an exotic story about queens and imperial confrontation, set no longer in Spain and England but now safely displaced to India and Bactria.

Clearly there lies within the plot and language of the play more than the stylistic elegance that Edmund Spenser and Samuel Johnson praised.[8] If the "content" of *Roxana* in both narrative and semiotic terms is the source for its denigration by earlier critics, I will suggest it, instead, as the site for remaking the play's challenge to both period and modern audiences. The basic outline of the story is as follows. The play is set at the royal court of Bactria (modern Afghanistan) where the king, Moleus, has been killed by his nephew, Oromasdes, who, in spite of a marriage to an Indian princess, Atossa, has taken Moleus's daughter, Roxana, as his mistress and has two children by her. To further his love for Atossa, Oromasdes' counselor, Bessus, tells Atossa of her husband's infidelity and brings Roxana and her children into Atossa's presence. After a disingenuous welcome, Atossa has Roxana tortured until she kills both herself and her children. Oromasdes has, in the intervening time, overheard Bessus boasting of his conquest of Atossa and had him executed. The play concludes with Atossa's invitation to Oromasdes to celebrate her birthday with a feast at which he is presented with the remains of Roxana and her children as the main dish. After the revelation of the events of the play, they murder each other with poisoned flowers and leave the chorus, senate, and audience to mourn the barbarisms.[9]

F. S. Boas concludes his commentary on *Roxana* with the detail from Fuller's contemporary assessment of the play which I have poached for my title, as being a summation appropriate to the play as a whole: "The soundest critic of *Roxana* is the nameless 'gentlewoman' who, we are assured, 'fell distracted' upon seeing it performed 'and never after recovered her senses.'"[10] While not accepting the patronizing rhetoric of the delicacy of female sensibility that this remark reflects (for after all Fuller also praises the play from the academic perspective of its male collegiate audience), I propose to connect this second, performatively excluded body, here foreign only in gender, with her counterparts on the page and stage who are foreign in both culture and ethnicity.

What might have caused one member of the audience to collapse and others to feel themselves academically edified by this savage little play that, in its marginal Cambridge setting, can place before its viewers' eyes images and interpretive challenges that both resonate with London's actualities and evade London's official censorship? The play in its special academic environment and its special academic language, uniquely combines a consideration of the representation of women, within the codes of marriage and diplomatic alliance, with an attempt to construct a view of "the East" for its English audience. Anticipating the comments of critics like Edward Saïd about the complicity of these two projects of subjugation and alienation, the play challenges its voyeuristic, and largely male, audience, who view these atrocities acted by and upon women necessarily within a perspective informed by the policies and self-construction of their own female monarch.

Edward Saïd and other critics like Gayatri Spivak have reminded us of the complicity of the twin projects of colonizing gender and race.[11] In an age that foretells the enormous imperialist expansions of the eighteenth and nineteenth centuries, Alabaster will challenge an audience deeply concerned with the questions of female rulership, marital autonomy, and the intimidating seductions of newly encountered alien cultures. Alabaster, like the great imperialists after him, was seduced by the twin Renaissance themes of knowledge and power that constitute the matrix for the fascination with the imperialist project.[12] Saïd would place Alabaster within the first wave of Orientalist appropriation, which included not only London's plays about the Ottoman empire but a thoroughgoing attempt to remake Western thought through the appropriation of Eastern Mediterranean philosophy and literature.[13] The Orient, in the early stages of imperialism, became "the stage upon which the whole East is confined . . . a closed field, a theatrical stage affixed to Europe."[14] Alabaster will even foreshadow Saïd's accounts of the eighteenth and nineteenth centuries as he maps foreign exoticism onto the construction of female identity, as both ruler and wife, at home in England. In the safely displaced and fascinatingly violent and exoticized setting of the Eastern Mediterranean, Alabaster will suggest a radical allegory of the contemporary conservative encroachments on the Tudor monarchy's attempts to modernize and liberalize the legal status of women through the existential presence of a female, unmarried monarch and an enlightened view of divorce.

The connection of academic drama to London politics is direct. Many of the plays addressed a London audience, even a female one. Within the exclusively male domain of the universities, at least one woman did consistently preside over and intervene in the dramatic productions of Oxbridge without fainting, and she often did so in eloquently idiomatic Latin:

> et ego quia nil nisi male agere possum, odi sane lucem, id est conspectum vestrum.
>
> [And I, because I can do nothing if not badly, wisely avoid the bright light, that is to say your faces.][15]

As she begins her royal address in 1566 to the assembled leaders of the University of Oxford, Elizabeth I adopts an iconography that she had systematically developed and caused to be associated with her person. As Roy Strong and Frances Yates have noted,[16] Elizabeth, through both her verbal and her iconographical articulations of herself as queen, emphasized her status as the Virgin Queen, as a modern day Diana or Cynthia who, like her mythological predecessor, could be immediately identified by her most recognizable attribute of chaste moonlight. And yet, in this self-introduction to the learned gentlemen of the University of Oxford the powerful virgin goddess/queen adopts a markedly self-

deprecating tone, perhaps not so far from the other and anonymous representative of her gender who fainted. This second woman, Elizabeth, herself empowered with a thorough education and eloquence in Latin, defers to the academicians and, instead of invoking the moon's purity, insists upon its reflected secondariness. Even encased in the safety of her double self-construction as both virginal and essentially English, she hesitates to be on display visually and verbally. The risk of deprecation will be far greater for those foreign, denuded, displayed, and sexually provocative women who will be offered to at least one Cambridge audience for visual consumption. With the increasing political and economic centralization of England in the capital encouraged by a powerful female monarch, the remark is more than polite; it is doubly startling. Elizabeth presents herself, the representative of real political events, as a mere foil to Oxford's learning and shrinks from the brightness of its light. At the same time, she insists that her effort should in some way reflect, in the public scene, the insights of these doctors far removed from London's daily events.

Such a staging of herself, emphasized by her reference to the faces of her spectators (*conspectum*), is not peculiar for Elizabeth who consistently made elaborate royal visits throughout England.[17] What is curious is her tone and the relationship that she implies between London and Oxford. Although many critics place the universities on the margins of Tudor England, her remarks offer them, not only an important, but even a central position. Just as the words of academics uttered in Tudor lecture halls are often relegated to a secondary role, so the spectacles viewed in the two great university towns of Oxford and Cambridge have not yet received the attention that Elizabeth herself insists upon as their due. The spectacle of the queen's several visits to the universities was hardly the only one available to their students and dons. The image of the queen both appeared and presented itself before the faces of her academic subjects, and those academic subjects presented to the royal eyes another sort of spectacle, one which formed a central part not only of university life and training but also of that raw material and experience that went into many of the London plays. I refer here to the dramatic performances that took place at the universities of Oxford and Cambridge in honor of particular religious holidays and royal visits.[18]

The products of the university included not only future parliamentarians but also a rich and ignored textual production whose most outrageous texts were in the form of plays presented by, and for, academic audiences. Often more incendiary than anything that could have been placed on the London stage, which was always under the threat of censure and dissolution by the Puritan City Council, these legitimate exercises in rhetoric were praised and funded by the authorities. Consistently politically irreverent and even subversive in their content, all the plays present challenges to modern critical expectations of what material and which attitudes were permitted a public hearing. In the context of the long period of female control represented by Elizabeth's reign and of the rapid international commercial expansion of the Elizabethan economy, *Roxana* stands out as a text presented in an entirely male performance context and yet, nevertheless, also presented to a queen.

Like the students of the last quarter of the sixteenth century, we must place before our eyes these academic plays.[19] We must take stock of what neoclassical material is being offered to reassure and orient these student interpreters, who will soon stage their own actual political dramas in London. We must assess what experiments in ideology and staging the sacred space of a university uniquely accorded to, and even encouraged in, its participants.[20]

Elizabeth's evident ill ease at staging her royal spectacle for academic eyes is thoroughly understandable. She addresses a highly trained audience accustomed not only to the witnessing of staged events but also to their evaluation and manipulation for particular social ends. The inheritance of the university drama derives both from the official classical curriculum of the universities and from the increasing availability of Italian neo-Senecan poetics and plays such as *La Dalida*. The academic audiences were not only aware of classical materials, they were also involved in their detailed study. A university play stands between the self-consciously academic humanist study of classical tragedy and the practice of commercial tragedy. It produces a uniquely powerful, irreverent, and classically trained collocation of writers, players, and viewers.

Traditionally fed by students aged fourteen or fifteen from grammar schools, the two universities grew greatly in the late sixteenth century. Moreover, their populations became increasingly elite and politicized.[21] Any consideration of activities at Oxford and Cambridge in this period thus must include an awareness not only of a growth in the size of the audience but also of the increasingly political and nonacademic nature of the university population. The many political and intellectual changes of the period, the increase of royal control, the influx of the sons of the nobility, and the growth of collegiate teaching and collegiate power within the university generated a lively intellectual environment, even if they did not radically alter the official curriculum. For the century of Tudor rule, the universities conformed far more to a materialist elitist description.

Nevertheless, what would emerge from the universities as a new radical politics in the seventeenth century was expressed in such controlled forms as academic drama in the sixteenth century. With the reinforcement of the

new suggestions of Ramist logic, which gave substantial importance to literary exempla, and the incipient politicization of the universities, the students and dons were able to explore many topics that would have been censored on the popular stage. At the universities, participation in the drama would be defended on both pedagogical and ethical grounds.

Oxbridge students were under constant scrutiny and discipline from the surrogate parental figures of senior fellows, as in the case of Corpus Christi College, Oxford.[22] Apart from private lessons in some sports and modest recreation, student dramatic productions for Christmas, royal visits, and other special events were one of their few diversions.[23] The performing of plays, both as an expression of the wealth of the college and a display of obedience to the royal patron in attendance,[24] and as a sort of Bakhtinian carnival to release the entropic energies of the students, especially over the long winter vacation, was typical until well into the eighteenth century. The symbolic representation of obedience to the monarch through the mounting of elaborate entertainments was especially important under Elizabeth I. These entertainments usually included the staging of several plays for the queen, whose fluency in Latin and flair for royal pageantry were well flattered by the university celebrations. Unlike the London stages, which were always under threat from the Puritan City Council and were finally closed in 1642, the university plays constituted sound pedagogy.[25] Plays were regularly commissioned and lavishly produced by the colleges, which spent enormous amounts of money on sets and were even permitted the use of Queen Elizabeth's own garments for costumes on occasion.[26] Indeed, some plays were accepted in partial fulfillment of the requirements for a degree.[27] While professional players had been banned in 1593 by the Privy Council, student players were rewarded as humanist rhetoricians. Furthermore, costumed in the ritual garments of real politicians and, at the same time, inspired by a saturnalian sense of irreverence and satire, they insisted upon the right to stage these spectacles.

This paradoxical role as the moment of release that later facilitates containment of subversive experimental ideas and images was well-known to the university authorities. Such contained radical content and performance ensured good behavior in the students for the rest of the academic year and, perhaps, even good citizenship for the rest of a political career. These "revels" were aimed at two sorts of political objectives. Ralph Holinshed describes Elizabeth's 1566 visit to Oxford as follows:

> The one and thirtieth of August the queenes majestie in her progress cam to the universite of Oxford and was of all the students which had looked for hir coming thither two yeares, so honorablie and joifully received as either loialness towards the queenes majestie or the expectation of their friends did require.[28]

The pair of objectives appear in the last clause: political loyalty and institutional harmony. On the one hand, the plays provided an outlet for the not-to-be-underestimated flamboyant and anarchic tendencies of university students and were far more effective than the attempts to impose penalties and rules on the students. The preserved text of *The Christmas Prince, A True and Faithful relation of the risinge and fall of Thomas Tucker, Prince of Alba Fortunata,* by Griffius Higgs (1607-08), St. John's College, Oxford, Ms. 52, gives a clear sense of the enormous destructive energy that was released in an only barely contained form at these performances and revels:

> But (as it often falleth out), the Freshmen, or patients, thinkinge the Poulderlings or agentes too busie and nimble. They them too dull and backwards in their duty, the Standers by findinge both of them too forwarde and violente, the sportes for that night for feare of tumults were broken upp, everye man betaking himself to his reste. . . . And wheras yt was hoped à nighte sleepe would have somewhat abated theyr rage, it contraryewise sett a greater edge on theyr fury.[29]

On the other hand, these performances were yet another example of the staging of the Elizabethan system of control. Elizabeth relied heavily upon display and pageant, upon her subjects receiving "honorablie and joifully as . . . their loialness . . . did require" the spectacle of the monarch that they had looked for so long.

It is in the context of these heavy burdens, of being an educative extracurricular student activity and serving a crucial double political role, that the academic drama must be seen. And yet, I do not wish to underestimate the entertainment value of these plays, with their sumptuous costumes from the Office of Revels and the lively interventions in Latin verse by the royal audience. Indeed, it is precisely because the plays are being used to so many different ends that they are so provocative and important. Each of the three goals, rather than discrediting the other two, emphasizes the interdependency of the three projects. All three must be kept in mind as we turn now to the play itself.

The appeal of a play such as *Roxana* was finally secured by its technically accomplished staging, which both dazzled the eyes and repeated the iconography of the real monarch in London. Like their counterparts in Italy and France, the English plays were always staged indoors.[30] According to Elliott,[31] for example, the stage at Christ Church was placed at the high table in the main hall and was highly raked, with the royal throne placed in the "Corridor" at the center of the hall with the courtiers in front of the stage and seated in boxes affixed to the side walls. The most advanced and fashionable dramatic technology, machinery, and later even set designers such as Inigo Jones were used for these lavish productions. This interior splendor not only matched the exterior display of the more overtly political royal entrances and progresses through the university towns but also conflated optically the two events. The real queen who entered Oxford or Cambridge at noon might very well watch a boy play another queen, perhaps an Indian one, in Elizabeth's own clothes, that same evening.

Only now, against this sketched background of the intensity of the intellectual, social, and political forces that converge upon the university drama, can such a play as *Roxana* be fully considered. Since it was not uncommon for the academic plays to assess particular current political and philosophical material, to offer in the safe space of festival entertainment and well-turned Latin verses scathing parodies or at least critiques of highly contested and even forbidden topics, *Roxana* suggests itself, with equal force albeit in a different genre, as an appropriate pair to *The Christmas Prince.* Its theatrically excessive violence, couched in the recognizably Senecan classical conceit of the myth of the Thyestean cannibalistic feast, appeals to more than a simple period taste for violence on the stage. It draws upon its audience's fascination with two threatening, unstable, and seductive terms, the eastern and the female. In a period replete with exotic and violent treatments of both of these topics,[32] *Roxana* brings them together in a particularly frightening way in which the "strangeness" (with its sixteenth-century meaning of both peculiar and other) of these women is not kept safely in the distance of a fictional eastern space but instead, in fact, negotiates crises all too familiar to the English audience itself.

Modern literary theory has only just begun to concern itself with preindustrial European culture and arts. A concern with an earlier period and with contemporary critiques of essentializing literary history that deifies either the author of his text or even the text itself as somehow hermeneutically self-contained and available to the modern reader, therefore, often involves an act of triangulation or at least adaptation. The modern model, intended to decode an artifact of the nineteenth or twentieth century, will demand adaptation to an earlier context. Fortunately, Edward Saïd's own text's discussion of later imperialist constructions of the "other" invites an interest in the textual production of the protoimperialist and yet already Orientalist period. Precisely because of the shared grand narrative of imperialism, whose beginnings in England occur under Elizabeth's rule, the suggestions of critics like Saïd, who are concerned with its height in the nineteenth century, enlighten the reading of its origins in the sixteenth. Far from a simple story of military domination and expansion, British imperial ideology spread by an apparently more benevolent method of cultural appropriation and alienation even as early as 1583. *Roxana,* with its combination of representing the East and speaking to England of its women, provides a prehistory to the Orientalism of the industrial age and hints at which attitudes might fill in the space between the crusades of feudal Europe and the great age of empire.

Indeed, the case for **Roxana** as a play especially suited to a reading through Saïd's lens becomes yet stronger if we look to the details of his account. Drawing upon Antonio Gramsci's work, which distinguishes the cultivation of the subaltern in the project of eighteenth- and nineteenth-century European imperialism from Europe's other brutally militaristic strategies of repression, Saïd suggests that there was, especially in the case of the Muslim Orient in which **Roxana,** too, is set, a systematic mapping of the characteristics of the feminine onto those of the Oriental so as to align both as objects of desire and domination.[33] For Saïd, nineteenth-century Orientalists, seduced by the exoticism of the East, consistently associated it with sex and the female, as well as with the culturally other:

> For Nerval and Flaubert, such female figures as Cleopatra, Salomé, and Isis have special significance; and it was by no means accidental that in their work on the East, as well as in their visits to it, they preeminently valorized and enhanced female types of this legendary, richly suggestive, and associative sort. . . . The Oriental woman is an occasion and an opportunity for Flaubert's musings; he is entranced by her self-sufficiency, by her emotional carelessness, and also by what, lying next to him, she allows him to think. . . . Like the Queen of Sheba . . . she could say . . . "je ne suis pas une femme, je suis un monde."[34]

There is an almost symbiotic (or should one say, parasitical) relationship between the European male constructions of European female identity and of the Oriental. Whatever is said of those gendered other is directly connected to those cultured other, and, in both cases, this mark of difference is the site of domination of that otherness, whether "she" is coerced or complicit. What will be important is the exact nature of the historical details that are in crisis for a given period in the development of European hegemonic power. Saïd carefully notes differences among the various European centers of imperial power and among their peripheries and does not suggest a monolithic, transhistorical, and rigid paradigm. I, too, hope to suggest that a very particular form of the experiment he describes occurs in **Roxana,** whose author and audience, like Flaubert lying by the side of the Egyptian dancer, Kuchak Hanem, are surprised by "what they are allowed to think."[35]

Like Gerard de Nerval and Flaubert after him, Alabaster capitalizes upon a deep period fascination with the culture and customs of the eastern Mediterranean, with its exotica, its fantastical luxury, and its danger. The play's first lines conjure, in the voice of the shade of

Moleus, a Tartarean nightmare of the sensually threatening East for the eyes of its scholarly audience. And yet the speaking voice is not that of the Western interpreter but of the sympathetically suffering Oriental who will soon speak of Bactria's pain and humiliation by sin and the gods:

> Utrumne noctis ille Tartareae vapor
> Depinxit oculos ludicri mundi noctis
> Vegetumq rerum examens errore implicat?
> An hoc quod oculis haurio late meis,
> Illa est scelesta et excreta Bactria?
>
> (1)[36]

> [Is it some exhalation of the Tartarean night
> Which has colored the eyes of the night in the sportive world
> And entangles a multitude of lively things in uncertainty?
> Or is it that which I everywhere devour with my eyes,
> That is, the evil and damnable Bactria?]

Bactria's savage history has reduced her spiritual representative to introspective self-doubt and self-hatred. By contrast, however, with the victory over the Spanish Armada, the period of 1588-99 was marked, not by a decrease in international economic ventures, but by an increase combined with a striking tone of "national isolationism," "narrow nationalism and militancy" especially in the drama of the London plays of the University Wits.[37] Alabaster's text also presents the spectacle of female foreign suffering to the voyeuristic *(oculos/ oculis)* future politicians of London, who will soon join the audiences of great Orientalist plays such as *The Wars of Cyrus* and *Friar Bacon and Friar Bungay,* not to mention *Tamburlaine* itself. And yet, I hope to suggest that Alabaster uses this fashionable proto-Orientalist setting against the grain, as a displaced locus not for English self-congratulation for military and imperialist successes, but rather as a safely distant environment in which to critique that same English society.

The play will both invoke and frustrate a second fashionable trope, for Bactria's national humiliation will be played out in the suffering and crimes of its most powerful women, Roxana and Atossa. The period taste for explicit violence against women, especially foreign ones, whether Roman like Shakespeare's Lavinia in *Titus Andronicus* or Damascan like the virgins in Marlowe's *Tamburlaine,* is satisfied by the savage murders of both women. But this exoticism, while pandering to popular fantasies of the violence of non-English societies, does not wholly distance the play's narrative or thematic content from the English context. It provides a pretext for the performative aggression of the play that will permit Alabaster's topical commentaries on women and marriage in England, as well as abroad.

Not altogether unlike London dramatists, who were in this same decade experimenting with conventional New

Comedy resolutions of family strife, especially of the conflict between father and daughter over the choice of a husband (here Moleus, Atossa, and Oromasdes) and representations of marriage in ethical and legal terms, Alabaster stages this same moment of crisis. He offers his student audience a double adultery and meditations on divorce. He explores this uniquely dangerous topic in the legal construction of familial and female identity in this period with unapologetic directness.

Rather than alienating us from the Bactrian context, he coerces us into this dark and unstable world, which reminds us of our own. No commentary on divorce, adultery, and the question of heirs is neutral in an Elizabethan context.[38] Again, it is the shade who will warn the audience of this content and of its chaotic consequences. The challenge to the viewer's preconceptions about marriage is presented in the unimpeachable voice of the prophetic ghost of a neo-Senecan revenge play. As he agonizingly foretells the death of Roxana, he constructs the scene as one of ideal maternity victimized by the gods:

> Quid hoc? video natae capit?
> Roxana salve: patris an amplexum veni
> Solvet perire mortuis formae decus:
> Sed crevit in te nata: quanto es pulchrior
> Defunta (si non judico nimis pater.)
> Et haec nepotum capita, de matre auguror
> Patro nec ablunudunt, habent et quiddam avi:
> Nepos generque gemina amicitiae nota.
>
> (8)

> [What is this? Do I see the head of my daughter?
> Greetings Roxana: If you come into your father's embrace
> It will allow you to die in a way worthy of the dead:
> But a daughter appears in you: how much more lovely you are
> Dead (if I do not judge too much as a father)
> And these heads of my grandchildren, I foretell, which neither by mother
> Nor by father shall be expiated, have some hope from their grandfather:
> A noble grandson and a twin-born sister famous for friendship.]

The move from the shade's speech to the play itself marks a move from the prophecy of a divine director to a scrupulous performance of just those events foretold. Even such conventional details as Counselor Bessus' later praise of Atossa's beauty [pulchra est (17)], and chastity [castitas moram dabit (17)], disorientingly recall descriptions of the conventionally idealized western female, whose worth is constituted through physical beauty and sexual purity. Even his sardonic and misogynist philosophy of love, which echoes 1

Corinithians 7 and reminds a modern audience of Hamlet's fiercely binary attack on Ophelia as a virgin/whore in the nunnery speech, confirms this stereotype by negation:

> Nulla amoris nescia est,
> Quae semel amavit: virgines quod non sciunt
> Amant, mulieres quod sciunt, et quod amant.
>
> (17)

> [No woman is innocent of love,
> When once she has been in love: virgins love what they
> Do not know; and wives love what they do know.]

Bessus' final connection of love to civil war which makes him "equally traitor to my king and myself" [regi et mihi / pariter rebellis (17)] again invokes a conventional metaphor, that of the battle of love, and emphasizes both the inconstancy of women and the Renaissance doctrine of the husband as lord of his household and wife, ideas whose most notorious expression is perhaps contained in Katherina's last speech to Petruchio in *The Taming of the Shrew* (5.ii.136-79). In other contexts, this conventionalized language, with its superficiality and its underlying misogyny, might go scarcely noticed. And yet Atossa's foretold brutality, which conflates the stories of the revenging Atreus of Seneca's *Thyestes* and Euripides' jealous Medea, destabilizes the whole code of proper female behavior that is both presented and dismantled as the play opens. Atossa, though childless, is, like Medea, sexually betrayed and seeks revenge through the unwomanly act of infanticide. And yet the act is moved from the realm of the purely personal to that of the political; Atossa does not kill her own children for she has none. Instead, she destroys another woman's children who represent the only hope, albeit an illegitimate one, for an heir for Oromasdes. The invocation of the Medea archetype is especially striking, since Alabaster reverses the female antagonists, making the legitimate wife into the childless revenger who kills not only her rival's children but herself and her husband as well. The innovation is important because it displaces the monstrous actions of a witch and mistress onto the legitimate wife. The resonances with Elizabeth's own history are alarming, given the consistent Catholic argument, forwarded most aggressively by Mary Stuart, that she was herself, as the daughter of Henry VIII's second marriage after his dissolution of a first, arranged and childless marriage, just such an illegitimate child. If Medea attacks the code of marriage from the outside, Atossa attacks it from within. This system of arranged marriage, and the knowledge of its necessary companion of adultery, has transformed one who was modest, faithful, and gentle [pudica, fida, lenis, innocens fui (23)] into one who, victimized by her father and state obligations [patriae, sceptra, throno], has now ceded her legitimate marriage bed [thoro] to another and is thrown into a fit of murderous rage that frightens even the chorus of her ladies (25).

Such is the traumatic environment that sympathetically prompts Atossa's less sympathetic course of revenge, whose obscene results will horrify especially the woman who fainted at its premier in the audience. Indeed, even Oromasdes exists in this same fiercely rigid world. Delighted with his affair with Roxana, whom he claims genuinely to love, and with their children, who sadly only simulate heirs to his throne, he has yet to resolve the nightmare of the future. While, like Henry VIII, he has chosen a second love, and she has proved fertile, he is still encumbered by the burden of a first and infertile wife, who both threatens the directness of succession and forecloses the possibility of a second marriage. He meditates on this injustice, peculiar to kings, who must both agree to arranged marriages and secure legitimate heirs (27). Interestingly, his counselor, Arsaces, insists that even children do not guarantee peace in either private or public life and cites the examples of Niobe, Belidus, Priam, Laius, and, prophetically, Thyestes. Children, he argues, are fragile and no cure for the king's nagging political fears (28).

The portrait is a horrifying one of instability and desperation, one that might well terrify an audience of the last years of the sixteenth century. Veiled under the exotica of Bactria, and apparently about an affair with the beautiful Bactrian, Roxana, not the elegantly francofied Anne Boleyn, Alabaster's play probes perhaps the greatest fear of the end of the Tudor period, the succession. There is a moment, however, which I have omitted so far, that linguistically betrays the analogy's exactness. The first solution that Oromasdes suggests to his dilemma invokes that word *divortium* (26), notorious for Elizabeth, whose claim to the throne hinged upon its legality. Unlike his English counterpart, however, this Bactrian king will be denied this option. Heeding the advice of his senate and religion, he will retreat from this desperate solution and give up his hopes of a happy second marriage and a cure to his sorrows.

And yet the word has been spoken in a period still divided as to the legality of divorce and concerned about the ramifications of their own queen being the product of a broken home. By the end of the sixteenth century, England was the only Protestant country that lacked some form of legalized divorce.[39] Five years after the writing of the play, the confusion in English divorce law, a result of the religious reversals of the century and perhaps of Elizabeth's own complex relationship to marriage, was only partially resolved by Archbishop Whitgift, who, while not directly stating that second marriages were adulterous, established a series of Latin ecclesiastical statutes which permitted separation but required of both parties a hundred-pound bond not to remarry during the lifetime of the spouse.[40] Lawrence

Stone goes further to argue that, in spite of the events of Henry VIII's reign, there was in this period a concerted effort on the part of conservative clergymen and laymen to discourage divorce, against the grain of developments in Scotland and on the European continent.[41]

If we are troubled by the conservatism of the portrayal of the particular women, divided somewhat facilely into caring and virtuous mother and revenging and adulterous fury, we must nevertheless be struck by the aggressive and exact treatment of the matter of divorce. Along with the sensual naïveté and innocent exoticism of Roxana's presentation and speeches as she prays to the gods of the Night (30) and the almost strident presentation of Atossa's anger and hypocrisy as she dupes Roxana, whom she calls "mater" four times in her speech (33), there is a radical and unorthodox commentary on the negotiation of heterosexual liaisons. Displaced to Bactria, Alabaster's play refutes the developing official attitudes. The play even perhaps stages this displacement and the violent potentials of Orientalism itself. The play contains its own embedded Orientalism. Bactria is obsessed with India as the decadent fictional space characterized by Atossa's sensuality, violence, and sterility from which Oromasdes escapes to experience illicit sexuality. It offers its viewers, if they look carefully, an account of its own process of construction. Roxana precedes Flaubert's Kuchak Hanem by centuries and yet functions as a *mise-en-abîme* of the whole project of the fantasy, found at the imperial center, about life in the peripheries. India is Bactria's mystified East just as Bactria is England's. Here, however, Bactria is more than a sensationalist tactic to attract an audience that dreams of Ottoman sexuality and violence; it is also used as a mask to hide a structural critique of England's own legal move to limit the possibilities for divorce.

Almost with too much care, Alabaster creates a legitimate case for Oromasdes to divorce Atossa so as to heighten the agony of this missed opportunity from which a conservative politician, not unlike those in Elizabethan London, dissuades the king. Both natural affection and, more importantly, the capacity to produce heirs endorse this second would-be marriage as not only desirable personally but crucial politically. Henry VIII's case for the succession is repeatedly invoked, as is the threat of a kingdom torn [divisa regna (35)] by civil war, should Oromasdes fail to bring his house into order. Moreover, Atossa's crimes are made to square with the grounds for divorce, as she takes up an affair with Bessus and commits her many murders, culminating in that of Oromasdes himself. Finally, she even openly threatens treason, a charge that appears against Anne Boleyn as well in her trial, as she assures the chorus that she prays for civil strife along with all others who contemplate making any wars [quid bella aliud faciunt], and hope thereby to transform a personal ruin into a public victory, calling it the king's victory [hac gloria / regis vocatur, (54)]. Not only are the king's personal body and biological family under attack, but even his political body is threatened by her jealous fury. With so exact a repetition not only of the events of Henry VIII's life but also of what divorce law did exist, Alabaster seems to insist upon a comparison. Oromasdes' plight highlights the wisdom of Henry's choice of divorce, which at least deferred the civil war for a century and ultimately ensured Elizabeth's ascension to the throne and a period of peace.

While complicit in invoking a binary stereotype of female behavior for Atossa and Roxana, the play nevertheless hybridizes both the ideal mother, who is now a mistress, and the revenging fury, who stages the costs of the obligation to remain within painful and politically unstable arranged marriages. The analogy is quite precise, as is the interpretive challenge to the academic audience, which is encouraged to assess these dangerous and provocative issues. In a nightmarish experimental world set abroad, Alabaster stages, in terms of the codes of marriage and divorce that most constrained female identity in Tudor England, a liberal theory of female self-determination that connects the autonomous selection of a spouse not only to the fates of one woman and her children but to the preservation of the integrity and stability of the very state itself. Indeed, in seeking to account for the fainting spell at the play's performance, one might even push Alabaster's critique further and suggest that it is a play of great sympathy, if not for Atossa, although she, too, is presented as wronged by the system of marriages of political alliance, at least for Roxana, and for the women whose lives are destroyed by this thoroughly English inflexibility and atavism on the matter of marriage. Dare we suggest that the play offers a certain criticism not only of Oromasdes' treatment by the legal system but also of the treatment of Roxana and Atossa, figuring forth dramatically that female other who sometimes witnessed these university plays? Even as two women's fates are staged, at least one actual representative of that society collapses at the witness of her own tragedy, a tragedy that will remain unrescued from its severity until the legal reforms of the mid-nineteenth century.[42]

Alabaster's experiment, his lesson in rhetoric offered to a sophisticated audience of academic and political spectators, is couched in its academic Latin and in the seductive exotica of a foreign landscape that dissolves into the darkness of an awful sunset at the moment of Atossa's death (62). He invokes both as protections from reproof by the authorities, should they care to scrutinize this among so many other entropic, pedagogical exercises. He critiques neither, however, and, instead, manipulates them so as sufficiently to alienate its story from its most immediate and obvious implica-

tions. Replicating rather than critiquing a proto-Orientalist fantasy of the East, Alabaster strives, like Nerval and Flaubert after him, not to understand its otherness, but rather to use it as an intellectual and dramatic landscape in which to interrogate the others, whether constructed through a difference of religion, politics, or gender, that are closer to home. Those others will, in the space of *Roxana,* force the whole audience to "recover its senses." As for that ultimate other, the other of the East, "her" story of recovery has yet fully to be written.

Notes

1. T. S. Eliot, "Hamlet," *Selected Prose of T. S. Eliot,* ed. Frank Kermode (New York: Harcourt Brace and Jovanovich, 1975), pp. 45-49. Eliot famously calls the play "most certainly an artistic failure" because of its "superfluous and inconsistent scenes" (47).

2. There is an ongoing controversy about the composition, in terms of class and gender, in particular, of the London theater-going audience. Alfred Harbage initiates the debate with *Shakespeare's Audience* (New York: MacMillan, 1941). Ann Jennalie Cook refutes Harbage's utopian construction of a thoroughly heterogeneously nonelitist audience in *The Privileged Playgoers of Shakespeare's London, 1576-1642* (Princeton: Princeton University Press, 1981), which is a development of her controversial article "The Audience of Shakespeare's Plays: A Reconsideration," *Shakespeare Studies* 7 (1974), pp. 283-305. Martin Butler explicitly rejects her arguments for a limited aristocratic, educated, and wealthy audience in Appendix II of *Theater and Crisis 1632-1642* (Cambridge: Cambridge University Press, 1984). Andrew Gurr carefully reconstructs, in sociological, literary, and historical terms, a complex audience that attended with varying frequency a highly diverse group of productions presented by a wide variety of companies in different sorts of performance contexts in his two studies *The Shakespearean Stage, 1574-1642* (Cambridge: Cambridge University Press, 1984) and *Playgoers in Shakespeare's London* (Cambridge: Cambridge University Press, 1987).

3. My argument here is that the *Riverside Shakespeare,* ed. G. Blakemore Evans (New York: Houghton Mifflin, 1974) constitutes a representative and frequent point of entry, especially for university students, to Shakespeare's plays and that it contains one page of particular interest. On the same page as the famous Johannes de Witt sketch of the Swan Theater (plate 8, after p. 494), it contains two woodcuts of particular stagings of minor plays, Nathaniel Richard's *Messalina* (1640) and

William Alabaster's *Roxana* (from the 1632 author's edition).

4. William Alabaster, *Roxana* (London, 1632). My description is of the remarkable title page to Alabaster's own edition of the play, printed by William Jones. He published this edition in response to a plagiarized edition of the play, issued earlier that year by R. Badger for Andrew Crook. The play had been acted at Trinity College, Cambridge, in 1592. The image is widely reproduced as one of the Renaissance English stage. Both this and all future citations from *Roxana* are taken from the copy of Jones' edition in the Bodleian Library, Oxford, Douce A 399(1). All future page numbers are from this edition and are given in parentheses.

5. F. S. Boas, *University Drama in the Tudor Age* (Oxford: Clarendon Press, 1914), p. 288.

6. Ibid., pp. 286-88.

7. Ibid., p. 286.

8. Johnson, according to Boas, mentions Alabaster's *Roxana* as a model of Latin versification in his *Lives of the English Poets.*

9. There is a complete plot summary (with regrettably few comments on details of diction and image) in George R. Churchill and Wolfgang Keller, "Die lateinischen Universitäts-Dramen in der Zeit der Königen Elisabeth," *Shakespeare Jahrbuch* 34 (1898): pp. 252-55. Boas also offers a brief, if evaluative, summary in the pages already noted.

10. Boas, *University Drama,* p. 288. The words in inside quotes are Fuller's exact period comments on the production as cited by Boas. Interestingly, the particular detail of the collapse of a female audience member during a performance is not unique to Alabaster's neo-Italian play. Perhaps the most influential of the Italian humanistic playwrights at Oxbridge, Giambattista Giraldi Cinthio, uses the same detail to initiate his account of the ethical and dramatic defense of the use of explicit horror in his seminal and notorious horror tragedy, *Orbecche.* To establish the performance context for his discussion of this play in his treatise on tragedy, *Discorso intorno al comporre delle comedie e delle tragedie,* (Venice: n.p., 1554), Cinthio recounts Fuller's scene almost exactly (202). What is surprising is that, in the midst of this persuasive and highly academic discussion, Cinthio's practical stage experience inserts itself in a startling little anecdote. At the premier performance of *Orbecche,* according to Cinthio, when the remnants of Oronte were brought on stage at the Thyestean climax of the play, the fiancée of the actor who had played the role was so overcome with horror at the sight that she fainted.

There is a modern Italian edition available in G. B. Giraldi Cinthio, *Scritti Critici,* ed. Camillo Guerrieri (Milan: Marzorati, 1973). The above page numbers, however, are from the 1554 edition. Boas, *University Drama,* p. 240.

11. See Edward Saïd, *Orientalism* (New York: Vintage Books, 1978), and Gayatri Chakravorty Spivak, *In Other Worlds: Essays in Cultural Politics* (New York: Methuen, 1987).

12. Saïd, *Orientalism,* p. 32.

13. Ibid., p. 60.

14. Ibid., p. 63.

15. This line appears early in Thomas Cole's compilation of documents from the 1566 visit of Queen Elizabeth to Oxford University, Bodleian Ms. Lat. misc. e. 105, ff 27-28.

16. Roy Strong, *Gloriana: The Portraits of Queen Elizabeth I* (London: Thames and Hudson, 1987), pp. 125-28; Frances A. Yates, *Astraea: The Imperial Theme in the Sixteenth Century* (original imprint, London: Routledge and Kegan Paul, 1975; second imprint, London, Boston, Melbourne, and Henley: Ark Paperbacks, 1985), pp. 29, 76-80.

17. Elizabeth visited Cambridge in 1564 and Oxford in 1566 and 1592. See Boas, *University Drama,* pp. 90-98, 98-108, 252-67. In addition to the plays and speeches presented to her, she always delivered an original speech in fluent Latin in the course of her reign.

18. I do not wish to suggest that the plays performed at the two universities represent the totality of academic drama in Britain in the Tudor period. Certainly, plays were produced at the Inns of Court in London, and some schools were involved in the mounting of civic pageants. I intend only by limiting this topic to indicate my concentration, not to form an evaluation of the plays with which I shall not be concerned.

19. Certainly still the most important work to date on English academic drama is Boas' *University Drama in the Tudor Age.* Of particular use in the study of the history of the universities have been the following works: Boas, *An Introduction to Tudor Drama* (New York: AMS Press, 1933); Kenneth Charlton, *Education in Renaissance England* (London: Routledge and Kegan Paul, 1965); David Cressy, *Education in Tudor and Stuart England* (London: Edward Arnold, 1975); M. H. Curtis, *Oxford and Cambridge in Transition, 1558-1642: An Essay on Changing Relations Between the English Universities and English Society* (Oxford: Clarendon Press, 1959); Hugh Kearney, *Scholars and Gentlemen, 1500-1700* (London: Faber and

Faber, 1970); J. K. McConica, *English Humanists and Reform Politics* (Oxford: Oxford University Press, 1965); Jan Morris, *The Oxford Book of Oxford* (Oxford: Oxford University Press, 1978); Joan Simon, *Education and Society in Tudor England* (Cambridge: Cambridge University Press, 1966); Lawrence Stone, ed., *The University in Society,* vol. 1: *Oxford and Cambridge from the 14th Century to the Early 19th Century* (Princeton: Princeton University Press, 1974). Of particular interest are Lawrence Stone's own essay "The Size and Composition of the Oxford Student Body, 1580-1909" (pp. 3-110) and James K. McConica's essay "Scholars and Commoners in Renaissance Oxford" (pp. 151-82). The work of two other scholars must here be mentioned particularly: Alan H. Nelson's encyclopedic edition and editorial apparatus for the Cambridge dramas, *Records of Early English Drama: Cambridge,* vols. 1: *The Records,* and 2: *Editorial Apparatus* (Toronto, Buffalo, London: University of Toronto Press, 1989) and the ongoing work of John R. Elliott, Jr., on both the Oxford drama and the Inns of Court plays. I have only seen this material in manuscript except for his article "Queen Elizabeth at Oxford: New Light on the Royal Plays of 1566," *English Literary Renaissance* 18:2 (Spring 1988): pp. 218-29.

20. I have offered a fuller account of the whole neo-classicist agenda of Oxbridge in this period in a chapter on the university drama that takes as its focus another Neo-Latin tragedy of the period, *Perfidus Hetruscus.* See Elizabeth Richmond-Garza, *Forgotten Cites/Sights: Interpretation and the Power of Classical Citation in Renaissance English Tragedy* (New York: Peter Lang, 1994), pp. 93-132. That chapter offers a diachronic reading of the relationship of these plays to earlier literary events, as well as a synchronic account of its political and literary context, both of which will be seen through the focus on a single text. With this reading of *Roxana,* I propose to shift the emphasis to a critique of particular ideologies as represented in a singular instance of this sort of theater to its academic audience.

21. Cambridge grew, for example, from 1,200 students in 1564, to 1,800 in 1573, to 2,000 in 1597, and 3,000 in 1620. See Charlton, *Education in Renaissance England,* pp. 136-37.

22. McConica, "Scholars and Commoners," pp. 151-82.

23. These events are briefly described in Boas, *University Drama* (see especially his fifth chapter on Queen Elizabeth's visits to Cambridge in 1564 and Oxford in 1566, pp. 89-108). Certainly the most recent and extensive account of the festivities for a royal visit, Elizabeth's to Oxford in 1566, is in John Elliott's article (see note 19). Elliott will also soon be publishing an extended study of sixteenth-century performance history and has kindly discussed with me much of the material for his chapter on college and university drama. All of the specific textual references in the section that will now follow, however, are a result of my own research in Oxford and Cambridge unless otherwise noted.

24. Unfortunately, although performances did continue under James I, the new king's lack of real capacity in Latin and far less compelling persona both reduced the opulence of the plays after 1613 and prompted a decline in the quality of the dramatic performances. James was even noted by one commentator to have fallen asleep during a production in 1605.

The accounts of Elizabeth's visit in 1566 by Twyne and Wood, Bodleian MS. Twyne 17, 161, and Bodleian MS. Wood F1/2, are both reprinted in Elliott's article (see note 19). Boas, *University Drama,* also has a long, but divergent, discussion of the various versions of the 1566 visit in his fifth chapter. Although the details of the accounts do not exactly coincide, they all seem to emphasize both the opulence and deference of the university productions and the energy and sophistication with which Elizabeth responded to them. There was a revival for the visits of Charles II in 1605 and 1636, however, and elaborate performances of both new plays and earlier Elizabethan ones were staged with elaborate set designs by Inigo Jones. See John Orrell, *The Theaters of Inigo Jones and John Webb* (Cambridge: Cambridge University Press, 1985), pp. 30 ff.

25. The London plays and drama in general were, in this period, being aggressively attacked by Puritan opponents such as Stephen Gosson and Joshua Reynolds. See Jonas Barish, *The Antitheatrical Prejudice* (Berkeley and Los Angeles: University of California Press, 1981), chapter 4. These criticisms went largely unheeded by university officials at Oxford and Cambridge. See John Barton, "The King's Readers," in *The Collegiate University,* ed. James K. McConica (Oxford: Oxford University Press, 1986), pp. 290-91, and McConica, "Elizabethan Oxford," p. 652. Even Leicester's letter to Congregation in July 1584, which endorsed various reforms at the universities, including the banning of professional players, made a specific exception for student plays. Leicester remarks that students' plays are "commendable and great furderances of Learning." He further recommends that the plays be "continued at set times and increased, and the youth of the

Universitye by good meanes to be incouraged in the decent and frequent setting forth of them." Robert Dudley, (*Oxford University Annals*, Register L, fol. 242v). Similarly, the Privy Council letters sent to Cambridge in 1575 and 1592 and to Oxford in 1593 (*Oxford University Annals*, Register L fols. 262-62v) make no mention of the academic drama (Penry Williams, "Elizabethan Oxford: State, Church, and University," in McConica, *The Collegiate University,* pp. 404, 427). Elliott (see note 19) concludes from this information that, not only was university drama exempt from the general censure of the drama, but also that the more frequent letters to Cambridge indicate a stronger hold there of Puritan attitudes. He further argues that Cambridge's more intense puritanism resulted in fewer plays being produced there. Although an interesting conjecture, such a claim, particularly about the numbers of plays, is hard to prove with only partial records.

26. Both Boas' (*University Drama*) and Elliott's (see note 19) discussions of the 1566 visit indicate that large sums were spent on the productions and that Elizabeth lent costumes to the university for the performances from her own wardrobe. A glance at any part of the financial records from the colleges indicates the expense of the productions. Nelson's edition of the records makes such information readily available. According to the college financial records, Christ Church College, Oxford, alone spent £148 2*s.* i3/4*d.,* on the royal visit of 1566 (Rawlinson C878, cited in Boas, *University Drama,* p. 106). Most of the plays were staged by colleges like Christ Church and Magdalen. Both of these colleges had large financial resources and large numbers of undergraduates.

27. Elliott has noted that in 1512 a certain Edward Watson, college or hall unknown, was admitted to teach in the School of Grammar provided that he submit "100 hundred songs (*carmina*) in praise of the university and a comedy (*comedia*)" (*Oxford University Annals,* Register G, fol. 143). Elliott has further noted that Martin Llewellyn of Christ Church College, Oxford, records in a poem that he received a degree as a result of staging a play for the Dean. See note 19.

28. Ralph Holinshed, *Chronicle* (1577), quoted in Jan Morris, ed. *The Oxford Book of Oxford* (Oxford: Oxford University Press, 1978), p. 56.

29. Higgs St. John's College, Ms. 52, fol. 5.

30. See John Orrell, "The Theater at Christ Church, Oxford, in 1605," *Shakespeare Survey* 35 (1982): pp. 129-40; and John Bereblock's *Commentarij siue Ephemerae actiones rerum illustrium Oxonij gestarum adventu Serenissimae Principis*

Elisabethae, Bodleian MS Add. A. 63, fols. 1-22 and Bodleian Ms. Rawlinson D1071, fols. 1-25.

31. See note 19.

32. Even Shakespeare provides many such examples of eastern themes that often included prominent treatments of the definition of appropriate female behavior. *Antony and Cleopatra, The Tempest, Othello,* and *The Merchant of Venice* are only the most obvious, and that most financially successful of all Elizabethan plays, Christopher Marlowe's *Tamburlaine,* is even set in the Ottoman context.

33. The argument that I shall be using is largely presented in Saïd's *Orientalism*: "Oriental Residence and Scholarship: The Requirements of Lexicography and Imagination," (pp. 149-166), and in his analysis of the texts of the end of the nineteenth century in Paris, especially those of Flaubert and Nerval (pp. 179-92). Much is being made of his suggestions in current subaltern studies, particularly of the largely nonaggressive presence of the British Raj in India.

34. Ibid., pp. 180, 187. I have taken material from several places in Saïd's text to foreground this particular issue, but I have not, I hope, distorted his original argument.

35. Interestingly, Saïd distinguishes English Orientalism from its continental counterparts by virtue of its "more pronounced and harder sense of what Oriental pilgrimages might entail," p. 192.

36. This and all other quotations are taken from the original edition of 1632. I have preserved the original idiosyncrasies in Latin orthography of the Renaissance text. This text is available through a modern microfilm of *Roxana* (New York: Readex Microprint, 1955). There is no published English translation of the text, and so I offer my own of this and future passages.

37. Gurr, *Playgoing,* p. 137. Gurr also singles out the two plays mentioned in the next sentence, one of which is set in Persia. Moreover many of the plays at Oxbridge choose as their settings the eastern Mediterranean either in classical or Ottoman times. Boas' Appendix IV includes more than a dozen such plays, most of which are tragedies, *University Drama,* pp. 385-90.

38. I need no source to make the case for Elizabeth I's own uneasiness about this terrifying triad: divorce, the Catholic ground for denying her the crown; adultery, the ground for her mother, Anne Boleyn's, execution; and inheritance, an insoluble problem for a virgin queen past the age for having children.

39. Lawrence Stone, *Road to Divorce, England 1530-1987* (Oxford: Oxford University Press, 1990), p. 301. With the rejection of the sacramental status

of marriage by the Protestant churches, all other Protestant countries had adopted a policy that allowed divorce on the three grounds of wifely adultery, willful desertion for a period of years, and life-threatening cruelty. Stone, in this study and in his more recent and specialized *Uncertain Unions, Marriage in England 1660-1753* (Oxford: Oxford University Press, 1992), emphasizes the extreme and unusual conservatism of English attitudes, in general, towards divorce and argues for the exceptional nature of the few famous divorces that were secured in this period.

40. Stone, *Road to Divorce,* p. 305.

41. Ibid., p. 306.

42. Ibid., pp. 317-82.

Ceri Sullivan (essay date April 2000)

SOURCE: Sullivan, Ceri. "Penitence in 1590s Weeping Texts." *Cahiers Élisabéthains* 57, no. 5 (April 2000): 31-47.

[*In the following excerpt, Sullivan studies the style and function of penitence in Alabaster's devotional sonnets in relation to other late Elizabethan writers.*]

> When without tears I look on Christ, I see
> Only a story of some passion . . .
> But if I look through tears Christ smiles on me . . .
> And from his side the blood doth spin, whereon
> My heart, my mouth, mine eyes still sucking be.[1]

Penitential writing such as William Alabaster's is opaque to the fastidious modern gaze in the literalism of its cannibal images, its depth of self-abasement, its spurts and tides of blood, sweat and tears—however these may be cauterized with conceits. The sparse critical commentary that has been devoted to the literature of repentance in sixteenth-century England tends to follow the lead given by G. R. Hibbard when he damned Thomas Nashe's *Christs Teares Over Jerusalem* as 'a monument of bad taste, literary tactlessness and unremitting over-elaboration, for which it is not easy to find a parallel'.[2]

Nevertheless, in the 1590s over a dozen texts, which were frequently reissued, wept over the sins of the nation and their author. This essay examines five such works: penitential sonnets and narrative poems by Alabaster, Robert Southwell, and Henry Constable, and prose weeping texts by Southwell, and Thomas Lodge. These works reverse expectations raised in the secular sonnet by the topos of the gaze, which much recent criticism treats as a means of controlling the beloved. In the devotional texts, however, the gaze cannot be constructed by their authors as a means of control; it turns against its initiating eyes. The topos used for human control has to be inflected when used in the context of the divine. Polythalamous blood, tears, sighs and glances are expressed from a variety of sites within the laments: sometimes the agent is Christ, sometimes the author, and sometimes the tears come of their own accord. Far from the gaze defining the poet by affording him a coherent view of an ideal object, he becomes the object of 'his' tears' attempts to cleanse him. The devotional texts transform Petrarchan pseudohumility into what seems like obsessive weeping, but is actually a cogent physiology of penance.[3] While the authors of these penance texts come from widely differing rank, education and occupation, all were Catholics in the process of affirming their faith at the point at which the works were written. It can be argued that this confessional background causes them to apply the same torque to the conceit.

In view of the disparate circumstances of Lodge, Alabaster, Constable, and Southwell, they cannot be said to form a socially cohesive group. The similarities lie in their faith. Constable, Alabaster, and Lodge were renowned in their own time as converts from Anglicanism to Catholicism (and in Alabaster's case, back again, twice), and Southwell was a Jesuit missionary. Some texts seem to have been written during the time of, or just after, their authors' conversions. In Southwell's case the drafts of *Saint Peters Complaint* date from the period of his novitiate at Rome. All four men had travelled on the continent, meeting the new passional verse and devotional forms sanctioned by the Council of Trent.[4] Flexing secular genres was one way they seem to have marked their move into the Catholic Church. As Southwell says in the preface to his poems,

> Prophane conceites and fayning fits I flie,
> Such lawlesse stuffe doth lawlesse speeches fit:
> With *David* verse to vertue I apply.[5]

The point is repeated by Alabaster:

> since my holy vows have undertook
> To take the portrait of Christ's death with me,
> Then let my love with sonnets fill this book,
> With hymns to give the onset as did he,

and by Constable,

> if thou change the object of my love,
> the wyng'd affection which men Cupid call
> may gett his syght, & lyke an Angell prove.[6]

The topos of the gaze was sufficiently formalized by the 1590s to allow flexibility in its application. In *As You Like* It a petulant Phoebe rounds on Silvius:

> Thou tell'st me there is murder in mine eye:
> 'Tis pretty, sure, and very probable,

That eyes, that are the frail'st and softest things,
Who shut their coward gates on atomies,
Should be call'd tyrants, butchers, murderers.[7]

Her impatience with his reading of the topos—too many of Orlando's graffiti—is unusual in being voiced. Recent commentary has suggested that a characteristic strategy of sonnet sequences such as *Astrophil and Stella, Delia,* and *Diana* is to privilege the peremptory gaze of the lover over the reactions of an immobilized and silenced beloved. Assembling or dismantling the ideal woman becomes a neat craft, as Sidney's menacing fifth song implies:

I said thine eyes were stars, thy breasts the milken way,
Thy fingers Cupid's shafts, thy voice the angels' lay
. . .
But now that hope is lost, unkindness kills delight
. . .
Think now no more to hear of warm fine-odoured snow,
Nor blushing lilies, nor pearls' ruby-hidden row.[8]

Michael Spiller sums up the rhetorical purpose of the Elizabethan sonnet as providing an 'analogy of desire', where love stands in 'for political success, for maximizing one's power'. 'Ritualized play' becomes a form of public self-display. There is a competitive use of *sprezzatura,* of concentration on trifling passions, which may manage private anxieties which are not about love.[9] The 'cureless wounds' inflicted by the 'beamy darts' from the beloved's eyes are a commonplace in the secular sequences of the 1580s. As with the first kiss or the first parting, the first glance was a topos with which every self-respecting sonneteer had to deal. Readers are taxed for praise of the writer's grace in varying the convention, not for their admiration of the sonneteer's beloved. Specifically concentrating on the eye in this context, critics such as Nancy Vickers, Joel Fineman, and Barbara Estrin argue that the sonneteer uses the gaze in two strategies which attack and defend.[10] In the one, the writer is said to anatomize his ideal as he catalogues her beauties. Sidney, for instance, reifies then disjoints the woman in describing 'Queen Virtue's court, which some call Stella's face'—the move is mocked by Shakespeare's 'My Mistres eyes are nothing like the Sunne'.[11] In the other strategy, these critics depict the object of the sonnet, the woman, as a site where the poet can mirror himself. Such moments of praise freeze the women, even, ironically, when the fragment chosen for celebration is the woman's own eye. Sidney's lines implore a look:

Soul's joy, bend not those morning stars from me . . .
Where love is chasteness, pain doth learn delight . . .
O look, O shine, O let me die, and see,

but the eyes of the woman stare back blankly.[12]

The tears texts appropriate the gaze, and its fashionable ethos, to themselves. The modish connotations of Con-stable's sonnet on 'the conspiracie of his Ladies eyes and his owne to ingender love', or Lodge's 'Sonnet 26',

Ile teach thee lovely *Phillis,* what love is,
It is a vision seeming such as thou
That flies as fast as it assaultes mine eies,

are transposed in context and value in devotional sonnets such as Constable's 'To our blessed Lady':

An earthlye syght doth onely please the eye,
and breedes desyre, but doth not satisfye:
thy sight, gyves ys possession of all ioye.[13]

Our no less formulaic and fashionable disparagement of the gaze as scopophiliac or narcissistic is challenged by the devotional sonnets on weeping. While they retain the topos of the gaze, they focus attention on the divine object and the medium of sorrow, tears, not on the sorrowing author. The obsessive self-praise exhibited by the sonneteer has to turn outward to God, given the logic in the position of praising the divine—though this in its turn could suggest to the suspicious critic an even finer, and therefore more competitive, discrimination by the sonneteers over the conventions of the genre.

The theological location of the five Catholic texts can be determined by asking the question 'who is weeping?' Each text is a vivid *effictio* of sorrow. The poems produce petitionary tears which cooperate in the weeper's salvation. Nonetheless, while such tears pour out of the writer at his request, devotional merit is seen as accuring from the exercise of producing the tears, not in the tears themselves. Whether one is afflicted by spiritual dryness or is actually granted tears by God does not affect the merit earned in asking for them. Indeed a popular Catholic devotional text of 1584, Diego de Estella's *The Contempte of the World and the Vanitie thereof,* warns against those who 'commit spirituall adulterie, in appointing with them selves to make sensible devotion, the uttermost end'.[14] Their initiator's position can be distinguished from the Calvinist's understanding of salvation which is gained by God's election, not by one's own meritous works. Richard Strier has explored the difference in Herbert's poems on repentance. He argues that such poems as 'Grief', 'Praise III', and 'Marie Magdalene' dismiss the Counter-Reformation literature of remorse, which maintains the absolute necessity of the sacrament of penance to salvation. Strier sees Herbert's Calvinism demonstrated in that his tears are given by God, not inspired by his own contrition; the remorse that Herbert feels does not guarantee his forgiveness.

Penitence is not Herbert's main concern, however. These poems are part of his analysis of the solafidian paradox in petitionary prayer, stated in 'The Dedication' to *The Temple*:

Lord, my first fruits present themselves to thee;

Yet not mine neither: for from thee they came,
And must return.[15]

By contrast, the Catholic texts make a sustained exploration of the role of penitence. They take the Catholic Church's view that one may earn absolution by requesting it from God with contrition, confessing, providing satisfaction, and purposing amendment, a view that had been clarified by the deliberations of session twelve of the Council of Trent. Tears in these texts are signs of contrition for sin, and also of certain absolution if the will activates and confirms the repentance. Tears here come from two different sites and signify both grace desired and grace conferred; tokens of human cooperation with salvation and of divine forgiveness granted. Southwell, Lodge, Constable, and Alabaster each exploit different aspects of the conceit of the gaze, as they explore the workings and representation of the sacrament of penance.

William Alabaster was certainly aware of the contemporary theological controversy over repentance, as a means or a sign of salvation. His first conversion was marked, in his own account, by a 'greater tendernes of harte towards Christes Crosse and Passion than . . . the protestantes weare wont to feele', and ratified by an aggressive desire to dispute publicly with the divines sent to rescue him from error (including his uncle the Bishop of Bath and Wells, the Master of Trinity College Cambridge, and Lancelot Andrewes, the Bishop of Winchester).[16] Alabaster's nineteen penitential sonnets were written while or shortly after he was given the Loyolan *Spiritual Exercises* by the Jesuit missionary John Gerard in 1597-8, as part of his conversion to Catholicism.[17] The *Exercises* promote the active production of sorrow over vividly-imagined penitential scenes, including the Crucifixion and the pains of hell. Alabaster, however, does not evoke such scenes in memory, nor do his sonnets confess the sins of the penitent. The subject of all nineteen sonnets, his self-possessed tears, have no identified cause and are surprised in mid-flow. Rather, each concentrates on contrition, expressed in tears, for unspecified sins.

Alabaster's *gradatio* of the stages of penance numbers off his tears without claiming them as his own:

The first are bitter, of compunction,
The second brinish, of compassion,
The third are sweet, which from devoutness rain.[18]

His tears are usually put into an intercessory role; they are moved by his prayer to them to flow and act as prayers themselves:

Then run, O run
Out of mine eyes tears of compunction,
One after other run for my soul's sake . . .
Until you come before his heavenly throne.
There beg of Christ grace for me to repent.[19]

The chain of devotional efficacy takes shape as a chiasmus here: Alabaster prays for tears to pray for Alabaster. At one point, Alabaster shields his soul from Christ's gaze with his tears, using the Augustinian terminology of imputed grace:

Then weep forth pearls of tears to spangle thee,
In tears draw forth thyself until there be
Sufficient for thee to be enrolled.[20]

The tears in this sonnet are Alabaster's (not Christ's, as they are in Herbert's 'Praise III', 'after thou hadst slipt a drop / From thy right eye . . . The glasse was full and more', confirming Strier's distinction discussed above).[21] The self-injunction to shed tears is described as meritorious:

So he which in his bitter thought's recall,
Draweth his soul by penance into tears,
His worthlessness to Christ thereby endears.[22]

What is interesting about Alabaster's sonnets is the way he does not claim ownership of the tears; he addresses them as though they are entities which have a will of their own: 'these conceits, digest by thoughts' retire, / Are turned into april showers of tears'.[23] For instance he describes his tears as a rain of penitence which settles the roots of his newly converted soul firmly into Christ's wound:

Why should the fruit look withered and unsound?
Is it for want of rain? It is, I know.
Then you two characters, drawn from my head,
Pour out a shower of tears upon my bed.[24]

The 'characters' are eyes which both are and produce the signs of penitence; they are being exhorted by the author as separate from himself.

Tears emerge here not as a Petrarchan issue of passion, but a site for a union between divinity and humanity. They act as a species of ambiguous sacrament: they are tears of contrition, and they are also outward signs of absolution which has been granted to Alabaster. His sonnets acknowledge the tears' differing qualities:

And these diversities they do obtain
By difference of place from which they run.
The first come from the meditation
Of all my sins, which made a bitter vein,
The next pass through the sea of others' tears,
And so that saltness in the taste appears,
The third doth issue from Christ's wounded side,
And thence such sweetness in them doth abide.[25]

There is an awkwardness here. On the one hand, Alabaster can claim the merit of desiring the tears to flow, but on the other, if he were to create such tears, how could they be from inward grace conferred on him? The paradox of the secular sonnets, that the poems exist because of the gap between the lover and the mistress which, ostensibly, they are working to close, here becomes the paradox of Alabaster producing a rhetoric which may only describe, not affect; it must not succeed in swaying his feelings if the 'otherness' of the tears is to be maintained. Thus, the problem of sincerity in secular sonnets, so acidly commented on by Sidney ('if I were a Mistres, would never perswade mee they were in love; so coldely they apply fiery speeches, as men that had rather red Lovers writings'), becomes a theological problem.[26] Alabaster may not produce his own tears, he may only pray for them. This, I think, is why Alabaster is chary of describing the circumstances surrounding the origin of his tears, allowing them to well from him of their own accord while he focuses on the meritorious desire for them. His tone in the sequence of sonnets is one of helpless amazement in the face of such active and self-possessed drops. When his sins 'in multitude to Christ are gone / Against my soul indictment for to make', it is the tears, not himself, who 'beg of Christ grace for me to repent'.[27] His assumed role of passively gazing at his own productions can be distinguished from the Niobean petrification of the secular lover before the awesome beloved, such as Donne's in 'Twicknam Garden', since the latter's tears make the poet himself a focus of pilgrimage by lovers, (thus overturning the poem's overt concentration on the woman).[28]

Alabaster's clear perception of theological decorum produces what seem to be conceits in dealing with his tears of remorse. He acknowledges the reversal of human expectations when dealing with the divine, so has to explain, as an oddity, the everyday.

> How it is then your tears the earth bedew,
> And go not straight to heaven? Indeed 'tis true,
> They take their race upon humility,
> And after without loss to heaven do fly.[29]

Alabaster's wit lies in seeing the literal truth of hyperbolic positions when dealing with the divine. George Puttenham puts it well: 'we cannot exhibit overmuch praise, nor belye [God] any wayes, unlesse it be . . . by scarsitie of praise'.[30] Human praise and contrition can only be an understatement when dealing with God. The complaint often made by Alabaster's contemporaries about the use of a conceited style in religious verse—that it draws attention away from the object of devotion towards pleasure in the writing—cannot be justified when using human language to describe the divine, since such conceits are the literal truth.

Crucially, it is the poet's sense of self which disintegrates in Alabaster's work when he stands before God. In the tears texts, far from the object of the praise being iconized by enumeration it is the gazer who must lose a sense of being able to see clearly, before the power of a stronger Eye:

> O dart one beam into that cloudy night
> That holds my heart, that melted heart may rain
> Grace to mine eyes. Now, lord, the way is plain,
> Glance through mine eyes, and to my heart go right.[31]

The eye of judgement dissolves the poet's sense of self, in a reversal of the secular sonnet's use of the gaze to solidify the sense of self:

> For love of Christ to tears mine eyes do turn,
> And melted tears do make my soul to burn,
> And burning love doth make my tears more deep,
> And deeper tears cause love to flame above.[32]

Thus the eye/I pun ceases to operate in devotional texts as a marker of concurrent identification with, and difference from, the object of its sight, as it does in secular sonnets. The formally central, productive position of the weeper is undercut by the hapless position Alabaster takes before his own effusions. Theological necessity, of course, dictates an abject position within the topos for the errant weeper standing before Christ. The covertly dismissive attitude towards the beloved which makes secular sequences into complexes of self—rather than other—display would be heretical in these devotional poems.

. . . . .

This essay has suggested that the control-based function of the sight in secular sonnets is reversed in a religious context. Five Catholic texts on penance use the emotions to move the will; their tears are petitionary prayers desiring contrition so that they may cooperate with God in the writer's own salvation. The tears, however, have a second source. The texts describe them as uncontrollable—they flow without ceasing or cannot be produced at will—so their appearance assures the weeper of their divine, not human, origin. Thus, the tears have two functions: to pray for, and to prove, the presence of God within. Heteroglossic tears and glances from different sites, both divine and human, strain against the obsessive form of the monologic sonnet and meditation. The speaker loses agency, is no longer the focus of attention, and moves into a series of humble and contingent positions. The preciosity of the conceit from the secular sonnet no longer functions to praise the praiser: the irony of the secular topos is removed by the infinite value of the object being praised. Thus the ironic wit, as well as the devotional truth, of these works lies in their deliberately literal handling of the genre's conventions. It is theologically decorous that the writer's soul in these texts is fragmented rather than integrated by the gaze.

Notes

1. William Alabaster, *The Sonnets of William Alabaster,* ed. G. M. Story and H. Gardner (Oxford: Oxford Univ. Press, 1959), p. 39. My article has

greatly benefitted from discussions with Lucie Armitt, Danielle Clarke, Tom Corns, Margaret Kean, and Michael Whitworth, whom I would like to thank.

2. G. R. Hibbard, *Thomas Nashe* (London: Routledge, 1962), pp. 122-3.

3. Previous criticism of these weeping texts has been largely biographical or bibliographical, with occasional mention in discussions of *fin-de-siècle* melancholy. Alabaster and Southwell's work has been discussed briefly as the result of Tridentine ideas about the use of the passions in devotion, or as a model of confession by desire only, suitable for isolated recusants. See R. V. Caro, 'William Alabaster: Rhetor, Meditator, Devotional Poet', *Recusant History* 19 (1988): 62-80, 155-70; Éliane Cuvelier, *Thomas Lodge, témoin de son temps (c.1558-1625)* (Paris: Didier Érudition, 1984), pp. 507-8; N. B. Paradise, *Thomas Lodge. The History of an Elizabethan* (New Haven: Yale Univ. Press, 1931), pp. 125-7; Christopher Devlin, *The Life of Robert Southwell, Poet and Martyr* (London: Longmans, Green and Co., 1956), pp. 258-73; Pierre Janelle, *Robert Southwell the Writer. A Study in Religious Inspiration* (London: Sheed and Ward, 1935), pp. 205-27; Joseph Scallon, *The Poetry of Robert Southwell, S.J.* (Salzburg: Universität Salzburg, 1975), pp. 151-219.

4. There is some slight evidence that earlier readers thought of these texts as forming a group. Alabaster's sonnets join those by Crashaw in Archbishop Bancroft's miscellany book (Bancroft died in 1610), and Alabaster and Southwell both appear in Peter Mowle's commonplace notebook, completed early in 1605.

5. Robert Southwell, *The Poems of Robert Southwell, S.J.,* ed. J. H. McDonald and N. P. Brown (Oxford: Clarendon, 1967), p. 2.

6. Alabaster, *Sonnets,* p. 1; Henry Constable, *The Poems of Henry Constable,* ed. Joan Grundy (Liverpool: Liverpool Univ. Press, 1960), p. 192.

7. William Shakespeare, *As You Like It,* ed. Agnes Latham (London: Methuen, 1975), III.v.10-14.

8. Philip Sidney, *Selected Poems,* ed. Katherine Duncan-Jones (Oxford: Clarendon, 1973), pp. 164-5.

9. Michael Spiller, *The Development of the Sonnet. An Introduction* (London: Routledge, 1992), pp. 124-6, 147-8.

10. On the defensive fragmentation of the idealized object of the sight, see Nancy Vickers, 'Diana Described: Scattered Woman and Scattered Rhyme', *Writing and Sexual Difference,* ed. Elizabeth Abel (Brighton: Harvester Press, 1982), pp. 95-109. On the opposition in the male gaze of scopophilia or desire for the Other, and narcissism or identification with the Star, see Laura Mulvey, *Visual and Other Pleasures* (Basingstoke: Macmillan, 1989), ch. 3. On the move from subjectivity created by specular idealization of the object of praise, to a fragmented subjectivity about the true and false word, see Joel Fineman, *Shakespeare's Perjured Eye. The Invention of Poetic Subjectivity in the Sonnets* (Berkeley: California Univ. Press, 1986), pp. 1-48, 86-129. Barbara L. Estrin's *Laura. Uncovering Gender and Genre in Wyatt, Donne and Marvell* (Durham: Duke Univ. Press, 1994) counters the argument of sonnet-as-fragmentation by focusing on the subjectivity allowed by the poems to the lady. Lynn Enterline, in *The Tears of Narcissus* (Stanford: Stanford Univ. Press, 1995) discusses the link between images of self-reflection and images of loss in Renaissance lyrics.

11. Sidney, *Poems,* p. 121.

12. Sidney, *Poems,* p. 140.

13. Constable, *Poems,* pp. 117, 190; Thomas Lodge, *The Complete Works of Thomas Lodge,* 4 vols. (London: The Hunterian Club, 1883), 2:43.

14. Diego de Estella, *The Contempte of the World, and the Vanitie thereof* (1584) (Ilkley: Scolar Press, 1975), S11 v.

15. George Herbert, *The English Poems,* ed. C. A. Patrides (Oxford: Clarendon, 1974), p. 32. See also A. D. Nuttall, *Overheard by God. Fiction and Prayer in Herbert, Milton, Dante, and St John* (London: Methuen, 1980), pp. 7-9.

16. Alabaster, Sonnets, p. XII-XV.

17. On the use of the *Spiritual Exercises* in poetry of this period, see L. L. Martz, *The Poetry of Meditation* (New Haven: Yale Univ. Press, 1962), especially on the literature of remorse, pp. 199-203. Neither Constable nor Alabaster had their poems printed while they were alive but their verse circulated in manuscript, Alabaster, Sonnets, pp. XVI, XXVII-IX.

18. Alabaster, *Sonnets,* p. 9.

19. Alabaster, *Sonnets,* p. 7.

20. Alabaster, *Sonnets,* p. 9.

21. Herbert, *Poems,* p. 166.

22. Alabaster, *Sonnets,* p. 9.

23. Alabaster, *Sonnets,* p. 8.

24. Alabaster, *Sonnets,* p. 7.

25. Alabaster, *Sonnets,* p. 9.

26. Philip Sidney, *An Apology for Poetry* (1595), in ed. G. G. Smith, *Elizabethan Critical Essays,* 2 vols. (Oxford: Oxford Univ. Press, 1904), i:201.

27. Alabaster, *Sonnets,* p. 7.

28. John Donne, *The Elegies and the Songs and Sonnets,* ed. Helen Gardner (Oxford: Clarendon, 1965), p. 83.

29. Alabaster, *Sonnets,* p. 8. Compare stanza four of Crashaw's 'The Weeper', *The Poems English Latin and Greek of Robert Crashaw,* ed. L. C. Martin (Oxford: Clarendon, 1957), pp. 79-83.

30. George Puttenham, *The Arte of English Poesie* (1589), in *Elizabethan Critical Essays,* 2:30.

31. Alabaster, *Sonnets,* p. 21.

32. Alabaster, *Sonnets,* p. 18.

FURTHER READING

Biographies

Guiney, Louise Imogen. "William Alabaster." In *Recusant Poets,* Vol. 1, pp. 335-346. New York: Sheed & Ward, 1939.

Provides an introductory overview of the poet's religious life.

Story, G. M. "Biographical Sketch." In the General Introduction to *The Sonnets of William Alabaster,* edited by G. M. Story and Helen Gardner, pp. xi-xxii. Oxford: Oxford University Press, 1959.

Places Alabaster in his literary and political context.

Criticism

Coldewey, John C. "William Alabaster's *Roxana*: Some Textual Considerations." In *Acta conventus neo-latini bononiensis,* edited by R. J. Schoeck, pp. 413-419. Binghamton, NY: Center for Medieval & Early Renaissance Studies, 1985.

Examines the textual history of *Roxana.*

Ottenhoff, John H. "The Shadow and the Real: Typology and the Religious Sonnet." *University of Hartford Studies in Literature* 15-16, no. 3-1 (winter 1984): 43-59.

Provides a brief and focused analysis of several sonnets from *Divine Meditations*

Additional coverage of Alabaster's life and career is contained in the following sources published by the Gale Group: *Dictionary of Literary Biography,* **Vol. 134;** *Literature Resource Center;* **and** *Reference Guide to English Literature,* **ed. 2.**

Philip Melanchthon
1497-1560

(Born Philip Schwarzerd) German theologian, philosopher, historian, and nonfiction writer.

INTRODUCTION

Melanchthon was among the most important figures in the German Reformation movement as well as a scholar of considerable influence throughout sixteenth-century Europe. He was largely responsible for composing the *Augsburg Confession* (1531), the main Lutheran statement of belief. His best-known work is the *Loci Communes rerum theologicarum seu Hypotyposes theologicae* (*The Common Places of Theology*; 1521), which sets forth the major teachings of the Bible in a systematic manner. This treatise became the chief theological textbook of the Reformation movement, and its many editions were embraced by the major Protestant scholars, including John Calvin. A prolific writer, Melanchthon published more than seven hundred treatises, essays, and books on grammar and science.

BIOGRAPHICAL INFORMATION

Melanchthon was born on February 14, 1497. His father was a master armorer in the town of Bretten in southern Germany. From an early age, Melanchthon was educated at home by a private tutor. In 1507 he went to Pforzheim to live with his grandmother Elizabeth, whose brother was the humanist thinker Johann Reuchlin. Melanchthon was much influenced by his grand-uncle, who persuaded him to translate his name Schwarzerd into the Greek Melancthon, both meaning "black earth." In 1509 Melancthon entered the University of Heidelberg and began to study rhetoric and astronomy, but he continued his reading of the ancient poets, historians, and the neo-Latins. After receiving his baccalaureate degree in 1511, Melanchthon went to Tübingen and became a pupil of the celebrated Latinist Heinrich Bebel as well as of the famous humanist Georg Simler. He also studied astronomy, astrology, jurisprudence, mathematics, and medicine. In 1514, at the age of seventeen, Melanchthon earned a master's degree and received a position as an instructor at the University of Tübingen, where he lectured on ancient literature. He also worked in the printing office of Thomas Anshelm, pursued his private studies, translated works of philosophy, and, eventually, turned to theology.

Upon his arrival at Wittenberg University in 1518 to teach Greek language and literature, Melanchthon met Martin Luther, and the two soon became friends. Melanchthon's cool, organized, and disciplined manner contrasted with and complemented Luther's brilliant, fiery temperament. In 1519, when Luther debated Johann Eck, the pope's representative, Melanchthon publicly supported Luther, establishing himself as an important spokesman for the Reformation movement; he would later take part in important theological disputations in Marburg (1529), Worms (1540), and Regensburg (1541). While at Wittenburg, Melanchthon also taught, studied, and earned a Bachelor of Theology degree. In 1520, at the urging of Luther, he married the daughter of the mayor of Wittenberg. The following year, he produced the first edition of his *Loci Communes,* and in the decade that followed he developed the educational program that was used to implement the Reformation in Germany. In 1527, Melanchthon played a key role in drawing up a manual, *Instructions for the Church Visitors,* to be used by the government to survey, and then supervise, religious and moral education in the Saxony parishes. He later helped to found universities at Marburg, Königsberg, and Jena, and to reorganize existing universities at Greifswald, Wittenberg, Cologne, Tübingen, Leipzig, Heidelberg, Rostock, and Frankfurt an der Oder. These and his other activities in education earned him the title of *Praeceptor Germaniae* ("Germany's teacher"). At the Diet of Augsburg in 1530, Melanchthon drew up the *Augsburg Confession,* recognized as one of the most significant documents of the Lutheran Church.

Melanchthon's later years were marked by misunderstanding and strife. When Luther died in 1546, Melanchthon assumed the role of leader of the Reformation, but the movement was already fragmented and he was unable to prevent it from splintering. The publication of his 1548 letter criticizing Luther caused many to view him with distrust and his attempts to arrange compromises with the Catholic Church were viewed with skepticism. Melanchthon was involved in a number of theological debates during his later years, with his last major effort to reconcile differences between Protestant and Catholic theologians occurring at the colloquy at Worms in 1557. He died on April 19, 1560, and is buried at Wittenberg in the Castle Church, next to Luther.

MAJOR WORKS

Almost all of Melanchthon's works were written in Latin for an educated, scholarly audience. As a young academic, he delivered two well-known addresses on education, *De artibus liberalis* (*On the Liberal Arts*; 1517) and *De corrigendis adulesecentiae studiis* (*On Correcting the Studies of Youth*; 1518), in which he extolled the new humanistic and scientific spirit. Another early work, *Loci Communes* deals principally with such practical religious issues as sin, grace, law, and regeneration. In the *Augsburg Confession* Melanchthon aimed to show that Protestants, despite their call for reform, still belonged to the Catholic Church and had a right to remain in her fold. The innovations of Protestantism, he claimed, were merely a reformation of abuses that had crept into the Church. While this document is generally associated with Luther, the tenor and wording were the work of Melancthon. The *Augsburg Confession* subsequently underwent numerous changes, and its final form was determined by common agreement of Protestant theologians. In addition to his religious writings, Melanchthon published manuals and guides to Latin and Greek grammar, rhetoric, ethics, physics, politics, and history, as well as editions of and commentaries on classical authors. Many of these works were still popular more than a century after Melanchthon's death—a fact scholars attribute to the author's lucid prose style.

CRITICAL RECEPTION

During his lifetime, Melanchthon was an important figure not only for his contributions to the Reformation movement but for his extensive non-religious writings as well. It is estimated that by 1600 over two and a half million copies of Melanchthon's writings circulated in Europe—a staggering figure considering that only a small percentage of the population was literate at all, and that few people could read Latin. Many of Melanchthon's works were frequently reprinted: his Greek grammar went through thirty-six editions and his *Grammatica latina* (1532) went through ninety-four editions by 1600. His *Loci Communes* became an instant success, going through eighteen Latin editions and numerous translations within four years; it was required reading at Cambridge University and Queen Elizabeth I is said to have virtually memorized it. However, although Melanchthon continued to be honored as a scholar and humanist, his popularity waned after the eighteenth century, most likely because the use of Latin in academic circles was declining. His collected works were edited in the 1800s, and supplementary volumes appeared in the early twentieth century, with further items coming to light in the 1970s. Nevertheless, his works have remained primarily of interest to theologians and specialists in theological history. Those who have studied Melanchthon's work have explored his friendship with Luther, his influence on Lutheranism, the controversies surrounding some of his scriptural interpretations, his expositions on rhetoric and grammar, his work as a humanist and reformer, and his scientific views. While Melanchthon's works are not familiar to most lay readers, his stature as a key figure in the Reformation inspires commentary to this day.

PRINCIPAL WORKS

De artibus liberalis [*On the Liberal Arts*] (nonfiction) 1517

De corrigendis adulesecentiae studiis [*On Correcting the Studies of Youth*] (nonfiction) 1518

Integra graeca grammatica institutiones (nonfiction) 1518

De rhetorica libri tres [*Three Books on Rhetoric*] (nonfiction) 1519

Institutiones rhetoricae [*The Art and Craft of Rhetoric*] (essay) 1521

Loci Communes rerum theologicarum seu Hypotyposes theologicae [*The Common Places of Theology*] (treatise) 1521

Epitome Renovatae ecclesiasticae doctrinae ad illustrissimum Principium Hessorum (treatise) 1524

Unterricht der Visitatoren [*Instructions for the Church Visitors*] (nonfiction) 1527

Adversus anabaptistas iudicium (treatise) 1528

Apologia Confessionis [*The Apology that is to say the Defense of the Confession*] (treatise) 1531

Confessio fidei exhibita invictissimo Imperatori Carolo V. [*The Confession of the Faith Exhibited to Emperor Charles V*; also known as *Augsburg Confession*] (nonfiction) 1531

Elementorum rhetorices libri duo (essays) 1531

Commentarii in Epistolam Pauli ad Romanos [*Commentaries on the Pauline Epistles and Romans*] (theology) 1532

Grammatica latina (nonfiction) 1532

Philosophiae moralis epitome [*Summary of Moral Philosophy*] (treatise) 1538

De ecclesia et de autoritate verbi Dei [*On the True Authority of the Church*] (treatise) 1539

Defensio coniugii sacerdotum pia [*The epistle of the famous and great clerk Philip Melanchthon made unto our late sovereign lord King Henry the eight, for the revoking and abolishing of the six articles set forth and enacted by the crafty means and procurement of certain of our prelates of the clergy*] (treatise) 1540

Erotemata Dialectices (nonfiction) 1547

Historia de vita et actis reverendiss. viri d. Martini Lutheri [*The History of the Life and Acts of Martin Luther*] (biography) 1548

Initia doctrinae physicae [*Introduction to Physics*] (nonfiction) 1549

Liber de anima [*On the Soul*] (treatise) 1553

CRITICISM

Franz Hildebrandt (essay date 1946)

SOURCE: Hildebrandt, Franz. "Prelude: The Friendship Between Luther and Melanchthon." In *Melanchthon: Alien or Ally*, pp. xv-xxvii. Cambridge: Cambridge University Press, 1946.

[*In the following essay, Hildebrandt examines the relationship between Melanchthon and Luther and discusses their opinions of each other.*]

The puzzle is not so much the mutual attraction of two very different tempers, but the entry by, and reception of, Melanchthon into the headquarters of the Reformation; we are not concerned with the dramatic narrative of 'how they got on with each other' during the thirty years of their common residence in Wittenberg, but with the riddle of how their doctrines could 'mix'; with the astonishing fact that ever since they figure as joint partners of the firm 'Luther and Melanchthon' in such a way as none other of Luther's many colleagues could claim to be associated with him (the only conceivable

comparison would be 'Luther and Calvin'). It remains to be seen whether the question which is obviously of modern origin will ever be properly answered; all we can try here is to find out how far it was felt to be a problem at the time of the Reformation, and to search what little material we have for hints in that direction.

We have the statement of a faithful Melanchthonian, Paul Eber, maintaining against the critics who 'equate Luther with gold, and much prefer this to Melanchthon's silver . . .; we know that Philippus, together with, and after Luther has produced optima fide integrum corpus doctrinae, bona et perspicua methodo et studio' ([**Corpus Reformatorum**, ed. Bredschneider, hereafter referred to as] *CR*, 9, 966). On the other hand, there is a man like the Chancellor Brück denouncing in a letter to the elector prince of Saxony the heresies which Melanchthon himself had concealed from Luther: 'Doctor Martinus says and confesses, he had never thought that Philippus was still so deeply involved in the "phantasies" . . . I think there is no harm in Martinus still pressing on and giving a serious hearty talk to Philippus' (*CR*, 3, 427). The prince himself, no wonder, is so seriously worried by the reports of the 'Zweyung' between Luther and Melanchthon[1] that he goes so far as to contemplate the closing of Wittenberg University, which would appear the lesser evil as compared with an open split in the faculty (*CR*, 3, 365 sqq.); at the same time he exerts the utmost pressure to prevent Luther from directly mentioning Melanchthon in his forthcoming pamphlet against the 'sacramentarians': 'Therefore it is our desire, and we want him to take our well-meant advice, that he should refrain from mentioning Philippus by name in his book . . . it is easy to see how the adversaries would rejoice over that and into what bad report the word of God would be brought' (*CR*, 5, 746 sq.). These three voices represent the views taken by the three parties in the Church struggles after Luther's death (the 'Philippists', the 'Gnesiolutherans' and the mediating statesmen) and echoed in all the subsequent literature on our subject.[2]

But what is the opinion of Luther and Melanchthon themselves? Consulting Luther's table-talks first, we find overwhelming evidence for the personal affection in which Melanchthon is held; the famous story that Luther prayed him back from death in a grave illness (*WA Ti*, 5, 5565, 5407) is of symbolic significance. So he won him over to Wittenberg in his youth and kept him by his spell; yet the impression which we are given is as if Luther was entirely in Melanchthon's debt: we learn, for example, 'that D. Philippus had compelled him to translate the New Testament into German' (1, 961). The laudation of the great friend is not infrequently expressed in superlative terms: 'noster Philippus Melanchthon, homo admirabilis, imo paene nihil habens, quod non supra hominem sit . . . Philippus, quem non secus habeo ac me ipsum, excepta eruditione ac integritate vitae, qua me pudefacit, nedum superat' (*Letters*, ed. De Wette, I, 197; II, 407). It sounds as if Luther wanted us to picture himself as the barbarous peasant *vis-à-vis* the learned professor—which, incidentally, leads most people to make the wrong guess when comparing their two handwritings! His admiration for Melanchthon's writings is almost unqualified, whether it is the ***Dialectica***,[3] the commentaries,[4] the ***Confessio Augustana***[5] and the ***Apologia***,[6] or, above all, the ***Loci Communes*** which Luther would like to translate himself (De Wette, II, 557) and which he does not hesitate to classify as the norm for all scripture reading.[7] 'Therefore who nowadays wants to be a theologian, has many advantages. First, he has the Bible made so plain that he can read it without any difficulty. Then he can read the ***Loci Communes***; he should read them well and diligently so as to have them firmly in his head. If he has these two things, he is a theologian immune from the devil and all heretics, and the whole of theology lies open to him. . . . You find no book among all his books which comprises the sum of religion or the whole of theology as well as the *Loci*. All the Fathers and Commentators are just as nothing compared with that. Non est melior liber post scripturam sanctam quam ipsius loci communes' (*WA Ti*, 5, 5511; cf. 5647, 5787, 5827, 6439, 6458).

Luther's only word of regret is about Melanchthon's habit of dedicating his books to the potentates in State and Church, as e.g. to Henry VIII (the 1535 edition of the *Loci*, cf. *CR*, 2, 920) and Albrecht von Mainz (the 1532 commentary on Romans, cf. *CR*, 2, 611): 'I regret that Magister Philippus has dedicated his best prefaces to the naughtiest boys' (*WA Ti*, 4, 4699). But at the same time he defends him passionately from the charge of corruptibility in connection with a royal donation received from England: 'Et multa expendit in suos et alienos. Distribuit eam pecuniam. Et dignus esset, cui regnum donaretur, tantus vir et tam bene meritus de Romano imperio et ecclesia in tota Germania et aliis regionibus!' (4, 4957). The friend in his eyes is 'nimis modestus' (4, 4577; cf. 5, 5781): 'No one can repay his labour. He must live in the alms house. Forsitan valeat ad promovendum evangelium. Verecundus est. God help him! He shall go to heaven, there he will be well rewarded; the world shall not pay for his labour and work' (2, 1545). To the question of a sceptic, 'si Philippus esset episcopus Saltzburgensis, an ita liberalis maneret?', Luther replies firmly: 'Maxime! Nam habet agnitionem Christi Jesu' (4, 4985).

Convinced of the essential soundness on the part of Melanchthon, Luther can afford to smile about some of his 'hobbies', such as astrology: 'M. Ph. holds fast to it, but has never been able to convince me' (1, 855). 'Neither Philippus nor anybody else will ever persuade me to believe that it is a science. . . . Illa tota res est contra philosophiam' (5, 6250)—a statement no less illuminating than the test of the two handwritings! The scholar in Luther insists: 'Ego dixi: Foris nihil habent argumenti pro astrologia nisi autoritatem Philippi. Tum Doctor: Ego saepe confutavi Philippum ita evidenter, ut diceret: Haec quidem vis est! Et concessit esse scientiam, sed quam ipsi non teneant. Quare ego sum contentus, si non tenent eam artem, so I allow him to play with it . . . their art is all rubbish' (4, 5013). The believer is even more outspoken: 'Ego puto, quod Philippus astrologica tractat, sicut ego bibo *ein starcken trunck birs,* quando habeo graves cogitationes' (1, 17). But the choice of the tonic by the two men is not irrelevant. Of course what is true of astrology is equally true of dreams: 'Luther praised that dream of Philippus and said he had the gift of dreams, but I, he added, do not attribute any weight to it. I do not care to have dreams and visions. Certiora habeo, verbum Dei' (4, 4444 b; cf. 5, 5494). Should this be the root of the problem, that the 'solum verbum' was not certain enough for Melanchthon?

But Luther continues to speak about a mere diversity of gifts ('varia dona', 1, 80), and to describe the difference in terms of biblical analogies. 'Ego credo Paulum fuisse personam contemptibilem, a poor, thin, little man such as Philippus' (2, 1245) must have sounded very flattering to Melanchthon, but fails to impress us. Another comparison is surely nearer the mark: 'I am Isaiah, Philippus is Jeremiah; he always worried that he scolded too much, just like Philippus!' (1, 887)—though again the similarity between Philippus and Jeremiah can hardly be pressed beyond this one point! More obvious is the parallel drawn from Acts xv: 'Then they talked about the very different minds of Luther and Melanchthon who had yet achieved the maximum of concord. Luther replied: in the Acts of the Apostles you have this picture: James denotes Philippus who with his modesty would gladly have retained the law; Peter signifies myself who brought it to fall. Why do you worry? Philippus proceeds in charity, and I in faith. Philippus suffers himself to be eaten up, I eat up everything and spare nobody. Et ita Deus in diversis operatur idem' (4, 4577). Here we touch upon a fundamental issue to which we shall have to come back: 'Multi valde sudant, ut concordent Jacobum cum Paulo, velut etiam Philippus in Apologia, sed non serio. Pugnantia sunt: fides iustificat—fides non iustificat. Whoever can rhyme these two, him will I decorate with my doctor's cap and let him call me a fool' (3, 3292). Again, the different doctrinal emphasis—to put it cautiously—corresponds to the divergence in the fields of action: 'Diversum facit Philippus. Is meis negotiis non movetur, sed movent eum illa grandia reipublicae et religionis. Me privata tantum premunt. Sic sunt varia dona' (1, 80).[8]

Thus a peculiar *modus agendi* is necessitated on which Luther makes some further observations. It occurs only once that he has to blame Melanchthon for too much rigidity, and that is, significantly enough, in his capacity as examiner.[9] In all other respects 'de Philippo omnium judicium hoc est: si peccat, tunc lenitate peccat. He is too easily taken in. His little scholarly instruments are not good enough; the trunks demand an axe' (5, 6443). As it fell upon Melanchthon to represent the Protestant cause in nearly all official negotiations, this became of crucial importance. Luther's criticism of the **Augustana,** 'I cannot tread so softly' (De Wette, IV, 17) is well known. It had to be repeated on more than one occasion. When he tarried at the Hagenau convent in 1540, Luther remarked: 'Philippus vult mori in hac synodo et fecit versum. Sed nostrum Paternoster erit fortius cogitationibus Philippi' (4, 5058; cf. 5062, 5096, 5091, 5054). Eventually Melanchthon seemed to be converted to Luther's methods: 'Ph. has finally fallen foul of the Papists. For a while he wanted to deal with the case according to his equity; now he sees that nothing will help with these scoundrels' (4, 4909). But Luther's reflection is based upon something more than the practical success when he turns to Melanchthon's manner of polemics: 'Philippus, too, pricks, but with needles only; the pricks hurt and are hard to heal; but I stab with boars' spears' (1, 348). Long after Luther's death experience confirmed his suspicion 'that Philippus too much indulges in affections and bears the cross more impatiently than becomes a disciple, or rather, such a master of so many' (De Wette, II, 29; see below, pp. 66, 79).

Leaving aside these wider moral and political implications, we must try to understand what it means that Luther and Melanchthon talk in two different languages. The fact at least was realized by both. 'In tractatione scripturae ego vehementior sum quam Philippus, etsi in libello de ecclesia (1539) acrior fuit. Sententia eius libri est vehemens, sed verba videntur mihi non esse similia rebus; sed non intelligo vim Latini sermonis' (WA Ti, 4, 5054). But we are faced not with the simple question of the 'vis Latini sermonis',[10] but with the fundamental problem whether in reality 'verba videntur non esse similia rebus'. Is it only the language which separates Melanchthon from Luther or does he say something altogether different? Luther's summary reply seems to leave no doubt and is striking both in matter and in form: 'Res et verba Philippus; verba sine re Erasmus; res sine verbis Lutherus; nec res nec verba Carolostadius' (3, 3619). And the final verdict runs: 'Ego hoc didici experientia: *Quotquot M. Philippo et mihi adversati* sunt e nostris, exciderunt a fide' (4, 4946; cf. 5, 5788). The solidarity with Melanchthon is so firmly established that his dissent from Amsdorf and Agricola can be dismissed in the uncommonly irenic phrase: 'I do not think much of this strife of words, particularly among the people' (De Wette, III, 215); that the Elector's clemency is pleaded for Philippus in a moment of grave mismanagement;[11] that even in the sacramental dispute the other side is rebuked for its impertinent claim 'se cum Philippo et Luthero sentire' (WA Ti,

3, 3231), as if there were but one mind and one mouth to consider. However inconspicuous and inconsistent may have been the part which the virtue of tolerance played in Luther's life, in the case of Melanchthon he acted literally and thoroughly according to his words: 'Ego soleo dissimulare et celare, quantum possum, ubi aliqui nostrum vere dissentiunt a nobis' (De Wette, II, 522).[12] The only possible explanation for that course must be sought in an amazing capacity to read his own 'res' into and behind Melanchthon's 'verba'. Was his trust justified? Was he right in his optimism: 'What do we lack, Philippus, I, Doctor Jonas, Major? Are we not getting on well?' (WA Ti, 5, 5476).[13] Or had he any sinister forebodings when he once asked: 'How is it that he is the worst deceiver whom one had trusted most?' and when Melanchthon answered: 'Optime scribit Xenophon: facis id, quod est facillimum, amico iniuriam . . .' (4, 3938). In another, more harmless and objective, table-talk the tragedy of the second generation is well described: 'But Phil. said to Luther: My dear Doctor, there are godly people who die in the knowledge of Christ, and particularly young people; for the older we become, the more foolish we are. The young folk stick simply to the articles of the Christian faith; as they have learnt them, so they believe them; but when we grow old, we begin to dispute, want to be clever, while we are the greatest fools' (5, 5563). That is the Reformation itself in the process of 'growing old'—and so we come to look at our problem with the eyes of Melanchthon.

The picture, for all its parallels, is different from the outset. Here, too, we have the symbolic incident of Melanchthon watching a serious illness of Luther, yet, notwithstanding Luther's emphatic tribute, 'Ph. me uno verbo erigit' (**CR,** 1, 360), he is not powerful enough to pray him back from death, but, 'when he looked at him dissolved into tears' (WA Ti, 3, 3543). There is a sigh of relief in his exclamation: 'so far, thank God, Martinus breathes, so pray that he may go on breathing, ille unicus θεολόγου διδασκαλίας vindex' (**CR,** 1, 208)— and the corresponding sigh of despair after Luther's death when a new and trying era of the Church is dawning (cf. 11, 783 ff.: 'De Luthero et aetatibus ecclesiae'). 'I would die rather than be separated from this man; nothing more trist could happen than to have to do without Martinus' (1, 160, 269) is the refrain of many testimonies which show a genuine sense of dependence upon 'hoc Hercule nostro' (1, 282). It is noteworthy that of all comparisons this comes first to Melanchthon's mind; he can never escape the impression of overpowering physical and spiritual strength. 'Martinus seems to me to be driven by a spirit . . . impossible for me not to fall in love with him' (1, 269, 96); but these almost naïve understatements soon give way to the flourish of his Latin rhetoric: 'ne ille opprimatur, vir unus, quem ego ausim et vere non modo omnibus huius aetatis, sed omnibus omnium seculorum, omnium temporum vel

Augustinis, vel Hieronymis, vel Nazianzenis praeferre' (1, 270). Solon, Themistocles, Scipio and Augustus, however great their empires, are far inferior to 'nostris ducibus Jesaia, Baptista, Paulo, Augustino, Luthero' (11, 728). And the praise of the man is the praise of his doctrine. 'For when we study Luther, we deal with the cause of true theology and Christian doctrine, which he, in the spirit of Elijah, has plainly asserted; I have never had any doubt whatsoever about Luther's integrity or the truth of his doctrine' (1, 287, 598); yes, even 'you grieve the Holy Spirit, not Luther, when you take offence at this' (1, 320; cf. 1002). All this appears to be strictly in line with the later orthodoxy of Wittenberg: 'God's Word and Luther's doctrine shall never pass away',[14] and with the tendency which leads certain dogmatics to the conception of a 'Locus de Vocatione Lutheri'.

Yet Melanchthon gives himself away when in the course of his necrologies on Luther he makes the confession: 'Cumque decesserit Lutherus ἐν εὐφημίᾳ bonos et amantes Deum etiam de viro tanto, qui certe aliquam doctrinae celestis partem illustravit, decet εὔφημα dicere' (*CR*, 6, 80). Thus the adherence to the master is qualified in two important ways. First, 'decet εὔφημα dicere'—in marked contrast to Luther's own deplorable manner of speaking. 'Nunquam ita amavi Lutherum, ut veluti instruxerim eius in disputatione vehementiam' (1, 946). The disputations and pamphlets themselves become a nightmare to him; more than once he unburdens his heart in letters to Camerarius, his 'intimus': 'you are quite right in guessing that these harsh addresses (sc. Lutheri dissidia cum Iurisconsultis de clandestinis sponsalibus) are a cause of great grievance to me. Many things trouble me. What is the use of it all to the people? How very inopportune is the moment, when big decisions seem to be pending' (5, 310 sq.). We seem to hear the gentle voice of a British critic when we read: 'this cause could be pleaded in a more civil way' (1, 1023). While defending Luther's superiority against a popular overestimate of Erasmus,[15] he cannot help holding, like the latter, Luther's polemics responsible for the drive of many people into the opposite camp:[16] and both in the sacramental issue and in the conflict 'de libero arbitrio' Melanchthon himself must vote for appeasement.[17] 'How this conflicts with your statement, I cannot see even now' (3, 68 sq.) is one of his typical sentences written to Erasmus, with whom he maintained an unbroken correspondence.

The second qualification is that Luther 'certe *aliquam* doctrinae celestis *partem* illustravit', and again Melanchthon's friendship with Erasmus is a striking reminder of that. 'I have, during and after Luther's lifetime, rejected the Stoic and Manichean "deliria", presented by Luther and others, that all works, good and evil, in all men, good and evil, had to come about by necessity. It is obvious that such phrases are against the word of God, harmful to all discipline, and blasphemous' (9, 766; similarly 8, 916). This criticism deserves attention, not so much because of its particular theme but because of its general principle. 'God's Word' and 'Luther's doctrine' are not simply identical; the latter is judged by the former. Now the laudations of Luther, without losing their weight and sincerity, must be viewed in a different light: 'I should not want you to favour Luther unless it is because you feel bound to favour the truth of the Gospel . . . while Montanus wanted people to believe him, Luther wanted not himself, but scripture in its evidence and perspicuity to be believed' (1, 287, 406); 'volebat enim Lutherus non detinere (nos) in suis scriptis, sed ad fontes deducere omnium mentes; ipsam vocem Dei audire nos voluit' (6, 170). Of course this is precisely what Luther himself had said and how he wanted to be understood; and it is also the criterion of Lutheranism as a whole, established in the preface to the *Formula Concordiae*.[18] But it is significant that Melanchthon should be the first to apply the criterion in terms of a censure on parts of Luther's own writings.

He did not do it with an easy mind. 'Non sum natura φιλόνεικος; I am a quiet bird' (6, 880; 5, 474). But Luther, he thought, fell under that ominous category of the φιλόνεικος, and he, Melanchthon, felt very much his victim. 'I have also borne the almost shameful servitude, since Luther often served his nature (in which there was no small φιλονεικία) rather than what was good for his own person or the community' (6, 880) is an outburst two years after Luther's death which no biographer of Melanchthon could fail to register. It was, however, not different while Luther was alive. 'Πολλάκις σημαίνει τὴν παλαιὰν ὀργήν' (3, 595); 'omissis igitur ἃ μετεχειρίζοντο nunc βροντᾶται καὶ ἀστράπτεται καθ' ἑτέρων τινῶν, interdum me quoque petendo' (5, 462). And Cruciger confirms his suspicions: 'Luther calls the mediators Erasmians, no doubt aiming at us, and most of all at Philippus' (3, 397). But worst of all was the agitation of the anti-Philippist party which began early and grew intolerable in his last lonely years. 'Amsdorf has written to Luther to say that he was nursing a snake in his bosom, denoting myself: I leave out the rest' (3, 503). The charges were both moral and doctrinal. 'Some suspect me of taking favours from the mighty . . . and to have been corrupted with money by Iulius, the Bishop of Naumburg' (5, 332; 7, 352); against which we remember Luther's fervent defence of Melanchthon (see above, p. xviii). More heavily than these 'falsissimae calumniae certorum sycophantarum' weighs the charge against the *Augsburg Confession* and *Apologia*: 'Dicor nimium laudare bona opera' (5, 754). The reply is: 'Utinam satis laudarem!' Although Melanchthon stoically quotes the story of Flavianus Antiochenus, who, accused before Theodosius, declared that he would suffer reproof of his doctrine or morals, but give up the fight when 'de dignitate καὶ περὶ προεδρίας est certamen' (3, 459), the atmosphere of Wittenberg made it hard enough for him to remain calm. 'Noster Cyzizensis,' writes Cruciger about Amsdorf, 'ut est rigidus, etiam τὸν ἡμέτερον διδάσκαλον (Lutherum) inflammavit. . . . Itaque constituit alter (Melanchthon), se potius recta pedibus egressurum esse urbem, quam sic assentiatur aut pugnet cum διδασκάλῳ' (5, 477; cf. 484). The question of emigration arose more than once: 'Which of us has a safe abode? For about fifteen years I have daily expected expulsion, and am still expecting it' (6, 860).

As the date of the fifteen years indicates, the position was all the more difficult since Luther was no longer there; in fact, it was ultimately the bond with him which held Melanchthon in Wittenberg.[19] This implied not only mutual loyalty and support in the sphere of personal relations, but an emphatic claim by Melanchthon to be the true and genuine representative of the Lutheran tradition: 'I have always maintained the contents of the **Commentarius Inspectionis Ecclesiarum** to be in complete accordance with Luther's doctrine . . . si quis Lutherum recantare aliquid in meo opere iudicat, is multipliciter insanit. Si quid scriptum est, quod videtur pugnare cum Lutheri doctrina, id ad me, non ad Lutherum pertinet' (1, 898). The real divergences are about some Adiaphora;[20] here Melanchthon feels free to make his own comments on 'aliquam doctrinae celestis partem', and here Luther seems to have agreed to disagree. 'Neither does Luther seem to bear us any hostility. Yesterday he spoke very amiably about these controversies with me . . . when I pointed out what a tragic spectacle it would be to see us fight with one another like the Cadmean brothers. You know that I speak less harshly about predestination, free will, necessity of obedience, and original sin. In all these matters as such, Luther, I know, thinks as I do, but the uneducated too much prefer some of his more vehement phrases, the point of which they do not understand. I do not think it is for me to fight them; they may use their own judgment. Mihi tamen concedant homini Peripatetico, et amanti mediocritatem, minus Stoice alicubi loqui. That is the sum of the matter' (**CR**, 3, 383). It is indeed the 'summa negotii' because it shows clearly that Melanchthon's 'contribution' to Lutheranism is both to complete and to polish what Luther said; the key lies in the references to the 'homo peripateticus' and to the 'modus dicendi': 'scis me quaedam minus horride dicere'; thus the defects of Luther's φιλονεικία are overcome. The next passage makes the same vital point in still more positive terms: 'When we in our first visitation of the churches found so many conflicting voices among the uneducated about many points, I drew up a summa doctrinae in one volume which Luther had delivered in various volumes of commentaries and addresses; et quaesivi genus verborum, quo ad proprietatem, quae ad perspicuitatem et concordiam utilis est, discentes assuefierent, ac semper omnia scripta

iudicio Ecclesiae nostrae et ipsius Lutheri permisi: de multis quaestionibus etiam diserte sciscitatus sum Lutherum, quid sentiret, ac multi pagellarum illarum exempla adhuc habent' (7, 479). In other words, Melanchthon describes his work as the quest for a new 'genus verborum' which is apt to summarize and harmonize the doctrines of the Reformation; his task, in succession to Luther, is to restate the case in the proper language.

In a letter from which we quoted [earlier], he uses the very distinction between 'res et verba' and 'res sine verbis' which we have heard from Luther.[21] 'Lenitas' was, as we have seen, Luther's only charge against him. So we are again left with the question whether or not they both said the same thing in different words. 'Rem ipsam semper retinui' (7, 756 sq.) was Melanchthon's defence in an argument about the 'sola fide'. But that he is on the defence all the time appears to be the decisive factor in his relation to Luther. It lends colour to all his utterances, and it places them in marked contrast to the corresponding words of Luther about Melanchthon. A scene reported in the table-talks may serve as illustration. 'D. Caspar (Cruciger) said to Philippus that he could hardly bear his presence in his lectures. Then said Luther: Neither am I very keen to have him in my lectures, but I cross myself and think: Philippus, Jonas, Pommer[22] are not in here, and I imagine that no wiser man stands on the cathedra than myself' (*WA Ti,* 3, 2954 b). Luther is so sure of his teaching that he can safely ignore the presence of his learned colleague, and again, he is so sure of Melanchthon that he can safely leave it to him what he makes of the lecture: 'Philippus non est docendus, nec ego propter illum doceo aut lego' (*WA Ti,* 4, 5047). Melanchthon's position is just the reverse. One could not imagine that he would have happily lectured in front of Luther. He would have felt that he had to prove his orthodoxy—as he repeatedly admits: 'semper omnia scripta iudicio Ecclesiae nostrae et ipsius Lutheri permisi'—and should Luther have taken notes, Melanchthon would most surely have corrected them. Certainty on his side is lacking in the same measure in which it abounds with Luther; he tests where Luther trusts; he takes control of the depositum fidei which Luther generously leaves to him, and so he comes to determine the future of Lutheranism. The change of language is therefore of the most far-reaching psychological and theological importance; and it is from this direction that the puzzle 'Luther and Melanchthon' which we leave now will have to be approached for its solution.

Notes

1. 'If discord should grow between Lutherus and Philippus, God help us! What would come of it, how would the Papists glory and say: a kingdom

divided against itself must perish. Also, no doubt, many Christian folk would take offence and stumble, even fall altogether away from the Gospel' (*CR,* 5, 502).

2. It may be as well here to introduce the main figures of the inter-Lutheran controversies whose names, not often mentioned outside Germany, will frequently occur on the following pages. On Melanchthon's side we find Caspar Cruciger (Wittenberg; collaborator in Luther's translation of the Bible; his son succeeded Melanchthon as Professor); Paul Eber (Professor, General-superintendent and Hymn-writer in Wittenberg); Georg Major (Magdeburg, Wittenberg, Eisleben; his statement that good works are necessary to salvation caused the so-called Majorist dispute). The leaders of the 'Gnesiolutherans' are Nikolaus von Amsdorf, the first Lutheran Bishop (of Naumburg; who countered Major's statement by declaring good works to be harmful to salvation), and Matthias Flacius (Magdeburg and Jena; the first great Church historian of Lutheranism, author of the *Magdeburger Zenturionen*). Both oppose Melanchthon sharply in his attempts to compromise with Rome by accepting, in the so-called 'Interim' of Leipzig, a number of constitutional and ceremonial matters as non-essential ('Adiaphora'; 'adiaphorist' dispute). But they side with him against Andreas Osiander (Nürnberg and Königsberg, an uncle of Cranmer's wife) in defending 'imputed' against 'inherent' righteousness. Johann Brenz, the reformer of Württemberg, while opposing the 'Interim', tries to save Osiander from misinterpretation. Justus Jonas (Wittenberg, Halle, etc.; preached Luther's funeral sermon), the translator of Melanchthon's *Loci* and *Apologia,* belongs, in the 'Interim' controversy, to the opposite camp. Johann Agricola (Eisleben, Wittenberg and Berlin) is known for the three 'antinomian' disputations in which Luther defends Melanchthon against him and forces him to recant. Martin Bucer needs no introduction to Cambridge.

3. 'Philippus fecit, quod nullus fecit in mille annis in dialectica. . . . Brevitatem et perspicuitatem I could not combine as well as Philippus. . . . Philippus superat omnes Graecos et Latinos in dialectica', *WA Ti,* 2, 1545, 1649, 2300.

4. Particularly on Romans and Colossians: *WA Ti,* 1, 369; 4, 5007; 5, 5511.

5. *WA Ti,* 2, 1481; De Wette, IV, 17.

6. 'Apologia Philippi praestat omnibus doctoribus ecclesiae, etiam ipso Augustino', *WA Ti,* 1, 252.

7. 'Ideo biblia sacra legenda iuxta locos communes Phil. Melanchthonis', *WA Ti,* 5, 6009; cf. 3, 3589, 3695.

8. Cf. 3, 3809: 'L. negabat se esse administratorem.'

9. 'Therefore I am pleased when the young people and students produce arguments, however good or bad they might be, and I dislike Philippus examining so strictly and sharply as to rush over the poor fellows; one must climb stairs step by step, nobody can be at once on top', 4, 4056.

10. In another passage Luther makes the distinction: 'Tu rhetor es scribendo, non dicendo . . . sed quae scripseram, Philippo non placebant' (2, 2068).

11. 'For they have maintained our dear Confession and did abide firmly by it, even if everything else went wrong' (De Wette, v, 357).

12. Melanchthon, on the other hand, had his moments when he could say: 'non soleo dissimulare, quid de controversia illa sentiam' (*CR,* 1, 946)!

13. Cf. Luther's remarks on the future of the Wittenberg faculty, ibid. 5, 5423; 4, 5126.

14. 'Gottes Wort und Luthers Lehr vergehen nun und nimmermehr.' On the origin of the famous formula see O. Ritschl, *Dogmengeschichte des Protestantismus,* II, 356, note 3; and R. Seeberg, *Dogmengeschichte,* IV, part II, p. 435.

15. 'Quae fortasse longe graviores tumultus aliquando excitatura fuerant, nisi Lutherus exortus esset.'

16. 'Tota illa tragoedia περὶ δείπνου κυριακοῦ ab ipso nata videri potest' (1, 1083); Erasmus's words.

17. Melanchthon to Erasmus: 'De scriptis contra te hic editis quod fuerit meum iudicium, eo nihil hic dico, quia non solum propter privata officia, sed etiam propterea displicuerunt, quia tanta scripta sunt inutilia reipublicae. Neque hoc iudicium meum dissimulavi unquam' (3, 69).

18. Cf. *Symbolische Bücher der Evangelisch-Lutherischen Kirche,* ed. J. T. Müller, and the corresponding preamble of the Barmen Declaration of the Confessional Church.

19. Cf. F. Galle, *Melanchthon, Versuch einer Charakteristik Melanchthons als Theologen,* Halle, 1845, p. 146, n. 2.

20. See above, p. xvi. 'De Adiaphoris ideo minus contendimus, quia alia maiora certamina sustinemus. . . . Obsecro te, concordiam inter vos tueamur, nec propter Adiaphora inter nos ipsi dimicemus', letter to Hardenberg, *CR,* 7, 357; cf. ibid. 9, 763 sq.: 'Bedenken auf das Weimarer Confutationsbuch.'

21. 'Tantum me hoc cavisse, ut sine acerbitate verborum, res nudae proponerentur. Multae mihi causae fuerunt eius lenitatis . . . mihi magis fuit

spectandum, quid Deo placeret, quam quando sycophantas illos mihi placarem, a quibus nunc ut hereticus, ut fanaticus traducor. Hanc meam epistolam potes exhibere quibus velis. . . . Et Lutherus mihi optimus testis est, me semper optasse in hac tota dissensione, ut summa lenitate nostri omnes uterentur' (*CR*, 1, 898).

22. 'Doctor Pommer' (Pomeranus), nickname for Bugenhagen, the chief Pastor of Wittenberg and Reformer of Denmark, in whose frequent absence Luther deputized in the pulpit of the Stadtkirche at Wittenberg.

Works Cited

Melanchthon's works have been quoted from the *Corpus Reformatorum,* ed. Bredschneider (*CR*); Luther's from the Weimarer Ausgabe (*WA*; the table-talks, Tischreden: *WA Ti*), in a few instances from Walch and the Erlanger Ausgabe (*EA*), his letters from De Wette's edition and his disputations from Drews. The Lutheran Confessions of Faith have been quoted from J. T. Müller's edition (Gütersloh, 1928); they contain, besides the three oecumenical symbols, the *Augsburg Confession* and *Apologia,* Luther's *Articuli Smalcaldici* (with Melanchthon's *Tractatus de Potestate ac Primatu Papae*), his *Minor* and *Major Catechisms,* and the *Formula Concordiae.*

Theodore G. Tappert (essay date 1961)

SOURCE: Tappert, Theodore G. "Melanchthon in America." In *Luther und Melanchthon,* edited by Vilmos Vajta, pp. 189-98. Göttingen: Vandenhoeck & Ruprecht, 1961.

[*In the essay below, Tappert explores the influence of Melanchthon in the United States in the twentieth century.*]

Any attempt to trace the interpretations and the influence of Philip Melanchthon in America must take into account the fact that he did not become an object of independent scholarly investigation until the very close of the nineteenth century. It was in 1898 that the first substantial life of the reformer was published.[1] This is not to suggest that Melanchthon was wholly unknown or remained entirely unmentioned before 1898, but it means that when he was cited or appealed to this was often done to secure the support of his authority for some preconceived position. Astonishing caricatures of Melanchthon sometimes appeared, not only in such polemical Roman Catholic literature as pictured him as a secret member of the Masonic Order[2] but also in such Protestant literature as meant to take him seriously. The

enigmatic character of Melanchthon and the ambivalent role he played in the Reformation of course contributed to the sometimes curious assessments that were made.

I

During the first half of the nineteenth century a kind of Melanchthon cult developed in America. The name of this reformer was attached to a movement. Disciples gathered about his memory and proudly called themselves "Melanchthonians." They advocated and promoted what they took to be Melanchthon's characteristic theological and ecclesiastical stance.

To understand this revival of Melanchthonianism in America during the first half of the nineteenth century it is necessary to observe something of the situation which then existed. The dominant influence in the Lutheran Church in America during the preceding century had been that of Halle Pietism. For about two generations, from the beginning of the American Revolution in 1775 to about 1830, immigration from Europe had come to a virtual standstill. Cut off to a large extent from continuing influence from Europe, most Lutherans in America adhered to at least the outward expressions of their inherited Pietism. At the same time they were increasingly adapting themselves to the language and customs in their American environment. The consequence was that Lutheran church life took on more and more of the color of general American Protestantism. To be sure, the pattern was not uniform. Where German Reformed people were numerous, there was a tendency to accommodate Lutheran and Reformed positions and practices. Where Presbyterians, Methodists, or others were present in large numbers, Lutherans were inclined to imitate these. The fusion between an Americanized German Pietism (whether Lutheran or Reformed) and an English Puritanism modified by American revivalism (whether Presbyterian, Methodist, or other) produced the characteristic features of what came to be called "American Lutheranism." This was the only type of Lutheranism, its adherents claimed, which would in the long run be acceptable in the New World, and a contemporary critic caustically referred to it as "a kind of mongrel Methodistic Presbyterianism,"[3] while a man who had been brought up under its influence more judiciously called it an "accommodation of Lutheranism to the dominant Calvinism or Puritanism of America."[4]

It was in such a situation that Melanchthon came to enjoy acclaim. He was hailed as the champion of a progressive spirit and as one who had been ready to adjust his opinions for the sake of overcoming the disunion of Protestant churches. "The peace-loving Philip Melanchthon," it was said, might have brought about a union of Reformed and Lutherans at Marburg in 1529 if it had not been for Luther's obstinacy. "Luther, Zwingli, Melanchthon, and Oekolampadius had it in their power to put an end to all controversy, for which Luther alone was especially to blame . . . Philip did all that he could to restore unity."[5]

To be sure, the readiness of Melanchthon to make concessions to the right as well as to the left was acknowledged. "The circumstances under which the *Augsburg Confession* was composed" in 1530 "were far from being favorable to a full and free exhibition of the deliberate views of the Reformers even at that date, and fully account for some of the remnants of Romanism still found in that confession." At Augsburg the "peace-loving Philip" had been transformed into the "fearful and trembling Melanchthon" who surrendered so much to Rome that Luther was led "to affirm what American Lutherans now maintain, that he had yielded too much to the papists in the *Augsburg Confession*."[6]

The teachings and practices in which Melanchthon had yielded too much to Rome were specified. First, "the name and some of the ceremonies of the Roman mass were retained in the *Augsburg Confession*" (Art.XXIV). Although Luther rejected the mass entirely, "both the name and accompanying ceremonies," yet "if the *Augsburg Confession* were strictly binding on us, we should be under necessity of adopting on sacramental occasions all the public ceremonies then and now usual in the Romish church in celebrating public mass."[7] Second, private confession and absolution were retained in the *Augsburg Confession* (Art. XI, XXV, XXVIII). Here it was conceded that Melanchthon agreed with Luther, but subsequently this practice was "almost universally rejected, . . . except by a few Old Lutherans."[8] Third, baptismal regeneration was a "remnant of papal superstition." "Melanchthon, whilst he by no means indulges in the extravagant and unscriptural views of a change in the water employed in baptism, by the Deity's pervading it, etc., seems however in substance to have entertained views of the efficacy of this ordinance amounting to baptismal regeneration" (Art. II, IX).[9] Fourth, Melanchthon, like Luther, "treats the Sabbath as a mere Jewish institution and supposes it to be totally revoked, whilst the propriety of our retaining the Lord's Day or Christian Sabbath as a day of religious worship is supposed to rest only on the agreement of the churches for the convenience of general convocation" (Art. XXVIII).[10] Fifth, in the *Augsburg Confession* Melanchthon so worded the Lutheran teaching concerning the Lord's Supper that it admitted a Roman interpretation. The Apology of the *Augsburg Confession* asserted that Lutherans believed what had "heretofore been believed in the Romish church . . . They believed as fully as did the Romanists in receiving the real body and blood of Christ."[11]

What is revealing about this whole interpretation of Melanchthon is not only the criticism of some of the positions he took at Augsburg in 1530 but also the com-

mendation of changes he made afterwards in some of his views. "Melanchthon himself," it was pointed out, "did not regard his Confession as perfect, for he made sundry alterations in it in his successive editions."[12] He "subsequently changed his views" and was represented as holding that "the glorified human nature of Christ is not substantially (essentially) present at all, but only influentially, efficaciously or virtually . . . This was probably the opinion of that distinguished ornament of the Lutheran church, Melanchthon, who rejected the doctrine of the substantial presence of the glorified human nature."[13] It was even regarded as Melanchthonian to hold that in the Lord's Supper communicants partake "of the emblems of his broken body and shed blood."[14] In similar fashion, it was said, Melanchthon originally supported Luther in teaching "the Augustinian view of predestination." Luther also "entertained other views inconsistent with this. Melanchthon, who had embraced Luther's unadjusted views of doctrine, led the way in the process of harmonizing their conflicting elements by the rejection of absolute predestination."[15]

It should be observed that opinions here ascribed to Melanchthon were not only based on a study of available literature on the Reformation but were also shaped in some measure by the historical situation in America during the first half of the nineteenth century. On the one hand, it was a time when, as a result of large Irish immigration, the Roman Catholic Church was for the first time making a real impact on American religious life, and Protestants reacted with a bitter anti-Catholic crusade which had political as well as social and ecclesiastical aspects. American Lutherans joined others in attacking the "multitude of doctrinal and practical corruptions" and the "dangerous principles" which were binding on Roman Catholics and "in conformity with which they may reasonably be expected to destroy the present liberties of both Protestants and Catholics."[16] On the other hand, this was a time when concern for Protestant church union, although gradually waning in some circles, was still alive among "American Lutherans." It was therefore of interest to demonstrate that "the opinions now generally entertained in the Lutheran Church as to the nature of the sacrament of the Lord's Supper differ in no material point from those entertained by the other Protestant churches on the same subject."[17] Similarly it was asserted that the Calvinistic doctrine of predestination "has long since been abandoned by the great body of the Reformed Church," and "the principal Congregational divines of New England are also unwilling to term these decrees of God unconditional or absolute."[18] "Melanchthonian Lutheranism" thus appeared to be well adapted to reconcile divided Protestants while removing the "remnant of papal superstition" which had once clung to Melanchthon.

There is an element of truth in the later charge that Melanchthon was treated "with wonderful versatility."

On the one hand, his *Augsburg Confession* was alleged to contain "unscriptural doctrines" and "remnants of Romish error." On the other hand, he was celebrated as the champion of a common Protestantism which was anti-Catholic and in which "every individual should be left to the free exercise of his own judgment." On the one hand, Luther was the true progressive and Melanchthon the reactionary; on the other hand, Luther was the ultra-conservative and Melanchthon the liberal.[19] Actually this charge does not do full justice to the perception of American theologians in the first half of the nineteenth century. They were distinguishing between the young and the old Melanchthon and were expressing a value judgment in favor of the latter. They were calling attention not to their own versatility in interpreting the reformer but to the versatility of Melanchthon, who in their eyes possessed the gift of shifting his position to meet changing situations and growing knowledge.

This alone can account for the fact that a Lutheran synod in America which had a twelve-year existence came to be officially named "The Melanchthon Synod." When "American Lutheranism" was on the wane and the Evangelical Lutheran Synod of Maryland defeated the Definite Synodical Platform (which included a proposed American Recension of the *Augsburg Confession*), some of its members withdrew from the Maryland Synod in 1857 to form a new synod. Made up largely of rural ministers and congregations in the western part of Maryland—although at times including individual ministers in Virginia, Pennsylvania, New York, and Nova Scotia—the new synod reflected the spirit and leadership of one of the most extreme "Melanchthonians," Benjamin Kurtz. Its doctrinal position was that of advanced "American Lutheranism," rejecting those parts of the *Augsburg Confession* which treated ceremonies of the mass, private confession, baptismal regeneration, the real or corporeal presence of Christ in the Lord's Supper, and denial of the divine obligation of the Lord's Day.[20] The synod encouraged revivals, those "most precious effusions of the Holy Spirit," and deplored the growing emphasis on costly church edifices, imposing ceremonies, and extended creeds.[21] Dancing was declared to be "contrary to the Word of God and morally and physically detrimental."[22] "The scriptural doctrine with reference to the use of spiritual liquors, wine, and cider is 'total abstinence,'" it was declared.[23] A president of the synod said, when exhorting his brethren, "I earnestly trust that all the friends of active and vital Christianity will set their faces like a flint against the inroads and encroachments of ritualism and formality."[24] Members of the Melanchthon Synod did not claim to find precedents for attitudes such as these in the writings of Melanchthon, to which they had only limited access; if they had, they might have been chagrined to discover that Melanchthon danced, drank alcoholic beverages, advocated creedal

subscription, and defended rites and ceremonies. But this was beside the point. They were "Melanchthonians" and called their organization the "Melanchthon Synod" not because they felt themselves bound to adopt his every opinion and practice but because they believed that he was the leading early Lutheran exponent of conciliation, progress, development, and adaptation.

II

If ever this type of "Melanchthonian Lutheranism" had an opportunity to establish itself in America it was just before the middle of the nineteenth century. Circumstances were favorable for it. "To fall into line with Puritan ways and Presbyterian teaching was easy, popular, almost irresistible." It seemed to be a part of the process of adaptation to the American scene to compress Lutheran patterns of life "into the mould of Puritanism and Methodism." But expectations were not realized in full measure. The sons of S. S. Schmucker, the standard bearer of American Lutheranism, abandoned their father's position. The Melanchthon Synod dissolved (1869) soon after its leader Benjamin Kurtz died, and although the constitution of Susquehanna University, which he founded, prohibited the teaching of the Lutheran doctrines of Baptism and the Lord's Supper, within a generation such doctrines were taught there. In his old age Samuel Sprecher, the third of the leaders of American Lutheranism, conceded that the movement was a mistake: "I thought at one time that a Lutheranism modified by the Puritan element would be desirable, but I . . . am convinced of its hopelessness."[25] The movement was too negative to maintain itself, especially after the influence of the confessional awakening in Europe had made itself felt in America through literature and vast new immigrations.

During the latter half of the nineteenth century Lutherans in America gradually recovered an appreciation of the Confessions. Not only were attempts to revise the *Augsburg Confession* given up, but the other Confessions included in the Book of Concord were restored to a place of honor and authority. It was perceived that denominational integrity in America, where the voluntaristic principle of church membership prevailed, required adhesion to unambiguous declarations of faith. Much was therefore made of the unaltered *Augsburg Confession,* and extended discussions of the problems involved in the text of the Confession continued to the beginning of World War I. It was argued on the one hand that "the thanks of the entire Lutheran Church are due to Melanchthon for his *variatae.* He represents progress and adaptation in the Lutheran Church."[26] This was an echo of the earlier "Melanchthonianism." On the other hand it was argued that "Confessions cannot be altered or improved after they have become the basis of action." By itself the "Melanchthonian principle" of adaptation can only lead to the absorption of Lutheranism in a "common Protestantism."[27] This was a warning against a relapse into "American Lutheranism."

Efforts were made to arrive at a juster assessment of Melanchthon with the help of better historical knowledge. It was suggested that a good balance between Luther and Melanchthon had been achieved in Pietism, which was described as "a revival of the principles and method of Luther as complemented by Melanchthon."[28] It was also contended that neither "Lutherism" nor "Melanchthonism" is the whole of Lutheranism. Luther the prophet worked in harmony with Melanchthon the preceptor. Luther was the more original, Melanchthon the more logical. Luther quickened and impelled Melanchthon while the latter restrained and moderated the former. The influence of both is necessary, it was said, if the Lutheran Church is to remain "both conservative and progressive."[29] Whatever balance might otherwise have been achieved was disturbed by the controversy over election and predestination which roiled the waters of the Lutheran Church in America from the close of the Civil War to World War I. The conciliatory Melanchthon was charged with having sowed the dragon's teeth of discord, for in deviating from Luther, it was said, he had lapsed into synergism and other errors which later bore fruit in Pietism, both in Europe and in America.[30]

In the course of the twentieth century another aspect of Melanchthon's influence was given increasing attention. During the preceding half-century, as we have suggested, "American Lutheranism" had been counteracted by a return to the Confessions. As a rule the Confessions were interpreted in the light of the later dogmaticians of the seventeenth century, whose works were diligently studied as if their conclusions were normative. This introduced a traditionalism which implied that "the whole development of doctrine had been terminated and had been fixated and set down in the symbols of the Lutheran Church." Instead of reading the symbols in the light of the Scriptures, the Scriptures tended to be read in the light of the symbols, and the symbols in turn to be read in the light of the later dogmatic authorities.[31] The defects in this procedure, which was followed in practice more than in theory, were not fully exposed until the twentieth century.

Melanchthon, it was now stated, gave Protestantism its inclination to intellectualize religion. He "impressed the dialectic and text-book stamp upon the form of Lutheran theology from its first beginning to the very end of its highly wrought-out orthodox and classic period in the seventeenth century. The complete departure of the early and later Lutheran theological form from the method and the more vital and germinal insight of Luther into the modified Aristotelian frame of logical definition" was ascribed to Melanchthon. He was responsible for the reintroduction of Aristotle into theology. He emphasized natural religion and natural law. Accordingly, when in later editions of his *Loci* he discussed the nature of God, Melanchthon started with Plato and then added revelation. It was this method and spirit of Melanchthon, not the spirit of Luther, that led to the "ultraorthodoxy of the seventeenth century."[32]

On the surface, to be sure, Melanchthon did not seem to diverge from Luther. He used similar expressions, but his orientation was different. He regarded the supernatural ingredient in Christianity as information, and information which could be apprehended by natural man. As Melanchthon put it, man comes to a knowledge of God through "principles" similar to those by which man attains other knowledge: experience, syllogistic reasoning, understanding of fundamental concepts. Thus the Gospel conquers the mind, and the Gospel is more a deterrent to sin than a dynamic for Christian life. It was not only as a humanist that Melanchthon was led in this direction, but above all as an educator and church administrator.[33] It was this Melanchthon, the forerunner of Lutheran Orthodoxism, who gained ascendancy in America. Lutheran theology was stored "in the containers of Melanchthonian orthodoxy," and in most catechetical literature to this day Luther's Small Catechism is interpreted not in the light of Luther himself but "with forms and pedagogical tools derived from Melanchthon."[34] Whereas the "Melanchthonians" of the early nineteenth century were accommodating Lutheranism to revivalism and puritanical pietism, the "Melanchthonians" of the later nineteenth and early twentieth centuries were repristinating the theology of the Protestant scholastics, who were later disciples of Melanchthon.

One additional influence of Melanchthon in America remains to be mentioned. Parallel to similar movements elsewhere, there has been a revival of liturgical interest in America which has evoked both commendation and criticism. Although it has earlier roots, the liturgical movement came to flower especially since the beginning of the twentieth century. In many of its recent expressions it betrays an Anglican cast, and consequently much is made of tradition and its authority in determining what is regarded as good practice. Attention has been focused on "restoration" of older rites and ceremonies, and there has been comparatively less concern about the relation of such forms to the current proclamation of the church.

It is not without significance in this connection that the Adiaphoristic Controversy is never discussed in liturgical literature in America. Insight into the dynamic connection between cultus and doctrine, which was so lacking in Melanchthon, seems to play no decisive role in contemporary treatments of public worship. In his own time Melanchthon maintained that because forms of worship are matters of indifference, neither commanded nor prohibited by God, Lutherans could observe Roman rites and ceremonies as long as "pure doctrine" was preserved. Here again he tended to intellectualize Christian faith. Matthias Flacius objected by declaring that things that are indifferent in themselves may nevertheless cease to be *adiaphora*. "If a doctrine is non-scriptural, then the ceremonies attached to it are non-scriptural. If a belief is idolatrous, then the ceremonies connected with it are idolatrous." The position of Flacius was in its essence later incorporated in the Formula of Concord, while the views of Melanchthon came more or less to prevail in England,[35] whence much of the impetus for the American liturgical movement stems. It would be an over-statement to suggest that there has been a conscious adoption of Melanchthon's views on *adiaphora*, but that the tendency is nevertheless Melanchthonian can hardly be denied.

Such has been the career of Melanchthon's influence in America. He has been claimed and blamed for many things by many different groups. In no small measure the reason for this lies in Melanchthon himself, for he was a man of admirable gifts and noble impulses who was compelled by circumstances to assume a role in history for which he was not temperamentally suited. In comparison with Luther he has been called "the feminine principle of the Reformation."[36] He has been credited with having had a significant formative influence on Luther's theology, and yet he has been assailed for his slightest departure from Luther.[37] A recent prophecy has been fulfilled: "American Lutheranism will not particularly note the anniversary of Melanchthon's death. The memory of the great reformer who himself needed reforming is too painful."[38]

Notes

1. James W. Richard, Philip Melanchthon, the Protestant Preceptor of Germany (New York, 1898). The only other full-length biography was published sixty years later: Clyde L. Manschreck, Melanchthon, the Quiet Reformer (Nashville, 1958).

2. Robert D. Cross, The Emergence of Liberal Catholicism in America (Cambridge, Mass., 1958), p. 3.

3. William M. Reynolds, in a letter (1850) quoted in Adolph Spaeth, Charles Porterfield Krauth, Vol. I (New York, 1898), p. 179.

4. Edmund J. Wolf, "Melanchthonian Lutheranism," in The Lutheran Evangelist, XV, No. 14 (Springfield, Ohio, Apr.3, 1891), p. 2. On the movement as a whole see Vergilius Ferm, The Crisis in American Lutheran Theology: A Study of the Issue Between American Lutheranism and Old Lutheranism (New York, 1927).

5. Joh. Aug. Probst, Die Wiedervereinigung der Lutheraner und Reformierten (Allentown, Pa., 1826), pp. 21, 50. For a Reformed view of Melanchthon's mediatorial role see James I. Good, The Origin of the Reformed Church in Germany (Reading, Pa., 1887), pp. 108-125.

6. Samuel Simon Schmucker, American Lutheranism Vindicated; or, Examination of the Lutheran Symbols on Certain Disputed Topics (Baltimore, 1856), pp. 53-55. Punctuation and the spelling of some proper names are somewhat altered here and in following quotations to avoid unnecessary disturbance to the reader.

7. S. S. Schmucker, The American Lutheran Church, Historically, Doctrinally, and Practically Delineated. Fifth ed. (Philadelphia, 1852), pp. 241, 242. Some neo-Romanticists interestingly use the same argument in reverse today.

8. Ibid., pp. 239, 240.

9. Ibid., p. 65; American Lutheranism Vindicated, pp. 138, 139.

10. Schmucker, American Lutheranism Vindicated, p. 110.

11. Schmucker, The American Lutheran Church, pp. 240, 241.

12. Schmucker, American Lutheranism Vindicated, p. 23. The reference is to the socalled altered or variatae editions of the Augsburg Confession.

13. S. S. Schmucker, Elements of Popular Theology. Third ed. (Baltimore, 1842), p. 250; The American Lutheran Church, p. 241.

14. Schmucker, American Lutheranism Vindicated, p. 179. Cf. A Liturgy for the Use of the Evangelical Lutheran Church, published by order of the General Synod (Baltimore, 1847), p. 126. The difference between Luther and Melanchthon on the Lord's Supper was grossly exaggerated, as it is by Manschreck when he writes of Luther's "semitransubstantiation" (op. cit., p. 230)!

15. Schmucker, The American Lutheran Church, p. 66.

16. S. S. Schmucker, Discourse Commemorating the Glorious Reformation of the Sixteenth Century (New York, 1838), pp. vi, 34-66. Nativist propaganda, including the legend of Maria Monk, is here rehearsed at length.

17. Discipline, Articles of Faith, and Synodical Constitution as Adopted by the Evangelical Lutheran Synod of South Carolina (Baltimore, 1841), p. 21.

18. Schmucker, Elements of Popular Theology, p. 87.

19. Adolph Spaeth, "Melanchthon in American Lutheran Theology," in The Lutheran Church Review, XVI (1897), pp. 104-106.

20. Minutes, Melanchthon Synod, 1856, pp. 9-16, 21; 1857, p. 9.

21. Ibid., 1864, pp. 6-10; 1865, p. 11.

22. Ibid., 1867, p. 25.

23. Ibid., 1867, pp. 25, 26.

24. Ibid., 1866, p. 7.

25. E. J. Wolf, "Melanchthonian Lutheranism," in The Lutheran Evangelist, XV, No. 14 (Apr. 3, 1891), p. 2; No. 15 (Apr. 10, 1891), p. 2. Cf. Sprecher in No. 18 (May 1, 1891), p. 1.

26. James W. Richard, The Confessional History of the Lutheran Church (Philadelphia, 1909), p. 232.

27. Theodore E. Schmauk, The Confessional Principle and the Confessions of the Lutheran Church (Philadelphia, 1911), pp. 604, 636, 883.

28. Samuel Sprecher, The Groundwork of a System of Evangelical Lutheran Theology (Philadelphia, 1879), p. 177.

29. Richard, Confessional History, pp. 305-307.

30. F. Bente, "Historical Introductions to the Symbolical Books," in Concordia Triglotta (St. Louis, 1921), pp. 105, 106, 112, 128, 180.

31. Cf. Georg J. Fritschel, ed., Quellen und Dokumente zur Geschichte und Lehrstellung der ev.-luth. Synode von Iowa (Chicago, 1916), pp. 207-223.

32. Schmauk, op. cit., pp. 618-620, 624.

33. Richard R. Caemmerer, "The Melanchthonian Blight," in Concordia Theological Monthly, XVIII (1947), pp. 321-338. Cf. also Jaroslav Pelikan, From Luther to Kierkegaard (St. Louis, 1950), pp. 24-48.

34. Robert C. Schultz, "Melanchthon after Four Hundred Years," in The Cresset (Valparaiso, Ind.), Apr., 1960, p. 13.

35. Clyde L. Manschreck, "The Role of Melanchthon in the Adiaphora Controversy," in Archiv für Reformationsgeschichte, XLVIII (1957), pp. 165-181; H. C. von Hase, "Occasions for Confession, 1548-1948," in The Lutheran World Review, Vol. I, No. 2 (1948), pp. 27-37. For a stimulating study of Melanchthon's inclination to substitute concessions for confessions see Franz Hildebrandt, Melanchthon: Alien or Ally? (Cambridge, 1946).

36. J. L. Neve, A History of Christian Thought, Vol. I (Philadelphia, 1943), p. 256.

37. Cf. Lowell C. Green, in Gerhard L. Belgum, ed., The Mature Luther, Martin Luther Lectures III (Decorah, Iowa, 1959), pp. 123-129, 137. Walter G. Tillmanns, World and Men about Luther (Minneapolis, 1959), p. 106, curiously ascribes the present revival of interest in Melanchthon to the kinship of modern theologians with humanism. Harold H. Lentz, Reformation Crossroads (Minneapolis, 1958), emphasizes the ambiguities in Melanchthon's positions after the fashion of the late nineteenth century.

38. Schultz, op. cit., p. 14.

Hans Engelland (essay date 1965)

SOURCE: Engelland, Hans. Introduction to *Melanchthon on Christian Doctrine: Loci Communes 1555,* translated and edited by Clyde L. Manschreck, pp. xxv-xlii. New York: Oxford University Press, 1965.

[*In this essay, Engelland compares Melanchthon's approaches to theology in his earlier and later works and considers some controversial questions of scriptural interpretation in Melanchthon's writings.*]

On the twenty-ninth of August, 1518, Philip Melanchthon, a small, slender, unpretentious, almost timid figure, entered the Wittenberg Castle Church, which served as the great hall of Wittenberg University, and walked to the rostrum to give his inaugural speech on the reform of university education, *De corrigendis adolescentiae studiis.* It inaugurated a career that was to influence not only higher education but theology and the Church as well, for Melanchthon's influence brought about a spiritual outlook in Germany's evangelical universities that lasted for one hundred and fifty years, until the time of Wolffianism. Through the universities and the secondary institutions of learning which he created, his influence extended throughout the spiritual life of Germany.

Melanchthon, the son of an armorer, George Schwartzerd, was born on February 16, 1497, at Bretten in the Palatinate. He was the great-nephew of the famous humanist Johann Reuchlin, on whose recommendation he had been called to Wittenberg to the faculty of arts, and therefore to philosophy, to teach the Greek language and literature. However, he turned toward Luther and, in doing so, to theology. Early in the first year he stepped out of his specialized field by undertaking to interpret the Letter of the Apostle Paul to Titus, in addition to teaching Homer, whom he especially loved. In the following year, on September 19, 1519, after he was granted the degree of Bachelor of Theology, he began lecturing more in theology than in his own field; he offered lecture courses on Genesis and the

Psalms, the Gospels of Matthew and John, Colossians, First and Second Corinthians, and, above all, Romans, a course which between 1519 and 1521 he offered three times. These theological lectures were well attended, the hall often being overcrowded, but he could draw only a few people to his philological courses, which the students often found hard to endure to the end of the semester. Yet in 1524, when Luther begged him to drop classical philology and to give full time to the theological faculty, of which he became a member in 1519, he refused to sever his dual faculty status, a sign from the beginning that he objected to faculty barriers.

Melanchthon enlarged his range of interests to include all the sciences, many of which he treated in his lectures. Like the later Leibnitz, he was a historian of many parts [*ein Polyhistor*]: he wrote many Latin speeches [*Declamationes*], which had historical content and revealed political understanding, as, for example, when he spoke on the election of Charles V; he revised the Chronicle of Carion, a world as well as a church history; and he edited the historical works of writers of antiquity, like Tacitus' *Germania,* which he valued highly. As a philologist he edited many Latin and Greek authors, often translating the Greek into Latin and interpreting it [*Ennarationes*], as he did some of the speeches of Demosthenes, passages from Homer, and the ethical and political writings of Aristotle. He dealt with juridical and medical themes and wrote on psychology, which he based on contemporary knowledge of anatomy. In the sphere of the natural arts, he delved into astronomy, geography, geometry, arithmetic, anatomy, and botany; he even wrote a book on physics, the focal point of which was astronomy. He did not acquire his medical knowledge in the lecture hall on anatomy or at the sickbed, for he studied Galen's works and other writings in accordance with the customary humanistic veneration of antiquity; nevertheless, he did not obtain all his knowledge from books. He knew the importance of personal observation, whether in the hall of anatomy or in the observatory. His lectures were enriched not only by the literary works which gave them a continuity with the past, but also by a vast exchange of letters with foreign scholars, princes, and kings. Thus Melanchthon personified the whole university in his time. In his person he became a symbol of the *universitas litterarum.* After his death this was even more evident, for his lectures on exegesis, ethics, philology, and history had to be divided among four men.

THE APPROACH TO THEOLOGY IN THE OLDER
MELANCHTHON

THE THEOLOGICAL TASK OF ALL THE SCIENCES

Melanchthon's interest in all the sciences was ultimately motivated, not by an interest simply in man, but by his belief that the sciences all have a common theological task. In their common obligation they encounter one another; each is obligated to lead mankind to the knowledge of God.

According to Melanchthon's *Physics* (1549), the exploration of nature allows us to discover guides for spiritual living, especially in medical science, where we find arguments for refuting not only the Epicurean denial of God and his providence but also stoical determinism.[1] Even in his textbooks on physics he treats the question of the existence and providence of God, beginning his proofs for God with a causal conclusion a posteriori from ascertainable effects in nature produced by God.[2] In his *Dialectics* (1547) Melanchthon holds that the main task of the art of correct, orderly, clear teaching is to instruct mankind in the knowledge of God, the virtuous life, and the contemplation of nature.[3] Arithmetic should point to the unity of God and so guard against polytheism. We should "discern numbers in such a way that, if we hear of the unity of the Holy Father and of our Lord Jesus Christ, we do not conclude there are innumerable gods."[4] In the same manner geometry, which is so closely connected with arithmetic, should not exhaust itself in its practical applications, but should lift our eyes from earth to heaven and indicate to us the wonderful work and management of the world.[5] To be complete, astronomy must go beyond a consideration of the heavens to a contemplation of creation and the providence of God, and from this to virtue: "The laws of motion bear witness to the fact that the world did not originate through accident but was created by an eternal Spirit, and human nature stems from the heart of this Creator."[6] In the same manner Melanchthon turned toward astrology not only for its utility in the curing of diseases and the guiding of states but also for its religious lessons, for he saw in the "heavenly signs" an oracle of God which should not be despised.[7] The study of geography is "necessary in order to know God's ordering of kingdoms, where and when he manifested himself, left his imprint and made known his testimony, so that we may recognize the truth of his teaching and appropriate it."[8] Historical science, to be sure, has "worldly utility" in view, but over and above this, in an ethical, pedagogical sense, the task of historical science is finally religious; we learn from historical science about the beginning and course of religion, and about such things as the Church's doctrinal controversies and how they were decided; and without historical science we can hardly comprehend the prophets and the Holy Scriptures.[9] The task of philology also extends beyond the communication of the spoken word, for the Latin and Greek languages are not only receptacles of earthly things, but also of "heavenly doctrines." Greek makes possible a talk with the Son of God, with the evangelists and apostles, "without an interpreter"; it alone opens the way to the history of the Christian Church and to doctrine in the first centuries; and the knowledge of Hebrew is requisite for the Old Testament.[10] And finally, philosophical ethics should not only lead to an external ordering of human life but also to the knowledge of God, to which it should conduct us by its distinctions between good and evil and questions about the goals of men.[11]

The sciences in their totality are somewhat like a huge mountain which from all sides aspires to and is complete in a single peak—the knowledge of God. The individual sciences have their specific places on the circle of knowledge, but all are turned to a common center—the knowledge of God. Thus they have a common spiritual orientation in which we can perceive their final unity, even though they approach it [the knowledge of God] from different directions. In the praise of God they unite to form one choir, the *integer artium chorus*.[12]

THE FOUNDATION OF THE KNOWLEDGE OF ALL THE SCIENCES

The synopsis of the sciences just given rests upon a common fundamental assumption, upon a certain theory of knowledge, derived from a Ciceronian concept, for Melanchthon developed his idea of knowledge on the basis of the "natural light" in man, *naturalis lux in intellectu,* or *lux humani ingenii,* or *lumen divinitus insitum mentibus.*[13] This "natural light" is the basis for certitude in all the sciences. It coincides with the general experience of man, the *experientia universalis,* which is perceived by the senses, and it is common to all men of sound mind in a similar manner. For example, fire is hot. Second, he developed his idea of knowledge on the basis of innate, ultimate presuppositions of knowledge, the *notitiae nobiscum nascentes,* the source of the individual sciences, through which they are known and made clear, and in which we concur without further confirmation.[14] Melanchthon divided the *notitiae nobiscum nascentes* into ultimate presuppositions of thought, the *principia speculabilia* of physics and mathematics (for example, the whole is greater than any of its parts); and the ultimate presuppositions of action, the *principia practica* of ethics, which direct the moral life and above all require distinctions between good and evil.[15] Third, the "natural light" renders possible syllogistic thought, through which we are able to bring together those things which belong together and to separate those which do not agree.[16]

From this spiritual predisposition the innate *notitiae* lead to a consciousness of God; for this reason Melanchthon considers the atheist a deliberate liar.[17] With the help of the "natural light" he attempts to establish proof of God, and actually sets forth nine arguments. By virtue of the *principia speculabilia* it is possible to reason a posteriori from perceptible effects to God as the cause, and by virtue of the *principia practica,* to take for granted an immediate consciousness of God, which consists in the natural faculty to distinguish between good and evil and in a consciousness that we should obey God and be punished for disobedience. This immediate consciousness of God should actually be as clear and certain in us as the principles of thought which remain immutable, but man's defection from God created a barrier between man's heart and mind, and the heart is now moved by impulses contrary to the innate judgments about good and evil; consequently, men hesitate to approve the innate judgments. However, as this "divine light in the soul" cannot be extinguished, it should be "strongly aroused and the sense of it fortified so that we recognize, assert and confirm that the practical principles are just as sure and certain as the principles of thought, or even the immutable judgments of God."[18]

Melanchthon perceives this ethical-religious predisposition in the idea of the image of God, which though distorted after the Fall, nevertheless found expression, especially in the idea of law. Melanchthon then distinguishes divine, natural, and human law. The divine law is the law that God has imprinted on the human spirit as an "external and immutable precept of the divine spirit, a judgment against sin,"[19] often proclaimed in God's word. The law of nature, which is given in the *principia practica* and which Melanchthon defines as a "natural knowledge of God and our guide in morality or judgment about good and evil, which is implanted by God in mankind like the knowledge of numbers," is the order in nature which corresponds with the moral part of God's law, summarized in the Decalogue. Thus Melanchthon can describe the law of nature as a "knowledge of divine law implanted in human nature."[20]

For his first proof for God Melanchthon turns to nature, where he beholds an order which, he says, could not have been brought about by an accident nor a development of matter, but only by an orderly Spirit. His second proof is derived from the rational nature of man, which he says can take its origin only from that which is rational. The third follows a posteriori from the natural power to distinguish between good and evil, order and number; a Spirit must be the architect of such power. Fourth, the existence of God follows (a posteriori) from the natural belief of all men in God, a *notitia naturalis.* Fifth, the conclusion (a posteriori) from the transgressor's qualms of conscience is that a Spirit has ordained this judgment. Sixth, the conclusion (a posteriori) from political society is that an "eternal Spirit has given man an orderly understanding for the sake of maintaining political community." Seventh, Melanchthon speculates on the sequence of cause and effect, and concludes that the causal series cannot infinitely regress because there would then be no necessary connection of causes; there must be a single first cause. Eighth, purposeful reasoning toward a goal implies the existence of concluding *causae finales,* with God as the originator. Ninth, prophetic announcements of future events indicate that a Spirit announces and points out the changes before they happen.

REASON AND REVELATION, PHILOSOPHY AND THEOLOGY

From this naturalistic approach of Melanchthon's theology it follows that the revelation of God as attested in the Holy Scriptures can have only supplementary significance. Revelation only adds something to that which man himself can and ought to say about God. This fusion of reason and revelation becomes plain in the discussion about the providence of God. The proofs of God should both convince us about the existence of God and indicate certain characteristics in his being, for example, his providential care.[21] However, because the actualities of life do not always appear to reflect God's providence,[22] accepting it is more difficult than accepting God's existence. Therefore, the Biblical word is necessary to awaken and strengthen faith in his providence.[23] Thus, to the knowledge of God's existence revelation adds the certainty of his providential care.

The same complementary relationship between reason and revelation meets us in the idea of God in the doctrine of atonement. Melanchthon starts from the Platonic idea of God, that God is an eternal Spirit and the source of all good in nature, and then explains that "another, clearer, and more conclusive definition of the idea of God must be sought," because he [Plato] still "does not describe God as he has revealed himself." It is necessary to add how God has revealed himself in the Trinitarian manner. In view of the atonement, man knows by virtue of the law of nature that God is just and kind to those who fulfill his will and that he is angry with those who do not. Through the gospel we first come to know that God for Christ's sake wants to be kind even to those who have not deserved it, for he justifies the sinner. This was hidden from Xenophon, Plato, Cicero, and Pompanius Atticus.[24]

Melanchthon co-ordinates revelation and the "natural light" in accordance with this complementary relationship. He says that in the Church, in addition to general experience, principles, and syllogisms, we have "still a fourth standard of certainty, namely, divine revelation, which occurs with clear and indubitable evidence in the prophetic and apostolic books."[25] Melanchthon here places reason and revelation in a coexistence, somewhat like two countries with a common border, living peacefully beside one another. Reason tolerates pretentions to something that is beyond its control and more than logic, something contrary to its knowledge, God; it tolerates a way of knowledge that is independent of general experience and logical axioms; for its part, revelation foregoes exclusive jurisdiction in questions about God and concerns itself with the function of completeness. Neither is limited, threatened, or repressed by the other.

Reason does not feel itself threatened by the fact that in its assertions revelation claims mathematical certainty. Just as every man of sound will should be certain that two times four equals eight, "so should the articles of faith, the divine warnings and promises, be for us certain and unshakable; and the one who does wrong should be just as certain that sins are forgiven for the sake of the Son of God, for whose sake he is heard and is an heir of eternal life. However, the grounds for the certainty are different. Reason grasps statements about numbers according to its own judgment. However the articles of faith are certain on account of the revelation which God has confirmed through sure and clear evidence, such as resurrection of the dead and many other wonders."[26]

This complementary relationship between reason and revelation consequently determines the relation of theology to philosophy as well as to all the sciences.[27] Theology, based in Biblical revelation, enlarges the natural knowledge of God in philosophy, and in this way *Heilsgeschichte* determines the construction of dogmatics.[28] But this revealed knowledge of God in history is removed from philosophy's method of proof, which always starts from experience and principles.[29] Therefore, theology and philosophy are to be differentiated; they may not be mixed together like broth in the kitchen.[30]

However, though one cannot demonstrate revelation, one need not renounce methodical thought; it gives theology its scientific character, and without it theology would become an *inerudita theologia,* "in which important things will not be developed in an orderly manner, in which things that should be separated will be mixed, and things that according to their natures should be combined will be separated, and in which conflicting things will often be said, the immediate seen as truth, and peculiarities affected. . . . Nothing will hang together in it. One will perceive neither the point of departure nor the steps of progress nor the conclusion."[31] For this reason, in its conceptualizing theology must be able to define, limit, compare, and deduce.[32] It requires primarily dialectics in order to obtain a *methodus et forma orationis,*[33] a method and style of speaking, but it also needs the other sciences, especially physics and philosophical ethics, both to form concepts and acquire the contents of their knowledge, for example, their views of the soul or the will. Philosophy thus becomes the helpmate of theology,[34] its sciences, the *adminiscula in doctrina coelesti,*[35] an admission to divine doctrine.

It is a fascinating spiritual structure which Melanchthon instituted and in which many generations of young people grew up. He projected it on one single goal of thought—knowledge of God. It served the schools and universities, and in it they saw their particular mission. And this structure was based on a single assumption, that "natural light" is capable of knowledge of God.

With this doctrine of "natural light" Melanchthon gave the university a firm spiritual foundation and united all its sciences as fully as possible with the Christian faith. He first became *Praeceptor Germaniae* through this system of science.

The question concerning the rightness or wrongness of this naturalistic approach in his theology is posed by Melanchthon himself through an original and different approach in his **Loci Communes** of 1521, the first systematic theology of the evangelical Church.

THE APPROACH TO THEOLOGY IN THE YOUNG MELANCHTHON

In the young Melanchthon we encounter a completely different approach, manifested, of course, in the chapter on sin in his **Loci Communes** of 1521, in the reaction of God to the Fall of man. The question is whether man's departure from God only weakened and wounded the religious capacities of man, or whether it destroyed the spiritual bond with God so that man in a natural sense has completely lost God as the Creator and Sustainer.

Melanchthon sees the reaction of God in the departure of God's Spirit. "When God created man without sin, he was with him through his Spirit in order to move him to the right actions. This Spirit would have guided all the descendants of Adam if Adam had not fallen. But after Adam fell, God immediately turned aside from man, and would not be his guide."[36] This departure of the Spirit put an end to the spiritual union between God and man and had the following consequences:

1. *For the knowledge of men.* Melanchthon speaks of the consequences of this departure for knowledge in the chapter on "justification and faith." The theological position of his assertions is very significant, for he indicates that the capacity for knowledge with regard to the departure of God's Spirit is also related to the capacity for will and action. Single-handedly among the reformers, the young Melanchthon destroys the strict equilibrium between all the natural sciences. He sees in the question about the activity of God, in contrast to his later viewpoint, a genuine, yes, a cardinal question, which he expresses in his explanation of Genesis in 1523: "Is there a God? Was this world created by a divine power? Is it regulated by a divine being?"[37]

Melanchthon's answer actually undercuts the two ways to a natural knowledge of God which were known to him in the philosophical and theological tradition, the way from nature and the way from men.

First, the knowing of God from nature: Man "cannot comprehend the creation and the guidance of the world, and he supposes that things happen, originate, perish,

and recur accidentally. Thus thinks the flesh in all." Or man thinks that "the ordered and regulated movements" are "but the course of nature which we see. What does God have to do with small and limited creatures? Each thing maintains itself by its own strength."[38] "Though you constantly read and reread, and even wallow in sacred books and doctrines, nevertheless reason [*Verstand*] will never thus believe that God exists, that he is merciful and just. You may hear the words and you may hypocritically imitate the words of Spirit, but in actuality you will not understand, and you will but uphold God's existence as poetic fiction. Human blindness is a deep abyss." After this Melanchthon comes to his basic declaration: "God's existence, God's anger, God's compassion are spiritual things, and therefore they cannot be known by the flesh."[39] For this reason, "the belief that everything is ruled through divine providence and that nothing happens accidentally undercuts our reason, which denies the existence of God and his care for us." To the being of God belongs not only "spiritual things" but also his existence. This means positively, "only as God affects our hearts and indicates with regard to creation that from him and in him and through him everything is can the heart receive trust in God."[40]

In the second place Melanchthon takes the possibility of the knowledge of God out of the natural conscience and thus denies that conscience is able by itself to know God and his will. Here emerges the problem of natural law. Melanchthon distinguishes three laws, the law requiring the honoring of God, the law prohibiting the harming of anyone, and the law enjoining the using of all things commonly. He draws the second and third law from the communal life of man, and the first, from Scripture, from Romans 1:20. Although he is convinced that Paul himself dealt with God's existence under the laws of nature, he considers it curiosity rather than piety to argue that God's existence can be concluded from a rational proposition. The meaning is still clearer in the altered second edition of the **Loci Communes** in 1522: "Human reason easily infers the last two laws, but how it could infer the first law, I cannot see, since reason was so darkened after the fall of Adam. . . . How the first law is to be included among the laws of nature, let others judge. Hebrews 11 says that creation is known through faith."[41] Melanchthon very plainly denies knowledge of God through natural law in the section on the gospel, in which he even takes away the aspects of natural law in the second law; indeed, he dispenses with the notion of natural law: "In addition to the natural law with which God impressed the spirit of man, God also, I believe, gave laws to Adam forbidding the taking of the fruit from the tree of knowledge and to Cain forbidding anger with or sin against his brother lest he murder him. In this manner the Spirit of God renews the knowledge of natural law that became obscured in nature because the spirit of man became blind through sin. Therefore, I would almost prefer to call the law of nature not a judgment which is innate or implanted or impressed on the spirit of man by nature, but commandments which we receive from our ancestors and then pass on, as it were from hand to hand, to our descendants. As Adam instructed his descendants with respect to the creation of the world and the honoring of God, so he admonished Cain not to kill his brother."[42] Adam did not simply awaken some remembrance of something that was in Cain from the beginning, something lying dormant in his nature. He did not revive a law of nature which had faded like an old writing; instead, he said something unknown and new. For certainty concerning God's activity Melanchthon looks back both to the certainty and the mystery of God, which need proclamation through the word.

Melanchthon goes a step further. He makes a sharp religious judgment on the value of all attempts of man to confirm the existence and will of God by means of the two ways of natural knowledge. They not only do not lead to the desired goal, but actually are an expression of revolt against God. "What is known about the nature of God without the Spirit of God, which renews and illuminates our hearts, is no more than cold thought, certainly not faith, and for this reason nothing but sham and hypocrisy, ignorance concerning God, and contempt, even though the eyes of flesh do not see this hypocrisy. The Spirit sets everything in order."[43] Proofs of God are but disdain and disbelief concerning the majesty of God. Neither belief nor disbelief can be substantiated or refuted by proofs.

2. *For the will and action of man.* In turning from God man turned to himself, and is now ruled by the basic emotion of self-love. This *amor sui* "is the first and strongest basic motive ruling the nature of man (*primus affectus et summus naturae hominis*); it overpowers him, and for its sake he seeks and desires only that which seems to his nature good, pleasant, sweet, and glorious; he hates and fears whatever appears hostile to him; he avoids whatever opposes or whatever dictates to him; he does not pursue and seek what is not pleasing to him."[44] Because man does not have this basic emotion under control, he cannot freely choose to hate and to love; his love ends when one whom he may have loved up to that moment injures him.[45]

From this necessarily followed an antithesis to the scholastic theology which at that time confronted the reformers, especially in William of Ockham and Gabriel Biel. Men thought that the nature of man was not injured through the departure of God, which meant that, as in the beginning, man still had the freedom in himself to call forth good acts, *actus bonos elicere,*[46] even the freedom to love God above all else.[47] This view said that man had to take the first steps on the way to justification and to dispose himself thereby for justification, as proclaimed in the classical sentence, "Do that which

is given to you to do, and then God will give you his grace."[48] Melanchthon answers that man's self-love engenders additional hatred of God, for God is like a consuming fire to man. Only the compassion of God is able to overcome this hate, a compassion which produces a new affection of love for God so that man cannot but love God and return his love (*redamare deum*). No one can hate sin and repent except through the Holy Spirit.[49]

Thus Melanchthon establishes the impotence of man apart from God both in his knowledge of God and in his ability to will and act in accordance with God's command. For this reason, only God, through his Spirit, can again restore man. The approach of Melanchthon is thus not to define ever more closely what is human so as to have an analogy of God, but to return to the Spirit of God, for only the Spirit of God as it speaks to man in the word is able to direct his knowledge and will and action back to God.

Looking in retrospect on the approach through the "natural light," we must confirm that Melanchthon in his later theology de-emphasized the activity of the Spirit of God in man. The contours of tradition, which at first faded and were obscured by the brilliant light of the new knowledge, later came forward again. The consequences of the Fall from God are no longer universally understood, instead the "natural light" in man is a kind of sphere attributed to the Holy Spirit, as we saw in the question about the knowledge of God. This shaking change clearly appears for the first time in Melanchthon's commentary on Romans in 1532. Here for the first time we meet the proofs of God presented above, but, as in the *Loci* of 1535, only the first six; in the revision of the *Loci* of 1543-44 the proofs are enlarged to nine. Melanchthon never explicitly expressed the reason for this turnabout. Perhaps it was a defense against the enthusiasts, with their doctrine of the Spirit apart from the word, or an ethical-pedagogical interest over against their hostility to education, or perhaps a demand for a starting point for the proclamation of the gospel or for the study of the ancient philosophers, or perhaps all these motives combined.

Controversial Questions in the Interpretation of Melanchthon

The Relation of the Acts of God and the Acts of Men

The return to an approach to theology through man, with which Melanchthon returned to tradition, poses first of all the question as to whether this affected the central article of the Reformation concerning justification, and whether, with regard to the fulfillment of the law and the appropriation of salvation, a synergism penetrated Melanchthon's thinking.

With regard to the Decalogue, which now is understood as a short explanation and interpretation of the law of nature, man in his natural strength can fulfill only the second table, and that only in an external sense as *iustitia civilis* or *disciplina externa*. But Melanchthon had many reservations about the practical realization of this, because he saw it threatened by the weakness of original sin and by the power of Satan,[50] so that man even in this *disciplina externa* might easily fall if God were not preserving him.[51] Man is not able fully, in an inward sense, to fulfill the will of God, not even able to begin to do so.[52] "Without the Holy Spirit he cannot bring about the spiritual affections, which God demands, namely true fear of God, true trust in the compassion of God, true love of God, and patience and bravery in affliction and death."[53]

From this it is not to be expected that Melanchthon would be able to concede to assimilating grace in the natural will. He made several statements which, though misunderstood, in any case occasioned the suspicion of synergism, especially in his assertion of the three causes concurrently working together—the word of God, the Holy Spirit, and the will of man, which agrees with and does not resist the word of God. Yes, he could take over the formula of the "old"; the will is free in its ability to conform to grace (*facultas applicandi se ad gratiam*), "that is, it hears the promise and tries to agree and to end its deliberate sinning against conscience."[54] However, Melanchthon is speaking in the first assertion about the three causes which concurrently work together, not of a natural will but of a will that agrees, and he is thinking in the second of one who is already reborn, as a conversation recorded by Jacob Runge shows.[55] Many similar remarks corroborate this. "Trust and joy in the heart are the immediate works of the Holy Spirit."[56] The will is active in conversion "in so far as God has healed it" (*quatenus sanari divinitus coepit*).[57] Any nonresistance of the will results from the inducement of the Holy Spirit.[58] Yes, God works during and after the conversion, and so the will is not active; it remains purely passive. "It is very useful to know this rule about the Holy Spirit, for it is true that God effects much wonderful enlightenment and activity in conversion and throughout the lives of saints, which the human will only accepts, in which it is not a co-worker but holds its own passively. Nevertheless, we must be taught in all our anxious temptations to consider the word of God; we must plead for his help and ask him to strengthen us with his word," and "in this struggle the will is not inactive" (*in hoc certamine voluntas non est otiosa*).[59]

These and similar assertions make it appear questionable that Melanchthon really advocates a form of synergism when he speaks of the activity of the will. The assertions in which he speaks unqualifiedly and mistakenly are to be understood in accordance with the context in which he stood. He himself names as adversaries the enthusiasts and the Manicheans who make the *ministerium evangelicum* useless, and he energetically

rejects the misunderstanding that the Holy Spirit deals with man as with a statue, a piece of wood, or a stone.[60] God works in man not only in time of crisis but at all times, which means that God works in ways that cannot be described in logical thought patterns but only paradoxically, with the result that faith in one dimension appears to be the decision of the Holy Spirit, and in the other dimension, the decision of man.[61] But in Melanchthon's speeches about the activity of man still another motive appears. Many assertions have a pastoral character; he intends them to help in time of despondency and resignation, to assist in a resolution unto faith. "I cannot, you say. On the contrary, you can, in a certain manner. When the voice of the gospel rises in you, then ask God for help and comfort yourself that the Holy Spirit is active in this, that in this way God wants to convert. In view of his promises we should make an effort, call on him, and struggle against our mistrust and other destructive emotions."[62]

THE RELATION OF JUSTIFICATION AND SANCTIFICATION

A second question is whether Melanchthon later gave up the unity of justification and sanctification,[63] which he originally taught when he joined Luther, thereby separating *regeneratio* from *iustificatio* and treating it as a second act of God, and understanding *iustificatio* itself as a mere *imputatio* of the *aliena iustitia Christi*, as mere forgiveness of sins.

Melanchthon often speaks of justification as mere forgiveness or imputation of the righteousness of Christ or acceptance by God or a declaration of righteousness—without even mentioning sanctification. However, he does not intend to exclude sanctification but to console the terrified conscience under the judgment of God (*conscientia perterrefacta*) and to avert any Roman Catholic misunderstanding.

That basically he did not separate sanctification from justification is plain from the manner in which he speaks of Christ's mission. In the editions of the *Loci* after 1543-44 he says Christ came "in order to forgive us our sins and to begin in us new righteousness and eternal life through the Holy Spirit."[64] "Christ is our righteousness, that is, we are not righteous because the Son of the Eternal is righteous, but because his merit is credited to us for the forgiveness of sins and for reconciliation, and because he works a renewal in us, which some day in the eternal life will be complete righteousness."[65] He is "our righteousness, sanctification, and redemption, namely through his merit, his presence, and his strong activity in us."[66]

Because Melanchthon maintains this unity of forgiveness and sanctification in the mission of Christ, it recurs also in many of his teachings about justification. The new obedience must begin "because we are justified and our sins are annulled, and with that the new and eternal life actually begins in us, which is a new light and obedience toward God."[67] However, sanctification is not only the goal of justification but also its content. "Justification itself always brings new life and obedience with it," and "the beginning of renewal always happens at the same time as justification."[68] Those who believe in the gospel "are justified, that is, through the Son and for the sake of the Son are received in faith and through him by virtue of the Holy Spirit are sanctified to eternal life." We are justified by faith "by virtue of the justice which God imputed for the sake of his Son and through the beginning of a new, pure life."[69] Righteousness is "reconciliation or imputation of righteousness through the God who declares us justified for the sake of his Son, and the gift and the activity of that righteousness and that life in us will be eternal." Thus Melanchthon includes sanctification in justification when he speaks with the Holy Scriptures of righteousness in the complete meaning of the word, *de toto beneficio*.[70] However, even if he had spoken only about forgiveness in the case of justification, sanctification would have been decided for him, for forgiveness means not only that God does not impute the sins, but also that it includes "at the same time the gift of the Holy Spirit, eternal life, and all the promises of the gospel that God grants to us as acceptors, assisting us and sheltering us. In short, all the benefits of the gospel (*omnia beneficia Evangelii*) are included in the idea of the forgiveness of sins."[71] Forgiveness and sanctification are like the light and warmth of the sun: "the world grows bright and warm in the sun; nevertheless, light and warmth are in themselves different."[72] Thus Melanchthon reproved Osiander only for his Catholic manner of speaking, not for his inclusion of sanctification in justification. In this way he protected the unity of justification and sanctification.

PREDESTINATION

A third question is whether Melanchthon later gave up predestination; originally he had joined with Luther in decisively advocating it.

Note first that he refers to the universality of the promises of salvation and blames man's debt on a miscarriage of the human will only, because God is not *causa peccati*, and in him is no *contradictoriae voluntates*. On the other hand, there seem to be assertions which do not fit within these limits. In the commentary on Romans in 1556 he answers the question, Why are so many men lost and so few saved, and why must the Church suffer in so many ways? "Not all the plans of God can be understood by human thought, but we must sustain ourselves in the revealed word of God. . . . Someday in the eternal school we will learn the reason for the divine plan."[73] In this connection he often speaks of a hidden decree of God (*arcanum dei decretum, consilium*

arcanum), or of the hidden majesty (*arcana maiestas*). In view of God's decision with respect to Esau and Jacob, he declares that the same measure for measure is to be given only in the case of an obligation. "In the case of a gift or of compassion, it is not necessary to grant in the same measure."[74] "The sentence which says that there is an eternal election is true, and nevertheless it also remains true that we are not to investigate election without the word of God or beyond the word of God."[75] "We should agree to the word, even if we are not able to see all the connections in what is presented contradictorily" (*quae se in contrarium offerunt*).[76] "You must know that you should not judge a priori about your election, but a posteriori, that is, you are not to search in the hidden counsel of God to discover whether you are elected, you are to search in the revealed word."[77]

These statements indicate that Melanchthon does not reject predestination in principle—even in the sense of reprobation, but admonishes practically and pastorally about it. This would mean that a responsible decision of man and a sovereign decision of God take place simultaneously in the acceptance or rejection of salvation. In this assertion of dual activity Melanchthon is speaking in a paradoxical way, as he does in the question about the relation of the acts of God and of man in the formation of faith.

Melanchthon, therefore, stands theologically nearer to Luther than the traditional view indicates. The important theological deficiencies of the time following Melanchthon are more the responsibility of students who fragmented what he had fused.

In the teaching of the Lord's Supper Melanchthon may be distinguished from Luther in the fact that he established the real presence of Christ as an ever-searching presence [*Multivolipräsenz*]. In his teachings on the Church, he vigorously clarified the Church's jurisdiction, so that afterward within orthodoxy the so-called pastoral churches could develop. And through raising the state to the guardianship of both tables of the Decalogue, he introduced a development that later expressed itself in the tenet "*Cuius regio eius religio*" and in the state church [*Staatskirchentum*]. And finally, the enlightenment of the school of Christian Wolff, with its proofs of God and its combination of reason and revelation, can be traced directly back to Melanchthon.

Notes

1. [*Corpus Reformatorum* (hereafter cited as *CR*)] 13:190.

2. *CR* 13:200.

3. *CR* 12:513.

4. *CR* 13:657.

5. *CR* 3:108.

6. *CR* 11:297.

7. *CR* 11:265.

8. *CR* 9:481.

9. *CR* 3:481, 877 f., 882.

10. *CR* 11:859, 709.

11. *CR* 16:166 ff., 171 f.

12. *CR* 11:414.

13. *CR* 13:150, 647; 21:712.

14. *CR* 13:647 f.

15. *CR* 13:649; 21:711.

16. *CR* 13:648.

17. *CR* 15:565.

18. *CR* 21:641 ff., 711 f.

19. *CR* 21:712, 686, 687.

20. *CR* 13:649 f.; 21:687 f., 712.

21. *CR* 21:643.

22. *CR* 13:203.

23. *CR* 21:641.

24. *CR* 21:610, 733, 291.

25. *CR* 13:150 f.

26. *CR* 21:604 f.

27. *CR* 12:689.

28. *CR* 21:605 f.

29. *CR* 21:603 f.

30. *CR* 11:282.

31. *CR* 11:280.

32. *CR* 7:577.

33. *CR* 11:654, 280.

34. *CR* 11:282.

35. *CR* 13:657.

36. *CR* 21:97.

37. *CR* 13:761.

38. *CR* 13:761, 767.

39. *CR* 21:94, 160.

40. *CR* 13:762.

41. *CR* 21:117 f.

42. *CR* 21:140.

43. *CR* 21:160.

44. *CR* 21:98.

45. *CR* 21:90.

46. *CR* 21:91.

47. *Melanchthons Werke*, II, 1, *Loci communes von 1521,* Hans Engelland, ed. (Gütersloh, 1952), 31, n. 19.

48. *Ibid.*, 33, n. 27.

49. *CR* 21:98, 154.

50. *CR* 21:392, 401, 655.

51. *CR* 25:328.

52. *CR* 15:950.

53. *CR* 21:656.

54. *CR* 21.658 f.

55. *Cf.* A. Herrlinger, *Die Theologie Melanchthons in ihrer geschichtlichen Entwicklung* (Gotha, 1879), 92; Fr. H. R. Frank, *Die Theologie der Konkordienformel* (Erlangen, 1858), 198.

56. *CR* 15:97.

57. *CR* 24:316.

58. *CR* 15:680.

59. *CR* 9:468; 21:658.

60. *CR* 21:659, 663; 15:329.

61. See "*gleichwohl*" in the quotation in *CR* 9:468.

62. *CR* 21:659.

63. See especially Karl Holl, *Die rechtfertigungslehre im Licht der Geschichte des Protestantismus* (Tübingen, 1923). *Cf.* Karl Holl, *The Cultural Significance of the Reformation,* tr. by Karl and Barbara Hertz and J. H. Lichtblau (New York, 1959).

64. *CR* 21:854.

65. *CR* 12:410, thesis 34.

66. *CR* 8:612.

67. *CR* 13:1342.

68. *CR* 21:442; 28:401.

69. *CR* 14:1185, 579.

70. *CR* 12:410, thesis 39; 7:678 f.

71. *CR* 15:429.

72. *CR* 24:815; 14:86.

73. *CR* 15:997 f.

74. *CR* 15:683, 981.

75. *CR* 25:681.

76. *CR* 24:921.

77. *CR* 24:478.

Wilhelm Pauck (essay date 1969)

SOURCE: Pauck, Wilhelm. "*Loci Communes Theologici*: Editor's Introduction." In *Melanchthon and Bucer,* The Library of Christian Classics, Volume XIX, edited by Wilhelm Pauck, pp. 3-17. Philadelphia: The Westminster Press, 1969.

[In the essay which follows, Pauck surveys Melanchthon's career before examining in detail the purpose and method, theological content, and significance of the Loci Communes.*]*

Philip Melanchthon's work *Loci communes rerum theologicarum (Fundamental Theological Themes)* was first published in December, 1521, in Wittenberg (a little later another edition appeared in Basel). Melanchthon had begun to work on it in 1520, at a time when Martin Luther, his friend and older colleague at the University of Wittenberg, was deeply involved in the conflict with the Roman Catholic Church that his Ninety-five Theses of October 31, 1517, had aroused. On June 15, 1520, Pope Leo X published the bull *Exsurge Domine,* which threatened Luther with excommunication unless he recanted his views. On December 10, 1520, Luther publicly burned a copy of the papal bull in order to demonstrate that he would defy papal authority to the end. Throughout this decisive year, in the course of which the role and responsibility of a reformer were forced upon him, he published the programmatic treatises that summed up his criticisms of the Roman Catholic Church, his conception of the Christian gospel, and his proposals for a reformation of the Church. Through these writings he definitely established himself as the leader of the quickly growing movement of the Reformation. Indeed, his power and influence were then so great that when he went to Worms in the early spring of 1521 in order to be given a hearing before the Diet of the Holy Roman Empire, presided over by the new emperor, Charles V, he was the hero of the German nation, despite the fact that in the meantime the papacy had placed the ban upon him.

During all this time, Melanchthon had been at work on his own compendium of theological fundamentals. Indeed, his printer sent him the galleys of the first parts of his work in April, 1521, when Luther was at Worms awaiting the imperial decision about his case after he had once more and with heroic clarity refused to recant his views. Before the Edict of Worms, which declared him an outcast, was published, Luther was secretly put in safety at Wartburg castle and thus removed from Wittenberg. He did not cease to write and, indeed, he composed some of his most influential works in his isolated retreat, including the German translation of the New Testament, but he could no longer exercise a direct, personal influence upon the affairs either of the town or the University of Wittenberg, though he was in lively touch by correspondence with his friends there. Thus, Melanchthon, who had become one of the staunchest defenders of Luther against his critics and enemies, was drawn into active participation in the first actual efforts for the realization of a reformation in the church. It was under these circumstances that, with considerable strain and difficulty, he completed his *Loci* and finally published the work.

Luther, who had been kept informed by Melanchthon about the progress of his work, hailed it with great enthusiasm, believing that it was one of the clearest statements of the Christian religion ever written. His judgment was to be shared by many, for, as we shall see, it proved to be a great success.

I. THE CAREER OF MELANCHTHON, 1497-1521

In 1521, Philip Melanchthon was a widely respected scholar who enjoyed a great reputation, but he was still a young man in his early twenties.

He was born the son of an armorer, on February 16, 1497, in Bretten in the Palatinate. His father died (probably as a result of having drunk poisoned water) when his son Philip was only eleven years old. Philip, who had received elementary education in the schools of his hometown, then was sent to Pforzheim where his maternal grandmother, a sister of the famous Humanist John Reuchlin, lived. There he completed his preparatory education at the well-known Latin school under the supervision and inspiration of his great-uncle Reuchlin. It was probably at Reuchlin's suggestion that he then adopted the Greek form of his family name Schwarzerd—namely, Melanchthon—as a sign that he wanted to become a Humanist scholar.

By October 14, 1509, he had matriculated at the University of Heidelberg and in less than two years he obtained the degree of Bachelor of Arts (June 18, 1511). It is said that because of his extreme youth he was denied the right to continue his studies at Heidelberg. But on September 17, 1512, he was registered at the University of Tübingen and there, again after an astonishingly short time, he was given the degree of Master of Arts (January 25, 1514). By then he had become an enthusiastic Humanist. Interested in all branches of knowledge, including mathematics and the natural sciences as well as philosophy and theology, he cultivated ancient languages and particularly Greek language and literature, always in the circle of like-minded friends, e.g., John

Oecolampadius and Ambrose Blaurer, the later Reformers of Basel and Constance respectively, and always under the influence of Reuchlin. He edited and translated ancient authors and became an expert Greekist. In May, 1518, when he was twenty-one years old, he published a Greek grammar that was to remain in constant demand as a textbook for many decades. He then planned to prepare a reliable Greek edition of the works of Aristotle.

In the meantime, the University of Wittenberg, founded at the beginning of the century on the frontier of German civilization and not at all famous like the older schools of Heidelberg and Tübingen, was becoming prominent—because of Martin Luther, who, even before he became widely known as the author of the Ninety-five Theses on Indulgences, had played a major role in the reform of theological studies on the basis of Biblical theology. In 1518, the Wittenbergers wanted to introduce the study of Greek and Hebrew into their curriculum. The founder and chief sponsor of the University of Wittenberg, Frederick the Wise, Duke of Saxony, turned to Reuchlin for advice, with the result that Melanchthon was recommended to him. "Among Germans," Reuchlin wrote about his grandnephew, "I know of none who is superior to him, except Erasmus."[1]

Thus Melanchthon was appointed the first professor of Greek at Wittenberg. On August 25, 1518, he arrived in the small town on the river Elbe that was to remain his home for forty-two years, or throughout the rest of his life. Four days later, on August 29, 1518, he delivered his inaugural lecture in the castle-church that served the university as the main assembly hall. He spoke on curriculum reform (*De corrigendis adolescentiae studiis*). Over against the methods of the Scholastics, he demanded the renewal of the old disciplines of dialectics and rhetorics according to the standards of humanistic learning. He made a plea for the study of Greek philosophy, particularly of Aristotle, and expressed the hope that true, authentic learning would bring about a broad moral reform of life. The audience, which included Luther, responded enthusiastically. Luther was full of admiration for Melanchthon's wide knowledge of languages and for the sharpness of his mind. Melanchthon, on his part, quickly came under the spell of Luther's powerful thought and person. In a short time he, the Humanist in whose eyes Erasmus was the greatest of scholars, identified himself with Luther's cause and supported him wholeheartedly.

In June, 1519, he accompanied Luther to Leipzig in order to give him support in his disputation with John Eck. Almost immediately after his return to Wittenberg from Leipzig he wrote and published a report on the discussion in the form of a letter addressed to his friend Oecolampadius—which was highly favorable toward Luther. Eck responded quickly in a tract that was full of contempt for the "grammarian" from Wittenberg. Its title was *Eck's Defense against what Philip Melanchthon, a grammarian from Wittenberg, has falsely ascribed to him concerning the Theological Disputation at Leipzig.*[2] Melanchthon immediately refuted the attack in a brief treatise entitled **Philip Melanchthon's Defense Against John Eck.**[3] It was eloquently written. Full of a biting sharpness, it contained a defense of Luther's rejection of papal authority as well as a forthright assertion of the supremacy of Scripture over all authorities in the church, including the fathers, an assertion that culminated in the exclamation "*Patribus enim credo, quia scripturae credo.*"[4]

Melanchthon, who in the meantime had become not only an ardent admirer but also a personal friend of Luther, thus showed himself to be a Biblical theologian who had adopted Luther's views, and as such a critic of Roman Catholicism and an advocate of the Reformation. He, the Humanist, chose to demonstrate his theological position publicly by preparing himself for the degree of Bachelor of Divinity. On September 9, 1519, he defended twenty-four theological theses[5] which again proved that he was a convinced "Lutheran"; he won the desired degree and with it the marveling plaudits of his friends.

In the same year, he edited Luther's commentaries on The Psalms and on the letter to the Galatians, providing each of them with a preface of his own. Then he began to direct his attention to the letter to the Romans and, in connection with this, to Pauline doctrine. On January 21, 1520, he delivered the oration at the annual academic feast in honor of the apostle Paul[6] (who was the patron of the theological faculty), and from then on he was a Paulinist. He hailed Paul as superior to all philosophers and theologians because, Melanchthon said, he gave the true understanding of Christ and his "benefits" and because his teaching would lead to a right "order of life" (*forma vitae*). In the summer semester of 1519 and in the summer and winter semesters of 1520, Melanchthon taught courses on the letter to the Romans and he wrote treatises on Pauline theology. It was his purpose not only to understand as clearly as possible Paul's theological tenets but also to set them over against and to compare them with the teachings of philosophers and the Scholastic theologians.

The earliest of these writings was *A Theological Introduction to Paul's Epistle to the Romans.*[7] It was characterized by a blanket rejection of philosophy, particularly Aristotelianism. "All philosophy," Melanchthon wrote, "is darkness and untruth" (*tenebrae et mendacia*). It also contained a summary (*summa*) of Paul's argument in Romans that was set over against the doctrines and statements in which Peter Lombard had attempted to summarize the Christian religion (in his *Four Books of Sentences,* which for centuries had been used in the schools as the basic textbook of theology). In 1520, some of Melanchthon's students published, without his knowledge, a "theological summary" that Melanchthon apparently had presented in the classroom as the result of his Pauline studies on the basis of the letter to the Romans. It bore the title *Rerum theologicarum capita seu loci*[8] (*Themes or Basic Topics of Theological Matters*).

Melanchthon was disturbed by this unauthorized and premature publication of what, in his judgment, represented merely a preparatory study or, as he put it, *lucubratiuncula,* i.e., lucubrations, i.e., "studies undertaken by lamplight." He decided, therefore, to publish a revised and enlarged version of such a summary of theology. Thus, after having written still another introductory piece, *De studio doctrinae Paulinae* (1520), he turned to the preparation of *Loci communes.*

It is clear that all these labors, pursued as they were in the context of the deep excitement which Luther's conflict with the authorities and spokesmen of the Roman Catholic Church had aroused, represented Melanchthon's attempt to explain his conversion to "Lutheran" thinking. In all his writings, he demonstrated that he had decided to abandon Scholastic theology in any form and he also gave clear indications of the fact that he had turned away from Humanism, especially its program of intellectual and moral reform, which before his coming to Wittenberg had commanded all his loyalty.

Yet it is an exaggeration to say this. It is true that, during this period of his life, he was as sharply critical of humanistic ideas as he was of Scholastic teachings. But, nevertheless, he continued to be engaged in peculiarly humanistic studies. This seems to prove that though he had transcended his earliest intellectual outlook, he had not given it up entirely. To be sure, he now rejected Aristotle, whose works he had planned to edit just a few years earlier and whose thought, as he stated in his inaugural lecture, he wanted to restore to its pristine power. But, precisely while he was steeped in Pauline studies, he was also involved in efforts to renew the disciplines of dialectics and rhetorics according to the ancient patterns that the leading Humanists, and especially Erasmus, had rediscovered. During the same years that he worked and lectured on Paul, he prepared and published texts on *Dialectics* (1519) and on *Rhetorics* (1520); also, *Institutiones Rhetoricae* (1521).[9] In his dialectical studies he relied chiefly on Aristotle and Cicero, and in his work on rhetorics he was dependent upon Cicero and Quintilian. He believed that the methods of these disciplines had to be applied to literary texts so that they could be properly understood.

As we shall see, in composing his *Loci* he made ample use of these conclusions and thus he remained attached to Humanism after all. We should not be surprised at this, for when he wrote his *Loci,* he was still a very young man, twenty-four years old. His learning and his intellectual accomplishment were amazing,[10] but his thinking was still in flux.

II. THE PURPOSE AND METHOD OF MELANCHTHON'S *LOCI COMMUNES*

In several places in his work, Melanchthon makes quite clear what purposes he had in mind in writing his *Loci.* He says, for example, that he does not want to present a detailed commentary on theological doctrines but is, rather, "sketching a common outline of the topics that you can pursue in your study of Holy Scripture" (p. 70). His major purpose is to "summon" students to the Scriptures and to supply them with "a list [or nomenclature] of the topics to which a person roaming through Scripture should be directed" (p. 19).

However, this purpose is coupled with another one, namely, to demonstrate "how corrupt are all the theological hallucinations of those [i.e., the Scholastics] who have offered us the subtleties of Aristotle instead of the teachings of Christ" (p. 19). Melanchthon is persuaded that the "nature of Christianity" (*forma Christianismi*) can be established only by an analysis of the Scripture for the purpose of finding its "main substance" and "scope" (p. 19) and not by a reliance upon "the judgment of human reason" (p. 19) or upon philosophy. "I think," he writes in concluding his work, "that the commentaries of men on sacred matters must be fled like the plague, because the teaching of the Spirit cannot be drunk in purity except from the Scripture itself" (p. 152). He is persuaded that Christianity has been greatly harmed by the fact that "philosophy has gradually crept" into it: Early Christianity "was weakened by Platonic philosophy" and later the Church "embraced Aristotle instead of Christ" (p. 23). Thus "Christian doctrine" gradually "degenerated into Scholastic trifling" (p. 20).

The fundamental themes that the Bible offers to men for their consideration are "sin, law, and grace" or simply "the law and the gospel." They cannot be dealt with philosophically and they must not be put into a philosophical context. This is what the fathers and the Schoolmen did—with the result that the true understanding of Christ was lost. According to Melanchthon, earlier theologians attempted to state fundamentals, but they failed. For example: Origen tended to allegorize and then developed a "philosophical jargon"; John of Damascus "philosophizes too much" and Peter Lombard "piles up the opinions of men" instead of setting forth "the meaning of Scripture" (p. 20). By contrast, Paul does not "philosophize about the mysteries of the Trinity, [and] the mode of the incarnation" (p. 22).

From all this, Melanchthon derives the conclusion that it is "better" for a theologian "to adore the mysteries of the Deity than to investigate them" (p. 21), and that if one wants to know Christ, one must "know his benefits" (pp. 21 f.).

Thus it can be understood why Melanchthon adopted such a negative attitude toward the Scholastics. It must be noted that he had a wide acquaintance with their writings. As his exposition of the *Loci theologici* shows, he had read Peter Lombard and he had also studied such diverse theologians as Thomas Aquinas and Gabriel Biel. While he was engaged in the preparation of *Loci communes,* he twice undertook to defend Martin Luther against spokesmen of the Roman Catholic Church and advocates of Scholasticism. In each case, he affirmed a Scriptural theology over against the philosophical tradition of the Schools. In February, 1521, he published a reply[11] to an attack that the Roman Dominican Tommaso Rhadino had directed against Luther under the title *Oration to the princes and people of Germany against Martin Luther who violates the glory of his nation.*[12] In October, 1521, Melanchthon spoke up once more in defense of Luther against Scholastic authorities. He wrote a spirited *Defense of Luther against the mad decree of the Parisian theologians,*[13] a condemnation of Luther chiefly directed against Luther's statements in *The Babylonian Captivity of the Church.* Melanchthon vigorously set the authority of the Scripture against that of the tradition which the theologians of Paris had invoked.

Melanchthon's anti-Scholastic attitude, so one must realize, was inspired by his identification with Luther. Hence it is not astonishing that Luther's ideas reverberate throughout the *Loci communes.* Melanchthon's Paulinism was Lutheran, i.e., inspired by Luther. One may legitimately raise the question whether Melanchthon did not depend also upon Augustine.[14] Now, it is characteristic of him that while he sharply criticized Origen, Ambrose, and Jerome, he upheld Augustine. However, he did this because, in his thinking, Luther's authority was coupled with Augustine's. In the latter part of the *Loci,* for example, he refers to Augustine's tract *On the Spirit and the Letter* (which had been so important in Luther's theological development) and he remarks in this connection that he would prefer his readers to consult both Augustine *and* Luther!

It is noteworthy that when Melanchthon refers in the *Loci* specifically to Luther, he quotes from or points to Luther's most recent writings, namely, the treatises (of 1520) on *The Babylonian Captivity of the Church,* on *Good Works,* and on *The Freedom of the Christian Man.* While he was completing his book he became acquainted with the defense that Luther had written of his own teaching on justification, *Against Latomus.* It is apparent that this writing made a deep impression upon Melanchthon, especially because it restated Luther's

thesis about the Christian as *simul peccator ac iustus,* which, as we shall see, caused him considerable difficulty.

In this connection, we should remark that it would be an error to assume that because Melanchthon was so closely attached to Luther, he agreed with him on everything. The differences between the two, which developed later but which, to be sure, were never allowed to bring about a separation, were indicated as early as the first edition of the *Loci,* despite the fact that this work as a whole was conceived as an enthusiastic endorsement of Luther's thought.

This difference of Melanchthon from Luther is due chiefly to the fact that Melanchthon was so deeply concerned with the problem of the right theological method. He was fascinated by the task of developing a "theology of definitions."[15] This interest enabled him to write *Loci communes,* an outline in which the basic teachings of the Lutheran Reformation were summarized and by the influence of which he became and remained for centuries *the* theological teacher of Lutheranism.

Now, this preoccupation with a "theology of definitions" was the result of his humanistic studies and particularly of his admiration for Erasmus and his dependence upon him. It was from Erasmus and other Humanists, perhaps including Rudolf Agricola,[16] that he had learned to rely on the ancient rhetoricians (Cicero) and dialecticians (Aristotle) in order to understand literary works by paying attention to the basic themes and fundamental concepts by which their content was determined. Thus he came to see that the meaning of an author's work cannot be truly comprehended unless one finds (discovers, not invents) the basic ideas which dominate and guide his thinking.

Such a method Erasmus had recommended in several of his writings, particularly in the work *De duplici copia, verborum ac rerum, comentarii duo* (1513) and in his basic treatise on Biblical exegesis, *Ratio seu methodus compendio perveniendi ad veram theologiam.*[17] Indeed, Erasmus had there formulated the following advice: "Organize for yourself collections of *loci theologici.* You can find in the Bible two hundred and even three hundred such concepts. Each one of these must be supported by Biblical passages. *Loci* are little nests in which you place the fruit of your reading."[18] For Erasmus and the Erasmians, this procedure was not only of hermeneutical and rhetorical importance; it was also morally significant. They were persuaded that linguistic and conceptual clarity would lead to or was closely connected with moral clarity—according to the common conviction of the Humanists that the liberal arts or study of the humanities would lead to the actualization of *humanitas.* As Melanchthon put it in his oration *De encomio eloquentiae* (*On the Praise of*

Eloquence) of 1523: "The knowledge of good authors forms not only expression and speech but also the heart (*pectus*)."[19] One is reminded of this when one reads in the Dedicatory Letter the sentence (p. 18): "*Indicantur hic Christianae disciplinae praecipui loci.*" We have translated this as follows: "In this book the principal topics of Christian teaching are pointed out" (pp. 18 f.). We should perhaps say "discipline" instead of "teaching." At any rate, what Melanchthon had in mind here is a teaching with practical, formative consequences. This is proved by the sentence which is part of the same context: "There is nothing I should desire more, if possible, than that all Christians be occupied in greatest freedom with the divine Scriptures alone and be thoroughly transformed into their nature (*indolem*)" (p. 19).

It is clear that Melanchthon was concerned to bring about an "improvement of life" (*emendatio vitae*). In his *Loci communes,* his basic theme was the question why the law is broken and how it can be fulfilled. He could have said then what, in his last letter to Erasmus, he remarked about the second version of the *Loci* (first published in 1535), that he had endeavored to formulate "a reliable doctrine, useful for morals as well as piety."[20]

In this respect, he was, throughout his life, an Erasmian, believing that one studies philosophy, literature, theology, etc., in order to improve life.

However, at least in the first edition of the *Loci,* i.e., during those years of his life when the Protestant Reformation was in the making and when he was most strongly under the influence of Luther, Melanchthon differed from Erasmus by basing his teaching and program on the Bible alone and by rejecting a moral universalism. Moreover, he shared Luther's conviction that human nature is such that if any man, even the best, relies on his own moral powers and on his own religious capacities, he cannot help revealing himself as an unrighteous sinner. This is why he inveighed so sharply against the Scholastics, or 'Sophists,' as he preferred to call them, because of their dependence upon natural morality (the "philosophical virtues") and their advocacy of Aristotle. For the same reason, he criticized Cicero for "deriving the standards for laws ['the laws of nature'] from the nature of man" (p. 50). Instead, he affirms that "the knowledge of these laws" of nature "is not the product of our own mental powers" but that it has "been impressed on our minds by God." Then he goes on to say (and this is the same man who not so long before he wrote this advocated a renewal of Aristotelian studies!): "I am not concerned to make this agree with the philosophy of Aristotle. For what do I care what that wrangler thought?" (p. 50).

In another passage he writes: "You see how deep, rather, how unfathomable, it is, this wickedness of the human heart. Yet our Sophists are not ashamed to teach works

righteousness, satisfactions, and the philosophical virtues. Let it be granted that in Socrates there was a certain constancy, that Xenocrates was chaste, and Zeno temperate. Nevertheless, because these characteristics were in impure minds, and further, because these simulated virtues arose from love of self and love of praise, they ought not to be considered real virtues but vices. Socrates was tolerant, but he was a lover of glory or surely was self-satisfied about virtue. Cato was brave, but because of his love for praise. . . . Cicero in his *De finibus* thinks that all motivation for virtue lies in love of ourselves or love of praise. How much pride and haughtiness are to be found in Plato! In my opinion a temperament lofty and forceful in itself could hardly escape taking on some vice from Plato's ambition if it chanced to read him. The teaching of Aristotle is in general a passion for wrangling, so that it is not appropriate to number him among the writers of hortatory philosophy, not even in the last place" (p. 34).

Such sentences, we must judge, were written in utter deviation from Erasmus. It is understandable why Erasmus turned away from Melanchthon and why in his *Diatribe on Free Will* he sharply attacked him (without, to be sure, identifying him by name).[21]

In the first version of the *Loci,* Melanchthon expressed the conviction that only the forgiveness of God as it is promised in the gospel, and of which one can become assured only through Christ by the Holy Spirit, is the sole source of man's renewal. This is why for him only a Scriptural theology was the true theology, for, as far as he could see, the Scripture alone was the "source" (p. 49) and "standard" (p. 63) of the truth by which men live and must live, and in it the "Holy Spirit expresses himself most accurately and most simply" (p. 46).

III. THE THEOLOGICAL CONTENT OF THE *LOCI COMMUNES*

In this Introduction we must not discuss the entire content of Melanchthon's work, for our purpose should be not to prejudge it for the reader but to help him in understanding it. We shall therefore point out merely those features of Melanchthon's thought which give his work a special character.

Anyone can plainly see that he let Pauline thought as it is expressed mainly in the letters to the Romans and the Galatians determine his teaching. His chief themes are sin and grace and the law and the gospel. Specific doctrines of God and of Christ are not presented (in contrast to later versions of the *Loci* where they reappear). The discussion lacks a certain unity and does not always follow a clearly organized outline. What is offered is not really a "systematic" theology, as it is often asserted.

As we have already indicated, in its constructive as well as its polemical parts the work was inspired by Luther. However, Melanchthon is much less profound and paradoxical, but generally much clearer, than Luther, not only when he deals with justification "by faith and not by works" but also when he is engaged in argument with the "Sophists."

There are some emphases in Melanchthon's teaching that give it a special character. They do not represent anything new or original but they lend a distinctive flavor to his thought. In his discussion of sin and the unfree will, he makes much of the "affections," "the emotions," or "the inner disposition" (*affectus*) (pp. 23, 27 ff.), and he asserts that they are not in the power of either intelligence or will and that they can be changed only by a divine action.

Grace is defined as "God's favor" (*favor Dei*) and as God's goodwill toward us. The Roman Catholic teaching, according to which it is or can be seen as a "quality" in (or infused into) the human soul, is vigorously rejected.

Faith is described as a personal trust in God's promise of forgiveness. As such, it is distinguished from any historical knowledge (p. 91) or opinion. It is seen as the sense of "the mercy of God" (p. 92), indeed, as "an affection of the heart" (p. 90).

What is most characteristic is that in Melanchthon's view the life of the Christian is pointed toward renewal. Hence he tends to see justification, which occurs when one knows that he is forgiven (p. 105), as regeneration under the living power of the Holy Spirit (p. 123). Thus the Christian is seen as being in the process of becoming sanctified (p. 130). The following passage may perhaps be regarded as representative of the basic teaching of Melanchthon as it is expressed in the first edition and version of the *Loci communes*: "Christianity is freedom. . . . Those who have been renewed by the Spirit of Christ now conform voluntarily even without the law to what the law used to command. The law is the will of God; the Holy Spirit is nothing else than the living will of God and its being in action (*agitatio*). Therefore, when we have been regenerated by the Spirit of God, who is the living will of God, we now will spontaneously that very thing which the law used to demand" (p. 123; cf. p. 127). This conception led him to affirm a certain perfectionism: A Christian must not go to court or litigate (p. 128); Christians ought to hold their property in common with all (p. 60). Indeed, Melanchthon regarded as "unhealthy" the view that "public affairs cannot be administered according to the gospel" (pp. 58 f.).

He later changed some of these ideas. Indeed, he was in process of changing them when he completed the writing of the first edition of the *Loci*, for then he was involved in the very practical difficulties and the great diversity of opinion concerning the course of action to be followed which attended the first attempts to actualize a reformation of the church in Wittenberg.

IV. The Publication of the Work and Its Impact

The printing of *Loci communes* was begun in April, 1521, but due to the fact that Melanchthon found himself unable to finish the writing of the text as soon as he had planned, it was not completed until September. Two printings appeared in Wittenberg and another one in Basel. In 1522, a new printing became necessary. Melanchthon introduced several changes into the text. By 1525, eighteen different printings of this edition had been made. A German translation, by Georg Spalatin, was also reprinted several times. A second edition of the work, now much revised and enlarged, appeared in 1535, in Wittenberg; it too was published in several printings by 1541; it was translated into German by Justus Jonas. In the early forties, Melanchthon went to work to rewrite his book completely. The new edition, which was almost four times the size of the first one, was first published (again in Wittenberg) in 1543-1544. It was issued in several printings during Melanchthon's lifetime, the last one of which appeared in 1559. Melanchthon himself translated this third and final version of his main work into German (1555).[22] The book remained alive after Melanchthon's death (1560). The last separate printing of it (apart from editions of Melanchthon's complete works and from modern editions) appeared in 1595.

As these many editions and printings of the *Loci communes* show, it was an extraordinarily successful and influential publication. It gained its great reputation from the first edition, for this was marked by a spirit of immediate enthusiasm, eloquence, and great clarity of diction reflecting the moving power that went forth from the person of Martin Luther.

It is remarkable how highly Luther throughout his life praised the book of his collaborator and friend. In his treatise against Erasmus, he hailed it as a work of immortal significance that deserved to be included in the canon of the church.[23] And, in order to give just one more example, in his Table Talk he said once at the end of his life: "You cannot find anywhere a book which treats the whole of theology so adequately as the *Loci communes* do. . . . Next to Holy Scripture, there is no better book."[24]

Notes

1. Robert Stupperich, *Melanchthon,* German Edition (Berlin, 1960), p 22; English translation (The Westminster Press, 1965), p. 30.

2. *Excusatio Eckii ad ea quae falso sibi Philippus Melanchthon grammaticus Wittenbergensis super Theologica Disputatione Lipsica adscripsit* (Leipzig, 1519).

3. *Melanchthons Werke in Auswahl,* ed. by Robert Stupperich, Vol. I (Gütersloh, 1951), pp. 13-22.

4. "For I believe the fathers because I believe the Scripture." (*Ibid.,* pp. 19, 34.)

5. *Ibid.,* pp. 24 f.

6. *Declamatiuncula in Divi Pauli doctrinam.* (*Ibid.,* pp. 27-43.)

7. *Theologica Institutio Phil. Mel. in Epistulam Pauli ad Romanos* (1519) (*CR,* Vol. 21, cols. 49 ff.).

8. *Ibid.,* cols. 11 ff.

9. Cf. Wilhelm Maurer, *Melanchthons Loci communes von 1521 als wissenschaftliche Programmschrift* in *Lutherjahrbuch* 27 (1960), p. 29.

10. Luther wrote to his mentor and friend Staupitz about Melanchthon's performance in defending his B.D. theses: "He responded in such a way that it seemed to all of us to be a miracle." (*Ita respondit, ut omnibus nobis esset id quod est scilicet miraculum*). Cf. *WA Br.* I, p. 514; also, Stupperich's introduction to the theses in *Melanchthons Werke,* Vol. I, p. 23.

11. *Didymi Faventini adversus Thomam Placentinum pro Martino Luthero theologo oratio* (*Melanchthons Werke,* Vol. I, pp. 56-140). It was at first believed that the author of the Roman writing was the Leipzig theologian Jerome Emser, an old foe of Luther's, and that he had chosen to hide his identity under a pseudonym. Hence, Melanchthon too used a pseudonym, Didymus Faventinus.

12. This is reprinted in *CR,* Vol. 1, cols. 212-262.

13. *Adversus furiosum Parisiensium theologastrorum decretum Phil. Melanchthonis pro Luthero apologia* (*Melanchthons Werke,* Vol. I, pp. 142-162). The declaration of the theological faculty of Paris, entitled *Determinatio theologorum Parisiensium super doctrina Lutheriana,* is reprinted in *CR,* Vol. 1, cols. 366-385.

14. Cf. the highly suggestive essay by Wilhelm Maurer, "Der Einfluss Augustins auf Melanchthons theologische Entwicklung," in *Melanchthon-Studien* (Gütersloh, 1964), pp. 67-102.

15. Cf. Ernst Troeltsch, *Vernunft und Offenbarung bei Johann Gerhard und Melanchthon* (Göttingen, 1891), p. 58.

16. Cf. Paul Joachimsen, *Loci communes. Eine Untersuchung zur Geistesgeschichte des Humanismus und der Reformation,* in *Lutherjahrbuch* 8 (1926), pp. 27-97; W. Maurer, *Melanchthons Loci communes von 1521,* in *Lutherjahrbuch* 27 (1960), pp. 1-50; and Adolf Sperl, *Melanchthon zwischen Humanismus und Reformation,* pp. 21-44, particularly pp. 37 ff.

17. Cf. Hajo Holborn, ed., Erasmus' *Ausgewählte Werke* (Munich, 1933). There is an English translation of *De Copia,* entitled *On Copia of Words and Ideas,* by Donald B. King and H. David Rix (Marquette University Press, 1963).

18. *Ibid.,* pp. 158, 33 ff.; 291, 13 ff. Cf. W. Maurer, *Lutherjahrbuch* 27 (1960), p. 35.

19. Cf. Wilhelm H. Neuser, *Der Ansatz der Theologie Ph. Melanchthons* (Neukirchen, 1957), p. 37.

20. "Firma doctrina et utilis moribus ac pietati," *Opus epistularum Erasmi,* ed. by P. S. Allen (Oxford, 1906 ff.), Vol. XI, p. 323.

21. Cf. Wilhelm Maurer, "*Melanchthons Anteil am Streit zwischen Luther und Erasmus*" in *Melanchthon-Studien,* pp. 137-162, particularly pp. 151 ff.

22. Melanchthon's German version of the *Loci* has been translated into English by Clyde L. Manschreck. It was published in The Library of Protestant Thought under the title *Melanchthon on Christian Doctrine: Loci Communes, 1555* by the Oxford University Press in 1965.

23. *Invictum libellum, meo iudicio non solum immortalitate, sed canone quoque ecclesiastico digno* (*WA* 18, 601,3).

24. *WA Tr,* Vol. V, No. 5511.

Bruce T. Moran (essay date 1973)

SOURCE: Moran, Bruce T. "The Universe of Philip Melanchthon: Criticism and Use of the Copernican Theory." *Comitatus* 4 (1973): 1-23.

[*In the following essay, Moran studies Melanchthon's intellectual background, particularly his ideas about physics and astronomy, and goes on to examine his attitude toward and understanding of Copernican astronomy.*]

In the statutes of 1582 for the University of Altdorf, founded 1578, it is left to the individual judgment of the *mathematici* to expound planetary theory according either to Ptolemy or Copernicus (*vel Ptolemaei vel Copernici*).[1] This concession, that the Copernican hypothesis, as a mathematical construct, is as useful for the description and prediction of planetary movement as the Ptolemaic model, is evidence of a tradition which had long viewed astronomical hypotheses merely as attempts to save appearances rather than as descriptions of the real nature of things. Such a view of the Copernican theory was openly advocated by Philip Melanchthon at the University of Wittenberg. Indeed, Melanchthon's intellectual influence, predominant throughout Lutheran Germany, is particularly apparent at the University of Altdorf. Of the two *Physici* employed in the Faculty of Arts of Altdorf, the first, according to the aforementioned statutes, is to read solely the works of Aristotle, while the second is to read a group of works known collectively as the *Philipus,* i.e., the works of Melanchthon. Such an influence in physics as well as in the interpretation of astronomical hypotheses, has led to the suggestion of a "Wittenberg legacy" which not only encouraged the mathematical utilization of the Copernican theory, but also stimulated astronomical interest and skill in Germany during the latter part of the sixteenth century.[2] The existence of this tradition demands a closer study of those themes which predominate within Melanchthon's own intellectual universe and which bear upon his initial criticism and subsequent utilization of the Copernican theory as a mathematical device.

EPISTEMOLOGY

Any inquiry into particular motives leading to the acceptance or rejection of a new idea must, initially, confront certain fundamental assumptions about the intellect or the natural world which forge the criteria of theory choice. Philip Melanchthon's attitude toward the nature of knowledge, when viewed collectively with his attitude toward the nature of the universe and his position concerning the Copernican hypothesis, reveals a basic component in any relation of a particular psychology to speculative ideas. What Ernst Cassirer has suggested in this regard seems elemental: all our statements about the physical as well as the intellectual world are about ourselves and the peculiarity of our own organization.[3]

For Melanchthon all knowledge is oriented toward a knowledge of God. To this end there is fixed in the mind of man a "natural light" (*naturalis lux in intellectu*)[4] which allows reason and revelation to merge so that divine understanding may be approached through contemplation of the natural world. It is this "natural light," as philosophical intuition, which becomes the arbiter of *both* rational and revealed truth.

"In philosophy and all the arts," writes Melanchthon, "in which the light of human nature judges through itself, there are three precepts of certainty: general experience; principles, or innate ideas within us; and the

knowledge of order in determining consequences."[5] General experience is regarded as ordinary sense perception. That wine and pepper have a certain power to make one hot, and that the motions of the heavens are circular, constitute such sense experiences which are common to all clear thinking persons.

Melanchthon's second precept of intellectual reliability, which he calls "principles," may be characterized as ideas which express *a priori* insight in both the physical and moral realms. They provide, in fact, the means by which all initial assumptions about these two areas of knowledge are formed. "As light is held in the eyes in order to perceive bodies, so like light are these ideas in the mind by which we understand numbers, order, proportions, figures; and by which we form and consider propositions such as: the whole is greater than any of its parts: the cause does not follow its own effect: God is eternal thought, wise, true, just, pure, kind, who preserves the order of things and punishes evil. Moreover, the human intellect was created in this likeness, so that it is said: everyone, in a small image, is a counterpart of God."[6]

Melanchthon now divides these "principles" into two parts: *principia speculabilia* and *principia practica.* *Principia speculabilia,* or visible principles,[7] are represented as the innate presuppositions of mathematics and physics: for instance, that all things equal to one factor are equal also among themselves, and that for one simple body, there is only one natural motion.[8] *Principia practica,* or practical principles, are characterized as inherent moral ideas or propositions "which govern behavior in men, so that human nature may recognize the difference between virtue and shame."[9]

Melanchthon described the third precept of certainty as syllogistic thought, through which similarities and distinctions are recognized, and order is maintained in the operations of the mind.[10]

Thus far, two themes have emerged in Melanchthon's epistemology which are useful in understanding his relation to the new theory of Copernicus. First, Melanchthon's structure of knowledge so closely resembles the "threefold nature of knowledge" found in Neo-Platonism as to be indistinguishable from it. For "general experience," read sense perception; for "the knowledge of order in determining consequences," read dialectical reasoning; and for "principles," read intellectual intuition of essences.[11] In both systems, the primacy of intuition allows the individual to interpret certain symbolic forms as manifestations of divine revelation. This assumption, moreover, permits Melanchthon to view the order of the planets as a projection of divine intent. Consequently, Melanchthon's universe is inherently astrological; and, I shall argue, it is the Aristotelian structure of the world which provides Melanchthon with a cohesive physical explanation of astrological causation. Second, when Melanchthon uses, as an example of *principia speculabilia,* the strict Aristotelian proposition that for one simple body there is only one natural motion, he gives this aspect of the Aristotelian theory of motion the immense power of an innate idea. Thus, since the earth is viewed as a simple body, Melanchthon is destined, from the foundation of his thinking, to collide with the Copernican physical model.

To these three standards of knowledge, Melanchthon adds a fourth. "In the Church," he writes, "we have a fourth precept of certainty, namely, divine revelation, brought about by the enlightened and infallible testimonies which exist in the prophetic and apostolic books. Although human thought more easily and firmly agrees with these revelations which it discerns by natural light, nevertheless all rational creatures ought, just as firmly, to agree with the revealed judgments of God, even if we (do not) for some reason see these truths and powers by that natural light. Indeed, just as we assert without doubt that two times four is eight, so (similarly) one ought to be convinced that God must needs call forth the dead, that the Church shall adorn (the pious) with eternal glory and the unjust shall be cast away into eternal punishment."[12] Revelation, therefore, becomes an extenuation of "natural light," and as such, philosophy and the sciences are viewed as legitimate instruments in the pursuit of divine knowledge.

Melanchthon admits that there are many differences between the teachings of physics and the Bible. "Nevertheless," he writes, "there are many things in the teachings of the Church which are not able to be explained without physics."[13] Melanchthon maintains that without philosophy and the sciences, all religious knowledge corresponds to a mere crude theology (*inerudita theologia*). "It (theology) becomes a disorderly teaching in which essential ideas are not expressed methodically; in which things which ought to be separated are mixed, and, on the other hand, in which those things which by nature demand to be joined are estranged . . . nothing in this system would cohere. Indeed, neither the fundamental elements, nor the progression of ideas, nor even the conclusion could be discerned. Such a doctrine would only produce an infinity of errors."[14]

This divine function of philosophy and the sciences is reminiscent of Thomas Aquinas, who saw that in their relation to theology, "other sciences are called the handmaidens of this one."[15] Indeed, Aquinas appears to have directly influenced Melanchthon's conception of innate principles. There are some sciences, Aquinas writes, "which proceed from principles recognized by the natural light of the intellect such as arithmetic and geometry."[16] The Thomist-realist tradition is fundamental to Melanchthon's epistemology and allows him to proceed, by means of "natural light," from the physical world to a knowledge of God.

Although he felt that certain parts of Aristotle, particularly the notion of the world's eternity,[17] needed to be harmonized with the teachings of the Church, Melanchthon, in general, considered himself an Aristotelian.[18] While at Tübingen, Melanchthon convinced his teacher, Franciscus Stadianus, that the medieval commentators had grossly distorted Aristotle's metaphysics. Consequently, the two set upon the monumental task of producing yet another edition of the *pure* Aristotle in the original Greek text. Before the project was completed, Johannes Reuchlin, Willibald Pirckheimer, Georg Simler, Wolfgang Fabricius Capito and Johannes Husgen (Oecolampadius) had assisted in the endeavor.[19]

But if Melanchthon, on the one hand, could compose an oration on Aristotle, glorifying his life and placing him first in a list of "best authors,"[20] Luther, on the other, could obstinately write: "The whole of Aristotle is to theology as darkness is to light."[21] To be sure, Luther's nominalism prevented any epistemological inferences leading from rational contemplation of natural phenomena to divine understanding. To this end neither reason nor Aristotle could replace the certain knowledge of revelation. Nevertheless, the naive faith in Scriptural revelation as the only source of certain knowledge, characteristic of the thought of Andreas Carlstadt, Gabriel Zwilling and Thomas Münster, led Melanchthon to open hostility. He writes: "I am not disturbed by the clamor of those hypocrites who, under the pretense of religion, censure the investigation of nature and propound aloud that minds are thereby led away from those testimonies which God delivered with his own voice."[22]

MELANCHTHON AND THE SCIENCES AT WITTENBERG

The new teachings of the reformation perplexed and confused many people who had formerly accepted the theological explanations of an established religious hierarchy. Now with spiritual distinctions removed, and each believer a priest unto himself, it became apparent that some type of guidance was necessary from within the reformed Church, not only in matters of Biblical interpretation, but also in the fundamentals of knowledge. But if dogmatism had been deposed, how was one to guide the laity without projecting doctrine? The best approach, Melanchthon thought, was to acquaint everyone with at least the foundations of scientific knowledge. Such knowledge, he believed, when correctly pursued, would inevitably lead to a clearer understanding of the nature of God. It was, however, just such scientific instruction, eclipsed by theological debate, which was missing in the schools. The situation was appalling to Melanchthon, and he designated it as the greatest evil of his time. No other period, he thought, had revolted so much against true education as his own.[23] Somehow, the sciences, which had been neglected at the universities, had to be preserved. Some sanctuary—Nürnberg, Prussia, Wittenberg—free from theological and scriptural prejudice, had to be found. Indeed, Melanchthon called upon all properly educated men to summon everything in their power so that the youth might once again become interested in these studies. For you see, we can almost hear him imploring, a certain degree of knowledge is required before we can grasp the relationship of the surrounding world to ourselves and learn the plan of the eternal creators—the Father, Son and Holy Spirit.[24]

It is undeniable that Melanchthon was greatly troubled by those who regarded the sciences as superfluous to the revealed word of the Bible; but it is also certain that these studies had been almost traditionally ignored in the schools. In a style typical of the *Praeceptor Germaniae,* he writes: "What other did Homer wish to indicate when he painted the heavenly bodies on the shield of Achilles and described the rotation of the heavenly vault, than that the investigation of these things was worthy of the most illustrious men. In the writings of Virgil, Iopas, at a royal banquet sings of the wandering moon and the labors of the sun. It is shameful, however, that these sciences were admired in military camps and at banquets while they were despised, scorned and neglected in the schools to which were entrusted the preservation of philosophy and the protection of the state."[25]

As for the significance of astronomical study, Melanchthon pointedly remarks in the preface to the *Tabulae Astronomicae Resolutae* of Johann Schoner, 1536:

> Let others admire wooden doves or other creations of automata: these tables which indicate the position of every heavenly body, not merely for a single year, but for many centuries, are much more deserving of wonder.

> So much have I written in order that I might remind those youths who have read this work, how much they owe to Schoner who, by the publication of such distinguished books which are indispensable in the schools, furthers public instruction . . . but Schoner himself did not think it necessary to admonish the studious lest they allow themselves to be deterred from these sciences by the most absurd opinions of the unlearned who deride, in every respect, this sort of astronomical discipline. For those who are even moderately educated in philosophy are easily able to judge the great worth, pleasantness and enormous benefit of the sciences concerning the movements of the heavens.[26]

Through their very beauty and order, Melanchthon observes, the celestial bodies beckon to the human intellect. Even so, it is arithmetic and geometry, viewed as "the wings of the human soul," which allow the intellect to take flight and "enter into the heavens to wander freely in the heavenly company."[27] Mathematics, therefore, aspires to astronomy. This is of such importance to Melanchthon, that when reforming the structure of education at Wittenberg in 1545, he instructed that the study of arithmetic be made obligatory for *all* students. "By having arithmetic," he writes, "the entrance immediately opens to the doctrine of the motions of the heavens; and although it seems abstruse, it will easily be able to be comprehended. Therefore, *in all the schools,* we instruct those who are acquainted with grammar and dialectics to join with them the study of arithmetic. Moreover, we order the teachers who govern the study of youths to bring those youths to arithmetical instruction and exercise."[28]

Because of Melanchthon's diligence, scientific studies at Wittenberg received a tremendous impulse. While nominally engaged as a professor of Greek, Melanchthon nevertheless lectured on Aristotle's *De Mundo* and the *Quadripartitum* of Ptolemy.[29] Indeed, the *Leges Academiae Witenbergensis,* written by Melanchthon in 1545, reorganized the Faculty of Arts to include two *mathematici,* one of whom was to instruct students in the "lower" mathematics of arithmetic and the *Sphere* of Sacro Bosco, while the other delivered lectures on Euclid, Purbach's *New Theories of the Planets* and Ptolemy's *Almagest.* Aristotle and Dioscorides were to be examined under the direction of the *physicus,* while two *Inspectores Collegii* were named—the first to lecture on dialectics and rhetoric, the second on physics and the second book of Pliny.[30] Moreover, Melanchthon himself formulated an introductory textbook in physics, ***Initia Doctrinae Physicae*** (1549), and combined his masterful Ciceronian style with a historical knowledge of science in numerous academic discourses and orations. In addition, Melanchthon edited and prefaced works by Sacro Bosco, Euclid, Ptolemy, Alfraganus, Purbachius, Regiomontanus, Johann Schoner, Erasmus Reinhold and Georg Joachim Rheticus, many of which he intended to be used in the schools. But perhaps the best indication of Melanchthon's effect on the status of science at Wittenberg can be discovered in his own admonition to students about to be examined in the Faculty of Arts: "The studious know that we will not consume examinations in sophistries . . . but in special subjects of the arts, in dialectics, and in physics, in arithmetic, in Euclid, in the *Sphere* (of Sacro Bosco), in the *Theories* (i.e., Purbach's *New Theories of the Planets*), in computing the distances of places from the longitude and latitude of their positions, and in the doctrines of the Church."[31]

Astrology

In 1512, Melanchthon matriculated at the University of Tübingen in order to continue his studies for the Masters Degree. During the following six years, three learned men particularly influenced him: the humanist

Heinrich Bebel von Justingen (1472-1516), the philosopher-dialectician Franciscus Stadianus, and the astronomer-astrologer Johannes Stöffler (1452-1531). It was Stöffler however, esteemed and remembered by Melanchthon throughout his life, who played a crucial part in forming Melanchthon's understanding of the universe by acquainting him with a coherent astrological theory based on a physically consistent concept of nature. Melanchthon's correspondence, in which he never tires of writing of the astrological implications of comets and the positions of the planets, bears witness to the immense influence of this Tubingen professor.[32]

From the moment of his birth Melanchthon had been exposed to astrology. At that time, his father commissioned Johann Virdung von Hassfurt, court astrologer of the Palatinate and later professor of astronomy at Heidelberg, to draw up his son's horoscope. It appears that in his later life, Melanchthon was sincerely convinced by Virdung's calculations which implied that a northerly journey would some day be harmful and that he would endure shipwreck in the Baltic Sea. In 1560, as he lay dying, Melanchthon is reported to have pointed to a map which hung not far from his bed, upon which a large body of water was depicted. Contemplating the map he said, "Virdungus once prophesied to me from the stars that I would suffer shipwreck on the sea, now I am not far from it."[33]

Essentially, Melanchthon views the celestial bodies as revealed images or symbols of God's wisdom and goodness. As such, they do not predetermine events, but rather manifest divine purpose. Thus, not only does God reveal himself through Scripture, but also through the symbolic motions of the heavens. The entire universe becomes an emblem of divine will in which God governs everything, ruling the course of the heavenly bodies and all of nature by an absolutely fixed law.[34] Order and harmony reign overall. This is the greatest appeal of astrology to Melanchthon. He writes: "It is not merely the utility of these arts which pleases me . . . but much more it is this: when I consider the extraordinary concord of the celestial and lower bodies, such (a condition of) order and harmony suggests to me, *in itself,* that the world was not brought about by accident, but is ruled by God."[35]

Melanchthon always considered astrology to be a true science. Indeed, it was to establish astrology as a particular science that he composed the **Oratio de Dignitate Astrologiae,** 1535. Here astrology is regarded as "that part of physics which teaches what effect the light of the stars has on simple and mixed bodies, and what sort of temperaments, changes and inclinations occasion these effects."[36] Just as we can easily see that the light of the sun imparts warmth and dryness, and that the appearance of the moon produces moisture, so too, in various ways, do the other heavenly bodies affect mankind and the world. Saturn brings melancholy, Jupiter affords tranquility. The Sun vivifies, Mercury brings drought, and Venus and the moon induce rain.[37]

As with other sciences, Melanchthon continues, astrology bases all its presuppositions upon specific observation. While an astrologer might recognize from the aspects of the planets at the time of the birth of Catiline that this man would cause unrest and come to a tragic end, he could not predict that Catiline would cause an insurrection during the Consulship of Cicero and would eventually be killed in a battle at the foot of the Apennines. If, Melanchthon observes, the predictions of astrologers are not always accurate, so it is also with the physician who is not able to diagnose every illness and the statesman who is not able to avoid all political crises. Indeed, these sciences—medicine and politics—are much more easily investigated than astrology because the objects of their study are always very near.[38]

In an astrological universe, each particular bears the mark of the whole. Thus the temperaments and inclinations of a single individual are not the result of an isolated planet, but arise from the entire order of stars in the universe. In this way, the microcosm reflects the macrocosm. Indeed, the very proportions of the heavens are reflected on earth. "The doctrines concerning the motions of the heavens and geography," writes Melanchthon, "are inseparably bound together and cannot be split apart."[39] The possibility of such an ordered and harmonic relation between the earth and the upper spheres is the main feature, for Melanchthon, of the Aristotelian universe. By allowing God to operate through these spheres, Melanchthon opposes any fatalistic conception of nature whereby all occurrences are seen as deriving from strictly natural causes emanating from the heavenly bodies themselves.

More significant, from the point of view of Melanchthon's encounter with the Copernican theory, is his justification of astrology from within the Aristotelian conceptual framework. Melanchthon was, in fact, totally committed to the Aristotelian physical theory of the universe; it provided him with a logically consistent and physically coherent system from which astrological causality could be directly explained. In his preface to **Liber Joannis de Sacro Busto libellus de Sphaera** (Wittenberg, 1531), Melanchthon remarks: "I am of the opinion that Aristotle was correct when he said that this lower world is ruled by the higher, and that the cause of motion (change) in this world comes from that superior part . . . Since the motion of the heavens is first, it follows that the motion of the heavens is the cause of all other motions."[40]

The question of causality demands a *physical* explanation of astrological influences which, for Melanchthon, must also be consistent with peripatetic metaphysics.

While the constructions of Ptolemy or Copernicus might be used to predict planetary positions, only the Aristotelian physical universe is viewed as in accord with experience and the real nature of things, even though it is less than satisfactory as a predictive instrument. The views of Melanchthon in this regard are very similar to those of Aquinas who, developing the opinion of Simplicius, concluded that astronomical hypotheses *qua* mathematical constructions might be used to describe the apparent motions of the planets but ought never to be considered as strictly true representations of reality.[41] To accept a theory, therefore, which denied the Aristotelian edifice would have required the articulation of a new physics sufficiently convincing to alter fundamental peripatetic assumptions of nature. This the heliocentric model of Copernicus, though harmonically ordered and mathematically compelling as a system of planetary motion, was not initially able to achieve.

ATOMISM AND EPICUREANISM

There may also be a philosophical issue involved in Melanchthon's attitude toward the new theory of Copernicus. Certain elements of the Copernican doctrine may have led Melanchthon to view the physical aspects of this hypothesis as inherently atomistic and therefore Epicurean in nature. Because, in the traditional sense, atomism does away with all distinctions in the universe, "it is no wonder," writes John Dillenberger in his study of *Protestant Thought and Natural Science,* "that to Melanchthon and others the notion that the earth was like other planets immediately suggested the revival of atomism."[42] Such a view, however, misinterprets the physical nature of the Aristotelian universe and seems to overlook the essentially anti-religious features of Epicureanism to which Melanchthon adamantly objected.

Professor Dillenberger's evaluation implies that the earth loses its preeminence in nature when moved from the center of the cosmos, and becomes indistinguishable from all other heavenly bodies. But Melanchthon, as an Aristotelian, could not have held that the earth itself maintained such a position of perfection. Viewed from within the Aristotelian conceptual scheme, the earth, subject to corruption and change, was outshone entirely by the changeless and quintessential superlunary spheres. It was not the physical place of the earth in space, but rather man's moral place in the hierarchy of being which was of significance; and this unique moral status could be maintained whatever the earth's spatial position.[43]

Moreover, when Melanchthon condemns Epicureanism, he does not cease until he has rejected much more than simple atomism. He writes: "The Epicurean system is full of horrible ravings. First, dialectics are neglected by them all. In physics, it constructs the world from at-

oms and imagines that other worlds are separately born and others are continually destroyed, it removes from the world two principle causes of things, efficient and final. It denies the existence of God and affirms that everything was created and brought about without divine providence, merely by accident. It absurdly teaches that the stars are not durable bodies, but that daily new vapors catch fire and are consumed which produces the appearances of the sun and all the other stars. It affirms that the soul of man is destroyed with the body . . . in ethics, it affirms that the goal of human nature is pleasure, that is, to be without pain. Therefore, since it prefers pleasure to virtue, there follow many false opinions."[44]

The ethical features of the Epicurean system were frequently discussed in the Renaissance. In contrast, however, with Erasmus and Thomas More who were able, at least implicitly, to recognize elements compatible with Christianity within the ethical doctrines of Epicurus, Melanchthon remained logically and ethically opposed to the Epicurean philosophy, directing his attack primarily against the Renaissance champion of that philodophy, Lorenzo Valla.[45] Yet, whatever his ethical objections to the Epicurean system, Melanchthon was particularly uneasy concerning the denial of the existence of God, and its religious consequences. The exclamation of Lucretius in the opening lines of *De Rerum Natura*—*Tantum religio potuit suadere malorum*[46]—could easily represent the attitude responsible for much of Melanchthon's disfavor toward the system of Epicurus. Lucretius' poem scoffed at religion as the necessary consequence of ignorance. It dispelled God from the natural world and replaced the deity with an autonomous array of "atoms." Surely Epicurus and his followers ("who make the soul share in the body's death"[47]) deserved to burn in the fiery iron tombs of hell's sixth circle to which Dante had condemned them.

Hence, it is not atomism *per se* which Melanchthon rejects, but rather the anti-religious and atheistic effects of the entire Epicurean system. Melanchthon's real view of atomism may be discerned from a poem which he composed on the flyleaf of his copy of Vesalius' *De Humani Corporis Fabrica*, 1543:

> Think not that atoms, rushing in a senseless, hurried flight
> Produced without a guiding will this world of novel form.
> The mind which shaped them, wise beyond all other intellects
> Maintains and fashions everything in logical design. . . .
> The ordered movements of the stars recurring in their course
> Bear witness that a deity intelligent and good
> Established these provisions and now holds them in control.[48]

It would appear that Melanchthon was much less interested in "atomism" than in maintaining the hand of God in the whole of nature. But since no theologically adaptable form of atomism existed in the sixteenth century, any reference to an atomist attitude smacked also of the anti-religious system of Epicurus. It is just such a reference, found in the *De Revolutionibus,* which might have repelled Melanchthon.

> As it is with the tiny and indivisible bodies which are called atoms, although they are not perceptible or even make up a visible body when duplicated several times: but are able to be multiplied to such an extent that they eventually coalesce into an observable magnitude: so also it is concerning the position of the earth, although it is not at the center of the world, still its own distance (from the center of the universe) is incomparable (to the distance) of the sphere of the non-wandering stars.[49]

As with the atom, so the earth—"The metaphor," writes Georg Christoph Lichtenberg, "is far more intelligent than its author. . . . He who has eyes sees something in everything."[50]

If Melanchthon's relation to the physical theory of Copernicus was made difficult by atomism, the cause is to be found in the inherent anti-religious doctrine of the Epicurean philosophy of nature. It was not that Copernicus made the earth like the other planets, but that he seemingly adopted a point of view which held the theological implication, for Melanchthon, of a renewal of the materialistic teachings of Epicurus. In Melanchthon's view, such a revival of materialism necessarily led to the materiality and therefore the mortality of the soul.

THE COPERNICAN MODEL AS A MATHEMATICAL DEVICE

In her survey, *The Scientific Renaissance,* Marie Boas points out that: "Protestants, especially Lutherans, had been quicker to condemn Copernicanism" because "they did not see it as an astronomical *hypothesis* . . . but as a system fatal to the truth of the Bible."[51] Such generalizations, however, neglect major intellectual and psychological differences between the reformers which ultimately determined their relation to the new ordering of the planets. Indeed, Melanchthon's world view was substantially different from Luther's. While Melanchthon was devoted to astrology, Luther referred to it as "his (Melanchthon's) airy fantasy."[52] Moreover, Melanchthon *did* accept the theory of Copernicus as a mathematical hypothesis, while his realist objections to the heliocentric model might have arisen from epistemological or physical obstructions regardless of his Biblical opposition.

Traditionally there are two instances in the correspondence and writings of Melanchthon which reveal his hostility toward the Copernican theory. The first, a letter written to Mithobius (October 16, 1541), refers to Copernicus only generally as "that Sarmatian astronomer, who moves the earth and fixes the sun. Wise rulers ought to control the petulance of such natures."[53] This is nevertheless only a spontaneous, although emphatic, response to the Copernican notion based solely on Rheticus' *Narratio Prima.* Of much more significance, is his apparent denunciation of the Copernican theory in the section *Quis est motus mundi* from the *Initia Doctrinae Physicae,* 1549. Here Melanchthon writes:

> But some dare say, either because of the love of novelties or in order to appear ingenious, that the earth moves, and contend that neither the eighth sphere nor the sun moves while they assign other movement to the celestial spheres and place the earth among the stars. The joke is not new. There is a book by Archimedes called *De Numeratione Arenae,* in which he reports that Aristarchus of Samos defended this paradox, that the sun remains fixed and the earth turns round the sun. And although clever workers investigate many questions to give expressions to their ingenuity, the young should know it is not decent to defend such absurd opinions publicly, nor is it honest or a good example.[54]

Nevertheless, in 1904, Emil Wohlwill discovered that this passage had been measurably altered in the 1550 edition of the *Initia* and in all subsequent publications of the work, omitting altogether such phrases as "the love of novelties," "the joke is not new," and exhibiting, generally, a more dispassionate attitude concerning the heliocentric model. Noting Melanchthon's own reference in the *Initia* that 5507 years had elapsed since the creation of the world to 1545, Wohlwill argues that this section of the treatise was written in 1545 although it was set aside and not published until 1549. Seeing the work in print, he suggests, and being no longer of such an adverse inclination concerning the work of Copernicus, Melanchthon rewrote this segment of the *Initia* and republished the treatise in the following year.[55] Consequently, it would appear that in the nine years which lay between the letter to Mithobius and the first republication of the *Initia Doctrinae Physicae,* Melanchthon began to consider more rationally the mathematical utility of the Copernican hypothesis. Indeed, two professors at Wittenberg, Georg Joachim Rheticus and Erasmus Reinhold, who advocated and made use of the Copernican model, were both actively supported by Melanchthon during this time.

It was Rheticus who finally was able to persuade Copernicus to publish the *De Revolutionibus,* 1543, by introducing the Copernican system in his *Narratio Prima,* 1540. In fact, Rheticus may properly be called the first *real* Copernican. Erasmus Reinhold came as a student to Wittenberg, where he matriculated at the beginning of the winter semester 1530-31, and developed a close association with his teacher Jacob Milichius, professor of mathematics. Very soon, however, Reinhold's academic proficiency came to the attention of Melanchthon and by the end of April 1536, he was accepted as a member of the Faculty of Arts at Wittenberg and began lecturing on Euclid, Archimedes and Ptolemy.[56] Along with his colleague, Georg Rheticus, Reinhold was very early impressed by the Copernican hypothesis. But it was due to the efforts of Melanchthon, who won for him financial assistance from the Duke of Prussia, that Reinhold was able to formulate and complete his *Tabulae Prutenicae,* 1551, which was based on the Copernican theory.

Melanchthon's letters to Duke Albrecht of Prussia on Reinhold's behalf reveal not only Melanchthon's high regard for the Wittenberg mathematician, but also expose the continual struggle for patronage which prevailed in every area of scientific investigation.

July 16, 1544:

If I, because of my numerous requests, seem obtrusive, I nevertheless dare to write again in the confidence of Your Princely Grace, for it concerns the promotion of the sciences. Now, very few study mathematics, and among those of influence there are only a trifling number who promote this study. Nevertheless, at present, there is among us a learned man, who has dedicated himself to this study and has undertaken a work which will contribute much to the spread of this knowledge. Our Prince, however, cares little for these studies . . . I therefore would ask you to promote this profitable work and his *Ephemerides . . . for Princes are the images of God who calls Himself the father of orphans.*[57]

(my italics)

October 18, 1544:

Private persons, without the aid of princes, are truly not able to make instruments for the observation of the sun, stars, eclipses, equinoxes etc. for it costs something.

Therefore, will Your Princely Grace, who is so graciously consoling, grant such a stipend to Master Erasmus (Reinhold) who is now occupied with several useful works, and is an honorable Christian man, learned in the whole of philosophy . . .

Moreover, he will show his humble gratitude with a few works which he will dedicate to Your Princely Grace.[58]

July 15, 1545:

The learned mathematician Master Erasmus Reinhold . . . has received from Your Princely Grace now on the feast of Peter and Paul, fifty florins, for which I along with him humbly thank you. He (Reinhold) will also prove to be thankful with his work.[59]

Melanchthon was well acquainted with the work of both Rheticus and Reinhold,[60] and it was, perhaps, their influence which led him to speak more approvingly of Copernicus. In a letter to Georg and Huldrich Fugger, which Melanchthon later used as the preface to the 1552 edition of Regiomontanus' *Tabulae Directionum,*

he notes that King Alfons (thirteenth century) had "opened the way, for many discerning and inquisitive men to a better (astronomical) knowledge; and a few of them, like Purbachius, Blanchius, Cusanus, Regiomontanus, Copernicus, have by their zeal and acumen . . . widened considerably the scope of astronomical understanding. Therefore we must not refrain from investigating the wisdom in the work of God and we must contemplate the light of divine knowledge which resides in our spirit. We cannot overlook the fact that the sciences are a gift of God in order to recognize Him and thereby to maintain life in a wiser order."[61] Indeed, in 1549, the same year as the first edition of the *Initia Doctrinae Physicae* with its open invective against the new hypothesis, Melanchthon wrote to Caspar Cruciger: "For this and similar observations of motion we begin rather to admire and love Copernicus."[62]

In the **Initia Doctrinae Physicae,** the physical aspects of the Copernican theory are always rejected. But if Melanchthon has recourse to the Psalms in this regard, he also stresses, much more, those arguments from Aristotle which rest on the notion that the earth is a simple body (*Terra est corpus simplex*) and therefore capable of only one natural motion.[63] Further, from Melanchthon's point of view, the heliocentric theory of Copernicus was not a new hypothesis at all, but rather a revival of the long subdued error of Aristarchus. The same Aristotelian physical arguments traditionally drawn up against Aristarchus, therefore, could be employed equally well against the physical aspects of the Copernican theory.

In conclusion I wish to note that while even in the first edition of the **Initia Doctrinae Physicae** Melanchthon makes use of the astronomical values of Copernicus, it becomes clear from the subsequent editions of the work that Melanchthon had largely reconciled the Copernican notion as a *hypothesis* which was suitable for the interpretation of the appearances of the heavens. According to this view, both the Ptolemaic and the Copernican hypotheses were regarded as equally useful instruments for the prediction of planetary movement. It is precisely this *instrumentalist interpretation* which was accommodated by the mathematical faculties of the universities and which, at least initially, provided the most rational incentive for the use of the Copernican theory.

Notes

1. Friedrich Klee, *Die Geschichte der Physik an der Universität Altdorf bis zum Jahre 1650* (Erlangen, 1908), p. 19.

2. Robert S. Westman, "The Wittenberg Interpretation of the Copernican Theory," *The Nature of Scientific Discovery,* ed. Owen Gingerich (Washington, D.C., forthcoming 1974).

3. Ernst Cassirer, *The Philosophy of the Enlightenment,* tr. Fritz C. A. Koelln and James P. Pettegrove (Boston, 1955), p. 116.

4. Philip Melanchthon, *Corpus Reformatorum,* ed. Carolus Gottlieb Bretschneider, XIII (Halle, 1834), p. 150. Cited hereafter as *CR.* For a very good discussion of Melanchthon's epistemology, see the introduction by Hans Engelland in *Melanchthon on Christian Doctrine,* ed. Clyde L. Manschreck (New York, 1965).

5. *CR* XIII, p. 647: "In Philosophia et omnibus artibus, de quibus lux humani per sese iudicat, tres sunt normae certitudinis: Experientia universalis, Principia, id est, noticiae nobiscum nascentes, et ordinis Intellectus in iudicanda consequentia."

6. Ibid.: ". . . ut lumen in oculis conditum est ad cernenda corpora, sic in mente quasi lumen sunt hae noticiae, quibus intelligimus numeros, ordinem, proportiones, figuras, et conteximus ac iudicamus has primas propositiones: Totum est qualibet sua parte: Causa non est posterior effectu suo: Deus est mens aeterna, sapiens, verax, iusta, casta, benefica, conditrix mundi, servans rerun ordinem, et puniens scelera. Mens humana ad hanc similitudinem condita est, ut dicitur: Exemplumque Dei quisque est in imagine parva."

7. Melanchthon's *principia speculabilia* are undoubtedly reflections of Aquinas' *scientiae speculativae.* I have, however, adopted a literal translation of Melanchton's terminology.

8. *CR* XIII, p. 649.

9. Ibid.: ". . . quae regunt hominum mores, ut natura humana intelligit discrimen honestorum et turpium."

10. *CR* XIII, p. 652.

11. For the Neo-Platonic theory of knowledge, see E. H. Gombrich, "*Icones Symbolicae*: The Visual Image in Neo-Platonic Thought," *Journal of the Warburg Institute,* XI (1948), 165-192: see particularly 168-171.

12. *CR* XIII, p. 151: "In Ecclesia habemus et quartam norman certitudinis, videlicet, patefactionem divinam, illustribus et non fallentibus testimoniis factam, quae extat in libris propheticis et apostolicis. Etsi autem facilius et firmius adsentitur mens humana iis, quae luce naturali cernit, tamen simili constantia omnes creaturas rationales adsentiri oportebat sententiis a Deo patefactis, etiansi luce naturali non videmus esse veras et firmas. Ut sine dubitatione adseveramus, bis 4 esse 8: ita statuendum est, Deum excitaturum esse homines mortuos, et Ecclesiam ornaturum aeterna gloria, et impios abiecturum in aeternas poenas."

13. *CR* XIII, pp. 190-191: ". . . tamen multa sunt in doctrina Ecclesiae, quae sine physicis explicari non possunt."

14. *CR* XI, p. 280: "Est enim confusanea doctrina, in qua magnae res non explicantur diserte, miscentur ea quae oportebat seiungi, rursus illa quae natura coniungi postulat, distrahuntur: . . . Nihil in ea cohaeret, non initia, non progressiones, non exitus cerni possunt. Talis doctrina non potest non gignere infinitos errores . . ."

15. Thomas Aquinas, *Summa Theologiae, cura et studio Petri Caramello* (Rome, 1952), Part I, question I, art. 5.

16. Ibid., Part I, question I, art. 2.

17. Essentially, Aristotle argues that the world must be eternal as nothing can come into being from nothing. Melanchthon replies that only God, as the first cause, is eternal with *infinite powers of realization.* All that is finite, therefore, is brought about through this infinite power. Consequently, the world is ultimately created from nothing. Once created however, nothing else arises from nothing; there only remain changes within the world itself. Melanchthon replies to five other arguments of Aristotle relating to the world's eternity; for these, see *CR* XIII, pp. 376-380; also Bernhardt, *Philipp Melanchthon als Mathematiker und Physiker* (Wittenberg, 1865), pp. 72-73.

18. *CR* VII, p. 1126; also Bernhardt, p. 10.

19. Karl Hartfelder, *Philip Melanchthon als Praeceptor Germaniae,* (1889; rpt. Nieuwkoop, 1964), pp. 39-40.

20. *CR* II, p. 815.

21. Etienne Gilson, *Reason and Revelation in the Middle Ages* (London, 1950), p. 93.

22. *CR* XI, p. 933: "Nec moveor histrionum quorundam clamoribus, qui simulatione religionis vituperant, naturae inquisitionem, et abduci mentes ab iis scriptis vociferantur, quae Deus sua voce tradidit."

23. Georg von Puerbach, *Theoricae novae planetarum cum praefatione Philippi Melanchthonis* (Vitebergae, 1535). Also, *CR* II, p. 819.

24. *CR* VII, p. 473.

25. *CR* II, p. 818: "Homerus cum in clypeo Achillis pingeret sidera, et coeli verticem ac motum describeret, quid aliud voluit significare, quam harum rerum inquisitionem summis heroibus dignam esse. Apud Virgilium Iopas in regio convivio canit errantem Lunam Solisque labores. Turpe est autem, in castris et in convivio in

admiratione fuisse has artes, et in scholis iacere spretas atque neglectas, quibus Philosophiae defensionem atque conservationem respublica commendavit."

26. *CR* III, p. 118: ". . . hae tabulae multo magis sunt dignae admiratione, quae omnium siderum positus ostendunt, nec unius tantum anni, sed multorum seculorum.

"Haec eo praefatus sum, ut admonerem iuvenes, qui haec lecturi sunt, et quantum debeant Schonero iuvanti publica studia editione talium librorum, quibus in scholis opus est, deinde ut utilitate harum tabularum, excitati ad discendum invitentur. Illa admonitione hoc loco non putavi opus esse, ne se ab his artibus studiosi deterreri sinant, insulsissimis iudiciis indoctorum, qui totum hoc genus doctrinae de rebus coelestibus superbissime derident."

27. *CR* XI, p. 288. Also, William Hammer, "Melanchthon, Inspirer of the Study of Astronomy: with a translation of his oration in praise of astronomy," *Popular Astronomy* (June 1951), 308-319.

28. *CR* X, p. 1015: "Tenentibus autem Arithmeticam, patet iam aditus ad motuum coelestium doctrinam, et quamvis abstrusa videtur, tamen comprehendi facile poterit. Praecipimus igitur omnibus Scholasticis qui Grammaticen et Dialecticen discunt, ut adiungant Arithmeticam, Magistris etiam mandamus qui regunt adolescentum studia, ut adigant eos ad audiendam et exercendam Arithmeticen."

29. Hartfelder, *Melanchthon als Praeceptor Germaniae,* pp. 561-565.

30. *CR* X, p. 1010. Also, Walter Friedensburg, *Geschichte der Universität Wittenberg* (Halle, 1917), pp. 216-217.

31. *CR* X, pp. 1014-1015: ". . . sciant studiosi nos examina non in cavillationibus, aut ociosis quaestionibus consumpturos esse, sed in praecipuis artium materiis, in Dialecticis, et Physicis, Arithmetica, Euclide, Sphaera, Theoricis, in locorum intervallis computandis ex longitudine et latitudine locorum, et in doctrina Ecclesiae."

32. Karl Hartfelder, "Der Aberglaube Philipp Melanchthons," *Historisches Taschenbuch* (Leipzig, 1889), pp. 233-269: see particularly pp. 243-245.

33. *CR* X, p. 278: "Virdungus hat mir einsmals prophezeiet aus der Sternguckerkunst, ich werde Schiffbruch leiden auf der See; jetzt bin ich nicht weit darvon . . ."

34. *CR* III, p. 114.

35. *CR* XI, p. 263: "Me quidem non solum utilitas in his artibus delectat . . . sed multo magis hoc, quod cum hunc mirificum consensum corporum coelestium et inferiorum contemplor, ipse me ordo et harmonia admonet, mundum non casu ferri, sed regi divinitus."

36. *Ibid.*: "Astrologia pars est Physices, quae docet, quos effectus astrorum lumen in elementis et mixtis corporibus habeat, qualia temperamenta, quas alterationes, quas inclinationes pariat."

37. *Ibid.*: pp. 264-265.

38. *Ibid.*: pp. 262-265.

39. *CR* XI, p. 296: "Coniunctae artes sunt doctrina, de motibus coelestibus et Geographia, nec divelli possunt."

40. *CR* II, p. 533: "Ideoque recte dixisse Aristotelem iudico, cum ait, hunc inferiorem mundum a superiore gubernari, et superiora causam motus in inferioribus esse . . . cum initium motus sit a coelo, consequi, motum coeli et reliquis causam motus esse."

41. Pierre Duhem, *To Save the Phenomena,* tr. Edmund Doland and Chaninah Maschler (Chicago, 1969), pp. 41-43.

42. John Dillenberger, *Protestant Thought and Natural Science* (New York, 1960), p. 40.

43. Arthur O. Lovejoy, *The Great Chain of Being* (New York, 1960), p. 104.

44. *CR* XIII, pp. 656-657: "Epicurea plena est horribilium furorum. Primum Dialecticen omnino praetermisit. In Physicis componit mundum ex atomis, et somniat subinde alios mundos nasci, et alios interire, removet ab universitate rerum duas praecipuas causas, Efficientem et Finalem. Negat esse Deum, et affirmat omnia sine providentia divina, tantum casu nata esse, et casu ferri. Stellas ridicule fingit non esse durabilia corpora, sed quotidie novos halitus accendi et deflagrare, qui speciem Solis et aliarum stellarum efficiant. Animas hominum affirmat interire cum corporibus. . . . In Ethicis finem humanae affirmat esse voluptatem, hoc est, vacare cruciatu. Inde, cum anteferat voluptatem virtuti, multa falsa sequuntur."

45. Concerning the Renaissance reaction to the ethical aspects of Epicureanism, see D. C. Allen, "The Rehabilitation of Epicurus and His Theory of Pleasure in the Early Renaissance," *Studies in Philology,* XLI (1944), 1-15: see particularly 10-12.

46. Lucretius, T. *Lucreti Cari De Rerum Natura Libri Sex,* ed. H. A. J. Munro (Cambridge, 1866), line 101. That Melanchthon came into contact with

this work seems unquestionable. Scattered copies of the poem already existed in manuscript in various libraries during the Middle Ages. The first printed edition was published at Brescia in 1473.

47. Dante Alighieri, *The Inferno*, tr. John Ciardi (New York, 1962), X.6.13-15.

48. Philip Melanchthon, "Observations on the Human Body," a poem written in Latin by Melanchthon on the cover of a copy of the first edition of Vesalius' *De Humani Corporis Fabrica*, 1543, tr. Dorothy M. Schullian (Los Angeles, 1949). The original of Vesalius' *De Humani Corporis Fabrica* with Melanchthon's poem is in the National Library of Medicine.

49. Nicolaus Copernicus, "De Revolutionibus Orbium Coelestium Libri Sex," *Nikolaus Kopernikus Gesamtausgabe,* II (München, 1949), Liber primus, Cap. VI. 17: "Quemadmodum ex aduerso in minimis corpusculis ac insectilibus, quae atomi vocantur, cum sensibilia non sint, duplicata vel aliquoties sumpta non statim componunt visible corpus; at possunt adeo multiplicari, ut demum sufficiant in apparentem coalescere magnitudinem. Ita quoque de loco terrae, quamuis in centro mundi non fuerit, distantiam tamen ipsam incomparabilem adhuc esse praesertim ad non errantium stellarum sphaeram."

50. Georg Christoph Lichtenberg, *Lichtenberg: Aphorisms and Letters,* tr. Franz Mautner and Henry Hatfield (London, 1969), p. 42.

51. Marie Boas, *The Scientific Renaissance* (New York, 1966), p. 125. Cf. Ernst Zinner, *Entstehung und Ausbreitung der Copernicanischen Lehre* (1943), p. 229: "The new theory was publicly promoted by the administration of the Catholic Church and repressed by the administration of the Protestant Church." Also, Thomas Kuhn, *The Copernican Revolution* (New York, 1959), p. 196: "Luther, Calvin and Melanchthon led in citing Scripture against Copernicus and in urging the repression of Copernicans."

52. Hartfelder, "Der Aberglaube Philipp Melanchthons," p. 256.

53. *CR* IV, p. 679: ". . . ille Sarmaticus Astronomus, qui movet terram et figit Solem."

54. Philip Melanchthon, *Initia Doctrinae Physicae,* 1549, in *CR* XIII, p. 216. Quoted in A. B. Wrightsman, *Andreas Osiander and Lutheran Contributions to the Copernican Revolution,* dissertation at the University of Wisconsin, Madison, 1970, p. 342.

55. Emil Wohlwill, "Melanchthon und Copernicus," *Mitteilungen zur Geschichte der Medizin und Naturwissenschaft,* III (1904), 260-267. Wohlwill's

discovery has been embellished by more recent scholarly activity including: Hans Blumenberg, "Melanchthons Einspruch gegen Kopernicus," *Studium Generale,* XIII (1960), 174-182. Wilhelm Maurer, "Melanchthon und die Naturwissenschaft seiner Zeit," *Archiv für Kulturgeschichte,* XLIV (1962), 218-226. Konrad Müller, "Philip Melanchthon und das Copernicanische Weltsystem," *Centaurus,* IX (1963), 16-28. I have also used the *Initia Doctrinae Physicae in Academia Vuitebergensi,* Johann Lufft (Witebergae, 1550), second edition. Here the revised passages which Wohlwill cites appear on 39^r-40^r.

56. Friedensburg, p. 232.

57. *CR* V, p. 444: "Etsi autem videri possum impudentior, quod de multis negociis ad Cels. v. scribo, tamen sapientia Cels. v. spem mihi facit, Celsitudinem vestram boni consulere si ea scribam quae ad provehendas honestas artes conducunt. Mathemata paucissimi nunc discunt, et pauciores ex potentibus ea studia adiuvant. Est autem apud nos vir doctus qui huic uni studio se dedidit, et quaedam opera inchoavit profutura ad earum artium propagationem. Sed aula nostra parum curat haec studia. Si celsitudo vestra quotannis aliquod seu munus, seu stipendium ei daret, ipsis artibus profuturum hanc liberalitatem sperarem. Et vellem esse hortator, ut opera utilia et Ephemeridas ederet. . . . Principes sint dei imagines, qui se vocat patrem orphanorum."

58. *CR* V, pp. 510-511: "Nu Können Wahrlich Privat-Personen ohne Hülff der Regenten nit Instrumenta zur Observation der Sonnen, Sternen, Eclipsum, Equinoctiorum etc. machen, denn es kost etwas.

"Darum wollen E. F. G. wie sie gnädiglich vertröst, dieses Stipendium auf Magistrum Erasmum wenden, der etliche nützliche Werk jetzund vorhat, und ist ein ehrlicher christlicher Mann, gelahrt in ganzer Philosophia . . .

"Dazu erbeut er sich zu unterthäniger Dankbarkeit, die er mit etlicher seiner Arbeit beweisen will, welche er E. F. G. zuschreiben wird . . ."

59. *CR* V, p. 791: "Der wolgelart Magister Erasmus Reinhold Mathematicus, . . . hat von E. F. G. jetzund auf Petri und Pauli funfzig Floren empfangen, derwegen ich neben ihm E. F. G. unterthaniglich danke, Er wird sich auch mit seiner Arbeit dankbar erzeigen."

60. Melanchthon possessed a copy of Rheticus' *Narratio Prima* since 1540, and by 1550, he had acquired Reinhold's *Prutenic Tables* a copy of which he saw fit to send along to Christoph Strathmion in the same year. *CR* VII, p. 683.

61. *CR* VII, p. 951: ". . . tamen aditum multis ingeniosis et discendi cupidis ad perfectionem huius doctrinae patefecerunt, quorum aliqui, ut Purbachius, Blanchius, Cusanus, Regiomontanus, Copernicus, postea ingeniorum acie et sua solertia . . . totum hunc orbem artium illustrarunt.

"Itaque non simus adeo seu ferrei, seu Cyclopici, ut nec artem in opificio Dei, nec radios divinae nec cogitemus, disciplinas esse dona Dei, tradita nobis, et ut ipsum agnoscamus, et ut ordinem vitae regant ac tueantur . . ."

62. *CR* XI, p. 839: "His et similibus observationibus moti, Copernicum magis admirari et amare coepimus."

63. *CR* XIII, pp. 217-221.

Stefano Caroti (essay date 1986)

SOURCE: Caroti, Stefano. "Melanchthon's Astrology." In "'*Astrologi hallucinati*': Stars and the End of the World in Luther's Time, edited by Paola Zambelli, pp. 109-121. Berlin: Walter de Gruyter, 1986.

[*In this essay, Caroti examines Melanchthon's fascination with astrology and the exposition of these ideas in his introductory text on physics and in other works.*]

The central role of divination in Melanchthon's thought has been emphasized by many scholars, notably by Johann Friedrich, Karl Hartfelder, Aby Warburg and Lynn Thorndike.[1] Nowhere is this better illustrated than in his letters, which, like a barometer, register precisely how his hopes and fears were fuelled by prophecies of future events foretold by stars, comets, monstrous births, by dreams and even everyday events.[2] Melanchthon combined absolute belief in an immanent, divine providence with a symbolic and—if we are to believe K. Hartfelder[3]—Neoplatonic interpretation of natural and historical phenomena. Accurate identification of his philosophical sources is therefore frequently difficult, all the more so given his wide reading and skill in combining ideas from sources as disparate as prophetic literature, astrology, oneiromancy and the "marvels of nature" (*mirabilia naturae*).

As far as the topic of our Colloquium is concerned, in Melanchthon's correspondance unfortunately there is not an explicit evidence of his involvement in the quarrel on the Flood foretold for 1524; we can not however exclude the possibility of such an involvement, chiefly because the documentary sources of the years about 1524 are notoriously meagre. There are, moreover, some meaningful hints that compel us to assume Melanchthon's high concern about the Flood. His ac-

quaintance with two of the leading actors, Johannes Stöffler and Johannes Carion, is well known. Melanchthon in fact dedicated to the first like to a beloved teacher his *Oratio de artibus liberalibus*.[4] Carion himself was in Tübingen to attend Stöffler's lessons just in the first years of Melanchthon's teaching.[5] The relevance of their friendly relations, well attested by the letters, is corroborated by the fact that Melanchthon was for Carion both a sort of privileged connection with the Lutheran field and more than an editor of his *Chronica*, notwithstanding Melanchthon's sharp opinion on him.[6]

The letters reveal how Melanchthon's lifelong fascination with predictions, even in popular form like almanacs, annual prognostications, *Flugschriften* on astrological phenomena, on monstrous births and other portents, was inspired by a conviction that the future could be predicted accurately. Some signs, of course, were more reliable than others. Astrological signs, in particular, were supposedly more reliable because predictions based on them could be verified rigorously by astronomical calculations and astrological rules expounded in scholarly books on astral divination. Indeed among divinatory arts astrology claimed a singularly privileged status since it boasted a secular and almost universally acknowledged "scientific tradition". And Melanchthon, far from denying this long established claim, exalted astrology as one of the most important of all sciences.

One of the most systematic expositions of Melanchthon's ideas on astrology is to be found in his *Initia doctrinae physicae,* a work intended as an introduction to various problems in physics. In the first book, second chapter, Melanchthon repeatedly emphasizes the importance of astral causality, evidently without being aware that this compromises his advocacy of "consideratio circa propinquas causas" as the central tenet of physics.[7] He also quotes a well known passage in which Aristotle apparently alludes to astrology[8], thus following a tradition stemming from the introduction of Aristotelian natural philosophy in the Latin West. Nor does Melanchthon intend to undermine this tradition when he mentions that Aristotle's general recognition of astral causality on sublunary matter should be substantiated with specific theories and facts:

> Hanc doctrinam de particularibus effectionibus siderum omittit haec aristotelica physica, contenta hac generali praemonitione quod astra sint universale efficiens, ciens et temperans materiam motu et lumine.[9]

By this reasoning also Melanchthon justifies his citations in the *Initia doctrinae physicae* of Ptolemy's *Tetrabiblos* and *Almagest* when discussing, respectively, astrological and astronomical problems.

For Melanchthon astrology was made all the more respectable by its connection with astronomy. He considered the two not as distinct disciplines but rather as different components of the same discipline, equal in dignity and importance. For this reason, too, Melanchthon was convinced that censures of astral influence attacked not only divination but also the entire science, including mathematical calculations of planetary motions and geometrical representations of the universe.[10] This fusion of astronomy and astrology is a recurrent theme. For instance, on several occasions Melanchthon praises the revival of astronomy in Germany, summarising its history and interweaving the fortunes of astrology with those of astronomy.[11] He justified this approach by citing the authority of Ptolemy, the author of the *Almagest* and *Tetrabiblos*. In these respects Melanchthon's ideas on astral influence differ little from those of medieval advocates of astrology. However, in one very significant way he does diverge from medieval tradition. In medieval astrology the contribution of Arabic writers had been of paramount importance. But Melanchthon, like other Renaissance authors, thought Arabic astrology was almost worthless by comparison with Ptolemy's, and restricted their astrological achievements to the supposedly unscientific part of the discipline, that is to illicit divination. His censure is absolute, as we can read in the preface to the *De sphaera* of 1531:

> Nam etsi Arabes desertam a Graecis possessionem magna vi invaserunt, adeo ut has artes in occidentem et Hispaniam usque propagaverint, tamen eorum scripta ostendunt, curiosam nationem non tam elaborasse in observandis motibus, quam in divinationibus, quarum adeo cupidi fuerunt, ut non contenti Ptolemaei Astrologia, quae pars quaedam Physices existimari potest, sortes etiam et alia multa praedictionum genera ἀναιτιόλογητα commenti sint.[12]

Melanchthon never doubted the scientific accuracy of astrology. For instance, in 1535 Joachim Camerarius' edition of Ptolemy's *Tetrabiblos* was warmly received by Melanchthon[13]; in the same year he began lecturing on Ptolemy's work at Wittenberg and stressed the scientific character of the work in his opening address.[14] And in the following year he commented on the second book, beginning with an exhortation to appreciate the philosophical arguments of the first book.[15]

The first two chapters of the *Initia doctrinae physicae* also allude repeatedly to the scientific nature and practical value of astral divination and explain how it may reveal, by decoding signs, the original design of God's providence and means of fulfilling it—to the limited degree, at least, that mankind can fulfil divine intentions:

> Non est enim verisimile haec pulcherrima corpora in coelo frustra condita esse, praesertim cum et maneant eadem et leges habeant motuum magno consilio ordinatas.[16]

In the second chapter of the first book Melanchthon recalls the dire predictions of a universal deluge in 1524 to prove astral efficiency over meteorological phenomenon, even though they had already been shown incorrect:

> Econtra humiditates auctas esse, largos fuisse imbres, exundationes magnas et diluvia, cum in signis humidis Cancro aut Piscibus congressi sunt Saturnus, Jupiter et Venus, ut meminimus anni 1524 coniunctionem auxisse humiditatem[17]

The presence of this reference to the deluge foretold in 1524 in a work conceived as an introduction to physics is a clear witness of the importance given by the author to the many predictions that appeared some years before. This reference, moreover, shows a concerned attitude towards the astrological pamphlets of 1524: Melanchthon in fact, far from denying the validity of such foretellings—that evidently resulted at least far-fetched—seems to legitimate the astrologers' warnings, adducing them as a clear corroboration of astral causality.

Melanchthon never distinguished clearly between an acceptable, scientific astrology and unscientific astrology, as earlier authors had done. I think he shied away from drawing this distinction for two, or perhaps, three reasons. First, he did not want to risk providing critics of astral divination, who had become increasingly vociferous since the publication of Pico's *Disputationes adversus astrologiam divinatricem* with further arguments.[18] Second, Melanchthon rejected contemporary criticisms of astrology—including Pico's—precisely because they surreptitiously ignored distinctions and condemned without discrimination both the unscientific, improper part of the science and its supposed scientific part. Third, he was convinced that all sciences were divine by origin, regardless the corruptions man had introduced into them; consequently, the imperfections of astrology, that is, illicit divination, were not part of the science proper and should be ignored in a textbook on astronomy.

In the chapters on the planets and their movements, Melanchthon carefully records different astrological *significationes,* establishing general rules for forecasting correctly from planetary positions.[19] That Melanchthon's ideas here had been formulated, to some degree at least, some years before the publication of the *Initia doctrinae physicae* in 1549 is abundantly clear. Indeed he appears to have been working methodically on a treatise on physics in the years around 1535, a period rich in astrological events and readings. In a letter of May 24th of that year, in which he thanked his friend Camerarius for a copy of his edition of Ptolemy's *Tetrabiblos,* Melanchthon remarked that he was studying problems of the soul.[20] In October he was writing on anatomy.[21] In a letter of 1548 Melanchthon informs his friend Martin Bucer that he has substantially corrected his work, a statement which implies nevertheless that the original structure had been retained. The most significant corrections apparently concerned the wealth of astrological examples in the first draft, which now, at a distance of more than 10 years, Melanchthon found excessive. Furthermore, by publishing his *Initia doctrinae physicae* in 1549 Melanchthon may well have been hoping to forestall a pirate edition of the first draft which, according to letters, had been circulating for some time. This hypothesis is supported by remarks in his letter to Bucer:

> Scripsit ad me quispiam cui nomen est Morelio de physicis edendis que ante annos XII scripsi. Ubicumque ille est aut ubicumque adparatur sive Argentinae sive Lutetiae quaeso cures prohibere editionem. Nam totam lucubrationem retextui et in veteri sunt exempla astrologica quae proferri etiam typographo periculosum esset[22]

Certainly, Melanchthon's absolute faith in the scientific nature of astral divination had not diminished over the decade, even if, as years went by, he felt compelled to reduce the number of astrological examples and eliminate those which were not meteorological. He still believed unswervingly in the divine origin of all signs, including astrological ones. In a letter of April 1538[23], in which he complained that only lack of time prevented him from compiling a thorough defence of astrology ("constitueram epistola copiosiore tibi iudicium meum de dignitate illarum artium quae coelestes effectus monstrant exponere, ad quam lucubrationem mihi aliquod vacuis diebus opus erat"), he warns that philosophy as a whole is the real target of those denigrating astrology:

> Nam qui nos calumniantur propter *astrologiam,* mihi crede, nihilo sunt aequiores universae phylosophiae. Sed astute hanc partem lacerant, cuius reprehensio est plausibilior. Saepe audio pariter damnantes divinatricem et demonstrationem de motibus.[24]

Melanchthon's belief in divine forces informing natural and historical events is also undoubtedly a mainspring of his educational programme and his philosophy. For instance, one of the most frequently acknowledged differences between the two champions of the Reformation, Luther and Melanchthon, was the latter's insistence that human endeavour was important for attaining the grace of God. Melanchthon's comments in his preface to John of Holywood's *De sphaera* in 1531 are pertinent here. Besides echoing traditional apologetic ("Quis est autem tam ferreus, tam sine sensu ullo ut non aliquando suspiciens coelum et pulcherrima in eo lumina intuens, admiretur tam varias vices quae motibus conficiuntur, ne cupiat quasi vestigia illorum motuum, videlicet certam rationem divinitus ostensam, cognoscere?"[25]), Melanchthon roundly condemns critics of astrology and, by implication, those belittling other disciplines. By finding fault with man's natural desire to know God's works, through which His providential

plans are revealed ("praesertim cum illa cognitio admnoneat etiam nos de Deo et immortalitate nostra"[26]), such critics deny His very existence and so must be denounced as atheists. By denying the significance of divinatory signs, they deny divine providence and so reduce the world to the level of material chaos and human nature, destitute of reason, to the level of matter. This argument is a *topos* in Melanchthon's thought and his target is usually those supposedly espousing Epicureanism. His attack was not obviously confined to Epicureans of antiquity; it was also directed against contemporary theologians:

> Sed sunt nonnulli epicurei theologi qui totum hoc doctrinae genus irrident nec solum praedictionibus fidem detrahunt, sed etiam vituperant motuum cognitionem, quos sinamus una cum Epicuro ineptire.[27]

This uncompromising rebuttal of extreme mysticism, nourished by Melanchthon's Christian humanism, was intended as a firm warning against blind intolerance towards the sciences.

The preface to the *De sphaera* demands attention for at least two further reasons. The first is its theological justification of science, a justification supported by quotations from *Genesis* and *Jeremiah,* and by an elaborate argument for the similarity of nature and prophecy: both of which are considered by Melanchthon, though in different ways, theophanies:

> Cum igitur et natura nos exsuscitet et hortentur divina oracula (quamquam ille etiam naturae sensus divinus quidam afflatus et quaedam quasi Dei vox est) et magnitudo utilitatum invitet ad hanc doctrinam, diligenter eam colere studiosi adolescentes debent.[28]

Second is Melanchthon's insistence on including astrology as a part of astronomy and his disregard for arguments to the contrary proposed by many authors, most notably Pico in his *Disputationes*. Without explicitly refuting them, Melanchthon declares himself dissatisfied with Pico's criticisms. The mere fact Melanchthon launches his attack on Pico's *Disputationes* immediately after his refutation of Epicureanism mentioned above suggests how strongly he condemns Pico's dismissal of divination. Pico's ghost, too, compels him to a thorough defense of astrology which occupies most of his preface and which, he claims, he would have preferred to omit ("ut maxime alteram illam partem divinatricem omitamus"). After initially stressing the high scientific level attained by astronomy, he comments:

> Quamquam mihi neque Picus neque quisquam alius persuaserit sidera nullos habere effectus in elementis et in animantium corporibus, praeterea nullas significationes in hac inferiori natura.[29]

Melanchthon's hesitation here between "causing" and "meaning" does not have theoretical significance. Preferring to leave as wide a scope as possible for his analysis, he avoids distinguishing these two ideas which he believes wholly compatible. More particularly, he prefers not to distinguish them because manifestations of God's will, which governs natural and historical events, are always concealed as natural causality.

Melanchthon's defence of astral divination was founded both on the data of natural phenomenon (warm planets in conjunction give rise to dry weather, cold ones increase moisture) and on the authority of Aristotle. He quotes a passage in the *Meterologica,* often cited by Mediaeval and Renaissance advocates of astrology, in which Aristotle explains sublunary motions are governed by circular, celestial ones. Astrology's reputation and wide following were, supposedly, further arguments:

> Idque interpretatur consensus omnium saeculorum, quo compertum est eclipses semper habuisse tristes eventus. Non est autem hominis bene instituti dissentire a consensu tot saeculorum.[30]

The most delicate problem was, however, the religious propriety of astronomy and astrology. But even here Melanchthon's response is unfaltering. While admitting "omnia divinitus gubernari", he retains that God "non tollit naturales actiones et significationes rerum". (I doubt Melanchthon's belief in astral efficiency is entirely consistent with the traditional distinction which he proposes between natural and supernatural human acts—the latter concern mental and voluntary faculties—but that need not worry us here). Astral influence affects man's inclinations *(inclinatio humana),* his behaviour and, albeit indirectly, his reason, and sometimes so forcefully that he is completely overwhelmed by his bodily constitution:

> Quid enim tam receptum apud medicos est, quam τὰ ἤθη χαὶ τὰ πάθη corporum dispositionem imitari? Idque res loquitur ipsa ἤθη in homine bilioso existere nulla posse, sed excitari in eo immoderatos impetus, quasi ventos, magna et vehementia πάθη, quae difficilime possit ratio regere aut flectere.[31]

Differences in physical and social characteristic between geographical regions corroborate astral influence on the sublunary sphere.[32] But astral influence on human inclinations, though theoretically tenable, had in the past encountered many difficulties in practice, particularly when the superiority of man's reason over his other faculties was insufficiently stressed. In the Middle Ages even Thomas Aquinas had faced the serious charge of having surreptitiously countenanced astral predestination by his espousal of planetary influence on man.[33]

In his preface Melanchthon does not in fact insist on this kind of superiority: when discussing miracles, he hastens to exclude from astral causality Biblical events like the crossing of the Nile by the Isrealites, Peter's liberation from prison and Paul's conversion. These are not standard examples in astrological literature but Melanchthon mentions them to refute astrological interpretations of Biblical miracles proposed by earlier astrologers, notably Pierre d'Ailly. Melanchthon was characteristically circumspect about the dangerous implications of these interpretations. His belief in astral determinism was by no means blind and uncritical.

For Melanchthon the problem of reconciling astral influences with free will had to be analyzed more subtly. Everything was part of God's providential plan and subject to His will, both natural events and laws, including astrological ones. Consequently the notion that man is subject to astral influences does not exclude him from God's providential plan because astral influences are themselves subject to God's will. By thus reducing the distinction between natural and divine law, Melanchthon could avoid the materialistic implications of astral determinism, implications entertained only by those who denied God's providence or, worse, by atheists and Epicureans who denied the very existence of God:

> Sicut igitur naturae vires in aliis partibus eatenus recipimus, ne regnum Christi tollant, ita suas vires lumini eatenus tribuimus, ne quid de gloria Christi detrahatur, cui cum omnia subiecta sint, iure etiam sentiendum est stellarum vires ei parere oportere.[34]

This supposed harmony between natural events and God's will permitted Melanchthon to interpret favourably a line from *Jeremiah* which Medieval and Renaissance authors usually read as an unequivocal condemnation of astral divination: "Nolite timere a signis coeli, quae timent gentes". This passage is especially pertinent to the theme of our colloquium. Though Melanchthon's letters do not explicitly mention predictions of a Flood in 1524, they are pervaded by premonitions of coming disasters prefigured in menacing conjunctions, dire portents and ominous dreams. He does not try to deny these grim prophecies; to do so would require a denial of divine providence, the consequences of which are more insidious than any temporal fears. Instead he believed human suffering could only be mitigated by complete trust in God's providence and particularly in His promise of man's everlasting salvation:

> Neque enim negat Propheta signa esse: sed cum signa nominet sentit ea res magnas atque tristes minari. Consolatur autem pios ne ea metuant, non quia nihil significent, sed ut confidant se divinitus inter illa pericula tegi ac servari . . . Erigenda igitur mens est supra universam hanc corporalem naturam, vel si fractus illabatur orbis, nec patiendum ut verbum Dei, ut fiducia erga Deum nobis excutiatur, qua sicut muniuntur piae mentes adversus praesentia pericula, ita muniendae erunt etiam adversus inimicas astrorum significationes.[35]

For Melanchthon, then, predictions based on astral and other signs, however dire they may be, strengthen the pious man in a faith which cannot be perturbed by even the direst prophecies. This idea is repeated throughout Melanchthon's works and explains why he constantly looked for forewarnings or corroborations of catastrophies, like the Peasant's War, the dramatic fate of the Smalcaldic Confederates or the ever impending Turkish invasion.

With the contradiction between astral divination and Christian faith reconciled, to his own satisfaction at least, Melanchthon's conclusion follows easily:

> Sicut igitur aliae partes physicae non laedunt religionem christianam ita neque astrologia (nam hanc quoque partem Physicae esse sentimus) officit pietati . . . nam illa doctrina de motibus cognitionem habet gravissimam et homine dignissimam. Et si quis adhibebit iudicium, intelliget alteram partem artis, divinatricem videlicet, perinde esse partem Physices, sicut medicorum praedictiones pars quaedam Physices esse existimatur.[36]

The religious propriety of astronomy and calculations of planetary motions follow from the divine character of celestial signs:

> Cum autem et hic admirabilis ordo ac positus deinde certissimae leges cursus testentur, hoc opificium summa ratione constare, non est consentaneum astra nullas significationes, nullos effectus habere.[37]

Elsewhere I have discussed the different kinds of divination found in Melanchthon's letters[38] and have chosen here to emphasize instead their religious foundations in Melanchthon's philosophy as articulated in his preface to John Holywood's *De sphaera*. The most conspicuous feature of all, I believe, is the theological origin of Melanchthon's conviction that natural and historical events have, besides their immediate natural and historical significance, a hidden symbolism relating them to God's providential design for man's salvation. This theophanic character of reality underpins both his faith in signs, even the most ominous, and his conviction that such signs could not be ignored without calling God's providence into question.

These ideas reappear, sometimes developed in greater detail, in other works, letters and prefaces—the *Preface* to Georg Peurbach's *Theoricae novae planetarum*[39] and the *Dedicatory epistle* to Erasmus Ebner of his Latin version of Ptolemy's *Tetrabiblos*[40] are just two of many examples. For example, in the latter Melanchthon returns to the theme of our Colloquium and attributes the rise of moisture in 1524 to a planetary conjunction in Pisces:

> In aeris et aquarum et terrae mutationibus videmus causam aliquam esse lumen et motus coelestes, ut in magna humiditate qualis fuit anno 1524, propter coniunctionem multorum planetarum in Piscibus, aut in magno aestu qualis fuit anno 1540[41]

In conclusion, then, I do not think that Melanchthon's reputation as a firm supporter of astral divination is overstated. Indeed he enjoyed the same reputation amongst his contemporaries. In 1549, the year in which the *Initia doctrinae physicae* was published, Gervasius Marstallerus published an anthology—dedicated to another significant figure in Renaissance astrology, the royal mathematician Oronce Fine—in which he collected "Artis divinatricis quam astrologiam seu iudiciariam vocant Encomia et Patrocinia". Of the authors he included the most conspicuous by far was Melanchthon.[42]

Notes

Quotations from Melanchthon's works in the following notes are from C. G. Bretschneider-H. E. Bindseil's edition: Philippi Melanchthonis *Opera quae supersunt omnia* (Corpus Reformatorum, 1-28; Halis Saxonum-Brunsvigae, 1843-1860 = *C.R.,* followed by the number of the volume, the number(s) of the column(s), and, for the letters, prefaces and dedicatory epistles, the progressive number).

1. J. Friedrich, *Astrologie und Reformation oder Die Astrologen als Prediger der Reformation und Urheber des Bauern-Krieges. Ein Beitrag zur Reformationsgeschichte* (München, 1864); K. Hartfelder, "Der Aberglaube Philipp Melanchthons", *Historisches Taschenbuch,* 6, 1889, pp. 233-269; A. Warburg, "Heidnisch-antike Weissagung in Wort und Bild zu Luthers Zeiten", in A. Warburg, *Gesammelte Schriften,* hrsg. von G. Bing, II, (Leipzig, 1932), pp. 487-558 (at pp. 536-539 an unpublished Melanchthon's letter to Carion on the Comet of 1531, on which see J. Rauscher, "Der Halleysche Komet im Jahre 1531 und die Reformatoren", *Zeitschrift für Kirchengeschichte,* 32, 1911, pp. 259-276). L. Thorndike, *A History of Magic and Experimental Science,* 5 (New York, 1941), pp. 378-405.

2. S. Caroti, "Comete, portenti, causalità naturale e escatologia in Filippo Melantone", in *Scienze, credenze occulte, livelli di cultura. Congresso Internazionale di Studi [Firenze 26-30 giugno 1980]* (Firenze, 1982), pp. 393-426.

3. More recently Wilhelm Maurer has stressed the importance of Renaissance Neoplatonism in Melanchthon's thought, W. Maurer, *Der junge Melanchthon. I: Der Humanist, II: Der Theologe* (Göttingen, 1967). Though it is undoubtely easy to find some echoes of Renaissance Neoplatonism in Melanchthon's works and letters, his faith in astrology has nevertheless a marked aristotelian inspiration. Even Maurer acknowledges this "medieval" component, *Ibid., I,* pp. 130, 136 and 156.

4. *C.R.,* I, 15, n. 6; *Melanchthons Briefwechsel, Bd. I (1510-1528),* hrsg. v. O. Clemen (Supplementa

Melanchthoniana, VI; Leipzig, 1926), pp. 24-25, n. 8a. On Stöffler see also W. Maurer, *Ibid., I*, pp. 129 ff.; at p. 138 we find a brief hint to the pamphlets on the Flood.

5. O. Tschirch, "Johannes Carion Kurbranderburgischer Hofastrolog", *Jahresbericht des historischen Vereins zu Brandenburg*, 26-27, 1906, pp. 54-62; H. F. W. Kuhlow, "Johannes Carion (1499-1537). Ein Wittenberger am Hofe Joachim I.", *Jahrbuch f. Berlin-Brandenburgische Kirchengeschichte*, 54, 1983, p. 54.

6. H. F. W. Kuhlow, "Johannes Carion", p. 56.

7. *C.R.*, XIII, 182-185.

8. Arist., *Meteor.*, I, 2, 339a 21-23.

9. *C.R.*, XIII, 185.

10. "Itaque studiosi adolescentes ament hanc doctrinam de motibus coelestibus, et vitae utilem esse iudicent, cum propter anni descriptione cum etiam propter alias causas. Nam quod nonnulli improbant τῇ μαντιχῇ, videmus indoctos eodem calculo etiam motuum doctrinam condemnare. Certe contemptus huius totius Philosophiae in rudibus confirmatur. Etsi autem de divinatrice hoc loco non disputabo, tamen si recte volumus aestimare, haec ipsa motuum doctrina vere est praecipua μαντιχή. Testatur enim esse aeternam mentem opificem et gubernatricem mundi, nosque ad agnitionem Dei et ad immortalitatem conditos esse. An haec μαντιχή aspernanda est? Quid verius convenit vatibus, quam confirmare in animis hominum veras et pias opiniones de Deo? Quare fateamur, hanc ipsam motuum doctrinam μαντιχήν esse utilem vitae et moribus. Sit sane fatidicum quiddam, ut est χράσεις corporum et ingenia iudicare ex aliqua siderum insigni coniunctione, aut tempestates praedicere . . . Magis tamen fatidicum est, monstratis certissimis motuum legibus confirmare mentes, ut vere statuant esse Deum, qui ordinarit, qui gubernet hos motus, qui agnosci velit ab hominibus, quorum utilitatis causa has varietates motuum condiderit; quique, cum nos ad sui agnitionem invitet, bonis praemia, impiis poenas proposuerit. Sed haec alias copiosius disputavi." Ph. Melanchthonis, *Praefatio Achilli Gassero* to *"Libellus Joannis de Sacro Busto, De anni ratione seu ut vocatur vulgo Computus Ecclesiasticus*, *C.R.*, III, 575, n° 1715.

11. "Suavissime enim a Platone dictum est: θεὸν ἄει γεωμετρεῖν, hoc est, ut ego quidem interpretor, gubernare omnia, et certissima lege cursus coelestes et totam naturam regere. Quare haud dubie probat studium eorum, qui, quasi observantes illius cursus lineas, gubernatorem ipsum agnoscunt et venerantur. Iacobus Milichius utili consilio coniunxit libellos Arithmeticos et Geometricos aptissimos scholis, scriptos a praestantibus artificibus, et in ea Academia, quae aliquot seculis praecipuum fuit domicilium harum artium. Nam Viennae, autore Purbachio, propemodum renata est haec Philosophia de rebus coelestibus, et nunc magna cum laude possessionem eius velut haereditariam retinent", Ph. Melanchthonis, *Praefatio in J. Vogelini libellum de geometricis elementis, C.R.*, III, 114, n° 1453.

12. *C.R.*, II, 532, n. 1002. On this important topic see P. Zambelli, "Fine del mondo o inizio della propaganda? Astrologia, filosofia della storia e propaganda politico-religiosa nel dibattito sulla congiunzione del 1524", in *Scienze, credenze occulte*, pp. 352 ff., and supra her *Introduction*, pp. 24ff.

13. "Maximam tibi gratiam habeo et mea et Reipublicae caussa, quod *Ptolemaeum* nobis edidisti. Etsi enim nos huic studio non sumus prorsus dediti, tamen erit mihi curae, ut commoveam et accendem iuvenum studia. Itaque pro elegam quaedam ut grammaticus tantum, ut plures in manibus habeant aureum libellum, et spero his, qui Philosophiam amant, etiam graecas litteras propterea gratiores fore", letter sent to Joachim Camerarius on October 5th 1535, *C.R.*, II, 951, n° 1339.

14. "Hoc consilio et animo institui interpretari *Ptolemaei librum de Judiciis,* in quo nihil nisi grammaticam interpretationem polliceor . . . Id autem eo faceo, ut optimus author fiat notior ac familiarior adolescentibus et ut aliqui foelicioribus ingeniis prediti accendantur ad studium illarum praestantissimarum artium. Et multa sunt Physica in his quae assequi omnes studiosi facile possunt et sunt utilia in vita.", *C.R.*, 964, n° 1342.

15. "Habuit primus liber utilissimas de fato, de causis physicis, deque aliis quibusdam locis sententias, quae ad multas res iudicandas in vita conducunt, et habent usum in reliqua Philosophia . . . Hodie, Deo volente, secundi libri enarrationem incipiam, qui habet gentium discrimina, causas tempestatum, eclipsium et cometarum significationes", *C.R.*, III, 220, n° 1507.

16. *C.R.*, XIII, 179. The strong connection between providence and astral efficiency is topic in Melanchthon's thought: see, for instance, what he affirms in the Preface to John Holywood's *Computus Ecclesiasticus*, quoted in n. 10.

17. *C.R.*, XIII, 182.

18. Pico is mentioned frequently in Melanchthon's letters and prefaces, and he is always sharply cen-

sured. See, for instance Melanchthon's Preface to Johann Schoner's *Tabulae astronomicae resolutae*: "Multa indicari possunt ex positu astrorum de valetudine corporum, de ingeniis et inclinationibus, deque multis in vita casibus, de tempestatibus, de mutationibus Rerumpublicarum. Plurimum autem tantarum rerum consideratio et animadversio conducit prudentibus. Nec pugnat religio Christiana cum hac sententia, nec damnant has praedictiones sacrae literae: sunt enim pars quaedam Physices, sicut Medicorum praedictiones: sumuntur enim a causis naturalibus. Divinitus alia vis est indita Soli, alia Lunae, ut vis est alia piperis, alia malvae, et pium est agnoscere opera Dei et observare vires illis inditas. Sed haec disputatio longior est, quam ut hic tractari tota possit, et extant libri eruditissime scripti multorum, qui Pici et aliorum similibus calumniis respondent. Illud tantum adiiciendum esse putavi, iniquum est pronunciare priusquam causam cognoveris. At illi vituperant hanc doctrinam, qui simpliciter eam ignorant: quare eorum iudicia merito deridentur." *C.R.*, III, 119, n° 1455.

19. *C.R.*, XIII, 179.

20. "Quaestiones habeo multas Physicas, de quibus utinam tecum et cum Medicis vestris confabulari liceret. Perveni enim, iam ed eam partem quae inscribitur de anima, in qua tota hominis natura nobis quantum quidem possumus, expondenda est." *C.R.*, II, 878, n° 1277.

21. "Nostra φυσικὰ etiam satis pulcre procedunt, nunc enim pervenimus ad Anatomen corporis humani" *C.R.*, II, 951, n° 1339.

22. *C.R.*, VII, 157, n° 4372.

23. *C.R.*, III, 515, n° 1668.

24. *Ibid.*, 516.

25. *C.R.*, II, 530-531, n° 1002.

26. *Ibid.*, 531.

27. *Ibid.*, 533.

28. *Ibid.*, 532.

29. *Ibid.*, 533.

30. *Ibid.*, 536.

31. *Ibid.*, 534.

32. "Si quis autem considerabit diversas regionum naturas et diversarum gentium ingenia, quam aliam causam huius dissimiltudinis ostendere poterit quam coeli naturam?" *Ibid.*, 534.

33. Th. Litt, *Les corps célestes dans l'univers de Saint Thomas d'Aquin,* (Philosophes Medievaux, VII; Louvain-Paris, 1963).

34. *C. R.*, II, 535, n° 1002.

35. *Ibid.*, 535.

36. *Ibid.*, 535.

37. *Ibid.*, 536.

38. See n. 2.

39. *C. R.*, II, 814-821, n° 1239.

40. *C. R.*, VIII, 61-63, n° 5362.

41. *Ibid.*, 63.

42. Gervasius Marstallerus (ed.), *Artis divinatricis quam astrologiam seu iudiciariam vocant Encomia et Patrocinia* (Parisiis: Christianus Wechelus, 1549).

Luther D. Peterson (essay date 1987)

SOURCE: Peterson, Luther D. "Melanchthon on Resisting the Emperor: The *Von der Notwehr Unterricht* of 1547." In *Regnum, Religio et Ratio: Essays Presented to Robert M. Kingdon,* edited by Jerome Friedman, pp. 133-144. Kirksville, Mo.: Sixteenth Century Journal Publishers, 1987.

[*In the following essay, Peterson shows how in his treatise* Instruction Concerning Self-Defense *Melanchthon finds justifications for resistance by lower magistrates and subjects against the tyranny of higher political authority.*]

From his earliest publications, Professor Robert M. Kingdon has drawn the attention of Reformation scholars to the problem of political resistance: whether a right or perhaps even an obligation exists to resist political authority, and, if so, by whom may this be done and under what circumstances.* In examining the sources of Huguenot resistance theory, Kingdon demonstrated that Theodore Beza had espoused resistance in the early 1550s, much earlier than had been previously thought, and that he was deeply influenced in this by the German Lutherans, particularly by the bold *Confession, Instruction and Admonition of the Pastors and Preachers of the Christian Church at Magdeburg* of 1550.[1]

The Magdeburg *Confession* was indeed an influential tract in its day and has rightfully received a good deal of scholarly attention in our century.[2] It appeared at a time when Magdeburg, still defiant of the emperor and Catholicism after the Protestant defeat in the Schmalkaldic War, faced an imperial army led by elector Moritz of Albertine Saxony. Not widely recognized, however, is the fact that the *Confession* brought to a climax more than a quarter century of Lutheran thought on political resistance. As its authors stated, it did not attempt to repeat all previous arguments in favor of resistance, but rather intended to present additional ones.[3] In the process they found occasion to deride those current enemies whom they labeled the "Adiaphorists"— Philipp Melanchthon and the other theologians of Wittenberg and Leipzig, who they believed were betraying the Evangelical faith by cooperating with Moritz's religious policy. In contrast to their present lack of courage, these were the very ones who during the war had publicly justified resistance: at that time these "proved such self-defense (*notwehr*) sufficiently, both from God's Word and natural recognition, which God has planted in the human heart."[4] The *Confession* spoke correctly here, for during the Schmalkaldic War (1546-47) Melanchthon and his colleague Johannes Bugenhagen printed tracts, disputations, and letters of Luther justifying resistance, with introductions to tie the Reformer's ideas to the present moment, and fellow theologian George Major and jurist Basilius Monner authored respectively a parody of the emperor's declaration of war and a study of the constitutional grounds for revolt.[5] Printed in the vernacular, they were intended to be read by a wide audience and to shore up Protestant resolve. Given the probable consequences of defeat, a modern scholar has labeled their efforts a case of "Evangelical courage."[6] Except for Monner's book, the arguments of these tracts were mainly from Scripture and natural law and supported a right and duty of defense, as the *Confession* stated. These arguments received their longest and most thorough expression in still another German tract from the Wittenberg presses, ***Von der Notwehr Unterricht, Nützlich zu Lesen*** (***Instruction Concerning Self-Defense, Necessary to Read***), printed in 1547 under the name of Justus Menius.[7] I suspect that more copies of this were printed than any other book on resistance prior to the *Confession*, and since it nevertheless has been little studied,[8] I wish to examine it in the following as a contribution to the theme for which we are so indebted to the work of Professor Kingdon.

* * *

Von der Notwehr exists in two quite different versions, the first based on Menius's manuscript with revisions by Melanchthon, particularly in the second half, and the second for which Melanchthon in correspondence took full credit. The second version was best known at the time, reprinted more than once, and translated into Latin,[9] and therefore is the text under examination here. Melanchthon's version at seventy-eight pages was four pages shorter than the first, but still is long, rambling, and repetitious. It retains the divisions of the first, with a preface followed by a part he entitled, "Instruction Concerning Self-Defense, by Justus Menius," and then sections labeled "First Part," "Second Part," a brief "How Self-Defense is a God-Pleasing Work," and

"Third Part." Some of the book will interest us little. The last part is a statement of Lutheran religious teachings, set out here so that "the God-fearing soldier may know that he fights or suffers for the sake of true, necessary things," with the result that he should be ready to risk his life for this doctrine according to his calling (*Beruff*).[10] An otherwise unremarkable preface rejoindered the right of self-defense to the "many disagreeable people" who told the Evangelicals that their princes could not resist the emperor: would these not protect their wives, daughters, and youth against the "unjust atrocities" of Italians, Spaniards, and Hussars? (A4a). This argument reappears (b4a), as do others sounded in the second chapter ("Instruction . . ."): that the pope caused the Schmalkaldic War to destroy the Evangelical church, and that the Protestant cities, princes, and electors had been obedient to the emperor in all temporal matters (B2a-b). Furthermore, the religious issues which the emperor and pope intended to resolve by the force of arms should be settled in a free general council (B2b), the convening of which contemporary readers would have known Martin Luther to have repeatedly demanded. The second chapter ends by announcing that the treatise will show how far one is obliged to obey superiors and that self-defense and protection are proper against unjust power (B3b).

Already one may observe hints of two different theoretical bases for disobedience and resistance. This first of these is suggested by the *Self-Defense* in the title. Here one need not take God and God's will into account, but rather self-preservation and protection are deemed simply rights of nature. Quentin Skinner has focused attention on a private-law theory of resistance espoused by some medieval jurists and theologians on the basis of Roman and canon law. The Roman Digest, they observed, justified the violent action of self-defense, which it considered a basic law of nature, in the case of adultery or in repelling unjust force. Canon law dealt with the case of an "unjust" judge: one who proceeded when the case in question was under appeal, who acted outside his lawful jurisdiction and the result was "notorious injury" (*atrox injuria*), or who within his jurisdiction acted unjustly and caused irreparable harm. In all these circumstances the judge lost his authority and could be resisted as a private person. In the fourteenth century William of Ockham and Jean Gerson appealed to these natural rights to assert that subjects could depose their rulers. In late 1530 the private-law arguments were taken up by the Lutheran theologians to justify the opposition of the Protestant princes and cities to the emperor. Early in the following year they appeared in Luther's somewhat evasive *Warning to his Dear German People* and over the next decade in a few of Melanchthon's Latin writings. But prior to the Schmalkaldic War these arguments appeared mainly in private opinions (*Gutachten*) which the theologians addressed to the Saxon court.[11]

The second basis, that soldiers had callings that involved defending their faith, unsurprisingly suggests that the Lutherans conceived of resistance within the religious context. To be sure, Luther and Melanchthon from their earliest reflections upon society stressed obedience to higher authority as a religious duty. Luther's conception of this world rested on an Augustinian idea of two kingdoms, with two regiments to effect God's purposes within the worldly kingdom: a church to gather and nurture God's own, and temporal government to maintain order and protect God's own. The fourth commandment's injunction to honor parents was for Luther the model for authority and obedience. He regarded this commandment as the link between the two tables of the Law, and thus a witness to God's will for society.[12] Hence his conviction that whereas equality existed in the spiritual kingdom, here inequality and hierarchy governed, with obedience demanded of child to parent and subject to ruler. He continually appealed to Romans 13:1-7 in support not only of the proper behavior of subjects, but also of the divine origins of the hierarchies: "Let every person be subject to the governing authorities" because they have been instituted by God (v. 1). By the late 1520s Luther had fused these images into the idea of the orders of creation. God had established in the beginning three hierarchies or orders—the family, the state, and the church—by which to structure society and further his purposes within the world. All people were set within the household order as parents or children or servants and the state as ruler or soldiers or officials or subjects, and Christians were also in the church as ministers or members of the congregation. "Orders" (*Ordnungen*), "hierarchies" (*Hierarchien*), "offices" (*Ämter*), "estates" (*Standen*), and "regiments" (*Regimenten*) testified to the static nature of the conception, and "calling" (*Beruf*) to the sense of duty to God with which one acted within these orders.[13] This conception of society placed the Lutherans among those whom Thomas Brady has recently labelled the "Augustinian rear-guard fighters" of history, still asserting a religious function to the state. These opposed an idea which would soon dominate: the state as "an omnipotent yet impersonal power," and as "a form of public power separate from both the ruler and the ruled, and constituting the supreme political authority within a certain defined territory."[14]

Although the conception was fundamentally conservative, placing each order's activity within divine purpose, it also had a radical corollary—each order also had limits beyond which it could not legitimately act. Also, it recognized in addition to clergy and magistrates another office involving authority within society, that of housefather or more generally parents. Luther discussed resistance in the context of the orders in a disputation of 1539,[15] but the argument first appeared on the popular scene in the wartime tracts of the Wittenbergers. The burden of *Von der Notwehr* was to justify resistance to

higher political authority without authorizing uncontrolled rebellion, and the orders of creation proved useful for the purpose. One does not find here a detailed theoretical discussion of the orders, but rather throughout the concept was presupposed, as such terms as order or ordinance, office, and calling indicates, and it formed the basis of the book's argument for defense and protection in the "Second Part." One final note: with its focus on the temporal order, the book gave rather little attention to the household order, nor very much to the church order.

Turning then to the two substantial chapters, the "First Part" on disobedience and the "Second Part" on resistance, the reader is confronted immediately with a typical Lutheran image of society and with a special pleading of innocence. God gave humankind the spiritual and temporal regiments. The office of preaching was the keystone to the spiritual, and the rest had to obey it (B4b-C1b). The temporal regiment, founded on law, existed to maintain discipline and peace (C2a) and to protect and sustain the church (a3a). It placed the ten commandments and other divine law before the people, and needed to make more specific laws for specific circumstances. Those regents who did this were to use sound reason, and the results had to concur with divine and natural law. The temporal regiment must then enforce external compliance to these laws (C2b-3a). Melanchthon next produced Romans 13 and insisted obedience here ought to stem not from mere fear of punishment, but rather from the dictates of conscience. Nobody in a thousand years stated this demand for obedience as clearly and forthrightly as we Lutherans, Melanchthon claimed,[16] and therefore he rejected the accusation (presumably from Catholic opponents) that the Evangelicals were rioters or taught revolution.

Melanchthon's temporal regiment was conceived in accordance with the Lutheran image of a divinely-ordered society, and was therefore expressed in the language of orders of creation. He then held the ideal up to the light of experience, finding that few rulers used their offices as they were ordained, but rather to further idolatry and engage in murder (C2a, 4a, a3b). Many, that is to say, contravened their obligations to one or both tables of the Law, and if their failures were thus seen in religious terms, then understandably the Bible would be Melanchthon's recourse in cases where they had ordered their subjects to follow them. When a ruler ordered one to do something forbidden in God's law, the latter for the sake of his soul could not obey, and *Von der Notwehr* here employed a by-now standard Lutheran text for justifying disobedience, "We must obey God rather than men" (Acts 5:29).[17] Should opponents maintain that there could not be limits to one's obedience to the ruler, or if a guideline was needed to ascertain that limit, Melanchthon was ready with another passage, the familiar "Give to Caesar the things that are Caesar's and to God the things that are God's" (Matt. 22:21)—Caesar was due *only* that which belonged rightly to his office.[18]

The arguments for disobedience in **Von der Notwehr** followed those Luther had used as early as his *Of Temporal Authority: to What Extent it Should be Obeyed* of 1523, and therefore were unexceptional. However, since the Reformers regarded interference by governments in the religious sphere as particularly serious, they often gave the impression that only in such cases was disobedience acceptable. Melanchthon's mention of murder reminds us that enforcing Mosaic law encompassed also what we think of as "purely" temporal, and thus that these religious grounds for disobedience were indeed broad. Also, he felt it necessary to oppose advice he attributed to "popes and Turks" that for the sake of peace and unity counseled toleration of the errors of parents and governments. Peace and unity were admirable ideals, and also God-given objectives of temporal authority, but could not be acceptable at the price of destruction of God's law and endangerment of the individual's soul (D1b). Simply put, where a superior in any order commanded something that contravened God's law or will, the inferior could not obey. Melanchthon's argument here, as was true of Luther in his early arguments for disobedience, remained solely within the religious framework of the orders of creation.

In the "Second Part" Melanchthon proposed to demonstrate that active defense, and not only disobedience, was proper under certain circumstances. But since active resistance so clearly contradicted Romans 13 in spirit as well as word, Melanchthon utilized both orders of creation and the private law argument to argue that one might oppose the emperor. More accurately, he employed private law arguments to bolster an argument based upon the concept of orders of creation. Then he added a brief nod to feudal law, and finally refuted four arguments of his opponents. In an unsystematic way he showed when a government or magistrate was no longer to be tolerated, and explained what acts were then permissible or in fact demanded. He did not address directly a third question, who may carry out this resistance, but his argument suggested answers to this as well.

"He who resists the authorities resists what God has appointed" (Rom. 13:2a, RSV). Luther gave expression to the orders of creation in translating this. He rendered the last words as *Gottes ordnung,* thus "resists God's order (or ordinance)," highlighting God's purpose in establishing government instead of those people in the governmental offices. Melanchthon pointed to Luther's translation to claim that only when the authorities ruled in accordance with godly order were they to be obeyed: "Therefore this statement [i.e., Rom. 13] should not be

extended beyond the office (*Ampt*) which is God's ordinance (*ordnung*) to the confirmation of all tyranny and evil." Private law concurred that obedience was proper only *in casu iustae iurisdictionis* (b1a). But Melanchthon's goal here was resistance, not merely disobedience. He found that the papacy had no legitimate jurisdiction in the temporal order, so that in claiming authority over king and princes the pope was openly against God's order and was a thief and tyrant. Therefore the Schmalkaldic League was correct in protecting itself (a4a). As if to reply to the obvious objection that the enemy, ostensibly at least, was the emperor, not the pope, Melanchthon next produced two examples of just resistance within the temporal realm. Trebonius stabbed his superior (Julius Caesar, as readers would have known), and in this was not opposing God's ordinance but rather atrocious evil and the devil's will.[19] Second, the wife of a ruler of Thessalonia who killed him because of his cruel torture of martyrs was also not resisting God's ordinance (a4b).

For Evangelicals the pope's political activities perverted and threatened destruction of the temporal order, and therefore demanded resistance. Temporal tyranny, as in the case of Caesar or the Thessalonian, could result in the same, and Melanchthon appealed to natural law, "a light planted in human reason," to justify active resistance. Reason enabled men to recognize when rulers inflicted atrocious injury (*atrox iniuria*) on their subjects. In such a circumstance, and if no magistrate should step in with help, natural law permitted (*erleubet*) one to defend himself and "there are many cases" where this commanded (*geboten*) husbands to protect wives, fathers their children, and magistrates their subjects.[20] Did the Gospel that told Christians to turn the other cheek contradict this natural right? No, Melanchthon claimed, the Gospel rather confirmed natural law, and also permitted to Christians those positive laws of a state which agreed with reason (b1a-b). Were the Gospel to tell Christians to suffer and not defend themselves, it would be a "political document" and further oppression and slavery (d1b). To be sure, to assert a *right* of self-defense Melanchthon would have had to call upon a natural right and to have insisted upon its independent jurisdiction, since Lutherans had generally counseled Christians to suffer. A *duty* of protection, however, stemmed more directly from Luther's conception of the redeemed Christian who made himself a servant of the needs of fellow humans (the ethic of "Christian love"). Here the religious idea of office—whether in the house or temporal order—involved its holder in obligations towards those in his or her charge, and among these was that of protection. In fact Melanchthon often referred to both a right of self-defense and a duty of protection, and in the other instances duty was a consequence of one's Christian obligations to fellow humans. Turning to the present situation, Melanchthon judged that the emperor had attacked the Schmalkaldic League with foreign troops and deceit with the intent of overcoming the Evangelicals, and that the elector and princes were protecting wives, children, clergy, schools, and subjects. "Protection is an ordained work"; the defense raised by the Protestant leaders was therefore according to order.[21]

Melanchthon felt obligated to distinguish between justifiable defense on the one hand and riot and rebellion on the other. The decision here hinged on judgments both of the inferior's intent in opposing a superior and of the latter's overall performance of his office. Justifiable resistance against ordained authority must be for purposes of protection. Unjustified rebellion for him was violence carried out without a calling (*Beruff*) and intended to raise oneself up. Absalom's opposition to his father David, for example, was prompted by "unmeasureable arrogance" and ambition instead of either self-defense or protection of others (b2a, see 2 Sam. 15-18). Also, one must tolerate occasional lapses or failures of otherwise good regents. David, Jehoshaphat, Hezechiah, Cyrus, and Augustus, despite faults, desired the good and more often than not did rightly in their office. Violence perpetrated to remove these from office for such faults was rioting (b2a-b). On the other hand, "A tyrant is that sort of regent whose will is not good; who devotes himself to atrocities or evil," even when some act of his may be beneficial. Caligula, Nero, Diocletian, and the like were his examples, and he continued by praising the two men who led the revolts against the thirty tyrants of Athens and Spartan control of Thebes, two fathers (William Tell was one) who acted to protect their children, and Obediah's hiding of priests from the evil designs of Queen Jezebel. He asked whether housefathers of Rhodes would not have acted properly in removing a tyrant for violating the wives of some subjects (b3a-c1a). By justifying resistance in his present moment, he implied Charles V's place among a most unsavory crowd!

Interestingly, in the midst of this argument Melanchthon took up the case of Uriah, Bathsheba's husband. Though subjects should tolerate the failures of rulers like David, had Uriah the opportunity to protect his wife he would have been right in so acting: "the *casu defensionis* of the subject (*Unterthan*) remains" (b2b). This remarkable exception to the argument here was couched strictly in terms of a husband's duty of protection. He has then an office, one which moreover must be regarded as without equal in his order and which justifies his opposition if need be to the highest authority in another order.

Melanchthon also employed the feudal relationship of lord and vassal to argue the rights of inferiors. His example was Emperor Trajan, who while handing a sword to a new marshal supposedly said, "I give you this sword to protect the empire and my body, if I do rightly,

and against me if I do wrongly" (c2b). Melanchthon was answering potential objections. Some might not accept the argument asserted in the orders of creation and private law, that the princes' authority was independent of the emperor, but rather insist that they must be considered his agents. Trajan's lesson was that still the princes must be ready to act independently, according to what they deemed best for the empire as a whole.[22]

Before ending the "Second Part," Melanchthon addressed three arguments for simple obedience drawn from Scriptures and one that called upon the example of Luther. While his answers repeated much already discussed, some of his comments are worth noting. The first was Jesus' words to Peter at Gethsemane, "All who take up the sword will perish by the sword" (Matt. 26:52b). This was God's judgment against murder, not defense, and one could judge the difference by determining intent and by considering office. One knew his own conscience, and though he could not read someone else's heart, he—and the courts—could judge that person's intent using reason. Also, those in the preaching office should not bear the sword. Thus Peter did wrongly in drawing the sword and the pope was wrong in raising up this war. On the other hand, God gave princes the sword of protection, so the Protestant leaders had not "taken" it up (c1b-3a). The second argument was 1 Peter 2:18: "Servants, be submissive to your masters with all respect, not only to the kind and gentle but to the overbearing." This gave occasion for Melanchthon to repeat the distinction between acts that were "notorious injury" and those whose burdens were not so great. The prime example of the former was a lord's violation of the wife or children of a servant (*Knecht*). This the servant should oppose "according to his calling and ability." Injury was quite literally a decisive criterion of what was not to be tolerated. A pious wife was to be patient with a rowdy husband, "but she is not obliged to be patient if his acts towards her are injurious, with hitting by which she would lose her health." The pattern of rights and duties was maintained. Whereas she had a right of self-defense, Melanchthon said the servant would sin if he did not defend his family (c3b-4a). The third argument was the example of David not killing King Saul when he had the opportunity. As far as Melanchthon was concerned, David had indeed suffered *notoria iniuria* at Saul's hand, giving him the right of self-defense, but he did not want to give an example of regicide in this first instance of monarchy. More importantly, David at this time had no office, and protection of others was not involved. Hence his patience was a "special act" and "a voluntary indulgence" done for the sake of general peace (c4a-b).

Finally, recalling his well-known demand for obedience, some claimed the Schmalkaldic League's actions contradicted Luther. This Melanchthon dismissed without discussion: "In the *Warning* [*to his Dear German*

People] and in other writings, Dr. Martin Luther declared that defense was just" (d1b). Those today who still write as if Luther taught obedience pure and simple, might take note of these words of his closest colleague.

* * *

Von der Notwehr is extraordinary in its support of resistance to civil superiors, and for that matter to household superiors also. Melanchthon here accepted a personal right of self-defense, which seems valid in all threatening circumstances, but over which *a la* David, one ought to exercise judgment. Furthermore, household or temporal office carries the duty of protecting those in its care. If the superior's acts are such that "tyranny" and "notorious injury" fit, he is to be opposed and removed from office, if possible. And those acts may be violations of either table of the Mosaic law, so it would not be correct to say that the Lutherans justified resistance solely for what we would label religious reasons. If the superior's acts are more generally good, the judgment about which Melanchthon trusts to the reason of the inferior officeholder, then apparently the inferior's opposition should be limited if possible to the bare act of protecting those oppressed, perhaps like Obediah. In Melanchthon's view, Pope Paul III and Emperor Charles V were both, if on varying grounds, guilty of tyranny and *atrox iniuria,* and all should join behind the Schmalkaldic League banner to oppose them. This was an incendiary tract befitting its wartime purposes.

Extraordinary also is the answer or answers readers were offered, had they asked the question "Who may lead resistance?" The book was addressed to the current conflict between an elector, princes, and cities against their superior. The primary and probably sole intended answer was that these inferior magistrates were justified in their actions, and the German people should lock arms behind them. Nevertheless, Melanchthon's examples praised even common subjects, men and women alike, who resisted authorities and in some instances had led movements of resistance. According to Quentin Skinner, Melanchthon "insist[s] that 'it is never permissible' for private individuals 'to engage in acts of sedition' on their own behalf against any legally constituted authority."[23] His evidence is a few Latin treatises written in the decade prior to the war. With respect to ***Von der Notwehr,*** his claim is not correct, for here there is no prohibition of violence on the part of subjects and plenty of examples to the contrary. The book thus appears seditious. But this is precisely where its orders of creation argument proves valuable, for according to that parents are not simply private individuals but, just as lower magistrates, are indeed legally constituted authorities. Thus although he offered no indication of office in the cases of the two opponents of tyranny in Athens and Thebes, usually Melanchthon did identify the household office of subjects whose resistance he supported. That is to say, William Tell, the wife of the Thessalonian tyrant, and the husbands of Rhodes are examples of just resistance because they held offices in the household order that obligated them to protecting others.

There was a dilemma posed by ***Von der Notwehr.*** The private law argument did in fact suggest that individual subjects may legally resist authority. Melanchthon did not back away from that consequence, hoping instead that the orders of creation would restrain its seditious thrust. But what if his readers did not take "office" and "order" and "calling" seriously? In the same moment Basilius Monner's book placed the constitutional argument, which specifically limited resistance to lower magistrates, into discussion.[24] The Magdeburg *Confession* three years later, while pointing in approval to the previous discussion and also utilizing private law theory, emphasized the constitutional duties of lower magistrates, and this was what the Calvinists took away from the Lutheran experience of resistance. So ***Von der Notwehr*** deserves our attention not merely because of its length and thoroughness, but also because it turned out to be the high water mark for an argument that perhaps was "too hot to handle."

Notes

1. See "The First Expression of Theodore Beza's Political Ideas," *ARG* 46 (1955): 88-100, and "Les idées politiques de Beza d'après son traitté de l'authorité du magistrat en la punition des hérétiques," *BHR* 22 (1960), 566-69. The *Confession* appeared in German and Latin: *Bekentnis Vnterricht vnd Vermanung / der Pfarrhern vnd Prediger / der Christlichen Kirchen zu Magdeburgk; CONFESSIO ET APOLOGIA PASTOrum & reliquorum ministrorum Ecclesiae Magdeburgensis.* Both eds.: Magdeburg: Michel Lotther, 1550. Nine pastors signed it; its principal author was Nicolaus Gallus.

2. For contemporary influence see Kingdon, "First Expression," 93-96 and n 20; idem, "The Political Resistance of the Calvinists in France and the Low Countries," *Church History* 27 (1958): 227-28; Quentin Skinner, *The Foundations of Modern Political Thought* (Cambridge: Cambridge University Press, 1978), 2:209-10; Esther Hildebrandt, "The Magdeburg *Bekenntnis* as a Possible Link between German and English Resistance Theories in the Sixteenth Century," *Archiv für Reformationsgeschichte* 71 (1980): 240-52. Notable recent studies are Skinner, 207-10, 217-19; Cynthia G. Shoenberger, "The Confession of Magdeburg and the Lutheran Doctrine of Resistance," (Ph.D. diss., Columbia University, 1972); Oliver K. Olson, "Theology of Revolution:

Magdeburg, 1550-1551," *Sixteenth Century Journal* 3 (1972): 56-79.

3. Three additional arguments, to be precise; see *Bekenntnis* K1b; *CONFESSIO*, F3a.

4. *Bekenntnis,* H3b; *CONFESSIO,* E4a. The "Adiaphorists" are labeled "enemies" on H2a (*Bekenntnis*) and E2b (*CONFESSIO*).

5. See Oskar Waldeck, "Die Publizistik des Schmalkaldischen Krieges," *ARG* 7 (1909/10), 37-49, and my "The Philippist Theologians and the Interims of 1548: Soteriological, Ecclesiastical, and Liturgical Compromises and Controversies within German Lutheranism" (Ph.D. Diss., The University of Wisconsin, 1974), 452-63.

6. Curt Christmann, *Melanchthons Haltung im schmalkaldischen Kriege,* Historische Studien, no. 31 (Berlin, 1902), 54.

7. See n10 below. Menius was a student of both Luther and Melanchthon who, spending most of his career in Eisenach and Gotha, is sometimes called "the Reformer of Thüringia"; for him see Gustav L. Schmidt, *Justus Menius: der Reformator Thüringens,* 2 vols. (Gotha: Perthes, 1867).

8. The treatise is briefly discussed in the following: Schmidt, *Justus Menius* II: 20-26; Christmann, "Melanchthons Haltung," 5, 52-53, 156-57, as well as references to Melanchthon's revisions in chap. 3; Waldeck, "Publizistik," 44-47; Schoenberger, "Confession," 52-55; and my "Philippist Theologians," 455-56.

9. *Von der Notwehr vnterricht: Nützlich zu lesen. Durch Justum Menium. Witteberg. M.D.XLVII.* Colophon: *Gedruckt zu Witteberg / bey Veit Creutzer. M.D.XLVII.* Signatures A(1a-4b)-D, a-f. Signature references in the text of this article are to this edition, which is a second, slightly revised printing of the second version. This was reprinted again in 1549 (n.p., n.pub.) and in both eds. of Friedrich Hortleder, *Keyser vnd Königlichen Maiestete / Auch dess heiligen Rö. Reichs / geistlicher vnd weltlicher Stände. . . .* vol. II: *Handlungen vnd Ausschreiben . . . Von Rechtmässigkeit / Anfang / For- vnd endlichen Außgang deß Teutschen Kriegs / Keyser Carls deß Fünfften / wider die Schmalkaldische Bundsoberste. . . .* (1st ed., Frankfurt/M., 1618, 2d ed., Gotha, 1645), Book 2, no. 29. Latin ed.: *DE DEFENSIONE CONCESSA HVMANO GENERI IVRE naturae, Scriptum Justi Menij, Ex Germanica lingua in Latinum conuersum. VITEBERGAE ANNO M.D.XLVII.* A distinguishing mark of the first German edition is its signatures: A(1a-4b)-L. I am preparing a brief article explicating the differences in the two versions and

Melanchthon's reasons for extensively editing Menius's manuscript.

10. B3b; the "Third Part" is pp. c2b-f3b.

11. Skinner, *Foundations,* 124-26, 197-204. For the *Gutachten,* see Heinz Scheible, ed., *Das Widerstandsrecht als Problem der Deutchen Protestanten, 1523-1546,* Texte zur Kirchen- und Theologiegeschichte, no. 10 (Gütersloh: Mohn, 1969), 89-94; see also Hans Lüthje, "Melanchthons Anschauung über das Recht des Widerstands gegen die Staatsgewalt," *ZKG* 47, n.s. 10 (1928): 525-35.

12. Ernst Kinder, "Luthers Ableitung der geistlichen und weltliche 'Oberkeit' aus dem 4. Gebot," in *Für Kirche und Recht: Festschrift für Johannes Heckel z. 70. Geburtstag,* ed. Siegfried Grundmann (Cologne & Graz: Böhlau, 1959), 272, 275-77.

13. The best discussion of orders of creation is Wilhelm Maurer, *Luthers Lehre von den drei Hierarchien und ihr mittelalterlicher Hintergrund,* Bayerische Akademie der Wissenschaften, Philosophisch-Historische Klasse, Sitzungsberichte, 1970, no. 4 (Munich, 1970); see also Thomas Brady, "Luther and the State: the Reformer's Teaching in Its Social Setting," in *Luther and the Modern State in Germany,* ed. James D. Tracy, Sixteenth Century Essays & Studies, no. 7 (Kirksville, Mo.: Sixteenth Century Journal Publ., 1986), 33-36.

14. Brady, "Luther," 31-32; the quotes are from Skinner, *Foundations,* 352, 358.

15. This was the "*Zirkulardisputation,*" in Scheible, *Widerstandsrecht,* 94-98, and *WA* 39/II:39-51. See Rudolf Hermann, "Luthers Zirkulardisputation über Matth. 19:21," *Lutherjahrbuch* 23 (1941): 35-93.

16. Luther had written the same, dating it from the apostolic age; Brady, "Luther," 32, n 4.

17. Luther used this text as early as *Of Temporal Authority* of 1523. See Skinner, *Foundations* 17, and Gunnar Hillerdal, "Der Mensch unter Gottes Regiment: der Unterthan und das Recht," in Günther Vogt, ed., *Luther und die Obrigkeit* (Darmstadt: Wissenschaftliche Buchgesellschaft, 1972), 36.

18. D2a; this text also appears in *Of Temporal Authority.*

19. Melanchthon here agreed with the republican interpretation of Caesar's death argued by the Florentine civic humanists ca. 1400; see Hans Baron, *The Crisis of the Early Italian Renaissance,* 2d ed. (Princeton: Princeton University Press, 1966), esp. chaps. 3, 5.

20. b1a; see also c1a, d3a. The condition that left first redress to a magistrate was repeated on p. b3b.

21. b1a, *ordentlichen defension;* b2a, "*schutz oder defensio ein geordnet werck ist.*"

22. c1a-b. Melanchthon apparently regarded this pre-feudal incident as an example of the feudal *diffidatio.* See also Richard Benert, "Lutheran Resistance Theory and the Imperial Constitution," *Il Pensiero Politico* 7 (1973): 28; Benert notes that Melanchthon used the example in the 1543 ed. of *Loci communes,* as did Luther and Monner also.

23. *Foundations,* 203.

24. For a discussion of the constitutional argument, see ibid., chap. 4, and pp. 195-96, 204-11.

Abbreviations

ARG Archiv für Reformationsgeschichte

BHR Bibliothèque d'Humanisme et Renaissance

SCJ Sixteenth Century Journal

WA D. Martin Luthers Werke: Kritische Gesamtausgabe. Weimar: Böhlau, 1883-.

ZKG Zeitschrift für Kirchengeschichte

Åke Bergvall (essay date 1994)

SOURCE: Bergvall, Åke. "Melanchthon and Tudor England." In *Cultural Exchange between European Nations during the Renaissance,* edited by Gunnar Sorelius and Michael Srigley, pp. 85-93. Stockholm: Uppsala University, 1994.

[*In this excerpt, Bergvall highlights Melanchthon's status as a literary presence in England during the sixteenth, seventeenth, and eighteenth centuries.*]

Edward Denny in 1580 asked his younger friend Philip Sidney to suggest a recommended program of studies. In his written reply Sidney placed great emphasis on the study of history and proposed that Denny read a broad range of works, from the Greek and Roman classics to European chronicles. Denny's first choice, however, Sidney intimated, should not be Herodotos or Livy but a near contemporary: "You shoold begin with Phillip Melanthons Chronology."[1] Melanchthon's *Chronicon* was an appropriate beginning, since in one broad sweep it covered the whole of history, from creation to recent times. Yet Sidney's choice of Melanchthon is also indicative of a more fundamental debt: the Lutheran reformer and humanist had for decades stood in the forefront of educational reform both on the Continent and in England. Indeed, Melanchthon's influence in northern Europe—both directly through his writings and indirectly through the schools and the scholars he molded—was second only to that of Erasmus. While everybody today rightly recognizes the Erasmian stamp on northern humanism, Melanchthon is largely forgotten. My paper is a small attempt to rectify this omission by highlighting Melanchthon's presence in Tudor England, especially in the writings of Sir Philip Sidney.

I

In 1518 Philip Melanchthon, the precocious grandnephew of Johannes Reuchlin, became at the age of 21 the first professor of Greek at the University of Wittenberg. Indebted to Erasmus, the young lecturer immediately set his stamp on the university with an inaugural address that blazoned the new learning and placed rhetoric at the center of a humanist curriculum.[2] He remained faithful to Wittenberg, yet by the time of his death in 1560 he was not simply the reformer of his own university but the "*Praeceptor Germaniae,*" the "Teacher of Germany." By then he had taught over 150 courses and written influential textbooks in almost every subject of the curriculum.[3] He had also helped to reorganize a number of German universities and secondary schools along humanistic lines. Yet all of that was only one side of his mission.

Immediately upon his arrival at Wittenberg he became involved with one of the other professors, Martin Luther, who was then only beginning to formulate his critique of the status quo in religion. In Melanchthon, Luther found a worthy co-worker that in the years to come was to complement his own hot-tempered enthusiasm with calm scholarship and an ecumenical and irenic spirit. While Luther was the born leader and wrote the trail-blazing tracts that spread the Reformation all over northern Europe, Melanchthon consolidated and systematized the new doctrine through his more scholarly writings.[4] What we now know as Lutheranism was indeed to a large extent documented not by Luther himself but by Melanchthon. In 1521 came the first of many editions of his Erasmian exercise in theology, the *Loci communes,* in which "commonplaces" such as "God, Unity, Trinity, Predestination, Sin, Law, Grace," etc. were explicated.[5] And in 1530 it was Melanchthon who penned the first draft of what was to become the central doctrinal document of Lutheranism, *The Augsburg Confession.* Both of these works were to play a crucial part in the continued spread of Protestantism, not just in Germany and not just among the Lutherans. Melanchthon was a long-time friend of Martin Bucer, who was to become a major Zwinglian influence in England, and he remained on friendly terms with John Calvin even after cracks developed in the relationship between Wittenberg and Geneva.[6] But what about Melanchthon and England? What role did he have to play in the religious and intellectual development of the insular kingdom?

II

Melanchthon never sat foot on the British Isles, yet that was not for lack of trying. Already in 1516, before the young prodigy moved to Wittenberg, Erasmus recommended him for a teaching position at Cambridge to John Fisher, the university chancellor.[7] While nothing came of it, the efforts to bring him to England were renewed more than once by Henry VIII himself in the 1530s. At that point it was the German princes who would not let Melanchthon go. And finally, when Melanchthon's old friend Martin Bucer died in his post as Professor of Theology at Cambridge in 1553, Edward VI personally selected and invited Melanchthon to fill the vacancy.[8] Yet that also was not to be. Within a few months the king was dead, and Mary Tudor preempted any Protestant post. It is anyway doubtful whether Melanchthon, who himself had only a few more years to live, would have responded to Edward's call.

But if he did not make it to England in person, Melanchthon's intellectual presence was felt to a large degree. When Henry in 1531 needed support for his contemplated divorce from Katherine of Aragon, Melanchthon was one of the Continental experts consulted. While the king could not have been too pleased with the answer—Melanchthon advocated bigamy rather than divorce—that did not prevent him from strengthening the ties with the Lutherans after his break with Rome a few years later. A delegation was sent to Wittenberg to discuss the matter with Melanchthon, and Henry and Thomas Cranmer both invited the reformer to England. Unable to come, Melanchthon responded by dedicating a new 1535 edition of the *Loci communes* to the English king, who in turn rewarded Melanchthon financially. In the same year the Royal Injunctions for Cambridge University prescribes Melanchthon's humanist textbooks (together with those of Aristotle, Rudolph Agricola, and Trapezuntius) instead of the "frivolous questions and obscure glosses" of the medieval schoolmen.[9] The following year the rapprochement between Germany and England increased as theologians from both countries agreed on the "Wittenberg Articles," which in turn influenced Henry's own cautiously reformist *Ten Articles*. To further strengthen the ties, *The Augsburg Confession* was translated into English.[10] Yet Henry got cold feet, and the last decade of his reign was characterized by a return to a more Catholic theology. The *Thirteen Articles* of 1538, written by Melanchthon and accepted by Henry's commissioners, were rejected by the king, who instead went on to establish the conservative *Six Articles* the following year. Melanchthon responded by writing a long letter to the king in which he pleaded continued reform.[11]

With the accession of Edward VI the contacts with Wittenberg were renewed. Cranmer in particular had been on good terms with Melanchthon even during Henry's reign; and when asked to put together the new Anglican formularies, the Wittenberg reformer and humanist contributed significant parts. "Melanchthonian formulas" can be detected in the Edwardian and Elizabethan *Articles of Religion* as well as in the homilies.[12] Furthermore, an Order for the Cologne church, drawn up by Melanchthon and Bucer in 1543, was used by Cranmer when he put together the *Book of Common Prayer.* In particular, Melanchthon's teaching on the *adiaphora,* the gray area of religious non-essentials such as the use of ceremonies or of bishops, became a cornerstone of Anglican defense against Puritan radicals. Melanchthonian doctrine was also spread to a larger public with the English translation of the *Loci communes.*[13]

The most important reader of the *Loci,* however, was a young lady that could read the original Latin: Princess Elizabeth. Roger Ascham, Elizabeth's tutor and an admirer of Melanchthon, in 1550 wrote Johannes Sturm (himself a former student and close associate of the Wittenberg reformer) about the princess's education: "To these [classical authors] I added Saint Cyprian and Melanchthon's Common Places, & c., as best suited, after the Holy Scriptures, to teach her the foundations of religion, together with elegant language and sound doctrine."[14] As a consequence of Ascham's choice of reading, Elizabeth, according to Carl Meyer, became "a Melanchthonian in theology and in political science."[15] She was later to tell the Spanish ambassador that she would have liked the *Augsburg Confession,* or something like it, to be adopted for her country.

But Melanchthon's influence was far from restricted to the religious sphere. The true gauge of his impact in Tudor England is the extent to which he combined his efforts as a Reformer with his humanist mission. And it has finally become possible to measure that impact in a more objective way. I am thinking of the 1986 publication of E. S. Leedham-Green's *Books in Cambridge Inventories.*[16] By documenting the two hundred inventories of people who died between 1535 and 1760 while being attached to Cambridge University, Leedham-Green has opened up a gold-mine of information about the reading habits at the university. By studying these lists (made random by death), we get a fairly good picture of what authors were actually owned (and presumably read) by students, teachers, and in a few cases, book-sellers. Of the 200 inventories, I have selected the 176 that were made in the sixteenth century. With this statistical material I have simply calculated *how many* of these 176 persons *owned at least one book* by any particular author. . . . After the Bible, which is in a category by itself, we find nothing surprising in the next three names: Erasmus (73%), Cicero (69%), and Aristotle (60%). But I think some will raise their eyebrows about the next author, who makes a strong runner-up. Half the academic population of Cambridge it seems, if this statistical material is anywhere near the truth, owned at least one book by Melanchthon. Together with Erasmus this places him way ahead of any other Renaissance author. And if we break down this figure into separate titles, we find that Melanchthon is read both as a religious and a humanist writer. Most widely owned are the ***Loci communes*** (17%, which makes it more common than Calvin's *Institutes,* at 14%), followed by the ***Dialectics*** (15%) and the ***Chronicles***—the ones recommended by Sidney (14%). Other common works include his ***Commentaries on Romans*** and other biblical commentaries,[17] as well as university textbooks in ***Grammar, Syntax, Rhetoric, Ethics,*** an ***Introduction to Physics,*** and a study in psychology, ***On the Soul.*** The common denominator of these textbooks is their strong neo-Aristotelian emphasis. Aristotle, as glossed by Melanchthon, seems to have been common fare at the university.[18]

III

Although Philip Sidney studied at Oxford rather than at Cambridge, we can be pretty certain he had met several of these Melanchthonian textbooks. But we do not have to base our surmises on Sidney's interest in Melanchthon on such general hypotheses. Although the Wittenberg reformer died soon after Sidney's birth, a bridge was established via two of Melanchthon's pupils: Sidney's cherished mentor Hubert Languet, and Johannes Sturm, at whose famous Academy in Strasbourg Sidney spent several months in 1572. That Sidney's interest in Melanchthon remained after his return to England is seen not only in the letter to Denny, but also in his support of the translation of Melanchthon into English. Richard Robinson, who translated two Melanchthonian works in the late 1570s, dedicated one of them to Sidney.[19] He later looked back on the generous support he had received over a period of time from both Philip and his father: "[Philip Sidney] gave me for his book [i.e., the book dedicated to him] 4 angels, and his honourable father gave me for his book ten shillings. These two honourable personages many times benevolent unto my poor study."[20] But to be absolutely certain we are not reading Melanchthon into Sidney's writings, I shall restrict myself to the one work we are sure Sidney had read: the ***Chronicon*** he recommended to Denny about the same time as he was writing both *The Defence of Poesie* and the *Arcadia.*[21]

The ***Chronicon,*** in two separate volumes, was published under Melanchthon's own name only at the end of the reformer's life, and he died while revising a third volume.[22] Melanchthon's interest in world history, however, was of long standing. Indeed, the work had been on the market in different German, French, Italian, English, and Latin editions since 1532, but ascribed to a different author: it had been *Carion's Chronicle.* Yet John Carion, a student of Melanchthon's, had only had

a smaller part in the making of the book, while Melanchthon all along had been its real, if hidden, author. This applies in particular to the preface of the work, "The vse of readynge hystoryes," which Melanchthon kept revising until the end of his life.[23] The title of the preface is pure Melanchthon, yet it also harks back to a classical precedent: Plutarch's influential essay, "How the Young Man Should Study Poetry."[24] As Plutarch, in Sidney's words, "teacheth the use to be gathered of [the poets]" (*Defence,* p. 109), so Melanchthon wants to teach his readers how to rightly read both sacred and secular historiographers. And as Sidney turns Plutarch's precepts around, by *writing* rather than reading poetry right, so he uses Melanchthon's advice in writing his own political and historical romance, the *Arcadia.* But we also find unmediated echoes of Melanchthon's preface in *The Defence of Poesie.*

Melanchthon begins by telling the rulers what they have to learn from history, and then he turns to the "examples" the ordinary subject can learn from. When Sidney came to write the *Arcadia* he places great weight on the same "examples" as those found in Melanchthon's preface:

> The magistrate must be obeyed. They, which rebelled against the higher powers, were neuer vnpunished, as Absalon, Catalina, Brutus, Cassius and such like that were therefore punished [cf. the judgement scene in the old *Arcadia,* and the mob scene in the new]. Of faithfulnesse of frendes, as Jonathas, which saved the life of Dauid [cf. Musidorus and Pyrocles]. Of the punishment for aduoutry and suche like wicked dedes, as it appeareth by the example of David [cf. Musidorus and Pyrocles's affairs with the young princesses].
>
> (***Chronicles,*** sig. * iiii[v])

In the continuation we recognize both the theory of the *Defence* and the practice of the *Arcadia:*

> So are in histories set forth & painted examples of al kind of vertues. Yee and in examples and thinges committed is more euidently sene the worthinesse of vertues, yea & also of what vnclennesse and dishonesty vices are, then in preceptes or doctrines: Because that examples being set before vs as images, do not only teache openly, but do also admonish, sturre, and inflame the myndes that are honestly brought vp, that they maye be kindled toward vertues and honesty with a certain plesur and loue.[25]

As Sidney was to phrase it, poetry "is that feigning notable images of virtues, vices, or what else" (*Defence,* p. 81). Sidney of course places the poet higher than both the philosopher and the historiographer, "the one giueth the precept and the other the example, . . . while the peerless poet perform both" (*Defence,* pp. 84-85), yet that does not prevent him from appropriating Melanchthon's views on the power of the *image:* the poet "giveth a perfect picture," says Sidney, "for he yieldeth to the powers of the mind an image of that whereof the philosophers bestoweth but a wordish description, which doth neither strike, pierce, nor possess the sight of the soul so much as that other doth" (*Defence*, p. 85).

Sidney's use of Aristotle in the *Defence* (novel in its day) was in line with the revitalization of Aristotelianism that to a large extent had been brought about through Melanchthon's efforts. Yet both Melanchthon and Sidney limit Aristotle's influence to the sphere of reason. This has repercussions on their views on politics, ethics, esthetics, *and* history. In accordance with the Protestant tendency to separate the categories of faith and reason into separate yet complementary spheres, Melanchthon distinguishes in the **Chronicon** between secular and sacred history; the latter, contained in the Bible, "do not only treat of politike matters, but do chefely shadowe and declare vnto vs Gods kingdome, that God geueth his worde, that frely and of mercye he will saue: the which thing the histories of the Gentiles can not speake of" (**Chronicles**, sig. * vᵛ). Yet that does not mean that a Christian cannot draw benefit from secular history: "And thoughe the hystoryes of the Gentyls do not teache vs that God careth for vs, or that God worketh wyth vs: a godlye harte neuerthelesse shall marke thys, namelye, how commune welthes are kept and preserued in the worlde from heauen" (**Chronicles**, sig. *vʳ). It is evident that Sidney took this advice to heart in his poetic recreation of historical events. Being a "right" poet, as defined in *The Defence of Poesie*, he did not presume to enter the religious sphere that was cut out for scriptural poets like David.[26] The *Arcadia* is therefore set in Greece, and no overtly Christian material is introduced.[27] Yet that does not mean that Sidney, in Melanchthon's words, is not interested in showing "how commune welthes are kept and preserued in the worlde from heauen." As S. K. Heninger has recently shown, the oracle that figures prominently in the old *Arcadia* and is still present in the revised version, is Sidney's principal means of achieving this oblique, non-scriptural reference to divine providence.[28]

On the face of it Sidney seems to have little faith in the efficacy of secular history. History, "being captived to the truth of a foolish world," he complains in the *Defence*, "is many times a terror from well-doing, and an encouragement to unbridled wickedness" (p. 90). Yet the disagreement with Melanchthon is more apparent than real. Unwittingly or not, they both followed St Augustine and prefigured Hayden White. According to R. A. Markus, it had been Augustine, in his *City of God* and the *Literal Meaning of Genesis*, that first had understood history "not as a series of events but as statements about the past, recording events. 'History,' in this sense, *tells* of what happened; it *is* not what happened,

but its record."[29] For Augustine, the unmediated "facts" of history are therefore of limited value. The same holds true for Melanchthon and Sidney. It takes eyes "cleared by faith" (*Defence*, p. 77) to reinscribe history as a didactic medium: for Melanchthon, through teaching "the vse of readynge hystories" as an introduction to his own carefully sifted world history; for Sidney, by means of "right" poetry. And that is of course why Sidney places the **Chronicon** first on his list to Denny. Seen through the spectacles of faith, provided by Melanchthon, Denny can then go on and draw the necessary benefit also from other non-Christian historiographers.

Notes

1. As cited in James M. Osborn, *Young Philip Sidney, 1572-1577* (New Haven: Yale UP, 1972) 539. Sidney mentions Melanchthon in *The Defence of Poesie* as well, this time as a patron of poetry (*Miscellaneous Prose of Sir Philip Sidney,* ed. Katherine Duncan-Jones and Jan van Dorsten [Oxford: Clarendon, 1973] 112). References to the *Defence* will hereafter be given in the text. On Melanchthon as a writer and a patron of neo-Latin poetry, see Manfred P. Fleischer, "Melanchthon as Praeceptor of Late-Humanist Poetry," *Sixteenth Century Journal* 20/4 (1989): 559-80.

2. Even if Erasmus and Melanchthon never met, they kept up their correspondence and their friendship even after Erasmus's break with Luther. See Carl S. Meyer, "Christian Humanism and the Reformation: Erasmus and Melanchthon," *Concordia Theological Monthly* 41 (1970): 637-47.

3. "During his forty-eight years of teaching, Melanchthon offered at least 159 courses," writes Lowell C. Green: "of these 46 were in theology, with the remaining 113 courses distributed as follows: Greek authors, 51 courses, including at least 11 dealing specifically with Aristotle, 42 in Latin authors, of which at least 11 were liberal arts courses in Dialectic or Rhetoric, 11 in natural science, and 8 in history, including world history" ("The Reformation and Education in the Sixteenth Century," *Bulletin of Appalachian State University* 67 [1970]: 37). I shall return to Melanchthon's writings below.

4. See *Luther and Melanchthon in the History and Theology of the Reformation,* ed. Vilmos Vajta (Philadelphia: Muhlenberg, 1961), and Lowell C. Green, *How Melanchthon Helped Luther Discover the Gospel* (Fallbrook, CA: Verdict, 1980).

5. Erasmus's *Ratio seu Methodus* had provided the theory: "You should make up for yourself [from the Bible] some kind of theological 'loci' or accept those already handed down by someone else.

Into these you can collect, as in nestlets, all that you read" (as cited in Timothy J. Wengert, *Philip Melanchthon's "Annotationes in Johannem" in Relation to its Predecessors and Contemporaries,* Travaux d'Humanisme et Renaissance, vol. 220 [Geneva: Droz, 1987] 133).

6. Melanchthon's ecumenical spirit led hard-core Lutherans to accuse him of selling out Luther's original vision.

7. Meyer 643.

8. See Barrett L. Beer, "Philip Melanchthon and the Cambridge Professorship," *Notes and Queries* ns 34 (June 1987): 185.

9. T. W. Baldwin, *William Shakspere's Small Latine and Lesse Greeke,* 2 vols. (Urbana: U of Illinois P, 1944) 2: 34. According to Claire Cross, "It seems very likely that Cromwell sent similar injunctions to Oxford which have not been preserved" (vol. 3 of *The History of the University of Oxford: The Collegiate University,* ed. James McConica [Oxford: Clarendon, 1986] 129).

10. Thomas Cromwell ordered Richard Taverner, the translator of Erasmus, to translate Melanchthon's work. It appeared in English as *The confessyon of the fayth of the Germaynes* (London, 1536). STC 17788.

11. Melanchthon's letter was surreptitiously translated into English almost at once, but no copies of this first edition are extant. It was, however, reprinted in 1547 as *The epistle of the famous and great clerke Philip Melancton made vnto kynge Henry the eight, for the reuokinge of the six articles,* trans. J. C. ([Antwerp], 1547). STC 17789. On Melanchthon's part in the Henrician reformation, see James H. Pragman, "The Augsburg Confession in the English Reformation: Richard Taverner's Contribution," *Sixteenth Century Journal* 11/3 (1980): 75-85. Henry's infatuation with Wittenberg, while cooling down, did not freeze completely. In 1538, for example, the king had Richard Taverner translate Sarcerius' *Commonplaces of Scripture,* a rewrite of Melanchthon's *Loci* for a less learned audience.

12. Ralph Keen, *A Melanchthon Reader* (New York: Peter Lang, 1988) 19.

13. John Rogers, one of the Marian martyrs, translated the whole of the *Loci,* yet no copies are extant. An excerpt, however, translated by N. Lesse, was published as *The iustification of man by faith only: An apologie or defence of the worde of God* (London, 1548). STC 17792.

14. As cited in Baldwin 1: 259.

15. Carl S. Meyer, "Melanchthon's Influence on English Thought in the Sixteenth Century," *Miscellanea Historiae Ecclesiasticae II, Bibliothèque de la*

Revue d'Histoire Ecclésiastique, fasc. 44 (Louvain: Publications Universitaires de Louvain, 1967) 177. Meyer's article, despite its inclusive title, is restricted to a (valuable) discussion of the Tudor translations of Melanchthon's works.

16. 2 vols. (Cambridge: Cambridge UP, 1986). No such work has been published on Oxford University, and would anyway not be as useful since the inventory-makers there worked with less care (especially after 1586), often lumping books together under one undifferentiated post (see vol. 3 of *The History of the University of Oxford* 470-71). Yet the Oxford inventories, as far as Melanchthon is concerned, does not seem to differ substantially from those at Cambridge. See Mark H. Curtis, "Library Catalogues and Tudor Oxford and Cambridge," *Studies in the Renaissance* 5 (1958): 111-21, and *Oxford and Cambridge in Transition, 1558-1642* (Oxford: Clarendon, 1959) 162.

17. Together with Luther Melanchthon covered virtually the whole New Testament in a series of commentaries published between 1522 and 1524. This collection was the first fruits of Protestant exegesis and proved immensely influential on subsequent commentaries. See Wengert.

18. One result of Leedham-Green's research is that we need to revise Charles Schmitt's contention that "while the educational reforms of Johannes Sturm and Philip Melanchthon reinstated a humanized Aristotelian learning to the very core of the Reformed universities in Germany, nothing similar happened in England" (*John Case and Aristotelianism in Renaissance England* [Kingston and Montreal: McGill-Queen's UP, 1983] 20). Schmitt places too much emphasis on books printed in England and underestimates the magnitude of the book-import from the Continent during much of the century.

19. Robinson dedicated to Sidney *Godly prayers, meete to be vsed in these later times: collected out of Philip Melancthon and others* (London, 1579). STC 17790.5. His next translation was of a more important work: Philip Melanchthon, *A godly and learned assertion in defence of the true church* (London, 1580). STC 17790. We can only speculate as to whether he did any of these translations at Sidney's behest.

20. As cited in Katherine Duncan-Jones, *Sir Philip Sidney, Courtier Poet* (London: Hamish Hamilton, 1991) 229.

21. I have to admit, however, that we do not know which of the many different editions of the *Chronicon* Sidney used.

22. Philip Melanchthon, *Chronicon Carionis* (Wittenberg, 1558), and *Secunda pars Chronici Carionis* (Wittenberg, 1560). The third part was finished by Caspar Peucer and published in 1562 (together with reprints of the first two parts). A fourth part was published by Peucer in 1565, while a one-volume folio edition of the complete work came out in 1572 (in addition to competing editions that were on the market soon after the Wittenberg imprints). For bibliographical information about these editions, and the numerous earlier printings published in Carion's name, see Philip Melanchthon, *Opera quae supersunt omnia,* ed. Carolus Gottlieb Bretschneider, Corpus Reformatorum, vol 12 (Halle, 1844) 707-10.

23. I am quoting the title of the preface from the Edwardian translation of the German edition: *Carion's Chronicle: The thre bokes of Cronicles,* trans. Gwalter Lynne (London, 1550). STC 4626. References to the English translation, abbreviated *Chronicles,* will be given in the text. The title of the original 1532 German preface was "Wozu Historien zu lesen nützlich ist," later translated into Latin as "De vsv lectionis historiarum." The title was retained until the 1558 Wittenberg edition, when Melanchthon's revised preface (to be read in conjunction with a new dedicatory letter to Archbishop Sigismund) omitted the heading. See Peter Fraenkel, *Testimonia Patrum* (Geneva: Droz, 1961) 53-54, on Melanchthon's contribution to the *Chronicles,* and on the similarities between the 1532 and the 1558 versions of the preface.

24. The debt is not surprising since Melanchthon had edited Plutarch; see Wengert 28.

25. For this central passage I want to give the equivalent Latin (since we do not know which edition Sidney had read): "Sed quid multa? quemadmodum in omnibus artibus paradigmata ad imitationem proponuntur, ita & in historiis exempla ob oculos depicta extant de omni genere uirtutum. Quin & in exemplis & factis cernitur longe clarius, quae dignitas sit uirtutum, & rursus quae turpitudo sit inhonestatis ac uitiorum, quàm in praeceptis, propterea quòd exempla tanquam imagines proposita, non solum docent apertè, sed & monent, commouent, et inflammant liberè eductos animos, ut uoluptate et amore quodam circa uirtutes & honestatem accendantur" (*Chronicorum libri tres* [Basle, 1557] 9). See also Melanchthon's *Oration on Aristotle:* "Nothing is sweeter than to look with your mind into men of outstanding virtue, in whom we can almost see the very image of the virtues. When we see Augustus [cf. Sidney's Cyrus] before us, we ponder the image and idea of the wise, just, moderate, constant, benevolent prince" (Keen 79).

26. Except by way of paraphrase, in his *Psalms of David.*

27. For the distinction between faith and reason as applied to Sidney, see my "Reason in Luther, Calvin, and Sidney," *Sixteenth Century Journal* 23/1 (1992): 115-27.

28. S. K. Heninger, Jr., "Spenser, Sidney, and Poetic form," *Studies in Philology* 88/2 (Spring 1991): 140-52.

29. R. A. Markus, *Saeculum: History and Society in the Thought of St Augustine* (Cambridge: Cambridge UP, 1970) 14. For the *City of God,* as for the *Chronicon,* "the meaning and structure of history derive from sacred history" (Markus 19). Melanchthon, certainly, was familiar with Augustine's views on history. The whole conceptual scheme of the *Chronicon*—the "four ages" presented in the preface as "the sayenge of Helias house" (*Chronicles,* sig. *vi^v)—is Augustinian (see, e.g., *The Enchiridion* 118). On Melanchthon's historical writings, see Fraenkel 52 ff.

Kees Meerhoff (essay date 1994)

SOURCE: Meerhoff, Kees. "The Significance of Philip Melanchthon's Rhetoric in the Renaissance." In *Renaissance Rhetoric,* edited by Peter Mack, pp. 46-62. New York: St. Martin's Press, 1994.

[*In the essay below, Meerhoff shows how Melanchthon applies the precepts of rhetoric to the task of reading and interpreting texts.*]

> *Magis affectibus quam argutiis.*
>
> Erasmus, *Methodus*

Since I am going to deal with so wide and complex a topic as 'the significance of Philip Melanchthon's rhetoric in the renaissance', I would prefer to begin with an analysis of an example from the huge corpus of Melanchton's writings, and to continue with a description of Melanchthon's teaching practice at the University of Wittenberg (Saxony), where students from all over Europe came to listen to this pale man with his awkward voice.

Philip Melanchthon played a major part in the reformation of the church, as an ally to Martin Luther, as a reformer of Christian education and as a leading humanist scholar. When he came to Wittenberg in 1518, he was already working on his first version of a rhetoric designed along humanist lines, which appeared the next year, very badly printed, in the same small town. Shortly afterwards it was reprinted in a better shape by Erasmus's friend John Froben, in Basel, Switzerland.

After his famous inaugural lecture *On Correcting the Studies of Youth,* he taught Homer and St Paul's *Letter to Titus,* and in the new year he commented on the Hebrew text of the *Psalms,* 'until', he writes, 'a more qualified person can be hired'.[1] We may assume that Reuchlin, his grand-uncle, was of some help to him in his hazardous enterprise. Melanchthon was only twenty-one years old at the time!

Some of the elements I have just mentioned reappear in my first example, his commentary on Cicero's *Topics.* As early as 1524, Melanchthon published in Wittenberg Cicero's text with its traditional companion-piece, the commentary of Boethius. He would have commented orally on the text in his classroom; at least, no written commentary from this period is extant. This was published only in 1533; as so often happened, lack of time prevented him from sending his lecture-notes to the press.[2]

The written commentary starts with some general remarks which are, I believe, very characteristic of his outlook. 'This book', says Melanchthon,

> belongs to that part of rhetoric which describes the method of finding arguments, and the ways in which discourse can be amplified. As such, it clearly parallels the second book of Erasmus's *De Copia*; in fact, the subject-matter of both books is identical, because there is no real difference between arguments and figures of thought. Indeed, one always needs to consider what part of a discipline a given work refers to; otherwise, it is no use studying. So, as I said before, the *Topics* contain precepts about the invention of arguments and a method of amplification. For an example, I might take the first Psalm [*Beatus vir*], which has the following proposition: 'Those who govern themselves according to God's word, are blessed.' The author could have limited himself to this one line. But he has created a whole text in such a way, that it fits in [*consentire*] with this proposition. So, right from the start, the proposition is amplified *a contrario,* and then *ab effectibus.* [Here, Melanchthon summarises the relevant lines.] The same could be said of the Psalm *Ecce quam bonum* [Ps. 133], 'Concord is a good thing'. This proposition is amplified with some very sweet [*amoeniores*] figures [He quotes]. . . . These examples suffice to show of what service this book can be.[3]

Clearly, Melanchthon considers Cicero's *Topics* mainly from a textual, even from a 'literary' point of view. Whereas Cicero presents the *Topics* as technical tools for the lawyer, Melanchthon stresses their use in the process of conceiving and analysing a text. It is for this reason that he refers almost instinctively to Erasmus's *De Copia,* and that he suggests in passing the common basis of arguments and rhetorical figures. In the *Elements of Rhetoric,* published in 1531, Melanchthon presents a scheme in which the figures, especially those which amplify discourse, all derive from the dialectical topics. For example, vivid description, or *hypotyposis,*

has its source in the topic of the circumstances, and so on. Since the importance of this chapter of the *Elements* has already been underlined in C. Vasoli's magnificent study of humanist dialectic and rhetoric, I simply point to the absolute identity of point of view in the rhetorical textbook and in the commentary.[4] Indeed, more than once Melanchthon expresses the same ideas in very different contexts; fundamental issues are treated like 'set pieces' which he inserts as vital elements in a variety of texts. These set pieces reflect without any doubt his teaching practice, and show the intimate bond between teaching and writing in Melanchthon's works. Another striking example of this procedure would be his ideas concerning imitation, which he expresses not only in the next chapter of the *Elements of Rhetoric,* but in an almost identical way in some of his major commentaries on Cicero and Quintilian.[5] In short, one can observe an intense circulation in Melanchthon's different texts, especially between textbooks and commentaries. This is the case in his rhetorical and dialectical works, but no less in his theological writings, to which we will return later.

In his introductory remarks to his commentary on Cicero's *Topics,* which remain my first point of reference, Melanchthon quite naturally illustrates the issue of topical invention and amplification with a twofold quotation taken from the Bible. We will see that for Melanchthon, the Scriptures have an essentially rhetorical orientation; and this presentation in the commentary shows that he considers the very lyrical texts of the Psalms to be constructed in exactly the same way as a forensic oration. In both cases, there is a point at issue which has to be developed and put into proper relief; in both cases, there is a rhetorical appeal to a public.[6]

The point I want to stress here is that it is very hard to say whether Melanchthon talks about the actual creation of the Psalm by King David himself, or simply about a convenient method for analysing this kind of text. We may surmise that in his mind, dialectical analysis comes close to the very process of creation.

This conjecture finds further support in Melanchthon's own teaching practice in which, as with so many other humanist scholars, imitation plays a vital part. In the stronghold of the reformation that was Wittenberg University, the study of the Bible and of theology constituted the final goal of the curriculum. Right from the start, Melanchthon was an essential helper to Luther in defending their new theological insights. We have seen that Melanchthon starts his career by lecturing on Paul's *Letter to Titus.* He refers to this analysis in the first version of his rhetoric, which I quoted earlier. Even here, while talking about techniques of interpretation and paraphrase of a biblical text, Melanchthon states that he urged his audience to use their own paraphrases to create a new text by quoting parallel examples, by adducing additional arguments, and so on. He ends his remarks on paraphrase by stating that when used as he suggested, paraphrase can be the source of *mirabilis copia*.[7]

Of course, the very fact that Melanchthon gives so much attention to the techniques of analysing texts in an elementary rhetorical textbook indicates very clearly that for him, analysis and production of texts form an inseparable whole. Indeed, his remarks on paraphrase are only the beginning of a long chapter entirely dedicated to the methodical interpretation of all kinds of texts. The exegesis of the Scriptures features prominently, but by no means exclusively, in these pages, which were read with passion all over Europe by Protestant reformers as well as by anti-Lutheran catholics like Alardus of Amsterdam, the editor of Rudolph Agricola's writings.[8] They are an essential element in the first book of the early **Rhetoric,** which Melanchthon rounds off by presenting his ideas on sermon-writing in a chapter headed '*de sacris concionibus*'. Thus, once again methodical analysis of scriptural texts and the rhetoric of preaching constitute a diptych.[9]

So far I have concentrated mainly on the beginnings of Melanchthon's career, during those crucial years from 1518 to 1524. As we have seen, in this period Melanchthon lectured on both biblical and profane texts, and published his first rhetorical textbook and his commentary on Cicero's *Topics,* among some eighty other texts.

Let us now consider briefly the period around the **Elements of Rhetoric,** the final version of which was published in Wittenberg in 1531. According to the list compiled by Carl Hartfelder one hundred years ago, Melanchthon lectured in 1529 on Paul's *Letter to the Romans,* a few months later on dialectic and the *Organon* of Aristotle, and finally on two Ciceronian orations, *Pro Murena* and *Pro Marcello*. In 1530 he taught Cicero's *De Oratore,* immediately followed by Cicero's *Pro Archia,* and perhaps by another Ciceronian oration. In 1531, he probably lectured on Homer's *Iliad,* and certainly on three Ciceronian orations, *Pro Caelio, Pro Sulla,* and the ninth *Philippic*. In 1532, he took up *Romans* again, as he did so many times before and after this period, then the *Ethics* of Aristotle, Book v, and a Ciceronian oration, *Pro Ligario*. Let us stop here, for the same pattern recurs more or less identically.

Evidently, the larger portion of Melanchthon's teaching activities during this period was dedicated to textual analysis, not to dialectical or rhetorical theory. When he taught Cicero's *De Oratore* or Aristotle's *Organon,* more often than not he illustrated his teaching by analysing an oration. The publisher of Melanchthon's famous analysis of the *Pro Archia* was a former student of his. When he issued the text with its commentary in

1533, he wrote a prefatory letter in which he recalls with enthusiasm the huge number of students who had attended the lecture on *De Oratore* some three years earlier, and specifies that Melanchthon added straight away an analysis of the oration, 'in order to confront theory with practice'. This testimony is confirmed by several others.[10] Behind it, we discover a basic principle of humanist education, which explains why most of the humanists' textbooks are relatively slim, and why they repeat so often *reliqua usus docebit,* 'practice will teach you the rest'. *Usus* is *not* doing exercises with formal rules, it is, first and foremost, reading texts.

It is my conviction that the essential aim of humanist dialectic and rhetoric is to be mere tools, first to read texts in a methodical way, and then, once the secrets of composition have been unveiled by textual analysis, to create new, coherent texts on the basis of this methodical reading. I also believe that this is what the humanists themselves considered to be the main difference between their outlook and that of their medieval predecessors. When one finds the rules of the syllogism explained in a humanist textbook in a way very similar to that of medieval manuals, one should bear in mind the very different use that is made of the theory of *iudicium* in both cases. For a humanist, a syllogism is ultimately important only as far as it can be used to test the logical coherence of a text; for a scholastic philosopher, on the other hand, the syllogism will also serve as a testing device, but mainly to test the validity of single propositions, and the formal correctness of the language used, within a theological system.

This very opposition is echoed in an eloquent way in Phrissemius' introductory letter to his commented edition of Agricola's *De Inventione Dialectica*: whereas Peter of Spain teaches you endless rules and pointless distinctions, Agricola will teach you how to deal with a text, either as a whole, or as a significant part of a whole; he will teach you how to read and how to write a Latin that is syntactically sound and logically coherent. Hoping to learn that from Peter of Spain, Phrissemius continues, is like trying to shear a donkey, or to squeeze water from a pumice-stone![11]

It certainly is one of the merits of Dr Peter Mack to have foregrounded this essential feature of Agricola's work. Its historical impact on later generations has been stressed quite correctly in a recent Dutch study and anthology (in translation) of Agricola's writings published by Dr Marc van der Poel.[12]

We know that for Melanchthon, reading Agricola in his student years was quite a shock and also a kind of liberation ([**Corpus Reformatorum,** hereafter referred to as] **CR,** vol. IV, 716); I would suggest that the sheer quantity of analyses of Ciceronian orations in the Wittenberg curriculum proves, among other things, the correct understanding of Agricola's message by his admirer and biographer.

What, then, is the relationship between these analyses of Cicero and the other highlight of the curriculum, the interpretation of Paul's *Letter to the Romans*? Undoubtedly, the reading of classical orations serves as a model for reading the latter. I think we can speak of a kind of 'moral' priority of Cicero, the method of reading being first practiced on profane speeches in order to avoid a confrontation with the holy texts without proper preparation; 'with unwashed hands', as Erasmus would put it.

Thus, in his earliest analyses of *Romans*, which have come down to us in the form of student's notes, Melanchthon intends to prove the rhetorical skills of Paul by comparing the *exordium* of *Romans* with that of Cicero's *Pro Marcello* and of *Pro Archia*. After all, only the technical abilities of Paul were at stake here, those of Cicero were beyond any possible discussion.[13]

The question of St Paul's rhetorical skills, which had been raised from the time of early Fathers of the church,[14] was of special importance to Melanchthon. Martin Luther proclaimed *Romans* to be the key to the Scriptures as a whole, because in this letter Paul speaks of justification by faith alone, *sola fide*, which soon became one of the cornerstones of the new theology. *Romans* also defines what both Luther and Melanchthon considered to be the basic issues of the biblical message, such as 'sin', 'law', 'mercy' and 'faith'. In their eyes, Paul offers all the definitions and distinctions, especially that between 'law' and 'gospel', which they regarded as essential to the correct interpretation of the entire Bible and called therefore *loci communes*, 'central headings', 'points of reference'. As early as 1520, Melanchthon contends that *Romans* offers *the* final method of interpreting the Scriptures, thus implying that Paul himself is the ultimate interpreter, the Christian Hermes.[15]

In short, Paul is an expert in methodical reading, who explains Christian doctrine *ordine et artificio plane rhetorico*. But he is more than a cold dialectician, as he does more than merely teach. He is a real orator, and as such he moves and seduces his reader with all possible means: *doctissimus est Paulus et facundus!*[16]

These ideas about Paul's rhetorical abilities are voiced in Melanchthon's earliest lectures on *Romans*, and are very eloquently expressed in the oratorical companion-pieces of these lectures, namely the declamations in which he advocates the study of Paul's letters. In these festive speeches, Melanchthon clearly aims at matching Paul's eloquence, at giving a living example of its elegance and effectiveness. Melanchthon thus becomes a kind of reincarnation of Paul, or at least of the Melanchthonian image of Paul. It is quite curious to see that in turn, his own orations came to be considered as 'classical' models of eloquence. In many classrooms in Wittenberg, Strasburg and elsewhere, they were read and analysed, and often provided with dialectical and rhetorical annotations in the margins, in order to reveal their subtle, Pauline *artificium*.[17]

But even in those early days, around the year 1520, Melanchthon's activities and conceptions are echoed with astonishing rapidity. We know, for instance, that John Phrissemius lectured in Cologne, that very year, not only on Erasmus's *De Copia* and Agricola's *De Inventione Dialectica*, but also on *Romans*; we know as well that in the same year, Maarten van Dorp, the other prominent editor of Agricola's writings, pronounced and published in Louvain an oration in which he announces his own lecture on St Paul and praises effusively the Apostle's divine eloquence.[18]

It is in this period that the image of Saint Paul as a fully fledged orator seems to prevail as far as Melanchthon is concerned. He will moderate his views later on, still stressing Paul's remarkable dialectical skills, but playing down the excellence of his style. What remains, is the idea of *Romans* as a *method*, a *compendiaria via* to the Scriptures, and the urgent need to analyse *Romans* in an adequate way, that is, a methodical way.

In fact, what we have here is quite a complex, reflective system, in which the issue of humanism versus scholasticism returns. Melanchthon, indeed, develops two complementary oppositions: on the one hand, that between a persuasive, eloquent mode of expression as against an arid, uninspired and technical machinery; on the other hand, an adequate, rhetorical *analysis* of a text, treating it as a coherent whole as against the scholastic approach, which chops a text into inarticulate little pieces, tearing it apart in order to proceed to a formal interpretation of the fourfold significance of a fragment. This is what Melanchthon calls *de quatuor sensibus in singulis prope syllabis nugari*. Both oppositions occur, for example, in his **Small Declamation concerning the Study of Paul** (1520), which I referred to above. Let us look into this more closely.

The first opposition recurs in many Melanchthonian writings, for instance in the famous **Reply** to Pico della Mirandola (**CR**, vol. IX, pp. 678-703). It can be summarised in a formula like 'persuasive elegance versus cold logic'. The 'pursuit of eloquence' (H. Gray) can be considered as one of the distinctive features of humanist theological thinking. It is already present in Agricola and is paramount in Erasmus's thought. The humanists all want to translate into the field of language their experience of the biblical message as primarily affective, as a direct appeal to a person's emotions. The

Pauline concepts of law and gospel, which Melanchthon uses as basic ingredients for his Protestant dogmatics in the *Loci Communes* (1521), both possess a two-way impact, on reason and on the emotions. Law furnishes both the knowledge of sin and the terrifying experience of God's anger; it is this emotional shock which paves the way for the reception of the gospel. Gospel, in turn, implies knowledge about God's will, about Christ and his gifts (*beneficia*) to mankind, about justice, and so on; it is also a promise, a vivifying force, as it dispenses hope and consolation. This twofold system, both rational and affective, also informs Melanchthon's homiletics, in which teaching and appealing to the emotions are the two complementary goals. In this case, Melanchthon tries to build his homiletic theory on Paul's remarks in his first *Letter to Timothy* (1 Tim. 4:13) to which he refers on at least ten different occasions; he even dedicates a formal oration to this very passage in 1546.[19] In this last text, Melanchthon gives an account of what he considers to be Paul's own preaching practice, as shown in his letters; and it goes without saying that Melanchthon again presents his hero as an expert in dialectical procedure while teaching the elements of Christian faith, and as an oratorical magician while stirring up his audience's emotions.[20]

Thus, both in theory—the twofold function of the basic topics of law and gospel—and in practice—preaching as appeal—Melanchthon attributes to non-rational processes a major part in Christian faith. The Bible, a most appealing message in itself, has found an eloquent interpreter in St Paul. As early as 1520, Melanchthon makes a dramatic contrast between Paul's stirring eloquence and the impurity and ugliness of scholastic quibbling, which offers no satisfaction whatsoever to the heart.[21] Of course, this whole passage in the *Small Declamation* has distinctly Erasmian overtones.

Let us now turn to the parallel opposition that is found in the same declamation of 1520: scholastic versus humanist interpretation of texts. It is concerned with what has been called, in a somewhat different context, 'medieval fragmentation' as opposed to 'renaissance reintegration'.[22] Melanchthon suggests that bad theology, bad preaching and inadequate textual analysis are all results of the same, basically cold and arrogant attitude, characteristic of scholasticism. Scholastic theologians like nothing better than tearing apart texts; they simply refuse to consider any other approach, insensible as they are to the beauty and harmony of a well-wrought text. When they have to analyse *Romans,* for instance, they totally ignore Greek sentence structure with its delicate rhythm and balance; so, firstly they distort the text by superimposing on it a completely non-classical syntax as a consequence of their bad Latin; after that, they pursue the grinding by analysing this already perverted text according to Aristotelian procedures, taking out little fragments in order to insert these in their frivolous systems. These systems are thus built out of scraps taken from many kinds of text, biblical as well as patristic, or even Aristotelian. Melanchthon implies that Protestant theology, on the other hand, is based on the respectful analysis of complete, unaltered texts, and, above all, on the careful interpretation of *Romans,* which offers the key to the Scriptures.[23]

A formal attack on scholasticism based on exactly the same opposition appears some ten years later, in 1529, in the prefatory letter which Melanchthon publishes as an introduction to his rhetorical analysis of *Romans*. In this violent letter Melanchthon compares the scholastics with people whose supreme joy consists in looking at some remnants of antique sculptures, and who do not care at all about the work of art as a whole, about the beauty which results from coherence and symmetry. People like that will never grasp the intention of Paul's letter, which one can understand only by paying close attention to the work as a whole, to its structure, to the skillful connections of its constituent parts.[24]

These two oppositions reveal the core of Melanchthon's rhetorical conception. The second one in particular offers the basic principle behind his own textual analyses. In this respect, his terminology is very revealing. The analysis of *Romans* (1529) that I have just mentioned can serve as an example. It is called *Dispositio*. In this name we discover once again the ambiguity I pointed out at the beginning of this chapter: is Melanchthon referring to the creation of a text or to its methodical analysis? I think we can safely assert now that it is both, in that *dispositio* is meant to reconstruct the actual process of creation and thus to disclose an author's fundamental intention.[25]

In order to re-create the author's intention, we must try to answer some elementary questions, such as: what is the author's basic goal in the broadest possible sense? Does he want to obtain something, or to teach, and so on? Let us stick to *Romans*. According to Melanchthon, Paul intends to teach us something, namely, what is the essence of the gospel. This essence is justification by faith alone, *not* by good works. To make this central issue clear, Paul introduces the opposition between gospel and law, and so on. Melanchthon translates these questions into rhetorical concepts. To ask for the general aim is to ask for the oratorical genre, *genus orationis,* in this case the so-called didactical genre. To ask for the central issue is to determine the *status causae*; in this case it is the *status finitivus,* for Paul wants to defend against those opponents who stress the importance of good works his idea concerning justification by faith. Finally, once these two basic questions have been answered, Melanchthon wants us to examine how Paul has developed this central thesis, how he defends his case. This boils down to asking how he backs up his thesis by argumentation, and how the arguments are connected logically.

In other words, *dispositio* is the uncovering of logical invention as a chain of arguments supporting one basic contention; it is, in fact, *inventio* and *dispositio* intertwined, and considered from the point of view of textual coherence.[26] Indeed, *Romans* can only serve as a key to the Scriptures as long as Paul is proven to be an impeccable logician.[27] And this is precisely Melanchthon's personal aim: to show by a methodical procedure that Paul's method to the Scriptures has been built up in a methodical way.

I have tried to show elsewhere how, with this in his mind, Melanchthon systematised some of Rudolph Agricola's intuitions and suggestions concerning the combination of dialectical and rhetorical concepts. As early as the 1519 **Rhetoric** he contended that the logical 'deep structure' of a text is reducible to an underlying syllogism, the conclusion of which coincides with the rhetorical *status causae*.[28] Reformers of the second generation such as Henry Bullinger, Zwingli's successor, John Calvin, and Martin Bucer, who eventually moved from Sturm's Strasburg to Cambridge, all used this very method for their exegesis of the Scriptures. They were all familiar not only with Erasmus and Melanchthon, but with Agricola as well, this founding father of textual analysis.

Outside the church, the method was widely used in classrooms all over Europe, either in purely Melanchthonian shape or faintly disguised by people such as Latomus and Peter Ramus.

When, in the early 1560s, a student and friend of Melanchthon's, David Chytraeus, delivers a solemn speech *Concerning the Proper Study of Dialectic,* he strongly insists on the importance of textual analysis according to the rules that Melanchthon formulated.[29] He also looks back, offering a kind of genealogy of dialectical studies. By way of conclusion, I will simply report the scholars he quotes, and whom he considers to constitute modern dialectic's golden chain. The first to be quoted is Melanchthon, because his dialectical textbook (the *Erotemata*) is still the most popular in Germany; after that, Chytraeus turns to R. Agricola, J. Willichius, J. Sturm, J. Caesarius, and finally—after mentioning in passing F. Titelmans (from Louvain), Lorenzo Valla and George of Trebizond—Peter Ramus. 'After Philip [Melanchthon], nobody has shown the use one can make of dialectic in analysing the works of eloquent poets and orators more clearly and fully than Peter Ramus'.

It is all the more unfortunate that Peter Ramus only wanted to have followers, and loathed the idea of predecessors. He preferred to come out of the blue, to struggle in single combat with Aristotle, guided only by an invisible Socratic demon. But that is another story; I do not intend to tell it now.[30]

Notes

1. On Melanchthon's first *Rhetoric,* see my 'Mélanchthon lecteur d'Agricola: rhétorique et analyse textuelle', in *Réforme-Humanisme-Renaissance,* vol. XVI, no. 30 (1990), pp. 5-22 (p. 8 and note 3). Melanchthon's first lectures in 'Verzeichnis der Vorlesungen Melanchthons' at the end of K. Hartfelder, *Philipp Melanchthon als praeceptor Germaniae* (Berlin, 1889), pp. 555-6. Cf. Melanchthon's correspondence in *Corpus Reformatorum* (hereafter *CR*), vol. I, 76 (3 April 1519) and vol. I, 81 (21 May 1519): 'Ego psalterium praelego, dum doctior aliquis conducitur.'

   For more information, see L. C. Green and Ch. D. Froehlich, *Melanchthon in English—New Translations into English with a Registry of Previous Translations,* Sixteenth-Century Bibliography, vol. 22 (Saint Louis, 1982); (P. Melanchthon) *A Melanchthon Reader. Translated by R. Keen,* American University Studies, series VII, vol. 41 (New York, 1988); R. Keen, *A Checklist of Melanchthon Imprints through 1560,* Sixteenth-Century Bibliography, vol. 27 (Saint Louis, 1988).

2. In 1524, Melchior Lotter the Younger prints in fact *two* Ciceronian texts, both preceded by a letter signed P. Melanchthon: the oration *Pro Milone* and the *Topica, cum commentariis Boe(thii).* See *VD,* 16: C.3319, C.3783; *Index aureliensis,* vol. VIII (1989), 137.739-740; *CR,* vol. I, 700; *CR,* vol. XVI, 805. The combination is highly instructive.

3. *CR,* vol. XVI, 807; cf. *CR,* vol. XIII, 479, *CR,* vol. XVI, 872. See also Melanchthon's commentary on the Psalms, 1553-1555, in *CR,* vol. XIII, 1019, 'Argumentum ac dispositio primi Psalmi' and ibid., *CR,* vol. XIII, 1224-5.

   The commentary on the *Topics* has been often republished in combination with others; see for example *Bibliotheca Belgica,* vol. VI, pp. 131 sqq.; *CR,* vol. XVI, 805; Keen, 1988, 147.

4. C. Vasoli, *La dialettica e la retorica dell' Umanesimo* (Milan, 1968), pp. 328-9. *Elementa Rhetorices,* 1531[1], chapt. 'tertius ordo figurarum', *CR,* vol. XIII, 479-80: '. . . Figurae supra traditae, etiam ab indoctis iudicari possunt, sed amplificatio singularem requirit artem atque usum. Ad hanc rem scripti sunt utilissimi libri *De Copia* Erasmi, quorum prior continet figuras quibus verba variantur, posterior continet figuras quae maiorem rerum copiam suppeditant. Idem nos in hoc tertio figurarum ordine docebimus quomodo crescat oratio, partim verbis, partim etiam rebus aucta. Sed nos breviores erimus, quia omnibus in manu sunt Erasmi libelli. . . . Cum enim res inventae

atque dispositae sunt, quae negotii substantiam continent, postea videndum est, ubi pluribus verbis in una re utendum sit, ut verbis tanquam pictae et illuminatae res fiant illustriores. Deinde ubi etiam prosit plus addere rerum. . . . Observet autem studiosus lector figuras omnes, praesertim has quae augent orationem ex locis dialecticis oriri, ad quos si quis prudenter sciet eas referre, plaeraque in causis subtiliter et acute iudicare, et definitas negotii regiones melius videre poterit. Nam iidem loci cum confirmandi aut confutandi causa adhibentur, argumenta sunt ac nervi, ut vocant. Cum adhibentur illuminandi causa, dicuntur ornamenta.' See also R. Agricola, *DID*, III, chs 1-7 (see note 11 below).

5. *CR*, vol. XIII, 492 sqq.; cf. *CR*, vol. XVI, 722 sqq., *CR*, vol. XVI, 858 sqq., *CR*, vol. XVII, 670 sqq. (Comm. Cic. *De orat., Part. Or.,* Quint. *Inst. Or. X*). Another 'set piece' would be the attacks on uncontrolled allegorical interpretation. See also note 28 below.

6. See note 25 below.

7. P. Melanchthon, *De rhetorica libri tres* (Basel, 1519), 30-1, 'cum sacram illam ad Titum epistolam praelegissem . . .'

8. See my article, 'Rhétorique néo-latine et culture vernaculaire', *Etudes littéraires* (Canada, Laval), vol. XXIV/3 (1991-2), pp. 63-85.

9. P. Melanchthon, *De rhetorica* (1519) pp. 29-41, on *enarratio*; ibid., pp. 103-7 (end of Book 1) on sermon writing.

10. K. Hartfelder (note 1 above), pp. 558-9; *CR*, vol. XVI, 895, the letter of the publisher in Haguenau (1533). For other testimonies, see my article referred to in note 1 above.

11. R. Agricola, *De inventione dialectica libri tres, cum scholiis J. M. Phrissemii* (Cologne, 1523) f. 7v. In the last chapter of *DID*, Agricola states explicitly: 'Usum duabus in his rebus fore accipio, scriptis autorum cuiusque generis expendendis, et nostris deinde ad illorum exemplum quantum datur effingendis' (Cologne, 1539), pp. 452-3. Carl Bullemer, *Quellenkritische Untersuchungen zum I Buche der Rhetorik Melanchthons* (Würzburg, 1902), p. 2ff, already stresses Agricola's influence on Melanchthon in this respect. This small thesis is still worth reading.

12. P. Mack, 'Rudolph Agricola's Reading of Literature', *Journal of the Warburg and Courtauld Institutes,* vol. XLVIII (1985), pp. 23-41; M. van der Poel (ed. and trans.), *Rudolf Agricola: Over Dialectica en humanisme* (Baarn, 1991), Introduction, esp. p. 36.

13. E. Bizer (ed.), *Texte aus der Anfangszeit Melanchthons* (Neukirchen-Vluyn, 1966), for example p. 50: 'Paulus si ineruditus homo fuisset, non potuisset tam ornatum contexere exordium [*sc. Rom.* 1:8] in quo magna verborum Emphasi utitur. In oratione aliqua primo aliquid proponitur, postea causa subjicitur, ut Cicero *pro Marcello* in principio: item *pro Archia*'. In his commentaries on these orations, Melanchthon will stress the coherence of their exordia, which results from the logical link between a proposition and what he calls *aetiologia.* See my article (note 8 above), and compare *CR*, vol. XVI, 897, 909, 925, 948.

14. See E. Norden, *Die Antike Kunstprosa,* vol. II (Darmstadt, 1971), pp. 492ff, 516ff on theories about the language of the New Testament.

15. *CR*, vol. I, 276 (1520): 'Porro autem rerum theologicarum summam, nemo certiore *methodo* complexus est, quam Paulus in Epistola, quam ad Romanos scripsit, omnium longe gravissima. In qua communissimos et quos maxime retulit Christianae philosophiae locos excussit . . . quibus cognitis nihil superest quod desideret Theologus'; *CR*, vol. II, 456 (1530): 'Haec [*sc.* Epist ad Rom.] enim propemodum est *methodus* totius scripturae, quia disputat de iustificatione, de usu legis, de discrimine legis et evangelii, qui sunt praecipui loci doctrinae Christianae.' *CR*, vol. II, 944 (1535): 'Talis [*sc.* methodus] est Pauli Epistola ad Romanos; quare decrevi, eam iterum enarrare'. In his preface to Luther's *Operationes in Psalmos* (March 1519), Melanchthon compares the letter to the Romans with 'Atticus Mercurius, ad reliquas iter indicat', *CR*, vol. I, 72.

16. P. Melanchthon, *Annotationes in Epistulam Pauli ad Rhomanos* (Nürnberg, 1521) folio A3r; cf. Bizer (note 13 above), pp. 45, 48.

17. The first editions of both speeches were printed by Melchior Lotter: *Declamatiuncula in D. Pauli doctrinam* (Wittenberg, 1520, see note 21 below) and *Adhortatio ad Paulinae doctrinae studium* (Wittenberg, 1520; *CR*, vol. XI, 34-41) published as an appendix to Erasmus's Latin translation of *Romans.* Lotter's address to the reader (*CR*, vol. I, 276) was written by Melanchthon and is quoted in note 15 above. See the important bibliography of Melanchthon's orations by H. Koehn, 'Philipp Melanchthons Reden. Verzeichnis der im 16. Jahrhundert erschenenen Drucke', *Archiv für Geschichte des Buchwesens,* vol. XXV (1984), col. 1323, no. 51 and col. 1325, no. 54.

As examples of orations with a rhetorical *artificium* in the margins I may quote the 1529 R. Estienne edition of *Encomium eloquentiae* (1523) Koehn, col. 1331, no. 71, and the *Adhortatio*

(1520) as reprinted in *Liber selectarum declamationum* (Strasburg, 1541), pp. 1-11 (cf. also the introduction, ff iii-iv) which constitutes the start of an impressive series of collected orations, mainly printed in Strasburg. See Koehn, col. 1302, no. 1 (1541), and nos 2-39.

18. On Phrissemius and Dorp, see my article (note 1 above), pp. 7, 9n, 14n. Dorp's orations have been edited by J. IJsewijn (Leipzig, 1986). The same pattern recurs ten years later, when John Sturm, at the request of a progressive Sorbonne Doctor writes in Paris a rhetorical analysis of *Romans,* which unfortunately is lost. See J. Sturm, *Epistola apologetica contra J. Andream alterum flagrum Aegyptium* (Strasburg, 1581) p. 3, quoted by Ch. Schmidt in *La vie et les travaux de Jean Sturm* (Strasburg, 1855; reprinted Nieuwkoop, 1970), p. 11. On the relationship between Melanchthon and Sturm see my article, 'Logic and Eloquence?', *Argumentation,* v (1991), pp. 357-74.

19. See the account of this in S. Wiedenhofer's outstanding study *Formalstrukturen humanisticher und reformatorischer Theologie bei Philipp Melancthon,* Regensburger Studien zur Theologie, vol. II (Berne, 1976) pp. 195 ff., 326 ff., Ibid., p. 66 ff., on Erasmus's 'affective theology', which inspired Melanchthon's.

20. P. Melanchthon, *Oratio de dicto Pauli 1 Timoth. IV,* in *CR,* vol. XI, p. 757: 'Cumque de totis libris primum dixit [*sc* Paulus], postea dividit partes materiarum, quas continent. Partim enim continent doctrinam, id est, dogmata seu articulos [fidei], quos ostendunt qualis sit Deus, et quomodo se patefecit, . . . quomodo et quo tempore filius Dei missus, crucifixus et resuscitatus sit, quae beneficia nobis donet; partim vero conciones divinae sunt adhortationes, traducentes animos ad adfectum aliquem . . .' 'Admonere tantum volui, ut cogitetis, prudentissime significari Pauli verbis, ad quos fines dirigendae sint studia, videlicet ad agnitionem veram Dei, deinde ad accendendos pios adfectus.' Cf. *CR,* vol. VI, 694-5 and *De modo et arte concionandi* (ca. 1538) where Tim. 4:13 is combined with 1 Cor. 14:3. Text in *Supplementa Melanchthoniana,* vol. V/2, P. Drews and F. Cohrs (eds), (Leipzig, 1929, reprinted Frankfurt, 1968), pp. 33-55. Ibid., p. 33: '(Nam) cuiuslibet concionis finis est proprie, ut vel doceat auditores de dogmatibus, vel ut traducat animos ad aliquem affectum.' For further details, see U. Schnell, *Die homiletische Theorie Philipp Melanchthons,* Arbeiten zur Geschichte und Theologie des Luthertums, vol. XX (Berlin, 1968).

21. P. Melanchthon, *Declamatiuncula in D. Pauli doctrinam* (1520), in *Melanchthons Werke in Auswahl,* ed. R. Stupperich, vol. I (Gütersloh, 1951), pp. 28-43 (also called 'Studienausgabe', abridged SA or MSA), and as an appendix to *Die Loci Communes Philipp Melanchthons in ihrer Uhrgestalt,* G. L. Plitt and Th. Kolde (eds) (Erlangen, 1890), pp. 262-77. Ibid., p. 273: 'scholae, quae miseris modis excarnificant afflictas conscientias per summas suas, quae adfectibus vitiorum adeo non medentur, frivolis et nugacibus disputationibus, ut et morbo morbum addant'; 'inter scholas et sacram Pauli doctrinam quantum intersit, facile cernent, qui vel hunc a limine salutaverint. Neque iam ago, quale sit in scholis sermonis genus, quam impura et sordidata docendi disserendique ratio . . . Ita nec in scholastica theologia animo satisfecerit pius quispiam, tot hominum argutiis, nugis, technis et traditiunculis conspurcata.'

22. B. Vickers, *In Defence of Rhetoric* (Oxford, 1988), chapters 4 and 5. Unfortunately, I cannot agree with Vickers's interpretation of Melanchthon, who in his Reply to Pico would have 'no taste for mock-encomium or irony', would have 'missed' Pico's irony, and so forth (ibid., pp. 192, 193). On the contrary, Melanchthon very well understood the passage quoted by Vickers, *l.c.,* p. 189. As early as 1523, Melanchthon states that he believes Pico was only playing: 'ludens, credo, in αδόζῳ argumento', that is, using the tricks of a mock encomium: *Encomium eloquentiae,* one of the most frequently reprinted orations (see Koehn, 1984), available in *CR,* vol. XI, 50 ff, and in *SA,* vol. III, pp. 43-62) as well as in other modern editions; passage quoted: *SA,* vol. III, p. 47. In a forthcoming article in *Archiv für Reformationsgeschichte* (1992), E. Rümmel shows that the *Reply* to Pico was written by one of Melanchthon's pupils. I should like to thank Judith Rice Henderson for drawing my attention to this article.

23. P. Melanchthon, *Declamatiuncula* (1520) *l.c.,* 1890, p. 274: 'Quod Paulina minus intelliguntur, debemus eximiis istis Magistris nostris, qui cum omnis veteris literaturae rectaeque eruditionis imperiti essent, divinam Pauli orationem et rhetoricis vinctam membris, et suis compactam articulis, primum novis interpunctionibus dissecuerunt, deinde suo more secundum Aristotelem enarraverunt: ita ut nusquam ne versus quidem cum versu conveniret. Ad haec non erat vulgaris hominis officium, de quatuor sensibus in singulis prope syllabis nugari. Nec puduit audaces homines in re tam seria ludos agere . . . etc.' Immediately afterwards, Melanchthon quotes Erasmus's *Methodus* (1516).

24. P. Melanchthon, Letter to Count Herman of Neuenahr (a pupil of Caesarius and a friend of Erasmus), Spring 1529, in *CR,* vol. I, 1043-5.

25. Ultimately rhetorical analysis reveals the principles of God's own rhetoric, especially in the Scriptures. See for example *CR*, vol. XIII, 1224-5, already referred to above: 'Cogitemus Psalmos sapientiam, et vocem Dei esse, et Deum fontem eloquentiae, sapienter, recte et ordine loqui. Ideo in singulis Psalmis quaeratur unum aliquod principale argumentum, ut in aliis carminibus erudite scriptis, et consideretur quomodo membra cohaereant . . . ; it et hic quaerimus propositionem, seriem partium, et accomodamus Psalmos, alios ad alia genera causarum, videlicet, ut iuxta puerilia praecepta diligentius consideretis, quis sit finis, quid velit efficere scriptum, an doceat, aut petat aliquid' (Comm. on Ps. 51). See also R. Schäfer, 'Melanchthons Hermeneutik im Römerbrief-Kommentar von 1532', in *Zeitschrift für Theologie und Kirche*, LX (1963), pp. 216-35 (p. 217): 'Melanchthon geht von dem fruchtbaren Grundsatz aus, dass man ein literarisches Werk allein dann richtig versteht, wenn man es nach denselben Gesichtspunkten interpretiert, mit deren Hilfe es erzeugt worden ist.'

26. P. Melanchthon, *Dispositio orationis in Epistola Pauli ad Romanos* (1529) in *CR*, vol. XV, 445, 450-1: 'Nunc demum pervenit ad principalem propositionem, quae est huius totius Epistolae status. Ut autem architectus totam aedificii formam in animo inclusam habet, et videt quomodo omnes inter se partes consentiant, ita nos in legendis gravibus disputationibus, omnium propositionum atque argumentorum seriem oportet animo complecti. In primis autem meminisse statum necesse est, qui continet negotii summam, ad quem omnia argumenta tanquam ad caput referentur.' *CR*, vol. XV, 482: 'Porro ut architectus totius formam aedificii in animo complecti solet, ita nos totius scripti tanquam ideam quandam in animam includere debemus, ut Apostoli sententiam penitus perspiciamus. . . . Semper autem in hanc Epistolam intueri nos oportet, semper oportet habere positam ob oculos hanc sententiam, quod fide in Christum iustificemur coram patre . . . Quoties orabimus, primum in hanc Epistolam intuendum est, ut erigamus nos ac sciamus nos exaudiri, si credimus in Christum non propter merita nostra.'

27. P. Melanchthon, in *CR*, vol. I, 1044 (see note 24 above): 'Cum autem epistola ad Romanos . . . veluti methodum universae Scripturae contineat, non satis est, unum atque alterum ex illa versiculum decerpere. Tota legenda est, et considerandum, quomodo omnes inter se partes, omnia membra cohaereant atque consentiant, et venanda certa, perpetua et simplex sententia Apostoli. . . . Ego igitur in hac epistola totius seriem disputationis breviter ostendi. . . . Sed me fortasse nonnulli ridebunt, quod orationem Pauli ad vulgaria dicendi praecepta exigam. Verum res loquitur ipsa, non sine certa ratione disputasse Apostolum.'

28. See my articles cited above (notes 1, 8 and 18). The final remarks of the *Topics* commentary summarise this procedure (*ad* Cic. *Top.* 25, 29): 'Unaquaeque causa habet unum aliquem principalem statum, ut 'Milo occidit Clodium iure.' Habet quoque unaquaeque causa firmum aliquod argumentum prae reliquis, ut hoc: 'Vim vi repellere licet' [=major], Milo vim vi repulit [=minor]: ergo iure occidit Clodium. Conclusio est status . . .': *CR*, vol. XVI, 832. This example is also a 'set piece'. See for example *CR*, vol. XIII, 430, 597, 643; *CR*, vol. XVI, 975, 982-3, 989-91, 1005-6, 1017-19 (*Dispositio* of the *Pro Milone*), etc. Compare with Agricola, *DID*, ed. 1539, pp. 242, 268, 280, 'tota pro Milone oratio in ratiocinationem coniecta est'.

29. J. Willichius, *Erotematum Dialectices libri III. Quibus accessit D. Chytraei De studio dialectices recte instituendo libellus* (Basel, 1568). The prefatory letter of the latter is dated from Rostock, March 1563. Chytraeus summarises with the following dialectical analysis: 'hoc modo, ut in omni autore bono . . . primum Quaestionem, seu Propositionem, totius scripti summam continentem, excerpamus. Deinde praecipua membra et argumenta, et ex quibus locis ea ducta sint, consideremus. Tertio nuda argumenta formis syllogismorum inclusa, et ad leges syllogismi accommodata iudicemus . . . Ornamenta vero quae accesserunt . . . praeceptis et legibus artis rhetoricae et grammaticae examinantur.

Habent autem Adolescentes illustria huius . . . generis exercitationum Dialecticae exempla, in omnibus disputationibus orationum Ciceronis, et epistolarum Pauli, et enarrationibus autorum, quos in scholis explicari quotidie audiunt': pp. 272-3. Ibid., p. 274, Agricola, *DID*, II, chs 19-21 in particular; p. 275, J. Willichius, *Erot. dial. lib. III*; pp. 275-6, J. Sturm, *Part. dial lib. IV*; p. 276, J. Caesarius, *Dial. lib. X*; pp. 276-7, cf. pp. 280-1, P. Ramus: 'Nemo autem post Philippum . . . usum artis Dialecticae, in disertorum poetarum et oratorum scriptis recte intelligendis et explicandis, facilius et uberius ostendit, quam Petrus Ramus'. At the beginning and the end of this genealogy figures Philip Melanchthon, 'reverendus praeceptor noster' (p. 280). *VD*. 16, C.2759.

30. See my article in *Argumentation,* vol. V (note 18 above). In a hitherto unknown letter to P. Ramus, dated from Rostock, 22 April 1570, Chytraeus expresses his admiration: 'Etsi igitur nulla inter nos consuetudo familiaris hactenus intercessit: tamen

multos iam annos, lectione librorum a te . . . editorum, in quibus velut Hercules, divinitus nostrae aetati donatus, totum orbem artium, a monstris inutilium et peregrinarum praeceptionum liberas, et suas cuique arti regiones ac fines certos attribuens, rectissimam singulis docendi et discendi viam demonstras: mirifico me tui amore et desiderio, et virtutis ac sapientiae admiratione accensum esse fateor', D. Chytraeus, *Epistolae . . . editae a D. Chytraeo authoris filio* (Hanau, 1614), pp. 547-8. Ramus was travelling in Germany at the time.

Charlotte Methuen (essay date July 1996)

SOURCE: Methuen, Charlotte. "The Role of the Heavens in the Thought of Philip Melanchthon." *Journal of the History of Ideas* 57, no. 3 (July 1996): 385-403.

[*In the following essay, Methuen argues that Melanchthon's interest in natural philosophy is related to his educational interest, which she says depends on his particular theological and cosmological view of the universe.*]

Philip Melanchthon has long been recognized as one of the central figures in the German Lutheran Reformation. His theological contribution to the Reformation may be found in his codifying of Lutheran theology in the **Confessio Augustana** and in the **Loci Communes,** the first major Lutheran theological textbook, which long remained a central text for the teaching of theology in Lutheran schools and universities. A teacher at the University of Wittenberg from 1518 until his death, Melanchthon was also involved in the reform of universities and the establishment of school systems throughout Lutheran Germany. These reforms facilitated the spread of the Reformation by encouraging the development of Lutheran educational principles and the establishing of Humanist education as the basis for the schools and universities of Lutheran Germany, and Melanchthon's role in this process has led to his being accorded the title *Praeceptor Germaniae.*[1] More recently, Melanchthon has also been hailed as the initiator of a new "Lutheran" approach to natural philosophy.[2] It is my contention in this article that Melanchthon's interest in natural philosophy is integrally connected to his educational interest and that these hang upon a particular theological and cosmological understanding of the universe, particularly the heavens, as becomes clear from his defense of astronomy.

I.

Despite his theological interests and his commitment to the dissemination of Lutheran theology, Melanchthon was reluctant to teach theology and remained primarily concerned with the teaching of the subjects which made up the curriculum of the arts faculty in a sixteenth-century university. It was as Professor of Greek that he was originally appointed to the University of Wittenberg, and he had a deep interest in the teaching of ancient languages, especially Greek, and in the study of ancient texts in their original form rather than through later commentators. His promotion of the trivium (grammar, logic, and rhetoric) led him to write a textbook in each of these areas; and these works continued to be used as prescribed works in many German universities into the seventeenth century.[3] As an educator Melanchthon was thus firmly in the humanist mold. However, Melanchthon's interests did not only take in the teaching of languages; he also promoted the teaching of both moral and natural philosophy.[4] Moreover, he was a strong advocate of the teaching of the mathematical sciences, particularly arithmetic, geometry, and astronomy. These, together with music, made up the quadrivium, which complemented the linguistic arts.

In Melanchthon's day the mathematical sciences had long been accepted as part of the arts curriculum,[5] even if in practice minimal attention had been paid them at many universities.[6] Their ambiguous status is reflected by the attitude taken by many humanist reformers, who did not regard arithmetic, geometry, astronomy, and music as an essential part of the curriculum. Thus Erasmus believed that music, arithmetic, and geography should be taught only to pupils who had a particular interest in these subjects[7] and that knowledge of nature, astrology, architecture, and other related subjects would come from reading the ancient authors.[8] In a similar vein Juan Luis Vives argued that mathematics tended to divorce the mind from the practical concerns of life and that its study was not, therefore, to be recommended.[9] In contrast Melanchthon seems to have recognized the value of the study of the mathematical sciences from the beginning of his scholarly career. Perhaps he was inspired by his professor of mathematics at Tübingen, Johannes Stöffler, a gifted mathematician who wrote his own *Arithmetic* and was also fluent in the praise of his subject.[10] In an early oration, **De artibus liberalis,** delivered in Tübingen in 1517, Melanchthon praises arithmetic as a principal part of philosophy; geometry for its role in producing the wonderful machines of war and the beautiful ornaments of cities; music for its elegance and harmony; and astronomy (very briefly) for its applications in medicine.[11]

This oration should almost certainly be read as part of the tradition of orations and odes which extolled each of the liberal arts for its practical (and often also theological) applications and which were often a feature of graduation ceremonies for those who had recently gained their *magister artium*. Therefore, it does not necessarily imply that Melanchthon was already convinced that the mathematical arts were to be regarded as a central part of the curriculum. Indeed, in *De corrigendis adolescentiae studiis,* his inaugural lecture given in Wittenberg in August 1518, the emphasis is on the teaching of theology, and mathematics warrants only a brief mention. This mention is, however, positive and suggests that at this early stage of his career Melanchthon regarded mathematics as more informative than Aristotle's philosophy.[12] By 1521 his perception of the importance of mathematics was such that he proposed replacing lectures on Aristotle's *Physica* with a course on mathematics.[13] From an early stage in his career, then, Melanchthon was more convinced of the value of studying mathematics than were some other humanists.

From the early 1530s he became an enthusiastic promoter of the mathematical sciences. Although he was never himself a particularly competent mathematician and never wrote a mathematical textbook of his own, Melanchthon became an important figure in Wittenberg's mathematical circles, and his correspondence often touches upon matters of mathematical, and particularly astronomical and astrological interest.[14] He was also the author of a number of prefaces to contemporary editions of important mathematical textbooks, including Sacrobosco's *De Sphaera,*[15] Georg Peurbach's *Theorae Novae Planetarum,*[16] Regiomontanus's *Tabulae Directionum*[17] and at least two editions of Euclid's *Elements,*[18] as well as to less well-known works of mathematical and astrological interest.[19] Besides these prefaces, Melanchthon wrote and gave orations which emphasized the importance of arithmetic, astronomy, and geography;[20] others which pointed out the role of mathematics in the lives of important personalities;[21] and yet others which discussed the merits of astrology and the proper interpretation of astronomical observations.[22] Here Melanchthon describes what he regards as the true importance of teaching arithmetic, geometry, and astronomy. Although these writings on mathematics span a period from the early 1530s to the end of Melanchthon's life, they display a remarkable unity of content and purpose; and little significant development in Melanchthon's approach to mathematics can be observed.[23]

To Melanchthon and his contemporaries it was clear that the mathematical sciences, especially arithmetic and geometry, had practical applications which meant that they were taught to all school children and not only to future university students. It was thus generally recognized that arithmetic was needed for all calculations, while geometry was required for making measurements or for building. Astronomy too had important practical uses because of the importance of the stars and planetary positions in defining geographical location and measuring time, a particularly important facility as the calendar controversies became entwined with the confessional and political conflicts of the sixteenth century.

Like most of his mathematically-minded contemporaries, Melanchthon was fully aware of such practical applications of the mathematical sciences and in his lectures and prefaces he frequently underlined the utility of mathematics in everyday life. He pointed out that arithmetic is needed to count anything, and is especially relevant in business transactions, that geometry is necessary for the construction of houses, bridges, and other such works and that without astronomy there would be no appreciation of time and, since the seasons are bound up with the rising and setting of certain stars, no way of measuring or ordering the passing of the year.

Nor could there be any historical understanding without astronomy, for it would be impossible to establish when important events had taken place. Astronomy is also necessary in navigation and for establishing the positions of geographical features and state borders, since position on the earth are determined by observation of the stars. Astronomy underpins both history and geography, which are in turn vital to the understanding of both politics and the church since they enable the history of religions and states and monarchs to be traced and the sites of important events, particularly those described in the biblical narratives, to be known.[24] Such affirmations of the practical and pragmatic applications of the mathematical sciences formed part of the conventional repertoire of praise for mathematics,[25] but they were not Melanchthon's central interest. Of far more importance to him was the use of the mathematical sciences as a foundation for philosophy. Here arithmetic and geometry are particularly important.

II.

According to Melanchthon, mathematics offers a good basis for philosophy because of the logical structure and certainty of its proofs. He defines philosophy to be "not all opinions about everything," but "that knowledge which can be proved," and he holds that true philosophy is that which departs least from proofs, commenting that the philosophy of Aristotle is superior to that of other philosophical schools because it is the most diligent in seeking proofs.[26] This emphasis on establishing proof means that any aid to learning logical thought is a useful tool in learning philosophy. This is just what arithmetic and geometry have to offer: arithmetic shows the order of things and demonstrates how confused things may be differentiated,[27] while geometry taught according to Euclid brings an understanding of the power of proof and teaches logical method.[28] The Greeks also recognized this and taught dialectics only after an introduction to arithmetic. They saw that

> dialectics takes its beginnings from arithmetic, and that practice in multiplication and division is the best preparation for syllogism. Thus the power of demonstration can be better understood when arithmetic is known, because this art has the most eloquent proofs.[29]

It is in this sense, he believes, that "the first understanding is of number." Arithmetic and geometry teach a sense of order which is essential to understanding philosophy. Melanchthon thinks this is what Pythagoras meant when he defined the mind as number: he was implying that "the soul is a reasoning being which understands things and observes order."[30] Geometry and arithmetic train this characteristic of the human mind and in doing so offer the best possible introduction to philosophy.

Melanchthon is drawing here on a long-standing recognition that when it comes to logical method, the mathematical sciences, especially arithmetic and geometry, cannot be bettered. However, for Melanchthon the central point seems to be the fact that mathematics is ordered, rather than the form that this order takes. Although he praises the clarity, logic, and certainty of mathematical method, he does not discuss that method in detail; neither does he pay any attention to the question of the origin of its certainty. Here he differs from, for instance, his friend Simon Grynaeus, who also emphasizes the exactness of mathematical method and its consequent importance in avoiding the kind of sophistry exhibited by scholastic philosophers with their misuse of words. Grynaeus, however, goes on to discuss the reasons for and attempts to define what that method might be actually be when applied outside the mathematical sciences per se.[31] Melanchthon seems simply to take for granted the logic and certainty of mathematical method; his interest in the use of geometry and arithmetic as a first step in teaching philosophy is not concerned with the actual proofs of arithmetic and geometry, but treats them as a means to an end.

This approach is entirely coherent with his understanding of philosophy as a whole. Gilbert has suggested that Melanchthon regarded dialectics primarily as didactic method, centering on the most appropriate ordering of the subject matter for effective teaching rather than upon the detail of actual philosophical or syllogistic proof.[32] Thus it appears that for Melanchthon the details of philosophy's logical proofs were less important than the fact that the teaching of an orderly, logical philosophy was actually taking place. What, then, are Melanchthon's reasons for encouraging the teaching of philosophy?

III.

Melanchthon's whole approach to the teaching of philosophy was driven by his conviction that through the study of the orderly thought of philosophy the importance of civil obedience and of living a morally upright life can be recognized. Arithmetic and geometry were important as a first step in learning philosophy, but philosophy was in turn important because it provided an authoritative foundation for morally correct behavior.

There is thus a sense in which he subsumed all philosophy under the heading of moral philosophy, and this was certainly one reason why he encouraged its teaching.[33]

Melanchthon's appeal to philosophy as a basis for ethical determination of right and wrong behavior was a direct result of the theological problem which had arisen from Luther's denial of the efficacy of good works and his questioning of the authority of the Roman Catholic Church. Luther's position, while theologically liberating, could be interpreted as leaving no defined authority against which correct civic behavior could be measured. The consequent lack of an ethical authority became a pressing problem in the mid-1520s, when civil unrest and peasant uprisings threatened the course of the Reformation. Luther responded by calling upon his doctrine of the two kingdoms and turning to the political strength of the German princes;[34] Melanchthon looked to the theological understanding of the law.[35] His response was to argue a third use of the law, a *usus paedagogicus,* besides the *usus theologicus* and the *usus politicus* or *civilis* and to emphasize the teaching of philosophy in an attempt to establish that the order of society was divinely ordained.[36] In his opinion the study of the law could guide the faithful in leading a correct, godly life and in gaining a purer knowledge of God's will.

Study of the law is bound up with the study of natural law in the form of philosophy; and this Melanchthon had come to consider vital, as a preparation for the study of theology, as a basis for morality and ethics, and as a training for a correct life. From the 1530s Melanchthon emphasized the importance of teaching moral philosophy in the form of Aristotle's *Ethica Nichomachea* (especially the fifth book which teaches that human excellence consists in respecting civil law) and began to lay a far greater weight on philosophy teaching as a whole.[37] Although acknowledging that neither living a correct life nor studying philosophy could bring about salvation (achieved only through faith), Melanchthon was convinced that the study of philosophy could be of positive help in preparing the mind and the soul to receive God by "inflaming their souls with love and enthusiasm for the truth and rousing them to understanding of the noblest things."[38] By teaching a logical, orderly way of thinking philosophy was able to lay the foundation for proper, orderly behavior; it was thus a prerequisite for a proper civil and moral life and, therefore, for the resolution of the problems facing the church and the state. It was the effective teaching of such philosophy which Melanchthon believed could be aided by teaching arithmetic and geometry.

But philosophy has another central aspect, and that is its ability to reveal the order which is present in the natural world. This aspect is related to the philosophy's function as a foundation of moral behavior through Melanchthon's theology of creation: he believed the order of the natural world to have been established by God, so that it represents a pattern for the order which God intends for society. Melanchthon saw true philosophy as the "observation of natural causes and effects," and argued that it was precisely this aspect which showed that philosophy must be the law of God.[39] His response to the "sophists" who had ensnared philosophy in endless discussions of terminology was to appeal to physics or natural philosophy as the basis for all true philosophy.[40] Yet, while the healing properties of plants, the wonder of the human body, and the order of society were certainly a part of this philosophy,[41] Melanchthon's appeal was not primarily to a natural philosophy which studied the world of nature as it can be seen in the sublunar sphere. For Melanchthon the order of the creation was exemplified by the order which may be perceived in the motions of the stars and planets, and he believed that society as a whole and the church in particular should take the order and regularity of the heavens as a model.[42] Thus, it was astronomy to which he directed the student of philosophy.

IV.

For Melanchthon astronomy is an essential component of philosophy—so important, in fact, that philosophy is "maimed and mutilated" without it.[43] He represents the pinnacle of the mathematical sciences and explains:

> Plato in *Phaedrus* represents two kinds of souls, one of which he says is winged; from the other he says the wings have departed. Furthermore he says that the winged ones fly to heaven, delighting in the company of and conversation with God and in the most beautiful spectacle of the heavenly courses, and that it contemplates the causes of all changes in lower nature, in the air, in living bodies, in human inclinations and habits and in the various downfalls of empires and cities. Those souls flying through the whole sky have been captivated by the beauty of divine things, and of that admirable order and by the sweetness of learning and virtue. They long to enjoy perpetually this one pleasure; nor do they burden their souls with obscene passions, which disturb the harmony of virtue in the soul, but they oppose the obscurity which prevents them from seeing heavenly things. And those souls from which the wings have departed wander on the ground and seek impure pleasures from terrestrial things; for they do not see the most beautiful light of celestial things. Although Plato interpreted the wings as the heroic impulses of the mind, these impulses alone do not bear the mind upwards: indeed skills are necessary to sustain those impulses. Arithmetic and geometry are, therefore, the wings of the human mind. . . . Raised to heaven by their might, you will be able to illuminate with your eyes the natural universe of things, to perceive the distances and measurements of the greatest bodies, to see the fateful conjunctions of the stars, in short to perceive the causes of the greatest things which happen in this human existence.[44]

By taking astronomy to be the highest of the mathematical sciences, Melanchthon reverses the traditional understanding that the purest forms of mathematics are those which apply only to noetic forms, that is, arithmetic and geometry in its pure, non-applied form, which would see astronomy as a mixed—and thus a lower—science, which attempts to apply the pure form of mathematics to physical reality.[45] For Melanchthon, in contrast, it is precisely astronomy's capability to interpret the natural world and to decode the motions of the heavens that gives it its value, for in doing so it is able to show the will of God. Astronomy can only do this because of the order and harmony in the celestial region it describes. These have been ordained by God; by unlocking the motions of the planets and stars for human understanding, astronomy is able to give an insight into God's intended order for the world.

This is a somewhat circular argument: the regularity of the heavens shows that they were created by God; the fact that they were created by God means that they can reveal God's intention that the world should be orderly. The practical applications of astronomy, which are only possible because the movements of celestial bodies are regular and can be observed and predicted, are thus a further demonstration that the celestial bodies were created by God and did not come about by chance. It is, therefore, an insult against God to assert, as Epicurus does, that "the sun is a vapour set alight and in motion by some chance . . . and that the stars are little clouds similarly illumined by chance."[46] And because God created the heavens, they can reveal God to human beings: the heavenly bodies and their movements reflect the beauty and regularity of a skilled mind, a *mens architectrix,* which is God's mind. It is because the heavens reveal God that they may be—and should be—read as a message from God to the world which tells how life should ideally be lived.[47] The regularity of the heavenly motions are intended by God both to help in the planning and fulfilling of human tasks and to remind human beings that "from [God] comes order both in our own minds and in wider society, and that there are penalties consequent on upsetting this order."[48]

Although Melanchthon argues that in general the "understanding about God and about providence" derived from the observation of the celestial order "arouses souls at once to goodness,"[49] it is clear from his comment about penalties that he shared the traditional view that the stars, particularly comets and planetary conjunctions, may also function as portents of disasters to come. Such disasters can be interpreted as God's punishment of a sinful people. But God is just and gives due warning that such punishments are about to occur; such warnings appear in the heavens and account for the apparently threatening influence of the light of the stars, sun and moon. Astronomy may, therefore, be able to give early warning of catastrophic events such as flood or famine, the death of a prince or the collapse of an empire; and such disasters may in turn be averted if people repent of their evil ways, turn to God and pray.[50] The true understanding of astronomical observations thus contributes to the increase of piety and strengthens the church, which is what God wants for the world. By demonstrating "divine causes and effects," astronomy can in this way be a force for good.

V.

Melanchthon himself recognizes that his attempt to read God's intentions from the heavens may be categorized as astrology and that it is, therefore, open to criticism.[51] The proper interpretation of celestial phenomena and the question of whether or not they could be seen as omens sent by God was a subject of intense debate in the sixteenth century, and it is surely no coincidence that Melanchthon's mature position on mathematics, astronomy, and astrology first appears in the early 1530s. Indeed, his interest in astronomy was probably initiated by his observation of the comet of 1531, and the anxieties which this comet provoked in himself and the people around him.[52]

Comets were traditionally known as portents of disaster, and—to judge by the number of tracts and pamphlets which such phenomena brought in their wake in the sixteenth century—they seem invariably to have unleashed a wave of speculation about their meaning and correct interpretation. Some kind of theological response to these phenomena must have seemed to Melanchthon at least desirable and probably absolutely necessary.[53] However, even among Lutherans there was no single interpretation of such phenomena; there was not even a consensus about whether they should be interpreted.[54] From Melanchthon's own references to other opinions it is clear that he was conscious that he was contributing to a debate, and he frequently referred to opponents who believed that the use of astrology or prediction (μαντικην) had no part to play in Christian theology or philosophy. Nevertheless, he remained convinced that the interpretation of astronomical observations could be a valuable tool for understanding the will of God.

This conviction is rooted in his understanding of physics and his understanding of astrology as a part of physics. It was important to him to distinguish astrology from superstition: he rejects the use of celestial observations in an attempt to predict particular aspects of the future—for instance, through the casting of individual horoscopes—which he rejects as superstition; superstition has no causes which can be derived from physics and makes no attempt to discover what has been ordained by God. Astrology, on the other hand, is based upon "observations of physical causes which are ordinances of God"; it "teaches what effects the light of the stars has on simple and mixed bodies, and what kind of

temperament, what changes and what inclinations it induces,"[55] and so it is a part of physics. Just as physics as a whole seeks causes and effects, so does astrology seek to establish the causes and effects implicit in God's ordinances for the world.[56] Physics and astrology related in such a way that physics may be said to "subserve" astrology because "the latter investigates more general causes from which the causes of the former can be deduced."[57]

In his *Physicae seu naturalis philosophiae compendium,* a manuscript dating from 1543, Melanchthon explicitly discusses the study of astrology.[58] In the *Initia Doctrinae Physicae,* written during the 1540s and first published in 1549, he chooses to avoid the terms "astrology" and astrologer"; but they still make up the content of his opening discussion. Here he gives a brief outline of the history of the "two so-called schools of physics in Greece." The first of these schools, instituted by Thales, considers the effects of the celestial bodies on sublunar material; that is, astrology. The other, as defined by Empedocles and Democritus and improved by Hippocrates, investigates the material and changes inherent in the sublunar material itself. Melanchthon recognizes that it is the latter tradition which is usually identified with the study of physics, but he maintains that it should be complemented through the study of the effects of the stars on the sublunar sphere,[59] and he is adamant that in doing so he can claim the authority of Aristotle, who taught that there was a continuity between the celestial and sublunar spheres.[60]

The chain of causes and effects which can be observed in the interactions of the matter of the sublunar sphere has its origins in causes in the supralunar sphere and the movements of the stars, and these in turn are caused by God. Because of this continuity a study of cause and effect which is restricted to the investigation of the "proximate causes" (*causae proximae*) within the sublunar sphere cannot be complete. It is necessary to take into account the vertical causal connections between the sublunar and celestial spheres, and beyond the celestial sphere to God. Although Melanchthon believes that the sublunar world displays an order which shows that it has been created by God and which results from that creation, he believes too this order points the observer in the first instance to the influence of the stars, and only indirectly to God.[61] It is the heavens and their motions that offer the clearest manifestation of the divine order.

This conclusion results in part from Melanchthon's hierarchical, Aristotelian view of the universe and in part from his theological understanding of the effects of the fall on creation. Taken together, these aspects of his thought leave the distinct impression that the heavens must be regarded as the pristine creation of God, more perfect than the sub-lunar sphere. Following Aristotle,

Melanchthon assumes that the heavens are not subject to generation or corruption and that the material of which they consist does not allow change.[62] The heavens are made not of elements, as is the sublunar sphere, but of a pure, perfect substance. The sublunar sphere, on the other hand, consists of imperfect elements which are rendered even more imperfect by the fact that they do not keep to their proper places but have become mixed and confused.[63] By implication the stuff of the heavens is closer to the divine because of its perfection. The heavens, says Melanchthon, thus reveal "vestiges of divinity" and it is these which are able to lead the observer to God. By virtue of the chain of causes described in Melanchthon's physics, there is, however, "a harmony and accord between the celestial and the lower [sublunar] bodies" which can and should be noted by the human observer,[64] and this does mean that there are also "vestiges of divinity" which remain to be found in the sublunar sphere.[65] Because of this it is possible to understand something of God's will by observing the events and the constitution of the sublunar sphere, particularly as it has been created by God at its most wonderful, that is, in the human body and soul.[66] However, it is the stars that speak most directly of God.

Although he never says so directly, Melanchthon's implication seems to be that the heavens have retained their pristine, prelapsarian state. Because he is convinced that God created a world which was only good and in which everything was ordered as it should be, he is able to state explicitly that human beings would originally have been directly illuminated by divine light as reflected in the light of the stars and heavenly bodies.[67] In this prelapsarian world, natural law, under which Melanchthon understands the knowledge which philosophy and reason can find out about the natural world, would have sufficed for human beings to achieve salvation.[68] The fallen, imperfect nature of the human mind and soul means that this is now no longer the case, and the most immediate consequence of this is that salvation is not possible without the gospel. However, although such philosophical knowledge can never bring salvation, it is possible for human minds to transcend their fallen natures to some extent by observing the natural, created world.

The discovery of the creative nature and the providence of God is not the exclusive preserve of the astronomer, and the student of "natural history" or of human anatomy will also be confronted with the order of God's creation. In practice, however, it seems that Melanchthon concentrated his own pleas for study of actual physical phenomena in two areas: medicine and the study of anatomy, and astronomy or astrology. Although these appear at first sight to be unrelated topics, they are in fact closely related, since the theory of sixteenth-century medicine was grounded in aristotelian physics and cosmology, and especially in the effects of the stars upon the "humours" in the human body and its practice was closely linked to astronomy. It depended heavily upon the analysis of the effect of the stars on the humours and character of any particular sick person for the establishment of both diagnosis and the treatment. Theologically speaking, the human being is the only inhabitant of the sublunar world to have been created "in the image of God," with an intellect and a will which reflect the mind of God and with a body which is a physical expression of the purpose for which God has designed it. The study of anatomy, like the study of astronomy, should reveal that purpose; in doing so it will, again like astronomy, lead the student to a better understanding of God's providence.[69] It is possible for the human observer to grasp something of the order of God's mind precisely because the human mind has been created as some kind of image of God's mind. The study of anatomy and the study of astronomy therefore have the same theological aim of helping the student understand the mind of God.

The heavens have a special status here, not only because of their role in medical practice, but because Melanchthon's understanding of sin apparently allows him to assume that the heavens are not fallen. Melanchthon understands sin to be either a direct result of human misuse of free will or a consequence of the perversion of the human will under the influence of the devil.[70] Natural disasters such as floods, storms, or earthquakes do not fall under the category of sin, but are better understood as punishments justly inflicted upon a sinful people. As has already been seen, Melanchthon believes that celestial phenomena may be interpreted as warnings that such punishments are in the offing, and should encourage people to repent and to pray. Such prayers can be effective because God is not bound to the celestial conjunctions but is always free to decide that a disaster will not happen. From this divine freedom to change the course of events by breaking through the chain of causes and effects manifested in the stars it can be seen that God's goodness is "higher and better than the nature of the stars."[71]

Its fallen state means that humankind has to make a conscious effort to understand what God is saying to it through the stars. This is why the study of philosophy, especially natural philosophy, is so necessary; for it is only through this study that the structures and order of the world can be so interpreted. But the perfection of the heavens means that it is most effective to transcend the sublunar sphere by observing God's works directly as they are laid out in the heavens. Thus sight is for Melanchthon the first of the five human senses: without sight it would be impossible for the human being to observe these most important and significant celestial motions at all.[72] However, understanding the motions requires more than sight alone, for sight cannot unlock or interpret what is observed. To describe and understand the celestial motions the human mind must apply reason in the form of physics and mathematics, or, more specifically, astronomy. Mathematics is thus of the utmost importance in freeing the human mind from the restrictions of its fallen nature, because it is the only means by which human reason can unlock the "vestiges of divinity" found in the heavens, that is, the regularity of the motions of the celestial bodies.

It is not only that the human mind is allowed to attain this freedom; such an endeavor is expected of and natural to human beings, so that to deny that the study of the heavens can lead the observer to God is to "wage war against human nature, which was clearly founded to understand divine things," as Melanchthon puts it. Indeed "God desires that knowledge of these wonderful courses and powers should lead us towards knowledge of the divine,"[73] so that the study of the heavens is "as appropriate to human nature as is swimming to a fish or singing to a nightingale."[74] Using another circular argument, he asserts that the fact that these motions are responsive to mathematical analysis is itself an indication that they reflect the nature of the mind of God, for, "as Plato says, God always geometrizes."[75] God therefore created the heavens along mathematical lines and made it possible for the human mind to reason mathematically, and so they should do so. But the very fact that the order of the heavens may be described mathematically shows that this order is more capable of illustrating God and God's intentions than is that of the sublunar world, which is less susceptible to mathematical analysis (at least in terms of the mathematics available to a sixteenth-century mathematician).

Because the human mind may be said to be number in its capacity to seek out order and regularity,[76] and because in this it reflects the mind of God, the study of mathematics offers a vehicle by which the human mind may transcend its restrictions and reach some understanding of God. Thus the human mind, created by God, reflects the structure of the heavens, also created by God, and in this way human observation of the heavens is able to offer a route to a better knowledge of God. Only the heavenly motions can be interpreted by mathematics, and thus mathematics offers the only sure way of transcending the natural world, for it is the sole means by which the human mind is led to the heavens and thence to God. Astronomy thus becomes the vital first step towards understanding the order which God intended for the world, and a cornerstone for Melanchthon's ethical authority.

VI.

Melanchthon's justification of the study of astronomy was rooted in a strongly Aristotelian cosmological understanding of the universe. As we have seen, he was happy to draw upon the writings of Plato to illustrate certain points of his argument, and his confidence that the human mind is a reflection of God's mind probably owes much to Plato. Melanchthon's praise of astronomy above "noetic" arithmetic is surely not Platonic, however, nor is his emphasis on the importance of interpreting the physical world. It is probably no coincidence that Melanchthon's integration of the study of the heavens into a physical and ethical system that allowed observations of the heavens to be used as a basis for ethical authority results in a theological, ethical astronomy very similar to that propounded in the introduction of Ptolemy's *Almagest,* a work which was almost certainly known to Melanchthon from his own days as a student in Tübingen and on which he himself lectured in 1541.[77] Perhaps it was here that Melanchthon found the ideas which led him to integrate the study of astronomy into his theological system and to promote it so fluently.

Melanchthon's promotion of astronomy does, however, have limits. The argument that astronomy can lead the observer to an understanding of God could logically be taken to imply that better, more accurate observations will result in a better understanding of God. In later generations this was indeed the conclusion which was drawn on the basis of such arguments. Melanchthon's ideas were taken to Tübingen by his student, Jacob Heerbrand, who taught theology to a number of the teachers of Johannes Kepler as well as to Kepler himself. In the hands of Michael Maestlin (Tübingen's professor of mathematics from 1583 to 1631) and of his pupil Johannes Kepler, this theological justification of astronomy became a theological justification for the exact study of the heavens which could legitimate the overthrow of traditional Aristotelian and Ptolemaic cosmology.[78] Melanchthon, however, saw such consequences of his praise of astronomy as going too far. On the one hand his theological, astrological application of astronomy did indeed require accurate observations and the precise prediction of astronomical conjunctions. On the other hand his appreciation of astronomy was, as we have seen, rooted in an Aristotelian cosmology which he was not prepared to—or was not able to—compromise on the basis of new observations.[79] In this sense his defense of mathematics and astronomy is merely rhetorical, as Breen has argued. The cosmological system was an integral part of Melanchthon's theological, teleological interpretation of the universe and with it his moral philosophy; it could not simply be discarded, for if it were, the whole edifice would collapse.[80]

Despite this reservation, which was to cause problems for later generations, Melanchthon's defense of astronomy ensured not only that it continued to be taught, but that its teaching could be defended as an integral part of theology. Although Melanchthon remained adamant that neither human reason nor the observation of the natural world or of the heavens could ever bring salvation or an appreciation of the salvific work of God, he was nevertheless convinced that the astronomy with its doctrine of the heavens, *doctrinae coelestium,* was a step on the road to understanding the heavenly doctrines, *doctrinae coelestae,* of theology. For only through astronomy was revealed the wonderful order of the heavens, established by God to benefit humankind and to guide its behavior.

Notes

1. See Heinz Scheible, "Melanchthon," *Theologische Realenzyklopädie* (Berlin, 1977-), XXII, 371-410, with up-to-date bibliography; Karl Hartfelder, *Philipp Melanchthon als Praeceptor Germaniae* (Berlin, 1889).

2. Sachiko Kusukawa, *The Transformation of Natural Philosophy: the Case of Melanchthon* (Cambridge, 1995). It seems doubtful, however, that Melanchthon's approach can really be categorized as specifically "Lutheran," especially since other Lutherans—including Luther—take a completely different attitude towards natural philosophy. Nevertheless, it does seem to be innovative.

3. In Württemberg, for instance, Melanchthon's works were the set-books for the teaching of grammar, dialectics, and rhetoric in schools and as a preparation for university courses from 1559 until well into the seventeenth century (Charlotte Methuen, "Securing the Reformation through Education: the Duke's Scholarship System of Sixteenth-Century Württemberg," *Sixteenth Century Journal,* 25 [1994], 841-51).

4. See Kusukawa, *Transformation.*

5. Charles B. Schmitt, "Philosophy and Science in Sixteenth Century Universities: Some Preliminary Comments," in *Studies in Renaissance Philosophy and Science* (London, 1981), 505. John M. Fletcher, "Change and Resistance to Change: A Consideration of the Development of English and German Universities during the Sixteenth Century," *History of Universities,* 1 (1981), 17, notes that in German universities of the sixteenth-century lectures in mathematics were held to attract students to universities.

6. See, e.g., Claudia Kren, "Astronomical Teaching at the Late Medieval University of Vienna," *History of Universities,* 3 (1983), 21.

7. Desiderius Erasmus, *De pueris statim ac liberaliter instituendis, The Collected Works of Erasmus* (hereafter *CWE*), ed. Craig R. Thompson (Toronto, 1975-), XXVI, 336.

8. Desiderius Erasmus, *De ratione studii, CWE,* XXIV, 574.

9. Allen G. Debus, *Man and Nature in the Renaissance* (Cambridge, 1978), 3.

10. Kusukawa, *Transformation,* 167, n. 196, notes that Stöffler praised astronomy as natural theology, or *theologia naturali.*

11. Melanchthon, *De artibus liberalibus* (1517), *Corpus Reformatorum* (hereafter *CR*), ed. C. G. Bretschneider (Halle, 1834-60), XI, cols. 10-12.

12. Melanchthon, *De corrigendis adolescentiae studiis* (1518), *CR* XI, 17: "Philosophia, non uti nunc, ex Aristotele petebatur, sed totum sini adserverant mathemata, quae magnae curae tum literati omnes habebant."

13. Melanchthon to Spalatin, 21 March 1521, *Melanchthons Briefwechsel* (hereafter *MBW*), ed. Heinz Scheible (Stuttgart, 1977-), 130 and 14 June 1521, *MBW,* 146. This suggestion was not in fact carried out (see Kusukawa, *Transformation,* 49).

14. Melanchthon consistently denied that he had any particular mathematical skills. See, e.g., Melanchthon, *Praefatio in arithmeticen Joachimi Rhetici* (1536), *CR,* XII, 285; and Kusukawa, *Transformation,* 135. For Melanchthon's interactions with other mathematicians, see Robert S. Westman, "The Melanchthon Circle, Rheticus, and the Wittenberg Interpretation of the Copernican Theory," *Isis,* 66 (1975), 164-93, and Lynn Thorndike, *History of Magic and Experimental Science* (New York, 1941), V, chap. 17.

15. *Praefatio in librum: Ioannis de Sacro Busto de sphaera* (Melanchthon to Simon Grynaeus, August 1531), *CR,* II, 530-37 (*MBW,* 1176).

16. *Praefatio in librum: Georgii Purbachii Theoricae nouae planetarum* (Melanchthon to Simon Grynaeus, January 1535), *CR,* II, 814-20 (*MBW,* 1509).

17. *Praemissa libro: Ioannis Regiomontani tabulae directionum* (Melanchthon to Georg and Huldrich Fugger, 25 February 1552), *CR,* VII, 950-53 (*MBW,* 6363).

18. *Praefatio in geometriam Iohanni Vogelini* (1536), *CR,* III, 107-14 (*MBW,* 1780); and (virtually identical) Preface to Euclid's *Elements* (Basel, 1537) (*MBW,* 1937) ("A Letter of Melanchthon to the Reader," tr. Marian A. Moore, in *Isis,* 50 [1959], 145-50).

19. *Praefatio in libros de iudiciis natiuitatum Ioannis Schoneri* (1545), *CR,* V, 818-24 (*MBW,* 3978); *Praemissa libro: Claudii Ptolomaei de praedictionibus astronomicis (Quadripartitum) libri IV* (ed. by Melanchthon himself) (Melanchthon to Erasmus Ebnerus March 1553), *CR,* VIII, 61-63; and *Praemissa libro: Procli paraphrasis in quatuor Ptolomaei libros de Siderum effectionibus* (Melanchthon to Hieronymus Commerstaedt, 1 September 1554), *CR,* VIII, 338-41.

20. See *De astronomia et geographia* (1542), *CR,* XI, 292-98 and Melanchthon, *Praefatio in arithmeticen* (a lecture given as an introduction to another by the mathematician Rheticus), *CR,* XII, 285-92.

21. See, e.g., Melanchthon, *De Casparo Crucigero* (1549), *CR,* XI, 833-41 and *De Iohanne Regiomontano* (1549), *CR,* XI, 817-26.

22. Melanchthon, *An leges damnant praedictiones astrologicas?* (1536), *CR,* X, 712-15, *De dignitate astrologiae* (1535), *CR,* XI, 261-66, and *De Orione* (1553), *CR,* XII, 46-52 ("Melanchthon: Inspirer of the Study of Astronomy," tr. William Hammer, *Popular Astronomy,* 59 [1951], 308-19).

23. Kusukawa, *Transformation,* 149, points out that Melanchthon's position on natural philosophy remained virtually unchanged after 1543.

24. Melanchthon discusses these aspects of mathematics in various prefaces and letters. See especially *In arithmeticen praefatio, CR,* XI, 287 and *De astronomia et geographia, CR,* XI, 294-97.

25. For other contemporary examples of praise of the utility of mathematics see Peter Dear, *Mersenne and the Learning of the Schools* (Ithaca, 1988), 43-47.

26. *De Discrimine Evangelii et Philosophiae* (undated, but probably written in the early 1530s), *CR,* XII, 690-91.

27. *In arithmeticen praefatio, CR,* XI, 290: "[Arithmetica] ostendit ordinem rerum, et monet confusa evolvenda et discernenda esse. Haec sunt initia ratiocinationis in hominibus." Melanchthon had used this argument, and those which follow, as early as 1517 in his oration *De artibus liberalibus.*

28. *Praefatio in Geometriam, CR,* III, 108: "Deinde cum demonstrationes Geometricae maxime sint illustres, nemo sine aliqua cognitione huius artis satis perspicit, quae sit vis demonstrationum; nemo sine ea erit artifex methodi."

29. *In arithmeticen praefatio, CR,* XI, 291: "Videbant enim Dialecticen initia sumere ab Arithmetica, et exercitatio multiplicationis et divisionis, optime praeparat ingenia ad Syllogismos. Item vis demonstrationis melius intelligi potest, cognita Arithmetica: quia haec habet maxime illustres demonstrationes."

30. *Ibid.,* 290: "Ideo prima est numerorum intelligentia, idque sensisse opinor Pythagoram, cum definivit, mentem esse numerum; significavit enim animam esse ratiocinatricem, quae discernit res, et ordinem animadvertit."

31. *Euclidis Elementa,* ed. Simon Grynaeus (Basel, 1533), preface, folio a2^r. Discussions of the status of mathematical proof seem to have been quite common. For example, the Tübingen professors Michael Maestlin (professor of mathematics), Martin Crusius (dean of the arts faculty) and Georg Liebler (professor for natural philosohy) all discussed this question and concluded that the certainty of arithmetic and geometry is in part a function of their noetic subject matter. See Charlotte Methuen, "Kepler's Tübingen: Stimulus to a Theological Mathematics" (Ph.D. thesis, Edinburgh, 1995), 180.

32. Neal W. Gilbert, *Renaissance Concepts of Method* (New York, 1960), 68-73.

33. See Hans-Georg Geyer, "Welt und Mensch: Zur Frage des Aristotelismus bei Melanchthon" (Ph.D. thesis, Bonn, 1959), and Kusukawa, *Transformation.*

34. See, e.g., Bernd Moeller, *Deutschland im Zeitalter der Reformation (Deutsche Geschichte,* IV) (Göttingen, 1988), 90-101.

35. See, e.g., Kusukawa, "*Aspectio divinorum operum*: Melanchthon and Astrology for Lutheran Medics," *Medicine and the Reformation,* eds. Ole Peter Grell and Andrew Cunningham (London, 1993), 43.

36. Bernhard Lohse, "Philipp Melanchthon in seiner Beziehungen zu Luther," *Leben und Werk Martin Luthers von 1526 bis 1546,* ed. Helmar Junghans (Berlin, 1983), 410. Also Gerhard Ebeling, *Word and Faith,* tr. James W. Leitch (London, 1963), 62-78, and Kusukawa, *Transformation,* 62-74.

37. Kusukawa, *Transformation,* 69-70.

38. Melanchthon, *Praefatio in Theoricae Novae Planetarum, CR,* II, 815: "Nam mihi quoque unum hoc remedium videtur publicarum calamitatum fore, si se nostri homines ad veram veteremque Philosophiam convertant: quae cum incendat animos amore ac studio veritatis, et ad intellectum atque admirationem optimarum rerum exsuscitet, una efficit viros bonos ac moderatos."

39. *De discrimine evangelii et philosophiae, CR,* XII, 690: "Quod autem philosophia sit lex Dei, hinc quoque intelligi potest, quia est noticia causarum et effectuum naturalium, quae cum sint res ordinatae ex Deo, sequitur philosophiam esse legem Dei, quae est doctrina de illa divina ordinata."

40. *De philosophia, CR,* XI, 281: "Magno instrumento destitutus est Theologus, qui nescit illas eruditissimas disputationes, de anima, de sensibus, de causis appetitionum et affectuum, de noticia, de

voluntate. Et arroganter faciet, qui se profitetur Dialecticum, si nescit illas causarum partitiones, quae traduntur tantum in Physicis, et intelligi non possunt nisi a Physicis."

41. Melanchthon, *Liber de anima* (1553), *CR*, XIII, 137, and compare *De dignitate arte medicinae* (1548), *CR*, XI, 808-9. In the *Loci Communes* (1542), *CR*, XXI, 641-43, Melanchthon offers nine arguments for proving the existence of God from the natural world; here the movements of the heavens are subsumed under those "from the order of nature" and "from the truth of knowledge about the natural world."

42. Melanchthon, *Praefatio in Theoricae Novae Planetarum, CR*, II, 815-17.

43. *Ibid.,* 816.

44. *In arithmeticen praefatio, CR*, XI, 288.

45. Grynaeus argued for the primacy of arithmetic, and this position was reflected by professors of the arts faculty in Tübingen later in the century (see Methuen, "Kepler's Tübingen," 176-77).

46. Melanchthon, *In arithmeticen praefatio, CR*, XI, 288-89.

47. See, e.g., *Praefatio in Theoricae Novae Planetarum, CR*, II, 816; *De astronomia et geographia, CR*, XI, 297.

48. *De astronomia et geographia, CR*, XI, 297.

49. *Ibid., CR*, XI, 297.

50. Melanchthon, *Praefatio in Theoricae Novae Planetarum, CR*, II, 817

51. See, e.g., *De astronomia et geographia, CR*, XI, 294, ". . . ac tantum de motuum doctrina et regionum metis dicam, omissa divinatrice parte, ne quod mihi certamen accersam." The terms astronomy and astrology were used almost interchangeably during the sixteenth century. Melanchthon usually (but not invariably) distinguishes between astronomy, which is responsible for the observations, and astrology, which deals with predictions, and the effects of the observed phenomena.

52. Kusukawa, *Transformation,* 124-27. A number of comets were observed in central Europe during the 1530s: one in 1531, two in 1532, and others in 1533, 1538, and 1539. See C. Doris Hellman, *The Comet of 1577: its Place in the History of Astronomy* (New York, 1944), 88-90.

53. See Jim Tester, *A History of Western Astrology* (Woodbridge, 1987); also Lynn Thorndike, "The True Place of Astrology in the History of Sci-

ence," *Isis,* 46 (1955), 273-78; and Robert S. Westman, "The Astronomer's Role in the Sixteenth Century: a preliminary study," *History of Science,* 18 (1980), 105-47. See also *Astrologi Hallucinati: Stars and the End of the World in Luther's Time,* ed. Paola Zambelli (Berlin, 1986) especially John D. North, "Celestial Influence—the Major Premiss of Astrology" (45-100); Krzysztof Pomian, "Astrology as Naturalistic Theology of History" (29-43); Helga Robinson Hammerstein, "The Battle of the Booklets: Prognostic Tradition and Proclamation of the Word in Early Sixteenth-Century Germany" (129-51); Stefano Caroti, "Melanchthon's Astrology" (109-21); and Ingetraut Ludolphy, "Luther und die Astrologie" (101-7).

54. See Methuen, "Kepler's Tübingen," 103-22.

55. Melanchthon, *De dignitate astrologiae, CR*, XI, 263: "Astrologia pars est Physices, quae docet, quos effectus astrorum lumen in elementis et mixtis corporibus habeat, qualia temperamenta, quas alterationes, quas inclinationes pariat."

56. *An leges damnant praedictiones astrologicas?, CR*, X, 713-14: "His legibus in codice non damnari praedictiones Astrologicas, sed tantum illas quae non habent causas aut rationes Physicas, quae vocantur a Ptolemaeo ἀναιτιολογηται quales sunt augurum paedictiones, et quales sunt multae admixtae Astrologicis, ut cum divinant ex interrogationis tempore, cum pollicenter se caedes, aut furtorum autores indicaturos esse, Quemadmodum in decretalibus iure damnatur sacerdos, qui simulabat se ex Astrolabio quaerere, quomodo deprehendi possent furta. Tales igitur supersticiosae praedictiones damnari illis legibus sentio, quas et ipsi Philosophi improbant. Sed quidam inepti in genere damnant praedictiones Astrologicas, hoc est, eas, quae habent Physicas causas, et rationes. Has hac ratione probamus: Ordinationes Dei in natura observare, pium et utile est, non est superstitiosum. Nam superstitiosa sunt, quae non habent causas Physicas, et ordinationes Dei. Sed observationes Astrologicae sunt observationes causarum Physicarum, quae sunt ordinationes Dei."

57. Kusukawa, *Transformation,* 147. Melanchthon's position here reflects the traditional Aristotelian view of the hiearchical relationship of what are usually termed "subalternate" sciences.

58. *Ibid.,* 144-47.

59. Melanchthon, *Initia Doctrinae Physicae, CR*, XIII, 183: "Quanquam autem adiunctio doctrinae de motibus et effectibus coelestibus ad hanc considerationem inferioris materiae, utilis est, . . . et collatio artium utrique lumen adfert, tamen quia

utraque ars magna est, et latissime patet, usitatum nunc est physicen vocare hanc doctrinam, quae causas mutationum in mixtis propinquas, quae oriuntur ab huius materiae inferioris motu et qualitatibus, patefacit, ut medicus in curanda pleuritide, materiae motum et qualitatem in aegro corpore considerat, intellegit adfluere sanguinem ad locum adfectum."

60. *Ibid., CR*, XIII, 184-85. See also Reijer Hooykaas, "Von der 'physica' zur Physik," *Humanismus und Naturwissenschaften,* eds. Rudolf Schmitz and Fritz Krafft (Boppard, 1980), 9-38.

61. Melanchthon, *Initia Doctrinae Physicae, CR*, XIII, 410-12: "Postremae sententiae in libro Aristotelis de Generatione maxime memorabiles hae sunt: Causa perpetuitatis generationum et corruptionum est motus Solis et Planetarum in Zodiaco. Adfirmat igitur aliquam esse actionem stellarum universalem, in fovenda natura, et in conservanda hac inferiore materia, et ciendis insignibus mutationibus materiae. Ideo addit: etiam omnium viventium certas vitae periodos esse. Sed cum mens hunc mirandum naturae ordinem considerat, videlicet ipsas motuum leges, et certas planetarum et animantium species, et modos generationis et periodos durationis, necesse est ratiocinari, aliam esse priorem et intelligentem causam, videlicet, Deum conditorem, cuius consilio totus hic ordo et institutus est, et gubernatur, et conservatur, sicut doctrina de Deo in Ecclesia clarius docet."

62. *Ibid., CR*, XIII, 223: "Adparet autem coelum non admittere tales alterationes, quia nulla pars corrumpitur. Igitur non est ex materia elementari."

63. *Ibid., CR*, XIII, 392-400.

64. *De astronomia et geographia, CR*, XI, 297.

65. For example, Melanchthon writes in the 1535 version of the *Loci Communes* (*CR* XXI, 370) of the *vestigia divinitatis* which are to be found throughout nature.

66. See Kusukawa, *Transformation,* 75-123.

67. Melanchthon, *Praefatio in De iudiciis nativitatum, CR,* V, 822-23: "Si hominum natura mansisset integra, fulsisset in nobis lux divina, gubernatrix omnium motuum, et stellae in materia non contaminata alias actiones habuissent. At nunc in his sordibus infeliciores sunt actiones et extincta est illa lux, quae rexisset omnes humanos motus." See also Dino Belluci, "Mélanchthon et la défense de l'astrologie," *Bibliothèque d'Humanisme et Renaissance,* 50 (1988), 587-622. For Melanchthon's views of creation as only good see *Loci Communes* (1542), *CR*, XXI, 610 and 643-52 ("De caussa peccati et de contingentia").

68. *Loci Communes, CR*, XXI, 711: "Ut lumen oculis divinitus inditum est, Ita sunt quaedam notitiae mentibus humanis inditae, quibus agnoscunt et iudicant pleraque. Philosophi hoc lumen vocant notitiam principiorum, vocant κοινὰς ἐννοίας et προλήψεις. Ac vulgaris divisio nota est, alia esse principia speculabilia, ut notitias numerorum, ordinis, syllogismi, principia Geometrica, Physica. Haec omnes fatentur esse certissima et fontes maximarum utilitatum in vita."

69. See *Liber de anima* (1553) and especially Melanchthon's discussions of human intellect and will, and of human beings as the image of God (*CR*, XIII, 138-72); and see Kusukawa, *Transformation,* 85-99.

70. *Loci Communes, CR*, XXI, 643-52; see also *Praefatio in libros De iudiciis navitatum, CR,* V, 820-21, where he argues that all actions are caused either by human will, God, or the devil, which may warp human minds and hearts.

71. *Praefatio in Theoricae Novae Planetarum, CR,* II, 817-18: "Saepe fatorum saevitiam lenit Deus, placatus piorum votis. Quare haec quoque gravis causa fuerit, rerum futurarum significationes animadvertendi. Prodest enim commonefieri homines atrocibus siderum minis, ut a Deo opem implorent; deinde ut bonitatem Dei magis agnoscant, cum viderint, aliquam esse superiorem ac meliorem naturam sideribus, quae tristes significationes mitigat."

72. *Liber de anima, CR*, XIII, 72: "Dominantur inter sensus Oculi, quos inquit Plato praecipue nobis duces esse ad agnitionem Dei, intuentes hanc pulcherrimam coeli machinam, ac notantes motuum varietatem, quae non alio sensu, nisi oculorum animadverti potuit. Est et hoc ingens beneficium, quod hoc sensu lucem agnoscimus, quae et mirandum Dei opus est, et magnam naturae partem praecipue ostendit. Et praestantissimas naturas lucidas esse certum est, Deum, angelos, animas, et in corpore spiritus vitales et animales."

73. *Praefatio in Theoricae Novae Planetarum, CR,* II, 816: "Nam Epicuraeos illos, qui neque pulcherrimos motus coelestium corporum admirantur, neque cognitionem eorum utilem esse contendunt, ne quidem apellatione hominum dignos iudico. Etenim non solum bellum gerunt cum humana natura, quae praecipue ad has divinas res adspiciendas condita est, sed etiam θεομαχοι sunt. Voluit enim Deus horum mirabilium cursuum ac virium notitiam, ducem nobis esse ad divinitatis cognitionem."

74. *De astronomia et geographia, CR*, XI, 297: "Sua cuique naturae propiissima actio iucundissima est, ut nare piscibus, modulari Lusciniae, ita homines

magna voluptate adfici necesse est, cum naturam totam rerum aspiciunt, cum numerorum et magnitudinum proportiones inveniunt, cum coelestium et inferiorum corporum harmoniam et consensum deprehendunt, cum vident omnia certa lege condita esse, ut nos de Architecto admoneant."

75. *Praefatio in Theoricae Novae Planetarum, CR,* II, 817: "Quin potius, ut Plato dixit, Deum semper γεωμετρειν, hoc est, certissimo motu omnia metientem gubenare haec inferiora."

76. Melanchthon, *In arithmeticen praefatio, CR,* XI, 290, see note 30 above.

77. Kusukawa, *Transformation,* 134-35, and see Liba Chaia Taub, *Ptolemy's Universe: the Natural Philosophical and Ethical Foundations of Ptolemy's Astronomy* (Chicago, 1993). The connections between Melanchthon's thought and that of Ptolemy would probably bear further investigation.

78. See Methuen, "Kepler's Tübingen," 159-94.

79. The tension between these two poles can be seen particularly vividly from Melanchthon's reception of the work of Copernicus. See Emil Wohlwill, "Melanchthon und Copernicus," *Mitteilungen zur Geschichte der Medizin und der Naturwissenschaften,* 3 (1904), 261-62, Hans Blumenberg, *The Genesis of the Copernican World,* tr. Robert M. Wallace (Cambridge, Mass., 1987), 324-27, and Methuen, "Kepler's Tübingen," 76-81.

80. Quirinius Breen, "The Subordination of Philosophy to Rhetoric in Melanchthon," *Archiv für Reformationsgeschichte,* 43 (1952), 13-28.

Euan Cameron (essay date October 1997)

SOURCE: Cameron, Euan. "Philipp Melanchthon: Image and Substance." *Journal of Ecclesiastical History* 48, no. 4 (October 1997): 705-22.

[*In the essay which follows, Cameron finds that Melanchthon's image as "hesitant, temporising, even shifty" is not entirely without basis in historical fact but concludes too that this picture does not do justice to the man or his ideas.*]

In conferences, symposia and a modest number of publications, 1997 is being marked as the Melanchthon-year. However excellent in their own kind the results of the year's commemoration may be, neither in quantity nor in diversity will they approach the tributes and analyses which greeted the five-hundredth anniversary of Luther's birth fourteen years ago. Philipp Melanchthon (1497-1560) is destined forever to occupy the second rank behind Martin Luther, and to be remembered in connection with his greater colleague. While more of his works have recently appeared in English translation, no equivalent to the great American edition of Luther's works is to be expected.[1] In some ways this place in the shadows may do his reputation, and the study of his life and ideas, more good than harm. He is spared the attention of the psychoanalysts, the dramatists, the generalists and the amateurs. Melanchthon studies are usually more professional and less wayward than much that is written about Luther.

On the other hand, constant comparison between Melanchthon and Luther can introduce two historical distortions, which one must hope the work of 1997 may correct. First, Melanchthon is too often judged by whether he was a 'good' or 'faithful' follower of Luther. This process began just after Luther's death in 1546 and has continued since; usually the verdict has gone against him. Yet Melanchthon aspired to be a scriptural Christian, not a 'Lutheran'. He displayed an independent, proprietorial attitude to the 'Lutheran' confessions, which he adapted at will. His theological legacy deserves to be evaluated on its own terms, as much as that of, say, Calvin or Zwingli.

Secondly, Melanchthon was far more than a religious leader and teacher. His output may have been less vast than Luther's, but his range was far greater. As a classical philologist, rhetorician, logician, historian and philosopher, Philipp Melanchthon wrote and taught more widely than any other single reformer.[2] On his death his lectures on biblical exegesis, ethics, philology and history had to be divided between four successors.[3] This range of activity does not merely attest the energy and versatility of a scholar who, besides his academic work, was also a religious negotiator, an educational consultant, a correspondent and a husband and father. It also highlights Melanchthon's unique, self-imposed task: to reconstruct education in the German Protestant world, virtually single-handed, so that the insights of reformed doctrine were supported rather than compromised by the teaching of ethics, natural philosophy, or other subjects.

Yet Melanchthon still labours under an image problem. Alongside Luther's obstinate and resilient confidence, Melanchthon can appear hesitant, temporising, even shifty. He was reputedly prepared to negotiate far too much of the essential reformed message, at Augsburg in 1530, at Regensburg in 1541, and at the time of the *Interim* in 1548-9.[4] His qualifications to the Protestant message were attacked as revisionist betrayals by his ultra-Lutheran opponents during the 1550s: in some areas he seemed too Catholic, in others almost Calvinist. With his Renaissance scholarly tastes, his penchant for astrology, even his status as an unordained layman, Melanchthon seems somehow not quite to belong in the company of the other reformers. There are good historical reasons for this image problem. However, a verdict based only on the image does little justice to Melanchthon, nor does it adequately explain him, as this piece will try to show.

I

An attempt to make sense of Melanchthon may well begin with his university affiliation, often overlooked and significant. By a conscious decision he remained first and foremost a member of the Arts Faculty in Wittenberg throughout his career. He gave lectures on biblical exegesis; he wrote the definitive manual of Lutheran systematic theology. Yet he remained, academically speaking, a scholar of the Arts and a philosopher. When Luther asked him to devote himself full-time to theological lectures and give up Greek, Melanchthon, in July 1522, asked to be allowed to give up theology instead. He repeated the request to Spalatin in March 1523, and again in September 1524, without success.[5] Paradoxically, this scholar who on paper treated theology with confidence and authority, was most reluctant to spend his entire career teaching it. In a most absorbing recent book on Melanchthon's work in natural philosophy, Sachiko Kusukawa has suggested that Melanchthon turned away from theology to philosophy after an 'identity crisis as a leader of reform', when the Zwickau prophets caused him to lose his nerve at Wittenberg during Luther's absence in 1521-2. He left theology, apparently, because he had lost the stomach for it, and did not feel that he was up to the task.[6] This career choice can then be cited as evidence of Melanchthon's weak moral fibre, especially when it came to handling doctrine: and as a portent of trouble to come.

One may read Melanchthon's reasons more sympathetically. True, he claimed to Spalatin that he was 'unequal to handling the greatest subjects, indeed I seem to myself to be, as the proverb says, a donkey bearing mysteries'.[7] This was formulaic humanist self-deprecation, as the proverb suggests. He also protested that there were simply too many lectures in theology already: 'there is such a crowd of theological lectures that young people are overwhelmed rather than taught. . . . Are not the audiences satisfied with four or more theological lectures each day?'[8] There are, no doubt, signs that Melanchthon found aspects of the academic theologian's life uncongenial. In his letters to Joachim Camerarius, the most frank and revealing of all his early correspondence, he remarked 'on theological matters, to be sure there are things I could write about; but as often as I think about these controversies, I am fearfully pained, almost exhausted. If only the things which Paul calls "foolish talk" could be set aside, and those

things urged which "build up consciences"'.[9] In so far as Melanchthon felt himself inadequate to anything, it was because his health would not stand up to more lecturing besides his existing teaching commitments, and that (as he remarked in another context) his speech lacked the flair and carrying power needed to address large audiences. The same reason had prevented him from becoming a preacher at Wittenberg during Luther's absence.[10]

However, far more positive reasons kept Melanchton in his classroom. He saw his vocation to teach the Arts as no less essential, and his functions in that sphere as harder to replace, than the work of any theologian. In a celebrated letter written in 1523, Eobanus Hessus had deplored the way in which the first heady flush of enthusiasm for Reformation theology led students and scholars to desert their studies in other fundamental disciplines. Philipp Melanchthon shared Hessus' horror at the prospect of Germany becoming filled with half-educated enthusiasts for controversial religious dogma. He wrote back to support Hessus: 'believe me, those who despise secular learning, think nothing better of theological studies; they only use their name to cover their idleness'.[11] For the sake of theology itself, a reformed, that is, restructured educational curriculum was urgently needed. Luther and Melanchthon had between them proved that the Aristotelian philosophy taught in the traditional curriculum militated against the Lutheran 'gospel'.[12] The old curriculum had to be abolished; so, as Kusukawa shows, Melanchthon set out to replace it with a new, reformed Aristotelianism. In *The transformation of natural philosophy,* Melanchthon is alleged to have been so shocked by the spectacle of radical, Anabaptist anti-intellectualism in religion, revealed by the 1527 visitations, that he saw the need for a 'correct' philosophy, whereas before he had seen only the vices of the old one.[13] This thesis is one of several instances where Kusukawa contends that specific events in Melanchthon's life and in church history dictated how his thought evolved. It may be a little too neat. Melanchthon, as his letter to Eobanus Hessus shows, did not need Müntzer or the Anabaptists to tell him that secular education was important. Indeed, he had steered through reform of one part of the traditional philosophical curriculum as early as 1521.[14] In December 1524 he wrote to Spalatin, somewhat playfully, that despite the long-standing war between theologians and philosophers, he took great pleasure in the writings of the latter; he grieved that such works were neglected, and wished Spalatin to share his pleasure in them.[15]

For Melanchthon, learning was a religious duty, and education, in all its branches, was a type of piety. He expressed this view repeatedly and publicly, in the prefaces to his textbooks. 'One cannot come to piety without education; God saw fit to commit the teaching of piety to letters, therefore, they are to be learned with the utmost care and vigilance.' 'There is no more splendid ornament of religion [than learning].'[16] If St John Chrysostom kept a copy of the plays of Aristophanes by him and used it as a pillow, how much more should pupils read the less obscene Terence.[17] Melanchthon's attribution of religious worth to literary and philosophical studies might have been merely the moralistic puffing, typical of a schoolmaster attracting pupils to his subject: but it was not. With no less zeal than an Aquinas, or the later sixteenth-century Spanish neo-Thomists, Philipp Melanchthon produced a university Aristotelianism which meshed precisely with his Protestant theology. While religious purpose is visible in nearly all Melanchthon's many secular works, two books best demonstrate this trait: his commentary on Aristotle's *De anima,* originally published in 1540 and revised in 1552, and his ***Initia doctrinae physicae*** of 1549. Appropriately, Kusukawa's study concentrates on these two works in its central chapters iii and iv.[18]

Anyone who has dabbled in the debates around Aristotle's doctrine of the soul in Italy and Paris in the early sixteenth century, and the storm of protest over the works of Pietro Pomponazzi or Francesco Vimercati,[19] may find Melanchthon's work on *De anima* somewhat disappointing. Melanchthon showed almost no interest in the hottest philosophical questions of his age. He discussed the natural immortality of the soul relatively briefly, and relied almost entirely on scriptural sources; opinions of ancient philosophers were discussed briefly, those of moderns not at all.[20] On the other hand, much new anatomical and physiological material was added to the discussion of the soul which had not traditionally formed part of the subject. Especially in the 1552 recension, Melanchthon used the discoveries of Vesalius to discuss the organs of sense and the brain in detail.[21] The real innovation in Melanchthon's treatment, however, lay in his blending Aristotelian psychology and Protestant dogma. The rational mind ought to be able to fulfil the moral law, but it was corrupted. Even in corrupt sinners there was an innate moral sense of what was evil. If human nature had not fallen, it would have seen God aright; but after the fall, doubts and the pursuit of pleasures clouded its vision.[22] Likewise typical of Melanchthon's thought was his discussion of free will. Although fallen humanity could not fulfil the divine law, there remained a power to restrain the body to a purely 'external' obedience to the law, that is, to avoid foul crimes. Yet as far as the Christian faith and its demand for an 'internal' obedience to divine law were concerned, only through rebirth in the light of the Gospel could the human mind attain to any sort of obedience, and then only with the presence of the Holy Spirit.[23] Melanchthon thus incorporated Protestant anthropology into his exegesis of Aristotle. This is the chief point; and it is surprising that Kusukawa instead emphasies a rather too ingenious link between Melanchthon's psychology and the imma-

nence of God in Lutheran theology, as opposed to his transcendence in the thought of Zwingli. We are told that this contrast between immanence and transcendence underlay the eucharistic dispute, and therefore shaped Melanchthon's treatment of body and soul.[24] If one wishes to find a polemical purpose in Melanchthon's *De anima,* surely a far more obvious theme is its rejection of 'Stoicism': the work denounced the Stoics' belief that all emotions are opinions and should be avoided altogether, and their absolute determinism, which made God the author of evil.[25] Elsewhere, when Melanchthon did attack Zwingli, it was for his alleged 'Stoic' attitudes.[26]

Theology, then, could and must inform natural philosophy. However, the reverse was also true: natural philosophy could and must confirm and demonstrate the truths of revelation. This conviction emerges most clearly in the ***Initia doctrinae physicae.*** Against the atomists, Melanchthon insisted that there must be certainty in the behaviour of physical elements, otherwise physical life would not demonstrate the presence of the divine architect. He saw a sound understanding of physics as useful to demonstrate divine providence. It refuted both the Epicureans' idea that matter moved and took shape at random, and the determinism of the Stoics.[27] When discussing physical causation, he began with the first cause, God. God's workings could be discerned in the 'traces of nature' in a way which was 'most pleasing to a good mind, and confirms honourable opinions about God'. As Melanchthon grew older this desire to trace the 'footprints of God' in nature grew in importance for his natural philosophy.[28] Not only did Melanchthon press the argument from design; he also believed that the causes of natural events passed down through the natural order in a demonstrable chain. This was not a simplistic system. Melanchthon accepted that some causes were not discernible, while some were very complex. In explaining human behaviour, he made room for human free will, temperaments, astral influences, God, the devil and external forces.[29] It is in the context of his natural philosophy that we can explain one of the most notorious of Melanchthon's personal peculiarities, his practical interest in astrology.

The structure of the ***Initia doctrinae physicae*** was skewed, even unbalanced, by this peculiarity. Book I was, unusually for a work on 'physica', largely given over to astronomy and astrology. Book II, on causes, said much about astral influences on temperaments. Book III, on matter and its combinations, was relatively the shortest and most concise section of the book.[30] The author clearly intended to make the point that the stars both illustrated and explained important principles of physical causation: 'I consider this to have been a most ancient wisdom, to ascribe the great changes in inferior matter to the positions of the stars.'[31] Melanchthon readily went beyond Aristotle, ascribing to the stars influence on weather, disease and also political upheavals.[32] To explain differences in aptitude and health in individual people, he did not hesitate to cast horoscopes. Johann Albrecht, the archbishop of Magdeburg, was sickly compared to his brother Albrecht, duke of Prussia, because the former's horoscope was full of signs of disease.[33] Different positions of the stars could explain modest differences in aptitude. Of Melanchthon's pupils, Stigel could write elegant Latin verses more easily than Ursinus, who made more effort. Individuals' horoscopes might explain portentous political factors, such as Emperor Freidrich III's ill fortune in war, or François I's imprisonment by Charles V.[34] Melanchthon felt able to grasp the nettle of responding to the critics of judicial astrology: he distinguished between the random or diabolical forms of divination, which were always sinful, and the purely natural (therefore licit) study of physical causes which he took astrology to be.[35]

From this perspective, one may regard Melanchthon's interest in astrology as a logical extension of his theory of nature and causation. However, the subject allows of a more personal, psychological explanation as well. Kusukawa points out that Melanchthon was especially perturbed by the comet of 1531, which was closely followed by the deaths of Zwingli and Oecolampadius, and suggests that this marked a turning-point in Melanchthon's interest in astrology.[36] This further instance of Kusukawa's 'crisis theory' of Melanchthon's development may overlook an event in his early life. In Melanchthon's infancy his father commissioned a horoscope for him from the Palatine astrologer, Johann Virdung of Hasfurt, in which the young Philipp was warned that he would suffer shipwreck in the Baltic Sea. Accordingly he refused invitations to England, and to Denmark, to avoid the risks.[37] Even if fear of unfavourable astral signs was increased by the crises of the Reformation, the foundations for the attitude were evidently laid in childhood and family.

Kusukawa interprets Melanchthon's natural philosophy in terms of his desire to prove specifically Lutheran positions on the nature of being, God and his relationship to creation; and claims this was done to uphold Lutheran doctrines on the presence of Christ in the eucharist. This argument does not convince me, partly because the reasons alleged for Melanchthon's positions are suppositious, rather than directly proven by the evidence. More significant, though, is that Kusukawa attributes to Melanchthon no greater independence of mind than the wish merely to prove, in the philosophical sphere, what Luther was saying in the theological one.[38] Yet surely his works show that Philipp Melanchthon had a religious agenda of his own; and that this agenda grew more, rather than less distinct from Luther's as the years passed. He spent far more time, in his mature works of philosophy and theology

alike, disproving 'Stoic' ideas, especially determinism, than he ever spent refuting 'sacramentarian' heresies. He had never been a zealot for Lutheran eucharistic theology; by the 1540s and 1550s he was definitely estranged from it. To make such ideas the final purpose of his philosophy is therefore implausible, if not paradoxical. Yet when these cavils have been registered, it remains an important achievement to have drawn such attention to Melanchthon the philosopher. He achieved almost single-handedly what the Coimbra commentators, Spanish Jesuits such as Benito Pereira, or the authors of the *cursus philosophicus* managed by the deployment of teams of scholars.[39] This 'natural philosophy', especially its astronomical lore, was of course doomed to obsolescence; but Melanchthon (despite his knowledge of Copernicus) could not have foreseen the advances in observation and higher mathematics which would supersede his Ptolemaic system. Nor should one forget that Melanchthon and his pupils, through the revision of Carion's *Chronicle* and the work which it inspired, also laid the foundations of reformed world and church history in the middle of the sixteenth century.[40] Melanchthon should never again be reduced to merely an unreliable mouthpiece for Lutheran religious teaching.

II

Traditionally, historians have explained some of Melanchthon's distinctness from Luther by saying that he was a more committed follower of Renaissance Christian humanism. The recent appearance of a further volume of edited texts in Heinz Scheible's *Melanchthons Briefwechsel,* covering 1523-6 and the debate between Luther and Erasmus, draws attention to some nuances of this question. To describe an early sixteenth-century figure as a 'humanist' often tells us little: it may mean only that he wrote in the one fashionable literary style of the age.[41] It goes without saying that Melanchthon was an enthusiastic and highly learned student of the ancient classics. Did 'humanist' values make Melanchthon a very different sort of reformer from what he would have been without them? In his relationships with other humanist figures, his distaste for public wrangles over doctrine, his concern with practical ethics, and his commitment to building a more humane Christian society, there is evidence that 'humanism' for Melanchthon, at least, did have a specific, positive content.

Melanchthon's references to Erasmus in his correspondence from the mid 1520s are revealing. He wrote to Johann Memminger at Torgau in mid 1524:

> I support Erasmus with love and loyalty, but only 'as far as the altars': what is the reason for you to praise him so much to me, given that he has not yet written anything to show clearly in what he really believes true piety and the 'righteousness of God' to consist? So

great a teacher ought to declare his opinion to the world, since Christ gave the command to 'preach the Gospel to every creature'. I do not ask of him what people commonly do, that he should write against the pope or the monks, for I myself hate these quarrels; rather, that he should explain what Christian righteousness really is.[42]

Accordingly, when Erasmus did produce *De libero arbitrio,* Melanchthon so far set aside any disappointment about its contents, as to say that he was 'almost pleased' that Erasmus had taken up the dispute; that he had long wished for Luther to have a 'prudent antagonist' on this subject.[43] On the other hand, Melanchthon's deep dislike of pamphlet wars, already suggested by a letter to Oecolampadius on the appearance of Erasmus' *Diatribe,* surfaced as the controversy became embittered. He asked his confidant Joachim Camerarius on 11 April 1526 if he had ever seen anything more bitterly written than Erasmus's *Hyperaspistes*; 'it really is a snake [*aspis*]'. He feared how Luther would take it, and quietly resented Erasmus blaming him for the severer passages in Luther's *De servo arbitrio.*[44]

Although Erasmus presented himself as one who wished for peace and concord, it is Melanchthon who emerges from the correspondence as the genuine mediator, occasionally disingenuous in his efforts to calm the disputants. Writing to Erasmus, Melanchthon drew a distinction between Luther and his tumultuous or iconoclastic supporters, for whose behaviour Luther could not be held responsible. He later asked the Basle humanist Sigismundus Gelenius to correct Erasmus' misconception that Luther used Melanchthon's help for his controversial pieces.[45] In contrast, Erasmus' letters to Melanchthon betray a prickly disputant, who had already shown a displeasing taste for invective in his polemic with von Hutten shortly before the latter's death in 1523. His letters tried both to defend his own position, and to divide his friends from his chosen enemies. Erasmus drove a wedge, as far as he could, between Melanchthon and humanist reformers of south Germany and Switzerland like Oecolampadius, with whom Melanchthon tried to keep on reasonable terms. Erasmus could also descend to school-yard insults: he repeatedly called Guillaume Farel 'Phallicus'. He complained to Melanchthon about the Basle reformers, whom he accused of rejecting Luther's authority at every turn, but for whose excesses he held Luther to blame. He wished that Melanchthon had stuck to classical literature; and expressed scepticism about whether Luther really felt that good will towards him that Melanchthon had claimed.[46]

In view of the contrast between these two characters, it is plainly absurd to describe Melanchthon as a 'follower' of Erasmus. There remains, moreover, a subtle but critical difference between the two men on the 'humanist' issue, of how far theological controversy should be disputed in public. Melanchthon can appear 'humanist', even 'Erasmian', when he preferred theological controversies not to be taken on to the public stage. For instance, he wrote to Thomas Blarer in October 1526, as the eucharistic dispute was taking fire, that he wished that the protagonists had dealt with the whole affair in private letters, before taking it into the public arena: he deplored the 'public dissension among those who support one Gospel'.[47] However, if one compares Erasmus writing to similar effect about Luther's own polemics, the tone and style are different. Erasmus lamented the spreading of anti-papal and anticlerical slogans among the 'unlearned mob' who took these messages 'in the worst sense'. Plato [in the *Republic*] saw that the multitude could not be governed without falsehoods; if Christians should abhor falsehoods, they still need not reveal the whole truth to the people by all means.[48] Where Melanchthon wished for dignified behaviour among the reformers, Erasmus regarded the entire business of the Reformation as a matter of internal Church management, to be kept from the profane multitude.

Yet in a more practical sense, Melanchthon was a Christian humanist. Besides his commitment to the Reformation message, he believed passionately that a better Church could be built up through education, and unrelenting stress on the call to lead a good, moral, disciplined life. Accordingly he gave much time to laying the foundations for a reformed educational system. The great imperial city of Nuremberg tried repeatedly to drag him from Wittenberg to lead its re-founded civic school. Melanchthon consistently refused to desert his university and his prince, but gave copious advice on the school's staffing and curriculum, and eventually visited the city to help put things in order.[49]

Melanchthon's practical work in building up a reformed 'house of learning' offers a striking contrast to an aspect of Luther's work. In an article entitled 'Martin Luther: forerunner of the Reformation', recently translated, Heiko Oberman has suggested that Luther, at least in his more apocalyptic moods, entertained no expectation of 'reforming' Church and society at all. He saw himself as a prophet, destined to preach the word, and thereby to provoke the devil and the AntiChrist to ever greater rage against the Gospel, until Christ appeared at the end of time.[50] This thesis has startling implications for Melanchthon's role in the Lutheran Reformation. If Luther was indeed profoundly reluctant to 'reform' church and society, as (for example) his delay in renewing the liturgy suggests, then Melanchthon may truly have to be seen as the 'reformer' who envisaged, and substantially saw through, the practical reshaping of the Lutheran churches.[51]

III

Yet, was the Reformation safe in Melanchthon's hands? The question persists, and for two closely related reasons. First, many have supposed, from the 1550s onwards if not before, that Melanchthon's concern for ethics led him to dilute, or to draw attention from, the Lutheran principle of salvation through faith alone. Secondly, Melanchthon was a diplomat and a compromiser, who was apparently ready to give up quite a lot of reformed practice, or even principle, for the sake of accommodating Rome and achieving peace in the Church. Those who distrusted Melanchthon's eirenicism, also thought they saw pro-Catholic revisionism in his theology. In consequence, a cloud of doubt has hung over Melanchthon in a way almost unique among the early leaders of the Reformation.

Ironically, one of the charges formerly made against Melanchthon's theology arose out of a misunderstanding. In the days of the 'Luther-Renaissance' led by historians of dogma such as Karl Holl, Melanchthon was accused of teaching a 'scholastic' doctrine of justification, which laid far too much stress on the 'forensic' imputation of the merits of Christ to the believer, too little on inner renewal or sanctification. Holl believed that Luther taught a theology of justification which did more justice to the inner renewal of the saved believer. One still meets this criticism of Melanchthon repeated occasionally.[52] However, as Paul Althaus showed many years ago, the fault for misunderstanding Luther lay not with Melanchthon, but with Karl Holl. Melanchthon's theology was so coolly, so lucidly phrased, that it did not leave room for Holl's interpretation—or misinterpretation—in the way that Luther's verbally rich, allusive rhetorical fireworks allowed. Melanchthon explained Luther too well: others did not like what they read, so they assumed that he had got his Luther wrong, and misjudged his place among the reformers on that basis.[53]

A much more common charge laid against Melanchthon (more or less the reverse of the last one!) has derived from his insistence on 'good works' in the life of the saved Christian. Melanchthon said that 'good works', that is, leading a pious and moral life, were a 'necessary' consequence of being justified by grace through faith. He also sometimes stated that they were 'rewarded' by God. Such remarks have led some commentators to question whether Melanchthon really held to the cardinal Protestant doctrine of justification by faith alone. Did he think that good works were not only 'necessary', but a 'necessary condition' of being justified, that is, declared righteous before God? This issue has been brought into focus by the recent appearance of Athina Lexutt's thesis, *Justification in dialogue,* a work based on a wider project led by Karl-Heinz Muehlen to produce a collected edition of all the papers relating to the

religious conferences of Hagenau and Worms. Lexutt explores the theologies of justification found in the writings of all the participants to the religious conferences, including Melanchthon's contributions in the three versions of the confession of Augsburg (the Latin original, the German translation and the 1540 *Variata*) and his contemporary revisions of the *Loci communes,* the '*Common Places of Theology*', his great theological textbook.[54]

It is unfortunate that Lexutt does not begin her review of Melanchthon's writings earlier, because the impression can be formed that he only wrote about the 'need' for good works in the 1530s. In fact as early as the *Instructions to the visitors,* published in 1528, he insisted strenuously that good works were a part of Christian life, which had to be rigorously instilled into the people.[55] To understand Melanchthon's religious thought one must see how well he resolved this paradox: Christians were to learn and believe that they were saved entirely through the mercy of God for Christ's sake; yet, as saved people, they were bound to produce the 'fruits of righteousness' in virtuous living. Where Erasmus had reduced Christianity almost entirely to ethics, Melanchthon reincorporated ethics into reformed dogmatics.

The key passages for this issue are the discussions of 'free will', 'justification', 'new obedience' and 'good works' in the unpublished 1533 manuscript revision of the *Loci communes,* the 1535 published edition of the same work, and the closely related sections of the *Confessio Augustana variata,* the revised version of the *Confession of Augsburg* produced for the religious conference at Worms in autumn 1540.[56] Melanchthon wrote of 'free will' at this period in the light of his increasing hostility to 'Stoic' determinism, which he associated with Zwingli and Lorenzo Valla. So he insisted, on one hand, that human nature was so corrupt that it could not fulfil the demands of the law of God. On the other, there remained just enough free will for one to refrain from serious public sins: one could achieve naturally an 'external righteousness', which nevertheless fell far short of the law's demands.[57] On the justification of sinners Melanchthon was clear, to the point of repetitiveness. Forgiveness of sins was given freely, and solely for Christ's sake. If it depended on the individual's sorrow for sin, then anyone might be driven to despair, through uncertainty as to whether he or she were sorry enough. Justification by free grace comforted the terrified conscience.[58] After the sinner was justified, there ought to follow 'good works' of obedience towards the law. These included not merely external law-abiding conduct, but spiritual works: faith itself, prayer, thanksgiving, confession, proclamation of the Gospel and worship.[59]

The most complex passages in all these documents answered two questions: in what way were these 'good works' pleasing to God? In what senses could they be said to be 'rewarded'? Melanchthon stated clearly, that the good works of the saints did not fulfil the law. Yet an 'inchoate and imperfect obedience' was pleasing to God, because the person of the sinner who was saved was already pleasing, for Christ's sake. Works done after justification were 'meritorious'; but as they were also done with the aid and presence of the Holy Spirit, their 'merit' did not in any way contribute to justification. The 'rewards' given were increases in spiritual virtues, in this life and especially in the next. The purpose of this rather tortuous formulation was made clear in the revisions to the *Loci*: it was to answer Catholic objections to 'faith alone'. Since the New Testament said that those who 'kept the commandments', who 'did the will of the Father in heaven', would be rewarded with eternal life, then these so-called 'legal promises' must be incorporated in Protestant theology.[60] The driving-force behind Melanchthon's doctrine of 'good works' was exegetical, and apologetic. He wished to show that reformed theology taught the whole Gospel, and did not just exaggerate a part of it; and thereby to refute Catholic critics, not curry favour with them. It would be a mistake to call this a doctrine of 'synergism', of human free will 'co-operating' in bringing justification about; especially because, for Melanchthon, a *synergon* [συνεργόν] was an instrumental cause of something, in the lowest order of causation, but a cause nevertheless.[61] Good works were the fruits of righteousness, never its cause.

> The only mercy and grace of the Father, promised freely unto us for his Son's sake, Jesus Christ, and the merits of his blood and passion, be the only sufficient and worthy causes [of our justification]; and yet that notwithstanding, to the attaining of the same justification, God requireth to be in us not only inward contrition, perfect faith and charity, certain hope and confidence, with all other spiritual graces and motions . . . after we be justified, we must also have good works of charity and obedience towards God, in the observing and fulfilling outwardly of his laws and commandments.

So said the Ten Articles of the Church of England issued in 1536, in a formula derived explicitly from Melanchthon's own wording.[62] When the section on justification in the Ten Articles is compared with Melanchthon's own language in the *Loci,* it becomes harder to see how the articles 'avoided' *sola fide,* or 'diluted' Lutheranism, as has been claimed.[63]

Athina Lexutt, like other sympathetic students of Melanchthon, concludes that, at worst, Melanchthon was not always as clear on the Lutheran *sola fide* as he might have been; that he did not, in fact, compromise on vital issues of faith.[64] The best proof that he was not about to dilute the Reformation, however, lies in the remaining clauses of the *Variata,* and in his conduct during the negotiations. When the original *Augsburg confession* and the *Variata* are laid side by side, the *Variata* often appears fiercer, not milder than the original in opposing the Catholic standpoint. The sections on church ministry and penance denounced those who taught a wrong (that is, Catholic) doctrine of justification. The clause on Church rites condemned the 'burdening [of consciences] with superstitious opinions' about the need for particular rituals. The discussion on the mass included a new, bitter attack on private masses and the idea that a mass was a 'good work' earning remission of sins.[65]

In certain other areas there is no doubt that Melanchthon moved steadily away from his earlier 'Lutheran' positions, while still remaining within the Protestant mainstream. He became progressively more convinced that the discussion of predestination had no place in the reformed teaching of justification. It was better to say that the promises of Christ applied to everyone. It was only in the final recensions of the *Loci,* however, that he explicitly linked his distaste for predestination to his long-standing rejection of 'Stoic determinism' in the choices of everyday existence.[66] One might even sum up Melanchthon's mature thought on conversion in these terms:

> [Man] was no stone or log, to which something had happened without his knowing or willing it, but on the contrary he made a decision, in the way in which men are accustomed to make decisions . . . but the fact that he did come to make this decision, that he really believed and that he actually had the freedom to enter this new life of obedience and hope—all this was not the work of his spirit, but the work of the *Holy Spirit.*

Yet these are not Melanchthon's words: they are the words of the most Protestant of neo-orthodox reformed theologians of this century, Karl Barth.[67]

If he was willing to incur Calvin's wrath over predestination,[68] Melanchthon actually drifted closer to Calvin in eucharistic doctrine. Even in the 1520s Melanchthon never showed the polemical fervour and theological ingenuity of, say, Johannes Brenz. He told Oecolampadius simply that 'he speaks simply, and often, of his "body" and "blood". Nor do these things seem to be able to be twisted into figures [of speech]. Therefore, unless I am compelled by some surer revelation, I shall not depart from the words.'[69] However, the point which Melanchthon pressed most strongly was that acrimonious theological disputes were not appropriate, where there was no clear guidance beyond Scripture, and where disputes were unedifying to the laity.[70] By the time of the religious conferences of 1540-1, Melanchthon had adopted an even more pragmatic, functional attitude. The eucharist, or any other sacrament, could only function within the terms of its own institution: in other words, it was there to be eaten and drunk, not be paraded, prayed to or worshipped. As he later recalled, Melanchthon argued thus against Johannes Eck at Regensburg, who was trying to defend carrying the sacrament in procession and adoring it. Luther approved of Melanchthon's stance; even Eck could not refute it.[71] The right use of the eucharist mattered far more for Melanchthon than contention over the precise nature of Christ's 'bodily' presence. He had no time for the so-called 'ubiquity' of Christ's risen body, which would become the theme of fierce, gleeful debate between Lutherans and Calvinists in Germany.[72] This attitude must explain, for example, Melanchthon's support for the beleaguered Bucerian Albert Hardenberg during the acrimonious eucharistic dispute at Bremen which ultimately led to Hardenberg's departure.[73] It may also explain his urging the city fathers of Frankfurt not to expel the French and English exile communities in 1557, despite their non-Lutheran eucharistic beliefs.[74]

There is an important difference between vehement dislike of futile theological controversy, and readiness to compromise on essentials. Because Melanchthon clearly expressed the first sentiment, it does not follow that he lapsed into the second attitude. His typical approach, for instance in the *Confession of Augsburg,* the *Apology* and the *Treatise on the power of the pope,* was to write mild, non-inflammatory, but none the less clearcut and resolute defences of the Protestant position.[75] Athina Lexutt observes that at critical junctures in the religious conferences, Melanchthon was actually the most inflexible of the Protestant delegates.[76] Since the Catholic group appeared at Regensburg to be far more divided, weak and incoherent than the Protestants, Melanchthon may have hoped to make real conversions among them, without sacrificing principles. This motive could also account for certain passages in the *Variata* where Melanchthon attacked a rather extreme, burlesque form of Catholic theology which Gropper and Pflug certainly would not have held.[77] When Melanchthon did become implicated in anything more ambiguous, for instance the 'Regensburg book' of 1541 or the mediating reform programme proposed for the archbishopric of Cologne in the early 1540s, it was Bucer and Gropper who were primarily responsible, and the ambiguity was almost certainly of their making.

IV

Melanchthon remains a somewhat elusive personality, either despite or because of the matter-of-fact, straightforward manner in which he wrote. His relationship to Martin Luther was complex. Luther hardly ever wavered in his approval and trust of his younger colleague, even in the 1540s when Melanchthon expected that his eucharistic theology would cause trouble.[78] This unstinting favour may partly explain the extreme personal jealousy with which Luther's lesser associates, especially Amsdorf and Flacius Illyricus, rounded on

Melanchthon after Luther's death. Yet it would seem wrong to regard Luther and Melanchthon as close friends. When Melanchthon wished to pour out his soul, especially in the 1520s, it was to Joachim Camerarius, his closest friend and ultimately the editor of his letters, that he wrote. As Melanchthon reported, when he felt depressed, although Luther was most friendly, Luther was himself so troubled that Melanchthon left their meetings more grieving for him than before.[79] When unable to visit Camerarius, he complained that only the latter's company could help him to bear with the pressure of work and other troubles.[80] Camerarius also received from Melanchthon that most notorious letter, the only one written almost entirely in Greek, which described the circumstances of Luther's hasty wedding and Melanchthon's reactions. It was so critical that Camerarius, editing the letter for publication, suppressed parts, and reorganised most of the remainder so as to draw out some of the sting from Melanchthon's remarks.[81] Melanchthon had not been told of the planned wedding, and was not invited to the evening supper where Luther concluded it in the presence of three witnesses, Bugenhagen, Lukas Cranach and Johann Apel. The affront offered by this sudden and unannounced marriage may help to explain Melanchthon's reaction:

> [Luther] is an exceptionally impulsive[82] man, and the nuns, having laid snares for him 'by every contrivance', reeled him in. Likewise, much association with the nuns, even though he was high-minded and magnanimous, softened and inflamed his nature. . . . Now that I see that Luther is grieved and troubled because of the change in his life, I endeavour with every effort and kindness to console him, since he has not done anything which seems worthy of reproach or inexcusable. . . . Then I was always praying rather that he should be made humble than exalted and magnified, which is dangerous, not only for those in the priesthood but for all people. . . . I also hope that this life will make him more dignified, so as to cast aside that 'buffoonery',[83] of which we have often found him to be at fault. . . . Of old God revealed to us many mistakes made by the saints, that it may please us to make proof of his word not by making the reputation or the appearance of men our counsellor, but only his word. Moreover, he would be a most impious person who would condemn the teaching because of the lapse of the teacher.[84]

After that, I shall never again refer to Melanchthon as a 'lieutenant' or 'second-in-command' to Luther.

Only when considered entirely in his own right, and not as a pallid humanist shadow of Martin Luther, can Philipp Melanchthon be judged fairly. He was certainly not the stuff of which heroes or cult figures were made. One cannot imagine students hanging on his every word at table, as happened in Luther's household: which is perhaps a good thing. He may have been fastidious, even prissy. Yet he had a clear idea of his vocation and his business. He never lost sight of his first calling, to be a teacher. Confronted with a text, whether the Bible, Aristotle, Terence or the **Augustana,** and a blank sheet of paper, Melanchthon wrote with authority and confidence. He responded realistically to the challenges of the moment, whether to devise a clearer-cut role for the princes in the Reformation, or to present lucid, palatable statements of Protestant belief, or to confront the unsteady stances of Catholic theologians around 1540. Without Luther's unworldly vision and obstinate apocalyptic conviction, there would have been no Lutheran Reformation. Without Melanchthon's independent wisdom, there would certainly not have been a Lutheran educational system; there might even have been no organised Lutheran Church.

Notes

CR = *Corpus Reformatorum,* Halle 1834-60; Manschreck, *Loci = Melanchthon on Christian doctrine: Loci communes 1555,* ed. and trans. C. L. Manschreck, New York 1965; *MBW = Melanchthons Briefwechsel,* ed. Scheible; *MWA = Melanchthons Werke in Auswahl: Studienausgabe,* ed. R. Stupperich and others, Gütersloh 1951-71; *TRE = Theologische Realenzyklopaedie*

1. See Philipp Melanchthon, *Commentary on Romans,* trans. Fred Kramer, St Louis 1992; *Loci communes . . . 1543,* ed. and trans. J. A. O. Preus, St Louis 1992; earlier English translations include the 1521 *Loci communes* in *Melanchthon and Bucer: Loci communes theologici,* ed. W. Pauck, London 1969, and Manschreck, *Loci.*

2. Of *Philippi Melanchthonis Opera quae supersunt omnia,* ed. C. G. Bretschneider and others (*CR* i-xxviii), vols xi-xii are given over to *Declamationes* and to the *Cronica Carionis*; xiii includes the works on the *De anima,* natural philosophy, rhetoric and dialectic; xvi contains his *Ethics* and annotations on Cicero; further works on classical literature and philology comprise most of vols xvii-xx.

3. See Hans Engelland's introduction to Manschreck, *Loci,* p. xxvi.

4. For the periods under discussion see, for example, my *The European Reformation,* Oxford 1991, 190, 342-5, 347 and refs.

5. *MBW,* nos 237 (T1, 492), 258 (T2, 57-8), 342 (T2, 178). See also H. Scheible, 'Melanchthon, Philipp (1497-1560)', in *TRE* xxii. 373. 23-6, and compare *MBW,* no. 432 (T2, 365. 1-9).

6. Kusukawa, *Transformation,* 51-6.

7. *MBW,* no. 268 (T2, 57. 13-15).

8. Ibid. nos 268 (T2, 57. 15-16), 342 (T2, 178. 24-5).

9. Ibid. no. 369 (T2, 235. 9-12).

10. Ibid. no. 432 (T2, 365. 5-6), 348 (T2, 189. 39-47); see Scheible, 'Melanchthon', 376. 1ff.

11. Eobanus Hessus, *Ecclesiae afflictae epistola ad Lutherum,* Hagenau 1523; Melanchthon's response is in *MBW,* no. 273 (T2, 63-4)—the passage quoted is on lines 18-19; cf. also no. 330 (T2, 144-5). Luther's very similar reaction, written like Melanchthon's on 29 Mar. 1523, is quoted in A. G. Dickens, *The German Nation and Martin Luther,* London 1974, 63; see also p. 150.

12. Kusukawa, *Transformation,* 36-49.

13. Ibid. 63ff.

14. Ibid. 49-51: for a summary of Kusukawa's theses see pp. 73-4.

15. *MBW,* no. 361 (T2, 218. 13-25).

16. Ibid. nos 298 (T2, 99. 4-7), 330 (T2, 145. 6).

17. Ibid. no. 365a (T2, 230. 29-34).

18. Kusukawa, *Transformation,* 75-173.

19. For an introduction see Charles B. Schmitt, Quentin Skinner and Eckhard Kessler (eds) *The Cambridge history of Renaissance philosophy,* Cambridge 1988, 490-527 and refs; Melanchthon's role in the subject is discussed ibid. 625ff.

20. *MWA* iii. 365-72, and discussion in Kusukawa, *Transformation,* 98-9.

21. *MWA* iii. 307-11, and discussion in Kusukawa, *Transformation,* 114ff.

22. *MWA* iii. 328-9, 335-7, 345-9.

23. Ibid. iii. 349-55.

24. Kusukawa, *Transformation,* 107, 113-14.

25. *MWA* iii. 319-24, 349-51.

26. Zwingli is criticised by name for his determinism in the unpublished 1533 draft revision of the *Loci communes,* in *CR* xxi, col. 275; he does not appear to be mentioned in the *De anima.*

27. *CR* xiii, cols 185, 190-1, 345; cf. Kusukawa, *Transformation,* 149ff.

28. *CR* xiii, col 292; cf. Engelland's introduction to Manschreck, *Loci,* pp. xxvi-xxviii. Melanchthon made the same point in his testimonial for Heinrich Bullinger the younger in *MBW,* no. 8212, in 8, 67, and *CR* ix cols 150-1; cf. also *MBW,* no. 8529.

29. *CR* xiii, cols 339-40.

30. Bk I occupies *CR* xiii, cols 179-292; bk II, cols 291-380; bk III, cols 381-412.

31. *CR* xiii, col. 182.

32. Ibid. col. 183.

33. Ibid. cols 324-5, 329, 340.

34. Ibid. cols 325-6, 345.

35. Ibid. cols 335ff. To see how unusual this attitude was for a theologian, contrast J. Gerson, *Triologium astrologiae theologizatae,* Lyon 1419, in *Opera,* ed. L. E. du Pin, 2nd edn, The Hague 1728, i, cols 189-203, or J. Calvin, *Avertissement contre l'astrologie judiciaire,* in *Joannis Calvini Opera quae supersunt omnia,* ed. G. Baum, E. Cunitz and E. Reuss (*CR* xxix-lxxxvii), Braunschweig-Berlin 1853-1900, vii. 509-44.

36. Kusukawa, *Transformation,* 124ff. See further D. Bellucci, 'Mélanchthon et la défense de l'astrologie', in *Bibliothèque d'humanisme et renaissance* l (1988), 587-622.

37. Letters to Johannes Mathesius and Joachim Camerarius, in *MBW,* nos 8288, 8297; *CR* ix, cols 189, 196.

38. For example, Kusukawa, *Transformation,* 188-9.

39. For the catholic 'scholasticism' of the later sixteenth century see *Cambridge history of Renaissance philosophy,* 512ff, 606ff.

40. The contributions made by Melanchthon and his pupils to the formation of a Protestant church history are discussed in my 'Protestant identities in the later Reformation in Germany', in O. P. Grell and Bob Scribner (eds), *Tolerance and intolerance in the European Reformation,* Cambridge 1996, 116-17, 120-1. See also E. C. Scherer, *Geschichte und Kirchengeschichte an den deutschen Universitäten: ihre Anfänge im Zeitalter der Humanismus und ihre Ausbildung zu selbständigen Disziplinen,* Freiburg im Breisgau 1927.

41. The significance of 'humanism' in the reformed context is further discussed in my 'The late Renaissance and the unfolding Reformation in Europe', in J. Kirk (ed.), *Humanism and reform: the Church in Europe, England and Scotland 1400-1643: essays in honour of James K. Cameron* (Studies in Church History, Subsidia viii), Oxford 1991, 15-36.

42. *MBW,* no. 332 (T2, 148. 46-53).

43. Ibid. no. 343 (T2, 179. 4-8).

44. Ibid. no. 459 (T2, 417-18. 1-10). There is a typical Melanchthon pun here: ἀσπίς in Greek means a shield, as in the title of Erasmus' tract (the 'Shield-bearer'); *aspis* in Latin means an asp.

45. *MBW,* nos 344 (T2, 181. 8ff), 474 (T2, 439. 40-2).

46. Ibid. nos 341 passim, 360.

47. Ibid. no. 503 (T2, 497. 7-11).

48. Ibid. no. 360 (T2, 211-12). Compare Erasmus writing to Justus Jonas in 1521: *Erasmi epistolae,* ed. P. S. Allen and H. M. Allen, Oxford 1906-58, iv. 487-93, no. 1202.

49. *MBW,* nos 347, 348, 349, 350, 357, 449, 452, 453, 457, 463, 493.

50. Heiko A. Oberman, *The Reformation: roots and ramifications,* trans. Andrew C. Gow, Edinburgh 1994, 27-40.

51. Oberman, *Reformation,* 50: 'For Melanchthon, the "amendment" . . . could turn into the "Reformation", in the sense that has determined our use of the word ever since.'

52. For example in Stephen Strehle, *Calvinism, federalism and scholasticism: a study of the reformed doctrine of covenant,* Bern 1988, 89-97, 391-2.

53. See C. L. Manschreck's preface to Manschreck, *Loci,* p. xix, and Engelland's introduction ibid. p. xxxix. See also Scheible, 'Melanchthon', 395. 29-35, and Franz Hildebrandt, *Melanchthon: alien or ally?,* Cambridge 1946, 44-55. For a careful analysis and rebuttal of Karl Holl's interpretation see P. Althaus, *The theology of Martin Luther,* trans. R. C. Schultz, Philadelphia 1966, 241-2 and refs.

54. Lexutt, *Rechtfertigung,* 50ff, 66ff, 69ff, 112ff.

55. In E. Sehling (ed.), *Die evangelischen Kirchenordnungen des xvi. Jahrhunderts,* Leipzig 1902-, i. 153, cf. 161-3.

56. The *Loci* of 1533 is found in *CR* xxi, cols 253-332; the *Loci* of 1535 in *CR* xxi, cols 331-560; the *Variata* in *MWA* vi. 12-79.

57. *CR* xxi, cols 274ff, 373ff; cf *MWA* vi. 34.

58. *CR* xxi, cols 420ff; *MWA* vi. 14-15, 27-30.

59. *CR* xxi, cols 308-13, 429, 436-7; *MWA* vi. 30-1.

60. *CR* xxi, cols 309ff, 313-30, 430-47; *MWA* vi. 32-3. On 'good works' see also Carl E. Maxcey, *Bona opera: a study in the development of the doctrine in Philipp Melanchthon,* Nieuwkoop 1980.

61. In the *Initia doctrinae physicae,* in *CR* xiii, cols 310-11.

62. For this text see A. G. Dickens and D. Carr (eds), *The Reformation in England to the accession of Elizabeth I,* London 1967, 74. See also *MBW,* no. 1714; Scheible, 'Melanchthon', 379. 5-7.

63. Compare A. G. Dickens, *The English Reformation,* London 1964, 175-6; Christopher Haigh, *English Reformations: religion, politics, and society under the Tudors,* Oxford 1993, 128-30.

64. Lexutt, *Rechtfertigung*, 125-7, 176-7, 274; cf. Scheible, 'Melanchthon', 391-2, and Engelland's introduction to Manschreck, *Loci*, pp. xxxvii-xxxviii.

65. *MWA* vi. 16-17, 19-21, 38-45.

66. For Melanchthon's discussions of predestination, compare the 1521 *Loci*, in *MWA* ii/i. 10-12, the 1533 and 1535 *Loci* in *CR* xxi, cols 330ff, 450ff, the 1555 *Loci* in Manschreck, *Loci* 187ff, and the final version in *CR* xxi, cols 912ff, and *MWA* ii/ii. 592-602. His active hostility to the doctrine itself surfaced in the 1540s.

67. Karl Barth, *The Knowledge of God and the Service of God according to the teaching of the Reformation*, London 1938, 108-9.

68. See Calvin's criticism of Melanchthon's stand (where his name is not mentioned), in *Institutes*, III. xxi. 3.

69. *MBW*, no. 370 (T2, 238. 9-12).

70. See ibid. nos 372, 477, 478, 483.

71. See ibid. nos 8226, 8227, 8494, 8498; *CR* ix, cols 156, 157, 409, 431.

72. For the strife over 'ubiquity' see, for example, A. Scultetus, *Annalium evangelii passim per Europam . . . renovati decades duae*, Heidelberg 1618-20, i. 226-7; B. Nischan, 'Confessionalism and absolutism: the case of Brandenburg', in A. Pettegree, A. Duke and G. Lewis (eds), *Calvinism in Europe, 1540-1620*, Cambridge 1994, 195-7.

73. For Melanchthon's letters to Hardenberg see *MBW*, nos 8111, 8195, and Scheible, 'Melanchthon', 379. 45; on Hardenberg see Wim Janse, *Albert Hardenberg als Theologe: Profil einer Bucer-Schuelers*, Leiden 1994, 32-89.

74. *MBW*, no. 8271; *CR* ix, cols 179-80.

75. The standard editions of these texts are found in *Die Bekenntnisschriften der evangelischlutherischen Kirche, herausgegeben im Gedenkjahr des Augsburgischen Konfession 1930*, Göttingen 1930; most recent edn 1986.

76. Lexutt, *Rechtfertigung*, 45, 231.

77. Ibid. 30; cf. *MWA* vi. 16-17, 19-21. For Gropper's position see R. Braunisch, *Die Theologie der Rechtfertigung im "Enchiridion" (1538) des Johannes Gropper: sein kritischer Dialog mit Philipp Melanchthon*, Münster 1974.

78. For Luther's continued support see Scheible, 'Melanchthon', 380-1; Manschreck's preface to Manschreck, *Loci*, pp. xvi-xvii.

79. *MBW*, no. 382 (T2, 265. 1-16).

80. Ibid. no. 476 (T2, 440. 1-9).

81. Ibid. no. 408 (T2, 323-31). Scheible presents the original in Greek and Camerarius' paraphrase in its Latin translation. Side-by-side comparison between the original and Camerarius' reorganised text is provided in *MWA* vii. 238-44. See also *Documents illustrative of the continental reformation*, ed. B. J. Kidd, Oxford 1911, 179-80, for the crucial passage.

82. εὐχερής: this can mean either 'reckless' or 'biddable'.

83. βωμολοχία: the Greek word referred to the vulgar sort of humour practised by those who hung around temple altars waiting for scraps.

84. *MBW*, no. 408 (T2, 327-9).

Timothy Wengert (essay date 1999)

SOURCE: Wengert, Timothy. "'We Will Feast Together in Heaven Forever': The Epistolary Friendship of John Calvin and Philip Melanchthon." In *Melanchthon in Europe: His Work and Influence beyond Wittenberg*, edited by Karin Maag, pp. 19-44. Grand Rapids, Mich.: Baker Books, 1999.

[*In the following essay, Wengert provides a corrective to earlier analyses of the relations between Melanchthon and Calvin.*]

In 1842, as the ninth and final volume of Melanchthon's correspondence in the *Corpus Reformatorum* rolled off the Schwetschke presses in Halle, researchers had at their disposal only six letters between the leading Reformers in Wittenberg and Geneva.[1] Within a generation the number had grown considerably as the addendum to Melanchthon's correspondence, edited by Heinrich Bindseil and published in 1874, contributed fourteen and Calvin's correspondence in the *Corpus Reformatorum* an additional four.[2] Counting descriptions of one letter and one conversation with Melanchthon contained in letters to William Farel and the mention of three lost letters among letters of Melanchthon and Calvin, we can now document twenty-nine exchanges between these two pillars of the Reformation.[3]

The publication of this wealth of new sources on the relation between Melanchthon and Calvin led to several writings at the time, none more important than an article by Philip Schaff in the *Papers of the American Society of Church History* in 1891, entitled "The Friendship of Calvin and Melanchthon." This article, which formed the basis of comments in Schaff's multi-volume *History of the Christian Church*, has had continuous influence over the past century, notably in an article by James T. Hickman, "The Friendship of Melanchthon and Calvin."[4] Both Schaff and Hickman argue that Melanchthon and Calvin had established a true friendship and, despite certain differences in theology, enjoyed fundamental agreement in the faith.

In fact, the *topos* of friendship is used to explain away many of the theological tensions between the two men. Schaff begins his address, "When God has a great work to do in his kingdom on earth he trains and associates congenial agents of different gifts, but of one spirit and aim, to carry out his purposes."[5] And near the end of his article, Hickman exclaims "This friendship demonstrates the possibility of harmony in spite of theological differences."[6] The ecumenical agenda of both writers is not hard to discern.

By far the most thorough assessment of the relationship of Calvin and Melanchthon was produced by Willem Nijenhuis.[7] Here, too, an ecumenical agenda may be seen, although the careful historical work makes this a far more balanced contribution. Nijenhuis views Calvin's correspondence with Melanchthon from within the larger framework of discussions with the Lutherans and divides Calvin's relations into several epochs (before Luther's death and before and after the Consensus Tigurinus).[8] In the end, however, Nijenhuis concludes that Calvin's correspondence witnesses to his "total personal dedication to the Church of Christ and its unity."[9]

The present study, by placing the correspondence between Melanchthon and Calvin within the context of Renaissance letter-writing etiquette and the theological struggles of the day, challenges older visions of an ecumenical friendship and uncovers the profound tensions between these two Reformers. To use the word "friendship" (especially without modifiers) to describe any historical relationship poses complicated historiographical problems. By calling any two historical figures "friends," historians often seek to overcome psychological and theological differences using classical, even biblical, *topoi*. The friendship of David and Jonathan (or Achilles and Ajax), like the conversion of St. Paul, possesses only limited usefulness as a category for historical research. Nevertheless, this commonplace has particularly plagued recent research on Melanchthon. On the one hand, to insure Melanchthon's commitment to humanism, scholars have declared Melanchthon and Erasmus friends—despite the fact that almost every letter exchanged between them includes biting criticism of the recipient.[10] On the other, scholars eager to unite Melanchthon's theology with Luther's have also declared them friends.[11] Ignoring for the moment the twentieth-century American habit of calling anyone with whom one has conversed for more than two minutes a friend—if the word friendship is carefully de-

fined as intimate attachment, esteem, and affection between two people, then perhaps only Joachim Camerarius, Veit Dietrich, and Caspar Cruciger, Sr. qualify as Melanchthon's friends.[12]

The relation between Calvin and Melanchthon, on the contrary, was no friendship in this sense. Instead, it was what one might more properly call an epistolary friendship, that is, a literary fiction imposed by the authors themselves, especially Calvin, onto a very complex web of interactions, not all of which were friendly. At first reading, Melanchthon's early declaration of affection ("I love you from my soul and I pray that Christ may rule you")[13] and Calvin's equally enthusiastic description of his relation to Melanchthon seem to describe an intimate friendship. Calvin wrote: "We are sustained by that blessed hope, to which your letters recall us: we will feast together in heaven forever, where we will enjoy our love and friendship."[14] Such professions, however, were the staple of Renaissance letters and were based upon classical models and biblical norms.[15] Historians must not confuse professions of intimacy for the actual, intimate sharing of one's thoughts and feelings, especially when reading the correspondence of the sixteenth century, where expressions of affections were the rule. Moreover, when we place such powerful metaphors as "feasting together in heaven" within the context of the eucharistic debates, then another construction of such comments becomes possible. It must also never be forgotten that, with rare exceptions, Renaissance letters were public events, meant to be shared with others.[16] Thus they contained public affections not private ones.

Even the oft-quoted reminiscence of Calvin regarding the recently departed Melanchthon must be seen strictly within the Renaissance and Reformation framework, where it appeared. Calvin wrote:

> O Philip Melanchthon! I appeal to thee who now livest with Christ in the bosom of God, and there art waiting for us till we shall be gathered with thee to that blessed rest. A hundred times when worn out with labors and oppressed with so many troubles, didst thou repose thy head familiarly on my breast and say: 'Would that I could die in this bosom!' Since then I have a thousand times wished that it had been granted to us to live together; for certainly thou wouldst thus have had more courage for the inevitable contest, and been stronger to despise envy, and to count as nothing all accusations. In this manner, also, the malice of many would have been restrained who, from thy gentleness which they call weakness, gathered audacity for their attacks.[17]

In fact, Calvin was alluding to certain strains in their relationship: Meanchthon's supposed tendency to capitulate and his failure to support Calvin directly, Calvin's presumed strength, and the maliciousness of Melanchthon's accusers. However, coming as it did within a tract on the eucharist, it was also Calvin's attempt to depict Melanchthon as a supporter of the Genevan's eucharistic theology, something he never was in his own lifetime.[18]

The twenty-nine known exchanges between Calvin and Melanchthon provide a window for examining a highly charged relationship over a twenty-year span, during which many of the basic contours of the Protestant churches and their theology were debated. Such expressions of affection remind us that the principals were themselves passionate, committed individuals, for whom companionship, harmony, and truth defined existence. By maintaining a correspondence, both men hoped to gain something from the other while maintaining at least the semblance of peace between them for the sake of the church.

I. First Encounters

Under what circumstances did this epistolary friendship arise? Martin Bucer probably fostered the relationship between Melanchthon and the newly arrived French refugee, Calvin; the Wittenberg Concord of 1536 (on which both Melanchthon and Bucer labored) created the necessary theological peace under which it could develop. Calvin arrived in Strasbourg during September 1538 at Bucer's insistence in order to serve the French-speaking congregation there.[19] By October he could report to Farel contacts with Melanchthon over the then raging issue of church property.[20] Four months later the same issue and the question of church discipline were discussed. Here Calvin also described for Melanchthon his understanding of the Lord's Supper.[21]

When Calvin arrived in Strasbourg its clergy had already signed the Wittenberg Concord. They agreed that Christ was not absent from the Supper, that the bread and wine were not empty symbols and that, distinguishing the earthly and heavenly aspects of the Supper, "with the bread and wine the body and blood of Christ are truly and essentially present, offered, and received." While rejecting transubstantiation, they also held that "with the bread the body of Christ is truly present and truly offered." The worthiness of the recipient did not determine the presence of Christ in the Supper.[22] It is in the light of this agreement that Calvin's second edition of the *Institutes,* published in 1539, must be read.[23] No wonder Luther had such kind words for Calvin's "Reply to Sadoleto"![24] "Consider the nobility of Luther," Calvin reported to Farel. According to Melanchthon's report, when someone tried to induce Luther to criticize Calvin's position on the Lord's Supper in the "Reply," Luther read the passages and praised Calvin despite them.[25] By this time Melanchthon and Calvin had met in Frankfurt am Main and had discussed, among other things, the Lord's Supper.[26] This encounter may well have convinced Melanchthon that Calvin held to the Wittenberg Concord in principle,[27] and it encouraged

Calvin to believe that Melanchthon approved of his understanding of the Lord's Supper.[28]

It is in the context of this encounter and these expressions of approval that the expressions of love must be placed. On the single most important issue dividing Protestants, Melanchthon and Calvin seemed, at this time anyway, to be united. Under the banner of that unity they then met in Worms and Regensburg for the colloquy with the Catholic representatives in 1540-41. Melanchthon's correspondence touched on Calvin in two instances: once when they collaborated on a letter to Francis I and once when they wrote letters of consolation to the father of the recently deceased Louis de Richebourg.[29] At Regensburg Calvin first became familiar with the ***Confessio Augustana Variata,*** the emended version of the ***Augsburg Confession*** written by Melanchthon to take the Wittenberg Concord into consideration.[30]

II. Free Will and Predestination

With Calvin's return to Geneva in September 1541, the correspondence between the two men, scarcely begun, suffered something of a breakdown as much because of logistical problems in communication as anything else. A now lost letter sent by Melanchthon from Wittenberg in October 1542 took four months to arrive in Geneva.[31] Calvin made up for these delays by writing his first public letter to Melanchthon: the preface to *The Bondage and Liberation of the Will,* his attack on the Catholic theologian Pighius.[32]

Calvin could hardly have been ignorant of Melanchthon's (and, he had to assume, Wittenberg's) shift on the issue of human bondage from Luther's 1525 attack against Erasmus in *De servo arbitrio*—Pighius himself had pointed it out.[33] Indeed, the eighteenth article of the ***Augsburg Confession*** emphasized a distinction between freedom in civil matters and weakness in spiritual things,[34] and the second edition of Melanchthon's ***Loci communes*** of 1535 spoke of three causes for salvation (the Word, the Holy Spirit and the human will [*voluntas*]) and glossed over predestination.[35] Thus, Calvin, in prosecuting his case against Pighius, sought to reclaim the authority of Melanchthon, whose own opinion on the topic was unclear. Calvin dedicated this book to Melanchthon, "because it contains a defence of the godly and sound teaching of which you are not only a most zealous supporter, but a distinguished and very brave champion."[36] Calvin proceeded to compare his brevity and clarity to Melanchthon's own, but again as an argument in favor of Calvin's own treatment of this topic—one which Melanchthon had, so to speak, declared off limits in the 1535 *Loci.*[37] Calvin even suggested that Melanchthon had urged him to refute Pighius.[38] Thus, this preface is a delightful example of the shrewdness of Renaissance polemics, where, because shifts in thought were a sign of weakness, the enemy of my enemy, who scarcely agrees with me, must be made my friend.

In the body of the text, Calvin for the first time referred to Melanchthon's moderation. However, this must not simply be taken at face value. On the contrary, as we shall see, Calvin employed this (Stoic) category consistently in order to ameliorate real differences between himself and Melanchthon. What better way to overcome divisions in a polemical situation than to invoke a favorite humanist virtue. In point of fact at two crucial points Melanchthon and Calvin disagreed. For one thing, Melanchthon began his discussion of human freedom and bondage in the distinction between human and divine righteousness. For another, he divided all questions of divine causality from predestination—discussing the former under God's governance and the latter under the gospel.[39]

Melanchthon's thank you note for the tract was sent on 11 May 1543 from Bonn, where he was assisting Bucer in the ill-fated attempt to reform the archdiocese of Cologne.[40] His response is a lesson in Renaissance diplomacy. He first thanked Calvin for complimenting his simplicity. However, just as Calvin had employed an appeal to similarity in style to gain Melanchthon's approbation for Calvin's approaching a subject declared off limits in the *Loci*, Melanchthon now took the compliment to attack the subject of Calvin's book. Calvin ought to use his gifts—as Melanchthon claimed he himself did—for explaining important evangelical doctrines (such as the teaching of the Son of God, human sin, repentance and faith, prayer, and the church) and not for intricate disputations.[41]

Turning to the topic of predestination itself, he then quoted his Tübingen teacher, Francis Kircher from Stadion (hence: Stadianus), who taught that divine providence and contingency could never be satisfactorily balanced. Out of regard for the weak, Melanchthon argued that David's guilt was his own fault, not God's, and that he also retained the Holy Spirit by the action of his will [*voluntas*]. Having refuted Calvin's arguments, Melanchthon then prevented open warfare with this clever conclusion: "I do not write these things as if handing down to you, a most erudite and skilful person in the exercise of piety, some dictates. Indeed, I know that these things harmonize with your ideas. However, mine are cruder, accommodated to use."[42] Here Melanchthon had turned Calvin's reference to moderation on its head. This virtue had at its heart the Christian concern for the weak and simple and an avoidance of sophistry. But it was not simply a humanist virtue but rather a pointed theological argument and hermeneutical tool for recognizing the limits of erudition. Thus, in Melanchthon's eyes Calvin's approach—for all its biblical sincerity—was by its very subtlety speculative.

The very next letter from Melanchthon's pen (Calvin's intervening response is lost) reiterated the two reformers' fundamental disagreement on the question of predestination. Here, however, Melanchthon asserted that at least the two agreed on their understanding of the power of original sin.[43] It seems that for Melanchthon the disagreement on predestination was secondary and should not hinder their underlying support of the gospel.

Calvin not only knew differences existed between him and Melanchthon, he did something about them in another public letter, one that Melanchthon did not see and could not have read: the 1546 preface to the French translation of Melanchthon's third edition of the *Loci communes*. In the first place, Calvin acknowledged Melanchthon's avoidance of subtleties. He was a man "of profound wisdom, who did not wish to enter into subtle disputes." His only regard was for the edification of his readers. "The greatest simplicity is the highest virtue when dealing with Christian doctrine."[44]

As an example Calvin mentioned first the doctrine of the freedom of the will, which Melanchthon discussed only in terms of Christian salvation. Calvin explained that Melanchthon allowed for "civil" freedom in "things below" so as to emphasize God's grace. By forewarning the readers about Melanchthon's intention, Calvin hoped that they would not be scandalized when reading the *Loci*.[45] Second, Calvin turned to predestination. Again Melanchthon wanted, according to Calvin, to avoid all curiosity by dealing only with those things that needed to be known about the subject. Finally, Calvin noted that Melanchthon employed the same approach for the sacraments. He concluded that by understanding Melanchthon's modesty the reader could truly profit from this book.[46]

This clever introduction accepted Melanchthon's own defense of his approach to these articles of faith as outlined in their private correspondence—but to Calvin's theological advantage. By emphasizing Melanchthon's modesty, Calvin actually made room for his own, opposing positions without thereby having to refute Melanchthon. Melanchthon's reserve, which in Melanchthon's view arose from not only pastoral concerns (Calvin acknowledged that) but also theological insight into the limits of theological discourse, became in Calvin's hands a psychological or literary shortcoming, which Calvin had to warn the readers about in order that they might still profit from Melanchthon's work.

Even this subtle construing of Melanchthon's theology, however, did not prevent Melanchthon's position on predestination from becoming caught up in a Genevan dispute. In 1551 Jerome Bolsec and Jean Trolliet had crossed Calvin on the question of predestination, resulting in the arrest of Bolsec in October.[47] When the matter came before the city council, Trolliet appealed in his written defense to Melanchthon's position as outlined in the French translation of the *Loci*.[48] Calvin, in turn, was forced publicly to explain the discrepancy between his position and Melanchthon's.[49]

Like Melanchthon, Calvin insisted God was not the author of sin. However, Calvin also admitted that he diverged from Melanchthon on this point.

> Melanchthon, being a timid man, and not wanting to give curious folk a reason for inquiring too deeply into the secrets of God, accommodated himself too much to people's common understanding. He has desired more to accommodate to people's common sense. In the present case he has by these means spoken more as a philosopher than a theologian.[50]

Moreover, Calvin insisted that he had letters from Melanchthon that proved his case. He also insisted that if Melanchthon's statements were accorded such authority, then, in accord with the *Loci communes,* a third sacrament, confession, would also have to be reinstated in Geneva.[51]

Here Calvin viewed Melanchthon's theology, in its refusal to probe God's mysteries revealed in Scripture, as having succumbed to philosophical speculation. This hermeneutical divide appeared already in Calvin's letter of 1 January 1552 to Lelio Sozzini, who had urged restraint on Calvin in these matters. Calvin succinctly outlined his position: he abhorred paradoxes, he insisted on professing what he had learned from the Word of God, and he found comfort in the Word's simple teaching.[52]

What was Melanchthon's reaction to Calvin's approach? In a private letter to his friend Camerarius, dated 1 February 1552, he reported on the debate in Geneva concerning "Stoic necessity" and the arrest of Bolsec.[53] He also knew of Sozzini's admonition. The Zurich theologians, Melanchthon commented, were milder. On the same day he wrote to his son-in-law, Caspar Peucer, "O what a terrible matter! The teaching of salvation is obscured by disputations foreign to it."[54] Thus for Melanchthon the dispute itself, not the content of the doctrine, indicated the importation of philosophy into theology.

In a letter of 28 November 1552 Calvin informed Melanchthon of the dispute and the *Loci*'s role in it.[55] He insisted that he had not attacked Melanchthon directly and thereby headed off any public dispute with the Wittenberg Reformer. On the question of predestination itself, Calvin acquiesced to Melanchthon's emphasis on the universality of God's promise (cf. the 1543 edition of the *Loci,* CR 21:451) but at the same time insisted that the efficacy of that promise was lim-ited to those with the gift of faith. Calvin also noted Melanchthon's objection to the Consensus Tigurinus on this point (article 16). In closing comments that were also aimed at preventing a public dispute, Calvin praised Melanchthon's moderation while stressing that only face-to-face conversation could resolve this potential conflict.[56] When Melanchthon failed to respond to this letter, Calvin sent yet another appeal for understanding on this issue.[57] By then, however, the most pressing issue had become the Lord's Supper.

Later in their correspondence this issue surfaced only tangentially. When Calvin complained about Melanchthon's silence on the Lord's Supper, Melanchthon responded by vowing to take up the fight in matters central to the faith—which he explained meant answering the attacks on him by Nicholas Gallus and others on original sin and free will (something that indirectly would have implicated Calvin as well).[58] Shortly thereafter Justus Velsius in Frankfurt am Main railed against Calvin and the godlessness of his denial of free will.[59] Calvin, also in Frankfurt at the time, reported the same thing to Melanchthon, pleaded with the Wittenberg Reformer to come to his defense, and commiserated with him over the attacks of the Flacians.[60] Despite appeals from both sides, Melanchthon said nothing.

III. ADIAPHORA

The correspondence between Calvin and Melanchthon occurred in fits and starts. After an initial spurt from 1538 to 1545, the next letter was written in 1550. After a hiatus of two years, the correspondence picked up again briefly during 1552 but then stopped until 1554. Another brief flurry at that time again was broken off, despite Calvin's attempts to restart it, until 1557. These four breaks point not so much to missing letters as to Melanchthon's pique—witnessed to in three instances within the correspondence itself. In 1545 Calvin urged Melanchthon to go public on his understanding of the Lord's Supper.[61] The result? Silence. In 1550 Calvin wrote a pointed letter upbraiding Melanchthon for his stance on adiaphora.[62] The result? Not only silence but a rumor that Melanchthon had ripped the letter up—the sixteenth-century equivalent of hanging up on someone.[63] After 1552 Melanchthon refused to respond immediately to Calvin's challenge on predestination and the Lord's Supper.[64] When Calvin again urged Melanchthon to be forthcoming about his position on the Lord's Supper, the older man did not respond for three years.[65]

One of the sharpest exchanges in their correspondence revolved around the question of adiaphora, indifferent matters in church practice. To begin with the Reformers seemed united on this issue. Calvin, plagued with people unwilling to change church practices, asked

Melanchthon for his and Luther's opinions of his recently published tracts, *De vitandis superstitionibus* and *Excusatio ad Pseudo-Nicodemitas.*[66] Melanchthon responded by refusing to give the tracts to Luther (given the looming controversy over the Lord's Supper with Zurich) and shared instead his own opinion alone.[67] The resulting memorandum, published in Calvin's 1550 edition of *De vitandis superstitionibus,* linked necessary practices to the first commandment and thereby (contrary to Luther's grudging toleration of transubstantiation in a letter to the Italian evangelicals)[68] rejected adoration of and processions with the bread in the Mass. Adiaphora embraced all those practices which, while subject to abuse, could nevertheless be tolerated within the church. Melanchthon's memo also included special advice against the Anabaptists, against the sophistic excuses of the Nicodemites, against the hasty rush toward martyrdom, and in favor of clear witness to the gospel among the churches in exile.[69]

Upon receiving this letter, Calvin immediately conveyed his thanks to Melanchthon.[70] Less than a month later, Jacob Bording wrote to Melanchthon from Antwerp, asking for specific advice in his situation, given Melanchthon's general advice to Calvin. Melanchthon's response demonstrates how central *moderatio* was for his theological program.[71] He refused to give advice because of its danger to the weak. "Advice for the firm [in faith] is harder and sharper, for the young recruits and those unable to fight, who must be drawn and not frightened off, milder. As St. Paul commands [in Romans 14:1] . . . As a rule I follow this principle in such advice."[72] The specific need of the individual for the gospel outweighed the possibility of giving general rules for dealing with this issue.

In 1547 the evangelical princes suffered defeat at the hands of the imperial forces, aided by the "Judas of Meissen," Maurice of Saxony.[73] When it became clear that the triumphant emperor intended to impose the interim agreement on religious practices—passed at the diet in Augsburg in 1548 and hence nicknamed the "Augsburg Interim," which only allowed the Protestants married priests and communion in two kinds—Maurice and his advisors, including the recently reconstituted faculty of the University of Wittenberg, struggled to formulate an evangelical response that avoided the direct imposition of the hated Interim in Saxon lands. The resulting document, which staked out a moderate position on the Lord's Supper and justification, allowed the reinstitution of certain "indifferent" Roman practices.

When this proposal, to which the electors of Brandenburg and Saxony had agreed in principle but which never came to a vote by the Saxon estates meeting in Leipzig (this despite its being named the "Leipzig Interim"), became public in late 1548, it and its principal author, Philip Melanchthon, were attacked in various circles. Already in January 1549 Georg Buchholzer of Berlin sent a friendly inquiry to Melanchthon on the matter after having heard it read out publicly by John Agricola of Eisleben, chief theological advisor to the Brandenburg court and co-author of the Augsburg Interim. A more serious challenge arose from Lutheran theologians holed up in Magdeburg, including Matthias Flacius and Nicholas von Amsdorf. They argued that in a time of persecution things that normally were adiaphora could not be changed; such times demanded instead confession of faith. This became the first in a series of disputes to rock Lutheranism at least until the Formula of Concord brought some semblance of peace in 1580.

At the height of this initial storm of controversy, John Calvin also staked out his position. First, he wrote against the Augsburg Interim itself.[74] We know from Melanchthon's correspondence that a copy of Calvin's work on the subject reached him in early 1549.[75] When in mid-1549 Melanchthon became embroiled in the adiaphoristic controversy, Calvin sent Melanchthon a less than friendly letter. He expressed his sadness over the controversy and invoked their friendship as the basis for his admonition to Melanchthon, who had to shoulder some of the blame for the dispute.[76] He summarized Melanchthon's position this way: "This is the sum of your defense: only the purity of doctrine is retained; concerning external things one must not fight stubbornly."[77] Such struggles, Calvin noted, were foreign to Melanchthon's *modestia.* However, Calvin insisted that so many things ought not be conceded to the papists because they contradict God's Word and capitulation simply gives more ammunition to the enemy. Calling on the blood of the martyrs and the example of St. Paul, Calvin attempted to overcome Melanchthon's timidity. "Who would be so insane as to hold everything to such an extreme as to neglect the heart of the gospel?"[78] No wonder this surprisingly sharp rebuke, arriving in Wittenberg in the midst of his paper war with the so-called Magdeburg Consistory, evoked silence and sparked the rumor (at the very least) that Melanchthon had ripped the letter up. When the correspondence resumed, Calvin was always quick to express his sorrow at the attacks from the Flacians, perhaps as an indirect way of mitigating the severity of his earlier remarks.

IV. THE LORD'S SUPPER

By far the most dominant theme in this correspondence was the Lord's Supper and its attendant controversies. Each Reformer played an important role in the eucharistic theology and political maneuvering of the other. After initial harmony on the issue described above, problems first surfaced in relation to the second public dispute over the Lord's Supper between Luther and the

Zurich theologians, which began in 1543.[79] A harsh condemnation of Zwingli by Luther in a letter to the printer Christopher Froschauer led to equally harsh threats from Zurich.

Calvin reported Bullinger's complaints to Melanchthon and urged him to restrain his belligerent colleague.[80] At the same time both Bucer and Melanchthon, fearful that the Wittenberg Concord might collapse, sought to restore calm among the warring parties. However, Luther was also rumored to be writing against Bucer and Melanchthon in his so-called "Shorter Confession" on the Lord's Supper. Calvin's next letter to Melanchthon, which contained copies of his writings against the Nicodemites, questioned whether a letter from him should be given to Luther (it was not) and described Calvin's upset with Luther's tract and Andreas Osiander's even sharper attack. In this connection even Calvin could invoke the virtue of moderation. "That man's [Osiander's] petulance displeases me . . . so that I desire instead moderation, prudence and even sanity."[81] He also mentioned he was working to calm Bullinger. In Melanchthon's response he suggested he needed Calvin's advice more than Calvin needed his, and he mentioned for the first time the threat of exile.[82]

Calvin immediately replied by criticizing the Zurich Confession as a poor defense of Zwingli.[83] He also criticized Luther's bombast. The Reformer had placed the church in a danger that had to be countered. In this context Calvin then urged Melanchthon to go public with his understanding of the Lord's Supper.[84] It would seem that this demand, coupled with the dislocations of the Smalcald War, Calvin's signing of the Consensus Tigurinus, and his rebuke of Melanchthon's position on adiaphora in 1550, contributed to Melanchthon's seven-year silence.

The subsequent mention of the Lord's Supper occurred in the middle of the next controversy over that doctrine: the dispute between Calvin and Joachim Westphal.[85] Again Calvin begged Melanchthon for a public word on the dispute. He also described his agreement with Luther's sacramentology in these terms. "In baptism the efficacious Spirit is present in order to wash and regenerate us. The Holy Supper is a spiritual banquet in which we truly feed upon the flesh and blood of Christ."[86] Here is Calvin's construal of the Wittenberg Concord.

In response Melanchthon expressed his support of Calvin's Trinitarian defense and his treatment of Servetus.[87] He claimed that people were attacking Calvin out of hatred for him, Melanchthon. He expected exile and hoped to speak with Calvin, "whom I know to be a lover of the truth."[88] This final comment, in the nuanced language of the time, must be understood as indicating to Calvin that the two men in fact differed on this doc-

trine. It mirrored precisely Calvin's own earlier language regarding predestination. It meant Melanchthon would not attack Calvin publicly, but it precluded his support.

Calvin realized what the score was. In his response he thanked Melanchthon for his support on Servetus and expressed the hope that Melanchthon had not taken his admonition (to speak out publicly on the Lord's Supper) badly. He was convinced they could work out an agreement on predestination.[89] This did not, however, prevent Calvin from demanding Melanchthon's public support on the doctrine of the Lord's Supper. He knew Melanchthon's mind! Moreover, Zurich had already responded.[90]

Melanchthon knew all along the public nature of these letters and how Calvin was likely to use his support. He steadfastly turned aside Calvin's request (Calvin could judge his own opponents and their theatrics) and prayed for the divided church.[91] But he also corrected Calvin's mistaken impression of his silence. He was prepared to respond directly to attacks where the gospel was at stake,[92] and he rejected Calvin's connection of his silence with a fear of exile or other dangers.[93] Calvin agreed that the opponents just wanted to fight, but he urged Melanchthon (borrowing phrases from the *Te Deum*) to join the chorus of the company of angels and the holy fathers in support of the church.[94] The result was three years of silence on Melanchthon's part.

Melanchthon was unwillingly caught in the middle of this controversy. At the same time as Calvin was urging him to speak out, others on the opposite side of the dispute were doing the same. Already in 1555 Johann Stigel begged Melanchthon to answer Calvin's attacks on Luther.[95] In a response to a request from Christopher Stathmion, a pastor at the Coburg, Melanchthon outlined his basic position.[96] He has often been asked about the "sure and certain form of the words" (*de forma certa verborum*). He rejected Osiander's claim that the bread is God and insisted rather on the Pauline use of *koinonia* in I Corinthians 10:16.

He clearly understood the differences between his and Calvin's theology, even describing how in Poland some followed Calvin's books while others preferred to order the church "according to the norm of our confession" (*iuxta normam confessionis nostrae*).[97] By this time Calvin's second response to Westphal had been printed.[98] It appealed directly to Melanchthon's description of Luther's support for Calvin (in connection with the "Reply to Sadoleto").[99] Melanchthon's (less than honest) response to Andrew Misenus in Altenburg a year later insisted that he had never said what Calvin claimed and that he had not read all that Calvin had written.[100] He again appealed for the use of sure forms of speech and rejected the Bremen city council's use in its condemnation of Hardenburg of such novel phrases as "the bread is the essential body of Christ." "Who has spoken this way? We say: 'With the bread the body of Christ is consumed.'"[101] This refusal to equate the bread with Christ's body, which Melanchthon construed as an invitation to bread worship, marked his entire eucharistic theology.[102] Christ's presence was with the bread and occurred during the proper use of the elements, not before or after. He contented himself with the sure and certain forms of speaking found in Paul.

This same search for "certain forms of speaking" appeared even near the end of Melanchthon's life. When some Hungarian evangelicals inquired about the Lord's Supper after one of their colleagues, Christopher Reuter, had written against Zwingli and Calvin, Melanchthon responded by pointing them to his statements in the *Examen ordinandorum* to prove that he himself was not a Calvinist. He refused to accept the book in order not to become sucked in to the conflict and emphasized that the presence of Christ was associated with its proper use, not with processions or adoration of the host.[103] Even Georg Buchholzer, while using what Melanchthon said in the *Examen* to prove Melanchthon was not a Calvinist, had pleaded with Melanchthon for a clearer public statement.[104]

In 1557 another flurry of letters surrounded the publication of Calvin's final response to Westphal and the impending colloquy in Worms.[105] Now Calvin urged Melanchthon to convince the princes to invite the Swiss to a religious colloquy or to hold one of his own.[106] Melanchthon finally responded in October.[107] He described the departure of the Gnesio-Lutheran party, praised the people sent by Calvin (a party that included Budaeus and Beza) and prayed for the church. He did not publicly support Calvin.

However, in a speech to the evangelical delegates at Worms delivered a month earlier, Melanchthon, while condemning Westphal's use of "new and unusual language" to defend transubstantiation and a localized presence of Christ's body within the bread, added that Calvin's language also needed further explanation—a sure sign that Melanchthon realized their views did not coincide.[108] It was also a sign that he stood closer to Calvin than to Westphal on this issue as far as the language itself was concerned. Melanchthon insisted that any discussion of Christ's presence in the Lord's Supper had to be limited to biblical expressions (especially 1 Corinthians 10:16) and patristic usage.[109]

Despite this moderation, or perhaps because of it, Calvin's patience had finally reached the breaking point. In his last letter from their correspondence, dated 19 November 1558, he drew a parallel between attacks on Geneva by Spain and France with Melanchthon's theological enemies and with Calvin's opponents within

Geneva and without (especially Westphal).[110] He then directly criticized Melanchthon's silence in the Lord's Supper controversy. Although he sought an unbroken friendship, he was hurt by the fact that Hubert Languet was spreading rumors (to Sebastian Castellio's delight) about Melanchthon's criticism of Calvin's teaching.[111] Only Melanchthon's death prevented a public breach and allowed for Calvin's less than realistic eulogy in 1561.

V. EXEGESIS

The correspondence between Calvin and Melanchthon also included an exegetical component. In the letter that was supposed to have accompanied the gift of Calvin's treatise on Pighius, he requested from Melanchthon a copy of his commentary on Daniel.[112] Apparently Melanchthon fulfilled that request, for in a letter sent the following year Calvin praised the Daniel commentary he had received.[113] Such praise was by no means disingenuous. In 1555 a French translation of Melanchthon's work was published in Geneva and included Calvin's own introduction to Daniel as well. Given these clear historical connections, it is quite disappointing that modern scholars have not seen fit to compare these two exegetes on this work. Both understood they were living in the last days; both tried, under the influence of Luther's own apocalyptic expectations, to interpret Daniel's visions for contemporary society.[114] It is unfortunate that with few exceptions investigation of Melanchthon's influence over Calvin's exegesis has been limited by Calvin's remarks in the preface to his commentary on Romans, in which he complains about Melanchthon's tendency to skip over verses when using the *loci* method in biblical interpretation.[115] In fact, the Reformers often read and used one another's exegetical insights.

This did not mean they always agreed in such matters. For example, attached to a private letter written in 1543 to Joachim Camerarius, Melanchthon sent a copy of his *Unterschied des Alten und Neuen Testaments* with instructions to give it to Bernard Ziegler, so that he might better discern the differences between Melanchthon and Calvin on this point.[116] This action indicates an important hermeneutical divide between the two Reformers. Melanchthon's law-gospel hermeneutic clearly contradicted, in his own eyes, the salvation-historical approach of his Genevan correspondent. It continues to divide Christians today.

VI. CONCLUSIONS

Predestination, church practices, free will, the Lord's Supper: the topics of Melanchthon and Calvin's correspondence touched on many of the burning issues of the day. Given the penchant for polemic in that day and ours, their epistolary friendship, for all its weaknesses, provides a an interesting model for theological discourse. Moderation and respect helped set a tone for discussion that allowed conversation to continue throughout their careers. They were not best friends; they were fierce, committed Christians, who struggled to right the church amid a storm sea of troubles and who understood the importance of the other man's help in this endeavor.

These letters also reveal the limits of such conversation. In the end Calvin misconstrued Melanchthon's moderation, as did many of his more vociferous opponents, and attempted to spur him on, especially in the questions of the Lord's Supper and predestination, to debate what in Melanchthon's mind was undebatable. The strict limitation that Melanchthon imposed on himself and his correspondents was, in his view at least, a biblical one. He refused to invent new language to describe Christ's eucharistic presence, and thus tolerated Calvin's view; he refused to speculate about the relation between divine causation and salvation. This moderation was thus not a character flaw, nor did it arise out of genuine fear in the face of persecution. It was a stubborn refusal to venture beyond the biblical and patristic witness in theological discourse. But Melanchthon also linked this moderation to one of Lutheranism's enduring hallmarks: the central concern for how the distinction between law and gospel provides comfort to the terrified conscience.

Calvin also developed a radically biblical theology. However, he insisted that the biblical witness itself set the limits not just of terminology but of content and that therefore any comfort had to be found within the totality of that witness. What appeared to Melanchthon as speculation was for Calvin faithfulness. And Melanchthon's *moderatio,* for all its appeal, could only be construed by Calvin as timidity or, worse yet, the result of philosophical scruples. It is finally this hermeneutical divide that continues to mark the differences between these two great streams of the Protestant tradition and between their ablest spokesmen.

Notes

1. [Philip Melanchthon. *Melanchthons Briefwechsel: Kritische und kommentiere Gesamtaugabe.* Edited by Heinz Schieble. 10 vols. to date. Stuttgart-Bad Cannstatt: Frommann-Holzboog, 1977-. Hereafter referred to as] MBW 3245 ([Philip Melancthon. *Corpus Reformatorum. Philippi Melanchthonis opera quae supersunt omnia.* Edited by Karl Bretschneider and Heinrich Bindsell. 28 vols. Halle: A Schwetschke and sons, 1834-60. Hereafter referred to as] CR 5:107-9; =[*Ioannis Calvini Opera Quae Supersunt Omnia.* Edited by Wilhelm Baum, E. Cunitz and E. Reuss. 59 vols. Brunswick: A. Schwetschke, 1863-97. Hereafter referred to as] CO 11:539-42), MBW 3886 (CR

5:734-39; =CO 6:621-24), MBW 6576 (CR 7:1085f.; =CO 14:368f.), MBW 7306 (CR 8:362f.; =CO 15:268f.), MBW 7489 (CR 8:482f.; =CO 15:615f.), and MBW 8384 (CR 9:328f.; =CO 16:659).

2. Bindseil's work, *Philippi Melanchthonis epistolae, iudicia, consilia, testimonia aliorumque ad eum epistolae quae in Corpore Reformatorum desiderantur* (Halle: Schwetschke, 1874), appeared in the midst of the publication of Calvin's correspondence and contained MBW 3157 (Bds. 165-69; =CO 6:229-32), MBW 3169 (Bds. 169-71; =CO 11:515-17), MBW 3803 (Bds. 214-18; =CO 12:9-12), MBW 3884 (Bds. 479f., not in CR 40), MBW 3885 (Bds. 219f.; =CO 12:61f.), MBW 3928 (Bds. 221-23; =CO 12:98-100), MBW 5830 (Bds. 310-13; =CO 13:593-96), MBW 6655 (Bds. 331-35; =CO 14:414-18), MBW 7273 (Bds. 364f.; =CO 15:215-17), MBW 7424 (Bds. 372-74; =CO 15:488f.), MBW 7562 (Bds. 379f.; =CO 15:737f.), MBW 7957 (Bds. 396-98; =CO 16:280-82), MBW 8293 (Bds. 417-19; =CO 16:556), and MBW 8782 (Bds. 435-38; =CO 17:384-86). The corresponding portions of Calvin's correspondence (CO 10-17), published by Schwetschke between 1871 and 1877, also included MBW 2366 (CO 11:17f.), MBW 3273 (CO 11:594f.), MBW 3531 (CO 11:696-98), and MBW 8331 (CO 16:604f.).

3. Calvin's letters to Farel are described in MBW 2103 (CO 10:276-80) and MBW 2152 (CO 10/2:322-32); mention of now lost letters are found in MBW 3169 (where Calvin referred to a letter written by Melanchthon around October 1542), MBW 3273 (where Melanchthon referred to a letter written by Calvin around June 1543 and brought by Johannes Sturm of Strasbourg to Melanchthon in Bonn), and MBW 8331 (where Calvin mentioned two letters sent "inter paucos dies," one of which was MBW 8293).

4. *Westminster Theological Journal* 38 (1976): 152-65. Besides Schaff's work, Hickman depends on John T. McNeill, Williston Walker, and Clyde Manschreck.

5. Philip Schaff, "The Friendship of Calvin and Melanchthon," in *Papers of the American Society of Church History,* 4 (1892): 143-63. Another early study was by Emile Doumergue, *Jean Calvin: Les hommes et les choses de son temps,* vol. 2 (Lausanne: G. Bridel, 1902), 545-61.

6. Hickman, "Friendship," 164.

7. Willem Nijenhuis, *Calvinus oecumenicus: Calvijn en de eenheid der kerk in het licht van zijn briefwisseling,* Kerkistorische Studien, 8 ('s-Gravenhage: Martinus Nijhoff, 1959), 12-14, 131-

99. Other, narrower studies include Rodolphe Peter, "Calvin, traducteur de Mélanchthon," in *Horizons européens de la Réforme en Alsace,* ed. Marijn de Kroon and Marc Lienhard (Strasbourg: Istra, 1980), 119-33, and Danièle Fischer, "Calvin et la Confession d'Augsbourg," in *Calvinus ecclesiae Genevensis custos,* ed. Wilhelm Neuser (Frankfurt am Main: Peter Lang, 1984), 245-71.

8. See Nijenhuis, *Calvinus,* 131-41, 141-54, 154-99, respectively, where the final section is subdivided into periods of polemic (1549-1556), working toward a colloquy (1556-1559), and resignation (1559-1564). The present research uncovered similar shifts.

9. Ibid., 314, quoting from the English summary.

10. See Timothy J. Wengert, *Human Freedom, Christian Righteousness: Philip Melanchthon's Exegetical Dispute with Erasmus of Rotterdam* (New York: Oxford University Press, 1997).

11. See the criticism by Heinz Scheible, "Luther and Melanchthon," *Lutheran Quarterly,* n.s., 4 (1990): 317-39.

12. Camerarius was Melanchthon's first biographer and an early publisher of his correspondence. He exchanged more letters with Melanchthon than anyone else. See Timothy J. Wengert, "'With Friends Like This . . .': The Biography of Philip Melanchthon by Joachim Camerarius," in *The Rhetorics of Life-Writing in Early Modern Europe: Forms of Biography from Cassandra Fedele to Louis XIV,* ed. Thomas F. Mayer and D. R. Woolf (Ann Arbor: University of Michigan, 1995), 115-31. Veit Dietrich was a student of Melanchthon and preacher in Nuremberg. Caspar Cruciger, also one of Melanchthon's students, taught at the University of Wittenberg. For him see Timothy J. Wengert, "Caspar Cruciger (1504-1548): The Case of the Disappearing Reformer," *The Sixteenth Century Journal* 20 (1989): 417-41. For other important students of Melanchthon see *Melanchthon in seinen Schülern,* Wolfenbütteler Forschungen, 73, ed. Heinz Scheible, (Wiesbaden: Harrassowitz Verlag, 1997).

13. MBW 2366 (CO 11:17). "Te ex animo amo et precor Christum ut te gubernet."

14. MBW 3169 (CO 11:515), dated 16 February 1543: "Sustineamur beata illa spe, ad quam nos literae tuae revocant: in coelis nos simul perpetuo victuros: ubi amore amicitiaque nostra fruemur."

15. See Danièle Fischer, "Calvin et la Confession d'Augsbourg," 248. No self-respecting biblical scholar would transform St. Paul's expressions of love for his congregations into intimate friendships. Even sixteenth-century exegetes understood the rules governing friendly letters. See Timothy J. Wengert, "Georg Major (1502-1574): Defender of Wittenberg's Faith and Melanchthonian Exegete," in Heinz Scheible, ed., *Melanchthon in seinen Schülern,* 150-51, regarding Major's understanding of Philippians as a friendly letter.

16. Two examples of this were Calvin's letter of 21 April 1544 (MBW 3531), which Melanchthon sent to Joachim Camerarius in Leipzig with instructions to distribute to others (MBW 3588; CR 5:415-16), and Melanchthon's memorandum of 17 April 1545 (MBW 3886; CO 6:621-24), which ended up in the Netherlands through the offices of Francis Dryander (MBW 3955; CR 5:794-95).

17. Cited without reference in Schaff, "The Friendship," 160. It is found in CO 9:461-62, taken from Calvin's "On the True Partaking of the Flesh and Blood of Christ" (1561).

18. Danièle Fischer, "Calvin et la Confession d'Augsbourg," 247-52, provides a partial list of their disagreements (including predestination, the Lord's Supper, adiaphora, Lutheran ceremonies) and mentions Melanchthon's praise for Castellio and Calvin's frustration at the Wittenberger's indecision. See below for further analysis of these issues.

19. For these biographical details, see T. H. L. Parker, *John Calvin: A Biography* (Philadelphia: Westminster, 1975).

20. MBW 2103 (CO 10:276-80). Cf. MBW 1853 (CR 3:288-90), dated 24 February 1537, where Melanchthon argued the case before the rapacious Philip of Hesse.

21. MBW 2152 (CO 10/2:322-32).

22. StL 17:2087f. See Mark U. Edwards, *Luther and the False Brethren* (Stanford: Stanford University Press, 1975), 149-55.

23. See Danièle Fischer, "Calvin et la Confession d'Augsbourg," 254-55, for an analysis of Calvin's preface, where he makes direct mention of the Concord. From the text itself see, for example, Inst. IV.xvii.7, where he rejects those who "make us partakers of the Spirit only," or IV.xvii.10, where he insists that "unless a man means to call God a deceiver, he would never dare assert that an empty symbol is set forth by him" and then concludes in IV.xvii.18 that "under the symbol of bread we shall be fed by his body, under the symbol of wine we shall separately drink his blood, to enjoy him at last in his wholeness." It was for Calvin "as if" Christ were present and a communion bestowed "by the power of his Spirit," but it was a communion with Christ nevertheless. In IV.xvii.40 he dealt with the *manducatio infidelium.*

24. WABr 8:568-70, a letter to Bucer dated 14 October 1539; here 569,29-30: "Bene vale, et salutabis D. Iohannem Sturmium et Ioh. Caluinum reverenter, quorum libellos cum singulari voluptate legi." MBW 2289 ([Martin Luther. *Luthers Werke. Kritische Gesamtasugabe.Briefwechsel.* 18 vols. Weimar: H. Böhlau, 1930-85. Hereafter referred to as] WABr 8:562-66) included the elector's suggestion to publish it in Saxony.

25. This was reported by Melanchthon to Bucer via the messenger. See MBW 2290 (CO 10/2:432), dated 14 October 1539. The passage from the "Reply to Sadoleto" may have been this (translated in *John Calvin and Jacopo Sadoleto: A Reformation Debate,* ed. John C. Olin [New York: Harper, 1966], 70-71): "In the case of the Eucharist, you blame us for attempting to confine the Lord of the universe . . . within the corners of a corporeal nature with its circumscribed boundaries. What end, pray, will there be to calumny? We have always distinctly testified, that not only the divine power of Christ, but His essence also, is diffused over all, and defined by no limits, and yet you hesitate not to upbraid us with confining it within the corners of corporeal nature! How so? Because we are unwilling with you to chain down His body to earthly elements. But had you any regard for sincerity, assuredly you are not ignorant how great a difference there is between the two things—between removing the local presence of Christ's body from bread, and circumscribing His spiritual power within bodily limits." Calvin went on to say, "We loudly proclaim the communion of flesh and blood, which is exhibited to believers in the Supper; and we distinctly show that that flesh is truly meat, and that blood truly drink—that the soul, not contented with an imaginary conception, enjoys them in very truth. That presence of Christ, by which we are engrafted in Him, we by no means exclude from the Supper, nor shroud in darkness. . . ."

26. MBW 2152 (CO 10/2:322-32), in a report to Farel dated 16 March 1539. Calvin expressed his respect for Melanchthon's exegesis and style and their differences in method in the preface to his commentary on Romans (dated 18 October 1539 to Simon Grynaeus; CO 10:402-406). His comments on Melanchthon's neglect of passages may have referred not only to the *Commentarii* of 1532 but to the *Dispositio* of 1530.

27. The question of Calvin's subscription to the Concord or to the Augsburg Confession, especially the *Variata* edited by Melanchthon for the 1541 Regensburg Colloquy, is a complicated one and best dealt with by Danièle Fischer, "Calvin et la Confession d'Augsbourg," 253-54. Fischer, citing

CO 9:841-46, concludes that Calvin "affirma haut et clair, que les positions eucharistiques de son *Institution Chrétienne* de 1539 n'allaient absolument pas à l'encontre de celles de la *Formule de Concorde.*"

28. Nijenhuis, *Calvinus oecumenicus,* 12, points to Calvin's comments to Farel (MBW 2152) and summarizes, "Hij deelt aan Farel mede, dat er overeenstemming bestaat tussen Melanchthon en hemzelf inzake de avondmaalsleer."

29. See MBW 2703 (CR 4:327f.), dated 23 May 1541, and MBW 2683 (CR 4:239—41; cf. CO 11:188-94), dated April 1541. For Calvin's contributions at the colloquies, see Wilhelm H. Neuser, *Calvins Beitrag zu den Religionsgesprächen von Haguenau, Worms und Regensburg* (Neukirchen: Erziehungsverein, 1969). Calvin was not pleased with Bucer and Melanchthon's compromise language on the eucharist. See Parker, *John Calvin,* 135.

30. See Danièle Fischer, "Calvin et la Confession d'Augsbourg," and the literature cited there. Despite Fischer's questioning (263) whether Calvin formally subscribed to the Variata, his language (CO 16:430: "Nec vero Augustanum Confessio repudio, cui pridem volens ac libens subscripsi, sicuti eam autor ipse interpretatus est") seems to indicate he did. The key word is "pridem" (long ago) and probably referred to the period just before his return to Geneva in 1541. The final phrase, "sicuti eam autor ipse interpretatus est," is a clear reference to the Variata, which even Melanchthon's *Corpus doctrinae* of 1560 viewed as an exposition of the original. For the later discussion of the Lord's Supper, see below.

31. Cf. MBW 3169 (CO 11:515-17), from Calvin, dated 16 February 1543.

32. CO 6:229-404. The preface was probably written in January 1543. See the arguments in MBW 3157.

33. CO 6:250-51 ([*Evangelische Theologie.* Hereafter referred to as] ET 28-29).

34. CA XVIII ([*Die Bekentnissschriften der evangelisch-lutherischen Kirche.* 10th. ed. Göttingen: Vandenhoeck and Ruprecht, 1986. Hereafter referred to as] BKS, 73-74). The small changes in the Variata underscore that God commands and forces carnal people to civil righteousness through the law.

35. CR 21:376, 428, 450-53.

36. CO 6:229-30 (ET, 3).

37. CO 6:229-30 (ET, 3-4): "The kind of defense which I employ is straightforward and honest. For as much as you shrink from crafty, sidelong de-

vices in argument which serve to draw darkness over things which are otherwise clear and open, in short from all pretence and sophistry, so you are pleased by an unembellished and frank clarity which, without any concealment, sets a subject before the eyes and explains it. This quality of yours has often stirred in me great admiration, just because it is so rarely found, for, although you are outstanding for your amazing insight, you still rank nothing above straightforwardness." For Melanchthon's comments on the subject, see CR 21:373, where on the issue of the free will (*liberum arbitrium*) Melanchthon stated, "Non quaeritur de arcano Dei consilio gubernantis omnia; non quaeritur de praedestinatione; non agitur de omnibus contingentibus." Given this debate, Melanchthon's later comments in the third edition of the *Loci* could be construed as a correction of his Genevan correspondent.

38. CO 6:229-30 (ET, 4): "Besides I remember that you once assigned me the task of writing something to restrain Pighius's insolence if he should continue to challenge us."

39. Both of these distinctions formed the heart of later Lutheran comments on predestination and free will in the Formula of Concord.

40. MBW 3245 (CR 5:107-9; =CO 11:539-42). He mentioned that he had not yet received the book but had looked at a copy in Bucer's possession.

41. CR 5:108. He cited Paul's exhortation to Timothy in 1 Timothy 4:14.

42. CR 5:109. That is, to use among the *rudes*. Erasmus had similarly complained that Melanchthon had wasted his talents, but he urged him to turn from theology back to the humanities. Here the debate is over how to teach in the church, not whether to teach there.

43. MBW 3273 (CO 11:594f.), dated 12 July 1543 and sent from Melanchthon in Bonn to Calvin in Strasbourg.

44. CO 9:848. "Et de faict, ce qui est bien à priser, ie voy que l'auteur, estant homme de profond savoir, n'a pas voulu entrer en disputes subtiles, ne traiter les matieres d'un artifice tant haut qu'il luy eut esté facile de faire, mais s'est abaissé tant qu'il a peu, n'ayant esgard qu'à la seule edification. C'est certes la façon et le style que nous aurions tous à tenir: sinon que les adversaires nous contraignissent par leurs cavillations à nous destourner de ce train. Tant y a que la plus grande simplicité est la plus grande vertu à traicter la doctrine Chrestienne."

45. CO 9:849. "Mais si a il esté bon d'en advertir les lecteurs, afin que nul ne fust scandalizé de peu de chose, voyant l'intention de l'auteur."

46. CO 9:850. "Quant les lecteurs garderont une telle modestie à iuger du livre qu'a eu l'auteur en le composant, tout ira bien, et n'y aura rien qui les empesche à y profiter beaucoup."

47. For details, see Parker, *John Calvin*, 112-16.

48. CO 14:374-77. Jerome Bolsec was also involved.

49. CO 381-82, dated 6 October 1552.

50. CO 11:381. Cest que Melancthon *[sic]*, estant homme craintif, pour ne point donner occasion a gens curieux de trop senquerir des secretz de Dieu, sest voulu par trop accommoder au sens commun des hommes. Et par ce moyen a plus parle en philosophe quen theologien, quant a la cause presente." Melanchthon had demonstrated this by referring to Plato's authority. At the same time, Calvin praised Melanchthon's wisdom, virtue, and faithful work for the gospel.

51. CO 11:382.

52. CO 14:229-30.

53. MBW 6322 (CR 7:930-31). He nicknamed Calvin "Zeno."

54. MBW 6324 (CR 7:931-32). "O rem miseram! Doctrina salutaris obscuratur peregrinis disputationibus."

55. MBW 6655 (CO 14:414-18). He was responding directly to MBW 6576 (CO 14:368-69), dated 1 October 1552, in which Melanchthon had resumed their correspondence.

56. CO 14:417-18. "Notus est mihi tuus candor, perspecta ingenuitas et moderatio: pietas vero angelis et toti mundo testata est. Ergo facile, ut spero, tota ea res inter nos expediretur." The appeal to face-to-face conversation in Renaissance letters must always be understood as an attempt to avoid a public dispute.

57. MBW 7273 (CO 15:215-17), dated 27 August 1554. His frustration with Melanchthon was aptly expressed in two other letters from the same time to Vermigli and Sleidan (CO 15:219-21). His charge: Melanchthon was too influenced by philosophy.

58. MBW 7489 (CR 8:482-83; =CO 15:615-16), dated 12 May 1555.

59. MBW 7958 (Hartfelder, [*Zeitschrift für Kirchengeschichte*. Hereafter referred to as] ZKG 12 [1891]: 205-6), dated 17 September 1556.

60. MBW 7957 (CO 16:280-82), dated 17 September 1556.

61. MBW 3928 (CO 12:98-100), dated 28 June 1545.

62. MBW 5830 (CO 13:593-96), dated 19 June 1550.

63. MBW 6655 (CO 14:414-18), dated 28 November 1552. Melanchthon blamed unreliable couriers (MBW 6576; CO 14:368-69).

64. MBW 7273 (CO 15:215-17), dated 27 August 1554.

65. Calvin's challenge came in MBW 7562 (CO 15:737-38), dated 23 August 1555. In a letter dated 3 August 1557, MBW 8293 (CO 16:556-58), he complained about not having heard from Melanchthon for three years.

66. CO 6:537-614. MBW 3803 (CO 12:9-12), dated 21 January 1545. See Francis Higman, "The Question of Nicodemism," in *Calvinus Ecclesiae Genevensis Custos,* ed. Wilhelm Neuser (Frankfurt am Main: Peter Lang, 1984), 165-70.

67. MBW 3884 (Bds. 479-80), Melanchthon's first draft of the letter, and MBW 3885 (CO 12:61-62), dated 17 April 1545.

68. WABr 10:330-31. Luther's comments in Melanchthon's view contradicted the Wittenberg Concord.

69. MBW 3886 (CR 5:734-39; =CO 6:621-24), dated 17 April 1545.

70. MBW 3928 (CO 12:98-100), dated 28 June 1545. He did, however, admit to some differences. P. 100: "Tametsi enim paululum est discriminis in particulis quibusdam, de re tamen ipsa optime inter nos convenit."

71. MBW 3955 (CR 5:794-95), dated 17 July 1545.

72. CR 5:794: "Consilia de firmis duriora καὶ ἀκριβέστερα, tyronibus et imbellibus leviora, qui provehendi sunt non deterrendi, ut Paulus iubet . . . Hanc fere rationem in his consiliis sequor."

73. For this material, see my article on "Adiaphora" in the *Oxford Encyclopedia of the Reformation* and the literature cited there.

74. CO 7:547-674: "Interim Adultero-Germanum: cui adiecta est vera Christianae pacificationis et ecclesiae reformandae ratio."

75. MBW 5434 (CR 7:328-30), a letter to Joachim Moller in Celle dated 4 February 1549.

76. MBW 5830 (CO 13:593-96), dated 19 June 1550. "In libera admonitione veri amici officio fungar."

77. CO 41:594. "Haec tuae defensionis summa est, modo retineatur doctrinae puritas, de rebus externis non esse pertinaciter dimicandum."

78. Co 41:595. "Cuius dementiae est, sic ad extremum tueri omnia, ut totius evangelii summa negligatur?"

79. For this debate, see Timothy J. Wengert, "Luther and Melanchthon, Melanchthon and Luther," *Luther-Jahrbuch* 65 (1998).

80. MBW 3531 (CO 11:696-98), dated 21 April 1544. To demonstrate the seriousness of the problem to Camerarius, Melanchthon sent him a copy of Calvin's letter (MBW 3588).

81. MBW 3803 (CO 12:9-12), dated 21 January 1545. Zurich's pastors responded with the Zurich Confession.

82. MBW 3884 (Bds. 479-80) and MBW 3885 (CO 12:61-62), dated 17 April 1545. Initially Melanchthon used this threat in anticipation of Luther's attack on him (which never materialized) in the "Shorter Confession" and stated it arose at his brother George's suggestion. By this time it had become a part of his ideal of moderation.

83. MBW 3928 (CO 12:98-100), dated 28 June 1545. The Confession was "puerilis, quum in multis pertinaciter magis quam erudite." Bucer, too, was not pleased, claiming that it was an attempt to twist the Wittenberg Concord in such a way as to set Bucer against Luther. See MBW 3854.

84. CO 12:99. "Ad hanc ergo plenam et solidam mentis tuae explicationem forte viam tibi patefacere nunc vult Deus, ne perpetuo haereant dubii, qui ab autoritate tua pendent, quos scis esse quam plurimos." The Wittenberg *Reformatio,* written by Melanchthon, did as much. However, its eucharistic theology would hardly have pleased Calvin.

85. See Parker, *John Calvin,* 137-39.

86. MBW 7273 (CO 15:215-17), dated 27 August 1554, here 217. "In Baptismo adesse Spiritus efficaciam, ut nos abluat, et regeneret. Sacram Coenam spirituale esse epulum, in quo vere Christi carne et sanguine pascimur." (The johannine language ["flesh of Christ"] indicates a very different understanding of Christ's presence than that in Wittenberg.) To get on Melanchthon's good side, Calvin also announced his willingness to discuss the issue of predestination and described his own hurt at the unfair attacks on Melanchthon by the "Osiandrists" in the question of justification.

87. MBW 7306 (CO 15:268-69), dated 14 October 1554. This approval was a constant theme throughout his correspondence of the time. See MBW 7558 (CR 8:523-24), to Heinrich Bullinger dated 20 August 1555, and MBW 8185 (CR 9:131-35), a public letter dated 10 April 1557.

88. CO 15:269: "quem scio amantem esse veritatis."

89. MBW 7424 (CO 15:488-89), dated 5 March 1555. The language (which could be construed as ques-

tioning Melanchthon's sincerity) is striking: "ut de gratuita piorum electione sincerior quam antehac docendi formam inter nos mutuo conveniunt."

90. CO 15:488-89. *"Peri tes artolateias* pridem interior animi tui sensus mihi cognitus est, quem etiam non dissimulas in tuis literis. Sed mihi displicet tua ista nimia tarditas. Nunc iudicium tuum avidissime exspecto."

91. MBW 7489 (CO 15:615-16), dated 12 May 1555.

92. Here he referred to Gallus' attack on free will, to which he promised to respond "simply and without ambiguity."

93. CO 15:616: "Nec in hac senecta pertimesco exsilia et alia pericula." Calvin's posthumous *laudatio* cited by Schaff would not have gained Melanchthon's approval.

94. MBW 7562 (CO 15:737-38), dated 23 August 1555.

95. MBW 7656 (CR 8:621), dated 1 December 1555.

96. MBW 7883 (CR 8:790-91), dated 4 July 1556.

97. MBW 8164 (CR 9:788), dated 23 March 1557. This may be based upon reports like that of Johann Crato in Breslau (MBW 6544).

98. CO 9:41-120, "Secunda Defensio piae et orthodoxae de sacramentis fidei contra Ioachimi Westphali Calumnias." The preface is dated 5 January 1556.

99. CO 9:52. "Quin etiam Lutherus ipse quum scripta mea inspexisset, quale de me iudicium fecerit, mihi per testes idoneos probare non difficile erit. Sed mihi unus pro multis erit Philippus Melanchthon."

100. MBW 8092 (CR 9:18-19), dated mid-January 1557.

101. CR 9:18-19. "Nuper huc Senatus Bremensis misit legatos. Erat propositio his verbis scripta: panis est essentiale corpus Christi. Quis sic locutus est? Dicimus: cum pane sumi corpus Christi."

102. It also meant that he would reject the notion of ubiquity.

103. MBW 9075 (unpublished), dated 27 September 1559 (cf. MBW 9123), and Melanchthon's response in MBW 9218 (CR 9:1038-39), dated 4 February 1560.

104. MBW 8996 (in G. Kawerau, *Johann Agricola von Eisleben: Ein Beitrag zur Reformationsgeschichte* (Berlin: Wilhelm Hertz, 1881), 347-49). In the *Examen,* published in 1552, Melanchthon asked what is distributed and received in the Lord's Sup-

per. He answered: "Warer Leib und Blut des HErrn Jhesu Christ. Der hat diese nießung eingesetzt, das er bezeuget, das er warhafftiglich und wesentlich bey uns und in uns sein wil und wil in den bekerten wonen, jnen seine güter mitteilen und in jnen krefftig sein. Wie er spricht Joh. 15[:4]. 'Bleibet in mir und ich in Euch.'"

105. MBW 8293 (CO 16:556-58), dated 3 August 1557, a lost letter, and MBW 8331 (CO 16:604-5), dated 8 September 1557. Calvin's tract, "Ultima admonitio ad Joachimum Westphalum," is published in CO 9:137-252 and called on Melanchthon for support.

106. Melanchthon had suggested as much to John Laski (MBW 7926 and MBW 7960).

107. MBW 8384 (CR 9:328-29; =CO 16:659), dated 8 October 1557. Cf. MBW 8380 to Heinrich Bullinger.

108. MBW 8332 (unpublished), dated 9 September 1557.

109. In that way his last public word on the subject, the "Iudicium de coena domini" of 1560, also demanded of Heshuss in Heidelberg the same restraint. See MSA 6:484-86, where his concerns remained the language ("de una forma verborum"), transubstantiation ("Non dicit, mutari naturam panis"), and the restriction of Christ's presence to its proper use and not "extra sumptionem." Christ is present "non propter panem sed propter hominem." He also accepted the use of the term symbol because of patristic testimony. Heshuss's simple rejection of this term was criticized because of the way it set Heshuss himself up as an unassailable authority ("quae est igitur tanta auctoritas Heshusii").

110. MBW 8782 (CO 17:384-86).

111. In his postscript to three sermons against Castellio from 1562, Calvin could angrily charge (CO 58:202): "Quant à Melancthon, si ce rustre ne s'arreste point à lui comme il le proteste, mais à l'Evangile, comment prouvera-il par l'Evangile que Dieu n'ordonne point de ses creatures?"

112. MBW 3169 (CO 11:515-17), dated 16 February 1543. Apparently the books were not ready in time for the Frankfurt book fair and were thus delayed.

113. MBW 3531 (CO 11:698), dated 21 April 1544. "Testor hoc tibi, nullo me huius aetatis scripto hactenus ita fuisse delectatum." For background on this commentary, see Hans Volz, "Beiträge zu Melanchthons und Calvins Auslegungen des Propheten Daniel," ZKG 67 (1955/6):93-118.

114. This spilled over into their correspondence. See, for example, Melanchthon's letter to Calvin on 12 July 1543 (MBW 3273; CO 11:594), where Melanchthon wrote:

". . . [commende]s filio Dei, quem Daniel inquit [in ex]tremo tempore dissipaturum ecclesiae [devast]atorem esse."

115. CO 10:402-6, dated 22 October 1539, addressed to Simon Grynaeus. Calvin's comments could possibly also refer to Melanchthon's *Dispositio* on Romans (CR 15:443—92) from 1530. For one of the only treatments of Melanchthon's influence on Calvin, see Richard Muller, "'Scimus enim quod les spiritualis est': Melanchthon and Calvin on the Interpretation of Romans 7:14-23," in *Melanchthon and the Commentary,* ed. M. Patrick Graham and Timothy J. Wengert (Sheffield, Sheffield Academic Press, 1997).

116. MBW 3387 (CR 5:243), dated 7 December 1543.

Deszo Buzogany (essay date 1999)

SOURCE: Buzogany, Deszo. "Melanchthon As Humanist and Reformer." In *Melanchthon in Europe: His Work and Influence beyond Wittenberg,* edited by Karin Maag, pp. 87-101. Grand Rapids, Mich.: Baker Books, 1999.

[In the essay below, Buzogany bridges the gap between the theological and philosophical positions taken by Melanchthon.]

Melanchthon is usually considered as both a humanist and a reformer. Many of the books and studies written about him present him as a theologian. It is also worthwhile studying the humanist intellectual components of his personality, since, after all, a great proportion of his works are ones which present him as a deep thinking, thorough intellectual, writing with sublime eloquence.

Both theological debates and the newly-organized church profited a great deal from his humanism; and one should mention in this regard the service he rendered in composing and compiling the confessions. Thus, everything that shapes Melanchthon's theological work with class, its intellectual nature and proper sublimation to the salvation doctrines, was taken from the so-called "pagan arts." He brought into the domain of the church and the faith the useful and usable parts of the enormous amount of classical knowledge and put them in the service of God's Word, while at the same time subordinating them to the Word.

Melanchthon the theologian is also always present in his works written on the topic of the seven liberal arts. To those who know him only through his theological works, his humanism seems exaggerated, and we are almost shocked by the fact that he often refers to these classical authors, expounding these disciplines, or writing eulogies about them. This was self-evident in that age, when scientific work meant quoting the traditions of the classics. The age was that of late humanism. But Melanchthon went further than praising and quoting the classics. He always checked carefully and explored the possibility of building these originally pagan disciplines into the values and education of the Protestant church. In Melanchthon's view they provide a useful service in the better understanding and clearer transmission of God's Word.

"Ut rosa adflorem, flos fructum, fructus odorem, sic schola dat morem, mos sensum, sensus honorem." (As the rose produces flowers, the flowers bear fruits, and the fruits give off a pleasant smell, this is how the school produces virtue, virtue leads to reason, and reason produces appreciation.) This handwritten note dated from the beginning of the 17th century, found on one of the pages of Melanchthon's *Grammar* brought by some traveling student to Transylvania, fits perfectly with his personality, because after all, he was a thorough educator and served education with his whole life, both within and outside the school. His textbooks played a crucial role in the development of Transylvanian Protestantism, and later, Reformed education in the 16th century. Hundreds of these textbooks are still found in several libraries in Transylvania.

The humanist Melanchthon knew that the disciplines of the trivium, the first section of the seven liberal arts, could only help the reviving Church, if they were used in the service of God's Word. As a result of this rule, the three disciplines of the trivium were integrated in the following way: Grammar gives us the meaning of the original text of Holy Scripture, Dialectic serves the understanding of the text and the consistency of the sermon's content, while Rhetoric gives us God's Word in a way that makes it vivid and effective.

But for the moment let us take a look at Dialectic alone as clear evidence of the humanist and reformer Melanchthon's sublime knowledge. But before we begin a detailed analysis, let us describe briefly the seven liberal arts, to which this discipline belongs.

I always ask my students at the Reformed Theological Seminary in Kolozsvár this trick question: Can you tell me what are the seven liberal arts? My students usually enumerate several art-type activities, like poetry, painting, film etc., which have something to do with the arts of today. So, what are the seven liberal arts?

In higher education in the middle ages, a student yearning for knowledge had to learn quickly this small verse, which would introduce him to the world of the arts (we call them disciplines today): "Gram[matica] loquitur, Dia[lectica] vera docet, Rhet / orica] verba colorat, Mus[ica] canit, Ar[itmetica] numerat, Ge[ographia] ponderat, Ast[rologia] colit astra." (Grammar speaks, dialectics teaches facts, rhetoric colors speech, music sings, arithmetic counts, geography measures, and astrology studies the stars). In the early middle ages the sciences were separated into two groups. Depending on the number and character of the disciplines, they called them "verbal arts" (trivium: grammar, dialectics, rhetoric), and mathematical sciences (quadrivium: arithmetic, music, geometry and astronomy). Obviously the Latin names of these sciences refer to the number of the disciplines in each group. But let us now examine the dialectics of Melanchthon which belongs to the first group, the trivium.

I. The Praise of Dialectics

Melanchthon wrote two essays about dialectics. We do not know when the first, **De Dialectica,** was written. He probably composed it in the earlier period of his life. After a general introduction, he emphasizes the significance of this discipline:

> Among all the arts of humanism, dialectics is the most important, not only because of its usefulness for studying other arts, but also for making judgments in court-trials and in many other matters we deal with in life. Nothing can be taught systematically or learned perfectly without dialectics, which creates methods for every case, shows the origin, development and the outcome of things. It reveals and searches out confused and ambiguous things, it enumerates and arranges sections, and if something is to be proved, it indicates the sources of the arguments.[1]

Dialectics helps us to define the correct relationship between things and helps us to separate disparate elements. Complicated contradictions cannot be solved even by the most intelligent person without this science. "That is why Plato says the following: the only way to teach and learn is transferred by Dialectic, which was given to mankind by the immortal gods, for the useful purpose of teaching each other, and learning from one another everything which is necessary during life."[2] Religion, justice, law and many other useful things must be taught to the people. These subjects, however, remain confusing and incomprehensible, unless they are correctly lined up (put in a correct relationship to each other), arranged and united by dialectics. Therefore, this science provides light to every other discipline because it clarifies obscure and unfamiliar things, with that "godly flame, which was brought to the people by Prometheus, as Plato said."[3] "Thus, the art of dialectics is like the *Hermes Trismegistos,*[4] which is the interpreter of the people and gods in the temples, public affairs, schools, the public forum, and the Senate."[5] Plato, in his works, always took the opportunity to encourage the sophists of his age to study this discipline, because, if they ignored it, the youth of future generations would learn only useless things.

Melanchthon did not like those who approached the higher sciences without systematic dialectical examination, and "stray as though they were wandering in the night on *terra incognita.*"[6] Theologians and jurists were those who brought dialectics from the background to the forefront (*ex umbra in aciem*), because they could not have defended themselves without this tool (*suas personas sine hoc instrumentum tueri possunt*).

> Paul taught the handling of the Word of God correctly. How can somebody do this, who does not know the correct method of distinguishing and systematizing things? What can be more monstrous for the doctrines of the Church than mixing and muddling heterogeneous things such as the doctrine of Law and Gospel, the spiritual and the civil duties, the sacraments and the sacrifices? Without a frequent and well timed practice of dialectics no one can study these things with sufficient safety.[7]

Melanchthon was concerned about the Church and theological science because of the frequent lack of system and regularity. Without method only empty stories can be told, not the clear and perfect doctrine (*perfecta doctrina*). At the end of his speech he again encouraged the youth to study dialectics actively and with persistence, approaching it as the instrument of every other higher science.

The date of his second study is known: he wrote it in 1528 for the graduation of Iacobus Milichius, who obtained the degree of Master of Arts in that year. "Since the customs of this school are quite familiar to you, I think, it is no longer necessary for me to prove with large explanations why I step up here to speak," he began. Later he stated that he was not led by his own purposes in making this speech, but by the instructions of previous wise men who introduced this custom. He felt that he was bound to explain the correct way and methods of studying, correcting at the same time an earlier dangerous mistake which made the studying process impossible because of its harmful method. "While granting Masters' degrees to these young men whose studies we know, we warn most of the students not to practice science without method and order."[8] In the end he followed a similar path to his first speech, only with new ideas and from new standpoints. "How can anyone judge complicated contradictions, who doesn't study deeply the useful sciences, but only tastes them briefly and hastily, like dogs drinking from the banks of the Nile?"[9] Order and method in study are what help all of us to get complete knowledge from our favorite science. Melanchthon emphasized frequently that the correct method of studying provides an important role in this information-gathering process, supported with a maxim taken from the work *Oeconomicus* by Xenophon: If something lacks order, it is not worthy of respect, and is useless.

Melanchthon concentrated his attention on pseudo-thinkers, who studied theology and justice without first mastering dialectics. They were like the man mentioned by Cicero, who tried to lift himself up by his own hair. "Plato," says Melanchthon, "in his work, *The Republic*, calls those who imagine that they get satisfaction from the other arts without dialectics illegitimate philosophers; and since illegitimate children have no right to inheritance, so much more should all who first break into the field of other disciplines without mastering this art, be forbidden, by some kind of praetorian decree, from studying all other sciences."[10] Continuing his analysis he also said that dialectics was useless if studied briefly by simply learning some of this art's rules. We need to master it precisely, and achieve some practice in it. And this practice is as important as the knowledge of a science's principles. "As nobody can be either a painter just by watching Dürer paint, or a musician just by seeing Adolph play on the strings, so nobody should believe that he is going to be a master in dialectics without composing something, or disputing, in a word who has no practice in this art."[11] Melanchthon gathered an endless scientific supply of classical writings which praise everything from the fables of Aesop through the wisdom of philosophers, jurists, or the brave and outstanding medical practitioners.

Finally Melanchthon reached the point where dialectics, as a science, could be used in the Church, expounding that, although the essence and content of the holy science was not rooted in philosophy, nevertheless the church sermon, as the external instrument of handling the Word, took its form and frame from dialectics and other arts, so that preaching could only be structured with their help. And because, from his point of view, the theologian needed to be the most informed and skilled in everything, and had to know everything in the best possible way, it was not proper for him to neglect studying these arts. For instance, when he was to speak clearly and intelligibly about the nature of man, comparing it to the parts of the human body, he needed to have knowledge of dissertations written on this subject.

> How much light can be shed on the holy sciences by somebody who puts the philosophical doctrine about the virtues next to the holy sciences, and does not show what does and does not link the two? I think personally that it is essential to define accurately the character of both sciences [theology and philosophy], to delimit their differences clearly, and to indicate precisely their bounds, in order to stop philosophy from trespassing onto the territory of Christian doctrines, as the jurists would say. If our ancestors had done this, the infection of Church doctrines would not have lasted until now.[12]

A theologian also needs to know history, and the movement of stars and celestial bodies, said Melanchthon, without further explanation. A speech should end with stimulation, illustrating how important the first step of the trivium is to progressing in the fields of the other sciences: "Starting well is to be already half-done, therefore you can also make progress in the higher sci-

ences [the *quadrivium*, e.g. theology] if you start studying it correctly, namely, if you take along with you for the mastering of the other arts the knowledge of the sciences I am speaking about [the *trivium*]. This warning is emphasized at least as well by me as by your other teachers."[13]

II. A TEXTBOOK ABOUT DIALECTICS

Given our limitations of space and time we cannot afford to present the ***Dialectics*** of Melanchthon in its entirety, so we will give you only a description of some specific parts of it.

Following the first edition of his ***Rhetoric*** Melanchthon immediately started to write his ***Dialectics.*** Analyzing the text of various editions, one can separate it into three stages, that of 1520, 1528 and 1547.

The first edition was published in 1520 in Leipzig under the title ***Compendiaria dialectices ratio.*** Melanchthon's name is not on the title page, but it appears at the end of the dedication letter addressed to Johannes Schwertfegerus, who taught law in Wittenberg, and died on May 10, 1524. Luther recommended Iustus Ionas to replace him. In the dedication Melanchthon referred to his ***Rhetoric*** published a year earlier, emphasizing the fact that it could not be treated exhaustively without knowing the dialectics. If dialectics were absent, the speakers could say nothing certain or acceptable. As for the reason for writing the ***Dialectics,*** he said that the students' persistent demand forced him to write it, because, as he stated, most teachers of the time neglected this science. "Therefore, taking time away from my other studies, I wrote out the method of discussing in the shortest way I could."[14] This version appeared in 1521 in three places (Basle, Leipzig, The Hague), in 1522 in two places (Basle, Paris), and also in 1523 in three places (Strasbourg, Basle, Augsburg). But other editions are known as well.[15] On June 26, 1529, Melanchthon wrote about his second version to Camerarius, stating that he had emended his ***Dialectics*** shortly before, rewriting and completing the last two chapters.[16] It seems that he started correcting the first version already in 1527, since Brettschneider seems to have known in a letter dated July 2, 1527 that Melanchthon had written that he had edited it and made it more complete. But there is no point in looking for that letter in that year because of some typographical mistake which caused a 6 to turn into a 7. Thus Melanchthon actually wrote the letter to Ioachim Camerarius in 1526 and mentioned correcting the ***Dialectics*** and giving the corrected version to his students, having decided to take them through the whole encyclopedia.[17] It seems that he had already finished correcting the book by June 1529, since in his letter dated June 10 he informed Fridericus Myconius that it was a serious test of strength revising the ***Dialectics,*** which now, in his words, would appear in a much better form.[18] The work thus enriched in content was published that very year *(Dialectices Phil[ippi] Mel[anchthonis] libri quatuor ab auctore ipse de integro in lucem conscripti ac editi. Item rhetorices praeceptiunculae doctissimae),* and later was published seven more times.[19] This version was the one which Paulus Eberus, one of Melanchthon's disciples, added to and published in 1544 in Wittenberg entitled: *Dialecticae praeceptiones collectae a Philippo Melanthone,* indicating in its introduction that it could hardly please the author, who would surely have rewritten it himself if he had had the time.

Melanchthon's *Dialectics* gained its final form in 1547, printed in the middle of the year under the title of *Erotemata dialectices, continentia fere integram artem, ita scripta, ut juventuti utiliter proponi possint. Edita a Philippo Melanthone. Viteb[ergae], 1547.* The book was highly successful, inasmuch as on October 18, 1547 Melanchthon wrote to his pastor, "The dialectics have been sold in 3000 copies. Now they are reprinting it, and it needs some correction."[20] As for pastor Casparus Aquila,[21] he wrote on November 10 of the same year that he could not send the *Dialectics* because he was out of town during its printing, and when he came back every single copy had been sold. "Therefore, there will soon be another edition, containing many corrections, since some parts of the material need more careful consideration. But I think, if God helps us, I can send you a copy of this edition within one month."[22]

We can find out about some of Melanchthon's rewriting from the letter he sent to Joannes Aurifaber.[23] He made essential and structural changes only in the chapter "De loco causarum," although he was not totally satisfied with the corrections. He was about to go to Leipzig, where he intended to discuss the question with Aurbachius. The small stylistic corrections did not affect the content of the other part of the book.[24] The corrected version was rapidly printed, because he wrote at the beginning of December to Hieronimus Baumgartner: "I send you a copy of the *Dialectics,* not as if I wanted you to read some trifles like this, but only because momentarily I have no other lecture to send you."[25] He also sent a copy of the newly-published book to Vitus Theodor's son in the middle of December.[26] This edition was very successful, since it was totally sold out in only two months. This is proved by Melanchthon's letter written to Mattheus Collinus at the academy of Prague, where he already spoke about the third edition of the book.[27] The *Dialectics* were finally published in more than ten editions.

III. Dedication

Melanchthon dedicated the *Dialectics* to Joachim Camerarius's son John, out of respect for his father. He told the young man that this science helped people to distinguish clearly the reasons and logical process of a text used for persuasion, steering audiences away from falseness by revealing the lies. Following the general introduction he explored more practical domains, pointing to the character of the dialectics to be used in the Church. First of all he wished to convince his colleagues and students not to speak against this use of the science of dialectics, "I encourage them, but also ask them for the sake of God's glory and the Church's salvation not to neglect Dialectics, and not to acclaim the silly speeches of people who revile this science and declare it useless for the Church."[28] He was convinced that this science became abominable and detested in the age when it was not taught as an art, but as an obscure shadow, or an incomprehensible and unexplainable labyrinth of rules, unfamiliar even to scholars. "But I," said Melanchthon, "teach the real, not the compromised, but the original Dialectics as taken partly from Aristotle, and partly from some of his very clever interpreters, like Alexander Aphrodiensis or Boetius. And I think it is very useful not only in the public forum and the court of justice, or in philosophy, but also in the Church."[29] He referred to the use of this discipline in the Church when he said that even if God's will, law, sin, the gospel and many other important things were evident from the holy books given by God, without dialectics one could hardly speak about them coherently and with structure. Besides, he saw the use of the science not only in clarifying a doctrine's meaning, but in providing understanding for the Church.[30] Therefore a discipline like this ought not to be used in the service of arguing, chattering or vanity, but had to be used for a high standard, clarity, science, and the love of truth. He was convinced that this way of intelligent speaking and teaching of the truth was given by God as a gift, and was extremely necessary in the explanation of the holy doctrines, and in the search for truth in other domains.[31] Again he defended Aristotle against those who attacked his work and thought it useless, recommending to his students to read Aristotle's works in Greek. He thought it useful for the students to reinforce the teachings of this great Greek thinker with the handbooks of Joannes Caesarius and Iodocius Willicchus, saying, "I also made every effort in this edition to include the whole art, therefore I think this discipline very useful for the youth to study. I also attached a bibliography to indicate the sources of my teachings."[32]

The texts of the following sections can be found in the book published in 1580, in Leipzig. It starts with a short δεφινιτιον of dialectics, "Dialectics is the art or the way of correct, exact and clear teaching, correct definition and division, the rebinding of wrong connections or disproving of errors.[33]

The word *dialectics* comes from the Greek word *dialegomai,* which means to speak with somebody while exchanging opinions. As a definition this is obviously a collage of the meanings of the Latin expressions *(disputo, dissero)*. This definition is expanded upon in the subtitle, as though in answer to the question, what does dialectics deal with? Melanchthon's answer is "with every topic and question which can be taught to people, like arithmetic, which deals with things concerning counting."[34] Man as a rational being was endowed by God with the notion of numbers, to be able to differentiate things without mixing them and without everything becoming a chaotic mixture *(in unum chaos miscenda)*. Therefore it is necessary to know that God is one, and the creature is one, substance is one and essence is one, while God and his enemy Satan are two different things. "Therefore dialectics does not create new things, it only teaches us the method and form of teaching" *("non nasci res in Dialectica, sed modum et formam docendi tradi in Dialectica")*. Melanchthon finished his work by praising the disciple with the maxim of Petrus Hispanus, a definition which Melanchthon fully supported,

> Dialectics is the art of arts, the science of sciences, which gives the way to the origin of every method. This is foolish praise, but you need to understand, dialectics is the art of arts, which is better not in its dignity, but in its usefulness to serve every art and discipline. . . . Finally says [Petrus Hispanus] it shows the way to the origin of every method, which means that it creates method, or teaches every discipline. . . . If some orator wants to speak about repentance, than he has to provide the definitions, the parts, the reasons, the effects.[35]

Melanchthon saw the difference between rhetoric and dialectics in the fact that dialectics presents the summary of things but rhetoric expounds them widely, and decorates them with new ideas. He tried to emphasize the importance of studying this discipline partly by means of two quotations taken from Plato and partly with the words of Paul concerning the selection of a bishop. Paul says concerning the selection of a bishop that he must be suitable as a teacher (idoneum ad docendum), "and he similarly warns the doctors to handle correctly the word of God, or as he says *orthotomein*, which surely means dialectics because it is the correct way of teaching and dividing."[36] Firstly, Melanchthon thought it necessary to be careful and not let different things get mixed. We must make a difference between the Law and the Gospel, the commandments and the promises, the outside order, or the common truth, and the inside order or the truth of the heart. "These show clearly enough that creating correct differentiations and definitions is very necessary, and this is done by dialectics. But this discipline must be taught with restraint, and the youth must get used to the simple explanation of truth, not through the rules of arguing or using finger-pointing and intrigue."[37]

We have examined how dialectics helps us to organize questions, and how it illuminates the world of notions.

The following is a perfect example of how Melanchthon harmonized the two disciplines. God, says Melanchthon's definition, is a formless substance, intelligent, almighty, wise and good, true, gracious, holy, fully independent, the final cause of all nature, order, and the good of nature. He demands that humanity behave according to his will, and punishes those who work against him. It is a definition which can also be made by people outside the church;[38] but in the church the following addition is necessary because we need to speak about God as He revealed himself in evident testimonies. Therefore we need to complete the definition with the methodical description of God's person, as follows: the eternal Father, whose son is his own image, and Son, who carries the image of his father, and Holy Spirit in whom God reveals himself, created the heaven and earth and everything in them, and gathers the eternal Church from the human race, and revealed his will in evident testimonies, as through the resurrection of the dead.[39]

From the point of view of the will another category comes to light, faith as knowledge.

> Faith is knowledge, Melanchthon again formulated, and through it we accept every teaching given by God to the Church with solid conviction including the promise of forgiveness, which if we accept it, gives us absolution for our sins. This promise also gives us trust in the Son of God, in whom, if we rest, we will reach high up to God, being sure that he will accept us and hear us; and we pray to him.[40]

On this level Melanchthon's systematic argumentation received an unusual impulse regarding Reformed doctrines. "Hope," he continued, "is the sure expectation of eternal life given by the Son of God, and awaiting the divine help and assistance during misfortunes. Faith and hope differ, because faith means also knowledge and above all also trust. . . . But hope is the expectation of the future salvation."[41] Love means obedience to God's commandments through true faith and joy. The apostle John defines love in his first epistle: love for God means submitting to his orders, "We understand this definition better when our heart is set on fire with a fervent love for God."[42] Fear of God, called servile fear, is the protector of order and skill, which leads us to fear God's anger, but when combined with faith it becomes a virtue like fear of parents. Patience is a virtue which shows up in obedience to God in hard times and teaches us to become perfect, and not to act against God's will when crushed by pain.[43] That was the way in which Melanchthon created a step by step science in God's service and for Reformation's goals.

I would like to end this contribution with a footnote which I think is appropriate at this point. On August 26, 1636 an unknown admirer of Melanchthon noted in one of his books in Debrecen, "*Frustra doctores sine me colluere sorores*" that is, "without this discipline no other science can really be practiced."

Notes

1. ". . . omnium artium humanarum Dialecticam maxime necessariam esse, non solum ad artes alias tractandas, sed etiam ad controversias forenses, et pleraque alia negotia in vita iudicanda. Nihil enim; ordine doceri, nihil perfecte disci potest, nisi adhibita Dialectica, quae in unaquaque causa methodum informat, ostendit initia, progressiones, et exitus rerum . . . Confusa et ambigua retexit et partitur, membra enumerat ac disponit, indicat argumentorum fontes, si quid est probandum." [Philip Melancthon. *Corpus Reformatorum. Philippi Melanchthonis opera quae supersunt omnia.* Edited by Karl Bretschneider and Heinrich Bindsell. 28 vols. Halle: A Schwetschke and sons, 1834-60. Hereafter referred to as] CR 10. 908-9.

2. "Itaque Plato gravissime dixit, unam hanc docendi ac discendi viam, quae in Dialectica traditur, a Deis immortalibus donatam esse generi humano, propter hanc summam utilitatem, ut docere homines inter se ac discere possent, quod in omni vita maxime necessarium est." CR 10. 909.

3. ". . . omnibus artibus lumen adfert [scil. dialectica—BD], sicut Plato inquit, a Prometheo aliquo divinitus ad homines perlatam esse, ἄμα φανοτάτῳ τινὶ πυρὶ." CR 10. 909.

4. The expression: κοινὸς ἑρμῆς used by Melanchthon was taken from Aristotle and Menandros, who use it with the following everyday meaning: the revealed thing must be shared with those present. Obviously Melanchthon wants to refer here to the sharing of spiritual things.

5. "Est igitur Dialectica veluti κοινὸς ἑρμῆς interpres Deorum atque hominum, in templis, in foro, in scholis, in iudiciis, in Senatu." CR 10. 909.

6. "Quo magis reprehendi sunt hoc tempore, qui sine Dialectica properant ad superiores artes, in quibus quoniam sine Dialectica methodum reperire nullam possunt, ita errabunt, ut si in ignotissimis regionibus nocte iter facerent." CR 10. 909.

7. "Paulus praecepit verbum Dei ὀρθοτομεῖν. Id quomodo faciet, qui nullam sciet apte distinguendi et partiendi racionem? Quid erit monstrosius, doctrina religionis, si diversi loci miscebuntur, et confundentur, quales sunt, doctrina legis et Evangelii, vitae spiritualis officia, et vitae civilis officia, sacramenta et sacrificia? Neque quisquam satis cautus erit in talibus locis, nisi multum ac diu exercitatus in Dialectica." CR 10. 909-10. Melanchthon refers here to the second letter of Paul to Timothy (2 Tim 2:15).

8. "Cum scholae consuetudo vobis nota sit, non arbitrabar mihi opus esse longa defensione, cur huc ad dicendum accesserim. . . . Nos itaque dum hoc tempore horum adolescentium, quibus Magisterii titulum concedemus, studia cognoscimus, animadvertimus magnam iuventutis partem, sine ratione atque ordine in literis versari." CR 11. 159-60.

9. "Quid autem iudicabit de obscurissimis controversiis is, qui non penitus introspexit bonas artes, sed obiter degustavit eas fugiens, velut canes e Nilo bibunt?" CR 11. 160.

10. "Plato in Repub. spurios Philosophos adpellat eos, qui sine Dialectica, satisfacere se aliis artibus existimabant, quare sicut spuriis non licet haereditatem petere, ita procul ab omnium literarum tractatione praetorio aliquo edicto submoveri debebant illi, qui ante irrumpunt in alias disciplinas, quam hanc artem perceperint." CR 11. 161.

11. "Sicut non statim pictor est qui Durerum pingentem vidit, nec cytharoedus, qui vidit Adolphum eruditissime tangentem fides: ita non putet se Dialecticam callere is, qui nihil scripsit, non disputavit, denique qui artem non exercuit." CR 11. 161.

12. "Quantum lucis adferet sacris literis, qui Philosophorum doctrinam de moribus cum illis conferet et ostendet, quae consentiant, quae non consentiant? Ego vero etiam necessarium esse iudico, ostendere utrunque doctrinae genus et intervalla certa regione describere, et fines eorum regere, ut jureconsulti loquuntur, ne possit iterum in Christianae doctrinae possessionem Philosophia irrumpere. Quod si fecissent veteres, non usque adeo contaminata esset ante haec tempora doctrina ecclesiastica." CR 11. 162.

13. "Quod si dimidium facti qui bene coepit habet, profecto et vos in superioribus disciplinis plus promovebitis, si recte coeperitis, hoc est, si earum literarum, de quibus dico, scientiam ad eas attuleritis. Haec quamquam sedulo praeceptores vestri moment, tamen et ego . . ." CR 11. 163.

14. "Neque enim rhetorica citra dialecticorum usum commode tractari absolvique possunt [. . .] Haec ut copiose tractarem, studiosi quidam a me contenderunt, quod eo sint loco nostris temporibus, ut et magna professorum pars artis usum ignoret. Suffuratus igitur horas aliquot studiis mei, disserendi rationem descripsi, idque quam potui brevissime." CR 1. 153-54. Nr. 67. It is worth comparing it with the letter addressed to Bernardus Maurus, in which he gives a fuller account of the relation between rhetoric and dialectics. CR 1. 62-66. Nr. 32.

15. CR 1. 509.

16. "Dialectica mitto Michaeli, quae nuper recognovi, et posteriores duos libellos retexui, et ita tractavi, ut totam artem complexum me esse putem." CR 1. 1084. Nr. 624. Preceding this, dated on July 15 we read that he restarted his lectures on dialectics at the request of new students, and that he wanted to complete it with Aristotle's *Organon*. CR 1. 1081. Nr. 622.

17. "Ego meam διαλεκτικὴ perpolio. Nunc enim pueris meis trado, quos per universam ἐγκυκλοπαίδεαν χειραγωγεῖν statui." CR 1. 803. For Brettschneider's reference see CR 13. 507-8.

18. In this period he worked at a feverish pace, and according to one of Luther's letters addressed to Iustus Ionas, even his health was at stake because of his exhausting public work. ("Philippus sese macerat cura rei ecclesiasticae et rei publicae usque ad periculum valetudinis." CR 1. 1074.)

19. Wittenberg, 1531; Paris, 1532; Wittenberg, 1533, in the same year in the same location again; Wittenberg 1536; Leipzig, 1536 and Strasbourg 1542. CR 13. 509.

20. "Vendita sunt tria millia exemplorum Dialectices. Nunc recuditur, et emendatione indiget." CR 6. 705.

21. Aquila was born August 7, 1488 in Augsburg, studied in Italy and Switzerland, in 1516 was elected pastor of Gengen, and from there he went to Wittenberg in 1520. His posts were: 1522 Sickingen, 1523 Eisenach, 1527 Saalfeld where he was elected bishop in 1528. He appears in 1548 in Schmalkalden as an exile and from there returned to Saalfeld in 1552. He died in 1560. CR 10. 334.

22. "Dialecticos libellos ideo non misi, quia cum ederentur, ego aberam in iugis Herciniis, et me reverso exemplaria omnia vendita erant. Mox igitur instituta est secunda editio, in qua multa erunt emendatiora; habui enim de quibusdam materiis δευτ έρας φροντίδας. Mittam igitur eius editionis exempla intra mensem Deo volente." CR 6. 722.

23. Aurifaber was born in 1517 in Bratislava. His original name was Goldschmid. He was Melanchthon's disciple, and later his friend. He began teaching as a lector in the University of Wittenberg. On June 16, 1550 he was awarded a doctorate and later was invited to teach theology at the Rostock Academy, thanks to the recommendation of Melanchthon. Aurifaber was in Regensburg already in 1554, where he also taught theology and led the Consistorium. In 1567 he returned to Bratislava, as the pastor of St. Elisabeth church and the inspector in charge of the supervision of church and schools. He also died there in 1568. CR 10. 336.

24. "In dialecticis περ ὶ ϛυνεκτικοῦ, in loco causarum a me erratum est. Mutavi eum locum etsi ne nunc quidem mihi aut tibi satisfactum est. Sed iam eo Lipsiam, cum Aurbachio ea de re disputaturus. In alliis partibus libelli, etsi quaedam emendavi, tamen res non sunt mutatae." CR 6. 725-26.

25. Baumgartner was a senator of Nürnberg, born there on March 9 to a wealthy noble family. He studied in his native town of Eittenberg, where he became acquainted with both Luther and Melanchthon. He continued as senator until his death in 1565. CR 10. 337. The fragment of the letter to him states: "Mitto tibi exemplum Dialectices, non quod has nugas a te legi velim, sed quia nunc alia iucundiora, quae mitterem, non habebam." CR 6. 749.

26. Vitus Theodor (formerly Dietrich) was a beloved disciple and friend of both Luther and Melanchthon. This is evidenced by the fact that Melanchthon wrote him 235 letters between 1530 and 1549. He became a pastor in Nüremberg, where he died on March 26, 1549. CR 10. 415. For the letter referring to the sending of the dialectics look at CR 6. 750.

27. "Dialecticam mitto, qualis nunc tertio edita est." CR 6. 816.

28. "Hos et adhortor, et propter gloriam Dei ac propter Ecclesiae salutem obtestor, ne Dialecticam negligant, nec applaudant insulsis sermonibus eorum, qui vituperant eam, et Ecclesiae inutilem esse clamitant" CR 6. 655.

29. "Ego veram, incorruptam, nativam Dialecticam, qualem et ab Aristotele, et aliquot eius non insulsis interpretibus, ut ab Alexandro Aphrodisiensi et Boetio accepimus, praedico. Hanc affirmo non modo in foro et in iudiciis, aut in philosophia, sed etiam in Ecclesia valde utilem esse." CR 6. 655.

30. "Imo Dialectica opus est, non solum ut doctrina lucem habeat, sed etiam ut sit concordiae vinculum." CR 6. 655.

31. . . . veram docendi et ratiocinandi viam sciamus Dei donum esse, et in exponenda doctrina coelesti et inquisitione veritatis in aliis rebus necessariam." CR 6. 656.

32. "Ego quoque in hac editione propemodum integram artem complexus sum, et hanc rationem tradendae artis utilem fore studiis iuventutis exsistimo. Et τεχνολογικὰ quaedam inserui, quae fontes praeceptorum ostendunt." CR 6. 657.

33. *Erotemata Dialectices, continentiae fere integram artes, ita scripta, ut iuventuti utiliter proponi possint, Edita a Philippo Melanch[tone].* Lipsiae. (In fine: Lipsiae, imprimebat Ioannes Steinmann Anno M.D.LXXX.) "Dialectica est ars seu via, recte, ordine, et perspicue docendi, quod fit recte definiendo, dividendo, argumenta vera connectendo, et male cohaerentia seu falsa retexendo et refutando." CR 13. 513.

34. "Circa omnes materias seu quaestiones, de quibus docendi sunt homines, sicut Arithmetica versatur circa omnes res numerandas." CR 13. 514. In some of the following explanatory sentences he makes a detailed presentation of the relationship between the two disciplines.

35. "Dialectica est ars artium, scientia scientiarum, ad omnium methodorum principia viam habens. Laudatio videtur ridicula, sed sic intelligatur: Dialectica est ars artium, id est non dignitate antecedens, sed usu serviens omnibus artibus et scientiis. . . . Deinde inquit, ad omnium methodorum principia viam habens, id est, in omnibus materiis methodos, hoc est, viam docendi instituens . . . Si concionatori dicendum erit de poenitentia, exponet et ipse definitiones, partes, causas, effectus." CR 13. 515.

36. CR 13. 517. Melanchthon combines here several quotations from the Bible. One is 1 Tim 3: 2, "oportet ergo episcopum . . . doctorem [esse]," the other Tit 1:9, "potens sit [scil. episcopus] et exhortari in doctrina sana et eos qui contradicunt arguere," and 2 Tim 2:15, "-recte tractandum [according to Melanchthon: secare] verbum veritatis [according to Melanchthon: verbum Dei]." The last one is worth quoting in Greek too, because it contains the expression used by Melanchthon:, "*orthomounta [orthotomein] ton logon* τϛζ αλτηειαϛζ."

37. "Hic satis apparet, valde necessariam esse diligentiam recte dividendi et definiendi, quae sunt opera Dialectices. Sed sobrie tradatur ars, et assuefiat adolescentia ad simplicem veritatis explicationem, non ad studium cavillandi, aut ad sycophanticam. Hactenus προλεγόμενα εψδὶε'α recitata sunt. Nunc, Deo iuvante, artem ipsam inchoabimus." CR 13. 517.

38. "Hanc descriptionem mentes humanae, etiam extra Ecclesiam, et sine singulari revolutione, discunt ex demonstrationibus, et membra praecipua sunt in hac tabella." CR 13. 530.

39. "Ideo in Ecclesia ad priora membra diserte adduntur personarum nomina: . . . et pater aeternus, qui genuit filium imaginem suam, et filius, qui est imago patris, et Spiritus Sanctus sicut patefecit se divinitas, qui condidit coelum et terram, et caetereas naturas in eis, et in genere humano sibi colligit aeternam Ecclesiam, et suam voluntatem illustribus testimoniis, ut resuscitatione mortuorum, declaravit." CR 13 530-31.

40. "Fides est noticia, qua firmo assensu amplectimur totam doctrinam a Deo traditam Ecclesiae, et is hac etiam promissionem reconciliationis, quam apprehendentes accipimus remissionem peccatorum fiducia filii Dei, et hac fiducia acquiescentes in filio Dei, accedimus ad Deum, et nos recipi et exaudiri statuimus, et eum invocamus." CR 13 538-39.

41. "Spes est expectatio vitae aeternae propter filium Dei certa, et expectatio auxilii et mitigationis calamitatum in hac vita, iuxta consilium Dei. Differunt fides et spes, quia fides et noticiam significat, et deinde fiduciam . . . Spes autem est expectatio futurae liberationis." CR 13 539.

42. "Sed si arderent corda nostra magno incendio amoris erga Deum, haec definitio magis intelligi posset." CR 13 539.

43. Timor Dei, qui vocatur servilis, et est custos disciplinae, est habitus, qui inclinat ut revera expavescamus agnitione irae Dei et poenarum. [. . .] Tolerantia est virtus obediens Deo in aerumnis, quas docet perferendas esse, ita, ne fracti dolore faciamus contra mandata Dei. . . ." CR 13 539.

John R. Schneider (essay date 1999)

SOURCE: Schneider, John R. "Melanchthon's Rhetoric As a Context for Understanding His Theology." In *Melanchthon in Europe: His Work and Influence beyond Wittenberg,* edited by Karin Maag, pp. 141-59. Grand Rapids, Mich.: Baker Books, 1999.

[In this essay, Schneider emphasizes the integration of Melanchthon's humanistic background with this theology, particularly through his study of rhetoric.]

I. THE UNKNOWN MELANCHTHON

It is well enough known that Philip Melanchthon's standing as a teacher of Protestant doctrine was controversial during most of his lifetime, and that it has remained so in the centuries since his death. As Robert Stupperich wrote in his book, *Der unbekannte Melanchthon,* it is a bitter irony that the "most peaceable man of his age" somehow became "the most embattled."[1] So heavily did the endless controversies weigh upon Melanchthon that, by the end, he really did long to die, so that he might be set free from "the furies of theologians."[2] Afterwards, however, he was not set free—not in name and reputation, anyway. Ferocious battles between "Philippists" and "Gnesio-Lutherans" divided the movement for the next three generations.[3] In later times, historians waged intense debates over the interpretation of his doctrines and over the final legacy of his theology as a whole.

In his book, *Melanchthon: Alien or Ally?*, Franz Hildebrandt observed that what has made Melanchthon so controversial is the great extent to which he strove to integrate classical humanism into Protestantism.[4] For it seems that the many controversies that burned all around him in his lifetime—on free will and predestination, on justification, the eucharist and the adiaphora, among others—were, at bottom, also (and perhaps even more deeply) about the nexus of "faith and reason" underlying his approach to those doctrines. Indeed, the debates that have raged among scholars of Melanchthon have been mainly over that delicate seam which he wished to sew into the whole fabric of his theology. In that light, the impassioned, perennial question of Hildebrandt's title is as much a comment on the nature of Protestantism as it is on Melanchthon.

Indeed, none of the other major framers of Protestant teaching was so thoroughly immersed in Greek and Latin letters as Melanchthon was. Nor was any so naturally disposed to love them as gifts from God, or so masterly in cultivating them, as he was. To put it in perspective, as E. Gordon Rupp suggested, in Melanchthon we get some inkling of what might have happened had Erasmus himself become an evangelical.[5] But to invert the hypothesis, had Melanchthon remained Catholic, things would have been much easier for him. He might well have assumed one of those prestigious university chairs they offered him, and become known primarily as the successor to Erasmus as the foremost scholar of Europe. Historians would no doubt classify him, too, as one of those esteemed Catholic "reformers." However, as it happened, his unexpected destiny as midwife to the birth of Luther's cause put him in an almost impossible position. For in the earliest throes of its nativity, the evangelical movement was prone to ominous anti-intellectual and (its twin) anti-nomian eruptions. Melanchthon understood better than anyone did (on his own side, at least) that these precipitous pitfalls were always just one misstep off the sheer precipice of Luther's teachings on justification and Scripture. He knew from history and by instinct that, unlike souls, traditions do not live by "grace alone." To endure, and to become viable in the world, the "bread" of culture is needed. Melanchthon's burden thus was not merely to forge what was the first Protestant summary of the faith, as is commonly acknowledged. It was (more profoundly) to hammer out its very first model of human culture—in relation to that faith. Under the circumstances, then, we do not wonder that his thought

has been so difficult to understand, or that it has been controversial for so long.

Making matters still more difficult, however, is the way in which Melanchthon's theology developed. From about 1527 onward, he began to make revisions that seemed to certain contemporaries to be dramatic departures from the original teachings of Luther and from his own earlier professions. These changes became manifest in his most important dogmatic work, the ***Loci communes theologici,*** which he subjected to successive revisions from the first edition in 1521[6] to the last one in 1559.[7] In the earliest one, Melanchthon came out boldly for the Wittenberg theology. In the introduction to that monumental work, a young and remarkably self-assured Melanchthon issued those now-famous and oft-quoted little manifestos against conventional methods in the schools: "the mysteries of heaven ought to be worshiped rather than investigated," he wrote; and, again: "to know Christ is to know his *benefits*."[8] Moreover, his handling of that cluster of connected themes—original sin, election, law, grace and justification, was unequivocally in line with Luther's. And sprinkled throughout the work was a fresh recognition, on his part, of the pretense of philosophers, the limits of human reason and the grave dangers of transgressing them.[9]

When we turn to the last editions, however, it almost seems that another person wrote them. To begin, the author gives a rigorous argument for *including* the very doctrines of God, the Trinity and the Incarnation that he had so forcefully warned about early on.[10] Moreover, his handling of predestination was modified now to bring human freedom, dignity and value into balance with the negative evangelical claims on the powers of sin, and on the bondage of the will.[11] Furthermore, he now stressed the value of philosophy on all sorts of levels—including proofs from nature that God exists.[12] And the entire style of the last writings is markedly more pedestrian, making its tone seem many years removed from those first high-spirited beginnings, when everything had seemed so fresh and full of promise.

Among scholars, the most common explanation for the changes has been that there was truth, more or less, in the objection of his critics that he had given away his first principles—that Melanchthon was neither a very strong man, nor thus a very great thinker. Historians have almost universally understood him as a person who never quite found his most basic place to stand, trying as he did (so they say) to straddle high fences. In the context of his biography, they have supposed (for various reasons) that his earliest humanism was straightforwardly Erasmian. Thus, his adoption of Luther's theology in the autumn of 1518 seems to have been a sudden conversion from one worldview to (at its core) the direct opposite. From this perspective, the natural explanation for the later changes is that he never quite really was the author of his own professed convictions. Rather, he inherited them from admired others—first Erasmus, then Luther—and he never really understood the dialectical conflict that thus existed deep inside him. Then, when things got difficult, as they did, Melanchthon resorted, as people often do, to older habits. The inner conflict became manifest in the ambivalence of his later thought.[13] The title of Sperl's influential book, *Melanchthon zwischen Humanismus und Reformation,* summarizes the categories and general thesis of this common (and largely negative) assessment.[14] It seems that Melanchthon lived in suspension "between" two antithetical realms, thus never finding rest in either one.

The role of Melanchthon's theology in the great debate between Protestant Modernists of the nineteenth century and their antagonists is useful as a point of reference for our own proposals. For this debate typifies the general picture of Melanchthon that has become commonplace. Modernists like Albrecht Ritschtl appealed constantly to the early slogans on method as laying precedent for their own attack on the metaphysics of orthodoxy.[15] They generally disregarded the older Melanchthon as having given way to the countervailing "intellectualism" that crept in from his pre-Lutheran past (and was indicative of his less-than-Luther-sized stature). As Troeltsch wrote, the final harvest of this fateful "first Protestant dogmatics" was really nothing more than to have offered "a theology of definitions."[16] As part of his powerful rebuttal of these theologians (and most deeply Schleiermacher, whom they followed), Barth ignored the obvious absurdity of the appeal itself and focused rather (again) upon the underlying hermeneutical problem of "faith and reason" in Melanchthon. Barth singled him out (in spite of the fact that Modernists appealed almost as often to Luther) as having implanted that deadly Ciceronian seed which now grew those twin deadly fruits of the modern age—"anthropocentrism" and "natural theology." The theology of the older Melanchthon was, to Barth, thus merely evidence in support of his revived Gnesio-Lutheran argument.[17] Melanchthon had corrupted the pure biblical Word by adding to it "the word of man." In the wider literature, while historians appreciate Melanchthon's manifest contributions to church, school and society, their understanding of his theology as a whole has been, until quite recently, almost universally one or another version of that dialectical sort. His work in theology has been noticed considerably less for its normative power than for the perennial problems of "Christ and culture" that it provokes.

The obvious influence of humanism on his theology, with the apparently uneven course of his evolution, does make the evangelical integrity of the whole very difficult to discern, much less to clarify. However, when one considers just how disciplined, careful and scrupu-lous Melanchthon always was with language (that this was his genius, in fact), and how very dutiful he was as a person, it is perhaps not surprising that scholarship might make the progress it has been making toward a more favorable image. One element of this change is a renewed focus on Melanchthon's beginnings. For, contrary to the view that he adopted Erasmus's philosophy wholesale, it seems certain now that Melanchthon, during his years as student and teacher in Tübingen (1512-1518), had already forged his own unique brand of humanism. And while Erasmus inspired him in the broadest sense (as he did all the young scholars), the most fundamental influences came from others (as will be noted), whose ideas he used and shaped with an originality that was largely unnoticed by historians.[18] But furthermore, this peculiar humanism was much more solidly on track with what he discovered Luther doing in Wittenberg than was previously understood. Although there was much in Luther's vision that was new and astonishing to him, it also seems that the substance of his Christian humanism (and not just the linguistics of it) prepared him, to an extent that is extraordinary, for receiving Luther's vision as his own. It thus also equipped him, without any lapse of time whatsoever, to begin giving Luther's insights the hermeneutical structure and theological form they were lacking. So it was that, in almost no time at all (which is otherwise impossible to explain), Melanchthon emerged as Luther's advocate, and the primary public voice of early Lutheranism, on an international stage.[19]

When one first becomes aware of these beginnings, a fresh image does begin to come clear. That "unknown Melanchthon" suggested by Stupperich's title emerges from the evidence as a figure of measurably greater vision, accomplishment and stature than he has generally been given credit for in the histories.

II. DIALECTICS AND HUMAN DISCOVERY

The most complete statement and application of this earliest philosophy is contained, not in a work of metaphysics or ethics, but in the books of rhetoric Melanchthon wrote while he was teaching at Tübingen. He had completed all but the final touches on his *De rhetorica libri tres* during his last year in Tübingen.[20] It came from the printer in January 1519.[21] As with his formal dogmatic work, the *Loci communes,* Melanchthon revised his *Rhetoric* in successive editions. They constitute phases that are somewhat in parallel to the course of his development in theology.[22] And there are, likewise, not dissimilar debates concerning what the progressive changes signified. Moreover, Melanchthon considered *De rhetorica* to be something much greater and more profoundly important than a mere lexicon, or manual of techniques and commonplaces on eloquence. The most complete recent studies agree that *De rhetorica* was in fact a systematic work of philosophy, or better, hermeneutics.[23] In its conception the writing was something very like what Ernesto Grassi deemed "rhetoric as philosophy," in reference to Florentine humanists such as Mirandella and Ficino.[24] Like theirs, Melanchthon's rhetoric was a challenge to the abstract, foundational rational systems that flourished in the schools of his time.

Melanchthon came to his philosophical position naturally. Fatherless at ten, his male mentors were all scholars who venerated Italian letters, and who passionately believed that ancient models of composition were linked inseparably to the discovery of truth. But furthermore, these "forerunners of the Reformation," to use Oberman's phrase, were all convinced that such models were the structures which enabled truth to take shape in the form of truly human civilization.[25] For all of them, to bring these arts to society north of the Alps was less a career in studies than it was a spiritual mission. It even included re-charistening—a kind of scholars' baptism. When the boy Philip Schwarzerd (who learned the Latin and Greek languages as if he had been born to them) brilliantly performed a play (*Henno*) at the Pforzheim grammar school in the presence of his famed great-uncle John Reuchlin, the esteemed man renamed him "Melanchthon."[26] Now he, too, was an apostle of this missionary movement that wished to hitch Pegasus, as it were, to the oxcart of the world.

Of all the many stimuli and influences upon him at this formative time, two stand out as by far the most powerful (and neither was Erasmus). The one was a book on dialectic, by the Dutch humanist John Agricola (1444-1485), which his older acquaintance Joachim Oecolampadius, no doubt sensing its timeliness and propriety for the younger man's formation, presented to him sometime in 1516.[27] Agricola (known as "the educator of Germany") named the work, *De inventione dialectica,* and we shall discuss its provocative title just below. The second influence, however, was an early Medieval commentary on the philosophy of Aristotle by one Themestius.[28] Melanchthon discovered this text while taking a course in dialectics from his colleague and mentor Franz Stadianus. The theories advanced in both these works were similar in substance, and Melanchthon made them the foundations on which he would erect a theory of his own—a rhetorical theory which he believed would revolutionize the art as it was taught in the schools.

The principal element of Agricola's book, as the title indicates, was that the art of dialectics must be formally reconnected with the art of rhetoric.[29] The main point of that linkage, which he believed was crucial to the great chain of ancient civilization, was the concept of "invention." Of course, as every student of rhetoric knows, "invention" is what one does in the initial stages of composition. It is a matter of "finding" the right forms for expressing whatever it is that one deems worth writing or speaking about. Agricola's point, however (and the notion that shaped Melanchthon forever after), was that "invention" is even more fundamentally the business of dialectics and dialecticians. This was most directly a challenge to colleagues in his own discipline, and only indirectly to rhetoricians. (Melanchthon would take up the torch in that realm.) In brief, the message was that dialecticians must not allow their craft to deteriorate, as they were prone to let it do, into disconnected games of logic. They must remain centered instead on the universal and perennial questions of meaning and purpose in human life. For the professor of dialectics, moreover, the proper place to begin was with the conventional method of applying standard "categories" of definition to one's chosen topic or theme. That way one forged something more than just a definition, and in doing so created the elementary stuff of a powerful oration—on death, for instance, or virtue. We cannot elaborate here, but the main idea of Agricola's humanism is clear enough. The use of traditional "categories," or "topics" in dialectics was envisioned as "invention" for building the framework of great composition.[30] Of all the ideas that shaped Melanchthon's early understanding of the world, before meeting Luther, this one was of absolutely first importance to the building of his own humanism and later theology.

But before going on, there was the influence of Aristotle also, through the commentary of Themistius. Melanchthon's letters and other written comments on this approach convey the sense of real astonishment he felt at believing he had uncovered something momentous.[31] In his inaugural speech at Wittenberg in 1518, he proclaimed, in contrast to the common understanding, that Aristotle's interest was not really in metaphysics at all, nor in abstract analytics and logic. On the contrary, his metaphysics, analytics, logic, ethics, politics—everything he wrote—served the aim of his rhetoric, which was to put truth in literary forms that would at last shape individuals and societies in the image of wisdom and virtue.[32] So captivated by these thoughts was Melanchthon, that when he came to Wittenberg his next major project was to have been to gather a team of experts—Reuchlin and Stadian among them—to manufacture a newly edited and glossed publication of Aristotle's writings.[33] Alas, the projected work never got going, for his life was rudely interrupted in 1519 by that small matter of his destiny with Luther. Nonetheless, the philosophical substance of his plan did come forth in his own rhetoric.

III. DIALECTICS AND RHETORIC: THE HERMENEUTIC'S HUMAN PURPOSE

We can but briefly look at the texts written by Melanchthon which give some light upon his progress on the way to his mature rhetoric. The main one is a very obscure declamation that it seems he gave in Tübingen sometime in 1517. Published in that year as *De artibus liberalibus,* it stands as a fairly comprehensive statement of his educational theory to that time.[34] For our present purpose, the declamation contains two key statements—one about dialectic, the other about rhetoric. The statements are important, because what would distinguish Melanchthon's rhetoric from all other models in his time (and perhaps in any time) is the thoroughly systematic integration of dialectics into it. The statement Melanchthon made about dialectics in the early oration, adumbrating his later method, was simply that it was "the mother of all the arts."[35] Secondly, though (no doubt making some brows furrow, not least his professor of rhetoric Heinrich Bebel), Melanchthon proceeded to state that rhetoric, on the other hand, was but "a part of dialectics."[36] We cannot go into the discussions that have begun on the course of his developmental path in these matters. It should be noted, however, in view of certain opinions to the contrary, that the statements in the declamation of 1517 are not in the least inconsistent with the views Melanchthon would advance in *De rhetorica,* and thereafter.[37] For assuming, as one must, that the "rhetoric" he disparaged in the speech was none other than the "rhetoric" which he would in his own works disparage in the schools, nothing changed but the terms. In truth, the hallmark of his theory (as will be clear) was that dialectics (as understood by Agricola) was philosophy in its most concentrated, seminal form, and then that rhetoric must grow from them.[38] He simply restated these very points in the inaugural address he was to give at Wittenberg only a year or so later.[39] And all together, they remained at the innermost core of his rhetorical theory to the end.[40]

The preface to *De rhetorica*—a dedication to his fellow student Bernhard Maurus—made this theoretical purpose—and Melanchthon's sense of its historic significance—as clear as could be. As he put it, in recent decades the two arts have become separated, so that the one, dialectics, is now "artless," "a maimed and paltry thing."[41] The once-noble art of rhetoric, likewise, has become little more than a supercilious tool of politicians, a means for "writing insincere praises of princes."[42] Concerned about this disintegration of the academic mind, a very young Melanchthon now aimed to bring dialectic and rhetoric back together, and thus salvage education in the schools. His main premise was obviously derived from Agricola: the two arts are essentially the same, differing only on the methodological surface. As he phrased it: "the one [dialectic] navigates with its sails more tightly drawn; the other [rhetoric] meanders more freely." But otherwise, he wrote, "the argument is the same."[43]

Added to this intuition, Melanchthon demanded complete focus upon the "common causes," as he called

them.[44] Again, in carrying Agricola's vision forward, he thus strove to keep education firmly linked together with the deepest experiences his students would have in life.[45] For in Melanchthon's view, when rightly formed by language, human reflection on these human causes (*caussae* rather than mere *res*) gave otherwise mere speaking (*verba*) the power of true speech (*oratio*). It was in this context, primarily, that he also expressed his debt to Erasmus, who wisely trained students to keep a store of commonplaces, or *loci communes,* on hand to assist in this noble purpose.[46]

As is useful to note, in the introduction to his own dialectics (published in 1520), Melanchthon (following convention) summed up the essential elements of that discipline as being three: definition, division and argumentation.[47] The primary concept, again, was that of the "categories" or "topics" that one used as the framework for all three operations. Explicitly following Agricola, he noted that the first parts of this work were a kind of "invention."[48] In listing the "topics" to be used, we note the deliberate progression from terms of "essence" to those of "effect" in the world. As Agricola and (so he believed) Aristotle did, he thus understood both the "topics" and this natural progression as basic sources, from which all composition ought to flow, "as it were from springs."[49] Melanchthon imported all these ideas, most basically the last one, into the methods of his rhetoric.

The main receptor in rhetoric for the techniques of dialectics was his revised notion of the classical *genus demonstrativum,* which he indicated was to be the model for the other types. From this one, so reformed into an incarnation of dialectics, he wrote: "the others draw their waters."[50] Going into some detail on Aristotle's "categories" (expanding them for his rhetorical purposes from three to nine), he laid the groundwork for what was to follow. To summarize: using these "topics" in their progression to define and otherwise work up a truly meaningful subject (such as his example, "justice"), a writer could not but produce a natural flow in composition from logical clarity to logical power. What is more, however, the aforesaid logical forces served the larger purpose of the theme, whose power was *human.* For the imperative when all three elements—dialectic, rhetoric and the world order—meshed perfectly was, all at once, cognitive, affective and moral. It was in that comprehensive sense that he wrote, "thus, the entire oration is absolved."[51]

Two other interrelated items in his rhetoric must be noted: the concept of the *scopus dicendi,* and his theory of *confirmatio.* These of course are ordinary rhetorical concepts. What is remarkable, however, is the way Melanchthon shaped them. Writing on the *genus deliberativum,* he explained that the *scopus* (or *status caussae*) was "the principal and chief theme of which the controversy consists, and to which all the arguments of the oration have to be referred."[52] Erasmus, likewise, was well known for stressing the importance of having a *scopus,* or main "sighting," as he sometimes called it, in view at all times.[53] However, for Erasmus this was not a dialectical technique as it entirely was for Melanchthon.[54] Indeed, the latter believed the *scopus* must be more than just a point of orientation for the whole. For him, it most generally was the thesis, the terms of which must be handled dialectically, its proposition then placed within a rhetorical structure that made it the inference of one or more arguments. To Melanchthon, the best way of proving one's thesis—the most powerful technique of *confirmatio*—was to make it come out as the conclusion of a syllogism. Hence, for him, the traditional practice of disposition might best be shaping an entire speech into an expanded syllogistic form.[55] That way (so he believed) one achieved, through perfect logical clarity and arguments, absolute certainty of truth.

With these ideas in view, we can now turn to the emergence of Melanchthon's evangelical hermeneutics, and to the controversial levels of his theology.

IV. THE RHETORIC OF PAUL, HOLY SCRIPTURE AND CHRISTIAN DOCTRINE

In 1519 Melanchthon committed himself to theology in earnest. He began writing commentaries based on lectures—on Genesis, Matthew and, of course, Romans. Indeed, his dogmatic work grew directly from study of this epistle. Lectures matured into what was at first to become a commentary on Lombard's *Sentences.* However, the work ripened quickly into an introduction to Christian doctrine. The ***Loci communes theologici*** came out in 1521.[56] Careful examination of this work in context reveals the extent to which his rhetoric supplied the framework for his hermeneutics on every level. This is most apparent in the brief outline of Romans that he used in writing the dogmatic work. The mechanical details appear most conspicuously in the rhetorical delineation of Romans, which he had prepared as the skeleton for the ***Loci communes.*** First published by Ernst Bizer in 1966, it reveals in detail how he was using his rhetoric to construe and interpret this crucial text.[57]

Melanchthon deemed the epistle was itself a work of rhetoric—in the *genus didacticus (demonstrativum)*—offering an "argument" by means of which to understand (dually) "what the Gospel is, and what is the use of Christ."[58] Paul thus forged a "status or proposition," which is that "the highest righteousness is faith," and thus, following an *exordium,* he used scores of conventional devices to set up his argument.[59] In the fourth chapter, Paul clinched his thesis with a "confirmation" consisting of a deduction in seven parts.[60] In a later, similar draft, Melanchthon classified the epistle as be-

longing rather to the *genus iudicale* and as thus comprising "an exordium, narration, confirmation—aptly composed."[61] The narrative (chapters one through three) established axioms on sin, law and righteousness out of sacred revealed tradition. The "confirmation" (mainly chapter four) contained "six arguments," each one being a simple deduction from the axioms given to prove the thesis in question, that we are justified by faith, apart from works of the law.[62] As a teacher of doctrine, then, Melanchthon thus clearly believed that Paul followed the very same rules of composition that shaped the traditions of antiquity.

In the preface that Luther invited him to write for his *Operationes in Psalmos* (1519), Melanchthon made the larger hermeneutical implications of this view clear.

> I am not saying this: that not all the sacred and canonical books are to me of the same rank. But certain ones are generally read more often, and such is their composition that they are able to act as interpreters, or commentaries on the rest. For example, among the Pauline epistles, the one to the Romans is a scopus—an Attic Mercury—which points the way into the rest.[63]

By Paul's method, then, his *status caussae* in Romans created a kind of *scopus* for understanding the sense of Scripture as a doctrinal whole.

In two orations on Paul, which the faculty appropriately invited him to give in 1520, he developed these ideas further.

> For since, some volumes prescribe laws, others narrate the history of past deeds, our Paul, by a certain methodological disputation, examines those *loci* without which it will not have profited at all to have learned laws. Neither the predictions of prophets nor the Gospels' histories can be entered into unless you follow his commentaries . . . serving as a method.
>
> In brief, for the sake of our redemption, indeed, we would not have known Christ himself, had God withheld Paul from the world.
>
> In vain you will have learned the evangelical history, unless you observe the *scope* and *use* of the history as demonstrated by him. [For] what else does he do but bring light to all Scripture as by a certain method?[64]

These passages indicate (besides much else) that in 1520 Melanchthon had already received and shaped Luther's doctrinal notion of Scripture in rhetorical terms. He did not imagine Scripture, conceptually, as a single, uniform writing, but as being a kind of purposeful literary tradition (similar to that of the classics), the deepest meaning and purpose of which was illumined by its greatest orators. Melanchthon's notion of Scripture (in the relevant doctrinal senses), then, had Paul's rhetoric as the literal *scopus* of the whole. In that deeper sense, it *was* the whole. But it also had the rest—the diverse laws, histories, sayings and songs—as parts that were always in a dynamic relation to the center. Thus Melanchthon gave quite a remarkable account of the sense, unity and diversity of the canon (we shall encounter his notion of Scripture's uniqueness in a moment). But furthermore, the passages also show that as a diverse but rhetorically unified whole, Scripture achieves that total complex of human purposes we encountered moments ago. Through Paul, it confronts human beings with both the scope (the "what") and the use (the "effects") of its great message. Further examination of Melanchthon's earliest theological writings reveals that this general vision of Scripture as *oration* (in his peculiar sense of that term)—oration that was *sacred*—was uppermost in his understanding of himself as a commentator and theologian. Both these ideas must now be kept in view as we seek to show their relevance to his principles of "faith and reason" in forging Protestant theology.

V. UNDERSTANDING MELANCHTHON'S THEOLOGY IN THE CONTEXT OF HIS RHETORIC

Melanchthon's use of these rhetorical thought-forms as a kind of first Protestant hermeneutics is immensely important as context for understanding the contested parts of his theology. In this last section, but briefly and in outline, we shall focus on questions about the integrity (with regard to the fundamental of *sola scriptura*) of his dramatic decisions to expand his doctrines as he did, and to begin stressing the virtues of philosophy to Christians. We shall also suggest an approach to disputes (with regard to the fundamental of *sola gratia*) over revisions he made in handling the doctrine of election. And, to conclude, we shall make some observations about his (rhetorical) theory of truth and how it illumines his vision of theology and his final legacy as a teacher of Protestant doctrine.

First, let us consider the issue of the expansion of topics. As noted, Ritschl, Barth and many others (for different reasons) have judged this expansion as indicating a disunity of clear principle, and a trend of degeneration in Melanchthon's theology as a whole. Some scholars, such as Wolf and Fraenkel, working carefully with the theological texts, have disputed this judgment.[65] Our understanding of the hermeneutical principles that Melanchthon used in forming these texts strongly supports their defense. For very simply, in 1521 he was obviously quite affected by the fresh realization that theology had lost its topical compass. In his terms, scholastic theologians had lost sight of the *scopus* of theology— Paul's teaching on the "benefits of Christ." To Melanchthon's way of thinking, no greater formal error was imaginable, for without knowing the *scopus* (of any oration, much less God's) we are left completely clueless. In that circumstance, focusing on this or that part of the speech only makes matters worse, for we see them as fragments rather than as the parts of a larger

whole that they are; and we import all the wrong meaning into them. In respect of the doctrines of God, Trinity and Incarnation, what could be more harmful than teaching about them (*Deus in se*) without reference to the very truths of our human purpose and destiny that this very God is most concerned to make known? It would be rather like studying one's benefactor's molecular composition instead of being interested foremost with his purposes. As Fraenkel rightly observed in Melanchthon, "the *loci praecipui* are the way to understanding the whole of Christian doctrine. They are not identical with the whole," and thus, on the eventual expansion to include the other topics: "This is an expansion within, not a transformation of the original doctrinal scheme."[66] Another way of stating the matter is that Melanchthon simply corrected the "invention" of theologians' rhetoric at the first, and completed its full "disposition" at the last. There was certainly nothing in the beginning to give warrant to Ritschl's appeal (to principles opposed to a real metaphysics), and Barth ought rather to have found in the ending something very like a precedent for his own Christ-centered Christian realism. It seems that Melanchthon's expansion of his dogmatics was not at all confused, or degenerative. It was rather the outgrowth and application of his very first principles toward completeness and maturity in doctrine.

Let us similarly consider the contrast between Melanchthon's earlier and later writing on philosophical wisdom and proofs of God's existence. In the early stages, he indeed placed his emphasis upon the failings and deadly dangers of philosophy, in contrast to Scripture and its Gospel. One could pick sentences like this one from almost any page of his essays of that time: "they are straying entirely from the path who think that the doctrines of the Christian life are helped by the literature of the philosophers."[67] He wrote with discernible passion that philosophers were "blind," that their writings were ineffective, and that he had personally incurred much damage to his soul in reading them.[68] In contrast, one could pick sentences like this second one from almost any page of his essays on the subject less than ten years later: "how great is the magnitude and power of the arts in doctrine."[69] That there was a reversal of his earlier strategy is obvious enough, but did the later statement also signify a contradiction of the evangelical principle underlying the earlier one? We think not.

For one thing, careful examination reveals that even in his most severe criticisms of philosophy were not as exclusionary as they might sound. For example, in his *Declamatiuncula* on Paul (1520) he wrote this typical statement: "Philosophers *also* [our emphasis] placed beatitude in perfect virtue and perpetual tranquillity of the soul."[70] In other words (in undertone) they had the right questions and larger sense of purpose. Furthermore, as he often noted (disparagingly), philosophers understood many good "laws for living," and they had among them many "fine examples."[71] What they did not understand was "whence they might find such a soul," for they did not have revealed to them, "the mystery hidden for so many ages—the benefits of Christ."[72] At first, Melanchthon's purposes clearly were to define precisely what it was that made philosophy inferior to Scripture, and then, in that light, to discriminate clearly between them. However, we see that both the definition he gave and the distinction he made left the way open, in principle, for that later strategy of integration. For the claim contained in his metaphor that philosophy was "blind" (rhetorically powerful as it was to his fellows) actually entailed the secondary one that philosophy "saw" basic things, especially in ethics, remarkably well. In view of his rhetorical concepts, it is not very hard to understand the agility of his thinking on the matter. Again, it was the *scopus* of Christian doctrine that counted as its essence, gave Scripture its qualities of unity, clarity and force—in sum, the most basic qualities contained in the expression, *sola scriptura*. Once made, however (especially once the uniquely Christian oration was expanded to completion), there could be no principled objection to placing the "orations" of human culture in (emergency) service of Christ.

More complex and difficult to discern, however, is coherence of principle (*sola gratia*) in Melanchthon's last teachings on predestination. For his earliest handling of the subject seems to have been straightforwardly deterministic and dialectical enough. In contrast, by the latest editions, Melanchthon had expanded things to include an entire chapter in qualified defense of belief in human freedom in that context.[73] In this discussion Melanchthon is careful to reject two extremes—a kind of Stoicism (which he feared was incipient in the growing influence of certain forms of Calvinism), and an ancient Pelagianism (the trend in Rome).[74] In sum, Philip affirmed the sovereignty of divine grace, but also warned that however it all happens a human being is no "piece of wood or a stone," which God merely acts upon.[75] He liked to cite the words of Chrysostom: "God draws, but he draws the one who is willing."[76] In this fashion, Melanchthon believed he was clearly in line with the best authorities that had written on the matter (including Luther).[77]

The criticism that Melanchthon was a "synergist" (and closet Erasmian) has been widely argued, and the intricate particulars of that debate cannot detain us here. Nevertheless, if we consider merely that Melanchthon imagined divine communication as rhetoric, and if we also consider what he supposed rhetoric in this instance was, perhaps we can gain some understanding of why he saw no conflict with his earlier notions, or with Luther's. Very simply, to Melanchthon, successful rhetoric (with its dialectical core) did two things with

respect to the human will. First it made the moral realities of a person's circumstances perfectly clear. At one and the same time, however, it also persuaded and (in a word) compelled the person, by intuition of judgment, to believe, and then to act. (Belief of this sort already was, in fact, the beginning of the action.) All this is wrapped together in Melanchthon's concept of truth, as actualized in rhetoric. The integration of dialectics thus spelled differences between him and Erasmus, not just in their humanism, but in the manner in which their respective humanisms would give shape to the intricacies of their doctrines of election. And it perhaps explains why he believed to the last that his position on human freedom was not, in the end, a departure from Luther's.

Melanchthon's concept of truth, in this form, is also very important as context for one last issue of concern. That is the reputation his theology has earned for what we may call its sense of vision and purpose— Melanchthon's understanding of himself and his mission. Troeltsch's phrase, "theology of definitions," sums up the general attitude of historians toward Melanchthon's place in history. He was to Luther what Boswell was to Johnson—a secretary and organizer of his master's ideas—but little more. Against this perception, it should suffice to consider again what Melanchthon's notion of definition was. For it was hardly that of a "Luther's lexicon," but was rather a dialectical and rhetorical notion with immense implications for human life. Properly formed "definitions" tapped into the greatest cosmic powers in the universe, and they unleashed those powers in the most perfect and humanly momentous manner possible. This rhetorical supposition was almost certainly behind what might otherwise seem a bland and pedestrian method in his *Loci communes,* particularly later on. Beginning always with the "what is it?" (*quid est?*), he progressed dutifully to the "What power?" (*quid vis?*) on each doctrine. While the result may have been excessively pedestrian, repetitive and a little dull (compared with the literary extravagances of a Luther or Calvin), we ought at the very least appreciate the vision at work. In its own terms, it was successful, and a good many people (including Luther and Calvin) found its harvest invaluable as a resource for their own lives and works.

In conclusion, in the context of his rhetoric, the general integrity of Melanchthon's theology as a whole begins to come into clearer light than otherwise. And his stature as a theologian of Protestantism and as a man of great ability and character only grows.

Notes

1. Robert Stupperich, *Der Unbekannte Melanchthon: Wirken und Denken des Praeceptor Germaniae in neuer Sicht* (Stuttgart: W. Kohlhammer, 1961), 9.

2. See text of the poem found near Melanchthon's deathbed, given in translation and discussed by E.

Gordon Rupp, "Philip Melanchthon and Martin Bucer," in Hubert Cunliffe-Jones with Benjamin Drewery, eds., *A History of Christian Doctrine* (Philadelphia: Fortress Press, 1978), 378.

3. Robert Kolb, "Philip's Foes, but Followers Nonetheless," in M. Fleischer ed., *The Harvest of Humanism in Central Europe: Essays in Honor of Lewis W. Spitz* (St. Louis: Concordia, 1992), 159-78.

4. Franz Hildebrandt, *Melanchthon: Alien or Ally?* (Cambridge: Cambridge University Press, 1946).

5. Rupp, 374.

6. In Latin we recommend the edition in [Phillip Melanchthon. *Melanchthons Werke in Auswahl. [Studienausgabe].* Edited by Robert Stupperich. 7 vols. Gütersloh: Gerd Mohn, 1951-75. Hereafter referred to as] MSA II/1, 15-185. For the 1521 edition in translation, see William Pauck, tr./ed., *Melanchthon and Bucer,* The Library of Christian Classics, XIX (Philadelphia: The Westminster Press, 1959).

7. For the 1559 edition in Latin, MSA II/1, 186-388. For the 1555 edition in translation, Clyde L. Manschreck (ed., tr.), introduction, Hans Engelland, *Melanchthon on Christian Doctrine: Loci Communes of 1555* (Grand Rapids, MI: Baker Book House, 1965).

8. See Pauck, 21, translation of Melanchthon's oft-cited words: "Mysteria divinitatis rectius adoraverimus, quam vestigaverimus." Also, 21: "cognoscere Christum, eius beneficia cognoscere est" (italics ours).

9. See, for example, ibid., 19-20.

10. See Manschreck, xlv-li.

11. Ibid., 51-69.

12. Ibid., 5-10.

13. On this view of Melanchthon's development being marked by "conversions" and sudden "breaks" and syntheses (rather than deliberate reflection), see Timothy J. Wengert, *Philip Melanchthon's Annotationes in Johannem in Relation to its Predecessors and Contemporaries,* Travaux d'Humanisme et Renaissance 220 (Geneva: Droz, 1987), 56-57.

14. Adolf Sperl, *Melanchthon zwischen Humanismus und Reformation: Eine Untersuchung über den Wandel des Traditionsverständnisses bei Melanchthon und die damit zusammenhängenden Grundfragen seiner Theologie,* Forschung zur Geschichte und Lehre des Protestantismus, 10, XV, (Munich: Chr. Kaiser, 1959).

15. For appeals to Melanchthon's principles as anti-metaphysical, see Albrecht Ritschl, *The Christian Doctrine of Justification and Reconciliation* (Clifton, NJ: Reference Book Publishers, 1966), 396.

16. Ernst Troeltsch, *Vernunft und Offenbarung bei Johann Gerhard und Philip Melanchthon* (Göttingen: Vandenhoeck & Ruprecht, 1891), 59.

17. Karl Barth, *Protestant Theology in the Nineteenth Century: Its Background and History* (Valley Forge: Judson Press, 1973), 76, 579.

18. On the very basic differences between Melanchthon and Erasmus, see especially Manfred Hoffman, "Rhetoric and Dialectic in Erasmus's and Melanchthon's Interpretation of John's Gospel," in Timothy Wengert and M. Patrick Graham, eds., *Philip Melanchthon (1497-1560) and the Commentery* (Sheffield: Sheffield Academic Press, 1997), 48-78.

19. John Schneider, *Philip Melanchthon's Rhetorical Construal of Biblical Authority: Oratio Sacra* Texts and Studies in Religion. vol. 51, (Lewiston/Queenston/Lampeter: The Edwin Mellen Press), 1990, 97-99.

20. See Schneider, "The Hermeneutics of Commentary: origins of Melanchthon's Integration of Dialectic into Rhetoric," in Wengert and Graham, *Melanchthon and the Commentary,* 20-47, esp. references on 22-23.

21. *Philippi Melanchthonis De rhetorica libri tres,* Wittenberg, 1519.

22. The best survey of the editions, if not the substance of their evolution, is in Joachim Knappe, *Philipp Melanchthons 'Rhetorik',* Rhetorik-Forschungen, 6 (Tübingen: Niemeyer, 1993).

23. See esp. Wengert, *Annotationes,* and Schneider, *Oratio Sacra.*

24. Ernesto Grassi, *Rhetoric as Philosophy: The Humanist Tradition* (University Park: The Pennsylvania State University Press, 1980).

25. On Melanchthon's first teachers, Schneider, *Oratio Sacra,* 13-50.

26. On this episode and its spiritual significance, Maurer, *Der junge Melanchthon zwischen Humanismus und Reformation* (Göttingen: Vandenhoeck & Ruprecht, 1967-69), I, 20-21.

27. Schneider, *Oratio Sacra,* 34.

28. Ibid., 29; on Themistius, Peter Mack, *Renaissance Argument: Valla and Agricola in the Traditions of Rhetoric and Dialectic* (Leiden: Brill, 1993), 135.

29. Mack, *Renaissance Argument,* esp., 320-33.

30. Ibid.

31. Discussion and references in Schneider, *Oratio Sacra,* 45, 56.

32. Melanchthon's inaugural speech, in MSA, III, 29-42.

33. Ibid., 35-36.

34. This speech occurs in full, *ibid.,* 17-28. See discussion in Schneider, *Oratio Sacra,* 38-43.

35. Ibid., 21.

36. Ibid., 22. On Melanchthon's view of Bebel, Schneider, *Oratio Sacra,* 29 and refs., n.31.

37. Knappe, *Melanchthons 'Rhetorik,'* 6, in our view is entirely mistaken, because Knappe's view is typically (in regard to Melanchthon) semantically presumptive in judging this part of the speech as "völlig unhumanistisch." "Un-Erasmian" would be a better term for it, but that illustrates the underlying error, here.

38. Knappe's comment that "Mit seinem Wechsel nach Wittenberg änderte Melanchthon seine Auffassung," ibid., is entirely unwarranted and only exemplifies the casual manner in which such dramatic shifts are attributed to Melanchthon with changes of climate and heroes.

39. MSA, III, 35-37.

40. Contrary to Wilhelm H. Neuser, see Schneider, *Oratio Sacra,* 69 and refs., n. 50.

41. *Philippi Melanchthonis De rhetorica libri tres,* Wittenberg, 1519.

42. Ibid.

43. Ibid. brackets ours.

44. Ibid., B1r.

45. Ibid., Hans-Jörg Geyer somewhat usefully compares these "common causes," which Melanchthon here lists as including "virtues, fortune, death, wealth, letters and the like," to the "existentials" of Heidegger, for the idea is not only ethical, it is about the whole scope of human meaning and purpose. Geyer, *Von der Geburt des wahren Menschen: Probleme aus den Anfängen der Theologie Melanchthons* (Neukirchen: Neukirchener Verlag des Erziehungsvereins, GmbH, 1965), 52.

46. *De rhetorica,* E3r-E4v.

47. *Compendaria·dialectica,* [Philip Melancthon. *Corpus Reformatorum. Philippi Melanchthonis opera quae supersunt omnia.* Edited by Karl Bretschneider and Heinrich Bindsell. 28 vols. Halle: A Schwetschke and sons, 1834-60. Hereafter referred to as] CR 20, 711.

48. Ibid., Also Mack, *Renaissance Argument,* discussion of Melanchthon's *loci dialectici,* 327-33.

49. CR 20, 749.

50. *De rhetorica,* A5r. Almost all of the book (84 percent) was devoted to integrating dialectics into the invention and disposition of rhetoric. See Knappe, *Melanchthons 'Rhetorik,'* 30.

51. *De rhetorica,* A3r.

52. Ibid., F1v.

53. M. O'Rourke Boyle, *Erasmus on Language and Method in Theology* (Toronto/Buffalo: [University of Toronto Press], 1977), esp. 76-78.

54. Ibid., on Erasmus's way of relating parts to the whole: "[not] a progressive mathematics of meaning, as in dialectics." Also, M. Hoffman, "Rhetoric and Dialectic in Erasmus's and Melanchthon's Interpretation of John's Gospel," esp. 75-78.

55. *De rhetorica,* B1r; and esp. E5v-E5r, and G2v.

56. On the early outlines of the *Loci communes,* see esp. Ernst Bizer, ed., *Texte aus der Anfangzeit Melanchthons* (Neukirchen/Vluyn: Neukirchener Verlag des Erziehungsvereins, 1966).

57. Bizer, *Texte,* 20-30.

58. Ibid., 20.

59. Ibid., 20-23.

60. Ibid., 23.

61. Ibid., 97.

62. Ibid., 98-99.

63. [Martin Luther. *Luthers Werke. Kritische Gesamtausgabe.[Schriften].* 65 vols. Weimar: H. Böhlau, 1883-1993. Hereafter referred to as] WA 5, 24. On this preface, Schneider, *Oratio Sacra,* 99-104.

64. CR XI, 38. On these orations, given in 1520, Schneider, *ibid.,* 163-87.

65. See Peter Fraenkel, *Testamonia Patrum: The Function of the Patristic Argument in the Theology of Philip Melanchthon* (Geneva: Droz, 1961), esp. 43-51 on the factors underlying the expansion, and for an analysis that independently supports our argument.

66. Ibid., 45.

67. MSA I, 34.

68. Ibid., 34-35; 41.

69. MSA III, 90.

70. MSA I, 32.

71. Ibid., 30.

72. Ibid., 32.

73. See Manschreck, 51-69.

74. Ibid., 51 (on Stoicism), 58 (on Pelagius).

75. Ibid., 60.

76. Ibid.

77. Ibid., 68.

FURTHER READING

Biographies

Manschreck, Clydge Leonard. *Melanchthon: The Quiet Reformer.* Nashville: Abingdon Press, 1958, 175 p.

Attempts to understand Melanchthon and his ideas in the context of the Renaissance and the Reformation.

Richard, James William. *Philip Melanchthon: The Protestant Preceptor of Germany, 1497-1560.* Philadelphia: The Westminster Press, 1965, 175 p.

Study of the life and theology of Melanchthon that is reconstructed largely from the reformer's own writings.

Stupperich, Robert. *Melanchthon.* Translated by Robert H. Fischer. Philadelphia: The Westminster Press, 1965, 175 p.

Sympathetic portrayal of Melanchthon and his work by a leading Melanchthon scholar.

Criticism

Classen, Carl Joachim. "Melanchthon's Rhetorical Interpretation of Biblical and Non-Biblical Texts." In *Rhetorical Criticism of the New Testament, pp. 99-177.* Tübingen: Mohr Siebeck, 2000.

Shows how Melanchthon applied rhetorical and dialectical theory to the texts of the Bible and other works.

Estes, James M. "The Role of the Godly Magistrates in the Church: Melanchthon as Luther's Interpreter and Collaborator." *The American Society of Church History* 67, no. 3 (September 1998): 463-83.

Explores the question of the relationship between Melanchthon's ideas on the office of the Christian magistrate and Luther's thoughts on the subject.

Fraenkel, Peter. *Testimonia Patrum: The Function of the Patristic Argument in the Theology of Philip Melanchthon.* Geneva: Librairie E Droz, 1961, 382 p.

Considers Melanchthon's thought in the light of his reading of the teachings of the Church Fathers.

Hildebrandt, Franz. *Melanchthon: Alien or Ally.* Cambridge: Cambridge University Press, 1946, 98 p.

Examination of the concessions made by Melanchthon to elements outside the "inner circle" of the evangelical faith.

Jensen, Kristian. "The Latin Grammar of Philipp Melanchthon." In *Aca Conventus Neo-Latini Guelpherbytani: Proceedings of the Sixth International Congress of Neo-Latin Studies,* edited by Stella P. Revard, edited by Fidel Räle and Mario A. Di Cesare, pp. 513-19. Binghampton, N.Y.: Medieval and Renaissance Texts and Studies, 1988.

Claims that Melanchthon's pedagogical attitude can be detected in his works on Latin grammar.

Jensen, Minna Skafte. "Melanchthon, the Muses, and Denmark." In *Renaissance Culture in Context: Theory and Practice,* edited by Jean R. Brink and William F. Gentrup, pp. 136-44. Aldershot, UK: Scolar Press, 1993.

Discusses Melanchthon's influence on Danish poets of the sixteenth century.

Kuspit, Donald B. "Melanchthon and Düer: The Search for the Simple Style." *Journal of Medieval and Renaissance Studies* 3, no. 2 (fall 1973): 177-202.

Offers an account of Melanchthon's consciousness of art understood in terms of his belief that the "simplicity" of Albrecht Dürer's art conveyed religious truth.

Maag, Karin, ed. *Melanchthon in Europe.* Grand Rapids, Mich.: Baker Books, 1999, 191 p.

Volume containing eight essays that examine various aspects of Melanchthon's work.

McNally, J. R. "Melanchthon's Earliest Rhetoric." In *Rhetoric: A Tradition in Transition,* edited by Donald C. Bryant, pp. 33-48. East Lansing: Michigan State University Press, 1974.

Describes the contents and emphases of Melanchthon's 1519 *De rhetorica libri tres.*

Quere, Ralph Walter. *Melanchthon's Christum Cognoscere: Christ's Efficacious Presence in the Eucharistic Theology of Melanchthon.* Nieuwkoop: B. De Graaf, 1977, 405 p.

Study of Melanchthon's eucharistic doctrine, comparing it with Luther's teaching.

Rogness, Michael. *Philip Melanchthon: Reformer Without Honor.* Minneapolis: Augsburg Publishing House, 1969, 165 p.
   Defines Melanchthon's place in the development of Lutheran theology.

Scheider, John R. *Philip Melanchthon's Rhetorical Construal of Biblical Authority: Oratio Sacra.* Lewiston, N.Y.: The Edwin Mellen Press, 1990. 191 p.
   Detailed study of Melanchthon's life and work that contends the reformer construed biblical scripture literally as sacred rhetoric.

Vajta, Vilmos. *Luther und Melanchthon in the History and Theology of the Reformation.* Philadelphia: Muhlenberg Press, 1961, 198 p.
   Collection of essays in English and German.

Wengert, Timothy J. *Law and Gospel: Philip Melanchthon's Debate with John Agricola of Eisleben*

Over Poenitentia. Grand Rapids, Mich.: Baker Book House, 1997, 232 p.
   Study of how Melanchthon, during the time his theology first came under attack in the 1520s by another Wittenberg-trained reformer, John Agricola, came to define the relation between *poenitentia* and law.

————. *Philip Melanchthon's Exegetical Dispute with Erasmus of Rotterdam.* New York: Oxford University Press, 1998, 238 p.
   Discusses Melanchthon's criticism of Erasmus's interpretation method.

Wengert, Timothy J., and Graham, M. Patrick, eds. *Philip Melanchthon (1497-1560) and the Commentary.* Sheffield, UK: Sheffield Academic Press, 1997, 304 p.
   Examines Melanchthon's commentary on ancient texts.

Additional coverage of Philip Melanchthon is contained in the following sources published by the Gale Group: *Dictionary of Literary Biography,* **Vol. 179; and** *Literature Resource Center.*

A Vindication of the Rights of Woman

Mary Wollstonecraft

The following entry provides criticism of Wollstonecraft's political treatise *A Vindication of the Rights of Woman* (1792). For additional information on Wollstonecraft's career, see *LC,* volumes 5 and 50.

INTRODUCTION

Wollstonecraft's *A Vindication of the Rights of Woman* (1792) is a declaration of the rights of women to equality of education and to civil opportunities. The book-length essay, written in simple and direct language, was the first great feminist treatise. In it Wollstonecraft argues that true freedom necessitates equality of the sexes; claims that intellect, or reason, is superior to emotion, or passion; seeks to persuade women to acquire strength of mind and body; and aims to convince women that what had traditionally been regarded as soft, "womanly" virtues are synonymous with weakness. Wollstonecraft advocates education as the key for women to achieve a sense of self-respect and a new self-image that can enable them to live to their full capabilities. The work attacks Enlightenment thinkers such as Jean Jacques Rousseau who, even while espousing the revolutionary notion that men should not have power over each other, denied women the basic rights claimed for men. *A Vindication of the Rights of Woman* created an uproar upon its publication but was then largely ignored until the latter part of the twentieth century. Today it is regarded as one of the foundational texts of liberal feminism.

BIOGRAPHICAL INFORMATION

Wollstonecraft was born in London in 1759, the second of six children. Her father, Edward John Wollstonecraft, was a tyrannical man, and as she was growing up Wollstonecraft watched her mother bullied and mistreated by him. At the age of nineteen Wollstonecraft left home to make her own way in the world. In 1783 she aided her sister, Eliza, escape an abusive marriage by hiding her from her husband until a legal separation was arranged. Wollstonecraft and her sister later established a school at Newington Green before she moved to Ireland to work as a governess to the family of Lord Kingsborough. In 1787 she returned to London and em-

barked on a literary career. The following year Wollstonecraft was hired as translator and literary advisor to Joseph Johnson, a publisher of radical texts. She soon became acquainted with prominent intellectuals in radical political circles. When Johnson launched the *Analytical Review,* Wollstonecraft became a regular contributor of articles.

In 1790, in response to Edmund Burke's *Reflections on the Revolution in France,* Wollstonecraft published *A Vindication of the Rights of Men,* in which she disputed Burke's conservative position and advocated for the rights of the poor and the oppressed. In 1791 two events took place that prompted Wollstonecraft to write her *A Vindication of the Rights of Woman.* The first was the writing of the new French Constitution, which excluded women from all areas of public life and granted citizenship rights only to men over the age of twenty-five. The second was the report on education given by Charles Maurice de Talleyrand-Périgord to the French National Assembly recommending that girls' education should be directed to more subservient activities. *A Vindication of the Rights of Woman* is dedicated to Talleyrand, and Wollstonecraft appeals to him to rethink his views. While she was working on the treatise, Wollstonecraft fell in love with the married painter and philosopher Henry Fuseli. When she was rejected by him, and after her newly published treatise caused a stir in England, she moved to France. There she witnessed Robespierre's Reign of Terror; she would later criticize the violence of the French Revolution in her history, *An Historical and Moral View of the Origins and Progress of the French Revolution, and the Effect It Has Produced in Europe* (1794). In Paris Wollstonecraft met Captain Gilbert Imlay, an American timber merchant, with whom she later had a daughter, Fanny. When Imlay deserted her, Wollstonecraft attempted suicide. Soon after she lived with the philosopher William Godwin, whom she eventually married. In August 1797 she gave birth to their daughter, Mary (later Mary Shelley, author of *Frankenstein*), and less than a month later she died.

PLOT AND MAJOR CHARACTERS

A Vindication of the Rights of Woman begins with a dedication to Talleyrand-Périgord, the Late Bishop of Autun, asking him to reconsider some of his ideas about the education of girls and women. In her dedication Wollstonecraft states that the main idea in her book is based on the simple principle that if woman is not prepared by education to become the companion of man, she will stop the progress of knowledge and virtue. Her argument in the thirteen chapters that follow is that rights are based on human reason and common human virtues, which are empowered by God. Because people have tended to use reason to justify injustice rather than promote equality, a vindication of the rights of women is needed. Her work begins with a discussion of sexual character, then offers observations on the state of degradation to which woman is reduced by various causes; presents critiques of writers who have rendered women objects of pity or contempt; shows the effect that an early association of ideas has upon the character; discusses the notion of modesty as it is applied to women; shows how morality is undermined by sexual notions of the importance of a good reputation; outlines the pernicious effects that arise from the unnatural distinctions established in society; discusses parental affection and one's duty to parents; comments on national education; presents examples of the folly that the ignorance of women generates; and concludes with reflections on the moral improvement that a revolution in female manners would produce.

In the course of *A Vindication of the Rights of Woman*, Wollstonecraft criticizes the ideas of Jean-Jacques Rousseau, who, she judges, has an inadequate understanding of rights and is wrong when he claims that humans are essentially solitary. Indeed, one of the principal projects and strategies of *A Vindication of the Rights of Woman* is to turn Rousseau's egalitarian principles against his negative characterization of women in *Emile* (1762). She challenges Burke also, who she views as having a mistaken conception of the nature of power. A great deal of her treatise attacks the educational restrictions and "mistaken notions of female excellence" that keep women in a state of "ignorance and slavish dependence." She argues that girls are forced into passivity, vanity, and credulity by lack of physical and mental stimulus and by a constant insistence on the need to please, and ridicules notions about women as helpless, charming adornments in the household. She sees women as too often sentimental and foolish, gentle domestic "brutes" whose fondness for pleasure has been allowed to take the place of ambition. Wollstonecraft suggests that it is only by encouraging the moral development of every individual to success and independence that a true civilization will work.

MAJOR THEMES

A Vindication of the Rights of Woman argues for equality for women and girls not only in the political sphere but in the social realm as well. It asks readers to reconsider prevailing notions about women's abilities. Some of the main issues that Wollstonecraft emphasizes are education, virtues, passion versus reason, and power. She argues that the current roles and education of women do women more harm than good and urges reform that would provide women with broader and deeper learning. She also discusses the virtues that will develop a "true" civilization. However, she rejects traditional notions of feminine "virtue" and sees virtues not as sexual traits but as human qualities. She also insists that intellect, or reason, and not emotion, or passion, be the guiding force in human conduct. Society's association of women with emotionality and thus vulnerability must to be countered, she argues, by the use of reason and engagement in strenuous mental activity. In *A Vindication of the Rights of Woman* Wollstonecraft talks a great deal about power—in terms of the status quo, in regards to women's position in society, and so on—but ultimately what she urges is for women to have power not over men but over themselves.

CRITICAL RECEPTION

A Vindication of the Rights of Woman was much acclaimed in radical political circles when it was published, but it also attracted considerable hostility. The statesman Horace Walpole, for example, called Wollstonecraft "a hyena in petticoats," and for most of the nineteenth century the book was ignored because of its scandalous reputation. Beginning in the late twentieth century, literary critics and philosophers began to take great interest in Wollstonecraft's treatise as one of the founding works of feminism. Some issues discussed by commentators of Wollstonecraft's treatise are the author's attitude toward sexuality, ideas about education, the role of reason versus passion, attitudes toward slavery, the relevance of the work to contemporary struggles for rights, the unflattering portrayal of women, and the status of the work as a foundational feminist text.

PRINCIPAL WORKS

Thoughts on the Education of Daughters: With Reflections on Female Conduct, in the More Important Duties of Life (essay) 1787

Mary: A Fiction (novel) 1788

Original Stories from Real Life; with Conversations, Calculated to Regulate the Affections, and Form the Mind to Truth and Goodness (children's stories) 1788

A Vindication of the Rights of Men, in a Letter to the Right Honourable Edmund Burke; Occasioned by His Reflections on the Revolution in France (essay) 1790

A Vindication of the Rights of Woman, with Strictures on Political and Moral Subjects (essay) 1792

An Historical and Moral View of the Origin and Progress of the French Revolution, and the Effect It Has Produced in Europe (essay) 1794

Letters Written during a Short Residence in Sweden, Norway, and Denmark (letters) 1796

The Wrongs of Woman; or, Maria (unfinished novel) 1798; published in *Posthumous Works of the Author of a Vindication of the Rights of Woman*; also published as *Maria; or, The Wrongs of Woman*, 1975

A Wollstonecraft Anthology [edited by by Janet M. Todd] (essays, novels, children's stories, and letters) 1977

Collected Letters of Mary Wollstonecraft [edited by Ralph M. Wardle] (letters) 1979

CRITICISM

James L. Cooper and Sheila McIsaac Cooper (essay date 1973)

SOURCE: Cooper, James L. and Sheila McIsaac Cooper. "Mary Wollstonecraft: Enlightenment Rebel." In *The Roots of American Feminist Thought*, pp. 15-24. Boston: Allyn and Bacon, 1973.

[*In the following essay, Cooper and Cooper offer a general introduction to Wollstonecraft's background and her interest in sexual equality before discussing the significance of* A Vindication of the Rights of Woman *as a foundational text for American feminist thought.*]

Mary Wollstonecraft (1759-1797) shocked genteel Englishmen and Americans "with the most indecent rhapsody . . . ever penned by man or woman." *A Vindication of the Rights of Woman* (1792) was nonetheless "so run after" that on occasion there was "no keeping it long enough to read it leisurely."[1] It attracted immediate public notice that ensured its author's fame and notoriety as a champion of women's equality through a "revolution in female education and manners."[2]

Shaken by the republican thought and revolutionary action of the emerging middle classes, British and American conservatives of the late eighteenth century had "had enough of new systems" proposed by "philosophizing serpents," such as Mary Wollstonecraft and Thomas Paine. Conservatives felt that attacks on tradition had promoted disruption of the British Empire in the American Revolution and demolition of established European institutions in the French Revolution. Reckless assaults on the political order threatened society by

altering the particular tasks which nature and tradition seemingly had assigned to each group. Thus careless or premeditated levelling of functional differences pierced the veneer of civilization and led immediately to either an absolute equality or anarchy. Attacks upon social institutions were numerous, intense, and serious before Mary Wollstonecraft, a "hyena in petticoats," proposed an equality between the sexes. Few things seemed more obvious to conservatives than that differences between the sexes were deeply rooted in physical nature and broadly reinforced by tradition. All evidence—from physiology to the Bible—supported the subordination of woman to man as a rightful and necessary condition for pursuit of the general welfare.[3]

Republicans and rationalists were about as interested in feminine equality as conservatives. Few carried their espousal of reason, questioning of tradition, and support of reform or revolution to feminist conclusions. Concerned primarily, if not explicitly, with the problems of white, bourgeois men, they rarely extended their social analyses to consider and challenge the traditional subordination of blacks or women. To the degree that they explored existing racial and sexual distinctions, they tended to find subordination essentially reasonable and consistent with the natural order. Republicans and rationalists did not always approve inequality with assurance and without qualification. But despite possible guilt, equivocation, or reservation, they generally found the principle of feminine equality uncongenial.[4]

Mary Wollstonecraft was not the first to raise the woman question in eighteenth-century England or America. Indeed, as the century passed, the number of newspaper articles, pamphlets, books, and sermons about woman's role gradually increased. The longer the discussion continued, the more the arguments for improving woman's condition gained cautious acceptance. Some writers advocated basic changes in woman's position, but the greater number and the better known recommended limited improvements. Wollstonecraft took issue with the most widely read commentators among the latter group. She paid special attention to the writings of Jean Jacques Rousseau, the famous French *philosophe,* and Dr. John Gregory, a medical professor closely associated with the leaders of the Scottish Enlightenment.[5]

Whether conservative or rationalist, these authors considered women physically inferior, domestic beings necessarily subordinate to their male protectors. Only in their hopes for heaven did women stand an even chance. Almost no one argued for civil or economic equality between the sexes. All sought improved education for women, but none believed in intellectual equality. The range of ideas on feminine education extended from training in advanced domestic arts to extensive reading (excluding such disciplines as classical language, philosophy, and science). Whatever the differences in program, however, most reformers sought to make women better companions for men and better teachers of children.

Mary Wollstonecraft constructed her argument for feminine equality upon commonplace principles of contemporary rationalist and republican thought. Associated after 1786 with such radical Enlightenment thinkers as William Godwin, Thomas Paine, Dr. Richard Price, and Joseph Priestley, she absorbed their protests against an authority based on revelation, precedent, or power. Extending from the physical to the social realm Isaac Newton's idea of a universe governed by natural law, she believed that human beings could discern through reason the absolute and unchanging law of nature and bring their conduct into harmony with it. Through science and education they could perfect society by assuring that each individual and group filled its appointed role in the natural order. But artificial authorities and hierarchies in church and state only obstructed human potential. Received doctrine and traditional institutions required testing, therefore, and deserved acceptance only if found in accord with the great rational design of the universe.

In the crowning events of the eighteenth century—the American and French Revolutions—lay both rationalist hopes for social institutions founded on natural law and conservative fears of the abyss of anarchy. Revolutionary statesmen and soldiers spoke eloquently of natural rights and republican liberties as opposed to the traditional prerogatives of monarchs, oligarchs, and aristocrats. In the flush of republican triumph, one of Mary Wollstonecraft's friends, Dr. Richard Price, enthusiastically endorsed the expected fruits of revolution. But his comments triggered the most devastating conservative attack on rationalist assumptions and revolutionary activity ever penned—Edmund Burke's *Reflections on the Revolution in France* (1790). Burke challenged the quick scrapping of a political system and the abstractions of the *philosophes*. Preferring historic privilege, he rejected the doctrine of natural rights as advanced by the revolutionary thinkers and admired the average Briton's continuing fear of God, awe of kings, affection for parliaments, duty to magistrates, reverence for priests, and respect for nobility.

Angered by Burke's assault on a good friend and an enlightened cause, Mary Wollstonecraft responded with the hastily written *Vindication of the Rights of Men* (1790), which established her reputation as a successful rationalist polemicist. This frequently emotional and vituperative reply attacked Burke's preference for tradition over theoretical or right reason. She thought that Burkean reverence for historic antecedents inevitably led to worship of the "savages, thieves, curates, or practitioners in the law" who founded states. Surely the admired British constitution had been "settled in the dark days of ignorance, when minds of men were shackled by the grossest prejudices and most immoral superstitions." "Somewhere," Wollstonecraft insisted, "implicit submission to authority . . . must stop, or we return to barbarism; and the capacity of improvement, which gives us a natural sceptre on earth, is a cheat." Only when human beings learn "to respect the sovereignty of reason" will they "discern good from evil" and "break the ignoble chain" of the past.[6]

Neither in her response to Burke nor in her *Vindication of the Rights of Woman* did Wollstonecraft endorse all the major positions of her radical rationalist friends. She allowed that Dr. Price's zeal carried him beyond "sound reason" to "utopian reveries." Unlike many of the radicals, she did not press beyond republicanism into open support of democracy or anarchy. Nor did she give up Christianity for deism, agnosticism, or atheism, although she was opposed to clerical establishments. Some of the radicals who considered human reason powerful enough to shape as well as discern nature looked forward to a state of social perfection in which absolute equality would be engineered. But Mary Wollstonecraft never expected "a heaven on earth." "I know that the human understanding is deluded with vain shadows, and that when we eagerly pursue any study, we only reach the boundary set to human enquiries."[7]

Thus she never asserted that the establishment of the natural order through reason would create an absolute equality between man and man or between man and woman. She accepted the existence of a "common law of gravity" which assigned to each individual or group an appropriate position in society. She admitted that women have less physical strength than men, a condition that no environmental effort could eradicate. And she acknowledged that greater physical strength made men better able to practice certain virtues. She also argued that women have a certain sphere of activity, particular duties, and a "maternal character" naturally different from men's. Furthermore, she conceded that historically women had always been subordinate to men.

Insisting that "it is justice, not charity, that is wanting in the world," Wollstonecraft demanded an equality of rights or opportunities for all human beings, even if such functional equality resulted in some groups or individuals being subordinate to others. Full access to the Creator through reason would free woman from the artificial stations arbitrarily assigned by man and allow her to find her God-ordained place in the natural order. Society could never achieve perfection until all groups or individuals functioned in harmony with the law of nature. But man assured woman's physical dependence and lowered her level of mental activity by denying her adequate physical exercise, providing inappropriate education, and permitting only a cramped sphere of activity. Denial of civil existence and work outside the home only extended woman's deficiencies, finally leaving her destitute of virtue. Man thereby created unnatural physical, intellectual, and moral inequalities between the sexes and sealed woman in an artificial inferiority.

Mary Wollstonecraft's belief in the essential rationality of mankind led her to place special emphasis upon the ability of correct education to overcome man-made degradation. She had initially ventured into print with *Thoughts on the Education of Daughters: with Reflections on Female Conduct, in the more important Duties of Life* (1787). Although *Thoughts* did not contain the greater feminist thrust of her later work, it indicated an early concern not only about women's education but also about their interest in "frippery" and their maternal negligence, points she later expanded in *Rights of Woman.* She also considered and bemoaned their limited career opportunities as well as the confining nature of the marriage relationship.

Wollstonecraft's thoughts about education of women were greatly influenced by Catherine Macaulay, author of a notable history of England, whose *Letters on Education* (1790) attributed much of woman's inferiority directly to faulty education.[8] Wollstonecraft thus supported an educational system with reduced sexual distinctions. She proposed the establishment of a national system of public and coeducational schools encouraging maximum student participation and self-regulation. By dedicating the *Rights of Woman* to Charles Talleyrand-Perigord, Mary Wollstonecraft publicly asked this French revolutionary leader to build more feminine equality into his country's most important social institution—its schools. Not until the demands of reason were more fully satisfied through education, Wollstonecraft argued, could women know what their natural function in society was.

Rationalist thought and republicanism effectively served the male bourgeois struggle to win freedom from aristocratic and feudal authorities. Mary Wollstonecraft hoped to extend similar freedom to bourgeois women as well. Few of the rationalists and republicans who preached "the rights of man" recognized the extent to which they were talking primarily about the privileges of the middle class. But Wollstonecraft openly acknowledged her "particular attention to those in the middle class." Indeed, her assertion that "the majority of mothers . . . leave their children entirely to the care of servants" offers one illustration of this class bias.

Equality of right or of opportunity would lift certain conventional restraints from all women. Yet functional equality was not of equal use to every woman, for all the disadvantages of poverty would prevent the lower classes from capitalizing effectively on the new freedoms. Since Wollstonecraft laid most stress upon edu-

cation to eradicate the worst sexual distinctions, the class implications of her educational reform have special importance. Critical of Talleyrand for advocating an identical education for boys and girls to age eight and ending formal feminine education then, she proposed to extend this absolute educational equality another year and allow women additional schooling. But her program for education beyond age nine allowed for rapidly increasing class and sexual differences. Although the benefits of the general attack on patriarchy and the proposed egalitarianism in early schooling spilled over to all classes, the *Rights of Woman* remained a feminine Declaration of Independence particularly for middle-class women.

Born into a middle-class home, Mary witnessed the desire for upward mobility and experienced the bitter taste of poverty which made rationalism and republicanism congenial. And having learned the meaning of social and economic displacement at the hands of man, she was likely to read a middle-class feminism into a middle-class rationalism. Surely her early experiences with men were too devastating and the roles thrust upon her as a youth too unconventional for her to equate the traditional position of women with the natural order.[9] Her father, a master weaver who squandered a sizeable inheritance attempting to become a gentleman farmer, failed miserably as protector and provider. His alcoholic bouts and abusive disposition rendered his timid wife cowering and ineffectual. Mary, the eldest daughter, provided financial and psychological support for her parents and most of her siblings for years.

An eighteenth-century adolescent girl with great drive but only a few years of day-school education had very limited resources for maintaining her own independence, let alone for supporting other people. At nineteen, Mary temporarily escaped from the oppressive family atmosphere to become a companion to an elderly woman. She returned home to nurse her ailing mother. Upon Elizabeth Wollstonecraft's death, Mary went to live with the family of her good friend Fanny Blood and sewed with the Blood women well into the night to supplement the meager income of another inadequate man. Mary, her sister Eliza, and Fanny opened a school which survived for three years. Then Mary served briefly as governess to the children of an Irish peer whose profligate wife neglected maternal duties, thereby accounting for much of Wollstonecraft's scorn for "ladies of fashion."

Mary Wollstonecraft determined in 1788 to make her living by the pen. But in spite of her extensive programs of self-education, she never overcame all the deficiencies which she attributed to inadequate schooling. Among the many causes which helped "to enslave women by cramping their understanding and shaping their senses," Mary thought "the disregard of order" did "more mischief than all the rest." An inadequate or misdirected education left women unable to generalize from observation and incapable of giving sufficient "vigor to the faculties and clearness to the judgment." She squeezed a modest living from translating and from writing essays, fiction, and review articles. But her treatises continued to lack that disciplined argument and logical organization characteristic of authors with an extended formal education or of radicals with an instinct for and commitment to theoretical consistency. She could not resist the temptation to dart off on tangents, to substitute polemic for argument, or to intrude parenthetical comments. Indeed after she became famous as a writer, Godwin appointed himself her grammar instructor.

While Mary tried in turn the occupations available to intelligent girls of her background and breeding, she did not consider that most popular alternative to autonomy—marriage. Too many of the marriages of relatives and close friends were disastrous. Her parents' example encouraged her to foreswear marriage at fifteen, and little that she saw thereafter shook her resolve. The ineffectual Mr. Blood depended first on his wife and later on Mary to support his family. And her dear friend Fanny died in childbirth in Lisbon, summoned there by the suitor who had originally rejected her. Mary had also spirited her distraught sister, Eliza, away from her husband and what Mary viewed as an emotionally disastrous union. Thus she despaired both for the single woman without support and the married woman who paid dearly for what support she received.

For all the apparent nonconformity of her life-style, Mary Wollstonecraft sought the substance of conventional relationships with men. A year after the publication of the *Rights of Woman,* she formed a liaison with Gilbert Imlay, an American painter then resident in France, where Mary was observing the Revolution. Becoming his mistress, she gave birth to a daughter. But Imlay tired of the relationship and took a new mistress in England. Distraught by this seeming betrayal, Mary attempted suicide. Within a year, however, she drifted into an affair with the noted radical, William Godwin.[10] He had argued in *Political Justice* for an end to matrimony as an institution, but he forsook this position in taking Mary as his legal wife. Neither in her life nor in her writing did she seek complete independence of woman from man. Unlike Godwin, she never renounced the institution of marriage, although she wanted to strip it of forms which had entrapped so many of her female friends and relatives. Recognizing certain essential functional differences between man and woman, she accepted the legitimacy of woman's domestic and maternal roles as long as they were not made enslaving. She and Godwin experimented with the appropriate degree of independence within the marriage bond by continuing to live and work in separate lodgings. But it was to

the maternal that she finally succumbed: Mary Wollstonecraft Godwin died in 1797 from the complications of childbirth. She left an autobiographical novel, *The Wrongs of Woman; or, Maria,* a sequel to the *Rights of Woman,* unfinished.

More sensitive to form than substance, the public noted those conventions which Mary Wollstonecraft flouted, not those she affirmed. She did not espouse many of the fundamental political, religious, or absolute egalitarian tenets of her radical rationalist friends. Yet she did not escape judgment by association, especially after her anarchist husband, Godwin, eulogized her in a widely read memoir which publicized her honest but unconventional arrangements with Imlay. Association with radicalism was not altogether unfashionable at the height of the revolutionary era, but Burke's stunning assault on revolutionary republicanism and rationalism and the continuing radicalization of the French Revolution turned the tide of opinion in Britain and America. Public openness to feminist and other proposals for social reconstruction decreased noticeably as the fortunes of republicanism, rationalism, and revolution waned.

Wollstonecraft's feminist attack on convention was nevertheless too telling to be completely ignored in the United States. Although the shift from seventeenth-century religious argument to eighteenth-century rationalism had not drastically affected many Americans' conception of woman's place, the popularity of Gregory, Rousseau, and others reflected a gradual improvement in social convention. However, not until Wollstonecraft's treatise appeared did Americans in any significant number face arguments for sexual equality directly. Even though the implications of her call for such equality immediately repelled most people, the issue had been effectively raised and a debate started that could not be dismissed easily.[11]

Charles Brockden Brown, the American novelist, discussed woman's rights in *Alcuin: A Dialogue,* published in 1798. Brown borrowed his ideas of sexual differences, education, and, to a lesser extent, marriage from Wollstonecraft. *Rights of Woman* also received serious attention from "Constantia" or Judith Sargent Murray, daughter of a prosperous and prominent Gloucester, Massachusetts, merchant. She published a three-volume collection of essays in 1798 dealing with several of Mary Wollstonecraft's themes. Brown and Mrs. Murray were not typical of their age, yet a few others shared their sentiments, including Aaron Burr, who considered the *Rights of Woman* a work of genius.[12]

A number of other Americans cited some of Mary Wollstonecraft's premises in the early nineteenth century. In *Observations on the Real Rights of Women* (1818), Hannah Mather Crocker found the "*Rights of*

Woman . . . replete with fine sentiments, though we do not coincide with her opinion respecting the total independence of the female sex." While not a radical, Cotton Mather's granddaughter desired freedom for her daughters to study "every branch of science, even jurisprudence." Mary's ideas also circulated among the more important British and American communitarian reformers of this period. Frances Wright, radical feminist and leader of the interracial Nashoba experiment, and Robert Owen and his son, Robert Dale Owen, of the New Lanark, Scotland, and New Harmony, Indiana, model communities, endorsed the *Rights of Woman.* Calling for a strike of mill girls in 1834, a still more militant young woman from Lowell, Massachusetts, delivered "a flaming Mary Wollstonecraft speech on the rights of women and the inequities of the 'monied aristocracy'" from atop the town pump.[13]

New editions of the *Rights of Woman* became available after 1833, and it was probably one of these that Lucretia Mott and Elizabeth Cady Stanton read. Shut out, along with other female delegates, from the 1840 World Anti-Slavery Convention, Mrs. Mott wandered the London streets with Mrs. Stanton discussing "Mary Wollstonecraft, her social theories, and her demands of equality for women." At this time they agreed to hold a woman's rights convention in America. If "the movement for woman's suffrage, both in England and America, may be dated from this World's Anti-Slavery Convention," then surely the spirit of Mary Wollstonecraft was present at its birth.[14]

Notes

1. The most accessible, complete edition of Mary Wollstonecraft, *A Vindication of the Rights of Woman with Strictures on Political and Moral Subjects,* is edited by Charles W. Hagelman, Jr. (New York: W. W. Norton & Co., Inc., 1967).

2. Contemporary English commentary on the *Rights of Woman* is quoted and summarized in Ralph M. Wardle, *Mary Wollstonecraft: A Critical Biography* (Lawrence: University of Kansas Press, 1951), 157-162. Emma Rauschenbusch-Clough, *A Study of Mary Wollstonecraft and the Rights of Woman* (London: Longmans, Green, and Co., 1898), 39-45, provides an extended formal analysis of Wollstonecraft's feminist ideas. See also Margaret George, *One Woman's "Situation": A Study of Mary Wollstonecraft* (Urbana: University of Illinois Press, 1970) and Eleanor Flexner, *Mary Wollstonecraft* (New York: Coward, McCann & Geoghegan, Inc., 1972) for fine contemporary examinations of Wollstonecraft's life and work.

3. Rauschenbusch-Clough, *Study of Wollstonecraft,* 43-45.

4. Excellent analyses of rationalist ambivalence toward blacks are developed in David Brion Davis,

Problems of Slavery in Western Culture (Ithaca: Cornell University Press, 1966), 391-421, and Winthrop D. Jordan, *White over Black: American Attitudes toward the Negro, 1550-1812* (Chapel Hill: University of North Carolina Press, 1968), 349-356, 429-481. For rationalism and women, see Mary S. Benson, *Women in Eighteenth Century America: A Study of Opinion and Social Usage* (Port Washington, New York: Kennikat Press, Inc., 1966 reissue of 1935 edition), 65-78, 127-171.

5. The best survey of eighteenth-century English and American thought about the position of women can be found in Benson, *Women in America,* 34-78.

6. Mary Wollstonecraft, *A Vindication of the Rights of Men, in a Letter to the Right Honourable Edmund Burke; Occasioned by His Reflections on the Revolution in France* (Gainesville, Florida: Scholars' Facsimiles & Reprints, 1960 reissue of 1790 edition), 19, 22-23, 61, 97. For analysis of this treatise, see Rauschenbusch-Clough, *Study of Wollstonecraft,* 71-86; Wardle, *Wollstonecraft,* 111-123; George, *Situation,* 87-89.

7. Wollstonecraft, *Rights of Men,* 33-35, 76-77.

8. For Wollstonecraft's debt to Macaulay, see Wardle, *Wollstonecraft,* 110, 144-145, 150-151.

9. For the details of Wollstonecraft's early life, see especially Wardle, *Wollstonecraft,* 3-110.

10. On Godwin and Wollstonecraft, see Rauschenbusch-Clough, *Study of Wollstonecraft,* 13-16, 176-185; Wardle, *Wollstonecraft,* 258-316; George, *Situation,* 149-168.

11. Benson, *Women in America,* 100-171.

12. Benson, *Women in America,* 172-187; Wardle, *Wollstonecraft,* 158, 357. Charles Brockden Brown's *Alcuin: A Dialogue* has been carefully edited by Lee R. Edwards and conveniently reprinted by Grossman Publishers (New York, 1970).

13. Aileen S. Kraditor, (ed.), *Up from the Pedestal: Selected Writings in the History of American Feminism* (Chicago: Quadrangle Books, Inc., 1968), 43; Wardle, *Wollstonecraft,* 334, 340; Rauschenbusch-Clough, *Study of Wollstonecraft,* 188; Eleanor Flexner, *Century of Struggle: The Woman's Rights Movement in the United States* (New York: Atheneum, 1968 reissue of 1959 edition), 55.

14. Wardle, *Wollstonecraft,* 340; Elizabeth Cady Stanton, Susan B. Anthony, Matilda J. Gage, and Ida H. Harper (eds.), *History of Woman Suffrage* (6 volumes, Rochester, New York, and New York, 1881-1922), I, 62.

Elissa S. Guralnick (essay date autumn 1977)

SOURCE: Guralnick, Elissa S. "Radical Politics in Mary Wollstonecraft's *A Vindication of the Rights of Woman*." *Studies in Burke and His Time* 18, no. 3 (autumn 1977): 155-66.

[*In the following essay, Guralnick argues that* A Vindication of the Rights of Woman *is much more than a feminist tract, and is a statement of extreme political radicalism that extends to criticizing, for example, the monarchy and the British educational system.*]

Since its publication in 1792, *A Vindication of the Rights of Woman* has been treated almost exclusively as a feminist manifesto, a simple defense of women's rights. Although critics have generally allowed that the *Rights of Woman* enlarges upon the political tenets expounded in the *Rights of Men,* little attention has been paid to the relationship between the two documents. It has been as if the warning implied in the March 1792 issue of the *Analytical Review* has been carefully and universally heeded: "It might be supposed that Miss W. had taken advantage of the popular topic of the 'Rights of Man' in calling her work 'A Vindication of the Rights of Woman,' had she not already published a work, one of the first answers that appeared to Mr. Burke, under the title of, 'A Vindication of the Rights of Men.' But in reality the present work is an elaborate *treatise of female education.*"[1] As the *Analytical* reviewer seems to have wished, *A Vindication of the Rights of Woman* has never been thoroughly examined as a political tract, a radical critique of society from broad egalitarian premises.

Yet the *Rights of Woman* is a radical political tract, even before it is a radical feminist tract. In fact, the feminism that animates the *Rights of Woman* is merely a special instance of the political radicalism that animates the *Rights of Men.* To ignore this fact is to misconstrue much of the basic character of *A Vindication of the Rights of Woman.* It is to fail, as Wollstonecraft's critics have usually done, to understand the propriety of the work's apparent digressions into such tenuously related material as the tyrannical abuse of power by kings and the effeteness of their courts, or the detrimental effects upon society of the existence of a standing army and navy, or the mistakes of educators who would lead boys too early into an understanding of the vices of the world. And it is to underestimate as well the full extent of the social reform that Wollstonecraft envisions as necessary to ameliorate the condition of women in her society. *A Vindication of the Rights of Woman* cannot be properly interpreted except as a statement of political radicalism—more bold, more uncompromising, and more intelligently argued than the earlier *Vindication of the Rights of Men.*

Indeed, for all its spirit, the *Rights of Men* is not an impressive political document. It was conceived far too

exclusively as a vituperative attack on the person and politics of Edmund Burke.[2] As the great British spokesman for conservative public polity, and as an apparent deserter from the cause of freedom he had espoused in approving the American Revolution, Burke was a natural butt for Wollstonecraft, committed as she was to egalitarian principles. But in his *Reflections on the Revolution in France,* Burke had offended Wollstonecraft on more than philosophical grounds. With an injustice that she could not allow to go unnoticed, Burke had maligned the Reverend Richard Price—dissenting minister, political radical, and friend to Wollstonecraft from her days as school-mistress in Newington Green. Price's sermon, *A Discourse on the Love of Our Country,* had served as the immediate provocation for the *Reflections,* and Burke had not concealed his scorn for the style or opinions of the eminent dissenter.[3] Wollstonecraft, only weeks after the publication of the *Reflections,* responded in kind, heaping on her opponent a wrath and a contempt she made no effort to disguise. Unabashedly, she characterized Burke as an unprincipled charlatan, given to wit above judgment, eloquence above honest simplicity, and opportunism above integrity.

In place of Burke's argument in defense of his political conservatism—an argument that Wollstonecraft thought to proceed from a spurious reliance upon supposed common sense[4]—Wollstonecraft offered an argument from reason. Reason tempered by passion, she contended, not only rejects Burke's appeal to tradition and the wisdom of antiquity, but also urges a spirit of revisionism founded on several clear truths: namely, that freedom is the birthright of all men; that the progress of virtue in civilization depends upon the equality of all men; that prescription and property are destructive of that equality and consequently injurious to the progress of virtue; that blind submission to authority is debasing to the men who kneel and ruinous to the men before whom the knee is bent. Elaboration of these truths vies with castigation of Burke as the principal focus of the *Rights of Men*; and the disorganization that follows from Wollstonecraft's divided purpose is compounded by the technique of free association that permits topic to succeed topic haphazardly throughout the text. In its incoherent organization, as in its rational and egalitarian premises, the *Rights of Men* looks ahead to its far more famous successor, *A Vindication of the Rights of Woman.*

The *Rights of Men* looks ahead, too, in the character of the figurative language that emerges from close reading of the text. Although Wollstonecraft was not a dedicated or inventive user of metaphor or simile in her prose, she does appear to be struggling in the *Rights of Men* to discover a particular figure—one fit to describe the condition of men (and women) who have been made deficient in their humanity by reason either of undue wealth and power or of staggering poverty and abjectness. From the first pages of her answer to Burke, Wollstonecraft shows herself to be at once interested in this problem of dehumanization and incapable of describing it fully. She is not content to say of the rich, who "pamper their appetites, and supinely exist without exercising mind or body," merely that "they have ceased to be men."[5] Groping after an expression harsh enough to describe their debasement, she calls them "artificial monster[s]," the deformed products of "hereditary property—hereditary honours."[6] A vivid metaphor, but not, it seems, a satisfactory one; for it is never used again. Sixteen pages later, the rich are spoken of together with the uneducated lower classes, both emerging in description as vulgar "creatures of habit and impulse."[7] The metaphor is ugly, particularly in its application to the poor, whom Wollstonecraft pitied; thus it, too, is abandoned. As the text proceeds, Wollstonecraft argues that sophistication, libertinism, servility, and depraved sensuality are unmanly;[8] but she finds no comprehensive figure by which to represent that unmanliness.

Not, at least, quite yet. But a figure is in the making—one that is at once startling and obvious, simple and extraordinary. That which is unmanly is, of course, womanly; and the realization that woman can be used as a general figure for the social and even political debasement of all mankind emerges sporadically but surely as the *Rights of Men* proceeds. As early as the third paragraph of the text, the possibility shyly obtrudes itself with Wollstonecraft's likening of a wit to a "celebrated beauty, [anxious] to raise admiration on every occasion, and excite emotion, instead of the calm reciprocation of mutual esteem and unimpassioned respect."[9] Later, "luxury and effeminacy" are identified as the curses of the aristocracy,[10] and "profligates of rank" are said to be "emasculated by hereditary effeminacy."[11] As Wollstonecraft's attention turns to and from the special problem of woman's place in society[12]—as woman becomes characterized as a flattered doll, vain, inconsiderate, intentionally weak and delicate, and designedly lacking in the "manly morals" of "truth, fortitude, and humanity"[13]—the metaphor urges itself more strongly upon Wollstonecraft and reader alike. Although not so insistent or complex in this text as in the *Vindication of the Rights of Woman,* the figure does reach a kind of climax in the *Rights of Men* when Wollstonecraft attacks the quality of Burke's patriotism and piety: "You love the church, your country, and its laws, you repeatedly tell us, because they deserve to be loved; but from you this is not a panegyric: weakness and indulgence are the only incitements to love and confidence that you can discern, and it cannot be denied that the tender mother you venerate deserves, on this score, all your affection."[14] Here in her description of the church as a weak, imprudent mother is the germ, already beginning to grow, of the figure which will animate and complicate the *Vindication of the Rights of Woman,* helping

to make this later text altogether as radical in its politics as in its sociology.

For if the *Rights of Woman* is a political treatise, it is so primarily by virtue of the fact that Wollstonecraft consciously describes political as well as social realities in England through and by means of the social condition of the country's women. In his biography of Mary Wollstonecraft, Ralph Wardle notes that the central thesis of the *Rights of Woman* is "that women as well as men are entitled by birthright to liberty and equality, and that if their rights are withheld, they will deter the progress of civilization. Truly Mary enjoyed at least one flash of genius, and that came when she recognized the similarity between the plight of oppressed womankind and that of oppressed mankind, and concluded that the solutions were identical."[15] The flash of genius Wardle identifies is genius indeed, but not accurately described; for the similarity he notes is more complex than he allows. Oppressed womankind serves in the *Rights of Woman* not merely as a figure for oppressed and impoverished mankind, but as a figure for all men, high as well as low, who are implicated in social and political contracts which condone inequality of rank, wealth, and privilege.

Indeed, it is significant that in the *Rights of Woman* Wollstonecraft more often likens women to the rich and powerful than to the poor and weak, as would seem most natural. Women are oppressed, it is true; but their oppression is, ironically, the consequence of their privileged status as pampered creatures of whom no mental competence or moral intelligence is expected. As Wollstonecraft argues in the course of her exposition, "birth, riches, and every extrinsic advantage that exalt a man above his fellows, without any mental exertion, sink him in reality below them. In proportion to his weakness, he is played upon by designing men, till the bloated monster has lost all traces of humanity."[16] Speaking primarily of middle-class women, but warning that "the whole female sex are, till their character is formed, in the same condition as the rich,"[17] Wollstonecraft argues that women are born to indulgence, and powerful in the very weakness that is the beauty and cunning by which they lord it over the men who imprison them. Thus, women can be seen to "act as men are observed to act when they have been exalted by the same means."[18] They are, in short, "either abject slaves or capricious tyrants"[19]—different sides of the same devalued coin.

So it is that Wollstonecraft can argue that women enjoy "illegitimate power" and receive "regal homage."[20] They are like Turkish bashaws,[21] like despots,[22] like kings,[23] like Roman emperors,[24] like "vicegerents allowed to reign over a small domain"[25]—and, conversely, all such tyrants are like women. When Wollstonecraft opines that it is impossible for any man, when the most favourable circumstances concur, to acquire sufficient knowledge and strength of mind to discharge the duties of a king, entrusted with uncontrouled power; how then must they be violated when his very elevation is an insuperable bar to the attainment of either wisdom or virtue; when all the feelings of a man are stifled by flattery, and reflection shut out by pleasure! Surely it is madness to make the fate of thousands depend on the caprice of a weak fellow creature, whose very station sinks him *necessarily* below the meanest of his subjects![26]

we can only understand that the regal character has been feminized in its degradation. Such is the inevitable conclusion to be drawn from the metaphoric pattern of the text.

That Wollstonecraft herself has drawn this very conclusion is evident from her discussion of the military. Soldiers, kings, and women, she contends somewhat disjointedly, are linked by similar, vicious characteristics. Soldiers, after all, by reason of their participation in a rigid military hierarchy, are types of the enslaved monarch: "Every corps is a chain of despots, who, submitting and tyrannizing without exercising their reason, become dead weights of vice and folly on the community."[27] And every individual within every corps is characterized by womanly indolence, polished manners, and love of ornamental dress. Officers, especially, are "particularly attentive to their persons, fond of dancing, crowded rooms, adventures, and ridicule. Like the *fair* sex, the business of their lives is gallantry.—They were taught to please, and they only live to please."[28] Lest we miss the point, Wollstonecraft concludes a long quotation from Rousseau—actually an extended comparison of the respective intellectual provinces of men and women—with the single comment, "I hope my readers still remember the comparison, which I have brought forward, between women and officers."[29] Officers, we are made to realize, have been emasculated, womanized, by their exalted position within the body politic; and war has become "rather the school of *finesse* and effeminacy, than of fortitude."[30]

Emasculated, too, are the rich; for "wealth and female softness equally tend to debase mankind."[31] Thus, the society of the great, like the society of women, is insipid.[32] "Women, in general, as well as the rich of both sexes, have acquired all the follies and vices of civilization, and missed the useful fruit";[33] for both "neglect the duties of humanity"[34]—women, by failing to cultivate their bodies and intellects for the benefit of their families; the rich, by failing to develop their physical and mental powers, in accordance with the laws of nature, for their own benefit and that of the state. Once again, Wollstonecraft drives home her point with a slyly framed quotation:

> When do we hear of women who, starting out of obscurity, boldly claim respect on account of their great

abilities or daring virtues? Where are they to be found?—'To be observed, to be attended to, to be taken notice of with sympathy, complacency, and approbation, are all the advantages which they seek.'—True! my male readers will probably exclaim; but let them, before they draw any conclusion, recollect that this was not written originally as descriptive of women, but of the rich. In Dr. Smith's Theory of Moral Sentiments, I have found a general character of people of rank and fortune, that, in my opinion, might with the greatest propriety be applied to the female sex. I refer the sagacious reader to the whole comparison.[35]

The effeminate rich, like the effeminate military, enjoy social and political status at the expense of their own masculinity.

So natural is it for Wollstonecraft to argue that women enjoy the degradation of the exalted, that she rarely likens them to the truly abject. Occasionally, they are compared to the "mass of mankind"—"obsequious slaves, who patiently allow themselves to be penned up";[36] occasionally, their condition is likened to that of the poor.[37] And in one outstanding instance, the wife who patiently drudges for her husband is said to be "like a blind horse in a mill."[38] But characteristically, woman is described as a privileged slave, an underling comfortable in a debasement of which she herself approves. Thus, she is very much like a courtier who grovels before the king and, as a reward for his congeniality, enjoys himself a certain amount of groveling from others:

> From whence arises the easy fallacious behavior of a courtier? From his situation, undoubtedly: for standing in need of dependents, he is obliged to learn the art of denying without giving offence, and, of evasively feeding hope with the chameleon's food: thus does politeness sport with truth, and eating away the sincerity and humanity natural to man, produce the fine gentleman.
>
> Women in the same way acquire, from a supposed necessity, an equally artificial mode of behaviour.[39]

Woman is that saddest of spectacles—a human being of possible merit, defrauded of her potential and trivialized. And in so far as men are like her in their positions within the body politic, they too are defrauded and trivialized.

It is for this reason, no doubt, that Wollstonecraft so closely associates the betterment of woman's plight with the rise of the classless society.[40] Effeminacy—with all its implications of weakness, vanity, and amorality—must be banished from the state, and from all social and political institutions within the state, even as it is banished from individuals. The *Vindication of the Rights of Woman* cannot be a feminist document without also being a radical political tract, if only because Wollstonecraft perceives the private and public problems of her country to be inextricably related. "A man has been termed a microcosm; and every family might also be called a state,"[41] she asserts. "Public virtue is only an aggregate of private."[42] So long, then, as private virtue permits the indulgence and the debasement of woman, the state and all the individuals in it will suffer from a similar degradation.

It can thus be argued that Wollstonecraft does not digress from her subject when she turns her attention to what appear to be tangential matters. Although her text could be organized more coherently and the connections among her points stated more clearly, she does not willfully wander from her just domain. The conduct of parents toward children, of teachers toward pupils, of bishops toward country vicars, of military officers toward underlings, of monarchs toward subjects—these are all, after their fashion, types of the conduct of husbands toward wives; and as such, all bear examination and criticism. Even such "episodical observations" as those in which Wollstonecraft mourns the demise of the British hero or decries the vicious self-interest of the British statesman[43] have their relevance. Such disgraces are intimately related to the paucity of virtue in British society, and virtue is condemned to moulder so long as woman is abused and happy in her abuse. As Wollstonecraft notes in her introduction to the ***Rights of Woman,*** "weak, artificial beings, raised above the common wants and affections of their race, in a premature unnatural manner, undermine the very foundation of virtue, and spread corruption through the whole mass of society!"[44] Women—especially those who are or who aspire to be ladies—are preeminently such beings; and the evidence of the corruption to which they contribute is as much Wollstonecraft's subject as the defense of their misappropriated rights.

Ultimately, it is the premise of Wollstonecraft's feminism that the establishment of women's rights must be allied to a complete transformation of society and the body politic. If the ***Rights of Woman*** seems less radical than such a premise would suggest, that is only because Wollstonecraft has had the tact merely to hint at the character society will assume when its transformation is complete. Reason, of course, will prevail; and a total leveling of distinctions among men (and women) will have been accomplished. More than any other end, Wollstonecraft desires the establishment of unexceptioned equality among all rational beings. She will allow a superior place in the order of things only to God, who merits homage by virtue of his wisdom and justice, not by virtue of his power. Even God himself cannot be a tyrant in Wollstonecraft's perfect society: he must be rational and virtuous, so that his character may serve as a foundation for human morality. Men, meanwhile, must regulate their behavior "according to . . . common laws," recognizing a lesson in the fact that "the eccentric orbit of the comet never influences astronomical calculations respecting the invariable or-

der established in the motion of the principal bodies of the solar system."[45] Eccentricity—even the eccentricity of the hero or the genius—is, for Wollstonecraft, unnecessary and perhaps detrimental to the common good.

> It is not for the benefit of society that a few brilliant men should be brought forward at the expence of the multitude. It is true, that great men seem to start up, as great revolutions occur, at proper intervals, to restore order, and to blow aside the clouds that thicken over the face of truth; but let more reason and virtue prevail in society, and these strong winds would not be necessary.[46]
>
> The welfare of society is not built on extraordinary exertions; and were it more reasonably organized, there would be still less need of great abilities, or heroic virtues.[47]

Three years later, in writing her history of the French Revolution, Wollstonecraft would return to this point, blaming the failure of the century's great social movement on those luminaries whose "patriotism expir[ed] with their popularity":

> It will be only necessary to keep in mind the conduct of all the leading men, who have been active in the revolution, to perceive, that the disasters of the nation have arisen from the same miserable source of vanity, and the wretched struggles of selfishness; when the crisis required, that all enlightened patriots should have united and formed a band, to have consolidated the great work; the commencement of which they had accelerated. In proportion as these desertions have taken place, the best abilities which the country contained have disappeared. And thus it has happened, that ignorance and audacity have triumphed, merely because there were not found those brilliant talents, which, pursuing the straight forward line of political economy, arrest, as it were, the suffrage of every well disposed citizen.—Such talents existed in France: and had they combined, and directed their views by a pure love of their country, to one point; all the disasters, which in overwhelming the empire have destroyed the repose of Europe, would not have occurred to disgrace the cause of freedom.[48]

If talent is to be an object of Wollstonecraft's respect, it must be employed for society's benefit by individuals indifferent to their own personal stake in the success they might achieve through largely individual endeavor. Talent, in other words—like wisdom, reason, and virtue—must be respected as an abstraction; and its possessors must be content to work for the common good without distinguishing themselves from the common man.[49]

How the perfect society of patriotic equals is to be established Wollstonecraft does not say, although there is evidence in the ***Rights of Woman*** that she believed its eventual establishment to be simply in the nature of things. "Every thing around us," she argues at one point, "is in a progressive state":[50] everything that survives the difficulties of existence develops from a weak and vulnerable infancy to a strong and dignified maturity. Society is no exception. In its infancy, it suffers the domination of an aristocracy that soon gives way, under the pressures of "clashing interests," to a monarchy and hierarchy; later, as civilization enlightens the multitude, the monarchy finds itself forced to maintain its unjustified power by means of a deception and a corruption which at once poison the populace and point out their own antidote—"the perfection of man in the establishment of true civilization."[51] Such, Wollstonecraft would later argue, was the experience of the French, whose

> revolution was neither produced by the abilities or intrigues of a few individuals; nor was the effect of sudden and short-lived enthusiasm; but the natural consequence of intellectual improvement, gradually proceeding to perfection in the advancement of communities, from a state of barbarism to that of polished society, till now arrived at the point when sincerity of principles seems to be hastening the overthrow of the tremendous empire of superstition and hypocrisy, erected upon the ruins of gothic brutality and ignorance.[52]

Nature, Wollstonecraft seems to assert, will provide for our own best interests in her own good time; we need only assist her by recognizing the character of those interests and working patiently on their behalf.

It is perhaps for this reason that Wollstonecraft poses so few practical solutions to the problems she identifies in the *Rights of Woman.* No measures she might suggest could possibly rival the wisdom of those measures that will naturally arise in the course of civilization's gradual development. Wollstonecraft need not attempt to incite revolution or even reform. She need only assist the slow, unalterable movement of progress by clarifying the character of those social problems which will demand solution in future years and by adumbrating the probable shape those solutions will take.[53] If, then, the *Rights of Woman* appears somewhat timid in the few proposals for reform that it offers, that appearance is largely misleading. As Wollstonecraft explains in the first chapter of her text, "Rousseau exerts himself to prove that all *was* right originally: a crowd of authors that all *is* now right: and I, that all will *be* right."[54] For Wollstonecraft, "all will *be* right" only when the whole of society has undergone a radical reordering. In the promise of that reordering lies the extreme political radicalism that is at once the premise and the sine qua non of *A Vindication of the Rights of Woman.*

Notes

1. *Analytical Review* 12 (1792): 248-249.

2. A perceptive analysis of style and rhetoric in the *Rights of Men* appears in James T. Boulton, *The Language of Politics in the Age of Wilkes and Burke* (London: Routledge and Kegan Paul, 1963), pp. 167-176. Boulton shows that Wollstonecraft's criticism of Burke—whose style she finds too much marked by passion and imagination and too little controlled by reason—is equally applicable to her own prose style in this emotional pamphlet. Boulton concludes that Wollstonecraft conveys the impression of being "a writer whose views were strongly felt and vigorously communicated; many of the strictures she directs at the *Reflections* are valid and telling; but the chief weakness is Wollstonecraft's inability to embody at all times in her prose those qualities of intellectual honesty and emotional discipline which she claimed were of prime importance to a political philosopher. She condemns Burke and, by the same token, is herself condemned" (pp. 175-176).

3. Edmund Burke, *Reflections on the Revolution in France,* in *Works,* 6 vols. (London: Bohn, 1854), 2: 285 ff.

4. For Wollstonecraft's discussion of Burke's premises, see *A Vindication of the Rights of Men* (1790), ed Eleanor Louise Nicholes (Gainesville: Scholars' Facsimiles and Reprints, 1960), p. 68.

5. Ibid., pp. 10-11.

6. Ibid., p. 12.

7. Ibid., p. 28.

8. Ibid., pp. 42, 47, 50, 116, respectively.

9. Ibid., p. 4.

10. Ibid., p. 51.

11. Ibid., p. 97.

12. Ibid., pp. 47-48, 52, 111-115.

13. Ibid., p. 112.

14. Ibid., p. 124.

15. *Mary Wollstonecraft: A Critical Biography* (Lawrence: University of Kansas Press, 1951), p. 157.

16. *A Vindication of the Rights of Woman, with Strictures on Political and Moral Subjects* (London, 1792), p. 91. A more readily available text—a reprint of the slightly revised second edition of the *Rights of Woman*—is the Norton Critical Edition, ed. Carol H. Poston (New York, 1975); in Poston's edition, the quotation is found on p. 45. All subsequent quotations from the *Rights of Woman* will be cited by two page numbers—the first a reference to the 1792 edition, the second a reference to Poston's.

17. Wollstonecraft, *Rights of Woman,* p. 122/57.

18. Ibid., p. 92/45.

19. Ibid., p. 92/45.

20. Ibid., p. 38/21.

21. Ibid., p. 80/40.

22. Ibid., pp. 80/40, 115/54.

23. Ibid., pp. 85/42, 119/56.

24. Ibid., p. 89/44.

25. Ibid., p. 98/48.

26. Ibid., pp. 24-25/16.

27. Ibid., p. 27/17.

28. Ibid., p. 43/24.

29. Ibid., p. 79/39.

30. Ibid., p. 332/145.

31. Ibid., p. 108/51.

32. Ibid., p. 107/51.

33. Ibid., p. 129/60.

34. Ibid., p. 138/64.

35. Ibid., pp. 122-123/57-58.

36. Ibid., p. 109/52.

37. Ibid., p. 134/62.

38. Ibid., p. 144/67.

39. Ibid., pp. 298-299/131.

40. See, for instance, ibid., pp. 38/22 and 74/38.

41. Ibid., p. 411/177.

42. Ibid., p. 445/192.

43. Ibid., pp. 327-329/143-144.

44. Ibid., p. 5/9.

45. Ibid., p. 307/134.

46. Ibid., pp. 372-373/162.

47. Ibid., p. 136/64.

48. *An Historical and Moral View of the Origin and Progress of the French Revolution* (London, 1794), pp. 301-302.

49. Early in the *French Revolution* (p. 7), Wollstonecraft announces the strength of her commitment to total equality among men by charging government with the responsibility of leveling natural inequalities: "Nature having made men unequal, by giving stronger bodily and mental powers to one than to another, the end of government ought to be, to destroy this inequality by protect-

ing the weak." Essentially, she wishes to maintain the advantages which accrue to society from men of superior intelligence and training, while diminishing the disadvantages which arise from the social and political privilege usually accorded them.

50. *Rights of Woman*, p. 242/108.

51. Ibid., pp. 29-31/18-19.

52. *French Revolution*, pp. vii-viii.

53. Indeed, the example of the French Revolution would later evoke in Wollstonecraft a firm commitment to gradualism. In her history of the Revolution, Wollstonecraft would argue that only an excessive degeneracy and tyranny of the aristocracy can justify a people's "having recourse to coercion, to repel coercion." For if the progress of reason is likely to bring about a melioration of conditions in government, "it then seems injudicious for statesmen to force the adoption of any opinion, by aiming at the speedy destruction of obstinate prejudices; because these premature reforms, instead of promoting, destroy the comfort of those unfortunate beings, who are under their dominion, affording at the same time to despotism the strongest arguments to urge opposition to the theory of reason" (*French Revolution*, pp. 69-70).

54. *Rights of Woman*, p. 22/15.

R. M. James (essay date April-June 1978)

SOURCE: James, R. M. "On the Reception of Mary Wollstonecraft's *A Vindication of the Rights of Woman*." *Journal of the History of Ideas* 39, no. 2 (April-June 1978): 293-302.

[*In the following essay, James discusses the early reviews of* A Vindication of the Rights of Woman, *which were largely favorable, and compares them to the later reviews after Wollstonecraft's reputation had collapsed.*]

It is popularly assumed that Mary Wollstonecraft's *A Vindication of the Rights of Woman* was greeted with shock, horror, and derision when it appeared early in 1792, that the forces of reaction massed against this bold attempt to assert the equality of woman and spattered the Amazon with their pens. Her biographers have repeatedly asserted that the first reviews and recorded reactions to the work were generally favorable, but they have had little impact on the popular misconception. The reasons for that scholarly ineffectuality are obvious enough. Later in the decade, Wollstonecraft was vilified by the press, and for much of the nineteenth century hers was a name to brandish at feminists as evidence of the horrific consequences of female emancipation. The furious clamorings of 1798 quite overwhelmed the calm approbation of 1792 in both intensity and duration. Since most writers on Wollstonecraft and the *Rights of Woman* are concerned primarily with the tardy progress of female emancipation, they expect a negative response to her and her work and have less than an active interest in the peculiarities of late eighteenth-century social thought. But the reception of Wollstonecraft's work and that of her followers, Mary Robinson and Mary Hays, illuminates an interesting moment in the historical transformation of women's status. Those works, part educational, part psychological, part political, appeared when the contest for improvement of women's education and their status in the family had been largely won, and the contest for enlarged political, civil, social liberties was about to be joined. The progressive intellectual circles represented by the leading reviews reacted positively to demands for intellectual equality, improved education, and reformed manners. Demands for political participation by women or for changes in women's social behavior were regarded as unessential and absurd. Those elements of the works in question that corresponded to changes that had been in train for half a century were approved; those that marked out the direction of more drastic social transformations were rightly though disapprovingly remarked as revolutionary and visionary, if they were seen at all.

With one important exception, every notice the *Rights of Woman* received when it first appeared was favorable. The reviews were split along party lines. Periodicals of radical inclination, sharing Wollstonecraft's philosophical assumptions, sympathetic towards the rights of man and events in France, distressed by Edmund Burke's lack of consistency, approved the work. Enthusiasts of the rights of man, they did not greet the rights of woman with horror. Wollstonecraft had written for the *Analytical Review* since 1788. Joseph Johnson who had published both the *Analytical* and the book, reviewed it positively, of course, as did the *Literary Magazine,* the *General Magazine,* the *New York Magazine,* the *Monthly Review,* and the *New Annual Register.* These periodicals had also favorably noticed her *Vindication of the Rights of Men,* one of the first answers to Burke's *Reflections on the Revolution in France.* The single journal that had favorably reviewed her *Rights of Men* and ignored the *Rights of Woman* was the *English Review.*[1] Although periodicals less politically or more conservatively committed did not in the main choose to review the work, the *Critical Review* attacked it in two passionate installments.

The contents of the reviews favorable to the work indicate why it was ignored rather than virulently attacked by most of those opposed to the political assumptions Wollstonecraft held. Most reviewers took it to be a sensible treatise on female education and ignored those recommendations in the work that might unsettle the re-

lations between the sexes. The *Analytical*'s response was typical. The work was catalogued for the year not under politics, but under "political economy," and the reviewer observed that "in reality the present work is an elaborate *treatise of female education.* . . . If the bulk of the great truths which this publication contains were reduced to practice, the nation would be better, wiser, and happier than it is upon the wretched, trifling, useless and absurd system of education which is now prevalent."[2] This ability to ignore the work's political implications crossed party lines. In an exchange between Horace Walpole and Hannah More, neither of whom had read the book and both of whom had "been much pestered to read" it, Walpole told More that he had been "assured it contains neither metaphysics nor politics. . . ." When Walpole flung his memorable phrase "that hyena in petticoats" at Wollstonecraft, the occasion was a political provocation to which the *Rights of Woman* was irrelevant. He objected to her attack on Marie Antoinette in the *Historical and Moral View of the Origin and Progress of the French Revolution* (1794), and his phrase reciprocates Wollstonecraft's hostility and contempt towards the French queen.[3] As in later attacks on Wollstonecraft, Walpole's hostility was directed against the female republican writer, and not against the vindicator of the rights of woman. In 1792 in Walpole and in More's circle, there were those who managed to find the work innocuous as a political tract and valuable as an educational and critical one.

In approving the work, the reviewers endorsed the view that the character of women at the present time needed to become more independent, more rational, more equal to men in mind and spirit; and they indicated how widespread the assumptions of earlier educational reformers had become. As is so often the case with British reformers, the benevolent, improving impulse sought to ameliorate the condition of the sex, not to alter relative positions between the sexes. Her demands for change in woman's spiritual condition approved, Wollstonecraft's hopes for social change earned from most of her reviewers the general reservation that "several of her opinions are fanciful, and some of her projects romantic."[4] The differences were specified by the most feminist of the reviewers, William Enfield.

Enfield was a dissenting minister with impeccable credentials; he had been associated with the Warrington Academy, was the memorialist of John Aikin, Mrs. Barbauld's father, and was memorialized in his turn by Aikin's son, Dr. John Aikin. Reviewing the *Rights of Woman* in Ralph Griffiths' *Monthly Review,* he refrained from chiding Wollstonecraft for her "challenge to the ancient wisdom that considered women to be inferior men," and rejoiced that "how jealous soever WE may be of our *right* to the proud preeminence which we have assumed, the women of the present age are daily giving us indubitable proofs that mind is of no sex, and that, with the fostering aid of education, the world, as well as the nursery, may be benefited by their instructions." He included her in the class of "philosophers" and would not offend her by styling her "authoress" (as the *Literary Magazine* had done). He copiously endorsed "the important business here undertaken . . . to correct errors, hitherto universally embraced, concerning the female character; and to raise woman, from a state of degradation and vassalage, to her proper place in the scale of existence; where, in the dignity of independence, she may discharge the duties and enjoy the happiness of a rational Being." The opinions that Enfield explicitly rejected are those that Wollstonecraft had anticipated would provoke laughter: the suggestions that women assume "an active part in civil government," that they abandon "the useful and elegant labours of the needle," and that the distinction of sexes be obliterated in social intercourse save where "love animates the behavior." The first and second Enfield considered of little importance in improving the condition and character of women, the third impracticable outside of heaven. In spite of his retreat at those points where feminist opinions might make a practical social difference, Enfield did fortify the lonely outpost of a rational asexual ideal: "Both men and women should certainly in the first place, regard themselves, and should be treated by each other, as human beings," and he concluded his remarks with a wish that English possessed "some general term to denote the species, like Ανθρωπος and *Homo* in the Greek and Roman languages. The want of such a general term is a material defect in our language."[5]

Enfield's position both typifies the limitations of the response to the *Rights of Woman* and corresponds to the order in which reforms were to be achieved in the nineteenth and twentieth centuries. Women were to be better educated, more respectable, and more useful as doctors, nurses, teachers before they were to be admitted to civic participation. They would have colleges before they had the vote, and the vote before the question of obliterating behavioral differences between the sexes was raised again. The principal difference between the pro- and anti-feminist positions at the end of the eighteenth century and the beginning of the nineteenth was less their attitude towards future change than their attitude towards past formulations. The *Critical Review,* which produced the only attack on the *Rights of Woman,* was also the only review to maintain the essential inferiority and the necessary subordination of women.

That the *Critical* should have picked up the volume at all is surprising, although Derek Roper has pointed out that the review went through a moderately liberal phase between 1774 and 1805. Robinson, the publisher of the *New Annual Register,* who was to be fined in 1793 for selling Paine's *Rights of Man,* had become a partner in 1774 and exerted a moderating influence on editorial

policies.[6] In spite of Robinson's association, the *Critical* reviewed Burke's *Reflections* favorably and scarified both Wollstonecraft and Paine on the rights of man. In the *Rights of Woman* the *Critical* saw the revolutionary implications of the social recommendations more clearly than the liberal reviews. As a consequence, it rejected explicitly the feminist premise that there is no characteristic difference in sex, but at the same time it endorsed educational premises that would have seemed actively and aggressively "feminist" fifty years earlier. Most disturbing to the reviewer was Wollstonecraft's attack on the idea of a sexual character.

The reviewer favored educating women for the same objects Wollstonecraft had suggested: women should possess knowledge so as to be more suitable companions to their husbands, better tutors to their children, more useful members of society. They should be able to examine a subject coolly, compare arguments, estimate degrees of evidence, and trace the evolutions of the human mind. And Wollstonecraft is praised for the force and conviction that her arguments on this score carry. The point of difference was not the cultivation of women's minds, but the relative roles of the sexes and the psychological characteristics that are and ought to be peculiar to each. The author stood firm on the intellectual inferiority of women: no women exist or have existed who are the intellectual equals of men, and demonstrate the same strength of reasoning or reach of intuitive perception. Even if women should possess the abilities that men do, it is not desirable that they should exercise them: "and when all are strong, to whom must the weaker operations belong? The female Plato will find it unsuitable to 'the dignity of her virtue' to dress the child, and descend to the disgusting offices of a nurse . . . and the young lady, instead of studying the softer and more amiable arts of pleasing, must contend with her lover for superiority of mind, for greater dignity of virtue; and before she condescends to become his wife, must prove herself his equal or superior." The utilitarian base of the argument is comical enough: the tasks allotted women are so disagreeable that if women possessed alternatives, no one would do them; the child would stop undressed, the weak unnursed. Contempt for feminine duties, fear of equality in relations between the sexes, conviction of the superiority of men and the masculine sphere of activity are all evident. At times the eighteenth-century fascination with polygamy seems to be lurking just under the surface of the prose, revelling in the grammar: we are told that "women [plural] are the companions of man [singular], and the companions of a rational creature should possess reason not totally uncultivated." Elsewhere the tendency to consider women as an undifferentiated herd and masculine achievement as singular turns up in the numbers used to refute Wollstonecraft's contention that women should have representatives in parliament: if they did, "the state would lose 10,000 useful domestic wives, in pursuit of one very indifferent philosopher or states-man." Although he faulted Wollstonecraft for discussing modesty and carnal appetites too freely, the reviewer was not afraid that the work would promote sexual license. Quite the contrary: "The precepts are calculated to form such women as we hope never to see; such as we are certain would waste their days in joyless celibacy, their sweets upon the desert air."[7]

When the *Rights of Woman* first appeared in 1792, reviewers and readers alike agreed with its recommendations for reform in women's education. If we take "feminism" to mean anxiety for the education of women and the improvement of their minds, there did not exist an anti-feminist in England in 1790. If we take feminism to mean restlessness with the subordinate position of women and a vague desire that women should be possessed of more "liberty" and more consequence, then public opinion was divided between those who thought that women had quite enough liberty as it was and those who thought the rhetoric of submission inappropriate to relations between men and women. If we take feminism to mean demands for specific changes in women's civil disabilities, including the right to vote, Wollstonecraft herself barely qualifies, and her followers, Hays and Robinson, do not even make the attempt. But although Wollstonecraft stayed securely enough within the established boundaries of educational writing not to terrify her first readers, she ventured out of bounds often enough to exhilarate them.

As should now be commonly known, Wollstonecraft's reputation collapsed as a consequence of two separate events: the course of the revolution in France and consequent repudiation of the vocabulary of revolution in England; and Godwin's publication of her posthumous works, including *Maria Or The Wrongs of Woman* and his *Memoirs of the Author of a Vindication of the Rights of Woman.* When she died in 1797, generous obituaries appeared in the *Gentleman's Magazine,* the *Monthly Magazine,* the *European Magazine,* and *New York Magazine.*[8] When Godwin's *Memoirs* appeared the following year, they were picked up for review by far more periodicals than had taken up the *Rights of Woman* itself.

The *Memoirs* revealed that Wollstonecraft had borne a child out of wedlock and then been deserted by her lover (Gilbert Imlay), that she had pursued him and had attempted suicide on two occasions, that she had found consolation with Godwin and had engaged in sexual relations with him before marriage. This series of actions found no approval at the time from any political persuasion. The periodicals that had been favorably disposed towards the *Rights of Woman* united in wishing the *Memoirs* unwritten, unpublished, and unread. If the *Memoirs* were "a singular tribute of respect to the memory of a well beloved wife,"[9] the vindication of

adultery in *Maria* was scarcely more palatable. The most sympathetic readings of the *Memoirs* attempted to palliate her acts by attributing them to virtuous though mistaken motives. Having shared Wollstonecraft's political principles, this set of reviewers did not insist upon a necessary connection between her politics and her sexual divagations.

For those opposed to her politics, the *Memoirs* and *Maria* served up a delicious evidence of the consequences of Jacobin principles in action. The anti-Jacobin attacks on Wollstonecraft took two forms: the merely scurrilous attack and the politically motivated scurrilous attack. The anti-Jacobin but professedly apolitical periodicals, displayed the scandals in detail but paid little attention to her works. The life alone testified to the consequences of adhering to the "new order" and provided an example which, "if followed, would be attended with the most pernicious consequences to society; a female who could brave the opinion of the world in the most delicate point; a philosophical wanton, breaking down the bars intended to restrain licentiousness; and a mother, deserting a helpless offspring, disgracefully brought into the world by herself, by an intended act of suicide."[10]

The reviews founded for polemical purposes, the *British Critic* and the *Anti-Jacobin Review,* gave her publications more attention and distinguished themselves by a particularly nasty use of the argument ad feminam. To the clergyman conducting the *British Critic* (Archdeacon Robert Nares and William Beloe), she appeared "in the strongest sense, a voluptuary and sensualist but without refinement." As had the *Gentleman's Magazine,* they remarked the contrast between the *Rights of Woman* and Godwin's version of Wollstonecraft's last hours: "The reader of the Vindication of the Rights of Woman, will perhaps be surprised when he is informed, that, during her last illness, no religious expression escaped the author's lips. In that work, the grand principle is, that woman is not the inferior of man, but his equal in moral rank, walking along with him the road of duty, in which "they are both trained for a state of endless improvement.""[11] With his version of the general proposition enforced by the *Rights of Woman* the reviewer has no quarrel, but it is clear that Wollstonecraft was led from the road of duty by the glimmerings of false philosophy. The *Anti-Jacobin* compared her to Messalina, denigrated the originality of her work, and isolated its political elements:

> Next succeeded her Rights of Woman, which the superficial fancied to be profound, and the profound knew to be superficial: it indeed had very little title to the character of ingenuity. Her doctrines are almost all obvious corollaries from the theorems of Paine. If we admit his principle, that all men have an equal right to be governors and statesmen, without any regard to their talents and virtues, there can be no reason for excluding women or even children.[12]

As had the *Critical* in 1792, the *Anti-Jacobian* located the vulnerability of the **Rights of Woman** in precisely those elements that account for the continuing interest in the work. The political features exaggerated for satiric purposes by eighteenth-century opponents are those isolated for praise by twentieth-century readers. Figure and ground have changed places.

To a considerable extent, it was the *Memoirs* rather than the **Rights of Woman** that shaped and colored Wollstonecraft's subsequent reputation. At the extremes of approval and disapproval were those like Godwin and the *Anti-Jacobin* who considered her acts an illustration of Jacobin morality in action. Between the ideologues were those like Matilda Betham who represented Wollstonecraft as an amiable eccentric who had refused to marry Imlay as a matter of principle, those who approved her principles and were embarrassed by her actions, and those who found both her life and principles reprehensible.[13] The range of attitudes has remained much the same from the beginning of the nineteenth century to the last quarter of the twentieth. The most obvious shift has been the replacement of moral disapproval by psychological disapproval: the lady was not evil, but certainly very odd, and not to be imitated.[14]

When the **Rights of Woman** first appeared, the attitude taken towards it varied directly with the political position of her reviewers, and the work was not generally regarded as politically significant. With the appearance of the *Memoirs,* the **Rights of Woman** came to seem more revolutionary than it had at first. Providing a vulnerable combination of sexual and political error, Wollstonecraft became the symbolic center for attacks on radical female writers. In certain circles, her name detached itself from her work and came to serve as a red flag for writers forgetful of what she had said. The influence of her name appears most strikingly in the reception accorded the works of her near followers Mary Robinson and Mary Hays.

Robinson's *Letter to the Women of England, on the Injustice of Mental Subordination, with Anecdotes* appeared in 1799 with the author disguised as "Anne Frances Randall," a self-proclaimed follower of Wollstonecraft.[15] The *New Annual Register, British Critic,* and *Critical Review* received the work without much hostility and without much respect. The *Critical* was admirably laconic in its complete notice: "Tolerable declamation in a cause which many will be inclined to support."[16] These reviews endorsed her educational recommendations and reserved judgment on the central question, the justice of mental (not social) subordination. The *Anti-Jacobin* took her off at more length, adverted as had all save the *Critical* to her being of "the school of Wollstonecraft, ironically emphasized Robinson's anecdote of the lady who shot her lover, and closed by reaffirming its purpose to root out the corruption the Wollstonecrafts spread in society. In effect, Robinson's work disappeared into the larger category dominated by Wollstonecraft's Amazonian figure.

In 1803 an anonymous work often attributed to Mary Hays, *A Defence of the Character and Conduct of the Late Mary Wollstonecraft Godwin* maintained with justice that Wollstonecraft's vilification was provoked by the passions raised by the revolution in France and by the asperity of tone adopted in the **Rights of Woman.** The author suggested that Wollstonecraft's tone had alienated many readers who would have been sympathetic to her views. If the work was by Hays, she knew whereof she spoke. She had abandoned work on her own feminist *Appeal to the Men of Great Britain in behalf of the Women* when the **Rights of Woman** appeared in 1792. In 1798, Johnson published her work anonymously. According to Claire Tomalin, the work found approval only at the *Analytical,* and like Wollstonecraft, Hays became "another butt for Tory sarcasm."[17] But Johnson's habit of anonymous publication to protect his authors and Hays' moderation of tone produced a paradoxical juxtaposition. In the *Anti-Jacobin* for September 1800, Elizabeth Hamilton's *Memoirs of Modern Philosophers* was reviewed enthusiastically for showing "that *all* the *female* writers of the day are not corrupted by the voluptuous dogmas of Mary Godwin, or her more profligate admirers." The novel's heroine, Bridgetina Botherim, is a parody of Mary Hays, and in the November installment, the reviewer tells us that the novel contains "an excellent imitation of that vicious and detestable stuff which has issued from the pen of M—y H—s." Couched cozily in between, there appeared in October a long and generally favorable review of an anonymous work entitled *Appeal to the Men of Great Britain in behalf of the Women.* While the reviewer has learned to "look with a suspicious eye upon demands" for rights by "advocates of the new philosophy . . . whether proceeding from the pen of a *Paine* or a *Wollstonecraft,*" this fair writer has no similar "sinister design" but advances a bold and fair specific appeal. Although the work contains some disputable propositions, "there will nothing occur offensive to the feelings of delicacy, nor injurious to the interests of religion and morality."[18] Similarly favorable though briefer readings were reported out by the *New Annual Register* and *Critical Review,* while the scorching attack was reserved for the *British Critic,* which assigned her to the party professing that "whatever is, is wrong" and charged her with illiteracy. As in 1792, the attitude towards a feminist work was shaped by the reviewer's perception of the writer's political stance, and in works after 1792 the presence of the name Wollstonecraft was a frequent though not necessary clue to the writer's position. Hays's work, sufficiently moderate in tone to earn the epithet "impotent" from William Thompson,[19] was protected by its mildness from the *Anti-Jacobin,* but fell an arbitrary sacrifice to the *British Critic,* which attacked a set of political views and contemptuously dismissed the work's author as not worth correction, an indignity not visited upon Wollstonecraft, who was afforded much correction.

While Wollstonecraft did indeed suffer "stoning by the mob," the cause was not "the reasonable and noble idea of woman's place in the family" presented in the *Rights of Woman.* Nor was the cause her assertion that "the sexes were equal, [her demand for] educational opportunities and even the franchise for women."[20] The stoning came well after the book and was not caused by a reaction to its specific content. Her educational proposals, when they were remembered, were widely approved. Her political and economic recommendations excited little negative or positive comment at the time of publication. The political hopes were too far from the possibility of realization to be seriously threatening, and the problem of work for women was a common theme when it concerned women of the lower classes or women educated beyond their means of support.[21] The emphasis on motherhood that was so striking to the nineteenth-century reader received almost no direct attention from contemporaries. Motherhood was one of the duties to be performed by women in their endeavor to be respectable and useful; it was not yet an object of adoration. The element that came disturbingly close to men's bosoms was the attack on the sexual character of women, the denial that a peculiarly feminine cast of mind was desirable. Men who were glad to agree that mind is of no sex were not pleased to acknowledge that manners ought to be of no sex. The shift in the treatment of feminist works between 1792 and 1798 indicates the continuing approbation of improved education for women and the solidifying opposition to works that seemed to threaten the established relations between the sexes.

Compared to her followers, Wollstonecraft's particular contribution was to state and to enact the major topics of feminist discourse. In the positions she articulated and the life she led, she touched upon almost every topic that has since been raised. Everything is there. Consequently, the reading of her work has varied directly with the concerns of that movement for which she was the first in England to speak. Modern readers light upon her specific proposals for social change and her insubordinate and combative tone. Those elements, dimly discomfortingly visible and politely ignored at the end of the eighteenth century, have been spotlighted by changes in the condition of women. Wollstonecraft's emphases on education and character (the latter might, however, be construed as an early demand for "assertiveness" training) have faded into the background as those demands have been met by actual social change. Although the needs and interests of her audience have determined the reading of her book, there is no discrepancy between the purposes of the work in its

original context and the uses to which it has been put. While the work's shape has been distorted, its intent has not been violated. One effect of the revival of the work, however, has been to distort the image present to its first viewers. Had Wollstonecraft argued specifically for the franchise, equal access to professions, equal treatment under the law, abolition of discrimination on the basis of sex, positions consistent with the book's argument but not developed, not central, or not present, her first readers might justly have thought her mad. Such recommendations would have borne no useful relation to the actual condition of women and the opportunities available to them. Instead, Wollstonecraft's abstract and general rhetoric provided for a variety of specific recommendations, and her specific recommendations were firmly in the forefront of eighteenth-century educational discussion, with some brief sorties to more dangerous terrain. Those elements of the work that modern readers tend to ignore ensured the work a respectful reception when it first appeared, and those elements that disturbed the work's first readers account for the continuing hospitality of its modern audience.

Notes

1. *The English Review* clarified its position in supporting Mirabeau's *Treatise of Public Education*, which restated Talleyrand's view that women should be confined to a domestic education "in opposition to some modern philosophers, or rather what the Italians call *filosofas iri,* who would wish to put into soft female hands the rod of government, and the sword of justice," XIX (1792), 56. The *Gentleman's Magazine* had a good laugh over the *Rights of Men*: "We should be sorry to raise a horse-laugh against a fair lady; but we were always taught to suppose that the *rights of woman* were the proper theme of the female sex; and that, while the Romans governed the world, the women governed the Romans" When the fair lady descended to her proper subject, the reviewer was not there to meet her. Both Wollstonecraft and the *Analytical* had anticipated the jocularity of the wits. *Gentleman's Magazine,* 61; pt. 1 (1791), 151; *Analytical Review,* 12(1792), 241-49, 13(1792), 481-89; *Literary Magazine,* 1(1792), 133-39; *General Magazine,* 6(1792), 187-91; *New York Magazine,* 4(1793), 77-81; *Monthly Review,* 8(1792), 198-209; *New Annual Register* (1792), p. [298]; Critical Review, N.S. 4(1792), 389-98, N.S. 5(1792), 132-41.

2. *Analytical Review,* 12(1792), 249; 13(1792), 530.

3. *Horace Walpole's Correspondence with Hannah More, et alii,* eds. W. S. Lewis, Robert A. Smith, Charles H. Bennett, XXXI (New Haven, 1961), 370, 373, 397.

4. *Monthly Review,* 8(1792), 209.

5. *Ibid.,* 198, 209.

6. "The Politics of the Critical Review 1756-1817," *Durham University Journal,* 53, N.S. 22(1961), 117-22.

7. N.S. 4(1792) 390, 396, 393; 5, 139. The *Critical* insisted on a characteristic difference in sex even against Catherine Macaulay Graham N.S. 2(1790), 618.

8. *Gentleman's Magazine,* 68, pt. 2 (1797), 894; *Monthly Magazine,* 4(1797), 232-33; *European Magazine,* 32(1797), 215; *New York Magazine,* N.S. 2(1797), 616.

9. *New Annual Register* (1798), p. [271]. The *Monthly Review* wisely considered the opinions on marriage and religion to be those of Godwin, not of his wife, 27(1798), 321-24.

10. *European Magazine,* 33(1798), 246-51. The original editor of the magazine was James Perry, a Foxite, who left after the first year, 1782. By 1798, the chief publisher of the magazine was J. Sewell, who, though he belonged to the Association at the Crown and Anchor in the Strand which busied itself in the distribution of anti-republican propaganda, had dismissed the business of compilation and had prohibited political talk on his premises in 1792 (notice dated Dec. 31, 1792, 22, last page).

11. *British Critic,* 12(1798), 228-33.

12. *Anti-Jacobin Review and Magazine,* 1(1798), 94-102.

13. Mary Matilda Betham, *Dictionary of Celebrated Women* (London, 1804), 374-77. Betham's principal source was the *Analytical Review* which, with the *Monthly Mirror,* had waxed rhapsodic about the letters to Imlay and had acclaimed their author another Werther. *Analytical Review,* 27(1798), 235-45; *Monthly Mirror,* 5(1798), 153-57. The *Monthly Mirror* is most familiar from its attempt to do a "cover story" on Wollstonecraft in its second issue for which a portrait was engraved, 1(1796), 131-33, but it was also conducted by Thomas Bellamy, hosier turned bookseller, who had conducted the *General Magazine,* one of the periodicals to review the *Rights of Woman* favorably on its first appearance. The *Critical Review* and *Gentleman's Magazine* disapproved of what they read, but were surprisingly restrained in their animadversions. The *Critical* even praised her genius and "undaunted and masculine spirit." *Critical,* N. S. 22(1798), 414-19; *Gentleman's Magazine* 68, pt. 1 (1798), 186-87. More injurious was Alexander Chalmers, *General Biographical Dictionary,* rev. and enl., XVI (London, 1814), 54-55.

That article followed the language of the *British Critic* in finding Wollstonecraft "a voluptuary and sensualist without refinement." Perhaps the pleasantest indication of the mix in attitudes towards Wollstonecraft appeared a few years later. Discussing the associations of Castletown Roche where Edmund Burke spent several of his earliest years, James Prior enumerated such luminaries as Essex, Raleigh, Spenser, and "the famed Mrs. Wolstoncroft," now in very respectable company; *Memoir of the Life and Character of the Right Honourable Edmund Burke,* 2nd ed. (London, 1826), I, 10.

14. The attacks on Wollstonecraft from the psychoanalytic point of view are familiar and have often been answered. Richard Cobb's comical hatchet job on Wollstonecraft as "impossible crazy lady" (*TLS,* Sept. 6, 1974, 941) has been severely rebuked by Janet M. Todd, "The Polwhelan Tradition and Richard Cobb," *Studies in Burke and his Time,* 16 (Spring, 1975); 271-78.

15. The *CBEL* lists the running title of Robinson's *Letter to the Women of England* as a separate work, *Thoughts on the Condition of Women,* n.d.

16. *New Annual Register,* 1799, p. [275]; *British Critic,* 14(1799), 682; *Critical Review* N.S. 27(1799), 360; *Anti-Jacobin Review* 3(1799), 144-46.

17. Claire Tomalin, *The Life and Death of Mary Wollstonecraft* (New York, 1974), 241.

18. Anti-Jacobin, 7 (1800), 39-46, 369-76 (Hamilton); 150-58 (Hays).

19. *Appeal of One Half the Human Race, Women, against the Pretensions of the Other Half, Men, to retain them in Political, and thence in Civil and Domestic, Slavery* (London, 1825), vii.

20. "Modern Ideal of Womanhood" (excerpts from *Rights of Woman*), in *A Library of the World's Best Literatures Ancient and Modern,* ed. Charles Dudley Warner, XXXIX (New York, 1897), 16131; Katherine B. Clinton, "Femme et Philosophie: Enlightenment Origins of Feminism," *Eighteenth-Century Studies,* 8 (1975), 283.

21. Mary Anne Radcliffe's *Female Advocate* (London, 1799) suggested restricting certain employments, such as toy and perfume sales, to women and establishing a magdalen to receive women; it was universally well received, though the *Critical* thought the style bad and the issues commonplace; N. S. 27 (1799), 479.

Anca Vlasopolos (essay date autumn 1980)

SOURCE: Vlasopolos, Anca. "Mary Wollstonecraft's Mark of Reason in *A Vindication of the Rights of Woman. Dalhousie Review* 60, no. 3 (autumn 1980): 462-71.

[*In the following essay, Vlasopolos claims that* A Vindication of the Rights of Woman *was written for "men of reason," whom Wollstonecraft recognized as being the owners of power and able to implement the ideals she espoused.*]

Underneath the tough talk of the speaking voice in *A Vindication of the Rights of Woman* hides a number of concessions to male readers and covert strategies for the defense of Wollstonecraft's sex and person. In a century in which philosophers and artists dissociated Reason and Sensibility and in which the upholders of Reason began to win important political victories, Wollstonecraft's awareness of audience shows astuteness. Moreover, her emphasis on Reason to the virtual exclusion of passions from human faculties serves to strengthen her credentials as thinker, to separate her from the general run of women, and to mask her own vulnerability to passionate impulses.

To an extent surprising for those of us primed to look upon *A Vindication* as a feminist manifesto, the book proves to be written for men. Its revolutionary import remains unquestionable (note Wollstonecraft's rapid overthrow of monarchy, army, navy, and clergy as institutions necessary for society[1]), yet *A Vindication* also occasionally upholds the sanctity of marriage, rigidly defined sex roles, class privileges in education, as well as a host of agelong prejudices about women's inferiority. The unevenness of the book, its unclear organization, and its repetition of arguments have less to do with Wollstonecraft's lack of formal education—she can be formidable in argument when she allows herself to be—than with her attempt to bring about a bloodless revolution.[2] She appeals to the men she hopes will be shaping the new world, but who, despite their ardent fight for men's rights, adhere to the same attitudes about women as those propagated by the outgoing order. Wollstonecraft seems to have decided to avoid alienating these men. Clearly, she cannot at all times hold back, and her mask drops, forcing her to retreat, recover, and start anew. To keep the mask she had to make certain concessions, but the mask allowed her to persuade by flattering and cajoling no less than by covertly threatening the men of Reason to whom the book is for the most part addressed.

In order to show herself worthy to be heard, Wollstonecraft adopts a tactic many women have been forced to use, namely, dissociating herself from other women. She legitimately saw herself as different from the common run, but she viewed her isolation with an ambivalent mixture of bravado and fear: "I am then going to be the first of a new genus—I tremble at the attempt,"[3] she wrote her sister after her arrival in London to begin earning her livelihood by her pen. In *A Vindication,* however, she consistently used the third-person plural to discuss women. Although there is one instance when she specifies, "reader, male or female" (p. 146), women are usually "they", not "we". When the author in the last chapter decides to "expostulate seriously with the ladies," though she does so with superstitious women, her tone is condescending, even insulting, and one can hardly suppose that she expected the ladies to read and approve of a work in which they are addressed as "ignorant women . . . in the most emphatical sense" (p. 180). Despite the rhetorical distance she creates, Wollstonecraft announces early in *A Vindication* that she abandons all pretenses to rhetoric; the simplicity of her style as well as the dignity of her purpose distinguish her writing from genres perceived as women's domain:

> Animated by this important object, I shall disdain to cull my phrases or polish my style;—I aim at being useful, and sincerity will render me unaffected. . . . I shall be employed about things, not words!—and, anxious to render my sex more respectable members of society, I shall try to avoid that flowery diction which has slided from essays into novels, and from novels into familiar letters and conversation.
>
> (p. 10)

The most important way in which Wollstonecraft attempts to dissociate herself from other women in order to be taken seriously as a thinker is through the argument she advances for the innate equality of the sexes. She seems to accept fully the premise that women exist in a state of mental retardation. To save her work from charges generally leveled at women and their enterprises, such as frivolity, sentimentality, sensuality, and cunning, Wollstonecraft exalts Reason as the supreme faculty, and, except in rare slips, derides the passions and emotions in the life of men and women and even in the relationship between parents and children. Reason, she writes, distinguishes humans from "brute creation" (p. 12). It is innate to all beings, and the stage of its development in the individual gives a just measure of his/her freedom (p. 121). All of woman's shortcomings stem from the system of education and of social intercourse which deprives women of developing and using Reason and hence deprives them of human rights (pp. 22, 64, 87, 92).

But, given her own context, can Wollstonecraft use her reason to advance such an argument and remain a woman? The question is not frivolous, for an examination of Wollstonecraft's tactics to establish her credibility reveals the extent to which she had to compromise her ideas about humanity. The bug-a-boo that haunts women's intellectual ventures—the charge of emotionalism—forced her to adopt the mask of tough reasoning from behind which she resorted to positions and theories which do not bear scrutiny in light of human experience, her own very much included. Love, particularly when involving sexual passion, falls victim to Wollstonecraft's insistence on Reason. She writes:

> . . . master and mistress of a family ought not to continue to love each other with passion . . . they ought not to indulge those emotions which disturb the order of society, and engross the thoughts that should be otherwise employed.
>
> (Pp. 30-31)

More outrageously, she proposes that "an unhappy marriage is often very advantageous to a family, and that the neglected wife, is, in general, the best mother" (p. 31).[4] She also argues that a woman whose reason is sufficiently developed will achieve the equanimity necessary to bear whatever character her husband might possess, even if "a trial . . . to virtue" (p. 32), a position she will later challenge in her unfinished novel, *The Wrongs of Woman*. At times the mask of Reason becomes so rigid as to reject the desire for "present happiness" (p. 32) as an acceptable motive for human actions.

Despite her attempts to present herself as a new genus—a woman of Reason persuading men of Reason—Wollstonecraft resorts to a variety of covert tactics for convincing her readers of the justice of her argument. Often she reasons plainly, particularly when in exasperation she sets aside the mask, but she is not above using the proverbial feminine weapons of flattery and dark hints involving issues about which men feel least secure. Wollstonecraft tries to establish her equality with men from the dedication to Talleyrand to the concluding apostrophe to "ye men of understanding." She makes men feel in control of the proposed "REVOLUTION in female manners" (p. 192). They are the "sagacious reader" (pp. 58, 191), "reasonable men" (p. 149), "men of understanding" (p. 194) who can be moved by appeals to reason.[5] Apart from flattering men's intellects,[6] Wollstonecraft makes it clear that her revolution will not challenge men in physical combat. She acknowledges the notion—cherished by many—of women's physical inferiority to men (p. 8) and goes so far as to assert that, "in some degree," such weakness makes women dependent on men (p. 11). She then turns to the men to whose intellectual and physical superiority she has bowed and asks them to become the liberators of women: "would men but generously snap our chains"; "I entreat them to assist to emancipate their companion, to make her a *help meet* for them" (p. 150);

"women must be allowed" (p. 173); "make them free" (p. 175); and finally "be just then . . . and allow her the privileges of ignorance, to whom ye deny the rights of reason" (p. 194).

At the same time that Wollstonecraft adopts a pleading tone to soften the resistance of her male readers and a stern tone in condemning the foolishness of her sex, she subtly awakens men's fears about women's dominance over them in a state of inequality and alleviates those fears in her visions of a freed humanity. One of the leitmotifs of *A Vindication* is the sheer ineptitude of unliberated women for the roles of wife and mother, and the improvement of domestic welfare, infant survival, and effective education of children attendant upon women's freedom to strengthen their minds and bodies. These arguments strike a note of modernity which makes *A Vindication* speak to readers almost two centuries later. But Wollstonecraft's appraisal of her male readership led her to think that a bit of terror mixed with optimism about perfectibility would give firmer ground to her argument than direct statement alone. She explains to men of Reason that as long as women are educated to be mentally deficient, they will fall for the "rakes" instead of men of solid character. She both consoles such men for their lack of amorous success and threatens them with the fact that a pretty girl may never look at them (p. 118) until women develop intellectual discernment. She proposes that women raised to please and attract men will continue to exercise their charms after marriage as well, especially after husbands' sexual passion has cooled. The desire for sexual attentions—the only measure of their worth—renders women unfaithful (p. 73). More frighteningly, their lapse from virtue produces a "half alive heir to an immense estate [who] came from heaven knows where" (p. 132). Wollstonecraft cautions men that "weak enervated women . . . are unfit to be mothers, though they may conceive," so that when the man of their choice—a libertine naturally—"wishes to perpetuate his name, [he] receives from his wife only a half-formed being that inherits both its father's and its mother's weakness" (p. 139). Even if submissive women are faithful, they prove either foolish mothers, who turn their children against the father, or spendthrifts or both (pp. 68, 73, 132, 152, 167).

Not content with awakening men's fears about the problematic nature of paternity, Wollstonecraft warns them against women who, taught that their sexuality is their only asset, use this weapon to obtain power over them:

> . . . the state of war which subsists between the sexes, makes them employ those wiles, that often frustrate the more open designs of force.
>
> When, therefore, I call women slaves, I mean in a political and civil sense; for, indirectly they obtain too

much power, and are debased by their exertions to obtain illicit sway.

(P. 167; see also p. 117)

By contrast, free women do not aim at vanquishing men: "I do not wish them to have power over men; but over themselves" (p. 62), declares Wollstonecraft.

One of the chief strengths of *A Vindication* resides in its vivid portrayals of women in straitened circumstances. These thrust upon our consciousness the absence of alternatives available to women without husbands. But for whom are these examples created? There's the widowed woman, the former feminine ideal of the docile wife, who left alone "falls an easy prey to some mean fortune-hunter, who defrauds the children of their paternal inheritance" so that the sons cannot be educated, or worse, "the mother will be lost in the coquette, and, instead of making friends of her daughters, view them with eyes askance, for they are rivals" (p. 49). Wollstonecraft again emphasizes the fate of the progeny rather than the psychological anguish of the widow. Men married to women who fulfill the feminine ideal may be supplanted after death by rakes, who will leave the children—the continuance of name and reputation—penniless and unprotected. Similarly, the example of the maiden sister forced to live with her brother and sister-in-law presents a vivid image of intolerable domestic tension between the two women, with the man helplessly caught between and swayed at last by his wife's connivances to throw his sister "on the world," "into joyless solitude" (p. 65). Both women, like the widow, appear in a less than favorable light. Our sympathy is with the poor man in the grave or the one caught between his affection for his sister and loyalty to his wife. The solutions Wollstonecraft proposes have less appeal for women than for the worried husbands. The widow educated in the principles of Reason "in the bloom of life forgets her sex—forgets the pleasure of an awakening passion, which might again have been inspired or returned" and devotes herself to managing the inheritance for the benefit of the children, working only for the reward beyond the grave (pp. 50-51). In the second illustration, "reason might have taught her [the wife] not to expect, and not even to be flattered by, the affection of her husband, if it led him to violate prior duties," while the sister might have been able to support herself and thus not disturb either the brother's domestic tranquility or his conscience (p. 66). Free women, Wollstonecraft tells her readers, make life easier for men.

But where behind the mask of Reason is Mary Wollstonecraft the "hyena in petticoats," the fiery revolutionary whose book eminent contemporary women refused to read? In *A Vindication* the mask of Reason slips off now and again and the author has to retreat, restate, and recover the ground she may have lost with

Mary Wollstonecraft (1759-1797)

her readers. The thread of the argument gets tangled, and we hear from biographers and critics the kind of criticism she tried to stave off: the charge of lack of intellect, of too much passion, of inability to organize and present an argument coherently.[7] Is Wollstonecraft wearing a mask at all? Her statements in letters, events of her life during the time she was composing *A Vindication,* and internal evidence show that she placed a much higher value on human relationships, on their passionate nature, than she allows for in her advocacy of Reason. Her indignation about the lot of women, her sympathy with them, and her disdain for men who wield power over other men and women are also greater than the mask allows her to express. Wollstonecraft's last works, *Letters Written during a Short Residence in Sweden, Norway, and Denmark* and *The Wrongs of Woman,* measure the growth of her confidence in herself as an author able to command a reader's interest regardless of sex; these works use few subterfuges, few poses in presenting conditions which cry out for reform.

In her writings as well as her life Mary reveals herself as a passionate, bright, impatient being who tries to use first the tenets of religion and then of Reason (without, however, discarding religion) as brakes upon her heedless impulses. With her customary imaginative acumen Virginia Woolf describes Mary as a dolphin rushing through the waters,[8] and we sense from her writings and glean from her life an indomitable life force which made her triumph over vicissitudes (among them two suicide attempts) that broke other women, and which kept her struggling for ten days, to the amazement of her physicians, against the puerperal fever to which she finally succumbed. From the earliest records of her thoughts—her letters to Jane Arden—we see a girl who craves affection (*Coll.,* p. 60). She reproaches her sister for turning pretty phrases in her letters instead of writing "one affectionate word . . . to the heart" (*Coll.,* p. 76). She devotes herself to the welfare of the Blood family to the detriment of her own interests for the love she bears her soulmate, Fanny Blood. She despises Fanny's half-hearted suitor for his lack of passion, and she acknowledges her own need of love (*Coll.,* pp. 93, 108), analyzing astutely her repression; in a letter in which she describes her literary endeavors, she writes:

> Many motives impel me besides sheer love of knowledge . . . it is the only way to destroy the worm that will gnaw the core—and make that being an isolé, whom nature made too susceptible of affections, which stray beyond the bounds, reason prescribes.
>
> (*Coll.,* p. 173)

But the worm whose existence she denied in *A Vindication* was, at the very time she was gathering her strength to reply to Burke and to compose the companion *Rights of Woman,* gnawing its way with a vengeance. Mary fell in love with the newly married Fuseli, continued to hope for reciprocal feelings from Fuseli for two years,[9] and finally went so far as to propose to Sophia Fuseli that she move in with the couple. In a letter which Wardle dates as immediately following Sophia's rejection, Mary agonizingly writes, "I am a mere animal, and instinctive emotions too often silence the suggestions of reason . . . There is certainly a great defect in my mind—my wayward heart creates its own misery" (*Coll.,* pp. 220-221). The mask of Reason in *A Vindication* clearly serves as a shield for her own vulnerability.

The internal evidence of *A Vindication* supports the split Mary perceives in her life between the dictates of Reason and the compelling motions of the heart. Despite her attempts to placate, entrap, and disarm the reader, she occasionally gives voice to her burning indignation. Following a particularly offensive excerpt from *Sermons to Young Women,* Wollstonecraft bursts out: "such a woman ought to be an angel—or she is an ass—for I discern not a trace of the human character, neither reason nor passion in this domestic drudge, whose being is absorbed in that of a tyrant's" (p. 96). Although throughout her argument she ascribes women's enslaved condition to their atrophied reason, Wollstonecraft cannot refrain from voicing at least once the envy women have felt for men's scope of action, for their freedom to go beyond the bounds "reason prescribes":

> . . . they [men] give a freer scope to the grand passions, and by more frequently going astray enlarge their minds. If then by the exercise of their own reason they fix on some stable principle, they have probably to thank the force of their passions, nourished by *false* views of life, and permitted to overleap the boundary that secures content.
>
> (P. 110)

Mary herself moved on to overleap practically every boundary prescribed by Reason and the society of her day. The stories of her affair with Imlay, her two pregnancies out of wedlock, and her liberated marriage to Godwin gave her a notoriety which made her work sink into near-oblivion for almost a century. But her experience, which encompassed more than many a man's scope, gave her the assurance to drop the mask and address the reader intimately and calmly in *Letters Written during a Short Residence in Sweden, Norway, and Denmark* and to turn finally to the large readership of women in her purposely didactic novel *The Wrongs of Woman.* She learned to turn a biting aside into a significant social comment about class and sex oppression by enhancing editorial statements with minute and eloquent details:

> . . . a man may strike a man with impunity because he pays him wages . . . Still the men stand up for the dignity of man, by oppressing women . . . In the winter, I am told, they [the women] take the linen down to the river, to wash it in the cold water; and though their hands, cut by the ice, are cracked and bleeding, the men, their fellow servants, will not disgrace their manhood by carrying a tub to lighten their burden.[10]

In the public *Letters* as well as her private correspondence in the years following the publication of her manifesto, Mary increasingly recognizes the role of emotions, of grand passions in shaping a human being's mind and experience.[11] *The Wrongs of Woman* portrays a heroine unthinkable in *A Vindication,* a woman who discovers her mistake in her choice of a mate after marriage, who rebels against the tyranny of wedlock, and who is not seduced but willingly plunges into a love affair with a man who proves to be less worthy than she had hoped. To a friend who ventures the opinion that Maria's situation is not "sufficiently important," Mary replies in the firm and confident manner of an author who knows that her choice of subject may limit her audience but who remains entirely committed to her cause, even if it alienates male readers:

> These appear to me (matromonial despotism of heart and conduct) to be the particular wrongs of woman; because they degrade the mind. What are termed great misfortunes may more forcibly impress the mind of

common readers, they have more of what might justly be termed *stage effect* but it is the delineation of finer sensations which, in my opinion, constitutes the merit of out best novels, this is what I have in view; and to shew the wrongs of different classes of women equally oppressive . . .

(*Coll.*, p. 392)

That last declaration of purpose not only moves Mary away from *A Vindication* with its pleas to men in power and its consideration of middle-class women only, but propels her as political thinker and feminist into our century, our very decade. It also taunts us with a promise of the works of Mary's maturity, whose fulfillment was prevented by her death at the age of thirty-eight.

A Vindication therefore remains Wollstonecraft's most solid monument, a work of extraordinary vision whose great strength the author dissipated somewhat by diverting the central argument into dead-end channels of audience watching and defensiveness about sex and self. Despite her efforts to placate her readers, Wollstonecraft's work suffered censure through judgments she tried to anticipate and answer, judgments that have more do with her life than her writing—emotionalism, immorality, extremism.[12] The parts of *A Vindication* which have withstood the test of time are those in which she drops the mask in order to speak freely of women's oppression and in which she prophetically envisages women entering careers, being represented politically, and, most importantly, being educated alongside men so that they may cease to be The Other and become human beings.

Notes

1. *A Vindication of the Rights of Woman,* ed. Carol H. Poston (New York: W. W. Norton and Co., Inc., 1975), pp. 16-18. All further references are to this edition.

2. Lest we, who in the last decades of the twentieth century still await the passage of ERA, consider her naive for having thought to tap men's good will be means of a mere book, we must consider that Mary was living in a time of two successful revolutions—the American and the French, the latter having not yet turned to terror. Civil rights had not yet been abridged in England as a consequence of fear of Jacobinism, and Mary associated with a group of visionaries who firmly believed that in time social justice might be achieved.

3. *Collected Letters of Mary Wollstonecraft,* ed. Ralph M. Wardle (Ithaca: Cornell University Press, 1979), p. 164. References to this edition will be cited in the text as *Coll.*

4. For the same argument see also pp. 27, 37, 50, 118-119.

5. Wollstonecraft covertly emasculates the men whom she attacks, such as Burke and Rousseau, by depriving them of Reason—the masculine trait—and endowing them with Sensibility, the province of women. For a detailed analysis of this aspect of *The Rights of Man* and *The Rights of Woman,* see Elissa S. Guralnick's "Radical Politics in Mary Wollstonecraft's *A Vindication of the Rights of Woman*," *Studies in Burke and His Time,* 18 (1977), 155-166.

6. Carol Poston notes that Wollstonecraft's language about respected men's works such as Lord Chesterfield's *Letters to His Son* changes from outright dismissal ("frivolous correspondence") to neutrality ("epistles") in revision (p. 106, n. 5), a move which could serve no other purpose than placating male readers.

7. Chief among Wollstonecraft's modern-day detractors is Richard Cobb, who in "Radicalism and Wreckage," *Times Literary Supplement,* 6 Sept. 1974, pp. 941-944, goes so far as to propose that her very name makes her unfit for study (for an analysis of the detractor tradition in Wollstonecraft studies see Janet M. Todd's "The Polwhelean Tradition and Richard Cobb," *Studies in Burke and His Time,* 16 [1975], 271-277). In the biographies, Margaret George, one of the most sympathetic of Mary's biographers, avoids discussion of anything but the main ideas in *A Vindication (One Woman's "Situation": A Study of Mary Wollstonecraft* [Urbana: University of Illinois Press, 1970], pp. 84-96); Eleanor Flexner in *Mary Wollstonecraft: A Biography* (1972; rpt. Baltimore; Penguin Books, Inc., 1973) roundly takes Mary to task for her shortcomings in logical argument (p. 164), as does Ralph M. Wardle in *Mary Wollstonecraft: A Critical Biography* (Lawrence: University of Kansas Press, 1951), who attributes the book's "worst fault"—its lack of organization—to Mary's "intense feelings," to "her usual want of mental discipline" (pp. 147, 156): Claire Tomalin dispenses with the method in *A Vindication* in *The Life and Death of Mary Wollstonecraft* (London: Weidenfeld and Nicolson, 1974) by declaring that it is "a book without any logical structure: it is more in the nature of an extravaganza" (p. 105); these biographers, with George's exception, follow Godwin's lead in his *Memoirs of the Author of A Vindication of the Rights of Woman* (1798; rpt. New York and London: Garland Publishing Inc., 1974), who declares the book to be "a very unequal performance, and eminently deficient in method and arrangement" (p. 83).

8. *The Second Common Reader* (New York: Harcourt, Brace & World, Inc., 1932; rpt. 1960) p. 145.

9. For the most recent account of the Fuseli episode and the extent to which it preoccupied Mary, see *Coll.*, p. 190, n. 1, p. 199, n. 5, pp. 202, 203, 205, 220 and 221, including n. 1 on p. 221.

10. *Letters Written during a Short Residence in Sweden, Norway, and Denmark,* ed. Carol H. Poston (Lincoln: University of Nebraska Press, 1976), p. 26. All references to this edition will be cited in the text as *Letters.*

11. See pp. 35, 55, 99, 109, 160 in *Letters* and pp. 263, 302, 308 in *Coll.* for Mary's changed

12. For an informative summary of contemporary resistance to *A Vindication* see Godwin, pp. 81-82, in which he fears the censure of Mary as political extremist rather than as an emotionalist. In *Revolution and Romanticism* (Cambridge: Harvard University Press, 1974), Howard Mumford Jones also separates Wollstonecraft's "revolutionary" thinking from "romantic individualism" only to satirize her emphasis on freedom by briefly listing her free actions as her becoming Imlay's mistress and giving birth to "an illegitimate daughter" (pp. 252-253). By contrast, Eleanor L. Nocholes in "Mary Wollstonecraft" (*Romantic Rebels: Essays on Shelly and His Circle,* ed. Kenneth Neill Cameron [Cambridge: Harvard University Press, 1973] maintains that Mary's writing style is intensely personal, and that she anticipates the "attitude and tone" of the Romantics (p. 45).

Orrin N. C. Wang (essay date fall 1991)

SOURCE: Wang, Orrin N. C. "The Other Reasons: Female Alterity and Enlightenment Discourse in Mary Wollstonecraft's *A Vindication of the Rights of Woman.*" *The Yale Journal of Criticism* 5, no. 1 (fall 1991): 129-49.

[*In the following essay, Wang argues against readings of* A Vindication of the Rights of Woman *as a text that represses female imagination in favor of male reason, seeing the work as a complex study about repression, reason, gender, and imagination.*]

It is uncannily fitting that Mary Shelley should dedicate her famous Romantic novel, *Frankenstein,* to her father, William Godwin, and not to her mother, Mary Wollstonecraft. The literal—and literary—gap between mother and daughter is an appropriate emblem for the discontinuity between Wollstonecraft's theoretical writing and the work of contemporary feminist literary critics. This discontinuity is largely due to a public monumentalization and disfigurement of Wollstonecraft by her contemporaries that is similar, I would suggest,

to the posthumous process that afflicted the writer she both admired and criticized, Jean-Jacques Rousseau.[1] Much of the initial hostility toward both figures was associated with English horror at the French Revolution. Just as counterrevolutionaries viewed Rousseau's social thought and the politics of the French Revolution as one and the same, so too did many people view Wollstonecraft's Protestant bourgeois radicalism as an irrevocable contamination of her feminist position.[2] In both cases, conservative critics saw the Reign of Terror as an inevitable consequence of each thinker's writing. A second, more important similarity was the extent to which late eighteenth- and early nineteenth-century readers connected each thinker's theory with his or her biography.[3] In each case, a theory associated with Enlightenment reason was subverted by a life of unrestrained passion and immoral activity. For such readers of Wollstonecraft and Rousseau, this subversion of theory by biography allegorized again what was occurring in France, a rational agenda of emancipation overcome by the uncontrollable demands of an irrational Reign of Terror. It is this early nineteenth-century monument of Wollstonecraft, as an individual aspiring to rational discourse while hopelessly repressing irrational emotion, that we have inherited and that has haunted even the most sympathetic perceptions of her by contemporary feminist critics.[4]

This is not to say that this reputation has remained completely the same since its inception. One change in this monument has been what exactly constitutes the "proof" of Wollstonecraft's unstable personal life. In its incarnation at the turn of the nineteenth century, Wollstonecraft's emotional instability was signified by every aspect of her lifestyle: her various love affairs, her illegitimate child, the "unconventional" form of her relationship to Godwin, and her attempted suicides. Today, only Wollstonecraft's attempted suicides can carry any of the same biographical weight. But just as the signs for her personal emotional life have changed, so too has the evaluation of those signs. Instead of seeing that life as a set of negative traits, a mark of Wollstonecraft's hypocrisy and limitations, most contemporary feminists see her private life as an emotional resource that Wollstonecraft heeded too little. For contemporary feminists, the emotional traces of Wollstonecraft's life are unstable, but in a positive sense; they represent needs and desires that have the potential to subvert patriarchal norms as much as Wollstonecraft's "reasoned" Enlightenment agenda. Indeed, they have become needs and desires tragically or inevitably *hampered* by that agenda.

Two things concerning Wollstonecraft's reputation, moreover, have remained relatively constant over the last two centuries. The first is the basic duality underwriting that reputation, reason versus imagination; the second, the genders assigned to the terms of that duality. No one has argued, in other words, with Mary Jacobus's description of the rational side of that duality as "the predominantly male discourse of Enlightenment Reason, or 'sense.'"[5] Opposing this discourse is the Otherness of Wollstonecraft's writing and biography, a chain of signifiers that links together such terms as femininity, imagination, irrationality, sensibility, and passion. In even the most sympathetic readings of Wollstonecraft, contemporary critics such as Cora Kaplan, Mary Poovey, and Mary Jacobus have portrayed her as trapped by this duality—at best, as reproducing the problems of this trap for our contemporary edification.[6] In all cases Wollstonecraft remains an individual experiencing an identity crisis; if she is no longer as the nineteenth century represented her, an unstable woman whose life proves her error, she remains an individual reacting to the interpellating textual and personal effects of two opposing discourses, male reason and female imagination.

Associated with this perception of Wollstonecraft's identity is a literary history that narrativizes her texts in terms of a progress from her critical work, ***The Rights of Woman,*** to her unfinished novel, ***The Wrongs of Woman; or Maria.*** The basic form of this narrative is one in which Wollstonecraft is more able, in her later works, to face the Otherness of her life—whether that be female desire or the "imaginative and linguistic excess" of female writing—that she represses or attacks in favor of male reason in ***The Rights of Woman.***[7] I want to argue against this view of ***The Rights of Woman*** as a text that is somehow blind to the insights of Wollstonecraft's other works. ***The Rights of Woman*** is a much more complex work about repression, reason, imagination, and gender, than the present monument of Wollstonecraft allows. My reading of Wollstonecraft differs from that expressed by the present monument in three ways. First, rather than seeing Wollstonecraft as being caught between the gender demands of male reason and female imagination, I see her text actively trying to disrupt that duality's assignation of gender, by strategically associating "woman" with a variety of local, contradictory identities.[8] The second difference is that I also see Wollstonecraft's text preempting that very duality by destabilizing the opposition between reason and the host of terms the text contrasts with reason. The complicated relationships between reason and those terms underwrite not only Wollstonecraft's critique of the "feminine" imagination but also her critique of that imagination's structure of repression. Those complex relationships also underwrite the very semantic and stylistic tensions of her text that contemporary critics have only been able to recognize *as* a repression of female Otherness by male reason. Finally, the third difference is that I see these textual tensions also pointing to a certain reflexivity within Wollstonecraft's work, a reflexivity for which ***The Rights of Woman*** is given too little credit. Far from being a text blind to the limits of

its own political and didactic discourse, ***The Rights of Woman*** carries out an ideological critique of its own teleological and millennial aspirations, precisely through its dissolution of the semantic identities that separate reason from passion.

I want to take up first the issue of what "woman" means in ***The Rights of Woman.*** Wollstonecraft is most famous for equating "woman" with "human," that beneficiary of both Enlightenment and post-Enlightenment theories of democratic principles. It is in that spirit of a humanistic, democratic discourse that Wollstonecraft addresses the beginning of her book to M. Talleyrand-Perigord, the influential member of the new Republic of France, the nation most strongly associated with those democratic, anti-monarchist ideals. It is also in the spirit of that same discourse that Wollstonecraft chastises Talleyrand for not extending, in a government pamphlet, the human rights of education to women as well as to men:

> I wish, Sir, to set some investigations of this kind afloat in France, and should they lead to a confirmation of my principles, when your constitution is revised the Rights of Woman may be respected, if it be fully proved that reason calls for this respect, and loudly demands JUSTICE for one half of the human race.[9]

As Wollstonecraft's words imply, the discourse she wants to enter primarily associates the human with the other half of the race, man. This fact has been turned against her, in that critics have accused Wollstonecraft of being blind to what happens to the feminine within such a discourse.[10] Such a critique argues that a universal term such as "human" hides inequality and sexual difference; by equating woman with human which equates with man, Wollstonecraft can only reproduce that elision. But this critique ignores the possibility of a metaleptic effect caused by Wollstonecraft's incursion, that she is in fact *introducing* the alterity of sexual difference into this supposedly universal discourse, and thus enabling, as Ernesto Laclau and Chantal Mouffe claim, "the birth of feminism through the use made of it in the democratic discourse, which was thus displaced from the field of political equality to the field of equality between the sexes."[11]

Nor does "woman" signify only democratic humanism in ***The Rights of Woman.*** Wollstonecraft associates the feminine with a variety of oftentimes contradictory qualities and positions. Because of these other significations, the equivalence between the feminine and democratic humanism does not reach the critical mass of an essential equation. Rather, this equivalence and the other instances of gender assignation operate as localized semantic moments, dependent upon the situational strategy of a fluid political polemic.

These local moments in ***The Rights of Woman*** comprise an argument by analogy, a strategy whose ubiquity must then be taken into account when we wish to determine the ontological status of those analogies. Yet, while the very number and variety of these analogies make them non-essentialist, they are not arbitrary. That is, all of Wollstonecraft's analogies are determined by the same theme; each analogy links women to a role of power—or powerlessness—at a different position within the socio-historic world of late eighteenth-century England. But while the theme of power thus structures Wollstonecraft's analogies, power itself is denied any essential signification. That is, in each example of women's empowerment or victimization, power is constituted by a different combination of codes of age, class, and gender. The result is a concrete depiction of the condition of women in the late eighteenth century that simultaneously repudiates the idea that there is any essential character to its catalogue of women's empowered and victimized identities.

In repudiating such a character, Wollstonecraft employs a linguistic method that denies what Laclau and Mouffe call "a fully sutured space" to both the patriarchy and the women it oppresses. Such a space posits an identity so sealed from outside signification that the identity achieves the "transparency of a closed symbolic order."[12] It is precisely this symbolic closure that the variety of Wollstonecraft's analogies denies. Yet, simultaneously, because of their role in articulating the position of women within eighteenth-century patriarchy, these analogies still deal with the brute fact of power and oppression.

Thus, while Wollstonecraft's polemic for women's rights utilizes the equation between woman and the human race, her critique of women's present condition associates women with the Others of democratic discourse: eastern princes, Roman emperors, monarchs and the aristocratic class. Here woman signifies a power that is not based on self-determination but on the analogy between the unearned, arbitrary trappings of despotic privilege and the equally capricious influence of physical beauty. Hence we have Wollstonecraft's rejection of such sexual influence in her famous reply to Rousseau: "I do not wish [women] to have power over men; but over themselves" (62; chap. 4).[13] But the tyrant's/woman's power over the people/man is also a powerlessness that must be constituted through *other* analogies, where the fact of women's limited opportunities and helplessness is signified by children and the lower class. Thus women are slaves oppressed by men who are tyrants, whose power is actually like that of women limited like children and the poor. Women *are* oppressed, but by a master/slave dialectic that resists any easy condensation of gender or class identities.

One might object that while women have been either "slaves or despots," *The Rights of Woman* still associates the utopian democratic ideal with the "manly." That opposition certainly does operate in

Wollstonecraft's text. Yet, that duality becomes a fundamentally reified part of Wollstonecraft's thought *only* when we ignore the other positions and roles of gender that crisscross that duality, such as the fact that the discourse of the monarch rests on examples of male despotism—for example, Louis XIV—and that the politically progressive concept of modesty is chiefly associated not with the masculine, but with the feminine. Likewise, Wollstonecraft disparages Lord Chesterfield's worldly letters to his son as "unmanly"—that is, effeminate—for their libertine exploitation of women (106; chap. 5), while at the same time she begins her attack upon Mrs. Piozzi's statement, that "all [women's] arts are employed to keep the hearts of man," by calling Piozzi's ideas "truly masculine sentiments" (102; chap. 5). Certainly Wollstonecraft does not want Piozzi to be less masculine in the way Chesterfield is, nor does she want Chesterfield to be more "manly" in the way Piozzi is. "Unmanly" and "truly masculine" do not constitute the intrinsic identities of gendered subjects, nor is Wollstonecraft downgrading them as such; rather, they are each a sign of a particular position within eighteenth-century English patriarchy, a position whose deadly denotative force Wollstonecraft dramatizes through the semantics—and politics—of gender.

By having the feminine and the masculine occupy, at different strategic moments, the key position of both her negative critique and utopian polemic, Wollstonecraft is, in effect, deconstructing the intrinsic identity of a gendered subject. Just as important, Wollstonecraft sees this deconstruction taking place within the context of an English androcentric society demanding the opposite of this deconstruction from its female population, so that

> a virtuous man may have a choleric or a sanguine constitution, be gay or grave, unreproved; be firm till he is almost over-bearing, or, weakly submissive, have no will or opinion of his own; but all women are to be levelled, by meekness and docility, into one character of yielding softness and gentle compliance.
>
> (95; chap. 5)

It is in this spirit, of an attack upon the "one character," that we should read Wollstonecraft's famous dictum that boys and girls should study together in order to produce "modesty without those sexual distinctions that taint the mind" (165; chap. 12). Wollstonecraft is not trying to efface sexual difference here; instead, she is attempting to disrupt the imprisoning codification of sexual identity as constructed in invidious social distinctions. Similarly, when Wollstonecraft criticizes the French educative system by saying, "[young girls] were treated like women [i.e., coquettes] almost from their very birth," she is not consigning "women" to an eternal identification with "coquetry" (81; chap. 5). Rather, she is trying to break up that singular identity imposed upon those girls, by exposing the identity's dependence upon linguistic and pedagogical structures: "they were treated *like* women almost from their very birth. . . ."

This strategy of gender *dis*identification is clear in one footnote commenting upon how men behave differently in front of women, depending upon the degree to which women stress their own "feminine" identity: "Men are not always men in the company of women, nor would women always remember that they are women, if they were allowed to acquire more understanding" (123; chap. 7). Upon which term of "men" or "women" should we confer originary status, to start this sentence's chain of signification? And who is the second "they"? Consider, also, how the meaning of the first clause and its relation to the rest of the sentence change, depending upon which, and how many, of the gender terms are placed in italics. This syntactical and grammatical indeterminacy succinctly dramatizes the dizzying spiral of signification that structures the absolute necessity and irreducible problem of sexual identity in *The Rights of Woman.* It is the text's consciousness of this indeterminacy that redirects the rage of sentences, such as the following one, away from an essential "woman" and toward the host of social, psychological, and linguistic forces that work to shore up the ontology of that identity: "This desire of being always women, is the very consciousness that degrades the sex" (99; chap. 5).[14]

By thus attacking the concept of a single feminine identity, *The Rights of Woman* escapes being located only within a duality of male reason and female imagination. It is precisely the hegemonic forces of that duality that Wollstonecraft disrupts, by deploying the feminine in a host of contradictory roles. But Wollstonecraft also disrupts this duality by subverting the unitary identities of imagination and reason. She emplots gender, repression, reason, and imagination in a narrative that is more complicated than the one that the duality of male reason and female imagination implies.

In order to understand this narrative, I want to examine two moments in *The Rights of Woman* in which Wollstonecraft appears explicitly to repress the female imagination in order to preserve male reason. One moment occurs when Wollstonecraft asserts that young children of the same sex should not be housed or educated together, so that they will not learn from each other the "vices, which render the body weak," specifically, masturbation (164; chap. 12).[15] Here, one can image the female imagination as a feminine interest in sexuality and pleasure, an interest which Wollstonecraft must repress in the name of a disembodied male rationality. The other moment occurs during Wollstonecraft's introductory remarks on style, when she promises not "to cull my phrases or polish my style . . . for wishing rather to persuade by the force of my arguments than dazzle by the elegance of my language, I shall not waste my time in rounding periods, or in fabricating the turgid bombast of artificial feelings . . ." (10; intro.). Here, the female imagination can be reinscribed within a feminine discourse of sensual and emotional rhetoric

that Wollstonecraft also dismisses in favor of a more masculine type of writing and style of reason. Thus, one could argue that, through these two instances in the text, *The Rights of Woman* attempts both thematically and formally to repress a feminine alterity in favor of a masculine ontology of Enlightenment reason. Seemingly disparate, Wollstonecraft's view on writing and her prohibition against masturbation *are* connected, but not by the particular model of repression that I sketched above.[16]

First, let us consider Wollstonecraft's words against masturbation. Her interdiction comes as part of a broader polemic, against the "wearisome confinement" women experience at school together, which is even worse than what young men suffer. In a passage just before the one on masturbation, Wollstonecraft describes the negative effect of this confinement in vivid terms.

> The pure animal spirits, which make both mind and body shoot out, and unfold the tender blossoms of hope, are turned sour, and vented in vain wishes or pert repinings, that contract the faculties and spoil the temper; else they mount to the brain, and sharpening the understanding before it gains proportionable strength, produce that pitiful cunning which disgracefully characterizes the female mind—and I fear will ever characterize it whilst women remain the slaves of power!
>
> (164; chap. 12)

We notice immediately that Wollstonecraft has, as she often does, characterized the female in negative terms. But more important is the specific way she characterizes the female as negative. In this passage, the "female mind" is the consequence of the "souring" of the "pure animal spirits"—"spirits" charged by a sensual articulation, verging on the explicitly sexual for both the male ("shoot out") and female ("tender blossoms") organs. How do we reconcile Wollstonecraft's positive evaluation of these terms with her words against masturbation? I would argue that, instead of a simultaneous acknowledgement and repression of sexuality, this passage is a parable that *warns* against the repression of sexuality—the "animal spirits." More precisely, Wollstonecraft's sexual language provides a biological metaphor for the process of social growth that Wollstonecraft opposes to the deforming and stunting socializing process women must undergo under England's contemporary educational system. The product of this system is "woman"—the "female mind"—whose essential consignment to this gender identity is undercut, not only by Wollstonecraft's visionary cry ("whilst women remain . . .") but also by the *male* configuration of masturbation and loss that structures the entire procedure ("animal spirits . . . turned sour"), which *itself* is undercut, in turn, by the biological gender of Wollstonecraft's subjects: ghettoized young girls who are "obliged to pace with steady deportment stupidly backwards and forwards . . . instead of bounding . . . in the various attitudes so conducive to health" (164; chap. 12).

These young girls, moreover, are not the sole victims of this oppressive system of single-sex confinement. For in the next paragraph, Wollstonecraft shifts her attention from the girls to the "boys [who] infallibly lose that decent bashfulness" in the setting of a single-sex school (164; chap. 12). Thus, while it is the confined group of girls whose "animal spirits" metaphorically "turn sour," it is the equally segregated group of boys who actually learn the "vices, which render the body weak."

Thus, masturbation functions not only as a sign for this whole pedagogical system of "souring" but also as the final figurative *and* literal consequence of this system: the vice that girls and boys will experience because of their isolation from one another.[17] By attacking that final consequence, Wollstonecraft is weighing in against the entire system, in which masturbation functions not as an expression but as a repression of the potential of mind *and* body. As such, the passage on masturbation exemplifies one particular target of Wollstonecraft's polemic, the repression of women's full emotional life by the schizophrenic identity men impose upon them: both coy mistress and chaste wife. (The fact that school boys specifically fall prey to masturbation stresses, for Wollstonecraft, how both sexes suffer the consequences of this repression.) Wollstonecraft's critique of this identity underscores the reason why she distinguishes between modesty and the desire for a good reputation. Modesty is the state of life one achieves after experiencing passion and the vicissitudes of life, whereas the desire for a good reputation is the hypocritical, deforming state that passes ignorance off as innocence, and whose end result is a titillation caused by the repression of desire. Thus Wollstonecraft does not repress passion in favor of a repressive reason; instead, she attacks passion when it *has* been repressed, when it is not allowed to become part of a lived experience, but instead is exploited as the fuel for what amounts to a solipsistic, masturbatory imagination.[18]

This is Wollstonecraft's critique of a certain type of "feminized" and "Romantic" imagination. By looking at this sensibility in *The Rights of Woman* more closely, we can understand more fully the implications of her introductory attack upon a writing style of supposed sensuality and feeling. Her emblem for this imagination is none other than Jean-Jacques Rousseau, who, as the writer of *Emile,* lays out in his education of Sophie the most specific blueprint for this particular kind of "feminization" of the female subject. But Rousseau is also the chief *example* of someone who indulges in this type of imagination:

> Even [Rousseau's] virtues also led him astray; for, born with a warm constitution and lively fancy, nature car-

ried him toward the other sex with such eager fondness, that he soon became lascivious. *Had he given away to these desires,* the fire would have extinguished itself in a natural manner; but virtue and a romantic kind of delicacy, made him practice self-denial; yet when fear, delicacy, or virtue, restrained him, he debauched his imagination, and reflecting on the sensations to which fancy gave force, he traced them in the most glowing colours, and sunk them deep into his soul.

(my emphasis, 91; chap. 5)

If Rousseau *had* given into his lasciviousness, if he had actually met, rather then just gone toward, the other sex, *his* "animal spirits" would not have gone "sour," and his imagination would not have been "debauched."[19] Here, virtue and self-denial are not continuous with modesty and reason; rather, the former terms are part of the moral ideology that is also responsible for the isolation of young girls in education and the specific type of "female mind" that is the result of such an isolation. Moreover, that literal isolation reminds us that the effects of feminine delicacy and virtue differ for Rousseau and for the women defined by this same code. For Wollstonecraft, Rousseau's Romantic imagination underwrites the identities of both women and men, but it assigns them to asymmetrical positions of power.

It is true that, for his contemporaries and later critics, Rousseau signified a sensibility that was always figured pejoratively in feminine terms.[20] We might then be tempted to see Wollstonecraft's critique of Rousseau's imagination as merely reproducing the hierarchy of gender values she is trying to attack. Our analysis of the circulation of gender in Wollstonecraft—especially in her interdiction against masturbation—should warn us against that temptation. But Wollstonecraft also subverts the temptation by assigning that sensibility to the premier patriarch of her day, Edmund Burke. Wollstonecraft's association between Burke and this sensibility goes back to her *A Vindication of the Rights of Men* (1790), which portrays Burke's *Reflections on the Revolution in France* (1790) as the reaction of an individual overcome by an unreasonable and emotional sensibility.[21] This emotional sensibility, like Rousseau's, victimizes women with a particular type of feminization, even as it exemplifies that feminization.[22] In much the same way, *The Rights of Woman* attacks the tautological reasoning of Burke's valorization of prejudice in the *Reflections* by likening that type of argument to "what is vulgarly termed a woman's reason" (113; chap. 5). Wollstonecraft's point is not that women essentially reason through prejudice but that Burke reasons in a way that patriarchy has "vulgarly" associated with the feminine.[23]

By identifying Burke and Rousseau with a "sensibility" that they and others have imposed on women, Wollstonecraft has, in effect, deconstructed their sexual politics, foregrounding the contradictions of their own logic of gender and identity. This is the context of Wollstonecraft's attack upon a writing style full of the "turgid bombast of artificial feeling." That is, Wollstonecraft and her contemporaries attacked Burke's *Reflections* on the very issue of a contradictory style, on how he described the French Revolution as a hysterical event, even though hysteria more aptly described his own emotional, oftentimes lurid prose. This sensational style of Burke's is the target of Tom Paine's *The Rights of Man* (1791, 1792) and Wollstonecraft's own *Rights of Men.*[24] By thus condemning a style of "sickly delicacy" and "false sentiments" at the beginning of **The Rights of Woman,** Wollstonecraft is not so much repressing a feminine style in favor of a male rationality as devaluing that style and disrupting its gender by associating it with one of the leading English fathers of the day.

One could still argue that, because of Wollstonecraft's own rambling and passionate style, she merely reproduces the irrational emotion she finds in Burke, even as she makes claims for the rational nature of her own work.[25] That argument would carry more force *if* the duality operating in Wollstonecraft's passage really was between reason and emotion. Yet she dismisses the "turgid bombast of artificial feeling" because it comes "from the head" and "never reach[es] the heart" (10; intro.). In fact, the duality dominating this passage is one between "*false* sentiments" and "*natural* emotions of the heart" (my emphasis, 10; intro.). Without the experience of such "natural emotions" one cannot become a "rational and immortal being"; instead, like the confined school girls, one's life—and writing—is stunted by the titillating "sickly delicacy" exemplified by the inflamed imagination of Rousseau. I would also stress that, for Wollstonecraft, these "natural emotions" must be experienced. Indeed, "false sentiments" are "false" only because they have not been experienced, since the purpose of the "natural emotions" is in fact to lead one to reason *through error.* Elsewhere, Wollstonecraft is explicit about how the experiential negativity of the passions is fundamentally involved in this dialectical progress toward reason, and how that progress has, in Wollstonecraft's time, been gender coded:

> I must therefore venture to doubt whether what has been thought as an axiom in morals may not have been a dogmatical assertion made by men who have coolly seen mankind through the medium of books, and say, in direct contradiction to them, that the regulation of the passions is not always wisdom—On the contrary, it should seem, that one reason why men have superior judgment and more fortitude then women, is undoubtedly this, that they give a freer scope to the grand passions, and by more frequently going astray enlarge their minds. If then by the exercise of their own reason they fix on some stable principle, they have probably to

> thank the force of their passions, nourished by *false* views of life, and permitted to overleap the boundary that secures content.

> (110; chap. 5)

Thus, "superior judgment and . . . fortitude" depend upon a prior experience of emotions that allows us to learn through our mistakes and our incorrect beliefs. One might argue, however, that such a schema accepts the passions as a fundamental part of life, only to relegate them still to a secondary role in relation to the final goal of this entire process, reason; that is, the passions are important only insofar as their negativity paves the way to our final attainment of reason. This critique is valid, insofar as it refers to one major aspect of *The Rights of Woman,* the utopian teleological impulse of the book, which images society and the individual as progressing toward the realization of their full potential, figured through the twin goals of God and reason. This Enlightenment diachronicity underwrites much of Wollstonecraft's polemic, insofar as Wollstonecraft opposes this diachronicity to a "propensity to enjoy the present moment" imposed upon and internalized by women, which stunts their political and social potential as much as their literal confinement in school (52; chap. 4). Yet this diachronicity and its politics do not exhaust Wollstonecraft's book. Her teleological movement toward reason is in direct tension with the epistemology structuring the critique that paradoxically pushes her teleological argument forward. Passion and reason imbricate this epistemology not diachronically but synchronically. That is, *at any given moment,* Wollstonecraft's feminist critique involves a reflexivity that resists any simple progress from passion to reason.

Wollstonecraft dramatizes this reflexivity, and the new complex dialectic between reason and passion it engenders, in the remarkable "Pisgah vision" she has right after the passage on the "regulation of the passions" I quoted at length above. "Pisgah" refers to the name of the mountain from which Moses was allowed to view the Promised Land; a Pisgah vision, then, was a mode of political prophecy that late eighteenth-century writers used to articulate their own feelings about the fate of the French Revolution and, by extension, the political future of Europe and England. One of the most famous visions of that period was that of Dr. Richard Price, an ardent supporter of the Revolution; Burke's *Reflections* is in large part a vehement attack upon Price's vision.[26] Wollstonecraft's own **Rights of Men** defends Price against Burke; Wollstonecraft's use of the vision is thus no mere Biblical allusion but her own contribution to a specific form of political discourse, with which she was intimately familiar. At once an elaboration and critique of this form, this contribution structures itself around Wollstonecraft's complex perception of the dialectical interplay between reason and passion.

After Wollstonecraft's statement on how reasonable men should actually thank the "force of their passions, nourished by false views of life," these lines follow:

> But if, in the dawn of life, we could soberly survey the scenes before as in perspective, and see every thing in its true colours, how could the passions gain sufficient strength to unfold the faculties?
>
> Let me now as from an eminence survey the world stripped of all its false delusive charms. The clear atmosphere enables me to see each object in its true point of view, while my heart is still. I am calm as the prospect in a morning when the mists, slowly dispersing, silently unveil the beauties of nature, refreshed by rest. In what light will the world now appear?—I rub my eyes and think, perchance, that I am just waking from a lively dream.
>
> (110; chap. 5)

Wollstonecraft has introduced a vision that apparently simulates the telos of her Christian diachronic narrative, in which she has reached—indeed, climbed to—a vantage point from which her perspective is influenced by neither "false delusive charms" nor "a lively dream." Instead, the "charms" of that "dream" will become the subject of her newly found, clear vision. By echoing the "*false* views of life," these "false delusive charms" present themselves as the erroneous but necessary catalysts for passion that will bring people to reason.

This is what Wollstonecraft first views:

> I see the sons and daughters of men pursuing shadows, and anxiously wasting their powers to feed passions which have not adequate object—if the very excess of these blind impulses, pampered by that lying, yet constantly trusted guide, the imagination, did not, by preparing them for some other state, render short-sighted mortals wiser without their own concurrence; or what comes to the same thing, when they were pursuing some imaginary present good.
>
> (110; chap. 5)

At first, this passage appears to reproduce Wollstonecraft's teleological narrative, with the "excess of these blind impulses" preparing people for the state of reason. Yet we can also read this passage another way, in which the exact moment of sublation from passion to reason is never clear; that is, the blind impulses and lying imagination "render short-sighted mortals wiser without their own concurrence"—while these mortals are *in* error and negativity. These mortals are not prepared for reason by realizing their error; rather, they reach preparation the more they are in error and the more they cannot see their error. Passion and reason still relate, but in a way that problematizes any easy shift from one to the other.

The next part of Wollstonecraft's vision reinforces this more problematic reading. The vision blasts "the ambitious man consuming himself by running after a phan-

tom" and observes how hard it would be for him to change his way *even* if he could clearly see the fallacy of his situation (111; chap. 5). Wollstonecraft then observes:

> But, vain as the ambitious man's pursuits would be, he is often striving for something more substantial than fame—that indeed would be the veriest meteor, the wildest fire that could lure a man to ruin.—What! renounce the most trifling gratification to be applauded when he should be no more! Wherefore this struggle, whether man be mortal or immortal, if that noble passion did not really raise the being above his fellows?
>
> (111; chap. 5)

Again, there is "something more substantial" in, not beyond, the ambitious man's pursuits—something that neither preempts nor coincides with the desire for fame, that which by itself would "lure a man to ruin." Here Wollstonecraft's irony folds in upon itself. Mocking both the pettiness of fame and those who would dismiss fame as only petty, she describes fame as the "trifling gratification" that deals with death. "That noble passion," then, neither works toward nor depends upon a release from the blindness of fame; instead, that passion raises the individual even as it works through its earthly double, the desire for fame.

The next part of Wollstonecraft's vision appears to retreat from this new problematic of passion's role. Discussing the follies of love, Wollstonecraft describes the process in which an individual creates a desired object with "imaginary charms." When those charms disappear—when the individual is no longer in error—it is reason that saves the mistaken passion from devolving into mere lust:

> And would not the sight of the object, not seen through the medium of the imagination, soon reduce the passion to an appetite, if reflection, the noble distinction of man, did not give it force, and make it an instrument to raise him above this earthy dross, by teaching him to love the centre of all perfection; whose wisdom appears clearer and clearer in the works of nature, in proportion as reason is illuminated and exalted by contemplation, and acquiring that love of order which the struggles of passion produce?
>
> (111; chap. 5)

Here, we are raised "above this earthy dross" and taught "to love the centre of all perfection" by reflection, contemplation, and reason, all of which appear at and beyond the level of passion's struggles. Wollstonecraft has apparently reverted to her teleological narrative of God and reason. Yet she then completely scrambles this narrative in her next paragraph:

> The habit of reflection, and the knowledge attained by fostering any passion, might be shewn to be equally useful, though the object proved equally fallacious; for they would all appear in the same light, if they were

not magnified by the governing passion implanted in us by the Author of all good, to call forth and strengthen the faculties of each individual, and enable it to attain all the experience that an infant can obtain, who does certain things, it cannot tell why.

> (111; chap. 5)

Wollstonecraft has, in effect, turned her teleological narrative inside out. First, she has transformed it into a *genetic* narrative, giving originary presence, moreover, not to reason but to "the governing passion implanted in us" by God. The process initiated and managed by this passion marginalizes reason even more so with the figure of the child, whose actions operate outside of the child's cognition, even as their existence calls forth Wollstonecraft's approval. While not simply erasing Wollstonecraft's teleological narrative, the genetic model does heighten the sense of disequilibrium the entire vision brings to bear on that teleological narrative, even at the moment when the vision appears most ready to fall back into that narrative.

Just as disorienting as the genetic model is the passage's doubling of passion. Not only does Wollstonecraft invoke the primary "governing passion," she also contrasts "any passion" and the knowledge (of passion? or reason?) it attains with the "habit of reflection"—only then to collapse the main difference between them. She associates *both* of these epistemological modes with error; both can be turned upon objects that are "equally fallacious," and both modes can still be productive, as long as they are redeemed—"magnified"—by the "governing passion."

It is this leveling of the hierarchy between reason and passion that Wollstonecraft finally recuperates out of the dizzying deployment of both these terms in her vision. Thus, even if we could foresee the error passion will bring, and

> had the cold hand of circumspection damped each generous feeling before it had left any permanent character, or fixed some habit, what could be expected, but selfish prudence and reason just rising above instinct? Who that has read Dean Swift's disgusting description of the Yahoos, and insipid one of Houyhnhnm with a philosophical eye, can avoid seeing the futility of degrading the passions, or making man rest in contentment?

> (112; chap. 5)

Yet Wollstonecraft's point does not seem to be that we can or should find a middle ground between, or a synthesis of, Swift's Yahoos and Houyhnhnms. Instead, the moral is the dialectical limit reason and passion impose on each other's perceptual powers. Wollstonecraft stresses this limit with startling force when she turns her moral upon the truth claims of the Pisgah vision she has just had. Thus, before the passage on Swift, she writes,

> I descend from my height, and mixing with my fellow-creatures, feel myself hurried along the common stream; ambition, love, hope, and fear, exert their wonted power, though we be convinced by reason that their present and most attractive promises are only lying dreams. . . .

> (111-12; chap. 5)

Several paragraphs later, she adds,

> The world cannot be seen by an unmoved spectator, we must mix in the throng, and feel as men feel before we can judge their feelings. If we mean, in short, to live in the world to grow wiser and better, and not merely to enjoy the good things of life, we must attain a knowledge of others at the same time that we become acquainted with ourselves—knowledge acquired any other way only hardens the heart and perplexes the understanding.

> (112; chap. 5)

Though Wollstonecraft recognizes that a descent from her vision will be into the error and "lying dreams" of passion she *still descends*. She does so not only because she must but also because of her recognition of the undependability of her position in that vision. What is her position in that vision but that of the "unmoved spectator" above the throng that she observes, but with whom she does not mix? The knowledge and wisdom that Wollstonecraft wants us to acquire echo those parts of her vision that imply that reason and insight are unknowingly found *in,* not through, passion and error. As such, the position of this knowledge and wisdom is radically antithetical to the epistemological position of the Pisgah vision—a vision that, for all intents and purposes, *is* the telos, the utopian vantage point of reason and clarity toward which Wollstonecraft's Enlightenment narrative moves.

Wollstonecraft's vision and its aftermath allegorizes a fundamental and irreducible tension in *The Rights of Woman* between a diachronic longing for an unambiguous political progress from passion to reason and a synchronic apprehension of the shifting epistemological boundaries between passion and reason, wherein reason functions not as a final goal but as a constant imperative toward critique, toward even the unmasking of its own dependency on the shadowed "wisdom" of passion. (We can recall that, much in the same way, the gender indeterminacy of the sentence, "Men do not always act like men . . . ," is set off by the intervention of "understanding.") As a reflexive meditation upon the exigencies and duplicities of vision, this passage is as powerful an example of "literariness," the insight into blindness and insight, as the one Paul de Man valorizes in the work of Wollstonecraft's own subject, Jean-Jacques Rousseau. More important, as an example of blindness and insight explicitly taking place within the context of a feminist politics, the passage at once powerfully acknowledges and critiques Wollstonecraft's text's own ideological inscription—a simultaneity given all the more force by Wollstonecraft's unreflective use of "man" as the human agent of the Pisgah vision.

Thus, Wollstonecraft's use of passion and reason, her critique of the Rousseauistic Romantic imagination, and her deployment of gender all resist her monumentalization as one who repressed her female Otherness in favor of a male identity of Enlightenment rationality. Indeed, the complex circulation of political, epistemological, and gender signs in *The Rights of Woman* reflect a discursive deftness that exceeds the aporia of writing Mary Jacobus finds only in Wollstonecraft's fragmentary *The Wrongs of Woman*, insofar as *The Rights of Woman* uses the errancy of language to press for an explicitly political, oftentimes didactic rhetoric. Perhaps the most uncanny thing about *The Rights of Woman* is that the text's (still unacknowledged) theoretical density and the text's given identity as political praxis occupy the same space without scandal. *That* is a doubling, repressed or unrepressed, from which we might do well to learn.

Notes

1. As Katherine M. Rogers writes, "Widely admired during her lifetime, Wollstonecraft shortly after her death was vilified by her enemies and her work was ignored by her friends. Her reputation was so bad by the nineteenth century that several leading feminists repudiated her. . . . Even Wollstonecraft's friend [Mary] Hays omitted her from her five-volume *Female Biography* in 1803" (*Feminism in Eighteenth-Century England* [Urbana, IL: University of Illinois Press, 1982], 3, 5).

2. Rogers, *Feminism in Eighteenth-Century England*, 3. See also Barbara Taylor, *Eve and the New Jerusalem: Socialism and Feminism in the Nineteenth Century* (New York: Pantheon, 1983), 9-12, and Alice Browne, *The Eighteenth Century Feminist Mind* (Detroit: Wayne State University Press, 1987), 170. Wollstonecraft, needless to say, saw a necessary continuum between her two positions. For a discussion of England's reception of Rousseau, see Edward Duffy, *Rousseau in England: The Context for Shelley's Critique of the Enlightenment* (Berkeley and Los Angeles: University of California Press, 1979), 37-53.

3. Just as Rousseau's *Confessions* affected the interpretation of his political and social theory, so too did Godwin's biography of Wollstonecraft provide anti-Jacobinists and anti-feminists with the tools to attack *The Rights of Woman*. For a discussion of the effects of the publication of Rousseau's autobiography in England, see Duffy, *Rousseau in England*, 32-53; for a discussion of how Godwin's biography of Wollstonecraft affected her intellectual and political reputation, see Browne, *The Eighteenth-Century Feminist Mind*, 170-73.

4. My notion of the historical "monument" develops out of Paul de Man's use of that term in his seminal essay, "Shelley Disfigured," in Harold Bloom et al., *Deconstruction and Criticism* (New York: Continuum, 1979), 39-73. See also Orrin N. C. Wang, "Disfiguring Monuments: History in Paul de Man's 'Shelley Disfigured' and Percy Bysshe Shelley's 'The Triumph of Life,' *ELH* 58, no. 3 (Fall 1991)—forthcoming.

5. Mary Jacobus, "The Buried Letter: *Villette*," in *Reading Women: Essays in Feminist Criticism* (New York: Columbia University Press, 1986), 59.

6. Thus Mary Poovey portrays Wollstonecraft's duality in the ideological terms of the two literary discourses open to her as a women, sentimental fiction and the "how to" texts of "the proper lady." Relying heavily on Wollstonecraft's biography, Poovey turns Wollstonecraft's life and texts into a seamless narrative of a figure— "Wollstonecraft"—who is, on the whole, blind to the limits of the discourses structuring her life and writing (*The Proper Lady and the Woman Writer: Ideology as Style in the Works of Mary Wollstonecraft, Mary Shelley, and Jane Austen* [Chicago: University of Chicago Press, 1984], 48-113). Likewise, Cora Kaplan sees in Wollstonecraft's supposed privileging of male reason over female sentiment a fear of the female body—a fear that duplicates current debates over the role of female sexuality and pleasure in contemporary feminist agendas ("Wild Nights: Pleasure/Sexuality/Feminism," in *Sea Changes: Culture and Feminism* [London: Verso, 1986], 31-57). Both Kaplan and Poovey primarily associate imagination in Wollstonecraft with a sexuality that the Romantic writer tries to occlude; in contrast, Mary Jacobus associates Wollstonecraft's imagination not only with passion but with the irreducible errancy—the "madness"—of language itself ("The Difference of View," in *Reading Woman*, 33-34). Thus, unlike Poovey, Jacobus looks for the repressed effects of imagination not in Wollstonecraft's biography but in the rhetorical effects of her writing. Still, Jacobus has not really altered the Wollstonecraft paradigm that she, like Poovey and Kaplan, has inherited. She merely transfers Wollstonecraft's subversive Otherness from Wollstonecraft's biography to her literary works.

An influential recent precursor of this critical plot that emphasizes the duality in Wollstonecraft as one between femininity and masculinity is Margaret Walters' "The Rights and Wrongs of Women: Mary Wollstonecraft, Harriet Martineau, and Simone de Beauvoir," in *The Rights and Wrongs of Women,* ed. Anne Oakley and Juliet Mitchell (London: Penguin, 1976), 304-29.

7. For a reading of Wollstonecraft's acknowledgement of female writing see Jacobus, "The Difference of View," 32-33; for a reading of female desire, see Kaplan, "Wild Nights," 35, 159. For Poovey the movement from *The Rights of Woman* to *The Wrongs of Woman* is both a progress and a decline. On the one hand Poovey sees *The Rights of Woman* as exhibiting a frustration over the split between Wollstonecraft's professional and sexual identities, a split that the later works confront more directly; yet Poovey also sees this later confrontation hampered by a reification of the bourgeois self that *The Rights of Woman* seeks to deny (*The Proper Lady and the Woman Writer,* 80-81, 94-113). For the argument that *The Wrongs of Woman* actually has more in common with *The Rights of Woman* than Wollstonecraft's first novel, *Mary, A Fiction* (1788), see Laurie Langbauer, "An Early Romance: Motherhood and Women's Writing in Mary Wollstonecraft's Novels," in *Romanticism and Feminism,* ed. Anne K. Mellor (Bloomington, IN: Indiana University Press, 1988), 209-11.

8. As Denise Riley points out, one can refute the essential nature of "woman" while still believing in some other hypostatized agent, such as "women." (See her *"Am I That Name?": Feminism and the Category of "Women" in History* [Minneapolis: University of Minnesota Press, 1988], 2-3.) In my critique, however, I do not distinguish between the terms "woman," "women," and the "feminine" precisely because I see Wollstonecraft's rejection of the gendered duality between reason and imagination as a rejection of the ontological assumptions that would allow for the reification of all three terms.

9. Mary Wollstonecraft, *A Vindication of the Rights of Woman,* ed. Carol H. Poston (New York: W. W. Norton, 1975), 6; intro. All further references to this work appear in the text. So that readers may easily locate my references in other editions, I have cited chapters as well as page numbers.

10. See Timothy J. Reiss, "Revolution in Bounds: Wollstonecraft, Women, and Reason," in *Gender and Theory: Dialogues on Feminist Criticism,* ed. Linda Kauffman (Oxford: Basil Blackwell, 1989), 12-21, 39-44. From the same book, see also Frances Ferguson's rebuttal to Reiss, "Wollstonecraft Our Contemporary," 51-62.

11. Ernesto Laclau and Chantal Mouffe, *Hegemony and Socialist Strategy: Towards a Radical Democratic Politics* (London: Verso, 1985), 154.

12. "Hegemonic practices are suturing insofar as their field of operation is determined by the openness of the social, by the ultimately unfixed character of every signifier. This original lack is precisely what the hegemonic practices try to fill in. A *totally* sutured society would be one where this filling-in would have reached its ultimate consequences and would have, therefore, managed to identify itself with the transparency of a closed symbolic order. Such a closure of the social is, as we will see, impossible" (Laclau and Mouffe, *Hegemony and Socialist Strategy,* 88). Also see *Hegemony and Socialist Strategy,* 127-34.

13. The quote by Rousseau that Wollstonecraft responds to is: "Educate [women] like men. The more women are like men, the less power they will have over men, and then men will be masters indeed" (Jean-Jacques Rousseau, *Emile,* trans. Barbara Foxely [London: J. M. Dent, 1911], 327).

14. I do not exaggerate when I claim that Wollstonecraft's analysis operates at the level of "forces"; the sentence I cite is in her chapter entitled "Animadversions on Some of the Writers Who Have Rendered Women Objects of Pity, Bordering on Contempt," which, as its title suggests, surveys and evaluates the cultural effect of a century's worth of literature aimed at conferring onto "woman" a single identity.

15. I am indebted to Richard A. Strier for pointing out to me that Wollstonecraft's reference to masturbation ("vices which render the body weak") is specifically aimed not at girls but at boys. Earlier, Wollstonecraft does refer to girls who might learn "nasty or immodest habits" from one another in nurseries and boarding schools (127; chap. 7).

16. While she does not refer to the same passage on masturbation that I analyze, the most vivid example of this model of repression, articulated at the level of both style and sexuality, is offered by Kaplan, "Wild Nights," 34-50.

17. After this passage Wollstonecraft once again refers to the "bad habits which females acquire when they are shut up together," thus stressing that masturbation is a literal fact for girls as well as boys (165; chap. 12).

18. Richard A. Strier has pointed out to me that, for someone like Wollstonecraft who came out of the Protestant tradition of dissent, this solipsistic imagination would also have been associated with a Catholic sensibility. For a recent reading of Wollstonecraft with a view on sexuality and expe-

rience similar to mine, see Langbauer, "An Early Romance," 210. Also, Wollstonecraft's critique of sentimental fiction is inscribed within the same polemic against female confinement and repression:

> There are the women who are amused by the reveries of the stupid novelists, who, knowing little of human nature, work up stale tales, and describe meretricious scenes, all retailed in a sentimental jargon, which equally tend to corrupt the taste, and draw the heart aside from its daily duties. I do not mention the understanding, because never having been exercised, its slumbering energies rest inactive, like the lurking particles of fire which are supposed universally to pervade matter.
>
> (183; chap. 13)

Thus, sentimental fiction actually keeps the mind from experience, confining understanding and rendering it passive, much like the way schools restrict the exercise and activities of young girls. (And while the negative view of fiction does privilege reason over emotion, the analogy between reason and the school girls disrupts any facile reification of the male reason/female emotion split.) In the same vein Wollstonecraft also argues that the reading of sentimental fiction is better than no reading at all, since such fiction at least gives women some experience, even if it is the wrong kind (184; chap. 13).

19. There is evidence that suggests that Wollstonecraft paints this picture of Rousseau with knowledge of his own literary references to masturbation. Consider, for example, this passage from a review of *The Confessions* in the *Analytical Review* which critics have attributed to Wollstonecraft:

> His most enthusiastic admirers must allow that his imagination was sometimes rampant, and breaking loose from his judgement, sketched some alluring pictures, whose colouring was more natural, than chaste, yet over which, with the felicity of genius, he has thrown those voluptuous shades, that, by setting the fancy to work, prove a dangerous snare, when the hot blood dances in the veins.
>
> (*Analytical Review* 11 [December 1791]; quoted in Duffy, *Rousseau in England*, 48)

As Duffy writes, "The *Analytical*'s critique of Rousseauean sensibility coincides exactly with the anti-Rousseauean message of [Wollstonecraft's] *Vindication of the Rights of Woman*" (48-49). We can also note the similarity between the *Analytical*'s passage, the Wollstonecraft quote, and this piece from *The Confessions,* in which Rousseau explicitly connects the imagination to masturbation:

> I had preserved my physical but not my moral virginity. . . . The progress of the years had told upon me, and my restless temperament had at last

made itself felt. . . . [I] learned that dangerous means of cheating Nature, which leads in young men of my temperament to various kinds of excesses, that eventually imperil their health, their strength, and sometimes their lives. This vice, which shame and timidity find so convenient, has a particular attraction for lively imaginations. It allows them to dispose, so to speak, of the whole female sex at their will, and to make any beauty who tempts them serve their pleasure without the need of first containing consent.

> (Jean-Jacques Rousseau, *The Confessions,* trans. J. M. Cohen [London: Penguin, 1953], 108-90)

The most thorough treatment of Rousseau and masturbation is, of course, Jacques Derrida's ". . . That Dangerous Supplement . . ." in *Of Grammatology,* trans. Gayatri Chakravorty Spivak (Baltimore: Johns Hopkins University Press, 1974), 141-64.

20. "There is indeed much in [Rousseau's] make-up that reminds one less of a man than a high-strung woman. . . . By subordinating judgment to sensibility Rousseau may be said to have made woman the measure of all things" (Irving Babbitt, *Rousseau and Romanticism* [1919; Boston: Houghton Mifflin; Cleveland: World Publishing, 1955], 130-32).

21. Throughout your letter [i.e., Burke's *Reflections*] you frequently advert to a sentimental jargon, which has long been current in conversation, and even in books of morals, though it never received the *regal* stamp of reason. A kind of mysterious instinct is *supposed* to reside in the soul, that instantaneously discerns truth, without the tedious labor of ratiocination. This instinct . . . has been termed *common sense,* and more frequently *sensibility*; and by a kind of *indefeasible* right, it has been *supposed,* for rights of this kind are not easily proved, to reign paramount over the other faculties of the mind, and to be an authority from which there is not appeal.

. . . [This sensibility] dips, we know not why, granting it to be an infallible instinct, and, though supposed always to point to truth, its pole star, the point is always shifting, and seldom stands due north.

> (Mary Wollstonecraft, *A Vindication of the Rights of Men* [Albany, NY: Delmar, Scholar's Facsimiles, 1975], 68-69)

For an extended analysis of Wollstonecraft's critique of Burke's emotional sensibility, see James T. Boulton, *The Language of Politics in the Age of Wilkes and Burke* (London: Routledge & Kegan Paul, 1963), 168-76.

22. Thus Wollstonecraft attacks the assumptions of gender that underwrite Burke's duality between a masculine sublime and feminine beautiful in his

Philosophical Enquiry into the Origin of Our Ideas of the Sublime and the Beautiful (1757), and then she asserts that Burke is himself actually inscribed not in the sublime but in the beautiful (*The Rights of Men,* 111-21, 138-42).

Wollstonecraft also associates Burke's sensibility with a "personal pique" and a "hurt vanity"—those very traits of egomania that Burke attacks in Rousseau (*The Rights of Men,* 110).

23. Elsewhere, in praising the writing of Catherine Macaulay, Wollstonecraft takes pains *not* to associate Macaulay's thought with the masculine:

> I will not call [Macaulay's] a masculine understanding, because I admit not of such an arrogant assumption of reason; but I contend that it was a sound one, and that her judgement, the matured fruit of profound thinking, was a proof that a woman can acquire judgement, in the full extent of the word.

> (105; chap. 5)

24. See Poovey, *The Proper Lady and the Woman Writer,* 58-59, and James K. Chandler, *Wordsworth's Second Nature: A Study of the Poetry and Politics* (Chicago: University of Chicago Press, 1984), 63. See also note 21.

25. This is exactly Boulton's final point about *The Rights of Men* (*The Language of Politics in the Age of Wilkes and Burke,* 172-76).

26. For a discussion of Price's vision and Burke's repudiation of it, see W. J. T. Mitchell, *Iconology: Image, Text, Ideology* (Chicago: University of Chicago Press, 1986), 144-46.

Steven Blakemore (essay date winter 1992)

SOURCE: Blakemore, Steven. "Rebellious Reading: The Doubleness of Wollstonecraft's Subversion of *Paradise Lost.*" *Texas Studies in Literature and Language* 34, no. 4 (winter 1992): 451-80.

[*In the following essay, Blakemore argues that in* A Vindication of the Rights of Woman *Wollstonecraft engages in a radical, systematic subversion of John Milton's* Paradise Lost *and, further, that she subverts the feminist myth she herself creates.*]

In 1784 Immanuel Kant published his famous essay in which he defined "enlightenment" as man's emergence from self-imposed nonage and challenged people to begin liberating themselves by pursuing knowledge instead of relying on tradition: "*Dare to know!* (*Sapere aude.*) 'Have the courage to use your own understanding,' is therefore the motto of the enlighten-

ment."[1] Kant's paradigmatic equation of childhood with ignorance and knowledge with liberation was one of the great cultural commonplaces celebrated by a variety of Enlightenment writers and repeated with special resonance by radical writers during the revolutionary era (1789-1815). Indeed, the French Revolution consummated a preexistent cleavage in Western thought. Revolutionary representations of knowledge, for instance, aggressively contested traditional texts that stressed the satanic dangers of epistemological curiosity. Mary Wollstonecraft and other revolutionary writers were, in this context, waging an intertextual war against a conservative canon that emphasized epistemological restraint. In England this canon consisted of a variety of works by, inter alia, Milton, Pope, Johnson, and Burke. With reference to Milton, both revolutionary and antirevolutionary writers intuited that *Paradise Lost,* particularly Book 9, was a core text providing the "terms" for the battle over the French Revolution's mythical meaning.

Revolutionaries, like Mary Wollstonecraft, were rebelling against the canonical readings of the traditional order. In contrast, such antirevolutionary writers as Edmund Burke equated what they envisioned as an epistemological revolution with Satan's revolt—the satanic presumption, pride, and lust for forbidden knowledge inscribed in the textual falls of rebellious angels and postlapsarian people. This counterrevolutionary allegory coincided with the subversive allegory that revolutionary readers were writing: Satan as revolutionary liberator or, as we shall see, Eve as feminist rebel in Wollstonecraft's *A Vindication of the Rights of Woman* (1792).

Contemporary criticism of Wollstonecraft's reading of Milton centers on, as does most Milton criticism, the ideological presentation of Eve *qua* woman in *Paradise Lost.* Sandra Gilbert and Susan Gubar, for instance, emphasize both a misogynistic Milton and Wollstonecraft's respondent antagonism, while Joseph Wittreich finds a "feminist" Milton, who Wollstonecraft and other eighteenth-century women sympathetically read in a "text torn by ideological contradictions that do not do irreparable damage and are evidence of Milton's subversion of stereotypical representations of Eve and of women generally, a Wollstonecraft determined to represent Milton's text in all its paradoxes and ambiguities."[2] In my essay, I propose to show, first, that Wollstonecraft, in fact, engages in a systematic and sustained subversion of *Paradise Lost* that is more radical and elaborate than has been previously maintained or documented and, second, that Wollstonecraft's text is itself "torn by ideological contradictions" that subvert the feminist myth she creates. Wollstonecraft not only subverts Milton's epic but his poem redounds upon her, so that she becomes a specter (or emanation) of Milton himself. I suggest that there is a doubleness inherent in rebellious reading—a doubleness that includes a counter-revolutionary reading that, in turn, subverts the revolutionary text by reconstructing the "terms" of rebellion. Wollstonecraft's reading of Milton entails this doubleness and has dialectic implications for the canonical texts of the revolutionary and Romantic eras.

1

One of Wollstonecraft's first allusions to Milton and *Paradise Lost* appears in chapter 2 of *A Vindication of the Rights of Woman.*[3] [*RW*] Questioning why women should "be kept in ignorance under the specious name of innocence?" (*Works,* 5:88), she alludes to both Eve's Edenic "innocence" and the knowledge that is withheld from her. In *Paradise Lost,* there is a masculine hierarchy of knowledge that Wollstonecraft, as will be seen, reads as a patriarchal plot to keep Eve in a state of ignorant "innocence" and hence in a state of "feminine" weakness. "Children," she notes, "should be innocent; but when the epithet is applied to men, or women, it is but a civil term for weakness" (5:89). Wollstonecraft hence makes a series of condemnatory connections between Milton's prelapsarian Eve and the postlapsarian women who are argued into debilitating ignorance by males using Milton's authoritative language.

After referring to women's "cunning, softness or temper, *outward* obedience" and evoking Milton's Eve, she makes the connection clear: "Thus Milton describes our first frail mother; though when he tells us that women are formed for softness and sweet attractive grace, I cannot comprehend his meaning, unless, in the true Mahometan strain, he meant to deprive us of souls, and insinuate that we were beings only designed by sweet attractive grace, and docile blind obedience, to gratify the senses of man when he can no longer soar on the wing of contemplation" (5:88).

Besides the reference to *Paradise Lost* ("For contemplation he and valour form'd / For softness she and sweet attractive Grace," *PL* 4.297-8), Wollstonecraft's sarcastic comment that she "cannot comprehend" Milton's meaning alerts us that she is commencing a strong rebellious reading of Milton, and her reference to "the true Mahometan strain" of his poem (i.e., "the widespread Christian misconception that Islam denied that women had souls," *Works,* 5:73, note a) connects Milton with Edmund Burke (in *The Rights of Men*), whom she also accused of stumbling into "the mussulman's creed" and laboring to prove "that one half of the human species, at least, have not souls" (*Works,* 5:45).

In addition, her contention that Milton's text turns woman into a sexual plaything "to gratify the senses of man" suggests, at this point, that woman's "fall" was and is sexual and not essentially epistemological, since knowledge is precisely the "forbidden fruit" prohibited by patriarchal oppressors who impose ignorance and define women's subordinate sexual roles. Wollstonecraft thus implies that woman's intellectual "innocence" is actually formulated in masculine terms of coercive prohibition.

Finally, the Miltonic libertine corrupted by his sensual desires, "when he can no longer soar on the wing of contemplation," alludes to all the Miltonic (and satanic) references to soaring in *Paradise Lost,* especially Milton's boast that he intends "to soar Above the Aonian Mount" (1.15). In *The Analytical Review* (vol. 7, 1790)—the journal in which she reviewed books, off and on, for nearly a decade—Wollstonecraft noted that "Milton slackened his flight when he entered heaven, for with drooping wing did he vainly attempt to soar where the boldest imagination is soon overwhelmed with silent despair," underscoring her preference for Milton's "satanic" books and reinforcing what had already become a cultural commonplace (*Works,* 7:250).

In this context, Wollstonecraft writes out both the fall of Milton and her correspondent feminist flight. She inverts, as will be seen, the biblical consequences of the Fall, resulting in woman's explicit subordination to man (see Genesis 3:16; *Paradise Lost* 10.195-6), and transforms Eve's eating of "knowledge" into an act of independence and empowerment. In a fallen world in which Wollstonecraft doubts whether "any knowledge can be attained without *labour and sorrow*" (*RW,* 182; my emphasis), she transforms the "curse" (84) of the Fall in Genesis (3:16-17) and *Paradise Lost* (10.194, 205) into the liberation of woman through the dolorous "labor" of knowledge.

Her vision of Milton's paradise as a state of ignorance corresponds to the postlapsarian European world where men keep women "in a state of perpetual childhood" (*RW,* 75; cf. 89, 99, 130, 178, 186, 190, 196). Wollstonecraft fleshes out the correlation between Miltonic "ignorance" and feminine "innocence" when she notes that when patriarchal "instructors" contend that women were created to be kept "innocent," they really mean "in a state of childhood" (*RW,* 130). By this logic, women "might as well never have been born," unless they were created "to enable man to acquire the noble privilege of reason, the power of discerning good from evil," while women, themselves, return to "the dust from whence we were taken, never to rise again" (*RW,* 130). By equating Miltonic innocence with political and psychological childhood (and the obedience and submission this entails), Wollstonecraft begins transforming the mythic act of feminine disobedience (the eating of forbidden knowledge) into a feminist act of liberation.

Thus, in Wollstonecraft's inversion of Milton, man eats first from the tree of knowledge and then prevents woman from doing the same—thus man becomes the "tempter" who provokes her cunning curiosity for the "forbidden fruit." The consequence is her "fall" into ignorance, metaphorically equivalent to "a knowledge of evil": ". . . if men eat of the tree of knowledge, women will come in for a taste; but, from the imperfect cultivation which their understandings now receive, they only attain a knowledge of evil" (*RW,* 89). Wollstonecraft hence suggests that by depriving women of authentically "good" knowledge (cf. 108: "But I still insist, that . . . the *knowledge* of the two sexes should be the same in nature, if not in degree"), men tempt them into a knowledge of evil, causing them to act out all those self-fulfilling stereotypes men deplore.

By making men the first mythic eaters of knowledge and, by extension, the first tempters of women—the tantalizing withholders of "true" knowledge—she reverses Milton's parable of original fault, for her metaphors equate the real "fatal fruit" with the "ignorance" with which men tempt women into falling. In this context, it is not Milton's paradigm of a fall into fatal knowledge (which critics of the French Revolution were using) but a fall out or away from the knowledge appropriated by masculine "tyrants." In *Paradise Lost,* Eve, after eating the forbidden fruit, initially considers withholding the "Knowledge in [her] power," so that she may be "Superior; for inferior who is free?" (9.820, 825). In contrast, Wollstonecraft switches the traditional positions of Adam and Eve and makes Adamic man the initiator of Eve's fall into false knowledge, or ignorance, while Eve's original sin is metaphorically posited as a positive act of self-assertion, even though she is subsequently punished by patriarchal authorities and "traditions." Writing at a time (1792) when the French Revolution was still being celebrated by most of Europe, a revolution she connects with a correspondent "revolution in female manners" (*RW,* 114; cf. 251, 265), Wollstonecraft rebels against the oppressive texts of patriarchal tradition and crystallizes a feminist version of the Enlightenment's challenge to the Old Order—*Sapere aude*!

2

Indeed, Wollstonecraft sees knowledge as the liberating power by which women can break out of their subordinate "orbits" and "turn" to their Creator: "For if . . . women were destined by Providence to acquire human virtues," then "they must be permitted to turn to the fountain of light, and not forced to shape their course by the twinkling of a mere satellite" (*RW,* 89). She suggests that women must break out of the reflected light of patriarchal tradition and turn to God, praised in *Paradise Lost* by angelic choirs as "Author of all being, / Fountain of light" (3.374-75). But Wollstonecraft again turns Milton's language against him, for she adds that "Milton . . . was of a different opinion; for he only

bends to the indefeasible right of beauty," quoting as evidence Eve's submission to Adam:

> To whom thus Eve with *perfect beauty* adorn'd.
> My Author and Disposer, what thou bidst
> *Unargued* I obey; so God ordains;
> God is *thy law; thou mine:* to know no more
> Is Woman's *happiest* knowledge and her *praise.*
>
> (*PL,* 4.634-38; Wollstonecraft's emphasis)

Wollstonecraft's italicization of the words underscores her critique ("these are exactly the arguments I have used to children") of what she believes is Milton's misogynous ideology expressed and parroted through the "fallen" words of prelapsarian Eve.[4] In chapter 6, she refers again to this Miltonic passage when she observes that it is not surprising that women are so ignorant, "considering the education they receive, and that their 'highest praise is to obey, unargued'—the will of man" (*RW,* 187).

Her linkage of Miltonic "beauty" with arguments used to coerce children into obedience and, by extension, the patriarchal texts keeping women in a state of political and psychological infantilism also suggests that in order to achieve "knowledge" and hence freedom and independence, women must rebel and disobey the patriarchal injunctions that equate knowledge with the forbidden province of "masculinity." Indeed, she subverts the very terms of *Paradise Lost,* celebrating satanic rebellion and disobedience, and, in doing so, begins entangling herself in a series of satanic positions, for rebellion against patriarchal authority is the sin of both Satan and Eve.

Many of her arguments, for instance, resemble both Satan's and Eve's rationalizations of rebellion against God's "tyranny." When she comments that the purpose of education is to "enable the individual to attain such habits of virtue as will render it independent" and that "it is a farce to call any being virtuous whose virtues do not result from the exercise of its own reason" (*RW,* 90), she begins an allusive turn reminiscent of Eve's contention (when she first exercises her reason against Adam) that the nature of labor in paradise requires their temporary separation and hence her initial independence (see *PL,* 9.205-384). In addition, her argument, throughout, that men have conspired to keep women weak by prohibiting them knowledge is also, mutatis mutandis, Satan's argument to Eve: God has forbidden "knowledge" in order "to awe" and keep His "worshippers" in a state of ignorance (*PL,* 9.703-04). Satan also equates knowledge with liberation and power—with "reason" and independence. His subversive question (*PL* 9.725-26), ". . . and wherein lies / Th' offense, that man [woman] should thus attain to know?" reverberates throughout Wollstonecraft's text.

Wollstonecraft is not unwittingly enmeshing herself in these satanic echoes; she is deliberately replicating them. She, in effect, takes the first act of female disobedience inscribed in the texts of patriarchal tradition and transforms it into an act of emancipation. She crystallizes the terms of female independence—the reason, labor, and knowledge that Milton qualifies.

But there are some redounding Miltonic ironies. For instance, Wollstonecraft argues that women are "drawn out of their sphere" by the intoxicating "regal homage" of male language, and hence it is difficult to convince them that their "illegitimate power" (male "homage" to female "beauty") actually degrades them and "is a curse" (*RW*, 90). Although this is a recurrent Wollstonecraftian theme (cf. 164, 169)—the language of "regal" beauty psychologically debilitates women by conditioning them to act out the enslaving stereotypes of a chivalric language disingenuously worshipful—the reader remembers that the first enactment of this language thematically occurs in Satan's linguistic deification of Eve in *Paradise Lost*:

> Empress of this fair World, resplendent Eve,
> . . . . .
> But all that fair and good in thy Divine
> Semblance, and in thy Beauty's heav'nly Ray
> United I beheld; no Fair to thine
> Equivalent or second, which compell'd
> Mee thus, . . . to come,
> And gaze, and worship thee of right declar'd
> Sovran of Creatures, universal Dame.
>
> (9.568, 606-12; cf. Eve's satanic dream in Book 5, 45-46, 74)

In *Paradise Lost,* Satan's linguistic deification of Eve is the deceptive idolatry that precipitates both her fall and her correspondent "curse."

Although Eve initially suspects the Serpent's "over-praising" (*PL,* 9.615), she is seduced through a language that glorifies her beauty and promises her empowerment through knowledge. Wollstonecraft hence unwittingly provides the terms for a subversive counter-revolutionary reading, in which she herself tempts woman to partake of "fallen" knowledge. If Satan and Eve are the real hero and heroine of her book, a counterrevolutionary reader would see them in and through the language of Milton.[5]

In her feminist reading, of course, the real satanic tempters are those Miltonic men who pay "regal homage" to the women they keep weak and "fallen." It is the seductive language of patriarchy that is one of the metaphoric "apples" of Wollstonecraft's book—a deceptive language that seemingly elevates woman but actually degrades her—and not the true knowledge that patriarchy prohibits. Wollstonecraft hence urges a return "to nature and equality" (both suppressed in the fallen patriarchal past) which she projects in a revolutionary future when even kings and nobles will "throw off their gaudy hereditary trappings" and women will transparently resign the "arbitrary power" of feeble beauty (*RW*, 90-91).

3

But Wollstonecraft's "paradisiacal" state has nothing in common with Milton's. In fact, she pointedly alludes to Adam and Eve's existence in the garden of Eden when she criticizes eighteenth-century sexual roles:

> . . . whoever has cast a benevolent eye on society, must often have been gratified by the sight of humble mutual love, not dignified by sentiment, or strengthened by a union in intellectual pursuits. The domestic trifles of the day have afforded matters for cheerful converse, and innocent caresses have softened toils which did not cause great exercise of mind or stretch of thought: yet, has not the sight of this moderate felicity excited more tenderness than respect? An emotion similar to what we feel when children are playing, or animals sporting, whilst the contemplation of the noble struggles of suffering merit has raised admiration, and carried our thoughts to that world where sensation will give place to reason.
>
> (*RW,* 94)

Two allusions are conflated in this passage. In *Paradise Lost,* Eve enjoys receiving Adam's "Grateful digressions, [that would] solve high dispute / With conjugal Caresses, from his Lip / Not Words alone pleas'd her." Later, Adam tries to convince her that prelapsarian labor does not preclude "sweet intercourse / Of looks and smiles, for smiles from reason flow" (8.55-57; 9.238-39). The theme of "domestic trifles" affording "matters for cheerful converse" and the "innocent caresses" that soften "toils" is the same (*RW*, 94), since Wollstonecraft is criticizing the childlike relations of both the prelapsarian pair and postlapsarian couples.

In her private correspondence, we can trace the evolution of this thought, since Milton's model of domestic bliss both attracted and repelled her. For instance, in a letter (23 August 1790) to her sister, Everina Wollstonecraft, she related her visit with Reverend Henry Dyson Gabell and his wife, Ann: ". . . after the various employments of the day they find most pleasure in each other's society—of which Milton has given a description, when he speaks of the first pair." She proceeds to note the couple's "domestic felicity," their pure "caresses," and the abundant "happiness and innocent fondness" that illuminates their eyes (*Letters,* 192).

On 10 September, she wrote another letter to Everina in which she qualifies her approval of the couple's apparent Edenic bliss:

> I did intend to have mentioned your situation [Everina was seeking employment] to the good folks here—but I have changed my mind—*happiness* is not a softener of the heart—and from them I should always expect little acts of kindness and grateful civilities [cf. *PL,* 8.600-01]—but never any great exertion, which might disturb, for a moment, the even tenor of their loves and lives. Whenever [I] read Milton's description of para-

dise—the happiness, which he so poetically describes fills me with benevolent satisfaction—yet, I cannot help viewing them, I mean the first pair—as if they were my inferiors—inferiors because they could find happiness in a world like this—A feeling of the same kind frequently intrudes on me here—Tell me, does it arise from mistaken pride or conscious dignity which whispering me that my soul is immortal & should have a nobler ambition leads me to cherish it?

(*Letters,* 195)

Wollstonecraft was undoubtedly thinking of the Gabells when she criticized "innocent" domestic bliss in **The Rights of Woman.** In the letter, the Gabells resemble, what to her is, Adam and Eve's thoughtless egotistic bliss as well as their immunity from "any great exertion" (*Letters,* 195) or, mutatis mutandis, "great exercise of mind or stretch of thought" (*RW,* 94). In addition, there are specific satanic echoes in both passages.

For instance, Wollstonecraft's condescending connection of "Edenic" domestic bliss with an "emotion similar to what we feel when children are playing, or animals sporting" (*RW,* 94), alludes to Satan's first view of Adam and Eve, who "dally" surrounded by "sporting" animals:

> Nor gentle purpose [discourse], nor endearing smiles
> Wanted, nor youthful dalliance as beseems
> Fair couple, linkt in happy nuptial League,
> Alone as they. About them frisking play'd
> All beasts of th' Earth, since wild, and of all chase
> In Wood or Wilderness, Forest or Den;
> Sporting the Lion ramp'd, and in his paw
> Dandl'd the Kid . . .

(*PL,* 4.337-44)

Since Satan is watching this scene, Wollstonecraft's correspondent "sight of this moderate felicity" (*RW,* 94) suggests that she is re-creating it in order to watch it with a subversive satanic eye. Indeed, her contrastable "admiration" for "the noble struggles of suffering merit" directly alludes to Satan's description of himself in Book 1 of *Paradise Lost*: ". . . that fixt mind / And high disdain, from sense of injur'd merit" (1.97-98). These intentional satanic echoes were initiated in her letter to Everina when, after asserting her superiority to Adam and Eve in "Milton's description of Paradise," she asks if this feeling arises "from mistaken pride or conscious dignity" (*Letters,* 195), since she realizes that these are supposed satanic characteristics (cf. *PL,* 2.428-29: Satan "with Monarchal Pride / Conscious of highest worth") and that Satan was the first subversive questioner of Adam and Eve's Edenic happiness.

All this impinges on Wollstonecraft's satanic reading—a reading she spells out in footnote 2, which follows the reference to the "emotion" we feel "when children are playing, or animals sporting": "Similar feelings has Milton's pleasing picture of paradisiacal happiness ever

raised in my mind; yet, instead of envying the lovely pair, I have, with conscious dignity, or Satanic Pride, turned to hell for sublimer objects" (*RW,* 94). The reference to her "conscious dignity" or "Satanic Pride" again connects her rebellious reading with the one initiated in the letter to Everina Wollstonecraft ("Tell me, does it arise from mistaken pride or conscious dignity?"), and even her distinction between Satan's envy of "the lovely pair" (see *PL,* 4.358-92) and her own superiority to them ("yet, instead of envying the lovely pair") reinforces her strong satanic reading, since she turns "to hell for sublimer objects."

She continues this reading in the same satanic footnote:

> In the same style, when viewing some noble monument of human art, I have traced the emanation of the Deity in the order I admired, till, descending from that giddy height, I have caught myself contemplating the grandest of all human sights;—for fancy quickly placed, in some solitary recess, an outcast of fortune, rising superior to passion and discontent.

(*RW,* 94)

There are a series of Miltonic echoes that she again subverts.

First, her qualified admiration for the work of art (i.e., *Paradise Lost*) emanating from "the Deity" is connected with her "view" of Adam and Eve and her correspondent criticism of their illusive "paradisiacal happiness." Her rejection of their paradise is hence linked to her turn from the Deity, or Milton's God ("till, descending from that giddy height"), and her superior contemplation of "the grandest of all human sights"—the satanic antagonist of God: "an outcast of fortune, rising superior to passion and discontent" (*RW,* 94). In *Paradise Lost,* Satan is "outcast from God" (2.694) and complains of his expulsion and "outcast" (4.106). In Wollstonecraft's rebellious reading, he rises superior "to passion and discontent"—precisely what he does not do in *Paradise Lost.* She, in effect, revises his rebellion into an act of imaginative liberation—"rising superior to passion and discontent."

Second, her reference to "descending from that giddy height" (*RW,* 94) evokes the Miltonic narrator who has soared over the Olympian hill and wishes to descend (see *PL,* 7.1-23) and who from the beginning has also intentionally entangled himself in a series of satanic resemblances,[6] as well as the postlapsarian Adam who descends the Hill of Speculation after receiving a "vision" of the future from Michael (see 12.588-89, 606-07).

Similarly, in chapter 5 (sec. 5), Wollstonecraft metaphorically ascends, like Michael and Adam in Book 12 of *Paradise Lost,* to survey the fallen world (cf. Poovey, 80): "Let me now as from an eminence survey the world stripped of all its false delusive charms" (*RW,* 179)—

with a secondary allusion to the opening of Samuel Johnson's "The Vanity of Human Wishes" ("Let Observation, with extensive view, / Survey mankind, from China to Peru"). She subsequently "descend[s] from my height" (**RW,** 181), alluding again to Adam's response to Raphael—"Therefore from this high pitch let us descend" (*PL,* 8.198)—and Michael's injunction to Adam—"Let us descend now therefore from this top / Of Speculation" (12.588-89).

But there are also satanic or "fallen" resemblances reminiscent of Eve's dream of apple eating, flying, and then falling (see *PL,* 5.28-94) or the many "descents" of Satan himself (see 2.14, 76; 9.163, 69; 10.394). In any case, her sympathetic identification with Satan underscores her subversive revision of Milton.

4

For instance, she suggests that there is a patriarchal conspiracy to keep women from the "tree of knowledge" by indoctrinating them with an ideology of sexual beauty: "But, according to the tenour of reasoning, by which women are kept from the tree of knowledge, the important years of youth, the usefulness of age, and the rational hopes of futurity, are to be sacrificed to render women an object of desire for a *short* time" (**RW,** 160). She traces, as will be seen, this ideological conspiracy back to the patriarchal authorities of *Paradise Lost*: Adam, Raphael, God, and, of course, Milton himself.

In this context, Milton's prelapsarian Eve is the implicit model for postlapsarian women's compelled ignorance, an ignorance that men translate as "innocence" in an effort to keep them weak and powerless: "Women are every where in this deplorable state; for, in order to preserve their innocence, as ignorance is courteously termed, truth is hidden from them, and they are made to assume an artificial character before their faculties have acquired any strength" (**RW,** 113). The contention that an oppressive order ideologically instills ignorance is, of course, an Enlightenment argument used repeatedly during the French Revolution. It is also, as has been seen, Satan's argument (*PL,* 9.703-06). Wollstonecraft's insight was to see that what was essentially a political and sociological explanation of "man's" fall had sexual and psychological implications for women as well.

Thus she argued that women acted out their debilitated roles in the very terms that patriarchy provided them. In **The Rights of Woman,** she confronts a series of "pestiferous" (87) texts in order to reveal how their misogynistic ideology contributes to women's psychological mutilation and hence their sociopolitical ignorance. Her equation of ignorance with innocence ("Why," she asks, should women "be kept in ignorance under the specious name of innocence?" *RW,* 88; cf. 82, 112-13, 18, 23, 30, 32, 203, 45) is specifically aimed at *Paradise Lost*

and the "innocence, that as a veil / Had shadow'd them [Adam and Eve] from knowing ill" (9.1054-55), as well as Milton's celebrations of Eve's Edenic innocence (4.388; 8.501; 9.373, 459). She criticizes, in a quotation from Vicesimus Knox, the contradictory equation of feminine ignorance with innocence in a fallen world where women need knowledge to resist temptation: "'Can anything,' says Knox, 'be more absurd than keeping women in a state of ignorance, and yet so vehemently to insist on their resisting temptation?'" (**RW,** 195). In Wollstonecraft's formulation, the patriarchal paradigm of innocence is a prescription for woman's fall.

Since Wollstonecraft is questioning the terms of what she believes is the dominant ideological and political order, she becomes the satanic subverter of the texts sustaining it. Hence, it is not surprising that, like Satan in *Paradise Lost,* she is a revisionist historian. Her argument that men have conspiratorially kept women from the "tree of knowledge" (i.e., "masculine" education) and hence kept them in a state of ignorance is, mutatis mutandis, the argument Satan uses to seduce Eve. In Book 4, after enviously seeing Adam and Eve's paradisiacal bliss, Satan begins rehearsing the arguments he will eventually use on Eve in Book 9:

> One fatal Tree there stands of Knowledge called,
> Forbidden them to taste: Knowledge forbidd'n?
> Suspicious, reasonless. Why should their Lord
> Envy them that? can it be sin to know,
> Can it be death? and do they only stand
> By Ignorance, is that their happy state,
> The proof of their obedience and their faith?
> . . .
> . . . Hence I will excite their minds
> With more desire to know, and to reject
> Envious commands, invented with design
> To keep them low whom knowledge might exalt
> Equal with Gods. . . .
>
> (*PL,* 4.514-20, 22-26)

The terms of Wollstonecraft's argument are similar to Satan's: the patriarchal order conspires to keep women weak by keeping them ignorant—only in Wollstonecraft's satanic reading, she herself is not the deceiver but the linguistic liberator of fallen woman.[7]

Like Satan, she subversively supplies the arguments that undermine traditional authority. In Book 9, Satan tells Eve why God has really forbidden the knowledge of good and evil ("Why then was this forbid? Why but to awe, / Why but to keep ye low and ignorant," *PL* 9.703-041), and this is essentially Wollstonecraft's argument in **The Rights of Woman,** where the knowledge of "evil" is actually the liberating power that men forbiddingly hide under the bogey word "masculine," and the fatal apple is the ideology of beauty through which men tempt women into their "fall."

Thus she insists that women's "hearts have not been debauched by knowledge, or their minds led astray by scientific pursuits" (**RW**, 239), but rather "paradisiacal reveries" (143), the "ignorance" that turns women into the "crafty" Eve-like tempters of *Paradise Lost* (239): patriarchal ideology again creates the women it deplores. Earlier she had noted that men scare women away from knowledge and exertion by exclamations "against masculine women," although she doubts their existence and suspects that men appropriate *human* virtues and selectively apply them to masculine or "manly" categories, in which case she wishes that women "may every day grow more and more masculine" (**RW**, 74; cf. *PL*, 9.803-04). Her subversive reading of Milton suggests that patriarchal prohibitors scare women away from the tree of knowledge by misnaming it "masculine" and insinuating that knowledge distorts woman's "femininity," transforming them into "masculine women" or the sexually ambiguous Sin in *Paradise Lost,* who "seemed Woman" but is "arm'd / With mortal sting" (2.650, 52-53). Like Satan, she suggests that "forbidden knowledge" is the hidden power that will release women from their subordinate roles.

On another level, her endeavor to desex virtue and demystify masculinity coincides with her suspicion that sexual love or passion seduces women into weakness, which resembles Milton's parable of a sexual fall: Satan's temptation of Eve is linguistically seductive; sexual lust is a consequence of the Fall, as is woman's mandatory obedience (see *PL,* 10.195-96). Wollstonecraft, consequently, warns against the "depravity of the appetite which brings the sexes together," a depravity that has a "fatal effect" (**RW,** 208), in her parable of sex as the fatal apple (cf. *PL,* 1.1-3, 9.889, 10.4). Later, the "feverish caresses of appetite" are connected to Milton's account of the first incestuous rape— "Sin embracing death" (**RW,** 264).[8] The word *appetite* is a thematic word in *Paradise Lost* through which Milton associates the eating of the apple with both sexual and epistemological lust (see 7.126-7, 546-47; 8.308; 9.580, 740; 10.565) and hence the sexually fallen Adam and Eve "both in subjection now / To sensual Appetite" (9.1128-29). In Wollstonecraft's reading, sex makes "ignorant" woman vulnerable to masculine manipulators, and sexual distinctions are part of the social distinctions that she and the French Revolution are rebelling against (see, e.g., **RW,** 241, 263, 265).

In chapter 9, her rebellion is specifically satanic, since the plight of contemporary women ("one half of mankind . . . chained to its bottom by fate," **RW,** 211) suddenly resembles that of Satan and the fallen angels, in *Paradise Lost,* "Chain'd on the burning Lake" (1.210, 2.169) and confined by "fate" (see 1.133, 2.197, 232, 393, 550). There is an allusive metaphoric inversion of the fallen angels into the "fallen" women kept down and in their "place" by their patriarchal oppressors, an

argument first used, mutatis mutandis, by Satan and the fallen angels (in Books 1 and 2, passim).

Indeed Wollstonecraft's linguistic identification with Satan reverberates throughout the first paragraph of chapter 7, which, as the editors of her *Works* note, resembles Milton's opening invocation in Book 3 of *Paradise Lost* (Todd and Butler, 191, note a). But Wollstonecraft's allusive invocation culminates in her satanic prayer that "Modesty . . . modulate for me the language of persuasive reason, till I rouse my sex from the flowery bed, on which they supinely sleep life away!" (**RW,** 191; cf. 136: "And can she [woman] rest supinely dependent on man for reason, which she ought to mount with him the arduous steeps of knowledge?"). In Book 1 of *Paradise Lost,* Satan also endeavors to rouse the fallen angels who "lie / Grovelling and prostrate on yon Lake of Fire" (1.279-80):

> . . . Princes, Potentates,
> Warriors, the Flow'r of Heav'n once yours, now lost,
> If such astonishment as this can seize
> Eternal spirits; or have ye chos'n this place
> After the toil of Battle to repose
> Your wearied virtue, for the ease you find
> To slumber here, as in the Vales of Heav'n?
> . . .
> Awake, arise, or be for ever fall'n.
>
> (*PL,* 1.315-21, 330)

Wollstonecraft's allusion implies that, like Satan's fallen angels, women can choose to rise from their "fallen" state and rebel against the patriarchal oppressor. Her identification with Satan's rebellious energy reverberates in the verb "rouse" ("til I rouse my sex from the flowery bed"). For instance, after Satan's rousing speech, the fallen angels "Rouse and bestir themselves ere well awake" (*PL,* 1.334), and Milton proceeds to name the devils who were "Rous'd from the slumber, on that fiery Couch, / At their great Emperor's call" (*PL,* 1.377-78). Wollstonecraft's allusion also suggests that "the flowery bed, on which" women "supinely sleep" (learned "female" behavior; cf. **RW,** 98) is actually the fallen region of "hell" to which they have been consigned by their triumphant oppressors. Similarly, she seeks to "raise" her sex out of their fallen state.

She hence repeatedly refers or returns to the scene of Eve's rebellion. She notes that in order to spread "enlightening principles":

> . . . women must be allowed to found their virtue on knowledge, which is scarcely possible unless they be educated by the same pursuits as men. For they are now made so inferiour by ignorance and low desires, as not to deserve to be ranked with them; or, by the serpentine wrigglings of cunning they mount the tree of knowledge, and only acquire sufficient to lead men astray.
>
> (**RW,** 245)[9]

Wollstonecraft's version of an epistemological Fall makes women cunning tempters not because they possess "knowledge" but because they only eat partially: their curiosity and desire for forbidden knowledge turns them into the satanic seducers, à la Eve, who "lead men astray." In other words, Wollstonecraft suggests that by withholding complete knowledge (another form of patriarchal temptation), men ironically turn women into the cunning creatures who haunt the misogynistic imagination. The implicit corollary is that full knowledge will restore woman to her proper ontological place, freeing both sexes from the sexual stereotypes perpetuated by patriarchal writers.

But it is again striking that Wollstonecraft's depiction of women's state ("for they are now made so inferior by ignorance and low desires") is precisely the language used by both Satan and Eve to rationalize their respective deceptions and rebellions. In Book 9, the serpentine Satan tells Eve that he was "at first as other Beasts that graze / The trodden Herb, of abject thoughts and low" until he ate the forbidden fruit (*PL*, 9.571-72), and Eve rationalizes her possession of "forbidden knowledge" in terms of her previous epistemological ignorance (*PL*, 9.820-22). In addition, Wollstonecraft's suggestion that it is the prohibition of true knowledge that tempts women into a fall into false knowledge echoes Eve's comment that God unwittingly commends "knowledge" by prohibiting it: "Thy praise hee also who forbids thy use, / Conceals not from us, naming thee the Tree of Knowledge . . . but his forbidding / Commends thee more" (*PL*, 9.750-54).[10] Moreover, Wollstonecraft conflates Eve and women with Satan by placing them in a compromising satanic position: "by the serpentine wrigglings of cunning," women "mount the tree of knowledge" (*RW*, 245)—since it is the serpentine Satan, in *Paradise Lost,* who "About the Mossy Trunk" wound himself (9.589). This illustrates the schizophrenic nature of her satanic ideology: Eve as satanic rebel coincides with Wollstonecraft as feminist revolutionary—yet she also depicts patriarchal men as satanic deceivers who trick innocent women into enacting Satan's and Eve's Ur-rebellion. Wollstonecraft's own role as feminist liberator—precisely the way Milton's duplicitous Satan casts and describes himself—complicates and begins subverting the feminist text she writes "out."

Wollstonecraft, in effect, does two things simultaneously: she appears to accept the pejorative terms of Milton's poem (woman as satanic seducer), but she inverts Milton's parable by suggesting that it is not the "illegal" possession of knowledge that causes women to fall but the patriarchal prohibition that tempts them into a fallen state of ignorance. It is not knowledge per se, but too little genuine knowledge that causes the sexes to fall—Adamic men apparently "misled" by seductive Eves, although her real subversive message is that the

patriarchal prohibition "misleads" women, who become, in turn, crafty creatures who try to compensate for their fallen condition. In this context, Wollstonecraft reinforces another theme specifically aimed at her male audience: women's ignorance paradoxically gives them too much power over men, that in compensating for their lack of authentic knowledge, women are forced to become the deceitful manipulators who create chaos in homes and states (see *RW*, 68, 113, 238-39, 245).[11] Assuring her male audience that knowledge will restore the "natural" relation between the sexes and make women more "reasonable," she creates her own mythic version of a fall "in the beginning" and redemption in a future presently aborning.

5

In arguing this, she also attempts to rescue Eve (as a symbol of woman) from Milton, since Eve, in Wollstonecraft's reading, is the misogynous emblem of patriarchy. Thus, if Eve is, at turns, the satanic seductress forced into her unnatural role by patriarchal prohibitors (after eating the fruit, Eve describes God as "Our great Forbidder," *PL*, 9.815), she is also the vulnerable victim of man and must be redeemed through "a revolution in female manners":

> It is time to effect a revolution in female manners—time to restore to them their lost dignity—and make them, as part of the human species, labor by reforming themselves to reform the world. . . . If men be demi-gods—why let us serve them! [cf. *PL*, 1.373, 796]. And if the dignity of the female soul be as disputable as that of animals—if their reason does not afford sufficient light to direct their conduct . . . [then] they are surely of all creatures the most miserable! [cf. *PL*, 1.157] and . . . must submit to be a *fair defect* in creation. But to justify the ways of Providence respecting them, by pointing out some irrefragable reason for thus making such a large portion of mankind accountable and not accountable, would puzzle the subtilest casuist.
>
> (*RW*, 114)

Wollstonecraft's call for "a revolution in female manners" (cf. 265) is perhaps a hostile reference to Burke's *Reflections* and his lament that a revolution in manners contributed to the French Revolution.[12] Wollstonecraft connects this ongoing revolution with a correspondent feminist revolution by suggesting that the political liberation of *mankind* impinges on the social liberation of women as well. Indeed, in her reading, women potentially become active agents of social and political change, reforming themselves as they reform the world. She suggests that their own psychological liberation is part and parcel of the apocalyptic revolution transforming Europe. Her reference to women's "labour" (it is time to make women, "as part of the human species, labour by reforming themselves to reform the world") allusively transforms the curse of the Fall (man to work by the sweat of his brow, woman to *labor*—conceive in sorrow) into the creative reformation of the fallen world.[13] In Milton's poem, restoration is initially projected in a Christian future already past—the Incarnation and Resurrection having already happened—and ultimately in a "future" outside of time. Wollstonecraft, in contrast, envisions the establishment of the *first* "unfallen" order in an egalitarian future she endeavors to justify.

Her subsequent comment that it is "time to restore to [women] their lost dignity" alludes to their Wollstonecraftian redeemer, who, like Christ in *Paradise Lost,* returns to "restore" postlapsarian women after the fall (see *PL,* 1.4-5). She continually locates woman's "fall" in the patriarchal texts she subverts, focusing on the consequences of Milton's fallen ideology—women "must submit to be a *fair defect* in creation"—Adam's misogynistic description of Eve after the Fall: "O why did God . . . create . . . this fair defect / Of Nature" (see 10.888-92). Throughout **The Rights of Woman,** Wollstonecraft angrily wars with this phrase (see 103, 107, 109, 124, 131, 136, 173, 185), and her subsequent allusion to Milton, who, in her reading, rationalizes women's inferior subordination by supposedly justifying "the ways of Providence" (cf. *PL,* 1.25-26) subverts a patriarchal logic that "would puzzle the subtilest casuist" (114). Even when he is not named, Milton's patriarchal presence permeates her revisionist myth.

She thus continues her critique of Milton's misogynous "creation." First, she attacks Milton's deceptive idealization of the first woman who, she maintains, is the submissive model for women, "outwardly ornamented with elaborate care, and so adorned to delight man, 'that with honour he may love'" (122). The quotation from Milton ("that with honour thou may'st love," 8.577) is in context of Raphael's admonition to Adam that Eve is to be cherished but not overly admired, since he is her superior (see 8.573-77). In addition, Wollstonecraft's reference to woman "outwardly ornamented with elaborate care" alludes to Adam's deflationary praise of Eve as "Too much of Ornament, in outward show / Elaborate, of inward less exact" (8.538-39; cf. 8.542-43).

Her subsequent comment that woman "is always represented as only created to see through a gross medium, and to take things on trust" (122) refers to Eve in *Paradise Lost,* who is placed in relation to her masculine intermediaries (Adam, Raphael, and Michael) who, in turn, explain, guide, and instruct her in the ways of God—the ultimate patriarchal authority. Indeed, Eve usually receives her instruction at second hand, seeing "through a gross medium," and Wollstonecraft's allusion to the Bible (1 Cor. 13:12) underscores the embedded patriarchal texts that perpetuate women's dependent "blindness."

She dismisses these traditional representations of woman as "fanciful theories," choosing to consider "woman as a whole . . . instead of a part of man" (*RW,* 122)—the "secondary" excrescence of Adamic man. Even patriarchal writers who "kindly restore the rib, and make one moral being of man and woman" (cf. *PL,* 4.483, 8.495, 9.915, and Genesis 2:23) are sure "to give her all the 'submissive charms'" (*RW,* 102)—Milton's description of Eve's embellished charms that cause Adam to smile "with superior Love" (see 4.498-99). Milton's submissive prelapsarian Eve is hence the thematic model for Wollstonecraft's weak and submissive woman. In a letter to William Roscoe (3 January 1792), she refers to Henry Fuseli's illustrations of *Paradise Lost,* adding that she doubts whether Fuseli can "produce an Eve" to please her—"unless it be after the Fall." Having just implied that Satan is the real "hero" of Milton's poem (*Letters,* 206), Wollstonecraft also suggests she prefers Milton's rebellious and fallen Eve as her feminist "heroine."

6

In attacking the sexual ideology embodied in assorted traditional texts, she traces the origin and source of this ideology back to Milton's God, and hence she engages in another satanic reading of Milton's poem. Questioning the ideological primogeniture by which patriarchal writers perpetuate and pass down restrictive images of female behavior ("written in the same strain"), she simultaneously attacks "the boasted prerogative of man— the prerogative that may emphatically be called the iron scepter of tyranny, the original sin of tyrants," as well as "all power built on prejudices, however hoary" (*RW,* 170). "Original sin" commences with man's tyrannous treatment and textual misrepresentation of woman, and his "iron scepter" evokes Satan's revisionist description of heaven's despotic God, seeking to extend "His [slave] Empire, and with Iron Scepter rule / Us here, as with his Golden those in Heav'n" (*PL,* 2.327-28). Wollstonecraft's allusion identifies her with Satan's characterization of Milton's God as Ur-tyrant—here the tyrant of women, rather than angels. She hence suggests subversively that the subordinate representation of woman was God and Adam's (i.e., man's) "original sin." But since her allusions are recognizably satanic, her text is open to counterrevolutionary readings that ironically reinforce her subversive identifications: a satanic Mary Wollstonecraft engaged in revisionist readings of history and seductive speeches that tempt women to fall into the *same* revolutionary knowledge as satanic, revolutionary men.[14]

Since she engages in a sustained satanic reading of Milton's text, even her distinction between a just God of light and love and Milton's God of custom and prejudice seems, at this point, to collapse: "I disclaim that specious humility which, after investigating nature, stops at the author. The High and Lofty One, who inhabiteth eternity, doubtless possesses many attributes of which we can form no conception; but reason tells me that they cannot clash with those I adore—and I am compelled to listen to her voice" (*RW,* 115). In her pursuit of true origins, Wollstonecraft refuses "that specious humility" that "stops" its investigation when it reaches the nature of God "the author," and hence she explicitly authorizes herself to proceed with her subversive writing. This opens her to conservative accusations of satanic presumption and arrogance—of wanting to transcend boundaries and hence "know" more than she should, linguistically enacting and hence repeating the Ur-rebellion. In this context, if there is a repressive Miltonic passage she is resisting, it is Raphael's espousal of epistemological restraint, "Of knowledge within bounds; beyond abstain / To ask" . . . "Heav'n is for thee too high / To know what passes there; be lowly wise" (*PL,* 7.120-21, 8.172-73). Like Satan, in Book 3, Wollstonecraft "explores" or investigates her way up to the precincts of light, and her reference to "the High [cf. *PL,* 1.40] and Lofty One" sounds slightly sarcastic, as if she is subverting the remote Miltonic Omnipotence by using, with mock humility, that "adulatory language" that, mutatis mutandis, she accuses Burke of using to deify kings (in *RM,* 20-21).

In addition, while apparently conceding that the "Lofty One" undoubtedly "possesses many attributes of which we can form no conception" (i.e., "know"), she negates the concession by declaring that "reason" tells her that "they" (God's unknown attributes) cannot clash with "those" (attributes) she "adores," that is, "knows." In other words, her "female" reason tells her that the attributes she admires in God are those that she already knows and adores. Milton's remote and hidden God suddenly surrenders to a reason that contradicts the conservative concession, and Wollstonecraft is "compelled to listen to her voice."[15]

Any doubt that she is investigating Milton's "Paternal Deity" (*PL,* 6.750) is dispelled in the subsequent paragraph:

> It seems natural for man to search for excellence, and either to trace it in the object he worships, or blindly to invest it with perfection, as a garment. But what good effect can the latter mode of worship have on the moral conduct of a rational being? He bends to power; he adores a dark cloud, which may open a bright prospect to him, or burst in angry, lawless fury, on his devoted head—he knows not why.
>
> (*RW,* 115)

The pejorative reference to "the latter mode of worship"—blindly investing "excellence" or God "with perfection, as a garment" alludes to Burke's "decent drapery"—his lament, in the *Reflections,* that the Revolution was stripping away civilization's beautiful traditions (see *Reflections,* 171).

This complements, I suggest, the subsidiary allusion to the romantic clichés of masculine "adoration": the worshipful lover doting on a piece of his absent mistress's clothing or "garment"—a conventional cliché lampooned throughout the eighteenth century. Milton, we will remember, "bends . . . to beauty" (*RW,* 89). Wollstonecraft's indictment is in the imagery of fetishistic idolatry. In this context, there is a thematic connection between man's sensual adoration of woman's "beauty" and the unreasonable glorification of an unapproachable "object" or God.

The ignorant man who "bends to power" evokes again *Paradise Lost* and the fallen angels who prostrate themselves and worship Satan: "Towards him they bend / With awful reverence prone; and as a God / Extol him equal to the highest in Heav'n" (*PL,* 2.477-79; cf. Eve's idolatrous worship of the forbidden tree, 9.834-38) or, more appropriately, the "subservient" angels' adoration of God and His Son in heaven: ". . . lowly reverent / Towards either throne they bow, and to the ground / With solemn adoration down they cast / Their Crowns . . ." (3.349-52). Indeed, her reference to the Deity as "a dark cloud" that idolatrous man "adores" alludes specifically to Milton's God in heaven who shades his glory "and through a cloud / Drawn round about thee like a radiant Shrine, / Dark with excessive bright thy skirts [robes] appear . . ." (3.378-80). In hell, Mammon remembers that God "amidst / Thick clouds and dark" resides and "with the Majesty of darkness round / Covers his throne" (see 2.263-68; cf. 10.32). Wollstonecraft's critique of God as the capricious patriarchal punisher (opening "a bright prospect" or bursting "in angry, lawless fury") is, of course, a critique of Milton himself, who also "blindly" ascends from hell, in a speech resonant with satanic echoes, and sees only "cloud instead, and ever-during dark" (3.45).

In chapter 11, referring to Burkean prescription, she again attacks Milton's God and poem: "The supporters of prescription . . . taking refuge in the darkness, which, in the language of sublime poetry, has been supposed to surround the throne of Omnipotence, . . . dare to demand that implicit respect which is only due to His unsearchable ways" (*RW,* 225). Although she distinguishes between the prescriptive pretenders who hide in the obscurant "darkness" (i.e., the ignorance) sanctioned by their textual God and the reasonableness of the true revolutionary God, Wollstonecraft's attack on prescription protected by the darkness "supposed to surround the throne of Omnipotence" resembles Satan's linguistic attack against the "Monarch in Heav'n" Who "Sat on his Throne, Upheld by old repute / Consent or custom" (see *PL,* 1.638-40). At any rate, Wollstonecraft's ambivalence culminates in her identification of Milton with the dark patriarchal oppressor, the supreme ideologist of male power.

7

But even more than Milton's God, Wollstonecraft's principal target is Adam, whom she sees as the primary patriarchal symbol of male appropriation—an appropriation originating in a fictional "beginning" created by patriarchs such as Moses and reinforced in a series of masculinist texts that valorize a tradition of female subordination: "The *rights* of humanity have been . . . confined to the male line from Adam downwards" (*RW,* 157). Hence, she argues that the fiction of woman's exclusive subordination is based on the patriarchal myth of Adam and his reincarnation in patriarchal texts as the origin and source of male superiority:

> Probably the prevailing opinion, that woman was created for man, may have taken its rise from Moses's poetical story; yet, as very few, it is presumed, who have bestowed any serious thought on the subject, ever supposed that Eve was, literally speaking, one of Adam's ribs, the deduction must be allowed to fall to the ground; or, only be so far admitted as it proves that man, from the remotest antiquity, found it convenient to exert his strength to subjugate his companion, and his invention to shew that she ought to have her neck bent under the yoke, because the whole creation was only created for his convenience or pleasure.
>
> (*RW,* 95)

Wollstonecraft's critique of Genesis (traditionally ascribed to Moses) also extends to *Paradise Lost,* since Milton is one of the "very few" to have "presumed" that "Eve was, literally speaking, one of Adam's ribs" (see *PL,* 8.465-71; 9.911-12, 1154; 10.884). In Wollstonecraft's reading, Milton's myth is based on Moses's tyrannical text.

"Moses's poetical story" is thus conflated with Milton's "myth," and the defeated "deduction" falls "to the ground" like the Adamic story she inters. The mythic locus of man and woman's birth (ground/bone) is consigned to the realm of fantasy, although she allows a subversive historical reading of Genesis as an allegory of man's original oppression of woman—oppression legitimized by the enslaving texts that justify misogynous tradition. Her concluding reference to woman's "yoke" alludes to the state of marriage (see *OED* meanings nos. 7b and 8b) and hence her parable of Eve/woman's Ur-enslavement. In Wollstonecraft's feminist reading, woman is oppressed from the beginning of a male "Creation," so that Milton's prelapsarian world is a prototype of the fallen one.

Later, she again traces the coercive cultural clichés of the writers that she discusses (Rousseau, Dr. Fordyce, Dr. Gregory, et al., as well as the women who reproduce patriarchal ideology) back to Moses and Milton's Adamic enslavement of Eve:

> Hapless woman! What can be expected from thee when the beings on whom thou art said naturally to depend for reason and support, have all an interest in deceiving thee! This is the root of the evil that has shed a corroding mildew on thy virtues; and blighting in the bud thy opening faculties, has rendered thee the weak thing thou art! It is this separate interest—this insidious state of warfare, that undermines morality, and divides mankind!
>
> (*RW,* 166)

The dependence of women on men, à la Eve on Adam, for "reason and support" is, of course, one of Milton's arguments throughout *Paradise Lost.*

In Wollstonecraft's reading, it is man's deceptive justification for woman's fallen condition (her supposed inferiority, and hence her subordinate dependence on him)—a restrictive rationale for woman's weakness disguised in the language of masculine support and help. She hence intends to reveal how Miltonic tradition is reified and reflected in contemporary patriarchal texts, for suddenly Adamic men are the satanic deceivers, and their covert "interest" in keeping women weak and "fallen" is the real "root of . . . evil," and not the forbidden fruit (cf. *PL,* 1.1-4, 9.645) or woman's "first" disobedience. Indeed, she again suggests that patriarchal empowerment is man's original sin, initiating the fragmentation of the sexes and provoking woman's correspondent rebellion and hence the sexual war that "divides mankind." Wollstonecraft effects a satanic reading of Milton in order to deconstruct *Paradise Lost* into a sourcebook of allusions for her new feminism.

Consequently, she engages in another subversive rewriting of Milton and Moses's "poetical story":

> . . . I . . . doubt whether woman were [*sic*] created for man: and, though the cry of irreligion, or even atheism, be raised against me, I will simply declare, that were an angel from heaven to tell me that Moses's beautiful, poetical cosmogony, and the account of the fall of man, were literally true, I could not believe what my reason told me was derogatory to the character of the Supreme Being: and, having no fear of the devil before mine eyes, I venture to call this a suggestion of reason, instead of resting my weakness on the broad shoulders of the first seducer of my frail sex.
>
> (*RW,* 148-49)

Doubting woman's "natural" subordination, Wollstonecraft refuses to be intimidated by patriarchal charges of irreligion or atheism, and hence she doubts the biblical account of Genesis as well as Milton's, since an "angel" (Raphael) appears, in Book 7, and relates to Adam Moses's "poetical cosmogony" (cf. *RW,* 91). Anticipating that she will be accused of a "satanic" reading, she has "no fear" of a bogey devil conjured up by patriarchal authorities to scare her back into an orthodox reading of Genesis and *Paradise Lost* and hence woman's natural "place."

But since Wollstonecraft herself raises the specter of a satanic reading by stating she has "no fear of the devil before my eyes," she creates a series of unintended, subversive ironies. While dismissing Milton and Moses's superstitious "account" and hence the "existence" of their demonized "bogey," the sentence can also be read to mean that she has no fear of the devil poised "before her eyes," and hence she places herself in the position of Eve in Book 9 of *Paradise Lost*. Indeed, Wollstonecraft's sentences resonate with rebellious satanic echoes—echoes that Milton himself reproduced in associating Eve's rebellious fall with Satan's. Thus, like Eve, she opposes her own "reason" to patriarchal authority and tradition. Just before Eve's fall, Adam warns her against relying on reason, since it can be deceived (see *PL,* 9.351-66), a warning that Eve subsequently ignores. Satan's temptation of Eve is appropriately in the language of seduced reason ("his persuasive words, impregn'd / With Reason, to her seeming, and with Truth," 9.737-38), which Eve subsequently replicates.

Moreover, Wollstonecraft's statement that she refuses to believe in traditional accounts of the Creation and the Fall and that, consequently, she refuses to believe what her "reason" tells her is "derogatory to the character of the Supreme Being" would certainly remind a traditional reader of Satan's seductive contention that God could not have forbid "knowledge," since that would have contradicted His goodness (see *PL,* 9.698-701; cf. 9.692-94, 5.71). Such a reader may accept Wollstonecraft's satanic subversions—her rebellious readings—as a redounding parodic repetition. Indeed, a subversive counterrevolutionary reader may suggest that her rebellious reading is, like Eve's rib, textually derivative.

In addition, Wollstonecraft's dismissal of a fictitious devil "as the first seducer of my frail sex"—and hence her refusal to "rest" woman's reputed "weakness" on his "broad shoulders," allusively conjures his satanic resembler—the "real" Satan of her revisionist book—Adam with "his shoulders broad" (*PL,* 4.303). Since Wollstonecraft has already referred to Adam as the first oppressor of the female sex, the possibility of a satanic reading resides in her exoneration of Satan. This suggests two possibilities: that having already provided intentional rebellious readings, Wollstonecraft provides another one here; or, that she reproduces, unwittingly, the satanic echoes reverberating throughout the passage.

In any case, Wollstonecraft continues her feminist critique of Adamic ideology:

> Again; men boast of their triumph over women, what do they boast of? Truly the creature of sensibility was surprised by her sensibility into folly—into vice; and the dreadful reckoning falls heavily on her own weak head, when reason awakes. For where art thou to find comfort, forlorn and disconsolate one? He who ought to have directed thy reason, and supported thy weakness, has betrayed thee! In a dream of passion thou

> [consented] to wander through flowery lawns, and heedlessly stepping over the precipice to which thy guide, instead of guarding, lured thee, thou startest from thy dream only to face a sneering, frowning world, and to find thyself alone in a waste, for he that triumphed in thy weakness is now pursuing new conquests; but for thee—there is no redemption on this side the grave!— And what resource hast thou in an enervated mind to raise a sinking heart?

(*RW,* 195-96)

Wollstonecraft's melodramatic presentation of woman's fall illustrates how she continues to return to Milton's poem.

Men's "triumphs" over women are in the satanic context of temptation, seduction, and betrayal, and hence she begins, as she has done before, a series of metaphoric equations of Adamic men with the satanic betrayer in *Paradise Lost*. When she writes that woman is "surprised by her sensibility into folly—into vice," the allusion is to Raphael's warning that man's "appetite" must be governed, "lest sin / Surprise thee, and her black attendant Death" (*PL,* 7.546-47). In Wollstonecraft's rewriting of Milton, sensibility—artificially emotional responses derived from sentimental, romantic texts and condemned throughout *The Rights of Woman*—is the "temptation" initiating woman's "fall," since it causes woman to trust her masculine betrayer.[16]

Her allegory of woman's seduced reason wakening to "the dreadful reckoning" that "falls heavily on her own weak head" suggests woman's postlapsarian realization that she has been betrayed by "man" and evokes the punitive patriarchal God who can "burst in angry, lawless fury, on" man's "devoted head" (*RW,* 115).

With all these Miltonic echoes, Wollstonecraft envisions woman as the vulnerably innocent Eve betrayed by Adamic man, whom she conflates with the satanic deceiver. But her allegory of woman as Eve is ironically sentimental, since she falls into the very language she has previously criticized: her disappointed anger that woman has been betrayed by her masculine protector—the Adamic "guide" who should have "directed" her "reason" and "supported" her "weakness"—the last clause linguistically sustaining the very "weakness" she has formerly deplored.

Wollstonecraft than proceeds with a revision of Eve's dream in Book 5 of *Paradise Lost*: In a dream, Wollstonecraft's vulnerable Edenic woman wanders "through flowery lawns" and then stumbles "over the precipice to which thy guide, instead of guarding thee, lured thee." In Book 5, Eve relates a "fallen" dream evoked by Satan, who has whispered it into her mind: a satanic voice awakes her which she mistakes for Adam's; she then proceeds to walk through Eden, searching for Adam, but she finds instead Satan, disguised as an angel, who tempts her to taste imaginatively the forbidden fruit that she fancies causes her to fly only suddenly to fall: "My Guide was gone, and I, methought, sunk down" (see 5.28-94). Eve, however, awakes and is relieved "to find this but a dream" (5.95); whereas, in Wollstonecraft's allegory, the forsaken woman wakes to find her dream of Adamic betrayal true. In Wollstonecraft's version, the satanic deceiver is really Adam (note how Wollstonecraft transcribes the "mistakes" in Eve's dream), who "lures" her into falling, and she awakes "only to face a sneering, frowning world, and to find thyself alone in a waste"—or a world very much like "The Limbo of Vanity" Satan alights on: "Dark, waste, and wild, under the frown of Night" (*PL,* 3.424).

It is telling that in this version of woman's fall, Wollstonecraft's Eve is vulnerably weak not only because she depends on man but because she has no Adamic man to depend on. Her allegory is sexually sentimental—Adamic man as the "first seducer" of the "frail sex"—the seducer who tempts and "lures" woman into her sexual fall (here the proverbial abandoned and "fallen woman")—the satanic Don Juan who betrays and deserts defenseless woman (and then proceeds to other "conquests"), leaving her "forlorn" and Adamless. Wollstonecraft reveals her own fear of sex and hence "falling," as her parable encapsulates another primal return to the origin and source of woman's fall in a patriarchal "beginning."

8

In retrospect, Wollstonecraft's inspired insight was to see how revolutionary arguments against coercive textual tradition applied to woman as well, for woman had also been assigned her "place" by the same oppressive powers that opposed the Revolution—the prohibitive, punitive powers of institutional patriarchy. Like men, women needed to be liberated from what Paine called "the Bastille of a word." Hence, Eve was the critical term in Wollstonecraft's revisionary critique. Mary Poovey notes that for Wollstonecraft, Milton's unfallen Eve is a "commentary not on woman but on the men from whose imagination she sprang—from Milton's Adam and, before him, from Milton himself" (72). But Wollstonecraft imagined another Eve supplied unwittingly by Milton and biblical tradition, for just as she sensed that Satan was the first revolutionary, she intuited that "fallen" Eve was the first feminist.

Similarly, she implied that Milton unwittingly liberated Satan from hell, that Milton did not "tremble when he led Satan far from the confines of his dreary prison" (*RW,* 108), and she recognized the subversive potential of a postlapsarian Eve, who after eating the forbidden fruit, proclaims that without it, "I had remain'd / In ignorance" (*PL,* 9.808-09). She endeavored to rescue Eve

from Milton, metaphorically equating her "first disobedience" with woman's epistemological liberation.

In this context, Wollstonecraft was also consciously miming Eve's rebellion through her own revolutionary reading of Milton—a reading that subversively rewrites the "myth" of patriarchy. The image of the reader as rebel or the writer as revolutionary—simultaneously interchangeable—inspired writers who were waging their own war against the textual tyranny of the old linguistic order.

But this created various ironies and complications. Wollstonecraft's own reading of Milton is not, of course, ideologically consistent: there are different versions of woman's fall, just as there are various "fruits" that cause it. In addition, Wollstonecraft sometimes engages in simple satanic inversions—God as tyrant, Satan as liberator, Eve as feminist rebel—while, at other times, she accepts Milton's demonization of the satanic order and simply applies it to Milton's prelapsarian progeny (Adam as the "real" Satan). The result, however, is also to create, exclude, and demonize a mythical "Other." In this context, the Manichaean readings of both revolutionary and counterrevolutionary writers begin to resemble each other.

Wollstonecraft's subversive reading is, likewise, just as vulnerable as the traditional writing she deconstructs. Her celebration of Satan and Eve's rebellion against authority is also susceptible to "reconstructive" readings by counterrevolutionary readers who would see her linguistically enacting Satan's temptation of Eve—resembling the arrogant Satan, who pridefully rebels against authority and deludes himself that he can create an antagonistic canon, in a writing that is incriminatory and mimetic. In celebrating the forbidden fruit of "knowledge"—fatal knowledge based on a false theory or understanding of human nature and society (i.e., "revolutionary" knowledge)—she could be seen tempting her sex with the *same* knowledge that was causing European man to fall.[17] This suggests that there are deconstructive dangers in embracing Satan too closely.

The conspicuous corollary is that subversive, satanic, deconstructive, and revolutionary readings can be reversed, reconstructed, returned, and "restored" (*PL,* 1.5) into the traditional terms they rebel against. In this rebellious reading, Wollstonecraft's subversive rewriting of *Paradise Lost* turns ironically into its opposite, since she exposes herself in the incriminatory language of Milton's critique and hence reveals herself, not as she intends, but in the language she both resists and embraces. Indeed, in this subversive counterrevolutionary reading, Wollstonecraft linguistically illustrates Milton's aesthetic critique of satanic rebellion: Satan and the fallen angels can only parody and invert their antagonistic models—they are essentially imitative and derivative, always returning to the "sources" and origins they rebel against. For in her "justification" of the "rights of woman," in her parable of the Fall, in her prophecy of woman's future redemption, she resembles the primary literary patriarch she rebels against.

In the *Reflections,* Burke had presented a similar counterrevolutionary reading of the French Revolution. He contended that revolutionary ideology creates its own opposition by turning into the very thing it resists. It reveals its secret attraction for the power and authority it demonizes. He suggested that revolutionaries impose their own authoritative traditions and canons and hence create inevitable rebellions against their authoritarian "readings." But Burke's revolutionary insight is, of course, also applicable to counterrevolutionary ideology upon which it can also "redound" (*PL,* 3.85, 9.128, 10.739).

The contradictions within Wollstonecraft's feminist text crystallize a crucial historical problem that confronts rebels and Romantics: How do you represent revolution when rebellion is written "out" (in the double sense of exposure and erasure) within the textual space of the tradition it resists? Since "tradition" even provides the "terms" of rebellion, revolutionaries write within the very system of representation they rebel against. They are profoundly implicated in the representations they react against. While Wollstonecraft and other radical readers subversively rewrite the traditional canon, their inversions are inscribed within a value system of good and evil, of fallen and unfallen worlds. Hence, they reproduce, mutatis mutandis, the same Manichaean readings of the traditional texts they subversively demonize. This contradiction, inscribed within traditional revolutionary texts, opens a rebellious "return"—a revolutionary reading that restores the ideological configurations of a reactive, reactionary text.[18] In this echoic intertextual juncture, Blake and Burke dialectically conflate, so that reading rebels and Romantics rereading Milton and the canon is to know again that they are, like the devils, complicit in the tradition they refuse to acknowledge.

Notes

1. Immanuel Kant, "What Is Enlightenment?" in *The Enlightenment: A Comprehension Anthology,* ed. Peter Gay (New York: Simon and Schuster, 1973), 384.

2. Sandra M. Gilbert and Susan Gubar, *The Madwoman in the Attic: The Woman Writer and the Nineteenth-Century Literary Imagination* (New Haven: Yale University Press, 1979), 205; Joseph Wittreich, *Feminist Milton* (Ithaca: Cornell University Press, 1987), 3.

3. Mary Wollstonecraft, *A Vindication of the Rights of Woman* (hereafter cited as *RW*), *The Works of Mary Wollstonecraft,* 7 vols., ed. Janet Todd and Marilyn Butler (Washington Square, N.Y.: New York University Press, 1989), 5:88; hereafter cited

as *Works.* John Milton, *Paradise Lost and Paradise Regained,* ed. Christopher Ricks (New York: New American Library, 1982).

4. Mary Poovey comments that Milton's cultural authority—"his preeminence in English literary, political, and religious traditions"—compels Wollstonecraft to "record her outrage . . . only by allusions and italicizing words in a quoted text (as in the passage just quoted)," suggesting "the extent to which she is still reluctant to take her aggression to its logical extreme" (*The Proper Lady and the Woman Writer: Ideology as Style in the Works of Mary Wollstonecraft, Mary Shelley, and Jane Austin* [Chicago: University of Chicago Press, 1984], 73). Wollstonecraft, however, had already critically named Milton (*RW,* 89)—the Bible is the intimidating cultural presence she is reluctant to name. The closest she comes to mentioning it pejoratively is in her critique of "Moses's poetical story" and Milton's unnamed God (see *RW,* 95, 115, 148-49, 225).

5. In a letter to William Roscoe (3 January 1792), Wollstonecraft, referring to the illustrations Henry Fuseli was making of *Paradise Lost,* noted that "like Milton he seems quite at home in hell—his devil will be the hero of the poetic series." Thus, like Blake, who was an acquaintance of hers, she was crystallizing a Romantic commonplace (see *Collected Letters of Mary Wollstonecraft,* ed. Ralph M. Wardle [Ithaca: Cornell University Press, 1979], 206; hereafter cited as *Letters*).

6. See Steven Blakemore, "'With No Middle Flight': Poetic Pride and Satanic Hubris in *Paradise Lost,*" *Kentucky Review* 5 (1985): 23-31.

7. Cf. Thomas Paine's critique of "priestcraft" in the *Prospect Papers* (1804): "As priestcraft was always the enemy of knowledge, because priestcraft supports itself by keeping people in delusion and ignorance, it was consistent with its policy to make the acquisition of knowledge a real sin. . . . Reason is the forbidden tree of priestcraft and may serve to explain the allegory of the forbidden tree of knowledge" (*The Complete Writings of Thomas Paine,* 2 vols., ed. Philip S. Foner [New York: Citadel Press, 1945], 2:800).

8. See *Paradise Lost,* 2.746-809. Mary Poovey notes, however, that "Wollstonecraft's Sin . . . seems much more obliging; indeed, syntactically, *she* is the aggressor: 'sin embracing death'" (76). Wollstonecraft apparently lost her correspondent fear of female sexuality (i.e., her own) after she became Gilbert Imlay's lover in 1793 (cf. her letter to William Godwin [13 November 1796, 360]).

9. Her seemingly awkward nominalization of the adjective *sufficient* (women "only acquire sufficient to lead men astray") emphasizes the deficiency of true knowledge, since the reader expects the sentence to read: "only acquire sufficient knowledge to lead men astray."

10. In Book 1, Satan formulated another version of the "concealment" that "tempts": God "his strength conceal'd, / Which tempted our attempt, and wrought our fall" (*PL,* 641-42). Cf. Wollstonecraft's criticism of Rousseau in her quotation from *Emile:* "Her [Sophie's] dress is extremely modest in appearance, and yet very coquettish in fact: she does not make a display of her charms, she conceals them; but in concealing them, she knows how to affect your imagination" (*RW,* 157).

11. For another version of this paradox, (cf. *RW,* 107, 133), see chapter 4 (*RW,* 128) where she quotes Adam's uxurious description of Eve (*PL,* 8.548-54) and contextually conjures up Raphael's correspondent rebuke to Adam with reference to the latter's intellectual and spiritual superiority to Eve (8.561-94). Hence, while her contention that masculine devotion to "feminine" beauty "changes the nature of things" (*RW,* 128) appeals to conservative readers with a clever argument that women's inferior beauty gives them too much seductive power over men, she simultaneously validates the patriarchal texts she subverts.

12. Edmund Burke, *Reflections on the Revolution in France,* ed. Conor Cruise O'Brien (Harmondsworth: Penguin, 1968), 175.

13. Throughout *RW,* man's "curse" (labor) is his *felix culpa,* enabling him to be free and independent through physical and intellectual exertion (see, e.g., 155). Gilbert and Gubar note that Adam's punishment "seems almost like a reward" (197), and they quote his own relieved response to God's punitive judgment: ". . . labour I must earn / My bread; what harm? Idleness had been worse" (*PL,* 10.1054-55). In contrast, weak women, in *RW,* are always in a state of fallen "relaxation." Wollstonecraft insists that women will remain sexually weak and vulnerable, "while they depend on man for a subsistence, instead of earning it by the exertion of their own hands or heads" (140). Pampered "gentlewomen are too indolent to be actively virtuous," while "many poor women maintain their children by the sweat of their brow [Adam's liberating curse], and keep together families that the vices of the fathers would have scattered abroad" (145).

14. A similar counterrevolutionary reading was in the offing, albeit as a sexual fall. In 1798 Richard Polwhele published *The Unsex'd Females,* a poem in which Wollstonecraft is attacked for desiring to unsex women through female reason; in 1801 "The Vision of Liberty" appeared in the ultraconservative *Anti-Jacobin Review.* Wollstonecraft was again depicted as the seducer of her sex (see Janet M. Todd, ed., *A Wollstonecraft Anthology* [Bloomington: Indiana University Press, 1977], 17).

15. Throughout her works, Wollstonecraft usually personifies *reason* as a feminine "she," but it is not clear whether she is making a feminist grammatical point or whether there is some precedent for her usage. Traditionally, reason was associated with masculinity (see, passim, Genevieve Lloyd, *The Man of Reason: 'Male' and 'Female' in Western Philosophy* [Minneapolis: University of Minnesota Press, 1984]).

16. For instance, in chapter 4, Wollstonecraft suggests that women, having "missed" the "useful fruit" (cf. 167: "useful knowledge"), fall when they succumb to the fatal "fruit" of sensibility: "Their senses are inflamed, and their understandings neglected, consequently they become the prey of their senses, delicately termed sensibility, and are blown about by every momentary gust of feeling" (*RW,* 129; in the Limbo of Vanity, the fanatic spirits of Catholic monks are blown "ten thousand Leagues awry," *PL,* 3.488). Here there are additional echoes, I suggest, of the consequences of Adam and Eve's fall ("for Understanding rul'd not, and the Will / . . . both in subjection now / To sensual Appetite," 9.1127-29) into postlapsarian sex ("Carnal desire inflaming"; "so inflame my sense," 9.1013, 9.1031). See *PL,* 9.786-94, 1008-15; cf. Rousseau's "duped" imagination and his writing "inflaming the imagination of his readers" (*RW,* 160-61).

17. In *Letters on the Female Mind* (London: 1793), Laetitia Matilda Hawkins, a conservative, antirevolutionary writer, made this point, passim, with reference to both Wollstonecraft and Helen Maria Williams.

18. A reading that exploits the semantic doubleness of *revolution* and its primary meaning of orbital, planetary motion—a restoration or return to an original point (see *OED,* nos. 1, 1b, 2). Cf. Burke's celebration of the Glorious Revolution of 1688 in the *Reflections* and Dr. Johnson's 1755 *Dictionary,* "revolution" (SV). In *The Eighteenth Brumaire of Louis Bonaparte,* Karl Marx sees partially the problem of revolutionary representation as a parodic repetition of *revolutionary* history.

Amy Elizabeth Smith (essay date summer 1992)

SOURCE: Smith, Amy Elizabeth. "Roles for Readers in Mary Wollstonecraft's *A Vindication of the Rights of Woman." Studies in English Literature* 32, no. 3 (summer, 1992): 555-70.

[*In the following essay, Smith examines* A Vindication of the Rights of Woman *to determine the intended audience of the work and argues that the treatise addresses both male and female readers.*]

Critics who have sought to characterize the implied audience for Mary Wollstonecraft's *A Vindication of the Rights of Woman* (1792) have been unable to reach a consensus. Most take one of two positions, arguing either for a primarily male or a primarily female audience.[1] Elissa S. Guralnick claims that the work's "rambling, uneven" nature results from being aimed at an audience "unused and unreceptive to rational discourse—an audience of middle-class women," and Cora Kaplan shares this position.[2] Having assessed Wollstonecraft's tone, textual examples, and the rhetorical distance she creates between herself and other women, Anca Vlasopolos argues instead that the work "proves to be written for men" and her argument has also been adopted by other critics.[3] In a political text a characterization of the implied audience is central for understanding the goals of the work. One must always exert caution when discussing an author's intentions, but questions of purpose and intention can be more safely broached with a text such as the *Vindication*. Primarily political in nature, it is clearly a voice in the debate spurred by the French Revolution, along with Burke's *Reflections on the Revolution in France* and Paine's *The Rights of Man*. Wollstonecraft's *Vindication* is shaped by a political agenda. But without a firmer conjecture about just whom she expected her readers to be, one cannot reach an understanding of how she may have hoped her text would function.

The first questions that must be asked about each of the arguments concerning audience, therefore, are strategic—why would Wollstonecraft write her *Vindication* to a female audience or to a male audience? What would be gained by a single gender focus? Most important, what did Mary Wollstonecraft want to achieve with her work? The last is answered clearly by the text—ultimately, she hoped for nothing less than to help stimulate conditions that would "improve mankind."[4] But as improvement was being impeded by the condition of most women, educated only enough to please and serve, what needed to be effected first was a "REVOLUTION in female manners" (317). Thus far the necessary audience to reach would seem to be women. But in Wollstonecraft's opinion, were women, in 1792, ready to carry on such a revolution by themselves?

The complexity of Wollstonecraft's attitudes toward other women calls for examination at a later point in this essay, but the text reveals her belief that women could not perform the revolution alone. Men, empowered legally and socially, were also needed to effect change. Yet they too could not work alone; then as now, women must be convinced that the revolution would be to their benefit, before they will take an active role. Thus, one can understand why Wollstonecraft needs to address readers of both genders. In this essay I argue that a close study of her *Vindication* reveals a text that clearly anticipates both male and female readers. The work's reputation for unevenness arises primarily from its being aimed at more than one audience—and at audiences who were each to play very different roles in the proposed revolution. Some of the problems with her text, such as the widely varying length of chapters and the apparent randomness of her subjects, can perhaps be accounted for by the speed with which it was reportedly written.[5] But what has often been seen as a lack of focus can be more accurately described as a double focus. The text's accommodation of a dual audience can be demonstrated through an analysis of the direct addresses and references to readers, the selection of examples, and the use of a semi-imperative mood, all of which shape and define the roles offered by the text for both male and female readers.

I. REFERENCES TO READERS

Although disagreement among critics might lead one to believe otherwise, Wollstonecraft makes a number of specific references to readers, beginning as early as her preface (see Table I).[6]

Middle-class women are the first audience specified: "The instruction which has hitherto been addressed to women, has rather been applicable to ladies, . . . but, addressing my sex in a firmer tone, I pay particular attention to those in the middle class, because they appear to be in the most natural state" (81). Early passages might lead one to believe that only a female audience is being addressed, but male readers too are anticipated. When Wollstonecraft describes the present deplorable state of the characters of most women, she "presume[s] that rational men will excuse me for endeavouring to persuade [women] to become more masculine and respectable" (83).

TABLE I: REFERENCES TO READERS

NON GENDER SPECIFIC REFERENCES (19; 41.3% OF TOTAL)		REFERENCES TO MALE READERS (11; 24% OF TOTAL)		REFERENCES TO FEMALE READERS (16; 34.7% OF TOTAL)	
P. 110 (2)*	P. 287	P. 83	P. 290	P. 81(2)	P. 234
148	290	112	316	127	239
188	294	148	319	145	249
207	304	233-34		190 (2)	308
208	305	263		196 (2)	
258	316 (2)	275		203 (2)	
				233	
SECOND PERSON SINGULAR		SECOND PERSON SINGULAR		SECOND PERSON SINGULAR	
P. 94-95 (NOTE 12)	P. 216	P. 261		PP. 301-303	
98	218	279			
212					

*PARENTHETICAL FIGURE INDICATES NUMBER OF OCCURRENCES ON PAGE.

Her preface clearly establishes both male and female readers.[7] In the body of the *Vindication* Wollstonecraft begins to define her audience more precisely, clarifying the separate roles that men and women are to play in the revolution. Male readers fall into two principal categories, the libertines and the men of reason. The first is typified by Lord Chesterfield, whom Wollstonecraft attacks for his licentiousness (147); in fact she traces the present lack of modesty in women directly to that of men, who, having been better educated, bear a heavier responsibility for improving general morals.[8] The attitudes of such men continue to be the largest impediments to female improvement. "Yes, let me tell the libertine of fancy when he despises understanding in woman—that the mind, which he disregards, gives life to the enthusiastic affection from which rapture, short-lived as it is, alone can blow!" (316-17). The reform of such men is too vital a part of Wollstonecraft's plan to let them read her work unadmonished.

The other primary group of men, addressed more frequently, provides a contrast to the libertines. These are the "reasonable men" (263), the "many superior men" (275), and "ye men of understanding" (319). Vlasopolos sees such addresses as part of the "flattering and cajoling" demeanor adopted by Wollstonecraft to please male readers.[9] But can one really assume Wollstonecraft believed there were no such men? A privileged female member of Joseph Johnson's "Academy" of writers, artists, and intellects, she was in steady contact with many of the most interesting and radical "men of understanding" of her day.[10] Her references to the libertine portion of her male audience, however, make clear that she knows not all men are "superior."

Yet even the men of superior judgment and intellect cannot effect changes in society unaided by women, and "how can woman be expected to co-operate unless she knows why she ought to be virtuous?" (86). The text's anticipation of a female audience is indicated by a variety of direct references and addresses. At two points she uses selective expressions of respect, echoing references to reasonable men, such as when she points out the hidden dangers of Dr. Gregory's *Legacy to his Daughters* which has "many attractions to recommend it to the notice of the most respectable part of my sex" (196). A more direct address is made later when she asks, "let not modest women start" (249) at the notion that sexual corruption on any level of society will inevitably permeate all levels. While the text implies some reasonable, respectable female readers, the majority of her references do not specify the character of the women being addressed.[11] Overall, however, Wollstonecraft's addresses to women are more complex than those to male readers and merit closer examination.

II. FEMALE READERS AND WOLLSTONECRAFT'S ROLE

As a female author, Wollstonecraft automatically achieves a certain distance when addressing her male audience. But as a woman, she is to some degree implicated when she examines the circumstances and behavior of other women. This situation causes Wollstonecraft to adopt language that critics have found troubling: "Where art thou to find comfort, forlorn and disconsolate one? He who ought to have directed thy reason, and supported thy weakness, has betrayed thee. In a dream of passion thou consented to wander through flowery lawns, and heedlessly stepping over the preci-

pice to which they guide, instead of guarding, lured thee" (233). Elevated language of this sort, not used consistently, raises questions concerning Wollstonecraft's attitudes toward her female readers.[12] Is she, as has been suggested, trying to establish a distance between herself and other women through the use of "artificial and abstract rhetoric"?[13] The chapter on "Modesty" ends with a further extended address to women: "Would ye, O my sisters, really possess modesty, ye must remember that the possession of virtue, of any denomination, is incompatible with ignorance and vanity! ye must acquire that soberness of mind, which the exercise of duties, and the pursuit of knowledge, alone inspire" (239). The plea continues, repeating the style of the former, but here she has clearly allied herself with women. What may appear to be a contradiction can be better understood by an examination of not just the language of the passages but also the subjects of each. When Wollstonecraft addresses the weaknesses that leave women "forlorn and disconsolate" she adopts a more distant stance and does not directly associate herself with her sex. In the latter passage, however, women who strive for modesty and virtue are her "sisters." Through her control of language she can create the distance that she has automatically from men and can selectively shape her relationship with female readers.

This vacillation between distance and solidarity manifests itself in other ways throughout the *Vindication*. Some critics claim that her use of pronouns—women are more often "they" than "we"—further indicates her desire to separate herself from other women.[14] The extent to which her pronoun usage is inconsistent, however, is generally overlooked. Her introduction offers an interesting example:

> But not content with this natural pre-eminence [of superior physical strength], men endeavour to sink us still lower, merely to render us alluring objects for a moment; and women, intoxicated by the adoration which men, under the influence of their senses, pay them, do not seek to obtain a durable interest in their hearts, or to become the friends of the fellow-creatures who find amusement in their society.
>
> (80)

A telling switch occurs here from "us" to "their." Wollstonecraft acknowledges that she too is a victim of attempted oppression but stops short of identifying with those who do fall prey to such men. An examination of the places throughout her work at which Wollstonecraft uses "we" and "us" reveals that she often does so to show herself the mutual victim of an insult without being a companion in folly.[15] Thus she can exclaim "How grossly do they insult us who thus advise us only to render ourselves gentle, domestic brutes!" (101) but generally excludes herself from statements that demonstrate feminine follies and weaknesses.

To understand why Wollstonecraft apparently determined such a stance to be beneficial to her argument we must understand her role in the work. Regina Janes argues that "since society is the enemy the speaker wants no part of, her identification is with no particular class or segment of that society, but with the position of the critic outside the established order."[16] To achieve, let alone maintain, such a privileged position would be impossible for any writer bound inescapably by class and gender, but Wollstonecraft makes the attempt. Her persona is not in general that of a woman speaking to her sisters in suffering—such a stance could, among other things, alienate male readers. The references she makes to her duty as an author provide an alternative voice. In her "Modesty" chapter she invokes this virtue and asks that it "modulate for me the language of persuasive reason, till I rouse my sex from the flowery bed, on which they supinely sleep life away" (227). One of the needs for her frequent dissociation from women becomes clearer. She must establish herself as above the present ignorant condition of most women if she is to be their champion.

Wollstonecraft is cautious, however, not to appear overly presumptuous and thus weaken her ethos. Her discussion of modesty not only deals with the sexual varieties but opens with a section that can justify her in the role she adopts: "A modest man often conceives a great plan, and tenaciously adheres to it, conscious of his own strength, till success gives it a sanction that determines its character" (227). Her "great plan" is to awaken women to the oppressive nature of their present relationships with men: "When women are once sufficiently enlightened to discover their real interest, on a grand scale, they will, I am persuaded, be very ready to resign all the prerogatives of love, that are not mutual, . . . for the calm satisfaction of friendship, and the tender confidence of habitual esteem" (205). The source of enlightenment will be, of course, Wollstonecraft herself.

Along with this definition of Wollstonecraft's role in the proposed "REVOLUTION in female manners" (317) must come a definition of the roles of her audience, which she determines by their abilities. Wollstonecraft deplores the artificial differences that have been constructed between genders. However, she must acknowledge those differences and address women as she finds them—guilty of "headstrong passions and grovelling vices," qualities that are the "natural effect" of little or no education (100). Wollstonecraft's criticisms of women are not a means of placating a male audience but a forthright assessment of what raw materials are available for the furtherance of her revolutionary plans.

Wollstonecraft's avowed primary objective with her female audience is to persuade them to relinquish the false power their culturally defined sexuality gives them over men: "I know that it will require a considerable length of time to eradicate the firmly rooted prejudices which sensualists have planted; it will also require some time to convince women that they act contrary to their real interest on an enlarged scale, when they cherish or affect weakness under the name of delicacy" (134). Wollstonecraft begins with the beginning. Women have no prospects for improvement until they stop degrading themselves. Temporary power can be obtained by acting the traditional role of the weak, delicate female, but when women employ these means, "virtue is sacrificed to temporary gratifications, and the respectability of life to the triumph of an hour" (125). Mary Poovey argues that, in regard to the revolution in female manners, "women are simply to wait for this revolution to be effected, for their dignity to be restored, for their reformation to be made necessary."[17] But however minor their role may seem to us now, they were being called upon to act—or in a sense, to stop acting. The traditional childlike role so many were playing, according to Wollstonecraft, was precisely what was impeding their progress as a sex, and indeed, all humanity's progress.

Throughout the *Vindication* Wollstonecraft warns women of the perilousness of any victory won by feminine wiles. Along with logical arguments, however, she paints distressing verbal portraits of neglected coquettes and appealing scenes of domestic bliss based on rational friendship. Other specific arguments are also strengthened with a variety of dramatic examples. Numerous and persuasive, these examples are one of the primary means by which the text shapes the roles anticipated for readers and thus they need to be examined in some detail.

III. ROLES FOR READERS AND WOLLSTONECRAFT'S CUES

Wollstonecraft's examples illustrate a variety of arguments, and not just those addressed to women. Vlasopolos accurately notes that "one of the chief strengths of *A Vindication* resides in its vivid portrayals of women in straitened circumstances."[18] She argues, however, that these examples are formed to create sympathy for the men who appear in them. Critics who disregard Wollstonecraft's anticipation of male readers fail to deal with the significant number of examples aimed primarily at male concerns. Depictions of unpleasant scenarios for men occur at many points in the text, serving to demonstrate the problems that result from female weaknesses:

> The weak enervated women who particularly catch the attention of libertines, are unfit to be mothers, though they may conceive; so that the rich sensualist, who has rioted among women, spreading depravity and misery, when he wishes to perpetuate his name, receives from his wife only an half-formed being that inherits both its father's and mother's weakness.
>
> (249)

Any attempt at reform must urge the necessity for that reform. With this example Wollstonecraft depicts the unhappy fruits of libertinism and the perpetuation of crippling "feminine" delicacy.

This tactic is complemented by portrayals of the domestic happiness a man will find with a properly educated woman unfettered by artificial, debilitating models of female behavior:

> I have seen [a good wife] prepare herself and children, with only the luxury of cleanliness, to receive her husband, who, returning weary home in the evening, found smiling babes and a clean hearth. My heart has loitered in the midst of the group, and has even throbbed with sympathetic emotion when the scraping of the well-known foot has raised a pleasing tumult.
>
> (255)

The lesson for male readers is clear. Frail and foolish women, however languid and appealing they appear, do not make good mothers; there are no real rewards for the encouragement of such behavior in females. Instead, sensible women will make a pleasing home and provide healthy, happy heirs. Despite the presence of women in each of the examples, the main appeal is made to men.

What is overlooked in Vlasopolos's argument, however, is that there is an equally strong network of examples in the *Vindication* that offer similar images of warning and reward to female readers (see Table II).

TABLE II: EXAMPLES*

EXAMPLES FOCUSED PRIMARILY TOWARD MALE READERS	EXAMPLES FOCUSED PRIMARILY TOWARD FEMALE READERS
P. 119 ("BUT TO VIEW THE SUBJECT . . .")	P. 111 ("I NOW SPEAK OF WOMEN . . .")
167 ("LOVE, CONSIDERED AS . . .")	135-37 ("BUT, SUPPOSING A WOMAN . . .")
181 ("OF WHAT MATERIALS . . .")	138-39 ("LET FANCY NOW PRESENT . . .")
188-89 ("THE MAN WHO CAN . . .")	159 ("BESIDES, HOW MANY WOMEN . . ."
249 ("TO SATISFY THIS GENIUS . . .")	165 ("A WOMAN WHO HAS LOST . . .")
254-55 ("COLD WOULD BE THE HEART . . .")	229-30 ("AND THUS HAVE I ARGUED . . .")
294-95 ("THE LIBERTINISM . . .")	

*THIS TABLE IS BY NO MEANS COMPREHENSIVE. MANY OF WOLLSTONECRAFT'S EXAMPLES HAVE A DOUBLE FOCUS AND ARE DIFFICULT TO CLASSIFY WITH CERTAINTY. THOSE CITED HERE ARE AMONG THE EXAMPLES IN WHICH THE GENDER FOCUS IS MORE OBVIOUS.

If a woman fails to cultivate her understanding and thinks only of setting a nice table and dressing well, her husband will soon tire of her:

> How many women of this description pass their days, or at least their evenings, discontentedly. Their husbands acknowledge that they are good managers and chaste wives, but leave home to seek for more agreeable—may I be allowed to use a significant French word—*piquant* society; and the patient drudge, who fulfils her task like a blind horse in a mill, is defrauded of her just reward.
>
> (159)

No good English woman could want to recognize herself in such a picture. And so, as with her examples for male readers, Wollstonecraft presents positive portrayals of women as well. The woman who concerns herself with being well educated, and subsequently educates her children, male and female, will find her happiness:

> I think I see her surrounded by her children, reaping the reward of her care. The intelligent eye meets hers, whilst health and innocence smile on their chubby cheeks, and as they grow up the cares of life are lessened by their grateful attention. She lives to see the virtues which she endeavoured to plant on principles, fixed into habits, to see her children attain a strength of character sufficient to enable them to endure adversity without forgetting their mother's example. The task of life thus fulfilled, she calmly waits for the sleep of death, and rising from the grave, may say—"Behold, Thou gavest me a talent, and here are five talents."
>
> (139)

Wollstonecraft consistently gives powerful form to her ideas and theories through examples, some of which make a general appeal to both men and women. Many, however, are tailored to stress points which have application either for men or for women. The text presents each gender with images that reinforce the rewards of adopting roles in the revolution; dutiful, respectable men and women will be each other's own rewards and will produce families of happy children. Libertinism in men and foolish calculated weaknesses in women injure both sexes. Overall, the many examples embody Wollstonecraft's abstract arguments, but more important, the fact that they target different portions of her audience allows her a means to illustrate her expectations from each. These expectations also find expression in another of Wollstonecraft's important rhetorical techniques, one that complements the subtler, more emotionally based appeal made through examples. Wollstonecraft employs a direct—although softened—imperative form.

Just as the examples indicate an anticipation of male and female readers and help to shape their roles, her use of a semi-imperative mood reveals more of the expectations she has from readers. Repeatedly throughout her text, requests and pleas are issued concisely but politely by her use of "let" joined with a noun or pronoun: "I would fain persuade my sex to act from simpler principles. Let them merit love, and they will obtain it" (200). The arguments that limit Wollstonecraft to a male or a female audience overlook the heavy use she makes of the semi-imperative, directed specifically at each sex, or at both together (see Table III).

This usage is inextricably tied with the roles assigned to her readers. Warnings that prompt women towards valuing rational relationships with men before short-lived reigns of coquettish tyranny often take the semi-imperative form: "Let them not expect to be valued when their beauty fades, for it is the fate of the fairest flowers to be admired and pulled to pieces by the careless hand that plucked them" (263). Combined with powerful imagery this rhetorical technique makes a strong appeal, presenting a voice firm but not strident.

TABLE III: SEMI-IMPERATIVE USAGE

Non Gender Specific Focus (27; 46.5% of total)		Male Focus (15; 26% of total)		Female Focus (16; 27.5% of total)	
P. 102	P. 205	P. 84	P. 181	P. 116	P. 200
108	212	112	193	134	201
109	230 (2)	119 (3)	296	182	235
110	233 (2)	132 (3)	311	190 (4)	238 (2)
115 (3)	269	144	319	191	249
121 (3)	274	160		198 (NOTE #6)	263
138	279				
160 (4)	286				
199	304				

This voice is also directed at male rea ders, reinforcing for them as well the messages conveyed through examples. While she makes use of full imperative also, the repeated usage of the "let" pattern allows for mnemonic ties between principal ideas. Wollstonecraft uses this semi-imperative form in a variety of ways, but primarily to issue warnings and challenges to her male audience. Often prefacing brief examples, the semi-imperative calls direct attention to what moral men are to extract from the portrait. In addressing, once again, the issue of a female education that emphasizes fawning servility at the expense of sincerity, Wollstonecraft warns: "Let the husband beware of trusting too implicitly to this servile obedience; for if his wife can with winning sweetness, caress him when angry, and when she ought to be angry, unless contempt has stifled a natural effervescence, she may do the same after parting with a lover" (181). The problem with teaching women dishonesty, Wollstonecraft demonstrates, is that men can be its dupes as well as its beneficiaries. By calling special attention to the brief example that follows, the use of the semi-imperative prepares the reader to expect an important lesson. Clearly, female manners are not just a female problem—men have a very real reason to take part in the revolution.

Wollstonecraft further strengthens her arguments advocating reformed female education by issuing challenges to men, also expressed in the semi-imperative mood. She argues that if what she is calling for is so unnatural—if women truly are not rational creatures—then educating them properly will be unproductive. But why not, she questions, try the experiment and find out? "When man, governed by reasonable laws, enjoys his natural freedom, let him despise woman, if she do not share it with him; and, till that glorious period arrives, in descanting on the folly of the sex, let him not over-

look his own" (132). Her usage of the semi-imperative provides her with a voice of reasonable stability that commands attention without seeming inflexible. When addressing male readers with this voice, she emphasizes reasons why they will benefit from the revolution in female manners and issues rational but memorable challenges, both inciting them to want change and pointing to how it can come about.

One important point that becomes apparent through a study of the semi-imperative addressed to men is the extent to which Wollstonecraft relies on male action for the revolution: "Let men take their choice. Man and woman were made for each other, though not to become one being; and if they will not improve women, they will deprave them" (296). A closer look needs to be taken at what the text can reveal of Wollstonecraft's expectations about the practical aspects of the revolution. She claims that "the improvement must be mutual" (296) yet an examination of her language seems to reveal that men are to perform the more active role in the revolution. One must, therefore, determine if and why Wollstonecraft has doubts about women's ability to take the lead.

IV. ROLES FOR THE REVOLUTION

Although she is consistent in her demands that women resign their reigns as "short-lived queens" (145), Wollstonecraft alternates between hope and despair regarding further expectations. At times, she is quite optimistic about what women should attempt and she is willing to ally herself with her sex: "Let us, my dear contemporaries, arise above such narrow prejudices. If wisdom be desirable on its own account, if virtue, to deserve the name, must be founded on knowledge, let us endeavour to strengthen our minds by reflection till our heads become a balance for our hearts" (190). Yet despite the encouraging tone of this passage a pessimism about women pervades much of the work. The real problem, Wollstonecraft realizes, is nothing less than the entire structure of society, firmly stratified according to class and gender. Thus the "romantic and inconstant" behavior of women is a result of the training they receive for their approved social role and "in the present state of society this evil can scarcely be remedied" (169). Difficulties, however, do not cause Wollstonecraft to give way to despair. An ambivalence towards women emerges strongly from the text, often suggesting frustration, and thus the role she assigns them is not one that would overturn the structure of society. The "men of understanding" must play the most active part in the proposed Revolution (319).

Why are men assigned the more active role? "Who can tell, how many generations may be necessary to give vigour to the virtue and talents of the freed posterity of abject slaves?" (171-72). At more than thirty points throughout the *Vindication,* Wollstonecraft directly likens women, in their present condition, to slaves—"slaves to their bodies" (130), "slaves of opinion" (139), "slaves to their persons" (257), and "the slaves of injustice" (313); in the present system, woman is made "the slave of her own feelings" (202) and "the slave of sensibility" (232).[19] Holding strong convictions about the lasting effects of education and the absolute necessity of the proper shaping of character, which in children is "fixed before their seventh year" (314), Wollstonecraft is dubious about the ability of the present generation of women to take the lead in a lasting revolution. Vlasopolos argues that through flattery Wollstonecraft "makes men feel in control of the proposed 'REVOLUTION in female manners.'"[20] But in fact, to a considerable extent she wants men to be in charge of the Revolution: "Would men but generously snap our chains, and be content with rational fellowship instead of slavish obedience, they would find us more observant daughters, more affectionate sisters, more faithful wives, more reasonable mothers—in a word, better citizens" (263). Appeals such as this are not mere fawning. Wollstonecraft repeatedly voices severe doubts about the ability of most women to overcome their faulty educations.

Women, however, are not the only party in need of reform. Miriam Brody notes that Wollstonecraft's logic can be thus reduced: "If men will not be reasonable, they will be sensualists. If they will be sensualists, women will be their slaves."[21] The corollary is that while women behave slavishly, men will not be reasonable. Clearly, what emerges is a vicious cycle that must be broken largely by those most capable of doing so. In 1792 that group was "ye men of understanding," to whom Wollstonecraft's final paragraph is addressed (319). Throughout her work she makes clear that women are oppressed by their faulty educations, not by any defect in their natures. She must acknowledge where power lies, but cautions men: "Let not men then in the pride of power, use the same arguments that tyrannic kings and venal ministers have used, and fallaciously assert that woman ought to be subjected because she has always been so" (132). Power, Wollstonecraft argues throughout her *Vindication,* corrupts, when exerted without reason. Because the problems between men and women take on a cyclic form both men and women must act to dispel them. Simultaneously, women must abdicate their short-lived reigns of superficial power, purchased at the price of their future happiness—they must become worthy of respect—and men must learn to value the truly virtuous, reasonable woman, abandoning the desire for "a meretricious slave to fondle" (204). Wollstonecraft is more optimistic about the ability of men to rectify the problems she examines and so she shapes for them a more active role in the revolution, asking them to grant women the powers, primarily those endowed by a better education, that can allow women to rise above their present frailties. Since

neither men nor women, however, can accomplish a complete revitalization of English society alone, her vision of social change entails, as Judith Lee argues, "a twofold process in which men and women evolve independently but reciprocally."[22] Without both halves of society acting together the nation cannot progress. "Rousseau exerts himself to prove that all was right originally" and "a crowd of authors that all is now right"; but Wollstonecraft envisions that when men and women can work and live harmoniously and reasonably, "all will be right" (95).

Unless the dual nature of the action needed to bring about the revolution is understood, Wollstonecraft's work cannot be fully appreciated. And the dual nature of this action cannot be understood until one realizes that Wollstonecraft's *Vindication* implies both male and female readers. Critics who believe that she wrote for men often depict her as insincere and confused—essentially charging her with the very traits she deplores so much in most women. The central problem with both of the existing critical stances, however, is that arguments limiting her to one audience or the other distort her complex work. To say that she wrote for women only is to underrate Wollstonecraft's abilities as a social analyst. She was well aware, as an examination of her work demonstrates, that society's problems have more than one source. Thus, she makes her powerful rhetorical appeals to both men and women as the best way to bring about her proposed "REVOLUTION in female manners."

Notes

1. Regina Janes states that Wollstonecraft addresses an audience that "constantly shifts," but, as this point is not central to her argument, provides no real textual support for this claim. "Mary, Mary, Quite Contrary, Or, Mary Astell and Mary Wollstonecraft Compared," *SECC* 5 (1976): 121-39, 133. Lucy Kelley Hayden cites brief examples indicating a mixed audience, but offers no analysis. "A Rhetorical Analysis of Mary Wollstonecraft's *A Vindication of the Rights of Woman,*" diss., University of Michigan, 1971 (pp. 135-38). Zilla Eisenstein claims that the work "was written to men as much if not more so than to women," in *The Radical Future of Liberal Feminism* (New York: Longman, 1981), p. 107.

2. Elissa S. Guralnick, "Rhetorical Strategy in Mary Wollstonecraft's *A Vindication of the Rights of Woman,*" *The Humanities Association Review* 30, 3 (1979): 174-85, 174, and Cora Kaplan, "Wild Nights: Pleasure/Sexuality/Feminism," in *The Ideology of Conduct: Essays on Literature and the History of Sexuality,* ed. Nancy Armstrong and Leonard Tennenhouse (New York: Methuen, 1987), pp. 160-83, 175.

3. Anca Vlasopolos, "Mary Wollstonecraft's Mask of Reason in *A Vindication of the Rights of Woman*," *DR* 60, 3 (Autumn 1980): 462-71, 462. Also see Laurie A. Finke, "'A Philosophic Wanton': Language and Authority in Wollstonecraft's *Vindication of the Rights of Woman*," in *The Philosopher as Writer: The Eighteenth Century,* ed. Robert Ginsberg (Selinsgrove, PA: Susquehanna Univ. Press, 1987), 155-76, 159; and Kathleen McCormack, "The Sybil and the Hyena: George Eliot's Wollstonecraftian Feminism," *DR* 63, 4 (Winter 1983-84): 602-14, 605.

4. Mary Wollstonecraft, *A Vindication of the Rights of Woman,* ed. Miriam Brody (London: Penguin, 1983), p. 317. All subsequent references are to page numbers in this edition and will be given parenthetically in the text.

5. Emily W. Sunstein, in *A Different Face: The Life of Mary Wollstonecraft* (New York: Harper, 1975), p. 208, describes how Wollstonecraft's publisher, Joseph Johnson, had a printer's devil at her door waiting for copy, giving her "little opportunity to correct or reorganize."

6. In Brody's edition, due to her lengthy introduction, the text of the *Vindication* does not begin until page 79.

7. One prospective reader is specified by name. In addition to the introduction, Wollstonecraft includes a dedication to Charles Maurice de Talleyrand-Périgord, in response to his 1791 work on education, *Rapport sur l'Instruction Publique, fait au nom du Comité de Constitution.* She does not, however, make further reference in the body of her work to suggest that Talleyrand is her primary audience.

8. "The little respect paid to chastity in the male world is, I am persuaded, the grand source of many of the physical and moral evils that torment mankind, as well as of the vices and follies that degrade and destroy women" (282; see also 233, 249, and 318).

9. Vlasopolos, "Mary Wollstonecraft's Mask of Reason," p. 462.

10. Gary Kelly, "Mary Wollstonecraft as '*Vir Bonus,*'" *English Studies in Canada* 5, 3 (Autumn 1979): 275-91, 275.

11. The final chapter contains a notable exception. Her most memorable and lengthy address, extending approximately two and one half pages, is harshly critical. Superstitious women, however, are the primary target of this section containing the infamous "O ye foolish women!" expostulation (302). While Wollstonecraft does claim that "I have throughout supposed myself talking to ignorant women," earlier references indicate that she does not believe herself to be addressing ignorant women exclusively.

12. Mary Wilson Carpenter's "Sibylline Apocalyptics: Mary Wollstonecraft's *Vindication of the Rights of Woman* and Job's Mother's Womb," in *Literature and History* 12, 2 (Autumn 1986): 215-28, discusses the biblical character of Wollstonecraft's prose, and Laurie A. Finke suggests that Wollstonecraft's deliberately archaic style is "a parody of feminine discourse" (p. 165). However, arguments that represent Wollstonecraft's use of archaic pronouns as biblical, ironic, or merely poetical do not entirely account for the effect the language has on her relationship with female readers.

13. Mary Poovey, *The Proper Lady and the Woman Writer: Ideology as Style in the Works of Mary Wollstonecraft, Mary Shelley, and Jane Austen* (Chicago: Univ. of Chicago Press, 1984), p. 78.

14. Vlasopolos, "Mary Wollstonecraft's Mask of Reason," p. 463; Finke, p. 159.

15. Uses of first person plural pronouns which refer exclusively to women occur on the following pages: 80 (2), 82, 100-101 (8), 111, 132, 153 (5), 182-83 (2), 190-91 (16), 201, and 263 (5).

16. Janes, "Mary, Mary, Quite Contrary," p. 133.

17. Poovey, p. 79.

18. Vlasopolos, "Mary Wollstonecraft's Mask of Reason," p. 466.

19. Further examples occur on the following pages: 82, 104, 107, 108, 117, 120, 121 (2), 122, 131, 132, 134, 144, 153, 171, 172, 179, 195, 204, 224, 256, 257 (2), 263, 265, 270 (3), 282, 285 (2), 286, and 294 (2).

20. Vlasopolos, "Mary Wollstonecraft's Mask of Reason," p. 464.

21. Miriam Brody, "Mary Wollstonecraft: Sexuality and Women's Rights," in *Feminist Theorists: Three Centuries of Women's Intellectual Traditions,* ed. Dale Spender (London: The Woman's Press, 1983), 40-59, 57.

22. Judith Lee, "Ways of Their Own: The Emanations of Blake's *Vala, or The Four Zoas*," *ELH* 50, 1 (Spring 1983): 131-53, 133. Lee demonstrates the influence of Wollstonecraft's social theories on Blake.

Moira Ferguson (essay date autumn 1992)

SOURCE: Ferguson, Moira. "Mary Wollstonecraft and the Problematic of Slavery." *Feminist Review* 42 (autumn 1992): 82-102.

[*In the following essay, Ferguson examines Wollstonecraft's discourse on slavery in* A Vindication of the Rights of Woman *and other works as it pertains to the "enslavement" of women as well as to colonial slavery.*]

> A traffic that outrages every suggestion of reason and religion . . . [an] inhuman custom.
>
> *A Vindication of the Rights of Woman*

> I love most people best when they are in adversity, for pity is one of my prevailing passions.
>
> *Collected Letters of Mary Wollstonecraft*

HISTORY AND TEXTS BEFORE *A VINDICATION OF THE RIGHTS OF WOMAN*

In 1790, Mary Wollstonecraft became a major participant in contemporary political debate for the first time, due to her evolving political analysis and social milieu. In contrast to *A Vindication of the Rights of Men* in 1790 which drew primarily on the language of natural rights for its political argument, *A Vindication of the Rights of Woman* (1792) favoured a discourse on slavery that highlighted female subjugation. Whereas the *Rights of Men* refers to slavery in a variety of contexts only four or five times, the *Rights of Woman* contains over eighty references; the constituency Wollstonecraft champions—white, middle-class women—is constantly characterized as slaves. For her major polemic, that is, Mary Wollstonecraft decided to adopt and adapt the terms of contemporary political debate. Over a two-year period that debate had gradually reformulated its terms as the French Revolution in 1789 that highlighted aristocratic hegemony and bourgeois rights was followed by the San Domingan Revolution that primarily focused on colonial relations.

Wollstonecraft's evolving commentaries on the status of European women in relation to slavery were made in response to four interlocking events: first, the intensifying agitation over the question of slavery in England that included the case of the slave James Somerset in 1772 and Phillis Wheatley's visit in 1773; second, the French Revolution in 1789; third, Catherine Macaulay's *Letters on Education* (1790) that forthrightly argued against sexual difference; and fourth, the successful revolution by slaves in the French colony of San Domingo in 1791.

This discourse on slavery employed by Wollstonecraft was nothing new for women writers, although it was now distinctly recontextualized in terms of colonial slavery. Formerly, in all forms of discourse throughout the eighteenth century, conservative and radical women alike railed against marriage, love, and education as forms of slavery perpetrated upon women by men and by the conventions of society at large.

WOLLSTONECRAFT'S EARLIER WORKS, RECEIVED DISCOURSE, AND THE ADVENT OF THE ABOLITIONIST DEBATE

Prior to the French Revolution, Mary Wollstonecraft had utilized the language of slavery in texts from various genres. In *Thoughts* (1786), an educational treatise,

Wollstonecraft talked conventionally of women subjugated by their husbands who in turn tyrannize servants, 'for slavish fear and tyranny go together' (Wollstonecraft, 1787: 63). Two years later, in *Mary, A Fiction* (1788), her first novel written in Ireland during trying circumstances as a governess, the heroine decides she will not live with her husband and exclaims to her family: 'I will work . . . , do anything rather than be a slave' (Wollstonecraft, 1788: 49).[1] Here as a case in point, Wollstonecraft inflects slavery with the orthodox conception of slavery that had populated women's texts for over a century—marriage was a form of slavery; wives were slaves to husbands.

Wollstonecraft's early conventional usage, however, in which the word slave stands for a subjugated daughter or wife was soon to complicate its meaning. From the early 1770s onward, a number of events from James Somerset's court case to Quaker petitions to Parliament and reports of abuses had injected the discourse of slavery into popular public debate.

The Abolition Committee, for example, was formed on 22 May 1787, with a view to mounting a national campaign against the slave trade and securing the passage of an Abolition Bill through Parliament (Coupland, 1933: 68). Following the establishment of the committee, abolitionist Thomas Clarkson wrote and distributed two thousand copies of a pamphlet entitled 'A Summary View of the Slave-Trade, and of the Probable Consequences of Its Abolition' (Clarkson, 1808: 276-85 and *passim*). Wollstonecraft's friend, William Roscoe, offered the profits of his poem 'The Wrongs of Africa' to the committee. The political campaign was launched on the public in full force (Craton, 1974: chapter 5).

Less than a year after the Abolition Committee was formed, Wollstonecraft's radical publisher, Joseph Johnson, co-founded a radical periodical entitled the *Analytical Review*. Invited to become a reviewer, Wollstonecraft's reviews soon reflected the new influence of the abolition debate (Sunstein, 1975: 171). One of the earliest books she critiqued in April 1789 was written by Britain's most renowned African and a former slave; Wollstonecraft was analyzing a text based on specific experiences of colonial slavery for the first time. Its title was *The Interesting Narrative of the Life of Olaudah Equiano, or Gustavus Vassa, the African Written by Himself,* in which Equiano graphically chronicles being kidnapped from Africa, launched on the notorious Middle Passage, and living out as a slave the consequences of these events.

While the *Analytical Review* acquainted the public with old and new texts on the current debate, Wollstonecraft was composing an anthology for educating young women that also reflected her growing concerns. Published by Joseph Johnson and entitled *The Female Reader: or Miscellaneous Pieces for the Improvement of Young Women,* the textbook cum anthology included substantial extracts promoting abolition. It included Sir Richard Steele's rendition from *The Spectator* of the legend of Inkle and Yarico, Anna Laetitia Barbauld's hymn-in-prose, 'Negro-woman', about a grieving mother forcibly separated from her child, and a poignant passage from William Cowper's poem, 'The Task', popular with the contemporary reading public:

> I would not have a slave to till my ground,
> To carry me, to fan me while I sleep,
> And tremble when I wake, for all the wealth
> That sinews bought and sold have ever earn'd.
> No: dear as freedom is, and in my heart's
> Just estimation priz'd above all price,
> I had much rather be myself the slave,
> And wear the bonds, than fasten them on him.

(Wollstonecraft, 1789: 29-31, 171, 321-2)

A series of events then followed one another in rapid succession that continued to have a bearing on the reconstitution of the discourse on slavery. In July 1789, the French Revolution erupted as the Bastille gaol was symbolically stormed and opened. Coinciding with the French Revolution came Richard Price's polemic, Edmund Burke's response, and then Wollstonecraft's response to Burke and her review of Catherine Macaulay's *Letters on Education.* Meanwhile, in September and the following months, Wollstonecraft reviewed in sections the antislavery novel *Zeluco: Various Views of Human Nature, Taken from Life and Manners, Foreign and Domestic,* by John Moore. Let me back up and briefly elaborate how all this attentiveness to colonial slavery affected public debate and Mary Wollstonecraft's usage of the term.

THE FRENCH REVOLUTION

On 4 November 1789, Wollstonecraft's friend, the Reverend Richard Price, Dissenting minister and leading liberal philosopher, delivered the annual sermon commemorating the 'Glorious Revolution' of 1688 to the Revolution Society in London. The society cherished the ideals of the seventeenth-century revolution and advocated Dissenters' rights. This particular year there was much for Dissenters to celebrate. Basically, Price applauded the French Revolution as the start of a liberal epoch: 'after sharing in the benefits of one revolution,' declared Price [meaning the British seventeenth-century constitutional revolution], 'I have been spared to be a witness to two other Revolutions, both glorious' (Price, 1790: 55). The written text of Price's sermon, *Discourse on the Love of Our Country,* was reviewed by Wollstonecraft in the *Analytical*'s December issue. A year later, on 1 November 1790, Edmund Burke's *Reflections on the Revolution in France* that attacked both Price and his sermon was timed to be published on the anniversary of Price's address. It soon became a topic of public debate. Several responses quickly followed.

As the first writer to challenge Burke's reactionary polemic, Wollstonecraft foregrounded the cultural issue of human rights in her title: *A Vindication of the Rights of Men.* It immediately sold out. Not by political coincidence, she composed this reply while evidence about the slave trade was being presented to the Privy Council during the year following the first extensive parliamentary debate on abolition in May 1789. *The Rights of Men* applauded human rights and justice, excoriated abusive social, church and state practices, and attacked Burke for hypocrisy and prejudice. She argued vehemently for a more equitable distribution of wealth and parliamentary representation. By 4 December the same year, Wollstonecraft had revised the first edition and Johnson rapidly turned out a second one in January 1791 (Tomalin, 1974).

In *The Rights of Men,* Wollstonecraft also frontally condemns institutionalized slavery:

> On what principle Mr. Burke could defend American independence, I cannot conceive; for the whole tenor of his plausible arguments settles slavery on an everlasting foundation. Allowing his servile reverence for antiquity, and prudent attention to self-interest, to have the force which he insists on, the slave trade ought never to be abolished; and, because our ignorant forefathers, not understanding the native dignity of man, sanctioned a traffic that outrages every suggestion of reason and religion, we are to submit to the inhuman custom, and term an atrocious insult to humanity the love of our country, and a proper submission to the laws by which our property is secured.

(Wollstonecraft, 1790: 23-4)

In *The Rights of Men,* Wollstonecraft explicitly argues for the first time that no slavery is natural and all forms of slavery, regardless of context, are human constructions. Her scorching words to Burke about his situating slavery 'on an everlasting foundation' (in the past and the future) sharply distinguishes her discourse from her more orthodox invocations of slavery in *Thoughts* and *Mary.* Contemporary events have begun to mark the discourse on slavery in a particular and concrete way.

In particular, Wollstonecraft challenges the legal situation. In *The Rights of Men,* she graphically represents slavery as 'authorized by law to fasten her fangs on human flesh and . . . eat into the very soul' (Wollstonecraft, 1790: 76). None the less, although she supports abolition unequivocally, she considers 'reason' an even more important attribute to possess than physical freedom. 'Virtuous men,' she comments, can endure 'poverty, shame, and even slavery' but not the 'loss of reason' (Wollstonecraft, 1790: 45, 59).

The same month that Wollstonecraft replied to Burke, she favourably reviewed Catherine Macaulay Graham's *Letters on Education.* Macaulay's argument against the accepted notion that males and females had distinct sexual characteristics was part of the evolving discourse on human rights that connected class relations to women's rights. Macaulay also expropriated the language of physical bondage and wove it into her political argument. Denouncing discrimination against women throughout society, *Letters* also rails against 'the savage barbarism which is now displayed on the sultry shores of Africa' (Ferguson, 1985: 399). Macaulay takes pains to censure the condition of women 'in the east'—in harems, for example—and scorns the fact that men used differences in 'corporal strength . . . in the barbarous ages to reduce [women] to a state of abject slavery' (Ferguson, 1985: 403-4). Macaulay's historical timing separates her from earlier writers who used this language; by 1790 slavery had assumed multiple meanings that included the recognition, implied or explicit, of connexions between colonial slavery and constant sexual abuse.

In **The Rights of Men,** however, Wollstonecraft had not exhibited any substantial attention to the question of gender. But, after she read Macaulay, her discourse on gender and rights shifted. Notably, too, as one edition after another of **A Vindication of the Rights of Men** hit the presses, Johnson was concurrently publishing Wollstonecraft's translation of Christian Gotthilf Salzmann's *Elements of Morality for the Use of Children.* In the preface to this educational treatise, Wollstonecraft pointedly inserted a passage of her own, enjoining the fair treatment of Native Americans. In terms of democratic colonial relations as they were then perceived, Wollstonecraft rendered Salzmann more up to date. There was, however, still more to come before Wollstonecraft settled into writing her second **Vindication** in 1792.

First of all, information about slavery continued to flow unabated in the press. According to Michael Craton, 'William Wilberforce was able to initiate the series of pioneer inquiries before the Privy Council and select committees of Commons and Lords, which brought something like the truth of slave trade and plantation slavery out into the open between 1789 and 1791' (Craton, 1974: 261). None the less, in April 1791, the Abolition Bill was defeated in the House of Commons by a vote of 163 to 88, a massive blow to the antislavery campaign.

Just as much, if not perhaps more to the point, in August of that year, slaves in the French colony of San Domingo (now Haiti) revolted, another crucial historical turning point. The French Caribbean had been 'an integral part of the economic life of the age, the greatest colony in the world, the pride of France, and the envy of every other imperialist nation' (James, 1963: ix).

The conjunction of these events deeply polarized British society. George III switched to the proslavery side, enabling faint-hearted abolitionists to change sides. Meanwhile, radicals celebrated. This triumphant uprising of the San Domingan slaves forced another angle of vision on the French Revolution and compounded the anxiety that affairs across the Channel had generated. Horrified at the threat to their investments and fearful of copycat insurrections by the domestic working class as well as by African Caribbeans, many panic-stricken whites denounced the San Domingan Revolution (Klingberg, 1926: 88-95).

Although no one spoke their pessimism outright, abolition was temporarily doomed. When campaigners remobilized in 1792, they were confident of winning the vote and refused to face the implications of dual revolutions in France and San Domingo. Proslaveryites, now quite sanguine, capitalized on the intense conflicts and instigated a successful policy of delay. A motion for gradual abolition—effectively a plantocratic victory—carried in the Commons by a vote of 238 to 85.

A VINDICATION OF THE RIGHTS OF WOMAN

The composition of **A Vindication of the Rights of Woman** started in the midst of these tumultuous events, its political ingredients indicating Wollstonecraft's involvement in all these issues. Indeed, Mary Wollstonecraft seems to have been the first writer to raise issues of colonial and gender relations so tellingly in tandem.

More than any previous text, the **Rights of Woman** invokes the language of colonial slavery to impugn female subjugation and call for the restoration of inherent rights. Wollstonecraft's eighty-plus references to slavery divide into several categories and subsets. The language of slavery—unspecified—is attached to sensation, pleasure, fashion, marriage and patriarchal subjugation. It is also occasionally attached to the specific condition of colonized slaves.

Wollstonecraft starts from the premise that all men enslave all women and that sexual desire is a primary motivation: 'I view, with indignation, the mistaken notions that enslave my sex. . . . For I will venture to assert, that all the causes of female weakness, as well as depravity, which I have already enlarged on, branch out of one grand cause—want of chastity in men' (1792: 37, 138).

Men dominate women as plantocrats dominate slaves: 'As blind obedience is ever sought for by power, tyrants and sensualists are in the right when they endeavour to keep women in the dark, because the former only want slaves and the latter a play-thing. . . . All the sacred rights of humanity are violated by insist-

ing on blind obedience; or, the most sacred rights belong *only* to man' (44, 83). In permeating the text with
the idea that women are oppressed by all men,
Wollstonecraft accords all women, including herself, a
group identity, a political position from which they can
start organizing and agitating.

However, when Wollstonecraft begins to argue at a concrete level, when she confronts, say, the 'foibles' of
women, that sense of group solidarity dissolves. Notable examples are women's too ready acceptance of inferior educations, female vanity and an excessive display of feeling, exemplified in the following passages
on: First, education:

> Led by their dependent situation and domestic employ-
> ments more into society, what they learn is rather by
> snatches; and as learning is with them, in general, only
> a secondary thing, they do not pursue any one branch
> with that persevering ardour necessary to give vigour
> to the faculties, and clearness to the judgment.
>
> (23)

Second, self-involvement:

> It is acknowledged that [females] spend many of the
> first years of their lives in acquiring a smattering of ac-
> complishments; meanwhile strength of body and mind
> are sacrificed to libertine notions of beauty, to the de-
> sire of establishing themselves,—the only way women
> can rise in the world,—by marriage. And this desire
> making mere animals of them, when they marry they
> act as such children may be expected to act:—they
> dress; they paint, and nickname God's creatures. Surely
> these weak beings are only fit for a seraglio!—Can
> they be expected to govern a family with judgment, or
> take care of the poor babes whom they bring into the
> world?
>
> (10)

With such attention to vain practices and little intellectual encouragement, women can scarcely be expected to
lead (nor do they lead) sensible lives:

> Nor can it be expected that a woman will resolutely
> endeavour to strengthen her constitution and abstain
> from enervating indulgencies, if artifical notions of
> beauty, and false descriptions of sensibility, have been
> early entangled with her motives of action.
>
> (43)

In censuring how white middle-class women act,
Wollstonecraft views them as a homogenized group—'I
view, with indignation, the mistaken notions that enslave my sex. . . . It is time to effect a revolution in
female manners' (37, 45). She separates herself off from
them as a mentor-censor.

Wollstonecraft's self-distancing arises from an understandably positive view she holds of her own ability to
transcend situations that she generally deplores in the
female population. Since she had broken through prescribed barriers in a rather independent fashion from an
early age, she deplores the same lack of resourcefulness
in other women; she sees no valid reason why other
women cannot act the same way, her sense of female
conditioning somewhat precarious. Or perhaps she understands her own social construction and her past inability to remove herself from certain scenarios—when
she worked as the irascible Mrs Dawson's companion,
for example. She could be projecting anger at her own
passivity in earlier situations.

This sense of herself as set apart comes out even more
clearly, though somewhat indirectly, in a footnote to the
second *Vindication.* In the text proper, Wollstonecraft is
referring to the length of time it will take for slaves—
like white women presumably—to gather themselves up
from the condition of slavery:

> Man, taking her body, the mind is left to rust; so that
> while physical love enervates man, as being his
> favourite recreation, he will endeavour to enslave
> woman:—and, who can tell, how many generations
> may be necessary to give vigour to the virtue and tal-
> ents of the freed posterity of abject slaves.
>
> (76-7)

In the footnote Wollstonecraft quotes herself, stating
that slavery always constitutes an untenable human
condition: 'Supposing that women are voluntary
slaves—slavery of any kind is unfavourable to human
happiness and improvement'. (77). Then she purportedly quotes from an essay by a contemporary, Vicesimus
Knox, as follows:

> The subjects of these self-erected tyrants [i.e., those
> who establish what norm of human affairs will be, ei-
> ther 'some rich, gross, unphilosophical man, or some
> titled frivolous lady, distinguished for boldness, but not
> for excellence'] are most truly slaves, though voluntary
> slaves; but as slavery of any kind is unfavourable to
> human happiness and improvement, I will venture to
> offer a few suggestions, which may induce the subju-
> gated tribes to revolt, and claim their invaluable birth-
> right, their natural liberty.
>
> (77)

However, as it turns out, Wollstonecraft has altered
Knox's quotation to underscore her own political orientation. In his essay, Knox was not talking of women, let
alone calling them slaves.

Wollstonecraft's fiery response to female domination
echoed in Knox's essay—that women should act independently and ignore strictures—is probably why the
essay appeals so much to her. Entitled 'On the fear of
appearing singular', one of the essay's most telling passages encourages such (singular) thought, no matter the
consequences or the social ridicule:

It may not be improper to premise, that to one individual his own natural rights and possessions, of whatever kind, are as valuable as those of another are to that other. It is his own happiness which is concerned in his choice of principles and conduct. By these he is to stand, or by these to fall.

In making this important choice, then, let the sense of its importance lead him to assert the rights of man. These rights will justify him in acting and thinking, as far as the laws of that community, whose protection he seeks, can allow, according to the suggestions of his own judgment. He will do right to avoid adopting any system of principles, or following any pattern of conduct, which his judgment has not pronounced conducive to his happiness, and consistent with his duties; consistent with those duties which he owes to his God, to his neighbour, to himself, and to his society. Though the small circle with whom he is personally connected may think and act differently, and may even despise and ridicule his singularity, yet let him persevere. His duty to freedom, his conscience, and his happiness, must appear to every man, who is not hoodwinked, superior to all considerations.

(Knox, 1782: 21-2)

This sense of importance that Wollstonecraft attached to independent or singular thought—a cornerstone of bourgeois individualist ideology—helps to explain her apparent lack of emotional solidarity with the white women she roundly castigates throughout the second *Vindication.* Although her intentions are unreservedly positive—to restore natural rights to all women—her approach is not entirely compassionate. She sees all around her that women 'buy into' societal norms. Because she has resisted these norms and short-circuited her own social construction, she deplores women who have not followed suit.

This separation that Wollstonecraft maintains from other women prevents her from seeing the implications of women's response, especially in the common frivolous practices she condemns. She cannot see that flirting and vanity could have a positive dimension, could sometimes be deployed by these very women as strategies of resistance, as devious ways of assuming a measure of power. Wollstonecraft, instead, sees the trope of the coquette, for example, as exclusive evidence that women accept their inferiority. The following passage on Rousseau's ideas about women as sexual objects illustrates Wollstonecraft's dislike of teasing behaviour. 'Rousseau declares that a woman should never, for a moment, feel herself independent, that she should be governed by fear to exercise her natural cunning, and made a coquetish slave in order to render her a more alluring object of desire' (1792: 25). Wollstonecraft sees women as slaves to men not just because of male sexual lust, but because women enslave themselves through an obsession with fashion and an eager acceptance of inadequate education. She cannot see female foibles in any other context than female self-trivialization.

Furthermore, the blame that Wollstonecraft attaches to white women for their vanity is complicated by her assessment of the relationship between African women and dress:

> The attention to dress, therefore, which has been thought a sexual propensity, I think natural to mankind. But I ought to express myself with more precision. When the mind is not sufficiently opened to take pleasure in reflection, the body will be adorned with sedulous care; and ambition will appear in tattooing or painting it.

> So far is this first inclination carried, that even the hellish yoke of slavery cannot stifle the savage desire of admiration which the black heroes inherit from both their parents, for all the hardly earned savings of a slave are expended in a little tawdy finery. And I have seldom known a good male or female servant that was not particularly fond of dress. Their clothes were their riches; and, I argue from analogy, that the fondness for dress, so extravagant in females, arises from the same cause—want of cultivation of mind.

(1792: 186-7)[2]

Wollstonecraft equates self-conscious dressing with lack of intellectuality. In doing so, she reveals her own acceptance (and construction) as a contemporary woman, bombarded by and receptive to such ideas about Africans as David Hume's:

> There never was a civilized nation of any other complexion than white, nor even any individual eminent either in action or speculation. No ingenious manufactures amongst them, no arts, no sciences. . . . Such a uniform and constant difference could not happen, in so many countries and ages, if nature had not made an original distinction betwixt these breeds of men.

(Hume, 1898: III, 252)[3]

Wollstonecraft does not take into account either white women's resentment about powerlessness, their displacement of anger, their projection of personal power and pleasure, or, in the case of Africans and African Caribbeans, some customary cultural practices.[4] Given, too, her protestations to Sophie Fuseli about her scrupulous conduct toward the Swiss painter, Henry Fuseli (and his toward Mary Wollstonecraft), her attack on coquetry might also betray a rather personal subtext.[5]

Wollstonecraft's views, then, of white women's behaviour in particular, and of sexual difference in general are complex and politically self-contradictory.[6] Justifiably, she thinks of herself positively breaking through social constraints while the vast majority of women conforms to a restrictive mandate. She sees this process continuing as a result of practices that reach back to antiquity:

> Man, from the remotest antiquity, found it convenient to exert his strength to subjugate his companion, and his invention to shew that she ought to have her neck bent under its yoke; she, as well as the brute creation, was created to do his pleasure.

(49)

These contentions parallel ideas expressed in Catherine Macaulay's *Letters on Education* where she argues that women are historically oppressed because of situation and circumstances; the only item distinctly separating men and women is physical strength which men have used to exercise freely their physical desires. The fine differences between them seem to be as follows: Catherine Macaulay wants women to stop being giddy but recognizes their social construction. At one level, Wollstonecraft concurs with this and even uses the language of 'circumstances' to explain vain and flirtatious female behaviour. But she seems much less patient—more desperate even—with women's situation. Catherine Macaulay is calmer, less rhetorically intense in her analysis, perhaps because with a certain amount of middle-class privilege in her life, the situation has affected her less.

Wollstonecraft's argument from antiquity has further implications, too. She contends that this age-old subjugation for unspecified reasons enables men's desire to transform women into tools for sexual lust. These beaten-down women with bent necks resemble the brute creation, brute a synonym in contemporary vocabulary for slaves. Thus, white women, slaves and oxen become part of a metonymic chain of the tyrannized; this association of colonial slavery with female subjugation opens up new political possibilities. The bent yoke, for example, suggesting excessive maltreatment also suggests insecurity on the part of the oppressor, a combination that precipitates insurrection. The question that permeates the image is: who will eternally bear a brutelike status? Remember, too, that the San Domingan Revolution is less than a year old so Wollstonecraft's words inscribe a threat of resistance in them: 'History brings forward a fearful catalogue of the crimes which their cunning has produced, when the weak slaves have had sufficient address to over-reach their masters' (167).

Moreover, Wollstonecraft deliberately uses the language of slavery to define women's status: 'When, therefore, I call women slaves, I mean in a political and civil sense; for, indirectly they obtain too much power, and are debased by their exertions to obtain illicit sway' (167). This imposed status, this condition of subjugation provokes women into the flirtatious behaviour she dislikes, but also provokes duplicitous strategies of gaining power. In histories of slave insurrections, the ear of the master—necessary for finding things out and for facilitating the timing of rebellions—was frequently obtained through such 'illicit sway'. While decrying the domestic sabotage of coquetry, she affirms a time-honoured slave strategy and the need for resistance. Perhaps more importantly, Wollstonecraft is suggesting collective opposition, but can only do so through positing the resistance of slaves and the London mob. Put bluntly, to

suggest that women politically resist—although she herself does—only seems possible for Wollstonecraft at an oblique level, given her social conditioning.

Wollstonecraft also re-emphasizes that the historical subjugation of women is linked to male desire for sexual as well as political and social power. In doing so, she fuses the oppression of white women and black female slaves as well as slaves in general. A striking passage from *The Rights of Woman* based on the trope of sexual abuse exemplifies the point. It includes one of the few specific references to contemporary African slaves in *The Rights of Woman,* or in any of Wollstonecraft's texts for that matter.

> Why subject [woman] to propriety—blind propriety, if she be capable of acting from a nobler spring, if she be an heir of immortality? Is sugar always to be produced by vital blood? Is one half of the human species, like the poor African slaves, to be subject to prejudices that brutalize them, when principles would be a sure guard, only to sweeten the cup of man?

> (Wollstonecraft, 1792: 82-3)

The passage announces that slaves and white women are subjected to tyrannical practices that have no purpose beyond the paltry one of 'sweeten[ing] the cup of man'. On the one hand, slaves should not be expected to give 'vital blood' to produce sugar and cater to white British colonial-patriarchal whim and profiteering. On the other hand, the 'cup of man' symbolically intimates that a female (opponent) is doing the filling. This sexual innuendo is consistent with Wollstonecraft's complex socio-sexual discourse throughout *The Rights of Woman.* Wollstonecraft's awareness of the generic use of *man* further problematizes her provocative phraseology and the relationship she hints at between sweetening men's cup and 'poor African slaves'. If only as faint shadows, black female slaves and the specific kind of sexual persecution they endure are ushered into view, interjecting themselves as sexual victims. Aware of political and personal levels, Wollstonecraft subtly denotes sexuality as one of the 'prejudices' that brutalize white and black women alike. As Cora Kaplan suggests, 'We must remember to read *A Vindication [of the Rights of Woman]* as its author has instructed us, as a discourse addressed mainly to women of the middle class. Most deeply class-bound is its emphasis on sexuality in its ideological expression, as a mental formation, as the source of woman's oppression' (Kaplan, 1986: 48).

Sex and resistance interact. A coquette's cunning that can overpower (manipulate) men, links to subterfuges and plots by slaves, especially by black female slaves who double as objects of desire. Or at least Wollstonecraft might unconsciously recognize that undue attentiveness to one's person means that desire is suppressed and life is lived on almost self-destructive, self-contradictory planes; excess vanity is not as foolish as she superficially thinks. Thus sexuality becomes the site of black female and by implication white female resistance. Women use the very object of desire—themselves, their bodies—to thwart those who desire.

Wollstonecraft knows, too, that external forces cause sexual and racial difference. She articulates this understanding in a positive review of Samuel Stanhope Smith's *An Essay on the Causes of the Variety of Complexion and Figure in the Human Species* (1787). She agrees with Smith that climate and social conditions are the principal causes of difference among men and women throughout the world, but that, above and beyond these differences, human beings constitute a unity (Johnson, 1788: Vol. 2, 431-9).[7] She again pinpoints superior male physical strength as the reason for this ongoing situation.

Thus she denies the conservative argument of innate difference and necessary cultural separations—that God created essentially distinct beings.[8] Such subjected people as African-Caribbean slaves and white Anglo-Saxon women are *prevented* from developing and exercising their reason; certain environments have precipitated their alleged propensity for passion. Once again, Wollstonecraft is arguing opposing sides of a question. Whereas attention to dress proves that Africans, conceived in a totalized way, are an unmeditative people, in this reading they became people historically cut off from intellectual pursuit. With a change in circumstances, she argues, reason can replace alleged naiveté and infantilism.[9]

Wollstonecraft's intervention regarding sexually abused female slaves is not surprising. Through reviews and personal reading, Wollstonecraft was well attuned to this phenomenon. In 1789, a review of Equiano's *Travels* centre-stages her horror at 'the treatment of male and female slaves, on the voyage, and in the West Indies, which make the blood turn its course' (Johnson, 1789: 28). Equiano categorically indicts 'our clerks and many others at the same time [who] have committed acts of violence on the poor, wretched, and helpless females' (Equiano, 1789: 69). In chronicling his feelings on finally leaving Montserrat, Equiano harrows readers by undergirding his despondency, disgust, and (silently) his sense of impotence: 'I bade adieu to the sound of the cruel whip and all other dreadful instruments of torture; adieu to the offensive sight of the violated chastity of the sable females, which has too often accosted my eyes' (Equiano, 1789: 121).

Besides her intimacy with Equiano's first-hand experiences, Wollstonecraft has presented a paradigm of slavery in an extract on Inkle and Yarico in *The Female Reader*. Shipwrecked British merchant Inkle is rescued and nursed back to health by islander Yarico. After they

fall in love, Inkle promises to take Yarico to London and treat her royally, but when a rescue ship appears, Inkle cavalierly sells her to slave traders when their ship docks in Barbados. To top off his inhumanity, after Yarico pleads for mercy on account of her pregnancy, Inkle 'only made use of that information to rise in his demands upon the purchaser' (Wollstonecraft, 1789: 31).[10]

Hence, Wollstonecraft's subtle approach to the sexual abuse of black women in the 'vital blood' passage, in reviewing Equiano, in spotlighting that last look at a pregnant Yarico in an anthology for adolescent girls. Since her discourse as a white woman is already shockingly untraditional, to speak sex, and of all things to speak openly of black women's sexuality and hint at abuse suffered at the hands of white planters, would be an untenable flouting of social propriety. She has to maintain a semblance of conventional gender expectations.

On the site of the body and sex, then, Wollstonecraft foregrounds the relationship between black and white women and their common point of rebellion. At one point even, referring to women as 'brown and fair', meaning dark and fair-haired white women most likely, slippage and connexion between black and white women reopen a fissure of sorts for comparing overlapping oppressions. Slave auctions and the marriage market, for example, are represented as variations on activities that are life-threatening to African-Caribbean and Anglo Saxon women (Wollstonecraft, 1792: 144). None the less, Wollstonecraft acknowledges by her loaded silences that the representation of others' sexuality as well as sexual self-representation is a tricky business (Jordan, 1968: 150-4). Thus, in one sense, equal rights and a self-denying sexuality go hand in hand, because sexuality for Wollstonecraft (dictated at large by men) imperils any chances of female autonomy. Not only that, Wollstonecraft recognizes dissimilar codings for white female and bondwomen's bodies, differences in complicity and coercion. In keeping with her sense of singularity, she is much harder on middle-class white women, in part because she is closer to them. She does not feel affected by or implicated in female social conditioning. Unlike Catherine Macaulay who argues that women will only waken up if they understand their oppression, Wollstonecraft implicitly recommends imitation of her own bold behaviour as the 'wakening up' device. To recap briefly: all women have the same choices available as she did and should forego vanity and self-indulgence; they should break their 'silken fetters'. If she can short-circuit subjugation, her brief goes, so can anyone.

Thus beyond a rhetorical appeal to effect a revolution in female manners, Wollstonecraft tends to eschew a group response to the absence of female rights. This aloofness, furthermore, permeates—even undercuts—her sense of vindication. A buried sense of identification and solidarity expresses itself, instead, in a displaced way.

Specifically, Wollstonecraft talks about resistance only by talking about slaves. The successful revolution by slaves in San Domingo taught the British public that slaves and freed blacks could collectively overthrow systematic tyranny. In the following passage, by equating slaves with labouring class 'mobs' and using highly inflated diction for rebels, Wollstonecraft censures slaves' reaction. 'For the same reason', states Wollstonecraft, quoting from Jean-Jacques Rousseau, 'women have, or ought to have but little liberty; they are apt to indulge themselves excessively in what is allowed them. Addicted in every thing to extremes, they are even more transported at their diversions than boys.' She continues this response to Rousseau: 'The answer to this is very simple. Slaves and mobs have always indulged themselves in the same excesses, when once they broke loose from authority.—The bent bow recoils with violence, when the hand is suddenly relaxed that forcibly held it' (Wollstonecraft, 1792: 144-5).

Yet since Wollstonecraft disdains passivity and servitude, she may be embedding an unconscious desire about female resistance that corresponds to her own. She could be hinting that women should emulate the San Domingan insurgents and fight back. The nuance is further stressed pictorially by the sexual overtones of female compliance in 'bent bow'. Just as importantly, the image resonates with the previous textual image of women from earliest times when necks bent under a yoke.

Put succinctly, what slaves can do, white women can do; or, as she asserts in *The Rights of Woman*, authority and the reaction to it push the 'crowd of subalterns forward' (Wollstonecraft, 1792: 17). Sooner or later, tyranny incites retaliation. San Domingo instructs women about the importance of connecting physical and moral agency. Struggle creates a potential bridge from ignorance to consciousness and self-determination. In the most hard-hitting sense, the San Domingan revolutionaries loudly voice by their bold example—to anyone ready to listen—that challenge to oppression is not an option but a responsibility. The social and political status quo is anything but fixed.

Wollstonecraft's metaphor of the bent bow also decrees a stern warning to men. It reminds readers that male tyrants and predators incite their own opposition; at some point those who are 'bowed' may uncoil themselves and assault the 'bender'.

This image of the bent bow further recalls Wollstonecraft's own situation in the last decade. Undeterred by an emotionally unnerving home life, she tried her hand at most of the humdrum occupations open to women, refusing to be moulded or deterred by social prescription. Befriending and being befriended by Dissenters like Richard Price only fortified Wollstonecraft's already firm opposition to women's lot. Moreover, her subtle, analogous and multiply voiced threats address at least two major audiences. She overtly advises women to educate themselves and warns men that vengeance can strike from several directions. The fierce, conservative reaction to *A Vindication of the Rights of Woman* is a response to the covert as well as the overt text.

In that sense, the wheel comes almost full circle. Wollstonecraft recognizes that all women are opposed by all men in a general group identity. However, because she privileges personal and political singularity and takes pride in independent thought and action, she identifies her own resistance to gendered tyranny as the means by which women should subvert domination. She projects outwards from her personal response to female domination, oblivious to more devious practices on the part of other females to assert themselves and gain at least some personal if not political power. In one sense, her bourgeois individualism prevents that insight since she sees herself outside customary female assimilation. Faced with oppression, women have simply made wrong choices. Consequently, Wollstonecraft can posit collective rebellion by white women to prescribed subordination only by analogy.

With this displaced reaction in mind, certain re-views of Wollstonecraft's diatribe against female reactions to males—their flirtatious behaviour—can be more sympathetically read. Just as Wollstonecraft can indict Africans for being neither intellectual nor reflexive while portraying a carefully executed and successful revolution, so, too, does she exhibit a conflictual stance toward women. Since slaves resist masters and since all men oppress all women, women will, by implication, resist their male masters. Thus indirectly, Wollstonecraft registers that through coquettish manipulation, however feebly or distortedly, a women's resistance could be enacted.[11]

This argument about slaves and mobs, that is, creates a fissure in the text. If we doubled back, say, on salient passages where Wollstonecraft condemns Rousseau—'Women should be governed by fear', he says, 'to exercise her natural cunning and made a coquettish slave' (47)—Wollstonecraft's view of slaves' and mobs' resistances becomes open to reinterpretation: even though she assaults these self-trivializing behaviours and deplores their forms, at some level she may recognize them as tropes of insurrection; she uses female reaction to male domination in a plural way. Deploring how women try to finesse and please men through sexual manoeuvring, she rhetorically conflates coquettish with cunning and makes sexual manipulation double as a form of resistance to tyranny. Women 'play at' blind obedience not only to get some of what they want, but unconsciously to ridicule their 'masters' to cancel out tyranny with emotional excess, with a mirror-image perversion of power. Frivolous giggling is also a signal act of mimicry whereby women seem to conform to expectations. Ironically, the artificiality of forced laughing marks male desire and orthodox prescriptions for female behaviour.

If Wollstonecraft is (unconsciously or not) subtly mocking the idea that fear works as a governing principle to produce obedience, she foregrounds the idea that forced obedience linked to sex is a practice that can turn into its opposite: women will mimic the master's desire with design, they will use conformist ideas about womanhood to gain power. At times, Wollstonecraft recognizes these strategies more openly. The state of warfare which subsists between the sexes (races), makes them (the tyrannized group) employ those ruses or 'illicit sway' that often frustrate more open strategies of force.

The aim of *The Rights of Women,* then, is to vindicate women's rights. Starting from the premise that all women are oppressed by all men, Wollstonecraft subscribes to a concept of overall group identity. This is undercut, however, when she probes particulars because her sense of a personally wrought self-determination causes her to find women culpable for their vanity, their acceptance of an inferior education, their emphasis on feeling. She locates herself outside what she deems self-demeaning behaviour.

So in the end, she posits a group response indirectly, only by looking at oppressed communities who have actively resisted—slaves in particular—and sometimes 'mobs'. Her suppressed sense of solidarity and identification with women express themselves through the rebellion of slaves whose bow (back) has been bent too far. This analogy also constitutes a threat against masters; contradiction is there from the beginning since all men are oppositional—within Wollstonecraft's political framework—to all women.

Put another way, Mary Wollstonecraft's construction within specific social and cultural boundaries that she resists produces a covert text. Her sense of personal singularity occludes her vision so she cannot always imagine or conceptualize flirtation as a tool of resistance. Despite a radical outlook, moreover, she still subscribes to a sense of class hierarchy that contradicts her demands for greater distribution of wealth and legal representation and for female independence and colonial emancipation. In that sense, her text brilliantly illuminates the bourgeois project of liberation. She embodies the liberal ideal of progress in demanding freedom in certain individuals but the shortcomings inherent in that ideal undercut it. The conditions that produced the

text, then, end up questioning the text itself and highlighting its gaps and incompletions, its long series of tensions between bourgeois values and issues of class, race, gender and desire. So deeply estranged from its internal conflicts is *The Rights of Woman* that it cannot ideologically fulfil itself; an authentic, workable solution to female subjugation is impossible. The text trips over itself, its variant vindications ideologically incompatible. As a result, contradiction emerges as a major textual coherence, problem-solving beyond reach.

Additionally, because the text invokes the French and San Domingan revolutions, the complexity of sexual difference, inequities perpetrated against Dissenters, and the abolition movement, textual implosions inevitably occur. Even while the text appears to dampen inflammatory ideas and underwrite the current system, liberating ideas erupt to refute the self-contradictory discourse of bourgeois feminism.

Thus the issues that Wollstonecraft avoids or bypasses end up hollowing and shaping the text into a new determination. She talks about disaffection, yet often blames women's alienation on their own behaviour; she poses the problem as one for which women bear responsibility. Her socio-cultural myopia leads her to misread resistance. Concurrently, she undermines her own argument through parallels between white women and black slaves. Moreover, the condition of women that she illumines pinpoints an important area of sexual difference and pushes the frontiers of this debate forward. Put baldly, the text ironically subverts the very bourgeois ideology it asserts (that creates alienation) and demands liberation despite the restrictive system it promotes.

Furthermore, Wollstonecraft's usage of colonial slavery as a reference point for female subjugation launches a new element into the discourse on women's liberation. No coincidence, then, that Charlotte Smith in *Desmond* (1792) and Mary Hays in *Memoirs of Emma Courtney* (1796) criticize colonial slavery along with discussions of women's rights; exploring popular controversies, they simultaneously allude to Wollstonecraft's innovative investigations and connexions. First of all, their inscription of colonial slavery presupposes the presence of women of colour and assumes a white, patriarchal class system as its common enemy. Second, it suggests unity among the colonized and their allies. Third, it centre-stages the question of sexuality in gender relations and stresses the ubiquity of sexual abuse in qualitatively different environments.

By theorizing about women's rights using old attributions of harem-based slavery in conjunction with denotations of colonial slavery, Wollstonecraft was a political pioneer, fundamentally altering the definition of rights and paving the way for a much wider cultural dialogue.

Notes

1. Writers as diverse as Katherine Philips, the Duchess of Newcastle, Aphra Behn, Mrs Taylor, Lady Chudleigh, Sarah Fyge Field Egerton, Anne Finch, the Countess of Winchelsea, Elizabeth Rowe, Elizabeth Tollett, and many more frequently employed the metaphor of slavery to express the subjugation of women; marriage was far and away the front-runner situation in which women described themselves or other women as 'enslaved'. Note also that Wollstonecraft refers to the Spartan's perpetual subjugation in Lacedaemonian society of the Helots, state serfs bound to the soil, with no political rights. See Shimron (1972: 96), Mitchell (1952: 75-84), and MacDowell (1986: 23-5, 31-42).

2. Wollstonecraft does not hold exclusively to those attitudes, however. In the *Analytical Review* somewhat later, for example, she argues that Hottentot people act in harmony with their situation (*Analytical Review* Vol. 25, May 1797, p. 466).

3. The essay was first published in 1742, but the passage quoted was added as a footnote in the edition of 1753-4. See Cook (1936) and Curtin (1964: 42).

4. Mary Prince, for example, as a slave in Bermuda and then in Antigua is described by a vitriolic writer in a pro-slavery newspaper article. The trunk of her only worldly possessions (containing unspecified items) that she took from her owner when she left is exaggerated by this writer to 'several trunks of clothes' to suggest excess vanity and even prostitution. 'She at length left his house, taking with her several trunks of clothes and about 40 guineas in money, which she had saved in Mr. Wood's service' (Zuill, 1937: 37).

5. Attentiveness to appearance, across cultures and stemming from different origins, infuriates Wollstonecraft. The fact that her own appearance is negatively commented upon at this time suggests itself as a factor that enters in. Apparently she spruced herself up when she became infatuated with Henry Fuseli, the Swiss painter. See Flexner (1972: 138-9).

6. For Wollstonecraft's views on Eros and her anger at women as sexual objects for men, see Blake (1983: 103-4).

7. See also Smith (1787).

8. Hannah More's renowned opinions on women constitute one of Mary Wollstonecraft's significant textual silences, but most notably in the second *Vindication*. When Wollstonecraft vociferously applauds women's assuming more prominent sociocultural roles, she implicitly intertextualizes More's opposition to this advice. See also Myers (1990: 260-2).

9. However, despite Wollstonecraft's argument that ethnic differences are due to climate and social conditions à la Stanhope Smith and her unilateral commitment to abolition, she remains ambivalent about black equality. Her acceptance of a system that operates on the differential between owners and workers and on the basis of certain assumptions about European superiority can never square with an absolute human liberation. Everything is measured against the model of a European society that regards African society as the other. Wollstonecraft may Eurocentrically contend that people in other cultures would be smart and civilized if they were raised as she was, but her review of Olaudah Equiano's narratives gives the lie even to that belief:

    We shall observe, that if these volumes do not exhibit extraordinary intellectual powers, sufficient to wipe off the stigma, yet the activity and ingenuity, which conspicuously appear in the character of Gustavus, [i.e., Equiano] place him on a par with the general mass of men, who fill the subordinate factions in a more civilized society than that which he was thrown into at his birth.

    (*Analytical Review* Vol. 4, May 1789, p. 28)

10. Aside from her commentary on Equiano's and Yarico's experiences, among others, Wollstonecraft also recognizes other ways that sexuality oppresses white women. She had dealt on a personal level with her sister Eliza's post-partum depression by effecting Eliza's separation from her husband, Hugh Skeys. She felt, it seems, as if Skeys were responsible for her sister's condition; she treated him, more or less, as a male predator, a villain of sorts. At the same time, the *Rights of Woman* appeared at a time in her life when she was immersed in a difficult personal situation; the choices open to a woman who wants to work and to love—she was discovering—were very limited.

11. Remember too that, psychologically, Wollstonecraft's attack on male sexuality could mark a displaced attack on Fuseli whose male sexuality has engendered inner turmoil. Mary Poovey's argument that 'men's [and not women's] unsatiable appetites' are Wollstoncraft's target is worth considering in the light of her passion for the Swiss painter (Poovey, 1984: 71-6 and *passim*). See also discussions of displacement in Freud (1966: 155-6 and *passim*).

References

Blake, Kathleen (1983) *Love and the Woman Question in Victorian Literature. The Art of Self-Postponement* Totowa, NJ: Barnes & Noble.

Burke, Edmund (1790) *Reflections on the Revolution in France* London: reprinted (1961); New York: Doubleday.

Clarkson, Thomas (1808) *The History of the Rise, Progress, and Accomplishment of the Abolition of the Slave-Trade by the British Parliament* Vol. 1, London: Longman, Hurst, Rees & Orme.

Cook, M. (1936) 'Jean Jacques Rousseau and the Negro' *Journal of Negro History* XXI, 294-303.

Coupland, Sir Reginald (1933) *The British Anti-Slavery Movement* London: Frank Cass & Co. Ltd.

Craton, Michael (1974) *Sinews of Empire. A Short History of British Slavery* New York: Anchor Books.

Curtin, Philip D. (1964) *The Image of Africa: British Ideas and Action, 1780-1850* Madison: University of Wisconsin Press.

Equiano, Olaudah (1789) *The Interesting Narrative of the Life of Olaudah Equiano or Gustavus Vassa, the African. Written by Himself* Vol. 1, London: by the author; reprinted in Edwards, Paul (1967) editor *Equiano's Travels. His Autobiography. The Interesting Narrative of the Life of Olaudah Equiano or Gustavus Vassa the African* London: Heinemann.

Ferguson, Moira (1985) *First Feminists: British Women Writers 1578-1799* Bloomington: Indiana University Press.

Flexner, Eleanor (1972) *Mary Wollstonecraft. A Biography* New York: Coward, McCann & Geohegan, Inc.

Freud, Anna (1966) *The Ego and the Mechanisms of Defence* New York: International Universities Press.

Graham, Catherine Macaulay (1974) *Letters of Education. With Observations on Religions and Metaphysical Subjects* intro. Gina Luria, New York and London: Garland Publishing Inc.

Green, T. H. and Grose, T. M. (eds) *Essays Moral, Political and Literary* Longmans, Green & Co.

Hume, David (1889) 'Of national character' in Green and Grose.

James, C. L. R. (1963) *The Black Jacobins. Toussaint L'Ouverture and the San Domingo Revolution* New York: Vintage.

Johnson, Joseph (1788, 1789) editor *The Analytical Review, or History of Literature, Domestic and Foreign, on an Enlarged Plan. Containing Scientific Abstracts of important and interesting Works, published in English; a general account of such as are of less consequence, with short characters; Notices, or Reviews of valuable foreign Books; Criticisms on New Pieces of Music and Works of Art; and the Literary Intelligence of Europe* London: Joseph Johnson.

Jordan, Winthrop D. (1968) *White Over Black: American Attitudes Toward the Negro, 1552-1812* Chapel Hill: University of North Carolina Press.

Kaplan, Cora (1986) *Sea Changes: Essays on Culture and Feminism* London: Verso.

Klingberg, Frank J. (1926) *The Anti-Slavery Movement in England. A Study in English Humanitarianism* New Haven: Yale University Press.

Knox, Vicesimus (1782) 'On the fear of appearing singular' *Essays Moral and Literary. A New Edition of Two Volumes* Vol. 1, No. 5, London: Charles Dilly.

Macdowell, Douglas M. (1986) *Spartan Law* Edinburgh: Scottish Academic Press.

Mitchell, H. (1952) *Sparta* London: Cambridge University Press.

Myers, Sylvia Harcstark (1990) *The Bluestocking Circle. Women, Friendship, and the Life of the Mind in Eighteenth-Century England* Oxford: Clarendon Press.

Poovey, Mary (1984) *The Proper Lady and the Woman Writer. Ideology as Style in The Works of Mary Wollstonecraft, Mary Shelley, and Jane Austen* Chicago: University of Chicago Press.

Price, Richard (1790) *A Discourse on the Love of Our Country, Delivered on Nov. 4, 1789, at the Meeting-House in the Old Jewry, to the Society for Commemorating the Revolution in Great Britain with an Appendix containing the Report of the Committee of the Society: an Account of the Population of France; and the Declaration by the National Assembly of France. Third Edition, with Additions to the Appendix, Containing Communications from France Occasioned by the Congratulatory Address of the Revolution Society to the National Assembly of France with the Answers to them* Dublin: T. Cadell.

Salzmann, Christian Gotthilf (1790) *Elements of Morality for the Use of Children* London: Joseph Johnson.

Shimron, Benjamin (1972) *Late Sparta. The Spartan Revolution 243-146 B.C.* Arethusa Monographs III, Buffalo: State University of New York, Department of Classics.

Smith, Samuel Stanhope (1787) *An Essay on the Causes of the Variety of Complexion and Figure in the Human Species. To which are added, Animadversions on certain Remarks made on the first edition of this Essay, by Mr. Charles White, in a series of Discourses delivered before the Literary and Philosophical Society of Manchester in England. Also, Strictures on Lord Kaims' Discourse on the Original Diversity of Mankind,* New York; second ed. New Brunswick: J. Simpson and Co.; New York: Williams & Whiting, 1810.

Sunstein, Emily (1975) *A Different Face. The Life of Mary Wollstonecraft* New York: Harper & Row.

Tomalin, Claire (1974) *The Life and Death of Mary Wollstonecraft* New York and London: Harcourt Brace Jovanovich.

Wollstonecraft, Mary (1787) *Thoughts on the Education of Daughters with Reflections on Female Conduct, in the more Important Duties of Life* London: Joseph Johnson.

————. (1788) *Mary, A Fiction* London: Joseph Johnson; reprinted as *Mary and the Wrongs of Women* (1976), editor Gary Kelly, Oxford: Oxford University Press.

————. (1789) *The Female Reader; Or Miscellaneous Pieces in Prose and Verse; Selected from the Best Writers, and Disposed Under Proper Heads; for the Improvement of Young Women. By Mr. Cresswick, Teacher of Elocution to Which is Prefixed a Preface, Containing Some Hints of Female Education* London: printed for Joseph Johnson.

————. (1790) *A Vindication of the Rights of Men, in a Letter to the Right Honorable Edmund Burke; Occasioned by His Reflections on the Revolution in France* 2nd. ed., London: printed for Joseph Johnson.

————. (1792) *A Vindication of the Rights of Women* London: Joseph Johnson.

Zuill, William (1937) *Bermuda Samples 1815-1850: Being a Collection of Newspaper Items, Extracts from Books and Private Papers, together with many Explanatory Notes and A Variety of Illustrations,* Bermuda: Bermuda Book Stores; rpt. Bungay, Suffolk: Richard Clay & Son.

Tom Furniss (essay date summer 1993)

SOURCE: Furniss, Tom. "Nasty Tricks and Tropes: Sexuality and Language in Mary Wollstonecraft's *Rights of Woman. Studies in Romanticism* 32, no. 2 (summer 1993): 177-209.

[*In the following essay, Furniss offers a deconstructionist reading of* A Vindication of the Rights of Woman *and questions its relevance for modern struggles for rights.*]

The following discussion of Mary Wollstonecraft's **Rights of Woman** necessarily raises general questions about the textual analysis of texts which have become important in the history of a political movement. It is intended as a deconstructive reading of **Rights of Woman** which traces and analyzes the contradictions of its project by situating it within a network of texts which constitutes one of its discursive contexts. In this way, it attempts to restage the text's crucial intervention in the Revolution Controversy and its bid to influence the deliberations of the National Assembly. But although the reading thereby suggests that Wollstonecraft's feminism can be partly understood as an extension of an essentially middle-class struggle for, and theory about, the "rights of man," this is not to judge the text from a historical moment which "knows better" (for one thing, "middle class" means differently now than it did at the end of the eighteenth century). One of the consequences of the following reading, therefore, is implicitly to question the supposition that **Rights of Woman** contains a "relevance" which can be unproblematically extracted and appropriated for contemporary struggles which are at once continuous with it and crucially different. To search this text for relevance is potentially to fail to recognize its *difference* (from itself as well as from ourselves), and hence overlook the challenges it can pose to sympathetic and unsympathetic readers alike. As Gillian Beer argues, "The encounter with the otherness of earlier literature can allow us to recognize and challenge our own assumptions" as well as "those of the society in which we live."[1]

One of the most significant political lessons we are still learning from deconstruction is that no position is immune from or able to stand outside of the unpredictable "tricks" of the textuality it encounters. It is especially important for the discourse and criticism of radical politics to open itself to this possibility, since it habitually claims to ground itself in some reality or truth outside discourse. Producing gaps and contradictions in the texts of the past which have been assigned the warning label "reactionary" has come to be seen as a radical reading practice, yet all too often such reading strategies are carried out as if from a place of safety—on the assumption, perhaps, that if we take the necessary precautions we will not be affected, or infected, by the texts we encounter. Beer suggests that such reading practices assume that we can stand outside history "like those late nineteenth-century doctors who described their patients and yet exempted themselves from the processes of disease and decay they described." We must ask ourselves, therefore, whether "Our necessary search for gaps, lacunae, as analytical tools may have the effect of privileging and defending us," allowing us to think that we read from a place of "authority and externality" (Beer 69). In other words, such guarded encounters with "reactionary" texts may end up repeating the reactionary position which they set out to read against and undo.

A radical reading, then, can neither simply condemn reactionary texts nor appropriate radical texts: "Radical reading is not a reading that simply assimilates past texts to our concerns but rather an activity that tests and de-natures our assumptions in the light of the strange languages and desires of past writing" (Beer 80). This is to acknowledge that texts actively affect the position from which they are read—that they might unsettle, or "read," the assumptions which are brought to bear upon them. This means that there are risks involved in producing radical readings of "reactionary" texts. Our reading of texts labelled "radical" will involve even greater risks in proportion to the extent that particular readings of such texts constitute the grounds of our own politics. But if we cannot avoid that risk (unless we abstain from reading and thinking altogether), and if we cannot limit these effects except by transforming our radicalism into a conviction criticism which unwittingly shares aspects of the conviction politics it seeks to criticize, then perhaps we ought to be alert to the ways a more "open" radicalism might result from such encounters with the otherness of other texts.[2]

To represent the relation between a reading and a text in terms of encounters and infections (and relations) is clearly to invoke, and be informed by, contemporary questions of sexuality and sexual politics. Such metaphors also inform—though in ways whose difference we must be open to—Wollstonecraft's reading of questions about sexuality and gender at the end of the eighteenth century. I will suggest that such metaphors come to inhabit Wollstonecraft's text partly through her encounter with the texts of Edmund Burke—in which, at different moments, women and revolutionary thought are figured and resisted as sources of an infection fatal to human and political constitutions. The irony, and the interest, of Wollstonecraft's critique of Burke is that while she identifies and criticizes this figurative pattern in Burke it also infects and energizes her attempt to isolate and resist it. A reading of Wollstonecraft's reading of Burke can therefore become an exemplary reading of the complexities of reading.

1. READING BURKE'S AESTHETICS AGAINST HIS POLITICS

One of the principal projects and strategies of Mary Wollstonecraft's *Vindication of the Rights of Woman* (1792) is to turn Rousseau's egalitarian principles against his negative characterization of women in *Emile* (1762).[3] The arguments of *Rights of Woman* are based on Wollstonecraft's answer to the recurrent question of whether inequality arises from nature or from culture. Wollstonecraft stresses throughout her text that the weakness and sensuality attributed to a certain class of women in eighteenth-century Europe are not part of their biological nature but the inevitable results of their education and social conditioning. She states her "profound conviction that the neglected education of my fellow creatures is the grand source of the misery I deplore, and that women, in particular, are rendered weak and wretched by a variety of concurring causes."[4] One of the central assumptions of *Rights of Woman* [*RW*] is that a transformation of education and social mores would bring about a transformation in women which would in turn transform the whole of social and politi-

cal life. Wollstonecraft thus offers her book as "a treatise . . . on female rights and manners" designed to counter the prevailing tendency to make women "alluring mistresses [rather] than affectionate wives and rational mothers" (*RW* 79).

But although the physical, intellectual, and moral debility of women is culturally produced and therefore susceptible of being transformed by cultural transformations, Wollstonecraft is at pains to stress that she does not intend to transgress the natural order of things:

> In the government of the physical world it is observable that the female in point of strength is, in general, inferior to the male. This is the law of Nature; and it does not appear to be suspended or abrogated in favour of woman. A degree of physical superiority cannot, therefore, be denied, and it is a noble prerogative! But not content with this natural preeminence, men endeavour to sink us still lower, merely to render us alluring objects for a moment.
>
> (*RW* 80)[5]

Not wishing to violate nature's law, Wollstonecraft wrestles with those cultural forces which extend and exploit natural differences through defining the feminine as a more than natural weakness. In thus attacking the predominant representation of women, Wollstonecraft implicitly concurs with the eighteenth century's negative valuation of the "feminine."[6] At the same time, however, she sets out to redefine "masculinity" as a set of "manly virtues" which, since they consist of "those talents and virtues, the exercise of which ennobles the human character," may be cultivated by both sexes. Since the acquisition of such virtues "raises females in the scale of animal being," Wollstonecraft expects that "all those who view [women] with a philosophic eye must, I should think, wish with me, that they may every day grow more and more masculine" (*RW* 80).

Although his name is relegated to the footnotes of *Rights of Woman,* the paradigms Wollstonecraft engages with and employs in these passages indicate that *Right of Woman* is a critical response to Edmund Burke as much as to Rousseau.[7] I want briefly to sketch how Wollstonecraft's *Vindication of the Rights of Men* (1790) exposes the way the politics of *Reflections on the Revolution in France* (1790) draws upon the aesthetics Burke develops in his *Philosophical Enquiry into the Origin of our Ideas of the Sublime and Beautiful* (1757/59). This will allow me to argue that Wollstonecraft's great insight in *Rights of Men* is that the political assumptions embedded in Burke's early aesthetics are inimical to the politics Burke appears to promote in *Reflections* towards the end of his life.[8]

In the *Philosophical Enquiry,* the aesthetic distinction between the sublime and the beautiful is underpinned by a distinction between masculine and feminine respectively. The beautiful (i.e. the feminine) is associated with relaxation and luxury and is represented as dangerously debilitating for the body. Burke claims that although beauty is alluring, it has potentially fatal effects on the human beings who cultivate or admire it. When we observe beauty, Burke argues, we experience "an inward sense of melting and languor"; this is because "beauty acts by relaxing the solids of the whole system."[9] The consequences of this relaxation are quite alarming since it "not only disables the members from performing their functions, but takes away the vigorous tone of fibre which is requisite for carrying on the natural and necessary secretions." Even more alarming is the suggestion that

> in this languid and inactive state, the nerves are more liable to the most horrid convulsions, than when they are sufficiently braced and strengthened. Melancholy, dejection, despair, and often self-murder, is the consequence of the gloomy view we take of things in this relaxed state of body.
>
> (*PE* 135)

Immediately prior to this, Burke argues that terror—the primary source of the sublime—induces "an unnatural tension and certain violent emotions of the nerves" which produces pain accompanied by a delight which is utterly different from the pleasure associated with the beautiful (*PE* 134). The bracing effects of the sublime (i e. the masculine) is thus constituted as the most effective preventative against the relaxing effects of the beautiful:

> The best remedy for all these evils is exercise or *labour*. . . . Now, as a due exercise is essential to the coarse muscular parts of the constitution, and that without this rousing they would become languid, and diseased, the very same rule holds with regard to those finer parts we have mentioned [i.e. the imagination and the other "mental powers"]; to have them in proper order, they must be shaken and worked to a proper degree.
>
> (*PE* 135)

Frances Ferguson shows how *Philosophical Enquiry* implicitly suggests that the beautiful is equally dangerous for the body politic and for the body, and that the antidote for both is the same—the "masculine" exertions involved in the sublime.[10] Reading between the lines here, Burke seems to be suggesting that society, and each member of that society, can only resist or prevent "horrid convulsions" by being "shaken and worked to a proper degree."

In *Reflections,* on the other hand (as Wollstonecraft was the first to point out), Burke seems to abandon the political position implicit in this aesthetics. The most well-known instance of this is his defense of monarchical beauty in the person of Marie Antoinette, whose treat-

ment by the revolutionary crowd at Versailles on 5-6 October 1789 becomes a micro-drama of the Revolution's violation of the *ancien régime.* Shortly before his celebration of the queen's beauty, Burke has her escaping "almost naked" from a "band of cruel ruffians and assassins" who invade her chamber.[11] This becomes the occasion for Burke's lament for the passing of the age of chivalry—a code of behavior which ought to be valued because,

> Without force, or opposition, it subdued the fierceness of pride and power; it obliged sovereigns to submit to the soft collar of social esteem, [and] compelled stern authority to submit to elegance.
>
> (170-71)

In other words, whereas the beautiful in *Philosophical Enquiry* is alluring but potentially fatal to body and body politic alike, in *Reflections* it is presented as a crucial corrective to the sublime aspects of political power. Curiously, the beautiful is explicitly presented as a set of "pleasing illusions" constituting a necessary supplement or fiction figured as a drapery which the Revolution threatens to tear away:

> All the decent drapery of life is to be rudely torn off. All the super-added ideas, furnished from the wardrobe of a moral imagination, which the heart owns, and the understanding ratifies, as necessary to cover the defects of our naked shivering nature . . . are to be exploded as a ridiculous, absurd, and antiquated fashion.
>
> (*Refs* 171)

If this passage makes an analogy between the fate of the queen at Versailles and that of European civilization as a whole (in that both are left exposed and vulnerable), the consequences of this are concentered in the change in the way men will henceforth regard women:

> On this scheme of things, a king is but a man; a queen is but a woman; a woman is but an animal; and an animal not of the highest order. All homage paid to the sex in general . . . is to be regarded as romance and folly.
>
> (*Refs* 171)

If a particular kind of woman (or way of regarding women) forms a paradigm of that which is being destroyed by the Revolution, another, seemingly very different, class of women epitomizes the most uncontrollable forces of destruction. As a prelude to his eulogy of Marie Antoinette and lament for the passing of the political culture she represents, Burke figures the Revolution's chief protagonists as a set of lower class women more brutal and inhuman than their male counterparts (*Refs* 159-65). In Burke's text, these women are not only the unrepresented (because of their class and sex), but the *unrepresentable*—an excess which society would overlook and exclude but which nevertheless returns with a vengeance. Since, for Burke (as for Rousseau), women's power over men ought to derive from weakness rather than strength (see *Emile* 322), the "brutal" behavior of these "masculine" women represents a terrifying revolution in manners.

I have reviewed these passages in *Reflections,* which are almost too well-known, in order fully to register how insightful Wollstonecraft's readings of Burke are and how these readings have a crucial impact on the feminist assumptions developed in **Rights of Woman.** In her two Vindications, Wollstonecraft directly encounters the sexualized nature of Burke's representation of *ancien régime* politics and aesthetics. Wollstonecraft endorses Burke's negative conception of feminine beauty in *Philosophical Enquiry* in order to remount the critique of the *ancien régime* which is implicit in that text, and to turn its aesthetic theory against the politics of *Reflections.* If, in *Reflections,* Burke laments the passing of the age of chivalry, Wollstonecraft celebrates and hastens that passing; if Burke is terrified by the prospect of "masculine" women and eulogizes Marie Antoinette as a feminine icon, Wollstonecraft would eliminate (through their own exertions) the "femininity" of monarchs, aristocracy, soldiers, and so on, as well as that of fashionable women.

Wollstonecraft's attempt to rewrite Burke's aesthetics is central to this project. Although her politics lead her to value the sublime as an aesthetic which promotes individual exercise and labor, the philosophical basis of that politics also impels her to claim that reason, far from being antithetical to the sublime, as Burke argues, is the most sublime of human faculties. In addition, she attempts to articulate a "good," almost neoclassical conception of the beautiful to set in opposition to "feminine" beauty. This radical recasting of Burke's aesthetics begins in the opening pages of **Rights of Men** [*RMen*]:

> truth, in morals, has ever appeared to me the essence of the sublime; and in taste, simplicity the only criterion of the beautiful.

> truly sublime is the character that acts from principle, and governs the inferior springs of action without slackening their vigour.[12]

Responding to Burke's anxiety that the revolution in manners which took place on 5-6 October 1789 exposes woman as an animal not of the highest order and transforms homage to women in general into romance and folly, Wollstonecraft counters that it is courtly homage itself, rather than revolutionary politics, which reduces women's humanity: "such homage vitiates them, prevents their endeavouring to obtain solid personal merit; and, in short, makes those beings vain inconsiderate dolls" (*RMen* 54). The feminine beauty cultivated by and characteristic of the *ancien régime* is, for Wollstonecraft, mere "animal perfection" (*RMen* 114).

One of the effects, she suggests, of *Philosophical Enquiry* is to induce women themselves to cultivate this debilitating image of the beautiful by convincing them "that *littleness* and *weakness* are the very essence of beauty" (*RMen* 112). But the crucial point here is that Wollstonecraft's understanding of both feminine beauty, which "relaxes the *solids* of the soul as well as the body" (*RMen* 115), and her antidote to it, concurs with Burke's in *Philosophical Enquiry*:

> you have clearly proved that one half of the human species, at least, have not souls; and that Nature, by making women *little, smooth, delicate, fair* creatures, never designed that they should exercise their reason to acquire the virtues that produce opposite, if not contradictory, feelings.

> (*RMen* 113-14)

In fact, as an antidote to feminine beauty, Wollstonecraft's "good" beauty might also be called "manly" beauty—since it is characterized and brought about, like the sublime, through exertion. Wollstonecraft points out that the logical consequence of Burke's analysis of the beautiful in *Philosophical Enquiry* ought to be that "we must endeavour to banish all enervating modifications of beauty from civil society" (*RMen* 115), but she imagines and sponsors a quite different kind of beauty to this which would be beneficial to human and political constitutions:

> should experience prove that there is a beauty in virtue, a charm in order, which necessarily implies exertion, a depraved sensual taste may give way to a more manly one—and *melting* feelings to rational satisfactions.

> (*RMen* 116)

This "manly" beauty, however, can only be achieved in an egalitarian society and so Wollstonecraft looks forward to what the members of the National Assembly can achieve through "active exertions that were not relaxed by a fastidious respect for the beauty of rank" (*RMen* 117).

Of particular importance for the following discussion of **Rights of Woman** is the way **Rights of Men** distinguishes these different kinds of beauty as the naked and the clothed:

> Is hereditary weakness necessary to render religion lovely? and will her form have lost the smooth delicacy that inspires love, when stripped of its Gothic drapery? . . . is there no beauteous proportion in virtue, when not clothed in a sensual garb?

> Of these questions there would be no end, though they lead to the same conclusion;—that your politics and morals, when simplified, would undermine religion and virtue to set up a spurious, sensual beauty, that has long debauched your imagination, under the specious form of natural feelings.

> (*RMen* 120-21)

Wollstonecraft seems, then, to share Rousseau's impulse to "strip man's nature naked."[13] This is driven by an anxiety that although the pleasing illusions of life may be figured as if they were merely clothes ("Gothic drapery," "sensual garb"), they work to surreptitiously "undermine" the human forms and/or institutions they seem to decorate or protect and to "debauch" the imagination which contemplates them.

2. DEFLOWERING THE LANGUAGE

The necessity of Wollstonecraft's celebration of the "manly" is clear in that it forms a paradigm by which radicalism can differentiate its political structures and theories of language from those corrupted and corrupting forms which it identifies as characteristic of the *ancien régime*. In the second Vindication the notion of the "manly" allows Wollstonecraft to rescue a certain class of women ("those in the middle class, because they appear to be in the most natural state" [*RW* 81]) from women's association with the corruptions of a feminized *ancien régime*—as well as from the regime of sexual difference itself. Such women are presented as being able to realize, through self-effort and through a different political system and culture, their "true" nature (which, like men's, is a "manly" blend of rationality and authentic feeling).

In defining her program to encourage women toward such attainments, and in her reasons for doing so, Wollstonecraft's reading of Burke's *Philosophical Enquiry* becomes apparent:

> I wish to persuade women to endeavour to acquire strength, both of mind and body, and to convince them that the soft phrases, susceptibility of heart, delicacy of sentiment, and refinements of taste, are almost synonymous with epithets of weakness, and that those beings who are only the objects of pity, and that kind of love which has been termed its sister, will soon become objects of contempt.
>
> (*RW* 82)

That reference to "soft phrases" indicates how much Wollstonecraft's project is bound up with questions of language and suggests that her conceptions about language are gendered according to the gender codes she inherits from reactionary and radical discourse alike. Unexpectedly concurring with Hamlet's vitriolic attack on women, Wollstonecraft asserts that they sacrifice "strength of body and mind . . . to libertine notions of beauty," that their desire merely to marry well makes animals of them, and that "when they marry they act as such children may be expected to act—they dress, they paint, and nickname God's creatures." The "pretty superlatives" current in fashionable society "vitiate the taste, and create a kind of sickly delicacy that turns away from simple unadorned truth" (*RW* 83, 82).[14] Thus it is possible to see that figurative analogies are being

developed in *Rights of Woman* between sexuality, political systems, and rhetorical language. All three domains are discussed in terms of the relationship between dress and body, and in all three Wollstonecraft's politics impel her to distrust the clothed and to valorize the unadorned.

This necessarily leads Wollstonecraft into a consideration of her own rhetorical practice:

> Animated by this important object, I shall disdain to cull my phrases or polish my style. I aim at being useful, and sincerity will render me unaffected; for wishing rather to persuade by the force of my arguments than dazzle by the elegance of my language, I shall not waste my time in rounding periods, or in fabricating the turgid bombast of artificial feelings, which, coming from the head, never reach the heart. I shall be employed about things, not words! and, anxious to render my sex more respectable members of society, I shall try to avoid that flowery diction which has slided from essays into novels, and from novels into familiar letters and conversations.
>
> (*RW* 82)

Wollstonecraft's concern to deflower her language here draws on a general set of assumptions about language and its relation to politics articulated in the discourse of radical politics at the end of the eighteenth century. We will see, however, that the claim to employ a straight-forward, transparent language as part of a critique of the "false" rhetoric through which the old order maintained power (a claim which has been reiterated by radical thought across history) is a founding rhetorical gesture in what is actually a densely and complexly rhetorical text—an enabling fiction which potentially undermines the distinction between radical and reactionary discourse it is used to establish.[15]

Although *Rights of Women* can be read as a critique of male-centered radicalism which turns its egalitarian principles against its failure to extend them to women,[16] there are many similarities between Wollstonecraft's Vindications and Paine's *Rights of Man*—the second part of which was published almost simultaneously with *Rights of Woman*. Both make the rhetorical gesture of discarding rhetoric in the process of criticizing the false rhetoric of the old order, and both figure the adornments of the *ancien régime* as feminine and dangerous. Both prescribe the same panacea—the masculinization of society through fundamental reforms in politics, language, aesthetics, and ethics. This process can be seen, for example, in Paine's critique of monarchy:

> what is called monarchy, always appears to me a silly, contemptible thing. I compare it to something kept behind a curtain, about which there is a great deal of bustle and fuss, and a wonderful air of seeming solemnity; but when, by any accident, the curtain happens to be open, and the company see what it is, they burst into laughter.
>
> (*RMan* 204)

In contrast to this,

> In the representative system of government, nothing of
> this can happen. Like the nation itself, it . . . presents
> itself on the open theatre of the world in a fair and
> manly manner. Whatever are its excellencies or its de-
> fects, they are visible to all. It exists not by fraud and
> mystery . . . but inspires a language, that, passing
> from heart to heart, is felt and understood.

> (*RMan* 204)

Paine's figuration of monarchy—in terms of its displacement of affect onto dress—aligns it with Burke's
and Rousseau's representation of femininity, whereas
representative government is at once "fair and manly."
The "manly" representative system stands naked on the
world's stage, openly displaying its own excellencies
and defects (in marked contrast to Burke's desire to
cover the "defects" of our naked shivering nature). Behind monarchy's implicitly feminine veils, on the other
hand, Paine hints that there is nothing to see at all.

For Paine and Wollstonecraft, then, "masculine" and
"feminine" are paradigms for two opposed systems of
thought and practice. The feminine characterizes the
ancien régime in a range of ways which become cor-
relatives of one another: its language is ornate and polished but lacks both force and a motivated relation to
"reality"; its political arrangements are said to be based
on little more than a conventional, though mysticized
relation between rulers and ruled (in which the masses
are seduced into submission by ceremonies and splendor, and in which the signs of authority—robes, ornamentation, custom—dazzle the sense and distract attention from the lack of substance behind them). The
converse and antidote of these is the "manly"—that
which is on open display, which says what it means,
and is genuinely representative without reserve or
equivocation.[17]

And yet the company's burst of laughter in Paine's text
is perhaps an uneasy one. For although representative
government is on open display, Paine's figure does not
quite reveal the whole truth about monarchy. We are assured that we would laugh if we accidentally saw behind the curtain, but we are not told what we would
laugh at. Paine's own figure thus turns out to conceal as
much as reveal, and his open, representational language,
"passing from heart to heart," seems unwittingly to repeat the deceptive structures it claims to expose. Paine's
language therefore retains its power of arousing speculation through a concealment analogous to the one he
criticizes. The attempt to distinguish the "sexual difference" of different governmental forms and between different rhetorical structures unexpectedly confuses the
difference between them. One of the concerns of the
present paper is to trace the way Wollstonecraft's texts
become entangled in their own particular version of this
endemic problem in late-eighteenth century radical
thought.

3. PRESCRIBING TO THE NATIONAL ASSEMBLY

We have seen that Wollstonecraft's argument is
grounded on the possibility that "masculine" and "feminine" are not anatomically determined, and that both
men and women are capable of achieving "manly" virtues through self-effort and education. The Protestant
work ethic, Enlightenment rationality, and the commercialization of society are combined in representing the
middle class capitalist ethos as a masculinization of society open to men and women alike. This is urgent for
Wollstonecraft, because the condition of women in
prerevolutionary societies is shown to be symptomatic
of an endemic cultural malaise. I want to begin this section by examining the way this set of assumptions informs Wollstonecraft's prescription for the National Assembly, in which she suggests that the continued
feminization of women would inevitably undermine the
new society being developed in France. This allows me
to argue that the repression of the feminine is for
Wollstonecraft both a means of liberating women and a
way of preventing women from undermining the bourgeois enterprise.

If the argument and concerns of **Rights of Woman** are
shaped by its response to Rousseau, Burke, and Paine,
Wollstonecraft's text also addresses itself to a still more
immediate political context. Wollstonecraft's dedication
of **Rights of Woman** to M. Talleyrand-Périgord shows
that her book is conceived not only as a treatise on female manners and language but as a practical political
intervention on behalf of women's rights. The National
Assembly was considering a national system of education with Rousseau as its principal inspiration, and
Talleyrand had prepared a report on public education
for the Constituent Assembly which had failed to extend Rousseau's egalitarian ideals to the equal education of women. This is why "In 1792 . . . between the
fall of the Bastille and the Terror when **A Vindication**
was written, it must have seemed crucial that Rousseau's
crippling judgement of female nature be refuted"
(Kaplan, "Pandora's Box" 156). Although
Wollstonecraft claims she has "read [Talleyrand's re-
port] with great pleasure," she finds it defective with regard to women's education and seeks to "induce" him
"to reconsider the subject and maturely weigh what I
have advanced respecting the rights of woman and national education" (**RW** 85).[18]

Wollstonecraft addresses the Assembly through
Talleyrand, thinking it "scarcely possible" that, having
read her treatise, "some of the enlarged minds who
formed your admirable constitution, will [not] coincide
with me" (**RW** 85). Indeed, Wollstonecraft's argument
in the dedication is eloquent and forceful; the principles
which make the rights of men irrefutable apply equally,
and with the same effect, to women:

> Consider, Sir, dispassionately, these observations, for a
> glimpse of this truth seemed to open before you when

you observed, "that to see one half of the human race excluded by the other from all participation of government, was a political phenomenon that, according to abstract principles, it was impossible to explain." If so, on what does your constitution rest? If the abstract rights of man will bear discussion and explanation, those of woman, by a parity of reasoning, will not shrink from the same test; though a different opinion prevails in this country, built on the very arguments which you use to justify the oppression of woman—prescription.

(*RW* 87)[19]

Thus, on the question of women's rights, even the Revolution seems to mimic Burke's recourse to the long usage of custom in order to justify things as they are. This style of argument is employed by "tyrants of every denomination," and "if women are to be excluded, without having a voice, from a participation of the natural rights of mankind," then "this flaw in your New Constitution will ever show that man must, in some shape, act like a tyrant" (*RW* 87 and 88). Thus, if the revolutionary government were to ignore the question of women's rights and education, it would build into its constitution the same "flaw" which had brought aristocratic society to its own crisis. This one prejudice (an opinion formed prior to reason) will necessarily prejudice (injure or impair) a constitution which claims to be formed upon principles of reason.[20] Thus Wollstonecraft closes her dedication with the request that "when your constitution is revised, the Rights of Woman may be respected" (*RW* 89).

4. Towards a Revolution in Female Manners

In the same moment that Wollstonecraft makes the unprecedented suggestion to the National Assembly that "women ought to have representatives" (which she expects will "excite laughter"), the potentially more radical implications of women's ambiguous place in prerevolutionary societies are touched upon:

> But, as the whole system of representation is now, in this country, only a convenient handle for despotism, [women] . . . need not complain, for they are as well represented as a numerous class of hard-working mechanics.

(*RW* 259, 260)

Such parallels between women and disenfranchised men continue throughout her text. Responding to Rousseau's suggestion that women should have "but little liberty [because] . . . they are apt to indulge themselves excessively in what is allowed them" (*Emile* 333), Wollstonecraft suggests that the reason for this tendency "is very simple":

> Slaves and mobs have always indulged themselves in the same excesses, when once they broke loose from authority. The bent bow recoils with violence, when the hand is suddenly relaxed that forcibly held it.

(*RW* 179)

Again answering Rousseau, Wollstonecraft says that his argument that some should not be educated like men is in "the same strain" as those of men who "argue against instructing the poor":

> "Teach them to read and write," say they, "and you take them out of the station assigned them by nature." An eloquent Frenchman has answered them, I will borrow his sentiments. "But they know not, when they make man a brute, that they may expect every instant to see him transformed into a ferocious beast."

(*RW* 154)

Elsewhere, and for similar reasons, Wollstonecraft likens women to "the poor African slaves," to "savages," and to "Butler's caricature of a dissenter" (*RW* 257, 311, 318). Regardless of which class they "properly" belong to, then, women have a political kinship with the most subjected or marginal groups in aristocratic societies. This is potentially to collapse the difference between queens and the women of the Revolution—though we will see that Wollstonecraft excludes both lower and upper class women from the revolution she envisages.

Wollstonecraft goes on to show that the analogy between women and the poor does not fully bring out the implications of Rousseau's objection to educating women:

> "Educate women like men," says Rousseau, "and the more they resemble our sex the less power they will have over us." This is the very point I aim at. I do not wish them to have power over men; but over themselves.

(*RW* 154; see *Emile* 327)

Women's "power" in Rousseau is paradoxically proportional to their educational inferiority to men. The relation between men and women is therefore not straightforwardly translatable into that between rich and poor because the sexuality of the relation introduces certain contradictions which subvert the apparent hierarchy.[21] For Patricia Parker the power which Sophie's weakness gives her over Emile "introduces . . . a crucial instability" into "the binary opposition of strength and passivity" (*Literary Fat Ladies* 203). In fact, Wollstonecraft's own text draws out the contradictory place of women in an aristocratic order, for if they are in many ways analogous to the oppressed and disenfranchised, women are also "a sex, who, like kings, always see things through a false medium"; a sex who "The passions of men have . . . placed . . . on thrones"; and a sex whose condition—since they are born "with certain sexual privileges"—is compared to that of "the rich" (*RW* 128, 146, 148). The situation and consequent effects of women and the rich are the same:

> Weak, artificial beings, raised above the common wants and affections of their race, in a premature unnatural

manner, undermine the very foundation of virtue, and spread corruption through the whole mass of society.

(*RW* 81)

As both Vindications recognize, and as Frances Ferguson theorizes, the danger of the beautiful—or of what Wollstonecraft identifies as "mistaken notions of beauty" (*RW* 182)—is that it can be contagious, surreptitiously recreating (and therefore undermining) the onlooker, and eventually a whole society, in its own image.[22]

Thus the obsessions and occupations women are educated to adopt allow parallels to be drawn between their condition and various central institutions of traditional society—including the monarchy, the aristocracy, military forces, and even the clergy.[23] In prerevolutionary societies, women occupy, precariously but perhaps subversively, the place at once of the highest and the lowest in society. They are equivalent both to the class which governs but does not represent, and to those classes which are unrepresented and unrepresentable. Dress, manners, custom, and chivalrous gallantry appear to keep up the distinction between women as monarchs and women as slaves, but are in fact precisely the means of enslaving women (and men) at one and the same time. These "pleasing illusions" seem to exalt women, but such exaltation is also their debasement. Such social mores render women equivocal, ambiguous, irresolvably oxymoronic—they are, Wollstonecraft ironically writes, "the fair defects in Nature" (*RW* 160).[24] Women so constituted are potentially disruptive of the society which constitutes them: akin at once to the monarchy and to the mob, they show how monarchy and mob might be mirror images of, or mutually implicated with, one another. By foregrounding and extrapolating the implications of such figurations of women, *Rights of Woman* thus shows how those images which have been identified as paradigmatic of aristocratic society also undermine its central institutions and hierarchies.

This is to offer a second opinion on Burke's diagnosis of the crisis in civilization facing Europe at the end of the eighteenth century. For Wollstonecraft, the disease is not French revolutionary thought (whose egalitarian principles are rather the antidote), but the maintenance of hierarchical institutions which have become prejudicial to society itself: "It is the pestiferous purple which renders the progress of civilization a curse," and the "baneful lurking gangrene is most quickly spread by luxury and superstition" (*RW* 99). This was Rousseau's diagnosis too, but he failed to realize that "the nature of the poison points out the antidote" (*RW* 99). In other words, for Wollstonecraft, the European crisis cannot be treated by reestablishing feminized institutions and manners, as Burke argued, nor by chaining women to femininity, as in Rousseau, but by instituting rational, egali-tarian—in a word, "manly"—political organizations and cultural codes. This radical revolution can only take place if it simultaneously transforms (through effort and education) gender roles as well as class divisions. This is why the burden of this text is to help "effect a revolution in female manners" in order that women might "labour by reforming themselves to reform the world" (*RW* 132).

5. Deconstructing Differences: Manners and Modesty

Part of Wollstonecraft's radical importance is that she tries to show that gender and sexuality—at least in the *ancien régime*—are not only socially constructed but have an unstable and shifting relation to biological sex. Femininity is neither a natural quality of the female sex, nor is it confined to that sex. Defined as an undue attachment to appearance (to pluming and plumage) rather than substance, femininity crosses gender divisions and begins to confuse them. It thus undermines the distinction between the sexes in a society which is in many ways founded on such distinctions. But although Wollstonecraft's antidote is to make women (and men) more "manly," her position is more ambivalent and potentially conservative than it would appear. Her description of sexuality in the *ancien régime* is an anxious one, but it is not clear that the problem would be resolved by introducing a different set of images or an alternative social structure. If "Riches and hereditary honours have made cyphers of women" (*RW* 106), then Wollstonecraft attempts utterly to distinguish between "secondary things," such as dress and ornamentation (*RW* 151), and that which ought to be primary and proper to women as human beings: women "have been stripped of the virtues that should clothe humanity, [and] have been decked with artificial graces that enable them to exercise a short-lived tyranny" (*RW* 121). But there are uncomfortable parallels here between the cause of the disease and its cure: for if women "have been *stripped* of the virtues that should *clothe* humanity" (my emphasis), virtue seems to be a custom or costume in much the same way as the "artificial graces" which women have been "decked with." Thus Wollstonecraft shies away from stripping woman naked—perhaps because she fears that behind the dress and before social conditioning there may be no essential self at all, merely (as Burke notoriously puts it) an animal not of the highest order.

Instead of simply stripping away the false ornaments which have corrupted them, then, Wollstonecraft also seeks to dress women more "wholesomely." In the dedication to Talleyrand, she distinguishes between manners and modesty: "a polish of manners . . . injures the substance by hunting sincerity out of society," while "modesty . . . [is] the fairest garb of virtue" (*RW* 86). According to this, neither manners nor morals—

neither "polish" nor "garb"—are intrinsic to the "substance" or "virtue" (of society or individual), but are *added to* it. Both, then, are supplements to what Burke calls "our naked . . . nature." For Wollstonecraft, the difference between modesty and manners is that the polish of manners "injures the substance," while the garb of modesty seemingly protects and reinforces it. Thus manners and modesty are distinguished in the way that Jacques Derrida finds Rousseau desperately trying to distinguish between the benign and the dangerous supplement.[25] Wollstonecraft is therefore caught up in the same problematic as Rousseau and Burke—though she would argue that both of them have offered the wrong solution by mistaking the dangerous for the benign supplement. For Wollstonecraft, such a "mistake" is peculiar to and characteristic of the historical and political moment she intervenes within:

> Manners and morals are so nearly allied that they have often been confounded; but, although the former should only be the natural reflection of the latter, yet, when various causes have produced factitious and corrupt manners . . . morality becomes an empty name.
>
> (*RW* 86)

In a healthy (middle class, egalitarian) society, then, manners are the "natural reflection" or authentic representation of morals and attain to a degree of naturalness in their own right. But although it is only in a diseased society that manners become "factitious and corrupt," the logic here suggests that such manners—making morality "an empty name"—are at once symptom and disease. Manners are presented as either a natural representation of morals or as destructive of morality. But it might be that this all-important distinction is one without a difference, since the relation of manners to morals, of representation to represented, is the same in each case. For dress is presented here as simultaneously that which undermines and that which defends body, mind, and state. Thus dress—and its range of equivalents: manners, decorum, habit, custom, modesty—functions according to the "strange economy of the supplement": "A terrifying menace, the supplement is also the first and surest protection; against that very menace."[26] In this way, the supplementary relation of dress to body—which society has made women's central obsession—means that women have become a paradigm for a whole cultural problematic.[27]

6. Maintaining Class and Sexual Difference in the Classroom

By recognizing that the *ancien régime* has made men "feminine" Wollstonecraft at once diagnoses its enervating effects and shows that "masculine" and "feminine" are not anatomically determined. Indeed, that "masculine" and "feminine" are political and ethical qualities is precisely why she can argue that women should be-

come more "masculine." But the possibility that masculine and feminine are not straightforward reflections of anatomy is one of the problems *Rights of Woman* wrestles with as well as being the enabling grounds of its argument. The fact that Wollstonecraft does not rigidly associate the manly with men or the feminine with women begins to appear uncannily like one of the symptoms she is trying to prescribe for rather than the basis of a remedy.[28] If there is nothing natural or anatomical which might legitimize gender roles and behavior, then Wollstonecraft's argument is based not on the distinction between the natural and the artificial, as she often claims, but on that between two sets of social conditioning which are *presented* as "artificial" and "natural." If gender roles and women's characters are formed discursively (through education, example, and the world's opinion), they are susceptible of being transformed through (and for) alternative ideological and aesthetic values. But this analysis also opens up the possibility that women (and men) have no essential character prior to social conditioning. Wollstonecraft attempts, therefore, to limit the transformations which her argument both depends upon and makes possible: "I do earnestly wish to see the distinction of sex confounded in society, unless where love animates the behaviour" (*RW* 147). Thus although Wollstonecraft argues that "the sexual distinction which men have so warmly insisted upon, is arbitrary" (*RW* 318), sexuality yet retains a differential function in the egalitarian society she envisages. Although she insists that there is no essential difference between men and women,[29] Wollstonecraft urgently reinscribes the difference when faced with what she believes to be monstrous transgressions of gender roles in sexual and political behavior. But if Wollstonecraft (like Burke in *Philosophical Enquiry*) would exclude femininity as negative, unstable, deceitful, we will see it return in her text as a troublesome problem which frustrates her efforts to establish an unequivocal politics, language, and gender.

The tensions and resistances within Wollstonecraft's text may be traced in moments where issues of education, sexuality, and class intersect. Consistent with her general argument for more openness and straight-talking—which is exemplified by her claim to have conversed "as man with man, with medical men on anatomical subjects" (*RW* 229)—Wollstonecraft suggests that young children should be given a basic education on sexual matters in order that the attempt to "obscure certain objects" might not "inflame their imaginations" (since "it is the modesty of affected modesty that does all the mischief"). And yet in her discussion of women's sexuality Wollstonecraft's text becomes secretive and obscure:

> In nurseries and boarding schools, I fear, girls are first spoiled, particularly in the latter. A number of girls sleep in the same room, and wash together. And though

I should be sorry to contaminate an innocent creature's mind by instilling false delicacy, or those prudish notions which early cautions respecting the other sex naturally engender, I should be very anxious to prevent their acquiring nasty or immodest habits; and as many girls have learned very nasty tricks from ignorant servants, the mixing them thus indiscriminately together, is very improper.

(*RW* 234)

Wollstonecraft's project, then, turns out to depend upon a crucial but problematic distinction between "false delicacy" (the modesty of affected modesty) and that true modesty needed to prevent "immodest habits." This distinction rests, in turn, upon maintaining what seem inherently unstable class divisions. The "indiscriminate" mixing of the classes and/or young girls (the syntax does not allow us to discriminate) leads to sexual impropriety, since the "very nasty tricks" learnt from "ignorant servants" are inevitably passed on, like diseases, to other girls. Far from stripping woman's nature naked, Wollstonecraft would prohibit girls from seeing each other without clothes. Her language correspondingly drapes its subject in mystery, introducing elements of obscurity and modesty in a text which originally set out to remove them. Faced with delicate, and indelicate, subjects, her text becomes delicate and evasive, taking on the very "feminine" traits it seeks to condemn, as if "manly language" were constitutionally incapable of broaching female sexuality.[30]

But if the improper mixing of the classes leads to sexual impropriety, there is no suggestion that the coming bourgeois order ought to erase class difference; however ignorant, servants will be necessary to free middle-class women from the chains of domestic duty. Thus in aristocratic and bourgeois society alike, differences and distances ought to be kept up—between young girls and between girls and their servants—for otherwise they might discover what makes them the same: if girls need assistance in washing, "let them not require it till that part of the business is over which ought never to be done before a fellow creature" (*RW* 235). "To say the truth," Wollstonecraft concludes, "women are in general too familiar with each other, which leads to that gross degree of familiarity that so frequently renders the marriage state unhappy" (*RW* 234). The representation of the female, here, seems in many ways to parallel that which Wollstonecraft is ostensibly writing against: girls, female servants, and women in general are presented as being in need of constant restraint; their sexuality is seen as tending almost irresistibly towards unspeakable corruptions. According to her own metaphor, Wollstonecraft seems to restring the bow in the very moment she seeks to relax the hand that holds it.[31]

In this moment of caution, the eighteenth-century's conception of the intimate relation between female sexuality and madness seems to resurface. This can be seen by juxtaposing Wollstonecraft's scene of female corruption with a passage Michel Foucault quotes concerning the correction wards of La Salpêtrière:

"The correction ward is the place of greatest punishment for the House, containing when we visited it forty-seven girls, most of them very young, more thoughtless than guilty. . . . And always this confusion of ages, this shocking mixture of frivolous girls with hardened women who can teach them only the art of the most unbridled corruption."[32]

Thus Wollstonecraft's concern to maintain women's "proper" sexuality for the marriage state seems compounded of an array of interrelated concerns—not only that women should form rational and virtuous companions for their husbands, but also that they might not be the vehicles for an outbreak of that madness which the age of reason lived in constant fear of.[33] Masturbation or lesbianism—practices which her "manly" language cannot openly speak of—are therefore regarded as "nasty tricks" which are dangerous not only for individual body, mind, and morality, but for the well-being of society as a whole. It is not that boys are incapable of getting up to similar kinds of tricks—Wollstonecraft also condemns the "nasty indecent tricks" which boys learn from each other in boarding schools, "not to speak of the vices, which render the body weak, whilst they effectually prevent the acquisition of any delicacy of mind" (*RW* 282)—but that, as this quotation shows, these unspeakable practices render the body and mind dangerously *weak*—i.e. "feminine." "Feminine" thus becomes associated with any kind of sexual activity which lies outside the procreative act. Although Wollstonecraft might want to confound sexual difference, this would require both sexes to become more "masculine" by limiting their sexuality to reproduction.

One way of attempting to impose such limitations is to intervene in that area which most encourages sensuality—women's reading habits. Wollstonecraft distinguishes between women's and men's imaginative activity by suggesting that while male artists are able to embody their imaginings in art objects or texts, "in women's imagination, love alone concentrates these ethereal beams" (*RW* 156 n. 8). Debarred from creative production, women's imagination is subject to and manipulated by the imaginative creations of other people:

Novels, music, poetry, and gallantry, all tend to make women the creatures of sensation. . . . This overstretched sensibility naturally relaxes the other powers of the mind, and prevents intellect from attaining that sovereignty which it ought to attain to render a rational creature useful to others.

(*RW* 152)

Reading "the unnatural and meretricious scenes sketched by the novel writers of the day" becomes an unnatural outlet for women's repressed sexuality (*RW*

309). With the "passions thus pampered, whilst the judgement is left unformed, what can be expected to ensue? Undoubtedly, a mixture of madness and folly!" (*RW* 152). Such novels provide women with a mere replica of human passion and a borrowed language:

> the reading of novels makes women, and particularly ladies of fashion, very fond of using strong expressions and superlatives in conversation; and, though the dissipated artificial life which they lead prevents their cherishing any strong legitimate passion, the language of passion in affected tones slips for ever from their glib tongues, and every trifle produces those phosphoric bursts which only mimic in the dark the flame of passion.
>
> (*RW* 309)

As Kaplan puts it, Wollstonecraft thus "sets up a peculiarly gendered and sexualized interaction between women and the narrative imaginative text, one in which women become the ultimately receptive reader easily moved into amoral activity by the fictional representation of sexual intrigue" ("Pandora's Box" 160). Once again, Foucault provides a discursive context: if women were thought to especially enjoy theatrical spectacles "that inflame and arouse them," novels were thought to be "a still more artificial milieu, and . . . more dangerous to a disordered sensibility":

> The novel constitutes the milieu of perversion, *par excellence,* of all sensibility . . . "The existence of so many authors has produced a host of readers, and continued reading generates every nervous complaint; perhaps of all the causes that have harmed women's health, the principal one has been the infinite multiplication of novels in the last hundred years . . . a girl who at ten reads instead of running will, at twenty, be a woman with the vapours and not a good nurse."[34]

Yet although this description of the impact of novels on women's sexuality, language, and health seems to identify the source of corruption as cultural rather than natural, Wollstonecraft can also appear to represent women's potential corruption as arising from the female anatomy and as being in need of cultural control. In her discussion of the results of over-familiarity between females the underlying concern seems to be about female genitals and their various processes and functions. That which ought to be kept covered is at once an anatomical part or process which should not be seen and a tale which should not be told:

> I could proceed still further, till I animadverted on some still more nasty customs, which men never fall into. Secrets are told where silence ought to reign; and that regard to cleanliness, which some religious sects have perhaps carried too far, especially the Essenes, amongst the Jews, by making that an insult to God which is only an insult to humanity, is violated in a beastly manner. How can *delicate* women obtrude on notice that part of the animal economy, which is so very disgusting?
>
> (*RW* 235)

Once again, an analogy is formed between women's sexuality and a secret which should not be told (even among women). And once again, Wollstonecraft's own text at once refers to female secrets and refuses to tell them. While Wollstonecraft prides herself on being able to talk as "man to man" about anatomy, she can also suggest that excessive familiarity between women is dangerous for women's moral being: "That decent personal reserve, which is the foundation of dignity of character, must be kept up between woman and woman, or their minds will never gain strength or modesty" (*RW* 326). Men never fall into these "nasty customs" not because they are more naturally modest, but because Wollstonecraft seems to be obliquely referring to processes characteristic of the female body. The reference to the Essenes is doubly suggestive in that this branch of the Pharisees "conformed to the most rigid rules of Levitical purity," being "particularly careful that women in the menstrual state should keep apart from the household," as well as adhering to the law which "enjoins modesty in regard to the covering of the body lest the Shekinah [i.e. the presence of God] be driven away by immodest exposure."[35] Woman's anatomy is her destiny here, making necessary an unremitting modesty and surveillance.

However ironic Wollstonecraft's "*delicate* women" might be, that irony rebounds back on the general tendency of her text to criticize the cultivation of delicacy in women. In wishing that these women would cultivate delicacy and cover up those parts of the "animal economy" which are so "disgusting" and "beastly," Wollstonecraft repeats Burke's anxieties that the stripping of Marie Antoinette reveals even the highest of women as "an animal not of the highest order" (*Refs* 171). If the Essenes go too far in conceiving female anatomy and its functions as an insult to God, Wollstonecraft still finds them "an insult to humanity"—a secret best kept hidden. Such anxiety spurs Wollstonecraft's text into a revealingly Burkean passage:

> Perhaps, there is not a virtue that mixes so kindly with every other as modesty. It is the pale moonbeam that renders more interesting every virtue it softens, giving mild grandeur to the contracted horizon. Nothing can be more beautiful than the poetical fiction, which makes Diana with her silver crescent, the goddess of chastity.
>
> (*RW* 327)

Rather than exposing the naked truth of women's sexuality, Wollstonecraft's text retreats into a set of beautiful poetic fictions in a way which seems to repeat Burke's recourse to the pleasing illusions of life. Tales which should not be told are displaced by an all-too-familiar tale about women and modesty. For this repeats Rousseau's view that while men are endowed with reason to control their desires, women, being by definition lacking in reason, have been given "modesty" with which to restrain their "boundless passions" (*Emile* 323). Thus Wollstonecraft unexpectedly cedes to Burke's and Rousseau's view that women must be kept within the bounds of modesty's "contracted horizon." Her resolution to be employed about things rather than words breaks down when confronted with female sexuality and retreats into a language and a representation of women (a "beautiful . . . poetic fiction") which it sets out to refute.

The restraint on the habits and nasty tricks women seem so prone to is linked, again, to a concern with language, since women's "sexual tricks" are associated with *double entendre*. Wollstonecraft objects to women's development of what she calls "bodily wit" which evolves from the "jokes and hoyden tricks" which are learnt while "shut up together in nurseries, schools, or convents," and which resemble "the double meanings which shake the convivial table when the glass has circulated freely" (*RW* 236). Breaking out in such enclosed female spaces, remote from the influence of men, "bodily wit" therefore seems to arise from women's potentially "corrupt" nature and is only then brought into society to engage men's wit and gallantry. What Wollstonecraft refers to by "bodily wit" is, like many of the terms in these passages, left obscure. A reading of Rousseau, however, suggests that "bodily wit" might refer to those bodily and sartorial signs through which women communicate the sexual messages which propriety denies to their verbal language. Rousseau advises the would-be lover to become proficient readers of this second language:

> Why do you consult their words when it is not their mouths that speak? Consult their eyes, their colour, their breathing, their timid manner, their slight resistance, that is the language nature gave them for your answer. The lips always say "No," and rightly so; but the tone is not always the same, and that cannot lie. Has not a woman the same needs as a man, but without the same right to make them known? Her fate would be too cruel if she had no language in which to express her legitimate desires except the words which she dare not utter.
>
> (*Emile* 348)

Thus woman becomes an equivocal sign composed of two contradictory messages (her words say "no" but her body sometimes says "yes"). Bodily wit is women's equivalent to verbal gallantry—allowing them to pursue "coquetry" yet keep "within bounds"—and men need all their wit to participate in the dialogue.[36] Women's body language thus emerges as the very reverse (or betrayal) of the manly language Wollstonecraft would have both men and women cultivate. These passages imply that such a double language is almost inevitable in women without the constraints of modesty, decorum, and delicacy. In other words, the (supposedly dangerous)

supplements Wollstonecraft would strip away from the body and the body politic are immediately replaced by another set of (supposedly benign) supplements indispensable to her own sociosexual ethics.[37] Yet the sheer complexity of Wollstonecraft's dilemma is indicated by the fact that, for Rousseau, women's bodily wit is produced precisely *because* they are subjected to the constraints of decorum.

Wollstonecraft is perhaps still more troubled about what she sees as the dangerous ambiguity introduced into gender by homosexuality, which she conceives to be the extension and inevitable result of a society whose sexuality has become a question of mere sensuality rather than of love and reproduction. Her analysis towards this conclusion is revealing. Nature—which "must ever be the standard of taste"—is "grossly . . . insulted by the voluptuary," whose "casual lust" reduces "a very considerable number of women" to "standing dishes to which every glutton may have access" (*RW* 248). But Wollstonecraft argues against the suggestion that prostitutes, by offering themselves to such gluttons, spare women in general. This is because prostitution and marriage are not mutually exclusive institutions but deeply implicated with one another. Married women are forced, by the false tastes which men develop through contact with prostitutes, "to assume, in some degree, the same character themselves" (*RW* 249). For the origin of prostitution, and of the weakness cultivated by married women in order to pander to their husbands' tastes, is one and the same: "want of chastity in men" (*RW* 249). But if this seems to counter the suggestion that women's sexuality is the "contagion" which debilitates society, in fact the feminine remains the problem in the form of the *feminization* of men. The appetite of unchaste men becomes so depraved "that a wanton stimulus is necessary to rouse it," and men are led to forget "the parental design of Nature" through a taste for "the mere person, and that for a moment" (*RW* 249). Once sexuality is separated from its reproductive purpose, the "person" of the object of desire entirely displaces the "natural meaning" of the act:

> So voluptuous, indeed, often grows the lustful prowler, that he refines on female softness. Something more soft than women is then sought for; till, in Italy and Portugal, men attend the levees of equivocal beings, to sigh for more than female languor.
>
> (*RW* 249)

Wollstonecraft's doubled emphasis on the "more than female" softness and languor of these "equivocal beings" underlines the anxiety that sexuality may become detached from its meaning (its basis in reproductive anatomy) and become pure excess or irreducibly ambiguous. The beautiful recreates men in its own image and more.

For Wollstonecraft, this leads in turn to yet further depravity, since women endeavor to recreate themselves in the more than female image held up to them—becoming ever more soft and languishing in order to gratify men's tastes, but in the process depriving themselves and sexual relations of their "proper" meaning. The result of this is to render women unfit for the role which their anatomy destines them:

> Women becoming, consequently, weaker in mind and body, than they ought to be, were one of the grand ends of their being taken into account, that of bearing and nursing children, [no longer] have . . . sufficient strength to discharge the first duty of a mother; and . . . either destroy the embryo in the womb, or cast if off when born.

> (*RW* 249)

Poston reads this as implying that "The lascivious father spreads syphilis to his wife, who for her part is so unhealthy and weak that the embryo is naturally aborted or the child is born blind and misshapen by venereal disease" (Norton 139). But to emphasize syphilis as the prime cause of these problems in generation is to overlook both the immediate context of the passage and the larger discursive network we have been tracing. Both these contexts suggest that the more pervasive "disease" is the enervating model of femininity developed by and characteristic of late eighteenth-century aristocratic culture. The effect of this endemic epidemic is to plunge that culture into a crisis which threatens its very survival:

> The weak enervated women who particularly catch the attention of libertines, are unfit to be mothers, though they may conceive; so that the rich sensualist, who has rioted among women, spreading depravity and misery, when he wishes to perpetuate his name, receives from his wife only an half-formed being that inherits both its father's and its mother's weakness.

> (*RW* 249)[38]

This is why Wollstonecraft is concerned both to eliminate femininity by making men and women more masculine and yet maintain the sexual difference involved in "proper," reproductive sexuality.[39]

In this way, Wollstonecraft extends Burke's analysis in *Philosophical Enquiry* of the dangerous, yet seductive, effects of the beautiful in order to show, by implication, that Burke's celebration of the beautiful in *Reflections* will inevitably precipitate a crisis in the hereditary principle which forms the very basis of the society he appears to defend. Wollstonecraft's analysis suggests that if, as C. B. Macpherson argues, Burke is actually seeking to institute bourgeois capitalism by introducing it under the guise of traditional forms (or by assimilating the new order to the old), then those forms would be just as inimical to the new as to the old order.[40] In the same way, for the Revolution to ignore the question of women's rights and education would be to build into its

constitution the same "flaw" which had brought aristocratic society to its own crisis. A concept of the masculine—constituted as the repression of sexuality and sensuality save for the supposedly "natural" function of reproduction—is thus developed and promoted as an antidote to the sexual confusion and debilitation which supposedly characterizes a feminized social order.

Taking advantage of the possibility that gender might have a conventional rather than natural relation to sexual anatomy in order to redefine masculinity as an ideal for both men and women, Wollstonecraft is nevertheless impelled to anchor her cultural and ideological project in "nature"—the biological reproduction of the species—and to limit the masculinization of woman through reference to "one of the grand designs of her being." This is achieved by distinguishing between "natural" reproductive functions and "unnatural" sensuality, and between aristocratic and bourgeois mores as sexual cultures which respectively impair and conform to nature. (This counters the suggestion sometimes made that Wollstonecraft was horrified by sensuality and argues instead that the repression of sensuality is inevitable to the logic of her text and the discursive network it intervenes and gets embroiled within.)

Although Wollstonecraft proposes the introduction of schools in which the sexes (and the social classes) would be educated, and dressed, alike—"to prevent any of the distinctions of vanity they [the classes? the sexes?] should be dressed alike"—she also suggests that,

> After the age of nine, girls and boys, intended for domestic employments, or mechanical trades, ought to be removed to other schools, and receive instruction in some measure appropriate to the destination of each individual, the two sexes being still together in the morning; but in the afternoon the girls should attend a school, where plain work, mantua-making millinery, etc., would be their employment.

> The young people of superior abilities, or fortune [of both sexes], might now be taught, in another school, the dead and living languages, the elements of science, and continue the study of history and politics, on a more extensive scale, which would not exclude polite literature.

> (*RW* 286, 287)

In other words, what in its context is an enlightened and innovative program of education is also a state apparatus for constructing new class and gender differences conducive to capitalist production. Children from the "lower orders"—those "intended" for domestic and mechanical trades—are educated into their "destined" places (a word which recalls Burke's rationale for class division), while the middle classes (marked by their "fortune" or "superior abilities") are correspondingly educated to fulfill their own "destiny." The division of education after the age of nine perpetuates, for a new political order, the different levels of language use which Olivia Smith identifies as one of the central distinctions of traditional society which radical politics set out to remove.[41] Literature (as well as advanced history and politics) is reserved for middle-class children in a way which anticipates the distinction in French schools between basic and literary uses of language which Etienne Balibar and Pierre Macherey suggest is fundamental to the institution and maintenance of the hegemony of the bourgeoisie in France.[42] Sex equality in secondary education is therefore reserved for middle class children—the girls of the "lower orders" being expected to learn skills "appropriate" to their "destined" adult lives (and appropriate, incidentally, to conventional ideas of women's "proper" employment). In this way, rather than dismantling the old order's ideology of destined or natural hierarchies, radical bourgeois capitalism—even in its feminist guise—simply reorganizes those hierarchies for a different political and economic interest. The revolution in female manners is reserved for middle class women—who "appear to be in the most natural state" (*RW* 81)—while those women who are most problematic for Burke and Wollstonecraft alike (aristocratic women and women from the "lower orders") are excluded as "unnatural" and irrecuperable. Nor is there an attempt, Wollstonecraft confesses, to "emulate masculine virtues" or "to invert the order of things" (*RW* 288, 109). In the end, she sums up her argument as follows: "Make women rational creatures and free citizens, and they will quickly become good wives and mothers" (*RW* 299). Rather than being equivocal figures (undermining sexual roles and the distinction between aristocracy and mob), female citizens will dutifully fulfill their natural destiny and meaning in a bourgeois society.

Notes

1. Gillian Beer, "Representing Women: Re-presenting the Past," *The Feminist Reader: Essays in Gender and the Politics of Literary Criticism,* ed. Catherine Belsey and Jane Moore (London: Macmillan, 1989): 63-80 (67). Beer suggests that reading the literature of the past for its contemporary "relevance" reproduces the attitude to the past, and to the texts of the past, currently adopted by the Conservative government in Britain (67-68). For an impressive reading of *Rights of Woman* which both traces its historical specificity and shows how it foregrounds for analysis the assumptions of a strand of feminism in the late 1980s, see Cora Kaplan, "Wild Nights: Pleasure/ Sexuality/Feminism," *Sea Changes: Essays on Culture and Feminism* (London: Verso, 1986) 31-56.

2. I am alluding here to Jacques Derrida's scattered remarks about the possibility of an "open Marx-

ism"—see, for example, James Kearns and Ken Newton, "An Interview with Jacques Derrida," *Literary Review* 14 (18 April-1 May 1980): 21-22; or Jacques Derrida, *Positions* (1972), trans. Alan Bass (Chicago: U of Chicago P, 1981; London: Athlone, 1987) 62-67. For a full-length study which attempts to develop the possibilities raised by these hints, see Michael Ryan, *Marxism and Deconstruction: A Critical Articulation* (Baltimore: Johns Hopkins UP, 1982).

3. Patricia Parker points out that "If the work of Rousseau is the first major attempt to justify equality among men . . . [*Emile*] also does much to elaborate . . . a justification of the inequality of men and women" (*Literary Fat Ladies: Rhetoric, Gender, Property* [New York: Methuen, 1987] 203). The significance of *Emile* in the constitution of bourgeois gender roles is still being reconstructed by feminist critics—see Parker 201-17, and Cora Kaplan, "Wild Nights," in *Sea Changes* 31-56, and "Pandora's Box: Subjectivity, Class, and Sexuality in Socialist Feminist Criticism," *Sea Changes* 147-76.

4. Mary Wollstonecraft, *Vindication of the Rights of Woman,* ed. Miriam Brody Kramnick (Harmondsworth: Penguin, 1982) 79. This text is based on the second edition of 1792. All quotations from *Rights of Woman* in the present article are taken from this edition, hereafter cited as *RW.*

5. The first edition reads "the female, in general, is inferior to the male. The male pursues, the female yields—this is the law of nature; and it does not appear to be suspended or abrogated in favour of women" (*A Vindication of the Rights of Woman,* ed. Carol H. Poston [New York: Norton, 1988] 8n).

6. For a discussion of Wollstonecraft's acceptance of the eighteenth century's degradation of the feminine, see Kaplan, "Pandora's Box," *Sea Changes* 157-59.

7. Wollstonecraft's only explicit mention of Burke in *Rights of Woman,* comes in a footnote (*RW* 216n). Poston discovers only two other allusions to Burke (34 and 64), but although it would certainly be possible to trace more allusions, I am arguing that *Rights of Woman* engages with Burke *intertextually* rather than simply through the occasional reference. The figuration of women which Wollstonecraft attacks in Rousseau is endemic to the seventeenth and eighteenth centuries (witness her guarded criticisms of Milton and Pope), but it is more urgent for Wollstonecraft to focus on *Emile* because of Rousseau's importance for late eighteenth-century radical thought. Even more troubling is that Rousseau's conception of women

appeared to coincide with that which had become so powerfully politicized in Burke's *Reflections.* Yet Rousseau's formulations about women and their education can also be strikingly similar to Wollstonecraft's—see, for example, Jean-Jacques Rousseau, *Emile* (1762), trans. Barbara Foxley (London: Dent and Dutton, 1947) 329, 330, 335. These similarities perhaps indicate that Wollstonecraft attacks those passages in Rousseau which most resemble Burke and quietly overlooks those which are akin to her own ideas.

8. For a more extended account of this, see Tom Furniss, "Gender in Revolution: Edmund Burke and Mary Wollstonecraft," *Revolution in Writing: British Literary Responses to the French Revolution,* ed. Kelvin Everest (Milton Keynes: Open UP, in press).

9. Edmund Burke, *A Philosophical Enquiry into the Origin of our Ideas of the Sublime and Beautiful* (1757/59), edited with an introduction by James T. Boulton (Oxford: Blackwell, 1987) 149-50, hereafter cited as *PE.*

10. See Frances Ferguson, "The Sublime of Edmund Burke, Or the Bathos of Experience," *Glyph: Johns Hopkins Textual Studies* 8 (1981): 62-78.

11. Edmund Burke, *Reflections on the Revolution in France* (1790), ed. Conor Cruise O'Brien (Harmondsworth: Penguin, 1968) 164, hereafter cited as *Refs.*

12. Mary Wollstonecraft, *A Vindication of the Rights of Men* (1790), introduced by Eleanor Louise Nicholes (Gainesville: Scholars' Facsimiles & Reprints, 1960) 2 and 6, hereafter referred to as *RMen.*

13. See Jean-Jacques Rousseau, *The Confessions* (1781), trans. J. M. Cohen (Harmondsworth: Penguin, 1953) 362.

14. See *Hamlet* III.i.146-47.

15. Miriam Kramnick points out that "In spite of Wollstonecraft's best intentions . . . her prose is an imitation, and not a particularly felicitous one, of the rounded sentences of eighteenth-century prose" (Introduction to *Rights of Woman* 41). For a discussion of the complexities of Paine's similar attempt to write a clear language as part of his response to Burke, see Tom Furniss, "Rhetoric in Revolution: The Role of Language in Paine's Critique of Burke," *Revolution and English Romanticism: Politics and Rhetoric,* ed. Keith Hanley and Raman Selden (New York: St. Martin's; Hemel Hempstead: Harvester, 1990): 23-48.

16. In the first volume of Thomas Paine's *Rights of Man* (1791), the distinction between the sexes—in contrast to that between classes—is presented as divinely ordained: "The Mosaic account of the creation," Paine writes in his counter-attack on Burke, "is full to this point, *the unity or equality of man.* The expressions admit of no controversy. 'And God said, Let us make man in our own image. In the image of God created he him; male and female created he them.' The distinction of sexes is pointed out, but no other distinction is even implied" (Thomas Paine, *Rights of Man* [1791/92], edited and introduced by Henry Collins [Harmondsworth: Penguin, 1969] 88-89, hereafter cited as *RMan*). Finding that Rousseau's egalitarianism is reserved for men and that he cultivates a "male aristocracy" ascendent over women, Wollstonecraft ruefully notes that "The *rights* of humanity have been . . . confined to the male line from Adam downwards" (*RW* 185). As Kaplan notes, "When feminists sought to appropriate liberal humanism for their own sex they had to contend with the double standard prominently inscribed within radical tradition, as well as with its suffocating and determining presence in dominant ideologies" ("Wild Nights" 33).

17. This conventional distinction between masculine and feminine is given its most powerful formulation for eighteenth-century readers, even as it is undone, in the description of sexual difference in *Paradise Lost* IV.295-318.

18. "*Rapport sur L'Instruction Publique, fait au nom du Comité de Constitution* (Paris, 1791). France's present system of compulsory free education owes a great deal to the model recommended over 150 years ago by Talleyrand" (Carol H. Poston, *RW* [Norton] 3, n. 2). Claire Tomalin records Talleyrand's visit to Wollstonecraft, in acknowledgement of her dedication, while he was in London in February 1792 (Claire Tomalin, *The Life and Death of Mary Wollstonecraft* [Harmondsworth: Penguin, 1977, first published by Weidenfeld & Nicolson, 1974] 146-47).

19. Poston suggests that the passage in quotation marks might be "a liberal translation from Talleyrand's *Rapport* . . . : 'sur quel principe l'un des deux pourroit-il en être désherité par la Societé protectrice des droits de tous?'" (*RW* [Norton] 5, n. 6). She also points out that "In France's Constitution of 1791 only males over twenty-five were citizens. Women were not to get the vote until 1944" (5, n. 7).

20. For Wollstonecraft's explicit attack on Burke's defense of prejudice in *Reflections,* see *RW* 216-17.

21. Rousseau talks of "the shame and modesty with which nature has armed the weak for the conquest of the strong" (*Emile* 322).

22. See Ferguson, "The Sublime of Edmund Burke" 76. Rousseau seems to recognize such a danger

when he says that "The exaggeration of feminine delicacy leads to effeminacy in men" (*Emile* 329). His antidote against such a danger (young girls should be encouraged to engage in "pleasant, moderate, and healthy exercise" [329-30]) suggests that Wollstonecraft exaggerates the tendency of Rousseau's prescriptions for women, and that in some instances the two writers are in concord.

23. In a phrase which ironically echoes Burke, for example, soldiers are said to be "a set of idle superficial young men, whose only occupation is gallantry, and whose polished manners render vice more dangerous, by concealing its deformity under gay ornamental drapery" (*RW* 97). Their "air of fashion . . . is but a badge of slavery," and "Like the *fair* sex, the business of [soldiers'] lives is gallantry; they were taught to please, and they live only to please" (*RW* 97, 106). In a footnote, she asks "Why should women be censured . . . because they seem to have a passion for a scarlet coat? Has not education placed [women] more on a level with soldiers than any other class of men?" (*RW* 106).

24. Wollstonecraft returns to such formulations throughout her text (see 118 and 145). Poston refers the reader to *Paradise Lost* X.891-92: "This fair defect / Of nature"; and to Pope, *Moral Essays* II: 44: "Fine by defect, and delicately weak" (Norton 34, n. 9). Burke's and Rousseau's representations of women in the same vein are much more disturbing and immediate for Wollstonecraft than Milton's or Pope's.

25. See Jacques Derrida, *Of Grammatology* (1967), trans. and introduced by Gayatri Chakravorty Spivak (Baltimore: John Hopkins UP, 1976) 163.

26. *Of Grammatology* 154. There is a suggestion, running through the texts of Rousseau, Burke, and Wollstonecraft, that woman is the supplement of society—that which both civilizes and endangers it, both its disease and its cure. If, in *Rights of Men,* Wollstonecraft would "grub up" the ivy which threatens the oak, in *Rights of Woman* she identifies Rousseau's conception of woman's relation to man as that of a "graceful ivy, clasping the oak that supported it" (104). Thus, women have "parasitical tendency" (153), and are treated as an "afterthought of creation" (178). Patricia Parker traces the way "the second sex" functions as a supplement in Genesis, Milton, Rousseau, and Freud (*Literary Fat Ladies* 178-233).

27. For Wollstonecraft's attack on the idea that women have an innate love of dress, see *RW* 111; but for her acknowledgement that women have been successfully conditioned into a harmful preoccupation with dress, see *RW* 170.

28. My analysis of the complicated relation between disease and cure in Wollstonecraft's reading of Burke is influenced by Derrida's discussion of "Plato's Pharmacy," in *Dissemination* (1972), trans. Barbara Johnson (Chicago: U of Chicago P, 1981) 61-171.

29. "I wish to sum up what I have said in a few words, for here I throw down my gauntlet, and deny the existence of sexual virtues, not excepting modesty. For man and woman, truth, if I understand the meaning of the word, must be the same" (*RW* 139; also see 105, 119, 121, 124, 128).

30. For Wollstonecraft's "refusal to acknowledge female sexuality," see Mary Poovey, "*A Vindication of the Rights of Woman* and Female Sexuality" (included in *RW* [Norton]: 343-55 [353]). Poovey suggests that "the surprisingly vitriolic language" of these passages reveals Wollstonecraft's "vehement disgust with female sexuality." This directly impinges on Wollstonecraft's language: "We can see one consequence of this evasion [of sexuality] in her own use of euphemisms and circuitous phrasing. Whenever Wollstonecraft approaches a subject that arouses her own volatile emotions, her language becomes both obscure and abstract; she shuns concrete nouns as if they were bodies she is trying to cover over" (350, 352).

31. Miriam Kramnick points out that although Wollstonecraft's "criticism of . . . aristocratic and would-be aristocratic ladies resembles the more scathing of the misogynist satirists of the eighteenth century," her anger arises over "what she perceived was a waste of potential and because she realized that it was women themselves who, by their ignorance and uselessness, provided the fuel for the traditional anti-feminists" (Introduction to *RW* 48). It is important to hold this in mind, but I am arguing that Wollstonecraft's project has a more complex relation to that which arouses its indignation than Kramnick allows. As Kaplan suggests, Wollstonecraft's use of the sexual metaphor of the bent bow recoiling with violence indicates that her figurative language, like the imaginary force of female sexuality itself, is "out of control" ("Wild Nights" 44).

32. Michel Foucault, *Madness and Civilization: A History of Insanity in the Age of Reason,* trans. Richard Howard (London: Tavistock, 1971) 208, quoting La Rochefoucauld-Liancourt.

33. It is suggestive that much of the action of Wollstonecraft's late, unfinished novel—which sets out to dramatize the issues of *Rights of Woman* in the same way that *Caleb Williams* does *Political Justice*—takes place during its heroine's unmerited incarceration in a madhouse. See *The*

Wrongs of Woman: Or, Maria (1798), reprinted in Mary Wollstonecraft, *Mary and The Wrongs of Woman,* ed. Gary Kelly (Oxford: Oxford UP, 1980).

34. Foucault 218-19, quoting Edmé-Pierre Beauchesne, *De l' influence des affections de l'âme dans les maladies nerveuses des femmes* (Paris, 1783) 31.

35. *The Jewish Encyclopedia* (New York: Funk and Wagnalls, 1903) v: 224-26.

36. See *Emile* 348. The analogy between "male wit" and "female beauty" is pursued throughout Wollstonecraft's two Vindications (see *RW* 146 and 311), while *Rights of Men* repeatedly condemns Burke as a wit (see *RW* 4, 7, 139, and 142).

37. "Delicacy" and "decorum" can mean opposite things in Wollstonecraft: she writes against that "decorum" which Rousseau suggests is the "constant and severe constraint" which women must be subject to all their lives (*RW* 178); she condemns decorum as a supplement harmful to women (197); yet she praises a "man of delicacy" for requiring "neither weakness nor sensibility" in women, but "affection" (232-33).

38. For a discussion of the contrasting effects of poverty and luxury on generation, see Adam Smith, *An Inquiry into the Nature and Causes of the Wealth of Nations* (1776), ed. R. H. Campbell, A. S. Skinner, and W. B. Todd in two volumes (Oxford: Oxford UP, 1979) 1: 96-97.

39. This is an anxiety Wollstonecraft shares with Rousseau—for whom the distinction between the sexes is vital to uphold civilization itself (*Emile* 326). Rousseau writes that "In the present confusion between the sexes it is almost a miracle to belong to one's own sex" (356). Foucault reveals how the transgression of gender boundaries—and especially men's imitation of female qualities and roles—is associated with madness in the eighteenth century. Foucault records one representation of the night-time activities of a house of confinement which is clearly influenced by De Sade: "'There, the most infamous excesses are committed upon the very person of the prisoner; we hear of certain vices practiced frequently, notoriously, and even publicly in the common room of the prison, vices which the propriety of modern times does not permit us to name. We are told that numerous prisoners, *simillimi feminis mores stuprati et constupratores*; that they return from this obscure, forbidden place covered over with their own and others' debaucheries, lost to all shame and ready to commit all sorts of crimes'" (Foucault 208, quoting H. Mirabeau, *Observations d'un*

voyageur anglais [Paris, 1788] 14). A tentative translation of Mirabeau's (appropriately) corrupt Latin would be "a manner very like the ravished and ravishers of women."

40. See C. B. Macpherson, *Burke* (Oxford: Oxford UP, 1980) 51-70 (69).

41. See Olivia Smith, *The Politics of Language 1791-1819* (Oxford: Clarendon, 1984) 1-34.

42. See Etienne Balibar and Pierre Macherey, "On Literature as an Ideological Form," *Untying the Text: A Post-Structuralist Reader,* ed. Robert Young (Boston: Routledge & Kegan Paul, 1981) 79-99.

Catriona MacKenzie (essay date fall 1993)

SOURCE: MacKenzie, Catriona. "Reason and Sensibility: The Ideal of Women's Self-Governance in the Writings of Mary Wollstonecraft." *Hypatia* 8, no. 4 (fall 1993): 35-55.

[*In the following essay, MacKenzie argues against interpretations of Wollstonecraft that stress her commitment to a liberal philosophical framework and valuation of reason over passion, claiming that in* A Vindication of the Rights of Woman *and other texts Wollstonecraft exposes the inadequacies of traditional liberalism.*]

When morality shall be settled on a more solid basis, then, without being gifted with a prophetic spirit, I will venture to predict that woman will be either the friend or slave of man. We shall not, as at present, doubt whether she is a moral agent, or the link which unites man with brutes.

(Wollstonecraft 1975, 120)

I.

In a letter written in 1795 while she was traveling in Scandinavia doing business on behalf of Gilbert Imlay, the man who had recently abandoned both her and her child by him, Mary Wollstonecraft wrote of herself: "For years have I endeavored to calm an impetuous tide—laboring to keep my feelings to an orderly course.—It was striving against the stream.—I must love and admire with warmth, or I sink into sadness" (Wollstonecraft 1977, 160). It is reflections such as these, as well as the tempestuous events of Wollstonecraft's personal life, that have led one of her biographers to suggest that Wollstonecraft was unable to live her own life by the ideal of self-governance that she proposed for women in *A Vindication of the Rights of Woman.*[2] The explanation proffered for this apparent discrepancy is that the *Vindication* was written when

Wollstonecraft was childless and inexperienced in sexual relationships with men. Her later experiences, however, taught her that passion cannot always, or cannot very easily, be governed by reason. More recent feminist commentators have rejected this rather patronizing view of the relationship between Wollstonecraft's life and her writings.[3] But the idea that Wollstonecraft defined self-governance in opposition to passion has not been challenged and still prevails even in feminist interpretations of her work.[4] Jane Martin, for example, argues that Wollstonecraft adopts a "sovereignty model of personality," which posits reason in opposition to feeling as the "ruling element" of the soul and which allows between reason and feeling "no give and take, no interaction, no sensitivity to context" (Martin 1985, Chap. 4).

In this essay I argue that the overriding preoccupations of Wollstonecraft's work, as well as of her life, were to articulate what it means for women to think and act as autonomous moral agents, and to envisage the kind of social and political organization required for them to do so. Although at times she seemed to identify autonomy with reason, defining it in opposition to passion, in a context in which woman was "always represented as only created to see through a gross medium, and to take things on trust" (Wollstonecraft 1975, 142). Wollstonecraft also struggled to develop an account of women's moral agency that would incorporate a recognition not only of women's capacity to reason but also of their right to experience and give expression to passion, including sexual desire. Of particular concern to her was the need to create the possibility for genuinely reciprocal friendships and love relationships between men and women. She was also vehement that women's bodies should be regarded neither as mere objects of use, pleasure, and exchange among men, nor by women as objects of narcissistic attention. Rather, respect for the body is an integral part of both self-esteem and respect for others. Wollstonecraft's view was that such reciprocity and respect could be realized only in a context in which women are able to exercise control of both the external—financial, educational, and political—circumstances of their lives and the direction of their own affections.

Such an interpretation need not deny that there are tensions within Wollstonecraft's account of women's autonomy, as well as difficulties with it for contemporary feminists. In particular, Wollstonecraft's treatment of the distinctions between reason/passion and public/private seems to raise problems from a feminist perspective for her understanding of self-governance. But I will suggest that these problems are not as clear-cut as they are sometimes made to seem. First, it is true that at many points in the *Vindication* Wollstonecraft is explicit that virtue must be founded on reason, not sensibility. She also ties virtue to the notion of the perfect-

ibility of the soul. This lends credence to the view that she regards self-governance as a matter of reason's control over unruly passions associated with the body. From a feminist perspective this is problematic because it allies Wollstonecraft's account of self-governance with hierarchical oppositions between soul/body, reason/passion, and masculine/feminine. The supposedly sex-neutral "self" that controls the body is thus implicitly associated with "masculine" virtues while downgrading "feminine" virtues associated with affectivity.[5] While not denying that Wollstonecraft does appeal to the idea of a "soul which knows no sex," I will try to show that, within the inevitable limits imposed by this idea, Wollstonecraft was also struggling to articulate a more subtle view of self-governance, one that would not pit women's reason in opposition either to their bodies or to affectivity. The outlines of this view are certainly present in the *Vindication,* but they are more fully developed in Wollstonecraft's posthumously published novel *The Wrongs of Woman* (Wollstonecraft 1980b) and in some of her travel writings and personal letters.[6]

Second, in the *Vindication* Wollstonecraft makes much of the claim that although virtue must be regarded as the same in both sexes, men and women have different "duties." Women's "duties," associated with the care of children and the running of the household, are considered by Wollstonecraft to follow "naturally" from women's role in reproduction. But as feminists have pointed out, this division of the sexes according to duties, as well as the idea that certain duties are "natural" to women, derives from and preserves the distinction between public and private that is at the root of women's subordination. Moira Gatens, for example, argues that Wollstonecraft's endorsement of a sexual division of labor is a consequence of her attempt to extend the liberal ideal of equality to women (Gatens 1991a).[7] According to Gatens, Wollstonecraft assumes that the liberal notion of equality, and the reason that grounds it, are sex-neutral. In fact, however, the characteristics of the "equal" liberal citizen are defined in opposition to, but also presuppose, those affective virtues associated with women. As a result, the liberal public sphere is a sphere of male equality that can function only through the subordination of women in the private sphere. Wollstonecraft's argument that women can fulfill dual roles as mothers-daughters-wives and as equal citizens thus overlooks the fact that within liberalism women's duties are necessarily tied to women's subordination. According to Gatens, Wollstonecraft attempts to deal with this difficulty by denying the ethical significance of women's embodiment and of those virtues associated with women, and by adopting a supposedly sex-neutral but in fact masculine ideal of virtue in both public and private spheres. But given the practical consequences of women's embodiment (in particular, the nature of women's involvement in reproduction), while the ethical significance of sexual difference is denied, difference re-emerges at the level of the division of labor. Because the sexual division of labor lies at the heart of women's social inferiority, the net effect of Wollstonecraft's account of virtue is to leave intact the structures of women's subordination.

While I do not deny that the idea that women have certain "natural" duties must be rejected, I do maintain that Wollstonecraft's views on the relation between public and private spheres are more complex than perhaps Gatens allows. Although Wollstonecraft certainly wants nothing to do with the Rousseauian idea of specific "feminine" virtues, she does not deny the ethical importance of the affections. Nor does she overlook the ethical significance of sexual difference.[8] Her concern is to understand the kind of moral character required in order to achieve justice in the public realm and genuine reciprocity in the private. But what motivates this concern is a recognition that male and female embodiment are different and that this difference has ethical and political significance. It was for this reason that she called for not only a "revolution in female manners" but also a complete transformation of the legal and economic relations of both public and private spheres.

It is certainly true that Wollstonecraft was not entirely successful in her effort to combat the representation of women's bodies as obstacles to women's moral agency, a view that came to dominate philosophical and cultural conceptions of femininity from the Enlightenment onward. At times she seems to take over the view that women's bodies are more "dependent" than men's bodies are and hence that women's bodies may be impediments to virtue. Particularly in *The Wrongs of Woman* and in some of her reflections on her own feelings for her daughter, she also seems to suggest that women are by nature more susceptible to the "attached affections" than are men. And, as I stated above, she seems to endorse the idea that certain duties are natural to women. But even here Wollstonecraft shows an awareness that perhaps her views, as well as her own susceptibilities, arise more from "the imperfect state of society" than from the nature of women's bodies.

II.

When reading Wollstonecraft it is important to try to disentangle her somewhat sketchy conception of self-governance from the arguments for equality out of which it arises. In her defense of equality she puts a great deal of stress on women's capacity to reason and on the idea that virtue must be founded on reason. This gives rise to the impression that for Wollstonecraft self-governance is equivalent to the rule of reason. I suggest, however, that Wollstonecraft does not straightforwardly endorse the extreme rationalism of the arguments for equality. Rather, these arguments serve the strategic function of directly answering the charges against women's equality that were raised by Enlightenment thinkers—but in particular, by Rousseau. Although the arguments for equality provide the necessary theoretical underpinning for her account of self-governance, in this account the role of reason figures more as a necessary part of a virtuous character than as the sole authority in all matters.

Wollstonecraft's argument in defense of women's equality works by extending the Enlightenment critique of sovereign power to relations between the sexes. Her claim is that if sovereign power is deemed illegitimate because it sanctions arbitrary power, then logical consistency requires that any exercise of arbitrary power be deemed illegitimate. What she seeks to show is that women's subordination to men is purely arbitrary, that is, it cannot be justified by reason. Wollstonecraft's main method of exposing the arbitrary nature of patriarchal power is via a critique of Rousseau's arguments against women's claims to equality. Her targets are, first, Rousseau's claim that women are by nature inferior to men with respect to those capacities that ground equality—namely reason, independence, and virtue—and, second, his claim that women's equality would subvert the social order.[9] In the *Vindication* Wollstonecraft presents two main arguments against the first claim, an environmental argument and an argument based on an appeal to the perfectibility of the soul. The environmental argument involves a straightforward appeal to empiricist psychology. Following Locke she argues that our capacities are developed and our characters formed in response to our environment, or what she terms "the effect of an early association of ideas." For Wollstonecraft, one of the most significant features of the environment is education or its lack, but environment also embraces customs, habits, opportunities, parental influences, and so on. Her response to Rousseau concedes that women "in the present state of society" do seem to be less capable of both reason and virtue than men are, but she seeks to show that this is simply a product of women's education and environment rather than a natural incapacity.

The environmental argument has, of course, been rehearsed repeatedly under a number of different guises by feminists since Wollstonecraft. A more interesting argument from the point of view of Wollstonecraft's concern with autonomy is the appeal to the perfectibility of the soul. At one level this argument works simply to challenge the coherence of any claim that certain groups of human beings can be naturally subject to others. Women, says Wollstonecraft, are either human beings or they are not—that is, they are either capable of reason and virtue or they are not, they either have an immortal soul or they do not. To postulate the possibility of a being that is neither one thing nor the other is to suggest that women are "beautiful flaws in nature. Let it also be remembered that they are the only flaw"

(Wollstonecraft 1975, 122). If women are *not* human beings, then they must be regarded as subject to their impulses and hence incapable of freedom of the will. If this is the case, then their subjection to the authority of others is perfectly justifiable. However, if women *are* human beings, then their subjection to the will of others is completely unjustifiable. Furthermore, if this is the case, it is morally requisite that women be given the liberty and the scope to perfect their souls through the exercise of their reason. Underlying this challenge is the idea that human beings have a duty to improve their souls, more than this, that the highest aim of human life is self-improvement.[10] Thus Wollstonecraft's argument against Rousseau is that by denying women equality, he undermines the foundation of morality because he denies women the possibility of undertaking what is in fact the sternest duty of beings accountable for themselves to God. Shortly we will see how this doctrine of perfectibility underpins Wollstonecraft's conception of self-governance.

In response to Rousseau's claim that women's equality would subvert the social order, Wollstonecraft seeks to show that precisely the reverse would be true.[11] Her argument to this effect focuses on Rousseau's conception of feminine virtue as founded not in reason but in modesty, which, she claims, is not virtue at all but a sham more likely to corrupt and degrade women and the social order than to improve either. The strategy of Wollstonecraft's argument is to concede to Rousseau certain assumptions but to deny the validity of the inferences he makes on the basis of those assumptions. First, she agrees that public virtue must be founded in private virtue, conceding also the importance of modesty and fidelity in relationships between men and women. However, she argues that Rousseau's recommendations for the education of women and his subjection of women to the authority of men will not bring about the desired result. According to Wollstonecraft, modesty must be founded in self-respect and in respect for the integrity of one's body, while fidelity is only a virtue if it arises out of genuine affection. Understood thus, modesty and fidelity are not sexually specific virtues at all. But Rousseau adopts a sexual double standard and makes modesty and fidelity the paramount virtues for women. Furthermore, he grounds these allegedly "feminine" virtues not in women's self-respect and capacity for affection but in male needs. It is clear that for Rousseau the function of so-called feminine virtue is to make women pleasing to men and to ensure that women's own needs are subordinated to this end. Wollstonecraft cites as evidence of this claim Rousseau's injunctions to Sophie to ensure that she is always alluring for Emile, while at the same time insisting that her chastity is her main asset. But pointing to the behavior of the leisured middle-class and aristocratic women whom Wollstonecraft so despised, she suggests that Rousseau's advice is more likely to pro-

duce infidelity, or at least sham fidelity, than genuine fidelity because it focuses women's whole attention on "corporeal embellishments" rather than on attaining genuine virtue.[12] The fact that feminine "virtue" must in the end be assured through force indicates that Rousseau was in fact aware of this.[13] Wollstonecraft's joking suggestion is that he abandoned logic on this issue because he succumbed to his own lasciviousness! Wollstonecraft is also outraged by Rousseau's insistence that it is not sufficient for a woman to be faithful; in addition, everyone must know of her fidelity. By making virtue a function of the opinions of others rather than of a person's own integrity and honesty, Rousseau deliberately undermines women's independence. More than this, he quite openly incites women to duplicity and cunning. But by depriving women of integrity and of every legitimate means of exercising power, Rousseau ensures that women will in fact create social disorder because despotism becomes the only path open to them. By being civil and political slaves women become private tyrants (Wollstonecraft 1975, esp. chaps. 4,5, and 12).[14] Wollstonecraft's conclusion is that Rousseau's recommendations teach women manners rather than morals—hardly an adequate basis for the virtue required to perfect the soul.

Rousseau's second argument in support of the claim that women's equality would subvert the social order is that women's primary function in life is to raise and educate children. Were women themselves to be educated to participate as equal citizens who would take responsibility for this crucial task? Wollstonecraft's response is simple but devastating. Once again she concedes certain assumptions to Rousseau, namely, that the family is indeed the foundation of social life and that women's primary *social* duty is to raise and educate children. However, she points out that if women are trained to be dependent on men, and required to base their judgements on the authority of men, then they will be incapable of raising and educating children. Wollstonecraft's argument is that the task of education demands independence of judgment. This in turn requires a capacity for reflection and generalization. But the education and social position that Rousseau recommends for women denies them the opportunity of developing these capacities. Furthermore, if women are ignorant of virtue and are themselves subjected to arbitrary authority, how likely is it that they will inculcate virtue in their own children? What is more likely is that they in turn will subject their children to arbitrary authority rather than teach them virtue through the use of reason. But having conceded that women's primary *social* duties are maternal duties, Wollstonecraft also argues that women have a duty to which their social duties must always be secondary. This is their duty to themselves as beings accountable to God.

III.

Wollstonecraft's views on the perfectibility of the soul are beautifully captured in one of her travel letters written in Tonsberg, Norway. This letter shows that Wollstonecraft's belief in the immortality of the soul did not prevent her from reflecting on the moral significance of human embodiment. In the letter, Wollstonecraft recounts her horror at discovering in the town's church a recess full of coffins containing embalmed bodies. Her horror arose from a sense that it degrades humanity to attempt to preserve the body when all active life has been extinguished, when "the enchantment of animation" is broken. In contrast to the "noble ruins" that are reminders of the exertions and efforts of earlier generations and that "exalt the mind," these futile attempts at prolonging life bring home the "littleness" and morality of the individual. Reflecting on her reaction, Wollstonecraft writes,

> Life, what art thou? Where goes this breath? this *I*, so much alive? In what element will it mix, giving or receiving fresh energy . . . I feel a conviction that we have some perfectible principle in our present vestment, which will not be destroyed just as we begin to be sensible of improvement.

> (Wollstonecraft 1977, Letter VII, 158-59)

Although at times Wollstonecraft's belief in the immortality of the soul led her to adopt an attitude of stoicism and resignation in the face of life's sorrows and injustices, her more considered view was that it is by learning from error and experience and by fighting injustice that the soul is improved.[15] As we will see, Wollstonecraft's views on what constitutes virtue or the perfection of the soul shifted somewhat from the *Vindication* to *The Wrongs of Woman*. But the idea that self-governance is essential to virtue and to the possibility of perfectibility or self-improvement remained a constant theme in her work, as did the idea that sexual inequality is immoral because it deprives women of self-governance.

Central to Wollstonecraft's notion of perfectibility and to her account of self-governance is a contrast—not accidentally echoing the same contrast in Rousseau—between independence and dependence. To be dependent is "to act according to the will of another fallible being, and submit, right or wrong, to power" (Wollstonecraft 1975, 135). However, independence, which Wollstonecraft calls "the grand blessing of life, the basis of every virtue" (Wollstonecraft 1975, 85), is not the mere converse of dependence, namely, being self-willed, but is a more complex virtue. In the *Vindication* Wollstonecraft lays great stress on the importance of reason to independence. She characterizes reason in the following terms:

> Reason is . . . the simple power of improvement; or, more properly speaking, of discerning truth. Every individual is in this respect a world in itself. More or less

may be conspicuous in one being than another; but the nature of reason must be the same in all, if it be an emanation of divinity, the tie that connects the creature with the Creator; for, can that soul be stamped with the heavenly image, that is not perfected by the exercise of its own reason?

> (Wollstonecraft 1975, 142)

According to Wollstonecraft, a person must exercise her reason in a number of different ways in order to achieve independence. The most important of these ways, and the one to which she remains committed throughout her writings, is that exercise of reason which counters the effects of prejudice and which refuses blind obedience to authority. Our actions can be free and virtuous, she wants to say, only if they are based on reasoned judgments, rather than arising out of conformity to social expectations or from notions of duty that require the individual to submit her own judgment to the arbitrary authority of others. In the *Vindication* this view leads Wollstonecraft to condemn military training and discipline as incompatible with freedom (Wollstonecraft 1975, 97).[16] In *The Wrongs of Woman* she has Darnford declare that "minds governed by superior principles . . . were privileged to act above the dictates of laws they had no voice in framing" (Wollstonecraft 1980b, 2: 187).[17] These "superior principles" are principles founded in respect for the rights of rational beings, including self-respect, as opposed to the principles of social utility that justify, among other things, the subordination of women and the exploitation of the poor. Her view was that a knowledge of such principles could only be arrived at by "enlarging the mind" through education, sensibility, and experience. By "cramping the understanding," women's education and social position, as well as Rousseau's recommendations on these matters, put the capacity for making independent judgments out of the reach of most women, condemning them to be slaves to the opinions of others.

In the *Vindication* Wollstonecraft seems to follow Rousseau in linking dependence on the opinions of others to being subject to one's own inclinations and passions.[18] In some places she therefore connects that exercise of reason which leads to independence of judgment and virtue with the control of the passions and with a kind of self-denying fortitude. Her complaint against the indolent women of the middle classes, for example, is that their senses are inflamed by the pursuit of pleasure and by momentary feelings. As a result, their reason is prevented from "attaining that sovereignty which it ought to attain to render a rational creature useful to others and content with its own station" (Wollstonecraft 1975, 152). In contrast, the virtuous widow Wollstonecraft depicts for us is a woman who subdues any passionate inclinations, selflessly devotes herself to educating and providing for her children, and then "calmly waits for the sleep of death" (Wollstonecraft

1975, 138-39). In a similar vein, Wollstonecraft also declares that "a master and mistress of a family ought not to love each other with passion. I mean to say that they ought not to indulge those emotions which disturb the order of society." (Wollstonecraft 1975, 114).

However, even in the *Vindication* Wollstonecraft seems to be ambivalent about this view. In a number of places she contrasts the "romantic, wavering feelings" that "inflame" the passions with those "strong, persevering passions" that "strengthen" the passions and so enlarge the understanding and ennoble the heart. (See, for example, Wollstonecraft 1975, 115, 152, 169.) Similarly she contrasts lust with love, sensuality with sensibility, parental self-love with parental affection, and so on, suggesting that although the first term in the pair undermines virtue the second term is essential to it. She also suggests that "the regulation of the passions is not, always, wisdom" and that the reason why men seem to be more capable of independent judgement than women are is because they have more scope to exercise "the grand passions" (Wollstonecraft 1975, 212). Even more surprising, she claims for women the right to sexual desire: "Women as well as men ought to have the common appetites and passions of their nature, they are only brutal when unchecked by reason: but the obligation to check them is the duty of mankind, not a sexual duty" (Wollstonecraft 1975, 238).

In the novel *The Wrongs of Woman,* the character Maria cautions her daughter in a letter to learn to distinguish genuine love and affection from passing infatuation but also urges her not to flee from pleasure and to open her heart to affection, even though that will also make her vulnerable to pain. In an important passage she deplores contemporary moral standards that require women to remain married to men for whom they have neither affection nor esteem: "woman, weak in reason, impotent in will, is required to moralize, sentimentalize herself to stone, and pine her life away, laboring to reform her embruted mate" (Wollstonecraft 1980b, 2: 154). Maria declares that, to the contrary, lack of passion and coldness of heart undermine virtue, and she argues that desire must be reciprocal and women must have the freedom to express "that fire of the imagination, which produces *active* sensibility, and *positive* virtue" (Wollstonecraft 1980b, 2: 153). Later she rails against the tyranny of laws that pit women's reason in opposition to their inclinations.

How should these apparent tensions be read, and what implications do they have for Wollstonecraft's conception of self-governance? In the *Vindication* Wollstonecraft does seem to waver between two different ways of thinking about self-governance. On the one hand, especially in her insistence on women's capacity to reason and in her scathing condemnation of the "manners" of contemporary women, she seems to regard the control of the passions by reason as essential to self-governance. On the other hand, she seems also to be moving toward the view that in a well-balanced, virtuous character, reason and sensibility should mutually strengthen and support each other rather than either dominating the other. This seems clearly to be the view of *The Wrongs of Woman.* Why, then, this ambivalence on Wollstonecraft's part? There may be some truth in the claim that the events of Wollstonecraft's own life helped confirm her in the latter view. However, there may also be other reasons for Wollstonecraft's wavering. A clue to these reasons is found in one of her travel letters. Reflecting on her fears and hopes for her daughter Fanny, Wollstonecraft writes:

> You know that as a female I am particularly attached to her—I feel more than a mother's fondness and anxiety, when I reflect on the despondent and oppressed state of her sex. I dread lest she should be forced to sacrifice her heart to her principles, or principles to her heart. With trembling hand I shall cultivate sensibility, and cherish delicacy of sentiment, lest, while I lend fresh blushes to the rose, I sharpen the thorns that will wound the breast I would fain guard—I dread to unfold her mind, lest it should render her unfit for the world she is to inhabit—Hapless woman! what a fate is thine.
>
> (Wollstonecraft 1977, Letter VI, 156)

In many other places in her writings Wollstonecraft qualifies her claims with a statement to the effect that what she describes characterizes the situation of women "in the current imperfect state of society." This indicates that Wollstonecraft's apparent devaluation of passion stems from a number of sources. As I argued above, it must be seen, in the context of Wollstonecraft's defense of equality and of women's capacity to reason, as a counter to the Rousseauian depiction of "feminine" virtue. But Wollstonecraft's anxiety about passion is also a response to a social situation that denied to women the scope for expressing desire and passion and hence gave rise to devastating conflicts between reason and sensibility. This is particularly evident in Wollstonecraft's reflections on Fanny quoted above and in her depiction of Maria's marriage to George Venables, a situation that Maria managed to tolerate for six years only by deadening her sensibility. A further reason for Wollstonecraft's ambivalence was her view that "in the current state of society" there was always the danger that women's sensibility was more likely to undermine than strengthen virtue by encouraging "romantic, wavering feelings" rather than "strong, persevering passions." As Maria reflects while gazing out of her asylum window hoping to catch a glimpse of Darnford, "how difficult it was for women to avoid growing romantic, who have no active duties or pursuits" (Wollstonecraft 1980b, 1: 87).

Wollstonecraft's attempt in the *Vindication* to distinguish between those passions that undermine and those that strengthen virtue echoes Rousseau's attempt to make a similar distinction. Like Rousseau, she feels that the very same faculties and capacities, under different circumstances, may give rise to virtue and generosity of heart or self-centered vice. She also shares Rousseau's views about the power of education to shape these faculties and capacities for good or ill. Where she differs from Rousseau is in her acute awareness that virtue and vice arise as much, if not more, from the character of our social and affective relations with others as from our individual dispositions, characteristics, and capacities. Although she often wants to make exceptions for individuals of "genius" and at times portrays herself as Rousseau's solitary walker, requiring solitude for reflection, Wollstonecraft's individuals are nevertheless much more embedded in their relations with others than are Rousseau's.[19] Despite the fact that she condemns the kind of obedient dependence characteristic of subordination, for Wollstonecraft independence is not defined in opposition to a mutually supportive dependence on others. In fact, the values of affection, reciprocity, and love for humanity are central to her account of self-governance. Wollstonecraft's view is that in the absence of genuine feelings for others, self-governance is most likely to be displaced by a kind of self-interested prudence. This was one of the aspects of Imlay that so wounded her, and which she blamed on his involvement with commerce.[20] In the *Vindication* she claims:

> The world cannot be seen by an unmoved spectator; we must mix in the throng and feel as men feel, before we can judge of their feelings . . . we must attain knowledge of others at the same time that we become acquainted with ourselves. Knowledge acquired any other way only hardens the heart and perplexes the understanding.
>
> (Wollstonecraft 1975, 215)[21]

And in *The Wrongs of Woman* Jemima is presented as a woman with a great capacity for virtue, but in her "virtue, never nurtured by affection, assumed the stern aspect of selfish independence" (Wollstonecraft 1980b, 1: 82) until Maria treats her with affection and respect.

Many of the tensions in her writings and the conflicts in her life bear testimony to Wollstonecraft's painful awareness that for women "in the current state of society" this kind of self-governance founded in generosity and affection was very difficult to achieve. On the one hand, she argues, women's subordination to men within the family, the idea that women's function is solely to please men, and the denial to women of the right to express or act in accordance with their affections all conspire to make love and friendship founded on respect just about impossible between men and women. This is because the effect of women's situation on *women* is to give rise either to an excess of affectionate sensibility—as Wollstonecraft felt was true of herself—or else

to coquetry, while its effect on *men* is to render them lascivious or tyrannical or both. In these circumstances it is highly unlikely that women will have sufficient self-respect, or command sufficient respect from men, to make reciprocity a genuine possibility. In this context it is interesting to note that Wollstonecraft's sometimes prudish remarks in the *Vindication* about the need for bodily modesty arise from the conviction that self-respect and respect for others is necessarily connected with respect for the integrity of one's own body and for the bodies of others. By the time of *The Wrongs of Woman* the prudish aspects of this conviction have disappeared, and Wollstonecraft's comments about marriage laws—"legal prostitution"—that make women and their children the property of men suggest that she regarded women's right to self-governance with respect to their bodies as integral to the demand for equality.

On the other hand, she continues, women's exclusion from the duties of citizenship tends to promote a kind of self-centeredness and leads to a lack of that sense of justice that is necessary if we are to treat others with respect. Here Wollstonecraft points to the behavior of those leisured women who show more concern for their dogs than for their servants. She also points to the kind of parental affection that is an extension of this kind of self-love: "Justice, truth, everything is sacrificed by these Rebekahs, and for the sake of their *own* children they violate the most sacred duties, forgetting the common relationship that binds the whole family on earth together" (Wollstonecraft 1975, 265). Wollstonecraft is adamant that the only solution is a transformation of women's situation in *both* private and public spheres.

IV.

One of the major themes of Wollstonecraft's work is that women will not be able to attain self-governance without a certain degree of material—particularly financial—independence. Wollstonecraft's concern with women's financial independence arises out of two firm convictions. The first is that women's emotional dependence and subjection to the tyranny of men will continue so long as women are financially dependent on men and so long as women's independence is not protected by the law. This conviction is articulated most forcefully in *The Wrongs of Woman,* where it is dramatized in the stories of Maria, Jemima, and the various women in whose houses Maria takes lodgings after leaving George Venables, all of whom are victims of the law's inequality. The second is that financial independence, but more importantly, work, is essential to self-esteem and to virtue. As Wollstonecraft remarks in the *Vindication,* "virtue, says reason, must be acquired by *rough* toils, and useful struggles with worldly *cares*" (Wollstonecraft 1975, 143, note 5). These convictions underlie her suggestion that women could very usefully be trained for a number of professions, including medicine, education, politics, and business.

Wollstonecraft was aware that women's financial independence could not be achieved without large-scale changes in the organization of society. To this end she advocated sweeping changes in marriage and property laws, urged the introduction of a system of public co-education, and suggested, even if somewhat tentatively, that it was not sufficient for women to be citizens, they must also be represented in government. Her view was that these were matters for public, not private, concern and felt that until such changes were introduced women would be unable to achieve self-governance in either their social or their affective relationships. However, Wollstonecraft had no clear proposals for how the changes she advocated might be compatible with the maternal "duties" that she seemed to think were natural to women. For this reason feminists recently have raised two serious objections to Wollstonecraft's conception of self-governance.

First, it is often claimed that Wollstonecraft's ideal of self-governance is an ideal attainable only by middle-class women. In the **Vindication,** for example, her description of a harmonious and fulfilling domestic scene includes reference to a woman "discharging the duties of her station with perhaps merely a servant-maid to take off her hands the servile part of the household business" (Wollstonecraft 1975, 254-55), and it is evident that without such domestic help Wollstonecraft herself would not have been able to devote much of her time to the business of writing.[22] The character of Jemima in *The Wrongs of Woman* indicates that Wollstonecraft became increasingly aware of this problem. Nevertheless, much of the narrative is occupied with the story of the middle-class Maria, who promises, in exchange for Jemima's support, to better her situation. Is the self-governance of educated middle-class women therefore to be achieved at the expense of working-class women who can relieve them of the "servile" aspects of their duties?[23] This question remains pertinent today.

Second, it is argued that despite the importance of Wollstonecraft's critique of property and marriage laws and of her argument that the rights of citizenship must be extended to women if they are going to be expected to fulfill what are after all social duties (the rearing of children), her critique of civil society works by trying to extend the contractual relations of civil society into the private sphere rather than by challenging the association between the masculine/feminine distinction and the tensions within the liberal public sphere between justice and love, contract and kinship, individuality and community. In other words, Wollstonecraft claims for women the capacities of the self-governing male citizen, arguing that relations within the family between men and women and parents and children must be founded on the same basis as relations between equal citizens within the public sphere. Given this starting point, Wollstonecraft can only acknowledge the ethical and political implications of women's specific embodiment by arguing that women have specific *social* duties—namely, their maternal duties—to which any activities in which they engage in the public sphere must be seen as secondary. Wollstonecraft's conception of self-governance thus compels her to preserve the distinction between public and private spheres and consequently to accept the oppressive representation implicit in this distinction of women's bodies as passive and bound to nature.[24]

These criticisms can begin to be addressed by first assessing Wollstonecraft's views on maternity. Wollstonecraft's remarks about women's maternal duties need to be read fairly carefully for the following reasons. First, it is clear that these remarks play a very important strategic function in her argument in defense of equality. For as was indicated above, what she seeks to show is that even granting the premises of the Rousseauian argument, the conclusions thought to follow from it do not in fact do so. It should not be assumed, however, that Wollstonecraft simply endorses these premises. Second, that Wollstonecraft does not straightforwardly endorse these premises is evident from a number of conflicting remarks she makes about maternity. It is true that she does claim that "the care of children in their infancy is one of the grand duties annexed to the female character by nature" (Wollstonecraft 1975, 265). However, she also claims that "natural affection, as it is termed, I believe to be a very faint tie, affections must grow out of the habitual exercise of a mutual sympathy" (Wollstonecraft 1975, 266). And in *The Wrongs of Woman* Maria remarks that "*in the present state of women* it is a great misfortune to be prevented from discharging the duties, and cultivating the affections" of a mother (Wollstonecraft 1980b, 2: 154 Italics added). These remarks suggest that Wollstonecraft's views on maternity pertain to a very specific context, one in which women had few options as far as contributions to society were concerned, apart from the raising of children; in which, given the lack of genuinely reciprocal relationships between men and women, the only outlet for women's affections was in their relationships with their children; in which women were by default primarily responsible for the raising of children because there was no legal or social obligation for men to do so; and in which many leisured women effectively abrogated their responsibilities toward their children.

Given the complexity of this context, Wollstonecraft's views on maternity need to be read on a number of different levels. At one level they are addressed to men, in particular to middle-class men, in the hope of convincing them that the education of their daughters and wives will in fact better enable them to perform those duties that she concedes are "annexed to the female character by nature." At another level, by distinguishing between affections and duties and by suggesting that maternity is a *social* duty, not a merely "natural affection," Wollstonecraft aims to contest the assumption that maternity and self-governance are incompatible virtues by showing that the kind of affections, responsibilities, and skills that arise in the context of child rearing are essential to self-governance. On this basis she can then argue that "maternal duties" are not incompatible with the duties of a citizen. At yet another level, this distinction also enables Wollstonecraft to suggest that women should be able to fulfill their obligations to society in ways other than, or additional to, maternity. Although Wollstonecraft was very well aware that this would not be possible without vast changes in the structure of society, it seems clear that she thought the difficulty was a question of social organization rather than of women's natures.

If this reading of Wollstonecraft's views on maternity is correct, what are its implications for the claim that her ideal of self-governance is an ideal attainable only by educated middle-class women? It is important to distinguish between the issue of whether class distinction is a necessary feature of Wollstonecraft's conception of self-governance and the issue of what she herself says on the matter. As far as Wollstonecraft herself is concerned, she seems to voice a number of somewhat conflicting views, probably reflecting the limited range of conceivable options that were available to her, indeed to all women. In a number of places she suggests that self-governance has less to do with what she calls a woman's "station" than with a woman's dignity and independence. In the **Vindication,** for example, she claims that virtue seems to be most prevalent among poor, uneducated working-class women (Wollstonecraft 1975, 171), and in *The Wrongs of Woman* Maria writes to her daughter: "I fondly hope to see you . . . possessed of that energy of character which gives dignity to any station; and with that clear, firm spirit that will enable you to choose a situation for yourself, or submit to be classed in the lowest, if it be the only one in which you can be the mistress of your own actions." (Wollstonecraft 1980b, 2: 149). Wollstonecraft was aware, however, that poor women, in addition to suffering the "wrongs of woman," also suffered the burdens of the poor more generally, and she believed that poor women were unlikely to be the mistresses of their own actions until both class and sex inequalities are abolished. Yet elsewhere Wollstonecraft seems to align self-governance with "cultivated sensibilities" and to take the existence of servants for granted, even though she is insistent that servants must be regarded and treated as fellow human beings. It is clear, though not surprising, that Wollstonecraft did not really come to terms with the question of who would care for the children of professional women. It is therefore quite possible that she assumed another woman, probably a servant, would

take up some of the responsibility. Despite this, I would deny that Wollstonecraft's conception of self-governance presupposes class distinction. For her ideal of self-governance is not committed to the idea that only professional women can achieve independence, even though she is adamant that a certain degree of education is essential for all women. Rather, at the heart of Wollstonecraft's concern with women's independence are the ideas that women must have the liberty and resources to assume responsibility for their own actions and that self-governance is not inconsistent with maternity, affection, or interdependence.

Where does this leave Wollstonecraft with respect to the public/private distinction and with respect to the alleged masculinity of her conception of self-governance? Again, Wollstonecraft's views need to be read carefully. On the one hand, she was aware that, "in the present imperfect state of society," men's equality and reason were achieved at the expense of women's liberty and autonomy and that reason and sensibility, justice and love, citizenship and kinship, and individuality and community seemed irreconcilable, particularly for women. I have tried to show that because she *was* concerned with the ethical implications of sexual difference, Wollstonecraft tried to articulate a conception of women's self-governance that does not simply identify self-governance with one side of these oppositions (the "masculine" side), but rather tries to reconcile them, as well as to disentangle them from their association with the masculine/feminine distinction.[25] I have also argued that Wollstonecraft was aware that her recommendations for women would require massive reorganization of the public sphere, including the political representation of women's interests. That Wollstonecraft in 1792 could not envisage the full extent of this reorganization should not lead us to conclude that she underestimated its difficulty or immensity.

But what is to be made of Wollstonecraft's agreement with Rousseau that the family is the foundation of civil life? And what is to be made of her concession that women's comparative physical weakness may make them more "dependent," and so perhaps less able to achieve virtue, than men? (Wollstonecraft 1975, 80, 109). To some extent this concession should be read as a response to Rousseau's attempt to link his claims about "feminine" reason and virtue to the supposed "natural" passivity and dependency of the female body. Wollstonecraft seeks once again to show that one may accept Rousseau's premises without accepting his conclusion—that virtue is different for the different sexes. This interpretation is supported by Wollstonecraft's frequent arguments to the effect that the physical incapacities to which many women are subject are the direct result of their subordination—in particular, of ideals of feminine beauty that actively discourage women from developing physical strength and skill. However, in light of the fact that Wollstonecraft's text wavers between the character ideal conception of self-governance that I have highlighted in this article and the idea that self-governance is a matter of reason's sovereignty over the body, this concession also indicates that Wollstonecraft was still struggling in the grip of the dominant cultural representation of women's bodies as passive, heteronomous bodies. This is perhaps why in the **Vindication** she could not see a clear solution to the problem of women's subordination except a transformation of the family. The events of Wollstonecraft's life after the publication of the *Vindication,* as well as her later writings, indicate that she became somewhat less optimistic about this solution. But the fact that feminists today are still coming to terms with the problem she so acutely diagnosed, and with some of her solutions, shows that many of the conflicts Wollstonecraft experienced and expressed in trying to articulate an adequate ideal of self-governance for women are still with us.

Notes

1. I use the terms "autonomy" and "self-governance" interchangeably in this article, although only the latter term was used by Wollstonecraft. My tendency, however, is to stick with Wollstonecraft's own term.

2. This view is expressed by Claire Tomalin (1974). Between the time of the publication of *Vindication of the Rights of Woman* in 1792 and her death following childbirth in 1797, Wollstonecraft had lived in revolutionary circles in Paris during the French Revolution; had had an affair with the American, Imlay, who was the father of her first child, Fanny; attempted suicide on two occasions following the break up of her relationship with Imlay; and lived with and then married William Godwin, who was the father of her second child, Mary (Shelley). By the standards of her time, and indeed even by our own, her life was extremely unconventional. It is partly because of this that the nature of her personal life has often provided the main context for the reception and interpretation of her work since the publication of *Vindication.*

3. See especially Miriam Kramnick's introduction to the 1975 edition of *Vindication,* and Moira Gatens (1991a). Although my interpretation of Wollstonecraft differs quite markedly from that of Gatens, her discussion in this article helped provoke a rethinking of my views on Wollstonecraft.

4. An exception to the standard contemporary feminist interpretation of Wollstonecraft's work is that of Jean Grimshaw (1989) which I discovered after writing this article. Grimshaw does not specifically discuss Wollstonecraft's views on autonomy, but she does argue that a careful reading of Wollstonecraft's other writings, apart from the *Vindication,* is essential if we are to understand the tensions and shifts in her views.

5. For a scholarly account of the changing associations within the history of philosophy between the reason/passion and public/private oppositions and ideals of masculinity and femininity, see Lloyd (1984).

6. This unfinished novel, which Wollstonecraft tells the reader is the story "of woman, rather than of an individual," is set in an asylum—Wollstonecraft's metaphor for women's "civil death" in eighteenth-century English society (see note 12 below). Its three central characters are Maria, a woman who has been committed and had her child abducted by an unfaithful and impecunious husband (George Venables) seeking to gain control of her inheritance; Jemima, Maria's warder, a working-class woman whose basically virtuous character has been deadened by poverty, sexual abuse, hard labor, and lack of affection; and the ambivalent Darnford, Maria's lover, who seems to embody both the virtues and the vices that Wollstonecraft discovered in men.

7. See also Moria Gatens (1986) and the discussion of Wollstonecraft in Chapter 1 Gatens (1991b).

8. Gatens' arguments in both her articles on Wollstonecraft (Gatens 1986, 1991a) seem to assume that a recognition of the ethical significance of sexual difference entails the idea of a specific feminine ethic. This assumption does not seem to me to be self-evident.

9. Rousseau's proposals concerning the education of women and his attempts to justify these proposals through an account of woman's "nature," occupy most of book V of *Emile* which is an account of the appropriate education for Sophie, Emile's future wife and helpmeet (Rousseau 1974). In book V it becomes clear that the concern with equality that preoccupies Rousseau in the *Social Contract* and the *Discourse on the Origin of Inequality* is a concern with men's equality only, as women are specifically excluded from the rights and duties of citizenship. In connection with this, feminist commentators have pointed out how Sophie's education is designed not around her own needs but around the idea that her role is to be Emile's complement and subordinate: "Nature herself has decreed that woman, both for herself and her children, should be at the mercy of man's judgment. . . . A woman's education must therefore be planned in relation to man" (Rousseau 1974, 328). For a sample of some of these commentaries see the discussions of Rousseau in Lloyd (1984), Martin (1985), Okin (1979), and Pateman (1988).

10. Wollstonecraft's interest in the doctrine of human perfectibility seems to be have been aroused by her association with the dissenting theologian and reformer Dr. Richard Price. For an account of this association at various periods of Wollstonecraft's life, see Tomalin (1974).

11. In contrast to Gatens (1991b, 23), who argues that Wollstonecraft's critique of the inequities of Rousseau's educational proposals for women does not take into account the integral role that these proposals play in Rousseau's overall social and political project, the following argument is intended to show that Wollstonecraft was well aware of this connection. In fact, what Wollstonecraft seeks to show is that Rousseau's proposals for women's education will actually undermine his social and political project.

12. In many places in the *Vindication* Wollstonecraft is quite scathing about the coquettish, pleasure seeking, self-obsessed behavior of these women who could take as long as five hours to get dressed! Her observations as well as her animosity arose from her experience working as governess to the children of a landed Irish aristocratic couple, the Kingsboroughs. Wollstonecraft felt that there was little hope, short of revolution, for changing the ways of the aristocracy. However, she hoped to influence the middle classes, to whom, she claims, her book is addressed. Wollstonecraft was appalled by the way in which the newly leisured middle-class women were attempting to emulate their aristocratic sisters, but, despite her scorn, the argument of the *Vindication* is that the behavior of these women has only one source—their social position. As Miriam Kramnick makes clear, (Wollstonecraft 1975), the social position of both middle- and working-class women and the opportunities open to them were dramatically different at the end of the eighteenth century from what they had been one hundred years previously. The rapid expansion of industrialization and mechanization in production had shifted much productive work out of the domestic economy and out of family-based businesses and into factories removed from the home. As a result, middle-class women, who previously had played a significant role in the economy, had become a leisured class dependent entirely on their husbands for economic support and "protection," while working-class women spent increasingly long hours outside the home, performing badly paid menial work with very little time left to care for their children. While working-class women thus ruined their health in factories, middle-class women ruined their health through idleness and through attempts to achieve ideals of "feminine" beauty. Women's economic disenfranchisement became "civil death" when Blackstone announced in 1757 that "the very being or legal existence of the woman is suspended during the marriage or at least is incorporated and consolidated into that of the husband" (quoted by Kramnick in Wollstonecraft 1975, 34). As I will suggest later in this article, sensitivity to this context makes more comprehensible some of Wollstonecraft's more drastic pronouncements against pleasure.

13. According to Rousseau, feminine virtue must be enforced in two ways: first, by ensuring that women not only remain in the private sphere but also lead retiring, almost reclusive lives: "the genuine mother of a family is no woman of the world, she is almost as much of a recluse as the nun in her convent" (Rousseau 1974, 350), and second, through the iron grip of social opinion. Rousseau asserts in *Emile*: "A man has no one but himself to consider, and so long as he does right he may defy public opinion; but when a woman does right her task is only half finished, and what people think of her matters as much as what she really is" (Rousseau 1974, 328).

14. Compare Wollstonecraft (1980b, 1: 137): "By allowing women but one way of rising in the world, the fostering the libertinism of men, society makes monsters of them, and then their ignoble vices are brought forward as proof of inferiority of intellect."

15. The attitude of stoic resignation is most evident in Wollstonecraft's early novel *Mary, A Fiction,* originally published in 1788 (Wollstonecraft 1980a). At the end of the novel the heroine's response to sorrow and sexual injustice is resignation mixed with joy at the prospect of death and the thought that "she was hastening to that world *where there is neither marrying,* nor giving in marriage" (Wollstonecraft 1980a, 68). Even here, however, Wollstonecraft's irony gets the better of her resignation.

16. Compare the following remarks, "Standing armies can never consist of resolute robust men; they may be well-disciplined machines, but they will seldom contain men under the influence of strong passions, or with very vigorous faculties; and as for any depth of understanding I will venture to affirm that it is as rarely to be found in the army as amongst women . . . The great misfortune is this, that they both acquire manners before morals, and a knowledge of life before they have from reflection any acquaintance with the grand ideal outline of human nature. The consequence is natural. Satisfied with common nature, they become a prey to prejudices, and taking all their opinions on credit, they blindly submit to authority" (Wollstonecraft 1975, 106).

17. Compare Maria's picture of her uncle who "inculcated, with great warmth, self-respect, and a lofty consciousness of acting right, independent of the censure of the world," (Wollstonecraft 1980b, 2: 128).

18. Compare Wollstonecraft (1975, 202) on woman "becoming the slave of her own feelings, she is easily subjugated by those of others."

19. In a footnote in the *Vindication* that anticipates contemporary feminist critiques of liberalism, Wollstonecraft suggests that Rousseau's picture of the solitary individual in the "state of nature" overlooks "the long and helpless state of infancy" and so the necessary sociality of human life (Wollstonecraft 1975, 94). Many contemporary feminists have argued that liberal political theory, particularly in its more libertarian guises, is deeply flawed because it assumes a mistaken conception of human subjectivity, namely, that human beings spring out of the earth fully developed like mushrooms, to paraphrase Hobbes. For a sample of these critiques, see Pateman (1988); Jaggar (1983); and Tapper (1986). Whether this characterization is applicable to contemporary forms of liberalism and social contract theory is, of course, the subject of considerable debate among liberals, communitarians, and feminists.

20. See, for example, her letter to him written in Hamburg en route to England from Scandinavia (Wollstonecraft 1977, Letter LXVII, 251). Wollstonecraft seemed to regard commerce as inherently corrupting. Compare her portraits of George Venables and the young Darnford in *The Wrongs of Woman* (Wollstonecraft 1980b).

21. Compare also Wollstonecraft (1977, Letter III, 150-51): "Mixing with mankind, we are obliged to examine our prejudices, and often imperceptibly lose, as we analyze them."

22. Wollstonecraft employed a French nursemaid named Marguerite to care for Fanny.

23. This objection is raised by Gatens (1991a), Martin (1985), and Eisenstein (1981, chap. 5).

24. As was mentioned earlier, this criticism is raised by Gatens (1986, 1991a, and 1991b). Carole Pateman also makes a similar criticism in Pateman (1988).

25. In this respect, her work anticipates some of the preoccupations of contemporary feminist philosophers interested in moral theory and theories of justice. See, for example, Benhabib (1987), Okin (1989); and Young (1990).

References

Benhabib, Seyla. 1987. "The generalized and the concrete other." In *Feminism as critique,* ed. Seyla Benhabib and Drucilla Cornell. Minneapolis: University of Minnesota Press.

Eisenstein, Zillah. 1981. *The radical future of liberal feminism.* New York: Longman.

Gatens, Moira. 1986. "Rousseau and Wollstonecraft: Nature vs. reason." In *Women and philosophy,* ed. Janna Thompson. Supplement to *Australasian Journal of Philosophy* 64 (June): 1-15.

———. 1991a. "The oppressed state of my sex: Wollstonecraft on reason, feeling and equality." In *Feminist interpretations and political theory,* ed. Carole Pateman and Mary Lyndon Shanley. Cambridge: Polity Press; University Park: Pennsylvania State University Press.

———. 1991b. *Feminism and philosophy: Perspectives on equality and difference.* Cambridge: Polity Press; Bloomington: Indiana University Press.

Grimshaw, Jean. 1989. "Mary Wollstonecraft and the tensions in feminist philosophy." *Radical Philosophy* 52 (Summer): 11-17.

Jaggar, Alison. 1983. *Feminist politics and human nature.* Totowa, NJ: Rowman and Allanheld; Brighton: Harvester.

Kittay, Eva, and Diana T. Meyers, eds. 1987. *Women and moral theory.* Totowa, NJ: Rowman and Littlefield.

Lloyd, Genevieve. 1984. *The man of reason.* London: Methuen; Minneapolis: University of Minnesota Press.

Martin, Jane Roland. 1985. *Reclaiming a conversation: The ideal of the educated woman.* New Haven: Yale University Press.

Okin, Susan. 1979. *Women in Western political thought.* Princeton, N.J.: Princeton University Press.

———. 1989. *Justice, gender and the family.* New York: Basic Books.

Pateman, Carole. 1988. *The sexual contract.* Cambridge: Polity.

Rousseau, Jean Jacques. [1755] 1973. "Discourse on the origins of inequality." In *"The Social Contract" and other discourses.* London: Dent (Everyman's Library).

———. [1762] 1974. *Emile.* London: Dent; New York Dutton (Everyman's Library).

———. [1762] 1983. *On the social contract; Discourse on the origin of inequality; Discourse on political economy.* Indianapolis, IN: Hackett.

Tapper, Marion. 1986. "Can a feminist be a liberal?" In *Women and philosophy,* ed. Janna Thompson. Supplement to *Australasian Journal of Philosophy* 64 (June): 37-47.

Tomalin, Claire. 1974. *The life and death of Mary Wollstonecraft.* New York: Harcourt, Brace, Jovanovich.

Todd, Janet M., ed. 1977. *A Wollstonecraft anthology.* Bloomington: Indiana University Press.

Wollstonecraft, Mary. [1792] 1975. *Vindication of the rights of woman,* ed. Miriam Kramnick. Harmondsworth: Penguin, 1975.

———. [1796] 1977. *Letters written during a short residence in Sweden, Norway, and Denmark.* In *A Wollstonecraft anthology,* ed. Janet M. Todd. Bloomington: Indiana University Press.

———. [1788] 1980a. *Mary, A Fiction.* In *Mary and "The Wrongs of Woman,"* ed. James Kinsley and Gary Kelly. Oxford: Oxford University Press.

———. [1798] 1980b. *The wrongs of woman; or, Maria: A fragment.* In *Mary and "The wrongs of woman,"* eds. James Kinsley, and Gary Kelly. Oxford: Oxford University Press.

Young, Iris. 1990. *Justice and the politics of difference.* Princeton: Princeton University Press.

Sally-Ann Kitts (essay date April 1994)

SOURCE: Kitts, Sally-Ann. "Mary Wollstonecraft's *A Vindication of the Rights of Woman*: A Judicious Response from the Eighteenth-Century Spain." *Modern Language Review* 89, no. 2 (April 1994): 351-59.

[*In the following essay, Kitts discusses a 1792 review of* A Vindication of the Rights of Woman *in a Spanish periodical that was very favorable but which played down the work's more revolutionary aspects.*]

Those familiar with Mary Wollstonecraft's radical feminist text, ***A Vindication of the Rights of Woman,*** may be surprised to discover that it received a lengthy and favourable review in a periodical published in the reactionary Spain of 1792. Following the outbreak of the French Revolution in July 1789, the government of Charles IV, headed by the Count of Floridablanca, had taken increasingly severe measures to curb the spread of revolutionary ideas from France, a country which had exerted a great influence on the development of Spanish culture and ideas throughout the eighteenth century. Beginning on a small scale with border seizures of books and prints, restrictive measures soon became more institutionalized: exactly a year after the storming of the Bastille, an updated index of prohibited and expurgated books, including revolutionary writings, was published; a severe press law was promulgated on 24 February 1791 forbidding the publication of any periodicals except the two official gazettes (*Mercurio histórico y político de España, Gaceta de Madrid*) and

the *Diario de Madrid,* and in June 1793 a blanket ban was declared on any mention, whether critical or favourable, of the events occurring in France.[1] The government was helped in establishing a 'cordón sanitario' between France and Spain by a renewed rapprochement with the Inquisition from September 1789 onwards, a notable change in policy following a period in which the power of the Church as a whole over Spanish society had been gradually restricted by the government of Charles III.[2]

One of the most wide-reaching and harmful of these measures, as far as the cultural and intellectual development of Spain was concerned, was the Royal Resolution of 24 February 1791 banning all private periodicals, except for the *Diario de Madrid,* 'por haber [en ellos] muchas especies perjudiciales'.[3] Indeed, the periodical press had become the major vehicle for the dissemination of new ideas in eighteenth-century Spain.[4] From its earliest polemical example, the *Diario de los literatos de España* (1737-42), through its first burgeoning in the decade of the 1760s with the essay-periodicals, modelled on Addison and Steele's earlier *Spectator,* the periodical press reached a period of daring and brilliance in the 1780s. The outspoken Madrid periodical *El censor* (1782-87) enlivened the early years, while the decade was to culminate in a burst of information and discussion of new ideas and advances in almost all fields of knowledge from 1786 until the untimely demise of periodicals in 1791.

Floridablanca's law caused irreparable damage to the periodical press, which was not to recover any real vigour until the death of Ferdinand VII in 1833, apart, that is, from two brief periods of activity during the liberal years of 1810-14 and 1820-23.[5] Those few journals which were able to publish in the last decade of the eighteenth century were forced to concentrate on issues of lesser importance, with no possible political significance. They were largely of commercial, agricultural, or scientific interest, or concentrated on the arts, publishing readers' poems and short articles together with bland reviews and tedious historical or geographical anecdotes.[6] Yet one topic which did continue to be aired was that of women's rights and role in society, a subject which had received much attention throughout the century in books, pamphlets, the theatre, and above all in the periodicals.[7] It was presumably seen by the government as a safe subject, offering no serious threat to either the political or the social stability of the country, a perception confirmed by the innocuous nature of the discussion in this period, which was largely limited to the question of the need for, nature, and aims of education for women, together with the possibility of enhancing their contribution to the welfare of society.[8]

While Mary Wollstonecraft's ***A Vindication of the Rights of Woman*** addresses both these apparently safe matters, it offers at the same time a radical review of the whole basis and structure of contemporary society.[9] Wollstonecraft was a staunch supporter of both the French Revolution and the egalitarian principles which underpinned it, and a vociferous and outspoken defender of women's rights at a time when the vast majority of women had virtually none. She stands out as one of the first women to work in a typically male profession, managing to support herself financially as a reviewer and editorial assistant to Thomas Christie on Joseph Johnson's journal, *The Analytical Review.* Her emotional life also set her apart from the accepted norm: in the Spring of 1793 she began a passionate affair with the American, Gilbert Imlay, and in May 1794 gave birth to their illegitimate daughter, Fanny. Learning of his faithlessness, she made the first of two attempts at suicide in May 1795, finally managing to break off with him later in 1795 after her second attempt at suicide failed. She began a relationship with William Godwin in 1796 and they were married in March 1797 following the discovery of her second pregnancy. Mary Wollstonecraft Godwin died following the birth of her second daughter in August 1797.[10]

First published in January 1792, *A Vindication of the Rights of Woman: With Strictures on Political and Moral Subjects* was swiftly translated into French. The French edition, entitled *Défense des droits des femmes,* is an accomplished, enthusiastic, and accurate translation of the original work.[11] The translator is an unnamed woman, who adds a number of footnotes to the text. They explain certain customs peculiar to English society or expand upon some of Wollstonecraft's arguments, calling at one point for better education and the right to divorce for women in France (pp. 448-49).[12]

The first part of the Spanish review of the French edition appeared in the *Diario de Madrid* on 6 September 1792, less than nine months after the publication of the first English edition.[13] The *Diario de Madrid,* a publication dating back to 1758, was the first daily newspaper to be published in Spain. The only non-governmental periodical allowed to continue publishing after Floridablanca's press ban, the *Diario de Madrid* is also noteworthy for its support of women writers and poets, publishing a large number of poems, letters, and short articles by women through to the first years of the nineteenth century.[14] This increase in the presence of creative writing by women in the last years of the eighteenth century may be seen as a positive and tangible effect of the debate in Spain on women's intellectual abilities which had begun with Feijoo's feminist essay, *Defensa de las mujeres* (1726). It reflects an increasing acceptance amongst the educated classes of woman's rationality and her ability to undertake intellectual pursuits and not just limit herself to domestic skills, an acceptance brought about by the substantial presence of writings about woman, both in the press and in books.

The review of Mary Wollstonecraft's *A Vindication of the Rights of Woman* is signed simply 'J. de V.', the initials of Julián de Velasco, co-editor of the *Diario de Madrid* with Pedro Salanova since the beginning of 1791.[15] Velasco's career in journalism appears to have begun in 1789 when, aged only twenty-five, he published the *Discursos literarios, políticos y morales,* a periodical which declared in the first issue that it was for 'las personas que se dedican al estudio de la moral, de la política y de la legislación'.[16] The periodical ran to only seven issues following the seizure of issue No. 6, a history of the Jesuits, and was condemned by the Inquisition in an edict of 10 May 1789.[17] Velasco is also known to have presented several requests to publish new periodicals, but these were not approved for publication: in 1787 for a *Mercurio filosófico,* together with his brother Bernardo who was a *Juez de Imprentas*; in 1802 for a *Diario de los teatros,* with Eusebio Alvarez; in 1803 for the *Efemérides de la instrucción de España,* thought to have been the inspiration behind Pedro Olivé's successful *Efemérides de la Illustración de España* (1804-05).[18] Velasco is also known to have been secretary to the Marqués de Valdelirio, a member of the Madrid Economic Society and would appear to have been an able French linguist.[19]

A forthright and politically radical text, *A Vindication of the Rights of Woman* would have suffered an immediate and probably total ban in Spain, from both the governmental and the inquisitorial censors, had its full contents been known. It is therefore not surprising to discover that the reviewer should have been selective in his choice of passages and arguments to highlight. Velasco paraphrases and translates extracts of around a paragraph in size, mostly taken from the beginnings and ends of chapters, which generally summarize the chief points made. Overall, the reviewer is very favourable to the book, providing an accurate summary of most of its arguments, although tempering their more revolutionary aspects. He also does not communicate the tone of anger and defiance and the feeling of personal involvement which come from the process of discussing a problem which the author shared with her readers and which characterizes Wollstonecraft's original text. The French edition gives the author's name as Mary Wollstonecraft and the text provides numerous indications of the sex of the author.[20] However, Velasco appears to wish the readers to think that Wollstonecraft is a man, since he assiduously avoids any reference to her as a woman. His Spanish version of the title gives her name as 'Marly Wollstone-craft' (p. 1043), and she is referred to variously throughout the review in either a male or a neutral fashion: as 'Wolstone Craft' (p. 1051), 'Wolstone' (p. 1051), 'Wolstonecraft' (p. 1052), 'Wollstonecraft' (p. 1179), 'M. W.' (p. 1180), 'Nuestro Filósofo' (p. 1183), 'Mr. Wolstonecraft' (p. 1185), and most frequently as 'el autor' or 'nuestro autor'.

Velasco begins by declaring that the fundamental idea of Wollstonecraft's work is 'explicada y discutida con mucha propiedad' (p. 1043) and he goes on to call it a 'sabia defensa de los derechos de las mujeres' (p. 1051). The review captures succinctly the general thrust of Wollstonecraft's argument, highlighting a number of important points. It states that the apparent improvement in the situation of women in Europe from the slavery of past centuries is deceptive, since women are in fact held in esteem by men only for their beauty, and this esteem lasts only as long as their good looks endure. This fictitious position of equality of men and women in European society exists at the expense of virtue, and it still remains the case that women have no rights whatsoever and no freedom. Rights for women can be obtained only by means of an education based on reason and which aims to enable women to exercise their mental faculties. It is only in this way that women will gain a precise knowledge of their obligations in and to society. Velasco notes that Wollstonecraft believes women cannot be criticized for failing to carry out their obligations, since no obligation can be said to bind if it is not backed by reason and the choice to fulfil it has not been freely and rationally made. Women's lack of education makes such a choice impossible for them. The reviewer draws a set of requirements from Wollstonecraft's text for the improvement of women's situation and society in general:

> Dar a las mujeres los mismos principios de educación que a los hombres, aficionarlas a sus obligaciones por el mismo conocimiento de estos deberes, dirigir su corazón y su espíritu por las luces de la razón, libertarlas de toda opresión que se oponga a los progresos de su espíritu y que suele ahogar todas las semillas de lo bueno, son otros tantos manantiales fecundos que producirán las mayores ventajas en la sociedad.

> (p. 1184)

Velasco writes that for Wollstonecraft, virtue is more than a superficial attitude projected onto the world and is common to both sexes. Real virtue is based on solid principles and rational reflection, and he notes that Wollstonecraft believes it is impossible for an individual to be virtuous in a state of total dependence on others, such as that in which women find themselves. Women, therefore, need the protection of civil laws to enable them to carry out their social and human obligations. To deny women education to develop their faculties of reason is a public waste of half the human race, since there are many occupations in which they could engage. If men were to treat women rationally and not as slaves, they would be better mothers, wives, sisters, and daughters, and have a true and real love for men once they were able to have respect for themselves. This would lead to true feelings of affection amongst families, and society as a whole would benefit. To achieve this harmonious state, women need a proper in-

tellectual and rational education, preferably in co-educational schools, as this will help to prepare them for coping in marriage and in society.

Velasco concludes his review with a quotation from Wollstonecraft:

> La virtud no prevalecerá en la sociedad, hasta que las virtudes de ambos sexos estén fundadas en la claridad de la razón, *después de estarlo en la religión* y hasta que se deje que los afectos que les son comunes adquieran la fuerza de que son capaces para poner en práctica sus mutuas obligaciones.

> (p. 1185, my italics)

The quotation comes from Chapter 12 of the **Vindication,** entitled 'On National Education', and reads in the French version:

> Le vertu ne prévaudra dans la société, que lorsque les vertus des deux sexes seront fondées sur la raison, et que lorsqu'on laissera les affections qui leur sont communes, acquérir la force dont elles sont susceptibles par la pratique de leurs mutuels devoirs.[21]

Velasco may well have added the reference to the primacy of religion to suit the requirements of Spanish Catholic readers and the Inquisition. The conclusion of the review corresponds with the middle of Chapter 12, which is the penultimate chapter of Wollstonecraft's text. Given that the French translation is complete, it appears that Velasco chose to ignore the authors' detailed recommendations in Chapter 12 for national public education for girls and omitted her final chapter, 'Some instances of the folly which the ignorance of women generates; with concluding reflections on the moral improvement that a revolution in female manners might naturally be expected to produce'.

The Spanish review of the translation of the **Vindication,** although (as can be seen from the above summary) for the most part a fair and detailed account of Wollstonecraft's arguments, is noticeably silent on one important aspect. Chapters 1 and 2 criticize the oppression of society exercised by the aristocracy, the army, and the Church. Wollstonecraft sees these authorities as tyrannical, arbitrary powers which subvert the natural order of equality and bar any possibility of social improvement and progress for women by inhibiting the development of reason. The overthrow of these institutions and the individuals who support them is a precondition for any real change in women's situation. Her criticism of the Church, and in particular of the aristocracy and monarchy, would assuredly have caused outrage and suffered the harshest censorship in the Spain of 1792.[22] It would seem reasonable to suggest, therefore, that Velasco may have chosen to operate a system of self-censorship and simply omit this aspect, in spite of it being a precondition to Wollstonecraft's later arguments. He presumably judged that it was better to disseminate successfully the particular idea on women's rights than to attempt to put forward the whole argument and thereby risk problems with the censors similar to those which he had experienced four years earlier with the *Discursos literarios, políticos y morales.*

A similar approach was adopted by a later Spanish translator of one of Wollstonecraft's texts, Francisca Ruiz de Larrea, the wife of Juan Nicolás Böhl de Faber. In his article on Francisca Ruiz de Larrea and Mary Wollstonecraft, Guillermo Carnero identifies a manuscript of travel letters, apparently written by Francisca, as being in fact a translation of Wollstonecraft's *Letters Written during a Short Residence in Sweden, Norway and Denmark,* published by Joseph Johnson in 1796.[23] A careful comparison with the original revealed to Carnero that certain deliberate changes had been made:

> Se trata de conscientes censuras. [. . .] En resumen: ha desaparecido todo lo que había en las *Letters* de Mary Wollstonecraft favorable a la crítica de los tópicos religiosos, o demonstrativo de comprensión hacia la Revolución Francesa. Y no falta en cambio, carta decimotercera, el ataque a Robespierre.

> (p. 141)

It would seem that Francisca Ruiz de Larrea also considered some of Wollstonecraft's views to be inappropriate for a prospective Spanish readership.

Yet Julián de Velasco's review of the *Vindication* was not unusual in its support of the case for women's rights, in its favourable reception of the work, or in its omitting the more radical aspects of the book. Spain was an increasingly reactionary country in 1792 and it is therefore both likely and understandable that the more radical aspects of Mary Wollstonecraft's work should have been excluded. It is surprising, however, to discover that they were also ignored by most of the English reviews of her work. Thus R. M. Janes notes that all except one of the first English reviews of the *Vindication* were favourable and that:

> The contents of the reviews favourable to the work indicate why it was ignored rather than virulently attacked by most of those opposed to the political assumptions Wollstonecraft held. Most took it to be a sensible treatise on female education and ignored those recommendations in the work that might unsettle the relations between the sexes.[24]

It would appear that the majority of reviewers, be they English or Spanish, emphasized the work as an educational treatise and may have considered that the views on political and social revolution were too extreme to be taken seriously. As Miriam Brody notes:

> Although the argument is inherently revolutionary, advocating the replacement of an aristocracy of inherited property and titles with a meritocracy based on reason,

the *Vindication* professes with such self-evident sincerity the values of a harmonious, affectionate family life, respect for faithfulness between husband and wife, and devotion to the welfare of children, that the traditional humanistic concern of women for family and children is satisfied.

> (p. 63)

Velasco's presentation of the work purely as a respectable treatise on women's upbringing and social role appears to be a standard interpretation for his time.

Velasco's particular focus and emphases are likely to be governed not only by common-sense expediency but also by an understanding of the needs and interests of his readership. Having been presented with a lengthy series of articles discussing the nature, education, and role of women in society in the periodical press of the 1780s, the literate Spanish public of 1792 could be assumed to be conversant with many of the central issues and arguments of the debate. A number of the points raised by Wollstonecraft and referred to by Velasco had already been articulated by Spanish authors in relatively recent popular discussion of female issues. For example, in 1786 a Spanish female intellectual, Josefa Amar y Borbón, writing in favour of the admission of women to the Madrid Economic Society, had highlighted the emphasis placed on appearance and on such so-called feminine qualities as delicacy and grace to the detriment of women's education.[25] Her answer was an education for women based on reason, and the later publication of a book permitted her to set out a detailed set of proposals for a comprehensive intellectual education for women.[26] A similar observation on the evanescence of beauty and the need for women to be educated in order to be virtuous had been made some twenty-five years earlier in José Clavijo y Fajardo's *El Pensador.*[27]

Similarly, Wollstonecraft's claim that women need to be freed from their state of dependence on men and given the protection of civil laws was forcefully put by 'D. J. G.', a contributor to the *Correo de Madrid,* in 1789.[28] The article compares the perceived slavery of women in Eastern harems with the deceptive freedom of European women in eighteenth-century society. In fact, D. J. G. argues, European women are frequently imprisoned by poverty, by the outcome of double moral standards which condemn them to lives of vice for a single sexual transgression, or by despotic husbands aided and abetted by a legal system which refuses to recognize women as having any independent status under the law.

The argument put forward by Wollstonecraft, that to deny women a rational education is a waste of a potential workforce of half of the human race, is one which had been articulated in September 1786 by another contributor to the debate on the admission of women to the Madrid Economic Society, Ignacio López de Ayala.[29]

The idea of using women as a workforce was very appealing to contemporary Spanish intellectuals, in particular politicians and those involved in the Economic Societies, who were faced with the task of rebuilding Spain's economy at a time when her world prestige was low and her impoverished industrial base could not compete with the tide of imports of manufactured goods which were draining further the national resources. Ayala states his case in simple but forceful terms:

> Trátese de saber si las mujeres españolas, esto es, si la mitad de España, han de permanecer inútiles como hasta aquí; o si, por el contrario, se les han de suministrar luces y conocimientos para que ayuden a los hombres y gobiernen con inteligencia sus caudales y familias. Trátese de saber si se puede sacar de este sexo utilidad o si es un gremio réprobo que debe quedar abandonado al capricho, a la inutilidad, ociosidad y desenvoltura; porque en sustancia esto se inquiere cuando se pregunta si han de tener parte en las Sociedades Económicas.

(p. 176)

Ayala exhibits a similar view to that expressed throughout her work by Wollstonecraft on the present degenerate state of much of womankind as a result of a deficient upbringing and education. His arguments are based on a premise shared with Wollstonecraft that men and women have mutual obligations founded on their equal capacities for rational thought and he too argues for a review of the relations between the sexes in order to achieve proper and natural harmony in human interaction: 'No miremos, pues, como máquinas o como estatuas a las mujeres, hagámoslas compañeras del hombre en el trabajo, hagámoslas racionales, y sepan lo que son y lo que pueden' (p. 178).

Velasco himself had contributed to the debate on woman in the *Diario de Madrid,* both as an author and as the editor of a periodical which published articles on female issues, as well as poems, letters, and essays by women. In June of 1792 he published an article on women's education, highlighting the important role which women have within the family, and extending from that, within the state.[30] He emphasized, as Wollstonecraft had, the need for both men and women to be properly educated so as to understand and acquire virtue, and he considered that without this understanding the moral character of society would suffer. The date of his article does not preclude his having been influenced in his writing by his awareness of Wollstonecraft's text.

Julián de Velasco was typical of a small but vociferous number of progressive Spanish writers of the 1780s and 1790s who supported an improved education and social status for women. He was clearly familiar with the current parameters of the debate on woman in Spain and may well have been influenced in his choice of which arguments to highlight from *A Vindication of the Rights of Woman* by his knowledge of what was acceptable and of current interest to his readership. His obvious acquaintance with the Spanish debate on women's rights and role in society enabled him to present a detailed and favourable review of the main thrust of those of Wollstonecraft's arguments which concentrated on feminist issues. At the same time his common sense and perception of the difficult times faced by Spanish intellectuals in the period following the French Revolution led him to keep a judicious silence on the radical elements which form the foundation for Wollstonecraft's vision of an egalitarian society. When these various implications and factors have been considered, it would appear that the publication in the Spain of 1792 of a favourable review of Wollstonecraft's most outspoken and well-known work may not be as strange and surprising as it might first have seemed.

Notes

1. On the measures taken to control the spread of revolutionary ideas in this period, see Lucienne Domergue, *Le livre en Espagne au temps de la Révolution Française* (Lyons: Presses Universitaires de Lyon, 1984), especially pp. 11-53; Lucien Dupuis, 'Francia y lo francés en la prensa periódica española durante la Revolución francesa', in *La literatura española del siglo XVIII y sus fuentes extranjeras,* ed. by Joaquín Arce, Nigel Glendinning, and Lucien Dupuis, Cuadernos de la Cátedra Feijoo, 20 (Oviedo: Facultad de Filosofía y Letras, 1968), pp. 95-127.

2. See Lucienne Domergue, *Tres calas en la censura dieciochesca (Cadalso. Rousseau. Prensa Periódica)* (Toulouse: Université de Toulouse-Le Mirail, 1981), pp. 79-81. She notes: 'A partir de la Revolución el Inquisidor General [fue el] nuevo aliado del ministerio contra el enemigo comun' (p. 179).

3. 'Cesen los papeles periódicos a excepción del Diario de Madrid', *Novísima recopilación de las leyes de España* (Madrid: Imprenta Real, 1805), Tomo IV, Libro VIII, Título XVIII, Ley V, pp. 151-52.

4. On the eighteenth-century Spanish press, see Paul-J. Guinard, *La presse espagnole de 1737 à 1791: Formation et signification d'un genre* (Paris: Centre de Recherches Hispaniques, 1973); Francisco Aguilar Piñal, *La prensa española en el siglo XVIII: Diarios, revistas y pronósticos,* Cuadernos Bibliográficos, 35 (Madrid: C.S.I.C., 1978); María Dolores Sáiz, *Historia del periodismo en España, 1: Los orígenes. El siglo XVIII* (Madrid: Alianza, 1983).

5. On the nineteenth-century press, see María Cruz Seoane, *Historia del periodismo en España, 2: El siglo XIX* (Madrid: Alianza, 1983).

6. On the periodicals of this period, see the relevant years' entries in Aguilar Piñal.

7. For a concise review of the debate on woman in Spain in the eighteenth-century press, see my 'La prensa y la polémica feminista en la España del siglo XVIII', *Estudios de Historia Social*, 52-53 (1990), 265-73.

8. For a detailed account of the writings on woman in this period see my 'The Debate on Woman in Spain, 1726-1808 (with Special Reference to Pamphlets and the Periodical Press)' (unpublished doctoral thesis, University of Sheffield, 1991), pp. 249-79.

9. On *A Vindication of the Rights of Woman*, see Miriam Brody's excellent introduction to Mary Wollstonecraft, *A Vindication of the Rights of Woman* (London: Penguin, 1988), in which she highlights the dual radical nature of the *Rights of Woman* as both a political and a feminist text; also Moira Ferguson and Janet Todd, *Mary Wollstonecraft* (Boston, MA: G. K. Hall, 1984), pp. 59-74.

10. For further information on Wollstonecraft's life and works, see *inter alia*, Ferguson and Todd, Claire Tomalin, *The Life and Death of Mary Wollstonecraft* (London: Weidenfeld & Nicholson, 1974), and *The Works of Mary Wollstonecraft*, ed. by Janet Todd and Marilyn Butler, 7 vols (London: Pickering & Chatto, 1989), 1, 7-28.

11. Mary Wollstonecraft, *Défense des droits des femmes, suivie de quelques considérations sur des sujets politiques et moraux* (Paris: Buisson; Lyon: Bruyset, 1792). A copy of this edition is held in the British Library.

12. Verbal agreement in a sentence in an earlier note indicates that the translator is, in fact, a woman: 'J'étois allée voir un petit garçon dans une école où l'on préparoit de jeunes enfans pour une école plus grande' (p. 438).

13. Claire Tomalin notes that the completed text was handed to the printer on 3 January 1792 (p. 105). The precise date of publication of the French translation is unknown. The title and publication details given in the *Diario de Madrid* are: '*Defensa de los derechos de las mujeres, a la que siguen algunas consideraciones sobre asuntos políticos y morales. Obra escrita en Inglés por Marly Wollstone-craft, [sic] traducida al francés, y dedicada al Illmo. Obispo de Autun: Paris, Buisson; Lyon, Bruyset, 1792'* (*Diario de Madrid*,

6 September 1792, p. 1043). The review was published in four parts: part 1, 6 September 1792, pp. 1043-45; part 2, 8 September, pp. 1051-52; part 3, 8 October, pp. 1179-81; part 4, 9 October, pp. 1183-85.

14. Manuel Serrano y Sanz, *Apuntes para una biblioteca de escritoras españolas desde el año 1401 al 1833,* 4 vols, Biblioteca de Autores Españoles, 268-71 (Madrid: Atlas, 1975), lists alphabetically by author a large number of poems, letters, and short articles published by women in periodicals during the eighteenth century, the majority of which are to be found in the *Diario de Madrid* in the 1790s. Francisco Aguilar Piñal also comments on the contribution of female poets to the periodical press in the introduction to *Indice de las poesías publicadas en los periódicos españoles del siglo XVIII*, Cuadernos Bibliográficos, 43 (Madrid: C.S.I.C., 1981), p. xiii.

15. Aguilar Piñal, *La prensa*, p. 36.

16. Aguilar Piñal, *La prensa*, p. 37. Lucienne Domergue, *Censure et lumières dans l'Espagne de Charles III* (Paris: Centre National de la Recherche Scientifique, 1982), gives Velasco's age as twenty-five in 1789 (p. 174).

17. Guinard, p. 221.

18. See Aguilar Piñal, *La prensa*, pp. 34, 41, 42. Domergue, in *Tres calas,* argues that Velasco was the originator of the idea which led to the *Efemérides* of Olivé (pp. 114-15).

19. Aguilar Piñal, *La prensa*, p. 37. Two works are credited to Velasco in Antonio Palau y Dulcet, *Manual del librero hispano-americano,* 28 vols (Barcelona: Palau, 1948-77), VII, 7, entries 357158 and 357159: an *Elogio del Rey* read at a prize-giving ceremony of the Madrid Economic Society on 17 March 1796 (Madrid: Sancha [1796]); *Historia maravillosa de la naturaleza y propiedades del elefante* (Madrid: Villalpando, 1806). He also translated a French play by a Monsieur Desforges, *La muger zelosa* (Madrid: Benito García, 1801), a copy of which is kept at the British Library and which names Velasco as the translator.

20. Apart from overt references ('Je plaide pour mon sexe' (Dedication, p. 1); 'J'espère trouver grace aux yeux de mon propre sexe' (Introduction, p. 8)) the very personal and informal nature of Wollstonecraft's text ensures that indications of the sex of the author abound through the feminine verbal agreements in its French version.

21. Wollstonecraft, *Défense,* p. 442. The English original reads: 'Virtue will never prevail in society till the virtues of both sexes are founded on rea-

son; and till the affections common to both are allowed to gain their due strength by the discharge of mutual duties' (Brody, p. 283).

22. For example, Wollstonecraft writes on monarchy in general:

    It is impossible for any man, when the most favourable circumstances concur, to acquire sufficient knowledge and strength of mind to discharge the duties of a king, entrusted with uncontrolled power; how then must they be violated when his very elevation is an insuperable bar to the attainment of either wisdom or virtue, when all the feelings of a man are stifled by flattery, and reflection shut out by pleasure! Surely it is madness to make the fate of thousands depend on the caprice of a weak fellow-creature, whose very station sinks him *necessarily* below the meanest of his subjects! (Brody, p. 96).

23. Guillermo Carnero, 'Francisca Ruiz de Larrea de Böhl de Faber y Mary Wollstonecraft', *Hispanic Review,* 50 (1982), 133-42.

24. R. M. Janes, 'On the Reception of Mary Wollstonecraft's *A Vindication of the Rights of Woman*', *Journal of the History of Ideas,* 39 (1978), 293-302 (p. 294).

25. Josefa Amar y Borbón, 'Discurso en defensa del talento de las mujeres, y de su aptitud para el gobierno y otros cargos en que se emplean los hombres', *Memorial literario, instructivo y curioso de la Corte de Madrid,* 8.32 (August 1786), 400-30. On the debate on the admission of women to the Madrid Economic Society, see Lucienne Domergue, *Jovellanos à la Société Economique des Amis du Pays de Madrid, 1778-1795* (Toulouse: Université de Toulouse-Le Mirail, 1969); Olegario Negrín Fajardo, *Ilustración y educación: La Sociedad Económica Matritense* (Madrid: Nacional, 1984); Paula de Demerson, *María Francisca de Sales Portocarrero: (Condesa de Montijo), Una figura de la Ilustración* (Madrid: Nacional, 1975); see also my 'The Debate on Woman', pp. 158-98.

26. Josefa Amar y Borbón, *Discurso sobre la educación física y moral de las mujeres* (Madrid: Cano, 1790).

27. José Clavijo y Fajardo, 'Carta del pensador a las damas', *El Pensador,* 1.2 (September 1762), 23-48.

28. D. J. G., 'Paralelo de la suerte feliz o desgraciada entre las mujeres asiáticas y africanas, y las europeas', *Correo de Madrid,* 5.299 (October 1789), 2403-05. I have been unable to ascertain the identity of D. J. G.

29. Ignacio López de Ayala, 'Papel sobre si las señoras deben ser admitidas como individuos de las sociedades', reprinted in Negrín, pp. 177-83.

30. J. de V., 'Sobre la educación', *Diario de Madrid,* 18 June 1792, pp. 835-36. His ideas were reiterated in a further article in the *Diario* on 21 June, pp. 847-48, when he emphasized that women's knowledge is for the betterment of society and must not be an end in itself. It gave rise to a positive reply in the issue published on 29 June, pp. 879-80.

Susan Gubar (essay date fall 1994)

SOURCE: Gubar, Susan. "Feminist Misogyny: Mary Wollstonecraft and the Paradox of 'It Takes One to Know One.'" *Feminist Studies* 20, no. 3 (fall 1994): 453-73.

[*In the following essay, Gubar analyzes Wollstonecraft's feminism and her often unflattering portraits of women in* A Vindication of the Rights of Woman *and other texts.*]

In a self-reflexive essay representative of current feminist thinking, Ann Snitow recalls a memory of the early seventies, a moment when a friend "sympathetic to the [women's] movement but not active [in it] asked what motivated" Snitow's fervor.

> I tried to explain the excitement I felt at the idea that I didn't have to be a woman. She was shocked, confused. *This* was the motor of my activism? She asked, "How can someone who doesn't like being a woman be a feminist?" To which I could only answer, "Why would anyone who likes being a woman *need* to be a feminist?"
>
> Quite properly my colleague feared woman-hating. . . . Was this, as [she] thought, just a new kind of misogyny?

Although Snitow eventually finds "woman-hating—or loving—. . . beside the point," she admits that she "wouldn't dare say self-hatred played no part in what I wanted from feminism," a remark that takes on added resonance in terms of her first reaction to consciousness raising: "'Woman' is my slave name," she felt back then; "feminism will give me freedom to seek some other identity altogether."[1]

"'Woman' is my slave name; feminism will give me freedom to seek some other identity altogether": Snitow's formulation dramatizes a curious contradiction feminism exhibits from its very inception to present times. The oxymoronic title of this essay—feminist misogyny—risks political incorrectness and implicitly asks us to pause, to consider the efficacy of the appellations "feminism" and "misogyny," not to derail our commitment to social justice but to make it more savvy, more supple. For when put to the test in the "Can you really tell?" game, current conceptualizations may not always help us distinguish feminist from misogynist claims.

On the one hand, can you judge the sexual politics of the thinker who wrote: "There is a pleasure, . . . an enjoyment of the body, which is . . . *beyond the phallus*"? What does it mean that this apparently liberated sentiment comes from Jacques Lacan (the same Lacan who boasted that "[women] don't know what they're saying, that's all the difference between them and me")?[2] On the other hand, can you surmise the ideology of the writer who declared that "woman is body more than man is" or of the theorist who stated that *"woman has sex organs more or less everywhere"*?[3] What does it mean that these two quotations, from feminist theorists Hélène Cixous and Luce Irigaray, eerily reiterate a proposition made by masculinist writers from Rousseau to Ambrose Bierce so as to deny women equal educational opportunities, specifically the idea that "to men a man is but a mind. . . . But woman's body *is* the woman"?[4]

Pursuing the same inquiry, we might ask why Denise Riley recently chose the allusive title *Am I That Name?* (1988) for a book advocating a poststructural approach to feminism, when the line (originally spoken in the femicidal atmosphere of Shakespeare's *Othello*) conflates the "name" woman with the name-calling that demotes woman to whore?[5] Finally, who would guess that this critique of Adrienne Rich—"The feminist dream of a common language . . . is a totalizing and imperialist one"—issues not from Lacan or some modern-day Iago but from the women's studies scholar Donna Haraway?[6] If the histories of feminism and misogyny have been (sometimes shockingly) dialogic, as I will try to suggest, what impact should that have on the ways in which we understand the once and future state of feminist theory?

The subtitle of my meditation may seem just as incongruous as its title, because we generally view Mary Wollstonecraft as a pioneer whose feminist efforts were tragically misunderstood by the misogynist society in which she lived. And, of course, as the aesthetic foremother of feminist expository prose, Wollstonecraft established a polemical tradition mined by such literary descendants as Olive Schreiner, Emma Goldman, and Virginia Woolf as well as by contemporary thinkers from Simone de Beauvoir to Kate Millett and, yes, Cixous and Riley. Indubitably, all of these theorists profited from and extended Wollstonecraft's insistence on righting the wrongs done to women. Paradoxically, however, they also inherited what I am calling her feminist misogyny. Indeed, the very troubling tenacity of this strain in feminist expository prose calls out for further thought.

That Wollstonecraft did, in fact, function as an effective advocate for women is probably self-evident, especially to anyone familiar with the political and literary culture into which she interjected her views. Although I will be examining a pervasive contradiction in her life and work, in no way do I mean to diminish or disparage her achievements. Quite rightly regarded as the founding feminist text in English, *A Vindication of the Rights of Woman* (1792) links the radical insurrection of the French Revolution to the equally radical insubordination of the feminist project. Nor do I think we should judge Wollstonecraft by late-twentieth-century definitions of feminism and find her wanting, "as if"—to quote Frances Ferguson—"Wollstonecraft would have turned out better work if she had had a word processor or a microwave oven."[7]

Although she has been faulted for adhering to a suspect faith in reason as an innate human characteristic,[8] Wollstonecraft exploited Enlightenment language to claim that—at least theoretically—women and men were alike in being endowed with reason, a divine faculty which only needed to be cultivated so as to perfect the human species. Many of the thinkers of her time emphasized the differences between the sexes, with the influential Rousseau demanding that women's education "should be always relative to the men. To please, to be useful to [men,] . . . to advise, to console us, to render our lives easy and agreeable: these are the duties of women at all times."[9] But Wollstonecraft believed that because both sexes shared an equal capacity for reason, women—considered as *human,* not as sexual, beings—should benefit from the educational programs historically only afforded men. In addition, Wollstonecraft's commitment to rationality made her especially sensitive to representations of female irrationality that enslaved women's hearts and minds.

From her meditations on the Bible and Milton's *Paradise Lost* to her interpretations of Pope's, Dr. Gregory's, and Rousseau's treatises, Wollstonecraft's analyses of debilitating female images assume that we are what we read and therefore these passage in *A Vindication of the Rights of Woman* constitute one of the earliest instances we have of feminist criticism. According to Wollstonecraft, female readers necessarily internalize male-authored and manifestly false impressions of who they are and what they should aspire to be, impressions that weaken rather than strengthen women's self-image. Confronting the socialization process effected by reading as well as by other child-rearing practices, Wollstonecraft used her expository prose and her two novels to theorize about the psychological and cultural engendering of femininity. None of her contemporaries devised as sophisticated a model for understanding the social construction of womanhood, speculations which laid the groundwork for Simone de Beauvoir's famous claim that "one is not born a woman, but rather becomes one."[10] Yet it is in this area—Wollstonecraft's analysis of the feminine—that we will find most striking evidence of the contradiction in her thinking that I am terming "feminist misogyny."

What image of woman emerges from the pages of *A Vindication of the Rights of Woman*? Repeatedly and disconcertingly, Wollstonecraft associates the feminine with weakness, childishness, deceitfulness, cunning, superficiality, an overvaluation of love, frivolity, dilettantism, irrationality, flattery, servility, prostitution, coquetry, sentimentality, ignorance, indolence, intolerance, slavish conformity, fickle passion, despotism, bigotry, and a "spaniel-like affection." The feminine principle, so defined, threatens—like a virus—to contaminate and destroy men and their culture. For, as Wollstonecraft explains: "Weak, artificial beings, raised above the common wants and affections of their race, in a premature unnatural manner, undermine the very foundation of virtue, and spread corruption through the whole mass of society."[11]

Here in *A Vindication of the Rights of Woman,* as in the next sentences I quote, femininity feels like a malady:

> [Women's] senses are *inflamed,* and their understandings neglected, consequently they become the *prey* of their senses, delicately termed sensibility, and are *blown about* by every momentary *gust* of feeling. Civilized women are, therefore, . . . *weakened* by false refinement. . . . Ever *restless* and *anxious,* their *over exercised* sensibility not only renders them *uncomfortable* themselves but *troublesome* . . . to others. . . . [T]heir conduct is *unstable,* and their opinions are *wavering.* . . . By *fits and starts* they are *warm* in many pursuits; yet this *warmth,* never concentrated into perseverance, soon *exhausts* itself. . . . *Miserable,* indeed, must be that being whose cultivation of mind has only tended to *inflame* its passions![12]

According to this passage, civilized women suffer from an illness, a veritable fever of femininity, that reduces them to "unstable" and "uncomfortable," "miserable," exhausted invalids. Wollstonecraft's description of women's restlessness, of the "warm gusts" of inflammation they suffer, sounds like nothing less than contemporary complaints about hot flashes and menopausal mood swings, as if the long disease of femininity has itself become a critical "change of life." At the close of the paragraph in which these words appear, Wollstonecraft takes to its logical conclusion the implications of women's "fits and starts": when "passions" are "pampered, whilst the judgment is left unformed," she asks, "what can be expected to ensue?" and she promptly answers, "Undoubtedly, a mixture of madness and folly!"

Elsewhere in a related series of metaphors, women operate like "gangrene, which the vices engendered by oppression have produced," and the mortal damage they inflict "is not confined to the morbid part, but pervades society at large." Even if she is not noxious, the female is obnoxious, a diminished thing which has dwindled, dehumanized, into something like a doll, providing merely an aimless leisure pastime for men: "She was created," Wollstonecraft claims, "to be the toy of man, his rattle, and it must jingle in his ears whenever, dismissing reason, he chooses to be amused."[13] Like a virus spreading corruption; like an illness condemning its victim to madness; like gangrene contaminating the healthy; like a jingling toy distracting irrational pleasure seekers: because femininity figures as, at best, frivolity and, at worst, fatality, the principle character emerging from the pages of *A Vindication of the Rights of Woman* is the femme fatale.

Wollstonecraft's derogations of the feminine, to be sure, are framed in terms of her breakthrough analysis of the social construction of gender. The above quotations, for instance, insist that women's "senses are inflamed" because "their understandings [are] neglected"; that women are artificially "raised" above the race; that the gangrene of their vices is "engendered" by oppression; and that they are "created" to be toys. Thus, her thesis—that a false system of education has "rendered [women] weak and wretched"—emphasizes the powerful impact of culture on subjectivity, the capacity of the psyche to internalize societal norms.[14] Indeed, Wollstonecraft stands at an originatory point in feminist thought precisely because she envisioned a time when the female of the species could shed herself of an enfeebling acculturation or feminization. Yet although (or perhaps because) *A Vindication of the Rights of Woman* sets out to liberate society from a hated subject constructed to be subservient and called "woman," it illuminates how such animosity can spill over into antipathy of those human beings most constrained by that construction.

Laying the groundwork for the first and second wave of the women's movement, *A Vindication of the Rights of Woman* implies that "'Woman' is my slave name; feminism will give me freedom to seek some other identity altogether." About the "few women [who] have emancipated themselves from the galling yoke of sovereign man," therefore, Wollstonecraft speculates that they are virtually transsexuals. Just as Newton "was probably a being of superior order accidentally caged in a human body," she imagines that "the few extraordinary women" in history "were *male* spirits, confined by mistake in female frames."[15] No wonder that, as Mary Poovey has pointed out, Wollstonecraft often speaks of herself "as a philosopher," "as a moralist," even "as [a] man with man," concluding her work with a plea to "ye men of understanding."[16] Rarely, in other words, does she present herself as a woman speaking to women.

Curiously, then, Wollstonecraft's radical stance nevertheless ends up aligning her with women's most fervent adversaries, as she herself admits. "After surveying the history of woman," she concedes, "I cannot help, agreeing with the severest satirist, considering the sex as the weakest as well as the most oppressed half of the species." And several passages in *A Vindication of the Rights of Woman* do seem to agree with "the severest satirist[s]" of women. While analyzing the "sexual weakness that makes woman depend upon man," for example, Wollstonecraft scorns "a kind of cattish affection which leads a wife to purr about her husband as she would about any man who fed and caressed her." If the female looks subhuman in her cattiness here, elsewhere she appears sinful in her cunning trickery. To castigate those made "inferiour by ignorance and low desires," Wollstonecraft describes "the serpentine wrigglings of cunning" that enable women to "mount the tree of knowledge, and only acquire sufficient [reason] to lead men astray."[17] Like their foremother, Eve, women bear the responsibility for the fall of man, and they do so because of their misuse of knowledge. Predictably, one of Wollstonecraft's favorite Greek allusions is to Eve's prototype, Pandora.

And a number of other passages in *A Vindication of the Rights of Woman* concur with the satirists of women, whom Wollstonecraft actually echoes. Take, for example, the following attack on the institution of marriage as a commodities market:

> It is acknowledged that [women] spend many of the first years of their lives in acquiring a smattering of accomplishments; meanwhile strength of body and mind are sacrificed to libertine notions of beauty, to the desire of establishing themselves,—the only way women can rise in the world,—by marriage. And this desire making mere animals of them, when they marry they act as such children may be expected to act:—they dress; they paint, and nickname God's creatures.— Surely these weak beings are only fit for a seraglio![18]

Not only does Wollstonecraft paraphrase Hamlet's angry speech to Ophelia—"You jig, you amble, and you lisp; you nickname God's creatures and make your wantonness your ignorance"; by relegating the feminine woman to a seraglio, she also glosses his refrain—"get thee to a nunnery": both nunnery and seraglio were common euphemisms for whorehouse. But the word "seraglio"—a Turkish or Eastern lodging for the secluded harem of Islamic noblemen—captures Wollstonecraft's disdain for a feminine lassitude so degenerate, so threatening to Western civilization that it must be marked as what Edward Said would call a kind of "Orientalism."[19]

If we compare Wollstonecraft's portrait of the feminine here with the notoriously severe eighteenth-century satirists of the weaker sex, it becomes clear that she shares with them Hamlet's revulsion. Judge Wollstonecraft's emphasis on libertine notions of beauty, for example, in terms of Pope's famous lines in his "Epistle to a Lady"—"ev'ry Woman is at heart a Rake" and "Most women have no characters at all"—as well as his insistence that the best woman is "a contradiction" in terms, "a softer man." Consider her picture of female animality and dilettantism in relation to Swift's monstrous Goddess of Criticism in *A Tale of a Tub,* a symbol of ignorance portrayed as part cat, part ass. Compare Wollstonecraft's vision of feminine hypocrisy and prostitution to Swift's attacks in his mock pastorals on dressing and painting, debased arts that conceal syphilitic whores; or place her indictment that unaccomplished women "nickname God's creatures" up against Dr. Johnson's comparison between a woman preaching and a dog dancing. Finally, examine Wollstonecraft's childish wives in terms of the earl of Chesterfield's definition of women as "children of a larger growth."[20]

Why does Wollstonecraft's text so eerily echo those composed by masculinist satirists?[21] A number of critics have noted problems, tensions, and repressions in the *oeuvre* produced by Wollstonecraft.[22] In particular, these scholars claim that, by appropriating an Enlightenment rhetoric of reason, Wollstonecraft alienated herself and other women from female sexual desire. Throughout *A Vindication of the Rights of Woman,* Wollstonecraft elevates friendship between the sexes over romantic and erotic entanglements (which she condemns as ephemeral or destructive). Yet I would view this motif not merely as a repression of sexuality but more inclusively as a symptom of the paradoxical feminist misogyny that pervades her work, only one sign of the ways in which Wollstonecraft's feminism operates vis-à-vis feminization and by no means an eccentric fault of her philosophizing. For, as Cora Kaplan has insightfully remarked: "There is no feminism that can stand wholly outside femininity as it is posed in a given historical moment. All feminisms give some ideological hostage to femininities and are constructed through the gender sexuality of their day as well as standing in opposition to them."[23]

If feminist expository prose necessarily situates itself in opposition to self-demeaning modes of feminization even as it is shaped by them, what Moira Ferguson describes as Wollstonecraft's propensity "to find women culpable of their vanity, their acceptance of an inferior education, their emphasis on feeling," her tendency to "locate herself outside what she deem[ed] self-demeaning behavior," takes on not only personal but also political and philosophical import.[24] Indeed, the tensions at work in Wollstonecraft's text dramatize, on the one hand, the ways in which "feminisms give some ideological hostage to femininities," as Kaplan puts it, and, on the other hand, the ironies embedded in the stage of patrilineal affiliation that Sandra Gilbert and I have examined in the aesthetic paradigm we call "the female affiliation complex."[25]

To take the first subject first, is it possible to view Wollstonecraft's description of the fever of femininity in *A Vindication of the Rights of Woman* as a portrait of any middle-class woman of her age, indeed as a *self-portrait*? Could the disgust at fallen, fated, or fatal females be *self*-disgust? In the words of Emma Goldman, the "sexually starved" Wollstonecraft was "doomed to become the prey of more than one infatuation" and her "insatiable hunger for love" led not only to a tragic desire for the married painter Fuseli but also to the two suicide attempts resulting from her tempestuous involvement with the philanderer Gilbert Imlay.[26] Wollstonecraft was so overcome by passion for Fuseli that she suggested a *mé-nage à trois* to his shocked wife; after discovering Gilbert Imlay's actress-mistress, she soaked her skirts so as to sink into the water after she threw herself from Putney Bridge. Did anyone better understand slavish passions, the overvaluation of love, fickle irrationality, weak dependency, the sense of personal irrelevance, and anxiety about personal attractiveness than Wollstonecraft herself?

Thus, Virginia Woolf, considering the various ways in which Wollstonecraft "could not understand . . . her own feelings," believed that the eighteenth-century polemicist made theories every day, "theories by which life should be lived," but "Every day too—for she was no pedant, no cold-blooded theorist—something was born in her that thrust aside her theories and forced her to model them afresh."[27] From the perspective of Goldman's and Woolf's essays, therefore, the misogyny of Wollstonecraft's work dramatizes the self-revulsion of a woman who knew *herself* to be constructed as feminine, and thus it exhibits a kind of "antinarcissism."[28] Indeed, what both Goldman and Woolf implicitly ask us to confront is the disparity between the feminist feats of *A Vindication of the Rights of Woman* and the gothic fates inflicted on Wollstonecraft's fictional heroines in *Mary, a Fiction* (1788) and *Maria* (1798).

Of course, the subtitle of *Maria—The Wrongs of Woman*—establishes it as a counterpart or extension of *A Vindication of the Rights of Woman,* as does the gloomy insight of its heroine when she asks, "Was not the world a vast prison, and women born slaves?"[29] Curiously, however, both novels negate or traverse the argument of *A Vindication of the Rights of Woman,* which, after all, condemns precisely the conventions of sentimental fiction *Mary* and *Maria* exploit. For the enflamed, volatile emotions Wollstonecraft castigates as weakness, folly, and madness in her polemic infuse, motivate, and elevate the heroines of both novels. After weeping, fainting, and bemoaning her love for a dead friend and a dead lover, the admirable paragon of sensibility who is the central character of *Mary* exclaims: "I cannot live without loving—and love leads to madness."[30] Just as rapturous and tearful, the heroine of

Maria exhibits the passion denounced throughout *A Vindication of the Rights of Woman* in a narrative that at moments seems not to caution against romance so much as to consecrate it: "So much of heaven" do the lovers of *Maria* enjoy together "that paradise bloomed around them. . . . Love, the grand enchanter, 'lapt them in Elysium,' and every sense was harmonized to joy and social extacy."[31]

But the startling slippages in Wollstonecraft's thinking about heterosexuality are accompanied by equally dramatic strains in her meditations on the bonds between women. Although historians of homosexuality have been led by Wollstonecraft's emotional relationships with Jane Arden and Fanny Blood to argue that the female intimacies celebrated in *Mary* should be situated on what Adrienne Rich calls a "lesbian continuum," several passages in *A Vindication of the Rights of Woman* inveigh against the "grossly familiar" relationships spawned in female communities.[32] Women "shut up together in nurseries, schools, or convents" engage in "nasty customs," share "secrets" (on subjects "where silence ought to reign"), and indulge in "jokes and hoiden tricks."[33] Wollstonecraft the novelist valorizes the nurturing comfort and intensity of female intimacies; however, Wollstonecraft the philosopher hints at the obscene debaucheries of such contacts.

The odd juxtapositions between *A Vindication of the Rights of Woman* and the novels imply that the misogynist portrait of the feminine penned by the feminist may, in fact, represent Wollstonecraft's efforts to negotiate the distance between desire and dread, what she thought she should have been and what she feared herself to be. In other words, *A Vindication of the Rights of Woman* presents a narrative voice of the feminist-philosopher and a fictive profile of femininity that interact to illuminate a dialogue between self and soul, the culturally induced schizophrenia of an antinarcissist. And in some part of herself, Wollstonecraft seemed to have understood this very well. In October 1791, after she had begun composing *A Vindication of the Rights of Woman* and while she was sitting for a portrait a friend had commissioned, she wrote that friend the following lines: "I do not imagine that [the painting] will be a very striking likeness; but, if you do not find me in it, I will send you a more faithful sketch—a book that I am now writing, in which *I* myself . . . shall certainly appear, head and heart."[34]

Just this dialectic—between head and heart, between a hortatory philosophic voice and a debased self-portrait of femininity—characterizes the feminist misogyny Wollstonecraft bequeathed to her literary descendants, including feminist polemicists writing today. Partially, it was informed by Wollstonecraft's inexorable entrapment inside a patrilineal literary inheritance. In *The War of the Words,* Sandra Gilbert and I argued that women writers before the late nineteenth century necessarily affiliated themselves with an alien and alienating aesthetic patrilineage. But this is even more true for the author of feminist expository prose than it is for the woman poet or novelist who, like Elizabeth Barrett Browning, "look[ed] everywhere for [literary] grandmothers and [found] none" because, instead of looking for aesthetic grandmothers, Wollstonecraft set out to debate the most powerfully paternal influences on her own culture: Moses and St. John, Milton and Rousseau, Pope and the authors of conduct and etiquette books.[35]

As a genre, feminist expository prose inevitably embeds itself in the misogynist tradition it seeks to address and redress. Representing the masculinist voice in order to controvert its messages, one chapter of *A Vindication of the Rights of Woman*—brilliantly analyzed by Patricia Yaeger—proceeds by lengthily quoting Rousseau's portrait of womanhood "in his own words, interspersing [Wollstonecraft's] comments and reflections."[36] Thus, another dialectic emerges beyond the one between the individual author's head and heart, specifically in *A Vindication of the Rights of Woman* the conversation between Wollstonecraft and Rousseau and more generally in the expository prose of her descendants the dialogic relationship between the histories of feminism and misogyny.

"It Takes One to Know One": the "One" in my subtitle is meant to indicate that it takes a feminist to know a misogynist, and vice versa. The terms of their engagement—as they bob and weave, feint and jab, thrust and parry in their philosophical fencing match or boxing ring—are particularly important to understand because, although feminism historically has not been the condition for misogyny's emergence, the pervasive threat of misogyny brought into being feminist discourse. To the extent that there can be (need be) no feminism without misogyny, the sparring of this odd couple—the feminist, the misogynist—takes on a ritualized, stylized quality as they stroll through the corridors of history, reflecting upon each other and upon their slam dancing. A full description of the choreography of their steps remains beyond the scope of this paper; however a brief study of the eccentric dips and swirls executed by these curiously ambivalent partners at the beginning and end of this century can begin the task Judith Butler sets feminist critique—namely, understanding "how the category of 'woman,' the subject of feminism, is produced and restrained by the very structures of power through which emancipation is sought."[37]

Like Mary Wollstonecraft's, Olive Schreiner's feminist prose stands in a vexed relationship to her fiction: specifically her polemical *Woman and Labour* (1911)—calling for "New Women" and "New Men" to enter "a new earth"—contrasts with a novel that obsesses over the self-pitying masochism of those who dream of al-

tered sexual arrangements, just as it broods with nauseated fascination on the horrible tenacity of traditional women.[38] The would-be author of an introduction to *A Vindication of the Rights of Woman,* Schreiner formulated her demands for female liberation as an attack not on men but on women and specifically on what she called "the human female parasite—the most deadly microbe . . . on the surface of any social organism."[39] In *Woman and Labour,* which functioned as "the Bible" for first wave feminists, the idle, consuming "parasite woman on her couch" signals "the death-bed of human evolution."[40] Strangely, too, Schreiner seems to blame the limits of evolution on female anatomy when she speculates that the size of the human brain could only increase "if in the course of ages the *os cervix* of women should itself slowly expand."[41]

Just as discomforting as the thought of an *os cervix* having to extend so as to produce larger human heads may be the less biologistic but comparable woman blaming in Schreiner's second wave descendants. Perhaps Ann Douglas's *Feminization of American Culture* (1977) furnishes the best case among the pioneers in women's studies. For here, nineteenth-century women's "debased religiosity, their sentimental peddling of Christian belief for its nostalgic value," and their "fakery" manage to "gut Calvinist orthodoxy" of its rigorous intellectual vitality. So aware was Douglas herself about faulting women for the fall (the "feminization") of American culture that she used her introduction to defend herself against the charge that she had "sid[ed] with the enemy." Although Douglas claimed to be motivated by a "respect" for "toughness," this (implicitly male) toughness seems entwined with self-hatred: "I expected to find my fathers and my mothers," she explains about her investigations into the past; "instead I discovered my fathers and my sisters" because "The problems of the women correspond to mine with a frightening accuracy that seems to set us outside the processes of history."[42]

About the immersion of Douglas's contemporaries in the literary history of the fathers, we might ask, what does it mean that a generation of readers was introduced to the works of Henry Miller and Norman Mailer through the long quotations that appeared in Kate Millett's important 1970 text, *Sexual Politics*? In this respect, Millett's work typifies a paradox that persists in a branch of feminist criticism which, following in the wake of Wollstonecraft's work, tackles the problematics of patriarchy by examining sexist authors (from Milton to Mailer) or by exploring male-dominated genres (pornography, the western, adventure tales, men's magazines, film noir). No matter how radical the critique, it frequently falls into the representational quandary of *A Vindication of the Rights of Woman*: replication or even recuperation. Throughout the feminist expository prose of the 1970s, the predominant images of women constellate around the female victim: foot binding and suttee, cliterodectomy and witch burning appear with startling frequency; the characters of the madwoman, the hysteric, the abused whore, the freak, and the female eunuch abound.

From *The Troublesome Helpmate* (1966), Katharine Roger's ground-breaking history of misogyny in literature, to my own work with Sandra Gilbert, moreover, feminist literary criticism has demonstrated that the most deeply disturbing male-authored depictions of women reveal with exceptional clarity the cultural dynamics of gender asymmetries. Thus, although Sandra and I usually focus on the female tradition, it seems striking that our most extended meditations on male authors center on such infamous masculinists as John Milton, H. Rider Haggard, Sigmund Freud, D. H. Lawrence, and T. S. Eliot, rather than, say, John Stuart Mill, George Meredith, or George Bernard Shaw, all self-defined friends of the women's movement. When questioned about our reliance on Freud, Sandra and I tend to respond by emphasizing how we have sought to disentangle the *de*scriptive powers of his insights into the sex/gender system from the *pre*scriptive overlay contained in the values he assigns aspects or stages of that system.

Perhaps this speculation tells us as much about the masculinist tradition as it does about the intervention of feminism. Can we extend it by proposing that misogynist texts often elaborate upon feminist insights but within structures of address or rhetorical frames that—in different ways, to different degrees—vilify, diminish, or dismiss them? For example, can it be that Shakespeare's portraits of femicidal heroes in *Hamlet,* or *Othello,* or *King Lear* lay bare the causes and dynamics of woman hating, albeit in plots that equivocate about the value placed upon such an emotion? To return to Freud, didn't his description of psychosexual development in Western culture make possible the radical revisions of a host of feminist theorists, ranging from Joan Riviere and Karen Horney to Shulamith Firestone, Juliet Mitchell, Gayle Rubin, Nancy Chodorow, and Adrienne Rich? In other words, if Wollstonecraft's *A Vindication of the Rights of Woman* embeds within it a misogynist text, do Shakespeare's *Hamlet,* Milton's *Paradise Lost,* Rousseau's *Confessions,* and Freud's "Female Sexuality" contain antithetical feminist subscripts?[43]

The idea of feminist misogyny might thereby explain a host of critical controversies over the ideological designs of individual authors or texts. For at the current time probably every "major" writer in the canon, possibly every touchstone work, has been claimed by one scholar or another as prototypically feminist *and* quintessentially masculinist. Nor is this surprising, given that each individual's "language," according to the foremost theorist of this issue, "lies on the borderline between oneself and the other." As M. M. Bakhtin's most evocative description of the "over-population" of language explains, "The word in language is half someone else's . . . it exists in other people's mouths, in other people's contexts, serving other people's intentions; it is from there that one must take the word, and make it one's own."[44] "[E]xpropriating" language from the purposes or designs of others, "forcing it to submit to one's own intentions and accents": this is the "complicated process" in which feminists and misogynists necessarily engage so their discourses necessarily intersect in numerous ways, undercutting or supplementing each other over time, contesting what amounts to a complex nexus of ideas, values, perspectives, and norms, a cultural "heteroglossia" of gender ideologies and power asymmetries. Like the concepts of Black self-hatred and Jewish anti-Semitism, feminist misogyny might bring to critical attention the interlocutionary nature of representation, that is, the crucially different effects of the sentence "I am this" and "You are that."[45]

Inevitably, as the interaction between "I am this" and "You are that" implies, feminist consciousness today still bears the marks of its having come into being through interactions with a masculinism that has been shaped, in turn, by women's independence movements, a phenomenon that explains a number of anomalies: that Mary Daly, not Norman Mailer, entitled a volume *Pure Lust* (1984) and coined the phrase "fembot," for instance; that Norman Mailer, not Kate Millett, wrote *The Prisoner of Sex* (1971); that after Kate Millett's *Sexual Politics*—an analysis of masculine domination, feminine subordination—she published *The Basement* (1979), a gothic meditation on the sexual subordination and ultimate annihilation of a young girl by a power-crazed, sadistic *woman.*[46] Similarly, feminist misogyny amplifies the eerie reverberations set in motion by Germaine Greer's decision to follow *The Female Eunuch* (1970) with *Sex and Destiny* (1984). The former sprinkles quotations from *A Vindication of the Rights of Woman* throughout a plea for a "revolution" in consciousness which requires that women refuse to bow down to "the Holy Family," reject the desexualization of their bodies, and protest against the manifold ways "our mothers blackmailed us with self-sacrifice."[47] However, the latter champions the family as the best social organization for women and children; touts chastity, coitus interruptus, and the rhythm method as optimal birth control methods; and nostalgically hymns the praises of the nurturance provided in so-called primitive cultures, specifically lauding "Mediterranean mothers [who] took their boy babies' penises in their mouths to stop their crying."[48]

Feminist misogyny in Mary Wollstonecraft's *oeuvre* may also help us understand why Andrea Dworkin has supplemented her antipornography expository prose with a gothic novel that could be said to be pornographic: *Ice and Fire* (1986) stands in as vexed a relation to *Intercourse* (1987) as **Mary** and **Maria** do to ***A Vindication of the Rights of Woman.*** Dworkin, the antipornography polemicist, condemns sexual intercourse in our culture as "an act of invasion and ownership undertaken in a mode of predation: colonializing, forceful (manly) or nearly violent."[49] However, her *Ice and Fire* includes two types of sexually explicit scenes that contravene this definition, one in which "a girl James Dean" uses men to invade or colonize herself—

> When a man fucks me, she says, I am with him, fucking me. The men ride her like maniacs. Her eyes roll back but stay open and she grins. She is always them fucking her, no matter how intensely they ride—

and the second in which the female narrator takes on the office of instructing her male lover on how to invade or colonize her:

> I teach him disrespect, systematically. I teach him how to tie knots, how to use rope, scarves, how to bite breasts: I teach him not to be afraid: of causing pain.

To be sure, when the masochistic speaker here explains about her abusive lover "Reader, I married him" and when "Reader, he got hard" metamorphoses into "he got hard: he beat me until I couldn't even crawl," we are meant to understand that Dworkin is returning to the romance tradition of Charlotte Brontë's *Jane Eyre* ("Reader, I married him") so as to uncover its abusive sexual politics.[50] Nevertheless, the question remains, if the antipornography ordinance Dworkin framed with Catharine McKinnon were deemed constitutional, would she be able to publish this kind of fiction? How can it be that her heroines resemble the actresses in the snuff films she seeks to outlaw, women bent on finding sexual fulfillment in their own destruction?

More generally, the feminist misogyny that pervades Dworkin's work typifies the uncanny mirror dancing that repeatedly links feminist polemicists to their rivals and antagonists. In 1975, the feminist-linguist Robin Lakoff published her groundbreaking *Language and Woman's Place,* a description of the genderlect she called "women's language": euphemism, modesty, hedging, polite forms of address, weak expletives, tag questions, empty adjectives and intensives, and hypercorrect grammar were said to characterize women's speech. Curiously, her findings accorded with those of Otto Jesperson, whose 1922 study, *Language: Its Nature, Development, and Origin,* proved that women were timid, conservative, even prudish language users and thus incapable of linguistic inventiveness. As I intimated earlier, another odd coupling could be said to exist between Jacques Lacan, who viewed women as inexorably exiled from culture, and the French feminists Luce Irigaray and Hélène Cixous, who valorize female fluidity, multiplicity, sensuality, and libidinal *jouissance.* Are all these feminists dancing with wolves?

"Feminism," Nancy Cott reminds us in much less heated or metaphorical terms, "is nothing if not paradoxical."

> It aims for individual freedoms by mobilizing sex solidarity. It acknowledges diversity among women while positing that women recognize their unity. It requires gender consciousness for its basis, yet calls for the elimination of prescribed gender roles.[51]

Just as aware of internal differences, Jane Gallop locates tensions within the psychology of feminism that explain the questions with which I began, the query of Ann Snitow's friend ("how can someone who doesn't like being a woman be a feminist?") as well as Snitow's response ("Why would anyone who likes being a woman *need* to be a feminist?"): "The feminist," according to Gallop, "identifies with other women but also struggles to rise above the lot of women. Feminism both desires superior women and celebrates the common woman."[52]

Over the past two decades, the stresses described by Cott and Gallop, along with professional competition inside the academy and social setbacks outside it, have given rise to internecine schisms in women's studies, divisions widened by feminists faulting other feminists as politically retrograde or even misogynist: activists and empiricists denounced theorists and vice-versa; lesbian separatists castigated integrationists; "prosex" and antipornography advocates clashed; class and race divided feminists, as did competing methodologies based on sexual difference or sexual equality, as did contested definitions of womanhood arising from cultural or poststructuralist thinkers.[53] Infighting reached a kind of apex in literary criticism as various histories began to appear, some featuring feminist critiques of feminism which served intentions not always hospitable to academic women. Here the Toril Moi of *Sexual/Textual Politics: Feminist Literary Theory* (1985) can officiate over feminist woman bashing: Moi dismisses American women's studies scholars as "patriarchal" because of their naive faith in the authority of the female subject and the unity of the work of art while she touts as her heroine Julia Kristeva, who "refuses to define 'woman'" and judges the belief that one "is a woman" to be "absurd."[54]

This atmosphere in which women need to beware women is probably what has led me to see feminist misogyny now and not, say, back in the seventies. As "constructionists" like Moi continue to vilify "essentialists," both groups segue into defensive and offensive steps that recall the rhythms of competing nationalities satirized in Sheldon Harnick's song, "The Merry Minuet":

> The whole world is festering with unhappy souls.
> The French hate the Germans, the Germans hate the
>   Poles,

Italians hate Yugoslavs, South Africans hate the Dutch,
And I don't like anybody very much.[55]

Does the price of institutionalization—of women's studies' inclusion in the academy—consist of our reduction to a plethora of jostling fields or approaches in which unhappy souls war for precedence with even more ferocity than they do in longer established areas or departments?

Have we attained our maturity in an age of ethnic purges and nationalistic frays that in our own domain take the form of battle dances which cause us to lose sight of our common aim to expropriate not only language but also society of overpopulated intentions hostile to women's health and welfare? When strutting our stuff with each other, among ourselves (and who, after all, are "we," given our institutional, generational, ethnic, and methodological differences?), have we lost sight of the ways in which unsympathetic outsiders or hostile institutions can appropriate or co-opt our internal debates, transforming self-critiques into assaults against our larger project? The recent brouhaha over Katie Roiphe's book epitomizes such difficulties. When in *The Morning After: Sex, Fear, and Feminism on Campus* Roiphe—a self-defined feminist—attacked Take Back the Night, antipornography, and sexual harassment activists for reenforcing Victorian stereotypes of predatory men and victimized women, it seemed eerily appropriate that she aligned herself with Ishmael Reed by entitling one of her chapters "Reckless Eyeballing." Just as Reed's masculinist novel *Reckless Eyeballing* lambastes Alice Walker for promoting a knee-jerk, racist suspicion about the criminality of African American men (and in the process illuminates the culturally diverse constructions of the feminist-misogynist dialogue), Roiphe's chapter presents contemporary feminists as retrograde zealot-puritans who would criminalize all men and indeed all forms of heterosexuality.[56]

Questioning another feminist critique of other feminists, namely constructionists' wholesale dismissal of essentialists, Diana Fuss has recently argued that "the political investments of the sign 'essence' are predicated on the subject's complex positioning in a particular social field, and . . . the appraisal of this investment depends not on any interior values intrinsic to the sign itself but rather on the shifting and determinative discursive relations which produced it."[57] Similarly, about feminist misogyny I think that—instead of furnishing us with yet another label to brand each other—it should make us sensitive to the proliferation of sexual ideologies, to the significance of who is deploying these ideologies and with what political effect, even as it breeds a healthy self-skepticism born of an awareness of our own inexorable embeddedness in history. Because we cannot escape how culture makes us know ourselves, we need to understand that even as our own theorizing engages with the social relations of femininity and masculinity, it is fashioned by them. Ultimately, then, the game of "Can you really tell?" reminds us that claims and counterclaims in the feminist-misogynist dialogue cannot be appraised without some consideration of the complex social identities, rhetorical frameworks, and historical contexts upon which they are predicated.

To adopt Gallop's words once again, "I am as desirous of resolving contradictions as the next girl, but I find myself drawing us back to them, refusing the separations that allow us to avoid but not resolve contradiction."[58] On the list of paradoxes she and other thinkers have enumerated, I would write the one so telling and compelling in the work of Mary Wollstonecraft. For the contradiction in terms that her life and letters dramatize continues to fashion the discourses through which many have struggled to vindicate the rights of women and men. As I think this, I seem to see them lining up for a succession of *pas de deux*; or is it a Virginia Reel? a do-si-do? a last tango? a merry minuet?—Rousseau and Wollstonecraft, Havelock Ellis and Olive Schreiner, Freud and Woolf, Sartre and Beauvoir, Mailer and Millett or Dworkin, Lacan and Irigaray or Cixous, Reed and Walker. But out of whose mouth does a voice issue to save the waltz by declaring, "Your turn to curtsy, my turn to bow"? And who takes the lead, if (when?) we turn to tap dance or shuffle along with one another?

Notes

1. Ann Snitow, "A Gender Diary," in *Conflicts in Feminism,* ed. Marianne Hirsch and Evelyn Fox Keller (New York: Routledge, 1990), 33, 9.

2. Both Lacan passages are discussed by Jane Gallop, *The Daughter's Seduction: Feminism and Psychoanalysis* (Ithaca: Cornell University Press, 1983), 34, 345.

3. Hélène Cixous in Hélène Cixous and Catherine Clément, *The Newly Born Woman,* trans. Betsy Wing (Minneapolis: University of Minnesota Press, 1986), 95; Luce Irigaray, *This Sex Which Is Not One,* trans. Catherine Porter with Carolyn Burke (Ithaca: Cornell University Press, 1985), 28.

4. Ambrose Bierce, in "Know Your Enemy: A Sampling of Sexist Quotes," in *Sisterhood Is Powerful: An Anthology of Writings from the Women's Liberation Movement,* ed. Robin Morgan (New York: Vintage, 1970), 34. Throughout this paragraph, I am grateful to Henry Louis Gates, Jr. who questions the efficacy of the "Can you really tell?" test with reference primarily to the ethnicity of the author in "'Authenticity,' or the Lesson of *Little Tree,*" *New York Times Book Review,* 24 Nov. 1991.

5. Denise Riley, *"Am I That Name?": Feminism and the Category of 'Women' in History* (Minneapolis: University of Minnesota Press, 1988). Tania Modleski cogently argues about this and other "postfeminist" theorists that "for many 'women' the very term arouses a visceral, even phobic reaction." See her *Feminism without Women: Culture and Criticism in a "Postfeminist" Age* (New York: Routledge, 1991), 16.

6. Donna Haraway, "A Manifesto for Cyborgs: Science, Technology, and Socialist Feminism in the 1980s," *Socialist Review,* no. 80 (March-April 1985): 92.

7. Frances Ferguson, "Wollstonecraft Our Contemporary," in *Gender and Theory: Dialogues on Feminist Criticism,* ed. Linda Kauffman (Oxford: Basil Blackwell, 1989), 60-61.

8. See Timothy J. Reiss, "Revolution in Bounds: Wollstonecraft, Women, and Reason," in *Gender and Theory,* 11-50.

9. Rousseau's infamous remark appears in Mary Wollstonecraft, *A Vindication of the Rights of Woman: An Authoritative Text, Backgrounds, the Wollstonecraft Debate, Criticism,* ed. Carol H. Poston (1792; New York: Norton Critical Edition, 1988), 79.

10. Sandra M. Gilbert and I have examined the seeming eccentricity of the literary women of Wollstonecraft's generation, the problem they pose to conventional definitions of the period, in "'But Oh! That Deep Romantic Chasm': The Engendering of Periodization," *Kenyon Review* 13 (summer 1991): 74-81. For an interesting discussion of de Beauvoir's much quoted point, as well as Monique Wittig's revisionary response to it, see Judith Butler, *Gender Trouble: Feminism and the Subversion of Identity* (New York: Routledge, 1990), 111-12.

11. Wollstonecraft, *Vindication,* 34, 9.

12. Ibid., 60-61 (emphasis mine).

13. Ibid., 178, 34.

14. Ibid., 7.

15. Ibid., 35. Equally telling, as Elissa S. Guralnick points out, Wollstonecraft couples the term "woman" with bashaws, despots, kings, emperors, soldiers, and courtiers, all of whom exercise "illegitimate power" and thus "enjoy the degradation of the exalted." See Elissa S. Guralnick, "Radical Politics in Mary Wollstonecraft's *A Vindication of the Rights of Woman,*" in Wollstonecraft, *Vindication,* 308-16.

16. Mary Poovey, *The Proper Lady and the Woman Writer: Ideology as Style in the Works of Mary Wollstonecraft, Mary Shelley, and Jane Austen* (Chicago: University of Chicago Press, 1984), 79-80. Along similar lines, Joan B. Landes argues that Wollstonecraft subscribes to an ideology of republican motherhood that views women's civic role as one performed inside the home, ascribes to men unbridled physical appetites, sets up a model of female duty, and displays an adherence toward male linguistic control that aligns her with the male philosophers of her day. See Joan B. Landes, *Women and the Public Sphere in the Age of the French Revolution* (Ithaca: Cornell University Press, 1988), 129-38.

17. Wollstonecraft, *Vindication,* 35, 175, 173.

18. Ibid., 10.

19. Edward Said, *Orientalism* (New York: Pantheon, 1978).

20. For a general discussion of the misogyny in these eighteenth-century texts, see my "The Female Monster in August Satire," *Signs* 3 (winter 1977): 380-94.

21. Ironically, then tragically, Wollstonecraft's detractors exploited precisely the images she shared with her philosophical opponents. She was depicted as one of the "philosophizing serpents in our bosom," a "hyena in petticoats," lampooned in *The Unsex'd Females: A Poem* as a "Poor maniac," ridiculed in a review in the *European Magazine* as a "philosophical wanton," and mocked in *The Shade of Alexander Pope on the Banks of the Thames* as "passion's slave." Similarly, her *Memoirs and Posthumous Works* was judged: "A Convenient Manual of speculative debauchery," and in 1801 the author of "The Vision of Liberty" intoned: "Lucky the maid that on her volume pores / A scripture, archly fram'd, for propagating w——s": see Ralph M. Wardle, *Mary Wollstonecraft: A Critical Biography* (Lawrence: University of Kansas Press, 1951), 318, 321, 322; as well as Janet Todd, "Introduction," in *A Wollstonecraft Anthology,* ed. Janet Todd (New York: Columbia University Press, 1990), 16-19.

22. Besides Poovey's and Landes's studies, see Mary Jacobus, "The Difference of View," in *Women Writing and Writing about Women,* ed. Mary Jacobus (London: Croom Helm, 1979), 16-17, as well as Cora Kaplan, "Pandora's Box: Subjectivity, Class, and Sexuality in Socialist Feminist Criticism," in *Making a Difference: Feminist Literary Criticism,* ed. Gayle Greene and Coppélia Kahn (London: Methuen, 1985), 157-60. Janet Todd reviews all these critics in *Feminist Literary History* (New York: Routledge, 1988), 103-10. On Wollstonecraft's making "genius a machismo male," see also Christina Battersby, *Gender and Genius: Towards a Feminist Aesthetics* (London: Women's Press, 1989), 98.

23. Cora Kaplan, "Wild Nights: Pleasure/Sexuality/Feminism," in Frederic Jameson et al., *Formations of Pleasure* (London: Routledge, 1983), 29.

24. Moira Ferguson, "Mary Wollstonecraft and the Problematic of Slavery," *Feminist Review* 42 (autumn 1992): 97.

25. Sandra M. Gilbert and Susan Gubar, *The War of the Words,* vol. 1 of *No Man's Land: The Place of the Woman Writer in the Twentieth Century* (New Haven: Yale University Press, 1988), chap. 4.

26. Emma Goldman, "Mary Wollstonecraft: Her Tragic Life and Her Passionate Struggle for Freedom," in Wollstonecraft, *Vindication,* 254-55.

27. Virginia Woolf, "Mary Wollstonecraft," in Wollstonecraft, *Vindication,* 269-70.

28. I am relying here on a term proposed by Hélène Cixous in "The Laugh of the Medusa," trans. Keith Cohen and Paula Cohen, *Signs* 1 (summer 1976): 878.

29. Mary Wollstonecraft, *Maria; or, The Wrongs of Women* (1798; New York: Norton, 1975), 27.

30. Mary Wollstonecraft, *Mary, a Fiction* (1788; New York: Schocken, 1977), 102.

31. Wollstonecraft, *Maria; or, The Wrongs of Women,* 51.

32. Adrienne Rich, "Compulsory Heterosexuality and Lesbian Existence," in *Women: Sex and Sexuality,* ed. Catharine R. Stimpson and Ethel Spector Person (Chicago: University of Chicago Press, 1980), 60-91. On Wollstonecraft, see Jeannette Foster, *Sex Variant Women in Literature* (1956; Baltimore: Diana Press, 1976), 56-60; and Lillian Faderman, "Who Hid Lesbian Theory?" in *Lesbian Studies: Present and Future,* ed. Margaret Cruikshank (Old Westbury, N.Y.: Feminist Press, 1982), 117. Interesting in this regard is the misogyny in lesbian literature that can be traced back to Radclyffe Hall's portraits of "feminine" women in *The Well of Loneliness,* many of whom strike her mannish Stephen Gordon as manipulative, materialistic, and frivolous. The words "grossly familiar" are from Wollstonecraft, *Vindication,* 127.

33. Wollstonecraft, *Vindication,* 128.

34. Mary Wollstonecraft, *Collected Letters of Mary Wollstonecraft,* ed. Ralph M. Wardle (Ithaca: Cornell University Press, 1979), 202-3.

35. Elizabeth Barrett Browning, *The Letters of Elizabeth Barrett Browning,* ed. Frederic G. Kenyon, 2 vols. (New York: Macmillan, 1897), 1: 231-32. In *The War of the Words,* Sandra Gilbert and I discuss the woman writer's "turn toward the father":

171-81. The two female precursors Wollstonecraft admires are Hester Mulso Chapone and Catharine Sawbridge Macaulay Graham, both discussed quite briefly in *A Vindication of the Rights of Woman,* 105-6 and 137.

36. Patricia Yaeger, "Writing as Action: *A Vindication of the Rights of Woman,*" *Minnesota Review* 29 (fall 1987): 74-75. See Wollstonecraft, *Vindication,* 77.

37. Butler, 2.

38. Olive Schreiner, *Woman and Labour* (1911; London: Virago, 1978), 272, 282. The long, slow death of the New Womanly Lyndall in *The Story of an African Farm* (1883) contrasts throughout the novel with the obesity, stupidity, voracity, racism, and cruelty of the traditional woman Tant' Sannie. Like Wollstonecraft, too, Schreiner publicly protested against female dependency on men but suffered repeated thralldom to men in her private life.

39. Schreiner, *Woman and Labour,* 82.

40. On Schreiner's plans to produce an introduction to *A Vindication of the Rights of Woman* and on *Woman and Labour* as a "Bible," see Joyce Avrech Berkman, *Olive Schreiner: Feminism on the Frontier* (St. Alban's, Vt.: Eden Women's Publications, 1979), 7, 10, 2. Schreiner's discussion of the "parasite woman on her couch" appears in *Woman and Labour,* 132-33.

41. Schreiner, *Woman and Labour,* 129-30.

42. Ann Douglas, *The Feminization of American Culture* (New York: Knopf, 1977), 6, 12, 8. See also 11.

43. In a recent essay, Sandra M. Gilbert explains her own attraction to D. H. Lawrence's works and that of women readers from Katherine Mansfield and H. D. to Anaïs Nin by envisioning Lawrence as "a proto French feminist." See her *Acts of Attention: The Poems of D. H. Lawrence,* 2d ed. (Ithaca: Cornell University Press, 1990), xix. In this regard Rachel Blau DuPlessis's often reprinted essay, "For the Etruscans," evokes D. H. Lawrence's *Etruscan Places.* See Rachel Blau DuPlessis, *The Pink Guitar: Writing as Feminist Practice* (New York: Routledge, 1990), 1-19.

44. M. M. Bahktin, "Discourse in the Novel," in *The Dialogic Imagination,* ed. Michael Holquist, trans. Caryl Emerson and Michael Holquist (Austin: University of Texas Press, 1981), 293-94.

45. According to Barbara Johnson, in a subtle analysis of the impact of racial stereotypes on racial identity, "questions of difference and identity are

always a function of a specific interlocutionary situation—and the answers matter of strategy rather than truth." See Barbara Johnson, "Thresholds of Difference: Structures of Address in Zora Neale Hurston," *Critical Inquiry* 12 (autumn 1985): 285.

46. On "fembot," see Mary Daly, *Pure Lust: Elemental Feminist Philosophy* (Boston: Beacon Press, 1984), 93.

47. Germaine Greer, *The Female Eunuch* (New York: Bantam, 1971), 335, 12, 157.

48. Germaine Greer, *Sex and Destiny: The Politics of Human Fertility* (New York: Harper & Row, 1984), 248.

49. Andrea Dworkin, *Intercourse* (New York: Free Press, 1987), 63.

50. Andrea Dworkin, *Ice and Fire* (New York: Weidenfeld & Nicolson, 1986), 72, 54-55, 101, 104-5.

51. Nancy Cott, "Feminist Theory and Feminist Movements: The Past before Us," in *What Is Feminism?* ed. Juliet Mitchell and Ann Oakley (New York: Pantheon, 1986), 49.

52. Jane Gallop, *Around 1981: Academic Feminist Literary Theory* (New York: Routledge, 1992), 138.

53. For background on such debates, see Joan Scott, "Deconstructing Equality-Versus-Difference"; and Theresa de Lauretis, "Upping the Anti (sic) in Feminist Theory," both in *Conflicts in Feminism*, 134-48 and 255-70.

54. Toril Moi, *Sexual/Textual Politics: Feminist Literary Theory* (London: Methuen, 1985), 62-63, 163. Later, Moi stated that her book was "written from a feminist perspective, or, in other words, from a perspective of political solidarity with the feminist aims of the critics and theorists I write about." In addition, she claims that after "the reactionary backlash of the eighties," she found it "far more difficult to be sanguine about one's feminist position" and "would now emphasize much more the risks of being a feminist." See her *Feminist Theory and Simone de Beauvoir* (Oxford: Basil Blackwell, 1990), 95, 102.

55. Quoted in Tom Glazer, ed., *Songs of Peace, Freedom, and Protest* (New York: McKay Press, 1970), 217-18. Here, as always and elsewhere, I am grateful for the help of Marah Gubar.

56. Katie Roiphe, *The Morning After: Sex, Fear, and Feminism on Campus* (Boston: Little, Brown & Co., 1993), 85. Significantly, Roiphe also aligns herself with John Irving and David Mamet (35 and 107). Yet in the opening of the book, she describes her own brand of feminism which she inherited from her mother. On *Reckless Eyeballing* and Alice Walker, see Ishmael Reed, "Steven Spielberg Plays Howard Beach," in *Writin' Is Fightin': Thirty-Seven Years of Boxing on Paper* (New York: Atheneum, 1988), 145-60.

57. Diana Fuss, *Essentially Speaking: Feminism, Nature, and Difference* (New York: Routledge, 1989), 20. See also Claire Goldberg Moses, "'Equality' and 'Difference' in Historical Perspective: A Comparative Examination of the Feminisms of French Revolutionaries and Utopian Socialists," in *Rebel Daughters: Women and the French Revolution*, ed. Sara E. Meltzer and Leslie W. Rabine (New York: Oxford University Press, 1992), 248, in which Moses points out: "The argument that feminist discourses of 'equality' and 'difference' are neither right nor wrong but relate to historically specific concerns or opportunities is further strengthened by noting the instability of these categories."

58. Gallop, 139.

Harriet Guest (essay date summer 1995)

SOURCE: Guest, Harriet. "The Dream of a Common Language: Hannah More and Mary Wollstonecraft." *Textual Practice* 9, no. 2 (summer 1995): 303-23.

[*In the following essay, Guest considers the similarities between the arguments in* A Vindication of the Rights of Woman *and Hannah More's* Structure, *noting especially the representation of the corruption perceived to be endemic among middle-class women.*]

I

'Have you read that wonderful book, The Rights of Woman', wrote Anna Seward to Mr Whalley, on 26 February 1792. 'It has, by turns, pleased and displeased, startled and half-convinced me that its author is oftener right than wrong.'[1] Seward's enthusiasm for Wollstonecraft's work, and sympathy for the trials of her life, seem to have endured despite her passionate antagonism to political radicalism in England. By August of 1792, she writes, with what is clearly a deeply felt sense of personal as well as political alarm, of:

Paine's pernicious and impossible system of equal rights, [which] is calculated to captivate and dazzle the vulgar; to make them spurn the restraints of legislation, and to spread anarchy, murder, and ruin over the earth.[2]

But neither Wollstonecraft's use of the discourse of natural rights, nor the scandal of her personal career, seem to have dismayed her. In 1798 she reports that

Wollstonecraft's 'death shocked and concerned me',[3] and, in a letter to Humphry Repton, she writes in praise of Godwin's *Memoirs* that:

> Bearing strong marks of impartial authority as to the character, sentiments, conduct, and destiny of a very extraordinary woman, they appear to be highly valuable. Since, on balancing her virtues and errors, the former greatly preponderate, it is no disgrace to any man to have united his destiny with hers.[4]

Seward seems to have found in Wollstonecraft's work and life principles she could continue to admire even though she recognized the sympathy between Wollstonecraft's political opinions and the radicalism she hated and feared. She went on to explain, in her discussion of the *Vindication* of 1792, that:

> Though the ideas of absolute equality in the sexes are carried too far, and though they certainly militate against St Paul's maxims concerning that important compact, yet they do expose a train of mischievous mistakes in the education of females;—and on that momentous theme this work affords much better rules than can be found in the sophist Rousseau, or in the plausible Gregory. It applies the spear of Ithuriel to their systems.[5]

What's intriguing about Seward's comments, I think, is the implication that Wollstonecraft's arguments about the education of women are somehow separable from the politics of her *Vindication* of their rights. Seward links her admiration for Wollstonecraft as an educational theorist with her feeling for her as a woman victimized by what she described as her 'basely betrayed attachment to that villain Imlay,' rather than with arguments for rights to sexual and political equality.[6] Now, I don't want to suggest that it was commonplace for women who rejected Wollstonecraft's political views to see her theories on the education of women as a distinct body of beliefs, uncoloured by her radicalism, and capable of being uncoupled from the claim to sexual equality. Writing in July 1792, Sarah Trimmer, for example, remembered the second *Vindication* exclusively as a claim for 'a further degree of liberty or consequence for women' within marriage; a claim which, she felt, threatened her own 'happiness in having a husband to assist me in forming a proper judgement, and in taking upon him the chief labour of providing for a family'. Trimmer regretted that Wollstonecraft had not employed her 'extraordinary abilities . . . to more advantage to society'.[7] In August of the same year, Horace Walpole wrote congratulating Hannah More on not having read the *Vindication.* Apparently confident of More's agreement, he observes that:

> I would not look at it, though assured it contains neither metaphysics nor politics; but as she entered the lists on the latter, and borrowed her title from the demon [Paine]'s book, which aimed at spreading the *wrongs* of men, she is excommunicated from the pale of my library.[8]

More herself claimed to find the notion of the rights of woman both absurd, and a regrettable staining of 'domestic manners . . . with the prevailing hue of public principles'.[9] Whether or not they had actually read the second *Vindication,* these writers clearly perceived it in the context of a polemical genre associated primarily with the discourse of rights—they perceived it as a political text.

What I do want to suggest, however, is that for a surprising range of readers the educational theories of Wollstonecraft's work did represent a common currency apparently uninflected by political differences. These readers seem to identify substantial parts of the text, at least, with a subgenre of educational conduct books and satires on social morality which they do not perceive to be appropriate to the articulation of political views. They seem, perhaps, to see gender as a category of concern that cuts across political differences. Mary Berry, the society hostess and correspondent of Walpole and More, acknowledges this possibility most directly. She writes, in a letter of 1799:

> I have been able . . . to go entirely through Hannah More, and Mrs Woolstonecraft immediately after her. It is amazing, but impossible, they should do otherwise than agree on all the great points of female education. H. More will, I dare say, be very angry when she hears this, though I would lay wager that she never read the book.[10]

In Hannah More's *Strictures on the Modern System of Female Education,* first published in 1799, and Wollstonecraft's *Vindication of the Rights of Woman: with strictures on political and moral subjects,* of 1792, Mary Berry detects an agreement on 'all the great points of female education' that would be amazing if it were not inevitable. And her observation may point up, I think, that aspect of the *Vindication* that seemed to Anna Seward to remove the text from political controversy, and to make it praiseworthy despite its arguments for sexual equality.

In a footnote to *The Unsex'd Females: A poem,* published in 1798, Richard Polwhele wrote that: 'Miss Hannah More may justly be esteemed, as a character, in all points, diametrically opposite to Miss Wollstonecraft.'[11] The polarization of the public and private characters of the two women is evident in the texts they produced, but nevertheless what seems to be common to them is the language, the discourse in which they characterize the corruptions of femininity. Their texts propose, on the whole, different remedies for that corruption, and identify its causes in markedly divergent terms. But the figure of the corrupt woman produced in these texts seems indistinguishable, and she seems characterized in terms that can stand independent of what Walpole and Polwhele saw as the absolute moral and political opposition of their views. That figure is, of course, familiar to any student of eighteenth-century writing on women. But I want now to examine her familiar features again, and to consider how they may illuminate the politics of feminism in the 1790s.[12]

II

Both More and Wollstonecraft allude, early in their arguments, to Hamlet's speech to Ophelia—'You jig, you amble, and you lisp, and nickname God's creatures.'[13] And the allusion seems to trigger, in their very different polemical texts, strikingly similar rehearsals of an apparently misogynistic discourse. Wollstonecraft argues that women—and particularly middle-class women—are encouraged to acquire 'a kind of sickly delicacy . . . a deluge of false sentiments and overstretched feelings, stifling the natural emotions of the heart' (10). More similarly believes that 'unqualified sensibility' has been cultivated in affluent women, 'till a false and excessive display of feeling became so predominant, as to bring into question the actual existence of . . . true tenderness' (VII, 79-80). It should be enough here to sketch only the outlines of the discursive construction of corrupt femininity that both texts then elaborate. In both, the feminine subject is represented as peculiarly the creature of her material circumstances, which absorb her perceptions and adapt or accommodate them to their own nature. More writes that:

> Women too little live or converse up to the standard of their understandings. . . . The mind, by always applying itself to objects below its level, contracts its dimensions, and shrinks itself to the size, and lowers itself to the level, of the object about which it is conversant.
>
> (VIII, 57)

As a result of their preoccupation with trivial and unconnected phenomena, women are unable to generalize their ideas, are peculiarly localized, and cannot maintain a coherent train of thought. They are enthralled by novels, fascinated by manners, superficial appearances, surface ornamentation, distracted by isolated incidents and random, occasional events. The desire for continual and easy stimulation that these habits of mind entail results in a debilitating absorption in the sensible body, in the addictive pleasures of luxury, the lowest forms of taste. Women are slaves to the demands of the fashionable body for adornment, for epicurean and sexual sensation, for an endless diet of ever novel and artificial stimuli. . . . More writes that:

> To attract admiration, is the great principle sedulously inculcated into [a woman's] young heart; and is considered as the fundamental maxim; and, perhaps, if we were required to condense the reigning system of the brilliant education of a lady into an aphorism, it might be comprised in this short sentence, *To allure and to shine.*
>
> (VII, 98)

Corrupted femininity is all surface, all display, lacking the detachment, the critical distance, necessary to the production of a continuous consciousness or integrity of identity capable of deferring its gratifications.

In Wollstonecraft's **Vindication** the analogy of travel provides a peculiarly revealing figure for the incoherence of feminine subjectivity. She argues that:

> A man, when he undertakes a journey, has, in general, the end in view; a woman thinks more of the incidental occurrences, the strange things that may possibly happen along the road; the impression that she may make on her fellow-travellers; and, above all, she is anxiously intent on the care of the finery that she carries with her, which is more than ever a part of herself, when going to figure on a new scene; when, to use an apt French turn of expression, she is going to produce a sensation.—Can dignity of mind exist with such trivial cares?
>
> (60)

It may be worth noting that, in this passage, Wollstonecraft's writing seems almost to yield to the pleasures of the narrative that's afforded by the feminine attraction to incidental events and details, and almost to acknowledge that the woman does have an 'end in view' in her desire to produce a sensation, though it's an end that could only be appropriate to genres more amenable to sentiment, such as travel letters or the novel. But the point is that feminine lack of purpose is represented here as producing a kind of dissipation of subjectivity into a succession of accidents, so that feminine identity becomes indistinguishable from the finery, the things which 'are more than ever a part' of what it is that constitutes its tenuous and apparent continuity. More argues, in an intriguingly similar image, that:

> The female . . . wanting steadiness in her intellectual pursuits, is perpetually turned aside by her characteristic tastes and feelings. Woman in the career of genius, is the Atalanta, who will risk losing the race by running out of her road to pick up the golden apple; while her male competitor, without, perhaps, possessing greater natural strength or swiftness, will more certainly attain his object, by direct pursuit, by being less exposed to the seductions of extraneous beauty, and will win the race, not by excelling in speed, but by despising the bait.
>
> (VIII, 31-2)

In the *Strictures,* the analogy of masculine direction and feminine aimlessness provides what is a much more explicit image of the feminine incapacity to regulate desire for tangible and immediate gratifications. But for both Wollstonecraft and More, corrupt femininity is characterized by its attachment to what is incidental or extraneous, and by the absence of the sense of purpose and direction that seems to them necessary to self-possession and moral control.

The image of corrupt femininity, abandoned beyond all coherence or control, is familiar enough. In the *Appeal to the Men of Great Britain in Behalf of Women* (which was published in 1798, but largely written earlier in the decade), for example, Mary Hays (who seems the most probable author[14]) implies that it is unnecessary to detail the character of immoral femininity again. It seems enough, on the whole, merely to allude to women's 'state of PERPETUAL BABYISM' (97), and occasionally to flesh out the fascination with dress, the slavery to fashion, the addiction to what she calls 'the idle vagaries of the present moment' (82), that characterize the image. In general terms, corrupt femininity represents the obverse side of all that is valued in the dominant moral discourses of the eighteenth century. But in the 1790s it has a distinctive character, the implications of which I want to consider. For it is peculiarly an image of the feminine role in commercial culture—of the feminine consumer. In what seems to me to be one of the more striking passages of the *Vindication,* Wollstonecraft writes:

> The conversation of French women . . . is frequently superficial; but, I contend, that it is not half so insipid as that of those English women whose time is spent in making caps, bonnets, and the whole mischief of trimmings, not to mention shopping, bargain-hunting, &c. &c.: and it is the decent, prudent women, who are most degraded by these practices; for their motive is simply vanity. The wanton who exercises her taste to render her passion alluring, has something more in view.
>
> (75-6)

The real crime here, Wollstonecraft is careful to emphasize, is that attention to 'the frippery of dress' weakens the mind, and distracts it from social duty. These women deprive the poor of employment, and themselves of the leisure necessary to self-improvement, for, she writes, they 'work only to dress better than they could otherwise afford' (75). But the most remarkable feature of this characterization must be that suggestion that the absorption in self-adornment, in the almost unmentionable folly of shopping and bargain hunting, is more contemptible and degrading than the behaviour of the sexually voracious woman, who at least has 'something more in view'.

What Wollstonecraft's comments here serve to confirm is that by the 1790s economic considerations have taken priority in the characterization of corrupted femininity. The problem is not that absorption in self-adornment may encourage an insatiable sexual rapacity disturbing to the social confidence placed in the system of propertied inheritance, though that remains an important ingredient of the discursive construction at issue. In these years, when fortunes may be more likely to be acquired through commercial speculation than as a result of inherited landed estates, the dangers of social disruption that cluster and find focus in the familiar figure of femi-

nine excess, at least in the context of the polemical genre of vindications, appeals and strictures, result from the vices of consumerism, rather than the more colourful sins of bad sexuality. The figure of corrupted femininity, I suggest, needs to be understood primarily as a set of gendered characteristics appropriated to the requirements of the discourse of commerce and its feared inverse, the anti-commercial horrors of profiteering, greed and consumerism run riot. In the late eighteenth century, the discourse of commerce projects out of itself the image of its own amoralism, producing the figure of insatiable feminine desire that shadows the morality of middle-class men and women, and that, in its confirmed and acknowledged immorality, works to consolidate the shaky moral values of commerce itself. The vices of commerce are embodied in the figure of immorally desirous femininity, which serves, as it were, to draw that poison off from the system of commerce itself. But in this context, of course, the poison is also the antidote—commerce needs the image of corrupt femininity to account for the consumption of its commodities, to represent the ceaseless stimulations to desire in the marketplace, and to figure, in its own shining form, the radiance of the commodity. It needs corrupt femininity to moralize and masculinize its own self-image.

Wollstonecraft's shoppers are caught up and implicated in the changing nature of the retail trade—they hunt for bargains in violation of the code of trust that was believed to have existed between tradesmen and their customers. They are implicitly promiscuous in awarding the favours of their custom, responding to the seduction of window displays and cut-price offers, undercutting traditional channels of supply with the industry of their busy fingers, rather than participating in those steady and trusting relationships of reciprocal recognition between consumer and supplier that are imagined to have characterized the more paternalist society of the past.[15] In Hays' *Appeal,* in particular, these shoppers and stitchers are reprimanded for their failure to fulfil the obligations of their class and gender, their failure to provide poor women with steady employment.[16] They are the counterpart of those men Wollstonecraft describes to Imlay in her *Letters written during a short residence in Sweden, Norway, and Denmark* (1796). She writes that:

> men entirely devoted to commerce never acquire, or [they] lose, all taste and greatness of mind. An ostentatious display of wealth without elegance, and a greedy enjoyment of pleasure without sentiment, embrutes them till they term all virtue, of an heroic cast, romantic attempts at something above our nature; and anxiety after others, a search after misery, in which we have no concern. But you will say that I am growing bitter, perhaps, personal. Ah! shall I whisper to you—that you—yourself, are strangely altered, since you have entered deeply into commerce . . . never allowing yourself to reflect, and keeping your mind, or rather passions, in a continual state of agitation.[17]

Imlay here is represented as partaking in those feminized qualities that the second *Vindication* attributes to corrupted femininity. What is personal, what strikes home to his self-image, she suggests, is the moralized and gendered discourse of anti-commerce, rather than the reflections produced by the discourses of sentiment, on the one hand, or civic humanism, on the other. Wollstonecraft's letter implies that Imlay the dealer in alum and soap will recognize and wish to reject the gendered and impassioned image of its own amoralism that commerce has produced.

Hannah More, it is no surprise to find, is prepared to locate value and virtue in the feminine image of the good consumer much more straightforwardly and explicitly than are Wollstonecraft and Hays—both of whom might be seen as more concerned to define middle-class women as something other than consumers. More's prose seems to register no flicker of doubt, none of the hesitancy that might point to a sense of incongruity, as she invests the figure of the good housewife with many of the virtues necessary to public spirit. She writes that:

> ladies whose natural vanity has been aggravated by a false education, may look down on *oeconomy* as a vulgar attainment, unworthy of the attention of a highly cultivated intellect; but this is the false estimate of a shallow mind. OEconomy . . . is not merely . . . the shabby curtailments and stinted parsimony of a little mind, operating on little concerns; but it is the exercise of a sound judgement exerted in the comprehensive outline of order, of arrangement, of distribution; of regulations by which alone well-governed societies, great and small, subsist. . . . A sound oeconomy is a sound understanding brought into action; it is calculation realized; it is the doctrine of proportion reduced to practice; it is foreseeing consequences, and guarding against them; it is expecting contingencies, and being prepared for them. The difference is, that to a narrow-minded vulgar oeconomist, the details are continually present. . . . Little events and trivial operations engross her whole soul.
>
> (VIII, 5-7)

The argument that the practice of the good consumer indicates that More identifies as 'real genius and extensive knowledge' (VIII, 8) can clearly only be supported in juxtaposition to the representation of the 'vulgar oeconomist', endowed with the narrow-minded absorption and capacity for engrossment in the physical that characterize corrupted femininity.

More writes of properly domesticated women that:

> Both in composition and action they excel in details; but they do not so much generalize their ideas as men, nor do their minds seize a great subject with so large a grasp. They are acute observers, and accurate judges of life and manners, as far as their own sphere of observation extends; but they describe a smaller circle. A woman sees the world, as it were, from a little eleva-

tion in her own garden, whence she makes an exact survey of home scenes, but takes not in that wider range of distant prospects which he who stands on loftier eminence commands.

> (VIII, 29-30)

The good domestic economist seems, on the one hand, to perceive with the kind of commanding and comprehensive grasp that distinguishes the vision of public men, from their loftier eminences. But on the other hand, within her 'smaller circle', she excels in her attention to detail. Her 'survey of home scenes', in other words, seems ambiguously 'exact'—it seems to be true and right, in the sense that the perceptions of great men are imagined to be true, disinterested and unbiased, and it seems to be exact in the sense that it is precise, and preoccupied with detail. Those qualities, I think, can only be represented as though they were compatible, and the notion that women do not generalize their ideas 'so much' as men can only be represented as though it made sense, as a result of the introduction of the contrasting figure of the vulgar economist, who as it were neutralizes the problem, by absorbing into herself what are seen as the more degrading implications of engrossment in the physical detail and menial drudgery of housekeeping.

III

The appropriation of the image of corrupted femininity to an anticommercial discourse is thoroughly problematic, as both More's *Strictures* and Wollstonecraft's *Vindication* demonstrate. The very currency, the power and resonance of the image in so many eighteenth-century texts serve to indicate the extent to which it has hoovered up the available languages of desire. It acts as a magnet for gendered characteristics in excess of those necessary to its function as a guarantee of the moral discourses from which it is projected and excluded. It can seem to have assumed the power to characterize not only what is excessive, corrupted, and feminized, but those qualities which seem in terms of the discourses of the period to be necessary to the distinction of gender, to be those essential to femininity itself. In the particular, anti-commercial form which I have suggested is specific to the 1790s, the image of corrupted femininity can seem to embrace and to represent all femininity, and thus to identify anti-commercial discourse as misogynistic. This can be seen in many of the polemical texts of the period, but is perhaps most unmistakably marked in More's *Strictures*. Writing of women's fashionable publicity, she argues:

> If, indeed, women were mere outside, form and face only . . . it would follow that a ball-room was quite as appropriate place for choosing a wife, as an exhibition room for choosing a picture. But, inasmuch as women are not mere portraits, their value not being determinable by a glance of the eye, if follows that a different

mode of appreciating their value, and a different place for viewing them antecedent to their being individually selected, is desirable. The two cases differ also in this, that if a man select a picture for himself from among all its exhibited competitors, and bring it to his own house, the picture being passive, he is able to *fix* it there: while the wife, picked up at a public place, and accustomed to incessant display, will not, it is probable, when brought home, stick so quietly to the spot where he fixes her; but will escape to the exhibition-room again, and continue to be displayed at every subsequent exhibition, just as if she were not become private property, and had never been definitively disposed of.

(VIII, 178-9)

More's argument is remarkable because of the twist, the change of direction that registers the problematic instability of discourses of gender. In the first place it seems that women are more valuable than portraits because they are more enigmatic, because they conceal hidden depths that cannot be known at a glance. The association of corrupt femininity with surface display seems to be what is established by portraiture, which can only paint the superficial appearance suitable for the exhibition room. But as More develops the image, that very addiction to surface, that sense in which femininity is fully manifested in its exhibitable and commodified form, becomes the valued and apparently uncorrupted site. Women who fail to recognize that they have become private property, which has been definitively disposed of, women who continue to desire to be seen, but unlike commodities do not apparently desire to be possessed, become identified as corrupt. They seem corrupt, shop-soiled, because of their suspect motivation and mobility—because, unlike portraits, they are not all surface. The analogy between women and their portraits, in More's argument, makes it clear that the identification of femininity with surface and display which is central to the discourse on feminized corruption has become ambiguous. The stable but superficial image which respects its status as private property is here a marker of relative purity and value.

Mary Hays' argument, in her *Appeal,* runs into similar difficulties in employing the analogy between women and works of art. She writes of corrupt women as 'mere automatans' [*sic*] who 'put on the semblance of every virtue', and may appear 'as captivating—perhaps even more so, than women of real sensibility'. She contrasts their 'varnish of surface' with 'real, unaffected, unassuming goodness', which is analogous to 'marble of the most exquisite quality,—which, without flaw or blemish, admits of an equal polish through all its parts as on its surface; and on which the sculptor may lastingly impress the sublimest efforts of his art' (255-6). What is curious about this contrast between automata and sculpture, what seems excessive to the familiar language of surface and depth, is the emphasis on the sculpted im-

age of virtuous femininity as a production, lastingly impressed by the hand of its maker. Both the automaton and sculpture, that emphasis on production serves to point up, afford pleasure to the spectator because of their visible surfaces and polished finish. The fact that marble statuary has a more enduring polish does not call into question the characterization of both corrupt and virtuous femininity in the desire to excite desire, in qualities common to commodities. What seem to distinguish corrupt from virtuous femininity are the aesthetic criteria which articulate discrimination between different kinds of art, between the value of different kinds of private property. The analogy between women and painting or sculpture makes explicit the commodification of femininity, while veiling that commercial form in the decent and acceptable drapery of aesthetic value, but the analogy also elides the distinction between virtue and corruption that it is apparently called upon to support. In this context, all femininity is identified as spectacle, and caught up in those transactions of desire that characterize both consumers and commodities.

The perceived erosion of what was imagined to have been the clear distinction between virtuous and corrupt femininity is a matter of explicit concern and alarm for conservative writers of the later eighteenth century. John Bowles, for example, in his *Remarks on Modern Female Manners* of 1802, laments that women of unblemished character 'No longer . . . pride themselves . . . on the distinction which separates them from the abandoned part of their sex'.[18] He argues that virtuous women should not tolerate the society of known adultresses—a point of etiquette that Hannah More also stressed in her *Strictures* of 1799, although in her *Essays for Young Ladies* of 1777 she had argued for the exercise of Christian forgiveness and tolerance. Bowles advances his case with an excessive strength of feeling that borders on panic. He writes that:

Honour, especially in women, can admit of no compromise with dishonour; no approaches from one towards the other must be suffered; the boundary between them must be considered as impassable; the line by which they are divided is the RUBICON of female virtue.[19]

His insistence can be taken as an indication of the frailty of definition, the discursive instability, of the categories of feminine virtue and corruption—categories which cannot be kept distinct by the mere device of social manoeuvring that he advocates. The blurring of these categories, he argues, represents 'a much more formidable enemy than Buonaparte himself, with all his power, perfidy, and malice'.[20] It indicates a social change which, he writes:

would be more tremendous than even the suspension of those wonderful powers of nature, which confine the planets to their respective orbs, and maintain, from age to age, the harmony of the universe.[21]

Bowles believes that apocalyptic chaos will result from virtuous women adopting immodest fashions of dress. Confronting the discursive confusion this represents, he exclaims that:

compared with such a woman, the bold and abandoned profligate, who with dauntless effrontery, appears publicly in her true character, is less disgraceful to her sex, and less injurious to society.[22]

Like Wollstonecraft contemplating the horrors of shopping, he finds himself welcoming the unambiguously scandalous woman as a more socially acceptable and useful figure than the fashionable woman of indeterminate morality. For, as I suggested earlier, it is the feminine image of corrupt desire, of bad sexuality, that is necessary to inoculate the morality of commercial culture. The danger represented by the confusion of the signs of vice and virtue, or by the possibility that anti-commerce might be recognized as a feature of commerce itself, is greater than the danger represented by the bold and abandoned face of bad sexuality or Napoleonic perfidy.

IV

The problem that I believe these texts of the late century respond to and articulate in their shared and apparently misogynistic discourse is clearly set out in Anna Laetitia Aikin or Barbauld's essay of 1773, 'Against Inconsistency in our Expectations'. She explains that:

We should consider this world as a great mart of commerce, where fortune exposes to our view various commodities, riches, ease, tranquillity, fame, integrity, knowledge. Every thing is marked at a settled price. Our time, our labour, our ingenuity, is so much ready money which we are to lay out to the best advantage. Examine, compare, choose, reject; but stand to your own judgement; and do not, like children, when you have purchased one thing, repine that you do not possess another which you did not purchase.[23]

It is perhaps apparent from this initial image of society that Barbauld's essay attempts to wed a moral discourse on the use of talents, on those differences of character that may result in tranquillity, fame, or integrity, to a discourse on the division of labour concerned to explain the diverse specializations of commercial society in a way that seems also to justify its inequalities. Barbauld concludes that:

There is a cast of manners peculiar and becoming to each age, sex, and profession. . . . Each is perfect in its kind. A woman as a woman: a tradesman as a tradesman. We are often hurt by the brutality and sluggish conceptions of the vulgar; not considering that some there must be to be hewers of wood and drawers of water, and that cultivated genius, or even any great refinement and delicacy in their moral feelings, would be a real misfortune to them.[24]

The inclusion of women here, as though gender were a category immediately comparable to occupation or class, is thoroughly problematic. What women in their capacity as The Sex bring to the great mart of commerce is, most obviously, their sexuality. They may figure in the great mart as consumers or commodities, but as I have tried to show, those roles are at least morally ambiguous.

What women are more commonly valued for by the late century is precisely their exclusion from the marketplace—the marginal position from which, according to John Bowles:

they soften, they polish, the rougher sex, which, without their mild and genial influence, would never exhibit any thing better than a race of barbarians. . . . They constitute the very ties of those family connections, those domestic societies, which can alone foster in the human heart those tender sympathies, the social affections. . . . In short, they adorn, they harmonize the world.[25]

That image of women as social glue is common to many of the polemical texts of the 1790s, including Wollstonecraft's and More's. But in Barbauld's essay it's clear that even this vague notion of a social function for virtuous femininity is incompatible with the model of society that the division of labour articulates. Barbauld laments that in modern society:

Every one is expected to have such a tincture of general knowledge as is incompatible with going deep into any science; and such a conformity to fashionable manners as checks the free workings of the ruling passion, and gives an insipid sameness to the face of society, under the idea of polish and regularity.[26]

The qualities that Barbauld here regrets, because they militate against specialization and against the division of labour on which the great mart of commerce is perceived to depend, are precisely those of polish and regularity which it is the business of women to instil. Barbauld acknowledges that the idea of society which it is the function of women to harmonize and polish is made redundant by the more powerful and persuasive model of the great mart described by political economy. In the context of that commercial model, there is no moral or professional language available to articulate feminine virtue. It has no place and no value. By the 1790s, I think, that perception has become inadmissible. The problem of feminine virtue, the problem of what women are wanted for, has become an issue capable of producing that anxiety about policing the division between good and bad women that John Bowles articulated—an anxiety that animates the spate of conservative and radical texts on the education of women in the 1790s. The most obvious function of women in the 1790s is to fuel the discourse of anti-commerce—a discourse that I have suggested shows an alarming tendency to become fully misogynistic, and to become the only available, or at least the dominant discourse on femininity.

V

Wollstonecraft, Hays, and More might all be understood, in their polemical writing, to respond to the impossible demands placed on femininity in commercial culture, and they all look to the possibility of professionalization to reclaim respectability for the notion of virtuous femininity. Hays and Wollstonecraft both argue strongly that the exclusion of women from the division of labour as anything but consumers means that the terms in which they can be represented are restricted almost completely to those of corrupt feminine desire made available by what I have called the discourse of anti-commerce. Emphasizing the dominance of the model of society produced by political economy, Wollstonecraft writes:

> Taught from their infancy that beauty is woman's sceptre, the mind shapes itself to the body, and, roaming round its gilt cage, only seeks to adorn its prison. Men have various employments and pursuits which engage their attention, and give a character to the opening mind; but women, confined to one, and having their thoughts constantly directed to the most insignificant part of themselves, seldom extend their views beyond the triumph of the hour.

> (44)

What women are perceived to be for, the character of femininity, is for Wollstonecraft produced by their allocated place and employment within the division of labour, which dictates that they will consume goods for their personal adornment, goods which the middle-class woman finds become 'more than ever a part of herself' (60), and constitute her social identity.[27] Hays' *Appeal* is more explicitly concerned than is the ***Vindication*** with the issues raised by differences of class. She argues that what she identifies as the 'misemployed talents' that middle-class women expend on 'ribbons, gauze, fringes, flounces and furbelows . . . might have placed thee on the woolsack, or have put a mitre on thy head, or a long robe on thy back, or a truncheon in thy hand' (79). The vanity of corrupt femininity is ambition misemployed, she claims. She argues strongly for the reappropriation to women of trades and professions that had become masculinized in the course of the eighteenth century. Significantly, Hays emphasizes that the masculinization of women's work had left prostitution as the only available professional course open to poor women obliged to compete in the marketplace.

More, in contrast, employs the language of professionalization to characterize both corrupt and virtuous femininity. The life of fashionable women, she argues, 'formerly, too much resembled the life of a confectioner', but 'it now too much resembles that of an actress; the morning is all rehearsal, and the evening is all performance' (VII, 120-1). The passions women bring to their public performances resemble those that 'might be supposed to stimulate professional candidates for fame and profit at public games and theatrical exhibitions' (VII, 123). More argues that:

> Most *men* are commonly destined to some profession, and their minds are commonly turned each to its respective object. Would it not be strange if they were called out to exercise their profession, or to set up their trade, with only a little general knowledge of the trades and professions of all other men, and without any previous definite application to their own particular calling. The profession of ladies, to which the bent of *their* instruction should be turned, is that of daughters, wives, mothers and mistresses of families. They should therefore be trained with a view to these several conditions, and be furnished with a stock of ideas, and principles, and qualifications, and habits, ready to be applied and appropriated, as occasion may demand, to each of these respective situations.

> (VII, 111-12)

More's suspicion of those who are equipped 'with only a little general knowledge' echoes Barbauld's distrust of the 'tincture of general knowledge' that is valued 'under the idea of polish and regularity'. It is a suspicion of what has come to seem an anachronistic lack of specialization, appropriate to an idea of society innocent of commercial progress. In More's *Strictures,* women can only become properly modern and professional by subjecting themselves to an extraordinary degree of restraint—by accepting the confinement of their different presence within the 'smaller circle' of domesticity. More argues that fashionable men are peculiarly subject to the allure of the ambiguously public world of clubs, which 'generate and cherish luxurious habits, from their perfect ease, undress, liberty, and inattention to the distinctions of rank' (VIII, 184). Clubs, she argues, 'promote . . . every temper and spirit which tends to *undomesticate*' (VIII, 185). It is the duty of the wife to correct what More represents as the democratical spirit of club life by cultivating in her husband the 'love of fireside enjoyments' (VIII, 186). By confining her own circle of understanding and activity to the domestic, More suggests that the wife will be able to produce in herself and her husband the belief that 'those attachments, which . . . are the cement which secure the union of the family as well as of the state' (VIII, 187) are those which are nourished in the asocial world of the family, of domesticity. The kind of limited publicity and professionalism to which Wollstonecraft and Hays wish to secure women access is associated in More's argument with 'inattention to the distinctions of rank', with the blurring of the boundaries of public and political space—boundaries which are for More secured by the polarization of family and state, and confirmed by the antagonism that she and John Bowles wish to see between virtuous and immoral women. Whereas for Wollstonecraft and Hays, women seem left with the possibility of entering more fully into the political and economic marketplace. As Wollstonecraft observes: 'The world cannot be seen by an unmoved spectator, we must mix in the throng, and feel as men feel' (112).

What is problematic about that statement is of course its apparent denial of the value of gendered difference. And that is a problem which, I hope to have shown, is produced by the specific historical moment in which the **Vindication** participates. The apparently misogynistic discourse that is common to both Wollstonecraft and More, and to a less marked extent to Hays, in their polemical texts if not in their writing in other genres, needs to be understood, I think, as peculiar to the late century. As I have mentioned, the general terms in which it characterizes corrupt femininity are common to writing about women throughout the eighteenth century. Mary Astell, for example, has some very similar things to say about fashionable women at the beginning of the century. But in Mary Astell's writing the image is not misogynistic, it is not a representation of all femininity. It is a set of terms appropriated, broadly speaking, to those women who are seen to be surplus to the marriage market, marriageable women who may be made redundant by the newly emerging relationship between the city and the landed gentry. By the late century, however, the requirements of anti-commercial discourse appropriate the image of corrupt femininity, and extend it into the nightmare of a language that represents all women, and all forms of feminine desire. It is important, I think, to recognize the specific uses to which the notion of feminine corruption is put, in the course of the eighteenth century. For if we accept its terms as common to all forms of femininity, then, in a sense, we accept their status as somehow essential to gender difference. We then tend to privilege from among the cluster of characteristics that make up the image those which we most nearly accept as essential to femininity ourselves—such as sexuality—and overlook the extent to which feminisms of the past have changed their nature to suit the specific historical circumstances in which they operate. We overlook the flexible self-image which is surely necessary to feminist polemical texts.

Notes

1. *Letters of Anna Seward: Written between the years 1784 and 1807. In six volumes* (Edinburgh: G. Ramsay & Co., 1811), III, p. 117.

2. To Lady Gresley, 29 August 1792, III. p. 160.

3. To Mrs Jackson of Turville-Court, 13 February 1798, V, p. 47.

4. 13 April 1798, V, p. 73.

5. To Mr Whalley, 26 February 1792, III, p. 117.

6. To Humphry Repton, 13 April 1798, V, p. 74.

7. *Some Account of the Life and Writings of Mrs Trimmer, with original letters, and meditations and prayers, selected from her journal. In two volumes* (London: R. & R. Gilbert, 1814, this 2nd edn 1816), To Mrs M., 12 July 1792, II, pp. 60-1.

8. *The Letters of Horace Walpole Earl of Orford,* 9 vols, ed. Peter Cunningham (London: Bohn, 1861), 21 August 1792, IX, p. 385. Walpole's remark about the absence of politics in the text implies the absence of direct or explicit comment on the political events of the day. In the preceding paragraph of the letter he describes. 'The *second* massacre of Paris' in some detail, and suggests that these events have confirmed his 'abhorrence of politics' (p. 384).

9. *Strictures on the Modern System of Female Education. With a view of the principles and conduct prevalent among women of rank and fortune* (1799), in *The Works of Hannah More. In eight volumes: Including several pieces never before published* (London: A. Strahan, 1801), VII, pp. 172-3.

10. *Extracts of the Journals and Correspondence of Miss Berry, from the year 1783 to 1852,* 3 vols., ed. Lady Theresa Lewis (London: Longmans, 1865), To Mrs Cholmeley, 2 April 1799, II, pp. 91-2. On perceptions of Wollstonecraft as an educational theorist see Regina M. Janes, 'On the reception of Mary Wollstonecraft's *A Vindication of the Rights of Woman',* Journal of the History of Ideas, 39 (1978), pp. 293-302, and Virginia Sapiro, *A Vindication of Political Virtue: The Political Theory of Mary Wollstonecraft* (Chicago: Chicago University Press, 1992), p. 28.

11. In Vivien Jones (ed.), *Women in the Eighteenth Century: Constructions of Femininity* (London: Routledge, 1990), p. 191.

12. The relation between More's *Strictures* and Wollstonecraft's second *Vindication* has been explored most fully by Mitzi Myers, in her important article, 'Reform or Ruin: "A revolution in female manners"', in *Studies in Eighteenth-Century Culture,* no. 11 (1982), pp. 199-216. Myers argues that Wollstonecraft and More are united, despite or across their political differences, in 'perceiving a society infected with fashionable corruption, [to which] both preach a militantly moral middle-class reform grounded in women's potentiality' (p. 211). As will I hope become apparent, my essay is concerned to unpack—to specify and complicate— what is involved in those rather generalized notions of fashionable corruption and middle-class morality. But I also question Myers's reading of

the second *Vindication* as primarily concerned with reforming women's domestic role, as well as her assumption that middle-class and affluent women are, in some sense, really corrupted by fashionable amusements. My approach is more extensively (if indirectly) indebted to Cora Kaplan's reading of Wollstonecraft in her brilliant and influential essay, 'Wild Nights: pleasure/sexuality/feminism', in *Sea Changes: Essays on Culture and Feminism* (London: Verso, 1986). Kaplan's essay (which was first published in 1983) argues that Wollstonecraft's text is 'interested in developing a class sexuality for a radical, reformed bourgeoisie' (p. 35), through the reform of something resembling Myers's 'fashionable corruption', but Kaplan argues that this reforming drive 'expresses a violent antagonism to the sexual' (p. 41). Her essay questions this 'negative construction of the sexual in the midst of a positive and progressive construction of the social and political' (p. 36). My essay attempts to extend this questioning, and to reconsider the polemical uses of the figure of negative sexuality, in the context of concerns about feminine morality that are, I think, specific to the cultural politics of the 1790s.

13. See *Strictures*, VII, pp. 78-9; and Mary Wollstonecraft, *A Vindication of the Rights of Woman*, ed. Carol H. Poston (New York: Norton, 1975), p. 10. The subtext here may be Burke's notorious use of Hamlet's speech. He writes that in 'sensible objects', 'so far is perfection . . . from being the cause of beauty; that this quality, where it is highest in the female sex, almost always carries with it an idea of weakness and imperfection. Women are very sensible of this; for which reason, they learn to lisp, to totter in their walk, to counterfeit weakness, and even sickness. In all this, they are guided by nature.' *A Philosophical Enquiry into the Origin of our Ideas of the Sublime and Beautiful*, ed. J. T. Boulton (London: Routledge & Kegan Paul, 1958), p. 110.

14. William Thompson attributed the *Appeal* to Mary Hays in the Introductory Letter to Mrs Wheeler, in their *Appeal of one-half of the human race, Women, against the pretensions of the other half, Men* (1825). The attribution may also be indirectly supported by the apology for writing in the first person that is appended to the *Appeal*. See *Appeal to the Men of Great Britain in behalf of Women* (London: J. Johnson, 1798), pp. 295-300. Wollstonecraft wrote to Mary Hays on 12 November 1792, commenting on a draft of her *Letters and Essays, Moral and Miscellaneous*, which was to be published in 1793. She argued that the text was 'too full of yourself . . . true modesty should keep the author in the back ground'. Ralph M. Wardle (ed.), *Collected Letters of Mary*

Wollstonecraft (Ithaca: Cornell University Press, 1979), p. 220.

15. On the changing nature of consumption see Neil McKendrik, 'Introduction. The birth of a consumer society: the commercialization of eighteenth-century England', and Chapter 1, 'The consumer revolution in eighteenth-century England', in Neil McKendrick, John Brewer and J. H. Plumb, *The Birth of a Consumer Society: The Commercialization of Eighteenth-Century England* (London: Europe, 1982); and E. P. Thompson's essay of 1971, 'The moral economy of the English crowd in the eighteenth century', reprinted in his *Customs in Common* (London: Merlin, 1991).

16. See, for example, *Appeal,* pp. 242-3.

17. In Janet Todd and Marilyn Butler (eds), *The Works of Mary Wollstonecraft* (London: Pickering, 1989), 7 vols. VI, pp. 340-1.

18. *Remarks on Modern Female Manners, as distinguished by indifference to character, and indecency of dress; extracted chiefly from 'Reflections political and moral at the conclusion of the war. By John Bowles, Esq.'* (London: Woodfall, 1802) p. 4.

19. Bowles, p. 6.

20. ibid., p. 16.

21. ibid., p. 20.

22. ibid., p. 15. Bowles's discussion may echo Hannah More's account of modern dress. She argues that as a result of excessive cultivation the arts have become 'agents of voluptuousness' (VII, p. 91), and comments: 'May we not rank among the present corrupt consequences of this unbounded cultivation, the unchaste *costume,* the impure style of dress, and that indelicate statue-like exhibition of the female figure, which, by its artfully disposed folds, its seemingly wet and adhesive drapery, so defines the form as to prevent covering itself from becoming a veil? This licentious mode, as the acute Montesquieu observed on the dances of the Spartan virgins, has taught us "to strip chastity itself of modesty"' (VII, p. 92).

23. In *The Works of Anna Laetitia Barbauld, With a Memoir by Lucy Aikin* (London: Longman, 1825), 2 vols, II, p. 185.

24. Barbauld, II, p. 194.

25. Bowles, p. 18.

26. Barbauld, II, pp. 193-4.

27. For a fuller discussion of Wollstonecraft's views on the employments appropriate to middle-class women, see Sapiro, pp. 158-61.

Cindy L. Griffin (essay date winter 1996)

SOURCE: Griffin, Cindy L. "A Web of Reasons: Mary Wollstonecraft's *A Vindication of the Rights of Woman* and the Re-weaving of Form." *Communication Studies* 47, no. 4 (winter 1996): 272-88.

[*In the following essay, Griffin proposes a nonlinear form of argument, based on the form of* A Vindication of the Rights of Woman, *which she believes will assist readers in recognizing the complexity of the work and the need to reconsider notions of effective rhetorical form.*]

Mary Wollstonecraft, recognized as one of the most influential feminists in history, strived to express her views in an age when the opinions and thoughts of women were seen as insignificant. At a time when the White, male, upper-class perspective was the dominant one and when women writers were scarce, Wollstonecraft emerged as a serious writer, philosopher, and advocate of the equality of women and men. Throughout her career in England in the late 18th century, Wollstonecraft challenged and ridiculed the common sentiment that women naturally were inferior to men, arguing that the prevailing system of reasoning and education, not women's "natural" subservience, kept them in positions of dependence and inferiority. In response to the common belief in women's lack of intelligence, their submissiveness, and their passivity, Wollstonecraft wrote and published her most influential work, *A Vindication of the Rights of Woman: With Strictures on Political and Moral Subjects* (1792)—a powerful and complex argument for women's rights and equality.[1]

Wollstonecraft's bold and important claims for women's independence have not received as much acclaim as might be expected. Although women prior to the 20th century praised her work,[2] only a few contemporary scholars speak in favor of Wollstonecraft. Todd suggests that Wollstonecraft's work is "so comprehensive that one may say that all feminists, radical and conservative, who followed Wollstonecraft are her philosophic descendants" (1976, p. xi); Sapiro argues that any "serious student of feminist theory or gender and political theory must have read *[A] Vindication of the Rights of Woman*" (1992, p. 280); Taylor considers Wollstonecraft a "pioneer" (1969, p. 19); Stuart (1978) explores Wollstonecraft's *A Vindication of the Rights of Men*; Griffin (1994) suggests that Wollstonecraft's arguments help explain the experience of alienation from a rhetorical rather than a strictly material perspective; and Huxman (1996) advocates that Wollstonecraft's work be considered a part of a symbolic convergence of early feminist discourse.

In contrast to this small group of supporters, however, the majority of responses to Wollstonecraft are grounded in a harsh rejection of her public image, her arguments, and her overall presentation of her ideas. Perhaps more than any other feminist on record, Wollstonecraft has been so harshly criticized, not only for what she said but for how she said it, that scholars would do well to consider the implications and foundations of this criticism.

Although both the content and form of Wollstonecraft's ideas have been scrutinized, shortly after her death in 1798, Wollstonecraft's character also came under attack. She was described as an "unsexed female" in Polwhele's poem, *The Unsex'd Females* (1800, pp. 23-35), and a "hyena in petticoats" by Walpole (1859, p. 452). Many years later, Lundberg and Farnham suggested that Wollstonecraft's theories came from a "tortured woman's soul"—they were "factually erroneous" and "socially mischievous" (1947, pp. 144-145). Wollstonecraft, Lundberg and Farnham suggested, wanted women to behave "as nearly as possible like men" (pp. 144-145). The content of her work also came under scrutiny shortly after her death, and her arguments were described as superficial (*Anti-Jacobin Review*, 1798) and as nothing more than "extravagant, absurd, and destructive theories" (*Anti-Jacobin Review*, 1801, p. 95).

In 1885, almost 100 years after her death, a reviewer for the *Eclectic Magazine* began the attack on the form of Wollstonecraft's arguments. This reviewer suggested that the work was "too long," lacking in arrangement, repetitive, "rambling," and disjointed (pp. 100-107). The intense attacks on her rhetorical form, however, did not take hold until the middle of this century. Beard argued that Wollstonecraft's style was "uninformed" and lacked the neatness and "athletic movement of Paine's English" (1946, p. 100). Kamm (1966, p. 19) criticized the manner in which *Vindication* was written, describing Wollstonecraft's work as "rambling" and a "book which shows every mark of having been hurriedly put together. . . . *[A] Vindication,* like its author, is flamboyant, passionate and sentimental." Nixon (1971, p. 97) suggested that Wollstonecraft's book was "not well planned. She reiterates her arguments without strengthening them, suddenly returning on her steps to insist on some point which previously she had not sufficiently stressed." Tomalin (1974, p. 136) suggested that the "book is without any logical structure"; Urbanski (1980, p. 55) described the book as "ill arranged," repetitive, and too full of digressions; and Brownmiller (1975, p. 4) argued that Wollstonecraft was possessed by the "furies" who "both impelled and choked her, . . . clogging her prose with gulping anger, roadblocks of venom, perilous flights of mannered scorn."[3]

The early rejections of Wollstonecraft's ideas seem to be grounded in questions of lifestyle and content, while later negative responses were based on the actual form of her arguments. This is not a new strategy for criticizing or even rejecting the arguments of feminist and minority rhetors; negative scrutiny regularly moves from what a rhetor says to how those ideas are presented (Spender, 1982, p. 28).[4] These criticisms of the form of a feminist rhetor's argument suggest that when the opposition no longer can refute the content of that argument, a refutation of the form of that argument begins. Although certain argument forms might be so complex or confusing as to be incomprehensible, Wollstonecraft's work clearly does not fall into this category. In this instance, the attacks regarding the proper form or arrangement of an entire argument and the disposition of an entire piece of discourse still are open for discussion.

The question of the nature of rhetorical form or style is not a new one in the communication discipline and has been addressed by several scholars in recent decades. Nelson (1972) argues for a fugal form in the rhetoric of Charles James Fox; McGuire (1977) suggests that critics understand Hitler's *Mein Kampf* as an encyclopaedic myth; Black (1978, 1992) advances the idea of a sentimental style; and Campbell (1980), Dow and Tonn (1993), and Blankenship and Robson (1995) argue for a lyric or feminine style of rhetoric. Recent scholarly efforts also have been directed at envisioning and teaching the complexity of arrangement or disposition in public speaking courses. Jaffe (1995) and Kearney and Plax (1996) advocate an intercultural perspective on form, and S. K. Foss and K. A. Foss (1994) propose a nonconfrontative, transformational model for presentational speaking that revisions the ways in which ideas are linked together. Taken as a whole, these attempts to advocate and explain the myriad patterns of argument are significant in that they suggest the complexity and diversity of argument forms available to rhetors. They do not, however, explain satisfactorily Wollstonecraft's rhetorical form.

I suggest that in order to understand Wollstonecraft's arguments and her rhetorical contribution more fully, scholars must consider the distinctive form or pattern of argument she advanced. Wollstonecraft's treatise illustrates the highly organic nature of an argument suggested by Toulmin (1988), or what Perelman (1970, p. 290) identifies as "a web [of ideas] formed from all the arguments and all the reasons that combine to achieve the desired result." Wollstonecraft's *Vindication* offers scholars an opportunity to scrutinize this web-like arrangement of ideas and to explore the implications of this arrangement for rhetors and rhetorical theory alike.

I propose that Wollstonecraft's arguments are understood best as a web of ideas, woven together through definition, redefinition, repetition, and a careful pattern of interconnection. Her pattern of arguing is web-like in form in that her overall argument begins with a central theme from which all other themes develop and to which all other themes connect. The web pattern continues as each theme is linked to the others by an intricate system of definition and redefinition and the interrelation of each of her ideas to the others. Wollstonecraft builds, in effect, a system in which all parts of her argument function symbiotically and in concert so that the taking apart of one strand of her argument requires addressing each of the other strands. The strength of this argument lies in the difficulty of refuting its entirety; its weakness, however, comes from its complexity and its web-like nature.

To assess Wollstonecraft's rhetorical form, I begin my analysis with a very brief discussion of *Vindication* and Wollstonecraft's perspective on women's rights. I then identify the web model of discourse by discussing her method of organization and illustrating the web pattern within the presentation of her arguments. I argue that Wollstonecraft's arguments create an interwoven pattern of ideas that ask the audience to participate in the argument process by building connection upon connection and relationship within relationship. This same pattern, however, can present difficulties for both the rhetor and the audience, and I address these as well. I conclude my analysis with a discussion of the ways in which Wollstonecraft's work illustrates the complex form an argument can assume when the issue under discussion is equally complex. I also address issues of the role of the audience and the process of argument construction itself, suggesting that the role of the rhetor, the form of an argument, and the task of the audience, at times, may be intimately interconnected.

WOLLSTONECRAFT'S ARGUMENTS AND AN ANALYSIS OF RHETORICAL FORM

In *Vindication,* Wollstonecraft attacked and challenged both male dominance and female acquiescence to that dominance. She offered a critique of and challenge to the prevailing system of education for women and proposed a reformed social order, particularly where women and men were concerned. Wollstonecraft argued against the influential theories and writings of Milton, Rousseau, Gregory, Fordyce, and Pope and challenged Biblical strictures, nobility, hereditary rule, and even common-sense notions regarding proper education and the natural social order. She turned arguments from each of these individuals and institutions against themselves, offering refutations of their claims and illustrating the harms done to women as a result. Her primary thesis was that were women to be properly educated, they would prove themselves to be morally and intellectually equal to men. To trivialize women and to keep them in a state of inferiority, according to Wollstonecraft, was antithetical to God's purpose. Wollstonecraft wanted women to have freedom to think rather than intellectual confinement, a chance for a stimulating education rather than lessons of obedience,

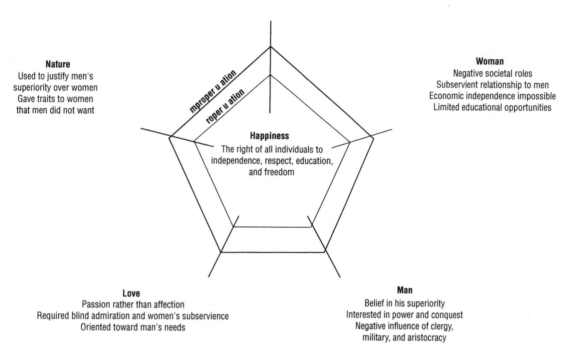

Virtue
Transvaluation of virtue with vice
Used to justify women's inferiority
Equivalent to ambition and power in men
Equivalent to submission and slavery in women

Nature
Used to justify men's
superiority over women
Gave traits to women
that men did not want

Woman
Negative societal roles
Subservient relationship to men
Economic independence impossible
Limited educational opportunities

mproper u ation
roper u ation

Happiness
The right of all individuals to
independence, respect, education,
and freedom

Love
Passion rather than affection
Required blind admiration and women's subservience
Oriented toward man's needs

Man
Belief in his superiority
Interested in power and conquest
Negative influence of clergy,
military, and aristocracy

Wollstonecraft's Web of Challenge

and strength of mind and body rather than flattering airs and a child-like nature. Women's character, Wollstonecraft surmised, was a product of oppression rather than nature; were society to alter its views of women as well as the restrictions placed on them, benefits would be reaped by all. Throughout *Vindication,* Wollstonecraft argued that women's position in society ought to improve so that women could become better wives and mothers, live lives of dignity and respect, and make more positive contributions to society as a whole.[5]

As Wollstonecraft argued from her notion of the established truth to examples of the folly of that truth and to a new definition of truth, she addressed one subject or topic, raised issues from another topic, asked the reader to branch out to yet another topic, and to see the relationships among and between each of her ideas. Through this series of connections and threads of relationships, Wollstonecraft developed a complicated system of definition and redefinition, cause and effect, and reasoning and refutation that is, perhaps, more complicated than either Perelman (1970) or Toulmin (1988) suggest. To understand Wollstonecraft's pattern of argument, I argue that the reader must envision the pattern of a web. This web has a central theme or center from which all strands of organization and thought extend. Each strand, as it moves away from the center of the

web, intersects with other strands, circling outward and developing or connecting with other themes or strands as the web increases in size. The result is that whether direct and confrontative or indirect and subtle, each idea in *Vindication* becomes an integral part of every other until a reader who might want to reject one of Wollstonecraft's theses can do so only by breaking apart the web and re-weaving a new one, leaving the web half-finished or rejecting the argument in its entirety.

Understanding how Wollstonecraft's pattern of arguments is constructed requires attention to three elements or components of this web pattern: (1) a central idea or theme, which Wollstonecraft identifies as happiness; (2) five strands or topics of argument that she develops throughout the book and that connect to her central idea—woman, man, virtue, nature, and love; and (3) a cross-strand theme of education that connects each of the five strands of argument together. What follows is a description of this web-like style of reasoning as it is developed in *Vindication,* also summarized in Figure 1.

THE CENTER AND FIVE STRANDS OF THE WEB

At the center of the web of reasons in *Vindication,* Wollstonecraft placed what she called a *first principle.* This principle rested on the conviction that God had ordained that all of mankind be happy. She included women in the definition of *mankind* and defined happiness as independence, respect, education, and freedom to grow (p. 91). Wollstonecraft stated this first principle in her opening sentences of the book, and the right of happiness was the theme to which she returned again and again throughout her work. Man's tyranny prevented women from achieving happiness because women failed to receive a proper education and were kept in a state of ignorance and dependence as a result of this tyranny (p. 121). Societal biases as well as inadequate education prevented women from attaining the respect Wollstonecraft saw as integral to this state of happiness (p. 233). The blind obedience to authority that was expected of women led to tyranny, unconditional submission, and the rejection of anything "new" that might bring women closer to this God-ordained happiness (pp. 264-265).

The right to happiness, which women had been denied, lay at the center of Wollstonecraft's arguments and at the center of the web. Each idea she developed in *Vindication* either connected directly or indirectly to this center, and a discussion involving any point in the web would send vibrations toward this center and call to mind this organizing principle. In this way, the reader repeatedly was reminded of this first principle and the focus toward increasing women's happiness. Surrounding this center idea and extending out from all sides were the five topics of woman, man, nature, virtue, and love. The topics were equal in emphasis, and all were connected in numerous ways to one another. As she proceeded through her work, Wollstonecraft articulated the current definition of each topic or strand and the negative impact it had on women, the social order in general, and the possibility of happiness. In arguing in this way, she illustrated the common view of each one of these topics, the ways in which this view had been constructed, and its ultimate impact on the center of the web—happiness.

Women.

In constructing the strand of woman, Wollstonecraft analyzed woman's role in society, her relationship to man, her range of choices for economic independence, and her educational opportunities. Wollstonecraft began by identifying the myriad ways that woman had been defined by the society at large, illustrating how far these definitions kept women from the center of the web and from happiness. *Woman* was defined as obedient; a "gentle, domestic brute" (p. 101); the slave of man (p. 122); subservient to love or lust (pp. 110, 204); a plaything, men's fancy; a lover of power; and a "toy of man, his rattle, and it must jingle in his ears whenever . . . he chooses to be amused" (pp. 107, 111, 118). Women were seen as submissive, docile and "spaniellike" in affection (pp. 117, 118, 179), and "naturally attentive" to dress and appearance (p. 129).

They were thought to be weak and frail (pp. 141, 153), by nature suited only for domestic duties, in a perpetual state of ignorance (pp. 131, 144-145, 154, 232), possessed of infantine airs (p. 154), and lacking in sensibility (pp. 173-175, 221).

Wollstonecraft argued that a woman, educated to be dependent on men, was to "endure injuries" silently, "smiling under the lash at which [she] dare not snarl" (pp. 117, 135, 180). She was to hide her good sense, should she be lucky enough to possess this quality, so that she did not appear superior to the men in her company (p. 198). Wollstonecraft suggested that because women never had received a useful education and because of the efforts of men to increase women's inferiority, "women are almost sunk below the standard of rational creatures" (p. 118). They were limited at every turn, "confined to the needle," and shut out "from all political and civil employments" (p. 288). The result of this confinement was boredom and a narrowness of mind that led to "cunning" behaviors and "sly tricks" designed to obtain some "foolish" pleasure that had caught women's attentions (p. 288).

Wollstonecraft argued that, in order to secure a husband, the primary goal in a woman's life (p. 116), women were taught to "feign a sickly delicacy" (p. 112) and to attend continually to their charms, dress, and appearance (pp. 170-172). The practice of "coming out," whereby a young girl was "taken from one public place to another, richly caparisoned," was little more than a marketplace for a "marriagable miss" (p. 289). This practice reinforced women's subservient role to men, emphasizing gaiety, attention to appearance, and little in the way of restraint or morality. The result, Wollstonecraft suggested, was disastrous. Women became accustomed to the gaiety and frivolity of a dazzling night life and, once married, soon lost interest in the drudgery of housekeeping. They began to act "audaciously" and in an "indolent" manner, to neglect their domestic duties, and to squander "away all the money which should have been saved for their helpless younger children" (pp. 241-242). Women soon lost their virtue as well as their reputations and, unlike men, could not gain their honor back again (p. 244).

The image of women presented by Wollstonecraft was harsh, unflattering, and even alarming. Her arguments suggested that women were ill prepared for carrying out domestic duties, finding contentment in marriage, or leading virtuous lives. Woman, Wollstonecraft summarized, had acquired little in the way of intellectual abilities and skills and, instead, had acquired all the "follies and vices of civilization, and missed the useful fruit" (p. 151). Throughout her analysis and vindication of women's rights, Wollstonecraft emphasized the harm done to women and to society by the prevailing definition or view of women. This construction of women,

Wollstonecraft continually reminded her readers, could not bring happiness to women or to men. Thus, the strand of argument representing woman consistently brought the reader back to the central theme, happiness, and to the myriad ways the prevailing definitions prevented women from achieving respect, independence, proper education, and freedom to grow.

Man.

In her attempt to vindicate the rights of women, Wollstonecraft offered a strand of argument that reflected her definition of *man*. The definition of *man* that Wollstonecraft offered was as negative as that of *woman* and was responsible for keeping men away from happiness as well. Wollstonecraft described men in general as arrogant, tyrants, rakes, sensualists, lovers of power, and dazzlers by riches (pp. 92, 106, 107, 113, 224). They were a mixture of "gallantry and despotism" (pp. 106-107) and took advantage of women, thinking only of conquest and sexual desire (p. 147). Men were disrespectful and, with an "impudent dross of gallantry thought so manly," men would "stare insultingly at every female" they met (p. 231). Wollstonecraft argued that this "loose behaviour" illustrated "such habitual depravity, such weakness of mind, that it [was] vain to expect much public or private virtue" from men. Until men could curb their "sensual fondness for sex" and their "impudence," neither women nor men could treat the other with respect (p. 231). Men might "boast of their triumphs over women," Wollstonecraft explained, but boasting of the ability to lure a woman into sin and then to abandon her to "face a sneering, frowning world" was an empty triumph (p. 233). Men then moved on to pursue "new conquests" and had done little more than engage in acts of betrayal (p. 233). The remedy, Wollstonecraft argued, was that "men ought to maintain the women whom they have seduced." This not only would "be one means of reforming female manners," but it would put a stop to "an abuse that has an equally fatal effect on population and morals" (p. 250).

Not only did the male character come under attack, but Wollstonecraft challenged the clergy, the military, and the aristocracy. Although she did not attack the clergy to the degree that she had in *A Vindication of the Rights of Men* (1790), which constituted her response to Burke's *Reflections on the Revolution in France* (1790), she did label the clergy as "indolent slugs," "relics of Popery," and "rapacious priests of superstitious memory" (1975, p. 276). The military also came under attack as it was full of "despots" and "idle superficial young men whose only occupation [was] gallantry"; soldiers, Wollstonecraft explained, were "dead-weights of vice and folly" (p. 97). The nobility received harsh scrutiny as well-they were a "pestilential vapour" that hovered over society (p. 96). Kings possessed "uncontrollable power," yet this very power was an "insuper-

able bar to the attainment of either wisdom or virtue," and no man could "acquire sufficient strength of mind" to carry out the duties of someone with such authority and control (p. 96). Kings were not educated to think or reason but were instructed in either "the invention of crimes, or the stupid routine of childish ceremonies." The result was that neither wisdom nor virtue governed the nation (p. 96).

In attacking three of the major institutions of her day— the church, the military, and the aristocracy— Wollstonecraft continued her challenge of male superiority and her development of the theme of man. She not only offered a discussion of her definition and view of man in general in *Vindication,* but she also questioned institutions that were male dominated and male governed, illustrating the ways that each prevented people in general from attaining the happiness she placed at the center of the web. Like the topic of woman, the topic of man also suggested to the reader the difficulties that lay in moving back to the central idea of happiness. As Wollstonecraft illustrated the ways in which the tyranny of male superiority prevented individuals from achieving respect, independence, education, and the freedom to grow, she reminded her readers of the connections among male superiority, oppression, and immorality. The strand of her argument relating to man, then, became directly linked to the central idea of happiness and to the strand of woman. These two were not the only strands of argument to be interconnected throughout *Vindication,* however. Wollstonecraft also argued for a third connection: virtue.

Virtue.

The topic of virtue also extended out from the center of the web in *Vindication,* and references to virtue can be seen in the preceding two categories. Wollstonecraft developed this strand of argument carefully, constructing yet another strand of reasoning that moved away from the center of her web. Virtue was a necessary part of civilization and could lead to happiness, Wollstonecraft argued, but it had become confused with vice (p. 91). Again, working from definition to redefinition, Wollstonecraft argued for the harms of the current definition of *virtue* and offered an alternative vision of this characteristic. Men's privileged positions, she suggested, enabled them to use their reason to justify women's inferiority and to perpetuate their prejudices, assigning to women the very qualities they themselves did not want (p. 91). Virtue in men thus had become power, ambition, and wealth; virtue in women consisted of happy submission, dependence, and the need for protection (p. 117). Even more absurd, Wollstonecraft suggested, was the belief that men were supposed to be more than happy to instruct or assist these ignorant creatures when necessary. If a "virtuous" woman could not even take care of herself, Wollstonecraft asked, then how was she to fulfill her duties as a wife and mother (p. 137)?

The result of man's unrestrained privilege was that virtue all but had disappeared, while the vices related to expedience and momentary gratification prevented individuals from achieving any real measure of happiness (p. 92). Were women more rationally educated, "human virtue" and "improvement in knowledge" would grow and expand, and virtue would resume its rightful place (pp. 121-122, 126). Unless virtue of any kind, Wollstonecraft summarized, "be built on knowledge, it will only produce a kind of insipid decency" (p. 242). Society, she suggested, must be organized and based on greater equality for virtue to gain its proper influence on human activities. If "one-half of mankind be chained" to the other, morality will never gain ground, and both men and women will continually "undermine" virtue "through ignorance or pride" (p. 252).

As Wollstonecraft developed the strand of virtue in *Vindication,* she linked it to her arguments for the right to happiness as well as to the damage done by defining women as subservient to men. She illustrated the ways in which virtue, as it had been constructed by male reasoning over time, prevented love from developing between men and women, kept women in positions of ignorance and dependence, and even tied men to roles of tyranny and power. Wollstonecraft's fourth topic, nature, follows this same pattern of interconnection and assists in the building of a complicated and tightly woven pattern of argument.

Nature.

"To account for, and excuse the tyranny of man, many ingenious arguments have been brought forward" that attempted to prove the natural superiority of the male over the female, Wollstonecraft asserted. The previously uncontested argument for women's natural abilities, dispositions, and characteristics was one of the arguments Wollstonecraft criticized (p. 100). Women's "natural" abilities very frequently were those traits that men did not want-traits that kept women in a state of dependence, servitude, and ignorance. The irony of the argument for women's natural tendencies, Wollstonecraft repeatedly suggested, was that while women were thought to possess certain characteristics or traits by virtue of their anatomy, their entire upbringing was spent making sure these were the qualities they developed. Women had been *defined* as women, and Wollstonecraft set out to challenge this definition.

Girls were thought to be naturally inclined to "sit still, play with dolls and listen to foolish conversation"; yet, their education and upbringing afforded them little else

in the way of activities (p. 177). They were said to be "from earliest infancy fond of dress," perpetually focused on "personal charms," and "hardly capable of understanding what is said to them" if it did not relate to their appearance; yet, they were discouraged from developing other traits (p. 176). As mothers, they were thought to be devoted to their children; as women, "they perceive themselves formed for obedience"; but without children and husbands, women would find themselves in the poor house for lack of employment and income (p. 179). Nature was supposed to have given women "fears and blushes," timidity, and a seductive "weakness" that guaranteed their dependence on men (p. 192), but were they to be freed from the "leading-strings" that made them this way, would women "be cajoled into virtue by artful flattery and sexual compliments" (p. 193)? Hardly, Wollstonecraft responded.

Nature was supposed to have provided women with the desire toward *"respectful observance"* of their husbands; the ability to study *"their humours,"* overlook *"their mistakes,"* submit *"to their opinions,"* and pass by "little instances of unevenness, caprice or passion"; give *"soft* answers to hasty words"; and complain "as seldom as possible." As the argument for women's natural traits accumulated, Wollstonecraft suggested, women's natural qualities sounded suspiciously like the "portrait of a house slave" and a "domestic drudge" (p. 195).

In identifying *nature* as a term that was used against women, rather than a term used to describe any inherent qualities held by women, Wollstonecraft challenged the belief in women's natural inferiority to men. What was seen as natural, she argued, was used to justify women's subservient role (p. 318). The prevailing definition of what was natural for women, Wollstonecraft's analysis suggested, kept women in positions of inferiority, denied them respect and self-determination, and assisted in perpetuating the prevailing definitions of *man, woman,* and *virtue.* This "natural" state prevented women from reaching the center of Wollstonecraft's web—happiness.

Love.

The final strand of argument Wollstonecraft developed in this portion of the web concerned the question of love. Here, Wollstonecraft addressed the prevailing opinion toward love, illustrated the ways in which love had been defined to oppress women, to meet the physical and emotional needs of men, and to transform vices into virtues. Wollstonecraft argued that love had been reduced to the state of perpetual passion rather than consistent affection. Love had become a woman's blind admiration for a man rather than women's and men's confidence in and respect for one another (p. 114). Love, which focused on pleasing the male only, had become more suited to the sensualist than to the long-term companion. In this state, love was but a fleeting shadow, unable to be maintained for any length of time and more akin to "chance and sensation" than to choice and reason (pp. 113, 115).

Love had been taken over by phrases of "pumped up passion" and by "artful flattery and sexual compliments" that led women astray as though they were nothing more than puppets (p. 193). Within marriage, Wollstonecraft added, love did not take the form of affection, admiration, and liking but, rather, resembled a relationship of dominance, deceit, and submission. In a marriage, love between a man and a woman had become the love of a master for his "trusty servant" rather than any real respect or friendship between individuals (p. 159). Love, in addition, was acquired through "affectation" rather than honesty, and it was guided by passion rather than genuine respect and admiration (pp. 112-113). The results were relationships and marriages between men and women founded on "momentary gratification" rather than on "compassionate tenderness" or long-lasting friendship (p. 115). Individuals, in this state of "love," spent their lives bounding "from one pleasure to another" and acquired neither "wisdom nor respectability of character" (p. 115).

As Wollstonecraft developed her arguments on the hazards and faults of the prevailing views toward love, she illustrated the various ways this definition of love connected with and affected women and men and prevented them from reaching the center of her argument. Love continued to channel women's energies toward subservience, while it perpetuated men's superiority. The result was that neither men nor women could behave in virtuous ways, nor could they attain happiness successfully. Both sexes were prevented from achieving respect by the other, both were dependent on the other for passion and momentary gratification, and both were prevented from growing together as whole and healthy individuals. What society viewed as the "natural" relationship between women and men, Wollstonecraft implied, was, at best, a sure path to unhappiness.

Cross Strands of Connection

Thus far, Wollstonecraft's rhetorical form suggests to the reader that the prevailing definitions of *woman, man, virtue, nature,* and *love* prevented individuals from achieving happiness. Her web, if the analysis were to stop at this point, would look like a wheel, with a central circle and five strands extending out from that center. The theme of education, however, indicates that her arguments are more fluid and complex and less rigid and mechanistic than the metaphor of a wheel suggests. Throughout her treatise on women's rights, Wollstonecraft repeatedly argued for the problematic nature of education as it then was conceived and for the

benefits of an improved educational system. In doing so, she created what might be envisioned as circles or rings that link each of the five strands to one another and make reaching the center of the web, realizing happiness, a very real possibility.

As she addressed the themes of woman, man, virtue, nature, and love, Wollstonecraft regularly called attention to the ways in which current societal definitions and assumptions regarding education directed each of these themes away from the center of the web—she created one connecting strand that focused on the effects of an inappropriate education. She also developed a second cross strand with her discussions of education that illustrated how redefining or redesigning the educational system could bring individuals and their behaviors closer to that center. The result is a sophisticated use of definition and redefinition, a fluid argument that depends on intricate connections among each of the five strands, and a move back to the center of her argument.

Improper Education.

The cross strand that takes the reader farthest away from the center of the web is Wollstonecraft's recurring argument for the problems of the current system of education. Her focus as the book begins is on the effects of an inadequate education on her theme of woman. Wollstonecraft argued that the contemporary system of education left women in a useless state and only functioned to keep women in positions of dependence and servitude. "The great advantages which naturally result from storing the mind with knowledge," she noted, are obvious (p. 219). Yet, women spent the first years of their lives "acquiring a smattering of accomplishments"—a little music, a little literature, and considerable instruction in methods of beauty—that directed them toward marriage rather than self-respect or independence (p. 83). The result was that women, prepared for marriage alone, could not support themselves or their children if an accident should befall their husbands (pp. 135-136, 289).

While she did address the issue of education for women as it related to women alone, Wollstonecraft consistently connected this theme to the effects of women's education on men and the relations between women and men. As noted above, men became tyrants and sensualists as a result of women's improper education. This happened, Wollstonecraft went on to explain, because, according to most writers of her generation, women's education should be "always relative" to the needs of men. So far did this notion go that, in the words of Rousseau, women were to be educated

> to please, to be useful to us [men], to make us love and
> esteem them, to educate us when young, and take care
> of us when grown up, to advise, to console us, to ren-

der our lives easy and agreeable—these are the duties of women at all times, and what they should be taught in their infancy.

(p. 175)

The discussion of improper education called attention to the link between the two themes of woman and man and to the ways in which it facilitated unhealthy individuals, unhealthy relationships, and unhappiness.

Wollstonecraft drew connections among an improper education, nature, and virtue. Education, as conceived in Wollstonecraft's era, was built on what she considered the ill-conceived principle that women lacked the ability to reason (p. 142). Wollstonecraft challenged those of her generation who insisted that knowledge was inconsistent with women's character (p. 144). Nature had not determined women to be incompetent, she argued, but an improper education had facilitated this tendency. The "narrowness of mind" so common to women, Wollstonecraft reasoned, was the result of "almost insuperable obstacles" placed in women's way "to prevent the cultivation of the female understanding"; nature had not done this—"the very constitution of civil governments" had (p. 144).

Faculty education, moreover, distorted conceptions of virtue. Education left women so "weakened by false refinement" that their "condition [was] much below what it would be were they left in a state nearer to nature" (p. 153). Education rendered women "innocent," "alluring and indulgent." Of what use, Wollstonecraft asked her readers, were these "virtues" beyond some foolish fancy designed by well-intentioned but misguided males (p. 187)?

Finally, an improper education did much to distort the relations between women and men. Love, as a result of women's lack of formal education, became the quest for marrying "advantageously," resulting in nothing more than legal prostitution (p. 151). For a "*short* time," Wollstonecraft reminded her audience, women became an "object of desire" (p. 189). All too soon, however, men lost interest because women, "kept from the tree of knowledge," had nothing in the way of intellect to offer them (p. 189). An attraction that could have developed into "natural fondness" soon burned out, and women often were discarded as their husbands went in pursuit of other pleasures (p. 189).

Woven throughout *Vindication* were Wollstonecraft's strong sentiments on the harms done to women by an improper education. So prevalent are these arguments that the reader can begin at any section in the book and soon will come to her critique of this faulty system. But Wollstonecraft also argued for a system of education that had the potential to bring individuals closer to the state of happiness she advocated. Although she hinted

at its content in the earlier pages of her document, she addressed it most fully in the latter half of her work. In this second cross strand, the strand that brings readers closer to the center of the web, Wollstonecraft continued to draw connections among her themes as she discussed the components and illustrated the benefits of an adequate education for women.

Proper Education.

Again, from the opening pages of her work, the reader senses the centrality of a proper education for reaching the state of happiness Wollstonecraft advocated. She dedicated her work to M. Talleyrand-Perigord, an advocate of a national system of education in France, explaining that a national system of education that included women as well as men "would advance, instead of [retard], the progress of those glorious principles that give a substance to morality" and virtue (p. 85). This national system would combine qualities of both private and boarding-school educations, and the effects of such an alternative form of education, Wollstonecraft argued, would be astounding: "It is plain from the history of all nations, that women cannot be confined to merely domestic pursuits, for they will not fulfill family duties, unless their minds take a wider range" (p. 294).

A proper education, Wollstonecraft reasoned, would redefine conceptions of woman, man, virtue, nature, and love. In this cross strand, however, Wollstonecraft began with the themes of man and virtue and then quickly incorporated the effects of a proper education for woman and love. A public education, she explained, would be "directed to form citizens; but if you wish to make good citizens, you must first exercise the affections of a son and brother" (p. 279). Wollstonecraft saw this attention to males as the only way to improve society; "public affections, as well as public virtue, must ever grow out of the private character" (p. 279). Children of both sexes must have room to move about and to "walk in a superb garden" in order that their minds and bodies might grow (pp. 281-292). They must learn "chastity" and "modesty"; personal habits, she reasoned, had "more effect on the moral character" than generally supposed, and a proper education could ensure that these habits were acquired (p. 282).

Education could improve the relations between women and men because, were they allowed to study together, "those graceful decencies might early be inculcated which produce modesty" (p. 283). Young people would learn lessons of "politeness" (p. 283), "friendship," "respect and confidence," (p. 284) and their minds would be "stored . . . with knowledge" (p. 285). Women's identity also would be strengthened by this system. Allowed to interact with others—to "mix with a number of equals"—young girls would be able to "form a just opinion" of themselves (p. 293). They would be taught to occupy their minds with a wide range of subjects beyond appearance and marriage and to "found their virtue on knowledge" (p. 294). Men's identity also would be enhanced because, as women develop their intellect and attain greater virtues, men also would become more virtuous, for the "improvement and emancipation" of both women and men "must be mutual" (p. 296).

More implicitly than explicitly, Wollstonecraft linked nature and education together. Nature, as it had been defined for both women and men, was the antithesis of a proper education in Wollstonecraft's web of argument because it defined women as everything that education would prevent. Wollstonecraft's arguments suggested that human nature actually was to be educated, to reason, and to participate fully in society. Human nature was to live in a state where equality existed between women and men, to honor and respect others, to pursue independence, and to live in a state of happiness. A proper education could alter this unnatural state quickly.

Education, whether positive or negative, affected the definition of *woman,* the relationships between men and women, and the images and ideals of virtue. The predominant notions of the qualities nature had given women, in addition, served as the foundation for their education. Healthy love and honest virtue could not exist without alterations in the prevailing views of education for women as well as men. Each topic of argument was linked to the organizing principle of happiness, and the topic of education moved the reader closer or further away from that center, depending on its framing. The result was that, throughout her analysis and discussion of woman, man, virtue, and nature, the reader must return time and again to the question of the right to happiness and the societal barriers that prevented individuals from attaining this right.

SUMMARY OF A WEB MODEL OF REASONING: RECONCEPTUALIZING RHETORICAL FORM

As Wollstonecraft argued for the vindication of the rights of women, she not only challenged women's position in society but she placed this challenge within a non-linear framework of argument. At the center of her claims lay her belief in a God-ordained right to respect, education, independence, and freedom to grow, which she labeled *happiness*. Individuals of both sexes had a right to this happiness, but numerous barriers lay in the way of reaching this state. In articulating these barriers, Wollstonecraft constructed five strands of arguments that extended out from her central idea of the right to happiness. Each strand represented a different topic-woman, man, love, virtue, and nature-and as she developed each one, she offered an analysis of the prevailing view of that topic and the implications of those views on men, women, and society at large. Her circular and interconnecting theme of education created cross

strands of arguments that assisted her in highlighting the interrelationships among her ideas. In doing so, she illustrated the cause-and-effect relationships within each of the strands and the need for increasing connections to be made within the prevailing system of reasoning.

A web model of reasoning necessitates a belief in and recognition of connectedness. Wollstonecraft's web reminds the reader of the connections among the prevailing system of reason and power, social structures and happiness, men and women, and even among seemingly disconnected ideas. Wollstonecraft's critics interpreted her work as rambling and disorganized, but this analysis of form suggests that her work was highly organized around patterns of connections that earlier critics overlooked. Organized as an intricate pattern of interconnections, *Vindication* presents not only a sophisticated rhetoric but an alternative framework for argument.

Several areas of interest worth pursuing are suggested for rhetorical scholars by a model of reasoning as a web. The web model itself, of course, needs further exploration and analysis. In order to refine and extend the model, it must be studied in other contexts and through other cases. A preliminary examination of the discourse of other rhetors—Douglass (1950), Nightingale (1992), Noggle (1983), and Le Guin (1989)—suggests that the web model is not unique to Wollstonecraft and that the traditional linear model of reasoning frequently can be inadequate or inappropriate in explaining the argumentative patterns employed by some rhetors.

This analysis also suggests the possibility of the existence of yet other ways of arguing.[6] Linear theories of arguing suggest that arguments require a distinct major premise, minor premise, and conclusion, or even, as Toulmin (1988) suggests concerning the field-invariant nature of arguments, that arguments proceed from a claim to grounds to warrant (incorporating the backing, modal qualifier, and rebuttal as well). Wollstonecraft's arguments, however, challenge this assumption.[7] The arguments in *Vindication* indeed may incorporate each of these components, but they do not always follow this linear pattern and frequently upset the order to which scholars have become accustomed. The web model used by Wollstonecraft reveals that arguments may have a center thesis with supporting arguments spinning out from this center that simultaneously act as rebuttals, qualifiers, backing, warrants, and claims. Each of these strands, in addition, contains elements of Toulmin's schema, but their use indicates a highly complex and intensely interconnected process of argument development.

A web model of reasoning also calls attention to the role of the audience in the process of arguing. Wollstonecraft's arguments, while not difficult to follow, are a great deal more complicated than some other forms of presentation, and the role of listeners or audiences in a web-like style is quite different from their roles when responding to a more linear form of arguing. A web form, which is more involved and interconnected, might require more work from the audience in order to process the arguments. Yet, the repetition of topics and ideas throughout the web and the continual reminders of connections to previous topics seem to ease some of the tension that might exist between intricacy and detail of reasoning and the processing of the arguments. Belenky, Clinchy, Goldberger, and Tarule (1986) have argued for a form of knowing or listening that might help explain the epistemology or the stance of the audience in this process. These researchers identify a form of knowing, which they call "connected knowing," that constitutes an epistemology that may be more consistent with Wollstonecraft's web pattern of argument. Connected knowing involves a process in which listeners store a variety of perspectives and ways of knowing in their minds—listeners hold all ideas as possibilities, assessing the implications of each. They then come to a decision that is highly contextual and interconnected, recognizing the power of each idea or possibility to influence others. Connected knowing encourages a view of the argument as a whole as opposed to a view of the isolated segments or parts of an argument, and Wollstonecraft's web suggests such a focus on the whole rather than the parts.

As a rhetor, Wollstonecraft seems to have made use of both connected and the more traditional form of separated knowing. In using the more familiar separate form of knowing, Wollstonecraft did challenge, doubt, refute, and argue against the views of the dominant framework. But she also asked her readers to keep in mind the whole of that dominant argument, suggesting a more connected stance or epistemology. Wollstonecraft located her argument against women's oppression within a larger interconnected framework of social codes and norms—something that had not been done as comprehensively before. She also wove a web of connections in support of women's emancipation for her audience. In this way, she relied more heavily on the connected stance and encouraged her listeners to follow in kind. Her work suggests that rhetors as well as audiences may use both of these stances productively.

Understanding an interconnected or web-patterned argument like Wollstonecraft's may be easier from a connected stance. From a connected stance, the listener can suspend judgment, store a series of arguments and connections, and then offer a response to or extension of the speaker's ideas or claims. From a position of separate knowing, listeners may experience a great deal more difficulty. With a focus on doubting the knowledge of another, a separate knower's task is disconnection as well as the isolation of ideas. Attempting to refute and challenge the myriad strands that a web pattern

presents as they are being developed might be frustrating, time consuming, and even a bit overwhelming, not to mention disruptive of the listening process.

An epistemology of connection implies a reconceptualization of patterns of argument and suggests yet another area of interest to rhetorical scholars. From a connected stance, listeners not only store and process arguments more comprehensively, but they also may be able to assist in the construction of the web. A web pattern of argument challenges traditional assumptions regarding the oppositional nature of argument and suggests the possibility of cooperative argument.[8] Traditional conceptualizations of argument focus on the process of convincing or persuading an individual or group to believe in a particular way, the attack of another's ideas, an adversarial or even "rapist/seducer/lover" stance, and the notion of participating in an argument as involving some kind of self-risk.[9]

A web model, however, suggests that participants might assume a more connected, cooperative, or collaborative stance. Participants in an argument might not challenge the claims of the other, hoping to prove the opponent wrong, but might instead engage in a process of contributing or adding their own connections and ideas in order to build an argument together. Participants in cooperative argument might adopt Gearhart's (1979) or S. K. Foss and Griffin's (1995) stance of a co-creator, working with another in order to construct a web. A cooperative argument, based on the web model, might involve a collaborative discovery of a perspective or plan of action, for example, and would emphasize the construction of the web and the various connections and themes that could be developed.

Finally, Wollstonecraft's method of reasoning in *Vindication* calls into question the issue of rhetorical form or style itself.[10] Her work suggests that definitions and attitudes toward form be re-evaluated and that the perimeters around rhetorical form be expanded. Specifically, what do scholars mean when they speak of form or style, and how do scholars determine the appropriateness or even effectiveness of a rhetor's form? Wollstonecraft's form or style has received much criticism since she failed to achieve the standards of appropriateness identified by rhetorical scholarship thus far; her arguments have been ignored or denigrated as a result. *Vindication* raises questions regarding the nature, function, and criteria used to determine appropriateness of form and suggests that discussions regarding the elements of rhetorical form be reintroduced into the ongoing debate over the nature of rhetoric itself.

As important and clear as her arguments were at the time she made them, the style and organization of Wollstonecraft's essay assume an equally important role. Wollstonecraft's entire argument was based on questioning the "natural" order and improving the position of women. She spoke to the larger truths of morality, virtue, and reason as a way of freeing women from the tyranny of men. Like feminists after her, Wollstonecraft illustrated the effect a change in women's status would have on society at large: children would receive a better education, relationships between men and women would be healthier, and marriage would be grounded in the firm bonds of friendship rather than the subservient ties of lust. While her work was considered powerful and angry at the time she wrote it, the arguments in *Vindication* remain bold, confrontative, and challenging even today. In questioning the predominant order, Wollstonecraft not only challenged the content of that order, but she altered conceptualizations of appropriate form with her web-like reasoning process. Recognized as the "first feminist declaration of independence," *A Vindication of the Rights of Woman* also might be seen as a first model for a feminist web of reasons.

Notes

1. Several women made arguments for women's rights, particularly in the arena of improved education for women, before Wollstonecraft. These arguments are as significant as Wollstonecraft's but are not as comprehensive. See, for example: Mary Astell, *A Serious Proposal to the Ladies* (1694) and *Some Reflections upon Marriage* (1700), both in Rogers (1979); Lady Mary Wortley Montagu, *Women Not Inferior to Man* (1739), *Woman's Superior Excellence over Man* (1740), and *Letters* (1718), all in Ferguson (1985); and Catherine Macaulay, *Letters on Education* (1790) in Luria (1974).

2. See, for example, Hays (1800), and Stanton and Anthony (in Spender, 1982).

3. I am offering only a small sample of the criticisms against Wollstonecraft and her arguments here. For a more comprehensive discussion of these criticisms, see Griffin (1992).

4. The phenomenon is not uncommon; Elizabeth Cady Stanton, Florence Nightingale, and Simone de Beauvoir, to name but a few, all have undergone the same treatment. See Spender (1982) for an assessment of this practice.

5. Wollstonecraft advocated a relational form of feminism (Offen, 1988) in which the family is taken as a primary organizing social structure and the necessary and appropriate starting point for a healthy social order. Women and men have clear and distinct roles in relational feminism, yet they are viewed as equals. For a critique of some of the pitfalls of Wollstonecraft's relational stance, see Gaten's (1991) discussion of the tensions between the public and the private and Wollstonecraft's construction of the "citizen/ husband/father and the citizen/wife/mother" (p. 121).

6. Gilligan (1982), for example, suggested a process for making ethical and moral decisions that relied on seeing the relationship among all parts of an issue and the various implications of each part as they related to one another. This relational process is much more complicated than reasoning in isolation—separating an issue into its parts and judging that issue or the basis of one of its parts alone. Dialectical reasoning, which entails the process of dividing a thing into its parts, offers a very different perspective from reasoning as a web. In the latter, connections, rather than divisions, are the focus, and truth grows out of the relationship among all connections rather than the synthesis of the many into one.

7. Classical conceptualizations of arrangement argue for this same general pattern. This pattern is reflected in Aristotle's call for an exordium, statement of case, proof, and epilogue in an argument. The author of *Ad Herennium* differs only slightly from this schema, suggesting that a rhetor must offer an introduction, statement of facts, division, proof, refutation, and conclusion.

8. The idea of cooperative argument is explicated by Makau (1990, 1991).

9. These conceptualizations are derived from the following research on the nature or position of the individual in an argument: Brockriede (1972), Hamblin (1970), and Natanson (1959).

10. S. K. Foss and K. A. Foss (1994) also suggest that scholars reconsider the nature of form in presenting ideas. In *Inviting Transformation*, they suggest that "the relationships among ideas" can take a number of nonlinear forms (p. 30).

References

Anti-Jacobin review and magazine or, monthly political and literary censor, I, (1798). Review of William Godwin's book *Memoirs of the author of the rights of woman*. 91-102.

"The vision of liberty." (1801). *Anti-Jacobin review and magazine or, monthly political and literary censor*, 9, 515-520.

Beard, M. (1946). *Woman as a force in history: A study in traditions and realities*. New York: Macmillan.

Belenky, M. F., Clinchy, B. M., Goldberger, N. R., & Tarule, J. M. (1986). *Women's ways of knowing: The development of self, voice, and mind*. New York: Basic.

Black, E. (1978). "The sentimental style as escapism, or the devil with Dan'l Webster." In K. K. Campbell & K. H. Jamieson (Eds.), *Form and genre: Shaping rhetorical action* (pp. 75-86). Falls Church, VA: Speech Communication Association.

Black, E. (1992). *Rhetorical questions: Studies of public discourse.* Chicago: University of Chicago Press.

Blankenship, J., & Robson, D. C. (1995). "A 'feminine style' in women's political discourse: An exploratory essay." *Communication Quarterly, 43,* 353-366.

Brockreide, W. (1972). "Arguers as lovers: A critical perspective." *Philosophy and Rhetoric, 5,* 1-11.

Brownmiller, S. (1975). *Against our will: Men, women and rape.* New York: Simon and Schuster.

Campbell, K. K. (1980). "Stanton's 'The solitude of self': A rationale for feminism." *Quarterly Journal of Speech, 66,* 304-312.

Douglass, F. (1950). *The life and writings of Frederick Douglass* (Vols. 1-4). (P. S. Forer, Ed.). New York: International.

Dow, B. J., & Tonn, B. M. (1993). "'Feminine style' and political judgment in the rhetoric of Ann Richards." *Quarterly Journal of Speech, 79,* 286-302.

Ecclectic Magazine of Foreign Literature, Science, and Art, 42. n. s. (1885). "Mary Wollstonecraft Godwin." 100-107.

Ferguson, M. (Ed.). (1985). *First feminists: British women writers 1578-1799.* Bloomington: Indiana University Press.

Foss, S. K., & Foss, K. A. (1994). *Inviting transformation: Presentational speaking for a changing world.* Prospect Heights, IL: Waveland.

Foss, S. K., & Griffin, C. L. (1995). "Beyond persuasion: A proposal for an invitational rhetoric." *Communication Monographs, 62,* 2-18.

Gaten, M. (1991). "'The oppressed state of my sex': Wollstonecraft on reason, feeling and equality." In M. L. Shanley & C. Pateman (Eds.), *Feminist interpretations and political theory* (pp. 112-128). University Park: Pennsylvania State University Press.

Gearhart, S. M. (1979). "The womanization of rhetoric." *Women's Studies International Quarterly, 2,* 195-201.

Gilligan, C. (1982). *In a different voice: Women's conceptions of self and of morality.* Cambridge, MA: Harvard University Press.

Griffin, C. L. (1992). *A feminist reconceptualization of form: A case study of Mary Wollstonecraft's three polemical works.* Unpublished doctoral dissertation, Indiana University, Bloomington.

Griffin, C. L. (1994). "Rhetoricizing alienation: Mary Wollstonecraft and the rhetorical construction of women's oppression." *Quarterly Journal of Speech, 80,* 293-312.

Hamblin, C. L. (1970). *Fallacies.* London: Methuen.

Hays, M. (1800). "Memoirs of Mary Wollstonecraft." *Annual Necrology for 1797-98,* 411-60.

Huxman, S. S. (1996). "Mary Wollstonecraft, Margaret Fuller, and Angelina Grimke: Symbolic convergence and nascent rhetorical vision." *Communication Quarterly, 44,* 16-28.

Jaffee, C. (1995). *Public speaking: A cultural perspective.* New York: Wadsworth.

Kamm, J. (1966). *Rapiers and battleaxes: The women's movement and its aftermath.* London: George Allen and Unwin.

Kearney, P., & Plax, T. G. (1996). *Public speaking in a diverse society.* Mountain View, CA: Mayfield.

Le Guin, U. K. (1989). *Dancing at the edge of the world: Thoughts on words, women, places.* New York: Grove.

Lundberg, F., & Farnham, M. F. (1947). *Modern woman: The lost sex.* New York: Harper.

Luria, G. (Ed.). (1974). *The feminist controversy in England 1788-1810.* New York: Garland.

Makau, J. M. (1990). *Reasoning and communication: Thinking critically about arguments.* Belmont, CA: Wadsworth.

Makau, J. (1991, November). *Resources and strategies for incorporating alternative perspectives in the communication classroom: Revised syllabus for argumentation.* Paper presented at the convention of the Speech Communication Association, Atlanta, GA.

McGuire, M. (1977). "Mythic rhetoric in *Mein Kampf*: A structuralist critique." *Quarterly Journal of Speech, 63,* 1-13.

Natanson, M. (1959). "The claims of immediacy." In M. Natanson & H. Johnstone (Eds.), *Philosophy, rhetoric and argumentation* (pp. 10-19). University Park: Pennsylvania State University Press.

Nelson, P. (1972). "The fugal form of Charles James Fox's 'Rejection of Bonaparte's overtures'." *Western Speech Communication Journal, 36,* 9-14.

Nightingale, F. (1992). *Cassandra and other selections from suggestions for thought to searchers after religious truth.* (M. Poovey, Ed.). New York: New York University Press.

Nixon, E. (1971). *Mary Wollstonecraft: Her life and times.* London: J. M. Dent.

Noggle, A. (1983). *Silver lining: Photographs by Anne Noggle.* Albuquerque: University of New Mexico Press.

Offen, K. (1988). "Defining feminism: A comparative historical approach." *Signs,* 14, 119-157.

Perelman, C. (1970). "The new rhetoric: A theory of practical reasoning." In R. M. Hutchins & M. J. Adler (Eds.), *The great ideas today* (pp. 272-312). New York: Encyclopedia Britannica.

Polwhele, R. (1800). *"The unsex'd females": A poem addressed to the author of the pursuits of literature.* New York: W. M. Cobbett.

Rogers, K. M. (Ed.). (1979). *Before their time: Six women writers of the eighteenth century.* New York: Frederick Ungar.

Sapiro, V. (1992). *A vindication of political virtue: The political theory of Mary Wollstonecraft.* Chicago: University of Chicago Press.

Spender, D. (1982). *Women of ideas, and what men have done to them.* London: Pandora.

Stuart, C. L. (1978). "Mary Wollstonecraft's *A vindication of the rights of men*: A rhetoric reassessment." *Western Journal of Speech Communication,* 41, 83-92.

Taylor, G. R. S. (1969). *Mary Wollstonecraft: A study in economics and romance.* New York: Haskell. (Original work published 1911.)

Todd, J. M. (1976). "The biographies of Mary Wollstonecraft." *Signs,* 1, 721-734.

Todd, J. M. (Ed.). (1990). *A Wollstonecraft anthology.* New York: Columbia University Press.

Tomalin, C. (1974). *The life and death of Mary Wollstonecraft.* New York: Harcourt Brace Jovanovich.

Toulmin, S. E. (1988). *The uses of argument.* New York: Cambridge University Press.

Urbanski, M. M. O. (1980). *Margaret Fuller's* Woman in the nineteenth century: *A literary study of form and content of sources and influence.* Westport, CT: Greenwood.

Walpole, H. (1859). *Letters of Horace Walpole, Earl of Oxford.* (Vol. 9), P. Cunningham (Ed.). London: Richard Bently.

Wollstonecraft, M. (1960). *A vindication of the rights of men, in a letter to the Right Honourable Edmund Burke.* Gainesville, FL: Scholars' Facsimiles and Reprints. (Original work published 1790.)

Wollstonecraft, M. (1975). *A vindication of the rights of woman.* M. B. Kramnick (Ed.). Baltimore, MD: Penguin. (Original work published 1792.)

Ewa Badowska (essay date fall 1998)

SOURCE: Badowska, Ewa. "The Anorexic Body of Liberal Feminism: Mary Wollstonecraft's *A Vindication of the Rights of Woman.*" *Tulsa Studies in Women's Literature* 17, no. 2 (fall 1998): 283-303.

[*In the following essay, Badowska analyzes the image of the "appetitive body" in* A Vindication of the Rights of Woman *and explores how Wollstonecraft links the image with notions of femininity in her work.*]

> Every day [Wollstonecraft] made theories by which life should be lived. . . . Every day too—for she was no pedant, no cold-blooded theorist—something was born in her that thrust aside her theories and forced her to model them afresh. . . . She whose sense of her own existence was so intense . . . died at the age of thirty six. But she has her revenge. . . . [A]s we . . . listen to her arguments and consider her experiments . . . and realise the high-handed and hot-blooded manner in which she cut her way to the quick of life, one form of immortality is hers undoubtedly: she is alive and active, she argues and experiments, we hear her voice and trace her influence even now among the living.
>
> Virginia Woolf, *The Second Common Reader*[1]

While we have always been willing to remember Mary Wollstonecraft as one who "made theories by which life should be lived," while we have described her as a defender of "rights," a producer of "arguments," a subject of self-inflicted "experiments" in unconventional living, we have often failed to remember her as one who shaped her theories and arguments in language, whose political discourse is embodied in metaphors and texts. But *A Vindication of the Rights of Woman* (1792)—a political manifesto written against the discourse of sensibility as a model for gender relations—is thoroughly suffused with the kind of language that is ordinarily regarded as marginal, or even inimical, to political discourse. Specifically, the manifesto is pervaded with the image of an appetitive body: its hungers, its tastes, as well as its (uncertain) boundaries. It is not the argumentative dimension of *A Vindication of the Rights of Woman* that produces the figural specter of bodies and appetites; rather, the drift of Wollstonecraft's metaphors and narrative digressions, their seemingly compulsive character, gives rise to this appetitive undercurrent: in Wollstonecraft's writing, women "eat the bitter bread of dependence" and become "standing dishes to which every glutton may have access."[2]

I will argue that a focus on these not strictly polemical aspects of Wollstonecraft's manifesto allows us to discern a riveting dimension of her text—one that reveals half-realized aspects of her argument and betrays an almost sibylline foreknowledge of the complicated nexus of issues linking femininity both with the body and with a renunciation of its appetites.[3] Wollstonecraft's theory of the Rational Woman—woman as subject of her own understanding—undergoes numerous crises in the course of *A Vindication of the Rights of Woman,* crises spawned by moments in the text that are not, strictly speaking, argumentative. For instance, the often discussed boarding-school crisis—since having "a number of [women] pig together in the same bedchamber" (p. 288) throws the narrator into a rhetorical passion—stems as much from the polemical argument against women's sentimental education as from the rhetoric of the dissolution of "proper" body boundaries ("that gross degree of familiarity" that should be counteracted by a "decent personal reserve," pp. 239-40). Wollstonecraft's argument discloses a narrative and rhetorical underside that bewilders her rational attempts at a rational theory of femininity.

With some reservations, I join a number of recent readers in arguing that "the female body which [Wollstonecraft] attempted to submerge surfaced in her text in spite of herself to disrupt and qualify her argument,"[4] but I show that the unconscious, uncontrollable surfacing of the body in Wollstonecraft's text is not a simple eruption of the material or the sexual that cannot be repressed. The bodies that so hauntingly populate the text are embroiled in another problematic: they are bodies produced in and by complex permutations of *metaphors* of femininity and sexuality, and they cannot be regarded as a purely material opposite of Wollstonecraft's preference for matters rational and asexual. In other words, this is not simply the question of a much debated opposition between disembodied reason and embodied female self. Instead, embodiment and disembodiment themselves are revealed in *A Vindication of the Rights of Woman* as intricate tropes. I want to argue that Wollstonecraft's theory of female identity, despite its manifest intention to speak on behalf of women as concrete political subjects, is embroiled in narratives that compel the understanding of the body as figural. In my reading of *A Vindication of the Rights of Woman,* I will consider the body as figure and examine the ways in which the body as figure complicates and disrupts Wollstonecraft's liberal feminism.

Even though in the minds of many readers Wollstonecraft's manifesto symbolically inaugurates political feminism, it is not, by virtue of this inaugural status, innocent of the kinds of conceptual rifts that we are used to diagnosing in contemporary articulations of political identity.[5] Wollstonecraft's writing, while it undoubtedly belongs to the moment of inception of feminist discourse in the West, already reflects the workings of a logic—the logic I refer to as anorexic—that parodies the liberal feminist figure of a self-possessed, autonomous female individual, as well as the structures of bourgeois femininity at their inception. The liberal *theory* of the rational female subject is from the very beginning in tension with the *stories* the manifesto implicitly tells about the dissolution of body boundaries. Wollstonecraft's figure of the woman keeps on disappearing: she resists stable definition, a definition without overflow, without boundary crossings—the kind of

feminine identity that a political manifesto written in the name of women would seem to command. But Wollstonecraft's woman disappears in other ways as well. She is a "standing dish" always in danger of being swallowed; while her physicality may at times immodestly obtrude on our senses (or so Wollstonecraft's narrator believes), its very lack of containment threatens to make the female subject elusively borderless.

The connection between the liberal ideal of the subject's self-possessed autonomy and the discourses of anorexia is made by Gillian Brown, in her excellent "Anorexia, Humanism, and Feminism," where she argues that "the anorexic dynamic" is "paradigmatic of the liberal self":

> liberal humanist expansionism is exactly what anorexia nervosa resists when it repudiates the basic site of femininity, the female body. . . . While Anglo-American feminism since Wollstonecraft would extend the rights and real estate of men to women, the anorectic would repudiate liberal property relations in favor of a radicalized form of self-proprietorship: dispossession. The disappearance of her body is thus an anti-humanistic liberation movement, a severance of female subjectivity from all social formations of self and body, including feminism.[6]

For Brown, Wollstonecraft's treatise exemplifies the liberal feminist tradition, the tradition that the twentieth-century anorexic woman sets herself against and parodies by embodying it *too* perfectly. But in my reading, the sense in which *A Vindication of the Rights of Woman* can be said to be *exemplary* is itself complicated, since anorexic figures that undermine the liberal ideal pervade the very text of liberal feminism from the start. What the anorexic woman will parody in the twentieth century is already present in the rhetoric of the liberal self as written by Wollstonecraft.

In addition to complicating the discourse of liberal feminism, the figure of the body also necessitates a rethinking of the category of "figure" as such. The metaphorical production of the body in Wollstonecraft's text instantiates a fascinating paradox: these textual bodies are products of a language that would erase its figurative status and pretend to pure literalness; but the bodies are as intensely signifying, as intensely encoded as what they purportedly negate—reason. The vicissitudes of Wollstonecraft's metaphors show a tantalizing tendency toward relentless concreteness, toward an "anorexic" translation of the metaphorical matters of taste and reason into matters of "digesting" and "swallowing," in a manner that questions the figurative status of "taste." In *A Vindication of the Rights of Woman,* the figurative language of "taste" is disarticulated: eating becomes the figure of no figure. The metaphor of "taste" cannot be carried off, and this deficiency reveals the alimentary troping that grounds—and performs—

the fiction of "taste.'"[7] The body in *A Vindication of the Rights of Woman* is not only figural, but also resists the possibility of a categorical distinction between the literal and the figural. I will begin my analysis by following the workings of the anorexic logic of intellect in Wollstonecraft's text, showing how she both denounces and longs for a femininity bound up with the retrenchment of appetite.

THE ANOREXIC LOGIC OF REASON

Considering the length of time that women have been dependent, is it surprising that some of them hunger in chains, and fawn like the spaniel?[8]

Mary Wollstonecraft, *A Vindication of the Rights of Woman* (p. 181)

A Vindication of the Rights of Woman is pervaded with images of a phantasmal appetitive body: the languages of taste and ingestion. This saturation may on some level be motivated by a familiar cliché, the metaphorical equivalence between sexuality and appetite.[9] Appetite in Wollstonecraft's text supervenes sexuality, almost threatening to supplant it: "Love, considered as an animal appetite, cannot long feed on itself without expiring" (p. 169). The ghostliness of appetite, its proclivity to appear uninvited—it sneaks into the text in sexuality's shadow—are the very reasons why impermeable barriers must be erected against it. Wollstonecraft's heavy investment in rationality for women drives her text's *anorexic logic*: reason seems to require a repudiation of sexuality, and thus also of appetite, sexuality's most prominent metaphorical double. Appetite's very correlation with the sexual exposes it to a threat of expulsion: like the sexual, appetite is in continual peril of being scapegoated, or even definitively abdicated.

Academic feminist readers of *A Vindication of the Rights of Woman* have been apt to emphasize, indeed censure, the opposition between feminine passion and masculine reason that they invariably detect in Wollstonecraft's oeuvre.[10] When feminist critics replay such oppositions—mind and body, reason and imagination, liberty and confinement—they participate, as did Wollstonecraft, in the tradition of Western dualism, in which the valorization of reason often leads to a strategic, systemic withdrawal from the cumbersome corporeal, a systemic distancing from the appetitive body that would trap the soaring intellect.[11] Many feminist philosophers and critics writing on representations of the female body—most importantly Susan Bordo and Leslie Heywood—have suggested that the Western emphasis on the primacy of rationality is structurally governed by the abjection of the body, of corporeality conceived as inherently feminine. Heywood, in her work on the anorexic logic of modernist textuality, describes

that process of cutting away, the mode of thought, the privilege given to rationality, the process of elimination that I have named "anorexic" for its similarity to the

logic of the disease. Anorexics enact with their bodies the process that Western logic inscribes: they physically demonstrate its subtext, the horror of the female flesh that is often the unconscious of discourse.[12]

Such readings tend to presume that the female body survived in hiding, bruised but victorious, the two-thousand-plus years of Western philosophy. Despite the theoretical ingenuity of her work on modernism, Heywood succumbs to the utopian desire to "restore the starved female text/*corps* and return to her the emotion and validity of a personal, embodied life," in which the perplexities of the body as well as of figuration could be resolved, and hopes for "a reconfiguration of the hierarchical relationship between the ideal, figurative body and the biological, literal body."[13] Though appealing, her reading shrinks from the body as figure. Even the "reconfiguration" Heywood postulates fails to address the troping inherent in the distinction between the literal and the figurative, between "body" and "discourse." It is only when sexuality and corporeality are read as outside language, as lodged in a biological, real body, that *A Vindication of the Rights of Woman* can be construed to pitch the intransigent body as a deplorable encumbrance against the faculty of reason. But there is more to Wollstonecraft's treatise than the usual difficulty of giving expression to a feminine corporeality within the rigid bounds of eighteenth-century literary discourse; what is at stake in these critical debates is not just the status of a literary convention. The body in Wollstonecraft's feminist manifesto is produced as literal and metaphorized as an encumbrance, but it is nonetheless figural.

A woman's "sexual character" (the primary guarantee of gender differences for Wollstonecraft's contemporaries) inheres, according to Wollstonecraft, in a consummate submission to corporeality, a corporeality that subsumes the totality of a woman's being. This assumption of unmitigated physicalness is for upper-class women in Wollstonecraft's numerous narrative vignettes a source of "glory": "genteel women are, literally speaking, slaves to their bodies, and glory in their subjection" (p. 131). Wollstonecraft describes an oxymoronic glorious enslavement, whose frisson proceeds from the illusion of achievement produced, perversely, at the very moment of subjugation. Genteel women are enslaved to their physical being, since such an enslavement is precipitated by the dictates of fashion and the demands of public opinion to which they submit. Yet, by a paradoxical turn of logic, they "glory in" these non-freedoms exacted by "opinion," for this "glory" is the only profit they derive from their enslavement: a submission to public opinion generates a mirage of freedom, a blindness to the state of submission in which they are trapped. The perils of embodiment for women consist, for Wollstonecraft, precisely in this paradox: to gain the transient feeling of power and freedom, a (genteel) woman is reduced to sheer physical-ness—an embodiment that is also an enslavement.[14] The passage continues thus:

> I once knew a weak woman of fashion, who was more than commonly proud of her delicacy and sensibility. She thought a distinguishing taste and puny appetite the height of all human perfection, and acted accordingly. I have seen this weak sophisticated being neglect all the duties of life, yet recline with self-complacency on a sofa, and boast of her want of appetite as a proof of delicacy that extended to, or, perhaps, arose from, her exquisite sensibility. . . .
>
> Such a woman is not a more irrational monster than some of the Roman emperors, who were depraved by lawless power.

(pp. 131-32)[15]

The "weak woman of fashion" is a paradigmatic sap: prey to opinion, she deceives herself into picturing so-phistication as restraint, as an "exquisite" withdrawal from what is available to her, as a member of the upper classes, in abundance: food. She practices, instead, a different kind of "exquisite" cuisine: the production of a classed female body. The irrational monstrosity of this icon—the "weak woman of fashion" is "not a more ir-rational monster than some of the Roman emperors"—consists, for Wollstonecraft, in the woman's perfor-mance of languor. Her reclining posture is more than physical weakness, a symptom of inanition; it is a spec-tacle signifying to the woman herself her ability to dis-play sophistication. In this display—she "recline[s] with self-complacency on a sofa"—she confirms that a re-trenchment of appetite is a small price to pay for a gain in "sophistication" and approval in the court of public opinion. For Wollstonecraft—"the first of a new genus," a professional woman writer, always on the brink of poverty[16]—anorexia is a distinctly aristocratic gender pathology, one that insulates aristocracy against the in-cursions of devouring bourgeois materialism.[17] Anorexia is aristocratic in that gestures of food refusal are mean-ingless in poverty: there is nothing there to refuse. The very spectacle of renunciation depends on the unques-tioned existence of plenty, on the assumption that re-fusal will be read as meaningful. The reclining aristo-crat stylizes herself as the inverted mirror image of a hungry materialist; she does not hunger after posses-sions, for she has risen beyond the need for acquisi-tion.[18] She performs a stylized version of self-imposed poverty, but the meaning of her histrionics crucially de-pends on her not being poor. The "weak woman of fashion" luxuriates in this renunciation: "like the Syba-rites, dissolved in luxury," she is "more than commonly proud of her delicacy and sensibility"; indeed, she en-joys renunciation *as* luxury. It is in passages such as this that disordered eating begins to signify disordered reason and thus locks the anorexic fashion addict back into the "sexual character"; the woman of fashion joins those women who are "standing dishes to which every glutton may have access" (p. 254).

Despite the sheer volume of scorn Wollstonecraft heaps on the fashion addict in her description of aristocratic anorexia, *A Vindication of the Rights of Woman* is suf-fused with a longing to salvage a version of this askesis, to resurrect it in the form of a middle-class morality.[19] We should not be taken in by the vehemence of Wollstonecraft's disparagements; indeed the excess of violent affect in the narrator's tone may alert us to the presence of a hidden, unsuspected identification. Para-doxically, Wollstonecraft wants to sustain what she can only conceive of as "monstrous" and preserve renuncia-tion as a meaningful gesture—on a different level: to imagine renunciation as a natural, non-performative condition, and yet practice withdrawal as an aesthetic and ethical gesture of identity formation. Wollstonecraft wants her rational middle-class heroines to practice re-nunciation for different reasons, and without seeming to perform either for the sake of public opinion or for their own self-complacency. Indeed, a form of renuncia-tion is necessary to the logic of Wollstonecraft's argu-ment from the first pages of her discourse: the passions are given to human beings so that "man by *struggling with them* might attain a degree of knowledge denied to the brutes," and about "appetites" she says that "they are only brutal when *unchecked by reason*" (pp. 91, 243, emphasis added).

The polarized class distinctions ("aristocratic" versus "middle-class") that characterize the logic of my analy-sis are indeed a productive fiction generated in Wollstonecraft's text to sustain a possibility of imagin-ing a "good" retrenchment. The logic of class consti-tutes, in *A Vindication of the Rights of Woman,* the most ideologically transparent form of emotional ap-peal: in the 1790s, merely to refer to "genteel" women was, in essence, to perform ostentatious self-definition by negation. Having disposed of the "bad" aristocratic performance of opinion-following languor, one could proceed to posit the "good," morally motivated and supposedly "natural," retrenchment. Whereas in Wollstonecraft's text aristocratic anorexia seems to sig-nify female subjugation ("genteel women are . . . slaves to their bodies"), middle-class askesis promises a transcendence of embodiment, and even individual lib-eration in the name of Reason. The aristocratic woman declines in the name of fashion; Wollstonecraft's ideal—a middle-class female ascetic, a born rational-ist—would practice renunciation in order to transcend the slavery precipitated by the dictates of "sexual char-acter." Essentially, Wollstonecraft ventures to preserve the signifier—renunciation—but hopes to control its meaning, indeed to radically alter and channel its po-tential significations. Ida, an anorexic girl described by Hilde Bruch, would indeed qualify as Wollstonecraft's model woman; she proclaimed: "My body became the *visual symbol* of pure ascetic and aesthetics. . . . Ev-erything became very intense and very intellectual, but absolutely untouchable."[20] Wollstonecraft embraces a version of this hyperintellectual transcendence of corporeality, the notion that bourgeois women should cultivate delicacy, understood as control of appetite and other bodily functions, while developing their capacity for reason.[21] To preserve the notion and the aesthetic of bourgeois femininity as renunciation Wollstonecraft attempts to divest the prescriptive control of appetite of its aristocratic, luxurious connotations; instead of ridiculing anorectic practices she now repudiates binge cycles:

> Luxury has introduced a refinement in eating, that destroys the constitution; and, a degree of gluttony which is so beastly, that a perception of seemliness of behaviour must be worn out before one being could eat immoderately in the presence of another, and afterwards complain of the oppression that his intemperance naturally produced. Some women, particularly French women, have also lost a sense of decency in this respect; for they will talk very calmly of an indigestion.
>
> (p. 253)

The shift from heaping scorn on anorexic aristocrats to ridiculing convivial dinner parties is a motivated one: under the guise of critiquing culinary excesses Wollstonecraft manages to present her own version of ideal retrenchment, her own version of a new bourgeois ethic. To abstain for aesthetic reasons—to demonstrate and acquire sensibility—is disparaged as inherently dissipated; abstemiousness as a sign of one's ethical uprightness and commitment to reason might, however, be welcome, and not devoid of its own aesthetic appeal, as an antidote to "intemperance." In the passage, the glutton "complain[s] of the oppression that his *intemperance naturally* produced" (emphasis added), suggesting that what is in accordance with nature is the ideal of temperance, of self-restraint and moderation. Wollstonecraft writes:

> I allow that it is easier to touch the body of a saint, or to be magnetised, than to restrain our appetites or govern our passions; but health of body or mind can only be recovered by these means, or we make the Supreme Judge partial and revengeful.
>
> (p. 311)

In Wollstonecraft's moral universe, gluttony is under negation, perhaps even under erasure. The potential of the self, especially the female self, for gluttony is perceived but immediately castigated; indiscriminate taking in—of substances, of accidental knowledges, of public opinions and gossip—is threatening to the purity of intellect, a purity guaranteed solely by the subject's self-restraint. The temperance of Wollstonecraft's projected "new women"—who "by reforming themselves . . . reform the world" (p. 133)—is a strategic measure, truly a revolutionary *tactic*. In Wollstonecraft's text, a teleological structure is at play: retrenchment seems to function as a catalyst, as what needs to exist

in order for a revolution to occur; the future utopia of rational domesticity is predicated upon such a relentless temperance. And yet, retrenchment is often a defensive strategy: "a defense against the original fear—that of eating too much, of not having control, of giving in to . . . biological urges."[22] From this vantage point, the energetic tone of optimism, so often heard in Wollstonecraft's call for "a revolution in female manners," may conceal a tremendous anxiety, perhaps the fear that appetite is gluttonous *by nature,* that there are no "natural" rules of temperance, of how much is "enough."

AN ECONOMY OF SCARCITY AND THE "DISH TO WHICH EVERY GLUTTON MAY HAVE ACCESS"

Tell me what you eat: I will tell you what you are.

Brillat-Savarin, *The Physiology of Taste*[23]

The rhetoric of appetite participates in, and is colored by, Wollstonecraft's attempt to work through the vexed question of sexual difference. The attribution of appetitiveness to men and of restraint to women is a rhetorical effect of the text's investment in the anorexic logic of reason rather than a simple "diagnosis" of a cultural configuration. The middle-class discipline of feminine restraint that Wollstonecraft projects arises in response to her conviction that "men are certainly more under the influence of their appetites than women; and their appetites are more depraved by unbridled indulgence and the fastidious contrivances of satiety" (pp. 252-53). Wollstonecraft repeatedly warns women not to be "intoxicated" by men's sexual advances; homage from men is described as "intoxicating" (p. 103), and so is indulgence in pleasure ("pleasure . . . mixes the intoxicating cup," p. 170). The danger of male appetite to women is thus textually associated with inebriation and also with infection by ingestion; the threat is substantial, since "disease and even death lurk in the cup or dainty that elevates the spirit or tickles the palate" (p. 170). Rational women, unimpressed by "homage," never "tickled" by vanity, and refusing to be "drunk" on men's praise, protect themselves against the threat posed by the predatory character of male passion. For Wollstonecraft's rational woman, renunciation becomes a protective, even preventive measure; it makes her stylize herself as the embodiment of a lack of appetite, as the very obverse of threatening male appetitiveness, all in an attempt to guard not only against the all too visible nature of male appetite but also against her own female self's potential, incipient gluttony. The more the text uses the rhetoric of appetite to characterize the threat of masculine power, the more women's defense against it assumes the character of appetitive restraint.

Wollstonecraft ascribes what she sees as men's twin vices—masturbation and homosexuality—to this association of men with unrestrained appetitiveness: men's attraction to "equivocal beings" results from an artificially produced fastidiousness that will not be satisfied with "bread, the common food of life" (p. 170)—good old femininity—and needs what Wollstonecraft calls "more than female languor" (p. 254) for its enjoyment. Claudia Johnson argues that, contrary to what is usually believed about Wollstonecraft's agenda in writing *A Vindication of the Rights of Woman,* Wollstonecraft actually "denounces the collapse of proper sexual distinction as the leading feature of her age."[24] What Johnson describes as Wollstonecraft's polemic against the "diffusion of unwholesome polymorphousness"[25] participates in what I would like to see, by contrast, as Wollstonecraft's critique of excessive (and thus "unnatural") appetitiveness, and her concomitant attempt to reinvent bourgeois femininity as a negation of gluttony and a new refinement of the body. Johnson's Wollstonecraft is obsessively preoccupied with the masculinity of men, and her feminist arguments are a mere aftereffect of her "real" interest in manhood. In Johnson's reading, Wollstonecraft blames the erosion of gender codes on the progressive sentimentalization of chivalric manhood (especially by Burke) and the resulting feminization of men. Johnson further detects in Wollstonecraft's *A Vindication of the Rights of Woman* the impulse to "hyperfeminize" women, maximizing sexual differences in order to preserve the masculinity of men; this impulse stems from the monstrosity—the enormity and perversion—of male tastes: "the taste of men is vitiated; and women, of all classes, naturally square their behavior to gratify the taste by which they obtain pleasure and power" (p. 254). The same "gross appetite, which satiety has rendered fastidious," is responsible for male authors' insistence on imposing the exigencies of excessive sensibility on female bodies and minds (p. 157). In the face of this hyperfeminization, "Wollstonecraft seems to advocate a converse asymmetry, whereby men's hypermasculinity is required to guarantee and ensure the possibility of female rationality."[26]

But Johnson's own agenda—to expose Wollstonecraft's terror of polymorphousness—makes her focus exclusively on the signified of Wollstonecraft's polemic, men's sexual predation, and to glide over the signifier, so often bound up with appetitiveness and debauched tastes. Johnson does not expose the logic—an economy of appetitive scarcity—upon which Wollstonecraft's metaphorics as well as her notion of "natural" temperance are founded. According to this logic of scarcity or temperance, there must be a correspondence between appetites and their satisfactions; hence, for men to appropriate more is for women to have less. In Wollstonecraft's gendered economy, there is only so much appetite to go around. Of course, such economic effects are presented in Wollstonecraft's text as "natural" and hence necessary. Indeed, Johnson's own argument operates according to a similar logic of scarcity:

she seems to argue that there is only so much masculinity to go around, and it is this assumption of a net amount of available masculinity that makes her argue as she does. While Johnson is certainly right to observe that men's sentimentality makes Wollstonecraft rigidly desire women's rationality, it is essential in my reading to expose the logic of scarcity on which such arguments depend: Wollstonecraft's insistence on women's appetitive retrenchment is strategic; it is only in the context of the ostensible monstrosity of male appetite that female askesis can appear natural.

The same gendered economy enables the polarization of the rhetoric of appetite in Wollstonecraft's discourse: if men's appetites can be described as "projective" (in Wollstonecraft's analogies, appetite makes men seek satisfaction outside the self, as it were), women's response to this appetite is of an introjective, assimilative kind: women's "thirsty ears eagerly drink the insinuating nothings of politeness" (p. 227). Yet a man's appetites, when they emerge out of the self, do not threaten the integrity of his subject. On the contrary, not only are women figured as the food that is to satisfy men's hunger—women are "standing dishes to which every glutton may have access" (p. 254)—but also they are figured as essentially porous creatures, vulnerable in the face of men's appetites because of their very permeability. Whenever Wollstonecraft wishes to satirize women's credulity and poor education, she talks about "imbibing" all kinds of pernicious notions and opinions (e.g., pp. 92, 119, 127); this "drinking in" (from Latin "in-" and "bibere") seems to account for the very possibility of thinking: in her account of "the effect which an early association of ideas has upon the character," Wollstonecraft explains that ideas are "taken in" and "assimilat[ed]" (p. 223). She then hastens to add that this process has "a more baneful effect on the female than the male character. . . . But females . . . have not sufficient strength of mind to efface the superinductions of art that have smothered nature" (pp. 224-25). These metaphorical patterns mark two different conceptions of subjectivity. The male subject constitutes a solid origin of appetites, a self-contained *cogito* from which appetite can issue forth without threatening the integrity of its source. The female subject, however, is rhetorically produced as *nothingness incarnate*: it exists only by means of this imbibing or devouring of the external world.[27] The female is imagined as a loose composite of imbibed opinions and the various "foods" of affection, vanity, and dependence. There is no essence to the female subject, only incorporation and excretion.

It is the threatened status of the boundaries of female subjectivity that makes Wollstonecraft anxious not to discern the physiology of the female body: "How can *delicate* women obtrude on notice that part of the animal economy, which is so very disgusting?" (p. 240). There is nothing there to discern except "disgusting" excretory processes and immodest bare skin. The heated passages concerning some "improprieties" prevalent in nurseries and boarding-schools testify to a similar fear: the free flow of introjection and ejection in enclosed spaces, characterized by a "gross degree of familiarity" (p. 239), threatens borders between men and women, as well as between women and women. The anxiousness of the narrator's tone may point to a species of homosexual panic, but it also testifies to what we might term "body" or "boundary" panic: a trepidation to reestablish safe body boundaries, boundaries that not only would guarantee the propriety of the relations between the sexes, but first of all, would contain the incorporative and excretory processes that threaten the integrity of the female person. Wollstonecraft's concept of "that decent personal reserve" that "must be kept between woman and woman" (p. 240) would not only act as a deterrent to those "nasty or immodest habits" and "very nasty tricks" that women acquire in boarding-schools (p. 239); it would also give the female person the solidity and boundaries that she lacks.

Wollstonecraft is particularly offended by "bodily wit" (p. 240), the kind of familiarity that breaks the boundaries between physicality and language, "almost on a par with the double meanings which shake the convivial table when the glass has circulated freely" (p. 240). "Bodily wit" becomes a paradigm for different kinds of critical boundary breakdowns: gluttony transgresses the rule of temperance ("the convivial table"), intoxication threatens reason ("the glass has circulated freely"), the boundaries between the literal and the figural are dangerously confounded in "double meanings," and "bodily wit" itself conflates an intellectual phenomenon with (gross) corporeality. I will now turn to such relays between bodies and words in Wollstonecraft's own text.

EATING WORDS: LANGUAGE AND INGESTION

> In dealing with anorexia nervosa we are dealing with *metaphor*—sometimes a startlingly apt form of metaphor. It is for this reason . . . that I propose to treat my patient as a text.
>
> Sheila MacLeod, *The Art of Starvation*[28]

Tracing the figures of taste and appetite enables a reconstruction of Wollstonecraft's conception of bourgeois femininity as renunciation. But we must also attend to the status of appetite itself as a problematic figure in the text of *A Vindication of the Rights of Woman* and this figure's role in producing the logic of rationality as anorexic. The figure of appetite, introduced by virtue of its synonymous relation with sexuality, appears to lose its metaphoricity in the course of Wollstonecraft's polemic. Barbara Johnson writes that if the opposition between an inside and an outside is the received model of conceiving the nature of a rhetorical figure, then "the vehicle, or surface meaning, is seen as

enclosing an inner tenor, or figurative meaning. This relation can be pictured somewhat facetiously as a gilded carriage—the vehicle—containing Luciano Pavarotti, the tenor."[29] In Wollstonecraft's *A Vindication of the Rights of Woman,* the vehicle breaks loose from the tenor, the gilded carriage ditches Pavarotti and runs amok. Appetite refuses to stand for sexuality, refuses to mean something other than itself: in the "weak woman of fashion" passage, it becomes a hero in its own right and displaces sexuality as the centerpiece of the drama of human difference. The rhetorical tendency of Wollstonecraft's text seems to support Maud Ellmann's passionate plea for the substitution of "a more encompassing poetics of starvation for the phallic poetics of desire."[30]

In *A Vindication of the Rights of Woman,* multiform inflections of hunger and appetite undermine the unquestioned primacy of "sexual character." But this literalization, the apparent breaking loose of appetite from its metaphorical ties, is nonetheless figurative. The process whereby feminine corporeality is *written* as literal—as pure, obdurate materiality, beyond the reach of rational discourse—is thematized by Wollstonecraft herself when she describes how "the mind shapes itself to the body, and roaming round its gilt cage, only seeks to adorn its prison" (p. 132); similarly, she describes how "false notions of beauty and delicacy stop the growth of their limbs and produce a sickly soreness, rather than delicacy of organs" (p. 225). Unwittingly, the text emphasizes the process of literalization that organizes its metaphorical structures: "genteel women are, *literally speaking,* slaves to their bodies, and glory in their subjection" (p. 131, emphasis added). "Literally speaking": there is an insistence here, an ardent desire to see "enslavement" of the body not just as a figure; "literally speaking" means perhaps that to be embodied for a woman *is* to be enslaved. Such sentences reduce abstract entities (a person, the mind, delicacy) to phenomena assumed to be primary, to be resistant to further analysis or decomposition, phenomena such as the physical "frame"—the body's cage, or sores and wounds. Their rhetorical effect is to produce corporeality as literal, as the bottom line to which all uncertainties and abstractions can be reduced. It is as if what the text purports to be about—reason, morality—is too elusive, too immaterial to grasp. The discourse uses vivid images of the body, but these images soon take over, and the discourse comes to be *about* the body. In its rhetorical patterns it "encrusts"—materializes and literalizes—such entities while denouncing the very process of "encrustation": Wollstonecraft can hardly contain her outrage at the prescriptive theory of a "grossly unnatural" femininity propounded by conduct book writers and sentimental authors, whose "specious poisons . . . *encrusting* morality eat away the substance" (p. 245, emphasis added). Wollstonecraft critiques the ostensible "sexual character" of women—their narcissistic interest in the accoutrements of their own persons and in the art of pleasing men—as a corrosive "crust" on the solid foundation of reason, an effect of their faulty, frivolous socialization. But her text itself rhetorically performs a continual "encrustation," a calcification of reason and morality.

The figure that captures this anorectic drive toward "literalization" or "encrustation" is *hypostasis*: a tendency—a compulsion, perhaps—to ascribe material existence to abstract entities, to prefer figures of tangibility to airy abstractions.[31] It is precisely through such a hypostatization that the anorexic "weak woman of fashion" comes to attach so much baleful importance to her body; she cannot imagine selfhood without making an immediate reference to "the body"—without hypostatizing her sense of identity. In "Interpreting Anorexia Nervosa," Noelle Caskey writes:

> It is the literal-mindedness of anorexia to take "the body" as a synonym for "the self" and to try to live in the world through a manipulation of "the body," particularly as it is reflected to the anorexic by the perceived wishes of others. . . . This type of thinking creates the predisposition to view the abstract entity of "the self" concretely, as a body, but it also stimulates the anorexic's other impulse, the impulse to escape the body entirely as a way of escaping the funnel of alien desires.[32]

Deliberately to confuse "the body" with "subjectivity" is to graft the abstract sense of self onto what is most materially available to one: one's body. It is to forget that in order to transcend the incomprehensible, daunting metaphor of selfhood, one engages in yet another daunting rhetorical move: the process of literalizing, of encrusting one's sense of self and making it coincide with the body, the body's cage. The twin processes, metaphorization and literalization, are profoundly interconnected; the attempt to escape from one into the other is a prototypical vicious circle. In the words of D. A. Miller, "Metaphorizing the body begins and ends with literalizing the meanings the body is thus made to bear."[33] My attempt to encompass and name the anorexic process rhetorically is, in a sense, predetermined: many texts on anorexia show an uncanny compulsion to invoke rhetorical figures in order to subsume the anorexic logic they describe under a single, figurative denomination. Anorexia has been most notably theorized as "metaphor" (Sheila MacLeod, Susie Orbach) and "prosopopeia" (Albaraq Mahbobah);[34] my own terms— "hypostasis," "literalization," or "encrustation"—are attempts to refine this list. "Anorexic figures"—both the women and the metaphors—are tantalizing precisely because they pose questions of figuration, of being a figure: a corporeal and rhetorical self.

Wollstonecraft's narrator declares herself averse to "words"—"I shall be employed about things, not words" (p. 83)—but cannot keep herself from digressing. Para-

doxically, the narrator of *A Vindication of the Rights of Woman* keeps producing excessive discourse about the need to retrench, in terms of both words and the body. Wollstonecraft's narrator may be read as a parodical embodiment of Bonnie Friedman's "Silence": in her moving meditation on writer's block, "Anorexia of Language: Why We Can't Write," Friedman asks us to imagine the allegorical figure of Silence, a personification of anorexia, with her teeth clamped against the world in a gesture of ultimate negativity. Silence is

> slim to the point of vanishing, with not a hair out of place as it gazes at me with lucid blue eyes. . . .
>
> Silence swallows. She stares at me in pain as if to say she cannot help herself. If she could—oh, the volumes she'd say! There'd be no stopping her. . . .
>
> Her restraint is perfect, virginal, absolute.[35]

Friedman's portrayal of Silence brings out the essential linkage between language and ingestion, as well as between restraint and excess, the linkage visible in *A Vindication of the Rights of Woman*. Like Friedman's Silence, Wollstonecraft's narrator suggests that there is a "strange affinity between askesis and excess,"[36] between renunciation and overabundance, in terms of both corporeality and language.

Characteristically for a text governed by the logic of anorexic literalization, Wollstonecraft's languid figures with a "puny appetite" are joined by a narrator vehemently set against "pretty feminine phrases" (p. 82). The text of *A Vindication of the Rights of Woman* associates the anorexic syndrome with a repudiation of figurative language; it is in Wollstonecraft's narrator's arguments concerning literary language that the tendency toward hypostasis is best discerned. Indeed, it is no mere coincidence that the twin oral phenomena— eating and language—exhibit disorders whose mechanisms appear essentially the same: the abandonment of everyday functionality in favor of an excess of signification. Already in the "Author's Introduction" Wollstonecraft's narrator announces her intention to "dismiss[] . . . those pretty feminine phrases," to negate her imbrication in figural paradoxes and declare herself free of "words":

> I shall disdain to cull my phrases or polish my style. I aim at being useful, and sincerity will render me unaffected; for wishing rather to persuade by the force of my arguments than dazzle by the elegance of my language, I shall not waste my time in rounding periods, or in fabricating the turgid bombast of artificial feelings, which, coming from the head, never reach the heart. I shall be employed about things, not words! and, anxious to render my sex more respectable members of society, I shall try to avoid that flowery diction which has slided from essays into novels, and from novels into familiar letters and conversations.
>
> These pretty superlatives, dropping glibly from the tongue, vitiate the taste, and create a kind of sickly delicacy that turns away from simple unadorned truth;

and a deluge of false sentiments and overstretched feelings, stifling the natural emotions of the heart, render the domestic pleasures insipid, that ought to sweeten the exercise of those severe duties, which educate a rational and immortal being for a nobler field of action.

(pp. 82-83)

Commenting on this passage, Tom Furniss observes that

it is possible to see that figurative analogies are being developed in *A Vindication of the Rights of Woman* between sexuality, political systems, and rhetorical language. All three domains are discussed in terms of the relationship between dress and body, and in all three Wollstonecraft's politics impel her to distrust the clothed and valorize the unadorned.[37]

While Furniss is correct to point out that the relation between rhetorical language and sexuality is mediated through yet another metaphor, our discussion of the anorexic logic that governs Wollstonecraft's representation of the female body allows us to discern a structure or a logic within what Furniss can only obliquely name "dress and body." Wollstonecraft's extended attack on metaphoricity is embroiled in the problematic of "literalization"—literalization as a figure that wishes to resolve, to do away with, its own figurative status—which in turn invokes the rhetorical connections between taste and language, the twin oral phenomena.

The passage from "Author's Introduction," built around a series of binarisms that seek to distinguish between the transparency of truth ("things") and the mediation of language ("words"), evinces Wollstonecraft's effort to produce the opposition between the language of affect and the language of affectation. It leads, however, into an almost obsessive series of oral metaphors. The language of affectation ("pretty superlatives") is characterized by its materiality and tangibility, and its production is represented as an easeful falling of drops from the tongue: "flowery diction" "drop[s] glibly from the tongue," bringing to mind small quantities of liquid, such as saliva. "The tongue" seems to veer unsteadily between various significations: we are repeatedly led from the organ of the mouth to the abstract organ of linguistic production and back again. The "dripping" impairs the sense of taste and creates a nauseating effect of "sickly delicacy." The danger of this linguistic proliferation is that the very prototype of pure affect—domestic affect—may be rendered "insipid." The languages of affectation and affect do not seem to be able to keep to their apportioned spheres: they travel back and forth like their prototype, the tongue.

The "sickly delicac[ies]" the passage refers to consist in this indeterminate traffic; they point in two directions, toward exaggerated affect but also toward nauseating confectioneries. With this surplus of oral metaphors, it

is no longer possible to disentangle the language of affect from the language of affectation. Initially, Wollstonecraft seems to be denouncing the feminine pretentious language in favor of a transparency, marked neither by linguistic mediation nor by gender. Further in the treatise, she thus comments on the writings of Catherine Macaulay: "Catherine Macaulay was an example of intellectual acquirements supposed to be incompatible with the weakness of her sex. In her style of writing, indeed, no sex appears, for it is like the sense it conveys, strong and clear" (p. 210). The opposition Wollstonecraft insists on, that between "feminine phrases" and writing unmarked by gender, is problematized by her verbal choices: pure truth and intellectual sense are marked by "strength" and "force," and we know from other parts of the treatise that these characteristics are always associated with male bodies. The narrator's implicit agenda is to masculinize women's bodies (she often recommends that women should acquire more muscular strength), as though building muscle strength could guarantee women access to the language of truth, unlike the orality of "feminine phrases" that expressly bars access to truth. "The converse and antidote of these [feminine phrases]," writes Furniss, "is the 'manly'—that which is an open display, which says what it means, and is genuinely representative without reserve or equivocation."[38]

Wollstonecraft's violent attack on metaphors participates in the dynamic of hypostasis and literalization. Becoming "literal" and thus "reasonable" is part of the dynamic of temperance. In warning against "those phosphoric bursts which only mimic in the dark the flame of passion" (p. 317), Wollstonecraft is reacting against Rousseau's equation of women's language with "taste,"[39] and criticizing literary language specifically in its supplemental, affective, appetitive qualities. It is an attempt to dismantle this equation that propels the text of *A Vindication of the Rights of Woman* toward the logic of anorexia: women's bodies and women's words become locked, in Wollstonecraft's text, in a struggle toward mutual elimination; they seem to stand, intransigent, in each other's way. As Ellmann shows, "Language and the body are locked in a struggle of attrition": "The thinner the body, the fatter the book."[40] When Wollstonecraft complains of "some women . . . [who] will talk very calmly of an indigestion" (p. 253), it is because in the anorexic logic of reason bodies are set against words, and Wollstonecraft cannot allow the possibility of verbalizing bodily processes. Words, in the anorexic logic of reason, are excessive in and of themselves; words are excess—essentially, a luxury, an extra, a supplement—precisely because they come from the mouth, because to produce them the teeth must be unclamped and the female subject's ideal self-possession must be breached, threatened by language's flickering, veering significations.[41] For women to talk about indigestion at all—and to talk about it calmly—is to transgress the boundary between bodies and words, to translate, too easily, a bodily state into a linguistic one. According to this logic, to talk about indigestion is actually to have or produce it: to speak is to have (eaten) too much. Wollstonecraft's attack on metaphors is an attack on such translations; and yet her text, as in the above sentence, often confuses eating with speaking: sentences seem to lose control over the difference between things and words about them. According to Wollstonecraft's argument, only a thorough separation of bodies from words—the very opposite of "bodily wit"—will allow us to gain access to writings supposedly unmarked by gender, writings that guarantee access to truth. Of course, hidden behind this is an assumption that women's bodies cannot help but infect their discourse, unlike men's bodies, which remain in hygienic isolation from men's words. The problematic relation between women's bodies and women's words is what disarticulates the text of liberal feminism from its very beginnings—and what disarticulates much feminist thought even now.

Notes

1. Virginia Woolf, *The Second Common Reader,* pp. 168-76, rpt. in Mary Wollstonecraft, *A Vindication of the Rights of Woman,* ed. Carol H. Poston (New York: Norton, 1988), pp. 270, 272.

2. Mary Wollstonecraft, *A Vindication of the Rights of Woman,* ed. Miriam Brody (Harmondsworth: Penguin, 1992), pp. 160, 254. Hereafter page references to this edition will appear parenthetically in the text.

3. Orrin N. C. Wang writes that Wollstonecraft's polemics "anticipate many of the theoretical aporias facing feminists and feminist Romanticists today. Recovering the legacy of those antinomies in Wollstonecraft reveals how she proleptically accomplishes what the theorization of Romanticism and gender together effects," in *Fantastic Modernity: Dialectical Readings in Romanticism and Theory* (Baltimore: Johns Hopkins University Press, 1996), p. 109. I would add that this "proleptic[] accomplish[ment]" is far from "rational" or conscious.

4. Miriam Brody, Introduction, *A Vindication of the Rights of Woman,* by Wollstonecraft, p. 69.

5. I have in mind the so-called problem of agency, whereby political agency seems to require the (liberal) notion of the subject as possessed both of coherence and intention, whereas our theoretical convictions seem to lead in the opposite direction, dispossessing the subject of any self-coincidence.

6. Gillian Brown, "Anorexia, Humanism, and Feminism," *The Yale Journal of Criticism,* 5, No. 1 (1991), 211-13, 194, 196-97.

7. See also Edmund Burke, *A Philosophical Enquiry into the Origin of Our Ideas of the Sublime and Beautiful,* ed. Adam Phillips (1757; Oxford: Oxford University Press, 1990). Although Burke defines "Taste" abstractly, as "those faculties of the mind which are affected with, or which form a judgment of the works of imagination and the elegant arts" (p. 13), he soon slides into examples that are not as abstract and that draw directly on the metaphorical potential of "taste": "All men are agreed to call vinegar *sour,* honey *sweet,* and aloes *bitter.* . . . They all concur in calling sweetness pleasant, and sourness and bitterness unpleasant" (p. 14, emphasis added).

8. Carol H. Poston's edition gives a variant reading: "Considering the length of time that women have been dependent, is it surprising that some of them *hug their chains,* and fawn like the spaniel?" in Wollstonecraft, *A Vindication of the Rights of Woman,* p. 82 (emphasis added).

9. David Hume, for instance, attributes "love betwixt the sexes" to "the bodily appetite for generation," in *A Treatise of Human Nature,* ed. P. H. Nidditch (1739-40; Oxford: Clarendon, 1978), pp. 394-96. But the pairing of sexuality and appetite may point to a latent structure: Maud Ellmann observes, "Since sexuality originates in eating, it is always haunted by the imagery of ingestion, having neither an object nor a territory proper to itself," in *The Hunger Artists: Starving, Writing, and Imprisonment* (Cambridge: Harvard University Press, 1993), p. 39.

10. Mary Poovey writes: "So intent is Wollstonecraft to reject the prevalent stereotype of women as *all* sexuality that she comes close to arguing that women have *no* innate sexual desires at all," in *The Proper Lady and the Woman Writer: Ideology as Style in the Works of Mary Wollstonecraft, Mary Shelley, and Jane Austen* (Chicago: University of Chicago Press, 1984), p. 74. In Poovey's own argument, however, "appetite" remains a largely unexamined figure of sexuality, blinding the author to the workings of this metaphor in Wollstonecraft's text. Poovey is seconded by Cora Kaplan who, in her excellent study of feminism's imbrication in battles over women's sexuality, describes Wollstonecraft as imposing "heartbreaking conditions for women's liberation—a little death, the death of desire, the death of female pleasure," in *Sea Changes: Essays on Culture and Feminism* (London: Verso, 1986), p. 39. In fact, Wollstonecraft writes that "true voluptuousness" is possible, as long as it proceeds "from the mind" (p. 325).

11. For an argument that connects the dualist tradition with the politics and pathologization of the female

body, see Susan Bordo, *Unbearable Weight: Feminism, Western Culture, and the Body* (Berkeley: University of California Press, 1993), pp. 144-48.

12. Leslie Heywood, *Dedication to Hunger: The Anorexic Aesthetic in Modern Culture* (Berkeley: University of California Press, 1996), p. 8.

13. Heywood, *Dedication to Hunger,* pp. 12, 57.

14. Wollstonecraft thus describes women's illusion of power: "Women have been duped by their lovers, as princes by their ministers, whilst dreaming that they reigned over them" (p. 107).

15. Wollstonecraft aims at disentangling some of the conundrums proposed by conduct books. Dr. Gregory writes that "luxury of eating" is "a despicable selfish vice in men, but in your sex it is beyond expression indelicate and disgusting. . . . We so naturally associate the idea of female softness and delicacy with a corresponding delicacy of constitution, that when a woman speaks of her great strength, her extraordinary appetite, her ability to bear excessive fatigue, we recoil at a description in a way she is little aware of," in Dr. Gregory, *A Father's Legacy to His Daughters,* in *The Young Lady's Pocket Library, or Parental Monitor,* intro. and ed. Vivien Jones (1774; London: Thoemmes, 1996), pp. 16, 20-21.

16. Wollstonecraft referred to herself as "the first of a new genus" in a letter to her sister Everina; see *The Collected Letters of Mary Wollstonecraft,* ed. Ralph M. Wardle (Ithaca: Cornell University Press, 1979), p. 164.

17. Hilde Bruch writes: "Most anorexic girls come from upper-middle-class and upper-class homes; financial achievement and social position are often high," in *The Golden Cage: The Enigma of Anorexia Nervosa* (New York: Random-Vintage, 1979), p. 25.

18. In her analysis of the twentieth-century culture of anorexia, *The Hunger Artists,* Ellmann observes: "To have it but not to eat it is a sign of class superiority, betokening an independence of necessity" (p. 7).

19. Self-starvation often has moral meanings in the anorectic's self-conception. Bruch writes: "These youngsters are frantically preoccupied with food and eating but consider self-denial and discipline the highest virtue and condemn satisfying their needs and desires as shameful self-indulgence" (p. x).

20. Bruch, p. 18.

21. Claudia Johnson notes that "wherever Wollstonecraft turns, she sees men and women both sinking into gross corporeality," in *Equivocal Beings: Politics, Gender, and Sentimentality in the 1790s: Wollstonecraft, Radcliffe, Burney, Austen,* Women in Culture and Society Series, ed. Catharine R. Stimpson (Chicago: University of Chicago Press, 1995), p. 41.

22. Bruch, p. 4.

23. Jean-Anthelme Brillat-Savarin, *The Physiology of Taste,* trans. Anne Drayton (New York: Penguin, 1994), p. 13.

24. C. Johnson, p. 23.

25. C. Johnson, p. 35.

26. C. Johnson, p. 45.

27. In essence, women have never grown up, and they still exhibit the characteristics of the Freudian pleasure-ego: "The original pleasure-ego wants to introject into itself everything that is good and to eject from itself everything that is bad"; see Sigmund Freud, "Negation," *The Standard Edition of the Selected Works of Sigmund Freud* (London: Hogarth, 1961), XIX, 237, for the classic formulation of this incorporative/excorporative binarism. Wollstonecraft often disparagingly describes women as children: "the overgrown child, his wife"; innocence is a "state of childhood"; narcissistic women are admonished for their "infantile airs" (pp. 114, 154, 155).

28. Sheila MacLeod, *The Art of Starvation* (London: Virago, 1981), p. 68.

29. Barbara Johnson, "Metaphor, Metonymy and Voice in *Their Eyes Were Watching God,*" *Black Literature and Literary Theory,* ed. Henry Louis Gates (New York: Methuen, 1984), p. 211.

30. Ellmann, p. 27.

31. My usage of "hypostasis" is very close to what Nicolas Abraham and Maria Torok call "antimetaphor," in "Mourning *or* Melancholia: Introjection *versus* Incorporation," in *The Shell and the Kernel: Renewals of Psychoanalysis,* ed. and trans. Nicholas T. Rand (Chicago: University of Chicago Press, 1994), pp. 125-38. Antimetaphor is "the figure of the active destruction of representation," "not simply a matter of reverting to the literal meaning of words, but of using them in such a way . . . that their very capacity for figurative representation is destroyed" (p. 132).

32. Noelle Caskey, "Interpreting Anorexia Nervosa," in *The Female Body in Western Culture: The Contemporary Perspectives,* ed. Susan Rubin Suleiman (Cambridge: Harvard University Press, 1986), p. 184.

33. D. A. Miller, "The Late Jane Austen," *Raritan,* 10, No. 1 (1990), 57.

34. MacLeod, p. 68; Susie Orbach, *Hunger Strike: The Anorectic's Struggle as a Metaphor for Our Age* (New York: Norton, 1986), p. 24; Albaraq Mahbobah, "Reading the Anorexic Maze," *Genders,* 14 (1992), 91.

35. Bonnie Friedman, "Anorexia of Language: Why We Can't Write," in *Writing Past Dark: Envy, Fear, Distraction, and Other Dilemmas in the Writer's Life* (New York: HarperPerennial, 1993), pp. 105-06.

36. Ellmann, p. 15.

37. Tom Furniss, "Nasty Tricks and Tropes: Sexuality and Language in Mary Wollstonecraft's *Rights of Woman,*" *Studies in Romanticism,* 32 (Summer 1993), 187. However, we have seen that Wollstonecraft indeed often distrusted the *un-clothed* (the naked female body). "Unadorned," in Furniss's argument, should be understood as "the natural."

38. Furniss, p. 189.

39. Wollstonecraft quotes Rousseau's dictum: "A man speaks of what he knows, a woman of what pleases her; the one requires knowledge, the other taste" (p. 186).

40. Ellmann, pp. 27, 22. For Ellmann, this claim seems to have a universal character. In my reading, the "struggle of attrition" is an effect of Wollstonecraft reacting against Rousseau.

41. I am playing upon the Derridean logic of supplementation here. Wollstonecraft insists that "words" and "phrases" are a mere supplement, an unnecessary extra, in her project to "be employed about things." Of course, they turn out, all too soon, to be a necessary complement without which "things" are not even conceivable. Interestingly, in a passage from Rousseau that Derrida quotes in his discussion of supplementation, it is a morsel of food swallowed in "Maman's" presence that shows supplementation to be a necessary complement. See Jacques Derrida, *Of Grammatology,* trans. Gayatri Chakravorty Spivak (Baltimore: Johns Hopkins University Press, 1974), p. 152.

Ruth Abbey (essay date summer 1999)

SOURCE: Abbey, Ruth. "Back to the Future: Marriage as Friendship in the Thought of Mary Wollstonecraft." *Hypatia* 14, no. 3 (summer 1999): 78-95.

[*In the following essay, Abbey analyzes Wollstonecraft's views on the political nature of the family and marriage in* A Vindication of the Rights of Woman *and her attitude toward sexuality in her unfinished novel,* Maria, or the Wrongs of Woman.]

According to the feminist political theorist Susan Moller Okin, the challenge facing liberal thinkers is to incorporate fully issues of gender and the family into their thinking about justice. She insists that "We can have a liberalism that fully includes women only if we can devise a theoretical basis for public policies that, recognizing the family as a fundamental political institution, extends standards of justice to life within it" (Okin 1989, 53). Those who share Okin's belief that for liberal theory to move forward it must take the political nature of family relations seriously should return to Mary Wollstonecraft's work to find the beginnings of such a liberalism. Wollstonecraft not only depicts the family as a fundamentally political institution but also applies liberal notions of justice to it. It is argued here that she brings the values that liberals believe should govern the public realm to the private world of love, romance, and family life by promoting the ideal of marriage as friendship.

Wollstonecraft extends her argument that women should exercise equal rights with men in the public sphere into a critique of the structural inequalities of marriage. Although a stern critic of "actually existing" marriages, she does not reject marriage as an institution altogether. Instead, she envisages a form of marriage that incorporates the major features of the classical notion of higher friendship such as equality, free choice, reason, mutual esteem and profound concern for one another's moral character.[1] The classical ideal of higher friendship provides a suitable model for her liberal approach to marriage because it represents the paradigmatic rational, equal, and free relationship. In such relationships, individuals exchange some of their independence for interdependence and are united by bonds of deep and lasting affection, as well as respect for and appreciation of one another's character and individuality. Wollstonecraft uses the idea that marriage should emulate many of the features of higher friendship to criticize the practices and values of romance and family life in eighteenth-century English society and to suggest a way in which marriage might be reconfigured to realize central liberal values.

To recast marriage in this way means that Wollstonecraft is applying liberal values to the world of romantic love and family life. That she thinks about marriage in political, and specifically liberal, terms and recommends a model of marriage that emulates many of friendship's salient features is an important feature of her work often overlooked in much of the secondary literature. Even those who note the idea's presence in her work do not attribute it the importance it assumes in this analysis. Diana Coole, for example, observes that Wollstonecraft favors the calmness of friendship over the passion of sexual love as a basis for marriage but does not link this to her later point about Wollstonecraft's belief in the relationship between domestic and public virtue (Coole 1988, 123). Karen Green refers to Wollstonecraft's idea that "marriage should be based on friendship between equals. A genuine regard of the genuine qualities of one's spouse should found a union between autonomous individuals united in their sense of duty towards their children" (Green 1995, 96). However, she does not make this idea central to Wollstonecraft's liberalism. Sylvana Tomaselli claims that Wollstonecraft's "ideal relationship between the sexes was one modelled on an idealized conception, which owed much to antiquity, of friendship between men" (Tomaselli 1995, xxvi). Yet the idea of marriage as friendship does not appear in her catalogue of Wollstonecraft's ideas that are relevant today (Tomaselli 1995, xxix). Finally, Virginia Sapiro says that Wollstonecraft had wanted friendship as "the ideal social relationship" to be extended into the family and the polity (Sapiro 1996, 36). I suggest, however, that friendship represents a different, albeit complementary, way of realizing liberal values in intimate relationships rather than providing the model for all social relationships.

In what follows, I briefly rehearse Wollstonecraft's critique of marriage and family life. Her alternative view of marriage, which draws on some of the features of the classical notion of higher friendship, is outlined. Her fear of arbitrary power provides the lynch pin for her analysis of power relations in both the public and the private realms. To minimize the exercise of arbitrary power, she promotes the extension of liberal values in both spheres. However, her model of marriage as friendship, which diminishes arbitrary power in the domestic sphere, seems unable to incorporate the possibility of robust and enduring sexual relations between the married partners. Before outlining Wollstonecraft's substantive position on these matters, I turn to the question of her place in the liberal canon.

Legacies For Liberalism

In judging the putatively private realm of love, marriage, and family life by the values that liberals believe should inform the public realm, such as equality, freedom, reason, consent, and the diminution of arbitrary power, Wollstonecraft threatens the traditional liberal distinction between public and private. As Martha Nussbaum writes, "Liberal thinkers tended to segment the private from the public sphere, considering the public sphere one of individual rights and contractual arrangements, the family a private sphere in which the state should not meddle" (Nussbaum 1996, 17). Yet despite their articulation in Wollstonecraft's best-known work, *Vindication of the Rights of Woman* (1985), both these elements—the questioning of the public/private separation within liberalism and the idea of reforming marriage along the lines of higher friendship—are typically associated with John Stuart Mill. Even

feminist scholars impute to Mill the belief that marriage should share the salient qualities of friendship and fail to recognize that Wollstonecraft advanced a similar position in the previous century.[2] Mary Shanley, for example, claims that Mill "made a most significant break with the past in adopting the language of friendship in his discussion of marriage" (Shanley 1981, 239). Nadia Urbinati holds that "it was only Mill who transformed this notion [of an ideal marriage, of a soul mate] into an instrument with which to denounce the reality of family life" (Urbinati 1991, 638). Perhaps because of Mill's recognized concern with the dynamics of the private realm, Nussbaum nominates him as the exception to the liberal tendency to distinguish the public from the private realm. Marilyn Friedman also describes Mill as "a noteworthy exception" to the liberal tradition's tendency to confine its attack on unjustified hierarchy to the public realm (Friedman 1993, 293). While Nussbaum's observation that "most of the liberal tradition did not follow Mill's lead" (Nussbaum 1996, 17) is correct, it is imperative to recognize that Wollstonecraft had challenged this separation in the previous century and promoted the idea of marriage as friendship. Only then can the importance of her contribution to the liberal tradition be appreciated.

However, while Wollstonecraft advocates the extension of liberal values into the household, she does not simply expand the reach of social contract thinking into the private realm. She does not impose the image of individuals as rights-bearers onto the domestic sphere nor assume that the only way for liberal values to be realized is through the mechanism of individual rights. She implies instead that there can be different models for liberal relationships, depending upon whether these occur among strangers in the public realm or among intimates in the household. Hers is both a comprehensive and a complex liberalism, suggesting that it is possible to promote liberal values without making the social contract model of human relations hegemonic[3] and without extending rights discourse to all areas of life. The nuanced character of her liberalism provides another reason why contemporary liberals should return to Wollstonecraft as a source for future thinking.[4]

Wollstonecraft's Critique Of Marriage

Notwithstanding the forward-looking aspects of her liberalism, Wollstonecraft accepts the traditional idea, expressed most recently in her time by Jean Jacques Rousseau, that marriage and motherhood are duties for women. Like Rousseau, she attacks the way women are socialized because it renders them unfit to perform their duties as wives and mothers. However, her qualifications and criteria for being a good wife and mother differ markedly from his. In contrast to his evocation of the cloistered wife and mother,[5] she insists that women engage with the wider world and its questions of politics and morality. Moreover, she claims that "this is the only way to make them properly attentive to their domestic duties. An active mind embraces the whole circle of its duties, and finds time enough for all" (Wollstonecraft 1985, 288, 253, 257). Her critique of women's socialization is two-pronged, for she claims that the feminine qualities promoted by her society and characterized in Rousseau's portrait of Sophie create women who are poor wives and dangerous mothers.[6] Conversely, she suggests that were marriage to emulate many of the features of friendship, marriage and parenthood would be vastly improved, as would the wider society, for marriage is "the foundation of almost every social virtue" (1985, 165).

Wollstonecraft points out that in her society, marriage alone brings women prestige and power. "[T]he only way women can rise in the world [is] by marriage" (Wollstonecraft 1985, 83, 151, 157), while men have more options open to them: "marriage is not the grand feature in their lives" (1985, 150). This immediately put an imbalance between the partners—one enters the relationship out of necessity while the other exercises greater choice. This asymmetry is a function of the vast differences between men's and women's legal, social, political, and economic power: as Wollstonecraft says, "the laws respecting women . . . make an absurd unit of a man and his wife" (1985, 257).[7] To acquire a husband, women are encouraged to be coquettes, to flirt, and to conceal their true feelings from the men who court them (Wollstonecraft 1985, 169-70). Wollstonecraft summarizes women's preparation for marriage: "Women are told from their infancy, and taught by the example of their mothers, that a little knowledge of human weakness, justly termed cunning, softness of temper, *outward* obedience, and a scrupulous attention to a puerile kind of propriety will obtain for them the protection of a man; and should they be beautiful, all else is needless; for at least twenty years of their life" (1985, 100).

In Wollstonecraft's society, part of becoming a woman is, therefore, a training in the art of pleasing (1985, 106, 147, 311), which is a training in deception. However, women trained in this modus operandi from a young age are unlikely to shed it as soon as they marry. Instead, to win male attention would remain their goal; they would go on flirting even after marriage, for "[a] husband cannot long pay those attentions with the passion necessary to excite lively emotions, and the heart, accustomed to lively emotions, turns to a new lover, or pines in secret, the prey of virtue or prudence" (Wollstonecraft 1985, 157, 111). As Wollstonecraft depicts it, the socialization of girls is inherently contradictory; it is geared toward finding a husband, yet the sort of woman so formed will be compelled to go on seeking attention from men other than her husband "for a lover the husband . . . cannot long remain" (1985, 224,

147, 167, 315). As such, girls are reared to be disloyal wives—in ambition, inclination, or imagination if not in practice.

Wollstonecraft castigates men who, like Rousseau, have designed an education for women that will make them "alluring mistresses rather than affectionate wives and rational mothers" (1985, 79). But women are not the only ones to suffer from this dispensation. Rational and virtuous men are also disadvantaged, for women are not educated to value their minds and merits. "[T]he modest merit of reasonable men has, of course, less effect on their [women's] feelings, and they cannot reach the heart by way of the understanding, because they have few sentiments in common" (Wollstonecraft 1985, 222). Thus, worthy men of moral substance would lose out to less worthy but more superficially attractive gallants (1985, 222-23). Wollstonecraft makes a similar point in her chapter on matrimony in "Thoughts on the Education of Daughters" (1989b), where one of the dangers of women marrying when they are young is that "should they be so fortunate as to get a good husband, they will not set a proper value on him; he will be found much inferior to the lovers described in novels, and their want of knowledge will make them frequently disgusted with the man" (1989b, 31).

The second prong of Wollstonecraft's critique of marriage was that feminine women make poor mothers: "the mother will be lost in the coquette" (1985, 137). Because women are not allowed to discover, let alone to develop, their rational potential and because their major aim in life is to make themselves pleasing to men, in Wollstonecraft's world, they become trivial creatures obsessed with appearances, games, and frivolity. Little more than children themselves, they are not fit to raise children, having nothing of value to pass on to them. Wollstonecraft asks rhetorically, "Can [these weak beings] be expected to govern a family with judgement, or take care of the poor babes whom they bring into the world?" (1985, 83, 119, 298, 313, 315). Socialization effectively incapacitates women for their important role as the child's first educator. This model of femininity particularly threatens the mother-daughter relationship because women trained as coquettes feel rivalry with, rather than friendship for, their maturing daughters (Wollstonecraft 1985, 137). Wollstonecraft thus shares Rousseau's premise about the central role women play as first educators of their children but develops vastly different recommendations for women's education from this starting point. She states that if society were to take this role seriously, it should produce women equal to this task (1985, 138-39).

Just as marriage and motherhood are duties for women, so Wollstonecraft believes that marriage and fatherhood are men's duties (1985, 249, 254).[8] Yet the influence of rational husbands alone would be minimal, "for unless

VINDICATION

OF THE

RIGHTS OF WOMAN:

WITH

STRICTURES

ON

POLITICAL AND MORAL SUBJECTS.

By MARY WOLLSTONECRAFT.

LONDON:

PRINTED FOR J. JOHNSON, N° 72, ST. PAUL'S CHURCH YARD.

1792.

Title page from a 1792 edition of Vindication of the Rights of Woman *by Mary Wollstonecraft.*

a mother concur, the father who restrains will ever be considered a tyrant" (Wollstonecraft 1985, 315). If women are more broadly educated, they would be better placed to carry out their educative duties as parents and to cooperate with men in this role. Part of Wollstonecraft's defense of female emancipation, therefore, consists of arguing that freedom, equality, and education would make women better mothers. As Coole says, Wollstonecraft "supplements her rights argument with an appeal to social utility" (Coole 1988, 124).

MARRIAGE AS FRIENDSHIP

Wollstonecraft's twin arguments about making women better wives and better mothers are mutually reinforcing, for she believes that if men and women marry by choice and for companionship, the husband is more likely to be at home and to be a better father to his children. Conversely, if women marry for friendship, coquetry and flirtation would not become a way of life. Not compelled to seek male approval and adoration, they could become dedicated wives and mothers. Wollstonecraft draws this portrait of friendly, rational family life when she writes, "The father of a family will not then weaken his constitution and debase his sentiments by visiting the harlot, nor forget, in obeying the call of appetite, the purpose for which it was implanted. And the mother will not neglect her children to practise the arts of coquetry, when sense and modesty secure her the friendship of her husband" (Wollstonecraft 1985, 89, 159, 254). Under current arrangements, however, women "do not seek to obtain a durable interest in their [men's] hearts, or to become the friends of the fellow-creatures who find amusement in their society" (Wollstonecraft 1985, 80). The way women are socialized "prevent[s] love from subsiding into friendship" (Wollstonecraft 1985, 115), yet "the noble mind that pants for and deserves to be respected" by a husband will never accept "[f]ondness [a]s a poor substitute for friendship" (Wollstonecraft 1985, 112). As these passages suggest, Wollstonecraft believes that if women are educated, allowed to expand their capacity for reason, and given greater freedom, independence, and choice, then marriage could become more like the classical notion of higher friendship: "When women are once sufficiently enlightened to discover their real interest, on a grand scale, they will, I am persuaded, be very ready to resign all the prerogatives of love, that are not mutual . . . for the calm satisfaction of friendship, and the tender confidence of habitual esteem" (1985, 205, 288).

A marriage suffused with "calm satisfaction" would liberate its partners from petty jealousies and allow them to channel their energies outward to the fulfillment of their duties (Wollstonecraft 1985, 288). Although such a relationship might not offer romantic love's grand passion and high excitement, the type of care it offers is precious: Wollstonecraft claims that when the passion of romance subsides into friendship there develops a "tender intimacy, which is the best refuge from care; yet is built on such pure, still affections" (1985, 224). Thus young people contemplating marriage should "look beyond the present moment, and try to render the whole of life respectable, by forming a plan to regulate friendship which only death ought to dissolve" (Wollstonecraft 1985, 167). A freer, more rational approach to marriage would produce stronger marriages because the people in them would be partners, indeed friends, who would value one another for their virtues of character rather than their physical beauty, status, wealth, or femininity or masculinity. "A man, or a woman, of any feeling, must always wish to convince a beloved object that it is the caresses of the individual, not the sex, that are received and returned with pleasure; and, that the heart, rather than the senses, is moved" (1985, 199).

Wollstonecraft concedes that if women had a proper education and could develop their reason and attain independence, they might not marry at all, but could still live happy, fulfilled lives (1985, 117). This signals that her aim is not simply to make women capable of more informed choices about who and why to marry but to give them the freedom to choose whether to marry at all. She observes that while the duty of motherhood calls most women by virtue of religion and reason, "women of a superior cast have not a road open by which they can pursue more extensive plans of usefulness and independence" (1985, 259). Nonetheless, she believes that the development of reason brings a clearer appreciation of, and capacity to carry out, one's duties: "the more understanding women acquire, the more they will be attached to their duty—comprehending it" (1985, 88, 91, 101, 103, 156, 160-61). This conviction, combined with her belief that motherhood is a natural duty for most women,[9] makes it unlikely that she envisages the majority of women remaining single.

It is important to underline what it means to impute to Wollstonecraft the belief, so typically associated with John Stuart Mill, that marriage should be modeled along the lines of higher friendship. It does not amount to claiming simply that Wollstonecraft recommends married partners to be fond of one another or to choose one another on the basis of character rather than status or wealth. Such recommendations had been made before Wollstonecraft; indeed, Rousseau thought love should be the foundation of marriage and family life. Earlier women writers, such as Mary Astell and Christine de Pisan had also pointed to the value of mutual affection in marriage. What distinguishes Wollstonecraft's position from these and brings it into line with the classical notion of friendship is her emphasis on equality between the marriage partners. By contrast, de Pisan[10] and Astell[11] accept that obedience is part of women's role in marriage while Rousseau, notwithstanding his claims about gender equality, urges women to submit to their husbands, even when they act unjustly (Rousseau 1966, 333). Wollstonecraft does not counsel wifely obedience just as Aristotle would not have talked about one partner in a higher friendship obeying another. When parties relate to one another as equals in a friendship, the language of obedience becomes obsolete.

Arbitrary Power

It seems surprising that in dedicating her *Vindication of the Rights of Woman* to the French statesman Talleyrand, Wollstonecraft expresses the hope that "marriage may become more sacred; your young men may choose wives from motives of affection, and your maidens allow love to root out vanity" (1985, 88). What unites the grand event of the French Revolution with the question of marriage and romance is the phenomenon of arbitrary power. Wollstonecraft, as a liberal, despises this form of power (1985, 99fn5, 107, 127, 143). As a liberal, she believes that if one human is to exercise power legitimately over another, such power must be based on rational consent. With the French Revolution, Wollstonecraft thinks that arbitrary power had begun to be expunged in the public sphere.[12] She insists, however, that before reason could spread and foster social progress, arbitrary power has to be eradicated in the household, too. "[T]yrants of every denomination, from the weak king to the weak father of a family . . . are all eager to crush reason. . . . Do you not act a similar part when you force all women, by denying them civil and political rights, to remain immured in their families groping in the dark?" (1985, 87).

As both genders are capable of reason, husbands' immense social power over their wives has no substantive basis. Hence Wollstonecraft's question: "Who made man the exclusive judge, if woman partake with him of the gift of reason?" (1985, 87). However, she does not conclude from this that men possess a monopoly on arbitrary power in the household. While women's socialization renders them weak and dependent, it does not render them helpless. Wollstonecraft exposes the dark side of women's enforced weakness by showing how it encourages them to abuse whatever power they can. Denied power through official, open avenues, they pursue it in clandestine ways, becoming sinister, calculating, and deceptive. In contrast to Rousseau's claim that "[c]unning is the natural gift of woman" (Rousseau 1966, 334), Wollstonecraft believes that women's inferiority to men—legally, economically, socially, physically, and psychologically—creates creatures who resent and resist their helplessness and who will resort to whatever means available to exercise power over others. "[T]his exertion of cunning is only an instinct of nature to enable them to obtain indirectly a little of that power of which they are unjustly denied a share; for, if

women are not permitted to enjoy legitimate rights, they will render both men and themselves vicious to obtain illicit privileges" (Wollstonecraft 1985, 89, 83-84, 111, 125-26, 257, 282, 288, 318).[13] Hence her clarification that "[w]hen therefore I call women slaves, I mean in a political and civil sense; for indirectly they obtain too much power, and are debased by their exertions to obtain illicit sway" (1985, 286).[14]

When refused power in any larger sense, women become tyrants in small matters. As they are forced to obey without being given any reason for their subjection, so they will compel others to conform to their will. "Powerless" wives tyrannize over children and servants (Wollstonecraft 1985, 135, 159).[15] Women who are forced to resort to arbitrary power are dangerous models for their children, for future citizens grow up in households witnessing the very power that liberals seek to expel from the public realm. Under the current conditions of marriage then, arbitrary power circulates between men and women and throughout the household, and the scourge of arbitrary rule is passed from generation to generation via household dynamics that form personalities unaccustomed to the possibility of free, rational and equal exchange among individuals.

Wollstonecraft's ideal of marriage as friendship would bring this situation to an end. If marriage united individuals as one another's equals and whose choice to live together is based on respect for one another's characters, children would grow up in quite a different domestic world. This would be an environment more conducive to the development of the virtues citizens need. Wollstonecraft suggests that the generation of good citizens begins at home, through children witnessing equal, rational relations between their parents and then having a good education to formalize these principles.[16] As she says, "If children are to be educated to understand the true principle of patriotism, their mother must be a patriot" (1985, 86). The political virtues of respect and affection for one's fellow citizens begin in the household: "if you wish to make good citizens, you must first exercise the affections of a son and brother . . . for public affections as well as public virtues, must ever grow out of private character. . . . Few, I believe, have had much affection for mankind, who did not first love their parents, their brothers, sisters and even the domestic brutes, whom they first played with. The exercise of youthful sympathies forms the moral temperature; and it is the recollection of these first affections and pursuits that gives life to those that are afterward more under the direction of reason" (Wollstonecraft 1985, 279).[17] In contrast then to Plato's famous suggestion in *The Republic* that particular family affection competes with the general love of the whole, Wollstonecraft believes that the love which begins in the family can expand to encompass one's fellow citizens and then humankind.

These claims about the connection between household and citizenry suggest that Wollstonecraft challenges any strong separation between the public and the private. Instead, she advocates ethical continuity between them, contending that the norms that govern the public realm should govern the private one, too. She seems to conceptualize the relationship between these two spheres as a series of concentric circles, beginning with the family and widening out to the public realm.[18] Challenging any rigid public/private separation, Wollstonecraft thinks of the family as political in four related ways: she is keenly aware that power relations circulate among household members; she is convinced that these relationships shape the sort of citizens that individuals become; she believes that relationships within the household should be reconfigured according to the same ethical ideals as govern public relations among citizens; and she believes that the quality of public life can only improve when this sort of change has occurred. As this section has shown, Wollstonecraft both recognizes the family as a fundamental political institution and extends standards of justice to life within it. As such, the challenge Okin poses requires liberals to go back to Wollstonecraft's work in thinking about future directions for liberalism.

SEXUALITY

The higher form of friendship that inspires Wollstonecraft's vision of reformed marriage has traditionally been thought of as existing between men only,[19] and its pleasures were not supposed to include sexual intimacy. This could help to explain why Wollstonecraft has trouble integrating corporeal love into the ideal of marriage modeled along the lines of friendship. This is not to suggest that she denies the sexual dimension of personality; on the contrary, her discussions of modesty and its role in directing and controlling sexual desire testify to its presence.[20] Nor does she underestimate the role sexual desire might play in a love relationship: rather, she admires the Danish practice of giving engaged couples considerable liberty in their courtship. Because young women are under the rule of neither father nor husband during this interregnum, she describes it as "the only period of freedom and pleasure that the women enjoy" (1987, 172). Such pleasure is often sexual: "the intimacy often becomes very tender: and if the lover obtain the privilege of a husband, it can only be termed half by stealth, because the family is wilfully blind. It happens very rarely that these honorary engagements are dissolved or disregarded . . ." (Wollstonecraft 1987, 172).[21] So while it would be misleading to say that Wollstonecraft has a prudish or negative view of sexuality, it is the case that her model of marriage as friendship seems unable to accommodate any robust and enduring sexual relationship between married partners.[22]

One illustration of Wollstonecraft's failure to incorporate ongoing sexual love into her model of marriage as friendship comes in her recommendation that, to fulfill their familial duties, mothers and fathers "ought not to continue to love one another with a passion" (1985, 114).[23] This belief seems to derive from a fear that sexual passion becomes all-consuming, distracting parents from their familial responsibilities. It also explains her conclusion that a neglected or widowed wife will always make the best mother (1985, 114, 138-39), because passionate love for her husband will not distract her from her parental duties.[24]

However, the advice that marriage partners not indulge their sexual appetites too frequently seems somewhat redundant given Wollstonecraft's many indications that sexual attraction is destined to diminish between marrieds. As she says, "Love, considered as an animal appetite, cannot long feed on itself without expiring. And this extinction in its own flame may be termed the violent death of love" (1985, 167). This echoes the imagery of an earlier vignette of a good marriage. In this scenario, the woman "secures her husband's respect before it is necessary to exert mean arts to please him and feed a dying flame, which nature doomed to expire when the object became familiar, when friendship and forbearance take place of a more ardent affection" (Wollstonecraft 1985, 138). If marriages were built on friendship or united people who can become friends, when the flames of sexual passion inevitably dwindle, something substantive would take their place (1985, 266).[25] Without the affection of friendship, marrieds eventually become bored with one another, mutually indifferent and perhaps even hostile (Wollstonecraft 1985, 114). Thus it seems that in the sort of companionate marriage she encourages, friendship and sexual desire are not ultimately compatible, let alone mutually strengthening.[26] As she writes, "Friendship is a serious affection; the most sublime of all affections, because it is founded on principle and cemented by time. The very reverse can be said of love. In a great degree, love and friendship cannot subsist in the same bosom; even when inspired by different objects they weaken or destroy each other, and for the same objects can only be felt in succession. The vain fears and fond jealousies, the winds which fan the flame of love / . . . are both incompatible with the tender confidence and sincere respect of friendship" (1985, 167-68).

Had Wollstonecraft lived longer, and had her marriage to William Godwin flourished, she might have offered further and perhaps different reflections on the place of sexuality in friendly marriages.[27] However, her untimely death challenges those who wish to take Wollstonecraft's thinking forward to incorporate robust and enduring sexual love into the model of marriage as friendship.

Such speculation about the direction of Wollstonecraft's thought raises the question of whether she adhered to the ideal of marriage as friendship outlined here throughout her career. It could be argued that the bleak depiction of marriage and heterosexual relations in general in her unfinished novel *Maria, or the Wrongs of Woman* (1975) suggests that she had been in the process of abandoning this ideal as naive and untenable. In that work, Maria Venables tries valiantly to become friends with her husband George, but her efforts founder on his cold indifference.[28] Discussing Maria's later relationship with Darnforth, Claudia Johnson argues that these "episodes finally judge male culture to be so corrupt as to make affective reciprocity between the sexes impossible" (Johnson 1995, 65). She concludes that "the emancipated, sturdy, purposive, mutually respecting, and rationally loving couple Wollstonecraft spent her career imagining is, finally, a female couple" (1995, 69). One response to the challenge Johnson's reading poses would be to delimit the relevance of the ideal of marriage as friendship by attaching it only to Wollstonecraft's *Vindication of the Rights of Woman* (1985). Periodizing the argument in this way does not threaten the claim that she preceded Mill in challenging the public/private separation and in adducing an ideal of marriage as friendship. However, if Wollstonecraft "outgrew" this ideal, how can it be relevant for contemporary liberals?

Several considerations are relevant here. Firstly there is the issue of sources; the ubiquitous difficulties of interpretation are multiplied when the writings being analyzed are unpublished, let alone unfinished. It is therefore difficult to identify the definitive logic of *Maria*, let alone to see it as superseding Wollstonecraft's position in her published writings. Secondly, because the ideal of marriage as friendship is predicated on gender equality, it is problematic to use material from *Maria* to discredit it. The protagonist's situation, incarcerated by her husband in an asylum and forcibly separated from her child, dramatizes women's structural inequality, and it is hard not to interpret her encounter with Darnforth in that light. Theirs is hardly the equal, freely chosen, and rational relationship the ideal of marriage as friendship embraces. Finally, if Johnson is right to detect a lesbian theme emerging in this work, then Wollstonecraft is effectively reinstituting the public/private separation she has earlier deconstructed. Nothing in *Maria* retracts Wollstonecraft's earlier insistence on the need for women to exercise the same rights as men in the public sphere; if anything, this work is more vociferous about the urgency of this. However, if free and equal private relations between the genders are as impossible as Johnson suggests, then different norms and dynamics must govern the realms of the public and private. On this reading, Wollstonecraft would fall into line with the separation of the spheres that has dominated liberal thinking.[29]

PAST AND FUTURE

Although the idea of modeling marriage along the lines of the classical notion of higher friendship is typically associated with John Stuart Mill, this ideal is present in Mary Wollstonecraft's best-known work, her *Vindication of the Rights of Woman* (1985). Accompanying her attack on the structural inequalities of marriage is an image of marriage modeled on the lines of higher friendship and based on equality, choice, complementarity, mutual esteem, and concern for character. This model for the reform of marriage highlights her comprehensive liberalism, for Wollstonecraft applies the values that liberals believe should govern the public realm, such as equality, autonomy, consent, reciprocity, and the diminution of arbitrary power, to the putatively private world of love, romance, and family life. Those who characterize the liberal tradition as perpetuating a strong distinction between public and private spheres thus overlook her feminist contribution to liberalism, which was made in the century prior to Mill's. Attention to this aspect of Wollstonecraft's thought should lead us to recount the history of liberalism in a slightly different way.

However, appreciating this aspect of Wollstonecraft's work has more than a retrospective relevance. Those who contend that in order for liberal political theory to move forward, the political nature of family relations must be taken seriously can return to her writing to find the beginnings of such a liberalism of the future. Liberals agreeing with Mary Shanley that "one of the aims of the liberal polity should be to promote the conditions which will allow friendship, in marriage and elsewhere, to take root and flourish" (Shanley 1981, 244) can also return to Wollstonecraft for assistance in this project. More generally, however, Wollstonecraft's model of marriage as friendship is valuable because it allows us to imagine how liberal values might be furthered without increasing the domination of the social contract model of human relations.[30]

Notes

1. Aristotle is an important source for this notion of higher friendship—see his *Nicomachean Ethics,* Books 8-9 (Aristotle 1980). Montaigne's essay on friendship (Montaigne 1965, 195-209) is another source.

2. Indeed, Jean Grimshaw claims that Wollstonecraft, "despite her own extremely difficult and unhappy experiences of marriage and childbearing, did not really ask questions about the institution of marriage as such" (Grimshaw 1986, 11).

3. This tendency is discussed in G. Davis, B. Sullivan, and A. Yeatman (1997).

4. Charles Taylor is just one example of political theorists who call for the recovery of a richer and more nuanced understanding of liberalism (Taylor 1996, 9; 1997, 287).

5. Rousseau's depiction of women's duties culminates in the claim that "the genuine mother of a

family is no woman of the world, she is almost as much of a recluse as the nun in her convent" (Rousseau 1966, 350).

6. As Catriona McKenzie notes, Wollstonecraft believes that it is possible to accept Rousseau's premises without accepting his conclusions (McKenzie 1993, 51).

7. This theme is explored further in *Maria or the Wrongs of Women* (1975), Wollstonecraft's work of fiction that was unfinished when she died.

8. See Karen Green (1995, 97). Wollstonecraft's distress at the thought that her first daughter might "never experience a father's care or tenderness" (Wollstonecraft 1987, 158) seems genuine, although its inclusion in a letter to the father, Gilbert Imlay, could also be designed to remind him of his parental duties.

9. Yet as Claudia Johnson says, for Wollstonecraft, "[t]he duties of maternity are striking precisely for what they do not signify: they are not binding upon all women, and they do not block women from participating in civic life any more than the equally important duties of fatherhood customarily inhibit men's circulation in the public sphere" (Johnson 1995, 48).

10. See *The Treasure of the City of Ladies* (de Pisan 1985) and *The Book of the City of Ladies* (de Pisan 1983). In the latter de Pisan writes, "And you ladies who are married, do not scorn being subject to your husbands" (1983, 255). As Green says, the noble woman's role involved obedience to her husband (Green 1995, 37). She draws a parallel between de Pisan's sexual and political ethics; both involve respect for authority and taking one's place in a just patriarchy (Green 1995, 42).

11. Although Astell wants marriage to become a more reasonable and friendly relationship, she does not see it as a partnership of equals. Women must still obey their husbands although in doing so they should be obeying the command of reason rather than arbitrary dictates (Astell 1986, 116). She also argues that women who suffer in this world because they are women will be rewarded in the next (1986, 128, 110, 112).

12. Even though it was not a republic, Wollstonecraft observes considerable freedom from arbitrary power in Norway: "the farmers not fearing to be turned out of their farms, should they displease a man in power, and having no vote to be commanded at an election for a mock representative, are a manly race" (Wollstonecraft 1987, 102). She describes the people in Denmark and Norway as "the least oppressed people of Europe" partly because they can freely discuss ideas "without fearing to displease the government" (1987, 105).

13. In a letter from Denmark, she continues to "harp on" to Imlay about the reciprocal exercise of arbitrary power in unequal marriages (Wollstonecraft 1987, 171).

14. My argument about women's exercise of arbitrary power differs from Moira Ferguson's interpretation. Ferguson claims that Wollstonecraft "cannot see that flirting and vanity could have a positive dimension, could sometimes be deployed by these very women . . . as devious ways of assuming a measure of power. Wollstonecraft, instead, sees the trope of the coquette, for example, as exclusive evidence that women accept their inferiority" (Ferguson 1992, 90). However, Ferguson's later claim that "this condition of subjugation provokes women into the flirtatious behaviour she dislikes, but also provokes duplicitous strategies of gaining power . . . she affirms a time-honoured slave strategy and the need for resistance" (1992, 92, 93) seems to go some way to challenge her former claim.

15. Contrast this notion to her advice in "On the Treatment of Servants": "The same methods we use with children should be adopted with regard to them. Act uniformly, and never find fault without a just cause; and where there is, be positive, but not angry" (Wollstonecraft 1989, 29).

16. This aspect of Wollstonecraft's thinking is more advanced than Mill's, for he pays little attention to the place of reproduction and children in friendly marriages. He seems to assume that individuals united in this sort of marriage contribute to the general social good in a diffuse way rather than discussing how such a relationship might transmit values to children. For a fuller discussion of this, see Abbey (1997, 93).

17. This is connected with her more general promotion of the social bonds of sympathy and benevolence. Although a discussion of these is beyond the scope of this paper, it is interesting to note that she expresses a sympathy with animals that echoes this image of children learning to feel and practice affection from their relationships with animals. In a letter from Sweden she writes "I like to see animals sporting, and sympathize in their pains and pleasures" (Wollstonecraft 1987, 84).

18. Sapiro's 1996 essay, which is based on her 1992 book, also points out that Wollstonecraft collapses the public/private separation at the ethical level (Sapiro 1996, 35, 37). As she notes when discussing Wollstonecraft's view of citizenship, "Virtue is founded on sociability, an ever-expanding circle of esteem and compassion" (in Falco 1996, 35, 43).

19. Discussing "the *great philosophical and canonical discourses* on friendship," Derrida asks, "Why can

one not account for feminine or heterosexual experiences of friendship within it?" (1993, 382, 383).

20. See, for example, Chapter Seven of *Vindication of the Rights of Woman* (1985). Compare Poston (1996, 96-98). Modesty also plays a role as Wollstonecraft recalls her sexual relationship with Imlay. Writing to him she says "if I blush at recollecting past enjoyment, it is the rosy hue of pleasure heightened by modesty; for the blush of modesty and shame are as distinct as the emotions by which they are produced" (Wollstonecraft 1987, 111).

21. See, too, her description of Maria and Darnforth's mutual sexual desire in *Maria* (Wollstonecraft 1975, 50-51).

22. Cora Kaplan finds a severe and repressive attitude to sexuality in Wollstonecraft's *Vindication of the Rights of Woman* (1985) and contrasts this with the approach taken in her fictional works (Kaplan 1986, 34-50, 158-161). Green's response is that Wollstonecraft's concern is not sexuality *per se* but the reduction of women to sex objects (Green 1995, 99-100).

23. One of Wollstonecraft's observations while traveling in Northern Europe suggests why her use of the term love includes a sexual component. She notes with dismay that "love here is merely an appetite, to fulfil the main design of nature, never enlivened by either affection or sentiment" (Wollstonecraft 1987, 157).

24. In the light of these passages, it is difficult to accept Grimshaw's conclusion that Wollstonecraft "did not ask questions about sexuality" (1986, 11).

25. As Poston describes Wollstonecraft's view, "In the mature and virtuous marriage, passion will be of short duration—no more than six months—and it will be succeeded by its far more dependable and virtuous cousin, friendship" (Poston 1996, 91).

26. Mill's model of marriage as friendship faces a similar difficulty. If anything, Wollstonecraft's attitude toward sexuality seems more positive than his. For a discussion of the role of sexuality in Mill's view of marriage, see Abbey (1997, 92-93).

27. Describing the beginning of their sexual intimacy, Godwin says "It was friendship melting into love" (in Wollstonecraft 1987, 13).

28. "With all my attention and affectionate interest, I perceived that I could not become the friend or confident of my husband. . . . I vainly endeavoured to establish, at our fire-side, that social converse, which often renders people of different characters dear to one another. Returning from the theatre, or any amusing party, I frequently began to relate what I had seen and highly relished; but with sullen taciturnity he soon silenced me" (Wollstonecraft 1975, 93).

29. How this image of the private realm could be reconciled with the reproduction of the species is another issue.

30. This seems especially valuable in the light of Carole Pateman's arguments that the social contract had been also a sexual contract (Pateman 1988; 1989). Her argument that the social contract had included the subordination of women has, however, been challenged. In the case of Hobbes, see Slomp (1994) and of Locke, see Butler (1991).

References

Abbey, Ruth. 1997. "Odd bedfellows: Nietzsche and Mill on marriage." *History of European Ideas* 23 (2-4): 81-104.

Aristotle. 1980. *Nichomachean ethics.* Trans. David Ross. Oxford: Oxford University Press.

Astell, Mary. 1986. *The first English feminist: Reflections upon marriage and other writings by Mary Astell.* Ed. Bridget Hill. Aldershot: Gower.

Butler, Melissa. 1991. "Early liberal roots of feminism: John Locke and the attack on patriarchy." In *Feminist interpretations and political theory,* ed. Mary Lyndon Shanley and Carole Pateman. Pennsylvania: Pennsylvania State University Press.

Coole, Diana. 1988. *Women in political theory.* Brighton: Wheatsheaf Books.

Davis, G., B. Sullivan, and A. Yeatman, eds. 1997. *The new contractualism?* Melbourne: Macmillan.

Derrida, Jacques. 1993. "Politics of friendship. *American Imago* 50 (3): 353-91.

Falco, Maria J., ed. 1996. *Feminist interpretations of Mary Wollstonecraft.* University Park: Pennsylvania State University Press.

Ferguson, Moira. 1992. "Mary Wollstonecraft and the problematic of slavery." *Feminist Review* 42: 82-102.

Friedman, Marilyn. 1993. "Feminism and modern friendship." In *Friendship: A philosophical reader,* ed. Neera Kapur Badhwar. Ithaca: Cornell University Press.

Green, Karen. 1995. *The woman of reason.* Cambridge: Polity Press.

Grimshaw, Jean. 1986. *Philosophy and feminist thinking.* Minneapolis: University of Minnesota Press.

Johnson, Claudia L. 1995. *Equivocal beings.* Chicago: University of Chicago Press.

Kaplan, Cora. 1986. *Sea changes: Essays on culture and feminism.* London: Verso.

McKenzie, Catriona. 1993. "Reason and sensibility: The ideal of women's self-governance in the writings of Mary Wollstonecraft." *Hypatia* 8 (4): 35-55.

Mendus, Susan. 1989. "The marriage of true minds: The ideal of marriage in the philosophy of John Stuart Mill." In *Sexuality and subordination,* ed. S. Mendus and J. Rendall. London: Routledge.

Montaigne, Michel de. 1965. *Essays.* Trans. John Florio. London: Dent.

Nussbaum, Martha. 1996. "The sleep of reason." *The Times Higher Education Supplement,* 2 February, 17-18.

Okin, Susan Moller. 1989. "Humanist liberalism." In *Liberalism and the moral life,* ed. N. L. Rosenblum. Cambridge: Harvard University Press.

Pateman, Carole. 1988. *The sexual contract.* Stanford: Stanford University Press.

———. 1989. *The disorder of women.* Stanford: Stanford University Press.

de Pisan, Christine. 1983. *The book of the city of ladies.* Trans. Earl Jeffrey Richards. London: Picador.

———. 1985. *The treasure of the city of ladies.* Trans. Sarah Lawson. London: Penguin.

Poston, Carol H. 1996. "Mary Wollstonecraft and 'the Body Politic'." In *Feminist interpretations of Mary Wollstonecraft,* ed. M. J. Falco. University Park: Pennsylvania State University Press.

Rossi, Alice S., ed. 1970. *Essays on sex equality.* Chicago: University of Chicago Press.

Rousseau, Jean Jacques. 1966. *Emile.* Trans. B. Foxley. London: Dent.

Sapiro, Virginia. 1992. *A vindication of political virtue: The political theory of Mary Wollstonecraft.* Chicago: University of Chicago Press.

———. 1996. "Wollstonecraft, feminism, and democracy: 'Being Bastilled'." In *Feminist interpretations of Mary Wollstonecraft,* ed. M. J. Falco. University Park: Pennsylvania State University Press.

Shanley, Mary Lyndon. 1981. "Marital slavery and friendship: John Stuart Mill's 'The subjection of women'." *Political Theory* 9 (2): 229-47.

Slomp, Gabriella. 1994. "Hobbes and the equality of women." *Political Studies* 42 (3): 441-52.

Taylor, Charles. 1996. "Communitarianism, Taylor-made." *Australian Quarterly* 68 (1): 1-9.

———. 1997. "Liberal politics and the public sphere." In *Philosophical arguments.* Cambridge: Harvard University Press.

Tomaselli, Sylvana, ed. 1995. *The vindication of the rights of men and the vindication of the rights of woman* by Mary Wollstonecraft. Cambridge: Cambridge University Press.

Urbinati, Nadia. 1991. "J. S. Mill on androgyny and marriage." *Political Theory* 19 (4): 626-48.

Wollstonecraft, Mary. 1975. *Maria or the wrongs of woman.* Ed. Moira Ferguson. New York: W. W. Morton.

———. 1985. *Vindication of the rights of woman.* Ed. M. Brody. London: Penguin.

———. 1987. *A short residence in Sweden.* Ed. Richard Holmes. London: Penguin.

———. 1989a. "On the treatment of servants." In *The works of Mary Wollstonecraft,* ed. Janet Todd and Marilyn Butler. Vol. 4. London: William Pickering.

———. 1989b. "Thoughts on the education of daughters." In *The works of Mary Wollstonecraft,* ed. Janet Todd and Marilyn Butler. Vol. 4. London: William Pickering.

Jenny Davidson (essay date winter 2000)

SOURCE: Davidson, Jenny. "'Professed Enemies of Politeness': Sincerity and the Problem of Gender in Godwin's *Enquiry Concerning Political Justice* and Wollstonecraft's *A Vindication of the Rights of Woman*." *Studies in Romanticism* 39, no. 4 (winter 2000): 599-615.

[*In the following essay, Davidson compares Wollstonecraft's treatment of insincerity in politics and social life in* A Vindication of the Rights of Woman *with William Godwin's less gendered political arguments in* An Enquiry Concerning Political Justice.]

Wollstonecraft's *Vindication of the Rights of Woman* (1792) identifies dissimulation as a specifically female problem. Attacking modesty as the embodiment of insincerity, Wollstonecraft aligns femininity with deceptiveness and suggests that as a consequence, women have an obligation to be not less but more truthful than their male counterparts: this is the ultimate "revolution in female manners" for which she calls.[1] Her call emerges from a historical moment characterized not just by its perception of a crisis in the manners and situation of women, however, but by what was widely understood to be a crisis of sincerity in the nation at large. The breakdown of honest and open communication between men and women is linked by Wollstonecraft to other failures—of political representation, of individual rights—and Wollstonecraft's call for women to become more sincere is also part of a larger political plan. Godwin is even more explicit than Wollstonecraft about the political evils of insincerity. While Wollstonecraft attacks politeness primarily insofar as it is a tool for the oppression of women, Godwin argues that insincerity is the most stubborn obstacle to social reform and political revolution in the broadest sense.

Godwin's philosophical argument against insincerity in *An Enquiry Concerning Political Justice* (1793) may be neither so persuasive nor so practical as Wollstonecraft's gendered and openly polemical attack on politeness. Yet *Political Justice* has the virtue of taking sincerity to its logical extreme, setting up the premise that only the complete lack of reserve between individuals will guarantee absolute freedom in the political sphere. By exploring the rhetorical and cultural contexts in which Godwin's argument for truth-telling is situated, I hope to show how and why the problem of insincerity had come to be perceived by writers of the 1790s as central to questions of power and exclusion. Godwin's arguments for sincerity in *Political Justice* can be read profitably in counterpoint with a body of writing, more sympathetic to politeness, authored by Hume, the Edgeworths and others. Godwin responds quite explicitly to several of these arguments; others are written in the wake of Godwin's own defense of absolute sincerity, and with the goal of undermining such a defense and preserving thereby the social and political stability that politeness secures.

The impossibility of thinking about politeness without also considering problems posed by relations between the classes is revealed by the fact that servants (both literal and metaphorical) figure in the two most prominent examples of insincerity available to writers on either side of the politeness debate: the letter signed "your most obedient and humble servant"; and the fashionable mode of excluding visitors by asking a servant to say that one is "not at home." The topic of servants offers writers across the political spectrum a way of managing anxiety or disposing of rhetorical excess at the boundaries where masters and servants interact. In his rejection of "the notorious hypocrisy of 'I am not at home.'" Godwin deliberately foregrounds politeness as a problem not of gender but of class relations.[2] This choice proves problematic, however, as the topic of gender continues to perplex social relations in a manner that Godwin cannot address within the framework of the *Enquiry,* though I will suggest that it is thematized in *Caleb Williams* (1794). Both servitude and politeness are for Godwin antithetical to justice, yet his commitment to sincerity is ultimately undermined by his awareness that the insincerities associated with gender will prove even harder to eradicate than miscommunication between members of different social classes.

1

For *Political Justice,* deception is not simply one kind of injustice. It is rather the dominant trope for repre-senting injustice of all kinds, so that the institution of government is described most damningly as organized deception and the institution of marriage as "a system of fraud" (3.453). Truth is the best weapon against injustice and coercion alike, since insincerity is no less damaging than inequality: "Sincerity is not less essential than equality to the well being of mankind" (3.338). Godwin's opposition to institutional hypocrisy arises in part from the specific applications of hypocrisy in eighteenth-century Britain, a list which begins with the government's use of oaths to enforce religious and political conformity and goes on to include measures such as "penal statutes, and licensers of the press, and hired ministers of falshood and imposture" (3.274). Oaths are administered and publications censored, Godwin argues, so that the government can prevent truth from annihilating prejudice "by any future penetration or any accidental discovery" (a phrase that seems to describe something like Caleb Williams' discoveries about Falkland, where truth is indeed unearthed by a combination of penetration and accident and then suppressed by Falkland's subsequent manipulations of the judicial system). Godwin is especially outraged by those who want to prove "the insufficiency of democracy" by "the supposed necessity of deception and prejudice for restraining the turbulence of human passion."[3] As a matter of political obligation, Godwin wants to vindicate democracy by refuting the Machiavellian argument for manipulation or dissimulation.

Political Justice's argument for sincerity is uncompromising. Godwin is offended by all conventional insincerities, however innocuous. He objects first to the Scottish jurist Lord Kames's defense of dishonesty in the case of the custom-house oath. It had become commonplace for merchants to swear falsely that no custom was owed, and Kames justifies the false oath on the basis that as "'the oath is only exacted for form's sake, without any faith intended to be given or received, it becomes very little different from saying in the way of civility, "I am, sir, your friend, or your obedient servant."'"[4] Godwin is even more disgusted, however, by the utilitarian moralist William Paley's catalogue of "'falsehoods which are not lies; that is, which are not criminal'" in his *Principles of Moral and Political Philosophy,* widely used as a college textbook. Paley's list includes the servant who says that his master is not at home, the prisoner who pleads not guilty, and the advocate who asserts the justice of his client's cause; Paley claims that in each of these cases, "no confidence is destroyed, because none was reposed."[5]

Godwin charges that both Paley and Kames are constrained—by virtue of conservatism, conventionality, or lack of imagination—to argue that deception is ethical in certain cases. They write, after all, under a system of government in which oaths had been regularly imposed for more than a century to ensure political and religious conformity among office-holders. Godwin's characteristically inflammatory description of a government that imposes "contradictory and impracticable oaths" on its subjects, with the consequence of "perpetually stimulating its members to concealment and perjury," however, foregrounds the political imperative in a manner that the more measured analyses of Kames and Paley do not (3.20). Godwin despises the argument, advanced earlier by Swift as well as by Kames, that such oaths are conducive to political stability. Just as political oaths force men to lie about their political allegiances, Godwin argues, so "the tendency of a code of religious conformity is to make men hypocrites" (3.325). Most catastrophic of all, he concludes, are oaths administered in a court of justice: "there is no cause of insincerity, prevarication and falshood more powerful" than the practice of administering oaths in court, he claims, a practice that "treats veracity in the affair of common life as a thing unworthy to be regarded" (3.340).

Godwin's visceral dislike for hypocrisy leads him to focus on the damage lying does to a man's own character, an emphasis somewhat different from that of Kant's closely contemporary and no less uncompromising argument against lying.[6] Kant's central example is that of the well-intentioned man who lies to the murderers at his door by telling them that his friend (whom they seek, and whom he believes to be upstairs) is not at home, a lie designed to preserve his friend's life. Yet if the friend should have gone out without the host's knowledge, Kant observes, and if the murderers should subsequently find and kill him in a place they would not have otherwise searched, the well-intentioned man is liable under civil law for the consequences of his lie. Kant's point is that one should always refrain from lying, not just for prudential reasons but because truth-telling is an absolute obligation. Where Kant is concerned with the idea that "a lie always harms another," however, Godwin argues that the liar first and foremost harms himself. In keeping with this point, Godwin emphasizes the necessity for unreserved communication on personal and political topics alike, to counter the fact that in the unjust world of Britain in the 1790s, "a cold reserve . . . keeps man at a distance from man" (3.120). This reserve results both from external factors (the government's movement to suppress free speech and public meetings) and from internal prohibitions (such as the internalized ethos of chivalry that destroys both Falkland and Caleb Williams).

Domestic symptoms of reserve alarm Godwin as much as or more than political ones. *Political Justice* includes an entire chapter "Of the Cultivation of Truth," as well as an appendix addressing the specific and pressing question "Of the Mode of Excluding Visitors."[7] Godwin's best illustration of the principle of "truth in the common intercourses of life" is "the familiar and trivial case, as it is commonly supposed to be, of a master directing his servant to say that he is not at home, as a means of freeing him from the intrusion of impertinent guests" (3.148). The sheer commonness of the occurrence renders it especially pernicious, Godwin argues, and the effects of this insincerity damage visitor, servant, and master alike. The visitor can tell that the servant's answer is false and therefore "feels in spite of himself a contempt for the prevarication of the person he visits" (3.149). The argument from the servant's point of view is even stronger, since giving a false answer is personally degrading:

> Whatever sophistry we may have to excuse our error, nothing is more certain than that our servants understand the lesson we teach them to be a lie. It is accompanied by all the retinue of falsehood. Before it can be gracefully practised, the servant must be no mean proficient in the mysteries of hypocrisy. By the easy impudence with which it is uttered, he best answers the purpose of his master, or in other words the purpose of deceit. Before this can be sufficiently done, he must have discarded the ingenuous frankness by means of which the thoughts find easy commerce with the tongue, and the clear and undisguised countenance which ought to be the faithful mirror of the mind. Do you think, when he has learned this degenerate lesson in one instance, that it will produce no unfavourable effects upon his general conduct?

(3.149)

This is a new way of thinking about servants, in contrast to a certain lack of sympathy that continues to be evident in the writing of contemporaries like Wollstonecraft and Edgeworth.[8] After emphasizing the importance of frankness in the abstract, however, Godwin makes a tactical appeal to the self-interest of the master, who will surely benefit from his servants' honesty. The clincher for Godwin is that the lie is unnecessary, it being just as easy to say that one is engaged or indisposed as to give "the universally suspected answer, the notorious hypocrisy of 'I am not at home'" (3.149).

Many of Godwin's arguments for sincerity derive from a wariness about conventional language that is built into British radical and dissenting tradition. The movement against ordinary professions of insincerity came about in seventeenth-century England, when members of radical religious sects like the Quakers began to refuse to swear oaths in court or to use honorifics and titles when addressing others.[9] Evangelical reformers had argued more recently that upper-class insincerity corrupted the manners of the lower classes, to whom they set a poor example in honesty as well as in matters like card-playing and Sunday travel.[10] Decades before Godwin's radical defense of truth-telling, Richardson had identified precisely the same case—that of the master who tells his servant to say he is not at home—as especially dangerous. Unlike his morally lax contemporaries (Richardson suggests), Sir Charles Grandison "never suffers his servants to deny him, when he is at home."[11] This statement appears in the context of a discussion not of servants—though the novel treats the proper government of servants in some detail—but of politeness. The paradox of true politeness (rather awkwardly expressed by Richardson) is that Sir Charles is at once "remarkable for his truth, yet . . . unquestionably polite": "He censures not others for complying with fashions established by custom; but he gives not in to them. He never perverts the meaning of words."[12] Where Sir Charles Grandison is paralyzed (like a donkey poised between two identical and equidistant bundles of hay) by the choice between truth and politeness, however, Godwin goes relentlessly for truth.

2

It should be clear by now that the example of the servant who says his master is not at home is more equivocal than Godwin admits; one might even say that it more naturally serves to *defend* conventional language. Godwin's use of the servant example to testify against linguistic convention is directly contrary to that of Hume, for instance, who concludes his most explicit argument in favor of hypocrisy with a provocative defense of this form of excluding visitors. Unpublished during Hume's lifetime, this private letter (written to a friend who had asked whether a man should remain in orders against his conscience) opens by rejecting sincerity outright. "It is putting too great a Respect on the Vulgar, and on their Superstitions, to pique one'self [*sic*] on Sincerity with regard to them," Hume says. "Did ever one make it a point of Honour to speak Truth to Children or Madmen?"[13] By this act of exclusion, Hume suggests that truth is a privilege, not a right, and that truth-telling is often a matter of convenience. Yet insincerity is not just a privilege for the select few but an essential part of ordinary life, and Hume goes on to deplore (perhaps ironically) his own lack of religious observance: he claims to wish that "it were still in my Power to be a Hypocrite in this particular" since "[t]he common Duties of Society usually require it." After suggesting that a clergyman who swears to his religious beliefs "only adds a little more to an innocent Dissimulation or rather Simulation, without which it is impossible to pass thro the World," Hume concludes with a sly rhetorical question: "Am I a Lyar, because I order my Servant to say I am not at home, when I do not desire to see company[?]" Hume defends this formula on the grounds of its conventionality. The phrase is not meant to deceive; it is merely a matter of courtesy or of convenience, depending on how one chooses to look at it. Yet by foregrounding the example of the servant who says his master is "not at home," Hume's argument for hypocrisy challenges the contemporary consensus on how to define the word "liar." The rhetorical question "Am I a Lyar" may expect the answer no, but it also allows for a qualified yes: yes, I am a liar when I tell my

servant to say that I am not at home; indeed (as Godwin might add) I am not simply a liar but a hypocrite in the worst sense, since I farm out the dirty work to my social inferior. While Hume would hardly endorse such an argument, it exists unspoken in the space between the lines.

The "innocent Dissimulation" of religious conformity that Hume identifies as one of the "common Duties of Society" is also central to Burke's *Reflections on the Revolution in France* (1790), where established religion is far more extensively defended. Consistent with Hume's emphasis, Burke seems to care less for religious belief as such than for religious observance, since "religion is the basis of civil society."[14] He follows this statement with an extravagant claim: "In England we are so convinced of this, that there is no rust of superstition, with which the accumulated absurdity of the human mind might have crusted it over in the course of ages, that ninety-nine in a hundred of the people of England would not prefer to impiety" (186-87/8: 141). The last word is perhaps the most surprising: if the word "truth" were substituted for "impiety," this could easily be a straightforward satire on religion in the Godwinian manner. In spite of the satirical tone here, however, Burke endorses the social benefits to England of that "rust of superstition." His commitment to religious observance is motivated by a belief that human psychology depends on prejudice, which "renders a man's virtue his habit; and not a series of unconnected acts" (183/8: 138). Johnson suggests something very similar in the *Rambler* when he says that "even [the hypocrite] might be taught the excellency of virtue, by the necessity of seeming virtuous."[15]

If Burke and Godwin lie at opposite ends of the spectrum on politeness, the Edgeworths' *Practical Education* (1798) falls somewhere in between. The book addresses both cases of insincerity, the servant who says his master is not at home and the insincere subscription to a letter (the latter is also the verbal crux of the argument in Burke's *Reflections* about civility and forms of address in Price's sermon). Like Paley and Kames, the Edgeworths defend certain practices on the grounds that they are not meant to deceive. Other practices, however, they attack. At times, the book sounds as though it might have been written by Godwin, as when it identifies "Honesty is the best policy" as the best maxim in education as in life: "We must not only be exact in speaking truth to our pupils, but to every body else; to acquaintance, to servants, to friends, to enemies."[16] Yet that point is immediately qualified by the authors' refusal "to enter any overstrained protest against the common phrases and forms of politeness":

> No fraud is committed by a gentleman's saying that he is *not at home*, because no deception is intended; the words are silly, but they mean, and are understood to

mean, nothing more than that the person in question does not choose to see the visitors who knock at his door. 'I am, Sir, your obedient and humble servant;' at the end of a letter, does not mean that the person who signs the letter is a servant, or humble, or obedient, but it simply expresses that he knows how to conclude his letter according to the usual form of civility. Change this absurd phrase, and welcome; but do not let us, in the spirit of Draco, make no distinction between errors and crimes.

(1: 193, original emphasis)

The very next move of *Practical Education* is to distinguish the accouterments of convention—that is, ordinary insincerities—from the crimes associated with what the Edgeworths call the "Chesterfieldian system of endeavouring to please by dissimulation," a system that they insist (protesting perhaps a little too much) "is obviously distinguishable by any common capacity from the usual forms of civility" (1: 195). Parents must be especially careful that their children do not catch them out in the kind of insincerity that Chesterfield recommends, the Edgeworths continue, where they "[pretend] to like the company, and to esteem the characters of those whom they really think disagreeable and contemptible." Yet it is hard to imagine where in practice this line will be drawn.

Godwin's own position on politeness to friends and acquaintances is characteristically extreme. In fact, he believes the lie of being "not at home" to be unnecessary in every possible sense, since "the existence of these troublesome visitors is owing to the hypocrisy of politeness" (3.150). If we told people what we really think of them, in other words, they would no longer visit us so often! In the 1797 essay "Of Politeness," Godwin develops this argument more fully.[17] The essay opens by imagining a remark "not unfrequently heard from the professed enemies of politeness": "I dislike such a person; why should I be at any pain to conceal it? . . . I feel in myself no vocation to be a hypocrite" (337). Godwin proceeds to examine this statement with scrupulous fairness, admitting that in such cases, sincerity is sometimes simply a cloak for self-gratification. The essay makes more concessions than *Political Justice* to the dictates of self-control: after all, Godwin says, "When I refuse to vent the feeling of bodily anguish in piercing cries, as the first impulse would prompt me to do, I am not therefore a hypocrite" (338).

This does not mean, however, that we should censor our criticism of friends and neighbors in the name of kindness. Godwin balances the claims of benevolence against those of sincerity and finds in favor of the latter, specifically with regard to the proposition "that I should speak of a man's character, when he is absent, and present, in the same terms" (341). As Godwin sees it, we live under an obligation actively to criticize our neighbours, and he suggests that "[g]reat inconveniences

arise from the prevailing practice of insincerity in this respect" (342). His target here is the "commonly received rule of civilised life, that conversation is not to be repeated, particularly to the persons who may happen to be the subject of it."[18] Lifting this rule means taking a step towards justice: greater truthfulness is needed, as insincerity "corrupts the very vitals of human intercourse" (344). When Godwin asserts finally that "politeness, properly considered, is no enemy to admonition," the statement conjures up nightmares of public denunciation in the style of the Cultural Revolution (346). Yet Godwin sincerely believes that one's responsibility to correct overrides the specious obligations of politeness. For the sake of consistency, his argument against insincerity demonizes conventional politeness as a watered-down version of the hypocrisy associated with Chesterfield, an unmanly and overly pliable concession to the vanity of others.[19]

An unforeseen consequence of the revolutionary commitment to absolute sincerity (at least in Burke's hostile summaries of arguments for sincerity by Godwin and others) is that absolute sincerity can topple paradoxically over the precipice into euphemism. While theorists of sincerity openly attack the code of civility for turning language into a tool of deception, their own rhetorical practice is deceptive in a different way (or so Burke charges), relying on a highly formalized and bureaucratic language to conceal the violence of their political practice. Where radical writers argue that all conventional language is euphemistic and therefore politically dangerous, then, and that Burke defends conventional language in order to enforce a system of dissimulation and domination, Burke presses countercharges of euphemism against the revolutionary writers themselves. His condemnation of radical and revolutionary perversions of language anticipates many of Orwell's charges against totalitarianism in "Politics and the English Language" (1946). In the *Preface to Brissot's Address to his Constituents* (1794), for instance, Burke observes that when Roland addresses the people "he can no longer be direct": "The whole compass of the language is tried to find synonimes [*sic*] and circumlocutions for massacre and murder" (8: 512). Brissot's language shows a similar obscurity, Burke argues, and he accounts for the translator's difficulty with the text by pointing out that "[Brissot's] language requires to be first translated into French, at least into such French as the academy would in former times have tolerated," adding as an afterthought that "the language, like every thing else in this country, has undergone a revolution" (8: 520-21). The language of the revolution's British sympathizers is also infected with euphemism. Burke claims that British apprehensions about the thing that he insists on denominating by the brutal term "Regicide Peace" are quieted only "by totally putting it out of sight, by substituting for it, through a sort of periphrasis, something of an ambiguous quality, and describing such a connection [a peace between Britain and France] under the terms of *'the usual relations of peace and amity.'"*[20] This blandness is more truly violent than even the bloodiest account of the war could be; Burke charges that the revolutionaries use insipid, impersonal language to disclaim any responsibility for violence.

Burke's attack on euphemism brings to mind Bataille's observation that "[c]ommon language will not express violence."[21] Bataille argues that de Sade's meticulous blow-by-blow accounts of torture are composed paradoxically in the language not of torturer but of victim: "As a general rule the torturer does not use the language of the violence exerted by him in the name of an established authority; he uses the language of the authority, and that gives him what looks like an excuse, a lofty justification." Yet while the language of Godwin's *Political Justice* certainly tends toward lofty justification, Godwin is no less desirous than Burke of avoiding euphemism. Near the beginning of *Political Justice,* Godwin quotes quite seriously the famous description from *Gulliver's Travels* of the causes of war, citing this catalog of violence as though it is straight political philosophy rather than satire.[22] Godwin applies the passage as a literal demonstration of the thesis that if violence were always described in factual language, war would simply disappear.

This trick of defamiliarization—an inherently satirical move that is often associated with Swift, Burke, and the generally conservative genre of satire—turns out to be almost as popular with radical writers as with writers defending the status quo. Elizabeth Inchbald uses a similar tactic against the authority of conventional language in *Nature and Art,* whose hero (a noble savage raised in Africa by his British father) "would call *compliments, lies*—*Reserve,* he would call *pride*—*stateliness, affectation*—and for the monosyllable *war,* he constantly substituted the word *massacre.*"[23] Inchbald and others thus charge Burke with being saturated in the common forms of language—a language that relies on conventional phrases like "defensive war" to mask rampant national aggression—even as he levels against the radicals a complementary charge that violence permeates their ordinary language.

3

It is virtually a commonplace to observe that the confrontation between Burke and Wollstonecraft over the morality of the French Revolution concerns manners as much as politics or morals. Neither Burke nor Wollstonecraft believes that manners can be considered in isolation, and for both writers, the term "manners" works as shorthand for a larger system of power. In the end, manners reflect moral objectives: just as the construct of female modesty is designed to secure female

virtue, so manners more generally secure moral or political ideals. Where Burke wants to strengthen the security of manners, Wollstonecraft calls for a revolution in manners that will transform relations between men and women by rescuing the latter from the forms of modesty that promote insincerity. In response to Burke's use in the *Reflections* of the word "chivalry" to describe the inherited body of manners on which social stability depends, Wollstonecraft identifies a related phenomenon called gallantry as the single most serious threat to morality and asks for a "revolution in female manners" to counter it (5.114). Yet while Wollstonecraft objects to the status of modesty as the first and foundational female virtue, she does not wish women to abandon modesty altogether: far from it. The problem is how to separate the kind of modesty that elicits respect from men and women alike—and that is related in turn to self-respect—from its false double, a quality only mistakenly called modesty. False modesty forces women to deceive others as well as themselves, bestowing power on women only within a system of tyranny and dependence.

In the **Vindication of the Rights of Woman,** which targets the conduct-book model of female chastity as a "system of dissimulation" that obliges women to sacrifice the substance of morality for the show of it (5.186), Wollstonecraft argues that women have been transformed by the pressures of chivalry, gallantry, and modesty into disgusting hypocrites. Her argument against female hypocrisy is extremely effective in countering the openly gendered model of chivalry that Burke endorses in the *Reflections*. By aligning Burke with the system of dissimulation that dominates female education, Wollstonecraft explodes Burke's argument that certain kinds of hypocrisy are a good thing.[24] Wollstonecraft's attack on female modesty as a system of dissimulation is simultaneously an attack on the deceitfulness of those who, like Burke, defend a status quo built on property and propriety. Once Wollstonecraft reveals chivalry's inherent bias against sincerity and against women, she maneuvers herself into a strong position from which to refute Burke's political arguments as well. It is Wollstonecraft's feminist argument against Burke that sounds most persuasive to readers two centuries later, rather than Paine's populist political arguments or Godwin's philosophic radicalism (in Godwin's ideal world, such things as wives and families would hardly seem to exist).

Where Wollstonecraft attacks modesty as a system of dissimulation, then, Godwin attacks all forms of insincerity without quarter, on the grounds that they destroy social integrity. Godwin's arguments are in this sense more extreme than either Burke's or Wollstonecraft's. Wollstonecraft makes partial concessions to decency and therefore to modesty, just as Burke makes partial concessions to sincerity and therefore to individual rights, and these equivocations blur the edges of their confrontation, which is more than simply an all-or-nothing contest in which Burke represents decency and Wollstonecraft sincerity (or Burke order and Wollstonecraft rights). Wollstonecraft's call for a revolution in female manners is radical and ambitious. But her choice to define her work in terms of women's rights, as opposed to political rights more generally, stops her deliberately short of a full critique of political insincerity. The limits of her analysis appear even within the second *Vindication*'s central argument about reputation. Wollstonecraft is eager to replace pernicious ideas about women's sexual reputation (ideas summed up by Hume's deadpan observation in the *Enquiry Concerning the Principles of Morals* that a woman's "smallest failure" with regard to sexual fidelity is "sufficient to blast her character") with a gender-neutral model borrowed from Adam Smith, where reputation depends only on the opinion of honest men and women.[25] Most, if not all readers will be persuaded by the *Vindication* that women's sexual modesty represents a disgusting kind of hypocrisy.[26] Yet Wollstonecraft's forceful challenge to the idea that sexual modesty is more important than common-or-garden varieties of honesty—and her claim that mistaken ideas about women's sexual reputation subvert morality—are partly mitigated by her own commitment to decency or true modesty, words given new definitions in the *Vindication* but borrowed nonetheless from the bad old vocabulary of sentimental virtue.

Another problem the *Vindication* chooses not to address directly concerns the fact that in the 1790s, the reputation of men seemed to have been recently reconstructed along the very same lines as the morally destructive and inherently hypocritical ideas about women's chastity that Wollstonecraft sought to eradicate. Wollstonecraft's rejection of a morality based on women's sexual reputation is both powerful and problematic: powerful, because it constitutes the single most compelling eighteenth-century challenge to the rule of civility; problematic, insofar as the specter of women's chastity continues to haunt not just the *Vindication* but many other radical texts of the 1790s. A great deal of evidence suggests that throughout the decade, radical writers (Godwin among them) saw the tyranny of sexual reputation, far from releasing women from oppression, instead extending its sway over men as well. Wollstonecraft argues that gallantry and modesty corrupt not just the morality of women but morality in general; consequently, the particular responsibility of radical women in a time of political revolution is to effect a revolution in female manners. But if men's manners have been corrupted as well, as Wollstonecraft's analysis implies, the task of reform will be truly Herculean.

Following this clue, radical men's writing of the same period tends not to contradict the fundamentals of Wollstonecraft's analysis but to suggest that an undue degree of attention to appearances has poisoned society far more extensively than even Wollstonecraft suggests. Propelling its characters by a force that resembles sexual guilt, Godwin's *Caleb Williams* (1794) attacks the ideologies of chivalry and reputation for their effects not on women but on men. Godwin's novels contain few female characters, and most readers would agree that the concerns of actual women are no more than peripheral to either his fiction or his philosophy. Yet *Caleb Williams* is characterized by a discourse on reputation and guilt so consistently sexualized that it is hard to see how even so effective an attack as Wollstonecraft's on the ideology of chastity will relieve the oppressive weight of "things as they are." Godwin depicts in the novel the nightmarish transferal of ideas about women's chastity or sexual "spotlessness," first to the relationship between master and servant and subsequently to all relationships between the individual and the other members of the society in which he must live. All the characters in the novel, not just the story's supposed villain, are seduced by the ideology of chivalry. The flawed hero Falkland is "too deeply pervaded with the idle and groundless romances of chivalry," "the fool of honour and fame," tainted with "the poison of chivalry": his excessive love of reputation is at the root of all his subsequent crimes.[27] Falkland's secret guilt is remorselessly investigated by his servant Caleb Williams, whose curiosity about the signs of Falkland's guilt will destroy both his master and himself. Yet Caleb does not set out deliberately to destroy Falkland's reputation and pull down the edifice of chivalry. Godwin suggests instead that Caleb himself is fatally smitten with the same ideas about honor that have destroyed Falkland.

In his 1832 account of the composition of *Caleb Williams,* Godwin emphasizes the novel's likeness to the Bluebeard story. Falkland is Bluebeard, Godwin says, and Caleb Williams "the wife, who in spite of warning persisted in his attempts to discover the forbidden secret, and, when he had succeeded, struggled as fruitlessly to escape the consequences as the wife of Bluebeard in washing the key of the ensanguined chamber . . ." (353). If the likeness of the male title character to the wife in this story were not strange enough, the character of Falkland—who Marilyn Butler has plausibly argued is modeled on Burke—is also strikingly feminine. Knowledge of his own guilt causes Falkland to blush and blanch throughout the novel, and Caleb compulsively reads these physical symptoms in the manner of a jealous husband policing his wife's behavior. After one especially provoking sally of Caleb's, for instance, Falkland shudders and storms out of the room, prompting Caleb to wonder whether these signs are "'the fruit of conscious guilt, or of the disgust that a man of honour conceives as guilt undeservedly imputed?'" (118). By putting both Falkland (for his guilt) and Caleb (for his resemblance to Bluebeard's wife) in the position of women scrutinized by their husbands for symptoms of sexual transgression, Godwin depicts a world entirely governed by the gendered logic of appearances.

The implication of *Caleb Williams* is that nothing can break the tyranny of reputation. A parodic redaction of the conventional debate about virtue and reputation appears late in the novel, after Caleb's naive new friend Laura hears the rumor that he robbed his great benefactor Falkland. She refuses to hear a word of Caleb's explanation. "True virtue refuses the drudgery of explanation and apology," she says: "True virtue shines by its own light, and needs no art to set it off" (310). "And can you imagine," Caleb asks desperately, "that the most upright conduct is always superior to the danger of ambiguity?" Laura's answer is uncompromising: "Exactly so. Virtue, sir, consists in actions, and not in words. The good and the bad are characters precisely opposite, not characters distinguished from each other by imperceptible shades." The reader is meant to understand that this idealistic rendition of the argument about reputation will always fail to withstand the pressure of things as they are. When Wollstonecraft attacks modesty as an assault on morality, it is the specificity of the problem to women that lets her argue that their situation can and must be changed. Godwin's novel shows that the false logic of sexual reputation governs so many aspects of human society that all political relations have been poisoned by insincerity. Though the goal of *Political Justice* is to show that a revolution in truthfulness will change everything, *Caleb Williams* suggests otherwise: that chivalric manners are here to stay.

Notes

1. *The Works of Mary Wollstonecraft,* ed. Janet Todd and Marilyn Butler with Emma Rees-Mogg, 7 vols. (London: Chatto and Windus; New York: New York UP, 1989) 5.114, 5.265. Subsequent references are to this edition and are cited parenthetically in the text by volume and page number.

2. *An Enquiry Concerning Political Justice,* ed. Mark Philp with Austin Gee, vol. 3 of *Political and Philosophical Writings of William Godwin,* ed. Philp (London: William Pickering, 1993) 149. All citations are from Philp's edition of *Political Justice,* whose text follows the 1793 version; subsequent references are given parenthetically in the text, by volume and page number. Where relevant, I note variants from the 1796 edition, published as volume four in the same series.

3. Godwin attributes this line of argument to Machiavelli; on eighteenth-century responses to Machiavelli, see the seminal work by J. G. A.

Pocock, *The Machiavellian Moment: Florentine Political Thought and the Atlantic Republican Tradition* (Princeton: Princeton UP, 1975). Godwin's target here is not necessarily Burke, who carefully distinguishes his argument for prejudice from the justifications of manipulative and deceptive behavior in the name of power that are associated with Machiavelli.

4. Cited in *Political Justice* 3.17n. For the full context of this argument, see [Henry Home, Lord Kames], *Loose Hints upon Education, Chiefly Concerning the Culture of the Heart* (Edinburgh: John Bell and John Murray, 1781) 360-65. Kames's larger argument is that while governments should be "tender in imposing oaths," political oaths do actually lead men to support the state and may therefore be considered a good thing (365). For another important discussion of the same topic, see Jeremy Bentham, *"Swear not at all:" Containing an Exposure of the Needlessness and Mischievousness, as well as Antichristianity of the Ceremony of an Oath* (London: R. Hunter, 1817). Other writers are more concerned to expose the self-serving invocation of such arguments for opportunistic ends, as when the wicked dandy in one of Edgeworth's novels attempts to justify his extramarital affairs by a reference to the same argument: "Marriage vows and custom-house oaths he classed in the same order of technical forms,—nowise binding on the conscience of any but fools and dupes." See *Vivian* (1812), in Maria Edgeworth, *Tales and Novels,* 10 vols. (London: George Routledge and Sons, Ltd., 1893) 5: 288.

5. *Political Justice* 3.17-18n; and see William Paley, *The Principles of Moral and Political Philosophy,* 5th ed., 2 vols. (London: J. Davis, 1788) 1: 184-86. Part of Paley's intention here is to excuse or justify the behavior of Jacobites who swear loyalty oaths to a monarch and subsequently betray him; after examining what is encompassed by an oath of allegiance, Paley concludes that resistance to the king is allowed in certain cases (1: 206).

6. Immanuel Kant, "On a Supposed Right to Lie From Benevolent Motives" (1797), in *The Critique of Practical Reason and Other Writings in Moral Philosophy,* ed. and trans. Lewis White Beck (Chicago: U of Chicago P, 1949) 346-50. See also the discussion of "offences by falsehood" in Jeremy Bentham, *An Introduction to the Principles of Morals and Legislation* (London: T. Payne, 1789) 218-21. I am indebted for several of these references to Sissela Bok, *Lying: Moral Choice in Public and Private Life* (1979; New York: Vintage, 1989).

7. This section of *Political Justice* underwent extensive revision for the 1796 edition, where the ap-

pendix I discuss here was rewritten and given the new title "Illustrations of sincerity"; see Godwin, *Political and Philosophical Writings* 4.161-80. For a later discussion of lying and conventional language that treats both religious oaths and "the reply that one is 'not at home,'" see Henry Sidgwick, *The Methods of Ethics,* 7th ed. (1907; Indianapolis: Hackett, 1981).

8. Part of Godwin's optimism about servants may have derived from his lack of involvement with them. Certainly both Edgeworth and Wollstonecraft are far more despairing about the morality of servants; on women's writing and the problem of servants during this period, see the excellent essay by Mitzi Myers, "'Servants as They are Now Educated': Women Writers and Georgian Pedagogy," *Essays in Literature* 16 (1989): 51-59.

9. Christopher Hill describes the longstanding practice "of refusing to remove the hat in the presence of social superiors, or to use the second person plural to them," tracing it from late-sixteenth-century usage through Quaker practice during the English revolution to its recurrence during the French Revolution; *The World Turned Upside Down: Radical Ideas during the English Revolution* (London: Temple Smith, 1972) 198-99. For a discussion of oaths, see Hill 281.

10. See for instance Samuel Richardson, *Pamela* (1740), 2 vols. (London: J. M. Dent & Sons Ltd.; New York: E. P. Dutton & Co. Inc., 1938) 2: 400; and Hannah More, *Thoughts on the Importance of the Manners of the Great to General Society* (London: T. Cadell, 1788). Wollstonecraft is also committed to the importance of setting a good example for the servants, particularly with regard to religion: "Above all, we owe [servants] a good example. The ceremonials of religion, on their account, should be attended to" (*Thoughts on the Education of Daughters,* in *Works* 4.38).

11. Samuel Richardson, *The History of Sir Charles Grandison,* ed. Jocelyn Harris, 7 vols. in 3 (London: Oxford UP, 1972) IV, letter XXVI (2: 388).

12. Austen's satire "Jack and Alice" (1787-90) targets this habit of Grandison's: one character is found "at home as was in general the Case, for she was not fond of going out, & like the great Sir Charles Grandison scorned to deny herself when at Home, as she looked on that fashionable method of shutting out disagreable [*sic*] Visitors, as little less than downright Bigamy." See *Minor Works,* vol. 6 of *The Works of Jane Austen,* ed. R. W. Chapman (1954; Oxford: Oxford UP, 1987) 15. (Chapman mistakenly cites *Grandison* IV, letter iii; the correct reference is as above.) Insofar as Austen's

early satires are compilations of absurd contemporary shibboleths, her use of the "not at home" example—a peccadillo ridiculously exaggerated here to the level of "downright Bigamy"—seems telling.

13. *New Letters of David Hume,* ed. Raymond Klibansky and Ernest C. Mossner (Oxford: Clarendon, 1954) 83.

14. Edmund Burke, *Reflections on the Revolution in France and On the Proceedings in Certain Societies in London Relative to That Event,* ed. Conor Cruise O'Brien (1968; London: Penguin, 1986) 186; *The French Revolution, 1790-1794,* ed. L. G. Mitchell, vol. 8 of *The Writings and Speeches of Edmund Burke,* ed. Paul Langford (Oxford: Clarendon, 1989) 141. Subsequent references to the *Reflections* are given parenthetically in the text, with page numbers for both O'Brien's widely available text and the Clarendon edition; Burke's other works are cited solely in the Clarendon edition. Machiavelli also places a utilitarian emphasis on religion; for a discussion of this point, see Maurizio Viroli, "Machiavelli and the republican idea of politics," in *Machiavelli and Republicanism,* ed. Gisela Bock, Quentin Skinner, and Maurizio Viroli (Cambridge: Cambridge UP, 1990) 157.

15. Samuel Johnson, *The Rambler,* 3 vols., ed. W. J. Bate and Albrecht B. Strauss (New Haven and London: Yale UP, 1969), no. 20, 26 May 1750 (1: 113).

16. Maria Edgeworth and Richard Lovell Edgeworth, *Practical Education,* 2 vols. (London: J. Johnson, 1798) 1: 193. Subsequent references are to this edition and are cited parenthetically in the text. Referring to the phrase "honesty is the best policy," Kingsley Amis observes that "what has become a bland near-platitude was once a disrespectful paradox meaning very nearly that honesty is the best trickery, and certainly that fair dealing will get you further than any clever strategem." See Amis, *The King's English: A Guide to Modern Usage* (New York: St. Martin's Griffin, 1997) 157.

17. William Godwin, "Of Politeness," in *The Enquirer: Reflections on Education, Manners, and Literature* (London: G. G. and J. Robinson, 1797) 326-50. Subsequent references are to this edition and are cited parenthetically in the text.

18. "Of Politeness" 343. Godwin disapprovingly notes that "the writers of comedy" have "seized" upon the gap between what we say to our neighbor and what we say of him "as a rich fund of humour" (343). An important instance can be found in

Austen's *Emma,* where Emma (in the words of one critic) "violates decorum by talking *to* Miss Bates as she might have spoken *of* her"; see Patricia Meyer Spacks, *Gossip* (New York: Knopf, 1985) 165, original emphasis. For another discussion of this moment that treats the relationship between hypocrisy and social superiority, see D. W. Harding, "Civil Falsehood in *Emma,*" in *Regulated Hatred and Other Essays on Jane Austen,* ed. Monica Lawlor (London and Atlantic Highlands, NJ: Athlone, 1998) 173.

19. Edgeworth's novel *Manœuvring* makes a very similar argument, although her fiction tends to portray Chesterfieldian manipulators as quintessentially not just feminine but female; see Maria Edgeworth, *Manœuvring,* in *Tales and Novels,* esp. 5: 98, 5: 130.

20. *First Letter on a Regicide Peace* 10: 277, original emphasis. Burke may have in mind Thucydides' account of similarly corrupt and self-serving linguistic phenomena in a time of civil war; see *History of the Peloponnesian War,* trans. Rex Warner (London: Penguin, 1972) 242. For a brief but suggestive discussion of "totalitarian euphemism," see David Bromwich, *Disowned by Memory: Wordsworth's Poetry of the 1790s* (Chicago and London: U of Chicago P, 1998) 84.

21. Georges Bataille, *Eroticism,* trans. Mary Dalwood (1962; London and New York: Marion Boyars, 1987) 186-87; and see also Gilles Deleuze, *Masochism: An Interpretation of Coldness and Cruelty,* trans. Jean McNeil (New York: George Braziller, 1971) 16-17.

22. Godwin, *Political Justice* 3.7; and see Jonathan Swift, *Gulliver's Travels,* vol. 11 of *Prose Works,* ed. Herbert Davis et al. (Oxford: Basil Blackwell, 1959) 246.

23. Elizabeth Inchbald, *Nature and Art,* 2 vols. in 1 (London: G. G. and J. Robinson, 1796; Oxford and New York: Woodstock Books, 1994) 1: 81, original emphasis.

24. Burke's own defense of hypocrisy in the abstract depends on the counterweight of a sustained attack on revolutionary hypocrisies; like all defenders of hypocrisy, Burke only wants to keep certain types. For specific attacks on revolutionary hypocrisy, see Burke, *Reflections* 155/8: 119, 204-5/8: 154, 247/8: 189.

25. See David Hume, *An Enquiry Concerning the Principles of Morals,* in *Enquiries Concerning Human Understanding and Concerning the Principles of Morals,* ed. L. A. Selby-Bigge, 3rd ed., rev. P. H. Nidditch (1975; Oxford: Clarendon, 1994) 238-39. For an important discussion of

Wollstonecraft's argument about reputation, see Carol Kay, "Canon, Ideology, and Gender: Mary Wollstonecraft's Critique of Adam Smith," *New Political Science* 15 (1986): 63-77.

26. Wendy Shalit's controversial recent book on modesty disagrees vehemently with Wollstonecraft's arguments in the *Vindication*; see *A Return to Modesty: Discovering the Lost Virtue* (New York: Simon and Schuster, 1999) 111.

27. William Godwin, *Things As They Are; or The Adventures of Caleb Williams,* ed. Maurice Hindle (Harmondsworth: Penguin, 1988) 101, 106, 336. Godwin's own attitude to chivalry is curiously ambivalent. See especially the discussion of "the mixed and equivocal accomplishments of chivalry," in *Political Justice* 3.253; and the nostalgia of *St Leon,* ed. Pamela Clemit, vol. 4 of *Collected Novels and Memoirs of William Godwin,* ed. Mark Philp (London: William Pickering, 1992) 361.

Lisa Plummer Crafton (essay date summer 2000)

SOURCE: Crafton, Lisa Plummer. "'Insipid Decency': Modesty and Female Sexuality in Wollstonecraft." *European Romantic Review* 11, no. 3 (summer 2000): 277-99.

[*In the following essay, Crafton explores Wollstonecraft's attitude toward female sexuality and her condemnation of artificial decorum and propriety in* A Vindication of the Rights of Woman.]

> Modesty must be equally cultivated by both sexes or it will ever remain a sickly hothouse plant whilst the affectation of it, the fig leaf borrowed by wantonness, may give a zest to voluptuous enjoyments.
>
> > Mary Wollstonecraft, *A Vindication of the Rights of Woman*

> And does my Theotormon seek this hypocrite modesty!
> This knowing, artful, secret, fearful, cautious, trembling hypocrite.
>
> > William Blake, *Visions of the Daughters of Albion*

> Modest Concealments please a Lover's Eye
> The Charms you hide, his Fancy will supply.
>
> > Thomas Marriott, *Female Conduct*

"The finest bosom in nature is not so fine as what imagination forms." With these words, Dr. Gregory, in giving *A Father's Legacy to His Daughters* (1774), typifies the kind of legacy of hypocrisy that paternalistic writers of the eighteenth century offered to all of whom Blake called the "daughters of Albion." Gregory's text parallels Thomas Marriot's *Female Conduct*

(1759) in representing a cultural model of what we might call an erotics of concealment. Such advice for female conduct codified the sexual mores that upheld rules of decorum, rituals that centered upon modesty and its variant related virtues: prudence, chastity, and propriety. Eighteenth and early nineteenth-century conduct book writers, in fact, seldom offered discourse on female behavior without extended attention to the virtue of modesty, and, as Yeazell's *Fictions of Modesty* points out, most novels of the period took the form of either courtship narratives with modesty as a required habit for heroines lucky enough to be in the marriage plot or gothic tales wherein the modest heroine served to enhance the villain/hero's already quite lurid aims. Within this context of sentimental fiction and conduct books for female propriety, even the first part of Mary Wollstonecraft's pronouncement in the epigraph above, her claim that modesty must be "equally cultivated by both sexes," challenges the specifically gendered nature of virtue assumed by most of eighteenth-century culture. When she further suggests that the presumed virtue is at present and will "ever remain a sickly hot-house plant," Wollstonecraft, satirized by Polwhele as the "unsex'd" female, challenges the assumption that modesty is a "natural" behavior for women, likening it instead to a flower grown under artificial conditions and diseased at that. Her extraordinary and radical demystification of this supposedly natural virtue of modesty has become a significant part of our construction of Wollstonecraft and sexuality, the topic about which she is most misunderstood. The final part of her quotation in the epigraph indicts hypocritical affectation of virtue, exposing its function as a "zest to voluptuous enjoyments." This part of her argument against propriety has been overlooked or subsumed in most critical readings of her major feminist polemic, *A Vindication of the Rights of Woman,* and the consequences for feminist studies of Romanticism have been a legacy with which we must grapple.

Critical assumptions and misreadings of Wollstonecraft's "rational feminism" with regard to female sexuality have obscured her passionate indictments of artificial decorum, what she terms "insipid decency." Wollstonecraft's exposure of the "hypocrite modesty," in fact, aligns her with Blake, whose quotation from *Visions of the Daughters of Albion*—his critique of racial, cultural, and gendered forms of slavery which was published in 1793, one year after the *Vindication*—forms the second epigraph for this essay. Like Blake's *Visions* with which it is in dialogue, Wollstonecraft's text radically represents culturally-defined virtues as diseased and perverted forms of morality. A recuperation of Wollstonecraft from exaggerated critical assumptions about her negation of passion reveals that her representation of sexuality is, in fact,

integral to and integrated with the avowedly moral aim of all of her political and cultural critiques; as she consistently argues, "Without knowledge there can be no morality."[1]

Wollstonecraft's views on female sexuality are pivotal in terms of how we interpret her program for a "REVOLUTION in female manners" (192). A reductive characterization of her text as "rationalist"—an effect of the genre of philosophical discourse as well as the text's clear emphasis on the necessity for the use of reason in becoming fully human and, conversely, the dangers of excessive passion—has created an uncomfortable positioning of Wollstonecraft within feminism, the one context in which she has consistently been a central figure.[2] Some critics feel a need to argue their way out of a corner formed by their representation of Wollstonecraft as an eighteenth-century feminist who, seemingly, vindicated women by urging them to give up erotic pleasure and sexual desire, which hardly seems a vindication. This apparent conundrum is, in fact, a product of a critical inability to accept the integration of sexuality and rationality for which Wollstonecraft's text actually argues. What is at stake in these misreadings of Wollstonecraft? The implications are significant both for the way we continue to privilege Wollstonecraft's rationalism, and thus the way we posit her participation in Romanticism, and the way we conceive women's writing in the eighteenth century to be antithetical to conceptions of a passionate, sexual female body.

Feminist critics of eighteenth-century and nineteenth-century literature have significantly contextualized the emphasis which Romantic women writers place on rationality as a consequence of and warning against a male sexual libertinism that exploits and then rejects women as sexual objects. Although many critics have pointed to this apparent disjunction between male and female Romantic writers, Anne Mellor, in her study *Romanticism and Gender* and in her edited collection *Romanticism and Feminism,* epitomizes this argument as she argues that for these writers, the powerful paeans to passion that characterize so many texts by male Romantic authors were, in fact, destructive to female autonomy, not to mention basic economic subsistence.[3] Mellor, for instance, counters Wordsworth's famous description, in the "Preface" to *Lyrical Ballads,* of good poetry as the "spontaneous overflow of powerful feelings: [that] takes its origin from emotion recollected in tranquility" (157) with the sobering revisionary point that the "overflow of passionate feeling in a female mind that has not thought long and deeply can be disastrous for the welfare of women" (*The Romantics and Us* 281). Inverting the order of the Wordsworthian maxim—it is not enough for a woman to follow her spontaneous overflows with *subsequent* deep thought, but rather she must think before she feels—Mellor's restatement functions to alert readers to the gendered nature of such pronouncements about emotion. By validating women writers' endorsement of reason, however, Mellor reproduces a one-sided view of Wollstonecraft, stating that Wollstonecraft's identification of the rational woman with the "repression, even elimination, of female desire" inaugurated a "legacy of female self-denial" (*Romanticism and Gender* 34) with which contemporary feminism is still grappling.[4] In "Pandora's Box: Subjectivity, Class and Sexuality in Socialist Feminist Criticism," Kaplan astutely summarizes the implications of this split between the rational and sexual woman for modern feminist thinking and blames Wollstonecraft for the legacy:

> It is interesting and somewhat tragic that Wollstonecraft's paradigm of women's psychic economy still profoundly shapes modern feminist consciousness. How often are the maternal, romantic-sexual and intellectual capacity of women presented by feminism as in competition for a fixed psychic space. Men seem to have a roomier and more accommodating psychic home, one which can, as Wordsworth and other Romantics insisted, situate all the varieties of passion and reason in creative tension. This gendered eighteenth-century psychic economy has been out of date for a long time, but its ideological inscription still shadows feminist attitudes toward the mental life of women.
>
> (158)

While Kaplan's assessment of some contemporary feminism's inability to accommodate passion and reason in "creative tension" is useful and, I believe, correct, it is disturbing how Wollstonecraft is credited as a spokesperson for the repression of female desire.

These misreadings of Wollstonecraft's text are not duplicated, interestingly enough, by critical analyses of Wollstonecraft's most infamous legacy, her own passion-driven life. The same critics who emphasize the text's cautions against passion note that these warnings against sexual desire in her texts do not transfer to her own life. Poovey's work is particularly important in showing that the rhetoric of the *Vindication* displays a tension between Wollstonecraft's attempts to deny that women are *essentially* sexual beings and her belief in women's need for sexual fulfillment. Even Poovey, however, misreads by overstating Wollstonecraft's denials, arguing that Wollstonecraft is so intent "to reject the prevalent stereotype of women as all sexuality that she comes close to arguing that women have no innate sexual desire at all . . . the closer we read Wollstonecraft's *Vindication,* the clearer it becomes that her defensive denial of female sexuality in herself and in women in general is just that—a defense against what she feared" (73-4). Statements like this one characterize Wollstonecraft as completely subject to the prevailing ideological fears about female appetite. Clearly, the conduct books which Wollstonecraft rejects prescribe decorous behaviors for women as a maneuver against the expression of female desire. Given this fact, Wollstonecraft's cautions about excessive female appetite reveal not so much a fear of female sexuality, as Poovey claims, but rather her keen awareness of how rhetorically difficult it is to vindicate women's right to sexual passion in a culture which already characterizes women as dominated by their appetites.[5] My argument—that Wollstonecraft's occasional rhetorical defensiveness regarding sexuality is a conscious maneuver to downplay female appetite for an audience all too eager to find evidence of Pope's statement that "every woman is at heart a rake"—is more valid when we take into account the scandal elicited by Godwin's *Memoirs,* published after her death, and the frenzied appetite with which readers relished accounts of her sexual indiscretion. Thus, Wollstonecraft's conflicting rhetorical maneuvers result from well-grounded fears, not about sexuality, but about the cultural responses to and hypocritical directives against female expression of desire. A revised reading of the *Vindication*'s argument about female sexuality proves, at the least, that Wollstonecraft's attitudes toward and representation of female sexuality are hardly the binary rejection of passion and embrace of rationality that even feminist critics, perhaps especially feminist critics, have reproduced.[6] Thus, it may be fair to say that Wollstonecraft deconstructs but fails to escape entirely what Vivien Jones calls the "normative ideology of propriety" ("Women" 180).

All these cross-currents of consideration serve to problematize any rigid identification of Wollstonecraft within Romanticism and feminism and rightly emphasize female sexuality as a central issue in coming to terms with Wollstonecraft's argument. Despite fine analyses of the tensions within the *Vindication,* however, most critics maintain Wollstonecraft's denial of female desire and distort her equally deliberate distrust and critique of restraint, prudence, and decorum. Wollstonecraft, in fact, argues that the full liberation of woman entails freedom not only from social and political restrictions that constitute virtual enslavement but also from orthodox moral codes of behavior. What emerges, in fact, from the *Vindication* is a very Blakean ethos that especially condemns modesty, and other rituals of dissimulation, and embraces instead an open and conscious nurturing of sexual desire within a framework of mutual respect between the sexes. This perception is decidedly not the one found in most critical studies of Wollstonecraft today, not even in comparative studies of Blake's *Visions* and Wollstonecraft's *Vindication.* A quick review of the ways in which scholars who have aptly linked the two writers have done so through critical misreadings of Wollstonecraft's views of female sexuality demonstrates the persistence of a critical myopia regarding Wollstonecraftian restraint and rationality.

Michael Ackland's study of Blake's *The Four Zoas* acknowledges the "conceptual links" between Wollstonecraft and Blake, but in doing so he refers to "Wollstonecraft's apparent neglect of women's sexuality" (173) and says that "Wollstonecraft's ideal woman approximates, not Oothoon, but the chaste and disciplined Jane Eyre" (172). Two studies of specific connections between Wollstonecraft's *Vindication* and Blake's *Visions* also duplicate this characterization of Wollstonecraft's text. Although Hilton offers a useful, succinct summary of the biographical relationship between Blake and Wollstonecraft and an interesting discussion of slavery as the master trope of Blake's myth, his deconstructive reading whereby Oothoon is relegated to "a figure (a figuration) of the text" (103) does not ultimately relate the poem to the agenda of cultural change to which Wollstonecraft is committed. Goslee's fine reflective study of the ambiguities of race and gender in Blake's use of the slavery trope also duplicates this reductive characterization of Wollstonecraft when Goslee argues that Blake "appears to correct Wollstonecraft" (119) by replacing her premise of universal reason with one of universal desire. Finally, Mellor emphatically avows, in her 1996 study, "Sex, Violence, and Slavery: Blake and Wollstonecraft," that "Wollstonecraft insisted on the necessity of curbing female sexual desire" and then posits Blake's celebration of open sexuality as a "direct criticism of Wollstonecraft" (363).[7]

Far from arguing the need to curb sexual desire, Wollstonecraft actually appropriates it within her rational feminism in order to indict repression as hypocrisy and ultimately perversion. Her central targets for this hypocritical perversion of natural human passion are, of course, the experts on manners, the writers of eighteenth-century conduct books. Realizing that the social norms that perpetuate female weakness are institutionalized by texts that purport to be "authorities," Wollstonecraft critiques the male-authored educational tracts for women, especially those of Rousseau, Gregory, and Fordyce, as described by the title of chapter five, "Animadversions on Some of the Writers Who Have Rendered Women Objects of Pity, Bordering on Contempt." Taking up her pen against these "glowing pens of genius," as she sarcastically refers to them, she links these female conduct manuals, referred to in chapter eight as "specious poisons" (131), to the tradition of male conduct books, associated most famously, of course, with the courtier tradition. Wollstonecraft builds on the analogy between the female and the courtier to point out that both kinds of conduct books are written for those who are completely dependant on others and who therefore must acquire "an equally artificial mode of behavior" (131).[8] Her rejection of their advice centers around these writers' reliance upon words like "decorum," "prudence" and "modesty."

Wollstonecraft must first point out that these conduct manuals ironically contradict their own doctrines in their very existence. Although these writers argue that modesty and other gendered virtues are "natural," the literature itself attests to the belief that they must be cultivated and codified for women by the writers themselves. Wollstonecraft pierces this hypocritical guise and exposes the confusion between behavior and morality central to these texts. Although her responses to Rousseau are the most well-known, her strategic exposure of the inconsistencies, immorality, and illicit voyeurism that characterize these conduct manuals is even more compelling in her treatment of Gregory's *A Father's Legacy to His Daughters*.[9] Rejecting Gregory's "advice respecting behavior" (131), Wollstonecraft explains that she entirely disapproves of his rules "because it appears to me to be beginning as it were, at the wrong end . . . without understanding, the behavior here recommended would be rank affectation" (98). In powerfully effective yet subtle rhetorical moves, Wollstonecraft's response to Gregory's text follows this trajectory: first, she invalidates the moralist's attempts to enshrine cultural, gendered virtues as "natural"; second, having proven that such virtues as modesty or prudence are, in fact, artificial, she goes on to condemn Gregory's calls for women to conceal their true affections; finally, she subtly implies an inversion of virtue/vice whereby the compensatory reward that moralists like Gregory gain from the erotics of concealment become the vice, and virtue is characterized as free and open expression of appetite. We can see this trajectory of argument in the following sections from chapter two of the *Vindication*.

First, the challenge to natural virtue:

> [Gregory] advises [women] to cultivate a fondness for dress, because a fondness for dress, he asserts, is natural to them. I am unable to comprehend what either he or Rousseau mean, when they frequently use this indefinite term. If they told us that in a pre-existent state the soul was fond of dress, and brought this inclination with it into a new body, I should listen to them with a half smile, as I often do when I hear a rant about innate elegance.—But if he only meant to say that the exercise of the faculties will produce this fondness—I deny it.—It is not natural; but arises, like false ambition in men, from a love of power.

(28)

Second, the condemnation of dissimulation:

> [Gregory] actually recommends dissimulation, and advises an innocent girl to give the lie to her feelings, and not dance with spirit . . . In the name of truth and common sense why should not one woman acknowledge that she can take more exercise than another . . . and why, to damp innocent vivacity, is she darkly to be told that men will draw conclusions which she little thinks of?—Let the libertine draw what inferences he

pleases; but, I hope, that no sensible mother will re-strain the natural frankness of youth by instilling such indecent cautions.

(28)

Finally, having set up for the inversion of virtue/vice by the phrase "indecent caution," the rejection of hypo-critical compensation and a defense of desire:

> I now allude to that part of Dr. Gregory's treatise, where he advises a wife never to let her husband know the extent of her sensibility or affection. Voluptuous precaution, and as ineffectual as absurd . . . as if it were indelicate to have the common appetites of hu-man nature.

(30, 32)

Rejecting by redefinition, Wollstonecraft finally sug-gests that Gregory's comments are "consistent with the cautious prudence of a little soul that cannot extend its views beyond the present minute division of existence" (32).[10] Gregory (and others like him) then becomes a figure for more than just a sin of omission as Wollstonecraft consistently emphasizes the narcissistic and diseased nature of such repressed moralists. Using Lord Chesterfield's *Letters* as an example, she points out the damage done by the belief that "children ought to be constantly guarded against the vices and follies of the world" (106 n.8). Wollstonecraft states that she never knew a youth educated by these "chilling suspi-cions . . . the hestitating *if* of age, that did not prove a selfish character" (106 n.8). The real culprit in this sys-tem of cautious education of children is the misguided tactic whereby one tries to substitute dogmatic abso-lutes for knowledge by experience, the kind of instruc-tion where "blind obedience[is] required" (108). As a result, Wollstonecraft asserts, parents may succeed in making children prudent but, "prudence, early in life, is but the cautious craft of ignorant self-love" (112). While, in this context, she argues that parents who force prudence upon the natural spontaneity of children are in fact crafting what will become a kind of systematic nar-cissism, Wollstonecraft makes the link between pru-dence and diseased sexuality clear. If humans are sim-ply mortal creatures—if, as she says wryly, our purpose after death is no more than to support "vegetable life and invigorate a cabbage" (109)—and our efforts of education directed toward that mortal life, she argues, "moderation in every pursuit would then be supreme wisdom; and the prudent voluptuary might enjoy a de-gree of content, though he neither cultivated his under-standing nor kept his heart pure" (109). If, however, we pursue knowledge beyond the conveniences of life, then the merely prudent one who lacks the courage to expe-rience life will never be complete: he may "avoid gross vices . . . but he will never aim at attaining great vir-tues" (110). By such oxymoronic phrases as "prudent voluptuary," Wollstonecraft insinuates that the system-

atic course of acquiring virtue results in a hypocritical posture of goodness that perverts what would be natural human appetites. A gendered system of virtue makes women especially vulnerable to this hypocrisy; linking female chastity to ill-guided prudence, she notes that "women are so often degraded by suffering the selfish prudence of age to chill the ardor of youth" (75). Such officious attention to decorous behavior leads to the de-struction not only of youthful energy but also one's genuine feelings; prudence is that which "teaches us to guard against the common casualties of life by sacrific-ing the heart" (109).

Wollstonecraft's representation of social virtue as moral vice stems from a rejection of moral absolutes in gen-eral, especially orthodox Christian precepts, and a be-lief that moral virtues must be embodied, not accepted as "precepts heaped upon precepts" (108), but rather gained "by the exertion of [one's] own faculties" (108). Utilizing a binary opposition between obedience to ab-stract virtues and an "embodied" morality, she distin-guishes between authentic modesty and humility, for example, by asserting, "Jesus Christ was modest, Moses was humble" (122). Here she sets up a dichotomy be-tween a New Testament incarnational morality versus an Old Testament theoretical and dogmatic standard of virtue, an interpretive maneuver common in radical Dissenting sects of the Revolutionary era.[11] This theo-logical distinction becomes a consistent part of her at-tack; she rejects the gendered social virtues because they are "pharisaical" (123). This label is one of her fa-vorite indictments of traditional moral categories, em-phasizing the Christian relationship between the Phari-sees and Christ, the letter versus the spirit of the law. Discounting the pursuit of reputation above all, she ex-plicitly acknowledges her use of the term in its Biblical context: "They who only strive for this paltry prize, like the Pharisees, who pray at the corner of streets to be seen of men, verily obtain the reward they seek" (34). Having applied this Biblical distinction to the pursuit of social manners, she boldly claims that for women to be-come virtuous requires, in fact, the rejection of tradi-tional orthodox moral codes. Virtue, she says, cannot simply be pursued to be "the stilts of reputation" and must not be "respected with pharisaical exactness be-cause 'honesty is the best policy'" (101).

Wollstonecraft's warnings against moral policies culmi-nates in a radical inversion of good/evil as she goes on to accuse the abstract virtues of, in fact, working in the opposite way, actually destroying innate tendencies to-ward virtue and encouraging hypocrisy and perversion, and it is in this move that she most conclusively and powerfully indicts the supposed moral discourse of the conduct manuals. With a conscious inversion of ortho-dox categories, Wollstonecraft, as Poovey has noted, in-tuits the dynamics of repression and compensation or perversion, reversing the categories of good/evil, purity/

sin. In the context of her suggestion that women's pursuit of knowledge should not differ from men's, she protests against "the absurd rules which make modesty a pharisaical cloak of weakness" (123).[12] This metaphorical image of a cloak which shields, masks, and distorts human desire and sexuality is both a symbolic and ideological indictment of the moral codes of the conduct manuals and becomes a persistent target for Wollstonecraft's exposure of diseased sexual behavior caused by the hypocritical postures used by men and women, especially under the "convenient cloke" of marriage.

Prudent voluptuaries or cautious moralists, the conduct book writers do, in fact, argue for a modesty which functions to augment male sexual desire. Rousseau, Gregory, and Fordyce—whose texts she counters at length in chapter five—all blatantly conflate modest behaviors and sexual attraction. Explaining to Sophia that what she gives up through her subservience to Emile will be compensated by being "the arbiter of his pleasures," Rousseau's *Emile* (1762) teaches woman how to "render [her] favours rare and valuable" (442-3). With more irony, Gregory, in *A Father's Legacy* (1774), confesses that what men say and what they want are two different things; recommending a perpetual reserve for women, he counsels that if men say they like a more direct woman, "trust me, they are not sincere when they tell you so" (37). Most directly, Fordyce's *Sermons to Young Women* (1766) instructs that "Modest Apparel" is a "powerful attractive" to a lover, for "we are never highly delighted where something is not left us to fancy" (1:53). Fordyce admits to what Yeazell wittily calls a "thermal model of female attraction . . . a well-insulated vessel retains the heat that a warm surface dissipates . . . the coquette would seem to have been imagined as an open fire, whose warmth is widely available and readily expended, while the modest woman was more like a dependable stove, whose regulated surface temperature might promise a higher heat within" (47).[13] Wollstonecraft acknowledges this "thermal model" when she says, "it is the immodesty of affected modesty, that does all the mischief; and this smoke heats the imagination by vainly endeavoring to obscure certain objects" (127 n.2). The desire to "obscure certain objects" is part of the erotic recompense of concealment echoed throughout the conduct manuals from Gregory's blunt statement that "The finest bosom in nature is not so fine as what imagination forms" to Moore's advice in the popular collection *Fables for the Female Sex* (1744): "The maid, who modestly conceals / Her beauties, while she hides, reveals; / Give but a glimpse, and fancy draws / Whate'er the Grecian Venus was" (62). This visual eroticism is especially clear in Marriott's *Female Conduct* (1760) whose epigraph at the beginning of this essay suggests the cultural target for Wollstonecraft's cloak metaphor: "Modest Concealments please a Lover's Eye, / The Charms you hide, his

Fancy will supply" (62). The kind of erotic concealment that these writers of the conduct books highlight belies the stated aim of the manuals, advice for virtuous and decent behavior.

Wollstonecraft's astute recognition of the erotically-charged admonitions against the expression of sexuality strongly influences her discussion of modesty; more than any other gendered virtue, she launches a clearly militant attack on it—"I here throw down my gauntlet and deny the existence of sexual virtues, not excepting modesty" (51)—and devotes a complete chapter to "Modesty—Comprehensively Considered and Not as a Sexual Virtue." The virtue so completed gendered, and eroticized, by the culture is one that Wollstonecraft attempts to reinscribe as gender-neutral, a requisite for moral character.[14] Such attempts to wrest the word away from "voluptuous men," as Yeazell suggests, were not very successful apparently because Wollstonecraft's chapter was so misunderstood as to be excerpted in popular ladies' magazines alongside the advice of Gregory that she attempts to undermine. It is no wonder then that her chapter has been misunderstood by contemporary critics as well, and we need to pay attention to her distinctions between true and false modesty, the relationship between modesty and chastity, female complicity in these behaviors, and ultimately the false morality, or "insipid decency," that produces the inversion of this virtue into vice.

At the opening of chapter seven, Wollstonecraft addresses modesty (and here, as throughout, she means the gendered female modesty ascribed to women in the social sphere) as the "sacred offspring of sensibility and reason" and as "true delicacy of mind" (121). Her style here, the use of what she would call "high-flown sentiments," makes it hard to interpret the tone;[15] in fact, many critics have completely misread this opening to the chapter. Kelly, for example, misses the text's careful discrimination between two kinds of modesty as Wollstonecraft takes pains to distinguish between that "purity of mind which is the effect of chastity" and a "simplicity of character that leads us to form a just opinion of ourselves" (121). Because the passage is so easily misunderstood, it is worth quoting in full:

> In speaking of the association of ideas, I have noticed two distinct modes; and in defining modesty, it appears to me equally proper to discriminate that purity of mind which is an effect of chastity, from a simplicity of character that leads us to form a just opinion of ourselves, equally distant from vanity or presumption, though by no means incompatible with a lofty consciousness of our own dignity.
>
> (121-2)

Kelly, in an otherwise astute understanding of the text, says that Wollstonecraft defines modesty as "that purity of mind which is the effect of chastity"; much more careful reading of the chapter demonstrates that she contrasts the first definition, associated with chastity, from an authentic "simplicity of character . . . by no means incompatible with a lofty consciousness of our own dignity," enabling us to see our strengths and weaknesses with a rational eye. Kelly's reading here is understandable; certainly, Wollstonecraft's attention to the virtue stems not just from a critique of the false, socially-defined quality but also a genuine, even evangelical belief in the importance of an authentic, Christ-like modesty as a virtue for both sexes. Critical misreadings of this quite radical distinction are pervasive and persistent; Mellor, for example, reads Blake's denouncement of "subtil modesty" (a socially-prescribed, false, pernicious, and perverted "virtue" in *Visions of the Daughters of Albion*) as a critique of Wollstonecraft, stating that Blake's false modesty is "that very rational modesty advocated by Wollstonecraft" ("Sex, Violence, and Slavery" 366), when, in fact, their indictment of such hypocrisies are the same. Reoccuring as a foundational premise throughout the chapter, her complex distinction between true and false modesty makes clear that "the regulation of the behavior is not modesty" (123-4). In fact, what "voluptuous men" argue for as the essence of modesty is "in fact its bane" (126). Thus, in her moral discourse, the definition of "simplicity of character" is the kind of authentic and valuable modesty that "teaches a man not to think more highly of himself than he ought to think" (122).[16] True virtues, as opposed to decorous behaviors, are not specific to the female sex alone as she directly clarifies when talking about the quality of reserve: "It is obvious, I suppose, that the reserve I mean has nothing sexual in it, and that I find it *equally* necessary in both sexes" (128). Rhetorically, of course, her statement that "it is obvious" only highlights that it is not and further emphasizes the importance of making critical distinctions; likewise, her acknowledgment of the link between modesty and chastity, present in that first definition of "that purity of mind which is an effect of chastity," underscores how traditional moral precepts conflate the two and usher in a kind of morality based only on female sexual purity.

Here we should clearly acknowledge that Wollstonecraft's moral vision is obviously exclusive of depraved animal appetite; the critical construction of Wollstonecraft as anti-sexual is based on what is clearly her rejection of overt expressions of lust. She warns women against being "the slaves of casual lust" (138) and, with cynicism and disgust, lashes out against those women who are "standing dishes to which every glutton may have access" (138). Yet, these heated rejections of what she sees as extreme and immodest sexual behaviors do not constitute a critique of female sexuality; on the contrary, they serve as part of a complex appropriation of sexuality and rationality, mutually nurturing each other. Rejecting the binary separation of these, she

states more emphatically, "the regulation of the passions is not, always, wisdom—On the contrary, it should seem, that one reason why men have superiour judgment, and more fortitude than women, is undoubtedly this, that they give a freer scope to the grand passions, and by more frequently going astray enlarge their minds" (110). That is, healthy passion leads to rational and moral virtue; rational thought leads one to healthy passion. Prescribed social virtues, however, have no place in this dialectic. Thus, Wollstonecraft can warn against sexual depravity and against chastity without inconsistency, saying honestly, "I doubt whether chastity will produce modesty though it may propriety of conduct" (124).[17] While she does not, of course, claim that chastity has no influence on moral character, she points out the discrepancy between stated moral absolutes and social courtship rituals which compelled women to play the game of dissimulation and suggests that in order "to render chastity the virtue from which unsophisticated modesty will naturally flow" (123), it would be necessary to make the female heart "beat time to humanity, rather than to throb with love" (123). Contextualizing sexual purity, then, within a holistic, embodied moral vision allows Wollstonecraft to use modesty as an example of the abuse of sexual virtues in general and, in particular, the abuse of sexuality inherent in the cultural institution of marriage.

It is this functional, intentional, and consistent use of modesty as a foundation for her representation of sexuality that drives the progression of Wollstonecraft's ***Vindication,*** a progression that needs to be marked carefully as the text exposes and indicts loveless marriage and mandated sexual complicity for females and reinscribes the social virtue of modesty as perversion. Asserting that modesty is itself, at the present state, destructive rather than beneficial to virtue, Wollstonecraft writes, "Modesty must be equally cultivated by both sexes or it will ever remain a sickly hothouse plant whilst the affectation of it, the fig leaf borrowed by wantonness, may give a zest to voluptuous enjoyments" (126). Here Wollstonecraft argues that the affectations of modesty actually serve to cover up the wanton desire that one refuses to express. The trope of the fig leaf—itself another image of the covering "cloak"—indicts the kind of Old Testament, Pharisaical version of shame and repression of sexuality. The image also echoes directly and reverses this passage from Moore's *Fables for the Female Sex*: "From's Eve's first fig-leaf to brocade, / All dress was meant for fancy's aid, / Which evermore delighted dwells / On what the bashful nymph conceals" (63). She, furthermore, undercuts both male and female postures of morality as she suggests that some who appear to be moral wives, who are technically "faithful to their husbands' beds" (124) are often actually the most immodest and that men who feign moral and modest behavior and yet secretly and perversely enjoy stolen moments of lewdness are much more immodest than the "immoral" libertine: "How much more modest is the libertine who obeys the call of appetite or fancy, than the lewd joker who sets the table in a roar" (125).[18]

It is significant that such erotic concealments are fostered by both men and women. While clearly indicting the patriarchal culture's insistence on the gendered systems of virtue, Wollstonecraft also adamantly emphasizes that to deny such gendered systems is also to deny a protected status; that is, she points to female complicity to these norms, most emphatically in her treatment of the artificial morality of contemporary sentimental novels.[19] Wollstonecraft singles out Richardson's narration of the plight of Clarissa Harlowe, deploring what she sees as Richardson's repetition and representation of gendered sexual systems for men and women: "When Richardson makes Clarissa tell Lovelace that he had robbed her of her honor, he must have had strange notions of honor and virtue. For miserable beyond all names of misery is the condition of a being who could be degraded without its own consent!" (72).[20] The "strange notions of honor and virtue" are, of course, the culturally-encoded ones of female virtue, vulnerable to attack by male sexual predators. But what would it mean to refuse to be "degraded without [one's] own consent"? Wollstonecraft suggests that sexual dishonor is no different from any kind of dishonor, denying the protected position of sexual virtue as somehow separate and judged differently than other acts of virtue. She directly confronts this issue of the double standard of reputation in chapter eight, "Morality Undermined by Sexual Notions of the Importance of a Good Reputation." Significantly, again using the trope of the covering cloak of hypocritical morality, she is angry that an innocent girl who becomes a "prey to love" is "degraded forever" even though her "mind was not polluted by the arts which [some] married women, under the convenient cloak of marriage, practise" (132).[21] This line should not be read out of context as a indictment of sexual appetite itself—the "polluted" secret activities of some wives are not simply sexual acts but the arts of depraved appetite, deceptively practiced with lovers. Serving as its own kind of "pharisaical cloak," marriage as a cultural institution serves to hide, and thus, maintain depraved behaviors.

Exposing this hypocritical posturing, Wollstonecraft consistently uses the cloak metaphor not only as a foundation for her argument in the *Vindication* but as a central part of the narrative of her novel *Maria, or the Wrongs of Woman.* Maria's realization of how marriage can cloak "polluted" behaviors comes dramatically as her husband George Venables offers her sexually (in terms of his "duty as a husband") to Mr. S—— for a loan of five hundred pounds. Thus selling his wife to prostitution, George urges her, paradoxically, to "act like a prudent woman" (101) and acknowledge that a

"husband [is] a convenient cloke" (101). The course of the novel plots Maria's growing independence of mind and virtue, one that allows her to live openly with her lover Darnford instead of choosing to "call into play a thousand arts" (127) which might have deceived people into believing her honorable, by their standards. The narrator forcefully and eloquently distinguishes between true virtue and mere behavior by denouncing "honorable" women who "avail themselves of the cloke of marriage, to conceal a mode of conduct, that would for ever have damned their fame, had they been innocent, seduced girls" (127).

Both *Maria* and the *Vindication* make this critique of women's immodesty not to indict woman's nature, but rather the institution of marriage as defined by eighteenth-century cultural norms. Her disgust at mere animal appetites is actually aimed at the culture that generates women's insatiable desire to establish themselves by marriage (out of economic necessity), for it this contest that dehumanizes women, as she declares in the *Vindication*: "And this desire making mere animals of them, when they marry they act as such children may be expected to act . . . Surely these weak beings are only fit for a seraglio" (10). In *Maria, or the Wrongs of Woman,* Wollstonecraft expounds even more dramatically on the same point: "By allowing women but one way of rising in the world, fostering the libertinism of men, society makes monsters of them, and then their ignoble vices are brought forward as proof of their inferiority of intellect" (72). It is not only the process of the marriage market that corrupts, for once married, women choose from two potential paths, both an affront to and an abuse of healthy sexuality. First, she may become a cunning woman who seeks to gain illicit power through sexuality; as Wollstonecraft says, "if women are not permitted to enjoy legitimate rights, they will render both men and themselves vicious, to obtain illicit privileges" (6). Cunning women are actually tyrants, perpetuating the cycle of power by which they have been formed, and Wollstonecraft admits that for these women, her project of reform would require them to actually lose power. A second path, just as grim, offers women the role of good, energetic housewives, "notable women" who will be a "trusty servant" for a man. Implicitly acknowledging that these relationships create unhealthy sexuality, indeed a lack of female sexuality, Wollstonecraft remarks of such women that their "husbands acknowledge that they are good managers and chaste wives; but leave home to seek for more agreeable, may I be allowed to use a significant French word, *piquant* society" (68). Clearly then, the apparent neglect of one's self as a sexual creature actually facilitates the cycle of men's infidelity. Wollstonecraft is no less assertive about the loss of sexual pleasure for the wife: using a metaphor deeply resonant in the age of Blake's "dark Satanic mills," she says that a wife in such an oppressive marriage "fulfills her task like a blind horse in a mill [and] is defrauded of her just reward; for the wages due to her are the caresses of her husband; and women who have so few natural resources in themselves, do not very patiently bear this privation of a natural right" (67).

Just as passionately as she condemns the pharisaical cloak and the fig leaf borrowed by wantonness, Wollstonecraft also indicts smug acts of restraint, which she links to vicarious sexual pleasure. Wollstonecraft's indictment of hypocritical morality twice uses the phrase "self-denial" in the contexts of compensation and perverse gratification. Immediately following her use of the fig leaf image, Wollstonecraft addresses part of her audience in complete denial, those men who "outwardly respect and inwardly despise the weak creatures whom they thus sport with" and sneers at them for their own hypocrisy: "They cannot submit to resign the highest sensual gratification nor even to relish the epicurism of virtue—self-denial" (126). She further suggests that hypocrisy is not limited to men, as women of fashion are especially subject to such false pleasures: "Did women really respect virtue for its own sake, they would not seek a compensation in vanity, for the self-denial which they are obliged to practice to preserve their reputation" (139-40).[22]

Wollstonecraft represents women enslaved in cultural models of sexuality and exposes the hypocrisy endemic to "moral" codes. Slowly drawing the curtain away from the conduct manuals' superficial "cloak of weakness," the text exposes Marriott's "Lover's eye" that feeds off of such concealment. What Wollstonecraft's **Vindications** points to is the necessity of em(body)ing morality and casting off the cloaks of deceptive systems of dissimulation, especially of female conduct. Significantly, this text asks the same of critical cloaks, of ideologies and methodologies which contribute to, or reify, binary distinctions between reason/passion, between male and female Romantic writers. These crude but polemically effective oppositions have shaped the way we position Wollstonecraft in the context of her contemporaries, but our attachment to this policy can be itself a kind of pharisaical, limiting critical perspective. Stripping ourselves of these preconceptions by which we have characterized Wollstonecraft's text offers us a naked multiplicity of perspectives about female responses to the cultural enslavement of women, allowing us to engage fully this seductive text which resists easy categorizations, and, most importantly, rejects reductionist identification of virtue with behavior. To do less is perhaps to say that one lives in a "decent" society but one that is a hollow substitute for virtue:

> Weak minds are always fond of resting in the ceremonials of duty but morality offers much simpler motives; and it were to be wished that superficial moralists had said less respecting behavior, and outward

observances, for unless virtue, of any kind, be built of knowledge, it will only produce a kind of insipid decency.

(133)

Notes

1. Mary Wollstonecraft, *A Vindication of the Rights of Woman,* ed. Carol Poston, 2nd ed. (NY: Norton, 1988), 63. All subsequent quotations from Wollstonecraft, unless otherwise noted, refer to this edition and are cited parenthetically in the text.

2. Claudia Johnson has aptly summed up feminist response to the text in this way: "Many discussions of Wollstonecraft's [text] . . . begin with apologies, and some conclude in frank disappointment . . . her censoriousness of women as well as her commitment to ostensibly masculinist, enlightenment values have disappointed those who expect feminism to produce, as she does not, a positive culture of the feminine and of female solidarity" (23). See *Equivocal Beings: Politics, Gender, and Sentimentality in the 1790s.*

3. See also Marlon Ross, *The Contours of Masculine Desire—Romanticism and the Rise of Women's Poetry.*

4. Mellor acknowledges the work of Cora Kaplan in this study; for the source of Mellor's comments, see Kaplan's *Sea Changes—Essays on Culture and Feminism.*

5. In contrast to these feminist misreadings, see Gary Kelly's seminal *Revolutionary Feminism: The Mind and Career of Mary Wollstonecraft* which examines both her life and all of her texts in terms of their participation in the cultural revolution in England in the 1790s and especially how the culture of sensibility developed the two divergent themes of subjectivity and domesticity in its construction of "woman." Although Kelly's treatment of sexuality in the Vindication is brief (see 125-8), he sharply observes that "Wollstonecraft is warning not against sexuality but against the construction of women around sexuality within court culture" (126).

6. See Virginia Sapiro's *A Vindication of Political Virtue: The Political Theory of Mary Wollstonecraft* for her clear and sharp observation, with regard to political beliefs, that Wollstonecraft's self is a dynamic unity in which the "passions must be infused with reason" (62).

7. My point is that what is a similarity between Blake's and Wollstonecraft's representation of sexuality is consistently misread because of our assumptions about Wollstonecraft's cautions

against passion; thus, the intertextual relationship between these two clearly dialogic texts, one that has been well documented, shifts markedly once we revise our understanding of Wollstonecraft.

8. Wollstonecraft in both *Vindications* conflates the status of women with that of a standing military and the aristocracy, all of whom adopt artificial poses because they are essentially idle. See Guralnick, 159-61.

9. See Poovey and Yeazell, especially, for Wollstonecraft's response to Rousseau. Also, see Jones' "The Seductions of Conduct: Pleasure and Conduct Literature" for a revisionist reading of how the conduct books' insistence on ideal virtues "open up spaces of fantasy and female desire which are potentially transgressive" (116).

10. The spatial metaphor, contrasting the "little" and "minute" view of prudence versus a soul's extended view "beyond" such division, highlights the difference between her text and these manuals. As Yeazell notes, the teleology of the conduct manuals is proper courtship and marriage whereas the teleology of Wollstonecraft's text is moral/spiritual fulfillment.

11. The best discussion of this dichotomy is in E. P. Thompson, *Witness Against the Beast: William Blake and the Moral Law,* which clearly delineates Blake's rejection of the Moral Law in favor of the Gospel of Mercy. Thompson does not discuss Wollstonecraft at all, but the study goes to great lengths to document the widespread radical interpolation of this dichotomy.

12. This phrase comes in a footnote to her remark that women who have improved their reason actually have the most modesty; in this note, she confesses that she has "conversed, as man with man, with medical men, on anatomical subjects, and compared the proportions of the human body with artists" without any sense of the "absurd rules which make modesty a pharisaical cloak of weakness."

13. My discussion of the conduct books' use of the metaphor of concealment is greatly indebted to Yeazell's thorough, interesting, and well-documented research.

14. See Yeazell's discussion of the etymology of the word, from "modestie" (humility) to "pudeur," a close French equivalent but with an erotic undertone, thus underscoring the fact that what seems "natural" in a given culture is in part linguistically determined.

15. Any critical study of her texts has to acknowledge her satirical rhetorical strategies that depend upon sarcasm, understatement, and ironic allusion to key signal words in the debate over the discourse of sensibility. Most importantly, Kelly's *Revolutionary Feminism* develops her manipulations of this discourse by showing how she "turns the tables" on writers who systematize oppression by adopting an innovative style, an "experiment in feminist writing," which makes the *Vindication* a "quasi-treatise" drawing upon philosophical works, the familiar essay, figurative language, the conduct books, devotional prose, and prose fiction. See 107-139, especially 108-20. See also Poovey's argument on Wollstonecraft's use of "circuitous phrasing" as evasiveness, 78, and Syndy Conger's more general discussion of Wollstonecraft's manipulation of this discourse, *Mary Wollstonecraft and the Language of Sensibility.*

16. Wollstonecraft's defense, indeed lavish encouragement, of modesty is emphatically for both sexes; I disagree with Yeazell's conclusions about this chapter as proving Wollstonecraft's complicity with her culture's attention to female modesty as in the following statement: "Like the writers she attacked, in other words, Wollstonecraft set out to discriminate true from false modesty in order to nurture the true—and in this connection, at least, her radical work belonged very much to the culture it criticized" (62).

17. Sometimes more clearly than recent scholars, Wollstonecraft's contemporaries realized her radical repositioning on the issue of female decorum. Although most parodic attacks centered on her unconventional lifestyle, as sensationalized in Godwin's *Memoirs,* some ridiculed the licentious nature of her texts; see the anti-Jacobin poem "The Vision of Liberty" whose author interpreted the Vindication as "Exhorting bashful womankind to quit / All foolish modesty." See Janet Todd's introduction to *A Wollstonecraft Anthology.*

18. She maintains this position in her fiction as well, suggesting in *Mary: A Fiction* that women barred from direct experience debauch their minds secretly and are actually more corrupt. See Laurie Langbauer for an excellent discussion of Wollstonecraft's novels, 211.

19. Wollstonecraft, at times, is critically suspicious of imaginative literature; she equates novels with sentimentality, as is evident in this list of things to avoid: "Novels, music, poetry, and gallantry" (61). She further berates the "stupid novelists" (183) in a review of 1789 where she offers a recipe for such a book: "unnatural characters, improbable incidents, tales of woe rehearsed in an affected, half-prose, half-poetical style, exquisite double refined

sensibility, dazzling beauty and elegant drapery." See Rev. of *Child of Woe,* by Elizabeth Norman, *Analytical Review* 3 (1789): 221-222.

20. Harriet Devine Jump summarizes some of the critical controversy over this intertextual reference in *Mary Wollstonecraft: Writer.* See 88.

21. Labeling the cultural institution of marriage a "convenient cloak" echoes the representation, in Wollstonecraft and other writers of the revolutionary decade, of cultural trappings as "drapery." Whereas Edmund Burke, in *Reflections on the Revolution in France,* lauds the "decent drapery of life" (171), radical writers of the 1790s expose the viciousness of it. Wollstonecraft twice directly responds to Burke's specious reasoning in his statement that the age of chivalry was one "under which vice itself lost half its evil by losing all its grossness" (170). First, Wollstonecraft rewrites Burke's equation in her description of military gallants as those "whose polished manners render vice more dangerous, by concealing its deformity under gay ornamental drapery" (17), She again responds to this specific phrase in her comment on Burke's description of the Versailles crowd of protesters as the "furies of hell, in the abused shape of the vilest of women"; in her response to his emphasis on the "vilest of women," she says, "Probably you mean women who gained a livelihood by selling vegetables or fish, who never had any advantage or education; or their vices might have lost part of their abominable deformity, by losing part of their grossness" (*The Works of Mary Wollstonecraft,* V, 30).

22. Blake, through Oothoon, echoes Wollstonecraft's condemnation of modesty very consciously in Visions when . . . the youth shut up from / The lustful joy. shall forget to generate. & and create an amorous image / In the shadows of his curtains and in the folds of his silent pillow. / Are not these the places of religion? the rewards of continence? / The self enjoyings of self denial? (7.5-9)). Both texts' use of the metaphor of concealment indicts the self-righteous moralist—Blake's youth "shut up from / The lustful joy" parallels Wollsonecraft's "prudent voluptuary"—and the "self enjoyings" that result from the secretive acts from behind the curtain or the cloak.

Works Cited

Ackland, Michael. "The Embattled Sexes: Blake's Debt to Wollstonecraft in *The Four Zoas.*" *Blake: An Illustrated Quarterly* 16.3 (1982-3): 172-83.

Bentley, G. E. "'A Different Face': William Blake and Mary Wollstonecraft." *Wordsworth Circle* 10 (1979): 349-50.

Blake, William. *The Complete Poetry and Prose of William Blake.* Ed. David V. Erdman. Rev. ed. NY: Doubleday, 1988.

Bracher, Mark. "The Metaphysical Grounds of Oppression in Blake's *Visions of the Daughters of Albion.*" *Colby Library Quarterly* 20 (1984): 164-73.

Burke, Edmund. *Reflections on the Revolution in France.* Ed. Conor Cruise O'Brien. London and New York: Penguin, 1968.

Cobbett, William. *Advice to Young Men and to Young Women* . . . London: Mills, Jowett, & Mills, 1829.

Conger, Syndy. *Mary Wollstonecraft and the Language of Sensibility.* London and Toronto: Associated UPs, 1992.

Erdman, David. *Blake: Prophet Against Empire.* Princeton: Princeton UP, 1954.

Ferguson, Moira and Todd, Janet. *Mary Wollstonecraft.* Boston: Twayne, 1984.

Fordyce, James. *Sermons to Young Women, in Two Volumes.* 3rd ed. London, Millar, 1766.

Goslee, Nancy Moore. "Slavery and Sexual Character: Questioning the Master Trope in Blake's *Visions of the Daughters of Albion.*" *ELH* 57 (1990): 101-28.

Gregory, Dr. [John]. *A Father's Legacy to His Daughters.* London: Strahan and Cadell, 1774.

Guralnick, Elissa. "Radical Politics in Mary Wollstonecraft's *A Vindication of the Rights of Woman.*" *Studies in Burke and His Time* 18 (1977): 155-66.

Hilton, Nelson. "An Original Story." *Unnam'd Forms: Blake and Textuality.* Ed. Nelson Hilton and Thomas Vogler. Berkeley: U of California P, 1986. 69-104.

Johnson, Claudia. *Equivocal Beings: Politics, Gender, and Sentimentality in the 1790s.* Chicago: U of Chicago P, 1995.

Jones, Vivien. "The Seductions of Conduct: Pleasure and Conduct Literature." *Pleasure in the Eighteenth Century.* Ed. Roy Porter and Marie Mulvey Roberts. NY: New York UP, 1996. 108-32.

———. "Women Writing Revolution: Narratives of History and Sexuality in Wollstonecraft and Williams." *Beyond Romanticism: New Approaches to Texts and Contexts 1780-1832.* Ed. Stephen Copley and John Whale. London: Routledge, 1992. 178-99.

Jump, Harriet Devine. *Mary Wollstonecraft: Writer.* London: Harvester Wheatsheaf, 1994.

Kaplan, Cora. "Pandora's Box: Subjectivity, Class and Sexuality in Socialist Feminist Criticism." *Making A Difference: Feminist Literary Criticism.* Ed. Gayle Green and Coppelia Kahn. NY: Routledge, 1985. 146-76.

————. *Sea Changes—Essays on Culture and Feminism.* London: Verso, 1986: 31-56.

Kelly, Gary. *Revolutionary Feminism: The Mind and Career of Mary Wollstonecraft.* NY: St. Martin's P, 1982.

Langbauer, Laurie. "An Early Romance: Motherhood and Women's Writing in Mary Wollstonecraft's Novels." *Romanticism and Feminism.* Ed. Anne K. Mellor. Bloomington: Indiana UP, 1988. 208-219.

Lee, Judith. "Ways of Their Own: The Emanations of Blake's *Vala, or The Four Zoas.*" *ELH* 50.1 (1983): 131-53.

Marriott, Thomas. *Female Conduct: Being an Essay on the Art of Pleasing To be Practiced by the Fair Sex, before, and after marriage. A Poem in Two Books* London: Newberry, 1760.

Mason, Michael, ed. *William Blake.* Oxford: Oxford UP, 1992.

Mellor, Anne K., ed *Romanticism and Feminism.* Bloomington: Indiana UP, 1988.

————. *Romanticism and Gender.* NY: Routledge, 1993.

————. "Sex, Violence, and Slavery: Blake and Wollstonecraft." *Huntington Library Quarterly* 58.3-4 (1996): 345-70.

————. "Why Women Didn't Like Romanticism." *The Romantics and Us.* Ed. Gene Ruoff. New Brunswick: Rutgers UP, 1999. 274-87.

Mitchell, Orm. "Blake's Subversive Illustrations to Wollstonecraft's *Original Stories.*" *Mosaic* 17.4 (1984): 17-34.

Moore, Edward. *Fables for the Female Sex.* London: Francklin, 1744.

Myers, Mitzi. "Reform or Ruin: 'A Revolution in Female Manners.'" *Studies in Eighteenth-Century Culture* 11 (1982): 199-216.

Nurmi, Martin. *William Blake.* Kent, Ohio: Kent State UP, 1976.

Poovey, Mary. *The Proper Lady and the Woman Writer.* Chicago: U of Chicago P, 1984.

Ross, Marlon. *The Contours of Masculine Desire: Romanticism and the Rise of Women's Poetry.* NY: Oxford UP, 1989.

Rousseau, Jean Jaques. *Emile.* Trans. Barbara Foxley. London, 1911.

Thompson, E. P. *Witness Against the Beast: William Blake and the Moral Law.* NY: New P, 1993.

Todd, Janet. "Introduction." *A Wollstonecraft Anthology.* Ed. Janet Todd. Bloomington: Indiana UP, 1977. 1-21.

Welch, Dennis. "Blake's Response to Wollstonecraft's *Original Stories.*" *Blake: An Illustrated Quarterly* 13 (1979): 4-15.

Wollstonecraft, Mary. *The Works of Mary Wollstonecraft.* Ed. Janet Todd and Marilyn Butler. 7 vols. NY: New York UP, 1989.

————. *A Vindication of the Rights of Woman.* Ed. Carol Poston. 2nd ed. NY: Norton, 1988.

Wordsworth, William. *Lyrical Ballads 1798,* Ed. W. J. B. Owen. 2nd ed. Oxford: Oxford UP, 1969.

Yeazell, Ruth. *Fictions of Modesty.* Chicago: U of Chicago P, 1991.

Daniel Engster (essay date September 2001)

SOURCE: Engster, Daniel. "Mary Wollstonecraft's Nurturing Liberalism: Between an Ethic of Justice and Care." *The American Political Science Review* 95, no. 3 (September 2001): 577-88.

[*In the following essay, Engster examines* A Vindication of the Rights of Woman *and* A Vindication of the Rights of Men *and shows how Wollstonecraft's ideas bear on the current debate in political and moral philosophy about justice and care.*]

In recent years, feminist scholars have proposed political theories based upon an ethic of care as an alternative to liberal theories of justice.[1] Although these scholars have paid little attention to the ideas of historical feminist authors, Mary Wollstonecraft (1759-97) provides important insights into the relationship between liberal justice and feminist care. In this article, I explore Wollstonecraft's views on the relationship between justice and care and outline her proposal for creating a nurturing form of liberalism based upon a synthesis of these concepts.

While contemporary scholars continue to debate the precise nature of justice and care theories, and some even question whether the two concepts are analytically distinct, most recognize certain distinguishing features between them (Gatens 1998; Held 1995a).[2] Justice theories are organized around formal and abstract rights and rules, whereas care theories emphasize the importance of nurturing activities, personal attentiveness, and the maintenance of human relationships. An important difference between the two is the high moral value that care theories place upon nurturing activities and the realms in which they traditionally occur, especially family life, friendships, and sexual and other close personal relationships (Friedman 1995, 147-8). Concomitant to this view is the belief that private and public spheres cannot be separated: The care provided in personal relationships and family life is essential for public activity and deserves public recognition and support (Katzenstein and Laitin 1987, 262-3).

Even if Okin (1989a, 1989b) is correct in arguing that justice theories can accommodate certain concerns of care theories, the latter may at least be distinguished from the former by their emphasis on care-giving activities.[3] More distinctive is their commitment to taking others' needs as the starting point for normative action (Ruddick 1990, 237; Tronto 1993, 105). In this respect, care theories are more flexible and contextual than theories of justice. Whereas justice theories mediate human relationships by applying abstract moral principles to particular cases, care theories start from the particular needs of individuals and attempt to address these needs in context (Friedman 1993, 70-1). They also tend to focus on the inherent and often unchosen responsibilities and duties that stem from human interdependence and relationships, while justice theories tend to stress individual autonomy and voluntary contractual obligations (Gatens 1998, xiv-xv).

The first generation of care theorists were primarily interested in differentiating the concepts of justice and care, but many recent discussions center around "how justice and care can appropriately be combined from a feminist point of view" (Held 1995a, 2; see also Card 1995; Clement 1996; Dillon 1992; Friedman 1993, 1995; Held 1995b; Hirschmann and Di Stefano 1996; Jaggar 1995; James 1992; Koehn 1998; Okin 1989b; Robinson 1999; Tronto 1993). Interest in this issue has been piqued by awareness of potential shortcomings in the original care ideal (Jaggar 1995). The focus of the care ethic on the particular raises questions about its applicability to public affairs and large social structures. (Mendus 1993). At the same time, care ethics has been criticized for ignoring the ways in which institutionally structured power inequities may compromise caring relationships (Friedman 1993). A number of theorists also point out that caring relationships can slide into paternalism or parochialism if not governed by some objective criterion of genuine care (Barry 1995, 252-6; Jaggar 1995; Koehn 1998; Narayan 1995; Sevenhuijsen 1998; Tronto 1993).

Wollstonecraft affords important insights into these debates, yet her writings have been ignored by contemporary care theorists. The neglect of Wollstonecraft's writings is perhaps understandable given her reputation as a conventional liberal feminist—one who simply added women to the classical liberal tradition and stirred. Indeed, several scholars suggest that Wollstonecraft's philosophy embodies all the inadequacies of liberal theories of justice when applied to women (Eisenstein 1981, 90; Gatens 1991; Jacobus 1979, 10; Pateman, 1989; Poovey 1984). The only thing that Wollstonecraft is said to have to offer "on the question of sexual equality

is that women are entitled to be treated 'like men' or 'as if they were men'" (Gatens 1991, 126-7). It is held that she incorporated women into the liberal public sphere without taking account of their concerns and perspective.

The problem with the liberal interpretation of Wollstonecraft's thought is that it disregards the important role she accords to caring relationships. Although she draws heavily upon the classical liberal tradition, she nonetheless identifies caring relationships as the foundation and end of society. She argues that the development of autonomous individuals begins in the family, with the particular attention of mothers and fathers to the needs of their children. In fact, family duties are central to her political philosophy. In her vision of society, the highest moral importance is given to the particular caring-giving duties of husbands, wives, fathers, mothers, sons, daughters, and citizens.

Within this framework of care Wollstonecraft does recognize an important role for justice. She asserts that equality and rights must be extended to women in political, social, and family affairs in order to foster the development of healthy caring relationships within the family and society at large. Her critique of society is intended to demonstrate that unjust family and social relations not only impede the development of care but actually promote uncaring and pathological relationships. Wollstonecraft is thus rightfully known for her strong advocacy of equality and rights, but it has been overlooked that she demanded equality and rights for women primarily to promote a more caring and dutiful citizen body. Her political philosophy is perhaps best described as a nurturing liberalism in which liberal justice provides the necessary backdrop for the development of virtuous care.

Wollstonecraft offers important insights into contemporary care/justice debates. Recent proposals for combining care and justice often minimize the moral and theoretical significance of care or limit its applicability to personal and private affairs (Held 1995b; Jaggar 1995). Wollstonecraft synthesizes justice and care without slighting either value. She embeds justice within the larger framework of care but demonstrates its importance for caring relationships. By her account justice is instrumental to care—an essential feature of caring relationships. She identifies caring duties, in turn, as the crux of a virtuous social order and the key to addressing many social problems. Wollstonecraft argues that many social problems are the result of unhealthy caring relationships that can only be corrected by extending justice to personal relationships and elevating the status of care-giving duties.

My main purpose is to explore the neglected element of care within Wollstonecraft's moral and political thought and to bring her ideas to bear on contemporary debates about care and justice. It may seem anachronistic to apply contemporary concepts to the ideas of an eighteenth-century thinker, but two points justify my interpretation. First, even if the concept of care is a recent discursive invention, the elements that define it (including a concern for nurturing relations, an emphasis on the particular needs of others, a desire to promote attentiveness, and responsibility among individuals) have long existed. Because Wollstonecraft was concerned with those elements, it is plausible to consider her an early care theorist even though she expressed her concerns in a different social and historical context.[4]

Second, and more important, Wollstonecraft stands at a critical historical juncture in the formation of the modern care ethic. In the late eighteenth century, philosophers began to shift notions of moral sentimentality and affection, which are quite similar to elements of the modern care ethic, from the public realm and humanity to the domestic sphere and women (Okin 1981; Tronto 1993). According to Tronto (pp. 25-59), this shift was driven primarily by large-scale economic and social transformations that made political theories based upon contextual morality and affective personal relations seem less relevant for public affairs. Wollstonecraft's writings may be read as an early protest against the domestication and segregation of caring activities as well as a warning about the pathologies of care that would result from it.

A secondary (albeit largely implicit) purpose of this article is to contribute to recent efforts to increase appreciation for Wollstonecraft's works in the canon of modern political philosophy (Falco 1996; Gunther-Canada 1997; Sapiro 1992, 280-300; Weiss 1996). Wollstonecraft remains a peripheral figure among political scientists. Too often her writings are assumed to advocate nothing more than the extension of liberal rights to women and are considered of historical but not theoretical interest. I suggest that Wollstonecraft articulated an innovative liberal theory that places nurturing and caring activities at the center of public affairs. She viewed liberal rights and freedoms as a means to promote the virtuous fulfillment of nurturing duties. That fulfillment, in turn, could protect against the selfishness and irresponsibility often associated with liberal society. Wollstonecraft aimed at the revolutionary transformation of society, not so much through restructuring macroeconomic and political institutions as through improving the quality of personal and domestic care. But before personal care can transform the political, she argues, political justice first must be extended to personal caring relations.

BURKEAN CARE AND *A VINDICATION OF THE RIGHTS OF MEN*

It is useful to begin the discussion of Wollstonecraft's philosophy with a brief discussion of Edmund Burke's *Reflections on the Revolution in France,* Wollstonecraft

dedicated her first major political work, *A Vindication of the Rights of Men* (1790), to the task of rebutting it. Scholars have proposed a variety of hypotheses to explain the vehemence of her response to Burke, but none has suggested that her reaction may have been provoked in part by the similarity of their ideas. Both wrote during a period when the contextual and affective moral and political philosophies of the Scottish Enlightenment thinkers, among others, were being replaced by universalistic and abstract moral and political philosophies, or at least were being pushed into the domestic sphere (Tronto 1993, 25-59). Both Burke and Wollstonecraft viewed this development with concern but addressed it in very different ways.

In *Reflections,* Burke criticizes the uncaring nature of universalistic philosophies and defends the traditional and patriarchal social structure as necessary for the preservation of caring relationships and the fulfillment of duties. Wollstonecraft apparently read *Reflections* as a twisted or pathological description of her own concern with nurturance and care-giving duties. She counters Burke's argument by claiming that universal rights are a necessary prerequisite for healthy caring relationships, and she dedicates much of her *Rights of Men* to highlighting the shortcomings of care ethics when treated in isolation from equality and rights.

Burke formulates some of his central criticisms of the French Revolution in terms reminiscent of care ethics. One clear example is his criticism of Enlightenment liberalism's commitment to abstract rights. The true rights of individuals, he declares, depend upon their particular wants and needs (Burke [1790] 1987, 51-3). In professing his love for liberty, for example, Burke notes that he would not therefore congratulate a mentally ill individual for escaping (or being cast out) from a psychiatric hospital (p. 7). The abstract perfection of natural rights is their practical defect. They ignore the special needs of different individuals. Burke asserts that the devotion to abstract rights can devolve into the most callous and uncaring sorts of policies and actions if not adapted to the particular and contextual needs of human beings:

> Though a pleasant writer said, *liceat perire poetis* [Let the poets perish], when one of them, in cold blood, is said to have leaped into the flames of a volcanic revolution, *ardentem frigidus Aetnam insiluit* [Coldly he jumped into burning Aetna], I consider such a frolic rather as an unjustifiable poetic license than as one of the franchises of Parnassus; and whether he was a poet, or divine, or politician that chose to exercise this kind of right, I think that more wise, because more charitable, thoughts would urge me rather to save the man than to preserve his brazen slippers as the monuments of his folly.

> (p. 55)

Burke claims it is the responsibility of each of us—and of governments more generally—to attend to the real and variable needs of individuals. The commitment to abstract rights is too simplistic and impersonal to treat all human beings in a truly humane manner.

Burke's concern with caring relationships is also evident in his criticism of the selfish individualism of Enlightenment society. Burke worried that liberal societies would strip away "all the pleasing illusions which made power gentle and obedience liberal" and reduce all human relations to matters of power and self-interest (p. 67). "On the scheme of this barbarous philosophy, which is the offspring of cold hearts and muddy understandings . . . laws are to be supported only by their own terrors and by the concern which each individual may find in them from his own private speculations or can spare to them from his own private interests" (p. 68). For Burke, the only way to preserve affectionate and attentive personal relationships is to maintain traditional feudal arrangements in which power differentials are mitigated by manners and customs and each individual occupies a status and role that defines his or her duties toward others. Kings behave toward subjects as loving fathers; the nobility feels obliged to care for the lower classes; men show special concern for women. The whole of society is arranged "so as to create in us love, veneration, admiration, or attachment" (p. 68).

Liberal theories of justice replace these affections with a base commitment to equality and freedom. They tear away all traditional and communal norms in favor of a calculating and isolated individualism. Burke foretells the coming of a society driven by "present convenience" and the "lust of selfish will" (pp. 77, 83). The French revolutionaries' rude treatment of King Louis XVI and Marie Antoinette is emblematic of the new social ethos devoid of humaneness (pp. 62-5). Burke's concern about the increasing equality and assertiveness of women, too, reflects his belief that universal morality will eventually degrade all relationships into mere contractual agreements (Gunther-Canada 1996, 65-6). "But the age of chivalry is dead," Burke decries. "That of sophisters, economists and calculators has succeeded; and the glory of Europe is extinguished forever. Never, never more shall we behold that generous loyalty to rank and sex, that proud submission, that dignified obedience, that subordination of the heart which kept alive, even in servitude itself, the spirit of an exalted freedom" (p. 66).

Wollstonecraft devoted *A Vindication of the Rights of Men* to a critique of Burke's *Reflections*. Probably more than any other work, it established her reputation as a traditional liberal theorist. She vehemently defends the Enlightenment ideals of freedom, equality, rights, and rationality against Burke's conservative defense of personal affection and moral sentimentality. Yet, it is misleading to characterize this work in terms of the simple contrast between affection and rationality, care and justice. Wollstonecraft expresses sympathy for many of

Burke's ideas and even observes that in different circumstances Burke might have been a "revolutionary" like herself (Wollstonecraft [1790] 1995, 5, 45-6). Above all, she expresses sympathy with his concern for affective and caring relationships, but she finds his account of these virtues to be distorted by his attachment to unequal social relations. *A Vindication of the Rights of Men* is not only a vindication of justice and equality but also, more accurately, a first vindication of her own vision of a just and caring society. She wants to demonstrate that the French revolutionaries' commitment to equality, rationality, and rights is not necessarily antithetical to the development of a caring and dutiful society but, indeed, the foundation of it.

Wollstonecraft ([1790] 1995) begins by ridiculing Burke's "pampered sensibility." His emotions and passions overwhelm his reason and subject him to pretty flights of imagination (pp. 6-7). Wollstonecraft portrays her own argument as an attempt to reinsert reason into the discussion about the French Revolution. "Quitting now the flowers of rhetoric, let us, Sir, reason together" (p. 7). Several scholars have commented upon the gender reversal implicit in Wollstonecraft's rhetoric (Gunther-Canada 1996; Johnson 1995, 23-46; Kelly 1992, 84-106). Wollstonecraft adopts the masculine language of reason to rebuke Burke's effeminate sentimentality and emotionalism.[5] This rhetorical strategy might appear antifeminine (indeed, Wollstonecraft has few good things to say about most of her female contemporaries), but her goal is to lead both women and men away from an artificial and conventional definition of the moral sentiments toward true human affection.

According to Wollstonecraft, feelings that are "ostentatiously displayed are often the cold declamation of the head, and not the effusions of the heart" (*Rights of Men,* p. 6). "When the heart speaks, we are seldom shocked by hyperbole, or dry raptures. I speak in this decided tone" (p. 29). She insists that her straightforward, unemotional prose indicates her true feelings; in contrast, Burke's fanciful and romantic prose is a sign of "false, or rather artificial, feelings" (p. 29). She even accuses Burke of "hard-hearted sophistry" (p. 59). He tries to manipulate his readers through fanciful images and appeals to the emotions. He sacrifices all true affection to stylized affectation.

Wollstonecraft's clearest statement on style appears in the opening pages of her *Vindication of the Rights of Woman* (1792), although a similar statement is found at the very beginning of *Rights of Men*: "I aim at being useful, and sincerity will render me unaffected; for, wishing rather to persuade by the force of my arguments, than dazzle by the elegance of my language, I shall not waste my time in rounding periods, or in fabricating the turgid bombast of artificial feelings, which, coming from the head, never reach the heart" (Wollstonecraft [1792] 1995, 77; VM, 5). We should not, of course, accept at face value Wollstonecraft's claim to speak without affectation. Her rhetoric is based upon the Rousseauean conceit that there is a true and natural language of the heart beneath the distorting layers of convention. The important point is that her rhetoric is not based, as sometimes supposed, upon the sharp distinction between reason and affection. She regards rational reflection as the truest road to uncovering the genuine feelings of the human heart.

Behind the poetic images and flowery rhetoric of Burke's *Reflections,* Wollstonecraft argues, there is a cold and uncaring philosophy. Burke exalts a constitution "settled in the dark days of ignorance" (**Rights of Men,** p. 11), when members of the peasantry were put to death for hunting on the nobility's lands or for defending their crops from the nobility's game. "How many families," she asks, "have been plunged, in the *sporting* countries, into misery and vice for some paltry transgression of these coercive laws, by the natural consequence of that anger which a man feels when he sees the reward of his industry laid waste by unfeeling luxury?—when his children's bread is given to dogs" (p. 16)! She notes that Burke's empathy seems to extend only to the rich and wellborn. His lack of concern for the needs of the poor exposes the indifference at the core of his philosophy:

> Misery, to reach your heart, I perceive, must have its cap and bells; your tears are reserved, very naturally considering your character, for the declamation of the theatre, or for the downfall of queens, whose rank alters the nature of folly, and throws a graceful veil over vices that degrade humanity; whilst the distress of many industrious mothers, whose helpmates have been torn from them, and the hungry cry of helpless babes, were vulgar sorrows that could not move your commiseration, though they might extort an alms. "The tears that are shed for fictitious sorrows are admirably adapted," says Rousseau, "to make us proud of all the virtues which we do not possess."
>
> (p. 14)

Wollstonecraft adds that not only the poor suffer under Burke's system. Feudalism stymies the development of healthy caring relationships. Burke assumes that "respect chills love" (**Rights of Men,** p. 6). Wollstonecraft counters that "affection in the marriage state can only be founded on respect" (p. 22). She explains that equal respect is necessary to appreciate the particular and unique characteristics of others and to love them as real individuals. Traditional social arrangements thwart genuine interpersonal relationships by encouraging people to take on false airs, to view others through artificial romantic ideals, and to marry according to status and wealth. "The respect paid to rank and fortune damps every generous purpose of the soul, and stifles the natural affections on which human contentment ought to be built" (p. 24).

In their efforts to emulate the manners of the nobility, the middle class similarly sacrifices personal intimacy to wealth and affectation. "The grand concern of three parts out of four is to contrive to live above their equals, and to appear to be richer than they are. How much domestic comfort and private satisfaction is sacrificed to this irrational ambition! It is a destructive mildew that blights the fairest virtues; benevolence, friendship, generosity, and all those endearing charities which bind human hearts together" (**Rights of Men,** p. 23). Feudal arrangements further undermine nurturing family relations by inclining parents to care more for the perpetuation of family name and estates than the well-being of their children. "The younger children have been sacrificed to the eldest son; sent into exile, or confined in convents, that they might not encroach on what was called, with shameful falsehood, the *family* estate. Will Mr. Burke call this parental affection reasonable and virtuous" (pp. 21-2)? In short, traditional social arrangements distort close personal relationships by subordinating them to romance, rank, and wealth.

Wollstonecraft defends the rights of men as the solution to this problem. Like Burke, she wants to avoid the development of a cold and calculating society. But in contrast to Burke, she claims the extension of rights and equality is necessary to this end. She suggests that a liberal political order based upon abstract and universal rights does not necessarily entail the demise of personal affection; on the contrary, it provides the basis for the development of more caring and dutiful relationships.

> The civilization which has taken place in Europe has been very partial, and, like every custom that an arbitrary point of honour has established, refines the manners at the expense of morals, by making sentiments and opinions current in conversation that have no root in the heart, or weight in the cooler resolves of the mind.—And what has stopped its progress?—hereditary property—hereditary honours. The man has changed into an artificial monster by the station in which he was born, and the consequent homage that benumbed his faculties like the torpedo's touch;—or a being, with a capacity of reasoning, would not have failed to discover, as his faculties unfolded, that true happiness arose from the friendship and intimacy which can only be enjoyed by equals; and that charity is not a condescending distribution of alms, but an intercourse of good offices and mutual benefits, founded on respect for justice and humanity.
>
> (**Rights of Men,** pp. 8-9)

In this passage, Wollstonecraft touches upon a number of themes that are central to both her **Vindications.** Following Rousseau, she claims that European civilization is corrupt because it is based upon unequal social relationships. This inequality has created a civilization of monstrous and unfeeling characters. The only way to develop true friendship and mutual care is to extend equality and justice to all. While she commends Burke's concern for relationships and care she suggests that he has not explored deeply enough what is necessary to promote these ends. He falls back upon the feudal hierarchy as the foundation of caring relationships and thus helps perpetuate the very thing he claims to detest: an impersonal and uncaring society.

Burke and Wollstonecraft approach the problem of promoting caring relationships in quite different ways. Burke looks back wistfully to the feudal social order in which caring duties are prescribed by the particular roles and status of individuals. Wollstonecraft looks ahead to the development of a more caring society based upon egalitarian social arrangements. Although Burke's concern for affection and care is more similar to the ideas of contemporary conservative theorists than to those of contemporary feminists, Wollstonecraft's critique nonetheless yields valuable lessons for contemporary feminist discussions about justice and care. Rather than jettison justice for care or draw a sharp distinction between them, she argues that the two concepts are integrally related. Without justice, the concern for care can justify paternalistic and oppressive social relationships, especially for women, children, and the poor. Indeed, she claims it is difficult if not impossible to actualize healthy caring relationships within an unjust social structure, since social inequality creates pathologies of care in the form of misplaced and artificial affections. It is this last point that Wollstonecraft elaborates at length in *A Vindication of the Rights of Woman.*

A VINDICATION OF THE RIGHTS OF WOMAN

After defending the principles of the French Revolution against Burke's conservative criticisms in her first *Vindication,* Wollstonecraft turns in *A Vindication of the Rights of Woman* to a criticism of the French revolutionaries for being too conservative. She charges them with betraying their ideals by reproducing elements of the feudal social order within their new constitution. Specifically, they exclude women from political rights and thus maintain the old patriarchal social system. "Who made man the exclusive judge, if woman partake with him the gift of reason" (Wollstonecraft [1792] 1995, 69)? Before the French Revolution, kings and nobles justified their rule by arguing that the people lacked the reason necessary to govern themselves. "Do you not act a similar part, when you *force* all women, by denying them civil and political rights, to remain immured in their families groping in the dark" (p. 69)? Although the revolutionaries were free from belief in the divine right of kings, they held fast to the "divine right of husbands" (p. 112). Denouncing both divine rights, Wollstonecraft demands the extension of civil and political rights to women.

This demand for women's rights solidified Wollstonecraft's reputation as a liberal feminist, but the liberal interpretation of her thought fails to capture the full complexity of her ideas. As noted above, in the *Rights of Men* Wollstonecraft criticizes not affection per se, but the heartless and unnatural affection that develops from unequal social relationships. In the *Rights of Woman,* she likewise defends the extension of rights to women primarily on the grounds that it will facilitate the development of more nurturing and caring relationships. In fact, she approaches the whole issue of governance from a care perspective, reformulating classical liberal theory to emphasize the importance of the family and nurturing relationships for the well-being of society at large.

Wollstonecraft's concern with care distinguishes her thought from classical liberal theory in several ways. Rather than simply appeal to the abstract dignity of all individuals, Wollstonecraft supports women's equality largely by emphasizing the ways in which it will facilitate the delivery of care. She also focuses on the importance of healthy family relationships for the public good and rejects the classical liberal distinction between public and private spheres. She claims justice must be brought to bear on the private sphere of family and social life in order to foster the development of care, and government must accord greater resources and respect to traditional nurturing activities, such as parenting and education. As Sapiro (1992, 183; 1996, 37) has written, Wollstonecraft "saw no clear distinction between public and private" but instead "saw 'public' and 'private' as integral parts of the same wholes, not just as different social spaces but, in some ways, as occupying the same space." Also distinct from classical liberal thought is Wollstonecraft's suggestion that the proper goal of government is the creation of a more virtuous citizen body devoted to fulfilling particular duties to one another and humanity at large.

Wollstonecraft is most often interpreted as a liberal theorist, but some scholars place her thought within the classical republican tradition and interpret her as a virtue theorist (Baker-Benfield 1989; Johnson 1995; Landes 1988; Sapiro 1992). There can be no doubt about the republican influences on her thinking. She argues that hierarchy and luxury invariably corrupt the morality of people, and she advocates an activist or participatory ideal of citizenship (Sapiro 1992, xix-xx, 77-116, 232-7). But her republicanism also is strongly influenced by her concern for caring relationships. She argues that public virtue depends upon particularized care relationships, and these depend upon social and political equality. She thus extends classical republican arguments about the corrupting effects of hierarchy and inequality into the private sphere and makes egalitarian family relations a central focus of her theory of a virtuous republic. At the same time, she associates virtue for both men and women not with military or political glory but with the fulfillment of family and social nurturing duties. In fact, she positively reviles the traditional republican valorization of the military and war (***Rights of Woman,*** pp. 92-3, 235-6; see Sapiro 1992, 102-3). Hers is a republic of care in which duty to children, spouses, friends, citizens, and humanity replaces the traditional republican ideal of the swaggering *vir virtutis.*

Wollstonecraft lays out the intellectual framework of her argument in the opening chapters of ***Rights of Woman.*** Criticizing Rousseau's account of the original isolation of human beings, she claims that God created human beings to progress toward moral perfection within and through society (pp. 79-82). She defines moral perfection as the development of reason, knowledge, and virtue (p. 79). Reason and knowledge provide human beings with the capacity to understand and control their social world and, more specifically, to comprehend their duties toward others. Virtue consists of the self-conscious fulfillment of these duties (Sapiro 1992, 74-5). The primary duties of women are their care-giving responsibilities as mothers, daughters, sisters, and wives. The primary duties of men are their care-giving responsibilities as fathers, sons, brothers and husbands. Beyond these primary duties exist broader social responsibilities to neighbors, other citizens, and all human kind.

For Wollstonecraft, the moral progress of society, which forms the entire backdrop of the argument in ***Rights of Woman,*** consists of progress toward a world in which men and women recognize the supreme importance of their care-giving duties within the family and society at large. Yet, she claims, everything depends upon women's equality. Without that, neither gender can satisfactorily fulfill its most basic care-giving duties, and society will remain stalled in a morally underdeveloped state. The following important passage from the prefatory letter to ***Rights of Woman*** aptly summarizes the underlying premises of Wollstonecraft's argument:

> Contending for the rights of woman, my main argument is built on this simple principle, that if she be not prepared by education to become the companion of man, she will stop the progress of knowledge and virtue; for truth must be common to all, or it will be inefficacious with respect to its influence on general practice. . . . If children are to be educated to understand the true principle of patriotism, their mother must be a patriot; and the love of mankind, from which an orderly train of virtues spring, can only be produced by considering the moral and civil interest of mankind; but the education and situation of woman, at present, shuts her out from such investigations.
>
> (p. 68)

Wollstonecraft makes clear from the outset of ***Rights of Woman*** that her central concern is the development of a more caring and nurturing society. She defends women's equality primarily on the grounds that it is prerequisite for the moral progress of humanity toward a more virtuous and dutiful state.

INEQUALITY AND THE PATHOLOGIES OF CARE

Wollstonecraft dedicates much of the argument in ***Rights of Woman*** to demonstrating how social and political inequality distorts women's natural affections and prevents them from effectively fulfilling their care-giving duties. On the most basic level, the unequal education given to most women leaves their minds suspended in a state of perpetual childhood. As a result, they are totally unfit for mature companionship and motherhood.

> The education of women has, of late, been more attended to than formerly; yet they are still reckoned a frivolous sex, and ridiculed or pitied by the writers who endeavour by satire or instruction to improve them. It is acknowledged that they spend many of the first years of their lives by acquiring a smattering of accomplishments; meanwhile strength of body and mind are sacrificed to libertine notions of beauty, to the desire of establishing themselves,—the only way women can rise in the world,—by marriage. And this desire making mere animals of them, when they marry they act as such children may be expected to act:—they dress; they paint, and nickname God's creatures.—Surely these weak beings are only fit for a seraglio!—Can they be expected to govern a family with judgement, or take care of the poor babes whom they bring into the world?
>
> (p. 77)

Wollstonecraft returns to this theme throughout ***Rights of Woman.*** Until women comprehend the importance of their care-giving activities for society and receive public recognition for them, they will not be fully attached to them or discharge them virtuously (p. 69). Trained to think primarily about their own beauty and marriage, many girls grow up to be "cold-hearted, narrow-minded," and self-centered women who neglect their duties (p. 142). Alternatively, those who remain attached to their duties tend to fulfill them in overly particular and arbitrary ways. "Mankind seem to agree that children should be left under the management of women during their childhood. Now, from all the observation that I have been able to make, women of sensibility are the most unfit for this task, because they will infallibly, carried away by their feelings, spoil a child's temper" (p. 145). Wollstonecraft is careful to note that her observations do not apply indiscriminately to all women (p. 136). Working women, in particular, tend to display more virtue than "gentlewomen" because they are less immersed within polite society and are more likely to engage in the sorts of practical employment that develop their "good sense" (pp. 154-5).[6] Wollstonecraft mainly worries about middle- and upper-class women, whose sentimental education renders them unfit for adult duties.

Wollstonecraft argues that gender inequality also disrupts close heterosexual relationships by encouraging women to tyrannize over men (***Rights of Woman,*** p.

78). She explains that all human beings innately desire recognition and respect from others (pp. 132, 231). Yet, social inequalities prevent women from attaining respect through legitimate social avenues. They are provided only the most superficial sort of education and are shut out from political activity and most occupations. Consequently, they resort to the only means available to them to achieve some power and respect. They use their feminine wiles to manipulate men to their will. "[Women's] exertion of cunning is only an instinct of nature to enable them to obtain indirectly a little of that power of which they are unjustly denied a share; for, if women are not permitted to enjoy legitimate rights, they will render both men and themselves vicious, to obtain illicit privileges" (p. 70). Women attempt to gain power vicariously by putting on "infantine airs" in order to excite men's desires (p. 78). Men respond with lavish and artificial displays of romantic affection. As a result, marriages are formed upon the weakest of foundations.

After the first flush of love passes, men usually became bored with their wives. "Their husbands acknowledge that they are good managers, and chaste wives; but leave home to seek more agreeable, may I be allowed to use a significant French word, *piquant* society" (*Rights of Woman,* p. 143). Women respond by redirecting their feminine arts toward new conquests or retiring into dreary bitterness.

> The woman who has only been taught to please will soon find that her charms are oblique sunbeams, and that they cannot have much effect on her husband's heart when they are seen every day, when the summer is passed and gone. Will she then have sufficient native energy to look into herself for comfort, and cultivate her dormant faculties? Or, is it not more rational to expect that she will try to please other men; and, in the emotions raised by the expectations of new conquests, endeavor to forget the mortification her love or pride has received? When the husband ceases to be a lover—and the time will inevitably come, her desire of pleasing will then grow languid, or become a spring of bitterness; and love, perhaps the most evanescent of all passions, gives place to jealousy or vanity.
>
> (p. 97)

Wollstonecraft hardly even considers the possibility that women might also turn to one another for support and refuge from their unhappy relations with men. Her silence on this subject seems to reflect her pessimism about it. She indicates that it is very difficult for women who grow up submitting to and tyrannizing over men ever to trust one another as true friends. Most view other women as rivals and reproduce the oppressions of patriarchal society in their female relationships (*Rights of Woman,* pp. 142, 286). In her last novel, *The Wrongs of Women, or Maria,* however, Wollstonecraft (1989) does provide the story of two women, Maria and Jemima, who are able to develop bonds of friendship through their common oppression (Johnson 1995, 47-69).[7]

The effects of inequality are even more pronounced in women's relations with their children. Wollstonecraft outlines a variety of ways in which inequality contributes to dysfunctional maternal-child relations. Being subject to the unjust rule of men within society, women often reproduce this injustice within their home. "It will not be difficult to prove that such delegates will act like men subjected by fear, and make their children and servants endure their tyrannical oppression. As they submit without reason, they will, having no fixed rules to square their conduct by, be kind, or cruel, just as the whim of the moment directs; and we ought not to wonder if sometimes, galled by their heavy yoke, they take a malignant pleasure in resting it on weaker shoulders" (*Rights of Woman,* p. 120).

Inequality also leads women to neglect their children. Because women associate their power and respect with their ability to control men, many of them show more concern for the arts of beauty and coquetry than the duties of motherhood (pp. 231-2). Alternatively, some women carry out a quiet revenge against their husband by "wanting their children to love them best, and take their part, in secret, against the father, who is held up as a scarecrow" (*Rights of Woman,* p. 243). Furthermore, social inequality often poisons even the most well-intentioned maternal affection with "perverse self-love" (p. 242). Women look to their children to be what they cannot be. They invest their children with their dreams and make them their source of power and pride. They forget that children, too, are human beings entitled to respect and independence.

> Woman, however, a slave in every situation to prejudice, seldom exerts enlightened maternal affection; for she either neglects her children, or spoils them by improper indulgence. Besides, the affection of some women for their children is, as I have before termed it, frequently very brutish: for it eradicates every spark of humanity. Justice, truth, every thing is sacrificed by these Rebekah's [sic], and for the sake of their *own* children they violate the most sacred duties, forgetting the common relationship that binds the whole family on earth together.
>
> (p. 243, emphasis in original)

Wollstonecraft recognizes far more clearly than many contemporary feminists the close links between social structures and the healthy delivery of care. Lacking a rational education and just social structure, women are likely express their affection in self-serving ways. They smother their children with affection but forget to recognize their humanity. Their love is just a more subtle form of their desire to tyrannize over others.

WOLLSTONECRAFT'S SYNTHESIS OF CARE AND JUSTICE

Wollstonecraft is well known for her defense of women's equality, but it is rarely noticed that the central reason she calls for equal rights is her desire to overcome the pathologies of care. She considers justice to be an integral aspect of a caring society and essential for encouraging women to fulfill their nurturing duties.

> Would men but generously snap our chains, and be content with rational fellowship instead of slavish obedience, they would find us more observant daughters, more affectionate sisters, more faithful wives, more reasonable mothers—in a word, better citizens. We should then love them with true affection, because we should learn to respect ourselves; and the peace of mind of a worthy man would not be interrupted by the idle vanity of his wife, nor the babes sent to nestle in a strange bosom, having never found a home in their mother's.
>
> (***Rights of Woman***, p. 241)

Wollstonecraft invokes friendship as her model of a natural and pure affection (***Rights of Woman***, pp. 98-101). Friendship is devoid of all coercion and romantic sentimentality and involves the respect of human beings for the unique and particular characteristics of one another, or what Wollstonecraft calls "mutual sympathy" (pp. 203, 241). She contrasts the "calm tenderness of friendship, the confidence of respect" with the "blind admiration, and the sensual emotions of fondness" (p. 99). Unless women are given the opportunity to develop their full capacities, however, they can never be the equal of their husband and never become their genuine friend. "The affection of husbands and wives cannot be pure when they have so few sentiments in common, and when so little confidence is established at home, as must be the case when their pursuits are so different. That intimacy from which tenderness should flow, will not, cannot subsist between the vicious" (p. 292).

Without social equality, women and men can never attain the highest form of personal intimacy—friendship. The lack of friendship between parents, in turn, undermines healthy child care: "Children will never be properly educated till friendship subsists between parents. Virtue flies from a house divided against itself—and a whole legion of devils take up their residence there" (***Rights of Woman***, p. 292). Wollstonecraft traces the ills of society from the political order to the family and back again. Without political and social equality, men and women will never achieve friendship within the family or provide the proper care for their children. As a result, children will grow up ill-equipped for the duties of citizenship, and political society will remain nothing more than an assemblage of selfish and isolated individuals.

Wollstonecraft outlines two sets of concrete proposals for equalizing the condition of women within society. First, she demands the extension of political and civil rights to women, including the rights to life, liberty, and property as well as the right to vote (***Rights of Woman***, pp. 230-41). Unique to her defense of these rights is her attention to their effects on family life. She claims political rights will expand women's understanding of their place within the web of social relations. They will come to see themselves as active citizens with responsibilities to others outside their immediate social sphere. This enlarged social understanding will make them more devoted and adept care givers because they will realize the importance of their nurturing activities for the public good. Lacking this enlarged social understanding, they will remain fixated on their petty concerns and will be incapable of fulfilling even their private family duties. "It is plain from the history of all nations, that women cannot be confined to merely domestic pursuits, for they will not fulfill family duties, unless their minds take a wider range, and whilst they are kept in ignorance they become in the same proportion the slaves of pleasure as they are the slaves of men" (p. 270).

Wollstonecraft argues in a similar vein about civil rights for women. They should be given a legal existence independent of their father, husband, and brothers and granted the right to divorce (Sapiro 1992, 149-52, 237). They also should have the right to own and inherit property as autonomous citizens (***Rights of Woman***, pp. 230-41). Furthermore, the government should work to open careers to women. At present, Wollstonecraft complains, too many women waste their life in idleness who might otherwise have been doctors, nurses, midwives, politicians, merchants, teachers, store owners, farmers, and more (pp. 238-9). Free access to careers will not only allow women to contribute their talents to the public good but also help them achieve economic independence from men. As a result, "women would not then marry for a support . . . and neglect the implied duties" (p. 239). Open careers, like engagement in the political realm, also will broaden women's understanding. They will approach their nurturing relationships with a wider understanding of social affairs rather than through their own private idiosyncrasies and desires.

Wollstonecraft claims that professional careers for women will strengthen family ties. People will marry from affection rather than convention, necessity, or passing romance. They will relate to one another as equals with common interests and aims rather than as master and servant. "In short, in whatever light I view the subject, reason and experience convince me that the only method of leading women to fulfill their peculiar duties, is to free them from all restraint by allowing them to participate in the inherent rights of mankind" (**Rights of Woman,** p. 272). Political and civil rights are, by Wollstonecraft's account, the foundation of a caring society.

Wollstonecraft's other major reform proposal is her plan for national education for girls. She claims the extension of equal rights and opportunities to women is inadequate for addressing the deep gender inequality within society, much of which stems from the manner in which women are socialized.[8] They are taught to feign weakness and innocence rather than to develop their reason. According to Wollstonecraft, women who are socialized in this manner would gain little from political and civil rights. She therefore argues that the government should assume direction of children's education in order to combat these social prejudices and especially the parochial views of parents. "For whilst schoolmasters are dependent on the caprice of parents, little exertion can be expected from them, more than is necessary to please ignorant people" (**Rights of Woman,** p. 257).

Wollstonecraft specifically calls for the establishment of public day schools to serve as a counterweight to the inequities within the family. Their purpose should be twofold: Educate the mind and heart, that is, cultivate both reason and care. She outlines several pedagogical reforms to meet this end. First, public schools should abolish all false distinctions of sex by educating girls and boys together in the same subjects and activities. In this way, they will be inculcated with a sense of mutual respect from a young age (**Rights of Woman,** p. 260). "I presuppose, that such a degree of equality should be established between the sexes as would shut out gallantry and coquetry, yet allow friendship and love to temper the heart for the discharge of higher duties" (p. 264). Second, pedagogical methods based upon obedience and hierarchy should be replaced by a system of active learning carried out through examples and conversation and designed to create students who exercise their reason independently of their teachers (p. 251; Sapiro 1992, 240-1).[9] Third, attention should be given to an education of the heart. "I am, indeed, persuaded that the heart, as well as the understanding, is opened by cultivation; and by, which may not appear so clear, strengthening the organs; I am not now talking of momentary flashes of sensibility, but of affections" (p. 142). The best means to accomplish this goal is to broaden children's understanding of the intimate links between their nurturing duties and the public good.

In discussing the education of women in particular, Wollstonecraft conjectures that they would not be drawn to petty pursuits "if political and moral subjects were opened to them; and I will venture to affirm, that this is the only way to make them properly attentive to their domestic duties.—An active mind embraces the whole circle of its duties, and finds time enough for all" (**Rights of Woman,** p. 265). Starting from small practical examples within the classroom, children can be taught the importance of care and respect in interpersonal relations. Later these particular affections can be related to larger political and moral concerns. Students then can be shown the important role of their care-giving duties for society at large. The point is to elevate the moral status of care-giving activities by teaching students about the central role of these activities in fostering a healthy and functioning society.

Wollstonecraft's fusion of justice and care is most evident in her account of healthy care-giving activities. Here she claims that justice is necessary not only in broad social affairs but also in the intimate relations among individuals. It is not only a prerequisite for the delivery of care but also provides an important check on it. The proper approach of the adult care giver to the child is one of respectful nurturing. Parents and teachers should devote their nurturing activities to transforming children into autonomous beings. They are to address their wards in the following manner: "It is your interest to obey me till you can judge for yourself; and the Almighty Father of all has implanted an affection in me to serve as a guard to you whilst your reason is unfolding; but when your mind arrives at maturity, you must only obey me, or rather respect my opinions, so far as they coincide with the light that is breaking in on your own mind" (**Rights of Woman,** p. 247). This passage aptly summarizes Wollstonecraft's vision of adult care. Parents and teachers are to direct their affections to the development of a child's reason and autonomy. Even if they cannot treat children as equals and hence as friends, they should think of them as friends in the making.

The following passage from *Original Stories,* as relayed by Mrs. Mason, the tutor, highlights Wollstonecraft's views.[10]

> [As] Mary had before convinced me that she could regulate her appetites, I gave her leave to pluck as much fruit as she wished; and she did not abuse my indulgence. On the contrary, she spent [the] most part of the time gathering some for me, and her attention made it sweeter. Coming home I called her my friend, and she deserved the name, for she was no longer a child; a reasonable affection had conquered an appetite; her understanding took the lead, and she had practiced a virtue.

> (Wollstonecraft [1788] 1989, IV, 400-1)

The test of healthy, as opposed to self-indulgent, parental care is whether it promotes the child's autonomy. Only after achieving autonomy can the child express genuine care for others. The goal of the parent or teacher is to graduate the child from a dependent to a friend.

Wollstonecraft has no illusions about the short-term effectiveness of her proposed reforms. Since "men and women must be educated, in a great degree, by the opinions and manners of the society they live in," she concludes that "till society be differently constituted, much cannot be expected from education" (*Rights of Woman,* p. 89). The first step toward reform is the extension of equal rights and education to women, but this is only a first step. A "revolution in female manners" must sweep through society in order to effect real change (p. 292). The success of this revolution depends not only on a change in women's consciousness but also on the transformation of men's consciousness. "For I will venture to assert, that all the causes of female weakness, as well as depravity, which I have already enlarged on, branch out of one grand cause—want of chastity in men" (p. 227). As long as men respond to coquetry, women will continue to play the flirt. "The two sexes mutually corrupt and improve each other. This I believe to be an indisputable truth, extending it to every virtue. Chastity, modesty, public spirit, and all the noble train of virtues, on which social virtue and happiness are built, should be understood and cultivated by all mankind, or they will be cultivated to little effect" (p. 229).

Although Wollstonecraft's revolution may start with equal rights and educational reform, it will not reach its end until the deep prejudices against women are rooted out of society. It likewise requires a revaluation of caring activities within society. These are to be viewed not as ancillary to business and political activities but as primary human and social virtues to be embraced by both men and women. The reward Wollstonecraft holds out for this revolution is the emergence of a more dutiful and virtuous society. "The conclusion which I wish to draw, is obvious; make women rational creatures, and free citizens, and they will quickly become good wives, and mothers; that is—if men do not neglect the duties of husbands and fathers" (*Rights of Woman,* p. 275). Wollstonecraft aims at the radical transformation of society not so much by effecting substantial change in political or economic institutions as by instigating a revolution in the status and nature of care.

WOLLSTONECRAFT'S NURTURING LIBERALISM

It should be evident from the foregoing just how misleading it is to characterize Wollstonecraft simply as a classical liberal feminist. She rejects the classical liberal distinction between public and private spheres, emphasizes the importance of care-giving activities, and sets her sights on creating a more dutiful and caring citizen body. On the one hand, she emphasizes the importance of involving women in public affairs for the sake of making them more virtuous care givers. "Females, in fact, denied all political privileges, and not allowed, as married women, excepting in criminal cases, a civil existence, have their attention naturally drawn from the interest of the whole community to that of the minute parts, though the private duty of any member of society must be very imperfectly performed when not connected with the general good" (*Rights of Woman,* pp. 281-2).

On the other hand, she asserts the importance of private care for the development of public virtue.

> Public education, of every denomination, should be directed to form citizens; but if you wish to make good citizens, you must first exercise the affections of a son and a brother. This is the only way to expand the heart; for public affections, as well as public virtues, must ever grow out of the private character, or they are merely meteors that shoot athwart a dark sky, and disappear as they are gazed at and admired. Few, I believe, have had much affection for mankind, who did not first love their parents, their brothers, sisters, and even the domestic brutes, whom they first played with. The exercise of youthful sympathies forms the moral temperature; and it is the recollection of these first affections and pursuits that gives life to those that are afterwards more under the direction of reason.
>
> (*Rights of Woman,* p. 256)

Wollstonecraft ultimately aims at a massive and long-term reform of both public and private affairs. She calls upon the government to extend equal rights to women and to work for their equality in the family and careers. She also calls upon government to take a direct role in educating a more egalitarian and caring citizen body. Most generally, she claims the mission of government goes beyond the abstract guarantee of equality and rights to all; its task is more particularly to balance power differentials within society by taking the side of the weak against the strong (Sapiro 1992, 182): "Nature having made men unequal, by giving stronger bodily and mental powers to one than to another, the end of government ought to be, to destroy this inequality by protecting the weak. Instead of which, it has always leaned to the opposite side, wearing itself out by disregarding the first principle of its organization" (Wollstonecraft [1794] 1989, VI, 17). In short, Wollstonecraft reformulates the classical liberal definition of government by placing it within the larger framework of care. One might say she took Burke's criticisms of Enlightenment liberalism seriously enough to recognize that liberal governments need to give special attention to caring activities if they are to avoid the selfish egoism and individualism associated with liberal justice.

Wollstonecraft's thought also does not fit neatly into the classical republican tradition. Landes (1988, 123-51), for example, has portrayed Wollstonecraft as an advocate of republican motherhood. Yet, most advocates of republican motherhood embrace a sharp distinction between the public and private spheres (Sapiro 1992, 178-

9). They suggest that men have a civic role in the public realm, whereas women's civic duties are confined to their domestic duties as mothers and housekeepers. Wollstonecraft, by contrast, argues that men should play a more active role within the family as fathers and husbands, since family affection is the foundation of public virtue. She likewise urges an independent civic existence for women as a means for broadening their private affections.

Wollstonecraft thus breaks down the traditional republican distinction between public men and private women. She argues that the cultivation of virtue depends upon drawing more men into the home and more women into the public sphere. The inegalitarian division of society into public and private realms is just as corrupting as the hierarchical public world of subjects and kings. She also abandons the classical republican association of human virtue with political and military glory. The main attribute of a virtuous individual by her account is the self-conscious fulfillment of one's responsibilities and duties to others. She calls upon both men and women to spend at least as much time and energy on domestic care as they devote to their political and business pursuits.

Once the important role of care within Wollstonecraft's philosophy is recognized, some of the contemporary criticisms of her thought are dispelled. Contemporary feminists claim, for example, that Wollstonecraft's argument for women's equality is contradictory (Gatens 1991; Pateman 1989). She defines the duties of women as those of "mothers and wives" but fails to realize that these roles are at the root of women's oppression. Pateman dubs this contradiction "Wollstonecraft's dilemma." That is, Wollstonecraft demands equal rights for women in the "gender-neutral" social world but simultaneously insists that women have special capacities and duties that differentiate them from men. The two demands are incompatible, according to Pateman (1989, 197), because they recognize "two alternatives only: either women become (like) men, and so full citizens; or they continue at women's work, which is of no value for citizenship."

Although Pateman highlights an important problem for most classical liberal theories, her criticism does not apply to Wollstonecraft, who redefines the public sphere as a space where care is to be accorded special prominence. She calls for a "revolution" in social thinking whereby the caring duties of both men and women are to be given equal respect with and made essential to the obligations of citizenship. Both men and women are called upon to share equally in the care-giving and civic functions of citizenship. Pateman is correct to observe that Wollstonecraft never considers the possibility of such radical policy initiatives as public subsidies for parenting activities, but this policy is not contrary to

her philosophy, given the role she envisions for government in fostering care. She identifies the reforms she considers most necessary to develop a society more attuned to the value of care, while admitting that her proposals are only "sketches" (*Rights of Woman,* p. 71). She leaves it to others to develop her ideas.

There is thus nothing contradictory about Wollstonecraft demanding equal rights for women and exhorting them to fulfill domestic duties. In her vision of society, domestic duties are every bit as deserving of respect as public occupations, and men are similarly expected to fulfill their domestic duties while engaging in public life. If liberal society is still confronted with the dilemma of incorporating women into the public sphere as full citizens, it is only because it has failed to implement reforms necessary to complete Wollstonecraft's revolutionary project. We still do not fully recognize the value of nurturing activities for public life or acknowledge the degree to which some of our most pressing social problems may stem from our neglect of care.

CONCLUSION

Wollstonecraft provides contemporary feminists with a model that combines justice and care. Throughout her writings, she identifies care as the foundation and end of social relations. She stresses the importance of nurturing family relations for creating autonomous individuals, and she defines moral progress as movement toward a more virtuous and dutiful society. At the same time, she argues that the development of nurturing relations depends upon a just social structure, for only in such a structure can care find healthy expression. Ultimately, she breaks down the dichotomy between justice and care as well as between the public and private spheres by arguing that justice is an essential feature of care. Justice facilitates the healthy expression of care and also provides a criterion for healthy care giving.

Few contemporary feminists examine the influence of larger social forces on the delivery and expression of care, but Wollstonecraft makes this theme the focus of her political philosophy. She argues that under conditions of social or economic inequality, the delivery and expression of care are often distorted. Men neglect their wives and children, and women tyrannize over men and neglect or overindulge their children. Children then grow up without the capacity for sympathy or care. The implications for social policy are far-reaching.

Wollstonecraft's thought suggests that feminists (and others) concerned with care should focus more attention on identifying and addressing the social inequalities that hinder the expression and delivery of care within society. Without a just social structure, care will be stymied, and duties will go unfulfilled. At the same time, a concerted effort should be made to elevate the status of caring activities within society. Wollstonecraft proposes public support for and direction of the education system, but her ultimate goal is to foster a revolution in thinking that will lead to equal respect for care-giving activities. In this regard, her thought also suggests that feminists (and others) concerned about care should focus more attention on identifying the institutions and conventions that diminish the importance of care-giving functions within our society and should explore the possibilities for instituting public policies that will give more support and respect to nurturing activities.

Wollstonecraft calls for a revolution in care but leaves it to others to identify the particular laws and policies that might be necessary to complete it. As women today struggle with the multiple demands of family, work, and civic activity, Wollstonecraft provides an inspirational vision of the interrelatedness of all these activities. Good mothers are, by her account, career women and politically active. The same is true of good fathers. The central tasks of government are to ensure that women and men have equal access to careers and politics and to encourage them to fulfill their care-giving duties. Although Wollstonecraft may not provide all the answers for promoting a nurturing liberal order, her writings direct us to consider important questions. In what ways might social injustices inhibit the delivery of care within our society, and how might government better support caring activities? If Wollstonecraft's analysis is correct, the answers to these questions may hold the key to addressing some of the central pathologies—including selfishness, indifference, and irresponsibility—that afflict contemporary liberal societies.

Notes

1. The foundational works include Chodorow 1978, Gilligan 1982, Noddings 1984, and Ruddick 1980, 1989. Among recent works that apply care ethics to politics are Clement 1996, Friedman 1993, Held 1993, Hirschmann 1992, Hirschmann and Di Stefano 1996, Sevenhuijsen 1998, and Tronto 1993.

2. The Held and Gatens books are anthologies of articles and book chapters that represent a diversity of approaches to justice and care.

3. For a very different view on the ability of justice theories to accommodate the concerns of care theorists, see Kittay 1997 and Sevenhuijsen 1998, 72-9.

4. Sapiro (1992, 258-9) dubs Wollstonecraft a feminist on the grounds that she shared with nineteenth- and twentieth-century feminist theorists "a minimal and flexible set" of common ideas and concerns. See also Kelly 1992, 1-2.

5. Because the first edition of *A Vindication of the Rights of Men* was published anonymously,

Wollstonecraft probably did not initially conceive of this gender reversal as part of her public rhetorical strategy.

6. Tronto (1993, 61-97) argues in this vein that care is linked not only with gender but also with class and race; lower-class individuals and people of color adopt this perspective more often than individuals with power and privilege.

7. Jemima is initially presented as a woman who, due to oppression and abuse throughout her life, is misanthropic and actually colludes with the corrupt society by working as a guard in an asylum. Over the course of the novel, Maria and Jemima develop a friendship based largely upon their common experiences and oppression as women.

8. Sapiro (1992, 237-9) emphasizes that Wollstonecraft defines education broadly in terms of socialization.

9. In an interesting contemporary parallel, Koehn (1998) suggests that the Socratic method provides an appropriate model for promoting principled and healthy caring relationships.

10. For the view that Mrs. Mason represents the ideas of Wollstonecraft, see Kelly 1992, 63-4.

References

Baker-Benfield, G. J. 1989. "Mary Wollstonecraft: Eighteenth-Century Commonwealthwoman." *Journal of the History of Ideas* 50 (January): 95-115.

Barry, Brian. 1995. *Justice as Impartiality.* Oxford: Oxford University Press.

Burke, Edmund. [1790] 1987. *Reflections on the Revolution in France,* ed. J. G. A. Pocock. Indianapolis, IN: Hackett.

Card, Claudia. 1995. "Gender and Moral Luck." In *Justice and Care,* ed. Virginia Held. Boulder, CO: Westview. Pp. 79-98.

Chodorow, Nancy. 1978. *The Reproduction of Mothering,* Berkeley: University of California Press.

Clement, Grace. 1996. *Care, Autonomy and Justice.* Boulder, CO: Westview.

Dillon, Robin. 1992. "Care and Respect." In *Explorations in Feminist Ethics: Theory and Practice,* ed. Eve Browning Cole and Susan Coultrap-McQuin. Bloomington: Indiana University Press. Pp. 69-81.

Eisenstein, Zillah. 1981. *The Radical Future of Liberal Feminism.* New York: Longman.

Falco, Maria, ed. 1996. *Feminist Interpretations of Mary Wollstonecraft.* University Park: Pennsylvania State University Press.

Friedman, Marilyn. 1993. *What Are Friends For? Feminist Perspectives on Personal Relationships and Moral Theory.* Ithaca, NY: Cornell University Press.

Friedman, Marilyn. 1995. "Beyond Caring: The De-Moralization of Gender." In *Justice and Care,* ed. Virginia Held. Boulder, CO: Westview. Pp. 61-77.

Gatens, Moira, ed. 1998. *Feminist Ethics.* Brookfield, VT: Ashgate.

Gatens, Moira. 1991. "'The Oppressed State of My Sex': Wollstonecraft on Reason, Feeling and Equality." In *Feminist Interpretations and Political Theory,* ed. Mary Lyndon Shanley and Carole Pateman. University Park: Pennsylvania State University Press. Pp. 112-28.

Gilligan, Carol. 1982. *In a Different Voice.* Cambridge, MA: Harvard University Press.

Gunther-Canada, Wendy. 1996. "Mary Wollstonecraft's 'Wild Wish': Confounding Sex in the Discourse on Political Rights." In *Feminist Interpretations of Mary Wollstonecraft,* ed. Maria Falco. University Park: Pennsylvania State University Press. Pp. 61-83.

Gunther-Canada, Wendy. 1997. "Teaching Mary Wollstonecraft: Women and the Canonical Conversation of Political Thought." *Feminist Teacher* 11 (Spring): 20-9.

Held, Virginia. 1993. *Feminist Morality: Transforming Culture, Society, and Politics.* Chicago: University of Chicago Press.

Held, Virginia, ed. 1995a. *Justice and Care.* Boulder, CO: Westview.

Held, Virginia. 1995b. "The Meshing of Care and Justice." *Hypatia* 10 (Spring): 128-32.

Hirschmann, Nancy. 1992. *Rethinking Obligation: A Feminist Method for Political Theory.* Ithaca, NY: Cornell University Press.

Hirschmann, Nancy, and Christine Di Stefano, eds. 1996. *Revisioning the Political.* Boulder, CO: Westview.

Jacobus, Mary. 1986. *Reading Woman: Essays in Feminist Criticism.* New York: Columbia University Press.

Jaggar, Alison. 1995. "Caring as a Feminist Practice of Moral Reason." In *Justice and Care,* ed. Virginia Held. Boulder, CO: Westview. Pp. 179-202.

James, Susan. 1992. "The Good-Enough Citizen: Female Citizenship and Independence." In *Beyond Equality and Difference,* ed. Gisela Bock and Susan James. New York: Routledge. Pp. 48-65.

Johnson, Claudia. 1995. *Equivocal Beings: Politics, Gender, and Sentimentality in the 1790s.* Chicago: University of Chicago Press.

Katzenstein, Mary Fainsod, and David Laitin. "Politics, Feminism, and the Ethics of Caring." In *Women and Moral Theory,* ed. Eva Kitty and Diana Meyers. Totowa, NJ: Rowman & Littlefield. Pp. 261-81.

Kelly, Gary. 1992. *Revolutionary Feminism: The Mind and Career of Mary Wollstonecraft.* New York: St. Martin's.

Kittay, Eva Feder. 1997. "Human Dependency and Rawlsian Equality." In *Feminists Rethink the Self,* ed. Diana Tietjens Meyers. Boulder, CO: Westview. Pp. 219-66.

Koehn, Daryl. 1998. *Rethinking Feminist Ethics.* New York: Routledge.

Landes, Joan. 1988. *Women and the Public Sphere in the Age of the French Revolution.* Ithaca, NY: Cornell University Press.

Mendus, Susan. 1993. "Different Voices, Still Lives: Problems in the Ethics of Care." *Journal of Applied Philosophy* 10 (1): 17-27.

Muller, Virginia. 1996. "What Can Liberals Learn from Mary Wollstonecraft?" In *Feminist Interpretations of Mary Wollstonecraft,* ed. Maria Falco. University Park: Pennsylvania State University Press. Pp. 47-60.

Narayan, Uma. 1995. "Colonialism and Its Others: Considerations On Rights and Care Discourses." *Hypatia* 10 (Spring): 133-40.

Noddings, Nell. 1984. *Caring: A Feminine Approach to Ethics and Moral Education.* Berkeley: University of California Press.

Okin, Susan. 1981. "Women and the Making of the Sentimental Family." *Philosophy and Public Affairs* 11 (1): 65-88.

Okin, Susan. 1989a. *Justice, Gender, and the Family.* New York: Basic Books.

Okin, Susan. 1989b. "Reason and Feeling in Thinking about Justice." *Ethics* 99 (2): 229-49.

Pateman, Carole. 1989. *The Disorder of Women: Democracy, Feminism and Political Theory.* Stanford, CA: Stanford University Press.

Poovey, Mary. 1984. *The Proper Lady and the Woman Writer: Ideology as Style in the Works of Mary Wollstonecraft, Mary Shelley and Jane Austen.* Chicago: University of Chicago Press.

Robinson, Fiona. 1999. *Globalizing Care: Ethics, Feminist Theory, and International Relations.* Boulder, CO: Westview.

Ruddick, Sara. 1980. "Maternal Thinking." *Feminist Studies* 6 (Summer): 342-67.

Ruddick, Sara. 1989. *Maternal Thinking.* Boston: Beacon.

Ruddick, Sara. 1990. "The Rationality of Care." In *Women, Militarism and War: Essays in History, Politics and Social Theory,* ed. Jean Bethke Elshtain and Sheila Tobias. Savage, MD: Rowman & Littlefield. Pp. 229-54.

Sapiro, Virginia. 1992. *A Vindication of Political Virtue: The Political Theory of Mary Wollstonecraft.* Chicago: University of Chicago Press.

Sapiro, Virginia. 1996. "Wollstonecraft, Feminism, and Democracy: 'Being Bastilled.'" In *Feminist Interpretations of Mary Wollstonecraft,* ed. Maria Falco. University Park: Pennsylvania State University Press. Pp. 33-45.

Sevenhuijsen, Selma. 1998. *Citizenship and the Ethics of Care: Feminist Considerations on Justice, Morality and Politics,* trans. Liz Savage. New York: Routledge.

Tronto, Joan. 1993. *Moral Boundaries: A Political Argument for an Ethic of Care.* New York: Routledge.

Weiss, Penny. 1996. "Wollstonecraft and Rousseau: The Gendered Fate of Political Theorists." In *Feminist Interpretations of Mary Wollstonecraft,* ed. Maria Falco. University Park: Pennsylvania State University Press. Pp. 15-32.

Wollstonecraft, Mary. [1790, 1792] 1995. *A Vindication of the Rights of Men and A Vindication of the Rights of Women,* ed. Sylvana Tomaselli. Cambridge: Cambridge University Press.

Wollstonecraft, Mary. 1989. *The Works of Mary Wollstonecraft,* ed. Janet Todd and Marilyn Butler. London: Pickering.

FURTHER READING

Biographies

Flexner, Eleanor. *Mary Wollstonecraft.* New York: Penguin Books, 1972, 307 p.

> Scholarly account of Wollstonecraft's life that emphasizes her early years.

George, Margaret. *"One Woman's Situation": A Study of Mary Wollstonecraft.* Urbana: University of Illinois Press, 1970, 174 p.

> Political and psychological study of Wollstonecraft that explores the connection between her life experience and her political ideas.

Godwin, William. *Memoirs of the Author of a Vindication of the Rights of Woman.* 1798. Reprint. Harmondsworth, England: Penguin Books, 1987, 224 p.

> Memoir of Wollstonecraft, written by her husband, that outlines the relation between Wollstonecraft's writings and her personal history, and offers candid analyses of her various relationships, including that with her husband.

Todd, Janet. *Mary Wollstonecraft.* London: Weidenfeld and Nicholson, 2000, 538 p.

> Vivid portrayal of Wollstonecraft that quotes extensively from her correspondence and notes the difference between the author's emotion-laden writing about her personal life and her reasoned tone in *A Vindication of the Rights of Woman.*

Tomalin, Claire. *The Life and Death of Mary Wollstonecraft.* London: Weidenfeld and Nicholson, 1974, 316 p.

> Account of Wollstonecraft's life and social context.

Wardle, Ralph M. *Mary Wollstonecraft: A Critical Biography.* Lawrence: University of Kansas Press, 1951, 366 p.

> Detailed study of Wollstonecraft's life and works, including *A Vindication of the Rights of Woman,* that examines the literary and social context in which the author worked.

Criticism

Barker-Benfield, G., "Mary Wollstonecraft: Eighteenth-Century Commonwealthwoman." *Journal of the History of Ideas* 50 (1989): 95-115.

> Views Wollstonecraft's achievement as extending the Commonwealth analysis of male corruption and program for male reform to women and discusses the elements of Commonwealth thought on which Wollstonecraft drew in her political writings, including *A Vindication of the Rights of Woman.*

Field, Corinne. "Breast-Feeding, Sexual Pleasure, and Women's Rights: Mary Wollstonecraft's *Vindication.*" *Critical Matrix: The Princeton Journal of Women, Gender, and Culture* 9, no. 2 (1995) 25-44.

> Explores Wollstonecraft's attitude toward female sexuality, motherhood, women's bodies, and women's rights as discussed in *A Vindication of the Rights of Woman.*

Gunther-Canada, Wendy. "Teaching Mary Wollstonecraft: Women and the Canonical Conversation of Political Thought." *Feminist Teacher* 11, no. 1 (spring 1997): 20-29.

> Examines the silence of women as authors in the canon of political writing and discusses the critic's own experience teaching Wollstonecraft in her classroom.

Khin Zaw, Susan. "The Reasonable Heart: Mary Wollstonecraft's View of the Relation Between Reason and Feeling in Morality, Moral Psychology, and Moral Development." *Hypatia* 13, no. 1 (winter 1990): 78-117.

Discusses Wollstonecraft's view of moral psychology, moral education, and moral philosophy in her early works, especially *A Vindication of the Rights of Woman*.

O'Quinn. "Trembling: Wollstonecraft, Godwin and the Resistance to Literature." *ELH* 64, no. 3 (fall 1997): 761-88.

Examines Wollstonecraft's polemic against literature in *A Vindication of the Rights of Woman* before discussing in detail her critique of the dangers of literature in *Maria; or The Wrongs of Woman*.

Robinson, Charles E. "A Mother's Daughter: An Intersection of Mary Shelley's *Frankenstein* and Mary Wollstonecraft's *A Vindication of the Rights of Woman*."

In *Mary Wollstonecraft and Mary Shelley: Writing Lives*, edited by Helen M. Buss, D. L. Macdonald, and Anne McWhir, pp. 127-38. Waterloo, Ontario: Wilfried Laurier University Press, 2001.

Examines Mary Shelley's life and works in relation to her mother, noting the influence of Wollstonecraft on Shelley's novel *Frankenstein*.

Sulloway, Alison G. "Emma Woodhouse and *A Vindication of the Rights of Woman*." *Wordsworth Circle* 7, no. 4 (autumn 1976): 320-32.

Discusses Jane Austen's indebtedness to *A Vindication of the Rights of Woman* as seen in her novel *Emma*.

Additional coverage of Mary Wollstonecraft's life and career is contained in the following sources published by the Gale Group: *British Writers Supplement*; *Concise Dictionary of British Literary Biography, 1789-1832*; *Dictionary of Literary Biography*, Vols. 39, 104, 158 and 252; *Feminist Writers*; *Literature and Its Times*, Vol. 1; *Literature Criticism from 1400 to 1800*, Vols. 5, 50; *Literature Resource Center*; *Reference Guide to English Literature*, ed. 2; *World Literature and Its Times*, Vol. 3.

How to Use This Index

The main references

Calvino, Italo
    1923-1985 .... **CLC 5, 8, 11, 22, 33, 39,
                                73; SSC 3, 48**
---

list all author entries in the following Gale Literary Criticism series:

AAL = *Asian American Literature*
BG = *The Beat Generation: A Gale Critical Companion*
BLC = *Black Literature Criticism*
BLCS = *Black Literature Criticism Supplement*
CLC = *Contemporary Literary Criticism*
CLR = *Children's Literature Review*
CMLC = *Classical and Medieval Literature Criticism*
DC = *Drama Criticism*
HLC = *Hispanic Literature Criticism*
HLCS = *Hispanic Literature Criticism Supplement*
HR = *Harlem Renaissance: A Gale Critical Companion*
LC = *Literature Criticism from 1400 to 1800*
NCLC = *Nineteenth-Century Literature Criticism*
NNAL = *Native North American Literature*
PC = *Poetry Criticism*
SSC = *Short Story Criticism*
TCLC = *Twentieth-Century Literary Criticism*
WLC = *World Literature Criticism, 1500 to the Present*
WLCS = *World Literature Criticism Supplement*

The cross-references

See also CA 85-88, 116; CANR 23, 61;
DAM NOV; DLB 196; EW 13; MTCW 1, 2;
RGSF 2; RGWL 2; SFW 4; SSFS 12
---

list all author entries in the following Gale biographical and literary sources:

AAYA = *Authors & Artists for Young Adults*
AFAW = *African American Writers*
AFW = *African Writers*
AITN = *Authors in the News*
AMW = *American Writers*
AMWR = *American Writers Retrospective Supplement*
AMWS = *American Writers Supplement*
ANW = *American Nature Writers*
AW = *Ancient Writers*
BEST = *Bestsellers*
BPFB = *Beacham's Encyclopedia of Popular Fiction: Biography and Resources*
BRW = *British Writers*
BRWS = *British Writers Supplement*
BW = *Black Writers*
BYA = *Beacham's Guide to Literature for Young Adults*
CA = *Contemporary Authors*
CAAS = *Contemporary Authors Autobiography Series*
CABS = *Contemporary Authors Bibliographical Series*
CAD = *Contemporary American Dramatists*
CANR = *Contemporary Authors New Revision Series*
CAP = *Contemporary Authors Permanent Series*
CBD = *Contemporary British Dramatists*
CCA = *Contemporary Canadian Authors*
CD = *Contemporary Dramatists*
CDALB = *Concise Dictionary of American Literary Biography*
CDALBS = *Concise Dictionary of American Literary Biography Supplement*
CDBLB = *Concise Dictionary of British Literary Biography*

CMW = *St. James Guide to Crime & Mystery Writers*

CN = *Contemporary Novelists*

CP = *Contemporary Poets*

CPW = *Contemporary Popular Writers*

CSW = *Contemporary Southern Writers*

CWD = *Contemporary Women Dramatists*

CWP = *Contemporary Women Poets*

CWRI = *St. James Guide to Children's Writers*

CWW = *Contemporary World Writers*

DA = *DISCovering Authors*

DA3 = *DISCovering Authors 3.0*

DAB = *DISCovering Authors: British Edition*

DAC = *DISCovering Authors: Canadian Edition*

DAM = *DISCovering Authors: Modules*

    DRAM: *Dramatists Module;* **MST:** *Most-studied Authors Module;*

    MULT: *Multicultural Authors Module;* **NOV:** *Novelists Module;*

    POET: *Poets Module;* **POP:** *Popular Fiction and Genre Authors Module*

DFS = *Drama for Students*

DLB = *Dictionary of Literary Biography*

DLBD = *Dictionary of Literary Biography Documentary Series*

DLBY = *Dictionary of Literary Biography Yearbook*

DNFS = *Literature of Developing Nations for Students*

EFS = *Epics for Students*

EXPN = *Exploring Novels*

EXPP = *Exploring Poetry*

EXPS = *Exploring Short Stories*

EW = *European Writers*

FANT = *St. James Guide to Fantasy Writers*

FW = *Feminist Writers*

GFL = *Guide to French Literature,* Beginnings to 1789, 1798 to the Present

GLL = *Gay and Lesbian Literature*

HGG = *St. James Guide to Horror, Ghost & Gothic Writers*

HW = *Hispanic Writers*

IDFW = *International Dictionary of Films and Filmmakers: Writers and Production Artists*

IDTP = *International Dictionary of Theatre: Playwrights*

LAIT = *Literature and Its Times*

LAW = *Latin American Writers*

JRDA = *Junior DISCovering Authors*

MAICYA = *Major Authors and Illustrators for Children and Young Adults*

MAICYAS = *Major Authors and Illustrators for Children and Young Adults Supplement*

MAWW = *Modern American Women Writers*

MJW = *Modern Japanese Writers*

MTCW = *Major 20th-Century Writers*

NCFS = *Nonfiction Classics for Students*

NFS = *Novels for Students*

PAB = *Poets: American and British*

PFS = *Poetry for Students*

RGAL = *Reference Guide to American Literature*

RGEL = *Reference Guide to English Literature*

RGSF = *Reference Guide to Short Fiction*

RGWL = *Reference Guide to World Literature*

RHW = *Twentieth-Century Romance and Historical Writers*

SAAS = *Something about the Author Autobiography Series*

SATA = *Something about the Author*

SFW = *St. James Guide to Science Fiction Writers*

SSFS = *Short Stories for Students*

TCWW = *Twentieth-Century Western Writers*

WLIT = *World Literature and Its Times*

WP = *World Poets*

YABC = *Yesterday's Authors of Books for Children*

YAW = *St. James Guide to Young Adult Writers*

Literary Criticism Series
Cumulative Author Index

Artsybashev, Mikhail (Petrovich)
1878-1927 .... **TCLC 31**
See also CA 170

Arundel, Honor (Morfydd)
1919-1973 .... **CLC 17**
See also CA 21-22; 41-44R; CAP 2; CLR 35; CWRI 5; SATA 4; SATA-Obit 24

Arzner, Dorothy 1900-1979 .... **CLC 98**

Asch, Sholem 1880-1957 .... **TCLC 3**
See also CA 105; EWL 3; GLL 2

Ash, Shalom
See Asch, Sholem

Ashbery, John (Lawrence) 1927- .. **CLC 2, 3, 4, 6, 9, 13, 15, 25, 41, 77, 125; PC 26**
See Berry, Jonas
See also AMWS 3; CA 5-8R; CANR 9, 37, 66, 102; CP 7; DA3; DAM POET; DLB 5, 165; DLBY 1981; EWL 3; INT CANR-9; MTCW 1, 2; PAB; PFS 11; RGAL 4; WP

Ashdown, Clifford
See Freeman, R(ichard) Austin

Ashe, Gordon
See Creasey, John

Ashton-Warner, Sylvia (Constance)
1908-1984 .... **CLC 19**
See also CA 69-72; 112; CANR 29; MTCW 1, 2

Asimov, Isaac 1920-1992 ..... **CLC 1, 3, 9, 19, 26, 76, 92**
See also AAYA 13; BEST 90:2; BPFB 1; BYA 4, 6, 7, 9; CA 1-4R; 137; CANR 2, 19, 36, 60; CLR 12, 79; CMW 4; CPW; DA3; DAM POP; DLB 8; DLBY 1992; INT CANR-19; JRDA; LAIT 5; LMFS 2; MAICYA 1, 2; MTCW 1, 2; RGAL 4; SATA 1, 26, 74; SCFW 2; SFW 4; SSFS 17; TUS; YAW

Askew, Anne 1521(?)-1546 .... **LC 81**
See also DLB 136

Assis, Joaquim Maria Machado de
See Machado de Assis, Joaquim Maria

Astell, Mary 1666-1731 .... **LC 68**
See also DLB 252; FW

Astley, Thea (Beatrice May) 1925- .. **CLC 41**
See also CA 65-68; CANR 11, 43, 78; CN 7; EWL 3

Astley, William 1855-1911
See Warung, Price

Aston, James
See White, T(erence) H(anbury)

Asturias, Miguel Angel 1899-1974 .... **CLC 3, 8, 13; HLC 1**
See also CA 25-28; 49-52; CANR 32; CAP 2; CDWLB 3; DA3; DAM MULT, NOV; DLB 113; EWL 3; HW 1; LAW; LMFS 2; MTCW 1, 2; RGWL 2, 3; WLIT 1

Atares, Carlos Saura
See Saura (Atares), Carlos

Athanasius c. 295-c. 373 .... **CMLC 48**

Atheling, William
See Pound, Ezra (Weston Loomis)

Atheling, William, Jr.
See Blish, James (Benjamin)

Atherton, Gertrude (Franklin Horn)
1857-1948 .... **TCLC 2**
See also CA 104; 155; DLB 9, 78, 186; HGG; RGAL 4; SUFW 1; TCWW 2

Atherton, Lucius
See Masters, Edgar Lee

Atkins, Jack
See Harris, Mark

Atkinson, Kate 1951- .... **CLC 99**
See also CA 166; CANR 101; DLB 267

Attaway, William (Alexander)
1911-1986 .... **BLC 1; CLC 92**
See also BW 2, 3; CA 143; CANR 82; DAM MULT; DLB 76

Atticus
See Fleming, Ian (Lancaster); Wilson, (Thomas) Woodrow

Atwood, Margaret (Eleanor) 1939- ... **CLC 2, 3, 4, 8, 13, 15, 25, 44, 84, 135; PC 8; SSC 2, 46; WLC**
See also AAYA 12, 47; BEST 89:2; BPFB 1; CA 49-52; CANR 3, 24, 33, 59, 95; CN 7; CP 7; CPW; CWP; DA; DA3; DAB; DAC; DAM MST, NOV, POET; DLB 53, 251; EWL 3; EXPN; FW; INT CANR-24; LAIT 5; MTCW 1, 2; NFS 4, 12, 13, 14; PFS 7; RGSF 2; SATA 50; SSFS 3, 13; TWA; YAW

Aubigny, Pierre d'
See Mencken, H(enry) L(ouis)

Aubin, Penelope 1685-1731(?) .... **LC 9**
See also DLB 39

Auchincloss, Louis (Stanton) 1917- ... **CLC 4, 6, 9, 18, 45; SSC 22**
See also AMWS 4; CA 1-4R; CANR 6, 29, 55, 87; CN 7; DAM NOV; DLB 2, 244; DLBY 1980; EWL 3; INT CANR-29; MTCW 1; RGAL 4

Auden, W(ystan) H(ugh) 1907-1973 . **CLC 1, 2, 3, 4, 6, 9, 11, 14, 43, 123; PC 1; WLC**
See also AAYA 18; AMWS 2; BRW 7; BRWR 1; CA 9-12R; 45-48; CANR 5, 61, 105; CDBLB 1914-1945; DA; DA3; DAB; DAC; DAM DRAM, MST, POET; DLB 10, 20; EWL 3; EXPP; MTCW 1, 2; PAB; PFS 1, 3, 4, 10; TUS; WP

Audiberti, Jacques 1900-1965 .... **CLC 38**
See also CA 25-28R; DAM DRAM; EWL 3

Audubon, John James 1785-1851 . **NCLC 47**
See also ANW; DLB 248

Auel, Jean M(arie) 1936- .... **CLC 31, 107**
See also AAYA 7; BEST 90:4; BPFB 1; CA 103; CANR 21, 64, 115; CPW; DA3; DAM POP; INT CANR-21; NFS 11; RHW; SATA 91

Auerbach, Erich 1892-1957 .... **TCLC 43**
See also CA 118; 155; EWL 3

Augier, Emile 1820-1889 .... **NCLC 31**
See also DLB 192; GFL 1789 to the Present

August, John
See De Voto, Bernard (Augustine)

Augustine, St. 354-430 .... **CMLC 6; WLCS**
See also DA; DA3; DAB; DAC; DAM MST; DLB 115; EW 1; RGWL 2, 3

Aunt Belinda
See Braddon, Mary Elizabeth

Aunt Weedy
See Alcott, Louisa May

Aurelius
See Bourne, Randolph S(illiman)

Aurelius, Marcus 121-180 .... **CMLC 45**
See Marcus Aurelius
See also RGWL 2, 3

Aurobindo, Sri
See Ghose, Aurabinda

Aurobindo Ghose
See Ghose, Aurabinda

Austen, Jane 1775-1817 ...... **NCLC 1, 13, 19, 33, 51, 81, 95, 119; WLC**
See also AAYA 19; BRW 4; BRWC 1; BRWR 2; BYA 3; CDBLB 1789-1832; DA; DA3; DAB; DAC; DAM MST, NOV; DLB 116; EXPN; LAIT 2; LATS 1; LMFS 1; NFS 1, 14; TEA; WLIT 3; WYAS 1

Auster, Paul 1947- .... **CLC 47, 131**
See also AMWS 12; CA 69-72; CANR 23, 52, 75; CMW 4; CN 7; DA3; DLB 227; MTCW 1; SUFW 2

Austin, Frank
See Faust, Frederick (Schiller)
See also TCWW 2

Austin, Mary (Hunter) 1868-1934 . **TCLC 25**
See Stairs, Gordon
See also ANW; CA 109; 178; DLB 9, 78, 206, 221, 275; FW; TCWW 2

Averroes 1126-1198 .... **CMLC 7**
See also DLB 115

Avicenna 980-1037 .... **CMLC 16**
See also DLB 115

Avison, Margaret 1918- .... **CLC 2, 4, 97**
See also CA 17-20R; CP 7; DAC; DAM POET; DLB 53; MTCW 1

Axton, David
See Koontz, Dean R(ay)

Ayckbourn, Alan 1939- ...... **CLC 5, 8, 18, 33, 74; DC 13**
See also BRWS 5; CA 21-24R; CANR 31, 59, 118; CBD; CD 5; DAB; DAM DRAM; DFS 7; DLB 13, 245; EWL 3; MTCW 1, 2

Aydy, Catherine
See Tennant, Emma (Christina)

Ayme, Marcel (Andre) 1902-1967 ... **CLC 11; SSC 41**
See also CA 89-92; CANR 67; CLR 25; DLB 72; EW 12; EWL 3; GFL 1789 to the Present; RGSF 2; RGWL 2, 3; SATA 91

Ayrton, Michael 1921-1975 .... **CLC 7**
See also CA 5-8R; 61-64; CANR 9, 21

Aytmatov, Chingiz
See Aitmatov, Chingiz (Torekulovich)
See also EWL 3

Azorin .... **CLC 11**
See Martinez Ruiz, Jose
See also EW 9; EWL 3

Azuela, Mariano 1873-1952 .. **HLC 1; TCLC 3**
See also CA 104; 131; CANR 81; DAM MULT; EWL 3; HW 1, 2; LAW; MTCW 1, 2

Ba, Mariama 1929-1981 .... **BLCS**
See also AFW; BW 2; CA 141; CANR 87; DNFS 2; WLIT 2

Baastad, Babbis Friis
See Friis-Baastad, Babbis Ellinor

Bab
See Gilbert, W(illiam) S(chwenck)

Babbis, Eleanor
See Friis-Baastad, Babbis Ellinor

Babel, Isaac
See Babel, Isaak (Emmanuilovich)
See also EW 11; SSFS 10

Babel, Isaak (Emmanuilovich)
1894-1941(?) .... **SSC 16; TCLC 2, 13**
See Babel, Isaac
See also CA 104; 155; CANR 113; DLB 272; EWL 3; MTCW 1; RGSF 2; RGWL 2, 3; TWA

Babits, Mihaly 1883-1941 .... **TCLC 14**
See also CA 114; CDWLB 4; DLB 215; EWL 3

Babur 1483-1530 .... **LC 18**

Babylas 1898-1962
See Ghelderode, Michel de

Baca, Jimmy Santiago 1952- . **HLC 1; PC 41**
See also CA 131; CANR 81, 90; CP 7; DAM MULT; DLB 122; HW 1, 2

Baca, Jose Santiago
See Baca, Jimmy Santiago

Bacchelli, Riccardo 1891-1985 .... **CLC 19**
See also CA 29-32R; 117; DLB 264; EWL 3

Bach, Richard (David) 1936- .... **CLC 14**
See also AITN 1; BEST 89:2; BPFB 1; BYA 5; CA 9-12R; CANR 18, 93; CPW; DAM NOV, POP; FANT; MTCW 1; SATA 13

Bache, Benjamin Franklin
1769-1798 .... **LC 74**
See also DLB 43

Bergelson, David 1884-1952 .... **TCLC 81**
See Bergelson, Dovid
Bergelson, Dovid
See Bergelson, David
See also EWL 3
Berger, Colonel
See Malraux, (Georges-)Andre
Berger, John (Peter) 1926- .... **CLC 2, 19**
See also BRWS 4; CA 81-84; CANR 51, 78, 117; CN 7; DLB 14, 207
Berger, Melvin H. 1927- .... **CLC 12**
See also CA 5-8R; CANR 4; CLR 32; SAAS 2; SATA 5, 88; SATA-Essay 124
Berger, Thomas (Louis) 1924- .. **CLC 3, 5, 8, 11, 18, 38**
See also BPFB 1; CA 1-4R; CANR 5, 28, 51; CN 7; DAM NOV; DLB 2; DLBY 1980; EWL 3; FANT; INT CANR-28; MTCW 1, 2; RHW; TCWW 2
Bergman, (Ernst) Ingmar 1918- ...... **CLC 16, 72**
See also CA 81-84; CANR 33, 70; DLB 257; MTCW 2
Bergson, Henri(-Louis) 1859-1941 . **TCLC 32**
See also CA 164; EW 8; EWL 3; GFL 1789 to the Present
Bergstein, Eleanor 1938- .... **CLC 4**
See also CA 53-56; CANR 5
Berkeley, George 1685-1753 .... **LC 65**
See also DLB 31, 101, 252
Berkoff, Steven 1937- .... **CLC 56**
See also CA 104; CANR 72; CBD; CD 5
Berlin, Isaiah 1909-1997 .... **TCLC 105**
See also CA 85-88; 162
Bermant, Chaim (Icyk) 1929-1998 ... **CLC 40**
See also CA 57-60; CANR 6, 31, 57, 105; CN 7
Bern, Victoria
See Fisher, M(ary) F(rances) K(ennedy)
Bernanos, (Paul Louis) Georges 1888-1948 .... **TCLC 3**
See also CA 104; 130; CANR 94; DLB 72; EWL 3; GFL 1789 to the Present; RGWL 2, 3
Bernard, April 1956- .... **CLC 59**
See also CA 131
Berne, Victoria
See Fisher, M(ary) F(rances) K(ennedy)
Bernhard, Thomas 1931-1989 ..... **CLC 3, 32, 61; DC 14**
See also CA 85-88; 127; CANR 32, 57; CD-WLB 2; DLB 85, 124; EWL 3; MTCW 1; RGWL 2, 3
Bernhardt, Sarah (Henriette Rosine) 1844-1923 .... **TCLC 75**
See also CA 157
Bernstein, Charles 1950- .... **CLC 142,**
See also CA 129; CAAS 24; CANR 90; CP 7; DLB 169
Berriault, Gina 1926-1999 .... **CLC 54, 109; SSC 30**
See also CA 116; 129; 185; CANR 66; DLB 130; SSFS 7,11
Berrigan, Daniel 1921- .... **CLC 4**
See also CA 33-36R; CAAE 187; CAAS 1; CANR 11, 43, 78; CP 7; DLB 5
Berrigan, Edmund Joseph Michael, Jr. 1934-1983
See Berrigan, Ted
See also CA 61-64; 110; CANR 14, 102
Berrigan, Ted .... **CLC 37**
See Berrigan, Edmund Joseph Michael, Jr.
See also DLB 5, 169; WP
Berry, Charles Edward Anderson 1931-
See Berry, Chuck
See also CA 115
Berry, Chuck .... **CLC 17**
See Berry, Charles Edward Anderson

Berry, Jonas
See Ashbery, John (Lawrence)
See also GLL 1
Berry, Wendell (Erdman) 1934- ... **CLC 4, 6, 8, 27, 46; PC 28**
See also AITN 1; AMWS 10; ANW; CA 73-76; CANR 50, 73, 101; CP 7; CSW; DAM POET; DLB 5, 6, 234, 275; MTCW 1
Berryman, John 1914-1972 ... **CLC 1, 2, 3, 4, 6, 8, 10, 13, 25, 62**
See also AMW; CA 13-16; 33-36R; CABS 2; CANR 35; CAP 1; CDALB 1941-1968; DAM POET; DLB 48; EWL 3; MTCW 1, 2; PAB; RGAL 4; WP
Bertolucci, Bernardo 1940- ...... **CLC 16, 157**
See also CA 106
Berton, Pierre (Francis Demarigny) 1920- .... **CLC 104**
See also CA 1-4R; CANR 2, 56; CPW; DLB 68; SATA 99
Bertrand, Aloysius 1807-1841 .... **NCLC 31**
See Bertrand, Louis oAloysiusc
Bertrand, Louis oAloysiusc
See Bertrand, Aloysius
See also DLB 217
Bertran de Born c. 1140-1215 .... **CMLC 5**
Besant, Annie (Wood) 1847-1933 ..... **TCLC 9**
See also CA 105; 185
Bessie, Alvah 1904-1985 .... **CLC 23**
See also CA 5-8R; 116; CANR 2, 80; DLB 26
Bethlen, T. D.
See Silverberg, Robert
Beti, Mongo .... **BLC 1; CLC 27**
See Biyidi, Alexandre
See also AFW; CANR 79; DAM MULT; EWL 3; WLIT 2
Betjeman, John 1906-1984 ...... **CLC 2, 6, 10, 34, 43**
See also BRW 7; CA 9-12R; 112; CANR 33, 56; CDBLB 1945-1960; DA3; DAB; DAM MST, POET; DLB 20; DLBY 1984; EWL 3; MTCW 1, 2
Bettelheim, Bruno 1903-1990 .... **CLC 79**
See also CA 81-84; 131; CANR 23, 61; DA3; MTCW 1, 2
Betti, Ugo 1892-1953 .... **TCLC 5**
See also CA 104; 155; EWL 3; RGWL 2, 3
Betts, Doris (Waugh) 1932- ..... **CLC 3, 6, 28; SSC 45**
See also CA 13-16R; CANR 9, 66, 77; CN 7; CSW; DLB 218; DLBY 1982; INT CANR-9; RGAL 4
Bevan, Alistair
See Roberts, Keith (John Kingston)
Bey, Pilaff
See Douglas, (George) Norman
Bialik, Chaim Nachman 1873-1934 .... **TCLC 25**
See also CA 170; EWL 3
Bickerstaff, Isaac
See Swift, Jonathan
Bidart, Frank 1939- .... **CLC 33**
See also CA 140; CANR 106; CP 7
Bienek, Horst 1930- .... **CLC 7, 11**
See also CA 73-76; DLB 75
Bierce, Ambrose (Gwinett) 1842-1914(?) ..... **SSC 9; TCLC 1, 7, 44; WLC**
See also AMW; BYA 11; CA 104; 139; CANR 78; CDALB 1865-1917; DA; DA3; DAC; DAM MST; DLB 11, 12, 23, 71, 74, 186; EWL 3; EXPS; HGG; LAIT 2; RGAL 4; RGSF 2; SSFS 9; SUFW 1
Biggers, Earl Derr 1884-1933 .... **TCLC 65**
See also CA 108; 153
Billiken, Bud
See Motley, Willard (Francis)

Billings, Josh
See Shaw, Henry Wheeler
Billington, (Lady) Rachel (Mary) 1942- .... **CLC 43**
See also AITN 2; CA 33-36R; CANR 44; CN 7
Binchy, Maeve 1940- .... **CLC 153**
See also BEST 90:1; BPFB 1; CA 127; 134; CANR 50, 96; CN 7; CPW; DA3; DAM POP; INT CA-134; MTCW 1; RHW
Binyon, T(imothy) J(ohn) 1936- .... **CLC 34**
See also CA 111; CANR 28
Bion 335B.C.-245B.C. .... **CMLC 39**
Bioy Casares, Adolfo 1914-1999 ... **CLC 4, 8, 13, 88; HLC 1; SSC 17**
See Casares, Adolfo Bioy; Miranda, Javier; Sacastru, Martin
See also CA 29-32R; 177; CANR 19, 43, 66; DAM MULT; DLB 113; EWL 3; HW 1, 2; LAW; MTCW 1, 2
Birch, Allison .... **CLC 65**
Bird, Cordwainer
See Ellison, Harlan (Jay)
Bird, Robert Montgomery 1806-1854 .... **NCLC 1**
See also DLB 202; RGAL 4
Birkerts, Sven 1951- .... **CLC 116**
See also CA 128; 133, 176; CAAE 176; CAAS 29; INT 133
Birney, (Alfred) Earle 1904-1995 .. **CLC 1, 4, 6, 11**
See also CA 1-4R; CANR 5, 20; CP 7; DAC; DAM MST, POET; DLB 88; MTCW 1; PFS 8; RGEL 2
Biruni, al 973-1048(?) .... **CMLC 28**
Bishop, Elizabeth 1911-1979 ..... **CLC 1, 4, 9, 13, 15, 32; PC 3, 34; TCLC 121**
See also AMWR 2; AMWS 1; CA 5-8R; 89-92; CABS 2; CANR 26, 61, 108; CDALB 1968-1988; DA; DA3; DAC; DAM MST, POET; DLB 5, 169; EWL 3; GLL 2; MAWW; MTCW 1, 2; PAB; PFS 6, 12; RGAL 4; SATA-Obit 24; TUS; WP
Bishop, John 1935- .... **CLC 10**
See also CA 105
Bishop, John Peale 1892-1944 ..... **TCLC 103**
See also CA 107; 155; DLB 4, 9, 45; RGAL 4
Bissett, Bill 1939- .... **CLC 18; PC 14**
See also CA 69-72; CAAS 19; CANR 15; CCA 1; CP 7; DLB 53; MTCW 1
Bissoondath, Neil (Devindra) 1955- .... **CLC 120**
See also CA 136; CN 7; DAC
Bitov, Andrei (Georgievich) 1937- ... **CLC 57**
See also CA 142
Biyidi, Alexandre 1932-
See Beti, Mongo
See also BW 1, 3; CA 114; 124; CANR 81; DA3; MTCW 1, 2
Bjarme, Brynjolf
See Ibsen, Henrik (Johan)
Bjoernson, Bjoernstjerne (Martinius) 1832-1910 .... **TCLC 7, 37**
See also CA 104
Black, Robert
See Holdstock, Robert P.
Blackburn, Paul 1926-1971 .... **CLC 9, 43**
See also BG 2; CA 81-84; 33-36R; CANR 34; DLB 16; DLBY 1981
Black Elk 1863-1950 .... **NNAL; TCLC 33**
See also CA 144; DAM MULT; MTCW 1; WP
Black Hawk 1767-1838 .... **NNAL**
Black Hobart
See Sanders, (James) Ed(ward)
Blacklin, Malcolm
See Chambers, Aidan

Booth, Martin 1944- .... **CLC 13**
See also CA 93-96; CAAE 188; CAAS 2;
CANR 92
Booth, Philip 1925- .... **CLC 23**
See also CA 5-8R; CANR 5, 88; CP 7;
DLBY 1982
Booth, Wayne C(layson) 1921- .... **CLC 24**
See also CA 1-4R; CAAS 5; CANR 3, 43,
117; DLB 67
Borchert, Wolfgang 1921-1947 .... **TCLC 5**
See also CA 104; 188; DLB 69, 124; EWL
3
Borel, Petrus 1809-1859 .... **NCLC 41**
See also DLB 119; GFL 1789 to the Present
Borges, Jorge Luis 1899-1986 ... **CLC 1, 2, 3,
4, 6, 8, 9, 10, 13, 19, 44, 48, 83; HLC 1;
PC 22, 32; SSC 4, 41; TCLC 109;
WLC**
See also AAYA 26; BPFB 1; CA 21-24R;
CANR 19, 33, 75, 105; CDWLB 3; DA;
DA3; DAB; DAC; DAM MST, MULT;
DLB 113; DLBY 1986; DNFS 1, 2; EWL
3; HW 1, 2; LAW; LMFS 2; MSW;
MTCW 1, 2; RGSF 2; RGWL 2, 3; SFW
4; SSFS 17; TWA; WLIT 1
Borowski, Tadeusz 1922-1951 .... **SSC 48;
TCLC 9**
See also CA 106; 154; CDWLB 4; DLB
215; EWL 3; RGSF 2; RGWL 3; SSFS
13
Borrow, George (Henry)
1803-1881 .... **NCLC 9**
See also DLB 21, 55, 166
Bosch (Gavino), Juan 1909-2001 ..... **HLCS 1**
See also CA 151; 204; DAM MST, MULT;
DLB 145; HW 1, 2
Bosman, Herman Charles
1905-1951 .... **TCLC 49**
See Malan, Herman
See also CA 160; DLB 225; RGSF 2
Bosschere, Jean de 1878(?)-1953 ... **TCLC 19**
See also CA 115; 186
Boswell, James 1740-1795 ... **LC 4, 50; WLC**
See also BRW 3; CDBLB 1660-1789; DA;
DAB; DAC; DAM MST; DLB 104, 142;
TEA; WLIT 3
Bottomley, Gordon 1874-1948 ..... **TCLC 107**
See also CA 120; 192; DLB 10
Bottoms, David 1949- .... **CLC 53**
See also CA 105; CANR 22; CSW; DLB
120; DLBY 1983
Boucicault, Dion 1820-1890 .... **NCLC 41**
Boucolon, Maryse
See Conde, Maryse
Bourget, Paul (Charles Joseph)
1852-1935 .... **TCLC 12**
See also CA 107; 196; DLB 123; GFL 1789
to the Present
Bourjaily, Vance (Nye) 1922- .... **CLC 8, 62**
See also CA 1-4R; CAAS 1; CANR 2, 72;
CN 7; DLB 2, 143
Bourne, Randolph S(illiman)
1886-1918 .... **TCLC 16**
See also AMW; CA 117; 155; DLB 63
Bova, Ben(jamin William) 1932- ...... **CLC 45**
See also AAYA 16; CA 5-8R; CAAS 18;
CANR 11, 56, 94, 111; CLR 3; DLBY
1981; INT CANR-11; MAICYA 1, 2;
MTCW 1; SATA 6, 68, 133; SFW 4
Bowen, Elizabeth (Dorothea Cole)
1899-1973 . **CLC 1, 3, 6, 11, 15, 22, 118;
SSC 3, 28**
See also BRWS 2; CA 17-18; 41-44R;
CANR 35, 105; CAP 2; CDBLB 1945-
1960; DA3; DAM NOV; DLB 15, 162;
EWL 3; EXPS; FW; HGG; MTCW 1, 2;
NFS 13; RGSF 2; SSFS 5; SUFW 1;
TEA; WLIT 4

Bowering, George 1935- .... **CLC 15, 47**
See also CA 21-24R; CAAS 16; CANR 10;
CP 7; DLB 53
Bowering, Marilyn R(uthe) 1949- .... **CLC 32**
See also CA 101; CANR 49; CP 7; CWP
Bowers, Edgar 1924-2000 .... **CLC 9**
See also CA 5-8R; 188; CANR 24; CP 7;
CSW; DLB 5
Bowers, Mrs. J. Milton 1842-1914
See Bierce, Ambrose (Gwinett)
Bowie, David .... **CLC 17**
See Jones, David Robert
Bowles, Jane (Sydney) 1917-1973 ..... **CLC 3,
68**
See Bowles, Jane Auer
See also CA 19-20; 41-44R; CAP 2
Bowles, Jane Auer
See Bowles, Jane (Sydney)
See also EWL 3
Bowles, Paul (Frederick) 1910-1999 . **CLC 1,
2, 19, 53; SSC 3**
See also AMWS 4; CA 1-4R; 186; CAAS
1; CANR 1, 19, 50, 75; CN 7; DA3; DLB
5, 6, 218; EWL 3; MTCW 1, 2; RGAL 4;
SSFS 17
Bowles, William Lisle 1762-1850 . **NCLC 103**
See also DLB 93
Box, Edgar
See Vidal, Gore
See also GLL 1
Boyd, James 1888-1944 .... **TCLC 115**
See also CA 186; DLB 9; DLBD 16; RGAL
4; RHW
Boyd, Nancy
See Millay, Edna St. Vincent
See also GLL 1
Boyd, Thomas (Alexander)
1898-1935 .... **TCLC 111**
See also CA 111; 183; DLB 9; DLBD 16
Boyd, William 1952- .... **CLC 28, 53, 70**
See also CA 114; 120; CANR 51, 71; CN
7; DLB 231
Boyle, Kay 1902-1992 .... **CLC 1, 5, 19, 58,
121; SSC 5**
See also CA 13-16R; 140; CAAS 1; CANR
29, 61, 110; DLB 4, 9, 48, 86; DLBY
1993; EWL 3; MTCW 1, 2; RGAL 4;
RGSF 2; SSFS 10, 13, 14
Boyle, Mark
See Kienzle, William X(avier)
Boyle, Patrick 1905-1982 .... **CLC 19**
See also CA 127
Boyle, T. C.
See Boyle, T(homas) Coraghessan
See also AMWS 8
Boyle, T(homas) Coraghessan
1948- .... **CLC 36, 55, 90; SSC 16**
See Boyle, T. C.
See also AAYA 47; BEST 90:4; BPFB 1;
CA 120; CANR 44, 76, 89; CN 7; CPW;
DA3; DAM POP; DLB 218, 278; DLBY
1986; EWL 3; MTCW 2; SSFS 13
Boz
See Dickens, Charles (John Huffam)
Brackenridge, Hugh Henry
1748-1816 .... **NCLC 7**
See also DLB 11, 37; RGAL 4
Bradbury, Edward P.
See Moorcock, Michael (John)
See also MTCW 2
Bradbury, Malcolm (Stanley)
1932-2000 .... **CLC 32, 61**
See also CA 1-4R; CANR 1, 33, 91, 98;
CN 7; DA3; DAM NOV; DLB 14, 207;
EWL 3; MTCW 1, 2

Bradbury, Ray (Douglas) 1920- ... **CLC 1, 3,
10, 15, 42, 98; SSC 29, 53; WLC**
See also AAYA 15; AITN 1, 2; AMWS 4;
BPFB 1; BYA 4, 5, 11; CA 1-4R; CANR
2, 30, 75; CDALB 1968-1988; CN 7;
CPW; DA; DA3; DAB; DAC; DAM MST,
NOV, POP; DLB 2, 8; EXPN; EXPS;
HGG; LAIT 3, 5; LATS 1; LMFS 2;
MTCW 1, 2; NFS 1; RGAL 4; RGSF 2;
SATA 11, 64, 123; SCFW 2; SFW 4;
SSFS 1; SUFW 1, 2; TUS; YAW
Braddon, Mary Elizabeth
1837-1915 .... **TCLC 111**
See also BRWS 8; CA 108; 179; CMW 4;
DLB 18, 70, 156; HGG
Bradford, Gamaliel 1863-1932 .... **TCLC 36**
See also CA 160; DLB 17
Bradford, William 1590-1657 .... **LC 64**
See also DLB 24, 30; RGAL 4
Bradley, David (Henry), Jr. 1950- .... **BLC 1;
CLC 23, 118**
See also BW 1, 3; CA 104; CANR 26, 81;
CN 7; DAM MULT; DLB 33
Bradley, John Ed(mund, Jr.) 1958- . **CLC 55**
See also CA 139; CANR 99; CN 7; CSW
Bradley, Marion Zimmer
1930-1999 .... **CLC 30**
See Chapman, Lee; Dexter, John; Gardner,
Miriam; Ives, Morgan; Rivers, Elfrida
See also AAYA 40; BPFB 1; CA 57-60; 185;
CAAS 10; CANR 7, 31, 51, 75, 107;
CPW; DA3; DAM POP; DLB 8; FANT;
FW; MTCW 1, 2; SATA 90, 139; SATA-
Obit 116; SFW 4; SUFW 2; YAW
Bradshaw, John 1933- .... **CLC 70**
See also CA 138; CANR 61
Bradstreet, Anne 1612(?)-1672 ...... **LC 4, 30;
PC 10**
See also AMWS 1; CDALB 1640-1865;
DA; DA3; DAC; DAM MST, POET; DLB
24; EXPP; FW; PFS 6; RGAL 4; TUS;
WP
Brady, Joan 1939- .... **CLC 86**
See also CA 141
Bragg, Melvyn 1939- .... **CLC 10**
See also BEST 89:3; CA 57-60; CANR 10,
48, 89; CN 7; DLB 14, 271; RHW
Brahe, Tycho 1546-1601 .... **LC 45**
Braine, John (Gerard) 1922-1986 . **CLC 1, 3,
41**
See also CA 1-4R; 120; CANR 1, 33; CD-
BLB 1945-1960; DLB 15; DLBY 1986;
EWL 3; MTCW 1
Braithwaite, William Stanley (Beaumont)
1878-1962 .... **BLC 1; HR 2**
See also BW 1; CA 125; DAM MULT; DLB
50, 54
Bramah, Ernest 1868-1942 .... **TCLC 72**
See also CA 156; CMW 4; DLB 70; FANT
Brammer, William 1930(?)-1978 ...... **CLC 31**
See also CA 77-80
Brancati, Vitaliano 1907-1954 .... **TCLC 12**
See also CA 109; DLB 264; EWL 3
Brancato, Robin F(idler) 1936- .... **CLC 35**
See also AAYA 9; BYA 6; CA 69-72; CANR
11, 45; CLR 32; JRDA; MAICYA 2;
MAICYAS 1; SAAS 9; SATA 97; WYA;
YAW
Brand, Max
See Faust, Frederick (Schiller)
See also BPFB 1; TCWW 2
Brand, Millen 1906-1980 .... **CLC 7**
See also CA 21-24R; 97-100; CANR 72
Branden, Barbara .... **CLC 44**
See also CA 148
Brandes, Georg (Morris Cohen)
1842-1927 .... **TCLC 10**
See also CA 105; 189

The Brothers Quay
  See Quay, Stephen; Quay, Timothy
Broughton, T(homas) Alan 1936- ..... **CLC 19**
  See also CA 45-48; CANR 2, 23, 48, 111
Broumas, Olga 1949- .... **CLC 10, 73**
  See also CA 85-88; CANR 20, 69, 110; CP
  7; CWP; GLL 2
Broun, Heywood 1888-1939 .... **TCLC 104**
  See also DLB 29, 171
Brown, Alan 1950- .... **CLC 99**
  See also CA 156
Brown, Charles Brockden
  1771-1810 .... **NCLC 22, 74, 122**
  See also AMWS 1; CDALB 1640-1865;
  DLB 37, 59, 73; FW; HGG; LMFS 1;
  RGAL 4; TUS
Brown, Christy 1932-1981 .... **CLC 63**
  See also BYA 13; CA 105; 104; CANR 72;
  DLB 14
Brown, Claude 1937-2002 ... **BLC 1; CLC 30**
  See also AAYA 7; BW 1, 3; CA 73-76; 205;
  CANR 81; DAM MULT
Brown, Dee (Alexander)
  1908-2002 .... **CLC 18, 47**
  See also AAYA 30; CA 13-16R; 212; CAAS
  6; CANR 11, 45, 60; CPW; CSW; DA3;
  DAM POP; DLBY 1980; LAIT 2; MTCW
  1, 2; SATA 5, 110; TCWW 2
Brown, George
  See Wertmueller, Lina
Brown, George Douglas
  1869-1902 .... **TCLC 28**
  See Douglas, George
  See also CA 162
Brown, George Mackay 1921-1996 ... **CLC 5,
  48, 100**
  See also BRWS 6; CA 21-24R; 151; CAAS
  6; CANR 12, 37, 67; CN 7; CP 7; DLB
  14, 27, 139, 271; MTCW 1; RGSF 2;
  SATA 35
Brown, (William) Larry 1951- .... **CLC 73**
  See also CA 130; 134; CANR 117; CSW;
  DLB 234; INT 133
Brown, Moses
  See Barrett, William (Christopher)
Brown, Rita Mae 1944- .... **CLC 18, 43, 79**
  See also BPFB 1; CA 45-48; CANR 2, 11,
  35, 62, 95; CN 7; CPW; CSW; DA3;
  DAM NOV, POP; FW; INT CANR-11;
  MTCW 1, 2; NFS 9; RGAL 4; TUS
Brown, Roderick (Langmere) Haig-
  See Haig-Brown, Roderick (Langmere)
Brown, Rosellen 1939- .... **CLC 32, 170**
  See also CA 77-80; CAAS 10; CANR 14,
  44, 98; CN 7
Brown, Sterling Allen 1901-1989 ...... **BLC 1;
  CLC 1, 23, 59; HR 2**
  See also AFAW 1, 2; BW 1, 3; CA 85-88;
  127; CANR 26; DA3; DAM MULT,
  POET; DLB 48, 51, 63; MTCW 1, 2;
  RGAL 4; WP
Brown, Will
  See Ainsworth, William Harrison
Brown, William Wells 1815-1884 ...... **BLC 1;
  DC 1; NCLC 2, 89**
  See also DAM MULT; DLB 3, 50, 183,
  248; RGAL 4
Browne, (Clyde) Jackson 1948(?)- ... **CLC 21**
  See also CA 120
Browning, Elizabeth Barrett
  1806-1861 ... **NCLC 1, 16, 61, 66; PC 6;
  WLC**
  See also BRW 4; CDBLB 1832-1890; DA;
  DA3; DAB; DAC; DAM MST, POET;
  DLB 32, 199; EXPP; PAB; PFS 2, 16;
  TEA; WLIT 4; WP

Browning, Robert 1812-1889 . **NCLC 19, 79;
  PC 2; WLCS**
  See also BRW 4; BRWR 2; CDBLB 1832-
  1890; DA; DA3; DAB; DAC; DAM MST,
  POET; DLB 32, 163; EXPP; LATS 1;
  PAB; PFS 1, 15; RGEL 2; TEA; WLIT 4;
  WP; YABC 1
Browning, Tod 1882-1962 .... **CLC 16**
  See also CA 141; 117
Brownmiller, Susan 1935- .... **CLC 159**
  See also CA 103; CANR 35, 75; DAM
  NOV; FW; MTCW 1, 2
Brownson, Orestes Augustus
  1803-1876 .... **NCLC 50**
  See also DLB 1, 59, 73, 243
Bruccoli, Matthew J(oseph) 1931- ... **CLC 34**
  See also CA 9-12R; CANR 7, 87; DLB 103
Bruce, Lenny .... **CLC 21**
  See Schneider, Leonard Alfred
Bruchac, Joseph III 1942- .... **NNAL**
  See also AAYA 19; CA 33-36R; CANR 13,
  47, 75, 94; CLR 46; CWRI 5; DAM
  MULT; JRDA; MAICYA 2; MAICYAS 1;
  MTCW 1; SATA 42, 89, 131
Bruin, John
  See Brutus, Dennis
Brulard, Henri
  See Stendhal
Brulls, Christian
  See Simenon, Georges (Jacques Christian)
Brunner, John (Kilian Houston)
  1934-1995 .... **CLC 8, 10**
  See also CA 1-4R; 149; CAAS 8; CANR 2,
  37; CPW; DAM POP; DLB 261; MTCW
  1, 2; SCFW 2; SFW 4
Bruno, Giordano 1548-1600 .... **LC 27**
  See also RGWL 2, 3
Brutus, Dennis 1924- ... **BLC 1; CLC 43; PC
  24**
  See also AFW; BW 2, 3; CA 49-52; CAAS
  14; CANR 2, 27, 42, 81; CDWLB 3; CP
  7; DAM MULT, POET; DLB 117, 225;
  EWL 3
Bryan, C(ourtlandt) D(ixon) B(arnes)
  1936- .... **CLC 29**
  See also CA 73-76; CANR 13, 68; DLB
  185; INT CANR-13
Bryan, Michael
  See Moore, Brian
  See also CCA 1
Bryan, William Jennings
  1860-1925 .... **TCLC 99**
Bryant, William Cullen 1794-1878 . **NCLC 6,
  46; PC 20**
  See also AMWS 1; CDALB 1640-1865;
  DA; DAB; DAC; DAM MST, POET;
  DLB 3, 43, 59, 189, 250; EXPP; PAB;
  RGAL 4; TUS
Bryusov, Valery Yakovlevich
  1873-1924 .... **TCLC 10**
  See also CA 107; 155; EWL 3; SFW 4
Buchan, John 1875-1940 .... **TCLC 41**
  See also CA 108; 145; CMW 4; DAB;
  DAM POP; DLB 34, 70, 156; HGG;
  MSW; MTCW 1; RGEL 2; RHW; YABC
  2
Buchanan, George 1506-1582 .... **LC 4**
  See also DLB 132
Buchanan, Robert 1841-1901 .... **TCLC 107**
  See also CA 179; DLB 18, 35
Buchheim, Lothar-Guenther 1918- .... **CLC 6**
  See also CA 85-88
Buchner, (Karl) Georg 1813-1837 . **NCLC 26**
  See also CDWLB 2; DLB 133; EW 6;
  RGSF 2; RGWL 2, 3; TWA
Buchwald, Art(hur) 1925- .... **CLC 33**
  See also AITN 1; CA 5-8R; CANR 21, 67,
  107; MTCW 1, 2; SATA 10

Buck, Pearl S(ydenstricker)
  1892-1973 .... **CLC 7, 11, 18, 127**
  See also AAYA 42; AITN 1; AMWS 2;
  BPFB 1; CA 1-4R; 41-44R; CANR 1, 34;
  CDALBS; DA; DA3; DAB; DAC; DAM
  MST, NOV; DLB 9, 102; EWL 3; LAIT
  3; MTCW 1, 2; RGAL 4; RHW; SATA 1,
  25; TUS
Buckler, Ernest 1908-1984 .... **CLC 13**
  See also CA 11-12; 114; CAP 1; CCA 1;
  DAC; DAM MST; DLB 68; SATA 47
Buckley, Christopher (Taylor)
  1952- .... **CLC 165**
  See also CA 139
Buckley, Vincent (Thomas)
  1925-1988 .... **CLC 57**
  See also CA 101
Buckley, William F(rank), Jr. 1925- . **CLC 7,
  18, 37**
  See also AITN 1; BPFB 1; CA 1-4R; CANR
  1, 24, 53, 93; CMW 4; CPW; DA3; DAM
  POP; DLB 137; DLBY 1980; INT CANR-
  24; MTCW 1, 2; TUS
Buechner, (Carl) Frederick 1926- . **CLC 2, 4,
  6, 9**
  See also AMWS 12; BPFB 1; CA 13-16R;
  CANR 11, 39, 64, 114; CN 7; DAM NOV;
  DLBY 1980; INT CANR-11; MTCW 1, 2
Buell, John (Edward) 1927- .... **CLC 10**
  See also CA 1-4R; CANR 71; DLB 53
Buero Vallejo, Antonio 1916-2000 ... **CLC 15,
  46, 139; DC 18**
  See also CA 106; 189; CANR 24, 49, 75;
  DFS 11; EWL 3; HW 1; MTCW 1, 2
Bufalino, Gesualdo 1920(?)-1990 ...... **CLC 74**
  See also CWW 2; DLB 196
Bugayev, Boris Nikolayevich
  1880-1934 .... **PC 11; TCLC 7**
  See Bely, Andrey; Belyi, Andrei
  See also CA 104; 165; MTCW 1
Bukowski, Charles 1920-1994 ... **CLC 2, 5, 9,
  41, 82, 108; PC 18; SSC 45**
  See also CA 17-20R; 144; CANR 40, 62,
  105; CPW; DA3; DAM NOV, POET;
  DLB 5, 130, 169; EWL 3; MTCW 1, 2
Bulgakov, Mikhail (Afanas'evich)
  1891-1940 .... **SSC 18; TCLC 2, 16**
  See also BPFB 1; CA 105; 152; DAM
  DRAM, NOV; DLB 272; EWL 3; NFS 8;
  RGSF 2; RGWL 2, 3; SFW 4; TWA
Bulgya, Alexander Alexandrovich
  1901-1956 .... **TCLC 53**
  See Fadeev, Aleksandr Aleksandrovich;
  Fadeev, Alexandr Alexandrovich; Fadeyev,
  Alexander
  See also CA 117; 181
Bullins, Ed 1935- ... **BLC 1; CLC 1, 5, 7; DC
  6**
  See also BW 2, 3; CA 49-52; CAAS 16;
  CAD; CANR 24, 46, 73; CD 5; DAM
  DRAM, MULT; DLB 7, 38, 249; EWL 3;
  MTCW 1, 2; RGAL 4
Bulosan, Carlos 1911-1956 .... **AAL**
  See also RGAL 4
**Bulwer-Lytton, Edward (George Earle
  Lytton)** 1803-1873 .... **NCLC 1, 45**
  See also DLB 21; RGEL 2; SFW 4; SUFW
  1; TEA
Bunin, Ivan Alexeyevich 1870-1953 ... **SSC 5;
  TCLC 6**
  See also CA 104; EWL 3; RGSF 2; RGWL
  2, 3; TWA
Bunting, Basil 1900-1985 ...... **CLC 10, 39, 47**
  See also BRWS 7; CA 53-56; 115; CANR
  7; DAM POET; DLB 20; EWL 3; RGEL
  2
Bunuel, Luis 1900-1983 ... **CLC 16, 80; HLC
  1**
  See also CA 101; 110; CANR 32, 77; DAM
  MULT; HW 1

Calisher, Hortense 1911- ..... **CLC 2, 4, 8, 38, 134; SSC 15**
See also CA 1-4R; CANR 1, 22, 117; CN 7; DA3; DAM NOV; DLB 2, 218; INT CANR-22; MTCW 1, 2; RGAL 4; RGSF 2

Callaghan, Morley Edward 1903-1990 .... **CLC 3, 14, 41, 65**
See also CA 9-12R; 132; CANR 33, 73; DAC; DAM MST; DLB 68; EWL 3; MTCW 1, 2; RGEL 2; RGSF 2

Callimachus c. 305B.C.-c. 240B.C. .... **CMLC 18**
See also AW 1; DLB 176; RGWL 2, 3

Calvin, Jean
See Calvin, John
See also GFL Beginnings to 1789

Calvin, John 1509-1564 .... **LC 37**
See Calvin, Jean

Calvino, Italo 1923-1985 .... **CLC 5, 8, 11, 22, 33, 39, 73; SSC 3, 48**
See also CA 85-88; 116; CANR 23, 61; DAM NOV; DLB 196; EW 13; EWL 3; MTCW 1, 2; RGSF 2; RGWL 2, 3; SFW 4; SSFS 12

Camara Laye
See Laye, Camara
See also EWL 3

Camden, William 1551-1623 .... **LC 77**
See also DLB 172

Cameron, Carey 1952- .... **CLC 59**
See also CA 135

Cameron, Peter 1959- .... **CLC 44**
See also AMWS 12; CA 125; CANR 50, 117; DLB 234; GLL 2

Camoens, Luis Vaz de 1524(?)-1580
See Camoes, Luis de
See also EW 2

Camoes, Luis de 1524(?)-1580 . **HLCS 1; LC 62; PC 31**
See Camoens, Luis Vaz de
See also RGWL 2, 3

Campana, Dino 1885-1932 .... **TCLC 20**
See also CA 117; DLB 114; EWL 3

Campanella, Tommaso 1568-1639 .... **LC 32**
See also RGWL 2, 3

Campbell, John W(ood, Jr.) 1910-1971 .... **CLC 32**
See also CA 21-22; 29-32R; CANR 34; CAP 2; DLB 8; MTCW 1; SCFW; SFW 4

Campbell, Joseph 1904-1987 .... **CLC 69**
See also AAYA 3; BEST 89:2; CA 1-4R; 124; CANR 3, 28, 61, 107; DA3; MTCW 1, 2

Campbell, Maria 1940- .... **CLC 85; NNAL**
See also CA 102; CANR 54; CCA 1; DAC

Campbell, Paul N. 1923-
See hooks, bell
See also CA 21-24R

Campbell, (John) Ramsey 1946- ..... **CLC 42; SSC 19**
See also CA 57-60; CANR 7, 102; DLB 261; HGG; INT CANR-7; SUFW 1, 2

Campbell, (Ignatius) Roy (Dunnachie) 1901-1957 .... **TCLC 5**
See also AFW; CA 104; 155; DLB 20, 225; EWL 3; MTCW 2; RGEL 2

Campbell, Thomas 1777-1844 .... **NCLC 19**
See also DLB 93, 144; RGEL 2

Campbell, Wilfred .... **TCLC 9**
See Campbell, William

Campbell, William 1858(?)-1918
See Campbell, Wilfred
See also CA 106; DLB 92

Campion, Jane 1954- .... **CLC 95**
See also AAYA 33; CA 138; CANR 87

Campion, Thomas 1567-1620 .... **LC 78**
See also CDBLB Before 1660; DAM POET; DLB 58, 172; RGEL 2

Camus, Albert 1913-1960 ...... **CLC 1, 2, 4, 9, 11, 14, 32, 63, 69, 124; DC 2; SSC 9; WLC**
See also AAYA 36; AFW; BPFB 1; CA 89-92; DA; DA3; DAB; DAC; DAM DRAM, MST, NOV; DLB 72; EW 13; EWL 3; EXPN; EXPS; GFL 1789 to the Present; LATS 1; LMFS 2; MTCW 1, 2; NFS 6, 16; RGSF 2; RGWL 2, 3; SSFS 4; TWA

Canby, Vincent 1924-2000 .... **CLC 13**
See also CA 81-84; 191

Cancale
See Desnos, Robert

Canetti, Elias 1905-1994 .. **CLC 3, 14, 25, 75, 86**
See also CA 21-24R; 146; CANR 23, 61, 79; CDWLB 2; CWW 2; DA3; DLB 85, 124; EW 12; EWL 3; MTCW 1, 2; RGWL 2, 3; TWA

Canfield, Dorothea F.
See Fisher, Dorothy (Frances) Canfield

Canfield, Dorothea Frances
See Fisher, Dorothy (Frances) Canfield

Canfield, Dorothy
See Fisher, Dorothy (Frances) Canfield

Canin, Ethan 1960- .... **CLC 55**
See also CA 131; 135

Cankar, Ivan 1876-1918 .... **TCLC 105**
See also CDWLB 4; DLB 147; EWL 3

Cannon, Curt
See Hunter, Evan

Cao, Lan 1961- .... **CLC 109**
See also CA 165

Cape, Judith
See Page, P(atricia) K(athleen)
See also CCA 1

Capek, Karel 1890-1938 .... **DC 1; SSC 36; TCLC 6, 37; WLC**
See also CA 104; 140; CDWLB 4; DA; DA3; DAB; DAC; DAM DRAM, MST, NOV; DFS 7, 11; DLB 215; EW 10; EWL 3; MTCW 1; RGSF 2; RGWL 2, 3; SCFW 2; SFW 4

Capote, Truman 1924-1984 . **CLC 1, 3, 8, 13, 19, 34, 38, 58; SSC 2, 47; WLC**
See also AMWS 3; BPFB 1; CA 5-8R; 113; CANR 18, 62; CDALB 1941-1968; CPW; DA; DA3; DAB; DAC; DAM MST, NOV; POP; DLB 2, 185, 227; DLBY 1980, 1984; EWL 3; EXPS; GLL 1; LAIT 3; MTCW 1, 2; NCFS 2; RGAL 4; RGSF 2; SATA 91; SSFS 2; TUS

Capra, Frank 1897-1991 .... **CLC 16**
See also CA 61-64; 135

Caputo, Philip 1941- .... **CLC 32**
See also CA 73-76; CANR 40; YAW

Caragiale, Ion Luca 1852-1912 ...... **TCLC 76**
See also CA 157

Card, Orson Scott 1951- .... **CLC 44, 47, 50**
See also AAYA 11, 42; BPFB 1; BYA 5, 8; CA 102; CANR 27, 47, 73, 102, 106; CPW; DA3; DAM POP; FANT; INT CANR-27; MTCW 1, 2; NFS 5; SATA 83, 127; SCFW 2; SFW 4; SUFW 2; YAW

Cardenal, Ernesto 1925- .... **CLC 31, 161; HLC 1; PC 22**
See also CA 49-52; CANR 2, 32, 66; CWW 2; DAM MULT, POET; EWL 3; HW 1, 2; LAWS 1; MTCW 1, 2; RGWL 2, 3

Cardozo, Benjamin N(athan) 1870-1938 .... **TCLC 65**
See also CA 117; 164

Carducci, Giosue (Alessandro Giuseppe) 1835-1907 .... **PC 46; TCLC 32**
See also CA 163; EW 7; RGWL 2, 3

Carew, Thomas 1595(?)-1640 . **LC 13; PC 29**
See also BRW 2; DLB 126; PAB; RGEL 2

Carey, Ernestine Gilbreth 1908- ...... **CLC 17**
See also CA 5-8R; CANR 71; SATA 2

Carey, Peter 1943- .... **CLC 40, 55, 96**
See also CA 123; 127; CANR 53, 76, 117; CN 7; EWL 3; INT CA-127; MTCW 1, 2; RGSF 2; SATA 94

Carleton, William 1794-1869 .... **NCLC 3**
See also DLB 159; RGEL 2; RGSF 2

Carlisle, Henry (Coffin) 1926- .... **CLC 33**
See also CA 13-16R; CANR 15, 85

Carlsen, Chris
See Holdstock, Robert P.

Carlson, Ron(ald F.) 1947- .... **CLC 54**
See also CA 105; CAAE 189; CANR 27; DLB 244

Carlyle, Thomas 1795-1881 ..... **NCLC 22, 70**
See also BRW 4; CDBLB 1789-1832; DA; DAB; DAC; DAM MST; DLB 55, 144, 254; RGEL 2; TEA

Carman, (William) Bliss 1861-1929 ... **PC 34; TCLC 7**
See also CA 104; 152; DAC; DLB 92; RGEL 2

Carnegie, Dale 1888-1955 .... **TCLC 53**

Carossa, Hans 1878-1956 .... **TCLC 48**
See also CA 170; DLB 66; EWL 3

Carpenter, Don(ald Richard) 1931-1995 .... **CLC 41**
See also CA 45-48; 149; CANR 1, 71

Carpenter, Edward 1844-1929 .... **TCLC 88**
See also CA 163; GLL 1

Carpenter, John (Howard) 1948- ... **CLC 161**
See also AAYA 2; CA 134; SATA 58

Carpenter, Johnny
See Carpenter, John (Howard)

Carpentier (y Valmont), Alejo 1904-1980 . **CLC 8, 11, 38, 110; HLC 1; SSC 35**
See also CA 65-68; 97-100; CANR 11, 70; CDWLB 3; DAM MULT; DLB 113; EWL 3; HW 1, 2; LAW; LMFS 2; RGSF 2; RGWL 2, 3; WLIT 1

Carr, Caleb 1955(?)- .... **CLC 86**
See also CA 147; CANR 73; DA3

Carr, Emily 1871-1945 .... **TCLC 32**
See also CA 159; DLB 68; FW; GLL 2

Carr, John Dickson 1906-1977 .... **CLC 3**
See Fairbairn, Roger
See also CA 49-52; 69-72; CANR 3, 33, 60; CMW 4; MSW; MTCW 1, 2

Carr, Philippa
See Hibbert, Eleanor Alice Burford

Carr, Virginia Spencer 1929- .... **CLC 34**
See also CA 61-64; DLB 111

Carrere, Emmanuel 1957- .... **CLC 89**
See also CA 200

Carrier, Roch 1937- .... **CLC 13, 78**
See also CA 130; CANR 61; CCA 1; DAC; DAM MST; DLB 53; SATA 105

Carroll, James Dennis
See Carroll, Jim

Carroll, James P. 1943(?)- .... **CLC 38**
See also CA 81-84; CANR 73; MTCW 1

Carroll, Jim 1951- .... **CLC 35, 143**
See Carroll, James Dennis
See also AAYA 17; CA 45-48; CANR 42, 115

Carroll, Lewis ... **NCLC 2, 53; PC 18; WLC**
See Dodgson, Charles L(utwidge)
See also AAYA 39; BRW 5; BYA 5, 13; CD-BLB 1832-1890; CLR 2, 18; DLB 18, 163, 178; DLBY 1998; EXPN; EXPP; FANT; JRDA; LAIT 1; NFS 7; PFS 11; RGEL 2; SUFW 1; TEA; WCH

Carroll, Paul Vincent 1900-1968 ...... **CLC 10**
See also CA 9-12R; 25-28R; DLB 10; EWL 3; RGEL 2

Chambers, James 1948-
    See Cliff, Jimmy
    See also CA 124
Chambers, Jessie
    See Lawrence, D(avid) H(erbert Richards)
    See also GLL 1
Chambers, Robert W(illiam)
    1865-1933 .... **TCLC 41**
    See also CA 165; DLB 202; HGG; SATA
    107; SUFW 1
Chambers, (David) Whittaker
    1901-1961 .... **TCLC 129**
    See also CA 89-92
Chamisso, Adelbert von
    1781-1838 .... **NCLC 82**
    See also DLB 90; RGWL 2, 3; SUFW 1
Chance, James T.
    See Carpenter, John (Howard)
Chance, John T.
    See Carpenter, John (Howard)
Chandler, Raymond (Thornton)
    1888-1959 .... **SSC 23; TCLC 1, 7**
    See also AAYA 25; AMWS 4; BPFB 1; CA
    104; 129; CANR 60, 107; CDALB 1929-
    1941; CMW 4; DA3; DLB 226, 253;
    DLBD 6; EWL 3; MSW; MTCW 1, 2;
    NFS 17; RGAL 4; TUS
Chang, Diana 1934- .... **AAL**
    See also CWP; EXPP
Chang, Eileen 1921-1995 .... **AAL; SSC 28**
    See Chang Ai-Ling
    See also CA 166; CWW 2
Chang, Jung 1952- .... **CLC 71**
    See also CA 142
Chang Ai-Ling
    See Chang, Eileen
    See also EWL 3
Channing, William Ellery
    1780-1842 .... **NCLC 17**
    See also DLB 1, 59, 235; RGAL 4
Chao, Patricia 1955- .... **CLC 119**
    See also CA 163
Chaplin, Charles Spencer
    1889-1977 .... **CLC 16**
    See Chaplin, Charlie
    See also CA 81-84; 73-76
Chaplin, Charlie
    See Chaplin, Charles Spencer
    See also DLB 44
Chapman, George 1559(?)-1634 . **DC 19; LC
    22**
    See also BRW 1; DAM DRAM; DLB 62,
    121; LMFS 1; RGEL 2
Chapman, Graham 1941-1989 .... **CLC 21**
    See Monty Python
    See also CA 116; 129; CANR 35, 95
Chapman, John Jay 1862-1933 .... **TCLC 7**
    See also CA 104; 191
Chapman, Lee
    See Bradley, Marion Zimmer
    See also GLL 1
Chapman, Walker
    See Silverberg, Robert
Chappell, Fred (Davis) 1936- .... **CLC 40, 78,
    162**
    See also CA 5-8R; CAAE 198; CAAS 4;
    CANR 8, 33, 67, 110; CN 7; CP 7; CSW;
    DLB 6, 105; HGG
Char, Rene(-Emile) 1907-1988 .... **CLC 9, 11,
    14, 55**
    See also CA 13-16R; 124; CANR 32; DAM
    POET; DLB 258; EWL 3; GFL 1789 to
    the Present; MTCW 1, 2; RGWL 2, 3
Charby, Jay
    See Ellison, Harlan (Jay)
Chardin, Pierre Teilhard de
    See Teilhard de Chardin, (Marie Joseph)
    Pierre

Chariton fl. 1st cent. (?)- .... **CMLC 49**
Charlemagne 742-814 .... **CMLC 37**
Charles I 1600-1649 .... **LC 13**
Charriere, Isabelle de 1740-1805 .. **NCLC 66**
Chartier, Emile-Auguste
    See Alain
Charyn, Jerome 1937- .... **CLC 5, 8, 18**
    See also CA 5-8R; CAAS 1; CANR 7, 61,
    101; CMW 4; CN 7; DLBY 1983; MTCW
    1
Chase, Adam
    See Marlowe, Stephen
Chase, Mary (Coyle) 1907-1981 .... **DC 1**
    See also CA 77-80; 105; CAD; CWD; DFS
    11; DLB 228; SATA 17; SATA-Obit 29
Chase, Mary Ellen 1887-1973 .... **CLC 2;
    TCLC 124**
    See also CA 13-16; 41-44R; CAP 1; SATA
    10
Chase, Nicholas
    See Hyde, Anthony
    See also CCA 1
Chateaubriand, Francois Rene de
    1768-1848 .... **NCLC 3**
    See also DLB 119; EW 5; GFL 1789 to the
    Present; RGWL 2, 3; TWA
Chatterje, Sarat Chandra 1876-1936(?)
    See Chatterji, Saratchandra
    See also CA 109
Chatterji, Bankim Chandra
    1838-1894 .... **NCLC 19**
Chatterji, Saratchandra .... **TCLC 13**
    See Chatterje, Sarat Chandra
    See also CA 186; EWL 3
Chatterton, Thomas 1752-1770 .... **LC 3, 54**
    See also DAM POET; DLB 109; RGEL 2
Chatwin, (Charles) Bruce
    1940-1989 .... **CLC 28, 57, 59**
    See also AAYA 4; BEST 90:1; BRWS 4;
    CA 85-88; 127; CPW; DAM POP; DLB
    194, 204; EWL 3
Chaucer, Daniel
    See Ford, Ford Madox
    See also RHW
Chaucer, Geoffrey 1340(?)-1400 .. **LC 17, 56;
    PC 19; WLCS**
    See also BRW 1; BRWC 1; BRWR 2; CD-
    BLB Before 1660; DA; DA3; DAB;
    DAC; DAM MST, POET; DLB 146;
    LAIT 1; PAB; PFS 14; RGEL 2; TEA;
    WLIT 3; WP
Chavez, Denise (Elia) 1948- .... **HLC 1**
    See also CA 131; CANR 56, 81; DAM
    MULT; DLB 122; FW; HW 1, 2; MTCW
    2
Chaviaras, Strates 1935-
    See Haviaras, Stratis
    See also CA 105
Chayefsky, Paddy .... **CLC 23**
    See Chayefsky, Sidney
    See also CAD; DLB 7, 44; DLBY 1981;
    RGAL 4
Chayefsky, Sidney 1923-1981
    See Chayefsky, Paddy
    See also CA 9-12R; 104; CANR 18; DAM
    DRAM
Chedid, Andree 1920- .... **CLC 47**
    See also CA 145; CANR 95; EWL 3
Cheever, John 1912-1982 ..... **CLC 3, 7, 8, 11,
    15, 25, 64; SSC 1, 38, 57; WLC**
    See also AMWS 1; BPFB 1; CA 5-8R; 106;
    CABS 1; CANR 5, 27, 76; CDALB 1941-
    1968; CPW; DA; DA3; DAB; DAC;
    DAM MST, NOV, POP; DLB 2, 102, 227;
    DLBY 1980, 1982; EWL 3; EXPS; INT
    CANR-5; MTCW 1, 2; RGAL 4; RGSF
    2; SSFS 2, 14; TUS

Cheever, Susan 1943- .... **CLC 18, 48**
    See also CA 103; CANR 27, 51, 92; DLBY
    1982; INT CANR-27
Chekhonte, Antosha
    See Chekhov, Anton (Pavlovich)
Chekhov, Anton (Pavlovich)
    1860-1904 ...... **DC 9; SSC 2, 28, 41, 51;
    TCLC 3, 10, 31, 55, 96; WLC**
    See also BYA 14; CA 104; 124; DA; DA3;
    DAB; DAC; DAM DRAM, MST; DFS 1,
    5, 10, 12; DLB 277; EW 7; EWL 3;
    EXPS; LAIT 3; LATS 1; RGSF 2; RGWL
    2, 3; SATA 90; SSFS 5, 13, 14; TWA
Cheney, Lynne V. 1941- .... **CLC 70**
    See also CA 89-92; CANR 58, 117
Chernyshevsky, Nikolai Gavrilovich
    See Chernyshevsky, Nikolay Gavrilovich
    See also DLB 238
Chernyshevsky, Nikolay Gavrilovich
    1828-1889 .... **NCLC 1**
    See Chernyshevsky, Nikolai Gavrilovich
Cherry, Carolyn Janice 1942-
    See Cherryh, C. J.
    See also CA 65-68; CANR 10
Cherryh, C. J. .... **CLC 35**
    See Cherry, Carolyn Janice
    See also AAYA 24; BPFB 1; DLBY 1980;
    FANT; SATA 93; SCFW 2; SFW 4; YAW
Chesnutt, Charles W(addell)
    1858-1932 .... **BLC 1; SSC 7, 54; TCLC
    5, 39**
    See also AFAW 1, 2; BW 1, 3; CA 106;
    125; CANR 76; DAM MULT; DLB 12,
    50, 78; EWL 3; MTCW 1, 2; RGAL 4;
    RGSF 2; SSFS 11
Chester, Alfred 1929(?)-1971 .... **CLC 49**
    See also CA 196; 33-36R; DLB 130
Chesterton, G(ilbert) K(eith)
    1874-1936 . **PC 28; SSC 1, 46; TCLC 1,
    6, 64**
    See also BRW 6; CA 104; 132; CANR 73;
    CDBLB 1914-1945; CMW 4; DAM NOV,
    POET; DLB 10, 19, 34, 70, 98, 149, 178;
    EWL 3; FANT; MSW; MTCW 1, 2;
    RGEL 2; RGSF 2; SATA 27; SUFW 1
Chiang, Pin-chin 1904-1986
    See Ding Ling
    See also CA 118
Chief Joseph 1840-1904 .... **NNAL**
    See also CA 152; DA3; DAM MULT
Chief Seattle 1786(?)-1866 .... **NNAL**
    See also DA3; DAM MULT
Ch'ien, Chung-shu 1910-1998 .... **CLC 22**
    See also CA 130; CANR 73; MTCW 1, 2
Chikamatsu Monzaemon 1653-1724 ... **LC 66**
    See also RGWL 2, 3
Child, L. Maria
    See Child, Lydia Maria
Child, Lydia Maria 1802-1880 .. **NCLC 6, 73**
    See also DLB 1, 74, 243; RGAL 4; SATA
    67
Child, Mrs.
    See Child, Lydia Maria
Child, Philip 1898-1978 .... **CLC 19, 68**
    See also CA 13-14; CAP 1; DLB 68; RHW;
    SATA 47
Childers, (Robert) Erskine
    1870-1922 .... **TCLC 65**
    See also CA 113; 153; DLB 70
Childress, Alice 1920-1994 . **BLC 1; CLC 12,
    15, 86, 96; DC 4; TCLC 116**
    See also AAYA 8; BW 2, 3; BYA 2; CA 45-
    48; 146; CAD; CANR 3, 27, 50, 74; CLR
    14; CWD; DA3; DAM DRAM, MULT,
    NOV; DFS 2, 8, 14; DLB 7, 38, 249;
    JRDA; LAIT 5; MAICYA 1, 2; MAIC-
    YAS 1; MTCW 1, 2; RGAL 4; SATA 7,
    48, 81; TUS; WYA; YAW

Craik, Dinah Maria (Mulock)
1826-1887 .... **NCLC 38**
See Craik, Mrs.; Mulock, Dinah Maria
See also DLB 35, 163; MAICYA 1, 2;
SATA 34

Cram, Ralph Adams 1863-1942 ..... **TCLC 45**
See also CA 160

Cranch, Christopher Pearse
1813-1892 .... **NCLC 115**
See also DLB 1, 42, 243

Crane, (Harold) Hart 1899-1932 .... **PC 3;**
TCLC 2, 5, 80; WLC
See also AMW; AMWR 2; CA 104; 127;
CDALB 1917-1929; DA; DA3; DAB;
DAC; DAM MST, POET; DLB 4, 48;
EWL 3; MTCW 1, 2; RGAL 4; TUS

Crane, R(onald) S(almon)
1886-1967 .... **CLC 27**
See also CA 85-88; DLB 63

Crane, Stephen (Townley)
1871-1900 ...... **SSC 7, 56; TCLC 11, 17,**
32; WLC
See also AAYA 21; AMW; AMWC 1; BPFB
1; BYA 3; CA 109; 140; CANR 84;
CDALB 1865-1917; DA; DA3; DAB;
DAC; DAM MST, NOV, POET; DLB 12,
54, 78; EXPN; EXPS; LAIT 2; LMFS 2;
NFS 4; PFS 9; RGAL 4; RGSF 2; SSFS
4; TUS; WYA; YABC 2

Cranshaw, Stanley
See Fisher, Dorothy (Frances) Canfield

Crase, Douglas 1944- .... **CLC 58**
See also CA 106

Crashaw, Richard 1612(?)-1649 .... **LC 24**
See also BRW 2; DLB 126; PAB; RGEL 2

Cratinus c. 519B.C.-c. 422B.C. ..... **CMLC 54**
See also LMFS 1

Craven, Margaret 1901-1980 .... **CLC 17**
See also BYA 2; CA 103; CCA 1; DAC;
LAIT 5

Crawford, F(rancis) Marion
1854-1909 .... **TCLC 10**
See also CA 107; 168; DLB 71; HGG;
RGAL 4; SUFW 1

Crawford, Isabella Valancy
1850-1887 .... **NCLC 12**
See also DLB 92; RGEL 2

Crayon, Geoffrey
See Irving, Washington

Creasey, John 1908-1973 .... **CLC 11**
See Marric, J. J.
See also CA 5-8R; 41-44R; CANR 8, 59;
CMW 4; DLB 77; MTCW 1

Crebillon, Claude Prosper Jolyot de (fils)
1707-1777 .... **LC 1, 28**
See also GFL Beginnings to 1789

Credo
See Creasey, John

Credo, Alvaro J. de
See Prado (Calvo), Pedro

Creeley, Robert (White) 1926- .. **CLC 1, 2, 4,**
8, 11, 15, 36, 78
See also AMWS 4; CA 1-4R; CAAS 10;
CANR 23, 43, 89; CP 7; DA3; DAM
POET; DLB 5, 16, 169; DLBD 17; EWL
3; MTCW 1, 2; RGAL 4; WP

Crevecoeur, Hector St. John de
See Crevecoeur, Michel Guillaume Jean de
See also ANW

Crevecoeur, Michel Guillaume Jean de
1735-1813 .... **NCLC 105**
See Crevecoeur, Hector St. John de
See also AMWS 1; DLB 37

Crevel, Rene 1900-1935 .... **TCLC 112**
See also GLL 2

Crews, Harry (Eugene) 1935- ..... **CLC 6, 23,**
49
See also AITN 1; AMWS 11; BPFB 1; CA
25-28R; CANR 20, 57; CN 7; CSW; DA3;
DLB 6, 143, 185; MTCW 1, 2; RGAL 4

Crichton, (John) Michael 1942- .... **CLC 2, 6,**
54, 90
See also AAYA 10, 49; AITN 2; BPFB 1;
CA 25-28R; CANR 13, 40, 54, 76; CMW
4; CN 7; CPW; DA3; DAM NOV, POP;
DLBY 1981; INT CANR-13; JRDA;
MTCW 1, 2; SATA 9, 88; SFW 4; YAW

Crispin, Edmund .... **CLC 22**
See Montgomery, (Robert) Bruce
See also DLB 87; MSW

Cristofer, Michael 1945(?)- .... **CLC 28**
See also CA 110; 152; CAD; CD 5; DAM
DRAM; DFS 15; DLB 7

Criton
See Alain

Croce, Benedetto 1866-1952 .... **TCLC 37**
See also CA 120; 155; EW 8; EWL 3

Crockett, David 1786-1836 .... **NCLC 8**
See also DLB 3, 11, 183, 248

Crockett, Davy
See Crockett, David

Crofts, Freeman Wills 1879-1957 .. **TCLC 55**
See also CA 115; 195; CMW 4; DLB 77;
MSW

Croker, John Wilson 1780-1857 .... **NCLC 10**
See also DLB 110

Crommelynck, Fernand 1885-1970 .. **CLC 75**
See also CA 189; 89-92; EWL 3

Cromwell, Oliver 1599-1658 .... **LC 43**

Cronenberg, David 1943- .... **CLC 143**
See also CA 138; CCA 1

Cronin, A(rchibald) J(oseph)
1896-1981 .... **CLC 32**
See also BPFB 1; CA 1-4R; 102; CANR 5;
DLB 191; SATA 47; SATA-Obit 25

Cross, Amanda
See Heilbrun, Carolyn G(old)
See also BPFB 1; CMW; CPW; MSW

Crothers, Rachel 1878-1958 .... **TCLC 19**
See also CA 113; 194; CAD; CWD; DLB
7, 266; RGAL 4

Croves, Hal
See Traven, B.

Crow Dog, Mary (Ellen) (?)- .... **CLC 93**
See Brave Bird, Mary
See also CA 154

Crowfield, Christopher
See Stowe, Harriet (Elizabeth) Beecher

Crowley, Aleister .... **TCLC 7**
See Crowley, Edward Alexander
See also GLL 1

Crowley, Edward Alexander 1875-1947
See Crowley, Aleister
See also CA 104; HGG

Crowley, John 1942- .... **CLC 57**
See also BPFB 1; CA 61-64; CANR 43, 98;
DLBY 1982; SATA 65; SFW 4; SUFW 2

Crud
See Crumb, R(obert)

Crumarums
See Crumb, R(obert)

Crumb, R(obert) 1943- .... **CLC 17**
See also CA 106; CANR 107

Crumbum
See Crumb, R(obert)

Crumski
See Crumb, R(obert)

Crum the Bum
See Crumb, R(obert)

Crunk
See Crumb, R(obert)

Crustt
See Crumb, R(obert)

Crutchfield, Les
See Trumbo, Dalton

Cruz, Victor Hernandez 1949- ... **HLC 1; PC**
37
See also BW 2; CA 65-68; CAAS 17;
CANR 14, 32, 74; CP 7; DAM MULT,
POET; DLB 41; DNFS 1; EXPP; HW 1,
2; MTCW 1; PFS 16; WP

Cryer, Gretchen (Kiger) 1935- .... **CLC 21**
See also CA 114; 123

Csath, Geza 1887-1919 .... **TCLC 13**
See also CA 111

Cudlip, David R(ockwell) 1933- .... **CLC 34**
See also CA 177

Cullen, Countee 1903-1946 .... **BLC 1; HR 2;**
PC 20; TCLC 4, 37; WLCS
See also AFAW 2; AMWS 4; BW 1; CA
108; 124; CDALB 1917-1929; DA; DA3;
DAC; DAM MST, MULT, POET; DLB 4,
48, 51; EWL 3; EXPP; LMFS 2; MTCW
1, 2; PFS 3; RGAL 4; SATA 18; WP

Culleton, Beatrice 1949- .... **NNAL**
See also CA 120; CANR 83; DAC

Cum, R.
See Crumb, R(obert)

Cummings, Bruce F(rederick) 1889-1919
See Barbellion, W. N. P.
See also CA 123

Cummings, E(dward) E(stlin)
1894-1962 .. **CLC 1, 3, 8, 12, 15, 68; PC**
5; WLC
See also AAYA 41; AMW; CA 73-76;
CANR 31; CDALB 1929-1941; DA;
DA3; DAB; DAC; DAM MST, POET;
DLB 4, 48; EWL 3; EXPP; MTCW 1, 2;
PAB; PFS 1, 3, 12, 13; RGAL 4; TUS;
WP

Cunha, Euclides (Rodrigues Pimenta) da
1866-1909 .... **TCLC 24**
See also CA 123; LAW; WLIT 1

Cunningham, E. V.
See Fast, Howard (Melvin)

Cunningham, J(ames) V(incent)
1911-1985 .... **CLC 3, 31**
See also CA 1-4R; 115; CANR 1, 72; DLB
5

Cunningham, Julia (Woolfolk)
1916- .... **CLC 12**
See also CA 9-12R; CANR 4, 19, 36; CWRI
5; JRDA; MAICYA 1, 2; SAAS 2; SATA
1, 26, 132

Cunningham, Michael 1952- .... **CLC 34**
See also CA 136; CANR 96; GLL 2

Cunninghame Graham, R. B.
See Cunninghame Graham, Robert
(Gallnigad) Bontine

Cunninghame Graham, Robert (Gallnigad)
Bontine 1852-1936 .... **TCLC 19**
See Graham, R(obert) B(ontine) Cunning-
hame
See also CA 119; 184

Curnow, (Thomas) Allen (Monro)
1911-2001 .... **PC 48**
See also CA 69-72; 202; CANR 48, 99; CP
7; EWL 3; RGEL 2

Currie, Ellen 19(?)- .... **CLC 44**

Curtin, Philip
See Lowndes, Marie Adelaide (Belloc)

Curtin, Phillip
See Lowndes, Marie Adelaide (Belloc)

Curtis, Price
See Ellison, Harlan (Jay)

Cusanus, Nicolaus 1401-1464 .... **LC 80**
See Nicholas of Cusa

Cutrate, Joe
See Spiegelman, Art

Cynewulf c. 770- .... **CMLC 23**
See also DLB 146; RGEL 2

de Andrade, Carlos Drummond
　　See Drummond de Andrade, Carlos
de Andrade, Mario 1892-1945
　　See Andrade, Mario de
　　See also CA 178; HW 2
Deane, Norman
　　See Creasey, John
Deane, Seamus (Francis) 1940- ...... **CLC 122**
　　See also CA 118; CANR 42
**de Beauvoir, Simone (Lucie Ernestine Marie
　　Bertrand)**
　　See Beauvoir, Simone (Lucie Ernestine
　　Marie Bertrand) de
de Beer, P.
　　See Bosman, Herman Charles
de Brissac, Malcolm
　　See Dickinson, Peter (Malcolm)
de Campos, Alvaro
　　See Pessoa, Fernando (Antonio Nogueira)
de Chardin, Pierre Teilhard
　　See Teilhard de Chardin, (Marie Joseph)
　　Pierre
Dee, John 1527-1608 .... **LC 20**
　　See also DLB 136, 213
Deer, Sandra 1940- .... **CLC 45**
　　See also CA 186
De Ferrari, Gabriella 1941- .... **CLC 65**
　　See also CA 146
de Filippo, Eduardo 1900-1984 ... **TCLC 127**
　　See also CA 132; 114; EWL 3; MTCW 1;
　　RGWL 2, 3
Defoe, Daniel 1660(?)-1731 .. **LC 1, 42; WLC**
　　See also AAYA 27; BRW 3; BRWR 1; BYA
　　4; CDBLB 1660-1789; CLR 61; DA;
　　DA3; DAB; DAC; DAM MST, NOV;
　　DLB 39, 95, 101; JRDA; LAIT 1; LMFS
　　1; MAICYA 1, 2; NFS 9, 13; RGEL 2;
　　SATA 22; TEA; WCH; WLIT 3
de Gourmont, Remy(-Marie-Charles)
　　See Gourmont, Remy(-Marie-Charles) de
de Hartog, Jan 1914-2002 .... **CLC 19**
　　See also CA 1-4R; 210; CANR 1; DFS 12
de Hostos, E. M.
　　See Hostos (y Bonilla), Eugenio Maria de
de Hostos, Eugenio M.
　　See Hostos (y Bonilla), Eugenio Maria de
Deighton, Len .... **CLC 4, 7, 22, 46**
　　See Deighton, Leonard Cyril
　　See also AAYA 6; BEST 89:2; BPFB 1; CD-
　　BLB 1960 to Present; CMW 4; CN 7;
　　CPW; DLB 87
Deighton, Leonard Cyril 1929-
　　See Deighton, Len
　　See also CA 9-12R; CANR 19, 33, 68;
　　DA3; DAM NOV, POP; MTCW 1, 2
Dekker, Thomas 1572(?)-1632 ..... **DC 12; LC
22**
　　See also CDBLB Before 1660; DAM
　　DRAM; DLB 62, 172; LMFS 1; RGEL 2
de Laclos, Pierre Ambroise Franois
　　See Laclos, Pierre Ambroise Francois
Delafield, E. M. .... **TCLC 61**
　　See Dashwood, Edmee Elizabeth Monica
　　de la Pasture
　　See also DLB 34; RHW
de la Mare, Walter (John)
　　1873-1956 . **SSC 14; TCLC 4, 53; WLC**
　　See also CA 163; CDBLB 1914-1945; CLR
　　23; CWRI 5; DA3; DAB; DAC; DAM
　　MST, POET; DLB 19, 153, 162, 255, 284;
　　EWL 3; EXPP; HGG; MAICYA 1, 2;
　　MTCW 1; RGEL 2; RGSF 2; SATA 16;
　　SUFW 1; TEA; WCH
de Lamartine, Alphonse (Marie Louis Prat)
　　See Lamartine, Alphonse (Marie Louis Prat)
　　de
Delaney, Franey
　　See O'Hara, John (Henry)

Delaney, Shelagh 1939- .... **CLC 29**
　　See also CA 17-20R; 67; CANR 30, 67; CBD;
　　CD 5; CDBLB 1960 to Present; CWD;
　　DAM DRAM; DFS 7; DLB 13; MTCW 1
Delany, Martin Robison
　　1812-1885 .... **NCLC 93**
　　See also DLB 50; RGAL 4
Delany, Mary (Granville Pendarves)
　　1700-1788 .... **LC 12**
Delany, Samuel R(ay), Jr. 1942- .... **BLC 1;
CLC 8, 14, 38, 141**
　　See also AAYA 24; AFAW 2; BPFB 1; BW
　　2, 3; CA 81-84; CANR 27, 43, 115, 116;
　　CN 7; DAM MULT; DLB 8, 33; FANT;
　　MTCW 1, 2; RGAL 4; SATA 92; SCFW;
　　SFW 4; SUFW 2
De la Ramee, Marie Louise (Ouida)
　　1839-1908
　　See Ouida
　　See also CA 204; SATA 20
de la Roche, Mazo 1879-1961 .... **CLC 14**
　　See also CA 85-88; CANR 30; DLB 68;
　　RGEL 2; RHW; SATA 64
De La Salle, Innocent
　　See Hartmann, Sadakichi
de Laureamont, Comte
　　See Lautreamont
Delbanco, Nicholas (Franklin)
　　1942- .... **CLC 6, 13, 167**
　　See also CA 17-20R; CAAE 189; CAAS 2;
　　CANR 29, 55, 116; DLB 6, 234
del Castillo, Michel 1933- .... **CLC 38**
　　See also CA 109; CANR 77
Deledda, Grazia (Cosima)
　　1875(?)-1936 .... **TCLC 23**
　　See also CA 123; 205; DLB 264; EWL 3;
　　RGWL 2, 3
Deleuze, Gilles 1925-1995 .... **TCLC 116**
Delgado, Abelardo (Lalo) B(arrientos)
　　1930- .... **HLC 1**
　　See also CA 131; CAAS 15; CANR 90;
　　DAM MST, MULT; DLB 82; HW 1, 2
Delibes, Miguel .... **CLC 8, 18**
　　See Delibes Setien, Miguel
　　See also EWL 3
Delibes Setien, Miguel 1920-
　　See Delibes, Miguel
　　See also CA 45-48; CANR 1, 32; HW 1;
　　MTCW 1
DeLillo, Don 1936- ..... **CLC 8, 10, 13, 27, 39,
54, 76, 143**
　　See also AMWS 6; BEST 89:1; BPFB 1;
　　CA 81-84; CANR 21, 76, 92; CN 7; CPW;
　　DA3; DAM NOV, POP; DLB 6, 173;
　　EWL 3; MTCW 1, 2; RGAL 4; TUS
de Lisser, H. G.
　　See De Lisser, H(erbert) G(eorge)
　　See also DLB 117
De Lisser, H(erbert) G(eorge)
　　1878-1944 .... **TCLC 12**
　　See de Lisser, H. G.
　　See also BW 2; CA 109; 152
Deloire, Pierre
　　See Peguy, Charles (Pierre)
Deloney, Thomas 1543(?)-1600 .... **LC 41**
　　See also DLB 167; RGEL 2
Deloria, Ella (Cara) 1889-1971(?) ..... **NNAL**
　　See also CA 152; DAM MULT; DLB 175
Deloria, Vine (Victor), Jr. 1933- ...... **CLC 21,
122; NNAL**
　　See also CA 53-56; CANR 5, 20, 48, 98;
　　DAM MULT; DLB 175; MTCW 1; SATA
　　21
del Valle-Inclan, Ramon (Maria)
　　See Valle-Inclan, Ramon (Maria) del
Del Vecchio, John M(ichael) 1947- .. **CLC 29**
　　See also CA 110; DLBD 9

de Man, Paul (Adolph Michel)
　　1919-1983 .... **CLC 55**
　　See also CA 128; 111; CANR 61; DLB 67;
　　MTCW 1, 2
DeMarinis, Rick 1934- .... **CLC 54**
　　See also CA 57-60, 184; CAAE 184; CAAS
　　24; CANR 9, 25, 50; DLB 218
de Maupassant, (Henri Rene Albert) Guy
　　See Maupassant, (Henri Rene Albert) Guy
　　de
Dembry, R. Emmet
　　See Murfree, Mary Noailles
Demby, William 1922- .... **BLC 1; CLC 53**
　　See also BW 1, 3; CA 81-84; CANR 81;
　　DAM MULT; DLB 33
de Menton, Francisco
　　See Chin, Frank (Chew, Jr.)
Demetrius of Phalerum c.
　　307B.C.- .... **CMLC 34**
Demijohn, Thom
　　See Disch, Thomas M(ichael)
De Mille, James 1833-1880 .... **NCLC 123**
　　See also DLB 99, 251
Deming, Richard 1915-1983
　　See Queen, Ellery
　　See also CA 9-12R; CANR 3, 94; SATA 24
Democritus c. 460B.C.-c. 370B.C. . **CMLC 47**
de Montaigne, Michel (Eyquem)
　　See Montaigne, Michel (Eyquem) de
de Montherlant, Henry (Milon)
　　See Montherlant, Henry (Milon) de
Demosthenes 384B.C.-322B.C. .... **CMLC 13**
　　See also AW 1; DLB 176; RGWL 2, 3
de Musset, (Louis Charles) Alfred
　　See Musset, (Louis Charles) Alfred de
de Natale, Francine
　　See Malzberg, Barry N(athaniel)
de Navarre, Marguerite 1492-1549 ..... **LC 61**
　　See Marguerite d'Angouleme; Marguerite
　　de Navarre
Denby, Edwin (Orr) 1903-1983 .... **CLC 48**
　　See also CA 138; 110
de Nerval, Gerard
　　See Nerval, Gerard de
Denham, John 1615-1669 .... **LC 73**
　　See also DLB 58, 126; RGEL 2
Denis, Julio
　　See Cortazar, Julio
Denmark, Harrison
　　See Zelazny, Roger (Joseph)
Dennis, John 1658-1734 .... **LC 11**
　　See also DLB 101; RGEL 2
Dennis, Nigel (Forbes) 1912-1989 ...... **CLC 8**
　　See also CA 25-28R; 129; DLB 13, 15, 233;
　　EWL 3; MTCW 1
Dent, Lester 1904(?)-1959 .... **TCLC 72**
　　See also CA 112; 161; CMW 4; SFW 4
De Palma, Brian (Russell) 1940- ...... **CLC 20**
　　See also CA 109
De Quincey, Thomas 1785-1859 ..... **NCLC 4,
87**
　　See also BRW 4; CDBLB 1789-1832; DLB
　　110, 144; RGEL 2
Deren, Eleanora 1908(?)-1961
　　See Deren, Maya
　　See also CA 192; 111
Deren, Maya .... **CLC 16, 102**
　　See Deren, Eleanora
Derleth, August (William)
　　1909-1971 .... **CLC 31**
　　See also BPFB 1; BYA 9, 10; CA 1-4R; 29-
　　32R; CANR 4; CMW 4; DLB 9; DLBD
　　17; HGG; SATA 5; SUFW 1
Der Nister 1884-1950 .... **TCLC 56**
　　See Nister, Der
de Routisie, Albert
　　See Aragon, Louis

Eastman, Charles A(lexander)
1858-1939 .... **NNAL; TCLC 55**
See also CA 179; CANR 91; DAM MULT;
DLB 175; YABC 1

Eaton, Edith Maude 1865-1914 .... **AAL**
See Far, Sui Sin
See also CA 154; DLB 221; FW

Eaton, Winnifred 1875-1954 .... **AAL**
See also DLB 221; RGAL 4

Eberhart, Richard (Ghormley)
1904- .... **CLC 3, 11, 19, 56**
See also AMW; CA 1-4R; CANR 2;
CDALB 1941-1968; CP 7; DAM POET;
DLB 48; MTCW 1; RGAL 4

Eberstadt, Fernanda 1960- .... **CLC 39**
See also CA 136; CANR 69

**Echegaray (y Eizaguirre), Jose (Maria
Waldo)** 1832-1916 .... **HLCS 1; TCLC 4**
See also CA 104; CANR 32; EWL 3; HW
1; MTCW 1

Echeverria, (Jose) Esteban (Antonino)
1805-1851 .... **NCLC 18**
See also LAW

Echo
See Proust, (Valentin-Louis-George-Eugene-
)Marcel

Eckert, Allan W. 1931- .... **CLC 17**
See also AAYA 18; BYA 2; CA 13-16R;
CANR 14, 45; INT CANR-14; MAICYA
2; MAICYAS 1; SAAS 21; SATA 29, 91;
SATA-Brief 27

Eckhart, Meister 1260(?)-1327(?) ... **CMLC 9**
See also DLB 115; LMFS 1

Eckmar, F. R.
See de Hartog, Jan

Eco, Umberto 1932- .... **CLC 28, 60, 142**
See also BEST 90:1; BPFB 1; CA 77-80;
CANR 12, 33, 55, 110; CPW; CWW 2;
DA3; DAM NOV, POP; DLB 196, 242;
EWL 3; MSW; MTCW 1, 2; RGWL 3

Eddison, E(ric) R(ucker)
1882-1945 .... **TCLC 15**
See also CA 109; 156; DLB 255; FANT;
SFW 4; SUFW 1

Eddy, Mary (Ann Morse) Baker
1821-1910 .... **TCLC 71**
See also CA 113; 174

Edel, (Joseph) Leon 1907-1997 .. **CLC 29, 34**
See also CA 1-4R; 161; CANR 1, 22, 112;
DLB 103; INT CANR-22

Eden, Emily 1797-1869 .... **NCLC 10**

Edgar, David 1948- .... **CLC 42**
See also CA 57-60; CANR 12, 61, 112;
CBD; CD 5; DAM DRAM; DFS 15; DLB
13, 233; MTCW 1

Edgerton, Clyde (Carlyle) 1944- ...... **CLC 39**
See also AAYA 17; CA 118; 134; CANR
64; CSW; DLB 278; INT 134; YAW

Edgeworth, Maria 1768-1849 .... **NCLC 1, 51**
See also BRWS 3; DLB 116, 159, 163; FW;
RGEL 2; SATA 21; TEA; WLIT 3

Edmonds, Paul
See Kuttner, Henry

Edmonds, Walter D(umaux)
1903-1998 .... **CLC 35**
See also BYA 2; CA 5-8R; CANR 2; CWRI
5; DLB 9; LAIT 1; MAICYA 1, 2; RHW;
SAAS 4; SATA 1, 27; SATA-Obit 99

Edmondson, Wallace
See Ellison, Harlan (Jay)

Edson, Russell 1935- .... **CLC 13**
See also CA 33-36R; CANR 115; DLB 244;
WP

Edwards, Bronwen Elizabeth
See Rose, Wendy

Edwards, G(erald) B(asil)
1899-1976 .... **CLC 25**
See also CA 201; 110

Edwards, Gus 1939- .... **CLC 43**
See also CA 108; INT 108

Edwards, Jonathan 1703-1758 .... **LC 7, 54**
See also AMW; DA; DAC; DAM MST;
DLB 24, 270; RGAL 4; TUS

Edwards, Sarah Pierpont 1710-1758 .. **LC 87**
See also DLB 200

Efron, Marina Ivanovna Tsvetaeva
See Tsvetaeva (Efron), Marina (Ivanovna)

Egoyan, Atom 1960- .... **CLC 151**
See also CA 157

Ehle, John (Marsden, Jr.) 1925- ...... **CLC 27**
See also CA 9-12R; CSW

Ehrenbourg, Ilya (Grigoryevich)
See Ehrenburg, Ilya (Grigoryevich)

Ehrenburg, Ilya (Grigoryevich)
1891-1967 .... **CLC 18, 34, 62**
See Erenburg, Il'ia Grigor'evich
See also CA 102; 25-28R; EWL 3

Ehrenburg, Ilyo (Grigoryevich)
See Ehrenburg, Ilya (Grigoryevich)

Ehrenreich, Barbara 1941- .... **CLC 110**
See also BEST 90:4; CA 73-76; CANR 16,
37, 62, 117; DLB 246; FW; MTCW 1, 2

Eich, Gunter
See Eich, Gunter
See also RGWL 2, 3

Eich, Gunter 1907-1972 .... **CLC 15**
See Eich, Gunter
See also CA 111; 93-96; DLB 69, 124;
EWL 3

Eichendorff, Joseph 1788-1857 .... **NCLC 8**
See also DLB 90; RGWL 2, 3

Eigner, Larry .... **CLC 9**
See Eigner, Laurence (Joel)
See also CAAS 23; DLB 5; WP

Eigner, Laurence (Joel) 1927-1996
See Eigner, Larry
See also CA 9-12R; 151; CANR 6, 84; CP
7; DLB 193

Einhard c. 770-840 .... **CMLC 50**
See also DLB 148

Einstein, Albert 1879-1955 .... **TCLC 65**
See also CA 121; 133; MTCW 1, 2

Eiseley, Loren
See Eiseley, Loren Corey
See also DLB 275

Eiseley, Loren Corey 1907-1977 .... **CLC 7**
See Eiseley, Loren
See also AAYA 5; ANW; CA 1-4R; 73-76;
CANR 6; DLBD 17

Eisenstadt, Jill 1963- .... **CLC 50**
See also CA 140

Eisenstein, Sergei (Mikhailovich)
1898-1948 .... **TCLC 57**
See also CA 114; 149

Eisner, Simon
See Kornbluth, C(yril) M.

Ekeloef, (Bengt) Gunnar
1907-1968 .... **CLC 27; PC 23**
See Ekelof, (Bengt) Gunnar
See also CA 123; 25-28R; DAM POET

Ekelof, (Bengt) Gunnar 1907-1968
See Ekeloef, (Bengt) Gunnar
See also DLB 259; EW 12; EWL 3

Ekelund, Vilhelm 1880-1949 .... **TCLC 75**
See also CA 189; EWL 3

Ekwensi, C. O. D.
See Ekwensi, Cyprian (Odiatu Duaka)

Ekwensi, Cyprian (Odiatu Duaka)
1921- .... **BLC 1; CLC 4**
See also AFW; BW 2, 3; CA 29-32R;
CANR 18, 42, 74; CDWLB 3; CN 7;
CWRI 5; DAM MULT; DLB 117; EWL
3; MTCW 1, 2; RGEL 2; SATA 66; WLIT
2

Elaine .... **TCLC 18**
See Leverson, Ada Esther

El Crummo
See Crumb, R(obert)

Elder, Lonne III 1931-1996 ..... **BLC 1; DC 8**
See also BW 1, 3; CA 81-84; 152; CAD;
CANR 25; DAM MULT; DLB 7, 38, 44

Eleanor of Aquitaine 1122-1204 ... **CMLC 39**

Elia
See Lamb, Charles

Eliade, Mircea 1907-1986 .... **CLC 19**
See also CA 65-68; 119; CANR 30, 62; CD-
WLB 4; DLB 220; EWL 3; MTCW 1;
RGWL 3; SFW 4

Eliot, A. D.
See Jewett, (Theodora) Sarah Orne

Eliot, Alice
See Jewett, (Theodora) Sarah Orne

Eliot, Dan
See Silverberg, Robert

Eliot, George 1819-1880 ...... **NCLC 4, 13, 23,
41, 49, 89, 118; PC 20; WLC**
See also BRW 5; BRWC 1; BRWR 2; CD-
BLB 1832-1890; CN 7; CPW; DA; DA3;
DAB; DAC; DAM MST, NOV; DLB 21,
35, 55; LATS 1; LMFS 1; NFS 17; RGEL
2; RGSF 2; SSFS 8; TEA; WLIT 3

Eliot, John 1604-1690 .... **LC 5**
See also DLB 24

Eliot, T(homas) S(tearns)
1888-1965 ...... **CLC 1, 2, 3, 6, 9, 10, 13,
15, 24, 34, 41, 55, 57, 113; PC 5, 31;
WLC**
See also AAYA 28; AMW; AMWC 1;
AMWR 1; BRW 7; BRWR 2; CA 5-8R;
25-28R; CANR 41; CDALB 1929-1941;
DA; DA3; DAB; DAC; DAM DRAM,
MST, POET; DFS 4, 13; DLB 7, 10, 45,
63, 245; DLBY 1988; EWL 3; EXPP;
LAIT 3; LATS 1; LMFS 2; MTCW 1, 2;
PAB; PFS 1, 7; RGAL 4; RGEL 2; TUS;
WLIT 4; WP

Elizabeth 1866-1941 .... **TCLC 41**

Elkin, Stanley L(awrence)
1930-1995 .. **CLC 4, 6, 9, 14, 27, 51, 91;
SSC 12**
See also AMWS 6; BPFB 1; CA 9-12R;
148; CANR 8, 46; CN 7; CPW; DAM
NOV, POP; DLB 2, 28, 218, 278; DLBY
1980; EWL 3; INT CANR-8; MTCW 1,
2; RGAL 4

Elledge, Scott .... **CLC 34**

Elliot, Don
See Silverberg, Robert

Elliott, Don
See Silverberg, Robert

Elliott, George P(aul) 1918-1980 .... **CLC 2**
See also CA 1-4R; 97-100; CANR 2; DLB
244

Elliott, Janice 1931-1995 .... **CLC 47**
See also CA 13-16R; CANR 8, 29, 84; CN
7; DLB 14; SATA 119

Elliott, Sumner Locke 1917-1991 ..... **CLC 38**
See also CA 5-8R; 134; CANR 2, 21

Elliott, William
See Bradbury, Ray (Douglas)

Ellis, A. E. .... **CLC 7**

Ellis, Alice Thomas .... **CLC 40**
See Haycraft, Anna (Margaret)
See also DLB 194; MTCW 1

Ellis, Bret Easton 1964- ...... **CLC 39, 71, 117**
See also AAYA 2, 43; CA 118; 123; CANR
51, 74; CN 7; CPW; DA3; DAM POP;
HGG; INT CA-123; MTCW 1; NFS 11

Ellis, (Henry) Havelock
1859-1939 .... **TCLC 14**
See also CA 109; 169; DLB 190

Ellis, Landon
See Ellison, Harlan (Jay)

Ellis, Trey 1962- .... **CLC 55**
See also CA 146; CANR 92

Exley, Frederick (Earl) 1929-1992 .... **CLC 6, 11**
   See also AITN 2; BPFB 1; CA 81-84; 138; CANR 117; DLB 143; DLBY 1981

Eynhardt, Guillermo
   See Quiroga, Horacio (Sylvestre)

Ezekiel, Nissim 1924- .... **CLC 61**
   See also CA 61-64; CP 7; EWL 3

Ezekiel, Tish O'Dowd 1943- .... **CLC 34**
   See also CA 129

Fadeev, Aleksandr Aleksandrovich
   See Bulgya, Alexander Alexandrovich
   See also DLB 272

Fadeev, Alexandr Alexandrovich
   See Bulgya, Alexander Alexandrovich
   See also EWL 3

Fadeyev, A.
   See Bulgya, Alexander Alexandrovich

Fadeyev, Alexander .... **TCLC 53**
   See Bulgya, Alexander Alexandrovich

Fagen, Donald 1948- .... **CLC 26**

Fainzilberg, Ilya Arnoldovich 1897-1937
   See Ilf, Ilya
   See also CA 120; 165

Fair, Ronald L. 1932- .... **CLC 18**
   See also BW 1; CA 69-72; CANR 25; DLB 33

Fairbairn, Roger
   See Carr, John Dickson

Fairbairns, Zoe (Ann) 1948- .... **CLC 32**
   See also CA 103; CANR 21, 85; CN 7

Fairfield, Flora
   See Alcott, Louisa May

Fairman, Paul W. 1916-1977
   See Queen, Ellery
   See also CA 114; SFW 4

Falco, Gian
   See Papini, Giovanni

Falconer, James
   See Kirkup, James

Falconer, Kenneth
   See Kornbluth, C(yril) M.

Falkland, Samuel
   See Heijermans, Herman

Fallaci, Oriana 1930- .... **CLC 11, 110**
   See also CA 77-80; CANR 15, 58; FW; MTCW 1

Faludi, Susan 1959- .... **CLC 140**
   See also CA 138; FW; MTCW 1; NCFS 3

Faludy, George 1913- .... **CLC 42**
   See also CA 21-24R

Faludy, Gyoergy
   See Faludy, George

Fanon, Frantz 1925-1961 .... **BLC 2; CLC 74**
   See also BW 1; CA 116; 89-92; DAM MULT; LMFS 2; WLIT 2

Fanshawe, Ann 1625-1680 .... **LC 11**

Fante, John (Thomas) 1911-1983 ..... **CLC 60**
   See also AMWS 11; CA 69-72; 109; CANR 23, 104; DLB 130; DLBY 1983

Far, Sui Sin .... **SSC 62**
   See Eaton, Edith Maude
   See also SSFS 4

Farah, Nuruddin 1945- ...... **BLC 2; CLC 53, 137**
   See also AFW; BW 2, 3; CA 106; CANR 81; CDWLB 3; CN 7; DAM MULT; DLB 125; EWL 3; WLIT 2

Fargue, Leon-Paul 1876(?)-1947 .... **TCLC 11**
   See also CA 109; CANR 107; DLB 258; EWL 3

Farigoule, Louis
   See Romains, Jules

Farina, Richard 1936(?)-1966 .... **CLC 9**
   See also CA 81-84; 25-28R

Farley, Walter (Lorimer)
   1915-1989 .... **CLC 17**
   See also BYA 14; CA 17-20R; CANR 8, 29, 84; DLB 22; JRDA; MAICYA 1, 2; SATA 2, 43, 132; YAW

Farmer, Philip Jose 1918- .... **CLC 1, 19**
   See also AAYA 28; BPFB 1; CA 1-4R; CANR 4, 35, 111; DLB 8; MTCW 1; SATA 93; SCFW 2; SFW 4

Farquhar, George 1677-1707 .... **LC 21**
   See also BRW 2; DAM DRAM; DLB 84; RGEL 2

Farrell, J(ames) G(ordon)
   1935-1979 .... **CLC 6**
   See also CA 73-76; 89-92; CANR 36; DLB 14, 271; MTCW 1; RGEL 2; RHW; WLIT 4

Farrell, James T(homas) 1904-1979 . **CLC 1, 4, 8, 11, 66; SSC 28**
   See also AMW; BPFB 1; CA 5-8R; 89-92; CANR 9, 61; DLB 4, 9, 86; DLBD 2; EWL 3; MTCW 1, 2; RGAL 4

Farrell, Warren (Thomas) 1943- ...... **CLC 70**
   See also CA 146

Farren, Richard J.
   See Betjeman, John

Farren, Richard M.
   See Betjeman, John

Fassbinder, Rainer Werner
   1946-1982 .... **CLC 20**
   See also CA 93-96; 106; CANR 31

Fast, Howard (Melvin) 1914-2003 .. **CLC 23, 131**
   See also AAYA 16; BPFB 1; CA 1-4R, 181; CAAE 181; CAAS 18; CANR 1, 33, 54, 75, 98; CMW 4; CN 7; CPW; DAM NOV; DLB 9; INT CANR-33; LATS 1; MTCW 1; RHW; SATA 7; SATA-Essay 107; TCWW 2; YAW

Faulcon, Robert
   See Holdstock, Robert P.

Faulkner, William (Cuthbert)
   1897-1962 .... **CLC 1, 3, 6, 8, 9, 11, 14, 18, 28, 52, 68; SSC 1, 35, 42; WLC**
   See also AAYA 7; AMW; AMWR 1; BPFB 1; BYA 5; CA 81-84; CANR 33; CDALB 1929-1941; DA; DA3; DAB; DAC; DAM MST, NOV; DLB 9, 11, 44, 102; DLBD 2; DLBY 1986, 1997; EWL 3; EXPN; EXPS; LAIT 2; LATS 1; LMFS 2; MTCW 1, 2; NFS 4, 8, 13; RGAL 4; RGSF 2; SSFS 2, 5, 6, 12; TUS

Fauset, Jessie Redmon
   1882(?)-1961 .. **BLC 2; CLC 19, 54; HR 2**
   See also AFAW 2; BW 1; CA 109; CANR 83; DAM MULT; DLB 51; FW; LMFS 2; MAWW

Faust, Frederick (Schiller)
   1892-1944(?) .... **TCLC 49**
   See Austin, Frank; Brand, Max; Challis, George; Dawson, Peter; Dexter, Martin; Evans, Evan; Frederick, John; Frost, Frederick; Manning, David; Silver, Nicholas
   See also CA 108; 152; DAM POP; DLB 256; TUS

Faust, Irvin 1924- .... **CLC 8**
   See also CA 33-36R; CANR 28, 67; CN 7; DLB 2, 28, 218, 278; DLBY 1980

Faustino, Domingo 1811-1888 ...... **NCLC 123**

Fawkes, Guy
   See Benchley, Robert (Charles)

Fearing, Kenneth (Flexner)
   1902-1961 .... **CLC 51**
   See also CA 93-96; CANR 59; CMW 4; DLB 9; RGAL 4

Fecamps, Elise
   See Creasey, John

Federman, Raymond 1928- .... **CLC 6, 47**
   See also CA 17-20R; CAAE 208; CAAS 8; CANR 10, 43, 83, 108; CN 7; DLBY 1980

Federspiel, J(uerg) F. 1931- .... **CLC 42**
   See also CA 146

Feiffer, Jules (Ralph) 1929- ...... **CLC 2, 8, 64**
   See also AAYA 3; CA 17-20R; CAD; CANR 30, 59; CD 5; DAM DRAM; DLB 7, 44; INT CANR-30; MTCW 1; SATA 8, 61, 111

Feige, Hermann Albert Otto Maximilian
   See Traven, B.

Feinberg, David B. 1956-1994 .... **CLC 59**
   See also CA 135; 147

Feinstein, Elaine 1930- .... **CLC 36**
   See also CA 69-72; CAAS 1; CANR 31, 68; CN 7; CP 7; CWP; DLB 14, 40; MTCW 1

Feke, Gilbert David .... **CLC 65**

Feldman, Irving (Mordecai) 1928- ..... **CLC 7**
   See also CA 1-4R; CANR 1; CP 7; DLB 169

Felix-Tchicaya, Gerald
   See Tchicaya, Gerald Felix

Fellini, Federico 1920-1993 .... **CLC 16, 85**
   See also CA 65-68; 143; CANR 33

Felsen, Henry Gregor 1916-1995 ..... **CLC 17**
   See also CA 1-4R; 180; CANR 1; SAAS 2; SATA 1

Felski, Rita .... **CLC 65**

Fenno, Jack
   See Calisher, Hortense

Fenollosa, Ernest (Francisco)
   1853-1908 .... **TCLC 91**

Fenton, James Martin 1949- .... **CLC 32**
   See also CA 102; CANR 108; CP 7; DLB 40; PFS 11

Ferber, Edna 1887-1968 .... **CLC 18, 93**
   See also AITN 1; CA 5-8R; 25-28R; CANR 68, 105; DLB 9, 28, 86, 266; MTCW 1, 2; RGAL 4; RHW; SATA 7; TCWW 2

Ferdowsi, Abu'l Qasem 940-1020 . **CMLC 43**
   See also RGWL 2, 3

Ferguson, Helen
   See Kavan, Anna

Ferguson, Niall 1964- .... **CLC 134**
   See also CA 190

Ferguson, Samuel 1810-1886 .... **NCLC 33**
   See also DLB 32; RGEL 2

Fergusson, Robert 1750-1774 .... **LC 29**
   See also DLB 109; RGEL 2

Ferling, Lawrence
   See Ferlinghetti, Lawrence (Monsanto)

Ferlinghetti, Lawrence (Monsanto)
   1919(?)- ..... **CLC 2, 6, 10, 27, 111; PC 1**
   See also CA 5-8R; CANR 3, 41, 73; CDALB 1941-1968; CP 7; DA3; DAM POET; DLB 5, 16; MTCW 1, 2; RGAL 4; WP

Fern, Fanny
   See Parton, Sara Payson Willis

Fernandez, Vicente Garcia Huidobro
   See Huidobro Fernandez, Vicente Garcia

Fernandez-Armesto, Felipe .... **CLC 70**

Fernandez de Lizardi, Jose Joaquin
   See Lizardi, Jose Joaquin Fernandez de

Ferre, Rosario 1938- ...... **CLC 139; HLCS 1; SSC 36**
   See also CA 131; CANR 55, 81; CWW 2; DLB 145; EWL 3; HW 1, 2; LAWS 1; MTCW 1; WLIT 1

Ferrer, Gabriel (Francisco Victor) Miro
   See Miro (Ferrer), Gabriel (Francisco Victor)

Ferrier, Susan (Edmonstone)
   1782-1854 .... **NCLC 8**
   See also DLB 116; RGEL 2

Ford, Jack
See Ford, John

Ford, John 1586-1639 .... **DC 8; LC 68**
See also BRW 2; CDBLB Before 1660; DA3; DAM DRAM; DFS 7; DLB 58; IDTP; RGEL 2

Ford, John 1895-1973 .... **CLC 16**
See also CA 187; 45-48

Ford, Richard 1944- .... **CLC 46, 99**
See also AMWS 5; CA 69-72; CANR 11, 47, 86; CN 7; CSW; DLB 227; EWL 3; MTCW 1; RGAL 4; RGSF 2

Ford, Webster
See Masters, Edgar Lee

Foreman, Richard 1937- .... **CLC 50**
See also CA 65-68; CAD; CANR 32, 63; CD 5

Forester, C(ecil) S(cott) 1899-1966 ... **CLC 35**
See also CA 73-76; 25-28R; CANR 83; DLB 191; RGEL 2; RHW; SATA 13

Forez
See Mauriac, Francois (Charles)

Forman, James
See Forman, James D(ouglas)

Forman, James D(ouglas) 1932- .... **CLC 21**
See also AAYA 17; CA 9-12R; CANR 4, 19, 42; JRDA; MAICYA 1, 2; SATA 8, 70; YAW

Forman, Milos 1932- .... **CLC 164**
See also CA 109

Fornes, Maria Irene 1930- . **CLC 39, 61; DC 10; HLCS 1**
See also CA 25-28R; CAD; CANR 28, 81; CD 5; CWD; DLB 7; HW 1, 2; INT CANR-28; MTCW 1; RGAL 4

Forrest, Leon (Richard)
1937-1997 .... **BLCS; CLC 4**
See also AFAW 2; BW 2; CA 89-92; 162; CAAS 7; CANR 25, 52, 87; CN 7; DLB 33

Forster, E(dward) M(organ)
1879-1970 ...... **CLC 1, 2, 3, 4, 9, 10, 13, 15, 22, 45, 77; SSC 27; TCLC 125; WLC**
See also AAYA 2, 37; BRW 6; BRWR 2; CA 13-14; 25-28R; CANR 45; CAP 1; CDBLB 1914-1945; DA; DA3; DAB; DAC; DAM MST, NOV; DLB 34, 98, 162, 178, 195; DLBD 10; EWL 3; EXPN; LAIT 3; LMFS 1; MTCW 1, 2; NCFS 1; NFS 3, 10, 11; RGEL 2; RGSF 2; SATA 57; SUFW 1; TEA; WLIT 4

Forster, John 1812-1876 .... **NCLC 11**
See also DLB 144, 184

Forster, Margaret 1938- .... **CLC 149**
See also CA 133; CANR 62, 115; CN 7; DLB 155, 271

Forsyth, Frederick 1938- .... **CLC 2, 5, 36**
See also BEST 89:4; CA 85-88; CANR 38, 62, 115; CMW 4; CN 7; CPW; DAM NOV, POP; DLB 87; MTCW 1, 2

Forten, Charlotte L. 1837-1914 .... **BLC 2; TCLC 16**
See Grimke, Charlotte L(ottie) Forten
See also DLB 50, 239

Fortinbras
See Grieg, (Johan) Nordahl (Brun)

Foscolo, Ugo 1778-1827 .... **NCLC 8, 97**
See also EW 5

Fosse, Bob .... **CLC 20**
See Fosse, Robert Louis

Fosse, Robert Louis 1927-1987
See Fosse, Bob
See also CA 110; 123

Foster, Hannah Webster
1758-1840 .... **NCLC 99**
See also DLB 37, 200; RGAL 4

Foster, Stephen Collins
1826-1864 .... **NCLC 26**
See also RGAL 4

Foucault, Michel 1926-1984 . **CLC 31, 34, 69**
See also CA 105; 113; CANR 34; DLB 242; EW 13; EWL 3; GFL 1789 to the Present; GLL 1; LMFS 2; MTCW 1, 2; TWA

Fouque, Friedrich (Heinrich Karl) de la Motte 1777-1843 .... **NCLC 2**
See also DLB 90; RGWL 2, 3; SUFW 1

Fourier, Charles 1772-1837 .... **NCLC 51**

Fournier, Henri-Alban 1886-1914
See Alain-Fournier
See also CA 104; 179

Fournier, Pierre 1916- .... **CLC 11**
See Gascar, Pierre
See also CA 89-92; CANR 16, 40

Fowles, John (Robert) 1926- . **CLC 1, 2, 3, 4, 6, 9, 10, 15, 33, 87; SSC 33**
See also BPFB 1; BRWS 1; CA 5-8R; CANR 25, 71, 103; CDBLB 1960 to Present; CN 7; DA3; DAB; DAC; DAM MST; DLB 14, 139, 207; EWL 3; HGG; MTCW 1, 2; RGEL 2; RHW; SATA 22; TEA; WLIT 4

Fox, Paula 1923- .... **CLC 2, 8, 121**
See also AAYA 3, 37; BYA 3, 8; CA 73-76; CANR 20, 36, 62, 105; CLR 1, 44; DLB 52; JRDA; MAICYA 1, 2; MTCW 1; NFS 12; SATA 17, 60, 120; WYA; YAW

Fox, William Price (Jr.) 1926- .... **CLC 22**
See also CA 17-20R; CAAS 19; CANR 11; CSW; DLB 2; DLBY 1981

Foxe, John 1517(?)-1587 .... **LC 14**
See also DLB 132

Frame, Janet .. **CLC 2, 3, 6, 22, 66, 96; SSC 29**
See Clutha, Janet Paterson Frame
See also CN 7; CWP; EWL 3; RGEL 2; RGSF 2; TWA

France, Anatole .... **TCLC 9**
See Thibault, Jacques Anatole Francois
See also DLB 123; EWL 3; GFL 1789 to the Present; MTCW 1; RGWL 2, 3; SUFW 1

Francis, Claude .... **CLC 50**
See also CA 192

Francis, Dick 1920- .... **CLC 2, 22, 42, 102**
See also AAYA 5, 21; BEST 89:3; BPFB 1; CA 5-8R; CANR 9, 42, 68, 100; CDBLB 1960 to Present; CMW 4; CN 7; DA3; DAM POP; DLB 87; INT CANR-9; MSW; MTCW 1, 2

Francis, Robert (Churchill)
1901-1987 .... **CLC 15; PC 34**
See also AMWS 9; CA 1-4R; 123; CANR 1; EXPP; PFS 12

Francis, Lord Jeffrey
See Jeffrey, Francis
See also DLB 107

Frank, Anne(lies Marie)
1929-1945 .... **TCLC 17; WLC**
See also AAYA 12; BYA 1; CA 113; 133; CANR 68; DA; DA3; DAB; DAC; DAM MST; LAIT 4; MAICYA 2; MAICYAS 1; MTCW 1, 2; NCFS 2; SATA 87; SATA-Brief 42; WYA; YAW

Frank, Bruno 1887-1945 .... **TCLC 81**
See also CA 189; DLB 118; EWL 3

Frank, Elizabeth 1945- .... **CLC 39**
See also CA 121; 126; CANR 78; INT 126

Frankl, Viktor E(mil) 1905-1997 ...... **CLC 93**
See also CA 65-68; 161

Franklin, Benjamin
See Hasek, Jaroslav (Matej Frantisek)

Franklin, Benjamin 1706-1790 .... **LC 25; WLCS**
See also AMW; CDALB 1640-1865; DA; DA3; DAB; DAC; DAM MST; DLB 24, 43, 73, 183; LAIT 1; RGAL 4; TUS

Franklin, (Stella Maria Sarah) Miles (Lampe) 1879-1954 .... **TCLC 7**
See also CA 104; 164; DLB 230; FW; MTCW 2; RGEL 2; TWA

Fraser, Antonia (Pakenham) 1932- . **CLC 32, 107**
See also CA 85-88; CANR 44, 65; CMW; DLB 276; MTCW 1, 2; SATA-Brief 32

Fraser, George MacDonald 1925- ...... **CLC 7**
See also AAYA 48; CA 45-48; 180; CAAE 180; CANR 2, 48, 74; MTCW 1; RHW

Fraser, Sylvia 1935- .... **CLC 64**
See also CA 45-48; CANR 1, 16, 60; CCA 1

Frayn, Michael 1933- .... **CLC 3, 7, 31, 47**
See also BRWS 7; CA 5-8R; CANR 30, 69, 114; CBD; CD 5; CN 7; DAM DRAM, NOV; DLB 13, 14, 194, 245; FANT; MTCW 1, 2; SFW 4

Fraze, Candida (Merrill) 1945- .... **CLC 50**
See also CA 126

Frazer, Andrew
See Marlowe, Stephen

Frazer, J(ames) G(eorge)
1854-1941 .... **TCLC 32**
See also BRWS 3; CA 118

Frazer, Robert Caine
See Creasey, John

Frazer, Sir James George
See Frazer, J(ames) G(eorge)

Frazier, Charles 1950- .... **CLC 109**
See also AAYA 34; CA 161; CSW

Frazier, Ian 1951- .... **CLC 46**
See also CA 130; CANR 54, 93

Frederic, Harold 1856-1898 .... **NCLC 10**
See also AMW; DLB 12, 23; DLBD 13; RGAL 4

Frederick, John
See Faust, Frederick (Schiller)
See also TCWW 2

Frederick the Great 1712-1786 .... **LC 14**

Fredro, Aleksander 1793-1876 .... **NCLC 8**

Freeling, Nicolas 1927- .... **CLC 38**
See also CA 49-52; CAAS 12; CANR 1, 17, 50, 84; CMW 4; CN 7; DLB 87

Freeman, Douglas Southall
1886-1953 .... **TCLC 11**
See also CA 109; 195; DLB 17; DLBD 17

Freeman, Judith 1946- .... **CLC 55**
See also CA 148; DLB 256

Freeman, Mary E(leanor) Wilkins
1852-1930 .... **SSC 1, 47; TCLC 9**
See also CA 106; 177; DLB 12, 78, 221; EXPS; FW; HGG; MAWW; RGAL 4; RGSF 2; SSFS 4, 8; SUFW 1; TUS

Freeman, R(ichard) Austin
1862-1943 .... **TCLC 21**
See also CA 113; CANR 84; CMW 4; DLB 70

French, Albert 1943- .... **CLC 86**
See also BW 3; CA 167

French, Antonia
See Kureishi, Hanif

French, Marilyn 1929- .... **CLC 10, 18, 60**
See also BPFB 1; CA 69-72; CANR 3, 31; CN 7; CPW; DAM DRAM, NOV, POP; FW; INT CANR-31; MTCW 1, 2

French, Paul
See Asimov, Isaac

Freneau, Philip Morin 1752-1832 .. **NCLC 1, 111**
See also AMWS 2; DLB 37, 43; RGAL 4

Freud, Sigmund 1856-1939 .... **TCLC 52**
See also CA 115; 133; CANR 69; EW 8;
EWL 3; LATS 1; MTCW 1, 2; NCFS 3;
TWA

Freytag, Gustav 1816-1895 .... **NCLC 109**
See also DLB 129

Friedan, Betty (Naomi) 1921- .... **CLC 74**
See also CA 65-68; CANR 18, 45, 74; DLB
246; FW; MTCW 1, 2

Friedlander, Saul 1932- .... **CLC 90**
See also CA 117; 130; CANR 72

Friedman, B(ernard) H(arper)
1926- .... **CLC 7**
See also CA 1-4R; CANR 3, 48

Friedman, Bruce Jay 1930- ...... **CLC 3, 5, 56**
See also CA 9-12R; CAD; CANR 25, 52,
101; CD 5; CN 7; DLB 2, 28, 244; INT
CANR-25

Friel, Brian 1929- .... **CLC 5, 42, 59, 115; DC
8**
See also BRWS 5; CA 21-24R; CANR 33,
69; CBD; CD 5; DFS 11; DLB 13; EWL
3; MTCW 1; RGEL 2; TEA

Friis-Baastad, Babbis Ellinor
1921-1970 .... **CLC 12**
See also CA 17-20R; 134; SATA 7

Frisch, Max (Rudolf) 1911-1991 ... **CLC 3, 9,
14, 18, 32, 44; TCLC 121**
See also CA 85-88; 134; CANR 32, 74; CD-
WLB 2; DAM DRAM, NOV; DLB 69,
124; EW 13; EWL 3; MTCW 1, 2; RGWL
2, 3

Fromentin, Eugene (Samuel Auguste)
1820-1876 .... **NCLC 10, 125**
See also DLB 123; GFL 1789 to the Present

Frost, Frederick
See Faust, Frederick (Schiller)
See also TCWW 2

Frost, Robert (Lee) 1874-1963 .. **CLC 1, 3, 4,
9, 10, 13, 15, 26, 34, 44; PC 1, 39;
WLC**
See also AAYA 21; AMW; AMWR 1; CA
89-92; CANR 33; CDALB 1917-1929;
CLR 67; DA; DA3; DAB; DAC; DAM
MST, POET; DLB 54, 284; DLBD 7;
EWL 3; EXPP; MTCW 1, 2; PAB; PFS 1,
2, 3, 4, 5, 6, 7, 10, 13; RGAL 4; SATA
14; TUS; WP; WYA

Froude, James Anthony
1818-1894 .... **NCLC 43**
See also DLB 18, 57, 144

Froy, Herald
See Waterhouse, Keith (Spencer)

Fry, Christopher 1907- .... **CLC 2, 10, 14**
See also BRWS 3; CA 17-20R; CAAS 23;
CANR 9, 30, 74; CBD; CD 5; CP 7; DAM
DRAM; DLB 13; EWL 3; MTCW 1, 2;
RGEL 2; SATA 66; TEA

Frye, (Herman) Northrop
1912-1991 .... **CLC 24, 70**
See also CA 5-8R; 133; CANR 8, 37; DLB
67, 68, 246; EWL 3; MTCW 1, 2; RGAL
4; TWA

Fuchs, Daniel 1909-1993 .... **CLC 8, 22**
See also CA 81-84; 142; CAAS 5; CANR
40; DLB 9, 26, 28; DLBY 1993

Fuchs, Daniel 1934- .... **CLC 34**
See also CA 37-40R; CANR 14, 48

Fuentes, Carlos 1928- .. **CLC 3, 8, 10, 13, 22,
41, 60, 113; HLC 1; SSC 24; WLC**
See also AAYA 4, 45; AITN 2; BPFB 1;
CA 69-72; CANR 10, 32, 68, 104; CD-
WLB 3; CWW 2; DA; DA3; DAB; DAC;
DAM MST, MULT, NOV; DLB 113;
DNFS 2; EWL 3; HW 1, 2; LAIT 3; LATS
1; LAW; LAWS 1; LMFS 2; MTCW 1, 2;
NFS 8; RGSF 2; RGWL 2, 3; TWA;
WLIT 1

Fuentes, Gregorio Lopez y
See Lopez y Fuentes, Gregorio

Fuertes, Gloria 1918-1998 .... **PC 27**
See also CA 178, 180; DLB 108; HW 2;
SATA 115

Fugard, (Harold) Athol 1932- . **CLC 5, 9, 14,
25, 40, 80; DC 3**
See also AAYA 17; AFW; CA 85-88; CANR
32, 54, 118; CD 5; DAM DRAM; DFS 3,
6, 10; DLB 225; DNFS 1, 2; EWL 3;
LATS 1; MTCW 1; RGEL 2; WLIT 2

Fugard, Sheila 1932- .... **CLC 48**
See also CA 125

Fukuyama, Francis 1952- .... **CLC 131**
See also CA 140; CANR 72

Fuller, Charles (H.), (Jr.) 1939- .... **BLC 2;
CLC 25; DC 1**
See also BW 2; CA 108; 112; CAD; CANR
87; CD 5; DAM DRAM, MULT; DFS 8;
DLB 38, 266; EWL 3; INT CA-112;
MTCW 1

Fuller, Henry Blake 1857-1929 .... **TCLC 103**
See also CA 108; 177; DLB 12; RGAL 4

Fuller, John (Leopold) 1937- .... **CLC 62**
See also CA 21-24R; CANR 9, 44; CP 7;
DLB 40

Fuller, Margaret
See Ossoli, Sarah Margaret (Fuller)
See also AMWS 2; DLB 183, 223, 239

Fuller, Roy (Broadbent) 1912-1991 ... **CLC 4,
28**
See also BRWS 7; CA 5-8R; 135; CAAS
10; CANR 53, 83; CWRI 5; DLB 15, 20;
EWL 3; RGEL 2; SATA 87

Fuller, Sarah Margaret
See Ossoli, Sarah Margaret (Fuller)

Fuller, Sarah Margaret
See Ossoli, Sarah Margaret (Fuller)
See also DLB 1, 59, 73

Fulton, Alice 1952- .... **CLC 52**
See also CA 116; CANR 57, 88; CP 7;
CWP; DLB 193

Furphy, Joseph 1843-1912 .... **TCLC 25**
See Collins, Tom
See also CA 163; DLB 230; EWL 3; RGEL
2

Fuson, Robert H(enderson) 1927- .... **CLC 70**
See also CA 89-92; CANR 103

Fussell, Paul 1924- .... **CLC 74**
See also BEST 90:1; CA 17-20R; CANR 8,
21, 35, 69; INT CANR-21; MTCW 1, 2

Futabatei, Shimei 1864-1909 .... **TCLC 44**
See Futabatei Shimei
See also CA 162; MJW

Futabatei Shimei
See Futabatei, Shimei
See also DLB 180; EWL 3

Futrelle, Jacques 1875-1912 .... **TCLC 19**
See also CA 113; 155; CMW 4

Gaboriau, Emile 1835-1873 .... **NCLC 14**
See also CMW 4; MSW

Gadda, Carlo Emilio 1893-1973 .... **CLC 11**
See also CA 89-92; DLB 177; EWL 3

Gaddis, William 1922-1998 ... **CLC 1, 3, 6, 8,
10, 19, 43, 86**
See also AMWS 4; BPFB 1; CA 17-20R;
172; CANR 21, 48; CN 7; DLB 2, 278;
EWL 3; MTCW 1, 2; RGAL 4

Gaelique, Moruen le
See Jacob, (Cyprien-)Max

Gage, Walter
See Inge, William (Motter)

Gaines, Ernest J(ames) 1933- .. **BLC 2; CLC
3, 11, 18, 86**
See also AAYA 18; AFAW 1, 2; AITN 1;
BPFB 2; BW 2, 3; BYA 6; CA 9-12R;
CANR 6, 24, 42, 75; CDALB 1968-1988;
CLR 62; CN 7; CSW; DA3; DAM MULT;
DLB 2, 33, 152; DLBY 1980; EWL 3;

EXPN; LAIT 5; LATS 1; MTCW 1, 2;
NFS 5, 7, 16; RGAL 4; RGSF 2; RHW;
SATA 86; SSFS 5; YAW

Gaitskill, Mary 1954- .... **CLC 69**
See also CA 128; CANR 61; DLB 244

Galdos, Benito Perez
See Perez Galdos, Benito
See also EW 7

Gale, Zona 1874-1938 .... **TCLC 7**
See also CA 105; 153; CANR 84; DAM
DRAM; DFS 17; DLB 9, 78, 228; RGAL
4

Galeano, Eduardo (Hughes) 1940- . **CLC 72;
HLCS 1**
See also CA 29-32R; CANR 13, 32, 100;
HW 1

Galiano, Juan Valera y Alcala
See Valera y Alcala-Galiano, Juan

Galilei, Galileo 1564-1642 .... **LC 45**

Gallagher, Tess 1943- .... **CLC 18, 63; PC 9**
See also CA 106; CP 7; CWP; DAM POET;
DLB 120, 212, 244; PFS 16

Gallant, Mavis 1922- ..... **CLC 7, 18, 38, 172;
SSC 5**
See also CA 69-72; CANR 29, 69, 117;
CCA 1; CN 7; DAC; DAM MST; DLB
53; EWL 3; MTCW 1, 2; RGEL 2; RGSF
2

Gallant, Roy A(rthur) 1924- .... **CLC 17**
See also CA 5-8R; CANR 4, 29, 54, 117;
CLR 30; MAICYA 1, 2; SATA 4, 68, 110

Gallico, Paul (William) 1897-1976 ..... **CLC 2**
See also AITN 1; CA 5-8R; 69-72; CANR
23; DLB 9, 171; FANT; MAICYA 1, 2;
SATA 13

Gallo, Max Louis 1932- .... **CLC 95**
See also CA 85-88

Gallois, Lucien
See Desnos, Robert

Gallup, Ralph
See Whitemore, Hugh (John)

Galsworthy, John 1867-1933 .... **SSC 22;
TCLC 1, 45; WLC**
See also BRW 6; CA 104; 141; CANR 75;
CDBLB 1890-1914; DA; DA3; DAB;
DAC; DAM DRAM, MST, NOV; DLB
10, 34, 98, 162; DLBD 16; EWL 3;
MTCW 1; RGEL 2; SSFS 3; TEA

Galt, John 1779-1839 .... **NCLC 1, 110**
See also DLB 99, 116, 159; RGEL 2; RGSF
2

Galvin, James 1951- .... **CLC 38**
See also CA 108; CANR 26

Gamboa, Federico 1864-1939 .... **TCLC 36**
See also CA 167; HW 2; LAW

Gandhi, M. K.
See Gandhi, Mohandas Karamchand

Gandhi, Mahatma
See Gandhi, Mohandas Karamchand

Gandhi, Mohandas Karamchand
1869-1948 .... **TCLC 59**
See also CA 121; 132; DA3; DAM MULT;
MTCW 1, 2

Gann, Ernest Kellogg 1910-1991 ..... **CLC 23**
See also AITN 1; BPFB 2; CA 1-4R; 136;
CANR 1, 83; RHW

Gao Xingjian 1940- .... **CLC 167**
See Xingjian, Gao

Garber, Eric 1943(?)-
See Holleran, Andrew
See also CANR 89

Garcia, Cristina 1958- .... **CLC 76**
See also AMWS 11; CA 141; CANR 73;
DNFS 1; EWL 3; HW 2

Garcia Lorca, Federico 1898-1936 ...... **DC 2; HLC 2; PC 3; TCLC 1, 7, 49; WLC**
See Lorca, Federico Garcia
See also AAYA 46; CA 104; 131; CANR 81; DA; DA3; DAB; DAC; DAM DRAM, MST, MULT, POET; DFS 4, 10; DLB 108; EWL 3; HW 1, 2; LATS 1; MTCW 1, 2; TWA

Garcia Marquez, Gabriel (Jose) 1928- .... **CLC 2, 3, 8, 10, 15, 27, 47, 55, 68, 170; HLC 1; SSC 8; WLC**
See also AAYA 3, 33; BEST 89:1, 90:4; BPFB 2; BYA 12; CA 33-36R; CANR 10, 28, 50, 75, 82; CDWLB 3; CPW; DA; DA3; DAB; DAC; DAM MST, MULT, NOV, POP; DLB 113; DNFS 1, 2; EWL 3; EXPN; EXPS; HW 1, 2; LAIT 2; LATS 1; LAW; LAWS 1; LMFS 2; MTCW 1, 2; NCFS 3; NFS 1, 5, 10; RGSF 2; RGWL 2, 3; SSFS 1, 6, 16; TWA; WLIT 1

Garcilaso de la Vega, El Inca 1503-1536 .... **HLCS 1**
See also LAW

Gard, Janice
See Latham, Jean Lee

Gard, Roger Martin du
See Martin du Gard, Roger

Gardam, Jane (Mary) 1928- .... **CLC 43**
See also CA 49-52; CANR 2, 18, 33, 54, 106; CLR 12; DLB 14, 161, 231; MAICYA 1, 2; MTCW 1; SAAS 9; SATA 39, 76, 130; SATA-Brief 28; YAW

Gardner, Herb(ert) 1934- .... **CLC 44**
See also CA 149; CAD; CD 5

Gardner, John (Champlin), Jr. 1933-1982 ...... **CLC 2, 3, 5, 7, 8, 10, 18, 28, 34; SSC 7**
See also AAYA 45; AITN 1; AMWS 6; BPFB 2; CA 65-68; 107; CANR 33, 73; CDALBS; CPW; DA3; DAM NOV, POP; DLB 2; DLBY 1982; EWL 3; FANT; LATS 1; MTCW 1; NFS 3; RGAL 4; RGSF 2; SATA 40; SATA-Obit 31; SSFS 8

Gardner, John (Edmund) 1926- .... **CLC 30**
See also CA 103; CANR 15, 69; CMW 4; CPW; DAM POP; MTCW 1

Gardner, Miriam
See Bradley, Marion Zimmer
See also GLL 1

Gardner, Noel
See Kuttner, Henry

Gardons, S. S.
See Snodgrass, W(illiam) D(e Witt)

Garfield, Leon 1921-1996 .... **CLC 12**
See also AAYA 8; BYA 1, 3; CA 17-20R; 152; CANR 38, 41, 78; CLR 21; DLB 161; JRDA; MAICYA 1, 2; MAICYAS 1; SATA 1, 32, 76; SATA-Obit 90; TEA; WYA; YAW

Garland, (Hannibal) Hamlin 1860-1940 .... **SSC 18; TCLC 3**
See also CA 104; DLB 12, 71, 78, 186; RGAL 4; RGSF 2; TCWW 2

Garneau, (Hector de) Saint-Denys 1912-1943 .... **TCLC 13**
See also CA 111; DLB 88

Garner, Alan 1934- .... **CLC 17**
See also AAYA 18; BYA 3, 5; CA 73-76; 178; CAAE 178; CANR 15, 64; CLR 20; CPW; DAB; DAM POP; DLB 161, 261; FANT; MAICYA 1, 2; MTCW 1, 2; SATA 18, 69; SATA-Essay 108; SUFW 1, 2; YAW

Garner, Hugh 1913-1979 .... **CLC 13**
See Warwick, Jarvis
See also CA 69-72; CANR 31; CCA 1; DLB 68

Garnett, David 1892-1981 .... **CLC 3**
See also CA 5-8R; 103; CANR 17, 79; DLB 34; FANT; MTCW 2; RGEL 2; SFW 4; SUFW 1

Garos, Stephanie
See Katz, Steve

Garrett, George (Palmer) 1929- .. **CLC 3, 11, 51; SSC 30**
See also AMWS 7; BPFB 2; CA 1-4R; CAAE 202; CAAS 5; CANR 1, 42, 67, 109; CN 7; CP 7; CSW; DLB 2, 5, 130, 152; DLBY 1983

Garrick, David 1717-1779 .... **LC 15**
See also DAM DRAM; DLB 84, 213; RGEL 2

Garrigue, Jean 1914-1972 .... **CLC 2, 8**
See also CA 5-8R; 37-40R; CANR 20

Garrison, Frederick
See Sinclair, Upton (Beall)

Garro, Elena 1920(?)-1998 .... **HLCS 1**
See also CA 131; 169; CWW 2; DLB 145; EWL 3; HW 1; LAWS 1; WLIT 1

Garth, Will
See Hamilton, Edmond; Kuttner, Henry

Garvey, Marcus (Moziah, Jr.) 1887-1940 .... **BLC 2; HR 2; TCLC 41**
See also BW 1; CA 120; 124; CANR 79; DAM MULT

Gary, Romain .... **CLC 25**
See Kacew, Romain
See also DLB 83

Gascar, Pierre .... **CLC 11**
See Fournier, Pierre
See also EWL 3

Gascoyne, David (Emery) 1916-2001 .... **CLC 45**
See also CA 65-68; 200; CANR 10, 28, 54; CP 7; DLB 20; MTCW 1; RGEL 2

Gaskell, Elizabeth Cleghorn 1810-1865 .... **NCLC 5, 70, 97; SSC 25**
See also BRW 5; CDBLB 1832-1890; DAB; DAM MST; DLB 21, 144, 159; RGEL 2; RGSF 2; TEA

Gass, William H(oward) 1924- . **CLC 1, 2, 8, 11, 15, 39, 132; SSC 12**
See also AMWS 6; CA 17-20R; CANR 30, 71, 100; CN 7; DLB 2, 227; EWL 3; MTCW 1, 2; RGAL 4

Gassendi, Pierre 1592-1655 .... **LC 54**
See also GFL Beginnings to 1789

Gasset, Jose Ortega y
See Ortega y Gasset, Jose

Gates, Henry Louis, Jr. 1950- ... **BLCS; CLC 65**
See also BW 2, 3; CA 109; CANR 25, 53, 75; CSW; DA3; DAM MULT; DLB 67; EWL 3; MTCW 2; RGAL 4

Gautier, Theophile 1811-1872 .. **NCLC 1, 59; PC 18; SSC 20**
See also DAM POET; DLB 119; EW 6; GFL 1789 to the Present; RGWL 2, 3; SUFW; TWA

Gawsworth, John
See Bates, H(erbert) E(rnest)

Gay, John 1685-1732 .... **LC 49**
See also BRW 3; DAM DRAM; DLB 84, 95; RGEL 2; WLIT 3

Gay, Oliver
See Gogarty, Oliver St. John

Gay, Peter (Jack) 1923- .... **CLC 158**
See also CA 13-16R; CANR 18, 41, 77; INT CANR-18

Gaye, Marvin (Pentz, Jr.) 1939-1984 .... **CLC 26**
See also CA 195; 112

Gebler, Carlo (Ernest) 1954- .... **CLC 39**
See also CA 119; 133; CANR 96; DLB 271

Gee, Maggie (Mary) 1948- .... **CLC 57**
See also CA 130; CN 7; DLB 207

Gee, Maurice (Gough) 1931- .... **CLC 29**
See also AAYA 42; CA 97-100; CANR 67; CLR 56; CN 7; CWRI 5; EWL 3; MAICYA 2; RGSF 2; SATA 46, 101

Geiogamah, Hanay 1945- .... **NNAL**
See also CA 153; DAM MULT; DLB 175

Gelbart, Larry (Simon) 1928- .... **CLC 21, 61**
See Gelbart, Larry
See also CA 73-76; CANR 45, 94

Gelbart, Larry 1928-
See Gelbart, Larry (Simon)
See also CAD; CD 5

Gelber, Jack 1932- .... **CLC 1, 6, 14, 79**
See also CA 1-4R; CAD; CANR 2; DLB 7, 228

Gellhorn, Martha (Ellis) 1908-1998 .... **CLC 14, 60**
See also CA 77-80; 164; CANR 44; CN 7; DLBY 1982, 1998

Genet, Jean 1910-1986 .. **CLC 1, 2, 5, 10, 14, 44, 46; TCLC 128**
See also CA 13-16R; CANR 18; DA3; DAM DRAM; DFS 10; DLB 72; DLBY 1986; EW 13; EWL 3; GFL 1789 to the Present; GLL 1; LMFS 2; MTCW 1, 2; RGWL 2, 3; TWA

Gent, Peter 1942- .... **CLC 29**
See also AITN 1; CA 89-92; DLBY 1982

Gentile, Giovanni 1875-1944 .... **TCLC 96**
See also CA 119

Gentlewoman in New England, A
See Bradstreet, Anne

Gentlewoman in Those Parts, A
See Bradstreet, Anne

Geoffrey of Monmouth c. 1100-1155 .... **CMLC 44**
See also DLB 146; TEA

George, Jean
See George, Jean Craighead

George, Jean Craighead 1919- .... **CLC 35**
See also AAYA 8; BYA 2, 4; CA 5-8R; CANR 25; CLR 1; 80; DLB 52; JRDA; MAICYA 1, 2; SATA 2, 68, 124; WYA; YAW

George, Stefan (Anton) 1868-1933 . **TCLC 2, 14**
See also CA 104; 193; EW 8; EWL 3

Georges, Georges Martin
See Simenon, Georges (Jacques Christian)

Gerhardi, William Alexander
See Gerhardie, William Alexander

Gerhardie, William Alexander 1895-1977 .... **CLC 5**
See also CA 25-28R; 73-76; CANR 18; DLB 36; RGEL 2

Gerson, Jean 1363-1429 .... **LC 77**
See also DLB 208

Gersonides 1288-1344 .... **CMLC 49**
See also DLB 115

Gerstler, Amy 1956- .... **CLC 70**
See also CA 146; CANR 99

Gertler, T. .... **CLC 34**
See also CA 116; 121

Gertsen, Aleksandr Ivanovich
See Herzen, Aleksandr Ivanovich

Ghalib .... **NCLC 39, 78**
See Ghalib, Asadullah Khan

Ghalib, Asadullah Khan 1797-1869
See Ghalib
See also DAM POET; RGWL 2, 3

Ghelderode, Michel de 1898-1962 ..... **CLC 6, 11; DC 15**
See also CA 85-88; CANR 40, 77; DAM DRAM; EW 11; EWL 3; TWA

Ghiselin, Brewster 1903-2001 .... **CLC 23**
See also CA 13-16R; CAAS 10; CANR 13; CP 7

Goebbels, (Paul) Joseph
1897-1945 .... **TCLC 68**
See also CA 115; 148

Goebbels, Joseph Paul
See Goebbels, (Paul) Joseph

Goethe, Johann Wolfgang von
1749-1832 .... **DC 20; NCLC 4, 22, 34, 90; PC 5; SSC 38; WLC**
See also CDWLB 2; DA; DA3; DAB; DAC; DAM DRAM, MST, POET; DLB 94; EW 5; LATS 1; LMFS 1; RGWL 2, 3; TWA

Gogarty, Oliver St. John
1878-1957 .... **TCLC 15**
See also CA 109; 150; DLB 15, 19; RGEL 2

Gogol, Nikolai (Vasilyevich)
1809-1852 .... **DC 1; NCLC 5, 15, 31; SSC 4, 29, 52; WLC**
See also DA; DAB; DAC; DAM DRAM, MST; DFS 12; DLB 198; EW 6; EXPS; RGSF 2; RGWL 2, 3; SSFS 7; TWA

Goines, Donald 1937(?)-1974 ... **BLC 2; CLC 80**
See also AITN 1; BW 1, 3; CA 124; 114; CANR 82; CMW 4; DA3; DAM MULT, POP; DLB 33

Gold, Herbert 1924- ... **CLC 4, 7, 14, 42, 152**
See also CA 9-12R; CANR 17, 45; CN 7; DLB 2; DLBY 1981

Goldbarth, Albert 1948- .... **CLC 5, 38**
See also AMWS 12; CA 53-56; CANR 6, 40; CP 7; DLB 120

Goldberg, Anatol 1910-1982 .... **CLC 34**
See also CA 131; 117

Goldemberg, Isaac 1945- .... **CLC 52**
See also CA 69-72; CAAS 12; CANR 11, 32; EWL 3; HW 1; WLIT 1

Golding, William (Gerald)
1911-1993 ..... **CLC 1, 2, 3, 8, 10, 17, 27, 58, 81; WLC**
See also AAYA 5, 44; BPFB 2; BRWR 1; BRWS 1; BYA 2; CA 5-8R; 141; CANR 13, 33, 54; CDBLB 1945-1960; DA; DA3; DAB; DAC; DAM MST, NOV; DLB 15, 100, 255; EWL 3; EXPN; HGG; LAIT 4; MTCW 1, 2; NFS 2; RGEL 2; RHW; SFW 4; TEA; WLIT 4; YAW

Goldman, Emma 1869-1940 .... **TCLC 13**
See also CA 110; 150; DLB 221; FW; RGAL 4; TUS

Goldman, Francisco 1954- .... **CLC 76**
See also CA 162

Goldman, William (W.) 1931- ...... **CLC 1, 48**
See also BPFB 2; CA 9-12R; CANR 29, 69, 106; CN 7; DLB 44; FANT; IDFW 3, 4

Goldmann, Lucien 1913-1970 .... **CLC 24**
See also CA 25-28; CAP 2

Goldoni, Carlo 1707-1793 .... **LC 4**
See also DAM DRAM; EW 4; RGWL 2, 3

Goldsberry, Steven 1949- .... **CLC 34**
See also CA 131

Goldsmith, Oliver 1730-1774 .... **DC 8; LC 2, 48; WLC**
See also BRW 3; CDBLB 1660-1789; DA; DAB; DAC; DAM DRAM, MST, NOV, POET; DFS 1; DLB 39, 89, 104, 109, 142; IDTP; RGEL 2; SATA 26; TEA; WLIT 3

Goldsmith, Peter
See Priestley, J(ohn) B(oynton)

Gombrowicz, Witold 1904-1969 .... **CLC 4, 7, 11, 49**
See also CA 19-20; 25-28R; CANR 105; CAP 2; CDWLB 4; DAM DRAM; DLB 215; EW 12; EWL 3; RGWL 2, 3; TWA

Gomez de Avellaneda, Gertrudis
1814-1873 .... **NCLC 111**
See also LAW

Gomez de la Serna, Ramon
1888-1963 .... **CLC 9**
See also CA 153; 116; CANR 79; EWL 3; HW 1, 2

Goncharov, Ivan Alexandrovich
1812-1891 .... **NCLC 1, 63**
See also DLB 238; EW 6; RGWL 2, 3

Goncourt, Edmond (Louis Antoine Huot) de
1822-1896 .... **NCLC 7**
See also DLB 123; EW 7; GFL 1789 to the Present; RGWL 2, 3

Goncourt, Jules (Alfred Huot) de
1830-1870 .... **NCLC 7**
See also DLB 123; EW 7; GFL 1789 to the Present; RGWL 2, 3

Gongora (y Argote), Luis de
1561-1627 .... **LC 72**
See also RGWL 2, 3

Gontier, Fernande 19(?)- .... **CLC 50**

Gonzalez Martinez, Enrique
1871-1952 .... **TCLC 72**
See also CA 166; CANR 81; EWL 3; HW 1, 2

Goodison, Lorna 1947- .... **PC 36**
See also CA 142; CANR 88; CP 7; CWP; DLB 157; EWL 3

Goodman, Paul 1911-1972 ..... **CLC 1, 2, 4, 7**
See also CA 19-20; 37-40R; CAD; CANR 34; CAP 2; DLB 130, 246; MTCW 1; RGAL 4

Gordimer, Nadine 1923- ...... **CLC 3, 5, 7, 10, 18, 33, 51, 70, 123, 160, 161; SSC 17; WLCS**
See also AAYA 39; AFW; BRWS 2; CA 5-8R; CANR 3, 28, 56, 88; CN 7; DA; DA3; DAB; DAC; DAM MST, NOV; DLB 225; EWL 3; EXPS; INT CANR-28; LATS 1; MTCW 1, 2; NFS 4; RGEL 2; RGSF 2; SSFS 2, 14; TWA; WLIT 2; YAW

Gordon, Adam Lindsay
1833-1870 .... **NCLC 21**
See also DLB 230

Gordon, Caroline 1895-1981 . **CLC 6, 13, 29, 83; SSC 15**
See also AMW; CA 11-12; 103; CANR 36; CAP 1; DLB 4, 9, 102; DLBD 17; DLBY 1981; EWL 3; MTCW 1, 2; RGAL 4; RGSF 2

Gordon, Charles William 1860-1937
See Connor, Ralph
See also CA 109

Gordon, Mary (Catherine) 1949- .... **CLC 13, 22, 128; SSC 59**
See also AMWS 4; BPFB 2; CA 102; CANR 44, 92; CN 7; DLB 6; DLBY 1981; FW; INT CA-102; MTCW 1

Gordon, N. J.
See Bosman, Herman Charles

Gordon, Sol 1923- .... **CLC 26**
See also CA 53-56; CANR 4; SATA 11

Gordone, Charles 1925-1995 .. **CLC 1, 4; DC 8**
See also BW 1, 3; CA 93-96, 180; 150; CAAE 180; CAD; CANR 55; DAM DRAM; DLB 7; INT 93-96; MTCW 1

Gore, Catherine 1800-1861 .... **NCLC 65**
See also DLB 116; RGEL 2

Gorenko, Anna Andreevna
See Akhmatova, Anna

Gorky, Maxim .... **SSC 28; TCLC 8; WLC**
See Peshkov, Alexei Maximovich
See also DAB; DFS 9; EW 8; EWL 3; MTCW 2; TWA

Goryan, Sirak
See Saroyan, William

Gosse, Edmund (William)
1849-1928 .... **TCLC 28**
See also CA 117; DLB 57, 144, 184; RGEL 2

Gotlieb, Phyllis Fay (Bloom) 1926- .. **CLC 18**
See also CA 13-16R; CANR 7; DLB 88, 251; SFW 4

Gottesman, S. D.
See Kornbluth, C(yril) M.; Pohl, Frederik

Gottfried von Strassburg fl. c.
1170-1215 .... **CMLC 10**
See also CDWLB 2; DLB 138; EW 1; RGWL 2, 3

Gotthelf, Jeremias 1797-1854 .... **NCLC 117**
See also DLB 133; RGWL 2, 3

Gottschalk, Laura Riding
See Jackson, Laura (Riding)

Gould, Lois 1932(?)-2002 .... **CLC 4, 10**
See also CA 77-80; 208; CANR 29; MTCW 1

Gould, Stephen Jay 1941-2002 .... **CLC 163**
See also AAYA 26; BEST 90:2; CA 77-80; 205; CANR 10, 27, 56, 75; CPW; INT CANR-27; MTCW 1, 2

Gourmont, Remy(-Marie-Charles) de
1858-1915 .... **TCLC 17**
See also CA 109; 150; GFL 1789 to the Present; MTCW 2

Govier, Katherine 1948- .... **CLC 51**
See also CA 101; CANR 18, 40; CCA 1

Gower, John c. 1330-1408 .... **LC 76**
See also BRW 1; DLB 146; RGEL 2

Goyen, (Charles) William
1915-1983 .... **CLC 5, 8, 14, 40**
See also AITN 2; CA 5-8R; 110; CANR 6, 71; DLB 2, 218; DLBY 1983; EWL 3; INT CANR-6

Goytisolo, Juan 1931- .... **CLC 5, 10, 23, 133; HLC 1**
See also CA 85-88; CANR 32, 61; CWW 2; DAM MULT; EWL 3; GLL 2; HW 1, 2; MTCW 1, 2

Gozzano, Guido 1883-1916 .... **PC 10**
See also CA 154; DLB 114; EWL 3

Gozzi, (Conte) Carlo 1720-1806 .... **NCLC 23**

Grabbe, Christian Dietrich
1801-1836 .... **NCLC 2**
See also DLB 133; RGWL 2, 3

Grace, Patricia Frances 1937- .... **CLC 56**
See also CA 176; CANR 118; CN 7; EWL 3; RGSF 2

Gracian y Morales, Baltasar
1601-1658 .... **LC 15**

Gracq, Julien .... **CLC 11, 48**
See Poirier, Louis
See also CWW 2; DLB 83; GFL 1789 to the Present

Grade, Chaim 1910-1982 .... **CLC 10**
See also CA 93-96; 107; EWL 3

Graduate of Oxford, A
See Ruskin, John

Grafton, Garth
See Duncan, Sara Jeannette

Grafton, Sue 1940- .... **CLC 163**
See also AAYA 11, 49; BEST 90:3; CA 108; CANR 31, 55, 111; CMW 4; CPW; CSW; DA3; DAM POP; DLB 226; FW; MSW

Graham, John
See Phillips, David Graham

Graham, Jorie 1950- .... **CLC 48, 118**
See also CA 111; CANR 63, 118; CP 7; CWP; DLB 120; EWL 3; PFS 10, 17

Graham, R(obert) B(ontine) Cunninghame
See Cunninghame Graham, Robert (Gallnigad) Bontine
See also DLB 98, 135, 174; RGEL 2; RGSF 2

Graham, Robert
See Haldeman, Joe (William)

Grimke, Angelina (Emily) Weld
1880-1958 .... **HR 2**
See Weld, Angelina (Emily) Grimke
See also BW 1; CA 124; DAM POET; DLB
50, 54

Grimke, Charlotte L(ottie) Forten
1837(?)-1914
See Forten, Charlotte L.
See also BW 1; CA 117; 124; DAM MULT,
POET

Grimm, Jacob Ludwig Karl
1785-1863 .... **NCLC 3, 77; SSC 36**
See also DLB 90; MAICYA 1, 2; RGSF 2;
RGWL 2, 3; SATA 22; WCH

Grimm, Wilhelm Karl 1786-1859 .. **NCLC 3,
77; SSC 36**
See also CDWLB 2; DLB 90; MAICYA 1,
2; RGSF 2; RGWL 2, 3; SATA 22; WCH

**Grimmelshausen, Hans Jakob Christoffel
von**
See Grimmelshausen, Johann Jakob Christoffel von
See also RGWL 2, 3

**Grimmelshausen, Johann Jakob Christoffel
von** 1621-1676 .... **LC 6**
See Grimmelshausen, Hans Jakob Christof-
fel von
See also CDWLB 2; DLB 168

Grindel, Eugene 1895-1952
See Eluard, Paul
See also CA 104; 193; LMFS 2

Grisham, John 1955- .... **CLC 84**
See also AAYA 14, 47; BPFB 2; CA 138;
CANR 47, 69, 114; CMW 4; CN 7; CPW;
CSW; DA3; DAM POP; MSW; MTCW 2

Grossman, David 1954- .... **CLC 67**
See also CA 138; CANR 114; CWW 2;
EWL 3

Grossman, Vasilii Semenovich
See Grossman, Vasily (Semenovich)
See also DLB 272

Grossman, Vasily (Semenovich)
1905-1964 .... **CLC 41**
See Grossman, Vasilii Semenovich
See also CA 124; 130; MTCW 1

Grove, Frederick Philip .... **TCLC 4**
See Greve, Felix Paul (Berthold Friedrich)
See also DLB 92; RGEL 2

Grubb
See Crumb, R(obert)

Grumbach, Doris (Isaac) 1918- . **CLC 13, 22,
64**
See also CA 5-8R; CAAS 2; CANR 9, 42,
70; CN 7; INT CANR-9; MTCW 2

Grundtvig, Nicolai Frederik Severin
1783-1872 .... **NCLC 1**

Grunge
See Crumb, R(obert)

Grunwald, Lisa 1959- .... **CLC 44**
See also CA 120

Gryphius, Andreas 1616-1664 .... **LC 89**
See also CDWLB 2; DLB 164; RGWL 2, 3

Guare, John 1938- .... **CLC 8, 14, 29, 67; DC
20**
See also CA 73-76; CAD; CANR 21, 69,
118; CD 5; DAM DRAM; DFS 8, 13;
DLB 7, 249; EWL 3; MTCW 1, 2; RGAL
4

Gubar, Susan (David) 1944- .... **CLC 145**
See also CA 108; CANR 45, 70; FW;
MTCW 1; RGAL 4

Gudjonsson, Halldor Kiljan 1902-1998
See Laxness, Halldor
See also CA 103; 164; CWW 2

Guenter, Erich
See Eich, Gunter

Guest, Barbara 1920- .... **CLC 34**
See also BG 2; CA 25-28R; CANR 11, 44,
84; CP 7; CWP; DLB 5, 193

Guest, Edgar A(lbert) 1881-1959 ... **TCLC 95**
See also CA 112; 168

Guest, Judith (Ann) 1936- .... **CLC 8, 30**
See also AAYA 7; CA 77-80; CANR 15,
75; DA3; DAM NOV, POP; EXPN; INT
CANR-15; LAIT 5; MTCW 1, 2; NFS 1

Guevara, Che .... **CLC 87; HLC 1**
See Guevara (Serna), Ernesto

Guevara (Serna), Ernesto
1928-1967 .... **CLC 87; HLC 1**
See Guevara, Che
See also CA 127; 111; CANR 56; DAM
MULT; HW 1

Guicciardini, Francesco 1483-1540 ..... **LC 49**

Guild, Nicholas M. 1944- .... **CLC 33**
See also CA 93-96

Guillemin, Jacques
See Sartre, Jean-Paul

Guillen, Jorge 1893-1984 . **CLC 11; HLCS 1;
PC 35**
See also CA 89-92; 112; DAM MULT,
POET; DLB 108; EWL 3; HW 1; RGWL
2, 3

Guillen, Nicolas (Cristobal)
1902-1989 .... **BLC 2; CLC 48, 79; HLC
1; PC 23**
See also BW 2; CA 116; 125; 129; CANR
84; DAM MST, MULT, POET; EWL 3;
HW 1; LAW; RGWL 2, 3; WP

Guillen y Alvarez, Jorge
See Guillen, Jorge

Guillevic, (Eugene) 1907-1997 .... **CLC 33**
See also CA 93-96; CWW 2

Guillois
See Desnos, Robert

Guillois, Valentin
See Desnos, Robert

Guimaraes Rosa, Joao 1908-1967 .... **HLCS 2**
See also CA 175; LAW; RGSF 2; RGWL 2,
3

Guiney, Louise Imogen
1861-1920 .... **TCLC 41**
See also CA 160; DLB 54; RGAL 4

Guinizelli, Guido c. 1230-1276 ...... **CMLC 49**

Guiraldes, Ricardo (Guillermo)
1886-1927 .... **TCLC 39**
See also CA 131; EWL 3; HW 1; LAW;
MTCW 1

Gumilev, Nikolai (Stepanovich)
1886-1921 .... **TCLC 60**
See Gumilyov, Nikolay Stepanovich
See also CA 165

Gumilyov, Nikolay Stepanovich
See Gumilev, Nikolai (Stepanovich)
See also EWL 3

Gunesekera, Romesh 1954- .... **CLC 91**
See also CA 159; CN 7; DLB 267

Gunn, Bill .... **CLC 5**
See Gunn, William Harrison
See also DLB 38

Gunn, Thom(son William) 1929- .. **CLC 3, 6,
18, 32, 81; PC 26**
See also BRWS 4; CA 17-20R; CANR 9,
33, 116; CDBLB 1960 to Present; CP 7;
DAM POET; DLB 27; INT CANR-33;
MTCW 1; PFS 9; RGEL 2

Gunn, William Harrison 1934(?)-1989
See Gunn, Bill
See also AITN 1; BW 1, 3; CA 13-16R;
128; CANR 12, 25, 76

Gunn Allen, Paula
See Allen, Paula Gunn

Gunnars, Kristjana 1948- .... **CLC 69**
See also CA 113; CCA 1; CP 7; CWP; DLB
60

Gunter, Erich
See Eich, Gunter

Gurdjieff, G(eorgei) I(vanovich)
1877(?)-1949 .... **TCLC 71**
See also CA 157

Gurganus, Allan 1947- .... **CLC 70**
See also BEST 90:1; CA 135; CANR 114;
CN 7; CPW; CSW; DAM POP; GLL 1

Gurney, A. R.
See Gurney, A(lbert) R(amsdell), Jr.
See also DLB 266

Gurney, A(lbert) R(amsdell), Jr.
1930- .... **CLC 32, 50, 54**
See Gurney, A. R.
See also AMWS 5; CA 77-80; CAD; CANR
32, 64; CD 5; DAM DRAM; EWL 3

Gurney, Ivor (Bertie) 1890-1937 ... **TCLC 33**
See also BRW 6; CA 167; DLBY 2002;
PAB; RGEL 2

Gurney, Peter
See Gurney, A(lbert) R(amsdell), Jr.

Guro, Elena 1877-1913 .... **TCLC 56**

Gustafson, James M(oody) 1925- ... **CLC 100**
See also CA 25-28R; CANR 37

Gustafson, Ralph (Barker)
1909-1995 .... **CLC 36**
See also CA 21-24R; CANR 8, 45, 84; CP
7; DLB 88; RGEL 2

Gut, Gom
See Simenon, Georges (Jacques Christian)

Guterson, David 1956- .... **CLC 91**
See also CA 132; CANR 73; MTCW 2;
NFS 13

Guthrie, A(lfred) B(ertram), Jr.
1901-1991 .... **CLC 23**
See also CA 57-60; 134; CANR 24; DLB 6,
212; SATA 62; SATA-Obit 67

Guthrie, Isobel
See Grieve, C(hristopher) M(urray)

Guthrie, Woodrow Wilson 1912-1967
See Guthrie, Woody
See also CA 113; 93-96

Guthrie, Woody .... **CLC 35**
See Guthrie, Woodrow Wilson
See also LAIT 3

Gutierrez Najera, Manuel
1859-1895 .... **HLCS 2**
See also LAW

Guy, Rosa (Cuthbert) 1925- .... **CLC 26**
See also AAYA 4, 37; BW 2; CA 17-20R;
CANR 14, 34, 83; CLR 13; DLB 33;
DNFS 1; JRDA; MAICYA 1, 2; SATA 14,
62, 122; YAW

Gwendolyn
See Bennett, (Enoch) Arnold

H. D. .... **CLC 3, 8, 14, 31, 34, 73; PC 5**
See Doolittle, Hilda

H. de V.
See Buchan, John

Haavikko, Paavo Juhani 1931- .. **CLC 18, 34**
See also CA 106; EWL 3

Habbema, Koos
See Heijermans, Herman

Habermas, Juergen 1929- .... **CLC 104**
See also CA 109; CANR 85; DLB 242

Habermas, Jurgen
See Habermas, Juergen

Hacker, Marilyn 1942- ...... **CLC 5, 9, 23, 72,
91; PC 47**
See also CA 77-80; CANR 68; CP 7; CWP;
DAM POET; DLB 120, 282; FW; GLL 2

Hadrian 76-138 .... **CMLC 52**

Haeckel, Ernst Heinrich (Philipp August)
1834-1919 .... **TCLC 83**
See also CA 157

Hafiz c. 1326-1389(?) .... **CMLC 34**
See also RGWL 2, 3

Haggard, H(enry) Rider
1856-1925 .... **TCLC 11**
See also BRWS 3; BYA 4, 5; CA 108; 148;
CANR 112; DLB 70, 156, 174, 178;
FANT; LMFS 1; MTCW 2; RGEL 2;
RHW; SATA 16; SCFW; SFW 4; SUFW
1; WLIT 4

Hagiosy, L.
See Larbaud, Valery (Nicolas)

Hagiwara, Sakutaro 1886-1942 .... **PC 18;
TCLC 60**
See Hagiwara Sakutaro
See also CA 154; RGWL 3

Hagiwara Sakutaro
See Hagiwara, Sakutaro
See also EWL 3

Haig, Fenil
See Ford, Ford Madox

Haig-Brown, Roderick (Langmere)
1908-1976 .... **CLC 21**
See also CA 5-8R; 69-72; CANR 4, 38, 83;
CLR 31; CWRI 5; DLB 88; MAICYA 1,
2; SATA 12

Haight, Rip
See Carpenter, John (Howard)

Hailey, Arthur 1920- .... **CLC 5**
See also AITN 2; BEST 90:3; BPFB 2; CA
1-4R; CANR 2, 36, 75; CCA 1; CN 7;
CPW; DAM NOV, POP; DLB 88; DLBY
1982; MTCW 1, 2

Hailey, Elizabeth Forsythe 1938- ..... **CLC 40**
See also CA 93-96; CAAE 188; CAAS 1;
CANR 15, 48; INT CANR-15

Haines, John (Meade) 1924- .... **CLC 58**
See also AMWS 12; CA 17-20R; CANR
13, 34; CSW; DLB 5, 212

Hakluyt, Richard 1552-1616 .... **LC 31**
See also DLB 136; RGEL 2

Haldeman, Joe (William) 1943- .... **CLC 61**
See Graham, Robert
See also AAYA 38; CA 53-56, 179; CAAE
179; CAAS 25; CANR 6, 70, 72; DLB 8;
INT CANR-6; SCFW 2; SFW 4

Hale, Janet Campbell 1947- .... **NNAL**
See also CA 49-52; CANR 45, 75; DAM
MULT; DLB 175; MTCW 2

Hale, Sarah Josepha (Buell)
1788-1879 .... **NCLC 75**
See also DLB 1, 42, 73, 243

Halevy, Elie 1870-1937 .... **TCLC 104**

Haley, Alex(ander Murray Palmer)
1921-1992 .... **BLC 2; CLC 8, 12, 76**
See also AAYA 26; BPFB 2; BW 2, 3; CA
77-80; 136; CANR 61; CDALBS; CPW;
CSW; DA; DA3; DAB; DAC; DAM MST,
MULT, POP; DLB 38; LAIT 5; MTCW
1, 2; NFS 9

Haliburton, Thomas Chandler
1796-1865 .... **NCLC 15**
See also DLB 11, 99; RGEL 2; RGSF 2

Hall, Donald (Andrew, Jr.) 1928- ...... **CLC 1,
13, 37, 59, 151**
See also CA 5-8R; CAAS 7; CANR 2, 44,
64, 106; CP 7; DAM POET; DLB 5;
MTCW 1; RGAL 4; SATA 23, 97

Hall, Frederic Sauser
See Sauser-Hall, Frederic

Hall, James
See Kuttner, Henry

Hall, James Norman 1887-1951 ..... **TCLC 23**
See also CA 123; 173; LAIT 1; RHW 1;
SATA 21

Hall, (Marguerite) Radclyffe
1880-1943 .... **TCLC 12**
See also BRWS 6; CA 110; 150; CANR 83;
DLB 191; MTCW 2; RGEL 2; RHW

Hall, Rodney 1935- .... **CLC 51**
See also CA 109; CANR 69; CN 7; CP 7

Hallam, Arthur Henry
1811-1833 .... **NCLC 110**
See also DLB 32

Halleck, Fitz-Greene 1790-1867 .... **NCLC 47**
See also DLB 3, 250; RGAL 4

Halliday, Michael
See Creasey, John

Halpern, Daniel 1945- .... **CLC 14**
See also CA 33-36R; CANR 93; CP 7

Hamburger, Michael (Peter Leopold)
1924- .... **CLC 5, 14**
See also CA 5-8R; CAAE 196; CAAS 4;
CANR 2, 47; CP 7; DLB 27

Hamill, Pete 1935- .... **CLC 10**
See also CA 25-28R; CANR 18, 71

Hamilton, Alexander
1755(?)-1804 .... **NCLC 49**
See also DLB 37

Hamilton, Clive
See Lewis, C(live) S(taples)

Hamilton, Edmond 1904-1977 .... **CLC 1**
See also CA 1-4R; CANR 3, 84; DLB 8;
SATA 118; SFW 4

Hamilton, Eugene (Jacob) Lee
See Lee-Hamilton, Eugene (Jacob)

Hamilton, Franklin
See Silverberg, Robert

Hamilton, Gail
See Corcoran, Barbara (Asenath)

Hamilton, Mollie
See Kaye, M(ary) M(argaret)

Hamilton, (Anthony Walter) Patrick
1904-1962 .... **CLC 51**
See also CA 176; 113; DLB 10, 191

Hamilton, Virginia (Esther)
1936-2002 .... **CLC 26**
See also AAYA 2, 21; BW 2, 3; BYA 1, 2,
8; CA 25-28R; 206; CANR 20, 37, 73;
CLR 1, 11, 40; DAM MULT; DLB 33,
52; DLBY 01; INT CANR-20; JRDA;
LAIT 5; MAICYA 1, 2; MAICYAS 1;
MTCW 1, 2; SATA 4, 56, 79, 123; SATA-
Obit 132; WYA; YAW

Hammett, (Samuel) Dashiell
1894-1961 .... **CLC 3, 5, 10, 19, 47; SSC
17**
See also AITN 1; AMWS 4; BPFB 2; CA
81-84; CANR 42; CDALB 1929-1941;
CMW 4; DA3; DLB 226; DLBD 6; DLBY
1996; EWL 3; LAIT 3; MSW; MTCW 1,
2; RGAL 4; RGSF 2; TUS

Hammon, Jupiter 1720(?)-1800(?) .... **BLC 2;
NCLC 5; PC 16**
See also DAM MULT, POET; DLB 31, 50

Hammond, Keith
See Kuttner, Henry

Hamner, Earl (Henry), Jr. 1923- ...... **CLC 12**
See also AITN 2; CA 73-76; DLB 6

Hampton, Christopher (James)
1946- .... **CLC 4**
See also CA 25-28R; CD 5; DLB 13;
MTCW 1

Hamsun, Knut .... **TCLC 2, 14, 49**
See Pedersen, Knut
See also EW 8; EWL 3; RGWL 2, 3

Handke, Peter 1942- .... **CLC 5, 8, 10, 15, 38,
134; DC 17**
See also CA 77-80; CANR 33, 75, 104;
CWW 2; DAM DRAM, NOV; DLB 85,
124; EWL 3; MTCW 1, 2; TWA

Handy, W(illiam) C(hristopher)
1873-1958 .... **TCLC 97**
See also BW 3; CA 121; 167

Hanley, James 1901-1985 ..... **CLC 3, 5, 8, 13**
See also CA 73-76; 117; CANR 36; CBD;
DLB 191; EWL 3; MTCW 1; RGEL 2

Hannah, Barry 1942- .... **CLC 23, 38, 90**
See also BPFB 2; CA 108; 110; CANR 43,
68, 113; CN 7; CSW; DLB 6, 234; INT
CA-110; MTCW 1; RGSF 2

Hannon, Ezra
See Hunter, Evan

Hansberry, Lorraine (Vivian)
1930-1965 ... **BLC 2; CLC 17, 62; DC 2**
See also AAYA 25; AFAW 1, 2; AMWS 4;
BW 1, 3; CA 109; 25-28R; CABS 3;
CAD; CANR 58; CDALB 1941-1968;
CWD; DA; DA3; DAB; DAC; DAM
DRAM, MST, MULT; DFS 2; DLB 7, 38;
EWL 3; FW; LAIT 4; MTCW 1, 2; RGAL
4; TUS

Hansen, Joseph 1923- .... **CLC 38**
See Brock, Rose; Colton, James
See also BPFB 2; CA 29-32R; CAAS 17;
CANR 16, 44, 66; CMW 4; DLB 226;
GLL 1; INT CANR-16

Hansen, Martin A(lfred)
1909-1955 .... **TCLC 32**
See also CA 167; DLB 214; EWL 3

Hansen and Philipson eds. .... **CLC 65**

Hanson, Kenneth O(stlin) 1922- .... **CLC 13**
See also CA 53-56; CANR 7

Hardwick, Elizabeth (Bruce) 1916- . **CLC 13**
See also AMWS 3; CA 5-8R; CANR 3, 32,
70, 100; CN 7; CSW; DA3; DAM NOV;
DLB 6; MAWW; MTCW 1, 2

Hardy, Thomas 1840-1928 .... **PC 8; SSC 2,
60; TCLC 4, 10, 18, 32, 48, 53, 72;
WLC**
See also BRW 6; BRWC 1; BRWR 1; CA
104; 123; CDBLB 1890-1914; DA; DA3;
DAB; DAC; DAM MST, NOV, POET;
DLB 18, 19, 135, 284; EWL 3; EXPN;
EXPP; LAIT 2; MTCW 1, 2; NFS 3, 11,
15; PFS 3, 4; RGEL 2; RGSF 2; TEA;
WLIT 4

Hare, David 1947- .... **CLC 29, 58, 136**
See also BRWS 4; CA 97-100; CANR 39,
91; CBD; CD 5; DFS 4, 7, 16; DLB 13;
MTCW 1; TEA

Harewood, John
See Van Druten, John (William)

Harford, Henry
See Hudson, W(illiam) H(enry)

Hargrave, Leonie
See Disch, Thomas M(ichael)

Harjo, Joy 1951- ..... **CLC 83; NNAL; PC 27**
See also AMWS 12; CA 114; CANR 35,
67, 91; CP 7; CWP; DAM MULT; DLB
120, 175; EWL 3; MTCW 2; PFS 15;
RGAL 4

Harlan, Louis R(udolph) 1922- .... **CLC 34**
See also CA 21-24R; CANR 25, 55, 80

Harling, Robert 1951(?)- .... **CLC 53**
See also CA 147

Harmon, William (Ruth) 1938- .... **CLC 38**
See also CA 33-36R; CANR 14, 32, 35;
SATA 65

Harper, F. E. W.
See Harper, Frances Ellen Watkins

Harper, Frances E. W.
See Harper, Frances Ellen Watkins

Harper, Frances E. Watkins
See Harper, Frances Ellen Watkins

Harper, Frances Ellen
See Harper, Frances Ellen Watkins

Harper, Frances Ellen Watkins
1825-1911 ..... **BLC 2; PC 21; TCLC 14**
See also AFAW 1, 2; BW 1, 3; CA 111; 125;
CANR 79; DAM MULT, POET; DLB 50,
221; MAWW; RGAL 4

Harper, Michael S(teven) 1938- ... **CLC 7, 22**
See also AFAW 2; BW 1; CA 33-36R;
CANR 24, 108; CP 7; DLB 41; RGAL 4

Harper, Mrs. F. E. W.
See Harper, Frances Ellen Watkins
Harpur, Charles 1813-1868 .... **NCLC 114**
See also DLB 230; RGEL 2
Harris, Christie 1907-
See Harris, Christie (Lucy) Irwin
Harris, Christie (Lucy) Irwin
1907-2002 .... **CLC 12**
See also CA 5-8R; CANR 6, 83; CLR 47;
DLB 88; JRDA; MAICYA 1, 2; SAAS 10;
SATA 6, 74; SATA-Essay 116
Harris, Frank 1856-1931 .... **TCLC 24**
See also CA 109; 150; CANR 80; DLB 156,
197; RGEL 2
Harris, George Washington
1814-1869 .... **NCLC 23**
See also DLB 3, 11, 248; RGAL 4
Harris, Joel Chandler 1848-1908 ..... **SSC 19;**
TCLC 2
See also CA 104; 137; CANR 80; CLR 49;
DLB 11, 23, 42, 78, 91; LAIT 2; MAI-
CYA 1, 2; RGSF 2; SATA 100; WCH;
YABC 1
Harris, John (Wyndham Parkes Lucas)
Beynon 1903-1969
See Wyndham, John
See also CA 102; 89-92; CANR 84; SATA
118; SFW 4
Harris, MacDonald .... **CLC 9**
See Heiney, Donald (William)
Harris, Mark 1922- .... **CLC 19**
See also CA 5-8R; CAAS 3; CANR 2, 55,
83; CN 7; DLB 2; DLBY 1980
Harris, Norman .... **CLC 65**
Harris, (Theodore) Wilson 1921- .... **CLC 25,**
159
See also BRWS 5; BW 2, 3; CA 65-68;
CAAS 16; CANR 11, 27, 69, 114; CD-
WLB 3; CN 7; CP 7; DLB 117; EWL 3;
MTCW 1; RGEL 2
Harrison, Barbara Grizzuti
1934-2002 .... **CLC 144**
See also CA 77-80; 205; CANR 15, 48; INT
CANR-15
Harrison, Elizabeth (Allen) Cavanna
1909-2001
See Cavanna, Betty
See also CA 9-12R; 200; CANR 6, 27, 85,
104; MAICYA 2; YAW
Harrison, Harry (Max) 1925- .... **CLC 42**
See also CA 1-4R; CANR 5, 21, 84; DLB
8; SATA 4; SCFW 2; SFW 4
Harrison, James (Thomas) 1937- ...... **CLC 6,**
14, 33, 66, 143; SSC 19
See Harrison, Jim
See also CA 13-16R; CANR 8, 51, 79; CN
7; CP 7; DLBY 1982; INT CANR-8
Harrison, Jim
See Harrison, James (Thomas)
See also AMWS 8; RGAL 4; TCWW 2;
TUS
Harrison, Kathryn 1961- .... **CLC 70, 151**
See also CA 144; CANR 68
Harrison, Tony 1937- .... **CLC 43, 129**
See also BRWS 5; CA 65-68; CANR 44,
98; CBD; CD 5; CP 7; DLB 40, 245;
MTCW 1; RGEL 2
Harriss, Will(ard Irvin) 1922- .... **CLC 34**
See also CA 111
Hart, Ellis
See Ellison, Harlan (Jay)
Hart, Josephine 1942(?)- .... **CLC 70**
See also CA 138; CANR 70; CPW; DAM
POP
Hart, Moss 1904-1961 .... **CLC 66**
See also CA 109; 89-92; CANR 84; DAM
DRAM; DFS 1; DLB 7, 266; RGAL 4

Harte, (Francis) Bret(t)
1836(?)-1902 ... **SSC 8, 59; TCLC 1, 25;**
WLC
See also AMWS 2; CA 104; 140; CANR
80; CDALB 1865-1917; DA; DA3; DAC;
DAM MST; DLB 12, 64, 74, 79, 186;
EXPS; LAIT 2; RGAL 4; RGSF 2; SATA
26; SSFS 3; TUS
Hartley, L(eslie) P(oles) 1895-1972 ... **CLC 2,**
22
See also BRWS 7; CA 45-48; 37-40R;
CANR 33; DLB 15, 139; EWL 3; HGG;
MTCW 1, 2; RGEL 2; SUFW 1
Hartman, Geoffrey H. 1929- .... **CLC 27**
See also CA 117; 125; CANR 79; DLB 67
Hartmann, Sadakichi 1869-1944 ... **TCLC 73**
See also CA 157; DLB 54
Hartmann von Aue c. 1170-c.
1210 .... **CMLC 15**
See also CDWLB 2; DLB 138; RGWL 2, 3
Hartog, Jan de
See de Hartog, Jan
Haruf, Kent 1943- .... **CLC 34**
See also AAYA 44; CA 149; CANR 91
Harvey, Gabriel 1550(?)-1631 .... **LC 88**
See also DLB 167, 213, 281
Harwood, Ronald 1934- .... **CLC 32**
See also CA 1-4R; CANR 4, 55; CBD; CD
5; DAM DRAM, MST; DLB 13
Hasegawa Tatsunosuke
See Futabatei, Shimei
Hasek, Jaroslav (Matej Frantisek)
1883-1923 .... **TCLC 4**
See also CA 104; 129; CDWLB 4; DLB
215; EW 9; EWL 3; MTCW 1, 2; RGSF
2; RGWL 2, 3
Hass, Robert 1941- ... **CLC 18, 39, 99; PC 16**
See also AMWS 6; CA 111; CANR 30, 50,
71; CP 7; DLB 105, 206; EWL 3; RGAL
4; SATA 94
Hastings, Hudson
See Kuttner, Henry
Hastings, Selina .... **CLC 44**
Hathorne, John 1641-1717 .... **LC 38**
Hatteras, Amelia
See Mencken, H(enry) L(ouis)
Hatteras, Owen .... **TCLC 18**
See Mencken, H(enry) L(ouis); Nathan,
George Jean
Hauptmann, Gerhart (Johann Robert)
1862-1946 .... **SSC 37; TCLC 4**
See also CA 104; 153; CDWLB 2; DAM
DRAM; DLB 66, 118; EW 8; EWL 3;
RGSF 2; RGWL 2, 3; TWA
Havel, Vaclav 1936- ..... **CLC 25, 58, 65, 123;**
DC 6
See also CA 104; CANR 36, 63; CDWLB
4; CWW 2; DA3; DAM DRAM; DFS 10;
DLB 232; EWL 3; LMFS 2; MTCW 1, 2;
RGWL 3
Haviaras, Stratis .... **CLC 33**
See Chaviaras, Strates
Hawes, Stephen 1475(?)-1529(?) .... **LC 17**
See also DLB 132; RGEL 2
Hawkes, John (Clendennin Burne, Jr.)
1925-1998 .. **CLC 1, 2, 3, 4, 7, 9, 14, 15,**
27, 49
See also BPFB 2; CA 1-4R; 167; CANR 2,
47, 64; CN 7; DLB 2, 7, 227; DLBY
1980, 1998; EWL 3; MTCW 1, 2; RGAL
4
Hawking, S. W.
See Hawking, Stephen W(illiam)
Hawking, Stephen W(illiam) 1942- . **CLC 63,**
105
See also AAYA 13; BEST 89:1; CA 126;
129; CANR 48, 115; CPW; DA3; MTCW
2

Hawkins, Anthony Hope
See Hope, Anthony
Hawthorne, Julian 1846-1934 .... **TCLC 25**
See also CA 165; HGG
Hawthorne, Nathaniel 1804-1864 ... **NCLC 2,**
10, 17, 23, 39, 79, 95; SSC 3, 29, 39;
WLC
See also AAYA 18; AMW; AMWC 1;
AMWR 1; BPFB 2; BYA 3; CDALB
1640-1865; DA; DA3; DAB; DAC; DAM
MST, NOV; DLB 1, 74, 183, 223, 269;
EXPN; EXPS; HGG; LAIT 1; NFS 1;
RGAL 4; RGSF 2; SSFS 1, 7, 11, 15;
SUFW 1; TUS; WCH; YABC 2
Haxton, Josephine Ayres 1921-
See Douglas, Ellen
See also CA 115; CANR 41, 83
Hayaseca y Eizaguirre, Jorge
See Echegaray (y Eizaguirre), Jose (Maria
Waldo)
Hayashi, Fumiko 1904-1951 .... **TCLC 27**
See Hayashi Fumiko
See also CA 161
Hayashi Fumiko
See Hayashi, Fumiko
See also DLB 180; EWL 3
Haycraft, Anna (Margaret) 1932-
See Ellis, Alice Thomas
See also CA 122; CANR 85, 90; MTCW 2
Hayden, Robert E(arl) 1913-1980 ..... **BLC 2;**
CLC 5, 9, 14, 37; PC 6
See also AFAW 1, 2; AMWS 2; BW 1, 3;
CA 69-72; 97-100; CABS 2; CANR 24,
75, 82; CDALB 1941-1968; DA; DAC;
DAM MST, MULT, POET; DLB 5, 76;
EWL 3; EXPP; MTCW 1, 2; PFS 1;
RGAL 4; SATA 19; SATA-Obit 26; WP
Hayek, F(riedrich) A(ugust von)
1899-1992 .... **TCLC 109**
See also CA 93-96; 137; CANR 20; MTCW
1, 2
Hayford, J(oseph) E(phraim) Casely
See Casely-Hayford, J(oseph) E(phraim)
Hayman, Ronald 1932- .... **CLC 44**
See also CA 25-28R; CANR 18, 50, 88; CD
5; DLB 155
Hayne, Paul Hamilton 1830-1886 . **NCLC 94**
See also DLB 3, 64, 79, 248; RGAL 4
Hays, Mary 1760-1843 .... **NCLC 114**
See also DLB 142, 158; RGEL 2
Haywood, Eliza (Fowler)
1693(?)-1756 .... **LC 1, 44**
See also DLB 39; RGEL 2
Hazlitt, William 1778-1830 ...... **NCLC 29, 82**
See also BRW 4; DLB 110, 158; RGEL 2;
TEA
Hazzard, Shirley 1931- .... **CLC 18**
See also CA 9-12R; CANR 4, 70; CN 7;
DLBY 1982; MTCW 1
Head, Bessie 1937-1986 ...... **BLC 2; CLC 25,**
67; SSC 52
See also AFW; BW 2, 3; CA 29-32R; 119;
CANR 25, 82; CDWLB 3; DA3; DAM
MULT; DLB 117, 225; EWL 3; EXPS;
FW; MTCW 1, 2; RGSF 2; SSFS 5, 13;
WLIT 2
Headon, (Nicky) Topper 1956(?)- ..... **CLC 30**
Heaney, Seamus (Justin) 1939- ...... **CLC 5, 7,**
14, 25, 37, 74, 91, 171; PC 18; WLCS
See also BRWR 1; BRWS 2; CA 85-88;
CANR 25, 48, 75, 91; CDBLB 1960 to
Present; CP 7; DA3; DAB; DAM POET;
DLB 40; DLBY 1995; EWL 3; EXPP;
MTCW 1, 2; PAB; PFS 2, 5, 8, 17; RGEL
2; TEA; WLIT 4
Hearn, (Patricio) Lafcadio (Tessima Carlos)
1850-1904 .... **TCLC 9**
See also CA 105; 166; DLB 12, 78, 189;
HGG; RGAL 4

Howard, Richard 1929- .... **CLC 7, 10, 47**
See also AITN 1; CA 85-88; CANR 25, 80; CP 7; DLB 5; INT CANR-25

Howard, Robert E(rvin) 1906-1936 .... **TCLC 8**
See also BPFB 2; BYA 5; CA 105; 157; FANT; SUFW 1

Howard, Warren F.
See Pohl, Frederik

Howe, Fanny (Quincy) 1940- .... **CLC 47**
See also CA 117; CAAE 187; CAAS 27; CANR 70, 116; CP 7; CWP; SATA-Brief 52

Howe, Irving 1920-1993 .... **CLC 85**
See also AMWS 6; CA 9-12R; 141; CANR 21, 50; DLB 67; EWL 3; MTCW 1, 2

Howe, Julia Ward 1819-1910 .... **TCLC 21**
See also CA 117; 191; DLB 1, 189, 235; FW

Howe, Susan 1937- .... **CLC 72, 152**
See also AMWS 4; CA 160; CP 7; CWP; DLB 120; FW; RGAL 4

Howe, Tina 1937- .... **CLC 48**
See also CA 109; CAD; CD 5; CWD

Howell, James 1594(?)-1666 .... **LC 13**
See also DLB 151

Howells, W. D.
See Howells, William Dean

Howells, William D.
See Howells, William Dean

Howells, William Dean 1837-1920 ... **SSC 36; TCLC 7, 17, 41**
See also AMW; CA 104; 134; CDALB 1865-1917; DLB 12, 64, 74, 79, 189; LMFS 1; MTCW 2; RGAL 4; TUS

Howes, Barbara 1914-1996 .... **CLC 15**
See also CA 9-12R; 151; CAAS 3; CANR 53; CP 7; SATA 5

Hrabal, Bohumil 1914-1997 .... **CLC 13, 67**
See also CA 106; 156; CAAS 12; CANR 57; CWW 2; DLB 232; EWL 3; RGSF 2

Hrotsvit of Gandersheim c. 935-c. 1000 .... **CMLC 29**
See also DLB 148

Hsi, Chu 1130-1200 .... **CMLC 42**

Hsun, Lu
See Lu Hsun

Hubbard, L(afayette) Ron(ald) 1911-1986 .... **CLC 43**
See also CA 77-80; 118; CANR 52; CPW; DA3; DAM POP; FANT; MTCW 2; SFW 4

Huch, Ricarda (Octavia) 1864-1947 .... **TCLC 13**
See also CA 111; 189; DLB 66; EWL 3

Huddle, David 1942- .... **CLC 49**
See also CA 57-60; CAAS 20; CANR 89; DLB 130

Hudson, Jeffrey
See Crichton, (John) Michael

Hudson, W(illiam) H(enry) 1841-1922 .... **TCLC 29**
See also CA 115; 190; DLB 98, 153, 174; RGEL 2; SATA 35

Hueffer, Ford Madox
See Ford, Ford Madox

Hughart, Barry 1934- .... **CLC 39**
See also CA 137; FANT; SFW 4; SUFW 2

Hughes, Colin
See Creasey, John

Hughes, David (John) 1930- .... **CLC 48**
See also CA 116; 129; CN 7; DLB 14

Hughes, Edward James
See Hughes, Ted
See also DA3; DAM MST, POET

Hughes, (James Mercer) Langston 1902-1967 ..... **BLC 2; CLC 1, 5, 10, 15, 35, 44, 108; DC 3; HR 2; PC 1; SSC 6; WLC**
See also AAYA 12; AFAW 1, 2; AMWR 1; AMWS 1; BW 1, 3; CA 1-4R; 25-28R; CANR 1, 34, 82; CDALB 1929-1941; CLR 17; DA; DA3; DAB; DAC; DAM DRAM, MST, MULT, POET; DFS 6; DLB 4, 7, 48, 51, 86, 228; EWL 3; EXPP; EXPS; JRDA; LAIT 3; LMFS 2; MAI-CYA 1, 2; MTCW 1, 2; PAB; PFS 1, 3, 6, 10, 15; RGAL 4; RGSF 2; SATA 4, 33; SSFS 4, 7; TUS; WCH; WP; YAW

Hughes, Richard (Arthur Warren) 1900-1976 .... **CLC 1, 11**
See also CA 5-8R; 65-68; CANR 4; DAM NOV; DLB 15, 161; EWL 3; MTCW 1; RGEL 2; SATA 8; SATA-Obit 25

Hughes, Ted 1930-1998 . **CLC 2, 4, 9, 14, 37, 119; PC 7**
See Hughes, Edward James
See also BRWR 2; BRWS 1; CA 1-4R; 171; CANR 1, 33, 66, 108; CLR 3; CP 7; DAB; DAC; DLB 40, 161; EWL 3; EXPP; MAICYA 1, 2; MTCW 1, 2; PAB; PFS 4; RGEL 2; SATA 49; SATA-Brief 27; SATA-Obit 107; TEA; YAW

Hugo, Richard
See Huch, Ricarda (Octavia)

Hugo, Richard F(ranklin) 1923-1982 .... **CLC 6, 18, 32**
See also AMWS 6; CA 49-52; 108; CANR 3; DAM POET; DLB 5, 206; EWL 3; PFS 17; RGAL 4

Hugo, Victor (Marie) 1802-1885 .... **NCLC 3, 10, 21; PC 17; WLC**
See also AAYA 28; DA; DA3; DAB; DAC; DAM DRAM, MST, NOV, POET; DLB 119, 192, 217; EFS 2; EW 6; EXPN; GFL 1789 to the Present; LAIT 1, 2; NFS 5; RGWL 2, 3; SATA 47; TWA

Huidobro, Vicente
See Huidobro Fernandez, Vicente Garcia
See also EWL 3; LAW

Huidobro Fernandez, Vicente Garcia 1893-1948 .... **TCLC 31**
See Huidobro, Vicente
See also CA 131; HW 1

Hulme, Keri 1947- .... **CLC 39, 130**
See also CA 125; CANR 69; CN 7; CP 7; CWP; EWL 3; FW; INT 125

Hulme, T(homas) E(rnest) 1883-1917 .... **TCLC 21**
See also BRWS 6; CA 117; 203; DLB 19

Hume, David 1711-1776 .... **LC 7, 56**
See also BRWS 3; DLB 104, 252; LMFS 1; TEA

Humphrey, William 1924-1997 .... **CLC 45**
See also AMWS 9; CA 77-80; 160; CANR 68; CN 7; CSW; DLB 6, 212, 234, 278; TCWW 2

Humphreys, Emyr Owen 1919- .... **CLC 47**
See also CA 5-8R; CANR 3, 24; CN 7; DLB 15

Humphreys, Josephine 1945- ..... **CLC 34, 57**
See also CA 121; 127; CANR 97; CSW; INT 127

Huneker, James Gibbons 1860-1921 .... **TCLC 65**
See also CA 193; DLB 71; RGAL 4

Hungerford, Hesba Fay
See Brinsmead, H(esba) F(ay)

Hungerford, Pixie
See Brinsmead, H(esba) F(ay)

Hunt, E(verette) Howard, (Jr.) 1918- .... **CLC 3**
See also AITN 1; CA 45-48; CANR 2, 47, 103; CMW 4

Hunt, Francesca
See Holland, Isabelle (Christian)

Hunt, Howard
See Hunt, E(verette) Howard, (Jr.)

Hunt, Kyle
See Creasey, John

Hunt, (James Henry) Leigh 1784-1859 .... **NCLC 1, 70**
See also DAM POET; DLB 96, 110, 144; RGEL 2; TEA

Hunt, Marsha 1946- .... **CLC 70**
See also BW 2, 3; CA 143; CANR 79

Hunt, Violet 1866(?)-1942 .... **TCLC 53**
See also CA 184; DLB 162, 197

Hunter, E. Waldo
See Sturgeon, Theodore (Hamilton)

Hunter, Evan 1926- .... **CLC 11, 31**
See McBain, Ed
See also AAYA 39; BPFB 2; CA 5-8R; CANR 5, 38, 62, 97; CMW 4; CN 7; CPW; DAM POP; DLBY 1982; INT CANR-5; MSW; MTCW 1; SATA 25; SFW 4

Hunter, Kristin 1931-
See Lattany, Kristin (Elaine Eggleston) Hunter

Hunter, Mary
See Austin, Mary (Hunter)

Hunter, Mollie 1922- .... **CLC 21**
See McIlwraith, Maureen Mollie Hunter
See also AAYA 13; BYA 6; CANR 37, 78; CLR 25; DLB 161; JRDA; MAICYA 1, 2; SAAS 7; SATA 54, 106, 139; WYA; YAW

Hunter, Robert (?)-1734 .... **LC 7**

Hurston, Zora Neale 1891-1960 .... **BLC 2; CLC 7, 30, 61; DC 12; HR 2; SSC 4; TCLC 121, 131; WLCS**
See also AAYA 15; AFAW 1, 2; AMWS 6; BW 1, 3; BYA 12; CA 85-88; CANR 61; CDALBS; DA; DA3; DAC; DAM MST, MULT, NOV; DFS 6; DLB 51, 86; EWL 3; EXPN; EXPS; FW; LAIT 3; LATS 1; LMFS 2; MAWW; MTCW 1, 2; NFS 3; RGAL 4; RGSF 2; SSFS 1, 6, 11; TUS; YAW

Husserl, E. G.
See Husserl, Edmund (Gustav Albrecht)

Husserl, Edmund (Gustav Albrecht) 1859-1938 .... **TCLC 100**
See also CA 116; 133

Huston, John (Marcellus) 1906-1987 .... **CLC 20**
See also CA 73-76; 123; CANR 34; DLB 26

Hustvedt, Siri 1955- .... **CLC 76**
See also CA 137

Hutten, Ulrich von 1488-1523 .... **LC 16**
See also DLB 179

Huxley, Aldous (Leonard) 1894-1963 .... **CLC 1, 3, 4, 5, 8, 11, 18, 35, 79; SSC 39; WLC**
See also AAYA 11; BPFB 2; BRW 7; CA 85-88; CANR 44, 99; CDBLB 1914-1945; DA; DA3; DAB; DAC; DAM MST, NOV; DLB 36, 100, 162, 195, 255; EWL 3; EXPN; LAIT 5; LMFS 2; MTCW 1, 2; NFS 6; RGEL 2; SATA 63; SCFW 2; SFW 4; TEA; YAW

Huxley, T(homas) H(enry) 1825-1895 .... **NCLC 67**
See also DLB 57; TEA

Huysmans, Joris-Karl 1848-1907 ... **TCLC 7, 69**
See also CA 104; 165; DLB 123; EW 7; GFL 1789 to the Present; LMFS 2; RGWL 2, 3

DLBY 1983; FANT; INT CANR-10;
MTCW 1, 2; RHW; SATA 62; SFW 4;
TCWW 2

James I 1394-1437 .... **LC 20**
See also RGEL 2

James, Andrew
See Kirkup, James

James, C(yril) L(ionel) R(obert)
1901-1989 .... **BLCS; CLC 33**
See also BW 2; CA 117; 125; 128; CANR
62; DLB 125; MTCW 1

James, Daniel (Lewis) 1911-1988
See Santiago, Danny
See also CA 174; 125

James, Dynely
See Mayne, William (James Carter)

James, Henry Sr. 1811-1882 .... **NCLC 53**

James, Henry 1843-1916 .... **SSC 8, 32, 47;**
TCLC 2, 11, 24, 40, 47, 64; WLC
See also AMW; AMWC 1; AMWR 1; BPFB
2; BRW 6; CA 104; 132; CDALB 1865-
1917; DA; DA3; DAB; DAC; DAM MST,
NOV; DLB 12, 71, 74, 189; DLBD 13;
EWL 3; EXPS; HGG; LAIT 2; MTCW 1,
2; NFS 12, 16; RGAL 4; RGEL 2; RGSF
2; SSFS 9; SUFW 1; TUS

James, M. R.
See James, Montague (Rhodes)
See also DLB 156, 201

James, Montague (Rhodes)
1862-1936 .... **SSC 16; TCLC 6**
See James, M. R.
See also CA 104; 203; HGG; RGEL 2;
RGSF 2; SUFW 1

James, P. D. .... **CLC 18, 46, 122**
See White, Phyllis Dorothy James
See also BEST 90:2; BPFB 2; BRWS 4;
CDBLB 1960 to Present; DLB 87, 276;
DLBD 17; MSW

James, Philip
See Moorcock, Michael (John)

James, Samuel
See Stephens, James

James, Seumas
See Stephens, James

James, Stephen
See Stephens, James

James, William 1842-1910 .... **TCLC 15, 32**
See also AMW; CA 109; 193; DLB 270,
284; RGAL 4

Jameson, Anna 1794-1860 .... **NCLC 43**
See also DLB 99, 166

Jameson, Fredric (R.) 1934- .... **CLC 142**
See also CA 196; DLB 67; LMFS 2

Jami, Nur al-Din 'Abd al-Rahman
1414-1492 .... **LC 9**

Jammes, Francis 1868-1938 .... **TCLC 75**
See also CA 198; EWL 3; GFL 1789 to the
Present

Jandl, Ernst 1925-2000 .... **CLC 34**
See also CA 200; EWL 3

Janowitz, Tama 1957- .... **CLC 43, 145**
See also CA 106; CANR 52, 89; CN 7;
CPW; DAM POP

Japrisot, Sebastien 1931- .... **CLC 90**
See Rossi, Jean Baptiste
See also CMW 4

Jarrell, Randall 1914-1965 .... **CLC 1, 2, 6, 9,**
13, 49; PC 41
See also AMW; BYA 5; CA 5-8R; 25-28R;
CABS 2; CANR 6, 34; CDALB 1941-
1968; CLR 6; CWRI 5; DAM POET;
DLB 48, 52; EWL 3; EXPP; MAICYA 1,
2; MTCW 1, 2; PAB; PFS 2; RGAL 4;
SATA 7

Jarry, Alfred 1873-1907 .... **SSC 20; TCLC 2,**
14
See also CA 104; 153; DA3; DAM DRAM;
DFS 8; DLB 192, 258; EW 9; EWL 3;
GFL 1789 to the Present; RGWL 2, 3;
TWA

Jarvis, E. K.
See Ellison, Harlan (Jay)

Jawien, Andrzej
See John Paul II, Pope

Jaynes, Roderick
See Coen, Ethan

Jeake, Samuel, Jr.
See Aiken, Conrad (Potter)

Jean Paul 1763-1825 .... **NCLC 7**

Jefferies, (John) Richard
1848-1887 .... **NCLC 47**
See also DLB 98, 141; RGEL 2; SATA 16;
SFW 4

Jeffers, (John) Robinson 1887-1962 .. **CLC 2,**
3, 11, 15, 54; PC 17; WLC
See also AMWS 2; CA 85-88; CANR 35;
CDALB 1917-1929; DA; DAC; DAM
MST, POET; DLB 45, 212; EWL 3;
MTCW 1, 2; PAB; PFS 3, 4; RGAL 4

Jefferson, Janet
See Mencken, H(enry) L(ouis)

Jefferson, Thomas 1743-1826 . **NCLC 11, 103**
See also ANW; CDALB 1640-1865; DA3;
DLB 31, 183; LAIT 1; RGAL 4

Jeffrey, Francis 1773-1850 .... **NCLC 33**
See Francis, Lord Jeffrey

Jelakowitch, Ivan
See Heijermans, Herman

Jelinek, Elfriede 1946- .... **CLC 169**
See also CA 154; DLB 85; FW

Jellicoe, (Patricia) Ann 1927- .... **CLC 27**
See also CA 85-88; CBD; CD 5; CWD;
CWRI 5; DLB 13, 233; FW

Jemyma
See Holley, Marietta

Jen, Gish .... **CLC 70**
See Jen, Lillian

Jen, Lillian 1956(?)-
See Jen, Gish
See also CA 135; CANR 89

Jenkins, (John) Robin 1912- .... **CLC 52**
See also CA 1-4R; CANR 1; CN 7; DLB
14, 271

Jennings, Elizabeth (Joan)
1926-2001 .... **CLC 5, 14, 131**
See also BRWS 5; CA 61-64; 200; CAAS
5; CANR 8, 39, 66; CP 7; CWP; DLB 27;
EWL 3; MTCW 1; SATA 66

Jennings, Waylon 1937- .... **CLC 21**

Jensen, Johannes V(ilhelm)
1873-1950 .... **TCLC 41**
See also CA 170; DLB 214; EWL 3; RGWL
3

Jensen, Laura (Linnea) 1948- .... **CLC 37**
See also CA 103

Jerome, Saint 345-420 .... **CMLC 30**
See also RGWL 3

Jerome, Jerome K(lapka)
1859-1927 .... **TCLC 23**
See also CA 119; 177; DLB 10, 34, 135;
RGEL 2

Jerrold, Douglas William
1803-1857 .... **NCLC 2**
See also DLB 158, 159; RGEL 2

Jewett, (Theodora) Sarah Orne
1849-1909 .... **SSC 6, 44; TCLC 1, 22**
See also AMW; AMWR 2; CA 108; 127;
CANR 71; DLB 12, 74, 221; EXPS; FW;
MAWW; NFS 15; RGAL 4; RGSF 2;
SATA 15; SSFS 4

Jewsbury, Geraldine (Endsor)
1812-1880 .... **NCLC 22**
See also DLB 21

Jhabvala, Ruth Prawer 1927- . **CLC 4, 8, 29,**
94, 138
See also BRWS 5; CA 1-4R; CANR 2, 29,
51, 74, 91; CN 7; DAB; DAM NOV; DLB
139, 194; EWL 3; IDFW 3, 4; INT CANR-
29; MTCW 1, 2; RGSF 2; RGWL 2;
RHW; TEA

Jibran, Kahlil
See Gibran, Kahlil

Jibran, Khalil
See Gibran, Kahlil

Jiles, Paulette 1943- .... **CLC 13, 58**
See also CA 101; CANR 70; CWP

Jimenez (Mantecon), Juan Ramon
1881-1958 .... **HLC 1; PC 7; TCLC 4**
See also CA 104; 131; CANR 74; DAM
MULT, POET; DLB 134; EW 9; EWL 3;
HW 1; MTCW 1, 2; RGWL 2, 3

Jimenez, Ramon
See Jimenez (Mantecon), Juan Ramon

Jimenez Mantecon, Juan
See Jimenez (Mantecon), Juan Ramon

Jin, Ha .... **CLC 109**
See Jin, Xuefei
See also CA 152; DLB 244; SSFS 17

Jin, Xuefei 1956-
See Jin, Ha
See also CANR 91

Joel, Billy .... **CLC 26**
See Joel, William Martin

Joel, William Martin 1949-
See Joel, Billy
See also CA 108

John, Saint 107th cent. -100 .... **CMLC 27**

John of the Cross, St. 1542-1591 .... **LC 18**
See also RGWL 2, 3

John Paul II, Pope 1920- .... **CLC 128**
See also CA 106; 133

Johnson, B(ryan) S(tanley William)
1933-1973 .... **CLC 6, 9**
See also CA 9-12R; 53-56; CANR 9; DLB
14, 40; EWL 3; RGEL 2

Johnson, Benjamin F., of Boone
See Riley, James Whitcomb

Johnson, Charles (Richard) 1948- .... **BLC 2;**
CLC 7, 51, 65, 163
See also AFAW 2; AMWS 6; BW 2, 3; CA
116; CAAS 18; CANR 42, 66, 82; CN 7;
DAM MULT; DLB 33, 278; MTCW 2;
RGAL 4; SSFS 16

Johnson, Charles S(purgeon)
1893-1956 .... **HR 3**
See also BW 1, 3; CA 125; CANR 82; DLB
51, 91

Johnson, Denis 1949- . **CLC 52, 160; SSC 56**
See also CA 117; 121; CANR 71, 99; CN
7; DLB 120

Johnson, Diane 1934- .... **CLC 5, 13, 48**
See also BPFB 2; CA 41-44R; CANR 17,
40, 62, 95; CN 7; DLBY 1980; INT
CANR-17; MTCW 1

Johnson, E. Pauline 1861-1913 .... **NNAL**
See also CA 150; DAC; DAM MULT; DLB
92, 175

Johnson, Eyvind (Olof Verner)
1900-1976 .... **CLC 14**
See also CA 73-76; 69-72; CANR 34, 101;
DLB 259; EW 12; EWL 3

Johnson, Fenton 1888-1958 .... **BLC 2**
See also BW 1; CA 118; 124; DAM MULT;
DLB 45, 50

Johnson, Georgia Douglas (Camp)
1880-1966 .... **HR 3**
See also BW 1; CA 125; DLB 51, 249; WP

Johnson, Helene 1907-1995 .... **HR 3**
See also CA 181; DLB 51; WP

Johnson, J. R.
See James, C(yril) L(ionel) R(obert)

Kafka, Franz 1883-1924 ... SSC **5, 29, 35, 60;**
  TCLC **2, 6, 13, 29, 47, 53, 112;** WLC
    See also AAYA 31; BPFB 2; CA 105; 126;
    CDWLB 2; DA; DA3; DAB; DAC; DAM
    MST, NOV; DLB 81; EW 9; EWL 3;
    EXPS; LATS 1; LMFS 2; MTCW 1, 2;
    NFS 7; RGSF 2; RGWL 2, 3; SFW 4;
    SSFS 3, 7, 12; TWA
Kahanovitsch, Pinkhes
  See Der Nister
Kahn, Roger 1927- .... CLC **30**
    See also CA 25-28R; CANR 44, 69; DLB
    171; SATA 37
Kain, Saul
  See Sassoon, Siegfried (Lorraine)
Kaiser, Georg 1878-1945 .... TCLC **9**
    See also CA 106; 190; CDWLB 2; DLB
    124; EWL 3; LMFS 2; RGWL 2, 3
Kaledin, Sergei .... CLC **59**
Kaletski, Alexander 1946- .... CLC **39**
    See also CA 118; 143
Kalidasa fl. c. 400-455 .... CMLC **9;** PC **22**
    See also RGWL 2, 3
Kallman, Chester (Simon)
  1921-1975 .... CLC **2**
    See also CA 45-48; 53-56; CANR 3
Kaminsky, Melvin 1926-
  See Brooks, Mel
    See also CA 65-68; CANR 16
Kaminsky, Stuart M(elvin) 1934- ..... CLC **59**
    See also CA 73-76; CANR 29, 53, 89;
    CMW 4
Kandinsky, Wassily 1866-1944 .... TCLC **92**
    See also CA 118; 155
Kane, Francis
  See Robbins, Harold
Kane, Henry 1918-
  See Queen, Ellery
    See also CA 156; CMW 4
Kane, Paul
  See Simon, Paul (Frederick)
Kanin, Garson 1912-1999 .... CLC **22**
    See also AITN 1; CA 5-8R; 177; CAD;
    CANR 7, 78; DLB 7; IDFW 3, 4
Kaniuk, Yoram 1930- .... CLC **19**
    See also CA 134
Kant, Immanuel 1724-1804 ..... NCLC **27, 67**
    See also DLB 94
Kantor, MacKinlay 1904-1977 .... CLC **7**
    See also CA 61-64; 73-76; CANR 60, 63;
    DLB 9, 102; MTCW 2; RHW; TCWW 2
Kanze Motokiyo
  See Zeami
Kaplan, David Michael 1946- .... CLC **50**
    See also CA 187
Kaplan, James 1951- .... CLC **59**
    See also CA 135
Karadzic, Vuk Stefanovic
  1787-1864 .... NCLC **115**
    See also CDWLB 4; DLB 147
Karageorge, Michael
  See Anderson, Poul (William)
Karamzin, Nikolai Mikhailovich
  1766-1826 .... NCLC **3**
    See also DLB 150; RGSF 2
Karapanou, Margarita 1946- .... CLC **13**
    See also CA 101
Karinthy, Frigyes 1887-1938 .... TCLC **47**
    See also CA 170; DLB 215; EWL 3
Karl, Frederick R(obert) 1927- .... CLC **34**
    See also CA 5-8R; CANR 3, 44
Kastel, Warren
  See Silverberg, Robert
Kataev, Evgeny Petrovich 1903-1942
  See Petrov, Evgeny
    See also CA 120
Kataphusin
  See Ruskin, John

Katz, Steve 1935- .... CLC **47**
    See also CA 25-28R; CAAS 14, 64; CANR
    12; CN 7; DLBY 1983
Kauffman, Janet 1945- .... CLC **42**
    See also CA 117; CANR 43, 84; DLB 218;
    DLBY 1986
Kaufman, Bob (Garnell) 1925-1986 . CLC **49**
    See also BG 3; BW 1; CA 41-44R; 118;
    CANR 22; DLB 16, 41
Kaufman, George S. 1889-1961 ...... CLC **38;**
  DC **17**
    See also CA 108; 93-96; DAM DRAM;
    DFS 1, 10; DLB 7; INT CA-108; MTCW
    2; RGAL 4; TUS
Kaufman, Sue .... CLC **3, 8**
  See Barondess, Sue K(aufman)
Kavafis, Konstantinos Petrou 1863-1933
  See Cavafy, C(onstantine) P(eter)
    See also CA 104
Kavan, Anna 1901-1968 .... CLC **5, 13, 82**
    See also BRWS 7; CA 5-8R; CANR 6, 57;
    DLB 255; MTCW 1; RGEL 2; SFW 4
Kavanagh, Dan
  See Barnes, Julian (Patrick)
Kavanagh, Julie 1952- .... CLC **119**
    See also CA 163
Kavanagh, Patrick (Joseph)
  1904-1967 .... CLC **22;** PC **33**
    See also BRWS 7; CA 123; 25-28R; DLB
    15, 20; EWL 3; MTCW 1; RGEL 2
Kawabata, Yasunari 1899-1972 ..... CLC **2, 5,**
  9, 18, 107; SSC **17**
  See Kawabata Yasunari
    See also CA 93-96; 33-36R; CANR 88;
    DAM MULT; MJW; MTCW 2; RGSF 2;
    RGWL 2, 3
Kawabata Yasunari
  See Kawabata, Yasunari
    See also DLB 180; EWL 3
Kaye, M(ary) M(argaret) 1909- .... CLC **28**
    See also CA 89-92; CANR 24, 60, 102;
    MTCW 1, 2; RHW; SATA 62
Kaye, Mollie
  See Kaye, M(ary) M(argaret)
Kaye-Smith, Sheila 1887-1956 .... TCLC **20**
    See also CA 118; 203; DLB 36
Kaymor, Patrice Maguilene
  See Senghor, Leopold Sedar
Kazakov, Yuri Pavlovich 1927-1982 . SSC **43**
  See Kazakov, Yury
    See also CA 5-8R; CANR 36; MTCW 1;
    RGSF 2
Kazakov, Yury
  See Kazakov, Yuri Pavlovich
    See also EWL 3
Kazan, Elia 1909- .... CLC **6, 16, 63**
    See also CA 21-24R; CANR 32, 78
Kazantzakis, Nikos 1883(?)-1957 .... TCLC **2,**
  5, 33
    See also BPFB 2; CA 105; 132; DA3; EW
    9; EWL 3; MTCW 1, 2; RGWL 2, 3
Kazin, Alfred 1915-1998 ... CLC **34, 38, 119**
    See also AMWS 8; CA 1-4R; CAAS 7;
    CANR 1, 45, 79; DLB 67; EWL 3
Keane, Mary Nesta (Skrine) 1904-1996
  See Keane, Molly
    See also CA 108; 114; 151; CN 7; RHW
Keane, Molly .... CLC **31**
  See Keane, Mary Nesta (Skrine)
    See also INT 114
Keates, Jonathan 1946(?)- .... CLC **34**
    See also CA 163
Keaton, Buster 1895-1966 .... CLC **20**
    See also CA 194

Keats, John 1795-1821 ...... NCLC **8, 73, 121;**
  PC **1;** WLC
    See also BRW 4; BRWR 1; CDBLB 1789-
    1832; DA; DA3; DAB; DAC; DAM MST,
    POET; DLB 96, 110; EXPP; LMFS 1;
    PAB; PFS 1, 2, 3, 9, 16; RGEL 2; TEA;
    WLIT 3; WP
Keble, John 1792-1866 .... NCLC **87**
    See also DLB 32, 55; RGEL 2
Keene, Donald 1922- .... CLC **34**
    See also CA 1-4R; CANR 5
Keillor, Garrison .... CLC **40, 115**
  See Keillor, Gary (Edward)
    See also AAYA 2; BEST 89:3; BPFB 2;
    DLBY 1987; EWL 3; SATA 58; TUS
Keillor, Gary (Edward) 1942-
  See Keillor, Garrison
    See also CA 111; 117; CANR 36, 59; CPW;
    DA3; DAM POP; MTCW 1, 2
Keith, Carlos
  See Lewton, Val
Keith, Michael
  See Hubbard, L(afayette) Ron(ald)
Keller, Gottfried 1819-1890 .... NCLC **2;** SSC
  26
    See also CDWLB 2; DLB 129; EW; RGSF
    2; RGWL 2, 3
Keller, Nora Okja 1965- .... CLC **109**
    See also CA 187
Kellerman, Jonathan 1949- .... CLC **44**
    See also AAYA 35; BEST 90:1; CA 106;
    CANR 29, 51; CMW 4; CPW; DA3;
    DAM POP; INT CANR-29
Kelley, William Melvin 1937- .... CLC **22**
    See also BW 1; CA 77-80; CANR 27, 83;
    CN 7; DLB 33; EWL 3
Kellogg, Marjorie 1922- .... CLC **2**
    See also CA 81-84
Kellow, Kathleen
  See Hibbert, Eleanor Alice Burford
Kelly, M(ilton) T(errence) 1947- ...... CLC **55**
    See also CA 97-100; CAAS 22; CANR 19,
    43, 84; CN 7
Kelly, Robert 1935- .... SSC **50**
    See also CA 17-20R; CAAS 19; CANR 47;
    CP 7; DLB 5, 130, 165
Kelman, James 1946- .... CLC **58, 86**
    See also BRWS 5; CA 148; CANR 85; CN
    7; DLB 194; RGSF 2; WLIT 4
Kemal, Yashar 1923- .... CLC **14, 29**
    See also CA 89-92; CANR 44; CWW 2
Kemble, Fanny 1809-1893 .... NCLC **18**
    See also DLB 32
Kemelman, Harry 1908-1996 .... CLC **2**
    See also AITN 1; BPFB 2; CA 9-12R; 155;
    CANR 6, 71; CMW 4; DLB 28
Kempe, Margery 1373(?)-1440(?) ... LC **6, 56**
    See also DLB 146; RGEL 2
Kempis, Thomas a 1380-1471 .... LC **11**
Kendall, Henry 1839-1882 .... NCLC **12**
    See also DLB 230
Keneally, Thomas (Michael) 1935- ... CLC **5,**
  8, 10, 14, 19, 27, 43, 117
    See also BRWS 4; CA 85-88; CANR 10,
    50, 74; CN 7; CPW; DA3; DAM NOV;
    EWL 3; MTCW 1, 2; NFS 17; RGEL 2;
    RHW
Kennedy, Adrienne (Lita) 1931- .... BLC **2;**
  CLC **66;** DC **5**
    See also AFAW 2; BW 2, 3; CA 103; CAAS
    20; CABS 3; CANR 26, 53, 82; CD 5;
    DAM MULT; DFS 9; DLB 38; FW
Kennedy, John Pendleton
  1795-1870 .... NCLC **2**
    See also DLB 3, 248, 254; RGAL 4

Kennedy, Joseph Charles 1929-
See Kennedy, X. J.
See also CA 1-4R; CAAE 201; CANR 4, 30, 40; CP 7; CWRI 5; MAICYA 2; MAICYAS 1; SATA 14, 86; SATA-Essay 130

Kennedy, William 1928- ... **CLC 6, 28, 34, 53**
See also AAYA 1; AMWS 7; BPFB 2; CA 85-88; CANR 14, 31, 76; CN 7; DA3; DAM NOV; DLB 143; DLBY 1985; EWL 3; INT CANR-31; MTCW 1, 2; SATA 57

Kennedy, X. J. .... **CLC 8, 42**
See Kennedy, Joseph Charles
See also CAAS 9; CLR 27; DLB 5; SAAS 22

Kenny, Maurice (Francis) 1929- ..... **CLC 87; NNAL**
See also CA 144; CAAS 22; DAM MULT; DLB 175

Kent, Kelvin
See Kuttner, Henry

Kenton, Maxwell
See Southern, Terry

Kenyon, Robert O.
See Kuttner, Henry

Kepler, Johannes 1571-1630 .... **LC 45**

Ker, Jill
See Conway, Jill K(er)

Kerkow, H. C.
See Lewton, Val

Kerouac, Jack 1922-1969 ...... **CLC 1, 2, 3, 5, 14, 29, 61; TCLC 117; WLC**
See Kerouac, Jean-Louis Lebris de
See also AAYA 25; AMWC 1; AMWS 3; BG 3; BPFB 2; CDALB 1941-1968; CPW; DLB 2, 16, 237; DLBD 3; DLBY 1995; EWL 3; GLL 1; LATS 1; LMFS 2; MTCW 8; NFS 8; RGAL 4; TUS; WP

Kerouac, Jean-Louis Lebris de 1922-1969
See Kerouac, Jack
See also AITN 1; CA 5-8R; 25-28R; CANR 26, 54, 95; DA; DA3; DAB; DAC; DAM MST, NOV, POET, POP; MTCW 1, 2

Kerr, Jean 1923- .... **CLC 22**
See also CA 5-8R; CANR 7; INT CANR-7

Kerr, M. E. .... **CLC 12, 35**
See Meaker, Marijane (Agnes)
See also AAYA 2, 23; BYA 1, 7, 8; CLR 29; SAAS 1; WYA

Kerr, Robert .... **CLC 55**

Kerrigan, (Thomas) Anthony 1918- .. **CLC 4, 6**
See also CA 49-52; CAAS 11; CANR 4

Kerry, Lois
See Duncan, Lois

Kesey, Ken (Elton) 1935-2001 ... **CLC 1, 3, 6, 11, 46, 64; WLC**
See also AAYA 25; BG 3; BPFB 2; CA 1-4R; 204; CANR 22, 38, 66; CDALB 1968-1988; CN 7; CPW; DA; DA3; DAB; DAC; DAM MST, NOV, POP; DLB 2, 16, 206; EWL 3; EXPN; LAIT 4; MTCW 1, 2; NFS 2; RGAL 4; SATA 66; SATA-Obit 131; TUS; YAW

Kesselring, Joseph (Otto) 1902-1967 .... **CLC 45**
See also CA 150; DAM DRAM, MST

Kessler, Jascha (Frederick) 1929- ...... **CLC 4**
See also CA 17-20R; CANR 8, 48, 111

Kettelkamp, Larry (Dale) 1933- .... **CLC 12**
See also CA 29-32R; CANR 16; SAAS 3; SATA 2

Key, Ellen (Karolina Sofia) 1849-1926 .... **TCLC 65**
See also DLB 259

Keyber, Conny
See Fielding, Henry

Keyes, Daniel 1927- .... **CLC 80**
See also AAYA 23; BYA 11; CA 17-20R, 181; CAAE 181; CANR 10, 26, 54, 74; DA; DA3; DAC; DAM MST, NOV; EXPN; LAIT 4; MTCW 2; NFS 2; SATA 37; SFW 4

Keynes, John Maynard 1883-1946 .... **TCLC 64**
See also CA 114; 162, 163; DLBD 10; MTCW 2

Khanshendel, Chiron
See Rose, Wendy

Khayyam, Omar 1048-1131 ... **CMLC 11; PC 8**
See Omar Khayyam
See also DA3; DAM POET

Kherdian, David 1931- .... **CLC 6, 9**
See also AAYA 42; CA 21-24R; CAAE 192; CAAS 2; CANR 39, 78; CLR 24; JRDA; LAIT 3; MAICYA 1, 2; SATA 16, 74; SATA-Essay 125

Khlebnikov, Velimir .... **TCLC 20**
See Khlebnikov, Viktor Vladimirovich
See also EW 10; EWL 3; RGWL 2, 3

Khlebnikov, Viktor Vladimirovich 1885-1922
See Khlebnikov, Velimir
See also CA 117

Khodasevich, Vladislav (Felitsianovich) 1886-1939 .... **TCLC 15**
See also CA 115; EWL 3

Kielland, Alexander Lange 1849-1906 .... **TCLC 5**
See also CA 104

Kiely, Benedict 1919- ... **CLC 23, 43; SSC 58**
See also CA 1-4R; CANR 2, 84; CN 7; DLB 15

Kienzle, William X(avier) 1928-2001 .... **CLC 25**
See also CA 93-96; 203; CAAS 1; CANR 9, 31, 59, 111; CMW 4; DA3; DAM POP; INT CANR-31; MSW; MTCW 1, 2

Kierkegaard, Soren 1813-1855 ..... **NCLC 34, 78, 125**
See also EW 6; LMFS 2; RGWL 3; TWA

Kieslowski, Krzysztof 1941-1996 .... **CLC 120**
See also CA 147; 151

Killens, John Oliver 1916-1987 .... **CLC 10**
See also BW 2; CA 77-80; 123; CAAS 2; CANR 26; DLB 33; EWL 3

Killigrew, Anne 1660-1685 .... **LC 4, 73**
See also DLB 131

Killigrew, Thomas 1612-1683 .... **LC 57**
See also DLB 58; RGEL 2

Kim
See Simenon, Georges (Jacques Christian)

Kincaid, Jamaica 1949- ...... **BLC 2; CLC 43, 68, 137**
See also AAYA 13; AFAW 2; AMWS 7; BRWS 7; BW 2, 3; CA 125; CANR 47, 59, 95; CDALBS; CDWLB 3; CLR 63; CN 7; DA3; DAM MULT, NOV; DLB 157, 227; DNFS 1; EWL 3; EXPS; FW; LATS 1; LMFS 2; MTCW 2; NCFS 1; NFS 3; SSFS 5, 7; TUS; YAW

King, Francis (Henry) 1923- .... **CLC 8, 53, 145**
See also CA 1-4R; CANR 1, 33, 86; CN 7; DAM NOV; DLB 15, 139; MTCW 1

King, Kennedy
See Brown, George Douglas

King, Martin Luther, Jr. 1929-1968 . **BLC 2; CLC 83; WLCS**
See also BW 2, 3; CA 25-28; CANR 27, 44; CAP 2; DA; DA3; DAB; DAC; DAM MST, MULT; LAIT 5; LATS 1; MTCW 1, 2; SATA 14

King, Stephen (Edwin) 1947- .... **CLC 12, 26, 37, 61, 113; SSC 17, 55**
See also AAYA 1, 17; AMWS 5; BEST 90:1; BPFB 2; CA 61-64; CANR 1, 30, 52, 76; CPW; DA3; DAM NOV, POP; DLB 143; DLBY 1980; HGG; JRDA; LAIT 5; MTCW 1, 2; RGAL 4; SATA 9, 55; SUFW 1, 2; WYAS 1; YAW

King, Steve
See King, Stephen (Edwin)

King, Thomas 1943- .... **CLC 89, 171; NNAL**
See also CA 144; CANR 95; CCA 1; CN 7; DAC; DAM MULT; DLB 175; SATA 96

Kingman, Lee .... **CLC 17**
See Natti, (Mary) Lee
See also CWRI 5; SAAS 3; SATA 1, 67

Kingsley, Charles 1819-1875 .... **NCLC 35**
See also CLR 77; DLB 21, 32, 163, 178, 190; FANT; MAICYA 2; MAICYAS 1; RGEL 2; WCH; YABC 2

Kingsley, Henry 1830-1876 .... **NCLC 107**
See also DLB 21, 230; RGEL 2

Kingsley, Sidney 1906-1995 .... **CLC 44**
See also CA 85-88; 147; CAD; DFS 14; DLB 7; RGAL 4

Kingsolver, Barbara 1955- . **CLC 55, 81, 130**
See also AAYA 15; AMWS 7; CA 129; 134; CANR 60, 96; CDALBS; CPW; CSW; DA3; DAM POP; DLB 206; INT CA-134; LAIT 5; MTCW 2; NFS 5, 10, 12; RGAL 4

Kingston, Maxine (Ting Ting) Hong 1940- .... **AAL; CLC 12, 19, 58, 121; WLCS**
See also AAYA 8; AMWS 5; BPFB 2; CA 69-72; CANR 13, 38, 74, 87; CDALBS; CN 7; DA3; DAM MULT, NOV; DLB 173, 212; DLBY 1980; EWL 3; FW; INT CANR-13; LAIT 5; MAWW; MTCW 1, 2; NFS 6; RGAL 4; SATA 53; SSFS 3

Kinnell, Galway 1927- ..... **CLC 1, 2, 3, 5, 13, 29, 129; PC 26**
See also AMWS 3; CA 9-12R; CANR 10, 34, 66, 116; CP 7; DLB 5; DLBY 1987; EWL 3; INT CANR-34; MTCW 1, 2; PAB; PFS 9; RGAL 4; WP

Kinsella, Thomas 1928- .... **CLC 4, 19, 138**
See also BRWS 5; CA 17-20R; CANR 15; CP 7; DLB 27; EWL 3; MTCW 1, 2; RGEL 2; TEA

Kinsella, W(illiam) P(atrick) 1935- . **CLC 27, 43, 166**
See also AAYA 7; BPFB 2; CA 97-100; CAAS 7; CANR 21, 35, 66, 75; CN 7; CPW; DAC; DAM NOV, POP; FANT; INT CANR-21; LAIT 5; MTCW 1, 2; NFS 15; RGSF 2

Kinsey, Alfred C(harles) 1894-1956 .... **TCLC 91**
See also CA 115; 170; MTCW 2

Kipling, (Joseph) Rudyard 1865-1936 . **PC 3; SSC 5, 54; TCLC 8, 17; WLC**
See also AAYA 32; BRW 6; BRWC 1; BYA 4; CA 105; 120; CANR 33; CDBLB 1890-1914; CLR 39, 65; CWRI 5; DA; DA3; DAB; DAC; DAM MST, POET; DLB 19, 34, 141, 156; EWL 3; EXPS; FANT; LAIT 3; LMFS 1; MAICYA 1, 2; MTCW 1, 2; RGEL 2; RGSF 2; SATA 100; SFW 4; SSFS 8; SUFW 1; TEA; WCH; WLIT 4; YABC 2

Kirk, Russell (Amos) 1918-1994 .. **TCLC 119**
See also AITN 1; CA 1-4R; 145; CAAS 9; CANR 1, 20, 60; HGG; INT CANR-20; MTCW 1, 2

Kirkland, Caroline M. 1801-1864 . **NCLC 85**
See also DLB 3, 73, 74, 250, 254; DLBD 13

Kirkup, James 1918- .... **CLC 1**
See also CA 1-4R; CAAS 4; CANR 2; CP
7; DLB 27; SATA 12
Kirkwood, James 1930(?)-1989 .... **CLC 9**
See also AITN 2; CA 1-4R; 128; CANR 6,
40; GLL 2
Kirshner, Sidney
See Kingsley, Sidney
Kis, Danilo 1935-1989 .... **CLC 57**
See also CA 109; 118; 129; CANR 61; CD-
WLB 4; DLB 181; EWL 3; MTCW 1;
RGSF 2; RGWL 2, 3
Kissinger, Henry A(lfred) 1923- ..... **CLC 137**
See also CA 1-4R; CANR 2, 33, 66, 109;
MTCW 1
Kivi, Aleksis 1834-1872 .... **NCLC 30**
Kizer, Carolyn (Ashley) 1925- ... **CLC 15, 39,
80**
See also CA 65-68; CAAS 5; CANR 24,
70; CP 7; CWP; DAM POET; DLB 5,
169; EWL 3; MTCW 2
Klabund 1890-1928 .... **TCLC 44**
See also CA 162; DLB 66
Klappert, Peter 1942- .... **CLC 57**
See also CA 33-36R; CSW; DLB 5
Klein, A(braham) M(oses)
1909-1972 .... **CLC 19**
See also CA 101; 37-40R; DAB; DAC;
DAM MST; DLB 68; EWL 3; RGEL 2
Klein, Joe
See Klein, Joseph
Klein, Joseph 1946- .... **CLC 154**
See also CA 85-88; CANR 55
Klein, Norma 1938-1989 .... **CLC 30**
See also AAYA 2, 35; BPFB 2; BYA 6, 7,
8; CA 41-44R; 128; CANR 15, 37; CLR
2, 19; INT CANR-15; JRDA; MAICYA
1, 2; SAAS 1; SATA 7, 57; WYA; YAW
Klein, T(heodore) E(ibon) D(onald)
1947- .... **CLC 34**
See also CA 119; CANR 44, 75; HGG
Kleist, Heinrich von 1777-1811 ...... **NCLC 2,
37; SSC 22**
See also CDWLB 2; DAM DRAM; DLB
90; EW 5; RGSF 2; RGWL 2, 3
Klima, Ivan 1931- .... **CLC 56, 172**
See also CA 25-28R; CANR 17, 50, 91;
CDWLB 4; CWW 2; DAM NOV; DLB
232; EWL 3; RGWL 3
Klimentev, Andrei Platonovich
See Klimentov, Andrei Platonovich
Klimentov, Andrei Platonovich
1899-1951 .... **SSC 42; TCLC 14**
See Platonov, Andrei Platonovich; Platonov,
Andrey Platonovich
See also CA 108
Klinger, Friedrich Maximilian von
1752-1831 .... **NCLC 1**
See also DLB 94
Klingsor the Magician
See Hartmann, Sadakichi
Klopstock, Friedrich Gottlieb
1724-1803 .... **NCLC 11**
See also DLB 97; EW 4; RGWL 2, 3
Kluge, Alexander 1932- .... **SSC 61**
See also CA 81-84; DLB 75
Knapp, Caroline 1959-2002 .... **CLC 99**
See also CA 154; 207
Knebel, Fletcher 1911-1993 .... **CLC 14**
See also AITN 1; CA 1-4R; 140; CAAS 3;
CANR 1, 36; SATA 36; SATA-Obit 75
Knickerbocker, Diedrich
See Irving, Washington
Knight, Etheridge 1931-1991 ... **BLC 2; CLC
40; PC 14**
See also BW 1, 3; CA 21-24R; 133; CANR
23, 82; DAM POET; DLB 41; MTCW 2;
RGAL 4

Knight, Sarah Kemble 1666-1727 .... **LC 7**
See also DLB 24, 200
Knister, Raymond 1899-1932 .... **TCLC 56**
See also CA 186; DLB 68; RGEL 2
Knowles, John 1926-2001 ... **CLC 1, 4, 10, 26**
See also AAYA 10; AMWS 12; BPFB 2;
BYA 3; CA 17-20R; 203; CANR 40, 74,
76; CDALB 1968-1988; CN 7; DA; DAC;
DAM MST, NOV; DLB 6; EXPN; MTCW
1, 2; NFS 2; RGAL 4; SATA 8, 89; SATA-
Obit 134; YAW
Knox, Calvin M.
See Silverberg, Robert
Knox, John c. 1505-1572 .... **LC 37**
See also DLB 132
Knye, Cassandra
See Disch, Thomas M(ichael)
Koch, C(hristopher) J(ohn) 1932- .... **CLC 42**
See also CA 127; CANR 84; CN 7
Koch, Christopher
See Koch, C(hristopher) J(ohn)
Koch, Kenneth (Jay) 1925-2002 .... **CLC 5, 8,
44**
See also CA 1-4R; 207; CAD; CANR 6,
36, 57, 97; CD 5; CP 7; DAM POET;
DLB 5; INT CANR-36; MTCW 2; SATA
65; WP
Kochanowski, Jan 1530-1584 .... **LC 10**
See also RGWL 2, 3
Kock, Charles Paul de 1794-1871 . **NCLC 16**
Koda Rohan
See Koda Shigeyuki
Koda Rohan
See Koda Shigeyuki
See also DLB 180
Koda Shigeyuki 1867-1947 .... **TCLC 22**
See Koda Rohan
See also CA 121; 183
Koestler, Arthur 1905-1983 ... **CLC 1, 3, 6, 8,
15, 33**
See also BRWS 1; CA 1-4R; 109; CANR 1,
33; CDBLB 1945-1960; DLBY 1983;
EWL 3; MTCW 1, 2; RGEL 2
Kogawa, Joy Nozomi 1935- ...... **CLC 78, 129**
See also AAYA 47; CA 101; CANR 19, 62;
CN 7; CWP; DAC; DAM MST, MULT;
FW; MTCW 2; NFS 3; SATA 99
Kohout, Pavel 1928- .... **CLC 13**
See also CA 45-48; CANR 3
Koizumi, Yakumo
See Hearn, (Patricio) Lafcadio (Tessima
Carlos)
Kolmar, Gertrud 1894-1943 .... **TCLC 40**
See also CA 167; EWL 3
Komunyakaa, Yusef 1947- .. **BLCS; CLC 86,
94**
See also AFAW 2; CA 147; CANR 83; CP
7; CSW; DLB 120; EWL 3; PFS 5; RGAL
4
Konrad, George
See Konrad, Gyorgy
See also CWW 2
Konrad, Gyorgy 1933- .... **CLC 4, 10, 73**
See Konrad, George
See also CA 85-88; CANR 97; CDWLB 4;
CWW 2; DLB 232; EWL 3
Konwicki, Tadeusz 1926- .... **CLC 8, 28, 54,
117**
See also CA 101; CAAS 9; CANR 39, 59;
CWW 2; DLB 232; EWL 3; IDFW 3;
MTCW 1
Koontz, Dean R(ay) 1945- .... **CLC 78**
See also AAYA 9, 31; BEST 89:3, 90:2; CA
108; CANR 19, 36, 52, 95; CMW 4;
CPW; DA3; DAM NOV, POP; HGG;
MTCW 1; SATA 92; SFW 4; SUFW 2;
YAW
Kopernik, Mikolaj
See Copernicus, Nicolaus

Kopit, Arthur (Lee) 1937- ...... **CLC 1, 18, 33**
See also AITN 1; CA 81-84; CABS 3; CD
5; DAM DRAM; DFS 7, 14; DLB 7;
MTCW 1; RGAL 4
Kopitar, Jernej (Bartholomaus)
1780-1844 .... **NCLC 117**
Kops, Bernard 1926- .... **CLC 4**
See also CA 5-8R; CANR 84; CBD; CN 7;
CP 7; DLB 13
Kornbluth, C(yril) M. 1923-1958 .... **TCLC 8**
See also CA 105; 160; DLB 8; SFW 4
Korolenko, V. G.
See Korolenko, Vladimir Galaktionovich
Korolenko, Vladimir
See Korolenko, Vladimir Galaktionovich
Korolenko, Vladimir G.
See Korolenko, Vladimir Galaktionovich
Korolenko, Vladimir Galaktionovich
1853-1921 .... **TCLC 22**
See also CA 121; DLB 277
Korzybski, Alfred (Habdank Skarbek)
1879-1950 .... **TCLC 61**
See also CA 123; 160
Kosinski, Jerzy (Nikodem)
1933-1991 .... **CLC 1, 2, 3, 6, 10, 15, 53,
70**
See also AMWS 7; BPFB 2; CA 17-20R;
134; CANR 9, 46; DA3; DAM NOV;
DLB 2; DLBY 1982; EWL 3; HGG;
MTCW 1, 2; NFS 12; RGAL 4; TUS
Kostelanetz, Richard (Cory) 1940- .. **CLC 28**
See also CA 13-16R; CAAS 8; CANR 38,
77; CN 7; CP 7
Kostrowitzki, Wilhelm Apollinaris de
1880-1918
See Apollinaire, Guillaume
See also CA 104
Kotlowitz, Robert 1924- .... **CLC 4**
See also CA 33-36R; CANR 36
Kotzebue, August (Friedrich Ferdinand) von
1761-1819 .... **NCLC 25**
See also DLB 94
Kotzwinkle, William 1938- ..... **CLC 5, 14, 35**
See also BPFB 2; CA 45-48; CANR 3, 44,
84; CLR 6; DLB 173; FANT; MAICYA
1, 2; SATA 24, 70; SFW 4; SUFW 2;
YAW
Kowna, Stancy
See Szymborska, Wislawa
Kozol, Jonathan 1936- .... **CLC 17**
See also AAYA 46; CA 61-64; CANR 16,
45, 96
Kozoll, Michael 1940(?)- .... **CLC 35**
Kramer, Kathryn 19(?)- .... **CLC 34**
Kramer, Larry 1935- .... **CLC 42; DC 8**
See also CA 124; 126; CANR 60; DAM
POP; DLB 249; GLL 1
Krasicki, Ignacy 1735-1801 .... **NCLC 8**
Krasinski, Zygmunt 1812-1859 .... **NCLC 4**
See also RGWL 2, 3
Kraus, Karl 1874-1936 .... **TCLC 5**
See also CA 104; DLB 118; EWL 3
Kreve (Mickevicius), Vincas
1882-1954 .... **TCLC 27**
See also CA 170; DLB 220; EWL 3
Kristeva, Julia 1941- .... **CLC 77, 140**
See also CA 154; CANR 99; DLB 242;
EWL 3; FW; LMFS 2
Kristofferson, Kris 1936- .... **CLC 26**
See also CA 104
Krizanc, John 1956- .... **CLC 57**
See also CA 187
Krleza, Miroslav 1893-1981 .... **CLC 8, 114**
See also CA 97-100; 105; CANR 50; CD-
WLB 4; DLB 147; EW 11; RGWL 2, 3
Kroetsch, Robert 1927- ... **CLC 5, 23, 57, 132**
See also CA 17-20R; CANR 8, 38; CCA 1;
CN 7; CP 7; DAC; DAM POET; DLB 53;
MTCW 1

Leskov, Nikolai (Semyonovich)
1831-1895 .... NCLC **25**; SSC **34**
See Leskov, Nikolai Semenovich

Leskov, Nikolai Semenovich
See Leskov, Nikolai (Semyonovich)
See also DLB 238

Lesser, Milton
See Marlowe, Stephen

Lessing, Doris (May) 1919- ... CLC **1, 2, 3, 6, 10, 15, 22, 40, 94, 170; SSC 6, 61; WLCS**
See also AFW; BRWS 1; CA 9-12R; CAAS 14; CANR 33, 54, 76; CD 5; CDBLB 1960 to Present; CN 7; DA; DA3; DAB; DAC; DAM MST, NOV; DLB 15, 139; DLBY 1985; EWL 3; EXPS; FW; LAIT 4; MTCW 1, 2; RGEL 2; RGSF 2; SFW 4; SSFS 1, 12; TEA; WLIT 2, 4

Lessing, Gotthold Ephraim 1729-1781 . LC **8**
See also CDWLB 2; DLB 97; EW 4; RGWL 2, 3

Lester, Richard 1932- .... CLC **20**

Levenson, Jay .... CLC **70**

Lever, Charles (James)
1806-1872 .... NCLC **23**
See also DLB 21; RGEL 2

Leverson, Ada Esther
1862(?)-1933(?) .... TCLC **18**
See Elaine
See also CA 117; 202; DLB 153; RGEL 2

Levertov, Denise 1923-1997 .. CLC **1, 2, 3, 5, 8, 15, 28, 66; PC 11**
See also AMWS 3; CA 1-4R, 178; 163; CAAE 178; CAAS 19; CANR 3, 29, 50, 108; CDALBS; CP 7; CWP; DAM POET; DLB 5, 165; EWL 3; EXPP; FW; INT CANR-29; MTCW 1, 2; PAB; PFS 7, 16; RGAL 4; TUS; WP

Levi, Carlo 1902-1975 .... TCLC **125**
See also CA 65-68; 53-56; CANR 10; EWL 3; RGWL 2, 3

Levi, Jonathan .... CLC **76**
See also CA 197

Levi, Peter (Chad Tigar)
1931-2000 .... CLC **41**
See also CA 5-8R; 187; CANR 34, 80; CP 7; DLB 40

Levi, Primo 1919-1987 ...... CLC **37, 50; SSC 12; TCLC 109**
See also CA 13-16R; 122; CANR 12, 33, 61, 70; DLB 177; EWL 3; MTCW 1, 2; RGWL 2, 3

Levin, Ira 1929- .... CLC **3, 6**
See also CA 21-24R; CANR 17, 44, 74; CMW 4; CN 7; CPW; DA3; DAM POP; HGG; MTCW 1, 2; SATA 66; SFW 4

Levin, Meyer 1905-1981 .... CLC **7**
See also AITN 1; CA 9-12R; 104; CANR 15; DAM POP; DLB 9, 28; DLBY 1981; SATA 21; SATA-Obit 27

Levine, Norman 1924- .... CLC **54**
See also CA 73-76; CAAS 23; CANR 14, 70; DLB 88

Levine, Philip 1928- .. CLC **2, 4, 5, 9, 14, 33, 118; PC 22**
See also AMWS 5; CA 9-12R; CANR 9, 37, 52, 116; CP 7; DAM POET; DLB 5; EWL 3; PFS 8

Levinson, Deirdre 1931- .... CLC **49**
See also CA 73-76; CANR 70

Levi-Strauss, Claude 1908- .... CLC **38**
See also CA 1-4R; CANR 6, 32, 57; DLB 242; EWL 3; GFL 1789 to the Present; MTCW 1, 2; TWA

Levitin, Sonia (Wolff) 1934- .... CLC **17**
See also AAYA 13, 48; CA 29-32R; CANR 14, 32, 79; CLR 53; JRDA; MAICYA 1, 2; SAAS 2; SATA 4, 68, 119; SATA-Essay 131; YAW

Levon, O. U.
See Kesey, Ken (Elton)

Levy, Amy 1861-1889 .... NCLC **59**
See also DLB 156, 240

Lewes, George Henry 1817-1878 ... NCLC **25**
See also DLB 55, 144

Lewis, Alun 1915-1944 .... SSC **40; TCLC 3**
See also BRW 7; CA 104; 188; DLB 20, 162; PAB; RGEL 2

Lewis, C. Day
See Day Lewis, C(ecil)

Lewis, C(live) S(taples) 1898-1963 .... CLC **1, 3, 6, 14, 27, 124; WLC**
See also AAYA 3, 39; BPFB 2; BRWS 3; CA 81-84; CANR 33, 71; CDBLB 1945-1960; CLR 3, 27; CWRI 5; DA; DA3; DAB; DAC; DAM MST, NOV, POP; DLB 15, 100, 160, 255; EWL 3; FANT; JRDA; LMFS 2; MAICYA 1, 2; MTCW 1, 2; RGEL 2; SATA 13, 100; SCFW; SFW 4; SUFW 1; TEA; WCH; WYA; YAW

Lewis, Cecil Day
See Day Lewis, C(ecil)

Lewis, Janet 1899-1998 .... CLC **41**
See Winters, Janet Lewis
See also CA 9-12R; 172; CANR 29, 63; CAP 1; CN 7; DLBY 1987; RHW; TCWW 2

Lewis, Matthew Gregory
1775-1818 .... NCLC **11, 62**
See also DLB 39, 158, 178; HGG; LMFS 1; RGEL 2; SUFW

Lewis, (Harry) Sinclair 1885-1951 . TCLC **4, 13, 23, 39; WLC**
See also AMW; AMWC 1; BPFB 2; CA 104; 133; CDALB 1917-1929; DA; DA3; DAB; DAC; DAM MST, NOV; DLB 9, 102, 284; DLBD 1; EWL 3; LAIT 3; MTCW 1, 2; NFS 15; RGAL 4; TUS

Lewis, (Percy) Wyndham
1884(?)-1957 .. SSC **34; TCLC 2, 9, 104**
See also BRW 7; CA 104; 157; DLB 15; EWL 3; FANT; MTCW 2; RGEL 2

Lewisohn, Ludwig 1883-1955 .... TCLC **19**
See also CA 107; 203; DLB 4, 9, 28, 102

Lewton, Val 1904-1951 .... TCLC **76**
See also CA 199; IDFW 3, 4

Leyner, Mark 1956- .... CLC **92**
See also CA 110; CANR 28, 53; DA3; MTCW 2

Lezama Lima, Jose 1910-1976 .... CLC **4, 10, 101; HLCS 2**
See also CA 77-80; CANR 71; DAM MULT; DLB 113; EWL 3; HW 1, 2; LAW; RGWL 2, 3

L'Heureux, John (Clarke) 1934- ...... CLC **52**
See also CA 13-16R; CANR 23, 45, 88; DLB 244

Liddell, C. H.
See Kuttner, Henry

Lie, Jonas (Lauritz Idemil)
1833-1908(?) .... TCLC **5**
See also CA 115

Lieber, Joel 1937-1971 .... CLC **6**
See also CA 73-76; 29-32R

Lieber, Stanley Martin
See Lee, Stan

Lieberman, Laurence (James)
1935- .... CLC **4, 36**
See also CA 17-20R; CANR 8, 36, 89; CP 7

Lieh Tzu fl. 7th cent. B.C.-5th cent.
B.C. .... CMLC **27**

Lieksman, Anders
See Haavikko, Paavo Juhani

Li Fei-kan 1904-
See Pa Chin
See also CA 105; TWA

Lifton, Robert Jay 1926- .... CLC **67**
See also CA 17-20R; CANR 27, 78; INT CANR-27; SATA 66

Lightfoot, Gordon 1938- .... CLC **26**
See also CA 109

Lightman, Alan P(aige) 1948- .... CLC **81**
See also CA 141; CANR 63, 105

Ligotti, Thomas (Robert) 1953- ...... CLC **44; SSC 16**
See also CA 123; CANR 49; HGG; SUFW 2

Li Ho 791-817 .... PC **13**

Liliencron, (Friedrich Adolf Axel) Detlev von 1844-1909 .... TCLC **18**
See also CA 117

Lille, Alain de
See Alain de Lille

Lilly, William 1602-1681 .... LC **27**

Lima, Jose Lezama
See Lezama Lima, Jose

Lima Barreto, Afonso Henrique de
1881-1922 .... TCLC **23**
See also CA 117; 181; LAW

Lima Barreto, Afonso Henriques de
See Lima Barreto, Afonso Henrique de

Limonov, Edward 1944- .... CLC **67**
See also CA 137

Lin, Frank
See Atherton, Gertrude (Franklin Horn)

Lincoln, Abraham 1809-1865 .... NCLC **18**
See also LAIT 2

Lind, Jakov .... CLC **1, 2, 4, 27, 82**
See Landwirth, Heinz
See also CAAS 4; EWL 3

Lindbergh, Anne (Spencer) Morrow
1906-2001 .... CLC **82**
See also BPFB 2; CA 17-20R; 193; CANR 16, 73; DAM NOV; MTCW 1, 2; SATA 33; SATA-Obit 125; TUS

Lindsay, David 1878(?)-1945 .... TCLC **15**
See also CA 113; 187; DLB 255; FANT; SFW 4; SUFW 1

Lindsay, (Nicholas) Vachel
1879-1931 .... PC **23; TCLC 17; WLC**
See also AMWS 1; CA 114; 135; CANR 79; CDALB 1865-1917; DA; DA3; DAC; DAM MST, POET; DLB 54; EWL 3; EXPP; RGAL 4; SATA 40; WP

Linke-Poot
See Doeblin, Alfred

Linney, Romulus 1930- .... CLC **51**
See also CA 1-4R; CAD; CANR 40, 44, 79; CD 5; CSW; RGAL 4

Linton, Eliza Lynn 1822-1898 .... NCLC **41**
See also DLB 18

Li Po 701-763 .... CMLC **2; PC 29**
See also WP

Lipsius, Justus 1547-1606 .... LC **16**

Lipsyte, Robert (Michael) 1938- ...... CLC **21**
See also AAYA 7, 45; CA 17-20R; CANR 8, 57; CLR 23, 76; DA; DAM MST, NOV; JRDA; LAIT 5; MAICYA 1, 2; SATA 5, 68, 113; WYA; YAW

Lish, Gordon (Jay) 1934- ... CLC **45; SSC 18**
See also CA 113; 117; CANR 79; DLB 130; INT 117

Lispector, Clarice 1925(?)-1977 .... CLC **43; HLCS 2; SSC 34**
See also CA 139; 116; CANR 71; CDWLB 3; DLB 113; DNFS 1; EWL 3; FW; HW 2; LAW; RGSF 2; RGWL 2, 3; WLIT 1

Littell, Robert 1935(?)- .... CLC **42**
See also CA 109; 112; CANR 64, 115; CMW 4

Little, Malcolm 1925-1965
See Malcolm X
See also BW 1, 3; CA 125; 111; CANR 82; DA; DA3; DAB; DAC; DAM MST, MULT; MTCW 1, 2; NCFS 3

Lucas, E(dward) V(errall)
  1868-1938 .... **TCLC 73**
  See also CA 176; DLB 98, 149, 153; SATA
  20
Lucas, George 1944- .... **CLC 16**
  See also AAYA 1, 23; CA 77-80; CANR
  30; SATA 56
Lucas, Hans
  See Godard, Jean-Luc
Lucas, Victoria
  See Plath, Sylvia
Lucian c. 125-c. 180 .... **CMLC 32**
  See also AW 2; DLB 176; RGWL 2, 3
Lucretius c. 94B.C.-c. 49B.C. .... **CMLC 48**
  See also AW 2; CDWLB 1; DLB 211; EFS
  2; RGWL 2, 3
Ludlam, Charles 1943-1987 .... **CLC 46, 50**
  See also CA 85-88; 122; CAD; CANR 72,
  86; DLB 266
Ludlum, Robert 1927-2001 .... **CLC 22, 43**
  See also AAYA 10; BEST 89:1, 90:3; BPFB
  2; CA 33-36R; 195; CANR 25, 41, 68,
  105; CMW 4; CPW; DA3; DAM NOV,
  POP; DLBY 1982; MSW; MTCW 1, 2
Ludwig, Ken .... **CLC 60**
  See also CA 195; CAD
Ludwig, Otto 1813-1865 .... **NCLC 4**
  See also DLB 129
Lugones, Leopoldo 1874-1938 .... **HLCS 2;**
    TCLC 15
  See also CA 116; 131; CANR 104; EWL 3;
  HW 1; LAW
Lu Hsun .... **SSC 20; TCLC 3**
  See Shu-Jen, Chou
  See also EWL 3
Lukacs, George .... **CLC 24**
  See Lukacs, Gyorgy (Szegeny von)
Lukacs, Gyorgy (Szegeny von) 1885-1971
  See Lukacs, George
  See also CA 101; 29-32R; CANR 62; CD-
  WLB 4; DLB 215, 242; EW 10; EWL 3;
  MTCW 2
Luke, Peter (Ambrose Cyprian)
  1919-1995 .... **CLC 38**
  See also CA 81-84; 147; CANR 72; CBD;
  CD 5; DLB 13
Lunar, Dennis
  See Mungo, Raymond
Lurie, Alison 1926- ..... **CLC 4, 5, 18, 39, 175**
  See also BPFB 2; CA 1-4R; CANR 2, 17,
  50, 88; CN 7; DLB 2; MTCW 1; SATA
  46, 112
Lustig, Arnost 1926- .... **CLC 56**
  See also AAYA 3; CA 69-72; CANR 47,
  102; CWW 2; DLB 232; EWL 3; SATA
  56
Luther, Martin 1483-1546 .... **LC 9, 37**
  See also CDWLB 2; DLB 179; EW 2;
  RGWL 2, 3
Luxemburg, Rosa 1870(?)-1919 ..... **TCLC 63**
  See also CA 118
Luzi, Mario 1914- .... **CLC 13**
  See also CA 61-64; CANR 9, 70; CWW 2;
  DLB 128; EWL 3
L'vov, Arkady .... **CLC 59**
Lydgate, John c. 1370-1450(?) .... **LC 81**
  See also BRW 1; DLB 146; RGEL 2
Lyly, John 1554(?)-1606 .... **DC 7; LC 41**
  See also BRW 1; DAM DRAM; DLB 62,
  167; RGEL 2
L'Ymagier
  See Gourmont, Remy(-Marie-Charles) de
Lynch, B. Suarez
  See Borges, Jorge Luis
Lynch, David (Keith) 1946- ...... **CLC 66, 162**
  See also CA 124; 129; CANR 111
Lynch, James
  See Andreyev, Leonid (Nikolaevich)

Lyndsay, Sir David 1485-1555 .... **LC 20**
  See also RGEL 2
Lynn, Kenneth S(chuyler)
  1923-2001 .... **CLC 50**
  See also CA 1-4R; 196; CANR 3, 27, 65
Lynx
  See West, Rebecca
Lyons, Marcus
  See Blish, James (Benjamin)
Lyotard, Jean-Francois
  1924-1998 .... **TCLC 103**
  See also DLB 242; EWL 3
Lyre, Pinchbeck
  See Sassoon, Siegfried (Lorraine)
Lytle, Andrew (Nelson) 1902-1995 ... **CLC 22**
  See also CA 9-12R; 150; CANR 70; CN 7;
  CSW; DLB 6; DLBY 1995; RGAL 4;
  RHW
Lyttelton, George 1709-1773 .... **LC 10**
  See also RGEL 2
Lytton of Knebworth, Baron
  See Bulwer-Lytton, Edward (George Earle
  Lytton)
Maas, Peter 1929-2001 .... **CLC 29**
  See also CA 93-96; 201; INT CA-93-96;
  MTCW 2
Macaulay, Catherine 1731-1791 .... **LC 64**
  See also DLB 104
Macaulay, (Emilie) Rose
  1881(?)-1958 .... **TCLC 7, 44**
  See also CA 104; DLB 36; EWL 3; RGEL
  2; RHW
Macaulay, Thomas Babington
  1800-1859 .... **NCLC 42**
  See also BRW 4; CDBLB 1832-1890; DLB
  32, 55; RGEL 2
MacBeth, George (Mann)
  1932-1992 .... **CLC 2, 5, 9**
  See also CA 25-28R; 136; CANR 61, 66;
  DLB 40; MTCW 1; PFS 8; SATA 4;
  SATA-Obit 70
MacCaig, Norman (Alexander)
  1910-1996 .... **CLC 36**
  See also BRWS 6; CA 9-12R; CANR 3, 34;
  CP 7; DAB; DAM POET; DLB 27; EWL
  3; RGEL 2
MacCarthy, Sir (Charles Otto) Desmond
  1877-1952 .... **TCLC 36**
  See also CA 167
MacDiarmid, Hugh .... **CLC 2, 4, 11, 19, 63;**
    PC 9
  See Grieve, C(hristopher) M(urray)
  See also CDBLB 1945-1960; DLB 20;
  EWL 3; RGEL 2
MacDonald, Anson
  See Heinlein, Robert A(nson)
Macdonald, Cynthia 1928- .... **CLC 13, 19**
  See also CA 49-52; CANR 4, 44; DLB 105
MacDonald, George 1824-1905 .... **TCLC 9,**
    113
  See also BYA 5; CA 106; 137; CANR 80;
  CLR 67; DLB 18, 163, 178; FANT; MAI-
  CYA 1, 2; RGEL 2; SATA 33, 100; SFW
  4; SUFW; WCH
Macdonald, John
  See Millar, Kenneth
MacDonald, John D(ann)
  1916-1986 .... **CLC 3, 27, 44**
  See also BPFB 2; CA 1-4R; 121; CANR 1,
  19, 60; CMW 4; CPW; DAM NOV, POP;
  DLB 8; DLBY 1986; MSW; MTCW 1, 2;
  SFW 4
Macdonald, John Ross
  See Millar, Kenneth
Macdonald, Ross ..... **CLC 1, 2, 3, 14, 34, 41**
  See Millar, Kenneth
  See also AMWS 4; BPFB 2; DLBD 6;
  MSW; RGAL 4

MacDougal, John
  See Blish, James (Benjamin)
MacDougal, John
  See Blish, James (Benjamin)
MacDowell, John
  See Parks, Tim(othy Harold)
MacEwen, Gwendolyn (Margaret)
  1941-1987 .... **CLC 13, 55**
  See also CA 9-12R; 124; CANR 7, 22; DLB
  53, 251; SATA 50; SATA-Obit 55
Macha, Karel Hynek 1810-1846 .... **NCLC 46**
Machado (y Ruiz), Antonio
  1875-1939 .... **TCLC 3**
  See also CA 104; 174; DLB 108; EW 9;
  EWL 3; HW 2; RGWL 2, 3
Machado de Assis, Joaquim Maria
  1839-1908 .... **BLC 2; HLCS 2; SSC 24;**
    TCLC 10
  See also CA 107; 153; CANR 91; LAW;
  RGSF 2; RGWL 2, 3; TWA; WLIT 1
Machen, Arthur .... **SSC 20; TCLC 4**
  See Jones, Arthur Llewellyn
  See also CA 179; DLB 156, 178; RGEL 2;
  SUFW 1
Machiavelli, Niccolo 1469-1527 ... **DC 16; LC**
    8, 36; WLCS
  See also DA; DAB; DAC; DAM MST; EW
  2; LAIT 1; LMFS 1; NFS 9; RGWL 2, 3;
  TWA
MacInnes, Colin 1914-1976 .... **CLC 4, 23**
  See also CA 69-72; 65-68; CANR 21; DLB
  14; MTCW 1, 2; RGEL 2; RHW
MacInnes, Helen (Clark)
  1907-1985 .... **CLC 27, 39**
  See also BPFB 2; CA 1-4R; 117; CANR 1,
  28, 58; CMW 4; CPW; DAM POP; DLB
  87; MSW; MTCW 1, 2; SATA 22; SATA-
  Obit 44
Mackay, Mary 1855-1924
  See Corelli, Marie
  See also CA 118; 177; FANT; RHW
Mackenzie, Compton (Edward Montague)
  1883-1972 .... **CLC 18; TCLC 116**
  See also CA 21-22; 37-40R; CAP 2; DLB
  34, 100; RGEL 2
Mackenzie, Henry 1745-1831 .... **NCLC 41**
  See also DLB 39; RGEL 2
Mackintosh, Elizabeth 1896(?)-1952
  See Tey, Josephine
  See also CA 110; CMW 4
MacLaren, James
  See Grieve, C(hristopher) M(urray)
Mac Laverty, Bernard 1942- .... **CLC 31**
  See also CA 116; 118; CANR 43, 88; CN
  7; DLB 267; INT CA-118; RGSF 2
MacLean, Alistair (Stuart)
  1922(?)-1987 .... **CLC 3, 13, 50, 63**
  See also CA 57-60; 121; CANR 28, 61;
  CMW 4; CPW; DAM POP; DLB 276;
  MTCW 1; SATA 23; SATA-Obit 50;
  TCWW 2
Maclean, Norman (Fitzroy)
  1902-1990 .... **CLC 78; SSC 13**
  See also CA 102; 132; CANR 49; CPW;
  DAM POP; DLB 206; TCWW 2
MacLeish, Archibald 1892-1982 ... **CLC 3, 8,**
    14, 68; PC 47
  See also AMW; CA 9-12R; 106; CAD;
  CANR 33; CDALBS; DAM POET;
  DFS 15; DLB 4, 7, 45; DLBY 1982; EWL
  3; EXPP; MTCW 1, 2; PAB; PFS 5;
  RGAL 4; TUS
MacLennan, (John) Hugh
  1907-1990 .... **CLC 2, 14, 92**
  See also CA 5-8R; 142; CANR 33; DAC;
  DAM MST; DLB 68; EWL 3; MTCW 1,
  2; RGEL 2; TWA

Manning, Olivia 1915-1980 .... **CLC 5, 19**
  See also CA 5-8R; 101; CANR 29; EWL 3;
  FW; MTCW 1; RGEL 2

Mano, D. Keith 1942- .... **CLC 2, 10**
  See also CA 25-28R; CAAS 6; CANR 26,
  57; DLB 6

Mansfield, Katherine . **SSC 9, 23, 38; TCLC**
  2, 8, 39; WLC
  See Beauchamp, Kathleen Mansfield
  See also BPFB 2; BRW 7; DAB; DLB 162;
  EWL 3; EXPS; FW; GLL 1; RGEL 2;
  RGSF 2; SSFS 2, 8, 10, 11

Manso, Peter 1940- .... **CLC 39**
  See also CA 29-32R; CANR 44

Mantecon, Juan Jimenez
  See Jimenez (Mantecon), Juan Ramon

Mantel, Hilary (Mary) 1952- .... **CLC 144**
  See also CA 125; CANR 54, 101; CN 7;
  DLB 271; RHW

Manton, Peter
  See Creasey, John

Man Without a Spleen, A
  See Chekhov, Anton (Pavlovich)

Manzoni, Alessandro 1785-1873 ... **NCLC 29,**
  98
  See also EW 5; RGWL 2, 3; TWA

Map, Walter 1140-1209 .... **CMLC 32**

Mapu, Abraham (ben Jekutiel)
  1808-1867 .... **NCLC 18**

Mara, Sally
  See Queneau, Raymond

Maracle, Lee 1950- .... **NNAL**
  See also CA 149

Marat, Jean Paul 1743-1793 .... **LC 10**

Marcel, Gabriel Honore 1889-1973 . **CLC 15**
  See also CA 102; 45-48; EWL 3; MTCW 1,
  2

March, William 1893-1954 .... **TCLC 96**

Marchbanks, Samuel
  See Davies, (William) Robertson
  See also CCA 1

Marchi, Giacomo
  See Bassani, Giorgio

Marcus Aurelius
  See Aurelius, Marcus
  See also AW 2

Marguerite
  See de Navarre, Marguerite

Marguerite d'Angouleme
  See de Navarre, Marguerite
  See also GFL Beginnings to 1789

Marguerite de Navarre
  See de Navarre, Marguerite
  See also RGWL 2, 3

Margulies, Donald 1954- .... **CLC 76**
  See also CA 200; DFS 13; DLB 228

Marie de France c. 12th cent. - ..... **CMLC 8;**
  PC 22
  See also DLB 208; FW; RGWL 2, 3

Marie de l'Incarnation 1599-1672 ...... **LC 10**

Marier, Captain Victor
  See Griffith, D(avid Lewelyn) W(ark)

Mariner, Scott
  See Pohl, Frederik

Marinetti, Filippo Tommaso
  1876-1944 .... **TCLC 10**
  See also CA 107; DLB 114, 264; EW 9;
  EWL 3

Marivaux, Pierre Carlet de Chamblain de
  1688-1763 .... **DC 7; LC 4**
  See also GFL Beginnings to 1789; RGWL
  2, 3; TWA

Markandaya, Kamala .... **CLC 8, 38**
  See Taylor, Kamala (Purnaiya)
  See also BYA 13; CN 7; EWL 3

Markfield, Wallace 1926-2002 .... **CLC 8**
  See also CA 69-72; 208; CAAS 3; CN 7;
  DLB 2, 28; DLBY 2002

Markham, Edwin 1852-1940 .... **TCLC 47**
  See also CA 160; DLB 54, 186; RGAL 4

Markham, Robert
  See Amis, Kingsley (William)

Markoosie .... **NNAL**
  See Markoosie, Patsauq
  See also CLR 23; DAM MULT

Marks, J
  See Highwater, Jamake (Mamake)

Marks, J.
  See Highwater, Jamake (Mamake)

Marks-Highwater, J
  See Highwater, Jamake (Mamake)

Marks-Highwater, J.
  See Highwater, Jamake (Mamake)

Markson, David M(errill) 1927- .... **CLC 67**
  See also CA 49-52; CANR 1, 91; CN 7

Marlatt, Daphne (Buckle) 1942- .... **CLC 168**
  See also CA 25-28R; CANR 17, 39; CN 7;
  CP 7; CWP; DLB 60; FW

Marley, Bob .... **CLC 17**
  See Marley, Robert Nesta

Marley, Robert Nesta 1945-1981
  See Marley, Bob
  See also CA 107; 103

Marlowe, Christopher 1564-1593 . **DC 1; LC**
  22, 47; WLC
  See also BRW 1; BRWR 1; CDBLB Before
  1660; DA; DA3; DAB; DAC; DAM
  DRAM, MST; DFS 1, 5, 13; DLB 62;
  EXPP; LMFS 1; RGEL 2; TEA; WLIT 3

Marlowe, Stephen 1928- .... **CLC 70**
  See Queen, Ellery
  See also CA 13-16R; CANR 6, 55; CMW
  4; SFW 4

Marmion, Shakerley 1603-1639 .... **LC 89**
  See also DLB 58; RGEL 2

Marmontel, Jean-Francois 1723-1799 .. **LC 2**

Maron, Monika 1941- .... **CLC 165**
  See also CA 201

Marquand, John P(hillips)
  1893-1960 .... **CLC 2, 10**
  See also AMW; BPFB 2; CA 85-88; CANR
  73; CMW 4; DLB 9, 102; EWL 3; MTCW
  2; RGAL 4

Marques, Rene 1919-1979 .. **CLC 96; HLC 2**
  See also CA 97-100; 85-88; CANR 78;
  DAM MULT; DLB 113; EWL 3; HW 1,
  2; LAW; RGSF 2

Marquez, Gabriel (Jose) Garcia
  See Garcia Marquez, Gabriel (Jose)

Marquis, Don(ald Robert Perry)
  1878-1937 .... **TCLC 7**
  See also CA 104; 166; DLB 11, 25; RGAL
  4

Marquis de Sade
  See Sade, Donatien Alphonse Francois

Marric, J. J.
  See Creasey, John
  See also MSW

Marryat, Frederick 1792-1848 .... **NCLC 3**
  See also DLB 21, 163; RGEL 2; WCH

Marsden, James
  See Creasey, John

Marsh, Edward 1872-1953 .... **TCLC 99**

Marsh, (Edith) Ngaio 1899-1982 .. **CLC 7, 53**
  See also CA 9-12R; CANR 6, 58; CMW 4;
  CPW; DAM POP; DLB 77; MSW;
  MTCW 1, 2; RGEL 2; TEA

Marshall, Garry 1934- .... **CLC 17**
  See also AAYA 3; CA 111; SATA 60

Marshall, Paule 1929- .. **BLC 3; CLC 27, 72;**
  SSC 3
  See also AFAW 1, 2; AMWS 11; BPFB 2;
  BW 2, 3; CA 77-80; CANR 25, 73; CN 7;
  DA3; DAM MULT; DLB 33, 157, 227;
  EWL 3; LATS 1; MTCW 1, 2; RGAL 4;
  SSFS 15

Marshallik
  See Zangwill, Israel

Marsten, Richard
  See Hunter, Evan

Marston, John 1576-1634 .... **LC 33**
  See also BRW 2; DAM DRAM; DLB 58,
  172; RGEL 2

Martha, Henry
  See Harris, Mark

Marti (y Perez), Jose (Julian)
  1853-1895 .... **HLC 2; NCLC 63**
  See also DAM MULT; HW 2; LAW; RGWL
  2, 3; WLIT 1

Martial c. 40-c. 104 .... **CMLC 35; PC 10**
  See also AW 2; CDWLB 1; DLB 211;
  RGWL 2, 3

Martin, Ken
  See Hubbard, L(afayette) Ron(ald)

Martin, Richard
  See Creasey, John

Martin, Steve 1945- .... **CLC 30**
  See also CA 97-100; CANR 30, 100;
  MTCW 1

Martin, Valerie 1948- .... **CLC 89**
  See also BEST 90:2; CA 85-88; CANR 49,
  89

Martin, Violet Florence 1862-1915 .. **SSC 56;**
  TCLC 51

Martin, Webber
  See Silverberg, Robert

Martindale, Patrick Victor
  See White, Patrick (Victor Martindale)

Martin du Gard, Roger
  1881-1958 .... **TCLC 24**
  See also CA 118; CANR 94; DLB 65; EWL
  3; GFL 1789 to the Present; RGWL 2, 3

Martineau, Harriet 1802-1876 .... **NCLC 26**
  See also DLB 21, 55, 159, 163, 166, 190;
  FW; RGEL 2; YABC 2

Martines, Julia
  See O'Faolain, Julia

Martinez, Enrique Gonzalez
  See Gonzalez Martinez, Enrique

Martinez, Jacinto Benavente y
  See Benavente (y Martinez), Jacinto

Martinez de la Rosa, Francisco de Paula
  1787-1862 .... **NCLC 102**
  See also TWA

Martinez Ruiz, Jose 1873-1967
  See Azorin; Ruiz, Jose Martinez
  See also CA 93-96; HW 1

Martinez Sierra, Gregorio
  1881-1947 .... **TCLC 6**
  See also CA 115; EWL 3

Martinez Sierra, Maria (de la O'LeJarraga)
  1874-1974 .... **TCLC 6**
  See also CA 115; EWL 3

Martinsen, Martin
  See Follett, Ken(neth Martin)

Martinson, Harry (Edmund)
  1904-1978 .... **CLC 14**
  See also CA 77-80; CANR 34; DLB 259;
  EWL 3

Martyn, Edward 1859-1923 .... **TCLC 131**
  See also CA 179; DLB 10; RGEL 2

Marut, Ret
  See Traven, B.

Marut, Robert
  See Traven, B.

Marvell, Andrew 1621-1678 .... **LC 4, 43; PC**
  10; WLC
  See also BRW 2; BRWR 2; CDBLB 1660-
  1789; DA; DAB; DAC; DAM MST,
  POET; DLB 131; EXPP; PFS 5; RGEL 2;
  TEA; WP

Marx, Karl (Heinrich)
  1818-1883 .... **NCLC 17, 114**
  See also DLB 129; LATS 1; TWA

McCorkle, Jill (Collins) 1958- .... **CLC 51**
See also CA 121; CANR 113; CSW; DLB
234; DLBY 1987

McCourt, Frank 1930- .... **CLC 109**
See also AMWS 12; CA 157; CANR 97;
NCFS 1

McCourt, James 1941- .... **CLC 5**
See also CA 57-60; CANR 98

McCourt, Malachy 1931- .... **CLC 119**
See also SATA 126

McCoy, Horace (Stanley)
1897-1955 .... **TCLC 28**
See also CA 108; 155; CMW 4; DLB 9

McCrae, John 1872-1918 .... **TCLC 12**
See also CA 109; DLB 92; PFS 5

McCreigh, James
See Pohl, Frederik

McCullers, (Lula) Carson (Smith)
1917-1967 .... **CLC 1, 4, 10, 12, 48, 100;**
SSC 9, 24; WLC
See also AAYA 21; AMW; BPFB 2; CA
5-8R; 25-28R; CABS 1, 3; CANR 18;
CDALB 1941-1968; DA; DA3; DAB;
DAC; DAM MST, NOV; DFS 5; DLB 2,
7, 173, 228; EWL 3; EXPS; FW; GLL 1;
LAIT 3, 4; MAWW; MTCW 1, 2; NFS 6,
13; RGAL 4; RGSF 2; SATA 27; SSFS 5;
TUS; YAW

McCulloch, John Tyler
See Burroughs, Edgar Rice

McCullough, Colleen 1938(?)- .. **CLC 27, 107**
See also AAYA 36; BPFB 2; CA 81-84;
CANR 17, 46, 67, 98; CPW; DA3; DAM
NOV, POP; MTCW 1, 2; RHW

McCunn, Ruthanne Lum 1946- .... **AAL**
See also CA 119; CANR 43, 96; LAIT 2;
SATA 63

McDermott, Alice 1953- .... **CLC 90**
See also CA 109; CANR 40, 90

McElroy, Joseph 1930- .... **CLC 5, 47**
See also CA 17-20R; CN 7

McEwan, Ian (Russell) 1948- .... **CLC 13, 66,**
169
See also BEST 90:4; BRWS 4; CA 61-64;
CANR 14, 41, 69, 87; CN 7; DAM NOV;
DLB 14, 194; HGG; MTCW 1, 2; RGSF
2; SUFW 2; TEA

McFadden, David 1940- .... **CLC 48**
See also CA 104; CP 7; DLB 60; INT 104

McFarland, Dennis 1950- .... **CLC 65**
See also CA 165; CANR 110

McGahern, John 1934- ... **CLC 5, 9, 48, 156;**
SSC 17
See also CA 17-20R; CANR 29, 68, 113;
CN 7; DLB 14, 231; MTCW 1

McGinley, Patrick (Anthony) 1937- . **CLC 41**
See also CA 120; 127; CANR 56; INT 127

McGinley, Phyllis 1905-1978 .... **CLC 14**
See also CA 9-12R; 77-80; CANR 19;
CWRI 5; DLB 11, 48; PFS 9, 13; SATA
2, 44; SATA-Obit 24

McGinniss, Joe 1942- .... **CLC 32**
See also AITN 2; BEST 89:2; CA 25-28R;
CANR 26, 70; CPW; DLB 185; INT
CANR-26

McGivern, Maureen Daly
See Daly, Maureen

McGrath, Patrick 1950- .... **CLC 55**
See also CA 136; CANR 65; CN 7; DLB
231; HGG; SUFW 2

McGrath, Thomas (Matthew)
1916-1990 .... **CLC 28, 59**
See also AMWS 10; CA 9-12R; 132; CANR
6, 33, 95; DAM POET; MTCW 1; SATA
41; SATA-Obit 66

McGuane, Thomas (Francis III)
1939- .... **CLC 3, 7, 18, 45, 127**
See also AITN 2; BPFB 2; CA 49-52;
CANR 5, 24, 49, 94; CN 7; DLB 2, 212;
DLBY 1980; EWL 3; INT CANR-24;
MTCW 1; TCWW 2

McGuckian, Medbh 1950- .... **CLC 48, 174;**
PC 27
See also BRWS 5; CA 143; CP 7; CWP;
DAM POET; DLB 40

McHale, Tom 1942(?)-1982 .... **CLC 3, 5**
See also AITN 1; CA 77-80; 106

McIlvanney, William 1936- .... **CLC 42**
See also CA 25-28R; CANR 61; CMW 4;
DLB 14, 207

McIlwraith, Maureen Mollie Hunter
See Hunter, Mollie
See also SATA 2

McInerney, Jay 1955- .... **CLC 34, 112**
See also AAYA 18; BPFB 2; CA 116; 123;
CANR 45, 68, 116; CN 7; CPW; DA3;
DAM POP; INT 123; MTCW 2

McIntyre, Vonda N(eel) 1948- .... **CLC 18**
See also CA 81-84; CANR 17, 34, 69;
MTCW 1; SFW 4; YAW

McKay, Claude .... **BLC 3; HR 3; PC 2;**
TCLC 7, 41; WLC
See McKay, Festus Claudius
See also AFAW 1, 2; AMWS 10; DAB;
DLB 4, 45, 51, 117; EWL 3; EXPP; GLL
2; LAIT 3; LMFS 2; PAB; PFS 4; RGAL
4; WP

McKay, Festus Claudius 1889-1948
See McKay, Claude
See also BW 1, 3; CA 104; 124; CANR 73;
DA; DAC; DAM MST, MULT, NOV,
POET; MTCW 1, 2; TUS

McKuen, Rod 1933- .... **CLC 1, 3**
See also AITN 1; CA 41-44R; CANR 40

McLoughlin, R. B.
See Mencken, H(enry) L(ouis)

McLuhan, (Herbert) Marshall
1911-1980 .... **CLC 37, 83**
See also CA 9-12R; 102; CANR 12, 34, 61;
DLB 88; INT CANR-12; MTCW 1, 2

McManus, Declan Patrick Aloysius
See Costello, Elvis

McMillan, Terry (L.) 1951- . **BLCS; CLC 50,**
61, 112
See also AAYA 21; BPFB 2; BW 2, 3; CA
140; CANR 60, 104; CPW; DA3; DAM
MULT, NOV, POP; MTCW 2; RGAL 4;
YAW

McMurtry, Larry (Jeff) 1936- .. **CLC 2, 3, 7,**
11, 27, 44, 127
See also AAYA 15; AITN 2; AMWS 5;
BEST 89:2; BPFB 2; CA 5-8R; CANR
19, 43, 64, 103; CDALB 1968-1988; CN
7; CPW; CSW; DA3; DAM NOV, POP;
DLB 2, 143, 256; DLBY 1980, 1987;
EWL 3; MTCW 1, 2; RGAL 4; TCWW 2

McNally, T. M. 1961- .... **CLC 82**

McNally, Terrence 1939- .... **CLC 4, 7, 41, 91**
See also CA 45-48; CAD; CANR 2, 56,
116; CD 5; DA3; DAM DRAM; DFS 16;
DLB 7, 249; EWL 3; GLL 1; MTCW 2

McNamer, Deirdre 1950- .... **CLC 70**

McNeal, Tom .... **CLC 119**

McNeile, Herman Cyril 1888-1937
See Sapper
See also CA 184; CMW 4; DLB 77

McNickle, (William) D'Arcy
1904-1977 .... **CLC 89; NNAL**
See also CA 9-12R; 85-88; CANR 5, 45;
DAM MULT; DLB 175, 212; RGAL 4;
SATA-Obit 22

McPhee, John (Angus) 1931- .... **CLC 36**
See also AMWS 3; ANW; BEST 90:1; CA
65-68; CANR 20, 46, 64, 69; CPW; DLB
185, 275; MTCW 1, 2; TUS

McPherson, James Alan 1943- . **BLCS; CLC**
19, 77
See also BW 1, 3; CA 25-28R; CAAS 17;
CANR 24, 74; CN 7; CSW; DLB 38, 244;
EWL 3; MTCW 1, 2; RGAL 4; RGSF 2

McPherson, William (Alexander)
1933- .... **CLC 34**
See also CA 69-72; CANR 28; INT
CANR-28

McTaggart, J. McT. Ellis
See McTaggart, John McTaggart Ellis

McTaggart, John McTaggart Ellis
1866-1925 .... **TCLC 105**
See also CA 120; DLB 262

Mead, George Herbert 1863-1931 . **TCLC 89**
See also CA 212; DLB 270

Mead, Margaret 1901-1978 .... **CLC 37**
See also AITN 1; CA 1-4R; 81-84; CANR
4; DA3; FW; MTCW 1, 2; SATA-Obit 20

Meaker, Marijane (Agnes) 1927-
See Kerr, M. E.
See also CA 107; CANR 37, 63; INT 107;
JRDA; MAICYA 1, 2; MAICYAS 1;
MTCW 1; SATA 20, 61, 99; SATA-Essay
111; YAW

Medoff, Mark (Howard) 1940- .... **CLC 6, 23**
See also AITN 1; CA 53-56; CAD; CANR
5; CD 5; DAM DRAM; DFS 4; DLB 7;
INT CANR-5

Medvedev, P. N.
See Bakhtin, Mikhail Mikhailovich

Meged, Aharon
See Megged, Aharon

Meged, Aron
See Megged, Aharon

Megged, Aharon 1920- .... **CLC 9**
See also CA 49-52; CAAS 13; CANR 1;
EWL 3

Mehta, Ved (Parkash) 1934- .... **CLC 37**
See also CA 1-4R; CAAE 212; CANR 2,
23, 69; MTCW 1

Melanchthon, Philipp 1497-1560 .... **LC 90**
See also DLB 179

Melanter
See Blackmore, R(ichard) D(oddridge)

Meleager c. 140B.C.-c. 70B.C. ...... **CMLC 53**

Melies, Georges 1861-1938 .... **TCLC 81**

Melikow, Loris
See Hofmannsthal, Hugo von

Melmoth, Sebastian
See Wilde, Oscar (Fingal O'Flahertie Wills)

Melo Neto, Joao Cabral de
See Cabral de Melo Neto, Joao
See also EWL 3

Meltzer, Milton 1915- .... **CLC 26**
See also AAYA 8, 45; BYA 2, 6; CA 13-
16R; CANR 38, 92, 107; CLR 13; DLB
61; JRDA; MAICYA 1, 2; SAAS 1; SATA
1, 50, 80, 128; SATA-Essay 124; WYA;
YAW

Melville, Herman 1819-1891 ..... **NCLC 3, 12,**
29, 45, 49, 91, 93, 123; SSC 1, 17, 46;
WLC
See also AAYA 25; AMW; AMWR 1;
CDALB 1640-1865; DA; DA3; DAB;
DAC; DAM MST, NOV; DLB 3, 74, 250,
254; EXPN; EXPS; LAIT 1, 2; NFS 7, 9;
RGAL 4; RGSF 2; SATA 59; SSFS 3;
TUS

Members, Mark
See Powell, Anthony (Dymoke)

Mrozek, Slawomir 1930- .... **CLC 3, 13**
See also CA 13-16R; CAAS 10; CANR 29;
CDWLB 4; CWW 2; DLB 232; EWL 3;
MTCW 1

Mrs. Belloc-Lowndes
See Lowndes, Marie Adelaide (Belloc)

M'Taggart, John M'Taggart Ellis
See McTaggart, John McTaggart Ellis

Mtwa, Percy (?)- .... **CLC 47**

Mueller, Lisel 1924- .... **CLC 13, 51; PC 33**
See also CA 93-96; CP 7; DLB 105; PFS 9,
13

Muggeridge, Malcolm (Thomas)
1903-1990 .... **TCLC 120**
See also AITN 1; CA 101; CANR 33, 63;
MTCW 1, 2

Muhammad 570-632 .... **WLCS**
See also DA; DAB; DAC; DAM MST

Muir, Edwin 1887-1959 .... **TCLC 2, 87**
See Moore, Edward
See also BRWS 6; CA 104; 193; DLB 20,
100, 191; EWL 3; RGEL 2

Muir, John 1838-1914 .... **TCLC 28**
See also AMWS 9; ANW; CA 165; DLB
186, 275

Mujica Lainez, Manuel 1910-1984 ... **CLC 31**
See Lainez, Manuel Mujica
See also CA 81-84; 112; CANR 32; EWL
3; HW 1

Mukherjee, Bharati 1940- ..... **AAL; CLC 53,
115; SSC 38**
See also AAYA 46; BEST 89:2; CA 107;
CANR 45, 72; CN 7; DAM NOV; DLB
60, 218; DNFS 1; EWL 3; FW; MTCW
1, 2; RGAL 4; RGSF 2; SSFS 7; TUS

Muldoon, Paul 1951- .... **CLC 32, 72, 166**
See also BRWS 4; CA 113; 129; CANR 52,
91; CP 7; DAM POET; DLB 40; INT 129;
PFS 3

Mulisch, Harry 1927- .... **CLC 42**
See also CA 9-12R; CANR 6, 26, 56, 110;
EWL 3

Mull, Martin 1943- .... **CLC 17**
See also CA 105

Muller, Wilhelm .... **NCLC 73**

Mulock, Dinah Maria
See Craik, Dinah Maria (Mulock)
See also RGEL 2

Munday, Anthony 1560-1633 .... **LC 87**
See also DLB 62, 172; RGEL 2

Munford, Robert 1737(?)-1783 .... **LC 5**
See also DLB 31

Mungo, Raymond 1946- .... **CLC 72**
See also CA 49-52; CANR 2

Munro, Alice 1931- .... **CLC 6, 10, 19, 50, 95;
SSC 3; WLCS**
See also AITN 2; BPFB 2; CA 33-36R;
CANR 33, 53, 75, 114; CCA 1; CN 7;
DA3; DAC; DAM MST, NOV; DLB 53;
EWL 3; MTCW 1, 2; RGEL 2; RGSF 2;
SATA 29; SSFS 5, 13

Munro, H(ector) H(ugh) 1870-1916 .... **WLC**
See Saki
See also CA 104; 130; CANR 104; CDBLB
1890-1914; DA; DA3; DAB; DAC; DAM
MST, NOV; DLB 34, 162; EXPS; MTCW
1, 2; RGEL 2; SSFS 15

Murakami, Haruki 1949- .... **CLC 150**
See Murakami Haruki
See also CA 165; CANR 102; MJW; RGWL
3; SFW 4

Murakami Haruki
See Murakami, Haruki
See also DLB 182; EWL 3

Murasaki, Lady
See Murasaki Shikibu

Murasaki Shikibu 978(?)-1026(?) ... **CMLC 1**
See also EFS 2; LATS 1; RGWL 2, 3

Murdoch, (Jean) Iris 1919-1999 ... **CLC 1, 2,
3, 4, 6, 8, 11, 15, 22, 31, 51**
See also BRWS 1; CA 13-16R; 179; CANR
8, 43, 68, 103; CDBLB 1960 to Present;
CN 7; CWD; DA3; DAB; DAC; DAM
MST, NOV; DLB 14, 194, 233; EWL 3;
INT CANR-8; MTCW 1, 2; RGEL 2;
TEA; WLIT 4

Murfree, Mary Noailles 1850-1922 .. **SSC 22;
TCLC 135**
See also CA 122; 176; DLB 12, 74; RGAL
4

Murnau, Friedrich Wilhelm
See Plumpe, Friedrich Wilhelm

Murphy, Richard 1927- .... **CLC 41**
See also BRWS 5; CA 29-32R; CP 7; DLB
40; EWL 3

Murphy, Sylvia 1937- .... **CLC 34**
See also CA 121

Murphy, Thomas (Bernard) 1935- ... **CLC 51**
See also CA 101

Murray, Albert L. 1916- .... **CLC 73**
See also BW 2; CA 49-52; CANR 26, 52,
78; CSW; DLB 38

Murray, James Augustus Henry
1837-1915 .... **TCLC 117**

Murray, Judith Sargent
1751-1820 .... **NCLC 63**
See also DLB 37, 200

Murray, Les(lie Allan) 1938- .... **CLC 40**
See also BRWS 7; CA 21-24R; CANR 11,
27, 56, 103; CP 7; DAM POET; DLBY
2001; EWL 3; RGEL 2

Murry, J. Middleton
See Murry, John Middleton

Murry, John Middleton
1889-1957 .... **TCLC 16**
See also CA 118; DLB 149

Musgrave, Susan 1951- .... **CLC 13, 54**
See also CA 69-72; CANR 45, 84; CCA 1;
CP 7; CWP

Musil, Robert (Edler von)
1880-1942 .... **SSC 18; TCLC 12, 68**
See also CA 109; CANR 55, 84; CDWLB
2; DLB 81, 124; EW 9; EWL 3; MTCW
2; RGSF 2; RGWL 2, 3

Muske, Carol .... **CLC 90**
See Muske-Dukes, Carol (Anne)

Muske-Dukes, Carol (Anne) 1945-
See Muske, Carol
See also CA 65-68; CAAE 203; CANR 32,
70; CWP

Musset, (Louis Charles) Alfred de
1810-1857 .... **NCLC 7**
See also DLB 192, 217; EW 6; GFL 1789
to the Present; RGWL 2, 3; TWA

Mussolini, Benito (Amilcare Andrea)
1883-1945 .... **TCLC 96**
See also CA 116

My Brother's Brother
See Chekhov, Anton (Pavlovich)

Myers, L(eopold) H(amilton)
1881-1944 .... **TCLC 59**
See also CA 157; DLB 15; EWL 3; RGEL
2

Myers, Walter Dean 1937- .. **BLC 3; CLC 35**
See also AAYA 4, 23; BW 2; BYA 6, 8, 11;
CA 33-36R; CANR 20, 42, 67, 108; CLR
4, 16, 35; DAM MULT, NOV; DLB 33;
INT CANR-20; JRDA; LAIT 5; MAICYA
1, 2; MAICYAS 1; MTCW 2; SAAS 2;
SATA 41, 71, 109; SATA-Brief 27; WYA;
YAW

Myers, Walter M.
See Myers, Walter Dean

Myles, Symon
See Follett, Ken(neth Martin)

Nabokov, Vladimir (Vladimirovich)
1899-1977 .... **CLC 1, 2, 3, 6, 8, 11, 15,
23, 44, 46, 64; SSC 11; TCLC 108;
WLC**
See also AAYA 45; AMW; AMWC 1;
AMWR 1; BPFB 2; CA 5-8R; 69-72;
CANR 20, 102; CDALB 1941-1968; DA;
DA3; DAB; DAC; DAM MST, NOV;
DLB 2, 244, 278; DLBD 3; DLBY 1980,
1991; EWL 3; EXPS; LATS 1; MTCW 1,
2; NCFS 4; NFS 9; RGAL 4; RGSF 2;
SSFS 6, 15; TUS

Naevius c. 265B.C.-201B.C. .... **CMLC 37**
See also DLB 211

Nagai, Kafu .... **TCLC 51**
See Nagai, Sokichi
See also DLB 180

Nagai, Sokichi 1879-1959
See Nagai, Kafu
See also CA 117

Nagy, Laszlo 1925-1978 .... **CLC 7**
See also CA 129; 112

Naidu, Sarojini 1879-1949 .... **TCLC 80**
See also EWL 3; RGEL 2

Naipaul, Shiva(dhar Srinivasa)
1945-1985 .... **CLC 32, 39**
See also CA 110; 112; 116; CANR 33;
DA3; DAM NOV; DLB 157; DLBY 1985;
EWL 3; MTCW 1, 2

Naipaul, V(idiadhar) S(urajprasad)
1932- .... **CLC 4, 7, 9, 13, 18, 37, 105;
SSC 38**
See also BPFB 2; BRWS 1; CA 1-4R;
CANR 1, 33, 51, 91; CDBLB 1960 to
Present; CDWLB 3; CN 7; DA3; DAB;
DAC; DAM MST, NOV; DLB 125, 204,
207; DLBY 1985, 2001; EWL 3; LATS 1;
MTCW 1, 2; RGEL 2; RGSF 2; TWA;
WLIT 4

Nakos, Lilika 1899(?)- .... **CLC 29**

Narayan, R(asipuram) K(rishnaswami)
1906-2001 . **CLC 7, 28, 47, 121; SSC 25**
See also BPFB 2; CA 81-84; 196; CANR
33, 61, 112; CN 7; DA3; DAM NOV;
DNFS 1; EWL 3; MTCW 1, 2; RGEL 2;
RGSF 2; SATA 62; SSFS 5

Nash, (Fredric) Ogden 1902-1971 . **CLC 23;
PC 21; TCLC 109**
See also CA 13-14; 29-32R; CANR 34, 61;
CAP 1; DAM POET; DLB 11; MAICYA
1, 2; MTCW 1, 2; RGAL 4; SATA 2, 46;
WP

Nashe, Thomas 1567-1601(?) .... **LC 41, 89**
See also DLB 167; RGEL 2

Nathan, Daniel
See Dannay, Frederic

Nathan, George Jean 1882-1958 .... **TCLC 18**
See Hatteras, Owen
See also CA 114; 169; DLB 137

Natsume, Kinnosuke
See Natsume, Soseki

Natsume, Soseki 1867-1916 .... **TCLC 2, 10**
See Natsume Soseki; Soseki
See also CA 104; 195; RGWL 2, 3; TWA

Natsume Soseki
See Natsume, Soseki
See also DLB 180; EWL 3

Natti, (Mary) Lee 1919-
See Kingman, Lee
See also CA 5-8R; CANR 2

Navarre, Marguerite de
See de Navarre, Marguerite

Naylor, Gloria 1950- ..... **BLC 3; CLC 28, 52,
156; WLCS**
See also AAYA 6, 39; AFAW 1, 2; AMWS
8; BW 2, 3; CA 107; CANR 27, 51, 74;
CN 7; CPW; DA; DA3; DAC; DAM
MST, MULT, NOV, POP; DLB 173; EWL
3; FW; MTCW 1, 2; NFS 4, 7; RGAL 4;
TUS

Neff, Debra .... **CLC 59**
Neihardt, John Gneisenau
1881-1973 .... **CLC 32**
See also CA 13-14; CANR 65; CAP 1; DLB
9, 54, 256; LAIT 2
Nekrasov, Nikolai Alekseevich
1821-1878 .... **NCLC 11**
See also DLB 277
Nelligan, Emile 1879-1941 .... **TCLC 14**
See also CA 114; 204; DLB 92; EWL 3
Nelson, Willie 1933- .... **CLC 17**
See also CA 107; CANR 114
Nemerov, Howard (Stanley)
1920-1991 .... **CLC 2, 6, 9, 36; PC 24;**
TCLC 124
See also AMW; CA 1-4R; 134; CABS 2;
CANR 1, 27, 53; DAM POET; DLB 5, 6;
DLBY 1983; EWL 3; INT CANR-27;
MTCW 1, 2; PFS 10, 14; RGAL 4
Neruda, Pablo 1904-1973 ... **CLC 1, 2, 5, 7, 9,**
28, 62; HLC 2; PC 4; WLC
See also CA 19-20; 45-48; CAP 2; DA;
DA3; DAB; DAC; DAM MST, MULT,
POET; DNFS 2; EWL 3; HW 1; LAW;
MTCW 1, 2; PFS 11; RGWL 2, 3; TWA;
WLIT 1; WP
Nerval, Gerard de 1808-1855 ... **NCLC 1, 67;**
PC 13; SSC 18
See also DLB 217; EW 6; GFL 1789 to the
Present; RGSF 2; RGWL 2, 3
Nervo, (Jose) Amado (Ruiz de)
1870-1919 .... **HLCS 2; TCLC 11**
See also CA 109; 131; EWL 3; HW 1; LAW
Nesbit, Malcolm
See Chester, Alfred
Nessi, Pio Baroja y
See Baroja (y Nessi), Pio
Nestroy, Johann 1801-1862 .... **NCLC 42**
See also DLB 133; RGWL 2, 3
Netterville, Luke
See O'Grady, Standish (James)
Neufeld, John (Arthur) 1938- .... **CLC 17**
See also AAYA 11; CA 25-28R; CANR 11,
37, 56; CLR 52; MAICYA 1, 2; SAAS 3;
SATA 6, 81; SATA-Essay 131; YAW
Neumann, Alfred 1895-1952 .... **TCLC 100**
See also CA 183; DLB 56
Neumann, Ferenc
See Molnar, Ferenc
Neville, Emily Cheney 1919- .... **CLC 12**
See also BYA 2; CA 5-8R; CANR 3, 37,
85; JRDA; MAICYA 1, 2; SAAS 2; SATA
1; YAW
Newbound, Bernard Slade 1930-
See Slade, Bernard
See also CA 81-84; CANR 49; CD 5; DAM
DRAM
Newby, P(ercy) H(oward)
1918-1997 .... **CLC 2, 13**
See also CA 5-8R; 161; CANR 32, 67; CN
7; DAM NOV; DLB 15; MTCW 1; RGEL
2
Newcastle
See Cavendish, Margaret Lucas
Newlove, Donald 1928- .... **CLC 6**
See also CA 29-32R; CANR 25
Newlove, John (Herbert) 1938- .... **CLC 14**
See also CA 21-24R; CANR 9, 25; CP 7
Newman, Charles 1938- .... **CLC 2, 8**
See also CA 21-24R; CANR 84; CN 7
Newman, Edwin (Harold) 1919- ...... **CLC 14**
See also AITN 1; CA 69-72; CANR 5
Newman, John Henry 1801-1890 . **NCLC 38,**
99
See also BRWS 7; DLB 18, 32, 55; RGEL
2
Newton, (Sir) Isaac 1642-1727 ...... **LC 35, 53**
See also DLB 252

Newton, Suzanne 1936- .... **CLC 35**
See also BYA 7; CA 41-44R; CANR 14;
JRDA; SATA 5, 77
New York Dept. of Ed. .... **CLC 70**
Nexo, Martin Andersen
1869-1954 .... **TCLC 43**
See also CA 202; DLB 214; EWL 3
Nezval, Vitezslav 1900-1958 .... **TCLC 44**
See also CA 123; CDWLB 4; DLB 215;
EWL 3
Ng, Fae Myenne 1957(?)- .... **CLC 81**
See also CA 146
Ngema, Mbongeni 1955- .... **CLC 57**
See also BW 2; CA 143; CANR 84; CD 5
Ngugi, James T(hiong'o) .... **CLC 3, 7, 13**
See also Ngugi wa Thiong'o
Ngugi wa Thiong'o
See Ngugi wa Thiong'o
See also DLB 125; EWL 3
Ngugi wa Thiong'o 1938- .... **BLC 3; CLC 36**
See also Ngugi, James T(hiong'o); Ngugi wa
Thiong'o
See also AFW; BRWS 8; BW 2; CA 81-84;
CANR 27, 58; CDWLB 3; DAM MULT,
NOV; DNFS 2; MTCW 1, 2; RGEL 2
Niatum, Duane 1938- .... **NNAL**
See also CA 41-44R; CANR 21, 45, 83;
DLB 175
Nichol, B(arrie) P(hillip) 1944-1988 . **CLC 18**
See also CA 53-56; DLB 53; SATA 66
Nicholas of Cusa 1401-1464 .... **LC 80**
See also DLB 115
Nichols, John (Treadwell) 1940- .... **CLC 38**
See also CA 9-12R; CAAE 190; CAAS 2;
CANR 6, 70; DLBY 1982; LATS 1;
TCWW 2
Nichols, Leigh
See Koontz, Dean R(ay)
Nichols, Peter (Richard) 1927- .... **CLC 5, 36,**
65
See also CA 104; CANR 33, 86; CBD; CD
5; DLB 13, 245; MTCW 1
Nicholson, Linda ed. .... **CLC 65**
Ni Chuilleanain, Eilean 1942- .... **PC 34**
See also CA 126; CANR 53, 83; CP 7;
CWP; DLB 40
Nicolas, F. R. E.
See Freeling, Nicolas
Niedecker, Lorine 1903-1970 ..... **CLC 10, 42;**
PC 42
See also CA 25-28; CAP 2; DAM POET;
DLB 48
Nietzsche, Friedrich (Wilhelm)
1844-1900 .... **TCLC 10, 18, 55**
See also CA 107; 121; CDWLB 2; DLB
129; EW 7; RGWL 2, 3; TWA
Nievo, Ippolito 1831-1861 .... **NCLC 22**
Nightingale, Anne Redmon 1943-
See Redmon, Anne
See also CA 103
Nightingale, Florence 1820-1910 ... **TCLC 85**
See also CA 188; DLB 166
Nijo Yoshimoto 1320-1388 .... **CMLC 49**
See also DLB 203
Nik. T. O.
See Annensky, Innokenty (Fyodorovich)
Nin, Anais 1903-1977 ..... **CLC 1, 4, 8, 11, 14,**
60, 127; SSC 10
See also AITN 2; AMWS 10; BPFB 2; CA
13-16R; 69-72; CANR 22, 53; DAM
NOV, POP; DLB 2, 4, 152; EWL 3; GLL
2; MAWW; MTCW 1, 2; RGAL 4; RGSF
2
Nisbet, Robert A(lexander)
1913-1996 .... **TCLC 117**
See also CA 25-28R; 153; CANR 17; INT
CANR-17

Nishida, Kitaro 1870-1945 .... **TCLC 83**
Nishiwaki, Junzaburo
See Nishiwaki, Junzaburo
See also CA 194
Nishiwaki, Junzaburo 1894-1982 .... **PC 15**
See also Nishiwaki, Junzaburo; Nishiwaki
Junzaburo
See also CA 194; 107; MJW; RGWL 3
Nishiwaki Junzaburo
See Nishiwaki, Junzaburo
See also EWL 3
Nissenson, Hugh 1933- .... **CLC 4, 9**
See also CA 17-20R; CANR 27, 108; CN
7; DLB 28
Nister, Der
See Der Nister
See also EWL 3
Niven, Larry .... **CLC 8**
See also Niven, Laurence Van Cott
See also AAYA 27; BPFB 2; BYA 10;
CAAE 207; DLB 8; SCFW 2
Niven, Laurence Van Cott 1938-
See Niven, Larry
See also CA 21-24R; CAAE 207; CAAS
12; CANR 14, 44, 66, 113; CPW; DAM
POP; MTCW 1, 2; SATA 95; SFW 4
Nixon, Agnes Eckhardt 1927- .... **CLC 21**
See also CA 110
Nizan, Paul 1905-1940 .... **TCLC 40**
See also CA 161; DLB 72; EWL 3; GFL
1789 to the Present
Nkosi, Lewis 1936- .... **BLC 3; CLC 45**
See also BW 1, 3; CA 65-68; CANR 27,
81; CBD; CD 5; DAM MULT; DLB 157,
225
Nodier, (Jean) Charles (Emmanuel)
1780-1844 .... **NCLC 19**
See also DLB 119; GFL 1789 to the Present
Noguchi, Yone 1875-1947 .... **TCLC 80**
Nolan, Christopher 1965- .... **CLC 58**
See also CA 111; CANR 88
Noon, Jeff 1957- .... **CLC 91**
See also CA 148; CANR 83; DLB 267;
SFW 4
Norden, Charles
See Durrell, Lawrence (George)
Nordhoff, Charles (Bernard)
1887-1947 .... **TCLC 23**
See also CA 108; DLB 9; LAIT 1; RHW 1;
SATA 23
Norfolk, Lawrence 1963- .... **CLC 76**
See also CA 144; CANR 85; CN 7; DLB
267
Norman, Marsha 1947- .... **CLC 28; DC 8**
See also CA 105; CABS 3; CAD; CANR
41; CD 5; CSW; CWD; DAM DRAM;
DFS 2; DLB 266; DLBY 1984; FW
Normyx
See Douglas, (George) Norman
Norris, (Benjamin) Frank(lin, Jr.)
1870-1902 .... **SSC 28; TCLC 24**
See also AMW; BPFB 2; CA 110; 160;
CDALB 1865-1917; DLB 12, 71, 186;
LMFS 2; NFS 12; RGAL 4; TCWW 2;
TUS
Norris, Leslie 1921- .... **CLC 14**
See also CA 11-12; CANR 14, 117; CAP 1;
CP 7; DLB 27, 256
North, Andrew
See Norton, Andre
North, Anthony
See Koontz, Dean R(ay)
North, Captain George
See Stevenson, Robert Louis (Balfour)
North, Captain George
See Stevenson, Robert Louis (Balfour)
North, Milou
See Erdrich, Louise

Olesha, Yuri (Karlovich) 1899-1960 . CLC 8;
TCLC 136
See Olesha, Iurii; Olesha, Iurii Karlovich;
Olesha, Yury Karlovich
See also CA 85-88; EW 11; RGWL 3

Olesha, Yury Karlovich
See Olesha, Yuri (Karlovich)
See also EWL 3

Oliphant, Mrs.
See Oliphant, Margaret (Oliphant Wilson)
See also SUFW

Oliphant, Laurence 1829(?)-1888 .. NCLC 47
See also DLB 18, 166

Oliphant, Margaret (Oliphant Wilson)
1828-1897 .... NCLC 11, 61; SSC 25
See Oliphant, Mrs.
See also DLB 18, 159, 190; HGG; RGEL
2; RGSF 2

Oliver, Mary 1935- .... CLC 19, 34, 98
See also AMWS 7; CA 21-24R; CANR 9,
43, 84, 92; CP 7; CWP; DLB 5, 193;
EWL 3; PFS 15

Olivier, Laurence (Kerr) 1907-1989 . CLC 20
See also CA 111; 150; 129

Olsen, Tillie 1912- ... CLC 4, 13, 114; SSC 11
See also BYA 11; CA 1-4R; CANR 1, 43,
74; CDALBS; CN 7; DA; DA3; DAB;
DAC; DAM MST; DLB 28, 206; DLBY
1980; EWL 3; EXPS; FW; MTCW 1, 2;
RGAL 4; RGSF 2; SSFS 1; TUS

Olson, Charles (John) 1910-1970 .. CLC 1, 2,
5, 6, 9, 11, 29; PC 19
See also AMWS 2; CA 13-16; 25-28R;
CABS 2; CANR 35, 61; CAP 1; DAM
POET; DLB 5, 16, 193; EWL 3; MTCW
1, 2; RGAL 4; WP

Olson, Toby 1937- .... CLC 28
See also CA 65-68; CANR 9, 31, 84; CP 7

Olyesha, Yuri
See Olesha, Yuri (Karlovich)

Olympiodorus of Thebes c. 375-c.
430 .... CMLC 59

Omar Khayyam
See Khayyam, Omar
See also RGWL 2, 3

Ondaatje, (Philip) Michael 1943- .... CLC 14,
29, 51, 76; PC 28
See also CA 77-80; CANR 42, 74, 109; CN
7; CP 7; DA3; DAB; DAC; DAM MST;
DLB 60; EWL 3; LATS 1; LMFS 2;
MTCW 2; PFS 8; TWA

Oneal, Elizabeth 1934-
See Oneal, Zibby
See also CA 106; CANR 28, 84; MAICYA
1, 2; SATA 30, 82; YAW

Oneal, Zibby .... CLC 30
See Oneal, Elizabeth
See also AAYA 5, 41; BYA 13; CLR 13;
JRDA; WYA

O'Neill, Eugene (Gladstone)
1888-1953 ... DC 20; TCLC 1, 6, 27, 49;
WLC
See also AITN 1; AMW; AMWC 1; CA
110; 132; CAD; CDALB 1929-1941; DA;
DA3; DAB; DAC; DAM DRAM, MST;
DFS 2, 4, 5, 6, 9, 11, 12, 16; DLB 7; EWL
3; LAIT 3; LMFS 2; MTCW 1, 2; RGAL
4; TUS

Onetti, Juan Carlos 1909-1994 ... CLC 7, 10;
HLCS 2; SSC 23; TCLC 131
See also CA 85-88; 145; CANR 32, 63; CD-
WLB 3; DAM MULT, NOV; DLB 113;
EWL 3; HW 1, 2; LAW; MTCW 1, 2;
RGSF 2

O Nuallain, Brian 1911-1966
See O'Brien, Flann
See also CA 21-22; 25-28R; CAP 2; DLB
231; FANT; TEA

Ophuls, Max 1902-1957 .... TCLC 79
See also CA 113

Opie, Amelia 1769-1853 .... NCLC 65
See also DLB 116, 159; RGEL 2

Oppen, George 1908-1984 ..... CLC 7, 13, 34;
PC 35; TCLC 107
See also CA 13-16R; 113; CANR 8, 82;
DLB 5, 165

Oppenheim, E(dward) Phillips
1866-1946 .... TCLC 45
See also CA 111; 202; CMW 4; DLB 70

Opuls, Max
See Ophuls, Max

Origen c. 185-c. 254 .... CMLC 19

Orlovitz, Gil 1918-1973 .... CLC 22
See also CA 77-80; 45-48; DLB 2, 5

Orris
See Ingelow, Jean

Ortega y Gasset, Jose 1883-1955 ...... HLC 2;
TCLC 9
See also CA 106; 130; DAM MULT; EW 9;
EWL 3; HW 1, 2; MTCW 1, 2

Ortese, Anna Maria 1914-1998 .... CLC 89
See also DLB 177; EWL 3

Ortiz, Simon J(oseph) 1941- .... CLC 45;
NNAL; PC 17
See also AMWS 4; CA 134; CANR 69, 118;
CP 7; DAM MULT, POET; DLB 120,
175, 256; EXPP; PFS 4, 16; RGAL 4

Orton, Joe .... CLC 4, 13, 43; DC 3
See Orton, John Kingsley
See also BRWS 5; CBD; CDBLB 1960 to
Present; DFS 3, 6; DLB 13; GLL 1;
MTCW 2; RGEL 2; TEA; WLIT 4

Orton, John Kingsley 1933-1967
See Orton, Joe
See also CA 85-88; CANR 35, 66; DAM
DRAM; MTCW 1, 2

Orwell, George . TCLC 2, 6, 15, 31, 51, 128,
129; WLC
See Blair, Eric (Arthur)
See also BPFB 3; BRW 7; BYA 5; CDBLB
1945-1960; CLR 68; DAB; DLB 15, 98,
195, 255; EWL 3; EXPN; LAIT 4, 5;
LATS 1; NFS 3, 7; RGEL 2; SCFW 2;
SFW 4; SSFS 4; TEA; WLIT 4; YAW

Osborne, David
See Silverberg, Robert

Osborne, George
See Silverberg, Robert

Osborne, John (James) 1929-1994 .... CLC 1,
2, 5, 11, 45; WLC
See also BRWS 1; CA 13-16R; 147; CANR
21, 56; CDBLB 1945-1960; DA; DAB;
DAC; DAM DRAM, MST; DFS 4; DLB
13; EWL 3; MTCW 1, 2; RGEL 2

Osborne, Lawrence 1958- .... CLC 50
See also CA 189

Osbourne, Lloyd 1868-1947 .... TCLC 93

Oshima, Nagisa 1932- .... CLC 20
See also CA 116; 121; CANR 78

Oskison, John Milton
1874-1947 .... NNAL; TCLC 35
See also CA 144; CANR 84; DAM MULT;
DLB 175

Ossian c. 3rd cent. - .... CMLC 28
See Macpherson, James

Ossoli, Sarah Margaret (Fuller)
1810-1850 .... NCLC 5, 50
See Fuller, Margaret; Fuller, Sarah Margaret
See also CDALB 1640-1865; FW; LMFS 1;
SATA 25

Ostriker, Alicia (Suskin) 1937- .... CLC 132
See also CA 25-28R; CAAS 24; CANR 10,
30, 62, 99; CWP; DLB 120; EXPP

Ostrovsky, Aleksandr Nikolaevich
See Ostrovsky, Alexander
See also DLB 277

Ostrovsky, Alexander 1823-1886 .. NCLC 30,
57
See Ostrovsky, Aleksandr Nikolaevich

Otero, Blas de 1916-1979 .... CLC 11
See also CA 89-92; DLB 134; EWL 3

Otto, Rudolf 1869-1937 .... TCLC 85

Otto, Whitney 1955- .... CLC 70
See also CA 140

Ouida .... TCLC 43
See De la Ramee, Marie Louise (Ouida)
See also DLB 18, 156; RGEL 2

Ouologuem, Yambo 1940- .... CLC 146
See also CA 111; 176

Ousmane, Sembene 1923- ... BLC 3; CLC 66
See Sembene, Ousmane
See also BW 1, 3; CA 117; 125; CANR 81;
CWW 2; MTCW 1

Ovid 43B.C.-17 .... CMLC 7; PC 2
See also AW 2; CDWLB 1; DA3; DAM
POET; DLB 211; RGWL 2, 3; WP

Owen, Hugh
See Faust, Frederick (Schiller)

Owen, Wilfred (Edward Salter)
1893-1918 ... PC 19; TCLC 5, 27; WLC
See also BRW 6; CA 104; 141; CDBLB
1914-1945; DA; DAB; DAC; DAM MST,
POET; DLB 20; EWL 3; EXPP; MTCW
2; PFS 10; RGEL 2; WLIT 4

Owens, Louis (Dean) 1948-2002 .... NNAL
See also CA 137; 179; 207; CAAE 179;
CAAS 24; CANR 71

Owens, Rochelle 1936- .... CLC 8
See also CA 17-20R; CAAS 2; CAD;
CANR 39; CD 5; CP 7; CWD; CWP

Oz, Amos 1939- .... CLC 5, 8, 11, 27, 33, 54
See also CA 53-56; CANR 27, 47, 65, 113;
CWW 2; DAM NOV; EWL 3; MTCW 1,
2; RGSF 2; RGWL 3

Ozick, Cynthia 1928- .... CLC 3, 7, 28, 62,
155; SSC 15, 60
See also AMWS 5; BEST 90:1; CA 17-20R;
CANR 23, 58, 116; CN 7; CPW; DA3;
DAM NOV, POP; DLB 28, 152; DLBY
1982; EWL 3; EXPS; INT CANR-23;
MTCW 1, 2; RGAL 4; RGSF 2; SSFS 3,
12

Ozu, Yasujiro 1903-1963 .... CLC 16
See also CA 112

Pabst, G. W. 1885-1967 .... TCLC 127

Pacheco, C.
See Pessoa, Fernando (Antonio Nogueira)

Pacheco, Jose Emilio 1939- .... HLC 2
See also CA 111; 131; CANR 65; DAM
MULT; EWL 3; HW 1, 2; RGSF 2

Pa Chin .... CLC 18
See Li Fei-kan
See also EWL 3

Pack, Robert 1929- .... CLC 13
See also CA 1-4R; CANR 3, 44, 82; CP 7;
DLB 5; SATA 118

Padgett, Lewis
See Kuttner, Henry

Padilla (Lorenzo), Heberto
1932-2000 .... CLC 38
See also AITN 1; CA 123; 131; 189; EWL
3; HW 1

Page, James Patrick 1944-
See Page, Jimmy
See also CA 204

Page, Jimmy 1944- .... CLC 12
See Page, James Patrick

Page, Louise 1955- .... CLC 40
See also CA 140; CANR 76; CBD; CD 5;
CWD; DLB 233

Page, P(atricia) K(athleen) 1916- ...... CLC 7,
18; PC 12
See Cape, Judith
See also CA 53-56; CANR 4, 22, 65; CP 7;
DAC; DAM MST; DLB 68; MTCW 1;
RGEL 2

Page, Stanton
See Fuller, Henry Blake

Page, Stanton
    See Fuller, Henry Blake
Page, Thomas Nelson 1853-1922 .... **SSC 23**
    See also CA 118; 177; DLB 12, 78; DLBD
    13; RGAL 4
Pagels, Elaine Hiesey 1943- .... **CLC 104**
    See also CA 45-48; CANR 2, 24, 51; FW;
    NCFS 4
Paget, Violet 1856-1935
    See Lee, Vernon
    See also CA 104; 166; GLL 1; HGG
Paget-Lowe, Henry
    See Lovecraft, H(oward) P(hillips)
Paglia, Camille (Anna) 1947- .... **CLC 68**
    See also CA 140; CANR 72; CPW; FW;
    GLL 2; MTCW 2
Paige, Richard
    See Koontz, Dean R(ay)
Paine, Thomas 1737-1809 .... **NCLC 62**
    See also AMWS 1; CDALB 1640-1865;
    DLB 31, 43, 73, 158; LAIT 1; RGAL 4;
    RGEL 2; TUS
Pakenham, Antonia
    See Fraser, Antonia (Pakenham)
Palamas, Costis
    See Palamas, Kostes
Palamas, Kostes 1859-1943 .... **TCLC 5**
    See Palamas, Kostis
    See also CA 105; 190; RGWL 2, 3
Palamas, Kostis
    See Palamas, Kostes
    See also EWL 3
Palazzeschi, Aldo 1885-1974 .... **CLC 11**
    See also CA 89-92; 53-56; DLB 114, 264;
    EWL 3
Pales Matos, Luis 1898-1959 .... **HLCS 2**
    See Pales Matos, Luis
    See also HW 1; LAW
Paley, Grace 1922- .. **CLC 4, 6, 37, 140; SSC
8**
    See also AMWS 6; CA 25-28R; CANR 13,
    46, 74, 118; CN 7; CPW; DA3; DAM
    POP; DLB 28, 218; EWL 3; EXPS; FW;
    INT CANR-13; MAWW; MTCW 1, 2;
    RGAL 4; RGSF 2; SSFS 3
Palin, Michael (Edward) 1943- .... **CLC 21**
    See Monty Python
    See also CA 107; CANR 35, 109; SATA 67
Palliser, Charles 1947- .... **CLC 65**
    See also CA 136; CANR 76; CN 7
Palma, Ricardo 1833-1919 .... **TCLC 29**
    See also CA 168; LAW
Pancake, Breece Dexter 1952-1979
    See Pancake, Breece D'J
    See also CA 123; 109
Pancake, Breece D'J .... **CLC 29; SSC 61**
    See Pancake, Breece Dexter
    See also DLB 130
Panchenko, Nikolai .... **CLC 59**
Pankhurst, Emmeline (Goulden)
    1858-1928 .... **TCLC 100**
    See also CA 116; FW
Panko, Rudy
    See Gogol, Nikolai (Vasilyevich)
Papadiamantis, Alexandros
    1851-1911 .... **TCLC 29**
    See also CA 168; EWL 3
Papadiamantopoulos, Johannes 1856-1910
    See Moreas, Jean
    See also CA 117
Papini, Giovanni 1881-1956 .... **TCLC 22**
    See also CA 121; 180; DLB 264
Paracelsus 1493-1541 .... **LC 14**
    See also DLB 179
Parasol, Peter
    See Stevens, Wallace
Pardo Bazan, Emilia 1851-1921 .... **SSC 30**
    See also EWL 3; FW; RGSF 2; RGWL 2, 3

Pareto, Vilfredo 1848-1923 .... **TCLC 69**
    See also CA 175
Paretsky, Sara 1947- .... **CLC 135**
    See also AAYA 30; BEST 90:3; CA 125;
    129; CANR 59, 95; CMW 4; CPW; DA3;
    DAM POP; INT CA-129; MSW; RGAL 4
Parfenie, Maria
    See Codrescu, Andrei
Parini, Jay (Lee) 1948- .... **CLC 54, 133**
    See also CA 97-100; CAAS 16; CANR 32,
    87
Park, Jordan
    See Kornbluth, C(yril) M.; Pohl, Frederik
Park, Robert E(zra) 1864-1944 ..... **TCLC 73**
    See also CA 122; 165
Parker, Bert
    See Ellison, Harlan (Jay)
Parker, Dorothy (Rothschild)
    1893-1967 .. **CLC 15, 68; PC 28; SSC 2**
    See also AMWS 9; CA 19-20; 25-28R; CAP
    2; DA3; DAM POET; DLB 11, 45, 86;
    EXPP; FW; MAWW; MTCW 1, 2; RGAL
    4; RGSF 2; TUS
Parker, Robert B(rown) 1932- .... **CLC 27**
    See also AAYA 28; BEST 89:4; BPFB 3;
    CA 49-52; CANR 1, 26, 52, 89; CMW 4;
    CPW; DAM NOV, POP; INT CANR-26;
    MSW; MTCW 1
Parkin, Frank 1940- .... **CLC 43**
    See also CA 147
Parkman, Francis, Jr. 1823-1893 .. **NCLC 12**
    See also AMWS 2; DLB 1, 30, 183, 186,
    235; RGAL 4
Parks, Gordon (Alexander Buchanan)
    1912- .... **BLC 3; CLC 1, 16**
    See also AAYA 36; AITN 2; BW 2, 3; CA
    41-44R; CANR 26, 66; DA3; DAM
    MULT; DLB 33; MTCW 2; SATA 8, 108
Parks, Tim(othy Harold) 1954- ...... **CLC 147**
    See also CA 126; 131; CANR 77; DLB 231;
    INT CA-131
Parmenides c. 515B.C.-c.
    450B.C. .... **CMLC 22**
    See also DLB 176
Parnell, Thomas 1679-1718 .... **LC 3**
    See also DLB 95; RGEL 2
Parr, Catherine c. 1513(?)-1548 .... **LC 86**
    See also DLB 136
Parra, Nicanor 1914- ... **CLC 2, 102; HLC 2;
PC 39**
    See also CA 85-88; CANR 32; CWW 2;
    DAM MULT; EWL 3; HW 1; LAW;
    MTCW 1
Parra Sanojo, Ana Teresa de la
    1890-1936 .... **HLCS 2**
    See de la Parra, (Ana) Teresa (Sonojo)
    See also LAW
Parrish, Mary Frances
    See Fisher, M(ary) F(rances) K(ennedy)
Parshchikov, Aleksei .... **CLC 59**
Parson, Professor
    See Coleridge, Samuel Taylor
Parson Lot
    See Kingsley, Charles
Parton, Sara Payson Willis
    1811-1872 .... **NCLC 86**
    See also DLB 43, 74, 239
Partridge, Anthony
    See Oppenheim, E(dward) Phillips
Pascal, Blaise 1623-1662 .... **LC 35**
    See also DLB 268; EW 3; GFL Beginnings
    to 1789; RGWL 2, 3; TWA
Pascoli, Giovanni 1855-1912 .... **TCLC 45**
    See also CA 170; EW 7; EWL 3
Pasolini, Pier Paolo 1922-1975 .. **CLC 20, 37,
106; PC 17**
    See also CA 93-96; 61-64; CANR 63; DLB
    128, 177; EWL 3; MTCW 1; RGWL 2, 3

Pasquini
    See Silone, Ignazio
Pastan, Linda (Olenik) 1932- .... **CLC 27**
    See also CA 61-64; CANR 18, 40, 61, 113;
    CP 7; CSW; CWP; DAM POET; DLB 5;
    PFS 8
Pasternak, Boris (Leonidovich)
    1890-1960 ...... **CLC 7, 10, 18, 63; PC 6;
SSC 31; WLC**
    See also BPFB 3; CA 127; 116; DA; DA3;
    DAB; DAC; DAM MST, NOV, POET;
    EW 10; MTCW 1, 2; RGSF 2; RGWL 2,
    3; TWA; WP
Patchen, Kenneth 1911-1972 .... **CLC 1, 2, 18**
    See also BG 3; CA 1-4R; 33-36R; CANR
    3, 35; DAM POET; DLB 16, 48; EWL 3;
    MTCW 1; RGAL 4
Pater, Walter (Horatio) 1839-1894 . **NCLC 7,
90**
    See also BRW 5; CDBLB 1832-1890; DLB
    57, 156; RGEL 2; TEA
Paterson, A(ndrew) B(arton)
    1864-1941 .... **TCLC 32**
    See also CA 155; DLB 230; RGEL 2; SATA
    97
Paterson, Banjo
    See Paterson, A(ndrew) B(arton)
Paterson, Katherine (Womeldorf)
    1932- .... **CLC 12, 30**
    See also AAYA 1, 31; BYA 1, 2, 7; CA 21-
    24R; CANR 28, 59, 111; CLR 7, 50;
    CWRI 5; DLB 52; JRDA; LAIT 4; MAI-
    CYA 1, 2; MAICYAS 1; MTCW 1; SATA
    13, 53, 92, 133; WYA; YAW
Patmore, Coventry Kersey Dighton
    1823-1896 .... **NCLC 9**
    See also DLB 35, 98; RGEL 2; TEA
Paton, Alan (Stewart) 1903-1988 ...... **CLC 4,
10, 25, 55, 106; WLC**
    See also AAYA 26; AFW; BPFB 3; BRWS
    2; BYA 1; CA 13-16; 125; CANR 22;
    CAP 1; DA; DA3; DAB; DAC; DAM
    MST, NOV; DLB 225; DLBD 17; EWL
    3; EXPN; LAIT 4; MTCW 1, 2; NFS 3,
    12; RGEL 2; SATA 11; SATA-Obit 56;
    TWA; WLIT 2
Paton Walsh, Gillian 1937- .... **CLC 35**
    See Paton Walsh, Jill; Walsh, Jill Paton
    See also AAYA 11; CANR 38, 83; CLR 2,
    65; DLB 161; JRDA; MAICYA 1, 2;
    SAAS 3; SATA 4, 72, 109; YAW
Paton Walsh, Jill
    See Paton Walsh, Gillian
    See also AAYA 47; BYA 1, 8
Patterson, (Horace) Orlando (Lloyd)
    1940- .... **BLCS**
    See also BW 1; CA 65-68; CANR 27, 84;
    CN 7
Patton, George S(mith), Jr.
    1885-1945 .... **TCLC 79**
    See also CA 189
Paulding, James Kirke 1778-1860 ... **NCLC 2**
    See also DLB 3, 59, 74, 250; RGAL 4
Paulin, Thomas Neilson 1949-
    See Paulin, Tom
    See also CA 123; 128; CANR 98; CP 7
Paulin, Tom .... **CLC 37**
    See Paulin, Thomas Neilson
    See also DLB 40
Pausanias c. 1st cent. - .... **CMLC 36**
Paustovsky, Konstantin (Georgievich)
    1892-1968 .... **CLC 40**
    See also CA 93-96; 25-28R; DLB 272;
    EWL 3
Pavese, Cesare 1908-1950 .... **PC 13; SSC 19;
TCLC 3**
    See also CA 104; 169; DLB 128, 177; EW
    12; EWL 3; RGSF 2; RGWL 2, 3; TWA

Phillips, Richard
See Dick, Philip K(indred)

Phillips, Robert (Schaeffer) 1938- .... **CLC 28**
See also CA 17-20R; CAAS 13; CANR 8;
DLB 105

Phillips, Ward
See Lovecraft, H(oward) P(hillips)

Piccolo, Lucio 1901-1969 .... **CLC 13**
See also CA 97-100; DLB 114; EWL 3

Pickthall, Marjorie L(owry) C(hristie)
1883-1922 .... **TCLC 21**
See also CA 107; DLB 92

Pico della Mirandola, Giovanni
1463-1494 .... **LC 15**
See also LMFS 1

Piercy, Marge 1936- .... **CLC 3, 6, 14, 18, 27,
62, 128; PC 29**
See also BPFB 3; CA 21-24R; CAAE 187;
CAAS 1; CANR 13, 43, 66, 111; CN 7;
CP 7; CWP; DLB 120, 227; EXPP; FW;
MTCW 1, 2; PFS 9; SFW 4

Piers, Robert
See Anthony, Piers

Pieyre de Mandiargues, Andre 1909-1991
See Mandiargues, Andre Pieyre de
See also CA 103; 136; CANR 22, 82; EWL
3; GFL 1789 to the Present

Pilnyak, Boris 1894-1938 . **SSC 48; TCLC 23**
See Vogau, Boris Andreyevich
See also EWL 3

Pinchback, Eugene
See Toomer, Jean

Pincherle, Alberto 1907-1990 ...... **CLC 11, 18**
See Moravia, Alberto
See also CA 25-28R; 132; CANR 33, 63;
DAM NOV; MTCW 1

Pinckney, Darryl 1953- .... **CLC 76**
See also BW 2, 3; CA 143; CANR 79

Pindar 518(?)B.C.-438(?)B.C. .... **CMLC 12;
PC 19**
See also AW 1; CDWLB 1; DLB 176;
RGWL 2

Pineda, Cecile 1942- .... **CLC 39**
See also CA 118; DLB 209

Pinero, Arthur Wing 1855-1934 .... **TCLC 32**
See also CA 110; 153; DAM DRAM; DLB
10; RGEL 2

Pinero, Miguel (Antonio Gomez)
1946-1988 .... **CLC 4, 55**
See also CA 61-64; 125; CAD; CANR 29,
90; DLB 266; HW 1

Pinget, Robert 1919-1997 .... **CLC 7, 13, 37**
See also CA 85-88; 160; CWW 2; DLB 83;
EWL 3; GFL 1789 to the Present

Pink Floyd
See Barrett, (Roger) Syd; Gilmour, David;
Mason, Nick; Waters, Roger; Wright, Rick

Pinkney, Edward 1802-1828 .... **NCLC 31**
See also DLB 248

Pinkwater, Daniel
See Pinkwater, Daniel Manus

Pinkwater, Daniel Manus 1941- .... **CLC 35**
See also AAYA 1, 46; BYA 9; CA 29-32R;
CANR 12, 38, 89; CLR 4; CSW; FANT;
JRDA; MAICYA 1, 2; SAAS 3; SATA 8,
46, 76, 114; SFW 4; YAW

Pinkwater, Manus
See Pinkwater, Daniel Manus

Pinsky, Robert 1940- .... **CLC 9, 19, 38, 94,
121; PC 27**
See also AMWS 6; CA 29-32R; CAAS 4;
CANR 58, 97; CP 7; DA3; DAM POET;
DLBY 1982, 1998; MTCW 2; RGAL 4

Pinta, Harold
See Pinter, Harold

Pinter, Harold 1930- .. **CLC 1, 3, 6, 9, 11, 15,
27, 58, 73; DC 15; WLC**
See also BRWR 1; BRWS 1; CA 5-8R;
CANR 33, 65, 112; CBD; CD 5; CDBLB
1960 to Present; DA; DA3; DAB; DAC;
DAM DRAM, MST; DFS 3, 5, 7, 14;
DLB 13; EWL 3; IDFW 3, 4; LMFS 2;
MTCW 1, 2; RGEL 2; TEA

Piozzi, Hester Lynch (Thrale)
1741-1821 .... **NCLC 57**
See also DLB 104, 142

Pirandello, Luigi 1867-1936 .. **DC 5; SSC 22;
TCLC 4, 29; WLC**
See also CA 104; 153; CANR 103; DA;
DA3; DAB; DAC; DAM DRAM, MST;
DFS 4, 9; DLB 264; EW 8; EWL 3;
MTCW 2; RGSF 2; RGWL 2, 3

Pirsig, Robert M(aynard) 1928- ... **CLC 4, 6,
73**
See also CA 53-56; CANR 42, 74; CPW 1;
DA3; DAM POP; MTCW 1, 2; SATA 39

Pisarev, Dmitrii Ivanovich
See Pisarev, Dmitry Ivanovich
See also DLB 277

Pisarev, Dmitry Ivanovich
1840-1868 .... **NCLC 25**
See Pisarev, Dmitrii Ivanovich

Pix, Mary (Griffith) 1666-1709 .... **LC 8**
See also DLB 80

Pixerecourt, (Rene Charles) Guilbert de
1773-1844 .... **NCLC 39**
See also DLB 192; GFL 1789 to the Present

Plaatje, Sol(omon) T(shekisho)
1878-1932 .... **BLCS; TCLC 73**
See also BW 2, 3; CA 141; CANR 79; DLB
125, 225

Plaidy, Jean
See Hibbert, Eleanor Alice Burford

Planche, James Robinson
1796-1880 .... **NCLC 42**
See also RGEL 2

Plant, Robert 1948- .... **CLC 12**

Plante, David (Robert) 1940- . **CLC 7, 23, 38**
See also CA 37-40R; CANR 12, 36, 58, 82;
CN 7; DAM NOV; DLBY 1983; INT
CANR-12; MTCW 1

Plath, Sylvia 1932-1963 ..... **CLC 1, 2, 3, 5, 9,
11, 14, 17, 50, 51, 62, 111; PC 1, 37;
WLC**
See also AAYA 13; AMWR 2; AMWS 1;
BPFB 3; CA 19-20; CANR 34, 101; CAP
2; CDALB 1941-1968; DA; DA3; DAB;
DAC; DAM MST, POET; DLB 5, 6, 152;
EWL 3; EXPN; EXPP; FW; LAIT 4;
MAWW; MTCW 1, 2; NFS 1; PAB; PFS
1, 15; RGAL 4; SATA 96; TUS; WP;
YAW

Plato c. 428B.C.-347B.C. ... **CMLC 8; WLCS**
See also AW 1; CDWLB 1; DA; DA3;
DAB; DAC; DAM MST; DLB 176; LAIT
1; LATS 1; RGWL 2, 3

Platonov, Andrei
See Klimentov, Andrei Platonovich

Platonov, Andrei Platonovich
See Klimentov, Andrei Platonovich
See also DLB 272

Platonov, Andrey Platonovich
See Klimentov, Andrei Platonovich
See also EWL 3

Platt, Kin 1911- .... **CLC 26**
See also AAYA 11; CA 17-20R; CANR 11;
JRDA; SAAS 17; SATA 21, 86; WYA

Plautus c. 254B.C.-c. 184B.C. ...... **CMLC 24;
DC 6**
See also AW 1; CDWLB 1; DLB 211;
RGWL 2, 3

Plick et Plock
See Simenon, Georges (Jacques Christian)

Plieksans, Janis
See Rainis, Janis

Plimpton, George (Ames) 1927- .... **CLC 36**
See also AITN 1; CA 21-24R; CANR 32,
70, 103; DLB 185, 241; MTCW 1, 2;
SATA 10

Pliny the Elder c. 23-79 .... **CMLC 23**
See also DLB 211

Plomer, William Charles Franklin
1903-1973 .... **CLC 4, 8**
See also AFW; CA 21-22; CANR 34; CAP
2; DLB 20, 162, 191, 225; EWL 3;
MTCW 1; RGEL 2; RGSF 2; SATA 24

Plotinus 204-270 .... **CMLC 46**
See also CDWLB 1; DLB 176

Plowman, Piers
See Kavanagh, Patrick (Joseph)

Plum, J.
See Wodehouse, P(elham) G(renville)

Plumly, Stanley (Ross) 1939- .... **CLC 33**
See also CA 108; 110; CANR 97; CP 7;
DLB 5, 193; INT 110

Plumpe, Friedrich Wilhelm
1888-1931 .... **TCLC 53**
See also CA 112

Po Chu-i 772-846 .... **CMLC 24**

Poe, Edgar Allan 1809-1849 ..... **NCLC 1, 16,
55, 78, 94, 97, 117; PC 1; SSC 1, 22,
34, 35, 54; WLC**
See also AAYA 14; AMW; AMWC 1;
AMWR 2; BPFB 3; BYA 5, 11; CDALB
1640-1865; CMW 4; DA; DA3; DAB;
DAC; DAM MST, POET; DLB 3, 59, 73,
74, 248, 254; EXPP; EXPS; HGG; LAIT
2; LATS 1; LMFS 1; MSW; PAB; PFS 1,
3, 9; RGAL 4; RGSF 2; SATA 23; SCFW
2; SFW 4; SSFS 2, 4, 7, 8, 16; SUFW;
TUS; WP; WYA

Poet of Titchfield Street, The
See Pound, Ezra (Weston Loomis)

Pohl, Frederik 1919- .... **CLC 18; SSC 25**
See also AAYA 24; CA 61-64; CAAE 188;
CAAS 1; CANR 11, 37, 81; CN 7; DLB
8; INT CANR-11; MTCW 1, 2; SATA 24;
SCFW 2; SFW 4

Poirier, Louis 1910-
See Gracq, Julien
See also CA 122; 126; CWW 2

Poitier, Sidney 1927- .... **CLC 26**
See also BW 1; CA 117; CANR 94

Pokagon, Simon 1830-1899 .... **NNAL**
See also DAM MULT

Polanski, Roman 1933- .... **CLC 16**
See also CA 77-80

Poliakoff, Stephen 1952- .... **CLC 38**
See also CA 106; CANR 116; CBD; CD 5;
DLB 13

Police, The
See Copeland, Stewart (Armstrong); Sum-
mers, Andrew James; Sumner, Gordon
Matthew

Polidori, John William 1795-1821 . **NCLC 51**
See also DLB 116; HGG

Pollitt, Katha 1949- .... **CLC 28, 122**
See also CA 120; 122; CANR 66, 108;
MTCW 1, 2

Pollock, (Mary) Sharon 1936- .... **CLC 50**
See also CA 141; CD 5; CWD; DAC; DAM
DRAM, MST; DFS 3; DLB 60; FW

Pollock, Sharon 1936- .... **DC 20**

Polo, Marco 1254-1324 .... **CMLC 15**

Polonsky, Abraham (Lincoln)
1910-1999 .... **CLC 92**
See also CA 104; 187; DLB 26; INT 104

Polybius c. 200B.C.-c. 118B.C. ...... **CMLC 17**
See also AW 1; DLB 176; RGWL 2, 3

Pomerance, Bernard 1940- .... **CLC 13**
See also CA 101; CAD; CANR 49; CD 5;
DAM DRAM; DFS 9; LAIT 2

Proust,
(Valentin-Louis-George-Eugene-)Marcel
1871-1922 .... **TCLC 7, 13, 33; WLC**
See also BPFB 3; CA 104; 120; CANR 110;
DA; DA3; DAB; DAC; DAM MST, NOV;
DLB 65; EW 8; EWL 3; GFL 1789 to the
Present; MTCW 1, 2; RGWL 2, 3; TWA

Prowler, Harley
See Masters, Edgar Lee

Prus, Boleslaw 1845-1912 .... **TCLC 48**
See also RGWL 2, 3

Pryor, Richard (Franklin Lenox Thomas)
1940- .... **CLC 26**
See also CA 122; 152

Przybyszewski, Stanislaw
1868-1927 .... **TCLC 36**
See also CA 160; DLB 66; EWL 3

Pteleon
See Grieve, C(hristopher) M(urray)
See also DAM POET

Puckett, Lute
See Masters, Edgar Lee

Puig, Manuel 1932-1990 .... **CLC 3, 5, 10, 28,**
65, 133; HLC 2
See also BPFB 3; CA 45-48; CANR 2, 32,
63; CDWLB 3; DA3; DAM MULT; DLB
113; DNFS 1; EWL 3; GLL 1; HW 1, 2;
LAW; MTCW 1, 2; RGWL 2, 3; TWA;
WLIT 1

Pulitzer, Joseph 1847-1911 .... **TCLC 76**
See also CA 114; DLB 23

Purchas, Samuel 1577(?)-1626 .... **LC 70**
See also DLB 151

Purdy, A(lfred) W(ellington)
1918-2000 .... **CLC 3, 6, 14, 50**
See also CA 81-84; 189; CAAS 17; CANR
42, 66; CP 7; DAC; DAM MST, POET;
DLB 88; PFS 5; RGEL 2

Purdy, James (Amos) 1923- .... **CLC 2, 4, 10,**
28, 52
See also AMWS 7; CA 33-36R; CAAS 1;
CANR 19, 51; CN 7; DLB 2, 218; EWL
3; INT CANR-19; MTCW 1; RGAL 4

Pure, Simon
See Swinnerton, Frank Arthur

Pushkin, Aleksandr Sergeevich
See Pushkin, Alexander (Sergeyevich)
See also DLB 205

Pushkin, Alexander (Sergeyevich)
1799-1837 .... **NCLC 3, 27, 83; PC 10;**
SSC 27, 55; WLC
See Pushkin, Aleksandr Sergeevich
See also DA; DA3; DAB; DAC; DAM
DRAM, MST, POET; EW 5; EXPS; RGSF
2; RGWL 2, 3; SATA 61; SSFS 9; TWA

P'u Sung-ling 1640-1715 .... **LC 49; SSC 31**

Putnam, Arthur Lee
See Alger, Horatio, Jr.

Puzo, Mario 1920-1999 .... **CLC 1, 2, 6, 36,**
107
See also BPFB 3; CA 65-68; 185; CANR 4,
42, 65, 99; CN 7; CPW; DA3; DAM
NOV, POP; DLB 6; MTCW 1, 2; NFS 16;
RGAL 4

Pygge, Edward
See Barnes, Julian (Patrick)

Pyle, Ernest Taylor 1900-1945
See Pyle, Ernie
See also CA 115; 160

Pyle, Ernie .... **TCLC 75**
See Pyle, Ernest Taylor
See also DLB 29; MTCW 2

Pyle, Howard 1853-1911 .... **TCLC 81**
See also BYA 2, 4; CA 109; 137; CLR 22;
DLB 42, 188; DLBD 13; LAIT 1; MAI-
CYA 1, 2; SATA 16, 100; WCH; YAW

Pym, Barbara (Mary Crampton)
1913-1980 .... **CLC 13, 19, 37, 111**
See also BPFB 3; BRWS 2; CA 13-14; 97-
100; CANR 13, 34; CAP 1; DLB 14, 207;
DLBY 1987; EWL 3; MTCW 1, 2; RGEL
2; TEA

Pynchon, Thomas (Ruggles, Jr.)
1937- ...... **CLC 2, 3, 6, 9, 11, 18, 33, 62,**
72, 123; SSC 14; WLC
See also AMWS 2; BEST 90:2; BPFB 3;
CA 17-20R; CANR 22, 46, 73; CN 7;
CPW 1; DA; DA3; DAB; DAC; DAM
MST, NOV, POP; DLB 2, 173; EWL 3;
MTCW 1, 2; RGAL 4; SFW 4; TUS

Pythagoras c. 582B.C.-c. 507B.C. . **CMLC 22**
See also DLB 176

Q
See Quiller-Couch, Sir Arthur (Thomas)

Qian, Chongzhu
See Ch'ien, Chung-shu

Qian Zhongshu
See Ch'ien, Chung-shu

Qroll
See Dagerman, Stig (Halvard)

Quarrington, Paul (Lewis) 1953- ..... **CLC 65**
See also CA 129; CANR 62, 95

Quasimodo, Salvatore 1901-1968 .... **CLC 10;**
PC 47
See also CA 13-16; 25-28R; CAP 1; DLB
114; EW 12; EWL 3; MTCW 1; RGWL
2, 3

Quatermass, Martin
See Carpenter, John (Howard)

Quay, Stephen 1947- .... **CLC 95**
See also CA 189

Quay, Timothy 1947- .... **CLC 95**
See also CA 189

Queen, Ellery .... **CLC 3, 11**
See Dannay, Frederic; Davidson, Avram
(James); Deming, Richard; Fairman, Paul
W.; Flora, Fletcher; Hoch, Edward
D(entinger); Kane, Henry; Lee, Manfred
B(ennington); Marlowe, Stephen; Powell,
(Oval) Talmage; Sheldon, Walter J(ames);
Sturgeon, Theodore (Hamilton); Tracy,
Don(ald Fiske); Vance, John Holbrook
See also BPFB 3; CMW 4; MSW; RGAL 4

Queen, Ellery, Jr.
See Dannay, Frederic; Lee, Manfred
B(ennington)

Queneau, Raymond 1903-1976 ..... **CLC 2, 5,**
10, 42
See also CA 77-80; 69-72; CANR 32; DLB
72, 258; EW 12; EWL 3; GFL 1789 to
the Present; MTCW 1, 2; RGWL 2, 3

Quevedo, Francisco de 1580-1645 .... **LC 23**

Quiller-Couch, Sir Arthur (Thomas)
1863-1944 .... **TCLC 53**
See also CA 118; 166; DLB 135, 153, 190;
HGG; RGEL 2; SUFW 1

Quin, Ann (Marie) 1936-1973 .... **CLC 6**
See also CA 9-12R; 45-48; DLB 14, 231

Quincey, Thomas de
See De Quincey, Thomas

Quinn, Martin
See Smith, Martin Cruz

Quinn, Peter 1947- .... **CLC 91**
See also CA 197

Quinn, Simon
See Smith, Martin Cruz

Quintana, Leroy V. 1944- ...... **HLC 2; PC 36**
See also CA 131; CANR 65; DAM MULT;
DLB 82; HW 1, 2

Quiroga, Horacio (Sylvestre)
1878-1937 .... **HLC 2; TCLC 20**
See also CA 117; 131; DAM MULT; EWL
3; HW 1; LAW; MTCW 1; RGSF 2;
WLIT 1

Quoirez, Francoise 1935- .... **CLC 9**
See Sagan, Francoise
See also CA 49-52; CANR 6, 39, 73; CWW
2; MTCW 1, 2; TWA

Raabe, Wilhelm (Karl) 1831-1910 . **TCLC 45**
See also CA 167; DLB 129

Rabe, David (William) 1940- ... **CLC 4, 8, 33;**
DC 16
See also CA 85-88; CABS 3; CAD; CANR
59; CD 5; DAM DRAM; DFS 3, 8, 13;
DLB 7, 228; EWL 3

Rabelais, Francois 1494-1553 .... **LC 5, 60;**
WLC
See also DA; DAB; DAC; DAM MST; EW
2; GFL Beginnings to 1789; LMFS 1;
RGWL 2, 3; TWA

Rabinovitch, Sholem 1859-1916
See Aleichem, Sholom
See also CA 104

Rabinyan, Dorit 1972- .... **CLC 119**
See also CA 170

Rachilde
See Vallette, Marguerite Eymery; Vallette,
Marguerite Eymery
See also EWL 3

Racine, Jean 1639-1699 .... **LC 28**
See also DA3; DAB; DAM MST; DLB 268;
EW 3; GFL Beginnings to 1789; LMFS
1; RGWL 2, 3; TWA

Radcliffe, Ann (Ward) 1764-1823 ... **NCLC 6,**
55, 106
See also DLB 39, 178; HGG; LMFS 1;
RGEL 2; SUFW 1; WLIT 3

Radclyffe-Hall, Marguerite
See Hall, (Marguerite) Radclyffe

Radiguet, Raymond 1903-1923 ...... **TCLC 29**
See also CA 162; DLB 65; EWL 3; GFL
1789 to the Present; RGWL 2, 3

Radnoti, Miklos 1909-1944 .... **TCLC 16**
See also CA 118; 212; CDWLB 4; DLB
215; EWL 3; RGWL 2, 3

Rado, James 1939- .... **CLC 17**
See also CA 105

Radvanyi, Netty 1900-1983
See Seghers, Anna
See also CA 85-88; 110; CANR 82

Rae, Ben
See Griffiths, Trevor

Raeburn, John (Hay) 1941- .... **CLC 34**
See also CA 57-60

Ragni, Gerome 1942-1991 .... **CLC 17**
See also CA 105; 134

Rahv, Philip .... **CLC 24**
See Greenberg, Ivan
See also DLB 137

Raimund, Ferdinand Jakob
1790-1836 .... **NCLC 69**
See also DLB 90

Raine, Craig (Anthony) 1944- .. **CLC 32, 103**
See also CA 108; CANR 29, 51, 103; CP 7;
DLB 40; PFS 7

Raine, Kathleen (Jessie) 1908- ..... **CLC 7, 45**
See also CA 85-88; CANR 46, 109; CP 7;
DLB 20; EWL 3; MTCW 1; RGEL 2

Rainis, Janis 1865-1929 .... **TCLC 29**
See also CA 170; CDWLB 4; DLB 220;
EWL 3

Rakosi, Carl .... **CLC 47**
See Rawley, Callman
See also CAAS 5; CP 7; DLB 193

Ralegh, Sir Walter
See Raleigh, Sir Walter
See also BRW 1; RGEL 2; WP

Raleigh, Richard
See Lovecraft, H(oward) P(hillips)

Rhine, Richard
　　See Silverstein, Alvin; Silverstein, Virginia
　　B(arbara Opshelor)
Rhodes, Eugene Manlove
　　1869-1934 .... **TCLC 53**
　　See also CA 198; DLB 256
R'hoone, Lord
　　See Balzac, Honore de
Rhys, Jean 1894(?)-1979 ...... **CLC 2, 4, 6, 14,**
　　　19, 51, 124; SSC 21
　　See also BRWS 2; CA 25-28R; 85-88;
　　CANR 35, 62; CDBLB 1945-1960; CD-
　　WLB 3; DA3; DAM NOV; DLB 36, 117,
　　162; DNFS 2; EWL 3; LATS 1; MTCW
　　1, 2; RGEL 2; RGSF 2; RHW; TEA
Ribeiro, Darcy 1922-1997 .... **CLC 34**
　　See also CA 33-36R; 156; EWL 3
Ribeiro, Joao Ubaldo (Osorio Pimentel)
　　1941- .... **CLC 10, 67**
　　See also CA 81-84; EWL 3
Ribman, Ronald (Burt) 1932- .... **CLC 7**
　　See also CA 21-24R; CAD; CANR 46, 80;
　　CD 5
Ricci, Nino 1959- .... **CLC 70**
　　See also CA 137; CCA 1
Rice, Anne 1941- .... **CLC 41, 128**
　　See Rampling, Anne
　　See also AAYA 9; AMWS 7; BEST 89:2;
　　BPFB 3; CA 65-68; CANR 12, 36, 53,
　　74, 100; CN 7; CPW; CSW; DA3; DAM
　　POP; GLL 2; HGG; MTCW 2; SUFW 2;
　　YAW
Rice, Elmer (Leopold) 1892-1967 ...... **CLC 7,**
　　　49
　　See Reizenstein, Elmer Leopold
　　See also CA 21-22; 25-28R; CAP 2; DAM
　　DRAM; DFS 12; DLB 4, 7; MTCW 1, 2;
　　RGAL 4
Rice, Tim(othy Miles Bindon)
　　1944- .... **CLC 21**
　　See also CA 103; CANR 46; DFS 7
Rich, Adrienne (Cecile) 1929- ... **CLC 3, 6, 7,**
　　　11, 18, 36, 73, 76, 125; PC 5
　　See also AMWR 2; AMWS 1; CA 9-12R;
　　CANR 20, 53, 74; CDALBS; CP 7; CSW;
　　CWP; DA3; DAM POET; DLB 5, 67;
　　EWL 3; EXPP; FW; MAWW; MTCW 1,
　　2; PAB; PFS 15; RGAL 4; WP
Rich, Barbara
　　See Graves, Robert (von Ranke)
Rich, Robert
　　See Trumbo, Dalton
Richard, Keith .... **CLC 17**
　　See Richards, Keith
Richards, David Adams 1950- .... **CLC 59**
　　See also CA 93-96; CANR 60, 110; DAC;
　　DLB 53
Richards, I(vor) A(rmstrong)
　　1893-1979 .... **CLC 14, 24**
　　See also BRWS 2; CA 41-44R; 89-92;
　　CANR 34, 74; DLB 27; EWL 3; MTCW
　　2; RGEL 2
Richards, Keith 1943-
　　See Richard, Keith
　　See also CA 107; CANR 77
Richardson, Anne
　　See Roiphe, Anne (Richardson)
Richardson, Dorothy Miller
　　1873-1957 .... **TCLC 3**
　　See also CA 104; 192; DLB 36; EWL 3;
　　FW; RGEL 2
Richardson (Robertson), Ethel Florence
　　Lindesay 1870-1946
　　See Richardson, Henry Handel
　　See also CA 105; 190; DLB 230; RHW

Richardson, Henry Handel .... **TCLC 4**
　　See Richardson (Robertson), Ethel Florence
　　Lindesay
　　See also DLB 197; EWL 3; RGEL 2; RGSF
　　2
Richardson, John 1796-1852 .... **NCLC 55**
　　See also CCA 1; DAC; DLB 99
Richardson, Samuel 1689-1761 ...... **LC 1, 44;**
　　　WLC
　　See also BRW 3; CDBLB 1660-1789; DA;
　　DAB; DAC; DAM MST, NOV; DLB 39;
　　RGEL 2; TEA; WLIT 3
Richardson, Willis 1889-1977 .... **HR 3**
　　See also BW 1; CA 124; DLB 51; SATA 60
Richler, Mordecai 1931-2001 .... **CLC 3, 5, 9,**
　　　13, 18, 46, 70
　　See also AITN 1; CA 65-68; 201; CANR
　　31, 62, 111; CCA 1; CLR 17; CWRI 5;
　　DAC; DAM MST, NOV; DLB 53; EWL
　　3; MAICYA 1, 2; MTCW 1, 2; RGEL 2;
　　SATA 44, 98; SATA-Brief 27; TWA
Richter, Conrad (Michael)
　　1890-1968 .... **CLC 30**
　　See also AAYA 21; BYA 2; CA 5-8R; 25-
　　28R; CANR 23; DLB 9, 212; LAIT 1;
　　MTCW 1, 2; RGAL 4; SATA 3; TCWW
　　2; TUS; YAW
Ricostranza, Tom
　　See Ellis, Trey
Riddell, Charlotte 1832-1906 .... **TCLC 40**
　　See Riddell, Mrs. J. H.
　　See also CA 165; DLB 156
Riddell, Mrs. J. H.
　　See Riddell, Charlotte
　　See also HGG; SUFW
Ridge, John Rollin 1827-1867 ...... **NCLC 82;**
　　　NNAL
　　See also CA 144; DAM MULT; DLB 175
Ridgeway, Jason
　　See Marlowe, Stephen
Ridgway, Keith 1965- .... **CLC 119**
　　See also CA 172
Riding, Laura .... **CLC 3, 7**
　　See Jackson, Laura (Riding)
　　See also RGAL 4
Riefenstahl, Berta Helene Amalia 1902-
　　See Riefenstahl, Leni
　　See also CA 108
Riefenstahl, Leni .... **CLC 16**
　　See Riefenstahl, Berta Helene Amalia
Riffe, Ernest
　　See Bergman, (Ernst) Ingmar
Riggs, (Rolla) Lynn
　　1899-1954 .... **NNAL; TCLC 56**
　　See also CA 144; DAM MULT; DLB 175
Riis, Jacob A(ugust) 1849-1914 ..... **TCLC 80**
　　See also CA 113; 168; DLB 23
Riley, James Whitcomb 1849-1916 .... **PC 48;**
　　　TCLC 51
　　See also CA 118; 137; DAM POET; MAI-
　　CYA 1, 2; RGAL 4; SATA 17
Riley, Tex
　　See Creasey, John
Rilke, Rainer Maria 1875-1926 .... **PC 2;**
　　　TCLC 1, 6, 19
　　See also CA 104; 132; CANR 62, 99; CD-
　　WLB 2; DA3; DAM POET; DLB 81; EW
　　9; EWL 3; MTCW 1, 2; RGWL 2, 3;
　　TWA; WP
Rimbaud, (Jean Nicolas) Arthur
　　1854-1891 .... **NCLC 4, 35, 82; PC 3;**
　　　WLC
　　See also DA; DA3; DAB; DAC; DAM
　　MST, POET; DLB 217; EW 7; GFL 1789
　　to the Present; LMFS 2; RGWL 2, 3;
　　TWA; WP

Rinehart, Mary Roberts
　　1876-1958 .... **TCLC 52**
　　See also BPFB 3; CA 108; 166; RGAL 4;
　　RHW
Ringmaster, The
　　See Mencken, H(enry) L(ouis)
Ringwood, Gwen(dolyn Margaret) Pharis
　　1910-1984 .... **CLC 48**
　　See also CA 148; 112; DLB 88
Rio, Michel 1945(?)- .... **CLC 43**
　　See also CA 201
Ritsos, Giannes
　　See Ritsos, Yannis
Ritsos, Yannis 1909-1990 .... **CLC 6, 13, 31**
　　See also CA 77-80; 133; CANR 39, 61; EW
　　12; EWL 3; MTCW 1; RGWL 2, 3
Ritter, Erika 1948(?)- .... **CLC 52**
　　See also CD 5; CWD
Rivera, Jose Eustasio 1889-1928 ... **TCLC 35**
　　See also CA 162; EWL 3; HW 1, 2; LAW
Rivera, Tomas 1935-1984 .... **HLCS 2**
　　See also CA 49-52; CANR 32; DLB 82;
　　HW 1; RGAL 4; SSFS 15; TCWW 2;
　　WLIT 1
Rivers, Conrad Kent 1933-1968 .... **CLC 1**
　　See also BW 1; CA 85-88; DLB 41
Rivers, Elfrida
　　See Bradley, Marion Zimmer
　　See also GLL 1
Riverside, John
　　See Heinlein, Robert A(nson)
Rizal, Jose 1861-1896 .... **NCLC 27**
Roa Bastos, Augusto (Antonio)
　　1917- .... **CLC 45; HLC 2**
　　See also CA 131; DAM MULT; DLB 113;
　　EWL 3; HW 1; LAW; RGSF 2; WLIT 1
Robbe-Grillet, Alain 1922- .... **CLC 1, 2, 4, 6,**
　　　8, 10, 14, 43, 128
　　See also BPFB 3; CA 9-12R; CANR 33,
　　65, 115; DLB 83; EW 13; EWL 3; GFL
　　1789 to the Present; IDFW 3, 4; MTCW
　　1, 2; RGWL 2, 3; SSFS 15
Robbins, Harold 1916-1997 .... **CLC 5**
　　See also BPFB 3; CA 73-76; 162; CANR
　　26, 54, 112; DA3; DAM NOV; MTCW 1,
　　2
Robbins, Thomas Eugene 1936-
　　See Robbins, Tom
　　See also CA 81-84; CANR 29, 59, 95; CN
　　7; CPW; CSW; DA3; DAM NOV, POP;
　　MTCW 1, 2
Robbins, Tom .... **CLC 9, 32, 64**
　　See Robbins, Thomas Eugene
　　See also AAYA 32; AMWS 10; BEST 90:3;
　　BPFB 3; DLBY 1980; MTCW 2
Robbins, Trina 1938- .... **CLC 21**
　　See also CA 128
Roberts, Charles G(eorge) D(ouglas)
　　1860-1943 .... **TCLC 8**
　　See also CA 105; 188; CLR 33; CWRI 5;
　　DLB 92; RGEL 2; RGSF 2; SATA 88;
　　SATA-Brief 29
Roberts, Elizabeth Madox
　　1886-1941 .... **TCLC 68**
　　See also CA 111; 166; CWRI 5; DLB 9, 54,
　　102; RGAL 4; RHW; SATA 33; SATA-
　　Brief 27; WCH
Roberts, Kate 1891-1985 .... **CLC 15**
　　See also CA 107; 116
Roberts, Keith (John Kingston)
　　1935-2000 .... **CLC 14**
　　See also CA 25-28R; CANR 46; DLB 261;
　　SFW 4
Roberts, Kenneth (Lewis)
　　1885-1957 .... **TCLC 23**
　　See also CA 109; 199; DLB 9; RGAL 4;
　　RHW

Roberts, Michele (Brigitte) 1949- ..... **CLC 48**
See also CA 115; CANR 58; CN 7; DLB 231; FW
Robertson, Ellis
See Ellison, Harlan (Jay); Silverberg, Robert
Robertson, Thomas William
1829-1871 .... **NCLC 35**
See Robertson, Tom
See also DAM DRAM
Robertson, Tom
See Robertson, Thomas William
See also RGEL 2
Robeson, Kenneth
See Dent, Lester
Robinson, Edwin Arlington
1869-1935 .... **PC 1, 35; TCLC 5, 101**
See also AMW; CA 104; 133; CDALB 1865-1917; DA; DAC; DAM MST, POET; DLB 54; EWL 3; EXPP; MTCW 1, 2; PAB; PFS 4; RGAL 4; WP
Robinson, Henry Crabb
1775-1867 .... **NCLC 15**
See also DLB 107
Robinson, Jill 1936- .... **CLC 10**
See also CA 102; INT 102
Robinson, Kim Stanley 1952- .... **CLC 34**
See also AAYA 26; CA 126; CANR 113; CN 7; SATA 109; SCFW 2; SFW 4
Robinson, Lloyd
See Silverberg, Robert
Robinson, Marilynne 1944- .... **CLC 25**
See also CA 116; CANR 80; CN 7; DLB 206
Robinson, Smokey .... **CLC 21**
See Robinson, William, Jr.
Robinson, William, Jr. 1940-
See Robinson, Smokey
See also CA 116
Robison, Mary 1949- .... **CLC 42, 98**
See also CA 113; 116; CANR 87; CN 7; DLB 130; INT 116; RGSF 2
Rochester
See Wilmot, John
See also RGEL 2
Rod, Edouard 1857-1910 .... **TCLC 52**
Roddenberry, Eugene Wesley 1921-1991
See Roddenberry, Gene
See also CA 110; 135; CANR 37; SATA 45; SATA-Obit 69
Roddenberry, Gene .... **CLC 17**
See Roddenberry, Eugene Wesley
See also AAYA 5; SATA-Obit 69
Rodgers, Mary 1931- .... **CLC 12**
See also BYA 5; CA 49-52; CANR 8, 55, 90; CLR 20; CWRI 5; INT CANR-8; JRDA; MAICYA 1, 2; SATA 8, 130
Rodgers, W(illiam) R(obert)
1909-1969 .... **CLC 7**
See also CA 85-88; DLB 20; RGEL 2
Rodman, Eric
See Silverberg, Robert
Rodman, Howard 1920(?)-1985 .... **CLC 65**
See also CA 118
Rodman, Maia
See Wojciechowska, Maia (Teresa)
Rodo, Jose Enrique 1871(?)-1917 .... **HLCS 2**
See also CA 178; EWL 3; HW 2; LAW
Rodolph, Utto
See Ouologuem, Yambo
Rodriguez, Claudio 1934-1999 .... **CLC 10**
See also CA 188; DLB 134
Rodriguez, Richard 1944- .... **CLC 155; HLC 2**
See also CA 110; CANR 66, 116; DAM MULT; DLB 82, 256; HW 1, 2; LAIT 5; NCFS 3; WLIT 1
Roelvaag, O(le) E(dvart) 1876-1931
See Rolvaag, O(le) E(dvart)
See also CA 117; 171

Roethke, Theodore (Huebner)
1908-1963 .... **CLC 1, 3, 8, 11, 19, 46, 101; PC 15**
See also AMW; CA 81-84; CABS 2; CDALB 1941-1968; DA3; DAM POET; DLB 5, 206; EWL 3; EXPP; MTCW 1, 2; PAB; PFS 3; RGAL 4; WP
Rogers, Carl R(ansom)
1902-1987 .... **TCLC 125**
See also CA 1-4R; 121; CANR 1, 18; MTCW 1
Rogers, Samuel 1763-1855 .... **NCLC 69**
See also DLB 93; RGEL 2
Rogers, Thomas Hunton 1927- .... **CLC 57**
See also CA 89-92; INT 89-92
Rogers, Will(iam Penn Adair)
1879-1935 .... **NNAL; TCLC 8, 71**
See also CA 105; 144; DA3; DAM MULT; DLB 11; MTCW 2
Rogin, Gilbert 1929- .... **CLC 18**
See also CA 65-68; CANR 15
Rohan, Koda
See Koda Shigeyuki
Rohlfs, Anna Katharine Green
See Green, Anna Katharine
Rohmer, Eric .... **CLC 16**
See Scherer, Jean-Marie Maurice
Rohmer, Sax .... **TCLC 28**
See Ward, Arthur Henry Sarsfield
See also DLB 70; MSW; SUFW
Roiphe, Anne (Richardson) 1935- .. **CLC 3, 9**
See also CA 89-92; CANR 45, 73; DLBY 1980; INT 89-92
Rojas, Fernando de 1475-1541 .... **HLCS 1; LC 23**
See also RGWL 2, 3
Rojas, Gonzalo 1917- .... **HLCS 2**
See also CA 178; HW 2; LAWS 1
Rolfe, Frederick (William Serafino Austin Lewis Mary) 1860-1913 .... **TCLC 12**
See Corvo, Baron
See also CA 107; 210; DLB 34, 156; RGEL 2
Rolland, Romain 1866-1944 .... **TCLC 23**
See also CA 118; 197; DLB 65, 284; EWL 3; GFL 1789 to the Present; RGWL 2, 3
Rolle, Richard c. 1300-c. 1349 ...... **CMLC 21**
See also DLB 146; LMFS 1; RGEL 2
Rolvaag, O(le) E(dvart) .... **TCLC 17**
See Roelvaag, O(le) E(dvart)
See also DLB 9, 212; NFS 5; RGAL 4
Romain Arnaud, Saint
See Aragon, Louis
Romains, Jules 1885-1972 .... **CLC 7**
See also CA 85-88; CANR 34; DLB 65; EWL 3; GFL 1789 to the Present; MTCW 1
Romero, Jose Ruben 1890-1952 .... **TCLC 14**
See also CA 114; 131; EWL 3; HW 1; LAW
Ronsard, Pierre de 1524-1585 . **LC 6, 54; PC 11**
See also EW 2; GFL Beginnings to 1789; RGWL 2, 3; TWA
Rooke, Leon 1934- .... **CLC 25, 34**
See also CA 25-28R; CANR 23, 53; CCA 1; CPW; DAM POP
Roosevelt, Franklin Delano
1882-1945 .... **TCLC 93**
See also CA 116; 173; LAIT 3
Roosevelt, Theodore 1858-1919 ..... **TCLC 69**
See also CA 115; 170; DLB 47, 186, 275
Roper, William 1498-1578 .... **LC 10**
Roquelaure, A. N.
See Rice, Anne
Rosa, Joao Guimaraes 1908-1967 ... **CLC 23; HLCS 1**
See also CA 89-92; DLB 113; EWL 3; WLIT 1

Rose, Wendy 1948- . **CLC 85; NNAL; PC 13**
See also CA 53-56; CANR 5, 51; CWP; DAM MULT; DLB 175; PFS 13; RGAL 4; SATA 12
Rosen, R. D.
See Rosen, Richard (Dean)
Rosen, Richard (Dean) 1949- .... **CLC 39**
See also CA 77-80; CANR 62; CMW 4; INT CANR-30
Rosenberg, Isaac 1890-1918 .... **TCLC 12**
See also BRW 6; CA 107; 188; DLB 20, 216; EWL 3; PAB; RGEL 2
Rosenblatt, Joe .... **CLC 15**
See Rosenblatt, Joseph
Rosenblatt, Joseph 1933-
See Rosenblatt, Joe
See also CA 89-92; CP 7; INT 89-92
Rosenfeld, Samuel
See Tzara, Tristan
Rosenstock, Sami
See Tzara, Tristan
Rosenstock, Samuel
See Tzara, Tristan
Rosenthal, M(acha) L(ouis)
1917-1996 .... **CLC 28**
See also CA 1-4R; 152; CAAS 6; CANR 4, 51; CP 7; DLB 5; SATA 59
Ross, Barnaby
See Dannay, Frederic
Ross, Bernard L.
See Follett, Ken(neth Martin)
Ross, J. H.
See Lawrence, T(homas) E(dward)
Ross, John Hume
See Lawrence, T(homas) E(dward)
Ross, Martin 1862-1915
See Martin, Violet Florence
See also DLB 135; GLL 2; RGEL 2; RGSF 2
Ross, (James) Sinclair 1908-1996 ... **CLC 13; SSC 24**
See also CA 73-76; CANR 81; CN 7; DAC; DAM MST; DLB 88; RGEL 2; RGSF 2; TCWW 2
Rossetti, Christina (Georgina)
1830-1894 .... **NCLC 2, 50, 66; PC 7; WLC**
See also BRW 5; BYA 4; DA; DA3; DAB; DAC; DAM MST, POET; DLB 35, 163, 240; EXPP; LATS 1; MAICYA 1, 2; PFS 10, 14; RGEL 2; SATA 20; TEA; WCH
Rossetti, Dante Gabriel 1828-1882 . **NCLC 4, 77; PC 44; WLC**
See also BRW 5; CDBLB 1832-1890; DA; DAB; DAC; DAM MST, POET; DLB 35; EXPP; RGEL 2; TEA
Rossi, Cristina Peri
See Peri Rossi, Cristina
Rossi, Jean Baptiste 1931-
See Japrisot, Sebastien
See also CA 201
Rossner, Judith (Perelman) 1935- . **CLC 6, 9, 29**
See also AITN 2; BEST 90:3; BPFB 3; CA 17-20R; CANR 18, 51, 73; CN 7; DLB 6; INT CANR-18; MTCW 1, 2
Rostand, Edmond (Eugene Alexis)
1868-1918 .... **DC 10; TCLC 6, 37**
See also CA 104; 126; DA; DA3; DAB; DAC; DAM DRAM, MST; DFS 1; DLB 192; LAIT 1; MTCW 1; RGWL 2, 3; TWA
Roth, Henry 1906-1995 ..... **CLC 2, 6, 11, 104**
See also AMWS 9; CA 11-12; 149; CANR 38, 63; CAP 1; CN 7; DA3; DLB 28; EWL 3; MTCW 1, 2; RGAL 4
Roth, (Moses) Joseph 1894-1939 ... **TCLC 33**
See also CA 160; DLB 85; EWL 3; RGWL 2, 3

Saunders, Caleb
See Heinlein, Robert A(nson)
Saura (Atares), Carlos 1932-1998 .... **CLC 20**
See also CA 114; 131; CANR 79; HW 1
Sauser, Frederic Louis
See Sauser-Hall, Frederic
Sauser-Hall, Frederic 1887-1961 ...... **CLC 18**
See Cendrars, Blaise
See also CA 102; 93-96; CANR 36, 62;
MTCW 2
Saussure, Ferdinand de
1857-1913 .... **TCLC 49**
See also DLB 242
Savage, Catharine
See Brosman, Catharine Savage
Savage, Thomas 1915- .... **CLC 40**
See also CA 126; 132; CAAS 15; CN 7;
INT 132; TCWW 2
Savan, Glenn (?)- .... **CLC 50**
Sax, Robert
See Johnson, Robert
Saxo Grammaticus c. 1150-c.
1222 .... **CMLC 58**
Saxton, Robert
See Johnson, Robert
Sayers, Dorothy L(eigh)
1893-1957 .... **TCLC 2, 15**
See also BPFB 3; BRWS 3; CA 104; 119;
CANR 60; CDBLB 1914-1945; CMW 4;
DAM POP; DLB 10, 36, 77, 100; MSW;
MTCW 1, 2; RGEL 2; SSFS 12; TEA
Sayers, Valerie 1952- .... **CLC 50, 122**
See also CA 134; CANR 61; CSW
Sayles, John (Thomas) 1950- . **CLC 7, 10, 14**
See also CA 57-60; CANR 41, 84; DLB 44
Scammell, Michael 1935- .... **CLC 34**
See also CA 156
Scannell, Vernon 1922- .... **CLC 49**
See also CA 5-8R; CANR 8, 24, 57; CP 7;
CWRI 5; DLB 27; SATA 59
Scarlett, Susan
See Streatfeild, (Mary) Noel
Scarron 1847-1910
See Mikszath, Kalman
Schaeffer, Susan Fromberg 1941- ..... **CLC 6,
11, 22**
See also CA 49-52; CANR 18, 65; CN 7;
DLB 28; MTCW 1, 2; SATA 22
Schama, Simon (Michael) 1945- ..... **CLC 150**
See also BEST 89:4; CA 105; CANR 39,
91
Schary, Jill
See Robinson, Jill
Schell, Jonathan 1943- .... **CLC 35**
See also CA 73-76; CANR 12, 117
Schelling, Friedrich Wilhelm Joseph von
1775-1854 .... **NCLC 30**
See also DLB 90
Scherer, Jean-Marie Maurice 1920-
See Rohmer, Eric
See also CA 110
Schevill, James (Erwin) 1920- .... **CLC 7**
See also CA 5-8R; CAAS 12; CAD; CD 5
Schiller, Friedrich von 1759-1805 ...... **DC 12;
NCLC 39, 69**
See also CDWLB 2; DAM DRAM; DLB
94; EW 5; RGWL 2, 3; TWA
Schisgal, Murray (Joseph) 1926- .... **CLC 6**
See also CA 21-24R; CAD; CANR 48, 86;
CD 5
Schlee, Ann 1934- .... **CLC 35**
See also CA 101; CANR 29, 88; SATA 44;
SATA-Brief 36
Schlegel, August Wilhelm von
1767-1845 .... **NCLC 15**
See also DLB 94; RGWL 2, 3
Schlegel, Friedrich 1772-1829 .... **NCLC 45**
See also DLB 90; EW 5; RGWL 2, 3; TWA

Schlegel, Johann Elias (von)
1719(?)-1749 .... **LC 5**
Schleiermacher, Friedrich
1768-1834 .... **NCLC 107**
See also DLB 90
Schlesinger, Arthur M(eier), Jr.
1917- .... **CLC 84**
See also AITN 1; CA 1-4R; CANR 1, 28,
58, 105; DLB 17; INT CANR-28; MTCW
1, 2; SATA 61
Schlink, Bernhard 1944- .... **CLC 174**
See also CA 163; CANR 116
Schmidt, Arno (Otto) 1914-1979 ...... **CLC 56**
See also CA 128; 109; DLB 69; EWL 3
Schmitz, Aron Hector 1861-1928
See Svevo, Italo
See also CA 104; 122; MTCW 1
Schnackenberg, Gjertrud (Cecelia)
1953- .... **CLC 40; PC 45**
See also CA 116; CANR 100; CP 7; CWP;
DLB 120, 282; PFS 13
Schneider, Leonard Alfred 1925-1966
See Bruce, Lenny
See also CA 89-92
Schnitzler, Arthur 1862-1931 ..... **DC 17; SSC
15, 61; TCLC 4**
See also CA 104; CDWLB 2; DLB 81, 118;
EW 8; EWL 3; RGSF 2; RGWL 2, 3
Schoenberg, Arnold Franz Walter
1874-1951 .... **TCLC 75**
See also CA 109; 188
Schonberg, Arnold
See Schoenberg, Arnold Franz Walter
Schopenhauer, Arthur 1788-1860 .. **NCLC 51**
See also DLB 90; EW 5
Schor, Sandra (M.) 1932(?)-1990 ..... **CLC 65**
See also CA 132
Schorer, Mark 1908-1977 .... **CLC 9**
See also CA 5-8R; 73-76; CANR 7; DLB
103
Schrader, Paul (Joseph) 1946- .... **CLC 26**
See also CA 37-40R; CANR 41; DLB 44
Schreber, Daniel 1842-1911 .... **TCLC 123**
Schreiner, Olive (Emilie Albertina)
1855-1920 .... **TCLC 9**
See also AFW; BRWS 2; CA 105; 154;
DLB 18, 156, 190, 225; EWL 3; FW;
RGEL 2; TWA; WLIT 2
Schulberg, Budd (Wilson) 1914- .. **CLC 7, 48**
See also BPFB 3; CA 25-28R; CANR 19,
87; CN 7; DLB 6, 26, 28; DLBY 1981,
2001
Schulman, Arnold
See Trumbo, Dalton
Schulz, Bruno 1892-1942 .. **SSC 13; TCLC 5,
51**
See also CA 115; 123; CANR 86; CDWLB
4; DLB 215; EWL 3; MTCW 2; RGSF 2;
RGWL 2, 3
Schulz, Charles M(onroe)
1922-2000 .... **CLC 12**
See also AAYA 39; CA 9-12R; 187; CANR
6; INT CANR-6; SATA 10; SATA-Obit
118
Schumacher, E(rnst) F(riedrich)
1911-1977 .... **CLC 80**
See also CA 81-84; 73-76; CANR 34, 85
Schuyler, George Samuel 1895-1977 .... **HR 3**
See also BW 2; CA 81-84; 73-76; CANR
42; DLB 29, 51
Schuyler, James Marcus 1923-1991 .. **CLC 5,
23**
See also CA 101; 134; DAM POET; DLB
5, 169; EWL 3; INT 101; WP
Schwartz, Delmore (David)
1913-1966 ... **CLC 2, 4, 10, 45, 87; PC 8**
See also AMWS 2; CA 17-18; 25-28R;
CANR 35; CAP 2; DLB 28, 48; EWL 3;
MTCW 1, 2; PAB; RGAL 4; TUS

Schwartz, Ernst
See Ozu, Yasujiro
Schwartz, John Burnham 1965- .... **CLC 59**
See also CA 132; CANR 116
Schwartz, Lynne Sharon 1939- .... **CLC 31**
See also CA 103; CANR 44, 89; DLB 218;
MTCW 2
Schwartz, Muriel A.
See Eliot, T(homas) S(tearns)
Schwarz-Bart, Andre 1928- .... **CLC 2, 4**
See also CA 89-92; CANR 109
Schwarz-Bart, Simone 1938- . **BLCS; CLC 7**
See also BW 2; CA 97-100; CANR 117;
EWL 3
Schwerner, Armand 1927-1999 .... **PC 42**
See also CA 9-12R; 179; CANR 50, 85; CP
7; DLB 165
**Schwitters, Kurt (Hermann Edward Karl
Julius)** 1887-1948 .... **TCLC 95**
See also CA 158
Schwob, Marcel (Mayer Andre)
1867-1905 .... **TCLC 20**
See also CA 117; 168; DLB 123; GFL 1789
to the Present
Sciascia, Leonardo 1921-1989 .. **CLC 8, 9, 41**
See also CA 85-88; 130; CANR 35; DLB
177; EWL 3; MTCW 1; RGWL 2, 3
Scoppettone, Sandra 1936- .... **CLC 26**
See Early, Jack
See also AAYA 11; BYA 8; CA 5-8R;
CANR 41, 73; GLL 1; MAICYA 2; MAI-
CYAS 1; SATA 9, 92; WYA; YAW
Scorsese, Martin 1942- .... **CLC 20, 89**
See also AAYA 38; CA 110; 114; CANR
46, 85
Scotland, Jay
See Jakes, John (William)
Scott, Duncan Campbell
1862-1947 .... **TCLC 6**
See also CA 104; 153; DAC; DLB 92;
RGEL 2
Scott, Evelyn 1893-1963 .... **CLC 43**
See also CA 104; 112; CANR 64; DLB 9,
48; RHW
Scott, F(rancis) R(eginald)
1899-1985 .... **CLC 22**
See also CA 101; 114; CANR 87; DLB 88;
INT CA-101; RGEL 2
Scott, Frank
See Scott, F(rancis) R(eginald)
Scott, Joan .... **CLC 65**
Scott, Joanna 1960- .... **CLC 50**
See also CA 126; CANR 53, 92
Scott, Paul (Mark) 1920-1978 ...... **CLC 9, 60**
See also BRWS 1; CA 81-84; 77-80; CANR
33; DLB 14, 207; EWL 3; MTCW 1;
RGEL 2; RHW
Scott, Sarah 1723-1795 .... **LC 44**
See also DLB 39
Scott, Sir Walter 1771-1832 .... **NCLC 15, 69,
110; PC 13; SSC 32; WLC**
See also AAYA 22; BRW 4; BYA 2; CD-
BLB 1789-1832; DA; DAB; DAC; DAM
MST, NOV, POET; DLB 93, 107, 116,
144, 159; HGG; LAIT 1; RGEL 2; RGSF
2; SSFS 10; SUFW 1; TEA; WLIT 3;
YABC 2
Scribe, (Augustin) Eugene 1791-1861 . **DC 5;
NCLC 16**
See also DAM DRAM; DLB 192; GFL
1789 to the Present; RGWL 2, 3
Scrum, R.
See Crumb, R(obert)
Scudery, Georges de 1601-1667 .... **LC 75**
See also GFL Beginnings to 1789
Scudery, Madeleine de 1607-1701 .. **LC 2, 58**
See also DLB 268; GFL Beginnings to 1789
Scum
See Crumb, R(obert)

Shaw, Robert 1927-1978 .... **CLC 5**
See also AITN 1; CA 1-4R; 81-84; CANR 4; DLB 13, 14

Shaw, T. E.
See Lawrence, T(homas) E(dward)

Shawn, Wallace 1943- .... **CLC 41**
See also CA 112; CAD; CD 5; DLB 266

Shchedrin, N.
See Saltykov, Mikhail Evgrafovich

Shea, Lisa 1953- .... **CLC 86**
See also CA 147

Sheed, Wilfrid (John Joseph) 1930- . **CLC 2, 4, 10, 53**
See also CA 65-68; CANR 30, 66; CN 7; DLB 6; MTCW 1, 2

Sheehy, Gail 1937- .... **CLC 171**
See also CA 49-52; CANR 1, 33, 55, 92; CPW; MTCW 1

Sheldon, Alice Hastings Bradley 1915(?)-1987
See Tiptree, James, Jr.
See also CA 108; 122; CANR 34; INT 108; MTCW 1

Sheldon, John
See Bloch, Robert (Albert)

Sheldon, Walter J(ames) 1917-1996
See Queen, Ellery
See also AITN 1; CA 25-28R; CANR 10

Shelley, Mary Wollstonecraft (Godwin) 1797-1851 ...... **NCLC 14, 59, 103; WLC**
See also AAYA 20; BPFB 3; BRW 3; BRWS 3; BYA 5; CDBLB 1789-1832; DA; DA3; DAB; DAC; DAM MST, NOV; DLB 110, 116, 159, 178; HGG; LAIT 1; LMFS 1, 2; NFS 1; RGEL 2; SATA 29; SCFW; SFW 4; TEA; WLIT 3

Shelley, Percy Bysshe 1792-1822 .. **NCLC 18, 93; PC 14; WLC**
See also BRW 4; BRWR 1; CDBLB 1789-1832; DA; DA3; DAB; DAC; DAM MST, POET; DLB 96, 110, 158; EXPP; LMFS 1; PAB; PFS 2; RGEL 2; TEA; WLIT 3; WP

Shepard, Jim 1956- .... **CLC 36**
See also CA 137; CANR 59, 104; SATA 90

Shepard, Lucius 1947- .... **CLC 34**
See also CA 128; 141; CANR 81; HGG; SCFW 2; SFW 4; SUFW 2

Shepard, Sam 1943- .... **CLC 4, 6, 17, 34, 41, 44, 169; DC 5**
See also AAYA 1; AMWS 3; CA 69-72; CABS 3; CAD; CANR 22; CD 5; DA3; DAM DRAM; DFS 3, 6, 7, 14; DLB 7, 212; EWL 3; IDFW 3, 4; MTCW 1, 2; RGAL 4

Shepherd, Michael
See Ludlum, Robert

Sherburne, Zoa (Lillian Morin) 1912-1995 .... **CLC 30**
See also AAYA 13; CA 1-4R; 176; CANR 3, 37; MAICYA 1, 2; SAAS 18; SATA 3; YAW

Sheridan, Frances 1724-1766 .... **LC 7**
See also DLB 39, 84

Sheridan, Richard Brinsley 1751-1816 .... **DC 1; NCLC 5, 91; WLC**
See also BRW 3; CDBLB 1660-1789; DA; DAB; DAC; DAM DRAM, MST; DFS 15; DLB 89; WLIT 3

Sherman, Jonathan Marc .... **CLC 55**

Sherman, Martin 1941(?)- .... **CLC 19**
See also CA 116; 123; CAD; CANR 86; CD 5; DLB 228; GLL 1; IDTP

Sherwin, Judith Johnson
See Johnson, Judith (Emlyn)
See also CANR 85; CP 7; CWP

Sherwood, Frances 1940- .... **CLC 81**
See also CA 146

Sherwood, Robert E(mmet) 1896-1955 .... **TCLC 3**
See also CA 104; 153; CANR 86; DAM DRAM; DFS 11, 15, 17; DLB 7, 26, 249; IDFW 3, 4; RGAL 4

Shestov, Lev 1866-1938 .... **TCLC 56**

Shevchenko, Taras 1814-1861 .... **NCLC 54**

Shiel, M(atthew) P(hipps) 1865-1947 .... **TCLC 8**
See Holmes, Gordon
See also CA 106; 160; DLB 153; HGG; MTCW 2; SFW 4; SUFW

Shields, Carol 1935- .... **CLC 91, 113**
See also AMWS 7; CA 81-84; CANR 51, 74, 98; CCA 1; CN 7; CPW; DA3; DAC; MTCW 2

Shields, David 1956- .... **CLC 97**
See also CA 124; CANR 48, 99, 112

Shiga, Naoya 1883-1971 ..... **CLC 33; SSC 23**
See Shiga Naoya
See also CA 101; 33-36R; MJW; RGWL 3

Shiga Naoya
See Shiga, Naoya
See also DLB 180; EWL 3; RGWL 3

Shilts, Randy 1951-1994 .... **CLC 85**
See also AAYA 19; CA 115; 127; 144; CANR 45; DA3; GLL 1; INT 127; MTCW 2

Shimazaki, Haruki 1872-1943
See Shimazaki Toson
See also CA 105; 134; CANR 84; RGWL 3

Shimazaki Toson .... **TCLC 5**
See Shimazaki, Haruki
See also DLB 180; EWL 3

Sholokhov, Mikhail (Aleksandrovich) 1905-1984 .... **CLC 7, 15**
See also CA 101; 112; DLB 272; EWL 3; MTCW 1, 2; RGWL 2, 3; SATA-Obit 36

Shone, Patric
See Hanley, James

Showalter, Elaine 1941- .... **CLC 169**
See also CA 57-60; CANR 58, 106; DLB 67; FW; GLL 2

Shreve, Susan Richards 1939- .... **CLC 23**
See also CA 49-52; CAAS 5; CANR 5, 38, 69, 100; MAICYA 1, 2; SATA 46, 95; SATA-Brief 41

Shue, Larry 1946-1985 .... **CLC 52**
See also CA 145; 117; DAM DRAM; DFS 7

Shu-Jen, Chou 1881-1936
See Lu Hsun
See also CA 104

Shulman, Alix Kates 1932- .... **CLC 2, 10**
See also CA 29-32R; CANR 43; FW; SATA 7

Shusaku, Endo
See Endo, Shusaku

Shuster, Joe 1914-1992 .... **CLC 21**

Shute, Nevil .... **CLC 30**
See Norway, Nevil Shute
See also BPFB 3; DLB 255; NFS 9; RHW; SFW 4

Shuttle, Penelope (Diane) 1947- .... **CLC 7**
See also CA 93-96; CANR 39, 84, 92, 108; CP 7; CWP; DLB 14, 40

Sidhwa, Bapsy (N.) 1938- .... **CLC 168**
See also CA 108; CANR 25, 57; CN 7; FW

Sidney, Mary 1561-1621 .... **LC 19, 39**
See Sidney Herbert, Mary

Sidney, Sir Philip 1554-1586 . **LC 19, 39; PC 32**
See also BRW 1; BRWR 2; CDBLB Before 1660; DA; DA3; DAB; DAC; DAM MST, POET; DLB 167; EXPP; PAB; RGEL 2; TEA; WP

Sidney Herbert, Mary
See Sidney, Mary
See also DLB 167

Siegel, Jerome 1914-1996 .... **CLC 21**
See also CA 116; 169; 151

Siegel, Jerry
See Siegel, Jerome

Sienkiewicz, Henryk (Adam Alexander Pius) 1846-1916 .... **TCLC 3**
See also CA 104; 134; CANR 84; EWL 3; RGSF 2; RGWL 2, 3

Sierra, Gregorio Martinez
See Martinez Sierra, Gregorio

Sierra, Maria (de la O'LeJarraga) Martinez
See Martinez Sierra, Maria (de la O'LeJarraga)

Sigal, Clancy 1926- .... **CLC 7**
See also CA 1-4R; CANR 85; CN 7

Sigourney, Lydia H.
See Sigourney, Lydia Howard (Huntley)
See also DLB 73, 183

Sigourney, Lydia Howard (Huntley) 1791-1865 .... **NCLC 21, 87**
See Sigourney, Lydia H.; Sigourney, Lydia Huntley
See also DLB 1

Sigourney, Lydia Huntley
See Sigourney, Lydia Howard (Huntley)
See also DLB 42, 239, 243

Siguenza y Gongora, Carlos de 1645-1700 .... **HLCS 2; LC 8**
See also LAW

Sigurjonsson, Johann 1880-1919 ... **TCLC 27**
See also CA 170; EWL 3

Sikelianos, Angelos 1884-1951 .... **PC 29; TCLC 39**
See also EWL 3; RGWL 2, 3

Silkin, Jon 1930-1997 .... **CLC 2, 6, 43**
See also CA 5-8R; CAAS 5; CANR 89; CP 7; DLB 27

Silko, Leslie (Marmon) 1948- .... **CLC 23, 74, 114; NNAL; SSC 37; WLCS**
See also AAYA 14; AMWS 4; ANW; BYA 12; CA 115; 122; CANR 45, 65, 118; CN 7; CP 7; CPW 1; CWP; DA; DA3; DAC; DAM MST, MULT, POP; DLB 143, 175, 256, 275; EWL 3; EXPP; EXPS; LAIT 4; MTCW 2; NFS 4; PFS 9, 16; RGAL 4; RGSF 2; SSFS 4, 8, 10, 11

Sillanpaa, Frans Eemil 1888-1964 ... **CLC 19**
See also CA 129; 93-96; EWL 3; MTCW 1

Sillitoe, Alan 1928- .. **CLC 1, 3, 6, 10, 19, 57, 148**
See also AITN 1; BRWS 5; CA 9-12R; CAAE 191; CAAS 2; CANR 8, 26, 55; CDBLB 1960 to Present; CN 7; DLB 14, 139; EWL 3; MTCW 1, 2; RGEL 2; RGSF 2; SATA 61

Silone, Ignazio 1900-1978 .... **CLC 4**
See also CA 25-28; 81-84; CANR 34; CAP 2; DLB 264; EW 12; EWL 3; MTCW 1; RGSF 2; RGWL 2, 3

Silone, Ignazione
See Silone, Ignazio

Silva, Jose Asuncion
See da Silva, Antonio Jose
See also LAW

Silver, Joan Micklin 1935- .... **CLC 20**
See also CA 114; 121; INT 121

Silver, Nicholas
See Faust, Frederick (Schiller)
See also TCWW 2

Silverberg, Robert 1935- .... **CLC 7, 140**
See also AAYA 24; BPFB 3; BYA 7, 9; CA 1-4R, 186; CAAE 186; CAAS 3; CANR 1, 20, 36, 85; CLR 59; CN 7; CPW; DAM POP; DLB 8; INT CANR-20; MAICYA 1, 2; MTCW 1, 2; SATA 13, 91; SATA-Essay 104; SCFW 2; SFW 4; SUFW 2

Silverstein, Alvin 1933- .... **CLC 17**
See also CA 49-52; CANR 2; CLR 25; JRDA; MAICYA 1, 2; SATA 8, 69, 124

Smith, Iain Crichton 1928-1998 .... **CLC 64**
See also CA 21-24R; 171; CN 7; CP 7; DLB 40, 139; RGSF 2

Smith, John 1580(?)-1631 .... **LC 9**
See also DLB 24, 30; TUS

Smith, Johnston
See Crane, Stephen (Townley)

Smith, Joseph, Jr. 1805-1844 .... **NCLC 53**

Smith, Lee 1944- .... **CLC 25, 73**
See also CA 114; 119; CANR 46, 118; CSW; DLB 143; DLBY 1983; EWL 3; INT CA-119; RGAL 4

Smith, Martin
See Smith, Martin Cruz

Smith, Martin Cruz 1942- .. **CLC 25; NNAL**
See also BEST 89:4; BPFB 3; CA 85-88; CANR 6, 23, 43, 65; CMW 4; CPW; DAM MULT, POP; HGG; INT CANR-23; MTCW 2; RGAL 4

Smith, Patti 1946- .... **CLC 12**
See also CA 93-96; CANR 63

Smith, Pauline (Urmson)
1882-1959 .... **TCLC 25**
See also DLB 225; EWL 3

Smith, Rosamond
See Oates, Joyce Carol

Smith, Sheila Kaye
See Kaye-Smith, Sheila

Smith, Stevie .... **CLC 3, 8, 25, 44; PC 12**
See Smith, Florence Margaret
See also BRWS 2; DLB 20; EWL 3; MTCW 2; PAB; PFS 3; RGEL 2

Smith, Wilbur (Addison) 1933- .... **CLC 33**
See also CA 13-16R; CANR 7, 46, 66; CPW; MTCW 1, 2

Smith, William Jay 1918- .... **CLC 6**
See also CA 5-8R; CANR 44, 106; CP 7; CSW; CWRI 5; DLB 5; MAICYA 1, 2; SAAS 22; SATA 2, 68

Smith, Woodrow Wilson
See Kuttner, Henry

Smith, Zadie 1976- .... **CLC 158**
See also CA 193

Smolenskin, Peretz 1842-1885 .... **NCLC 30**

Smollett, Tobias (George) 1721-1771 ... **LC 2, 46**
See also BRW 3; CDBLB 1660-1789; DLB 39, 104; RGEL 2; TEA

Snodgrass, W(illiam) D(e Witt)
1926- .... **CLC 2, 6, 10, 18, 68**
See also AMWS 6; CA 1-4R; CANR 6, 36, 65, 85; CP 7; DAM POET; DLB 5; MTCW 1, 2; RGAL 4

Snorri Sturluson 1179-1241 .... **CMLC 56**
See also RGWL 2, 3

Snow, C(harles) P(ercy) 1905-1980 ... **CLC 1, 4, 6, 9, 13, 19**
See also BRW 7; CA 5-8R; 101; CANR 28; CDBLB 1945-1960; DAM NOV; DLB 15, 77; DLBD 17; EWL 3; MTCW 1, 2; RGEL 2; TEA

Snow, Frances Compton
See Adams, Henry (Brooks)

Snyder, Gary (Sherman) 1930- . **CLC 1, 2, 5, 9, 32, 120; PC 21**
See also AMWS 8; ANW; BG 3; CA 17-20R; CANR 30, 60; CP 7; DA3; DAM POET; DLB 5, 16, 165, 212, 237, 275; EWL 3; MTCW 2; PFS 9; RGAL 4; WP

Snyder, Zilpha Keatley 1927- .... **CLC 17**
See also AAYA 15; BYA 1; CA 9-12R; CANR 38; CLR 31; JRDA; MAICYA 1, 2; SAAS 2; SATA 1, 28, 75, 110; SATA-Essay 112; YAW

Soares, Bernardo
See Pessoa, Fernando (Antonio Nogueira)

Sobh, A.
See Shamlu, Ahmad

Sobol, Joshua 1939- .... **CLC 60**
See Sobol, Yehoshua
See also CA 200; CWW 2

Sobol, Yehoshua 1939-
See Sobol, Joshua
See also CWW 2

Socrates 470B.C.-399B.C. .... **CMLC 27**

Soderberg, Hjalmar 1869-1941 ...... **TCLC 39**
See also DLB 259; EWL 3; RGSF 2

Soderbergh, Steven 1963- .... **CLC 154**
See also AAYA 43

Sodergran, Edith (Irene) 1892-1923
See Soedergran, Edith (Irene)
See also CA 202; DLB 259; EW 11; EWL 3; RGWL 2, 3

Soedergran, Edith (Irene)
1892-1923 .... **TCLC 31**
See Sodergran, Edith (Irene)

Softly, Edgar
See Lovecraft, H(oward) P(hillips)

Softly, Edward
See Lovecraft, H(oward) P(hillips)

Sokolov, Alexander V(sevolodovich) 1943-
See Sokolov, Sasha
See also CA 73-76

Sokolov, Raymond 1941- .... **CLC 7**
See also CA 85-88

Sokolov, Sasha .... **CLC 59**
See Sokolov, Alexander V(sevolodovich)
See also CWW 2; EWL 3; RGWL 2, 3

Sokolov, Sasha .... **CLC 59**

Solo, Jay
See Ellison, Harlan (Jay)

Sologub, Fyodor .... **TCLC 9**
See Teternikov, Fyodor Kuzmich
See also EWL 3

Solomons, Ikey Esquir
See Thackeray, William Makepeace

Solomos, Dionysios 1798-1857 .... **NCLC 15**

Solwoska, Mara
See French, Marilyn

Solzhenitsyn, Aleksandr I(sayevich)
1918- .. **CLC 1, 2, 4, 7, 9, 10, 18, 26, 34, 78, 134; SSC 32; WLC**
See Solzhenitsyn, Aleksandr Isaevich
See also AAYA 49; AITN 1; BPFB 3; CA 69-72; CANR 40, 65, 116; DA; DA3; DAB; DAC; DAM MST, NOV; EW 13; EXPS; LAIT 4; MTCW 1, 2; NFS 6; RGSF 2; RGWL 2, 3; SSFS 9; TWA

Solzhenitsyn, Aleksandr Isaevich
See Solzhenitsyn, Aleksandr I(sayevich)
See also EWL 3

Somers, Jane
See Lessing, Doris (May)

Somerville, Edith Oenone
1858-1949 .... **SSC 56; TCLC 51**
See also CA 196; DLB 135; RGEL 2; RGSF 2

Somerville & Ross
See Martin, Violet Florence; Somerville, Edith Oenone

Sommer, Scott 1951- .... **CLC 25**
See also CA 106

Sondheim, Stephen (Joshua) 1930- . **CLC 30, 39, 147**
See also AAYA 11; CA 103; CANR 47, 67; DAM DRAM; LAIT 4

Sone, Monica 1919- .... **AAL**

Song, Cathy 1955- .... **AAL; PC 21**
See also CA 154; CANR 118; CWP; DLB 169; EXPP; FW; PFS 5

Sontag, Susan 1933- .... **CLC 1, 2, 10, 13, 31, 105**
See also AMWS 3; CA 17-20R; CANR 25, 51, 74, 97; CN 7; CPW; DA3; DAM POP; DLB 2, 67; EWL 3; MAWW; MTCW 1, 2; RGAL 4; RHW; SSFS 10

Sophocles 496(?)B.C.-406(?)B.C. .... **CMLC 2, 47, 51; DC 1; WLCS**
See also AW 1; CDWLB 1; DA; DA3; DAB; DAC; DAM DRAM, MST; DFS 1, 4, 8; DLB 176; LAIT 1; LATS 1; LMFS 1; RGWL 2, 3; TWA

Sordello 1189-1269 .... **CMLC 15**

Sorel, Georges 1847-1922 .... **TCLC 91**
See also CA 118; 188

Sorel, Julia
See Drexler, Rosalyn

Sorokin, Vladimir .... **CLC 59**

Sorrentino, Gilbert 1929- .. **CLC 3, 7, 14, 22, 40**
See also CA 77-80; CANR 14, 33, 115; CN 7; CP 7; DLB 5, 173; DLBY 1980; INT CANR-14

Soseki
See Natsume, Soseki
See also MJW

Soto, Gary 1952- ... **CLC 32, 80; HLC 2; PC 28**
See also AAYA 10, 37; BYA 11; CA 119; 125; CANR 50, 74, 107; CLR 38; CP 7; DAM MULT; DLB 82; EWL 3; EXPP; HW 1, 2; INT CA-125; JRDA; MAICYA 2; MAICYAS 1; MTCW 2; PFS 7; RGAL 4; SATA 80, 120; WYA; YAW

Soupault, Philippe 1897-1990 .... **CLC 68**
See also CA 116; 147; 131; EWL 3; GFL 1789 to the Present; LMFS 2

Souster, (Holmes) Raymond 1921- .... **CLC 5, 14**
See also CA 13-16R; CAAS 14; CANR 13, 29, 53; CP 7; DA3; DAC; DAM POET; DLB 88; RGEL 2; SATA 63

Southern, Terry 1924(?)-1995 .... **CLC 7**
See also AMWS 11; BPFB 3; CA 1-4R; 150; CANR 1, 55, 107; CN 7; DLB 2; IDFW 3, 4

Southey, Robert 1774-1843 .... **NCLC 8, 97**
See also BRW 4; DLB 93, 107, 142; RGEL 2; SATA 54

Southworth, Emma Dorothy Eliza Nevitte
1819-1899 .... **NCLC 26**
See also DLB 239

Souza, Ernest
See Scott, Evelyn

Soyinka, Wole 1934- .. **BLC 3; CLC 3, 5, 14, 36, 44; DC 2; WLC**
See also AFW; BW 2, 3; CA 13-16R; CANR 27, 39, 82; CD 5; CDWLB 3; CN 7; CP 7; DA; DA3; DAB; DAC; DAM DRAM, MST, MULT; DFS 10; DLB 125; EWL 3; MTCW 1, 2; RGEL 2; TWA; WLIT 2

Spackman, W(illiam) M(ode)
1905-1990 .... **CLC 46**
See also CA 81-84; 132

Spacks, Barry (Bernard) 1931- .... **CLC 14**
See also CA 154; CANR 33, 109; CP 7; DLB 105

Spanidou, Irini 1946- .... **CLC 44**
See also CA 185

Spark, Muriel (Sarah) 1918- ..... **CLC 2, 3, 5, 8, 13, 18, 40, 94; SSC 10**
See also BRWS 1; CA 5-8R; CANR 12, 36, 76, 89; CDBLB 1945-1960; CN 7; CP 7; DA3; DAB; DAC; DAM MST, NOV; DLB 15, 139; EWL 3; FW; INT CANR-12; LAIT 4; MTCW 1, 2; RGEL 2; TEA; WLIT 4; YAW

Spaulding, Douglas
See Bradbury, Ray (Douglas)

Spaulding, Leonard
See Bradbury, Ray (Douglas)

Spelman, Elizabeth .... **CLC 65**

Spence, J. A. D.
See Eliot, T(homas) S(tearns)

Tartt, Donna 1964(?)- .... **CLC 76**
See also CA 142

Tasso, Torquato 1544-1595 .... **LC 5**
See also EFS 2; EW 2; RGWL 2, 3

Tate, (John Orley) Allen 1899-1979 .. **CLC 2, 4, 6, 9, 11, 14, 24**
See also AMW; CA 5-8R; 85-88; CANR 32, 108; DLB 4, 45, 63; DLBD 17; EWL 3; MTCW 1, 2; RGAL 4; RHW

Tate, Ellalice
See Hibbert, Eleanor Alice Burford

Tate, James (Vincent) 1943- ..... **CLC 2, 6, 25**
See also CA 21-24R; CANR 29, 57, 114; CP 7; DLB 5, 169; EWL 3; PFS 10, 15; RGAL 4; WP

Tauler, Johannes c. 1300-1361 ...... **CMLC 37**
See also DLB 179; LMFS 1

Tavel, Ronald 1940- .... **CLC 6**
See also CA 21-24R; CAD; CANR 33; CD 5

Taviani, Paolo 1931- .... **CLC 70**
See also CA 153

Taylor, Bayard 1825-1878 .... **NCLC 89**
See also DLB 3, 189, 250, 254; RGAL 4

Taylor, C(ecil) P(hilip) 1929-1981 .... **CLC 27**
See also CA 25-28R; 105; CANR 47; CBD

Taylor, Edward 1642(?)-1729 .... **LC 11**
See also AMW; DA; DAB; DAC; DAM MST, POET; DLB 24; EXPP; RGAL 4; TUS

Taylor, Eleanor Ross 1920- .... **CLC 5**
See also CA 81-84; CANR 70

Taylor, Elizabeth 1932-1975 ..... **CLC 2, 4, 29**
See also CA 13-16R; CANR 9, 70; DLB 139; MTCW 1; RGEL 2; SATA 13

Taylor, Frederick Winslow 1856-1915 .... **TCLC 76**
See also CA 188

Taylor, Henry (Splawn) 1942- .... **CLC 44**
See also CA 33-36R; CAAS 7; CANR 31; CP 7; DLB 5; PFS 10

Taylor, Kamala (Purnaiya) 1924-
See Markandaya, Kamala
See also CA 77-80; NFS 13

Taylor, Mildred D(elois) 1943- .... **CLC 21**
See also AAYA 10, 47; BW 1; BYA 3, 8; CA 85-88; CANR 25, 115; CLR 9, 59; CSW; DLB 52; JRDA; LAIT 3; MAICYA 1, 2; SAAS 5; SATA 135; WYA; YAW

Taylor, Peter (Hillsman) 1917-1994 .. **CLC 1, 4, 18, 37, 44, 50, 71; SSC 10**
See also AMWS 5; BPFB 3; CA 13-16R; 147; CANR 9, 50; CSW; DLB 218, 278; DLBY 1981, 1994; EWL 3; EXPS; INT CANR-9; MTCW 1, 2; RGSF 2; SSFS 9; TUS

Taylor, Robert Lewis 1912-1998 .... **CLC 14**
See also CA 1-4R; 170; CANR 3, 64; SATA 10

Tchekhov, Anton
See Chekhov, Anton (Pavlovich)

Tchicaya, Gerald Felix 1931-1988 .. **CLC 101**
See Tchicaya U Tam'si
See also CA 129; 125; CANR 81

Tchicaya U Tam'si
See Tchicaya, Gerald Felix
See also EWL 3

Teasdale, Sara 1884-1933 .... **PC 31; TCLC 4**
See also CA 104; 163; DLB 45; GLL 1; PFS 14; RGAL 4; SATA 32; TUS

Tecumseh 1768-1813 .... **NNAL**
See also DAM MULT

Tegner, Esaias 1782-1846 .... **NCLC 2**

Teilhard de Chardin, (Marie Joseph) Pierre 1881-1955 .... **TCLC 9**
See also CA 105; 210; GFL 1789 to the Present

Temple, Ann
See Mortimer, Penelope (Ruth)

Tennant, Emma (Christina) 1937- .. **CLC 13, 52**
See also CA 65-68; CAAS 9; CANR 10, 38, 59, 88; CN 7; DLB 14; EWL 3; SFW 4

Tenneshaw, S. M.
See Silverberg, Robert

Tenney, Tabitha Gilman 1762-1837 .... **NCLC 122**
See also DLB 37, 200

Tennyson, Alfred 1809-1892 ... **NCLC 30, 65, 115; PC 6; WLC**
See also BRW 4; CDBLB 1832-1890; DA; DA3; DAB; DAC; DAM MST, POET; DLB 32; EXPP; PAB; PFS 1, 2, 4, 11, 15; RGEL 2; TEA; WLIT 4; WP

Teran, Lisa St. Aubin de .... **CLC 36**
See St. Aubin de Teran, Lisa

Terence c. 184B.C.-c. 159B.C. ...... **CMLC 14; DC 7**
See also AW 1; CDWLB 1; DLB 211; RGWL 2, 3; TWA

Teresa de Jesus, St. 1515-1582 .... **LC 18**

Terkel, Louis 1912-
See Terkel, Studs
See also CA 57-60; CANR 18, 45, 67; DA3; MTCW 1, 2

Terkel, Studs .... **CLC 38**
See Terkel, Louis
See also AAYA 32; AITN 1; MTCW 2; TUS

Terry, C. V.
See Slaughter, Frank G(ill)

Terry, Megan 1932- .... **CLC 19; DC 13**
See also CA 77-80; CABS 3; CAD; CANR 43; CD 5; CWD; DLB 7, 249; GLL 2

Tertullian c. 155-c. 245 .... **CMLC 29**

Tertz, Abram
See Sinyavsky, Andrei (Donatevich)
See also CWW 2; RGSF 2

Tesich, Steve 1943(?)-1996 .... **CLC 40, 69**
See also CA 105; 152; CAD; DLBY 1983

Tesla, Nikola 1856-1943 .... **TCLC 88**

Teternikov, Fyodor Kuzmich 1863-1927
See Sologub, Fyodor
See also CA 104

Tevis, Walter 1928-1984 .... **CLC 42**
See also CA 113; SFW 4

Tey, Josephine .... **TCLC 14**
See Mackintosh, Elizabeth
See also DLB 77; MSW

Thackeray, William Makepeace 1811-1863 .... **NCLC 5, 14, 22, 43; WLC**
See also BRW 5; CDBLB 1832-1890; DA; DA3; DAB; DAC; DAM MST, NOV; DLB 21, 55, 159, 163; NFS 13; RGEL 2; SATA 23; TEA; WLIT 3

Thakura, Ravindranatha
See Tagore, Rabindranath

Thames, C. H.
See Marlowe, Stephen

Tharoor, Shashi 1956- .... **CLC 70**
See also CA 141; CANR 91; CN 7

Thelwell, Michael Miles 1939- .... **CLC 22**
See also BW 2; CA 101

Theobald, Lewis, Jr.
See Lovecraft, H(oward) P(hillips)

Theocritus c. 310B.C.- .... **CMLC 45**
See also AW 1; DLB 176; RGWL 2, 3

Theodorescu, Ion N. 1880-1967
See Arghezi, Tudor
See also CA 116

Theriault, Yves 1915-1983 .... **CLC 79**
See also CA 102; CCA 1; DAC; DAM MST; DLB 88; EWL 3

Theroux, Alexander (Louis) 1939- .... **CLC 2, 25**
See also CA 85-88; CANR 20, 63; CN 7

Theroux, Paul (Edward) 1941- ..... **CLC 5, 8, 11, 15, 28, 46**
See also AAYA 28; AMWS 8; BEST 89:4; BPFB 3; CA 33-36R; CANR 20, 45, 74; CDALBS; CN 7; CPW 1; DA3; DAM POP; DLB 2, 218; EWL 3; HGG; MTCW 1, 2; RGAL 4; SATA 44, 109; TUS

Thesen, Sharon 1946- .... **CLC 56**
See also CA 163; CP 7; CWP

Thespis fl. 6th cent. B.C.- .... **CMLC 51**
See also LMFS 1

Thevenin, Denis
See Duhamel, Georges

Thibault, Jacques Anatole Francois 1844-1924
See France, Anatole
See also CA 106; 127; DA3; DAM NOV; MTCW 1, 2; TWA

Thiele, Colin (Milton) 1920- .... **CLC 17**
See also CA 29-32R; CANR 12, 28, 53, 105; CLR 27; MAICYA 1, 2; SAAS 2; SATA 14, 72, 125; YAW

Thistlethwaite, Bel
See Wetherald, Agnes Ethelwyn

Thomas, Audrey (Callahan) 1935- .... **CLC 7, 13, 37, 107; SSC 20**
See also AITN 2; CA 21-24R; CAAS 19; CANR 36, 58; CN 7; DLB 60; MTCW 1; RGSF 2

Thomas, Augustus 1857-1934 .... **TCLC 97**

Thomas, D(onald) M(ichael) 1935- . **CLC 13, 22, 31, 132**
See also BPFB 3; BRWS 4; CA 61-64; CAAS 11; CANR 17, 45, 75; CDBLB 1960 to Present; CN 7; CP 7; DA3; DLB 40, 207; HGG; INT CANR-17; MTCW 1, 2; SFW 4

Thomas, Dylan (Marlais) 1914-1953 ... **PC 2; SSC 3, 44; TCLC 1, 8, 45, 105; WLC**
See also AAYA 45; BRWS 1; CA 104; 120; CANR 65; CDBLB 1945-1960; DA; DA3; DAB; DAC; DAM DRAM, MST, POET; DLB 13, 20, 139; EWL 3; EXPP; LAIT 3; MTCW 1, 2; PAB; PFS 1, 3, 8; RGEL 2; RGSF 2; SATA 60; TEA; WLIT 4; WP

Thomas, (Philip) Edward 1878-1917 .... **TCLC 10**
See also BRW 6; BRWS 3; CA 106; 153; DAM POET; DLB 19, 98, 156, 216; EWL 3; PAB; RGEL 2

Thomas, Joyce Carol 1938- .... **CLC 35**
See also AAYA 12; BW 2, 3; CA 113; 116; CANR 48, 114; CLR 19; DLB 33; INT CA-116; JRDA; MAICYA 1, 2; MTCW 1, 2; SAAS 7; SATA 40, 78, 123, 137; WYA; YAW

Thomas, Lewis 1913-1993 .... **CLC 35**
See also ANW; CA 85-88; 143; CANR 38, 60; DLB 275; MTCW 1, 2

Thomas, M. Carey 1857-1935 .... **TCLC 89**
See also FW

Thomas, Paul
See Mann, (Paul) Thomas

Thomas, Piri 1928- .... **CLC 17; HLCS 2**
See also CA 73-76; HW 1

Thomas, R(onald) S(tuart) 1913-2000 .... **CLC 6, 13, 48**
See also CA 89-92; 189; CAAS 4; CANR 30; CDBLB 1960 to Present; CP 7; DAB; DAM POET; DLB 27; EWL 3; MTCW 1; RGEL 2

Thomas, Ross (Elmore) 1926-1995 .. **CLC 39**
See also CA 33-36R; 150; CANR 22, 63; CMW 4

Thompson, Francis (Joseph) 1859-1907 .... **TCLC 4**
See also BRW 5; CA 104; 189; CDBLB 1890-1914; DLB 19; RGEL 2; TEA

Thompson, Francis Clegg
See Mencken, H(enry) L(ouis)

Townshend, Pete
See Townshend, Peter (Dennis Blandford)
Townshend, Peter (Dennis Blandford)
1945- .... **CLC 17, 42**
See also CA 107
Tozzi, Federigo 1883-1920 .... **TCLC 31**
See also CA 160; CANR 110; DLB 264;
EWL 3
Tracy, Don(ald Fiske) 1905-1970(?)
See Queen, Ellery
See also CA 1-4R; 176; CANR 2
Trafford, F. G.
See Riddell, Charlotte
Traill, Catharine Parr 1802-1899 .. **NCLC 31**
See also DLB 99
Trakl, Georg 1887-1914 .... **PC 20; TCLC 5**
See also CA 104; 165; EW 10; EWL 3;
LMFS 2; MTCW 2; RGWL 2, 3
Tranquilli, Secondino
See Silone, Ignazio
Transtroemer, Tomas Gosta
See Transtromer, Tomas (Goesta)
Transtromer, Tomas
See Transtromer, Tomas (Goesta)
Transtromer, Tomas (Goesta)
1931- .... **CLC 52, 65**
See also CA 117; 129; CAAS 17; CANR
115; DAM POET; DLB 257; EWL 3
Transtromer, Tomas Gosta
See Transtromer, Tomas (Goesta)
Traven, B. 1882(?)-1969 .... **CLC 8, 11**
See also CA 19-20; 25-28R; CAP 2; DLB
9, 56; EWL 3; MTCW 1; RGAL 4
Trediakovsky, Vasilii Kirillovich
1703-1769 .... **LC 68**
See also DLB 150
Treitel, Jonathan 1959- .... **CLC 70**
See also CA 210; DLB 267
Trelawny, Edward John
1792-1881 .... **NCLC 85**
See also DLB 110, 116, 144
Tremain, Rose 1943- .... **CLC 42**
See also CA 97-100; CANR 44, 95; CN 7;
DLB 14, 271; RGSF 2; RHW
Tremblay, Michel 1942- .... **CLC 29, 102**
See also CA 116; 128; CCA 1; CWW 2;
DAC; DAM MST; DLB 60; EWL 3; GLL
1; MTCW 1, 2
Trevanian .... **CLC 29**
See Whitaker, Rod(ney)
Trevor, Glen
See Hilton, James
Trevor, William .. **CLC 7, 9, 14, 25, 71, 116;**
SSC 21, 58
See Cox, William Trevor
See also BRWS 4; CBD; CD 5; CN 7; DLB
14, 139; EWL 3; LATS 1; MTCW 2;
RGEL 2; RGSF 2; SSFS 10
Trifonov, Iurii (Valentinovich)
See Trifonov, Yuri (Valentinovich)
See also RGWL 2, 3
Trifonov, Yuri (Valentinovich)
1925-1981 .... **CLC 45**
See Trifonov, Iurii (Valentinovich); Tri-
fonov, Yury Valentinovich
See also CA 126; 103; MTCW 1
Trifonov, Yury Valentinovich
See Trifonov, Yuri (Valentinovich)
See also EWL 3
Trilling, Diana (Rubin) 1905-1996 . **CLC 129**
See also CA 5-8R; 154; CANR 10, 46; INT
CANR-10; MTCW 1, 2
Trilling, Lionel 1905-1975 .... **CLC 9, 11, 24**
See also AMWS 3; CA 9-12R; 61-64;
CANR 10, 105; DLB 28, 63; EWL 3; INT
CANR-10; MTCW 1, 2; RGAL 4; TUS
Trimball, W. H.
See Mencken, H(enry) L(ouis)

Tristan
See Gomez de la Serna, Ramon
Tristram
See Housman, A(lfred) E(dward)
Trogdon, William (Lewis) 1939-
See Heat-Moon, William Least
See also CA 115; 119; CANR 47, 89; CPW;
INT CA-119
Trollope, Anthony 1815-1882 .... **NCLC 6, 33,**
101; SSC 28; WLC
See also BRW 5; CDBLB 1832-1890; DA;
DA3; DAB; DAC; DAM MST, NOV;
DLB 21, 57, 159; RGEL 2; RGSF 2;
SATA 22
Trollope, Frances 1779-1863 .... **NCLC 30**
See also DLB 21, 166
Trotsky, Leon 1879-1940 .... **TCLC 22**
See also CA 118; 167
Trotter (Cockburn), Catharine
1679-1749 .... **LC 8**
See also DLB 84, 252
Trotter, Wilfred 1872-1939 .... **TCLC 97**
Trout, Kilgore
See Farmer, Philip Jose
Trow, George W. S. 1943- .... **CLC 52**
See also CA 126; CANR 91
Troyat, Henri 1911- .... **CLC 23**
See also CA 45-48; CANR 2, 33, 67, 117;
GFL 1789 to the Present; MTCW 1
Trudeau, G(arretson) B(eekman) 1948-
See Trudeau, Garry B.
See also CA 81-84; CANR 31; SATA 35
Trudeau, Garry B. .... **CLC 12**
See Trudeau, G(arretson) B(eekman)
See also AAYA 10; AITN 2
Truffaut, Francois 1932-1984 ... **CLC 20, 101**
See also CA 81-84; 113; CANR 34
Trumbo, Dalton 1905-1976 .... **CLC 19**
See also CA 21-24R; 69-72; CANR 10;
DLB 26; IDFW 3, 4; YAW
Trumbull, John 1750-1831 .... **NCLC 30**
See also DLB 31; RGAL 4
Trundlett, Helen B.
See Eliot, T(homas) S(tearns)
Truth, Sojourner 1797(?)-1883 ...... **NCLC 94**
See also DLB 239; FW; LAIT 2
Tryon, Thomas 1926-1991 .... **CLC 3, 11**
See also AITN 1; BPFB 3; CA 29-32R; 135;
CANR 32, 77; CPW; DA3; DAM POP;
HGG; MTCW 1
Tryon, Tom
See Tryon, Thomas
Ts'ao Hsueh-ch'in 1715(?)-1763 .... **LC 1**
Tsushima, Shuji 1909-1948
See Dazai Osamu
See also CA 107
Tsvetaeva (Efron), Marina (Ivanovna)
1892-1941 .... **PC 14; TCLC 7, 35**
See also CA 104; 128; CANR 73; EW 11;
MTCW 1, 2; RGWL 2, 3
Tuck, Lily 1938- .... **CLC 70**
See also CA 139; CANR 90
Tu Fu 712-770 .... **PC 9**
See Du Fu
See also DAM MULT; TWA; WP
Tunis, John R(oberts) 1889-1975 ..... **CLC 12**
See also BYA 1; CA 61-64; CANR 62; DLB
22, 171; JRDA; MAICYA 1, 2; SATA 37;
SATA-Brief 30; YAW
Tuohy, Frank .... **CLC 37**
See Tuohy, John Francis
See also DLB 14, 139
Tuohy, John Francis 1925-
See Tuohy, Frank
See also CA 5-8R; 178; CANR 3, 47; CN 7
Turco, Lewis (Putnam) 1934- ..... **CLC 11, 63**
See also CA 13-16R; CAAS 22; CANR 24,
51; CP 7; DLBY 1984

Turgenev, Ivan (Sergeevich)
1818-1883 ..... **DC 7; NCLC 21, 37, 122;**
SSC 7, 57; WLC
See also DA; DAB; DAC; DAM MST,
NOV; DFS 6; DLB 238, 284; EW 6;
LATS 1; NFS 16; RGSF 2; RGWL 2, 3;
TWA
Turgot, Anne-Robert-Jacques
1727-1781 .... **LC 26**
Turner, Frederick 1943- .... **CLC 48**
See also CA 73-76; CAAS 10; CANR 12,
30, 56; DLB 40, 282
Turton, James
See Crace, Jim
Tutu, Desmond M(pilo) 1931- .. **BLC 3; CLC**
80
See also BW 1, 3; CA 125; CANR 67, 81;
DAM MULT
Tutuola, Amos 1920-1997 ..... **BLC 3; CLC 5,**
14, 29
See also AFW; BW 2, 3; CA 9-12R; 159;
CANR 27, 66; CDWLB 3; CN 7; DA3;
DAM MULT; DLB 125; DNFS 2; EWL
3; MTCW 1, 2; RGEL 2; WLIT 2
Twain, Mark .. **SSC 34; TCLC 6, 12, 19, 36,**
48, 59; WLC
See Clemens, Samuel Langhorne
See also AAYA 20; AMW; AMWC 1; BPFB
3; BYA 2, 3, 11, 14; CLR 58, 60, 66; DLB
11; EXPN; EXPS; FANT; LAIT 2; NFS
1, 6; RGAL 4; RGSF 2; SFW 4; SSFS 1,
7; SUFW; TUS; WCH; WYA; YAW
Tyler, Anne 1941- . **CLC 7, 11, 18, 28, 44, 59,**
103
See also AAYA 18; AMWS 4; BEST 89:1;
BPFB 3; BYA 12; CA 9-12R; CANR 11,
33, 53, 109; CDALBS; CN 7; CPW;
CSW; DAM NOV, POP; DLB 6, 143;
DLBY 1982; EWL 3; EXPN; LATS 1;
MAWW; MTCW 1, 2; NFS 2, 7, 10;
RGAL 4; SATA 7, 90; SSFS 17; TUS;
YAW
Tyler, Royall 1757-1826 .... **NCLC 3**
See also DLB 37; RGAL 4
Tynan, Katharine 1861-1931 .... **TCLC 3**
See also CA 104; 167; DLB 153, 240; FW
Tyutchev, Fyodor 1803-1873 .... **NCLC 34**
Tzara, Tristan 1896-1963 ..... **CLC 47; PC 27**
See also CA 153; 89-92; DAM POET; EWL
3; MTCW 2
Uchida, Yoshiko 1921-1992 .... **AAL**
See also AAYA 16; BYA 2, 3; CA 13-16R;
139; CANR 6, 22, 47, 61; CDALBS; CLR
6, 56; CWRI 5; JRDA; MAICYA 1, 2;
MTCW 1, 2; SAAS 1; SATA 1, 53; SATA-
Obit 72
Udall, Nicholas 1504-1556 .... **LC 84**
See also DLB 62; RGEL 2
Uhry, Alfred 1936- .... **CLC 55**
See also CA 127; 133; CAD; CANR 112;
CD 5; CSW; DA3; DAM DRAM, POP;
DFS 11, 15; INT CA-133
Ulf, Haerved
See Strindberg, (Johan) August
Ulf, Harved
See Strindberg, (Johan) August
Ulibarri, Sabine R(eyes) 1919- .... **CLC 83;**
HLCS 2
See also CA 131; CANR 81; DAM MULT;
DLB 82; HW 1, 2; RGSF 2
Unamuno (y Jugo), Miguel de
1864-1936 . **HLC 2; SSC 11; TCLC 2, 9**
See also CA 104; 131; CANR 81; DAM
MULT, NOV; DLB 108; EW 8; EWL 3;
HW 1, 2; MTCW 1, 2; RGSF 2; RGWL
2, 3; TWA
Undercliffe, Errol
See Campbell, (John) Ramsey
Underwood, Miles
See Glassco, John

Waters, Mary C. .... **CLC 70**

Waters, Roger 1944- .... **CLC 35**

Watkins, Frances Ellen
   See Harper, Frances Ellen Watkins

Watkins, Gerrold
   See Malzberg, Barry N(athaniel)

Watkins, Gloria Jean 1952(?)-
   See hooks, bell
   See also BW 2; CA 143; CANR 87; MTCW
   2; SATA 115

Watkins, Paul 1964- .... **CLC 55**
   See also CA 132; CANR 62, 98

Watkins, Vernon Phillips
   1906-1967 .... **CLC 43**
   See also CA 9-10; 25-28R; CAP 1; DLB
   20; EWL 3; RGEL 2

Watson, Irving S.
   See Mencken, H(enry) L(ouis)

Watson, John H.
   See Farmer, Philip Jose

Watson, Richard F.
   See Silverberg, Robert

Waugh, Auberon (Alexander)
   1939-2001 .... **CLC 7**
   See also CA 45-48; 192; CANR 6, 22, 92;
   DLB 14, 194

Waugh, Evelyn (Arthur St. John)
   1903-1966 .. **CLC 1, 3, 8, 13, 19, 27, 44,**
   107; SSC 41; WLC
   See also BPFB 3; BRW 7; CA 85-88; 25-
   28R; CANR 22; CDBLB 1914-1945; DA;
   DA3; DAB; DAC; DAM MST, NOV,
   POP; DLB 15, 162, 195; EWL 3; MTCW
   1, 2; NFS 17; RGEL 2; RGSF 2; TEA;
   WLIT 4

Waugh, Harriet 1944- .... **CLC 6**
   See also CA 85-88; CANR 22

Ways, C. R.
   See Blount, Roy (Alton), Jr.

Waystaff, Simon
   See Swift, Jonathan

Webb, Beatrice (Martha Potter)
   1858-1943 .... **TCLC 22**
   See also CA 117; 162; DLB 190; FW

Webb, Charles (Richard) 1939- .... **CLC 7**
   See also CA 25-28R; CANR 114

Webb, James H(enry), Jr. 1946- ...... **CLC 22**
   See also CA 81-84

Webb, Mary Gladys (Meredith)
   1881-1927 .... **TCLC 24**
   See also CA 182; 123; DLB 34; FW

Webb, Mrs. Sidney
   See Webb, Beatrice (Martha Potter)

Webb, Phyllis 1927- .... **CLC 18**
   See also CA 104; CANR 23; CCA 1; CP 7;
   CWP; DLB 53

Webb, Sidney (James) 1859-1947 .. **TCLC 22**
   See also CA 117; 163; DLB 190

Webber, Andrew Lloyd .... **CLC 21**
   See Lloyd Webber, Andrew
   See also DFS 7

Weber, Lenora Mattingly
   1895-1971 .... **CLC 12**
   See also CA 19-20; 29-32R; CAP 1; SATA
   2; SATA-Obit 26

Weber, Max 1864-1920 .... **TCLC 69**
   See also CA 109; 189

Webster, John 1580(?)-1634(?) ...... **DC 2; LC**
   33, 84; WLC
   See also BRW 2; CDBLB Before 1660; DA;
   DAB; DAC; DAM DRAM, MST; DFS
   17; DLB 58; IDTP; RGEL 2; WLIT 3

Webster, Noah 1758-1843 .... **NCLC 30**
   See also DLB 1, 37, 42, 43, 73, 243

Wedekind, (Benjamin) Frank(lin)
   1864-1918 .... **TCLC 7**
   See also CA 104; 153; CDWLB 2; DAM
   DRAM; DLB 118; EW 8; EWL 3; LMFS
   2; RGWL 2, 3

Wehr, Demaris .... **CLC 65**

Weidman, Jerome 1913-1998 .... **CLC 7**
   See also AITN 2; CA 1-4R; 171; CAD;
   CANR 1; DLB 28

Weil, Simone (Adolphine)
   1909-1943 .... **TCLC 23**
   See also CA 117; 159; EW 12; EWL 3; FW;
   GFL 1789 to the Present; MTCW 2

Weininger, Otto 1880-1903 .... **TCLC 84**

Weinstein, Nathan
   See West, Nathanael

Weinstein, Nathan von Wallenstein
   See West, Nathanael

Weir, Peter (Lindsay) 1944- .... **CLC 20**
   See also CA 113; 123

Weiss, Peter (Ulrich) 1916-1982 .. **CLC 3, 15,**
   51
   See also CA 45-48; 106; CANR 3; DAM
   DRAM; DFS 3; DLB 69, 124; EWL 3;
   RGWL 2, 3

Weiss, Theodore (Russell) 1916- ... **CLC 3, 8,**
   14
   See also CA 9-12R; CAAE 189; CAAS 2;
   CANR 46, 94; CP 7; DLB 5

Welch, (Maurice) Denton
   1915-1948 .... **TCLC 22**
   See also BRWS 8; CA 121; 148; RGEL 2

Welch, James 1940- ... **CLC 6, 14, 52; NNAL**
   See also CA 85-88; CANR 42, 66, 107; CN
   7; CP 7; CPW; DAM MULT, POP; DLB
   175, 256; LATS 1; RGAL 4; TCWW 2

Weldon, Fay 1931- . **CLC 6, 9, 11, 19, 36, 59,**
   122
   See also BRWS 4; CA 21-24R; CANR 16,
   46, 63, 97; CDBLB 1960 to Present; CN
   7; CPW; DAM POP; DLB 14, 194; EWL
   3; FW; HGG; INT CANR-16; MTCW 1,
   2; RGEL 2; RGSF 2

Wellek, Rene 1903-1995 .... **CLC 28**
   See also CA 5-8R; 150; CAAS 7; CANR 8;
   DLB 63; EWL 3; INT CANR-8

Weller, Michael 1942- .... **CLC 10, 53**
   See also CA 85-88; CAD; CD 5

Weller, Paul 1958- .... **CLC 26**

Wellershoff, Dieter 1925- .... **CLC 46**
   See also CA 89-92; CANR 16, 37

Welles, (George) Orson 1915-1985 .. **CLC 20,**
   80
   See also AAYA 40; CA 93-96; 117

Wellman, John McDowell 1945-
   See Wellman, Mac
   See also CA 166; CD 5

Wellman, Mac .... **CLC 65**
   See Wellman, John McDowell; Wellman,
   John McDowell
   See also CAD; RGAL 4

Wellman, Manly Wade 1903-1986 ... **CLC 49**
   See also CA 1-4R; 118; CANR 6, 16, 44;
   FANT; SATA 6; SATA-Obit 47; SFW 4;
   SUFW

Wells, Carolyn 1869(?)-1942 .... **TCLC 35**
   See also CA 113; 185; CMW 4; DLB 11

Wells, H(erbert) G(eorge)
   1866-1946 .... **SSC 6; TCLC 6, 12, 19,**
   133; WLC
   See also AAYA 18; BPFB 3; BRW 6; CA
   110; 121; CDBLB 1914-1945; CLR 64;
   DA; DA3; DAB; DAC; DAM MST, NOV;
   DLB 34, 70, 156, 178; EWL 3; EXPS;
   HGG; LAIT 3; LMFS 2; MTCW 1, 2;
   NFS 17; RGEL 2; RGSF 2; SATA 20;
   SCFW; SFW 4; SSFS 3; SUFW; TEA;
   WCH; WLIT 4; YAW

Wells, Rosemary 1943- .... **CLC 12**
   See also AAYA 13; BYA 7, 8; CA 85-88;
   CANR 48; CLR 16, 69; CWRI 5; MAI-
   CYA 1, 2; SAAS 1; SATA 18, 69, 114;
   YAW

Wells-Barnett, Ida B(ell)
   1862-1931 .... **TCLC 125**
   See also CA 182; DLB 23, 221

Welsh, Irvine 1958- .... **CLC 144**
   See also CA 173; DLB 271

Welty, Eudora (Alice) 1909-2001 .. **CLC 1, 2,**
   5, 14, 22, 33, 105; SSC 1, 27, 51; WLC
   See also AAYA 48; AMW; AMWR 1; BPFB
   3; CA 9-12R; 199; CABS 1; CANR 32,
   65; CDALB 1941-1968; CN 7; CSW; DA;
   DA3; DAB; DAC; DAM MST, NOV;
   DLB 2, 102, 143; DLBD 12; DLBY 1987,
   2001; EWL 3; EXPS; HGG; LAIT 3;
   MAWW; MTCW 1, 2; NFS 13, 15; RGAL
   4; RGSF 2; RHW; SSFS 2, 10; TUS

Wen I-to 1899-1946 .... **TCLC 28**
   See also EWL 3

Wentworth, Robert
   See Hamilton, Edmond

Werfel, Franz (Viktor) 1890-1945 ... **TCLC 8**
   See also CA 104; 161; DLB 81, 124; EWL
   3; RGWL 2, 3

Wergeland, Henrik Arnold
   1808-1845 .... **NCLC 5**

Wersba, Barbara 1932- .... **CLC 30**
   See also AAYA 2, 30; BYA 6, 12, 13; CA
   29-32R, 182; CAAE 182; CANR 16, 38;
   CLR 3, 78; DLB 52; JRDA; MAICYA 1,
   2; SAAS 2; SATA 1, 58; SATA-Essay 103;
   WYA; YAW

Wertmueller, Lina 1928- .... **CLC 16**
   See also CA 97-100; CANR 39, 78

Wescott, Glenway 1901-1987 .. **CLC 13; SSC**
   35
   See also CA 13-16R; 121; CANR 23, 70;
   DLB 4, 9, 102; RGAL 4

Wesker, Arnold 1932- .... **CLC 3, 5, 42**
   See also CA 1-4R; CAAS 7; CANR 1, 33;
   CBD; CD 5; CDBLB 1960 to Present;
   DAB; DAM DRAM; DLB 13; EWL 3;
   MTCW 1; RGEL 2; TEA

Wesley, John 1703-1791 .... **LC 88**
   See also DLB 104

Wesley, Richard (Errol) 1945- .... **CLC 7**
   See also BW 1; CA 57-60; CAD; CANR
   27; CD 5; DLB 38

Wessel, Johan Herman 1742-1785 .... **LC 7**

West, Anthony (Panther)
   1914-1987 .... **CLC 50**
   See also CA 45-48; 124; CANR 3, 19; DLB
   15

West, C. P.
   See Wodehouse, P(elham) G(renville)

West, Cornel (Ronald) 1953- .... **BLCS; CLC**
   134
   See also CA 144; CANR 91; DLB 246

West, Delno C(loyde), Jr. 1936- .... **CLC 70**
   See also CA 57-60

West, Dorothy 1907-1998 .. **HR 3; TCLC 108**
   See also BW 2; CA 143; 169; DLB 76

West, (Mary) Jessamyn 1902-1984 ... **CLC 7,**
   17
   See also CA 9-12R; 112; CANR 27; DLB
   6; DLBY 1984; MTCW 1, 2; RGAL 4;
   RHW; SATA-Obit 37; TCWW 2; TUS;
   YAW

West, Morris L(anglo) 1916-1999 ..... **CLC 6,**
   33
   See also BPFB 3; CA 5-8R; 187; CANR
   24, 49, 64; CN 7; CPW; MTCW 1, 2

West, Nathanael 1903-1940 .. **SSC 16; TCLC**
   1, 14, 44
   See also AMW; AMWR 2; BPFB 3; CA
   104; 125; CDALB 1929-1941; DA3; DLB
   4, 9, 28; EWL 3; MTCW 1, 2; NFS 16;
   RGAL 4; TUS

West, Owen
   See Koontz, Dean R(ay)

Wilhelm, Kate .... **CLC 7**
See Wilhelm, Katie (Gertrude)
See also AAYA 20; CAAS 5; DLB 8; INT
CANR-17; SCFW 2

Wilhelm, Katie (Gertrude) 1928-
See Wilhelm, Kate
See also CA 37-40R; CANR 17, 36, 60, 94;
MTCW 1; SFW 4

Wilkins, Mary
See Freeman, Mary E(leanor) Wilkins

Willard, Nancy 1936- .... **CLC 7, 37**
See also BYA 5; CA 89-92; CANR 10, 39,
68, 107; CLR 5; CWP; CWRI 5; DLB 5,
52; FANT; MAICYA 1, 2; MTCW 1;
SATA 37, 71, 127; SATA-Brief 30; SUFW
2

William of Malmesbury c. 1090B.C.-c.
1140B.C. .... **CMLC 57**

William of Ockham 1290-1349 ..... **CMLC 32**

Williams, Ben Ames 1889-1953 ..... **TCLC 89**
See also CA 183; DLB 102

Williams, C(harles) K(enneth)
1936- .... **CLC 33, 56, 148**
See also CA 37-40R; CAAS 26; CANR 57,
106; CP 7; DAM POET; DLB 5

Williams, Charles
See Collier, James Lincoln

Williams, Charles (Walter Stansby)
1886-1945 .... **TCLC 1, 11**
See also CA 104; 163; DLB 100, 153, 255;
FANT; RGEL 2; SUFW 1

Williams, Ella Gwendolen Rees
See Rhys, Jean

Williams, (George) Emlyn
1905-1987 .... **CLC 15**
See also CA 104; 123; CANR 36; DAM
DRAM; DLB 10, 77; IDTP; MTCW 1

Williams, Hank 1923-1953 .... **TCLC 81**
See Williams, Hiram King

Williams, Hiram Hank
See Williams, Hank

Williams, Hiram King
See Williams, Hank
See also CA 188

Williams, Hugo 1942- .... **CLC 42**
See also CA 17-20R; CANR 45; CP 7; DLB
40

Williams, J. Walker
See Wodehouse, P(elham) G(renville)

Williams, John A(lfred) 1925- . **BLC 3; CLC
5, 13**
See also AFAW 2; BW 2, 3; CA 53-56;
CAAE 195; CAAS 3; CANR 6, 26, 51,
118; CN 7; CSW; DAM MULT; DLB 2,
33; EWL 3; INT CANR-6; RGAL 4; SFW
4

Williams, Jonathan (Chamberlain)
1929- .... **CLC 13**
See also CA 9-12R; CAAS 12; CANR 8,
108; CP 7; DLB 5

Williams, Joy 1944- .... **CLC 31**
See also CA 41-44R; CANR 22, 48, 97

Williams, Norman 1952- .... **CLC 39**
See also CA 118

Williams, Sherley Anne 1944-1999 ... **BLC 3;
CLC 89**
See also AFAW 2; BW 2, 3; CA 73-76; 185;
CANR 25, 82; DAM MULT, POET; DLB
41; INT CANR-25; SATA 78; SATA-Obit
116

Williams, Shirley
See Williams, Sherley Anne

Williams, Tennessee 1911-1983 . **CLC 1, 2, 5,
7, 8, 11, 15, 19, 30, 39, 45, 71, 111; DC
4; WLC**
See also AAYA 31; AITN 1, 2; AMW;
AMWC 1; CA 5-8R; 108; CABS 3; CAD;
CANR 31; CDALB 1941-1968; DA;

DA3; DAB; DAC; DAM DRAM, MST,
DFS 17; DLB 7; DLBD 4; DLBY 1983;
EWL 3; GLL 1; LAIT 4; LATS 1; MTCW
1, 2; RGAL 4; TUS

Williams, Thomas (Alonzo)
1926-1990 .... **CLC 14**
See also CA 1-4R; 132; CANR 2

Williams, William C.
See Williams, William Carlos

Williams, William Carlos
1883-1963 .... **CLC 1, 2, 5, 9, 13, 22, 42,
67; PC 7; SSC 31**
See also AAYA 46; AMW; AMWR 1; CA
89-92; CANR 34; CDALB 1917-1929;
DA; DA3; DAB; DAC; DAM MST,
POET; DLB 4, 16, 54, 86; EWL 3; EXPP;
MTCW 1, 2; NCFS 4; PAB; PFS 1, 6, 11;
RGAL 4; RGSF 2; TUS; WP

Williamson, David (Keith) 1942- ..... **CLC 56**
See also CA 103; CANR 41; CD 5

Williamson, Ellen Douglas 1905-1984
See Douglas, Ellen
See also CA 17-20R; 114; CANR 39

Williamson, Jack .... **CLC 29**
See Williamson, John Stewart
See also CAAS 8; DLB 8; SCFW 2

Williamson, John Stewart 1908-
See Williamson, Jack
See also CA 17-20R; CANR 23, 70; SFW 4

Willie, Frederick
See Lovecraft, H(oward) P(hillips)

Willingham, Calder (Baynard, Jr.)
1922-1995 .... **CLC 5, 51**
See also CA 5-8R; 147; CANR 3; CSW;
DLB 2, 44; IDFW 3, 4; MTCW 1

Willis, Charles
See Clarke, Arthur C(harles)

Willy
See Colette, (Sidonie-Gabrielle)

Willy, Colette
See Colette, (Sidonie-Gabrielle)
See also GLL 1

Wilmot, John 1647-1680 .... **LC 75**
See Rochester
See also BRW 2; DLB 131; PAB

Wilson, A(ndrew) N(orman) 1950- .. **CLC 33**
See also BRWS 6; CA 112; 122; CN 7;
DLB 14, 155, 194; MTCW 2

Wilson, Angus (Frank Johnstone)
1913-1991 . **CLC 2, 3, 5, 25, 34; SSC 21**
See also BRWS 1; CA 5-8R; 134; CANR
21; DLB 15, 139, 155; EWL 3; MTCW 1,
2; RGEL 2; RGSF 2

Wilson, August 1945- ... **BLC 3; CLC 39, 50,
63, 118; DC 2; WLCS**
See also AAYA 16; AFAW 2; AMWS 8; BW
2, 3; CA 115; 122; CAD; CANR 42, 54,
76; CD 5; DA; DA3; DAB; DAC; DAM
DRAM, MST, MULT; DFS 3, 7, 15, 17;
DLB 228; EWL 3; LAIT 4; LATS 1;
MTCW 1, 2; RGAL 4

Wilson, Brian 1942- .... **CLC 12**

Wilson, Colin 1931- .... **CLC 3, 14**
See also CA 1-4R; CAAS 5; CANR 1, 22,
33, 77; CMW 4; CN 7; DLB 14, 194;
HGG; MTCW 1; SFW 4

Wilson, Dirk
See Pohl, Frederik

Wilson, Edmund 1895-1972 .. **CLC 1, 2, 3, 8,
24**
See also AMW; CA 1-4R; 37-40R; CANR
1, 46, 110; DLB 63; EWL 3; MTCW 1, 2;
RGAL 4; TUS

Wilson, Ethel Davis (Bryant)
1888(?)-1980 .... **CLC 13**
See also CA 102; DAC; DAM POET; DLB
68; MTCW 1; RGEL 2

Wilson, Harriet
See Wilson, Harriet E. Adams
See also DLB 239

Wilson, Harriet E.
See Wilson, Harriet E. Adams
See also DLB 243

Wilson, Harriet E. Adams
1827(?)-1863(?) .... **BLC 3; NCLC 78**
See Wilson, Harriet; Wilson, Harriet E.
See also DAM MULT; DLB 50

Wilson, John 1785-1854 .... **NCLC 5**

Wilson, John (Anthony) Burgess 1917-1993
See Burgess, Anthony
See also CA 1-4R; 143; CANR 2, 46; DA3;
DAC; DAM NOV; MTCW 1, 2; NFS 15;
TEA

Wilson, Lanford 1937- ... **CLC 7, 14, 36; DC
19**
See also CA 17-20R; CABS 3; CAD; CANR
45, 96; CD 5; DAM DRAM; DFS 4, 9,
12, 16; DLB 7; EWL 3; TUS

Wilson, Robert M. 1944- .... **CLC 7, 9**
See also CA 49-52; CAD; CANR 2, 41; CD
5; MTCW 1

Wilson, Robert McLiam 1964- .... **CLC 59**
See also CA 132; DLB 267

Wilson, Sloan 1920- .... **CLC 32**
See also CA 1-4R; CANR 1, 44; CN 7

Wilson, Snoo 1948- .... **CLC 33**
See also CA 69-72; CBD; CD 5

Wilson, William S(mith) 1932- .... **CLC 49**
See also CA 81-84

Wilson, (Thomas) Woodrow
1856-1924 .... **TCLC 79**
See also CA 166; DLB 47

Wilson and Warnke eds. .... **CLC 65**

Winchilsea, Anne (Kingsmill) Finch
1661-1720
See Finch, Anne
See also RGEL 2

Windham, Basil
See Wodehouse, P(elham) G(renville)

Wingrove, David (John) 1954- .... **CLC 68**
See also CA 133; SFW 4

Winnemucca, Sarah 1844-1891 .... **NCLC 79;
NNAL**
See also DAM MULT; DLB 175; RGAL 4

Winstanley, Gerrard 1609-1676 .... **LC 52**

Wintergreen, Jane
See Duncan, Sara Jeannette

Winters, Janet Lewis .... **CLC 41**
See Lewis, Janet
See also DLBY 1987

Winters, (Arthur) Yvor 1900-1968 .... **CLC 4,
8, 32**
See also AMWS 2; CA 11-12; 25-28R; CAP
1; DLB 48; EWL 3; MTCW 1; RGAL 4

Winterson, Jeanette 1959- .... **CLC 64, 158**
See also BRWS 4; CA 136; CANR 58, 116;
CN 7; CPW; DA3; DAM POP; DLB 207,
261; FANT; FW; GLL 1; MTCW 2; RHW

Winthrop, John 1588-1649 .... **LC 31**
See also DLB 24, 30

Wirth, Louis 1897-1952 .... **TCLC 92**
See also CA 210

Wiseman, Frederick 1930- .... **CLC 20**
See also CA 159

Wister, Owen 1860-1938 .... **TCLC 21**
See also BPFB 3; CA 108; 162; DLB 9, 78,
186; RGAL 4; SATA 62; TCWW 2

Witkacy
See Witkiewicz, Stanislaw Ignacy

Witkiewicz, Stanislaw Ignacy
1885-1939 .... **TCLC 8**
See also CA 105; 162; CDWLB 4; DLB
215; EW 10; EWL 3; RGWL 2, 3; SFW 4

Wittgenstein, Ludwig (Josef Johann)
1889-1951 .... **TCLC 59**
See also CA 113; 164; DLB 262; MTCW 2

Yates, Richard 1926-1992 .... **CLC 7, 8, 23**
See also AMWS 11; CA 5-8R; 139; CANR 10, 43; DLB 2, 234; DLBY 1981, 1992; INT CANR-10

Yeats, W. B.
See Yeats, William Butler

Yeats, William Butler 1865-1939 .... **PC 20; TCLC 1, 11, 18, 31, 93, 116; WLC**
See also AAYA 48; BRW 6; BRWR 1; CA 104; 127; CANR 45; CDBLB 1890-1914; DA; DA3; DAB; DAC; DAM DRAM, MST, POET; DLB 10, 19, 98, 156; EWL 3; EXPP; MTCW 1, 2; NCFS 3; PAB; PFS 1, 2, 5, 7, 13, 15; RGEL 2; TEA; WLIT 4; WP

Yehoshua, A(braham) B. 1936- .. **CLC 13, 31**
See also CA 33-36R; CANR 43, 90; EWL 3; RGSF 2; RGWL 3

Yellow Bird
See Ridge, John Rollin

Yep, Laurence Michael 1948- .... **CLC 35**
See also AAYA 5, 31; BYA 7; CA 49-52; CANR 1, 46, 92; CLR 3, 17, 54; DLB 52; FANT; JRDA; MAICYA 1, 2; MAICYAS 1; SATA 7, 69, 123; WYA; YAW

Yerby, Frank G(arvin) 1916-1991 ..... **BLC 3; CLC 1, 7, 22**
See also BPFB 3; BW 1, 3; CA 9-12R; 136; CANR 16, 52; DAM MULT; DLB 76; INT CANR-16; MTCW 1; RGAL 4; RHW

Yesenin, Sergei Alexandrovich
See Esenin, Sergei (Alexandrovich)

Yesenin, Sergey
See Esenin, Sergei (Alexandrovich)
See also EWL 3

Yevtushenko, Yevgeny (Alexandrovich) 1933- ...... **CLC 1, 3, 13, 26, 51, 126; PC 40**
See Evtushenko, Evgenii Aleksandrovich
See also CA 81-84; CANR 33, 54; CWW 2; DAM POET; EWL 3; MTCW 1

Yezierska, Anzia 1885(?)-1970 .... **CLC 46**
See also CA 126; 89-92; DLB 28, 221; FW; MTCW 1; RGAL 4; SSFS 15

Yglesias, Helen 1915- .... **CLC 7, 22**
See also CA 37-40R; CAAS 20; CANR 15, 65, 95; CN 7; INT CANR-15; MTCW 1

Yokomitsu, Riichi 1898-1947 .... **TCLC 47**
See also CA 170; EWL 3

Yonge, Charlotte (Mary) 1823-1901 .... **TCLC 48**
See also CA 109; 163; DLB 18, 163; RGEL 2; SATA 17; WCH

York, Jeremy
See Creasey, John

York, Simon
See Heinlein, Robert A(nson)

Yorke, Henry Vincent 1905-1974 ..... **CLC 13**
See Green, Henry
See also CA 85-88; 49-52

Yosano Akiko 1878-1942 .... **PC 11; TCLC 59**
See also CA 161; EWL 3; RGWL 3

Yoshimoto, Banana .... **CLC 84**
See Yoshimoto, Mahoko
See also NFS 7

Yoshimoto, Mahoko 1964-
See Yoshimoto, Banana
See also CA 144; CANR 98; SSFS 16

Young, Al(bert James) 1939- ... **BLC 3; CLC 19**
See also BW 2, 3; CA 29-32R; CANR 26, 65, 109; CN 7; CP 7; DAM MULT; DLB 33

Young, Andrew (John) 1885-1971 ...... **CLC 5**
See also CA 5-8R; CANR 7, 29; RGEL 2

Young, Collier
See Bloch, Robert (Albert)

Young, Edward 1683-1765 .... **LC 3, 40**
See also DLB 95; RGEL 2

Young, Marguerite (Vivian) 1909-1995 .... **CLC 82**
See also CA 13-16; 150; CAP 1; CN 7

Young, Neil 1945- .... **CLC 17**
See also CA 110; CCA 1

Young Bear, Ray A. 1950- ... **CLC 94; NNAL**
See also CA 146; DAM MULT; DLB 175

Yourcenar, Marguerite 1903-1987 ... **CLC 19, 38, 50, 87**
See also BPFB 3; CA 69-72; CANR 23, 60, 93; DAM NOV; DLB 72; DLBY 1988; EW 12; EWL 3; GFL 1789 to the Present; GLL 1; MTCW 1, 2; RGWL 2, 3

Yuan, Chu 340(?)B.C.-278(?)B.C. . **CMLC 36**

Yurick, Sol 1925- .... **CLC 6**
See also CA 13-16R; CANR 25; CN 7

Zabolotsky, Nikolai Alekseevich 1903-1958 .... **TCLC 52**
See Zabolotsky, Nikolai Alekseevich
See also CA 116; 164

Zabolotsky, Nikolay Alekseevich
See Zabolotsky, Nikolai Alekseevich
See also EWL 3

Zagajewski, Adam 1945- .... **PC 27**
See also CA 186; DLB 232; EWL 3

Zalygin, Sergei -2000 .... **CLC 59**

Zamiatin, Evgenii
See Zamyatin, Evgeny Ivanovich
See also RGSF 2; RGWL 2, 3

Zamiatin, Evgenii Ivanovich
See Zamyatin, Evgeny Ivanovich
See also DLB 272

Zamiatin, Yevgenii
See Zamyatin, Evgeny Ivanovich

Zamora, Bernice (B. Ortiz) 1938- .. **CLC 89; HLC 2**
See also CA 151; CANR 80; DAM MULT; DLB 82; HW 1, 2

Zamyatin, Evgeny Ivanovich 1884-1937 .... **TCLC 8, 37**
See Zamiatin, Evgenii; Zamiatin, Evgenii Ivanovich; Zamyatin, Yevgeny Ivanovich
See also CA 105; 166; EW 10; SFW 4

Zamyatin, Yevgeny Ivanovich
See Zamyatin, Evgeny Ivanovich
See also EWL 3

Zangwill, Israel 1864-1926 ... **SSC 44; TCLC 16**
See also CA 109; 167; CMW 4; DLB 10, 135, 197; RGEL 2

Zappa, Francis Vincent, Jr. 1940-1993
See Zappa, Frank
See also CA 108; 143; CANR 57

Zappa, Frank .... **CLC 17**
See Zappa, Francis Vincent, Jr.

Zaturenska, Marya 1902-1982 ..... **CLC 6, 11**
See also CA 13-16R; 105; CANR 22

Zeami 1363-1443 .... **DC 7; LC 86**
See also DLB 203; RGWL 2, 3

Zelazny, Roger (Joseph) 1937-1995 . **CLC 21**
See also AAYA 7; BPFB 3; CA 21-24R; 148; CANR 26, 60; CN 7; DLB 8; FANT; MTCW 1, 2; SATA 57; SATA-Brief 39; SCFW; SFW 4; SUFW 1, 2

Zhdanov, Andrei Alexandrovich 1896-1948 .... **TCLC 18**
See also CA 117; 167

Zhukovsky, Vasilii Andreevich
See Zhukovsky, Vasily (Andreevich)
See also DLB 205

Zhukovsky, Vasily (Andreevich) 1783-1852 .... **NCLC 35**
See Zhukovsky, Vasilii Andreevich

Ziegenhagen, Eric .... **CLC 55**

Zimmer, Jill Schary
See Robinson, Jill

Zimmerman, Robert
See Dylan, Bob

Zindel, Paul 1936-2003 ...... **CLC 6, 26; DC 5**
See also AAYA 2, 37; BYA 2, 3, 8, 11, 14; CA 73-76; CAD; CANR 31, 65, 108; CD 5; CDALBS; CLR 3, 45, 85; DA; DA3; DAB; DAC; DAM DRAM, MST, NOV; DFS 12; DLB 7, 52; JRDA; LAIT 5; MAICYA 1, 2; MTCW 1, 2; NFS 14; SATA 16, 58, 102; WYA; YAW

Zinov'Ev, A. A.
See Zinoviev, Alexander (Aleksandrovich)

Zinoviev, Alexander (Aleksandrovich) 1922- .... **CLC 19**
See also CA 116; 133; CAAS 10

Zoilus
See Lovecraft, H(oward) P(hillips)

Zola, Emile (Edouard Charles Antoine) 1840-1902 ...... **TCLC 1, 6, 21, 41; WLC**
See also CA 104; 138; DA; DA3; DAB; DAC; DAM MST, NOV; DLB 123; EW 7; GFL 1789 to the Present; IDTP; LMFS 1, 2; RGWL 2; TWA

Zoline, Pamela 1941- .... **CLC 62**
See also CA 161; SFW 4

Zoroaster 628(?)B.C.-551(?)B.C. ... **CMLC 40**

Zorrilla y Moral, Jose 1817-1893 .... **NCLC 6**

Zoshchenko, Mikhail (Mikhailovich) 1895-1958 .... **SSC 15; TCLC 15**
See also CA 115; 160; EWL 3; RGSF 2; RGWL 3

Zuckmayer, Carl 1896-1977 .... **CLC 18**
See also CA 69-72; DLB 56, 124; EWL 3; RGWL 2, 3

Zuk, Georges
See Skelton, Robin
See also CCA 1

Zukofsky, Louis 1904-1978 ... **CLC 1, 2, 4, 7, 11, 18; PC 11**
See also AMWS 3; CA 9-12R; 77-80; CANR 39; DAM POET; DLB 5, 165; EWL 3; MTCW 1; RGAL 4

Zweig, Paul 1935-1984 .... **CLC 34, 42**
See also CA 85-88; 113

Zweig, Stefan 1881-1942 .... **TCLC 17**
See also CA 112; 170; DLB 81, 118; EWL 3

Zwingli, Huldreich 1484-1531 .... **LC 37**
See also DLB 179

Literary Criticism Series
Cumulative Topic Index

This index lists all topic entries in Gale's *Classical and Medieval Literature Criticism* (CMLC), *Contemporary Literary Criticism* (CLC), *Drama Criticism* (DC), *Literature Criticism from 1400 to 1800* (LC), *Nineteenth-Century Literature Criticism* (NCLC), *Short Story Criticism* (SSC), and *Twentieth-Century Literary Criticism* (TCLC). The index also lists topic entries in the Gale Critical Companion Collection, which includes the following publications: *The Beat Generation* (BG), and *Harlem Renaissance* (HR).

Topic Index

LC Cumulative Nationality Index

AFGHAN

Babur **18**

AMERICAN

Bache, Benjamin Franklin **74**
Bradford, William **64**
Bradstreet, Anne **4, 30**
Edwards, Jonathan **7, 54**
Edwards, Sarah Pierpont **87**
Eliot, John **5**
Franklin, Benjamin **25**
Hathorne, John **38**
Henry, Patrick **25**
Hopkinson, Francis **25**
Knight, Sarah Kemble **7**
Mather, Cotton **38**
Mather, Increase **38**
Morton, Thomas **72**
Munford, Robert **5**
Occom, Samson **60**
Penn, William **25**
Rowlandson, Mary **66**
Sewall, Samuel **38**
Stoughton, William **38**
Taylor, Edward **11**
Washington, George **25**
Wheatley (Peters), Phillis **3, 50**
Winthrop, John **31**

BENINESE

Equiano, Olaudah **16**

CANADIAN

Marie de l'Incarnation **10**

CHINESE

Lo Kuan-chung **12**
P'u Sung-ling **3, 49**
Ts'ao Hsueh-ch'in **1**
Wu Ch'eng-en **7**
Wu Ching-tzu **2**

DANISH

Holberg, Ludvig **6**
Wessel, Johan Herman **7**

DUTCH

Erasmus, Desiderius **16**
Lipsius, Justus **16**
Spinoza, Benedictus de **9, 58**

ENGLISH

Addison, Joseph **18**
Alabaster, William **90**
Amory, Thomas **48**
Andrewes, Lancelot **5**
Arbuthnot, John **1**
Askew, Anne **81**
Astell, Mary **68**
Aubin, Penelope **9**

Bacon, Francis **18, 32**
Bale, John **62**
Barker, Jane **42, 82**
Beaumont, Francis **33**
Behn, Aphra **1, 30, 42**
Boswell, James **4, 50**
Bradstreet, Anne **4, 30**
Brome, Richard **61**
Brooke, Frances **6, 48**
Bunyan, John **4, 69**
Burke, Edmund **7, 36**
Burton, Robert **74**
Butler, Samuel **16, 43**
Camden, William **77**
Campion, Thomas **78**
Carew, Thomas **13**
Cary, Elizabeth, Lady Falkland **30**
Cavendish, Margaret Lucas **30**
Caxton, William **17**
Centlivre, Susanna **65**
Chapman, George **22**
Charles I **13**
Chatterton, Thomas **3, 54**
Chaucer, Geoffrey **17, 56**
Churchill, Charles **3**
Cibber, Colley **66**
Cleland, John **2, 48**
Clifford, Anne **76**
Collier, Jeremy **6**
Collier, Mary **86**
Collins, William **4, 40**
Congreve, William **5, 21**
Coventry, Francis **46**
Coverdale, Myles **77**
Crashaw, Richard **24**
Daniel, Samuel **24**
Davenant, William **13**
Davies, John **85**
Davys, Mary **1, 46**
Day, John **70**
Day, Thomas **1**
Dee, John **20**
Defoe, Daniel **1, 42**
Dekker, Thomas **22**
Delany, Mary (Granville Pendarves) **12**
Deloney, Thomas **41**
Denham, John **73**
Dennis, John **11**
Devenant, William **13**
Donne, John **10, 24**
Drayton, Michael **8**
Dryden, John **3, 21**
Elyot, Thomas **11**
Equiano, Olaudah **16**
Etherege, George **78**
Fanshawe, Ann **11**
Farquhar, George **21**
Fielding, Henry **1, 46, 85**
Fielding, Sarah **1, 44**
Finch, Anne **3**
Fletcher, John **33**
Ford, John **68**
Foxe, John **14**

Garrick, David **15**
Gay, John **49**
Gower, John **76**
Gray, Thomas **4, 40**
Greene, Robert **41**
Greville, Fulke **79**
Hakluyt, Richard **31**
Harvey, Gabriel **88**
Hawes, Stephen **17**
Haywood, Eliza (Fowler) **1, 44**
Henry VIII **10**
Herbert, George **24**
Herrick, Robert **13**
Heywood, John **65**
Hobbes, Thomas **36**
Hoccleve, Thomas **75**
Holinshed, Raphael **69**
Howell, James **13**
Hunter, Robert **7**
Johnson, Samuel **15, 52**
Jonson, Ben(jamin) **6, 33**
Julian of Norwich **6, 52**
Kempe, Margery **6, 56**
Killigrew, Anne **4, 73**
Killigrew, Thomas **57**
Kyd, Thomas **22**
Langland, William **19**
Lanyer, Aemilia **10, 30, 83**
Lead, Jane Ward **72**
Leapor, Mary **80**
Lilly, William **27**
Locke, John **7, 35**
Lodge, Thomas **41**
Lovelace, Richard **24**
Lydgate, John **81**
Lyly, John **41**
Lyttelton, George **10**
Macaulay, Catherine **64**
Malory, Thomas **11, 88**
Mandeville, Bernard **82**
Manley, (Mary) Delariviere **1, 42**
Marlowe, Christopher **22, 47**
Marmion, Shakerley **89**
Marston, John **33**
Marvell, Andrew **4, 43**
Massinger, Philip **70**
Middleton, Thomas **33**
Milton, John **9, 43**
Montagu, Mary (Pierrepont) Wortley **9, 57**
More, Henry **9**
More, Thomas **10, 32**
Munday, Anthony **87**
Nashe, Thomas **41, 89**
Newton, Isaac **35, 52**
Parnell, Thomas **3**
Parr, Catherine **86**
Pepys, Samuel **11, 58**
Philips, Katherine **30**
Pix, Mary (Griffith) **8**
Pope, Alexander **3, 58, 60, 64**
Prior, Matthew **4**
Purchas, Samuel **70**
Raleigh, Walter **31, 39**

471

LC- 90 Title Index